ROUTLEDGE HANDBOOK C
AND POST-MARXISM

In the past two decades, Marxism has enjoyed a revitalization as a research program and a growth in its audience. This renaissance is connected to the revival of anti-capitalist contestation since the Seattle protests in 1999 and the impact of the global economic and financial crisis in 2007–8. It intersects with the emergence of Post-Marxism since the 1980s represented by thinkers such as Jürgen Habermas, Chantal Mouffe, Ranajit Guha and Alain Badiou.

This handbook explores the development of Marxism and Post-Marxism, setting them in dialogue against a truly global backdrop. Transcending the disciplinary boundaries between philosophy, economics, politics and history, an international range of expert contributors guide the reader through the main varieties and preoccupations of Marxism and Post-Marxism. Through a series of framing and illustrative essays, readers will explore these traditions, starting from Marx and Engels themselves, through the thinkers of the Second and Third Internationals (Rosa Luxemburg, Lenin and Trotsky, among others), the Tricontinental, and subaltern and postcolonial studies, to more contemporary figures such as Huey Newton, Fredric Jameson, Judith Butler, Immanuel Wallerstein and Samir Amin.

The *Routledge Handbook of Marxism and Post-Marxism* will be of interest to scholars and researchers of philosophy, cultural studies and theory, sociology, political economics and several areas of political science, including political theory, Marxism, political ideologies and critical theory.

Alex Callinicos is Emeritus Professor of European studies at King's College London and was editor of *International Socialism* from 2009 to 2020. His most recent books are *Deciphering Capital* (2014), *Bonfire of Illusions* (2010) and *Imperialism and Global Political Economy* (2009).

Stathis Kouvelakis taught political theory at King's College London. He has published on Marxism, contemporary critical theory and French and Greek politics. His recent publications include *La critique défaite: Emergence et domestication de la Théorie critique* (Amsterdam, 2019) and *Philosophy and Revolution: From Kant to Marx* (2nd edition, 2017).

Lucia Pradella is Senior Lecturer in international political economy at King's College London. Her publications include *Globalization and the Critique of Political Economy: New Insights from Marx's Writings* (Routledge, 2015), *L'attualità del capitale: Accumulazione e impoverimento nel capitalismo globale* (2010) and *Polarizing Development: Alternatives to Neoliberalism and the Crisis* (co-edited, 2015).

"This handbook is an outstanding contribution to Marxist scholarship. The chapters dealing with the various authors or issues are all of exceptional intellectual and political quality. Anyone interested in the Marxist tradition and on the present debates cannot miss reading this remarkable collection."

Michael Löwy, *Emeritus Research Director National Center for Scientific Research, Paris*

"The analysis of Marxism alongside the many currents of critical thought that have engaged with it over the years could not be more urgent. This splendid volume offers both the perfect introduction to the topic, and nuanced philosophical analyses of the relationship between Marxism and post-Marxist critiques of injustice based on gender, race and ethnicity. This is an intelligent and erudite book that shows us not only how to read Marx but also how to place the struggle against capitalism at the heart of a historically-sensitive, philosophically rigorous, genuinely intersectional, and decolonised, collective enterprise."

Lea Ypi, *Professor of Political Theory, London School of Economics and Political Science*

ROUTLEDGE HANDBOOK OF MARXISM AND POST-MARXISM

Edited by Alex Callinicos, Stathis Kouvelakis and Lucia Pradella

Routledge
Taylor & Francis Group
NEW YORK AND LONDON

First published 2021
by Routledge
605 Third Avenue, New York, NY 10017

and by Routledge
2 Park Square, Milton Park, Abingdon, Oxon, OX14 4RN

First issued in paperback 2022

Routledge is an imprint of the Taylor & Francis Group, an informa business

Library of Congress Cataloging-in-Publication Data
A catalog record for this book has been requested

ISBN 13: 978-1-138-55552-5 (hbk)
ISBN 13: 978-0-367-65374-3 (pbk)
ISBN 13: 978-1-315-14960-8 (ebk)

DOI: 10.4324/9781315149608

Typeset in Bembo
by Apex CoVantage, LLC

CONTENTS

ABBREVIATIONS

CI	Marx, Karl. 1976. *Capital*, I. Harmondsworth: Penguin.
CII	Marx, Karl. 1978. *Capital*, II. Harmondsworth: Penguin.
CIII	Marx, Karl. 1981. *Capital*, III. Harmondsworth: Penguin.
G	Marx, Karl. 1973. *Grundrisse*. Harmondsworth: Penguin.
LCW	Lenin, V I. 1960–78. *Collected Works*. 45 vols, Moscow: Progress.
MECW	Marx, Karl, and Friedrich Engels. 1975–2005. *Collected Works*. 50 vols, Moscow: Progress.

CONTRIBUTORS

Yousuf Al-Bulushi is an Assistant Professor in the Department of Global and International Studies at the University of California, Irvine. He received his PhD in Geography from the University of North Carolina at Chapel Hill, and his BA in the Program in Literature with a certificate in Marxism and Society from Duke University.

Kieran Allen lectures at the School of Sociology in University College Dublin. He is a member of People Before Profit.

Jason Barker is Associate Professor of English at Kyung Hee University. He is the author of *Alain Badiou: A Critical Introduction* and translator of Badiou's *Metapolitics*, writer-director of *Marx Reloaded*, and author of the novel *Marx Returns*.

Pietro Basso has been Associate Professor of Sociological Theory at the Ca' Foscari University of Venice. He is the author of *Razzismo di stato. Stati Uniti, Europa, Italia*, (2015), *Le racisme européen. Critique de la rationalité institutionnelle de l'oppression* (Syllepse, 2016), and *Tempos modernos, jornadas antigas. Vidas de trabalho no início do século XXI* (Editora Unicamp, 2018); and the editor of *The Science and the Passion of Communism: Selected Writings of Amadeo Bordiga 1912-1965* (2020).

Riccardo Bellofiore teaches Political Economy at the University of Bergamo.

Tithi Bhattacharya is a Professor of History and the Director of Global Studies at Purdue University. Her recent publications include *Social Reproduction Theory. Remapping Class, Recentering Oppression* (2017) and co-authored with Nancy Fraser and Cinzia Arruzza *Feminism for the 99%: A Manifesto* (2019).

Roland Boer is a Professor of Philosophy in the Faculty of Marxism, Dalian University of Technology, Dalian, China. His research focus concerns comparative Marxist philosophy (between "east" and "west").

Bianca Imbiriba Bonente is a Lecturer in Political Economy at the Universidade Federal Fluminense, Niteroi, Brazil, and member of the Interdisciplinary Center for Studies and Research on Marx and Marxism (NIEP-Marx).

Geoff Boucher lectures at Deakin University and has written several books on Marxism and post-Marxism, including *Understanding Marxism* (2012) and *The Charmed Circle of Ideology* (2008), both of which discuss Laclau and Mouffe in some detail. He is currently engaged in the development of a Marxist general theory of social antagonism that incorporates insights from some of the most important currents in post-Marxism.

Alex Callinicos is Emeritus Professor of European Studies at King's College London and was editor of *International Socialism* 2009-20. His most recent books are *Imperialism and Global Political Economy* (2009), *Bonfire of Illusions* (2010), and *Deciphering **Capital*** (2014).

Terrell Carver is Professor of Political Theory at the University of Bristol. He has published widely on Marx, Engels, and Marxisms, and on sex, gender, and sexualities. He is co-author of *Judith Butler and Political Theory* for Routledge (2008), and author of *Marx* in the Polity Press series "Classic Thinkers" (2018).

Brett Clark is Professor of Sociology, Environmental Humanities, and Environmental and Sustainability Studies at the University of Utah. Along with Stefano B. Longo and Rebecca Clausen, he is the author of *The Tragedy of the Commodity: Oceans, Fisheries, and Aquaculture* (2015).

Noel Castree is a Professor of Geography at Manchester University, England, and an Honorary Professorial Research Fellow at the University of Wollongong, Australia. His main interest is in the political economy of environmental change and the politics of environmental expertise. He has published many articles on Marxism in journals such as *Antipode, Capital & Class* and *New Political Economy*. He is co-author of David *Harvey's Marxism: A Critical Introduction* (2021)

Sam Coombes is Senior Lecturer in the Department of European Languages and Cultures at the University of Edinburgh. He is the author of *The Early Sartre and Marxism* (2008) and *Edouard Glissant A Poetics of Resistance* (2018) and numerous articles in the fields of political thought, postcolonial theory, and alter-globalization studies.

Hugo F. Corrêa is Professor at Universidade Federal Fluminense, Brazil, and Researcher of the Interdisciplinary Center for Studies and Research on Marx and Marxism (NIEP-Marx).

Alex Demirović is a Supernumerary Professor at the Goethe-University Frankfurt/M; research fields: critical social theory and Marxism, intellectuals, regulation theory, theory of democracy (economic democracy).

Marcelo Dias Carcanholo is Professor at Universidade Federal Fluminense, Brazil, and Researcher of the Interdisciplinary Center for Studies and Research on Marx and Marxism (NIEP-Marx).

Allison Drew is an Honorary Professor at the University of Cape Town Centre for African Studies and a Professor Emerita at the University of York.

Arnold L. Farr is Professor of Philosophy at the University of Kentucky. He has written extensively on German idealism, philosophy of race, critical theory, and especially Herbert Marcuse. Arnold is also founder and president of the International Herbert Marcuse Society.

John Bellamy Foster is Professor of Sociology at the University of Oregon and editor of *Monthly Review* in New York. He is the author of *The Theory of Monopoly Capitalism* (1986,

2004), *Marx's Ecology* (2000), and *The Endless Crisis* (2012, with Robert W. McChesney), and *The Return of Nature* (2020), along with many other works.

James Furner teaches philosophy, politics and international studies at the Independent Institute of Education, MSA campus, Johannesburg. He is the author of *Marx on Capitalism: the Interaction-Recognition-Antinomy Thesis* (2019), and *Rescuing Autonomy from Kant* (forthcoming).

Daniel Gaido is a researcher at the National Research Council (Conicet), Argentina. He is co-editor, with Richard Day, of *Witnesses to Permanent Revolution* (2009), *Discovering Imperialism* (2009) and *Responses to Marx's* ***Capital*** (2018).

Mike Gonzalez is Emeritus Professor of Latin American Studies at Glasgow University. He has written widely on Latin American history, politics and culture. He is the author of *The Ebb of the Pink Tide; the Decline of the Left in Latin America* (2018) and *In the Red Corner: the Marxism of José Carlos Mariátegui* (2019).

Jukka Gronow is an Emeritus Professor of Sociology at the University of Helsinki and the author of *On the Formation on Marxism* (2016).

Christian Høgsbjerg is a Lecturer in Critical History and Politics in the School of Humanities at the University of Brighton. He is the author of *C.L.R. James in Imperial Britain*, which appeared as part of the C.L.R. James Archives series, and he has edited or co-edited other titles for this series including *The Black Jacobins Reader*, *World Revolution* and *Marxism, Colonialism and Cricket: C.L.R. James's Beyond a Boundary*.

Peter Hudis is Professor of Humanities and Philosophy at Oakton Community College in Illinois and is General Editor of *The Complete Works of Rosa Luxemburg*, which will make all of her writings available in English translation. Three volumes of a planned 17, in addition to *The Letters of Rosa Luxemburg*, have appeared so far.

Feyzi Ismail teaches at SOAS, University of London, and is active in the British anti-war and anti-austerity movements.

Dhruv Jain has a PhD in Social and Political Thought at York University, Ontario. His dissertation, *The Atomic Prince: A Lucretian Interpretation of Machiavelli*, examines the influence of the late Roman atomist philosopher, Lucretius, on the political thought of Niccolò Machiavelli. He also publishes on historical and contemporaneous Maoist movements in India, and post-war French political philosophy.

Bob Jessop is Distinguished Professor of Sociology at Lancaster University, UK. His research interests include radical social theory, critical political economy, and materialist state theory. His definitive study of Nicos Poulantzas was published in 1985 and he continues to work on questions of state and state power.

Stathis Kouvelakis taught political theory at King's College London. He has published on Marxism, contemporary critical theory, French and Greek politics. His recent publications include *Philosophy and Revolution. From Kant to Marx* (2nd edition, 2017) and *La critique défaite. Emergence et domestication de la Théorie critique* (2019).

Rick Kuhn is an honorary Associate Professor of Sociology at the Australian National University and a member of Socialist Alternative in Australia.

Andrew T. Lamas teaches urban studies and critical theory at the University of Pennsylvania and is on the board of the International Herbert Marcuse Society

Davide Gallo Lassere, PhD in Philosophy, is a member of the Sophiapol laboratory at the University of Paris Ouest. He works on the theories and on the history of capitalism.

Paul Le Blanc, Professor of History at La Roche University, has produced a broad range of studies on the labor and socialist movements. His works include: *A Short History of the US Working Class; Lenin and the Revolutionary Party; The Living Flame: The Revolutionary Passion of Rosa Luxemburg; October Song: Bolshevik Triumph and Communist Tragedy, 1917–1924; and Leon Trotsky.*

Lars T. Lih lives and works in Montreal, Quebec. His recent publications include *Lenin Rediscovered* (2006) and *Lenin* (2011). Lately he has been examining the Bolshevik outlook in 1917 and its relation to other parties. At present, he is preparing a collection of his articles under the title *Deferred Dreams*.

Stefano B. Longo is Associate Professor of Sociology at North Carolina State University. Along with Brett Clark and Rebecca Clausen, he is the author of *The Tragedy of the Commodity: Oceans, Fisheries, and Aquaculture* (2015).

João Leonardo Medeiros is a Lecturer in Political Economy at the Universidade Federal Fluminense, Niterói, Brazil, and member of the Interdisciplinary Center for Studies and Research on Marx and Marxism (NIEP-Marx).

Frédéric Monferrand holds a Ph.D. in Philosophy from Nanterre University (Sophiapol) and is a post-doctoral researcher at the university of Liège (Belgium). His research interests focus on Hegel, Marx, social ontology and the critique of capitalism.

Timothy S. Murphy is Houston-Truax-Wentz Professor and Regents Professor of English at Oklahoma State University. He is the author of *Wising Up the Marks: The Amodern William Burroughs* (1997) and *Antonio Negri: Modernity and the Multitude* (2012) and the translator of Negri's *Subversive Spinoza* (2004), *Books for Burning* (2005), *Trilogy of Resistance* (2011) and *Flower of the Desert* (2015).

John Narayan is a Lecturer in European and International Studies at King's College London. His current research focuses on the global politics of Black Power. He is the author of *John Dewey: The Global Public and its Problems* and co-editor of *European Cosmopolitanism: Colonial Histories and Post-Colonial Societies*.

Alf Gunvald Nilsen is Professor of Sociology at the University of Pretoria. He is the author of *Dispossession and Resistance in India: The River and the Rage* (2010), *We Make Our Own History: Marxism and Social Movements in the Twilight of Neoliberalism* (2014) and *Adivasis and the State: Subalternity and Citizenship in India's Bhil Heartland* (2018).

Henry Pickford is Professor of German and Philosophy at Duke University. He is the author of: *The Sense of Semblance: Philosophical Analyses of Holocaust Art; Thinking with Tolstoy and Wittgenstein:*

Expression, Emotion and Art; co-author of *In Defense of Intuition: A New Rationalist Manifesto*; editor and translator of Theodor W. Adorno, *Critical Models* (from the German) and *Selected Early Poems of Lev Loseff* (from the Russian); co-editor of *Der aufrechte Gang im windschiefen Kapitalismus*, and has published over twenty articles and book chapters. He is currently writing with Gordon Finlayson *Adorno: A Critical Life* and editing with Martin Shuster the *Oxford Handbook of Theodor W. Adorno*.

Lucia Pradella is a Senior Lecturer in International Political Economy at King's College London. She is the author of *L'attualità del capitale. Accumulazione e impoverimento nel capitalismo globale* (2010) and *Globalization and the Critique of Political Economy: New Insights from Marx's Writings* (2015) and co-editor of *Polarizing Development: Alternatives to Neoliberalism and the Crisis* (2015). She is currently working on the relationship between imperialism, the global reserve army of labour, and migration.

Vijay Prashad is the Executive Director of Tricontinental: Institute for Social Research, Chief Editor of LeftWord Books and Chief Correspondent for Globetrotter.

Manuel Quiroga is a PhD Research Fellow at CIECS (Conicet-National University of Córdoba), Argentina. He is currently writing his dissertation comparing debates on imperialism in German, French and Italian Social Democracy during the pre-WWI period

Darren Roso is a socialist writer based in Melbourne.

Camilla Royle recently completed a PhD in Geography at King's College London. She was deputy editor of the journal *International Socialism* between 2013 and 2020.

Kohei Saito is Associate Professor of Political Economy at Osaka City University. His book *Karl Marx's Ecosocialism* was awarded the Isaac and Tamara Deutscher Memorial Prize for 2018.

Ryuji Sasaki is Associate Professor of Economics at Rikkyo University, Tokyo.

George Souvlis holds a PhD in history from the European University Institute in Florence. Recently, he published the book *Voices on the Left, Challenging Capitalist Hegemony* (2019) and is co-editor of the forthcoming volume, *Back to the '30's? Crisis, Repetition and Transition in the 20th and 21th Centuries* (2019).

Colin Sparks taught media studies at Hong Kong Baptist University. His Ph.D. is from the University of Birmingham's Centre for Contemporary Cultural Studies.

Gayatri Chakravorty Spivak teaches at Columbia University. She has been working on Marxism, Feminism, and Deconstruction for the last 50 years.

Intan Suwandi is an Assistant Professor of Sociology at Illinois State University and author of *Value Chains: The New Economic Imperialism* (2019).

Robert T. Tally Jr. is the NEH Distinguished Teaching Professor in the Humanities and Professor of English at Texas State University. His books include *Topophrenia: Place, Narrative, and the Spatial Imagination*; *Fredric Jameson: The Project of Dialectical Criticism*; *Spatiality*; and, as editor, the *Routledge Handbook of Literature and Space* and *Teaching Space, Place, and Literature*.

André Tosel (1941–2017) was Professor of Philosophy at the university of Nice (France). He was the leading specialist in France on Gramsci and has also published extensively on Spinoza, Marx, Italian thought, and contemporary Marxism.

Enzo Traverso is Susan and Barton Winokur Professor in the Humanities at Cornell University. His works include *The Jewish Question: History of a Marxist Debate* (1994; new edition 2018), *The Origins of Nazi Violence* (2003), *Fire and Blood: The European Civil War 1914–1945* (2016), *The End of Jewish Modernity* (2016), *Left-Wing Melancholia: Marxism, History and Memory* (2017), and *The New Faces of Fascism: Populism and the Far Right* (2019).

Maria Turchetto taught history of economic thought and epistemology of social sciences at the Ca' Foscari University of Venice. She carried out research in the economic field with particular interest in the thought of Marx; in the field of epistemology on the relationships between social sciences and life sciences; in the field of philosophy on the thought of Louis Althusser. She has published numerous essays in Italian and foreign volumes and magazines (*Science & Society*, *Historical Materialism*, *Actuel Marx*, *Marxist Criticism*, *Quaderni Materialisti*). She is currently president of the cultural association "Louis Althusser" and directs the Althusseriana and Epistemology series at the Mimesis publishing house in Milan.

Marcel van der Linden is a Fellow and former Research Director of the International Institute of Social History, and emeritus professor of Social Movement History at the University of Amsterdam.

Leo Zeilig is a writer and researcher. He has written on African politics and history, including books on working-class struggle and the development of revolutionary movements and biographies on some of Africa's most important political thinkers and activists.

INTRODUCTION

Alex Callinicos, Stathis Kouvelakis and Lucia Pradella

The past decades have seen the interweaving of two closely connected phenomena: the emergence of Post-Marxism and the intellectual revitalization of Marxism. Post-Marxism emerged as a self-adopted label in the 1980s to characterize a particular means of escape from the widely proclaimed "crisis of Marxism" that followed the decline of the 1960s radical movements in the mid-1970s and that was reinforced by the collapse of the Communist regimes in 1989–91. To be a Post-Marxist is to pursue questions in part inherited from Marxism in a theoretical and political framework that simultaneously is itself influenced by Marxism but seeks to go decisively beyond it. Thus, for example, Ernesto Laclau and Chantal Mouffe argue that "[it] is no longer possible to maintain the conception of subjectivity and classes elaborated by Marxism, nor its historical vision of the historical course of capitalist development, nor, of course, the conception of communism as a transparent society," but nevertheless acknowledge that their own work has involved "the development of certain intuitions and discursive forms constituted within Marxism" (Laclau and Mouffe 1985, 4). Among the leading exemplars of this approach are, apart from Laclau and Mouffe themselves, Alain Badiou, Judith Butler, Jürgen Habermas and Axel Honneth, but in many ways it has affinities with the critiques of the domination of North by South developed by *Subaltern Studies* and postcolonialism. Thinkers of this kind tend to be in dialogue with mainstream approaches such as liberalism as well as the body of thought that has come to be known as poststructuralism (for example, Gilles Deleuze, Jacques Derrida and Michel Foucault), which takes its distance from both liberalism and Marxism and is influenced by Nietzsche's critique of the Enlightenment.

But Marxism remains a powerful reference point for Post-Marxists: the evolution of Slavoj Žižek at the end of the 1990s toward a more clearly defined Marxist (even idiosyncratically Leninist) position is exemplary in this respect. Indeed, as time has passed, the boundary between Marxism and Post-Marxism has become more blurred. This is partly because some important contemporary Marxist theorists have themselves drawn heavily on poststructuralism (the influence of Deleuze, himself a careful reader of Marx, on Negri is a case in point). But some Post-Marxists have moved back toward Marxism: the most important example is provided by Badiou's recent exploration of the "communist hypothesis" and even occasional self-description as a Marxist. This is a tribute to the continued intellectual and political power of Marxism, but it in no way settles the disputes that led to the crystallization of Post-Marxism as a distinct intellectual current.

These developments need to be understood against the backdrop of the revitalization of Marxism as a research program and the growth in its audience in the wake of the revival of anti-capitalist contestation since the Seattle protests of November 1999 and the impact of the global economic and financial crisis that started in 2007–8. The effort to re-articulate and develop Marxist perspectives in part involves established figures such as David Harvey, Fredric Jameson and Terry Eagleton, and long-standing research networks (for example, those contributing to the vast *Marx-Engels Gesamtausgabe* [MEGA^2], the publication of Marx's and Engels's complete writings). But we also see the entry of a new generation of younger scholars, who are beginning to offer their own distinctive take on the Marxist problematic, often shaped by experiences of precarious employment and new forms of political movement. It is distinctive in being far more isolated from mass political parties of the left (to the extent that these survive) than, not only the so-called classical Marxists of the Second and Third Internationals (for example, Kautsky, Luxemburg, Lenin, Trotsky), but the majority of the postwar generation (Althusser, Colletti, Sartre). The intellectual actuality of Marxism has been reaffirmed by the development in 2007–8 of the greatest systemic crisis that capitalism had experienced since the 1930s, even though its main political consequence – the implosion of the neoliberal political order – has so far favored the racist and fascist right.

Our Handbook is a response to this intellectual and political conjuncture. It presents the main traditions and preoccupations of Marxism from the vantage point of a present where Marxism is simultaneously less fragile intellectually than during the 1980s and 1990s but the connections between theory and practice are less clear than they have ever been. The richness but also the uncertainties with which the Marxist problematic is pursued are best captured by presenting it in dialogue with Post-Marxism: not only the origins but also the future of these currents of thought are in fact closely interdependent. This is necessarily an interdisciplinary undertaking. Marx's founding definition of his object of study as "a rich totality of many determinations and relations" meant his own critique of political economy transcended the disciplinary boundaries between philosophy, economics, politics and history (*G*: 100). The most creative work has continued in this spirit. At the same time, our Handbook escapes the tendency of many presentations of Marxism to treat it as a purely European tradition. Today, as in the past, much original work comes from outside the metropolis and in dialogue with movements against the domination of the North.

We have therefore organized the Handbook to trace the trajectory of Marxism and Post-Marxism through the crises and debates that have punctuated their interwoven histories. Longer contextual chapters are followed by clusters of shorter chapters devoted to individual thinkers or specific currents. (In planning the Handbook and commissioning the chapters we have been painfully aware of the numerous injustices we have been forced to commit and the many fine and original thinkers we have been unable to include.) The first three contextual chapters follow a chronological order, addressing Marx himself, and then the Marxisms that arose against the background of the Second and Third Internationals; thereafter we have more thematic treatments, which deal with areas that Marxism is often accused of neglecting – struggles in the Global South, the oppression of women and ecology, for example, mingle with assessments of 1968 and the "thousand Marxisms" that emerged in its aftermath, and the closely related development of Post-Marxism, before we conclude with explorations of how Marx's critique of political economy has been continued, and responses to the global crisis precipitated by the COVID-19 pandemic.

Communism, the Critique of Political Economy and the Proletariat

But what is Marxism? In order to answer this question, we need to go back to the work of the two founders of what was later to become one of the most influential modern ideologies.[1] Karl

Marx and Friedrich Engels were not the only intellectuals in mid-19th-century Europe to conclude that a radical-democratic break with the old regime could be only be realized through the achievement of communism. Nor were they alone in resorting to political economy for support for a communist diagnosis of the ills of capitalism. But they went beyond their contemporaries in two crucial respects: their critique of political economy and its organic connection with the emerging workers' movement.

The critique of political economy – inaugurated by Engels in 1844 but brought to maturity by Marx in the great cycle of manuscripts between the early 1850s and 1867 and culminating in *Capital* volume I – made three decisive moves. First, implicitly in Marx's *Economic and Philosophic Manuscripts of 1844* and explicitly from *The Poverty of Philosophy* (1847) onwards, political economy was radically historicized. Where classical political economists such as Adam Ferguson and Adam Smith had ended up portraying the emerging "commercial society" of the 18th and early 19th centuries as the "mode of subsistence" fully corresponding to the requirements of human nature, Marx demoted what he and Engels initially called "bourgeois society" to the status of a historically contingent and transitory economic system that developed the productive potential inherent in the human capacity to labor in a distorted and alienated form.

This historicization of political economy implied a theory of history that Marx rarely set out systematically (mainly in the chaotic collection of drafts written in the mid-1840s and edited and published much later as *The German Ideology* and in a pregnant paragraph in the 1859 Preface to *A Contribution to the Critique of Political Economy*). This theory portrayed history as a succession of modes of production, each based on a specific combination of the productive forces (the historically developed productive powers of humankind, expressed in the prevailing levels of knowledge and technique) and the social relations of production (the relations of economic control over these productive forces). The move from one mode to another is governed by two motors – the tendency for growing productive forces to come into conflict with the existing production relations and, where the productive forces are in the hands of a minority, the class struggle between exploiters and exploited. But it would be in what Marx called the "superstructure," consisting primary of law, politics and ideology, that "human beings become conscious of this conflict and fight it out" (*MECW* 29: 263; translation modified).

Second, during the decisive decade of 1857–67, Marx worked and re-worked the categories of political economy to develop a systematic analysis of the economic logic of the capitalist mode of production. Though never completed (Engels edited volumes II and III of *Capital* from manuscripts after Marx's death, publishing them in 1885 and 1894 respectively), this analysis presented capitalism as constituted by two main antagonisms – between capital and wage-labor, based on the exploitation of workers in production, and among the competing "many capitals" into which the capitalist class is itself divided. The interaction of these antagonisms – mediated by the competitive pressure that compels capitals to accumulate, that is, to reinvest profits in improved and expanded production – is responsible for the pattern of regular and destructive economic crises that Marx was among the first to discern. The presence of terms such as "antagonism" register the influence of Hegel's dialectical philosophy on Marx's project, though commentators argue endlessly over whether this influence was a help, a hindrance or a source of support from which he had eventually to liberate himself.

Third, the object of this analysis is capitalism as an actually existing and historically evolving world system. Already in their most famous text, the *Manifesto of the Communist Party* (1848), Marx and Engels offered a brilliant sketch of how 19th-century industrial capitalism was transforming the world through the creation of a single global economy and the subordination of every society to its rhythms. In his economic and historical studies from the mid-1840s onwards, Marx explored the concrete forms this process was taking, and in particular sought to understand how European colonial expansion helped to promote capital accumulation – an analysis taken further by one of the most brilliant of his successors, Rosa Luxemburg, in *The Accumulation of Capital* (1913). After Marx began his long exile in London following the defeat of the 1848 revolution, he looked not only into the impact of capitalist expansion on pre-capitalist societies but also started to investigate communal property relations and forms of resistance to colonial expansion, and to explore the history of the family, of women's condition and culture (see Chapter 1, "Foundation").

Marx therefore distinguished himself from his contemporaries in the first instance through the intellectual depth and the sheer scale of his critique of political economy. Second, however, the political content of this critique implied an organic connection with the emerging workers' movement. In the tradition of German classical philosophy in which Marx and Engels were formed intellectually, the term "critique" implies not simply negative or destructive criticism, but an attempt to identify the limits ignoring which leads to error. Thus Marx's lengthy critique of the political economists, notably in *The Economic Manuscript of 1861–63*, traces the limits of the insights they offer in their identification of capitalism as natural. But Marx goes further in that his critique works through the concepts and theories of political economy to reconstruct the economic logic of the capitalist system that these simultaneously reveal and conceal. This is possible because, from the early 1840s onwards, he shows an impatience with any purely theoretical critique and strongly links his own intellectual work to the actual, practical critique of the existing system. "The weapon of criticism" – he wrote in 1844 – "cannot, of course, replace criticism of the weapon . . . theory also becomes a material force as soon as it has gripped the masses." This is why the proletariat, "a class with *radical* chains," if guided by philosophy, could carry though a "universal emancipation" transcending the purely political changes achieved by the French Revolution (*MECW* 3: 182, 183, 186).

With the development of the critique of political economy the proletariat ceases to be a philosophical postulate and becomes both the object of capitalist exploitation and the active subject of communist transformation. This evolution reaches its climax in *Capital*, I. British socialists had already in the 1820s and 1830s taken over the labor theory of value systematically formulated by David Ricardo, who argued that commodities exchange in proportion to the labor required to produce them. They concluded that if capital is merely accumulated labor, then, as Thomas Hodgskin put it, "the best means of securing the progressive improvement, both of individuals and nations, is to do justice and allow labor to possess and enjoy the whole of its produce" (Hodgskin 1922, 109). In *Capital* Marx seeks to disjoin this argument from a normative problematic of injustice, and argues that, since living labor is the sole source of value, profits are surplus-value appropriated by capital. This is made possible by wage-labor's bargaining disadvantage, since to the exchange with capital the worker brings only his or her labor-power, which can only be activated by the access to the means of production controlled by capital. But capital's dependence on the exploitation of workers gives them the structural power not merely to resist, but to overthrow the system altogether. Marx argues that the long-term result of the accumulation process, the polarization of society as, across successive crises, economic power is concentrated in the hands of an ever-narrower group of capitalists, will create the conditions for socialist revolution:

> Along with the constant decrease in the number of capitalist magnates, who usurp and monopolize all the advantages of this process of transformation, the mass of misery, oppression, slavery, degradation and exploitation grows; but with this there also grows the revolt of the working class, a class constantly increasing in numbers, and trained, united, and organized by the very mechanism of the capitalist process of production.
> *(CI: 929)*

The critique of political economy thus issues in a political project of working-class self-emancipation (Callinicos 2018). Marx wrote *Capital*, I, in the mid-1860s, when he was playing a leading role in the International Working Men's Association, or First International. This was a coalition of trade unionists, mainly in Britain, and of Continental socialist political groupings. As was shown by its eventual destruction as a result of conflicts between Marx and the followers of his great rivals Mikhail Bakunin and Pierre-Joseph Proudhon, the International provided a terrain where different ideological currents could compete to influence the emerging European workers' movement. Nevertheless, Marx's prominence in the International derived in part from his intellectual commitment to helping form a political project distinctively of and for the working class (in very different ways Bakunin and Proudhon were oriented to a more loosely delimited mass of small producers of town and country). The importance of this project to his and Engels's self-understanding is indicated in this passage from a circular letter (17–18 September 1879) they wrote to the leaders of the German Social Democratic Party (SPD) against an attempt to move this new party in the direction of left liberalism:

> For almost 40 years we have emphasized that the class struggle is the immediate motive force of history and, in particular, that the class struggle between bourgeoisie and proletariat is the great lever of modern social revolution; hence we cannot possibly co-operate with men who seek to eliminate that class struggle from the movement. At the founding of the International we expressly formulated the battle cry: The emancipation of the working class must be achieved by the working class itself. Hence we cannot co-operate with men who say openly that the workers are too uneducated to emancipate themselves, and must first be emancipated from above by philanthropic members of the upper and lower middle classes.
>
> (MECW *45: 408)*

Marx and Marxisms

The intrinsic connection Marx and Engels posited between the critique of political economy and a politics of working-class self-emancipation offers a way of thinking about the trajectory of Marxism after its founder's death in 1883. Of course, the diversity of Marxisms and the range of thinkers who can be identified with them is too rich to be accommodated in any simple framework. Nevertheless, it is helpful to think about four great rendezvous that have taken place between Marxism and mass movements. The first came in the late 19th century with the emergence of mass socialist parties and the invention of a popularized Marxism as the most systematic version of socialist ideology. Challenged from both right and left from the beginning of the new century, this particular junction cracked wide open with the outbreak of the First World War in August 1914. The second rendezvous followed with the Russian Revolution of October 1917 and the associated polarization of the labor movement between revolutionary and social-democratic wings. This created the conditions for a third rendezvous, between the new Communist movement and national liberation struggles. Finally, 1968 marked a fourth rendezvous, between a revolutionary left impatient with official Communism and social democracy alike and a wave of working-class insurgency.

This is a political reading of the history of Marxism. This doesn't mean that everything pursued within a Marxist framework can be reduced to specifically political problems of analysis, strategy and organization. This is particularly so as the ties between Marxist intellectual research and left parties have loosened in the contemporary "era of a thousand Marxisms" (Wallerstein 1986, 1302; see also Tosel 2005). Most of these Marxisms are located primarily in the academy, and they can be driven by preoccupations internal to it. But the relationship between theory and practice – so central to Marx's understanding of his own project – has haunted his successors to this day. Perry Anderson famously drew a contrast between the "classical Marxism" of the founders and the Second and Third Internationals, whose practitioners were political activists, often party leaders, as well as theorists, and the "Western Marxism" that developed in Western Europe after the Second World War, whose main characteristic was "the structural divorce of this Marxism from political practice," leading to a displacement of intellectual focus from political economy and strategic debates to philosophy and aesthetics (Anderson 1976, 29).

This diagnosis seems overstated. As Anderson himself acknowledges, in France and Italy, the two countries that produced the most fertile developments of Marxism between the 1940s and the 1970s, leftist intellectuals, even if academics such as Louis Althusser or writers like Jean-Paul Sartre, operated in a political environment dominated by mass Communist parties whose ideological initiatives and strategic problems provided the key reference point, whether negative or positive, for socialist theory. The Frankfurt School, whether in American exile or after some returned to Germany, were preoccupied with how to continue the critique of capitalism when, as they saw it, the working class had definitively lost its capacity to act as a revolutionary subject. In strongholds of social democracy such as Britain and West Germany, Marxists probed the economic and political limits of the Keynesian welfare state, whether they started by rereading the *Grundrisse* and *Capital*, as German value-form theorists did, or chose the more empirical mode native to Ralph Miliband's adopted British home. And the most arcane theoretical writings achieved mass readerships at the height of the radicalizations of the 1960s and the 1970s. In the post-1989 period the popularity of Tony Negri's work, and somewhat more recently, of the writings and online lectures of Alain Badiou, David Harvey and Slavoj Žižek has to be seen against the waves of anti-capitalist mobilization that followed the Seattle protests in 1999 and the 2008 crash.

So Marxism, for all its plurality, has been marked by the interplay of theoretical and political preoccupations. It has also been punctuated by widely perceived moments of internal crisis – starting in the late 1890s with the publication of Eduard Bernstein's *Preconditions of Socialism*, but again during the First World War, in the 1930s, and at the end of the 1970s. Indeed, one of us has written, "Marxism is *constitutively*, from Marx's contribution onwards, . . . crisis theory" (Kouvelakis 2005, 25). Perhaps there are two main reasons for this succession of crises. First, Marxism is inherently tied to capitalism, at once the object of the critique of political economy and an enemy to be vanquished. But since, as Marx and Engels showed in the *Communist Manifesto*, it is also a dynamic system constantly transforming itself, Marxism constantly falls victim to the anxiety that it is not adequate to its Protean antagonist, that it must run to keep up with the metamorphoses of bourgeois society. This is then connected to a second source of anxiety, namely that capitalism continues to exist, and that therefore the communist project remains unrealized, two centuries now after Marx's birth.

First Rendezvous: Marxism and the Second International

In the first junction between Marxism and the workers' movement, in the late 19th and early 20th centuries, what was at stake was this very relationship itself. The emergence of the SPD as a mass workers' party with a growing electoral presence provided the context in which Marxism as a systematic socialist doctrine was formulated and popularized. Engels played a key role here. Though he and Marx had little influence over the party's actual direction, especially after the latter's death, Engels offered a key source of ideological legitimacy for the SPD and the other parties of a growing international socialist movement. His polemic *Anti-Dühring* (1878) presented the first concise and integrated account of his and Marx's understanding of history, political economy and socialist transformation. Part was spun off as a pamphlet, *Socialism, Utopian and Scientific*, that offered a highly influential statement of what Engels presented as Marxism's unique and incontestable claim to be based on a distinctively scientific approach to the understanding of human history.

In a move that Marx certainly did not oppose, though he might not have chosen it himself, Engels also inserted the "materialistic conception of history," as he called it, in a broader ontology. Most fully expounded in the posthumously published *Dialectics of Nature*, this was formed by extracting from Hegel's philosophy three "laws of the dialectic," understood as universal laws of nature instantiated in the physical as well as the social world. Engels integrated into this "dialectical materialism" some of the great intellectual developments of the day – for example, Darwin's theory of evolution by natural selection and the discovery of the laws of thermodynamics. Sometimes Engels's writings on science are mistakenly criticized for reducing Marx's original insights to a form of determinism. In fact, they seek to develop a sophisticated understanding of nature as a complex historical process and to avoid both the Romantic philosophy of nature associated with Schelling and other post-Kantian idealists and the mechanical materialism prevalent especially in mid-19th-century Germany.[2]

Engels's conceptualization of Marxism as simultaneously scientific socialism and a naturalistic ontology was taken much further by Karl Kautsky, who, thanks to his position as editor of the SPD weekly *Die neue Zeit*, educated an entire generation of Marxists. Reflecting the intellectual environment of the late 19th century, he cast Marxism as an evolutionary theory. Contrasting his intellectual formation with that of Marx and Engels, Kautsky wrote: "They started out with *Hegel*; I started out with *Darwin*" (Kautsky 1988, 7). In fact, Kautsky preferred Lamarck's more teleological version of evolutionary theory to Darwin's theory of evolution by natural selection. Socialism became in Kautsky's version of historical materialism the culmination of a process of social evolution, arising (in a phrase Kautsky frequently repeated) by "natural necessity." In one of his most influential texts, expounding the SPD's 1891 Erfurt program, Kautsky wrote:

> The capitalist social system has run its course. Its dissolution is now only a question of time. Irresistible economic forces lead with the certainty of doom to the shipwreck of capitalist production. The substitution of a new social order for the existing one is no longer desirable, it is inevitable.
>
> *(Kautsky 1910, 117)*

Kautsky did not think this conception of social evolution incompatible with human agency: class struggles and mass movements had their place in helping to accomplish the historical outcomes dictated by economic forces. Marxism itself had its part, in helping to make conscious the union of the workers' movement and socialism that was a necessary precondition of the overthrow of capitalism (Kautsky 1910, 189–90).

By the end of the 19th century, this union seemed close to achievement in Germany at least, with the advance of the SPD in mass membership and parliamentary representation. But it was precisely at this point that the first "crisis of Marxism" erupted, as Bernstein in *The Preconditions of Socialism* (1899) challenged the evolutionary progression to socialism conjured up by Kautsky from the right. Bernstein also shrewdly pointed to the gap between the SPD's revolutionary rhetoric and its much more cautious tactics, arguing that the party should embrace its practice as a progressive party of social reform. From the mid-1900s onwards this gap was also contested increasingly from the left, with Luxemburg emerging as the most eloquent and rigorous spokesperson of the party's revolutionary wing. The atmosphere of intense controversy in the international socialist movement over a variety of related questions – the relative weight of electoral politics and mass strikes in socialist strategy, imperialism and the growing tensions among the Great Powers, the meaning of the Russian Revolution of 1905 – did not prevent, or perhaps stimulated, the appearance of a series of major theoretical works that sought to develop Marxism by applying it to specific topics that the founders hadn't addressed – for example, Kautsky's *The Agrarian Question* and *The Foundations of Christianity*, V.I. Lenin's *The Development of Capitalism in Russia*, Otto Bauer's *Social Democracy and the National Question*, Rudolf Hilferding's *Finance Capital* and Luxemburg's *The Accumulation of Capital*. Whatever their limitations, these works set a benchmark for later Marxist inquiry.

Second Rendezvous: The Russian Revolution and the Ruptures of Marxisms

The outbreak of the First World War and the support given to their respective belligerent states by the SPD and the other main parties of the Second International turned the previous divisions into an open split. Lenin, one of the leading opponents of this policy, argued that genuine Marxists should seek to turn "the present imperialist war into a civil war" between classes (*LCW* 21: 34). This became a reality at the end of the war, as the Bolsheviks under Lenin's leadership sought to hang onto power in Russia, and as Luxemburg alongside many other militants of the new German Communist Party were murdered by right-wing militias backed by an SPD government. The Marxism of the new Communist International launched by the Bolsheviks in 1919 was a Marxism in arms, the ideology of a protagonist in what more than one historian has called the "European civil war" that raged between 1914 and 1945. The attempt by the Comintern to remodel its constituent parties under a quasi-military discipline fitted the practical experience of the millions that rallied to this new militant Marxism with its headquarters in Moscow.

The resulting polarization between pro- and anti-war socialists and the Russian Revolution of October 1917 made possible a second rendezvous, the reinvention of Marxism as a theory of revolutionary militancy. This is the historical moment when Marxism becomes a genuinely planetary force as the leaders of the new Soviet state sought to rally the masses of the colonial world against a shared imperialist enemy. But this moment also marks the fracturing of Marxism – partly because of the political competition between the old social-democratic Second International and the new Communist International, but also because the evolution of the Soviet Union into an industrialized Great Power built on and maintained by coercion stimulated the formulation of alternative versions of Marxism, whether to contest with Moscow the mantle of revolutionary orthodoxy (the followers of Leon Trotsky and Amadeo Bordiga, for example) or to articulate a sense of disappointment, even despair (above all, the Frankfurt School).

The catastrophe of 1914 and the revolutionary upheavals of 1917–18 also stimulated an unpicking of the evolutionary synthesis forged by Engels and Kautsky. This had happened sporadically before 1914. In *Reflections on Violence* (1908) Georges Sorel offered an intellectual as well as a political challenge to Kautsky's confidence in historical progress, arguing that capitalism was sinking into a decadence that affected bourgeoisie and proletariat alike and from which outbursts of mass revolutionary violence offered the only rescue (Sorel 1999). The title of another of Sorel's books, *The Illusions of Progress*, summed up his distance from Kautsky. In the philosophical background to this intervention lay a swelling current of anti-naturalistic thought that represented a reaction to the naturalism associated particularly with the impact of Darwin. Neo-Kantianism in Germany, Henri Bergson in France and Benedetto Croce in Italy epitomized this reaction, which after the First World War found expression among a new generation of revolutionary intellectuals – most prominently György Lukács and Antonio Gramsci – who simultaneously rallied to the Russian Revolution and the Comintern and sought to rethink Marxism theoretically to give a proper place to the role of subjectivity and practice in the Bolshevik achievement.

Plainly, politics was a driving force in this reconfiguration of Marxism. Kautsky's conceptualization of the attainment of socialism as occurring by "natural necessity" through an evolutionary process could claim a degree of support from Marx and Engels themselves. Contesting, in the aftermath of the defeated revolutions of 1848, voluntarist versions of communism that conceived the overthrow of capitalism "not as the product of realities of the situation but as a result of an effort of *will*," they had insisted: "We say to the workers: You have 15, 20, 50 years of civil war to go through to alter the situation and to train yourselves for the exercise of power" (*MECW* 10: 626). So revolution was a process for Marx and Engels as well. Indeed, in *Capital* Marx wrote that "capitalist production begets, with the inexorability of a natural process [*mit der Notwendigkeit eines Naturprozess*], its own negation" (*CI*: 929). But the experience of war and revolution after 1914 undermined any certainty in the triumphant union of socialism and the workers' movement that Kautsky had posited. Although Lenin before 1914 conceived his project as realizing in the particular conditions of Tsarist Russia the Second International Marxism most fully theorized by Kautsky (Lih 2006), the actual practice of the Bolsheviks effectively problematized this union, treating it, not as an ineluctable necessity but as the contested outcome of a struggle in which organized revolutionaries intervened in the class struggle to give it a conscious and communist direction. This implied a different practice of party-building, which the Comintern sought to systematize, particularly in the years of revolutionary turbulence following its formation. But what was the theory of this different practice? This was the question that Lukács and Gramsci sought to answer by drawing in innovative but also provocative ways on, respectively, the sociology of Georg Simmel and Max Weber and Croce's neo-Hegelian philosophy.

This kind of rethinking was bound to be controversial, and particularly so in the circumstances of the 1920s. The Marxism in arms of the Third International consolidated itself around its fortress, the new state that had emerged from the October Revolution. Indeed, whereas in the Comintern's early years the focus of the Third International was on the extension of the revolution, above all to Germany between 1918 and 1923, its *raison d'être* increasingly became the defense of the Soviet Union itself. This was formalized, during the succession struggles after Lenin's death in 1924 and Josef Stalin's rise to dominance, in the doctrine of Socialism in One Country, according to which it would be possible to build socialism in the Soviet Union prior to the overthrow of capitalism globally. This doctrine was quite different from Marx's own views and from the assumptions on which Lenin had advocated seizing power in 1917. The resulting ideological transformation was resisted by Stalin's defeated opponent Trotsky, who argued instead that socialism could only be achieved through a process of permanent revolution in which victories on the national scale could be secured only through the defeat of the capitalist world system. But Trotsky's supporters represented only a small and marginal current in a workers' movement dominated by social democracy and, as the threat of fascism grew in the 1930s, by growing Communist parties.

The consolidation of the Stalinist system involved the concentration of economic and political power in the hands of a central political bureaucracy ruling in the name of the Communist Party of the Soviet Union (as the Bolsheviks renamed themselves). The Communist Party itself claimed to rule on behalf of the working class – a working class first atomized and diminished in the years of civil war following the October Revolution and then reconstituted by the forced industrialization of the late 1920s and early 1930s as a much larger but thoroughly subordinated laboring class. The consolidation of Stalinism also involved the transformation of Marxism into a state ideology, a process that began with the invention of "Leninism" after its putative founder's death. As Valentino Gerratana puts it, the "systematic construction of 'Leninism,'" which involved "adoption of two closely related cults – one of Lenin, the infallible, charismatic leader, and one of the omnipotent party," "succeeded in blocking for half a century any development or renewal of the extraordinary revolutionary experience embodied in Lenin's theoretical work" (Gerratana 1977, 64, 71). The content of this "Marxism-Leninism" effectively took over Engels's and Kautsky's naturalistic ontology and flattened it out into a dogmatic catechism, most notably in Stalin's 1938 text "Dialectical and Historical Materialism" (Stalin 1943). But more important were the doctrine's perlocutionary functions in defining orthodoxy, legitimizing Soviet policy and justifying the exclusion (and, particularly during the Great Terror of 1936–38, mass murder) of heretics. The polarization of the world during the Cold War (1945–91) into rival geopolitical and ideological blocs headed respectively by the US and the USSR reinforced the performative role of Marxism-Leninism. It was in this era that Isaac Deutscher explicitly posited the plurality of Marxisms, pointing to

> a striking, and to a Marxist often humiliating, contrast between what I call classical Marxism – that is, the body of thought developed by Marx, Engels, their contemporaries, and after them by Kautsky, Plekhanov, Lenin, Trotsky, Rosa Luxemburg – and the vulgar Marxism, the pseudo-Marxism of the different varieties of European social-democrats, reformists, Stalinists, Khrushchevites, and their like.
>
> *(Deutscher 1971, 18)*

In this environment the kind of creative rethinking of Marxism that had flourished in the years immediately after the Russian Revolution could find no place in the orthodox Communist movement. The great exception to this – Gramsci – was able to pursue his researches precisely because he was confined to a Fascist prison that freed him from party control and indeed made him a symbol of Communist endurance (Anderson 2017). Divergences were, however, unavoidable even in the Stalinist era, which was one of wars where Communist parties often played an important role – in China and Spain in particular before the apocalypse of 1939–45.

Third Rendezvous: Marxism and National Liberation Struggles

The most important of these divergences concerned the issue of national liberation. One of Lenin's most creative contributions was to recognize the potential for revolts by oppressed nations to act as an ally for socialist revolution. Initially pursued as part of a strategy for overthrowing Tsarist absolutism, this understanding was generalized in response to the First World War. Lenin's pamphlet *Imperialism, the Highest Stage of Capitalism* (written in 1916) portrayed a capitalist world system dependent on the super-profits deriving from the exploitation of colonial labor. After 1917 he projected an alliance between the Comintern and anti-colonial nationalist movements even if their leadership was in social character or aspiration bourgeois. As Trotsky pithily put it, "[w]hat characterizes Bolshevism on the national question is that in its attitude towards oppressed nations, even the most backward, it considers them not only the object but also the subject of politics" (Trotsky 1971, 203). Perhaps the most remarkable expression of this attitude came in September 1920, at the First Congress of the Peoples of the East, convened by the Comintern in Baku, Azerbaijan, to promote the development of anti-imperialist movements throughout Asia (Riddell 1993).

This orientation, combined with the strains suffered by an expanding but internally antagonistic imperialist system at the end of the First World War, encouraged the development of Communist parties in the colonies and semi-colonies of European and American imperialism.

But its leaders had to grapple with the problem of how to combine the more immediate objective of national liberation with the fundamental goal of socialism, and in particular whether to ally with bourgeois nationalists who might share opposition to imperial domination but represented antagonistic class forces (the Irish Marxist James Connolly, one of the leaders of the 1916 Easter rising, had already had to confront this). The orthodox Communist solution became by the mid-1920a a stages strategy of achieving national liberation first and then pursuing socialism. This led to disaster in China during the 1925–27, when the Communist Party subordinated itself to the nationalist Kuomintang, which massacred Communist activists when they had served their purpose. The strategy was subjected to stringent critique by Trotsky for failing to grasp the interweaving of capitalist development and imperial domination in colonized societies. He argued that, especially after Stalin emerged as the winner of the internal Bolshevik struggle, the Comintern had been reduced to an instrument of the foreign policy of the Soviet Union.

But the Chinese Communist Party under Mao Zedong's leadership was able later to use a version of the same strategy to take power in 1949, by building up its own increasingly formidable army, exploiting the disruption caused by Japan's attempt to conquer China during the 1930s and evading Stalin's efforts to direct and restrain it for his own geopolitical reasons; by contrast, to secure Soviet dominance of Central and Eastern Europe at the end of the Second World War, Stalin pushed the armed Communist movements that dominated the resistance to the German and Italian occupation of southern Europe to acquiesce in the restoration of order on liberal capitalist terms (Claudin 1975). The eventual political break between Beijing and Moscow in 1960 implied the pluralization even of orthodox Communism, with important long-term implications. Along with the Cuban Revolution of 1958, this also indicated that Marxism might take different forms in the South. Maoism became a powerful political and ideological force with an international influence that continues to the present (Lovell 2019).

The salience of anti-imperialist strategy for the Comintern also encouraged it to confront the issue of race. Marx had championed the North in the American Civil War (1861–65), which he saw as a revolutionary struggle between rival social systems, capitalism and slavery. He also described the racialized division between native British workers and Irish migrant laborers as "the *secret of the impotence of the English working class*, despite its organization. It is the secret of the maintenance of power by the capitalist class" (*MECW* 43: 475). Irish independence was therefore in the interests of the British workers' movement; Marx also supported the first anti-colonial revolts in China and India. But only in the era of the Comintern did it become an explicit theme of socialist strategy to treat the victims of racial oppression as political subjects, notably in those great strongholds of segregation settler-colonial South Africa and the American South in the era of Jim Crow. And on the heretical fringe of the tiny world of Trotskyist groupuscules, the Trinidadian Marxist C.L.R James forged together Black self-emancipation and permanent revolution in his masterpiece on the Haitian Revolution, *The Black Jacobins* (1938). In the era of the postwar colonial revolution, it was another revolutionary from the Caribbean, Frantz Fanon, who most powerfully diagnosed the dynamics of racism and rebellion, in critical dialogue with both orthodox Communism and Sartre's fusion of existentialism and Marxism.

Fourth Rendezvous: 1960s and 1970s

James's achievement underlines the extent to which creative thinking that sought to escape what Mario Tronti called "the petrified forest of vulgar Marxism" (Tronti 2006, 11) took place at the margins. Nevertheless, it was there that serious attempts developed to continue Marxism as both critical intellectual project and revolutionary socialist politics. Indeed, for most (though not all) of these undertakings the two aspects were inseparable as they sought to rescue Marxism from the impasses of Soviet state philosophy and what seemed to be the final triumph of Bernstein in the social democratic parties of postwar Keynesian welfare capitalism.

This work took place in three main venues. First, as in James's case, the increasingly fragmented and ultra-marginalized Trotskyist movement provided the context in which critical thinking about the fate of Marxism could take place, typically through reflection on the failure of Trotsky's own predictions that the Second World War would see the collapse of what he saw as the temporary aberration represented by Stalinism and a repeat of the revolutionary crisis that had gripped capitalism in 1917–19: the writings of Tony Cliff in Britain and Cornelius Castoriadis in France are exemplary in this respect (Callinicos 1990).

Second, there was, as Anderson emphasizes, the academy. In the immediate postwar era, the most important case was provided by the Frankfurt School in Germany and the United States. The experience of exile from National Socialism in America and the actual outcome of the Second World War – the longest and strongest boom in the history of capitalism and the expansion of Stalinism from the Elbe to Northeast Asia – confirmed the leaders of the Frankfurt Institute for Social Research in the intuition that they had already developed before leaving Germany, namely that the processes of reification that Lukács had analyzed in *History and Class Consciousness* were so fragmenting the consciousness of the working class as to prevent it developing into the revolutionary subject whose necessity he had posited. From the early 1940s onwards, Max Horkheimer and Theodor Adorno took this argument much further, simultaneously portraying capitalist culture high and low as subjecting individuals to the rhythms of commodity fetishism and treating fetishism itself as symptomatic of a much broader, indeed transhistorical process in which nature is reduced to the object of human domination. Horkheimer and Adorno took inspiration from the fragmentary, brilliant writings of Walter Benjamin. Benjamin, however, never abandoned the project of socialist revolution, which he conceived, not as the product of Kautskyan "natural necessity," but the desperate irruption of the oppressed and exploited into the linear progress of capitalist historical time (Löwy 2005).

The third venue for the critical renewal of Marxism was provided by the mass Communist parties of Western Europe, above all in Italy and France. Sartre through the 1950s pursued a highly individual path, defined by two reference points – the tortuous and interconnected evolution of the Stalinist system and of the Communist parties, and the possibilities of revolution, which he increasingly located in the South. But as the 1960s dawned, these parties themselves seemed to offer more space for creative thinking, thanks in part to the ideological competition between the Soviet and Chinese versions of Communism, but also to the first stirrings of the mass movements that eventually became the great social, political and cultural upheaval that we call "the sixties," though it lasted till the mid-1970s (Harman 1988). At the fringes of the Italian Communist Party (PCI), which was the first to begin cautiously to distance itself from Moscow, there crystallized one of the most influential Marxist currents of the past fifty years, *operaismo* (workerism), as well as the more abstruse anti-Hegelian Marxism developed by Galvano della Volpe and his leading pupil Lucio Colletti. And it was within the considerably more rigid French Communist Party (PCF) that in the mid-1960s Louis Althusser and his pupils undertook what they intended to be a rigorous philosophical rereading of Marx's key texts, most famously *Capital* (Althusser et al. 2015). This rereading was with varying degrees of openness linked to the Maoist critique of Soviet Communism, which Mao now identified as the kind of "revisionist" restoration of capitalism that the Chinese Cultural Revolution (1966–76) sought to defeat.

The explosive development of mass student and worker insurgency, first in France (May–June 1968) and then in Italy (the "hot autumn" of 1969), brought all these different Marxisms out of the very narrow intellectual circles where they had hitherto developed and provide them with mass audiences concerned to renew the unity of theory and practice first posited by Marx himself. This doesn't mean that the highly sophisticated, indeed often arcane works of Sartre or Althusser became political primers. But they could find much larger audiences. For example, the Chilean Marxist Marta Harnecker wrote an introduction to historical materialism in Spanish that popularized the reinterpretation of Marxism developed by Althusser and his collaborators in *For Marx* and *Reading Capital* to a huge primarily Latin American readership (Harnecker 1969: our copy, published in 1976 in Spain as it emerged from the Francoist dictatorship, claims to be the 36th printing! Althusser's Latin American influence is discussed in de Ípola 2018). This phenomenon was driven by the appetite of newly radicalized students and young workers for Marxist theory, but it also reflected the efforts of at least some of the theorists themselves to think through what a revolutionary socialist strategy might mean in the late 20th century. This is true, for example, for the work of the Greek political theorist Nicos Poulantzas. According to Bob Jessop, his best known book, *Political Power and Social Class*, "appeared a few days before the occupation of the Sorbonne in the May events of 1968 and sold several thousand copies to the students involved in this struggle against the French state" (Jessop 1985, 13–14). The careful study of classic Marxist texts – particularly *Capital*, which became the subject of innumerable reading groups – that the newly radicalized tended to regard as mandatory provided a stimulus for new theoretical elaborations and the critique of established ones.

The far left political organizations that enjoyed a phase of explosive growth at the height of the upheavals of the late 1960s and early 1970s typically held allegiance to some version of Maoism or Trotskyism, of widely varying degrees of sophistication. Nevertheless, the fates of this renewed Marxist left and of the high theory that flourished alongside it proved to be closely connected. Thus Poulantzas's successive theorizations were closely related to his efforts to puzzle out a strategy for the left wing of the Communist movement. By the time he published his last book, *State, Power, Socialism*, in 1978, the Marxist left found itself under increasing intellectual and political pressure. The mainstream Communist parties reached the apogee of their influence in the mid-1970s, thereby limiting the effectiveness of their challengers on the far left. The defeat of the Portuguese Revolution in November 1975 and the PCI's effective rescue of the Italian state through its "historic compromise" with Christian Democracy were signs that the radicalization had passed its high water mark. Foucault's writings of the mid-1970s represented a frontal challenge to Marxism for what he contended was its failure to conceptualize power as an original phenomenon constitutive of the social field. While developed as an alternative form of critique to that elaborated by Marx, this perspective could be appropriated by more conventional forms of liberalism – politically in the ascendant with the coming to office of Ronald Reagan and Margaret Thatcher – that condemned Marxism as a totalitarian ideology. Althusser's announcement of yet another "crisis of Marxism" in 1977 was driven by his own sense of intellectual impasse but it registered a broader reality (Althusser 1994).

Diversifying Critique

A driving force in this crisis was the very nature of the radicalization that had provided the context for the fourth rendezvous between Marxism and the workers' movement. This involved a spectrum of movements – not just strikes and other sorts of workplace resistance, but opposition to the wars in Algeria and Vietnam, the struggle for civil rights in the United States and the Black Power movement it gave rise to, and what has come to be known "second-wave" feminism. The heterogeneity of the different forms of domination being contested and a growing sense that they couldn't be made to fit into the Marxist schema of class struggle were a major factor in the rise of poststructuralism. The 1970s in particular were marked by rich debates about the relationship between class exploitation and the oppression of women, but by the end of that decade, many feminists were drawing the conclusion that what Heidi Hartmann famously called the "Unhappy Marriage of Marxism and Feminism" had ended in divorce (Hartmann 1979). Ironically, this was at the very time when the most creative Marxist contributors to the debate were converging on a materialist interpretation of women's oppression under capitalism as arising from the role played by women in the privatized reproduction of labor power in households now structurally separated (as had not been true of precapitalist family forms) from production (German 1981; Vogel 2014; Brenner and Ramas 1984).

But, amid a left already in full retreat, these arguments had little chance of finding a large audience. Poststructuralism seemed to offer a more plausible theoretical framework in which non-class forms of domination could be interrogated (see Choat 2010 on the dialogue between Marxism and poststructuralism). Common to the otherwise quite different thought of Deleuze, Derrida and Foucault was a critique of the subject as the founding moment of knowledge as it had been conceived in modern Western philosophy since Descartes and an interest in the discursive and institutional processes through which individuals are formed into apparently coherent subjects. Both these themes were explored by Althusser as well, but what was widely seen as the incoherence of his attempt to think society as an integrated but internally complex totality (a "structure in dominance," as he put it) opened the door to the dissolution of structures into the infinite play of difference thematized in different ways by Deleuze and Derrida. Foucault's explorations of power-knowledge and governmentality during the 1970s renewed the critique of modernity developed by Nietzsche in the late 19th century. The 1980s, with Marxism in disarray, marked the moment of postmodernism, as the more vulgarized versions of poststructuralism marketed in the American academy became known (though ironically it was a Marxist, Fredric Jameson, who offered the most influential interpretation of postmodernism as a cultural phenomenon: Jameson 1991). Jean-François Lyotard articulated the spirit of the times when he defined the postmodern as "incredulity toward metanarratives," for example, the "grand narratives" weaving history together that Hegel and Marx had constructed, and preached "a war on totality" (Lyotard 1984, xxiv, 82).

This was also the moment of Post-Marxism: as early as 1983 Stuart Hall sardonically observed:

> *Post*-Marxism remains one of our largest and most flourishing contemporary theoretical schools. The Post-Marxists use Marxist concepts while constantly demonstrating their inadequacy. They seem, in fact, to continue to stand on the shoulders of the very theories they have just definitely destroyed.
>
> *(Hall 1983, 57)*

Their leading figures had widely differing attitudes to poststructuralism, Laclau and Mouffe, for example, drawing heavily on Derrida, Habermas devoting some of his best work to a stringent critique of this entire current of thought (Habermas 1987). The phenomenon of Post-Marxism is not unprecedented – to some extent at least Croce played a somewhat analogous role at the end of the 19th century, developing a dialogue with Marxism as interpreted by Antonio Labriola before rejecting it for liberalism. Gramsci praised Croce's thought because it

> has forcefully drawn attention to the study of the factors of culture and ideas as elements of political domination, to the functions of the great intellectuals in state life, to the moment of hegemony and consent as the necessary form of the concrete historical bloc

and thereby served as a corrective to Second International Marxism (Gramsci 1995, 332; Gramsci 1975, II, 1211; Q10 (XXXII)). But he argued that Croce's version of Hegelianism presented intellectuals as

> the arbiters and mediators of real political struggles, as personifying the "catharsis" – the passage from the economic aspect to the ethico-political one – ie the synthesis of the dialectical process itself, a synthesis that they 'manipulate' in a speculative fashion in their mind.
>
> *(Gramsci 1995, 343; Gramsci 1975, II, 1222; Q10 (XXXII) §7)*[3]

Whereas Croce's opposition to Marxism became more pronounced over time, the boundaries between contemporary Post-Marxism and Marxism proper remain blurred, reflecting the ambiguities expressed even by as strong-minded figures as Badiou and Negri as to how to position themselves with respect to these two lines of thought.

Gramsci himself was a major inspiration of a somewhat analogous phenomenon, though those involved don't seem to have applied the label "Post-Marxist" to their project – the group of scholars of colonial and postcolonial South Asia associated with the occasional publication *Subaltern Studies*. Reacting against the triumphalist portrayal of the Indian national movement perpetrated by supporters of the long dominant Congress and of the orthodox Communist parties, *Subaltern Studies* drew initially on British Marxist historians such as Edward Thompson and Eric Hobsbawm as well as on Gramsci (whose concept of the subaltern provided them with their collective name). But the most original figure in this group, Ranajit Guha, is unclassifiable intellectually. In his master-work, *Elementary Aspects of Peasant Insurgency in Colonial India*, though clearly taking much inspiration from Gramsci, he relies on structural linguistics to decode the actual forms of consciousness displayed by peasant rebellions – the very title of the book echoes that of Claude Lévi-Strauss's *The Elementary Structures of Kinship* (Guha 1983, especially 52–63). For others such as Partha Chatterjee, Foucault provided a more fruitful reference, though Chatterjee still drew on Gramscian concepts such as passive revolution (Chatterjee 1993).

The tendency of *Subaltern Studies* scholars to focus particularly on recovering specific forms of discourse led to controversy over its direction. For some, for example, the leading historian of modern India Sumit Sarkar, the group's initial Marxist orientation had become lost (1997). For others such as Dipesh Chakrabarty, a move toward a poststructuralist interrogation of Marxism was implicit from the start:

> In thus critiquing historicism and Eurocentrism and using that critique to interrogate the idea of the nation, in emphasizing the textual properties of archival documents, in considering representation as an aspect of power relations between the elite and the subaltern, Guha and his colleagues moved away from the guiding assumptions of the "history from below" approach of English Marxist historiography. With Guha's work, Indian history took, as it were, the proverbial linguistic turn. From its very beginning, *Subaltern Studies* positioned itself on an unorthodox territory of the Left.
>
> *(Chakrabarty 2000, 24)*

The emergence of a major group of critical historians from and working on the South dovetailed with a broader interrogation of Eurocentrism; its founding text was the Palestinian-American Edward Said's great work *Orientalism* (Said 1985), which diagnoses the discursive forms in which Asia was reduced to Europe's passive, sensual Other. Postcolonialism, as it came to be known, is, according to Robert J.C. Young, postcolonialism, a response to

> the long, violent history of colonialism. . . . Postcolonial cultural critique involves the reconsideration of this history, particularly from the perspectives of those who suffered

> its effects, together with the defining of its contemporary social and cultural impact. This is why postcolonial theory always intermingles the past with the present, why it is directed towards the active transformations of the present out of the clutches of the past
>
> *(Young 2016, 4)*

Particularly strong in literary studies in US and British universities, though its practitioners often came from the South (once again especially South Asia), postcolonialism inevitably drew heavily on poststructuralist concepts and motifs. Indeed, for some theorists, postcolonialism represented the truth of poststructuralism, whose deconstruction of totalizing ways of thinking offered tools for the critique of Eurocentrism (for example, Spivak 1988a; Bhaba 1994). As Young put it at the height of the postmodern craze, when postcolonial theory was just emerging, "[p]ostmodernism can best be defined as European culture's awareness that it is no longer the unquestioned and dominant center of the world" (Young 1990, 19). This could mean an antagonistic relationship with Marxism. Said takes Marx's 1853 article "The British Rule of India" (*MECW* 11: 125–33) as a prime example of "pure Romantic Orientalism" (Said 1985, 154). Young develops a more systematic critique, arguing that "Marxism's universalizing narrative of the unfolding of a rational system of world history is simply a negative form of the history of European imperialism" (Young 1990, 2). More recently, and representing the kind of confluence of *Subaltern Studies* and postcolonialism that he has promoted, Chakrabarty criticized Marx's *Capital* as inherently Eurocentric, portraying "capital in the image of a unity that arises in one part of the world at a particular period and then develops globally over historical time, encountering and negotiating historical differences in the process" (Chakrabarty 2007, 47).

Marxists have vigorously contested this critique (for example, Ahmad 1992; Pradella 2017). But in any case, the relationship between Marxism and postcolonialism isn't necessarily a conflictual one. "Can the Subaltern Speak?" by Gayatri Chakravorty Spivak is undoubtedly one of the founding texts of postcolonial theory. In this rich and complex chapter Spivak takes Foucault and Deleuze to task for "[t]he reduction of Marx to a benevolent but dated figure" and argues that

> the relationship between global capitalism (exploitation in economics) and nation-state politics (domination in geopolitics) is so macrological that it cannot account for the micrological texture of power. To move toward such an accounting one must move toward theories of ideology – of subject formations that micrologically and often erratically operate the interests that congeal the macrologies.

Developing such theories, she suggests, can benefit particularly from Derrida's more focused textual explorations, which "suggest a critique of European ethnocentrism in the constitution of the Other" (Spivak 1988b, 279, 293; see also Spivak 1999). In Spivak's thought, Marxism, deconstruction, postcolonialism and feminism can play off each other productively. More recently, Young has acknowledged that

> postcolonial theory depends on the far larger body of political and cultural theory about colonialism and imperialism developed by the many anti-colonial Marxisms of the twentieth century. Postcolonial theory implicitly presupposes a whole range of Marxist critical and theoretical concepts, and is therefore best situated within that larger body of theory.
>
> *(Young 2016, 73)*

An Agenda of Problems

But such theoretical nuances did not alter the very difficult situation the Marxist left found itself in the 1980s and 1990s. The onset of neoliberalism under Thatcher and Reagan morphed into an apparently even darker conjuncture, the collapse of the Communist regimes in the Soviet Union and in central and eastern Europe. The triumph of liberal capitalism received a famous apotheosis as the End of History in the writings of Francis Fukuyama (1989, 1992). Since Fukuyama meant by the End of History (in his own idiosyncratic version of Hegel's philosophy of history) the disappearance of systemic ideological alternatives to liberalism, his thesis implied the end of Marxism as well. And certainly the organized Marxism left was in disarray and retreat – the auto-destruction of the PCI, once the largest mass party in the West and the center of a dense and complex political culture radiating far into Italian working-class life, was symptomatic. It was at this moment that Fredric Jameson struck a powerful note of defiance:

> Capital and labor (and their opposition) will not go away under the new dispensation nor can there possibly exist in the future, any more than in the past, any viable "third way" between capitalism and socialism, however tainted the rhetoric and conceptuality of this last may have become for people to whom bureaucrats fed it by rote. . . . Whether the word Marxism disappears or not, therefore, in the erasure of the tapes in some new Dark Ages, the thing itself will inevitably reappear.
>
> *(Jameson 1990, 251)*

In the three decades since these words were published, Jameson's basic point has been vindicated. Largely stripped of its institutionalization in various kinds of left party, large or small, Marx's thought has been reduced to its theoretical essentials, as the critique of political economy – that is, of the ideological representations of capitalism offered by its intellectual apologists, and of the economic system that these simultaneously present and conceal. The post-1989 world has indeed been dominated by capitalism. This has been a classical story of hubris – the neoliberal triumphalism flourishing especially during the 1990s, to which Fukuyama gave voice – followed by nemesis in the shape of the 9/11 attacks and then the 2007–8 financial crash and its long and difficult aftermath. In other words, capitalism and Marxism are bound together as eternal antagonists. The travails of the former have renewed the audience for the latter. Harvey's engagement with *Capital* – as simultaneously critic, continuator and popularizer – make him the emblematic Marxist of these years.

But Marxism is now pursued in a very different context from those of the past. In the first place, there are no signs yet of a new rendezvous with the workers' movement. The experience of neoliberalism has generated powerful waves of contestation – most notably the mass movements that developed around the Seattle (1999) and Genoa (2001) protests, the campaigns against the Iraq War and the occupation of town squares that spread in the course of 2011 from Cairo across the Mediterranean and as far as Manhattan. But, ever since the defeats inflicted by Reagan and Thatcher in the first half of the 1980s, the organized workers' movement in the North has continued to be in retreat and generally in decline numerically, though the picture is more complex and promising elsewhere. This has reinforced the tendency already noted by Anderson for Marxist intellectual work to be located in the academy. This has been accompanied by a geographical shift (also highlighted in Anderson 1983), as the center of gravity moved toward the English-speaking world. As neoliberalism entrenched itself ideologically, continental European universities became increasingly inhospitable to Marxism, while the vast and wealthy American university system offered niches for Marxists from the US itself and (like Anderson and Harvey) from Europe as well. Even critical theorists based in Europe – for example, Žižek and Badiou – found their main audience in the US. It is symptomatic of this shift that the most influential Marxist book of recent decades – Michael Hardt's and Toni Negri's *Empire*, though co-authored by one of the leading Italian Marxists of the 1960s, was first published in English by Harvard University Press (Hardt and Negri 2000).

The picture becomes more complicated once we look beyond Europe and North America. India is home to two important Communist parties, the larger of which, the China-leaning Communist Party of India (Marxist), governed the important state of West Bengal between 1977 and 2011, and to a substantial Maoist movement sections of which wage armed struggle in parts of the countryside. Versions of traditional Marxism-Leninism predominate in these parties, but a highly sophisticated left intelligentsia has strong links with the Anglophone academy and contributes to all the varieties of critical theory, Marxism and postcolonialism especially. Other societies in the South that experienced substantial workers' and student movements in the 1970s and 1980s have produced serious Marxist intellectual cultures with bases in the organized left and footholds in the academy; this is true, for example, of Brazil, South Africa and South Korea. Latin America more generally experienced a powerful swing to the left in the 2000s, most notably in the shape of Hugo Chávez's Bolivarian revolution in Venezuela and Evo Morales and the Movement for Socialism in Bolivia, which have had intellectual effects as well. And in China, dynamo of the contemporary world economy, Marxism remains the official ideology and a compulsory item in the university curriculum, taught by over a hundred schools of Marxism (interestingly, the first was set up at Peking University as recently as 1992). The content of this Marxism is a meld of Marxism-Leninism and traditional forms of Chinese thought, notably Confucianism, but it is contested by more critical currents opposed to China's marriage with the market either on the basis of a strict interpretation of Cultural Revolution Maoism or from a perspective influenced by some version of Marxism in the West.

Contemporary Marxist theory is inevitably shaped by its positioning predominantly in the academy. Lukács and Gramsci in the era of the October Revolution saw, each in his own way, revolutionary political organization as the necessary mediating factor in the interplay between theory and practice posited by Marx. Some of the most outstanding Marxists of the 1960s generation – Daniel Bensaïd and Chris Harman, for example – showed it was still feasible to pursue Marxism creatively according to this model (see on the latter Callinicos 2020). But it has become harder. On the one hand, the shift to the Anglophone academy means the center of inquiry is located in societies in which the Marxist left has always been relatively weak. On the other hand, the organized left has in any case declined in the neoliberal era – not surprisingly, given the difficulties experienced by the workers' movement. This doesn't mean that there is no longer any connection between Marxist (or Post-Marxist) theory and anti-capitalist practice. The impact of Hardt's and Negri's book on the movement for another globalization of the early 2000s is one example; the influence of Laclau and Mouffe on new "left populist" formations like Podemos and La France Insoumise is another. But there is very little sense in which theoretical work is held to the test of practice – or political activity to the critique of theory. Mention of Laclau and Mouffe underlines another difference – Marxism can no longer claim to have, as it did for much of the 20th century, the monopoly of critical thought. Marxist work develops in competition and/or dialogue with Post-Marxism (as well as with poststructuralism and with more conventional left liberalism) and sometimes, as we have noted, it is hard to draw a dividing line between the two strands of thought (Negri and Žižek are cases in point).

Do these differences mean that there is no longer anything distinctive to Marxism? On the contrary, as we have seen, the critique of political economy has been renewed in the past generation, as Marxists attend to the new forms taken by capitalism and have sought to interrogate and refine the conceptual apparatus that Marx left behind, aided or hindered by the wealth of manuscripts that have become available through MEGA². From this central strand we can move upstream to more philosophical questions, or downstream to more empirical and political preoccupations. On the terrain of high theory, the problem of economic base and politico-ideological superstructure, already an issue in Engels's last years, retains its actuality. It is a question that has received sophisticated theoretical treatment by thinkers as diverse as Gramsci, Althusser and G.A. Cohen, but it is also the gateway to more concrete issues. Some of these are perennial: the problem of the capitalist state, the subject of immense debate in the 1970s, remains of the first importance, both because it's inseparable from any broader appreciation of the system's development and because it lies at the heart of any attempt to think through a political strategy. Similarly, the problem of ideology – that is, of how the representations of class societies tend to reproduce or subvert them – has been revitalized, partly thanks to the poststructuralist challenge, partly thanks to the uses made of Lacan's reinterpretation of psychoanalysis by Althusser, Jameson, Žižek and Badiou.

But the relationship between economic and non-economic social relations and institutions is also critical to the question of what Marxism has to say about the forms of oppression at the center of so many contemporary liberation struggles – race, gender, LGBT+, national and religious identities. But of course these different kinds of non-class oppression can't be seen primarily as symptoms of a philosophical problem; they require detailed attention in their own right for political and moral reasons. Understanding the relationship between class, race and gender is of particular importance. This issue was, as we have seen, central to the crisis of Marxism that developed in the 1970s, and the discussion has been resumed under the pressure of a renewed feminism, Black Lives Matter and the new trans politics. Racism itself takes new forms with the rise of Islamophobia in Western societies, against the background of the successive wars waged by the United States and its allies in the Greater Middle East, but, as is shown by the protests and wider political polarization sparked in the US by George Floyd's killing by Minneapolis police officers in May 2020, the older forms retain their vigor. How Marxism addresses this nexus of questions will be explored in some of the chapters that follow. Similar issues arise with the problem of humankind's relationship to nature – of the utmost practical importance because of climate change. Recent scholarship has shown that Marx and Engels were well aware of this problem, and of capitalism's destructive impact on the environment, but the thread was lost, only to be taken up again more recently in a growing and increasingly rich Marxist literature that traces the relationship between capital accumulation and environmental destruction (Foster 2000; Burkett 2014; Saito 2017; Foster 2020). We return to Marxism's conceptualization of nature in the context of the COVID-19 pandemic in the concluding part of this Handbook.

In the era of "a thousand Marxisms" there can be no agreement on the agenda of problems, let alone on how to answer them. The dominant sense nevertheless is one of intellectual vitality accompanied by political uncertainty. They are connected. Marxism has regained its breath by seeking use the analytical tools forged in *Capital* to make sense of where contemporary capitalism is going. A vast number of keystrokes have been devoted to, for example, understanding the process of financialization that is widely held to have transformed capitalism in the neoliberal era, exploring the extent to why the dynamics of economic crisis can be best interpreted starting from Marx's famous tendential law for the rate of profit to fall, or ascertaining whether contemporary capitalism can be seen as imperialism in terms similar to those used by Luxemburg or Lenin. But in the classical Marxism of Marx and their successors, the development of capitalism was inseparable from the formation of the working class, whose exploitation made them not simply the victims but, as the *Communist Manifesto* famously puts it, the gravediggers of capitalism. The Marxist critique of political economy was internally connected to a theory of revolutionary class subjectivity that began to be articulated explicitly in the era of the Russian Revolution.

Today capitalism remains, for all the changes since Marx's time, recognizably the beast he anatomized and sought to destroy. But, in the greatest systemic crisis bourgeois society has experienced since the inter-war years the working-class response was comparatively muted. How to explain this? Is it simply a matter of the traditional ideological and political mechanisms for containing resistance working effectively? Or has the neoliberal transformation of capitalism so atomized the working class and weakened its organizations that it has lost its capacity to act as a collective subject? And if so, is this loss permanent or temporary – in the latter case merely a phase in the recomposition of a working class that will eventually find its modes of organization and struggle? Or is capitalism so reconfiguring social relations that resistance will take qualitatively different forms that no longer have a recognizable resemblance to the working class in its traditional forms? Or, finally, was the very idea of class subjectivity, of economic antagonisms acting as the basis of collective political action always a mistake? All these diagnoses find their champions in the contemporary conversation among Marxists and Post-Marxists. Establishing which is right is partly dependent on the kind of economic and political inquiry distinctive to Marxism – what Lenin called "the very gist, the living soul of Marxism, a concrete analysis of a concrete situation" (*LCW* 31: 166). But it is also a matter of the shape taken by future social and political struggles. At stake here is not just how to apply Marxism but what kind of future it can have.

Notes

1. Heinrich (2019) is the first volume in what looks set to be the definitive biography of Marx. Engels is less well served in Hunt (2010).
2. See the important discussion of the Marx-Engels relationship in Liedman (2018), ch. 12.
3. The work of Jacques Bidet, who has developed a general theory of modernity from a close reading of Marx's *Capital*, can also be seen as a form of Post-Marxism, albeit very much still in dialogue with Marxism: for example, Bidet (1999, 2007).

Bibliography

Ahmad, Aijaz. 1992. *In Theory: Classes, Nations, Literatures*. London: Verso.

Althusser, Louis. 1969. *For Marx*. London: Allen Lane.

Althusser, Louis. 1994. "Marx dans ses limites." In Louis Althusser, *Écrits philosophiques et politiques*, edited by François Matheron, Tome 1, 359–524. Paris: Stock/IMEC.

Althusser, Louis, Étienne Balibar, Roger Establet, Pierre Macherey, and Jacques Rancière. 2015 (1965). *Reading Capital: The Complete Edition*. London: Verso.

Anderson, Perry. 1976. *Considerations on Western Marxism*. London: NLB.

Anderson, Perry. 1983. *In the Tracks of Historical Materialism*. London: Verso.

Anderson, Perry. 2017 (1977). *The Antinomies of Antonio Gramsci*. London: Verso.

Bernstein, Eduard. 1993 (1899). *The Preconditions of Socialism*. Cambridge: Cambridge University Press.

Bhaba, Homi. 1994. *The Location of Culture*. London: Routledge.

Bidet, Jacques. 1999. *Théorie générale: Théorie du droit, de l' économie et de la politique*. Paris: Presses universitaires de France.

Bidet, Jacques. 2007 (1985). *Exploring Marx's Capital: Philosophical, Economic and Political Dimensions*. Leiden: Brill.

Brenner, Johanna, and Maria Ramas. 1984. "Rethinking Women's Oppression." *New Left Review* 1(144): 33–71.

Burkett, Paul. 2014 (1999). *Marx and Nature: A Red and Green Perspective*. Chicago: Haymarket.

Callinicos, Alex. 1990. *Trotskyism*. Minneapolis: University of Minnesota Press.

Callinicos, Alex. 2018. "Marx's Politics." *International Socialism* 2(158): 35–63.

Callinicos, Alex. 2020. "Chris Harman and the Critique of Political Economy." *International Socialism* 2(165): 37–55.
Chakrabarty, Dipesh. 2000. "*Subaltern Studies* and Postcolonial Historiography." *Nepantia: Views from the South* 1(1): 9–32.
Chakrabarty, Dipesh. 2007. *Provincializing Europe: Postcolonial Thought and Historical Difference*. Princeton: Princeton University Press.
Chatterjee, Partha. 1993. *The Nation and Its Fragments*. New Delhi: Oxford University Press.
Choat, Simon. 2010. *Marx Through Post-Structuralism*. London: Continuum.
Claudin, Fernando. 1975. *The Communist Movement: From Comintern to Cominform*. 2 vols. New York: Monthly Review Press.
De Ípola, Emilio. 2018 (2002). *Althusser, the Infinite Farewell*. Durham, NC: Duke University Press.
Deutscher, Isaac. 1971. *Marxism in Our Time*. San Francisco: Ramparts Press.
Foster, John Bellamy. 2000. *Marx's Ecology: Materialism and Nature*. New York: Monthly Review Press.
Foster, John Bellamy. 2020. *The Return of Nature: Socialism and Ecology*. New York: Monthly Review Press.
Fukuyama, Francis. 1989. "The End of History?" *The National Interest* 16: 3–18.
Fukuyama, Francis. 1992. *The End of History and the Last Man*. Princeton: Princeton University Press.
German, Lindsey. 1981. "Theories of Patriarchy." *International Socialism* 2(12): 33–51.
Gerratana, Valentino. 1977. "Stalin, Lenin, and Leninism." *New Left Review* 1(103): 59–71.
Gramsci, Antonio. 1975. *Quaderni del carcere*. Edited by Valentino Gerratana. 4 vols. Turin: Einaudi.
Gramsci, Antonio. 1995. *Further Selections from the Prison Notebooks*. London: Lawrence and Wishart.
Guha, Ranajit. 1983. *Elementary Aspects of Peasant Insurgency in Colonial India*. New Delhi: Oxford University Press.
Habermas, Jürgen. 1987. *The Philosophical Discourse of Modernity: Twelve Lectures*. Cambridge: Polity.
Hall, Stuart. 1983. "The Problem of Ideology: Marxism without Guarantees." In *Marx: A Hundred Years On*, edited by Betty Matthews, 57–86. London: Lawrence and Wishart.
Hardt, Michael, and Antonio Negri. 2000. *Empire*. Cambridge: Harvard University Press.
Harman, Chris. 1988. *The Fire Last Time: 1968 and After*. London: Bookmarks.
Harnecker, Marta. 1976 (1969). *Les conceptos elementales del materialismo historico*. Madrid: Siglo veintiuno editores.
Hartmann, Heidi. 1979. "The Unhappy Marriage of Marxism and Feminism: Towards a More Progressive Union." *Capital and Class* 8: 1–34.
Heinrich, Michael. 2019. *Karl Marx and the Birth of Modern Society: The Life of Marx and the Development of His Work, Volume I: 1818–1841*. New York: Monthly Review.
Hodgskin, Thomas. 1922 (1825). *Labor Defended against the Claims of Capital*. London: The Labor Publishing Company.
Hunt, Tristram. 2010. *Marx's General: The Revolutionary Life of Friedrich Engels*. New York: Picador.
James, C.L.R. 2001 (1938). *The Black Jacobins: Toussaint L'Ouverture and the San Domingo Revolution*. London: Penguin.
Jameson, Fredric. 1990. *Late Marxism: Adorno, or, the Persistence of the Dialectic*. London: Verso.
Jameson, Fredric. 1991. *Postmodernism, or, the Cultural Logic of Late Capitalism*. London: Verso.
Jessop, Bob. 1985. *Nicos Poulantzas: Marxist Theory and Political Strategy*. Basingstoke: Palgrave.
Kautsky, Karl. 1910 (1892). *The Class Struggle: Erfurt Program*. Chicago: Charles H. Kerr & Co.
Kautsky, Karl. 1988 (1927). *The Materialist Conception of History*. Edited by J.H. Kautsky. abr. edn. New Haven: Yale University Press.
Kouvelakis, Stathis. 2005. "Crises of Marxism and the Transformations of Capitalism." In *Critical Companion to Contemporary Marxism*, edited by Jacques Bidet and Stathis Kouvelakis, 23–38. Leiden: Brill.
Laclau, Ernesto, and Chantal Mouffe. 1985. *Hegemony and Socialist Strategy*. London: Verso.
Lenin, V.I. 1964 (1917). "Imperialism, the Highest Stage of Capitalism." *LCW* 22: 185–304.
Liedman, Sven-Eric. 2018. *A World to Win: The Life and Works of Karl Marx*. London: Verso.
Lih, Lars T. 2006. *Lenin Rediscovered: What Is to Be Done? In Context*. Leiden: Brill.
Lovell, Julia. 2019. *Maoism: A Global History*. London: Bodley Head.
Löwy, Michael. 2005. *Fire Alarm: Reading Walter Benjamin's "On the Concept of History."* London: Verso.
Lukács, György. 1971 (1923). *History and Class Consciousness: Studies in Marxist Dialectics*. London: Merlin.
Luxemburg, Rosa. 2015 (1913). "The Accumulation of Capital: A Contribution to the Economic Theory of Imperialism." In *The Complete Writings of Rosa Luxemburg, Volume II, Economic Writings 2*, edited by Peter Hudis and Paul Le Blanc. London: Verso.
Lyotard, Jean-François. 1984 (1979). *The Postmodern Condition: A Report on Knowledge*. Minneapolis: University of Minnesota Press.

Poulantzas, Nicos. 1973 (1968). *Political Power and Social Classes*. London: NLB.
Poulantzas, Nicos. 1978. *State, Power, Socialism*. London: Verso.
Pradella, Lucia. 2017. "Marx and the Global South: Connecting History and Value Theory." *Sociology* 51(1): 146–61.
Riddell, John, ed. 1993. *To See the Dawn: Baku, 1920: First Congress of the Peoples of the East*. New York: Pathfinder.
Said, Edward W. 1985 (1978). *Orientalism*. Harmondsworth: Penguin.
Saito, Kohei. 2017. *Karl Marx's Ecosocialism: Capitalism, Nature, and the Unfinished Critique of Political Economy*. New York: Monthly Review Press.
Sarkar, Sumit. 1997. *Writing Social History*. New Delhi: Oxford University Press.
Sorel, Georges. 1999 (1908). *Reflections on Violence*. Cambridge: Cambridge University Press.
Spivak, Gayatri Chakravorty. 1988a. "Subaltern Studies: Deconstructing Historiography." In *Selected Subaltern Studies*, edited by Ranajit Guha and Gayatri Chakravorty Spivak, 3–32. New York: Oxford University Press.
Spivak, Gayatri Chakravorty. 1988b. "Can the Subaltern Speak?" In *Marxism and the Interpretation of Culture*, edited by Cary Nelson and Lawrence Grossberg, 271–313. Basingstoke: Macmillan.
Spivak, Gayatri Chakravorty. 1999. *A Critique of Postcolonial Reason: Towards a History of the Vanishing Present*. Cambridge, MA: Harvard University Press.
Stalin, J.V. 1943 (1938). "Dialectical and Historical Materialism." In *History of the Communist Party of the Soviet Union (Bolsheviks)*, 105–31. Moscow: Foreign Languages Publishing House.
Tosel, André. 2005. "Development of Marxism: From the End of Marxism to a Thousand Marxisms: France-Italy 1975–2005." In *Critical Companion to Contemporary Marxism*, edited by Jacques Bidet and Stathis Kouvelakis, 39–78. Leiden: Brill.
Tronti, Mario. 2006 (1966). *Operai e capitale*. Roma: DeriveApprodi.
Trotsky, Leon. 1939. "Once Again on the 'Crisis of Marxism.'" *The New International* 5(5): 133–34. www.marxists.org/archive/trotsky/1939/03/marxism.htm
Trotsky, Leon. 1971. *The Struggle against Fascism in Germany*. New York: Pathfinder Press.
Vogel, Lise. 2014 (1983). *Marxism and the Oppression of Women: Toward a Unitary Theory*. Chicago: Haymarket Books.
Wallerstein, Immanuel. 1986. "Marxisms as Utopias: Evolving Ideologies." *American Journal of Sociology* 91(6): 1295–308.
Young, Robert J.C. 1990. *White Mythologies: Writing History and the West*. London: Routledge.
Young, Robert J.C. 2016. *Postcolonialism: An Historical Introduction*. Chichester: Wiley Blackwell.

PART I

Foundation

1
FOUNDATION: KARL MARX (1818–83)

Lucia Pradella

Introduction

The history of Marxism is studded with attempts to go back to its foundations. Since Marx sees capital as a system that constantly recreates its own foundation, it is no wonder that his critique of political economy has become an inexhaustible source of answers to what seem to be the new questions of the present.

One of such questions concerns the idea of "globality." Did Marx develop a critique of capitalism as a global system? And does he provide us with tools for opposing imperialism, racism and gender oppression today? The prevalent answer within contemporary Marxist and Post-Marxist debates is that, despite its global potential, Marx's critique of political economy did not ascend to the level of the world market, and thus failed to overcome Eurocentrism and fully to recognize the agency of non-Western people (Chaturvedi 2010). While postcolonial scholars like Edward Said (1985), Gayatri Spivak (1999) and Dipesh Chakrabarty (2007) recognize emancipatory elements in Marx's work – his *intuition* of globality (see Spivak in this Handbook) – Marxist historical sociologists like the late Giovanni Arrighi (2007) and Andre Gunder Frank (1998) were more dismissive, up to the point of the latter denouncing Marx as a complicit supporter of Western imperialism.

If we read some passages from the *Manifesto* we could think that these criticisms are correct. How else can we judge Marx and Engels praising the role of the bourgeoisie drawing even the most "barbarian" nations into civilization, or Engels's view of Slavic peoples as "people without history"? A new body of Marxist scholarship seeks to differentiate this early Marx from a non-Eurocentric "late Marx" (e.g., Anderson 2010). Especially from the late 1850s, they argue, Marx broke away from the Eurocentrism of *The German Ideology* and *The Manifesto*, and supported anti-colonial movements in India and Ireland, and the emancipation of the slaves in the United States and Russia. This interpretation draws on writings that have been largely overlooked in many postcolonial and Marxist debates, including Marx's and Engels's notebooks published in the new historical-critical edition of their complete writings (the *Marx-Engels Gesamtausgabe*, MEGA^2). But it raises two main questions, concerning, respectively, the status of historical materialism and the critique of political economy. Are the founding texts of the Marxist tradition irremediably Eurocentric? And did Marx break with Eurocentrism only in his late political writings or in his overall critique of political economy?

These questions are linked to a second area of debate between Marxist, postcolonial and feminist scholars, concerning the relevance of Marx for conceptualizing gender relations. It is widely assumed that women's work is the blind spot of Marx's critique of political economy (Werlhof 1988; Mies 1998). Marx's *Capital* would not address the antagonism between capital and reproductive labor but would be mainly concerned with abstract labor, labor-power in the form in which it is useful to capital. This narrow focus on exploitation would close off the analysis of spaces of resistance (Bhattacharya 2017; Lebowitz 2003). We would thus need to expand our understanding of anti-capitalist struggles beyond the "traditional Marxist" canon. "Not just struggles between labor and capital at the point of production – for Nancy Fraser (2014, 71) – but also boundary struggles over gender domination, ecology, imperialism and democracy." This view resonates with David Harvey's (2017, 48) recent argument that we need to shift our focus from struggles at the point of valorization to those at the point of realization, which "trigger fights against predatory practices and accumulation by dispossession in the market place (e.g. against gentrification and foreclosures)." But what if it is the "traditional" struggle between wage labor and capital that has been insufficiently theorized or even understood?

This entry seeks to answer these questions by going back, again, to the foundations. It investigates what Engels deemed to be Marx's two main discoveries: the materialist conception of history and the theory of surplus value. As is well-known, the first inaugurated a new way of looking at history that shifted the focus from politics, religion, science and art onto the relations of production and reproduction of social life. Despite the limited results of Marx's and Engels's concrete application of this approach in the mid-1840s, in the next section I argue that the lifelong research program they inaugurated then laid the basis for overcoming the problem of Eurocentrism. This point is relevant fully to grasp the scope of Marx's theory of surplus value. By explaining how the exploitation of labor works within capitalism, for Marx, the theory of surplus value was the "pivot" of his critique of political economy (*CI*: 132), the Cartesian point that revolutionizes our understanding of capitalism as a global system. In the third section, I challenge narrow interpretations of the antagonism between wage labor and capital, and argue that, for Marx, this antagonism shapes the overall relationship between humankind and nature. His analysis of capitalist reproduction, I argue in the fifth and sixth sections, provides us with tools for conceptualizing the imperialist and gendered nature of processes of capital accumulation on a global scale. These aspects of Marx's work, I conclude, are crucial to thinking about the class struggle, both yesterday and today.

Historical Materialism

In the collection of manuscripts that then became the founding text of historical materialism, *The German Ideology*, Marx and Engels sought to "settle accounts with [their] former philosophical conscience" (*MECW* 29: 264). Through different paths, they came to recognize both the centrality of production relations and the validity of the labor theory of value. Marx's and Engels's personal trajectories reflect broader historical and intellectual developments. As Ronald Meek (1976) highlighted, the materialistic approach to history was elaborated within the Scottish Enlightenment alongside the labor theory of value. The revolution in production relations from the late 18th century onwards pushed the theorists of the French and Scottish Enlightenment to understand the impact of different "modes of subsistence" on human societies. By looking at capitalism (or commercial society) as a specific mode of subsistence among others, classical political economists like Adam Smith and David Ricardo were able to conceptualize its historical specificity. They thus grasped the role of labor in determining the value of commodities and the importance of class antagonisms in history. Because of their own class interests, however, classical economists did not push this analysis further and ended up naturalizing bourgeois relations, smuggling them in "as the inviolable natural laws" of society in the abstract (*G*: 87). Europe appeared as the *telos* and endpoint of historical progress, in a teleological framework that deeply informs also Hegel's philosophy of history (Pradella 2015).

Even when Marx embraced Ludwig Feuerbach's attempt to "put Hegel on his feet," he did so in a way that was deeply influenced by Hegel's critique of immediacy. Marx did not take as his starting point the human essence as revealed in sense-experience, as Feuerbach suggested: such human essence, Marx believed, is created through labor and our sense-experience is mediated by the totality of social relations. While Marx initially grounded his analysis of capitalist social relations in his critique of the alienation of workers from their activity and species being (*MECW* 3: 270–71), *The German Ideology* shifted the focus onto the spheres of production and reproduction of social life. It is "the mode of production of material life," a given society's "forms of intercourse" (*Verkehrsform*) – Marx and Engels there proclaimed – that "conditions the general process of social, political and intellectual life," not vice versa (*MECW* 29: 263).[1] Different "forms of intercourse," in their view, give rise to different "forms of ownership." This new approach marked a real turning point. By historicizing private property, in fact, Marx and Engels undermined the naturalization of capitalism by the classical political economists and reclaimed society as an object of study transcending capitalism and the state, bringing back class antagonisms into the picture (*MECW* 5: 46, 89; Levine 1987, 433, 436).

In *The German Ideology* Marx and Engels already traced a relationship between class antagonisms and gender oppression. "Civil society," in their view, stemmed out of the family, in its simple and more complex forms, the so-called tribal order. "The latent slavery in the family, though still very crude, is the first form of property" (*MECW* 5: 51–52), followed by the ancient (Greek–Roman) "communal and state property," the "feudal and estate property" and the capitalist one (*MECW* 5: 32–35). Although in their further studies Marx and Engels questioned the idea of the patriarchal origin of the family and a "natural" division of labor between the sexes, it is remarkable that *The German Ideology* already established a link between relations of production and reproduction (Brown 2012, 43). Even if their sequence of "forms of ownership" is focused on Europe, moreover, this does not imply a Eurocentric approach (see, for example, John Hobson's critique in Hobson 2013). As Eric Hobsbawm (1964, 28) argued, in fact, Marx and Engels do not suggest any logical connection between Roman and tribal (German) institutions and the feudal form, but only note a relation of succession, whereby "feudalism appears to be an *alternative* evolution out of primitive communalism." *The German Ideology* rather contains an embryonic attempt to contextualize the emergence of capitalism in Europe within a unified process of human development in ways that anticipate studies of global and connected histories (e.g., Subrahmanyam 1997; Washbrook 1997; Williams 1944).

Marx and Engels were so convinced of the necessity of adopting a global perspective that they understood historical materialism itself as an approach to world history made possible by the development of global interconnections. "The more the original isolation of the separate nationalities is destroyed by the advanced mode of production, by intercourse and by the natural division of labor between various nations arising as a result," they argued, "the more history becomes world history" (*MECW* 5: 50–51). It is thus no surprise that the development of the class struggle would push this global approach further. Already in the mid-1840s Marx paid great attention to the relationship between capitalism and colonialism, situating the industrial revolution in Britain within a global context. He investigated the role of Atlantic slavery and the Triangular Trade in financing the European commercial presence in the Indian Ocean between the 16th and the 19th centuries, when protective measures were crucial to defending British manufacturing from Asian competition (*MECW* 12: 148–56; *CI*: 921–22). Marx not only considered the importance of Indian and Chinese markets to the development of capitalism in Europe. He also paid great attention to the global consequences of the industrial revolution, tracing the social effects of deindustrialization from America to Africa, the Middle East to Asia (Marx 1983, 99, 318, 326–27, 477).

In these notebooks, however, Marx mainly studied the capitalist mode of production, only looking at how pre-capitalist societies were affected by its development. This focus depended, in my view, on Marx's and Engels's belief at the time that industrial development inevitably depressed the wages of the industrial working class (Lapides 1998). Since trade union mobilization could not do anything against this "iron law of wages," workers' economic struggles were bound to radicalize and aim at overthrowing the system. If capitalism was impoverishing workers worldwide and subordinating entire nations under its system of division of labor, the same system had laid the conditions for its supersession. The industrial proletariat was a revolutionary class not mainly because of its negative position within the system, but because of the power deriving from its role in production. By concentrating workers in large-scale industries and urban centers, the bourgeoisie was producing its own "grave-diggers": the men and women who were to put an end to class society, emancipating the entire humankind, including the colonies. Marx and Engels now saw the revolutionary process as the result of the contradiction between the development of the productive forces and the social relations in which such development takes place. This does not mean that social revolution was seen as the necessary outcome of these contradictions but that it is against this crisis-ridden backdrop that the class struggle, and the role of the communist party, need to be understood (Callinicos 2004, 106).

Things changed after 1848. The economic boom that followed the 1847 economic crisis in Europe and the defeat of the 1848 revolutions put in question Marx's and Engels's economic pessimism. At the same time, the growth of anti-colonial movements throughout Asia undermined their passive view of non-European peoples, pushing them to widen their gaze beyond Europe. In their *Neue Rheinische Zeitung* Review at the beginning of 1850 Marx and Engels welcomed the prospect of social upheaval in China (*MECW* 10: 266–67). In his 1853 articles for the *New York Tribune*, Marx for the first time supported popular struggles in Asia against colonial domination, and enthusiastically welcomed the "formidable revolution" of the Taiping (1850–64). In the London Notebooks (1850–53), moreover, he developed the materialistic method and applied it to the study of pre-capitalist societies (Rein 1988, 9). He investigated communal property relations and forms of resistance to colonial expansion, and studied the history of the family, women's condition and culture. This shows that Marx's materialist approach did not disregard culture and gender relations (Pradella 2015). Thanks to his investigations into the structure and politics of the Indian communities, moreover, Marx challenged the dualistic conception of a despotic "East" and a democratic "West" that prevailed at the time in Europe. Questioning the view, which he had himself entertained, that in the "East" the sovereign was the absolute owner of the land, Marx came to the conclusion that the Asiatic mode of production was based on a kind of common ownership more resistant to the evolution of private property than the Greek, Roman and Germanic forms (Marx's letter to Engels of 14 June 1853 in *MECW* 39: 344; Sperl 2004). This was true not only for Asian societies but also for pre-Columbian and European societies, including Slavic societies and Moorish Spain (*G*: 882).

Interestingly, Marx's position on the structure of Indian society changed just before he wrote his much contested articles on the "double mission" of British colonialism in India. In "The Future Results of British Rule in India" (written on 22 June 1853), Marx wrote that, despite the devastation it caused, British colonialism had also played a positive role in India by politically unifying the Subcontinent and creating the economic, social and political conditions for a common anti-colonial uprising of the Indian people against colonial domination (*MECW* 12: 217–22). The fact that Marx wrote this despite his open support for the Taiping revolution in China shows that this position does not depend on a deeply rooted Orientalism, but on his assessment – surely questionable – of the political conditions for a unified anti-colonial movement in India. Over time, moreover, Marx became aware of the strength of the mode of production in countries like China, where the power of the state had not been seized by the colonizers like in India (*MECW* 12: 218; Marx's letter to Engels of 8 October 1858 in *MECW* 40: 347). He changed his mind and came to the conclusion that Western colonialism was unlikely to expand in China.

Marx's interest in forms of social organization and resistance in non-Western societies, therefore, long predates his late notebooks (1879–83), which have been the focus of recent scholarship on the late Marx (e.g., Anderson 2010; Smith 2002). But it is certainly true, as David Smith argues (2002, 79–80), that these notebooks show Marx's attempt to study even more concretely and also in cultural terms the challenges capital would confront in its global expansion. As Raya Dunayevskaya (1985, 218–19) noted, they document Marx's increasing hostility to colonialism, racism and gender oppression. Marx investigated communal social forms from Russia and Ireland to Asia, Latin America to North Africa. In his *Notes on Indian History* (1986), he traced the country's long history of resistance to different colonizers. He also paid great attention to the emerging disciplines of archaeology, ethnology and anthropology, denouncing the influence of imperialist interests on their development. In the notebooks published by Lawrence Krader under the title of *Ethnological Notebooks*, for example, Marx criticizes the use of categories like "feudalism," which were deduced from European development, in the analysis of Indian society (Marx 1976, 420). Drawing on the works of Lewis Henry Morgan and Johann Bachofen he argued for the historical priority of the *gens* and the matrilineal lineage, ridiculing the view that the patriarchal family was the original form of family. Imperialist interests, he denounced, projected forms of despotism into primitive institutions in order to naturalize them (Marx 1976, 430, 479). Engels partially drew on these notebooks to write *The Origin of the Family, Private Property and the State* (1884). In them, Marx rejected racial theories of social progress and refuted the view of the Indo-Europeans as a single race, racial categories and the concept of the Aryan race itself.

Wage Labor and Capital

This brief overview of Marx's historical studies challenges the idea that the founding texts of the materialistic conception of history are inherently Eurocentric. Given the crucial role that this new approach played in the development of Marx's critique of political economy, this is relevant also for our discussion of the theory of surplus value. Differently from the classical economists, Marx consistently applied the labor theory of value to the wage-labor relation, and thus understood that this relation is based on "exploitation," that is, on a lack of equivalence between the value produced and the value appropriated by the workers in the form of the wage. Increasing the extraction of this "surplus value" is the driving force of capitalist accumulation. The relationship between wage labor and capital is inherently antagonistic, and this antagonism shapes the capitalist system as a whole, completely overthrowing the relationship between humankind and nature.

Labor in general, for Marx, is an *organic metabolism* between humankind and nature, through which humankind, as a part of nature, changes its external nature thus simultaneously changing its own (*CI*: 283).[2] In Marx's view, wealth derives from humankind *and* nature, not from labor alone (*MECW* 29: 278). But by selling their labor power in exchange for a wage, workers transfer onto capital their whole living power as species being; they put the organic metabolism between humankind and nature in the hands of capital. Marx's theory of exploitation, therefore, entails an important ecological dimension, which has been rediscovered by contemporary scholars like Elmar Altvater (1993), John Bellamy Foster and Paul Burkett (see Camilla Royle's entry in this Handbook).

This is why, for Marx, in the accumulation process workers cannot but impoverish themselves, both in qualitative and quantitative terms. In *Capital* he assumes for the purpose of argument that the wage corresponds the value of the workers' necessary means of subsistence and reproduction, even if he argues that it is in many cases well below it (*CI*: 582). He shows that the value represented by the wage is always lower than the value workers produce in the production process. From the moment they enter the production sphere, the capitalists consume their labor power with the exclusive goal of expanding the surplus working time, that is, the part of the working day in which the worker produces the value exceeding the value of their labor power (which corresponds to the necessary working day). In order to increase the extraction of surplus value, the development of the productive forces aims at creating a uniform and continuous time of valorization. This renders labor a purely abstract and mechanical activity, indifferent to its particular form and content.

In order to achieve this goal, capitalism gives rise to possibly the most important historical transformation in the process of production: it breaks the isolation of independent producers and makes them cooperate. Cooperation takes place "when numerous workers work together side by side in accordance with a plan, whether in the same process, or in different but connected processes" (*CI*: 443). For Marx, only when workers cooperate does the law of valorization come fully into motion. Cooperation is not just a specific phase in the development of capitalism but the "fundamental form of the capitalist mode of production" (*CI*: 441, 454), the condition for the division of labor and the development of the productive forces. By cooperating, for Marx, workers become members of a "collective worker" (*CI*: 451, "*gesellschaftlicher Arbeiter*" in the German original); they strip "off the fetters of [their] individuality, and [develop] the capabilities of [their] species" (*CI*: 447). Within capitalism, however, this unprecedented development of human capabilities empowers capital, a force that dominates the workers and both controls and exploits the social labor process.

Tracing the developments from simple cooperation to manufacturing and large-scale industry, volume I highlights the main contradictions of the development of the productive forces within capitalism. Aiming exclusively at increasing the exploitation of living labor, such development renders work a source of mortification rather than human fulfillment. It is a process of separation that impoverishes the collective worker, turns them "into a fragment of [themselves]," separates manual and intellectual tasks, and enslaves science under capital (*CI*: 482–83). This is why the development of the productive forces can only take place by repressing workers' resistance, which, for Marx, grows with their cooperation (*CI*: 449). With large-scale industry the tasks of the collective worker – both the manual and intellectual tasks into which their activity is divided into – are deprived of their content and become purely abstract and mechanical (*CI*: 549). The reduction of concrete to abstract labor is complete. This is why, for Marx, "in proportion as capital accumulates, the situation of the worker, be his payment high or low, must grow worse" (*CI*: 799). All progress in the means of production within capitalism is achieved at the expense not only of the worker but also of the environment (*CI*: 638).

> Instead of a conscious and rational treatment of the land as permanent communal property, as the inalienable condition for the existence and reproduction of the chain

of human generations, we have the exploitation and the squandering of the powers of the earth.

(*CIII*: 948–49)

Globalization and Imperialism

Marx's analysis of labor exploitation, therefore, is not concerned mainly with abstract labor, as some critics maintain, but uncovers the violent process through which concrete labor is reduced to abstract labor in the production process, at the expense both of the worker and the environment. This antagonism is global in scope, and draws in broader and broader swaths of the world's population. While in volume I of *Capital* Marx initially assumes that the money advanced by the capitalist pre-exists any exchange with wage-labor, he then shows that the repetition of the exchange dissolves the appearance that capital and labor are autonomous social forces. The value that the capitalist anticipates is entirely replaced by the newly produced value. Capital exchanges with labor-power the very value this created, appropriating other's labor without equivalent. Capital thus appears to be the product of wage labor, which produces itself as lacking wealth and produces wealth as capital (*CI*: 724).

The global scope of this dynamic becomes clear is we properly examine the process of capital reproduction. Classical economists, for Marx, were incapable of doing so because they maintained that capitalist production meets the needs of the population. But capitalist production is production for the sake of production, not consumption, and thus knows no boundaries. This is why, in his own analysis of reproduction, Marx treats the world of commerce as one nation and presupposes the full worldwide development of the capitalist mode of production, that is, a completely globalized capitalist system (*CI*: 727). The incorporation of new lands, the control over a larger population and the application of science – he argues – allow for an expansion of the field of accumulation of capital independent of its actual dimension (*CI*: 758). This field expands further through the displacement of less competitive producers and the *concentration* of capital, that is, the concentration of the means of production in fewer and fewer hands. The *centralization* of capital, on the other side, is the fusion of the already existing capital through, for example, mergers and acquisitions or the formation of joint stock companies (*CI*: 779). This process of concentration of property, for Marx, is facilitated by the credit system and the growth of what was later called finance capital.

We can therefore find in *Capital* a systematic analysis of processes of imperialist expansion that became the center of Marxist debates during the Second International (see Chapter 3 in this Handbook by Daniel Gaido and Manuel Quiroga). Grasping the global scope of the distinct but intertwined processes of concentration and centralization of capital helps explain different historical paths of imperialist expansion. While British and Dutch capital was mobile abroad well before significant levels of concentration at home, for example, the internationalization of German and US capital took place after a process of concentration at home and through the fusion of industrial and banking capital (Wilkins 1988). Despite not being the most common form of internationalization before the First World War, the latter path became paradigmatic in Marxist debates on imperialism. Marx's analysis escapes some of the rigidities of these debates, and also addresses the link between expansionism and profitability that they largely overlooked (Callinicos 2009, 55). For Marx, investment in the colonies, where the value of the labor power and the organic composition of capital are lower, is a major factor that helps counteract the tendency of the rate of profit to fall (*CIII*: 344–46). Likewise, finding sources of cheap raw materials becomes more important with the growing role of constant over variable capital in production (*CIII*: 203–4).

This helps explain why capitalism gives rise to an international system of division of labor that tends to concentrate higher value-added production activities and centralize capital in its center. This polarizing tendency of the system, along with colonization and the repatriation of profits extracted abroad, are for Marx among the causes of persisting international inequalities, as are international value transfers. These take place because at the international level competition does not compel a nation's more productive capital to reduce market prices to the level of production prices (*CI*: 702). Productivity increases thus become a source of surplus-profits, forcing capitalists in less developed countries to increase the exploitation of their labor force by lengthening the working day and depressing wages, also to below the value of the labor power. Interestingly, Marx's manuscripts anticipate some aspects of Ruj Mauro Marini's (1973) analysis of super-exploitation: a point that has remained largely unnoticed in contemporary debates. Marx affirms, just to mention one example, that wages in India were depressed even below the worker's modest needs (*MECW* 31: 251), and also noted this happening in English domestic industries, sweatshops *ante litteram* that developed alongside factory production (*MECW* 33: 348).

All this should dispel the widespread belief that for Marx capital accumulation has equalizing tendencies throughout the system. It rather helps explain why every phase of capitalist globalization has reproduced in new forms the most violent aspects of the process of so-called primitive accumulation of capital. As is well-known, this was an international process. In Britain, the state-supported dispossession of direct producers created a class of workers deprived of their means of production, while a terrorist legislation forced them to sell their labor-power on the market and helped impose workplace discipline. This happened alongside the colonial plunder, extermination, expropriation and exploitation of the population in the colonies: "idyllic processes" through which world money was concentrated and then invested in industrial production back in Britain. This so-called primitive accumulation generated international inequalities, which were largely non-existent between the main regions of the world before colonization. Such inequalities were further exacerbated after the Industrial Revolution also because of the continuing expansion of the European empires (Bairoch 1971). Contrary to the view that for Marx the violence of "primitive accumulation" would recede with the maturing of capitalism (e.g., Federici 1998; Harvey 2003), industrial accumulation subsumes previous forms of exploitation and plunder, as well as state violence. For Marx, these are part and parcel of the process of capital accumulation on a global scale.

But in the industrial era the violence of economic coercion reaches previously inconceivable levels, making direct violence secondary. This is because of the perverse tendencies of the system, which pushes more and more people into the reserve army of labor. For Marx this process takes place both in England and the colonies, where the "profound barbarism of bourgeois civilization . . . goes naked" (*MECW* 12: 222; see also *CI*: 916). In the colonies, capital concentration as well as the violent dispossession of direct producers are crucial factors that expand the reserve army of labor. For example, Marx believed that the "agricultural revolution" in Ireland was crushing the population with unprecedented force, forcing them out of the countryside and replacing them with sheep, cattle and pigs: a form of oppression no less destructive than earlier attempts by Elizabeth I and Cromwell to exterminate the Irish and replace them with English settlers. Similarly, for Marx, while in the period of so-called primitive accumulation British colonialism had only hit the surface of Indian society, it then destroyed the very foundations of this "great workshop of cotton manufacture for the world" by inundating it with its cheap industrial commodities (*MECW* 12: 154). In 1834, he noted, the bones of the cotton-weavers were "*bleaching the plains of India*" (*CI*: 558). In his articles and writings on colonialism, Marx also denounced the ecological devastation caused by imperialism, showing the global and imperial dimension of the metabolic rift (Foster and Clark 2018).

This devastation, for Marx, is a consequence of the very process of capital accumulation. This process, in his view, constantly feeds the "traffic in human flesh" (*CI*: 379) that is the properly capitalist labor market. Irish small and medium farmers, for example, constantly added new recruits to the global reserve army of labor, emigrating both to England and to America and Australia, where they joined peasants and workers from England unable to survive mechanization (*CI*: 862). British expansion in Asia allowed capitalists to organize large-scale migration of workers in semi-slavery conditions, derogatorily called "coolies," toward British colonies in the West Indies that were in dire need for workers after the abolition of slavery (Emmer 1986). Marx, therefore, did not ignore the peasantry, but rather analyzed the interrelationship between the conditions of workers and peasants in different national contexts (see, for example, his illustration of the general law of capital accumulation in chapter 25 of volume I). The expansion and contraction of the reserve army of labor, he argues, has a direct impact on the movements of wages (*CI*: 792). Capitalists use the global reserve army of labor as a weapon to put pressure on employed workers and limit their resistance, creating the conditions for reducing wages and lengthening the working day, thus further increasing the ranks of the reserve army of labor. The working population "produces the means by which it is itself made relatively superfluous . . . to an extent that is always increasing" (*CI*: 783). Capital accumulation is thus always, at the same time, "accumulation of misery, the torment of labor, slavery, ignorance, brutalization and moral degradation" for the working class (*CI*: 799).

Gender and Capital

So far our discussion has highlighted the global scope of the antagonism between wage labor and capital. Capital accumulation appears to be an imperialist process based on the exploitation of labor and nature that produces inequalities, national oppression and colonial violence. But does Marx have anything to say about gender oppression? In this section I argue that Marx's analysis of capital reproduction in volume I is much more relevant to conceptualizing social reproduction than generally believed. For Nancy Fraser (2014), for example, Marx left social reproduction out of the picture, making it an abode even more hidden than production. Lisa Vogel (2014, 72) assumes that Marx dealt with total social reproduction only in *Capital* volume III, while for Tithi Bhattacharya (2017, 33) Marx "leaves undeveloped or undertheorized the production and reproduction of labor power," looking at labor power only from the perspective of capital.

In volume I, however, it is Marx himself who points to the failure on the part of the classical political economists to consider the question of social reproduction. In more than one passages he describes capital as "an animated monster which begins to 'work,' 'as if its body were by love possessed'" (*CI*: 302) and uses biblical metaphors of parthenogenesis: money "differentiates itself as original value from itself as surplus-value, just as God the Father differentiates himself from himself as God the Son, although both are of the same age and form, in fact one single person" (*CI*: 256; see also *CI*: 727–28). These metaphors reflect critically the abstract and gender-neutral approach of the classical economists who reduce economic relations to market relations between private individuals and thus take their existence for granted, leaving social reproduction out of the picture. In line with the division between commodity production and social reproduction that characterizes capitalist social relations, they relegate social reproduction into the "private" sphere of the family. Since the determination of the value of the labor power presupposes the existence of such labor power, the wage form itself systematically conceals reproductive activities (Meilassoux 1975).

In *Capital* Marx puts forward a completely different perspective. He shows that by selling their labor power workers transfer onto capital their entire productive power as species being, including their reproductive power. But just as the productive forces of social labor appear as the productive forces of capital, so does "this natural power of labor appear as a power incorporated into capital for the latter's own self-preservation" (*CI*: 755–56). This mystification dissolves if we look at the process of capitalist production in its continuous flow and from a social point of view. Throughout their lives workers exchange with capital their entire labor power. The fact that capital does not buy this labor power *en bloc*, but in a discontinuous way, puts the workers in a condition of precarity and dependence. Although workers apparently own their "private life," their entire existence is someone else's property. Formal freedom conceals a relationship of wage slavery. Like the slaves, who had to face the agony of seeing their children taken away and sold, the working class substantially belongs to capital even before they sell themselves to the capitalists (*CI*: 724; cf. Davis 1981).

> From the standpoint of society . . . the working class, even when it stands outside the direct labor process, is just as much an appendage of capital as the lifeless instruments of labor are. Even its individual consumption is, within certain limits, a mere aspect of the process of capital's reproduction.
>
> *(CI: 719)*

According to Lisa Vogel (2014, 145), *Capital* volume I does not address the total social reproduction of capital because it is confined within the national level, and social reproduction can take place both in the family unit and through immigration, collective dormitories and the like. But if it is true that Marx examined capitalism as a global system, then reproductive activities, including those taking place outside of the national level, are part and parcel of the process of capital reproduction. And it is at this level, at the level of the total social reproduction of the system that, as Vogel argues, the question of the reproduction of the species is brought in. The antagonism between capital and wage labor concerns the totality of social relations, including the sphere of life-making activities and social needs (Brown 2012, 73). Through its exchange with wage labor, capital incorporates these activities. Although they are the pre-condition of the capitalist production process and are not under capitalist direct control, they are still subsumed under capital.

At the level of the total social reproduction of capital the biological difference between women and men in childbearing becomes relevant. Given the special role working class women perform with respect to the generational replacement of labor power, they face a specific condition of oppression within capitalism (Vogel 2014, 150, 154). Although Marx does not delve into the analysis of women's oppression in volume I, he makes it possible to understand its various forms against the backdrop of the overall antagonism between capital and wage labor. This approach systematically excludes naturalistic interpretations of gender inequality. Marx shows that if value-producing labor is labor that is abstracted from the natural and human conditions of production, capital develops in a complete antagonism with such conditions, threatening the very foundations of life.[3] The gendered dimension of the antagonism between capital and wage labor became even clearer in the industrial period, because "The labor of women and children was . . . the first result of the capitalist application of machinery!" (*CI*: 517). In *Capital*, Marx describes the terrible exploitation of women and children in the factories, and sheds some light on the crisis of social reproduction caused by industrialization, when capital "usurped the family labor necessary for consumption" (*CI*: 518, n38). The "feminization" of the workforce, he argues, caused the physical, moral and intellectual deterioration of women and children; it greatly increased infant mortality because of the lack of maternal care and the corruption caused by exploitation (*CI*: 520–23) and led to forms of commodified domestic labor.[4]

Although volume I presupposes the formal freedom of the worker, this does not mean that Marx believed that the extension of the wage-labor relationship takes place under conditions of formal freedom or that distinctions based on gender and age would dissipate (see Federici 2017, 20). On the contrary, Marx argues, "previously the worker sold his own labor-power, which he disposed of as a free agent, formally speaking. Now he sells wife and child. He has become a slave-dealer" (*CI*: 519). Capitalism built itself upon the power relations of the patriarchal pre-capitalist household economy, while undermining such relations and reducing the patriarchal family to the "private sphere" where the reproduction of labor power takes place. For Marx, it is not the patriarchal family as such that determines the social inferiority of women within capitalism, but the capitalist mode of production that undermines the economic foundations of the patriarchal family while relying on it for its own reproduction (see *CI*: 620; German 1981). Silvia Federici's (1998) historical reconstruction of the link between so-called primitive accumulation and the erosion of women's productive and reproductive power is therefore, in my view, a fertile development of Marx's own insights.

The social inferiority of women and the devaluation of their labor in capitalist society is essentially different from their subordination in the patriarchal family: it reflects the specifically capitalist appropriation of the workers' reproductive power. But, for Marx, by acting as a factor of disintegration of the patriarchal family and giving to everyone a role in production, industrial labor was the condition for overcoming the patriarchal division of labor and radically transforming the nature of housework. The participation of women and children in wage labor was a source of empowerment and liberation from privatized domestic activities, paternal/male domination and gender conventions. It thus entailed a huge emancipatory potential, sowing the seeds for a new form of cooperative association and human development (*CI*: 621).

Revolution

This brings me back to the initial question on Marx's conception of the class struggle. Often overlooked in contemporary debates is that in *Capital* Marx emphasizes power, not only injustice, in identifying the limits of capital: "Capitalism is seen as simultaneously producing growing mass misery and growing proletarian power" (Silver 2003, 18). With the development of capitalism, for Marx, "there also grows the revolt of the working class, a class constantly increasing in numbers, and trained, united and organized by the very mechanism of the capitalist process of production" (*CI*: 929). This is because capital accumulation is based on labor cooperation, which favors working class consciousness and organization. Thus, at a certain point, "the centralization of the means of production and the socialization of labor . . . become incompatible with their capitalist integument. . . . The expropriators are expropriated" (*CI*: 929).

These passages have been the object of much criticism for their apparent linear interpretation of the dynamic of working class power: industrialization would lead to the concentration of workers in big factories, this would translate in their growing class consciousness and revolt, making social revolution inevitable. This more sophisticated but still deterministic version of the contradiction between the development of the productive forces and capitalist social relations, so goes the criticism, would be obsolete given the shift of industrial production toward East Asia and the declining power of the working class in the West.

To see if that's really the case, let's trace Marx's argument in volume I. There he argues that the movement for the reduction of the working day is the premise for any advancement of the working class. Workers overcome their divisions and unify their separate struggles into "a movement of the *class*, with the object of achieving its interests in a general form, in a form possessing general, socially binding force." And "every movement in which the working class comes out as a class against the ruling classes and attempts to coerce them by pressure from without," Marx argues, "is a political movement" (Letter to Friedrich Bolte 23 November 1871, *MECW* 44: 258). The demand for the reduction of the working day is so crucial because it targets the link between exploitation and impoverishment at the center of capital accumulation. It thus creates the conditions to build solidarity between workers in employment and the reserve army, native-born and immigrant workers, and between genders and generations. This is a demand that the labor movement put forward in different national contexts and became part of an international struggle. Working time is also key to linking struggles around production and reproduction, with the ultimate goal of abolishing the capitalist division of labor in all its forms, including the sexual division of labor (Dunayevskaya 1964, 94).

For Marx, in fact, the *nature* of modern industry makes it possible to overcome the patriarchal family and achieve a superior form of relationships between genders and generations. As capitalism develops, women and children become more important as members of the employed working class both in numerical and organizational terms. While male workers could assume "characteristics that are truly revolting and thoroughly like slave-dealing," Marx also notes the "great fact" that it was their struggle that achieved the shortening of working hours for women and children in English factories (*CI*: 519). And in some cases, these limitations were extended also to the male adult workforce (*CI*: 394–95). This shows that support for the most oppressed workers is crucial for the advancement of the working class as a whole (Brown 2012, 93). As women became more involved in the workers' movement, as we shall see, Marx will discuss more explicitly their important role in it.

This diverse and multifaceted labor movement, for Marx, is not a secondary factor in the development of capitalism, but helps shape it. In Britain, for example, it was both technological change and working class organization that reinforced the process of concentration of production in big factories. The extension of factory legislation put an end to the most extreme forms of exploitation in domestic industry, where capitalists relied on the patriarchal family to exploit an isolated workforce mainly composed of women and children. Given the interplay of technological and political factors here, the process of concentration of industrial production in big factories is not definitive. Marx was well aware of this. In the 1867 Address written on behalf of the General Council of the International Workingmen's Association to its Lausanne congress, for example, he argues that "in order to oppose their workers, the employers [in England] either bring in workers from abroad or else transfer manufacture to countries where there is a cheap labor force" (*MECW* 20: 422).

By presupposing capital's field of action to be fully globalized, Marx's *Capital* makes it possible to understand the "dialectic between workers' resistance to exploitation at the point of production and the efforts of capital to overcome that resistance by constantly revolutionizing production and social relations" (Silver 2003, 19). It also makes it possible to understand that, since it is based on labor cooperation, this constant process of spatial reorganization creates new sources of structural power for workers (see Silver 2014). Workers, in fact, cooperate even if they do not work side by side, in a single workplace, but in diverse and connected locations. Within capitalism, they are brought together by capital control over their labor power, not necessarily by physical proximity (*CI*: 439). Cooperation is also made possible by the development of the means of transportation, which, for Marx, is part of the direct production process (*G*: 524). This means that the spatial condition is subsumed under the process of accumulation. By continuously expanding its field of action to overcome its contradictions, capital brings these contradictions to an even wider sphere, connecting laborers who work in different plants, firms and fields, and even from home. While making their conditions more precarious, this inter-connectedness also empowers the working class.

Over the years, Marx and Engels became increasingly aware of the complexity of the process of working-class organization internationally, and recognized the centrality of struggles against imperialism and dispossession. After welcoming the Taiping revolution, Marx unconditionally supported the Indian uprising in 1857–58, and saw both movements as part of a broader uprisings of the "great Asiatic nations" against British colonialism. Anti-colonial movements, for Marx, could have a reaction on Europe itself, accelerating the tendency toward crisis and the possibility of a revolutionary outcome.[5] This created new possibilities for anti-colonial and proletarian struggles to link up and reinforce each other. But if such connection did not take place, he argued in the case of India, anti-colonial revolutions could be the starting point for the capitalist national development of these countries. The social conditions of the mass of the population would depend on their appropriation of the fruits of that development (*MECW* 12: 221). It is no wonder, therefore, that Marx became such an inspiration for anti-colonial movements throughout the 20th century (see Chapter 14, Vijay Prashad's entry in this Handbook).

Marx also followed enthusiastically the development of the Civil War in the United States. As he forcefully put forward in his articles and writings at the time, the mobilization of African Americans was the condition for the victory of the North and the emancipation of the slaves, which was, in turn, the starting point for any further progress of the labor movement in the country. If, for Marx, "labor in white skin cannot emancipate itself when it is branded in a black skin, . . . a new life immediately arose from the death of slavery" (CI: 414). The movement for the 8-hour day started in the United States and then expanded to Europe. When Marx discusses the movement for the reduction of the working day, therefore, he does not have in mind a "pure" class struggle between bourgeoisie and proletariat proceeding in linear ways in separate national contexts, but an international movement of resistance to exploitation and oppression. Such was the revolutionary potential of the anti-slavery movement in the US, in his eyes, that in the 1867 Preface to *Capital* he declared that the American Civil War "sounded the tocsin" for the European working class (CI: 91).

This international movement was crucial to the birth of the First International and, as Raya Dunayevskaya showed, shapes *Capital* volume I in its entirety. Thanks to his involvement in the First International, Marx further deepened his perspective on international revolution even after the publication of volume I. At the end of the 1860s he changed his mind on the relationship between proletarian and anti-colonial struggles, and came to the conclusion that the independence of Ireland was the *premise* for the emancipation of the working class in England (cf. letter to Engels, 10 December 1869: *MECW* 43: 396–99). Irish independence would have undermined a bastion of the power of the English ruling class. Working class support for it was the condition for opposing the anti-Irish racism sparked by the ruling classes and for building real solidarity between Irish and English workers in England. Marx's writings on the Irish question in the 1870s contain deep insights into the link between colonial and racialized violence and the need to build anti-racist solidarity upon working class anti-imperialism and internationalism. In the early 1880s, Marx and Engels argued that if a peasant-based revolution in Russia became a signal for a social, anti-capitalist revolution in Western Europe, and if these revolutions were to complete each other, the Russian commune could represent the basis for the transition of Russian society toward socialism (*MECW* 24: 426). In his first draft letter to Vera Zasulich (written between late February and early March 1881), however, Marx repeatedly distinguished the commune in India from that in Russia, which had not been invaded by a foreign power and where the commune was still widespread at a nationwide scale (*MECW* 24: 349, 352). Despite his later in-depth studies of communities and anti-colonial resistance in India, it seems unlikely that, as Kevin Anderson argues (2010, 236), in the early 1880s Marx discerned in India similar revolutionary possibilities as in Russia.

It is evident however that, by then, Marx had become much more cautious about the social, economic and political consequences of colonialism, and more aware of the challenges to international working class solidarity in the context of imperialism and racialized violence. Already in the late 1850s Marx and Engels had discussed the danger that Britain's exploitation of the world would create a "bourgeois proletarian" silent or complicit with it (*MECW* 40: 342). In the 1870s, Marx came to the conclusion that anti-colonial struggles had a primary role in the development of the labor movement in imperialist countries themselves. His view of the connection between proletarian, anti-colonial and peasant-based struggles grounded a radical critique of stageist conceptions of history. International solidarity, Marx came to believe, was the true weapon that could undermine racist divisions among the working class. In the same period, he also came to the conclusion that "great social revolutions are impossible without the feminine ferment" (Marx to Kugelmann, 12 December 1868, *MECW* 43: 184). He argued in favor of women's equality within the First International and praised the "noble and prominent part" women workers played in the strikes in France in 1868 (Brown 2012, 116; General Council of the First International Minutes [1868–70] 1964, 336; Vogel 2014, 75). In the *Civil War in France*, moreover, he praised "the women of Paris," who, during the Commune, "joyfully give up their lives at the barricades and on the places of execution" (*MECW* 22: 350). Marx also contributed to the drafting of France's 1880 Workers' Party program, which included demands for the end of women's inferiority in relation to men and for societal responsibility for the care of the elderly and disabled (Brown 2012, 99).

Conclusion

Tracing the foundations of Marx's critique of political economy helps shed light on the real scope of his conception of the class struggle. If in his early writings Marx argued that our sensuous, inter-personal experience is always mediated by the totality of social relations, his investigation of production relations sought to make sense of this experience. Marx's focus on production relations does not mean that he underestimated processes located outside the immediate process of production but rather attempted to grasp the links between different spheres within the process of total reproduction of capital. Marx's analysis of capital reproduction in *Capital* further developed his initial insights on the materialistic conception of history. By examining the process of capital accumulation as an inherently international process, deeply gendered and racialized, Marx's *Capital* helps make sense of the experiences of specifically located workers, bringing their collective agency into the picture.

Marx's critical analysis of exploitation, in fact, is not conducted from the point of view of capital. It rather shows the contradictions inherent in the development of productive forces within capitalism, thus disclosing the new spaces of resistance emerging within the system. Marx's view of the permanent role of the methods of "primitive accumulation," moreover, points to the fact that expropriation and state violence do not only continue alongside exploitation, they are also deeply shaped by it. The antagonism between wage labor and capital is a global, gendered antagonism in which struggles over wages, working conditions and the duration of the working day are organically linked to struggles over dispossession, social reproduction, ecology, imperialism and racism. Not only, for Marx, is every movement that puts forwards the demands of the working class as a class a political movement, support for the demands and struggles of its most oppressed sections is crucial for the advancement of the working class as a whole. It is actually here, on the terrain of struggle, that the deeper unity between production and reproduction comes to light, when diversity becomes solidarity, strength and political radicalism.

Marx's *Capital* itself is a force within this global antagonism. It seeks to provide tools to advance the struggles of workers in the city and the countryside, in factories and households, the movements of peasants and indigenous peoples impoverished and decimated by colonial wars, dispossession and ecological disasters, slaves fighting for emancipation, and peoples resisting imperialist oppression. In so doing, Marx increasingly recognized the centrality of anti-racism and anti-imperialism for building the International, and came to appreciate the central role of women and demands for gender equality and for the socialization of reproductive activities in the program of the communist movement. Marx sought to show to this global working class, torn apart by competition and divisions, that there is a deeper dynamic that brings them together, allowing them to re-appropriate their own collective power. Marx's *Capital* thus provides us not only with possibly the most lucid analysis of the workings of the capitalist mode of production, but discloses the antagonism between two different social systems, the potential for a free society growing amid the misery of the present. Only by placing *Capital* in between these opposing systems, by using it as a tool of political organization and social emancipation, can we grasp its "globality" both in theory and practice.

Notes

1. *Verkehrsform* here means approximately "communication, commerce and intercourse," a broader concept than "relations of production," which emerged in *The Poverty of Philosophy* (1847) to denote the connection between different types of organization of labor and different economic and social systems (Therborn 1976, 362–63, 365–75).
2. In the *Economic and Philosophic Manuscripts of 1844* Marx argued that labor, "*life activity, productive life* itself. . . is the life of the species. It is life-engendering life" (*MECW* 3: 276).
3. This is why, as Marx put it in the 1844 *Economic and Philosophic Manuscripts*, women's position in a society reveals the overall level of development of humankind (*MECW* 3: 296).
4. For a discussion of Marx's view of the "moral position" of women, see Brown (2012, 104).
5. See, for example, Marx's article "Revolution in China and in Europe" (14 June 1853) in *MECW* 12: 93–100.

Bibliography

Altvater, Elmar. 1993. *The Future of the Market*. London: Verso.
Anderson, Kevin B. 2010. *Marx at the Margins: On Nationalism, Ethnicity, and Non-Western Societies*. Chicago: University of Chicago Press.
Arrighi, Giovanni. 2007. *Adam Smith in Beijing: Lineages of the Twenty-First Century*. London: Verso.
Bairoch, Paul. 1971. *Le Tiers-Monde dans l'impasse*. Paris: Gallimard.
Bhattacharya, Tithi, ed. 2017. *Social Reproduction Theory: Remapping Class, Recentering Oppression*. London: Pluto.
Brown, Heather A. 2012. *Marx on Gender and the Family: A Critical Study*. Leiden: Brill.
Callinicos, Alex. 2004 (1987). *Making History: Agency, Structure, and Change in Social Theory*. Leiden: Brill.
Callinicos, Alex. 2009. *Imperialism and Global Political Economy*. Cambridge: Polity.
Chakrabarty, Dipesh. 2007. *Provincializing Europe: Postcolonial Thought and Historical Difference*. Princeton: Princeton University Press.
Chaturvedi, Vinayak, ed. 2010. *Mapping Subaltern Studies and the Postcolonial*. London: Verso.
Davis, Angela. 1981. *Women, Race & Class*. New York: Vintage Books.
Dunayevskaya, Raya. 1964. *Marxism and Freedom . . . from 1776 Until Today*. New York: Twayne Publishers.
Dunayevskaya, Raya. 1985. *Women's Liberation and the Dialectics of Revolution: Reaching for the Future*. Atlantic Highlands, NJ: Humanities Press International.
Emmer, Piet C. 1986. *Colonialism and Migration: Indentured Labour Before and After Slavery*. Dordrecht: Martinus Nijhoff Publishers.
Federici, Silvia. 1998. *The Caliban and the Witch: Women, the Body, and Primitive Accumulation*. Brooklyn: Autonomedia.
Federici, Silvia. 2017. "Notes on Gender in Marx's *Capital*." *Continental Thought and Theory* 1(4): 19–37.
Foster, John Bellamy. 2000. *Marx's Ecology*. New York: Monthly Review Press.
Foster, John Bellamy, and Brett Clark. 2018. "Women, Nature, and Capital in the Industrial Revolution." *Monthly Review* 69(8): 1–24.

Frank, Andre Gunder. 1998. *ReORIENT: Global Economy in the Asian Age*. Berkeley: University of California Press.
Fraser, Nancy. 2014. "Behind Marx's Hidden Abode: For an Expanded Conception of Capitalism." *New Left Review* 2(86): 55–72.
General Council of the First International. 1964. *Minutes [1868–70]*. Moscow: Foreign Languages Publishing House.
German, Lindsey. 1981. "Theories of Patriarchy." *International Socialism* 2(12): 33–51.
Harvey, David. 2003. *The New Imperialism*. Oxford: Oxford University Press.
Harvey, David. 2017. *Marx, Capital, and the Madness of Economic Reason*. New York: Oxford University Press.
Hobsbawm, E.J. 1964. "Introduction." In Karl Marx, *Pre-Capitalist Economic Formations*, edited by E.J. Hobsbawm, 9–65. New York: International Publishers.
Hobson, John M. 2013. "Part 1: Revealing the Eurocentric Foundations of IPE: A Critical Historiography of the Discipline from the Classical to the Modern Era." *Review of International Political Economy* 20(5): 1024–54.
Lapides, Kenneth. 1998. *Marx's Wage Theory in Historical Perspective: Its Origin, Development, and Interpretation*. Westport: Praeger.
Lebowitz, Michael. 2003. *Beyond Capital: Marx's Political Economy of the Working Class*. London: Palgrave Macmillan.
Levine, Norman. 1987. "The German Historical School of Law and the Origins of Historical Materialism." *Journal of the History of Ideas* 48(3): 431–51.
Marini, Ruj Mauro. 1973. *Dialéctica de la dependencia*. Mexico DF: Ediciones Era.
Marx, Karl. 1976. *Die ethnologische Exzerpthefte*. Edited by Lawrence Krader. Berlin: Suhrkamp.
Marx, Karl. 1983. "Exzerpte und Notizen: September 1846 bis Dezember 1847." In Karl Marx and Friedrich Engels, *Gesamtausgabe, Fourth Section*. Vol. 6. Berlin: Dietz [*MEGA2* IV/6].
Marx, Karl. 1986. *Notes on Indian History (664–1858)*. Moscow: Progress Publishers.
Meek, Ronald L. 1976. *Social Science and the Ignoble Savage*. Cambridge: Cambridge University Press.
Meilassoux, Claude. 1975. *Femmes, greniers et capitaux*. Paris: Maspero.
Mies, Maria. 1998. *Patriarchy and Accumulation on a World Scale: Women in the International Division of Labour*. London: Zed.
Pradella, Lucia. 2015. *Globalization and the Critique of Political Economy: New Insights from Marx's Writings*. London: Routledge.
Rein, Wolfgang. 1988. "Marx' Studien zu den asiatischen Grundeigentumsverhältnissen im Heft XXII der 'Londoner Hefte 1850–53.'" *Arbeitsblätter zur Marx-Engels-Forschung* 23: 4–11.
Said, Edward W. 1985 (1978). *Orientalism*. Harmondsworth: Penguin.
Silver, Beverly. 2003. *Forces of Labor: Workers' Movements and Globalization since 1870*. Cambridge: Cambridge University Press.
Silver, Beverly. 2014. "Theorising the Working Class in Twenty-First-Century Global Capitalism." In *Workers and Labour in a Globalised Capitalism, edited by Maurizio Atzeni, 46–69*. Basingstoke: Palgrave Macmillan.
Smith, David N. 2002. "Accumulation and the Clash of Cultures: Marx's Ethnology in Context." *Rethinking Marxism* 14(4): 73–83.
Sperl, Richard. 2004. "Die Vierte Abteilung (Exzerpte, Notizen, Marginalien) – immanenter Bestandteil oder bloßes Additivum der Marx-Engels-Gesamtausgabe?" In Richard Sperl, *"Edition auf hohem Niveau": Zu den Grundsätzen der Marx-Engels- Gesamtausgabe (MEGA)*, 68–87. Hamburg: Argument.
Spivak, Gayatri C. 1999. *A Critique of Postcolonial Reason: Towards a History of the Vanishing Present*. Cambridge, MA: Harvard University Press.
Subrahmanyam, Sanjay. 1997. "Connected Histories: Notes towards a Reconfiguration of Early Modern Eurasia." *Modern Asian Studies* 31(3): 735–62.
Therborn, Göran. 1976. *Science, Class, and Society: On the Formation of Sociology and Historical Materialism*. London: Verso.
Vogel, Lise. 2014 (1983). *Marxism and the Oppression of Women: Toward a Unitary Theory*. Chicago: Haymarket.
Washbrook, David A. 1997. "From Comparative Sociology to Global History: Britain and India in the Pre-History of Modernity." *Journal of Economic and Social History of the Orient* 40(4): 410–43.
Werlhof, von Claudia. 1988. "Women's Work: The Blind Spot in the Critique of the Political Economy." In *Women, the Last Colony*, edited by Maria Mies, Veronika Bennholdt-Thomsen, and Claudia von Werlhof, 13–26. London: Zed Books.
Wilkins, Mira. 1988. "European and North American Multinationals, 1870–1914: Comparisons and Contrasts." *Business History* 30(1): 8–45.
Williams, Eric. 1944. *Capitalism and Slavery*. Chapel Hill: The University of North Carolina Press.

2
FRIEDRICH ENGELS (1820–95)

Roland Boer

Friedrich Engels's reputation has often not fared well. Regarded as the lesser intellect in relation to Marx, he is sometimes dismissed as the one who distorted Marx's thought and derailed the socialist tradition. Not only did he make a mess of his editing work with the second and third volumes of *Capital*, but he also distorted the later tradition by means of his *Dialectics of Nature* (1873–82) and his very popular *Anti-Dühring* (1877–78). With such distortion, so the criticism goes, it is no surprise that those dependent on Engels – even if they believed he represented a true and clear exposition of Marx's thought – betrayed the spirit of Marx's own thought. This assumption can be found among the many different strands of Marxism, from Europe, through North America to Australia (Berlin 1963, 103–4; Levine 1975, 2006; Carver 1983, 1990, 259–60; Hunt 1985; Howard and King 1989, 6–7; Arthur 1996; Steger and Carver 1999; Heinrich 1996; Roth 2002, 65; Musto 2009, 265–66),[1] although this is far less so in China (Zang 2015).

In what follows, I seek to redress this perception somewhat, focusing on three topics: relations between the military and social formations; Engels's early works on political economy; and his arguments concerning the revolutionary role of religion. Before doing so, let me address the issue of collaboration. I take the position that Marx and Engels worked together in such a way that it is often difficult to separate their ideas. After their first serious meeting in 1844, they came to correspond regularly when they were not physically together. This correspondence became even more frequent after Engels settled in Manchester and the Marxes in London. When Engels was finally able to divest himself of responsibilities at the family firm in Manchester and settle in London in 1870, Marx and Engels would meet almost daily in the afternoons. Their endless discussions took place while pacing Marx's study. Engels smoked his pipe and Marx his cigars, as they drank coffee or – more often – glasses of beer. They would start in different corners and then stride toward the middle, where they crossed and ended in their respective corners, only to repeat the process countless times. In this context, nearly all of their ideas were shared. If one or the other had come up with an idea, he would test it on the other for comment, and then the discussion would delve deeper. Although it is frequently difficult to discern distinct contributions, even in work attributed to one or the other, I focus on three insights that can with reasonable certainty be attributed primarily to Engels.

Military Insights

As an energetic and indeed athletic young man, in 1842 Engels grasped an opportunity and enlisted in the 12th Foot Company of the Guards Artillery Brigade in Berlin. He used the time to full advantage, attending lectures by Schelling and others, participating in the late-night debates at the Hippel Café (where he first encountered Marx), and gaining much from the discipline of military training. This discipline would stand him in good stead. For example, he took to the field during the failed revolutions of 1848. At first, he volunteered to join the rebel armies in Elberfeld and Barmen (his home) and a little later led and attempted to train a militia in the Palatinate and Baden. The experience of being under fire, as well as seeing how terribly untrained were the forces with which he worked, taught him much about himself, the importance of a good military force for any revolutionary movement, and the need for decisive action at the opportune moment.

Not long afterwards, Engels turned his experience into correspondence for a number of English newspapers. He covered military operations during the European revolutions of 1848–49 (focusing on the Hungarian Revolution), the Crimean War, the Franco-German War, the Indian uprising against the British and so on.[2] He developed a keen eye for strategic developments, identifying before others the direction of a war. Engels had found a distinct niche, turning his attention to more systematic analyses of military training, equipment, discipline, tactics and even uniforms.[3]

Through all of this attention to military matters, Engels developed a telling insight into the nature of revolutionary armies (which has been neglected in the intellectualization of Marxism of late). He argued that a communist revolutionary movement or party should always pay attention to the condition, training and discipline of their armed forces. Indeed, a communist revolution would never succeed without an able armed force, which included winning over significant sectors of a state's army to the revolutionary cause. Further, a revolutionary intervention requires not merely a unified and disciplined party, but also a crack armed force ready to act decisively and boldly. More importantly, he identified a crucial social dimension: the nature of the military indicates very well the nature of class and social formation in a society at large. So, he argued that a militia drawn from the whole population is appropriate to a communist society and that guerrilla warfare is a significant factor in a revolutionary movement (Engels 1986). These studies constitute a body of unique work that became extraordinarily relevant in the Russian Revolution (Lenin 1962, 1963; Stalin 1954). When the Battleship Potemkin mutinied in favor of the communists after the 1905 revolution, the latter delved into Engels's works. It soon dawned on the Bolsheviks that armed force was crucial to the revolution. They began to form the Red Guards, made up of workers trained in the tactics of guerrilla warfare. It should be no surprise that Engels's nickname became "The General."

Political Economy

The second major contribution concerns political economy. Since this work has been analyzed by others, I draw on some aspects of these studies, especially in the way Engels's first period in England (1842–44) led to his incisive pieces on political economy. This work led to what Stathis Kouvelakis calls the empirical and theoretical "discovery of the proletariat" (2003, 167–231).[4]

As Kouvelakis points out, Engels's insight was to translate the notable paradox of English backwardness (in terms of politics, society and intellectual life) and forwardness (in economics) into a German philosophical framework.[5] The key becomes contradiction, understood in terms of the dialectic and materialized in a spate of oppositions: division of labor, class, competition, wage-labor and capital, pauperization and concentration of wealth, the social and the economic, objective and subjective, and then the necessary process of intensification and the simplification of the dialectic in terms of revolution.

A key text is "Outlines of a Critique of Political Economy," in which Engels criticizes the moral framework of Adam Smith's benign view of the "market." Engels argues that capitalism does not arise gradually, until it attains its true form and thereby generates national wealth, but rather that capitalism is constituted by a fundamentally antagonistic relation that grows ever stronger. For Engels, the English economists simply miss the antagonistic nature of all that they touch. "Division of labor" is not a wonderful development, as they argued, but the basis of class and class conflict between wage-labor and capital. "Competition" does not lead to the desirable outcome of lower prices, but to struggle and crime. "Free trade" means new forms of monopoly, despotism, violence and degradation. "Private property" means the appropriation of wealth and the pauperization of those who miss out. "National wealth" is anything but national, for it is held increasingly in the hands of the relatively few capitalists, while the mass of workers is excluded: "The 'national wealth' of the English is very great, and yet they are the poorest people under the sun" (*MECW* 3: 421).

Engels goes much further on a number of points. The chronic instability and crisis-ridden nature of the capitalist market emerges in his writings, along with the role of the reserve army of the unemployed in the spiral of crises, the falling rate of wages and thereby standards of living, an articulation of the concentrations of capital, and an awareness of the influences of technological change in response to this self-destabilizing nature of capitalist economics. Further, the "market" in question is not an entity unto itself, ideally operating in terms of *laissez faire*, but is rather socially determined so that the revolution to come will be a social revolution. Even more, the materialist realities of social dualism cannot be understood without the ideological features of consciousness that are manifested in classes. The ideological and the social may be based on the material, but they are then transformed into instruments that will realize their own material aims. The dialectic, of course, has its own dynamic, in which antagonisms must be exacerbated and then simplified into two great warring camps through a spiral of crises, before the resolution of the antagonisms. In Engels's argument the first implicit articulation of objective and subjective factors in revolution emerges. As the tensions grow and the socio-economic conditions ripen, the working class becomes unavoidably conscious of its mission and engages in confrontation and then revolution. Crucially, these insights were developed first by Engels, with Marx taking up his insights and developing them further.

Apart from the inherent contradictions of capitalism, Engels also identified the working class as a practical and theoretical category. But what does he mean by the working class? Here *The Condition of the Working-Class in England* (1845) is crucial, not so much for its first-hand detail of the barbaric conditions of the Manchester working class districts (revealed to Engels under the guidance of Mary Burns), but for its theoretical breakthrough. The key is twofold: to understand the proletariat in terms of its enemy and to see it transformed into a movement. On the first point, the proletariat comes into being through this opposition, which is generated not only by the objective economic conditions of capitalism, but also by the sense of who the bourgeoisie is and why the bourgeoisie is an implacable opponent and oppressor. The bourgeoisie, *Mittelklasse* or middle-class, is implacably opposed by the working class, like two opposed camps or armies that must come to open battle – the military metaphors should not be unexpected.

Second, the working class moves from being an empirical reality to a workers' movement (*MECW* 4: 500). This entails subjective resistance to intolerable conditions: "The workers, the great majority of the nation, will not endure it" (*MECW* 4: 507). This rebellion against the class enemy may initially take the crude form of individual "crime" against the oppressors, but soon enough it is transformed into "association." It appears in myriad forms: initially "secret" and then the hard-won right to "free association"; in educational activities; in unions and strikes; in the persistent resistance that keeps "alive the opposition of the workers to the social and political omnipotence of the bourgeoisie" (*MECW* 4: 507). The perpetual drive of these associations is to challenge and ultimately destroy competition, which makes the everyday lives of workers a misery. Here the specific and immediate campaigns of workers' associations – higher wages, less hours, better conditions – are also part and parcel of the future communist society:

> If the competition among the workers is destroyed, if all determine not to be further exploited by the bourgeoisie, the rule of property is at an end. . . . The moment workers resolve not to be bought and sold no longer, when . . . they take the part of men possessed of a will as well as of working-power, at that moment the whole Political Economy of today is at an end.
>
> (MECW *4: 507)*

This pattern of political association is endemic to the nature of the working class, so much so that it cannot help organizing itself as a class, becoming unified and drawing together all the different currents of organized resistance.

In closing these observations concerning Engels's early insights, we face a paradox. Engels predicted with absolute confidence that the revolution would first happen – and soon – in England, due to the exacerbation of the contradictions in capitalism and the growth of the working-class movements. He was spectacularly wrong, as the repressive measures after the 1842 Chartist uprising came into effect and elements of the working class were bourgeoisified. Indeed, the working-class movements had already begun a process of decline at the time he did his research, so much so that they hardly made an impression during the revolutionary period of 1848 and would take a long time indeed to recover. Yet the paradox is that it was precisely this situation that provided Engels with his crucial insights into economics and the nature of the proletariat, insights that would have ramifications later and in – for both him and Marx – unexpected revolutions.

We can go further with this argument (which I have initially drawn from Kouvelakis). The dialectical nature of Engels's argument led eventually to another conclusion, first broached by Lenin's "weakest link" (1964). Instead of an advanced economic situation, it would turn out to be the specific "backwardness" of Russia's (and then China's, if not Asia's more generally) economic situation that would produce the conditions for revolutionary intervention. In this context, the "non-contemporaneity" (*Ungleichzeitigkeit*) of the present creates the possibility for socialist revolution, in which the unattained hopes of earlier forms link with present anticipations. In dialectical parlance, the revolutionary impulse of the present, which emerges from class struggle and generates expectations of a "prevented future" and the unleashing of the forces of production, gains "*additional revolutionary force* precisely from the *incomplete* wealth of the past" (Bloch 1991, 115–16). This philosophical elaboration by Ernst Bloch provides a significant argument, with its call for a multi-temporal and multi-spatial dialectic, that not merely makes sense of the successful socialist revolutions in supposedly "backward" countries rather than "advanced" capitalist ones, but rather reveals the necessity of socialist revolution in precisely in such places.

Back to Engels: it is not for nothing that his early work, especially his "Outlines of a Critique of Political Economy," was acknowledged by Marx as a "brilliant essay on the critique of economic categories." However, it is worth noting that Marx fully acknowledges that Engels "arrived by another road" to the same conclusions (*MECW* 29: 264). What Marx fails to say here is that Engels did so before him in an original way, not least because of Engels's direct experience in the family enterprise and his long residence and research in England. Yet, the contribution of Engels did not stop with his early work, for his close involvement with *Capital* ensured that Marx had access to practical and theoretical insights drawn from Engel's involvements in Manchester. Indeed, it can be argued that the second and third volumes of *Capital* benefitted from Engels hard work in editing them (Hollander 2011, 285–92).

Revolutionary Religion

Engels's third original contribution concerns the potential for a religion like Christianity to become revolutionary. This argument developed over a lifetime, being first glimpsed as a devout young man and finally explained only a few months before his death. Let me begin with a summary of the complete argument:

> It is now, almost to the year, sixteen centuries since a dangerous party of overthrow was likewise active in the Roman empire. It undermined religion and all the foundations of the state; it flatly denied that Caesar's will was the supreme law; it was without a fatherland, was international; it spread over the whole empire, from Gaul to Asia, and beyond the frontiers of the empire. It had long carried on seditious activities underground in secret; for a considerable time, however, it had felt strong enough to come out into the open. This party of overthrow . . . was known by the name of Christians.
>
> (MECW *27: 523)*

The proposal has both theoretical and theoretical dimensions, which emerged over time and intersect with one another. Let me set the context: as a young man of Reformed (Protestant) persuasion, he attended church, reflected on the preaching, read the Bible carefully (the New Testament in Greek) and debated with his friends and pastors, the Graeber brothers. However, the deepening influence of new philosophical currents biblical criticism led him to a profound struggle, in which he was unable to reconcile a conservative theological outlook with the challenges thrown up by the newer criticism. Painfully he gave up his faith, although in the process he wrote some insightful pieces that formed the basis of his later reflections on religion.

In particular, he noticed both the hypocrisy between piety and economic exploitation in his home town of Elberfeld-Barmen and the potential for political ambivalence. Here the theoretical insight already begins to emerge, although it is often implicit rather than explicit. Thus, the question of political ambivalence first appears in Engels's early observations on the famous Reformed preacher, Friedrich Wilhelm Krummacher, at whose feet Engels sat. On one occasion, Engels notes that the latter

> speaks of the contradiction between earthly riches and the humility of Christ, or between the arrogance of earthly rulers and the pride of God. A note of his former demagogy very often breaks through here as well, and if he did not speak in such general terms the government would not pass over his sermons in silence.
>
> (MECW *2: 15)*

What was this former demagogy? "As a student he was involved in the demagogy of the gymnastic associations, composed freedom songs, carried a banner at the Wartburg festival, and delivered a speech which is said to have made a great impression" (*MECW* 2: 15). The point is implicitly dialectical: through a radical transcendence revolutionary options may emerge.

This theoretical insight would reemerge from time to time in Engels's writings. On the one hand, he inveighs against the conservative, if extremely reactionary expressions of religion. They are nothing less than springs of endless deception, mystification and misery, so that the struggle for communism must overcome the resistance of religion: "We too attack the hypocrisy of the present Christian state of the world; the struggle against it, our liberation from it and the liberation of the world from it are ultimately our sole occupation" (*MECW* 3: 462). On the other hand, he also begins to cite religiously inspired revolutionary figures such as Thomas Müntzer et al. (Engels 1975d). Indeed, the full study of Müntzer would become the first historical materialist analysis of a religious revolutionary moment, *The Peasant War in Germany* (1850). In this study – and now we move to the historical dimension of Engels's contribution – he may have argued that theological language was a cloak for the political core, but he also observes that Luther's own teaching provided the radical impulse for Müntzer (only for Luther to backtrack and condemn the outcome of his teaching). Engels continued to develop his historical arguments, focusing now on early Christianity and the work of Bruno Bauer. In the early 1880s, he penned a couple of preparatory pieces (Engels 1989b, 1990a) on Bauer's approach and the biblical book of Revelation, before finally laying out his full historical argument.

This appeared in "On the Early History of Christianity" (1894–95), where he proposed that Christian origins were revolutionary for three main reasons. First, its followers came from exploited and poor peasants, slaves and unemployed urban poor. Second, this movement was in form very similar to the communist movement, with its false prophets, sects, conflicts and financial problems. Third, from its marginal origins it conquered the Roman Empire. The final point is a little problematic, for Christianity easily became a religion of empire – a point that actually indicates the political ambivalence of Christianity. Engels also observes that Christianity tended to offer other-worldly solutions to earthly problems, but the structure of his argument indicates a very this-worldly focus: the New Jerusalem would be as much of this world as the next.

Apart from the influence of this argument on biblical scholars and subsequent Marxists, I note here Marx's awareness of this position. In a report from 1882, the following appears:

> The persecutions of the governments against the International were like the persecutions of ancient Rome against the primitive Christians. . . . The persecutions of Rome had not saved the empire, and the persecutions of the present day against the International would not save the existing state of things.
>
> (MECW *22: 633; see also* MECW *46: 67)*

Conclusion

I have focused on three distinct contributions by Engels: his insightful work on military matters; his initial discoveries and continuing contributions to key points of Marx's economic analysis; and his argument for the revolutionary possibilities of religion. Yet so often Engels put himself at the service of Marx's projects, fostering, encouraging, cajoling and castigating the undisciplined Marx to get his work done. This self-created image has left its mark on subsequent impressions. But it was Engels who provided the primary guiding hand and theoretical impulse to the next generation of socialists. He saw with immense pleasure the massive growth of the German Social-Democratic Party, along with socialist movements throughout Europe, Russia and the rest of the globe. Nearly every socialist was introduced to Marxism by two of Engels's later texts: *Anti-Dühring* and the extract published as *Socialism: Utopian and Scientific*. One may quibble with some of his formulations, but they were the main works read, studied and cited, since Engels was able to write clearly and succinctly. Above all, they provided the path to the denseness of Marx's texts.

Notes

1. Hollander (2011, 1–2), describes the different ways of denigrating Engels in relation to Marx in terms of: operator versus the thinker; vulgar mechanist versus the humanist Hegelian; revisionist versus the brilliant originator; "His Master's Voice" versus the Master. See also Kircz and Löwy (1998) and Hunt (2010, 5).
2. The articles begin in *MECW* 11 and continue for many years afterwards.
3. A significant number appears in *MECW* 18.
4. The following draws in part on Kouvelakis (2003), as well as Hollander (2011), who has argued for the crucial role of Engels in the development of Marx's thought. Engels drew upon his direct experience in the Manchester firm, but also continually challenged Marx to make his theoretical arguments stronger.
5. The contradiction is enhanced when we recall that Germany's backwardness in political and economic forms had already begun producing a distinct forwardness in philosophy (as well as critical inquiry into ancient texts like the Bible).

Bibliography

Arthur, Christopher. 1996. "Engels as Interpreter of Marx's Economics." In *Engels Today: A Centenary Appreciation*, edited by Christopher Arthur, 173–210. Basingstoke: Macmillan.
Berlin, Isaiah. 1963. *Karl Marx: His Life and Environment*. 3rd edn. Oxford: Oxford University Press.
Bloch, Ernst. 1991 (1935). *Heritage of Our Times*. London: Polity.
Carver, Terrell. 1983. *Marx and Engels: The Intellectual Relationship*. Bloomington: Indiana University Press.
Carver, Terrell. 1990. *Friedrich Engels: His Life and Thought*. London: Macmillan and Co.
Engels, Friedrich. 1975a (1839). "Letters from Wuppertal." *MECW* 2: 7–25.
Engels, Friedrich. 1975b (1842). "The English View of the Internal Crises." *MECW* 2: 368–69.
Engels, Friedrich. 1975c (1842). "The Internal Crises." *MECW* 2: 370–74.
Engels, Friedrich. 1975d (1843). "Progress of Social Reform on the Continent." *MECW* 3: 392–408.
Engels, Friedrich. 1975e (1844). "The Condition of England I: The Eighteenth Century." *MECW* 3: 469–88.
Engels, Friedrich. 1975f (1844). "The Condition of England II: The English Constitution." *MECW* 3: 489–513.
Engels, Friedrich. 1975g (1844). "The Condition of England: *Past and Present* by Thomas Carlyle, London, 1843." *MECW* 3: 444–68.
Engels, Friedrich. 1975h (1844). "Outlines of a Critique of Political Economy." *MECW* 3: 418–43.
Engels, Friedrich. 1975i (1845). "The Condition of the Working-Class in England." *MECW* 4: 295–596.
Engels, Friedrich. 1978 (1850). "The Peasant War in Germany." *MECW* 10: 397–482.
Engels, Friedrich. 1986 (1870). "Prussian Francs-Tireurs." *MECW* 22: 198–202.
Engels, Friedrich. 1987a (1877–78). "Anti-Dühring: Herr Eugen Dühring's Revolution in Science." *MECW* 25: 3–309.
Engels, Friedrich. 1987b. "Dialectics of Nature." *MECW* 25: 313–588.
Engels, Friedrich. 1989a (1880). "Socialism: Utopian and Scientific." *MECW* 24: 281–325.
Engels, Friedrich. 1989b (1882). "Bruno Bauer and Early Christianity." *MECW* 24: 427–35.
Engels, Friedrich. 1990a (1883). "The Book of Revelation." *MECW* 26: 112–17.
Engels, Friedrich. 1990b (1894–95). "On the Early History of Christianity." *MECW* 27: 446–69.
Engels, Friedrich. 1990c (1894–95). "Introduction to Karl Marx's *The Class Struggles in France*." *MECW* 27: 506–24.
Heinrich, Michael. 1996. "Engels' Edition of the Third Volume of *Capital* and Marx's Original Manuscript." *Science and Society* 60: 452–66.
Hollander, Samuel. 2011. *Friedrich Engels and Marxian Political Economy*. Cambridge: Cambridge University Press.
Howard, M.C., and J.E. King. 1989 (1989, 1992). *A History of Marxian Economics*. 2 vols. London: Macmillan.
Hunt, Ronald. 1985. "Marx's Unseen Hand: Friedrich Engels and the Rise of Historical Determinism." *Polity* 18(2): 340–49.
Hunt, Tristram. 2010. *Marx's General: The Revolutionary Life of Friedrich Engels*. New York: Picador.
Kircz, Joost, and Michael Löwy, eds. 1998. "Friedrich Engels: A Critical Centenary Appreciation." *Science and Society* 62(1).

Kouvelakis, Stathis. 2003. *Philosophy and Revolution: From Kant to Marx*. London: Verso.
Lenin, V.I. 1962 (1905). "Between Two Battles." *LCW* 9: 457–65.
Lenin, V.I. 1963 (1906). "Lessons of the Moscow Uprising." *LCW* 11: 171–78.
Lenin, V.I. 1964 (1917). "The Chain Is No Stronger Than Its Weakest Link." *LCW* 24: 519–20.
Levine, Norman. 1975. *Tragic Deception: Marx Contra Engels*. Oxford: Clio.
Levine, Norman. 2006. *Divergent Paths: Hegel in Marxism and Engelsism, Volume 1: The Hegelian Foundations of Marx's Method*. Lanham: Lexington Books.
Musto, Marcello. 2009. "Marx-Engels: Gesamtausgabe (MEGA2)." *Review of Radical Political Economics* 41: 265–68.
Roth, Regina. 2002. "The Author Marx and His Editor Engels: Different Views on Volume 3 of *Capital*." *Rethinking Marxism* 14: 59–72.
Stalin, I.V. 1954 (1905). "Armed Insurrection and Our Tactics." In *Works*. Vol. 1, 133–39. Moscow: Foreign Languages Publishing House.
Steger, Manfred, and Terrell Carver. 1999. "Introduction." In *Engels After Marx*, edited by Manfred Steger and Terrell Carver, 1–16. University Park: Pennsylvania State University Press.
Zang, Fengyu. 2015. *Wannian Engesi zhexue jingdian wenben de neizai luoji yanjiu*. Beijing: Zhongguo Renmin Daxue Chubanshe.

PART II

Empire

3

MARXISM IN THE AGE OF IMPERIALISM – THE SECOND INTERNATIONAL

Daniel Gaido and Manuel Quiroga

It has become commonplace to refer to the Marxism of the Second International (1889–1914) as the embodiment of an economistic and mechanical interpretation of Marxism. Many factors have contributed to this misleading perception: the identification of the whole Second International with its reformist wing; the evolution of some of its main theoreticians, such as Kautsky and the Austro-Marxists, to anti-Bolshevik and non-revolutionary positions; and, finally, the long shadow of Stalinism, whose leaders developed an interpretation, aimed at fostering their revolutionary credentials, which described the Second International as a mainly reformist-led organization to which only a small left wing, led mainly by Lenin, presented an alternative from the very first hour.

However, a sober analysis of the main writings of the Second International Marxists tends to dispel such interpretations. First, because the production of that period was so vast, encompassing so many subjects and authors, and involving such different theoretical and political positions, that it is extremely difficult to prove such general and oversimplifying assertions. Second, because the Second International grouped organizations that operated mostly in the framework of a single class party, with political differences expressing themselves as tendencies and currents of opinion. Any analysis must take into account this diversity if it pretends to be scholarly rigorous.

This chapter will introduce the reader to some of the main debates of Second International Marxism on the subject of imperialism, placing them against the background of the major political debates of the time. It will challenge another commonplace claim about Second International Marxism, namely that its focus was exclusively Eurocentric. While this claim fits perfectly with many Social Democrats of that period, there were also many who consistently opposed this view and argued for an anti-imperialist policy and a sympathetic view toward the struggles of the indigenous peoples trampled by European expansion.

While the Social Democratic Party of Germany (SPD) was undoubtedly the backbone of the Second International and the model for the rest of its national sections, we will try to avoid an exclusively German vision of the debates on imperialism by referring to the analyses of some of the main Congresses and debates of the Second International, as well as to two lesser-known, non-German national parties that had a particular relationship with their own national imperialisms: the French and Italian socialist parties.

The First Socialist Writings and Debates on Imperialism

One of the first socialist analyses of colonial policy was written by Karl Kautsky (1883). The article compared the different kinds of colonies, favorably contrasting the settlement colonies developed by England, which had autonomy and parliamentary institutions, with the grim record of "exploitation-colonies" (such as India and the German colonies in Africa), where the natives were exploited by a small group of European merchants, civil servants and military officials. The article was meant to encourage opposition to German colonial ventures, but its disregard of the genocide practiced in settlement colonies is striking to a modern reader.

The first major debate on colonialism in the Second International occurred during the revisionist debate (1898–1903), which opposed Eduard Bernstein, the theoretician of reformism, to Karl Kautsky, Rosa Luxemburg and Belfort Bax, among others.[1] Bax, an English socialist who had already published an essay on "Imperialism vs. Socialism" in *The Commonweal* back in February 1885, started the debate with Bernstein with an article where he argued against any type of colonialism, stating that socialists should support the armed struggles of the colonized peoples (Bax 1896a). Bernstein developed the opposite view in an article in *Die neue Zeit*, arguing that socialists could not defend the rights of savages against (capitalist) higher culture (Bernstein 1896).

The debate continued with further articles by both writers. Bax ironically commented on the alleged incapacity for civilization of the African peoples, who resisted the lure of "Lancashire 'shoddy,' adulterated spirits, and other exhilarating products of the *höhere Kultur* [higher culture] with the aid of the Maxim gun." He stated that not all societies had to pass through the capitalist stage, and that under no circumstances could socialists support the subjugation of peoples standing at precapitalist stages of development (Bax 1896b, 61–62).

Kautsky, for his part, rejected Bernstein's pro-colonialist positions with the claim that, rather than promoting historical progress, modern colonial policy was being pursued by precapitalist reactionary strata: Junkers, military officers, bureaucrats, speculators and merchants (overlooking the role of German banks and heavy industry, Kautsky 1898). This view of colonialism as the product of precapitalist strata was widespread during the first stage of the debate on imperialism.

Two events marked the entry of imperialism into mainstream socialist debate in 1898–99: the Spanish-American War and the South African (or Boer) War.[2] A few years later, the English writer John A. Hobson, who covered the Boer War as a journalist, published a book that summarized the ideas of liberal anti-imperialism. According to Hobson's under-consumptionist views, the driving force for imperialism was the need for capital-exports, which originated in excessive saving at home. He recommended a policy of wealth redistribution through trade unionism and progressive taxation to reduce excessive saving by the capitalists, thus eliminating the need for foreign markets (Hobson 1902). The impact of Hobson's book on the socialist press was scarce at first, but it had a big influence on Lenin's famous work on imperialism, where Hobson's statistical data on the disparities in the growth rates of the different empires were used to refute Kautsky's theory of ultra-imperialism (Lenin 1964; Kautsky 1914).

New Positions and Debates in the Second International (1900–1907)

A resolution drafted by Luxemburg was approved by the Second International Congress held in Paris in 1900, which described imperialism as "the same militarism, naval policy, the same hunt for colonies, the same reaction everywhere, and above all a permanent international war danger." The proletariat had to "set against the alliance of imperialist reaction an international protest movement" (Luxemburg 2000, 807–9).

Among German Social Democrats, the first full-scale debate on imperialism took place at a party congress held in Mainz in September, 1900. The topic was "world-policy" (*Weltpolitik*), and the interventions dealt mainly with the implications of the South African War and of Germany's colonial policy in China. Specific issues were the creation of a German protectorate in Kiautschou (Jiaozhou), the repression of the Boxer Rebellion by the Western powers and German military intervention in China, allegedly in retaliation for the assassination of the German ambassador. At this congress, Luxemburg emerged as the most perceptive critic of imperialism and its catastrophic potential, portraying the struggle for colonies in world-historical terms (Luxemburg 2000, 800–4). The resolution adopted by the Mainz congress declared that Social Democracy was "an enemy of any oppression and exploitation" and protested against the "policy of robbery and conquest," calling for peaceful relations between all peoples (SPD 1900, 245). The resolution also recommended the study of the colonial question by the socialist parties, the creation of socialist parties in the colonies and the establishment of relations between them.[3] This represented a defeat for the Bernstein-like revisionist positions in international Social Democracy, something Bernstein himself admitted (Bernstein 1900). An article by Heinrich Cunow (1900), published in *Die neue Zeit* in the same year, denounced the "imperialist expansion policy" in Asia.

The next major forum for debating the issue of colonialism was the Dresden Congress of the SPD, held in September 1903, at which the party officially condemned Bernstein's revisionism and pledged "to carry on more vigorously than ever the fight against militarism, against the colonial and imperialist policy, against injustice, oppression and exploitation of every kind" (De Leon 1904, 96–97). A new debate on the colonial question took place at the International Socialist Congress held in Amsterdam in 1904, which was mostly similar to the Paris debate. The Amsterdam Congress also condemned the participation of socialist ministers in bourgeois governments, referring specially to the example of Millerand in France (see following section).

The year 1905 witnessed the radicalization of the workers' movement everywhere under the impact of the Russian Revolution. In Germany it was also a year of big labor disputes. In this scenario the left pushed for the adoption by the SPD of the political mass strike as a weapon in the struggle for power. This gave rise to a dispute among the union and the party leaderships that ended at the SPD Congress held in Mannheim in September 1905, where a resolution was adopted stating that the final decision over launching a general strike would belong to the union leadership, thus giving it effective veto power over party initiatives (Schorske 1955, 51). The radical push ended in a conservative backlash led by "the triple alliance of trade-unionists, party revisionists, and party executive" (Schorske 1955, 85).

Another element pushing for conservatism was the result of the "Hottentot elections" held in Germany on 25 January 1907, against the background of the genocide of the Namas and Hereros by German soldiers in present-day Namibia. A chauvinist outburst led to a massive vote by previously indifferent citizens, which reduced the SPD fraction in the Reichstag from eighty-one to forty-three deputies, although its number of voters actually increased. It was in this context that Parvus (Alexander Helphand), Trotsky's partner in the development of the theory of permanent revolution, published a brochure on *Colonial Policy and the Collapse of Capitalism* (Parvus 1907).

These events are crucial to explain the German delegation's behavior at the International Congress held in Stuttgart in August 1907. Most of the SPD delegates supported a draft resolution submitted by the Dutch socialist Henri Van Kol that did not "reject in principle every colonial policy" and argued that "under a socialist regime, colonization could be a force for civilization." The Second International should advocate "a positive socialist colonial policy," because the "ultimate consequence" of "the utopian idea of simply abandoning the colonies" would be "to give the United States back to the Indians" (International Socialist Congress 1907, 27–29).

Many left delegates attacked the idea of a "socialist colonial policy" as a contradiction-in-terms, among them Kautsky, who went against the majority of his own party, astonished to witness this division of mankind into "two peoples, one meant to rule and the other to be ruled," an idea that he called an argument of slavers and the ruling classes. Finally, a resolution was adopted at Stuttgart stating that by its "inherent nature, capitalist colonial policy must lead to enslavement, forced labor, or the extermination of the native population"[4]; although it was only approved by a slim majority of 128 votes against 108, thanks to the combined votes of the delegates of small nations.

An equally important debate on national defense took place at the Stuttgart Congress, where the SPD leader August Bebel stated that Social Democrats (even, by implication, those of the imperialist countries) should participate in wars of national defense. Gustave Hervé, from the French delegation, accused Bebel of going over to revisionism and stated that in a war the capitalist press would "unleash such a storm of nationalism that we will not have the strength to counteract it," making it impossible to distinguish between defensive and offensive wars. The intervention of delegates such as Lenin and Luxemburg was crucial to produce a "consensus" resolution that emphasized the demand of substituting the standing army by a citizen's militia, and declared:

> Should war break out in spite of all this, it is their [the Socialists'] duty to intercede for its speedy end, and to strive with all their power to make use of the violent economic and political crisis brought about by the war to rouse the people, and thereby to hasten the abolition of capitalist class rule.[5]

This was the first formulation of what would later become the central idea of the Zimmerwald Left: turning the imperialist war into civil war.[6]

The debate on socialist colonial policy was later downplayed by some of the revisionists and by some members of the SPD executive. In response, Kautsky wrote an important work (Kautsky 1907), where he argued against Van Kol's mechanical analysis, pointing out that modern colonialism, based on capital exports, made the different countries leap over stages of development. In no way could it be argued, according to Kautsky, that the spread of capitalism to countries that found themselves at other stages of development was an absolute prerequisite for the victory of socialism: this idea stemmed from "European pride and megalomania" that divided "mankind into lower and higher races" (Kautsky 1907, 46–59). After repeating his problematic distinction between progressive "work-colonies" and "exploitation-colonies," Kautsky stated that socialists "must support equally energetically all native colonial independence movements" (Kautsky 1907, 130). However, he also said that many colonial uprisings, despite the sympathy that socialists had for the rebels, should not be encouraged, in the same way as socialists did not support pointless proletarian putsches in Europe. Socialists should resist the extension of colonies and work for the expansion of self-government by the natives (Kautsky 1907, 76).

In the same year, an influential theoretical work by the Austro-Marxist Otto Bauer (1907) on the national question came out. Bauer's analysis of colonialism ("capitalist expansionism") was secondary to the main theme of his work. His position was ambiguous: on one hand, he thought imperialism was beneficial for the capitalist economy by better structuring the relationship between productive and unproductive capital, fostering exports and thus enabling a greater level of domestic activity. On the other hand, imperialism increased prices in the domestic market through commercial tariffs and negatively affected income distribution at the expense of the proletariat, while at the same time promoting racism, militarism and the limitation of parliamentary government.[7]

National Developments

France

The history of French Socialism was characterized by fragmentation and the presence of numerous tendencies. In the 1890s there were five groups: Blanquists, Guesdists, Possibilists, Allemanists and a number of Independent deputies, all of which, despite their differences, tended at that time to fall into a parliamentary and reformist mold, including collaboration with center-left republican forces, although the situation was very complex and positions shifted greatly over time (Moss 1976, 135; Noland 1970, 31).

One of the first major statements on colonialism was made by Jules Guesde's *Parti ouvrier français* (POF), which described colonial policy as "one of the worst forms of capitalist exploitation" and protested "against the colonial filibustering expeditions" (POF 1897, 47–48). In contrast with this schematic but clear condemnation, the positions of Jean Jaurès were ambiguous. He wrote many articles on Algeria in which he defended the Muslims against colonial abuses, but only to recommend a policy of assimilation and gradual granting of political rights to the natives educated in the French school system (Ageron 1963, 29). He argued that, deplorable as colonialism was, it was an unavoidable phenomenon: "all peoples are engaged in colonial expansion . . . [this] seems as irresistible as a natural law." His two main recommendations were that socialists should try to prevent these conflicts from unleashing a war in Europe by fighting their governments' "disproportionate" aspirations, as well as struggle for a better treatment of the natives, mainly through press and public campaigns (Jaurès 1896).

In 1899 Paul Louis, who became one of the main French specialists on the colonial question,[8] published an article that contains one of the first French uses of the word "imperialism," referring to the protectionist program for the British Empire. Louis emphasized that imperialist policy had become a common ground of British bourgeois parties. Although he was skeptical about its chances of success, he considered the mere existence of the imperialist program a great danger, inasmuch it was "a principle of reorganization for civilized humanity as a whole" (Louis 2011a, 131).

With the coming of the new century, French Socialism went through a new split when Alexandre Millerand, an Independent socialist, participated in Waldeck-Rousseau's cabinet of "republican defense" as Minister of Commerce. The ministerialist fraction included most Independents, Possibilists, as well as some Allemanists, whose fraction was decomposing. The Guesdists and Blanquists opposed Millerand's ministerialism, turning away from their own previous policy of collaboration with republican forces. This led to the failure of two socialist unity Congresses in 1900 and 1901 (Noland 1970, 115–37).

Two parties eventually emerged: the ministerialist *Parti Socialiste Français* and the anti-ministerialist *Parti Socialiste de France* (Willard 1965, 546). In its general statements, this latter party had a rather schematic vision of colonialism as the "necessary product" of capitalism, as well as contradictory views on nationalism, fostering at the same time national defencist and antipatriotic tendencies (Willard 1965, 557). However, some interesting works were produced by militants of that party. Paul Lafargue (1903) wrote a book on trusts in America, where he argued that the appearance of trusts was the result of a dialectical process by which competition destroyed itself, leading to "industrial integration through a unitary banking organization" (Lafargue 1903, 98–103). The immobilization of capital and the need to maintain production going despite market fluctuations led to an overabundance of means of production (Lafargue 1903, 104–5). The trusts, which acquired growing political power, therefore pushed for imperial expansion (Lafargue 1903, 14–19). The same year Louis wrote a small article on trusts, emphasizing how cartels could sell overseas at low prices, inferior even to production costs, in order to conquer new markets and dispose of excess production (Louis 1903, 662).

In 1904, Louis wrote a major article on imperialism, using the term to define a historical phase and arguing that "imperialism and socialism to a very large extent constitute the fundamental opposition of our age" (Louis 2011b, 292). Louis emphasized the modern character of imperialism by noticing that it could appeal to old militaristic and dynastic factors to justify its aspirations, but that those were not its essential trait; its real driving force was the need to overcome overproduction and crises. To this end, imperialism combined colonialism and protectionism. He concluded that "imperialism has its remedy in itself. If it must breed war, everything indicates that the armed conflicts of the future will, immediately or gradually, deal irreparable blows to the social institutions of the participating countries" (Louis 2011b, 299). An extract of this article appears in Lenin's *Notebooks on Imperialism* (*LCW* 39: 250–51).

In those years, the journal *Le Mouvement socialiste* published a few articles with different views on colonialism. The Dutch Van Kol presented a paternalist view of the colonial peoples, whom he described as "so sweet and so pacific." He argued against assimilationist attempts in Algeria, recommending greater administrative autonomy and relying on traditional Muslim institutions for the governance of Arabs (Van Kol 1903). From a different perspective on assimilation, *Le mouvement socialiste* published an article by Joseph Lagrosillière, a mixed-blood Socialist from Martinique, who protested against a number of corruption scandals and capitalist abuses in Martinique but adopted a strictly assimilationist position, defending participation in French political life (Lagrosillière 1902). In later years he became the main Socialist spokesman in defense of the rights and of the autonomy obtained by the "old" French colonies, and for the extension of this system to the new ones.

In 1905, French Socialism was unified in a single party, the *Section française de l'Internationale ouvrière* (SFIO), after the defeat of the ministerialists at the Amsterdam Congress (Noland 1970, 165–84). In that year Louis published what became the most popular study of colonialism in French (Louis 1905). Louis's brochure was a propaganda tract that stated that the search for markets, outlets for idle money and new resources, indistinctly, were the driving forces of colonization (Louis 1905, 21). Louis emphasized the growing tendency of the colonial peoples to rebellion (Louis 1905, 60–69). Seeking to counteract popular colonialist discourse, he stated that the costs of the colonies were greater than the returns they offered, stressing that they were paid mostly by the proletariat (Louis 1905, 47–86). His political conclusion was that class contradictions were sharpened by colonialism, through the proletarianization of the colonial peoples and the disappearance of the smaller capitalist enterprises. Socialists should show their support for the colonial peoples by emphasizing the solidarity of interests of all "the suffering, the humiliated of the world, despite the differences in race, colour and tongue" (Louis 1905, 108–10).

In those years the socialist deputy Gustave Rouanet conducted a strong press campaign from the journal *L'Humanité* against colonial scandals and abuses. After the elections of 1906, interest in colonial issues within party circles declined: at the 1907 SFIO Congress in Nancy, two reports on the subject were presented, one by Rouanet on the indigenous peoples' condition and another by Louis (a summary of his book); both were adopted without debate (Haupt and Rebérioux 1963, 16–17).

An exception to this indifference was the journal edited by Gustave Hervé, *La Guerre sociale*, which centered on antipatriotic and anticolonial agitation. One of its first issues featured a report by "socialist Kabyle" on the expropriation, low salaries and general oppression of Algeria's indigenous peoples (Rebérioux 1964, 94). On the second diplomatic crisis over Morocco in 1911, which threatened to lead to war between France and Germany, the journal was openly defeatist on the French side, and defended the patriotism of the indigenous peoples as a necessary stage in their development. The journal built a large network of correspondents, subscribers and donors among the Arabs of North Africa (Rebérioux 1964, 97). However, its rather puerile political stand (it routinely called for insurrection at home) did not help the journal build a real political base, and after 1912 Hervé began to slide into more and more right-wing nationalist positions.[9] In contrast with Hervé, Jaurès defended a "solution" for Morocco based on a joint exploitation of the country by all European powers (Jaurès 1907).

In the years before the war, French socialism developed the most disparate positions on colonialism, amidst a diminution of press campaigns and meetings dedicated to that issue (Rebérioux 1964, 97). In 1912, the SFIO saw Guesde position himself to the right of Jaurès and Vaillant, when he supported a project for "socialist colonization" by French workers in Morocco, finally dropped due to the pressure exerted by his opponents within the party (Bédarida 1974: 31–32).

In those years a polemic took place between Jaurès and Charles Andler, a curious figure known for his opposition to Marxism and his advocacy of socialism based on consumer-cooperatives (Prochasson 1989). In that discussion, Andler accused the German socialists of having sold out to German imperialism. At the same time, he reproached Jaurès for being blind toward that development.[10]

The SFIO Congress held in Brest in 1913 witnessed a clash between the different tendencies on the colonial question, which showed how little a coherent position on the question had crystallized in its ranks. If Édouard Vaillant offered an outright condemnation of colonial enterprises, and Bracke (Alexandre Desrousseaux) demanded the abandonment of the colonies, Francis de Pressensé argued that the positions of the socialists should be based on the old policy of assimilation and autonomy for the old colonies, aimed at peoples who were "still in an infantile period" of their development (Bédarida 1974, 31–32). At the same time, in the International arena the main SFIO spokesmen (Jaurès and Vaillant) were active in peace initiatives, including propaganda for the general strike in case of war.[11] With the assassination of Jaurès on 31 July 1914 and the outbreak of the First World War, the party fell prey to the chauvinist propaganda against the "German peril," a development symbolized by the inclusion of the "orthodox Marxist" Guesde as a Minister without Portfolio in the "national unity" government of René Viviani.

Italy

A peculiarity of the debates on colonialism in Italy, both in bourgeois and socialist circles, was that they tended to conflate under the term "colonization" both pacific emigration, mostly to South and North America, and the conquest of colonies, because colonialism was usually referred to by its apologists as an outlet for emigration (Choate 2003).

The real involvement of the Italian socialists with the colonial question came after the foundation of the Socialist Party in 1892, particularly as a result of Italy's attempt to conquer Ethiopia, which ended with a sound defeat of the Italian army in the battle of Adwa in 1896 (although Italy retained Eritrea). In this context an interesting debate took place in *Critica Sociale*, the most theoretically oriented Italian socialist journal edited by Filippo Turati, leader of a tendency that would eventually define itself as reformist. An article by "D'A" (1896) claimed that Italy had embarked in a useless military adventure at the expense of the Italian and Abyssinian proletarians' blood, since emigration would not be diverted to Africa and no significant outlet for industry would be created. Turati (1896) argued that the adventure was led by backward strata, such as the speculative bourgeoisie and the monarchy, while the industrial bourgeoisie was mostly opposed to the initiative owing to its scarce development. A later article in *Critica Sociale* compared favorably the pacific emigration to South and North America with the bloody African adventures, emphasizing the unnecessary character of African colonies (Solari 1899).

The first debate on Imperialism proper came a few years later. A correspondent for *Critica Sociale* in London, Olindo Malagodi, wrote two articles on American and British imperialism. Analyzing the British "Khaki Election" of 1900, when the Unionist government won a landslide by stirring up chauvinism over the South African War, he argued that the results and the tone of the campaign proved that imperialism in Britain was no longer associated with the aristocracy; if the old imperialism had been fought against by the bourgeoisie as an obstacle to capitalist development, there was now a new imperialism, because the bourgeoisie resorted to militarism and expansion to extend capitalism (Malagodi 1900). Malagodi extended this analysis to the United States, which, he argued, had turned from an egalitarian society of settlers into a plutocracy of monopolies. He concluded that imperialism was a new solution to the contradictions of capitalism, by means of which the bourgeoisie tried to attract the proletariat to a policy of conquest with the lure of higher wages derived from surplus profits (Malagodi 1900).

The editors of *Critica Sociale* published a critique by Luigi Negro. Negro's general analysis was that colonial expansion could prevent capitalist crises but only temporarily, until the new markets were also saturated, a point where a world crisis would inexorably break out (Negro 1901). Imperialism was not a new solution to the contradictions of capitalism, but only its development to its furthest conclusion. He questioned the link between protectionism and imperialism: in Britain protectionism was defensive, while in the United States it was a relic of old times: the development of trusts showed that protectionism was no longer needed; on the contrary, free markets to dispose of the overabundance of capital were required. This analysis was a sort of anticipation of the Centrist arguments, a little more extreme in its denial of a necessary relationship between Imperialism and protectionism.

Following the Italian elections in 1900, a general strike in Genoa in protest against the closure of the city's Chamber of Labour brought down the government. The new government led by Giovanni Giolitti implemented a policy of nonintervention in labor disputes, which led the Italian Socialist Party conditionally to support it (Davis 1989, 191). The left-wing tendencies within the Italian Socialist Party developed during this period of working-class militancy in opposition to this class-conciliation policy toward the Giolitti government (Riosa 1976, 31–39).

During that period a public discussion arose in Italy over the possible conquest of Libya. In this context, one of the first openly pro-colonialist positions appeared in Italian socialism, in an interview given by the famous Marxist and Hegelian scholar Antonio Labriola to *Giornale D'Italia*, where he deplored the opportunities that the Italian state had missed for occupying Egypt and Tunisia, and advocated the occupation of Libya with the usual argument about the need for securing an outlet for emigration in a land that, unlike Eritrea, offered actual opportunities for development. This position was rejected in the party journal *Avanti* in a series of articles that stressed the meagre economic utility of Libya (Arfé 1967, 205–6).

A second moment of prolific theoretical and political production on the question of Imperialism came with the Italo-Turkish War of 1911 and the conquest in Tripoli. The party leadership did not think that the war would actually start. An example of this attitude was an article by Turati (1911), which attributed the crisis to the ambition "of a few under-secretaries" that "sought to realize their ambitions and free themselves both from Giolitti and from socialist parliamentary influence." He declared himself confident that "the farce would not end in drama."

When the war actually started, the party leadership conducted a campaign against it, but was overcome by events when the expedition gave place to an economic crisis that turned the agitation against war into actual class struggle (Degl'Innocenti 1972, 470). In the course of the war the reformists tended to divide into two fractions, the "Left Reformists" led by Turati and the "Right Reformists" led by Ivanoe Bonomi. The left launched an attack against both fractions from the pages of the journal *Soffita* (subtitled *Giornale della Frazione Rivoluzionaria Intransigente*), which contained many articles on the war, whose content, however, was mostly of agitation, with little theoretical analysis.[12]

This situation stimulated intellectual production on imperialism and the colonial question. Many syndicalist intellectuals slid into chauvinism, like Arturo Labriola (Arfé 1967, 206) and Robert Michels (Trocini 2007), by arguing that Italy was a "proletarian" nation and therefore had the right to participate in the partition of the world.

In this context a study on Eritrea was published by Alessandro Schiavi (1912). He made a thorough survey of the literature on colonialism, noting the contradiction between the public discourse about the need for colonies as an outlet for emigration and more realistic works that pointed out that indigenous labor was required; others admitted that most of the money acquired through colonial exploitation was actually employed in keeping the colony. The budget was mostly provided by the state, always pushing for increases in military spending. Spontaneous emigration to the colonies had halted, because of the competence of the much cheaper indigenous labor and because South America was a much more alluring destination. Capital exports to the colonies had also almost ceased after mining prospects proved illusory. Italian colonialism was a failure on its own terms.

Another article in *Critica Sociale* by Ugo Mondolfo summarized the ideas of a work by Gennaro Mondaini, a colonialist that had managed to survive in the margins of the Socialist Party. Mondaini's book, published in 1911, presented an apologetic view of colonialism after the example of Van Kol, defending colonial expansion. Mondaini considered pacific penetration in the colonies an illusion, and defended armed intervention. Mondolfo retorted that the main goal of colonialism was to secure outlets against competitors. Socialists did not oppose the pacific penetration of capitalism; their opposition to colonialism was due to the fact that the needs satisfied by colonialism could just as well be satisfied by free trade. This response is an example of the weakness of some left reformist condemnations of colonialism as a product of protectionism (Mondolfo 1912).

In this situation, the left gained the upper hand among the party youth and finally in the party leadership itself, at a time when the right-wing reformist deputies were voting for the treaty of Libyan annexation. At the Congress of Reggio Emilia held in 1912, the maximalist left took over the leadership of the Italian Socialist Party (the old leftist Costantino Lazzari was named Party Secretary) and the right reformists (including Bonomi and Mondaini) were expelled (Craver 1996). When the First World War broke out, the Italian Socialist Party was one of the few sections of the Second International to declare itself neutral and non-supportive of the war effort.

The International Confronts the Approaching War

The Center-Left Rift

In 1910 a split between two tendencies, with profound international consequences, took place within the Social Democratic Party of Germany. A mass struggle was developing at that time over the demand for equal universal suffrage in Prussia, were a three-class voting system was in place. A sort of repetition of the debate of 1905 occurred, with Luxemburg calling for the employment of the mass political strike to achieve that demand. This time, however, Kautsky was her opponent, arguing against direct action and in favor of a "strategy of attrition," which he saw as the only correct policy in a situation where the proletariat did not have the mass of the people behind it. According to Kautsky, Social Democracy should concentrate in winning the next Reichstag elections rather than engaging in imprudent strikes. Kautsky called his position a center one, opposed both to the "statesman's impatience" of the revisionists and the "rebel's impatience" of the left (Schorske 1955, 173–85). This happened at a period of growing war danger in Europe, with conflicts like the Italo-Turkish War (1911–12), the Second Moroccan crisis (1911) and the Balkan Wars (1912–13).

In terms of the debate on imperialism and the war, the center began to argue that imperialism was not an inevitable stage in the development of capitalism, but a policy pursued by only a part of the bourgeoisie; following this line of reasoning, the Congress of the International that met in Copenhagen from 28 August to 3 September 1910 approved a resolution that argued that the reformist demands for general disarmament agreements and international courts of arbitration for international disputes should be made mandatory.[13] In 1911 the SPD deputies in the Reichstag proposed a new disarmament agreement. Kautsky supported this initiative with an article that asserted the existence of anti-war sections of the bourgeoisie with which the proletariat should make a common front in order to effectively oppose war; he explicitly attacked the idea that war "is strictly linked to the nature of capitalism and is therefore inevitable" (Kautsky 1911, 99). Luxemburg responded with an article that argued that imperialism was "the highest and last stage of capitalist development"; the task of Social Democracy was therefore to demonstrate the impracticable nature of disarmament agreements and warn against illusions regarding the alleged pacifism of sections of the bourgeoisie (Luxemburg 2011).

The Second Moroccan Crisis

The second Moroccan crisis erupted in 1911, when both France and Germany sent troops to the country, allegedly to protect their citizens and interests during a rebellion against the Sultan. The Bureau of the International consulted Bebel on the convenience of convening an international meeting of socialist parties of the countries involved in the crisis, but his secretary (Bebel was absent) responded emphasizing the inconvenience of taking action on that subject in an election year, when the issue could be used against the SPD in the midst of a chauvinist outburst in Germany. Luxemburg, who as a member of the International Secretariat had received a copy of the letter of Bebel's secretary, published it in the *Leipziger Volkszeitung*, creating a scandal in the German SPD. The Party Executive finally called for a demonstration, but too late, because the conflict ended in an agreement that delivered Cameroon to Germany in exchange for leaving Morocco to France (Schorske 1955, 198–201). The crisis was seen by many as an example of the SPD leadership's impotence in the face of a real war crisis.

The Chemnitz Congress

The debate on imperialism had a new chapter at the Chemnitz congress of the SPD, held against the background of the elections of 12 January 1912: Social-Democratic candidates received approximately 4,250,000 votes (34.8 percent of the total votes), dramatically increasing the party's representation in the Reichstag from 43 to 110 deputies. The debate on imperialism at the Chemnitz congress centered around Hugo Haase's draft resolution and his speech on behalf of the executive, where he argued that imperialism's tendency to lead to a war between the major capitalist powers went alongside a series of counter-tendencies, including economic integration, international cartels and the growing power of the proletariat. The sole fact of the existence of bourgeois politicians and governments that strived for disarmament, like the English government, proved, according to Haase, that war was not an inescapable consequence of capitalism. The domestic consequences of imperialism, protectionism and the rising cost of living, had to be countered through a struggle of the proletariat in favor of free trade.

Since Luxemburg absented herself from the congress, the main polemicist for the left was Paul Lensch, who argued that, while war was indeed not absolutely inevitable, the only real countertendency was the proletariat's struggle. The other tendencies mentioned by Haase were reactionary, because the British government did not pursue disarmament selflessly but as a reaction to the growth of German military power; Social Democrats should not strive to preserve the era of British supremacy and free trade already overcome by economic development. At the same time, Lensch countered the reformist demand for disarmament with the left demand for the militia: in all imperialist countries big mass armies had developed, which created the conditions for their transformation into citizens' militias; disarmament was not only utopian but reactionary, because its realization would lead to the appearance of small armies of "praetorian guards." Haase's resolution, however, was finally approved by the Chemnitz congress (Haase et al. 2011).

The Balkan Wars and the Basle Congress

The Balkan Wars, a struggle of the emerging European nation-states of the peninsula both against the remnants of Ottoman rule in Europe and among themselves (in the Second Balkan War 1913) gave rise to a political shift in international socialism. If traditionally the International had supported the *status quo* in the Balkans, the First Balkan War (1912–13) led to a mostly Austrian-led move toward a new position, supporting the Balkan peoples' independence while rejecting any demand that could compromise Austrian territorial integrity (Roebke-Berens 1981). An emergency Congress held in Basle in November 1912 approved a Manifesto that contained a precise analysis of the situation and the imperial rivalries involved, as well as a call for political action and demonstrations to prevent the outbreak of a European war.[14]

After the conflict ended, however, a feeling began to spread among the Social Democratic parties that Haupt called the "illusion of *détente*": the idea that, as the war crises were overcome in 1913, a durable agreement between the imperialist powers had been reached, and that the task of Social Democracy was to support this understanding to avert World War (Haupt 1972, 103–8). The leading organizations and currents of Social Democracy therefore came to expect a repetition of the Balkan events; that is to say, a similarly short and manageable crisis. The rise of theoretical and political Centrism was crucial to elaborating and spreading this prognosis. The socialist parties were thus left unprepared for the state of siege, the suppression of democratic freedoms and the chauvinist outbursts that followed the declaration of war in August 1914; conditions that led most of those parties to support their "own" governments in the war effort.

The Major Theoretical Works

The book of the Austro-Marxist Rudolf Hilferding, *Finance Capital* (1910), was the major theoretical contribution of the period: a very complex work that is the subject of intense debate to this very day. Hilferding's book stressed that the concentration of capital tended to create larger combinations in which the displacement of labor by machinery tied up capital for a steadily lengthening turnover period. Since fixed capital could not be readily reallocated elsewhere in the event of falling prices, large firms became more dependent on the banks in order to adjust to short-run market changes, while the banks in turn protected their growing investment in industry by collaborating in the formation of trusts and cartels. Thus "finance capital" emerged from the fusion of money-capital and industrial capital. The centralized control of output meant that organized capital could artificially raise its own profits at the expense of the unorganized firms in the home market, making the latter carry most of the burdens of crises. As an unlimited expansion in output would lower the rate of profit, strict constraints on investment in the home-market tended to arise: that was the fundamental cause of the capital-export drive, the ultimate cause of imperialism.

Hilferding thought cartels could not modify capitalism's crisis-pone nature; indeed they even intensified the tendency to overproduction. At the same time, Hilferding analyzed the possibility of the development of an international "general cartel" that would regulate the entire production. But if the idea was economically conceivable, it was, according to Hilferding, "in social and political terms . . . impossible" (Hilferding 1981, 296–97), because of the instability of international agreements between cartels, which were a "truce rather than an enduring community of interest, since . . . every variation in the market relations between states alters the basis of the agreement" (Hilferding 1981, 313). Hilferding's critique of imperialism appears in the last section of his book, where he dealt with the export of capital and the struggle for economic territory and with the changes in commercial policy, class structure and class struggles brought about by imperialism.

Hilferding's work was regarded as a decisive economic refutation of revisionism, winning the praise of both center and left authors.[15] However *Finance Capital* left open the door for turning the analysis of the mere likelihood of a general cartel into a concrete forecast for the future: that step was taken by Kautsky (2011). With the war already under way, Kautsky predicted that the end of the conflict would usher in a phase of "ultra-imperialism," characterized by the extension of cartelization into foreign policy and resulting in the creation of a federation of the strongest capitalist states that would thereby renounce armed conflicts. In that way, Kautsky defined imperialism as a *policy* that could be pursued or not by the developed capitalist states, rather than as an inevitable result of capitalist development.

Rosa Luxemburg's *The Accumulation of Capital* (1913) was the other major attempt to provide a comprehensive theoretical account of imperialism. She tried to substantiate the left's main idea, namely that imperialism was an unavoidable consequence of capitalism rather than a reversible policy, but in an idiosyncratic way: she criticized Marx's schemes of expanded reproduction, arguing that they did not account for real capitalist production conditions (in particular, rising productivity), and thus could not explain how a growing demand, necessary for the realization of the accumulated part of surplus-value, came into being. She reached the conclusion that this part of surplus-value necessarily needed an external buyer to be realized. According to Luxemburg, capitalism therefore had a permanent need for expansion, and the destruction of pre-capitalist "natural economy" (based on the expropriation of land, the forced proletarianization of indigenous labor and the replacement of peasant by capitalist production in the countryside) created the conditions for expanded markets, in a never-ending primitive accumulation process. The imperialist phase was the moment when competition for the remaining places of the Earth still in conditions of "natural economy" intensified, resulting in conflicts between the major capitalist powers and, ultimately, a world war.

Although Luxemburg's work contained valuable historical and economic insights, its basic economic argument failed to convince almost all the important theoreticians of the Second International, from the right, the center and the left (with a few exceptions, such as Franz Mehring). Lenin saw in her argument a revival of the Narodnik theories that he had fiercely fought against years before.[16] For his own evaluation, Lenin in *Imperialism, the Highest Stage of Capitalism* (1917) drew on Hilferding's analysis, emphasizing the emergence of finance capital, the falling rate of profit, the export of capital and the uneven development of capitalism as the driving forces of imperialism.

Conclusion

The writings of Marx and Engels did not contain a theory of imperialism; it therefore had to be developed by Marx's disciples of the Second International period, under the impact of a series of events that started with the Spanish-American and South African wars and ended with the First World War. In this chapter we have surveyed the political debates surrounding imperialism, from the clash between revisionism and Marxism in the first years of the International, to the center-left rift and the rise of Centrism in the years before the war, to the particular national forms that these differences assumed in France and Italy. We have also traced the gradual and contradictory origins of the theory of imperialism, which began as a series of empirical analyses of particular events and finally crystallized as a unified and theoretically grounded theory in the works of Hilferding and Lenin.

Notes

1. See Tudor and Tudor (1988).
2. For British socialist writings see the articles in *The Social Democrat* (1900, 1901, 1902). For an index: www.marxists.org/history/international/social-democracy/social-democrat/index.htm
3. See Day and Gaido (2011, 21–2), for an English version of the resolution.
4. See Day and Gaido (2011, 28), for an English version of the resolution.
5. See an English version of the resolution in Joll (1974, 206–8).
6. See Nation (1989) and Gankin and Fisher (1940) for the story of this idea.
7. See Quiroga and Scattolini (2016) for a detailed analysis.
8. A more detailed study of Louis can be found in Quiroga (2016).
9. See Loughlin (2001) for fuller account of his trajectory.
10. The documents would be later published in Andler (1918).
11. This is developed in detail in Haupt (1972).
12. *Soffita* can be consulted online at http://digitale.alessandrina.it/PeriodicoScheda.aspx?id_testata=33
13. The full resolution is in Riddell (1984, 70).
14. See www.marxists.org/history/international/social-democracy/1912/basel-manifesto.htm for an English version.
15. See Bauer (2011) and Karski (Marchlewski) (2011).
16. See Gaido and Quiroga (2013) for a detailed interpretation.

Bibliography

Ageron, Charles-Robert. 1963. "Jaurès et les socialistes français devant la question algérienne (de 1895 à 1914)." *Le Mouvement social* 42 (January–March): 3–29.

Andler, Charles. 1918. *Le socialisme impérialiste dans l'Allemagne contemporaine: dossier d'une polémique avec Jean Jaurès (1912–1913).* Paris: Bossard.

Arfè, Gaetano. 1967. "Italie: Les socialistes, l'Ethiopie et la Libye." In Haupt and Rebérioux 1967, 193–211.

Bauer, Otto. 2000 (1907). *The Question of Nationalities and Social Democracy.* Minneapolis: University of Minnesota Press.

Bauer, Otto. 2011. "Finance Capital." In Day and Gaido 2011, 413–40.

Bax, Ernest Belfort. 1896a. "The True Aims of 'Imperial Extension' and 'Colonial Enterprise.'" *Justice* (1 May): 7–8.

Bax, Ernest Belfort. 1896b. "Our German Fabian Convert; or, Socialism According to Bernstein." *Justice* (7 November). In Tudor and Tudor 1988, 61–64.

Bédarida, François. 1974. "Perspectives Sur Le Mouvement Ouvrier et L'imperialisme En France Au Temps de La Conquete Coloniale." *Le Mouvement Social* 86 (January).

Bernstein, Eduard. 1896. "Amongst the Philistines: A Rejoinder to Belfort Bax." *Justice* (14 November). In Tudor and Tudor 1988, 65–68.

Bernstein, Eduard. 1900. "Paris und Mainz." *Sozialistische Monatshefte* 4(11) (November): 709–18.

Choate, Mark I. 2003. "From Territorial to Ethnographic Colonies and Back Again: The Politics of Italian Expansion, 1890–1912." *Modern Italy* 8(1): 65–75.

Craver, Earlene. 1996. "The Third Generation: The Young Socialists in Italy, 1907–1915." *Canadian Journal of History* 31(2): 199–226.

Cunow, Heinrich. 2011 (1900). "Trade Agreements and Imperialist Expansion Policy." In Day and Gaido 2011, 177–94.

D'A., G. 1896. "Becchi e bastonati: l'impresa d'Africa e la borghesia italiana." *Critica Sociale* 6(2): 17–18.

Davis, John A. 1989. "Socialism and the Working Classes in Italy before 1914." In *Labour and Socialist Movements in Europe Before 1914*, edited by Dick Geary, 198–207. Oxford: Berghahn.

Day, Richard B., and Daniel Gaido, eds. 2011. *Discovering Imperialism: Social Democracy to World War I*. Leiden: Brill.

Degl'Innocenti, Maurizio. 1972. "La guerra libica, la crisi del riformismo e la vittoria degli intransigenti." *Studi Storici* 13(3): 466–516.

De Leon, Daniel. 1904. *Flashlights of the Amsterdam International Socialist Congress*. New York: New York Labor News.

Gaido, Daniel, and Manuel Quiroga. 2013. "The Early Reception of Rosa Luxemburg's Theory of Imperialism." *Capital & Class* 37(3): 437–55.

Gankin, Olga H., and Henry F. Harold. 1940. *The Bolsheviks and the World War: The Origin of the Third International*. Stanford: Stanford University Press.

Haase, Hugo, et al. 2011 (1912). "SPD Party Congress at Chemnitz, 'Debate and Resolution on Imperialism.'" In Day and Gaido 2011, 623–74.

Haupt, Georges, and Madeleine Rebérioux. 1963. "L'attitude de l'Internationale." *Le Mouvement Social* 45 (October): 7–37.

Haupt, Georges, and Madeleine Rebérioux. 1967. *La Deuxième internationale et l'Orient*. Paris: Éditions Cujas.

Haupt, Georges. 1972. *Socialism and the Great War: The Collapse of the Second International*. Oxford: Clarendon Press.

Hilferding, Rudolf. 1981 (1910). *Finance Capital: A Study of the Latest Phase of Capitalist Development*. London: Routledge.

Hobson, John A. 1902. *Imperialism: A Study*. London: James Nisbet.

International Socialist Congress. 1907. *Internationaler Sozialisten-Kongress zu Stuttgart, 18. bis 24. August 1907*. Berlin: Buchhandlung Vorwärts.

Jaurès, Jean. 1896. "Les compétitions coloniales." *La Petite République* (17 May).

Jaurès, Jean. 1907. "France and Morocco." *Social Democrat* (May): 295–96.

Joll, James. 1974. *The Second International, 1889–1914*. London: Routledge and Kegan Paul.

Karski [Marchlewski, Julian]. 2011 (1910). "Rudolf Hilferding's *Finance Capital: A Study of the Latest Phase of Capitalist Development*." In Day and Gaido 2011, 425–40.

Kautsky, Karl. 1883. "Auswanderung and Kolonisation." *Die neue Zeit* 1: 365–70, 395–404.

Kautsky, Karl. 1898. "Ältere und neuere Kolonialpolitik." *Die neue Zeit* 16(1) (March): 769–81, 801–16.

Kautsky, Karl. 1907. *Sozialismus und Kolonialpolitik. Eine Auseinandersetzung*. Berlin: Vorwärts. English version: *Socialism and Colonial Policy: An Analysis*. Belfast: Athol Books, 1975.

Kautsky, Karl. 1911. "Krieg und Frieden. Betrachtungen zur Maifeier." *Die neue Zeit* 29 (April): 97–107.

Kautsky, Karl. 1912. "Der erste Mai und der Kampf gegen den Militarismus." *Die neue Zeit* 30(2): 97–109.

Kautsky, Karl. 2011 (1914). "Imperialism." In Day and Gaido 2011, 753–74.

Lafargue, Paul. 1903. *Les trusts américains: leur action-économique-sociale-politique*. Paris: V. Giard & E. Brière.

Lagrosillière, Joseph. 1902. "Les scandales capitalistes et administratifs de la Martinique." *Le Mouvement socialiste* 108, 109 and 110 (November/December).

Lenin, V.I. 1964 (1917). "Imperialism, the Highest Stage of Capitalism." In *LCW* 22: 185–304.

Loughlin, Michael B. 2001. "Gustave Hervé's Transition from Socialism to National Socialism: Another Example of French Fascism?" *Journal of Contemporary History* 36(1): 5–39.

Louis, Paul. 1903. "Les bases de l'impérialisme." *La Renaissance Latine* 3(2) (15 Septembre): 644–78.

Louis, Paul. 1905. *Le colonialisme*. Paris: Société nouvelle de librairie et d'édition.

Louis, Paul. 2011a (1899). "Anglo-Saxon Imperialism." In Day and Gaido 2011, 129–46.

Louis, Paul. 2011b (1904). "Essay on Imperialism." In Day and Gaido 2011, 291–300.

Luxemburg, Rosa. 2000. *Gesammelte Werke*. Band 1.2. Edited by Annelies Laschitza, et al. Berlin: Dietz Verlag.

Luxemburg, Rosa. 2011 (1911). "Peace Utopias." In Day and Gaido 2011, 441–58.

Luxemburg, Rosa. 2015 (1913). "The Accumulation of Capital: A Contribution to the Economic Theory of Imperialism." In *The Complete Writings of Rosa Luxemburg, Volume II, Economic Writings 2*, edited by Peter Hudis and Paul Le Blanc. London: Verso.
Malagodi, Olindo. 1900. "Trionfi imperialisti I: Le elezioni inglesi, Trionfi Imperialisti II: Le elezioni americane." *Critica Sociale* X(22) (Novembre): 338–9, and (24) (Dicembre): 373–5.
Mondolfo, Ugo G. 1912. "Politica coloniale e socialismo." *Critica Sociale* 22(7): 102–5.
Moss, Bernard H. 1976. *The Origins of the French Labor Movement, 1830–1914: The Socialism of Skilled Workers*. Berkeley: University of California Press.
Nation, R. Craig. 1989. *War on War: Lenin, the Zimmerwald Left, and the Origins of Communist Internationalism*. Durham, NC: Duke University Press.
Negro, Luigi. 1901. "Nuova soluzione sociale? L'imperialismo americano e O. M." *Critica Sociale* 11(1): 7–9.
Noland, Aaron. 1970. *The Founding of the French Socialist Party (1893–1905)*. New York: H. Fertig.
Parvus [Alexander Helphand]. 2011 (1907). "Before the Hottentot Elections" (Selections). In Day and Gaido 2011, 331–46.
POF [Parti Ouvrier Français]. 1897. *Quinzième congrès national du Parti ouvrier tenu à Paris du 10 au 13 juillet 1897*. Lille: P. Lagrange.
Prochasson, Christophe. 1989. "Sur La Réception Du Marxisme En France: Le Cas Andler (1890–1920)." *Revue de Synthèse* 110(1): 85–108.
Quiroga, Manuel. 2016. "Teorías del imperialismo y marxismo en el socialismo francés temprano: El caso de Paul Louis (1896–1907)." *Izquierdas* (Chile) 27: 342–67.
Quiroga, Manuel, and Darío Scattolini. 2016. "Teoría y política de Otto Bauer sobre el imperialismo y las crisis (1904–1914)." *Izquierdas* (Chile) 30: 258–87.
Rebérioux, Madeleine. 1964. "La gauche socialiste française: 'La Guerre Sociale' et 'Le Mouvement Socialiste' face au problème colonial." *Le Mouvement Social* 46 (January): 91–103.
Rebérioux, Madeleine. 1967. "France: Diversité des options à la veille de la guerre." In Haupt and Rebérioux 1967, 136–65.
Riddell, John, ed. 1984. *Lenin's Struggle for a Revolutionary International*. New York: Monad.
Riosa, Alceo. 1976. *Il sindacalismo rivoluzionario in Italia e la lotta politica nel Partito socialista dell'età giolittiana*. Bari: De Donato.
Roebke-Berens, Ruth. 1981. "Austrian Social Democratic Peace Policy and the Balkan Crises of 1912–1913." *Peace & Change* 7(1–2): 17–27.
Schiavi, Alessandro. 1912. "Dall'Eritrea alla Libia." *Critica Sociale* 22(6): 83–5; (7): 99–102.
Schorske, Carl E. 1955. *German Social Democracy, 1905–1917: The Development of the Great Schism*. Cambridge, MA: Harvard University Press.
Solari, Gioele. 1899. "L'espansione coloniale italiana: a proposito di una recente pubblicazione." *Critica Sociale* 9(13): 203–4.
SPD [Sozialdemokratische Partei Deutschlands]. 1900. *Protokoll über die Verhandlungen des Parteitages abgehalten zu Mainz vom 17. bis 21. September: 245: Resolution zum Referat über Weltpolitik*.
Trocini, Federico. 2007. *Tra internazionalismo e nazionalismo: Robert Michels e i dilemmi del socialismo di fronte alla guerra e all'imperialismo (1900–1915)*. Roma: Aracne.
Tudor, Henry, and J.M. Tudor, eds. 1988. *Marxism and Social Democracy: The Revisionist Debate 1896–1898*. Cambridge: Cambridge University Press.
Turati, Filippo. 1896. "Becchi e bastonati: l'impresa d'Africa e la borghesia italiana." *Critica Sociale* 7(2): 18–19.
Turati, Filippo. 1911. "Da Jena al Marocco e a Tripoli passando per Roma." *Critica Sociale* 21(18): 273–75.
Van Kol, Henri. 1903. "L'Algérie et la politique coloniale." *Le Mouvement socialiste* 119 (April): 1–23 and 120 (May): 96–117.
Willard, Claude. 1965. *Les guesdistes: le mouvement socialiste en France, 1893–1905*. Paris: Éditions sociales.

4
KARL KAUTSKY (1854–1938)

Jukka Gronow

Introduction

Karl Kautsky was for several decades before the First World War, during the Second International, a leading, if not the leading theoretician of the Social Democratic Party of Germany (SPD) who had a decisive impact on socialist thinking and policy in Europe and elsewhere too (Salvadori 1979; Steenson 1978; Steinberg 1973; Lewis 2020). Kautsky was a prolific writer who published tens of books and hundreds of articles on various themes of social and economic theory as well as on actual politics. For thirty-four years, he was the editor in chief of *Die neue Zeit*, the theoretical organ of the SPD, the most influential Social Democratic Party of the Second International, and its most regular contributor from its very founding in 1883 till 1917, when Kautsky left the party. In 1890 Kautsky was commissioned to draft the party program, to become known as the Erfurt Program, which the German Social Democratic Party adopted in the following year. The program acted as a model for many social democratic parties. Kautsky's extensive commentary on the program, known in English as *The Class Struggle* (1910), became the Catechism of Socialism, which, together with his work *The Economic Doctrines of Karl Marx* (1936), set the theoretical foundations to socialist, revolutionary thinking and critique of capitalism at the turn of the 20th century. A whole generation of Marxists learned their Marxism through these works.

Kautsky was, in the eyes of both the friends and enemies of socialism, thought to represent genuine Marxism and to express the theoretical legacy of Karl Marx and Friedrich Engels. He collaborated closely Engels during the latter's final years. Kautsky edited and published many of Marx's posthumous works, including the first published version of *Theories of the Surplus Value* (1904, 1905, 1910). Kautsky's Marxism was during his lifetime the target of many critiques and disputes both from the left and the right of the party. The best-known dispute was the full-scale attack on all the main theorems of his Marxism, the so-called revisionism dispute, put forward by his close friend and collaborator, Eduard Bernstein, at the very end of the 19th century. This dispute is often referred to as the starting point of social democratic reformism. Neither Bernstein nor Kautsky's later critics could seriously shatter Kautsky's faith in the basic truths of Marxism or challenge his position as the acknowledged theoretician of the labor movement before the First World War.

Kautsky's Theory of Capitalism and the Socialist Revolution

Kautsky laid the foundations for the Marxist theory of capitalism as it became known in the labor movement of his time through his influential interpretation of Marx's economic doctrine. Kautsky understood Marx's *Capital* as a historical work that presented the historical laws of the development of capitalism, for example, the evolution of capitalism from simple commodity production, where producers owned their own means of production and exchanged their products according to the law of equal exchange, to a fully-fledged capitalism in which the means of production were monopolized in the hands of the capitalist class who exploited wage workers by appropriating the surplus product of their labor. The general law of capitalist accumulation was a central law of capitalism. To Kautsky it was a historical, empirical law predicting the future development of capitalism toward the increasing concentration of capital in the hands of the capitalist class. As a result, the increasing numbers of wage workers who constituted the great majority of the population faced diminishing numbers of capitalists who accumulated increasing amounts of capital in their hands. Together with its other side, the immizeration of the working class, the law predicted the polarization of the bourgeois society into two antagonistic social classes. (Kautsky 1907–08). This became the basic doctrine of the inevitability of the coming socialist revolution.

In Kautsky's understanding, Marx's *Capital* was not a historical study in the sense of presenting a detailed historical account of these developments in any concrete country, but put forward the theoretical laws of capitalist development reached through generalization. In his opinion, the difficulty of understanding Marx's *Capital* was partly due to the fact that, in particular in its first chapters in which Marx introduced his concepts of commodity, value and money, he did not present concretely enough the historical facts supporting his claims. (Kautsky 1906, IX–X). Kautsky's selective reading of *Capital* neglected Marx's analyses of the value form of the commodity and labor power and paid hardly any attention to the reification of social relations in capitalism. Kautsky's theoretical understanding was in a sense closer to classical political economy than to Marx's critique of it. Marx's critique of political economy was immanent, showing that bourgeois society did not hold its promise of a reasonable society guaranteeing the freedom and equality of its members and the human existence and well-being of the greatest number of humankind, whereas Kautsky's was a more straightforward critique of capitalist exploitation, the appropriation of the products of alien labor by the capitalist class, which violated the right of the worker to the products of his own labor.

The third cornerstone of Kautsky's (1936, 244) theory of capitalism and the socialist revolution was the contradiction between the social character of production and the private mode of appropriation. The thesis makes sense intuitively in claiming that due to the increasing centralization of production and accumulation of capital the products of labor were no longer the products of any individual laborer but incorporated the past and present work of thousands of individual workers. This short-hand formula for the conditions of socialism ripening within capitalism is however not totally harmless because it gives the impression that since the production process in capitalism is in fact socially organized all one has to do in order to establish socialism was to appropriate the appropriators and end the capitalist extraction of the surplus value. Its logical conclusion is Rudolf Hilferding's idea of organized capitalism (1973), which was an extrapolation of the concept of a general cartel in his *Finance Capital* (1981), hailed by Kautsky as the fourth volume of *Capital*. In organized capitalism not only had the capitalist anarchy of production come to an end, but so had competition among capitalist firms due to the total centralization of capital in the hands of a small number of capitalists. The only remaining antagonism was the antagonism of distribution. Moreover, the social organization of capitalist production proved that capitalist profits could not possibly be justified as originating from the labor of the private owners of the means of production, as they had in the – imaginary – stage of simple commodity production (Gronow 2015, 22–26).

In his full-scale critique of orthodox Marxism in what became known as the revisionism dispute, Eduard Bernstein (1993) in fact shared his friend's interpretation of Marx's doctrine of capitalism. What he questioned instead was its empirical validity. Bernstein agreed in principle that if the capitalist mode of production would, as Kautsky claimed, lead to the increasing concentration and centralization of capital accompanied by the growing immizeration of the working class, then socialist revolution would be the only realistic alternative to it. They both seemed to agree that one of the decisive questions was the fate of the middle classes, small-scale independent producers, merchants, artisans and peasants. If they were doomed to disappear, the laboring masses would have no alternative other than to become wage workers exploited by the big capitalists. Immizeration was their predestined fate in capitalism. If on the other hand, as Bernstein claimed, increasing polarization and immizeration were not inevitable, then socialist revolution would not be the only alternative to capitalism. Both Bernstein and Kautsky presented statistical evidence to support their positions. From today's perspective the empirical evidence could not possibly prove anything of the sort. It was also partly overshadowed by Bernstein's more fundamental accusations against Kautsky of historical determinism or fatalism. But even Bernstein admitted that if capitalism developed as Kautsky and Marx predicted then the death knell of capitalism would soon ring. Kautsky defended his own position vehemently against Bernstein's critical claims in a book that came out in the same year as Bernstein's (1899a, see also 1899b) by arguing that Bernstein's critique was either based on misunderstandings or rested on unconvincing empirical evidence.

Imperialism and Its Alternatives

Kautsky's concept of ultra-imperialism (2011a, 2011b) has become famous as the target of Lenin's critique in *Imperialism the Highest Stage of Capitalism*. According to Kautsky, the concentration of capital and annexations of colonies by the great colonial powers would lead to a worldwide organized capitalism as its logical end-product when the big monopolies and cartels would divide the whole world among themselves. What caused Lenin's anger was that Kautsky did not recognize the inevitable aggressive and reactionary nature of imperialism but believed instead in the prospect of a peaceful coalition of democratic nations as an antidote. As a matter of fact Lenin's critique was too polemical, since Kautsky thought that capitalism would, long before any such stage of ultra-imperialism or organized capitalism, collapse into its internal conflicts and contradictions. In this sense his ultra-imperialism was a hypothetical thought-construction in line with Hilferding's projection of a general cartel.

Neither Kautsky nor Lenin were particularly original thinkers of imperialism. Lenin relied heavily on Hilferding's and Hobson's works as well as on Kautsky's writings. The evaluation of Kautsky's contribution to the theoretical discussion of imperialism is difficult because he changed his position with regard to the driving forces and basic nature of imperialism (Kautsky 1907a, 1907b, 1908–9, 1911b). Kautsky's writings can, in line with his other commentary on actual political issues, be understood as the main party ideologist's reactions to the challenges posed by international politics and the war. Two main approaches to imperialism, following each other, can however be discerned in his writings. The first one explained colonial policy and international competition between the leading capitalist states resulting from the natural, uneven development of the agrarian and industrial sectors of production. The second, reminiscent of

Luxemburg's conception, was based on the theory of the over-accumulation of capital and the consequent under-consumption and overproduction. These approaches were not necessarily contradictory but differed in their emphasis. Colonial policy was the outcome of the advanced capitalist countries' chronic need for agrarian imports and new markets for their own industrial products.

Kautsky was, arguably, the first to develop a theory of the historical stages of the development of imperialism in a series of articles published in 1897–98 (see Macnair 2013). The first stage was that of feudal exploitative colonies followed by the "work colonies" (North America and South Africa) that enriched both Britain and the colonies themselves. The next stage was that of free trade, or Manchesterism, after the Industrial Revolution in Britain. It was finally followed by the real exploitative stage of colonialism as a consequence of the new protectionist policy adopted in Continental Europe as an antidote to British supremacy. Kautsky's stages distinguished themselves from each other mainly by the international trade policy that dominated them, as was typically the case with the later protectionist policy. (Kautsky (2011b, 757). In his writings he discussed at length the beneficiaries and the victims of imperial policy. Kautsky looked for political alternatives to imperialism and colonial policy that would be more democratic and favorable both to the working class at home and those exploited in the colonies. The democratic union of states is the best known of these. Other Marxist theorists of imperialism at the beginning of the 20th century were more inclined to look for the increasing economic contradictions and concentration of capital as the main causes of imperialism (see however Kautsky 1911b, 40–41). Like Lenin, they emphasized its aggressive nature and did not see any other alternatives to it than the socialist revolution that would put an end both to imperialism and to the whole exploitative nature of capitalism.

Parliamentary Democracy and the Socialist Revolution

After his dispute with Eduard Bernstein at the turn of the 20th century, Kautsky could state that the challenge had left both the Party and its revolutionary program intact. The official declarations of German Social Democracy hardly changed before the outbreak of the First World War and Kautsky could quite safely regard his position of its main ideologist unthreatened. However, the more reformist trade union representatives gained in power in the party in the Copenhagen Congress of the Second International in 1910 (Gaido 2008, 133). This change went largely unnoticed and without any critical comments by Kautsky. He was already balancing between his leftist and rightist challengers in the party. His position has become known as centrist. He believed that, since the working class would inevitably become the overwhelming majority in capitalism within a short time, it could accomplish its historical task and the socialist revolution through parliamentary elections. This demanded however that the party could freely mobilize and organize the working masses in labor unions as well as in a political party and also propagate its revolutionary program. This was possible under the conditions of universal suffrage, freedom of assembly and organization as well as the free press, which had become at least a partial reality in Germany after the abolition of Bismarck's socialist laws in 1890. Kautsky could speak in the name of Friedrich Engels (Engels 1990) who in his Introduction to Karl Marx's *The Class Struggle in France, 1848 to 1850* had written that the time of the old kind of political struggles, "barricade fighting," typical of the revolutions of the 19th century had become obsolete. Engels also praised parliamentary elections and actions as effective means of mobilizing the working class and measuring its political power. Just like Engels, Kautsky (1909, 1911a) understood the coming political transformation to be a genuine social revolution that would lead to a radical upheaval and restructuring of the whole political, social and economic order.

Kautsky's (1914) political caution became evident in the disputes over the use of the general strike as a political weapon and in his critique of Rosa Luxemburg (Luxemburg 2004a, 2004b) and Anton Pannekoek (Pannekoek 1911–12, 1912–13). In the minds of these radical critics of Kautsky, the general strike was valuable as a means of propagating and mobilizing the working class by showing them both their enemies and allies and revealing their real interests in the coming, final revolutionary struggle. They also accused Kautsky of not taking into account the response of the reactionary political forces and the previous ruling classes. Kautsky was however obviously fully aware that the bourgeoisie would not be all that willing to hand over their power to the workers' government without any resistance (Nygaard 2009). He presented also some concrete ideas for the economic transition and the new kind of working-class self-organization needed to manage economic production and distribution when faced with the – unsuccessful – German revolution in 1919 (Kautsky 1918a, 1919a).

Kautsky's political position has with certain truth been characterized as "revolutionary attentisme" relying on the strategy of attrition that he defended against Luxemburg and Pannekoek since he was careful in warning for any kind of adventurism that could endanger the main power base of the Social Democrats, the party organization with millions of members. This combination of revolutionary vigor and practical caution was highlighted by Mathias (1957; see also Lichtheim 1964, 259–64; Groh 1973). All the working class had to do was to wait and see until its organizations had grown sufficiently in size and strength to take over state power (Bronner 1980, 597–98). His opponents ridiculed the tactic as ballot box revolution. Recent scholarship, based on exploring Kautsky's conception of socio-political change and its development throughout his career (Day and Gaido 2009; Lewis 2011, 2020), has pointed out that Kautsky was from the Erfurt program onwards, a principled advocate of radical democratic republicanism who understood that a genuine parliamentary regime necessitates, in addition to universal suffrage, the election of judges and other state officials as well as a people's army.

The Russian Revolution and the "Renegade" Kautsky

Kautsky is probably best known to many Marxists as the Renegade, the verdict that Lenin announced after the Russian Revolution. The immediate reason for this verdict was Kautsky's vehement critique of the Bolshevik Revolution and of the political dictatorship the Bolsheviks had established in Russia (Kautsky 1918b, 1919b). This well-known confrontation, which sealed or rather spoiled Kautsky's reputation as a Marxist in the Soviet Union and among Soviet-minded Communists, has almost totally obscured the fact that Lenin was a most ardent admirer and pupil of Kautsky's until World War I. Kautsky's and Lenin's views about the perspectives of the Russian Revolution were closest during the first Russian Revolution in 1905 (Kautsky 1906; Lih 2006, 155–56). They both welcomed it as the first, democratic stage of the expected two-stage revolutionary process, the second stage of which would be the final socialist revolution, but only after a long period of bourgeois rule during which both the economic and social conditions as well as the working-class organizations could mature enough to make the next, socialist stage of the revolution possible.

Both Kautsky and Lenin shared the opinion that since the bourgeoisie and its political forces had become reactionary they were not any more the natural adherents of a bourgeois, democratic revolution and could not anymore be relied to accomplish the historical task that had fallen naturally on their shoulders during the political struggles of the previous century. Therefore the working class and its political organization, the Social Democratic Party, had to accomplish this historical mission of establishing and defending a genuinely democratic constitution.

They could however, as the doctrine went, by their political activity also speed up the historical process of the maturing of the conditions of socialism within capitalism, thus shortening the period between the two revolutions. As far as the Russian case was concerned, both Kautsky and Lenin relied on the idea that socialist revolutions would soon break out in Germany and other more advanced European countries that could create favorable conditions for the socialist transformation in Russia too.

The other European revolutions failed but even if they had succeeded it would have been difficult to any serious Marxist to defend the October Revolution that followed the February one only half a year after as the genuine socialist stage of a revolution. Kautsky was determined in his condemnation of Lenin's Bolshevik dictatorship, which he thought to be an inevitable consequence of the untimely and premature take-over of state power in Russia, a country that was populated by backward peasants and the industrial proletariat of which was small in numbers and undeveloped. One could therefore claim that, if anyone was a renegade from Marxism, it was Lenin, because he had abandoned the Marxist two-stage revolutionary formula and defended the Bolshevik dictatorship of the proletariat as socialism. Kautsky published several pamphlets after the Bolshevik coming to power that condemned Bolshevik rule as a dictatorship of a minority and demanded a democratic transition.

Some commentators and critics of Lenin, most notably John H. Kautsky (1994, 2001), have claimed that Kautsky and Lenin understood the relations between the intellectuals, or professional revolutionaries, and the working class in a totally different light. According to this interpretation, Lenin relied on the professional revolutionaries, who, armed with the right Marxist doctrine and possessing socialist consciousness, formed the core of his revolutionary party. Without them the working masses could only develop a trade-union consciousness. Lenin's analysis of the workers' aristocracy, whom the capitalists had bought over to their side by higher wages and other privileges, as well as the sharp distinction he made between the spontaneous trade-union consciousness and the real socialist or revolutionary consciousness of the wage workers is often presented to support the thesis that Lenin's party was a party of professional revolutionaries. Kautsky, in his turn, could never imagine any radical break between the party and the ordinary members of the working class. Lih (2006, 2011) has challenged this interpretation by arguing convincingly that Lenin was a most ardent follower of the revolutionary formula of Kautsky's Erfurt program until the Russian Revolution. Both Kautsky and Lenin thought that it was the historical mission of the organized working class to accomplish the socialist revolution. The main task of the Social Democratic Party and its "intellectuals" was to propagate Marx's and Engels's teachings among the workers, a task to which Kautsky diligently committed himself for the best part of his life. He believed firmly in the power of the scientific nature of Marxism expressed in the general laws of capitalism and the socialist revolution.

The Eclipse of Kautsky

Karl Kautsky lived twenty years after the First World War and the great social and political upheavals that followed it. His position as the main ideologist of the party and the Second International had however lost its momentum already during the war. The decline in his status was a dramatic one. It was certainly connected to the inability of the Second International to prevent the outbreak of war and the nationalistic revival in the belligerent countries with the resulting massacre of millions of workers on the battlefields. Many radical Social Democrats, Lenin among them, thought that Kautsky had personally betrayed their cause by not distancing himself publicly from the majority of his party voting for the war credits in the Reichstag. There are however other reasons for the decline of Kautsky's star in the German and international labor movement. After the death of the highly respected leader of the German Social Democratic Party, August Bebel, in 1913, Kautsky lost his closest contact to day-to-day politics. In 1917 Kautsky left his old party and joined the new Independent Social Democratic Party, USPD, at the same time as losing his position as the editor in chief of *Die neue Zeit*. Such concrete historical events played a role in directing his future life course and literary activity but it is presumably safe to conclude that Kautsky's theoretical – centrist – position did not fit any more with either sides in a labor movement that was divided between reformist Social Democracy and revolutionary Communism. His position was too far to the right for the Communists, too far to the left for the Social Democrats. Kautsky's thinking was also of rather little help in understanding the emergence of the National Socialist Party and its appeal among German workers. (In this Kautsky was certainly not alone.) He did however contribute to the unification of the two Social Democratic parties in Germany and some of his ideas were taken over in the new party program of 1925 (Morgan 1989, 61; Lewis 2020).

Kautsky did not give up his literary activity after the war. On the contrary, he wrote and published extensively after having moved to Vienna in 1924 to a scholarly retirement. Few of his later works are known or read today beyond a small circle of specialists. The magnum opus of his later years was the two-volume *Materialist Conception of History* (1927), which was influenced by evolutionist thinking. *Sozialisten und Krieg* (1937, Socialists and War) was a continuation of a theme that he had started in *Krieg und Demokratie* (1932, War and Democracy). These works did not get much of a response.

Kautsky died in Amsterdam, the Netherlands, in 1938, after Germany had annexed Austria. To many Marxist thinkers, Kautsky remains the renegade of Marxism. To Social Democrats he is merely of historical interest as a figure from the party's "pre-history." Reflecting on his life, Kautsky (2017, 40) was adamant: "So I will die as I have lived, an incorrigible Marxist."

Bibliography

Bernstein, Eduard. 1993 (1899). *The Preconditions of Socialism*. Cambridge: Cambridge University Press.

Bronner, Stephen E. 1982. "Karl Kautsky and the Twilight of Orthodoxy." *Political Theory* 10(4): 580–605.

Day, Richard B., and Daniel Gaido, eds. 2009. *Witnesses to Permanent Revolution: The Documentary Record*. Leiden: Brill.

Donald, Moira. 1983. *Marxism and Revolution: Karl Kautsky and the Russian Marxists 1900–1924*. New Haven: Yale University Press.

Engels, Friedrich. 1990. "Introduction to Karl Marx's *The Class Struggles in France, 1848 to 1850*." *MECW* 27: 506–24.

Gaido, Daniel 2008. "Marxism and Union Democracy: Karl Kautsky on Samuel Gompers and German Trade Unions." *Historical Materialism* 16: 115–36.

Groh, Dieter. 1973. *Neqative Integration und revolutionärer Attentismus. Die deutsche Sozialdemokratie am Vorabend des Ersten Weltkrieges*. Frankfurt am Main, Berlin and Wien: Ullstein.

Gronow, Jukka. 2015. *On the Formation of Marxism: Karl Kautsky's Theory of Capitalism, the Marxism of the Second International and Karl Marx's Critique of Political Economy*. Leiden: Brill.

Hilferding, Rudolf. 1973 (1927). "Organisierter Kapitalismus. Referat und Diskussion." In *Sozialökonomische Studientexte*. Vol. 10. Giessen: Rotdruck.

Hilferding, Rudolf. 1981 (1910). *Finance Capital: A Study of the Latest Phase of Capitalist Development*. London: Routledge.

Hobson, J.A. 1902. *Imperialism: A Study*. London: James Nisbet.

Kautsky, John H. 1994. *Karl Kautsky: Marxism, Revolution, Bureaucracy*. New Brunswick and London: Transaction Publishers.

Kautsky, John H. 2001. *Marxism and Leninism: Different Ideologies*. New Brunswick and London: Transaction Publishers.

Kautsky, Karl. 1883. "Auswanderung and Kolonisation." *Die neue Zeit* 1: 365–70, 395–404.

Kautsky, Karl. 1898. "Ältere und neuere Kolonialpolitik." *Die neue Zeit* 16(1): 769–81, 801–16.

Kautsky, Karl. 1899a. *Bernstein und das sozialdemokratische Programm. Eine Antikritik.* Stuttgart: J.H.W. Dietz Nachf.

Kautsky, Karl. 1899b. *Die Agrarfrage. Eine Uebersicht über die Tendenzen der modernen Landwirtschaft und die Agrarpolitik der Sozialdemokratie.* Stuttgart: J.H.W. Dietz Nachf.

Kautsky, Karl. 1906. "Treibkräfte und Aussichten der russischen Revolution." *Die Neue Zeit* 25(1): 88–82.

Kautsky, Karl. 1907a. "Die Nutzen der Kolonien für die Arbeiter." I–III. *Vorwärts* 11, 13, 17(13): 16.

Kautsky, Karl. 1907b. *Sozialismus und Kolonialpolitik. Eine Auseinandersetzung.* Berlin: Vorwärts. English version: *Socialism and Colonial Policy: An Analysis.* Belfast: Athol Books, 1975.

Kautsky, Karl. 1907–08. "Verelendung und Zusammenbruch." *Die Neue Zeit* 2: 540–51, 607–12.

Kautsky, Karl. 1908–09. "Sozialistische Kolonialpolitik." *Die Neue Zeit* 2: 33–43.

Kautsky, Karl. 1909. *Der Weg zur Macht. Politische Betrachtungen über das Hineinwachsen in die Revolution.* Berlin: Buchhandlung Vorwärts.

Kautsky, Karl. 1910 (1892). *The Class Struggle: Erfurt Program.* Chicago: Charles H. Kerr & Co.

Kautsky, Karl. 1911a. *Parlamentarismus und Demokratie.* Stuttgart: J.H.W. Dietz Nachf.

Kautsky, Karl. 1911b. *Handelspolitik und Sozialdemokratie. Populäre Darstellung der handelspolitischen Streitfragen.* Berlin: Buchhandlung Vorwärts, Paul Singer.

Kautsky, Karl. 1914. *Der politische Massenstreik. Ein Beitrag zur Geschichte der Massenstreikdiskussionen innerhalb der deutschen Sozialdemokratie.* Berlin: Vorwärts, Paul Singer.

Kautsky, Karl. 1918a. *Die Diktatur des Proletariats.* Wien: Volksbuchhandlung I. Brand.

Kautsky, Karl. 1918b. *Sozialdemokratische Bemerkungen zur Uebergangswirtschat.* Leipzig: Leipziger Buchdruckerei.

Kautsky, Karl. 1919a. *Terrorismus und Kommunismus. Ein Beitrag zur Naturgeschichte der Revolution.* Berlin: Verlag Neues Vaterland.

Kautsky, Karl. 1919b. *Die Sozializierung und die Arbeiterräte. Bericht, erstattet dem 2. Kongressder Arbeiter-, Soldaten und Bauernräte Deutschlands am 14. April 1919.* Wien: Volksbuchhandlung, I. Brand.

Kautsky, Karl. 1927. *Die materialistische Geschichtsauffassung.* l–2. Bd. Berlin: J.H.W. Dietz.

Kautsky, Karl. 1932. *Krieg und Demokratie.* Berlin: J.H.W. Dietz.

Kautsky, Karl. 1936 (1906). *The Economic Doctrines of Karl Marx.* New York: Macmillan.

Kautsky, Karl. 1937. *Sozialisten und Krieg.* Prague: Orbis Verlag.

Kautsky, Karl. 2011a (1914). "Imperialism." In Day and Gaido, eds. 2011, 753–74.

Kautsky, Karl 2011b (1915). "National State, Imperialist State and Confederations." In Day and Gaido, eds. 2011, 791–848.

Kautsky. Karl. 2017 (1924). "The Development of a Marxist." *Historical Materialism* 25(3): 148–90.

Lenin, V.I. 1964a (1902). "What Is to Be Done? Burning Questions of Our Movement." *LCW* 5: 347–529.

Lenin, V.I. 1964b (1917). "Imperialism, the Highest Stage of Capitalism." *LCW* 22: 185–304.

Lenin, V.I. 1964c (1918). "The State and Revolution: The Marxist Theory of the State and the Tasks of the Proletariat in the Revolution." *LCW* 25: 385–497.

Lenin, V.I. 1964d (1918). "The Proletarian Revolution and the Renegade Kautsky." *LCW* 28: 227–325.

Lewis, Ben. 2011. "Kautsky. From Erfurt to Charlottenburg." *Weekly Worker* (10 November).

Lewis, Ben, ed. 2020. *Karl Kautsky on Democracy and Republicanism.* Leiden: Brill.

Lichtheim, Georg. 1964. *Marxism: A Historical and Critical Study.* London: Routledge.

Lih, Lars T. 2006. *Lenin Rediscovered: What Is to Be Done? In Context.* Leiden: Brill.

Lih, Lars T. 2011. *Lenin.* London: Reaktion Books.

Luxemburg, Rosa. 2004a. "Social Reform or Revolution." In *The Rosa Luxemburg Reader*, edited by Peter Hudis and Kevin B. Anderson, 128–67. New York: Monthly Review Books.

Luxemburg, Rosa. 2004b. "The Mass Strike, the Political Party, and the Trade Unions." In *The Rosa Luxemburg Reader*, edited by Peter Hudis and Kevin B. Anderson, 168–99. New York: Monthly Review Books.

Luxemburg, Rosa. 2015 (1913). "The Accumulation of Capital: A Contribution to the Economic Theory of Imperialism." In *The Complete Writings of Rosa Luxemburg, Volume II, Economic Writings 2*, edited by Peter Hudis and Paul Le Blanc. London: Verso.

Macnair, Mike. 2013. "Kautsky and the Myths of Manchesterism." In *Kautsky on Colonialism.* London: November Publications.

Mathias, Erich. 1957. "Kautsky und der Kautskyanismus. Die Funktion der Ideologie in der deutschen Sozialdemokatie vor den ersten Weltkrieg." In *Marxismus-Studien.* 2 Folge, edited by I. Fetscher, 155–59. Tübingen: J.C.B. Mohr (Paul Siebeck).

Morgan, David W. 1989. "The Eclipse of Karl Kautsky, 1914–1924." *International Journal of Comparative Sociology* 30(1–2): 57–67.

Nygaard, Bertel. 2009. "Constructing Marxism: Karl Kautsky and the French Revolution." *History of European Ideas* 35(4): 450–64.
Pannekoek, Anton. 1911–12. "Massenaktion und Revolution." *Die neue Zeit* 2: 541–50, 589–93, 609–16.
Pannekoek, Anton. 1912–13. "Marxistische Theorie und revolutionäre Taktik." I–II. *Die neue Zeit* 1: 272–81, 365–73.
Salvadori, Massimo. 1979. *Karl Kautsky and the Socialist Revolution 1880–1938*. London: New Left Books.
Steenson, Gary P. 1978. *Karl Kautsky 1854–1938: Marxism in the Classical Years*. Pittsburgh: University of Pittsburgh Press.
Steinberg, H.-J. 1973. *Sozialismus und deutsche Sozialdemokratie. Zur Ideologie der Partei vor dem I. Weltkrieg*. Bonn and Bad Godesberg: Verlag für Litteratur und Zeitgeschehen.

5

ROSA LUXEMBURG (1871–1919)

Peter Hudis

Rosa Luxemburg's contributions as thinker, activist and original personality cannot be understood apart from the lifeworld of the Second International. It was the terrain in which she emerged as an aspiring Marxist economist and political activist in the late 1880s and 1890s and became an internationally recognized thinker in the years that followed. That lifeworld, defined by mass parties that assumed socialism would inevitably arise through the forward march of history, is far removed from what faces us today. Nevertheless, her legacy speaks directly to us – perhaps more than any other revolutionary of her generation. This is because she developed a distinctive concept of revolution that raised the question "what happens after the revolution" *before* it occurs. This led her to polemicize against numerous figures in the Second International as well as issue a searing critique of those who founded the Third International in its place.

Since her death, Marxists have had to face the inefficacy of Social Democracy and the disasters of Stalinism – and the difficulty of developing an alternative to both that wins the support of masses of people. Luxemburg did not anticipate this state of affairs and she offers no blueprint for how to overcome it, but her distinct perspective, developed in response to the reformist and revolutionary currents of her time, help explain the worldwide resurgence of interest in her work over the past decade (see Datta Gupta 2015).

Reform or Revolution

Crucial in this regard was her battle against Eduard Bernstein's reformism, in 1898–99. A fiercely independent mind is clearly manifest as this young, unknown Polish-Jewish woman takes on a leading figure of a party she had only joined shortly beforehand. And the object of her critique was none other than the person Engels had anointed literary executor of Marx's writings. Undeterred, she took aim at revisionism on both political and economic grounds – a consideration worth keeping in mind, given that many pay insufficient attention to her work as a Marxist economist.[1] Politically, she attacked Bernstein for claiming that the objective situation rendered Marx's advocacy of revolutionary transformation obsolete. Economically, she attacked his adoption of bourgeois marginal utility theory to question the labor theory of value. And she critiqued his rejection of dialectical thought as "an attempt to shatter the intellectual arm with the aid of which the proletariat . . . is yet enabled to triumph over the bourgeoisie" (Luxemburg 2004a, 162). Luxemburg never held that the objective contradictions of capital would automatically lead to a post-capitalist society; an essential precondition for the emancipation of the working class, she held, is its *mental and spiritual* development. It is not without reason that wrote to her closest colleague, "I do not agree with the view that it is foolish to be an idealist in the German movement" (Luxemburg 2011a, 118). This "idealism," however, was firmly rooted in a *materialist* grasp of the objective contradictions of capitalism.

Her most important insight contra Bernstein (and reformism generally) came in response to his claim that "the final goal of socialism is nothing to me, the movement is everything" (Bernstein 1993, 190). The tendency to disavow the *telos* of struggle in favor of struggle itself is a recurring theme to this day.[2] Luxemburg held that this renders not just the future unknowable, but also the present. She writes in *Social Reform or Revolution*,

> The secret of Marx's theory of value, of his analysis of money, his theory of capital, his theory of the rate of profit, and consequently of the whole existing economic system is . . . the final goal, socialism. And precisely because, *a priori*, Marx looked at capitalism from the socialist's viewpoint, that is, from the historical viewpoint, he was enabled to decipher the hieroglyphics of capitalist economy.
>
> *(Luxemburg 2004a: 150–51)*

She restated this in a review of Marx's *Theories of Surplus Value* in 1905:

> It was Marx who utterly transformed the position *vis a vis* his object of investigation – the position of the socialist, who glances over the *boundaries* of the bourgeois economic form from a higher viewpoint. In short, it was the *dialectic* method of Marx that created the possibility of bringing analysis to bear on the particular problems of economics.
>
> *(Luxemburg 2000b, 469)*

"Dialectics" is here posed as inseparable from viewing the present from the vantage point of the future. There is nothing utopian about this. Marx himself asks us in *Capital* to "imagine, for a change, an association of free men, working with the means of production held in common" (*CI*: 171). Although Luxemburg's discussions of a socialist future lack the depth of Marx's (as seen in her repeated posing of capitalist "market anarchy" and socialist "planned production" as absolute opposites),[3] she did not separate revolutionary critique from the need to envision a postcapitalist alternative.

The Impact of the 1905 Russian Revolution

This becomes clear from her response to the 1905 Russian Revolution. Now that the full scope of her writings on the 1905 are finally fully available,[4] it becomes possible to discern its impact on her conception of revolutionary transformation.

In 1905 Luxemburg provided a veritable daily account of the revolution in dozens of articles and essays. Most appeared in *Vorwärts*, the SPD's daily newspaper that she became chief editor of in October 1905 following a dispute over the party's attitude toward the revolution. In addition to contributing to a daily column entitled "The Revolution in Russia,"[5] she also published many pieces in the Polish revolutionary press, especially *Czerwony Sztandar* (the organ of her party, the Social Democracy of the Kingdom of Poland and Lithuania [SDKPiL]). These writings provide a rare opportunity to see how a major Marxist theoretician makes sense of a social revolution as it actually unfolds.

Luxemburg focuses on how the masses created new forms of democratically organized grass-roots committees, clubs, unions and parties to advance the revolution, noting how this extended to professionals as well as soldiers, sailors, students and peasants. The appreciation of mass spontaneity is evident throughout. She wrote in March 1905:

> The first wave of general strike and workers' uprising, which flowed from Petersburg through the entire empire, including through our country, was to a large extent spontaneous. Not in the sense that the workers rose up blindly, without any understanding of what was going on. On the contrary, the slogans and ideas of the struggle, which were circulated widely by Social Democracy, were so much "in the air," were such a natural expression of the workers' needs and had so much entered into the flesh and blood of the proletariat, that the only thing needed was an initial nudge for the entire mass of workers instinctively to rise up to do battle in response to the news from Petersburg.
>
> *(Luxemburg 1905, 3)*

Note that she does not counterpoise spontaneity to organization. Although political parties are incapable of producing a revolutionary upsurge through an act of will, they play an important role in instilling ideas in the masses that can inspire them to rise up against existing conditions. She suggests at numerous points that were it not for the patient work over many years of Social Democrats, the spontaneous upsurge that engulfed Russia in 1905 might never have happened.

> Now there has begun an important second phase of the revolution, one in which Social Democracy must aim at meeting events head on in a planned way, to try as much as possible to take in its hands the helm to steer the movements of the masses and give direction to the next revolutionary action. And we can cope with these tasks only by the most persistent and strenuous *work of organization and agitation*. . . . The more effectively and vigorously the revolutionary core succeeds now in building a road for the *party organization* to reach the masses, the quicker the victory and the fewer the casualties we will suffer in the next confrontation with absolutism.
>
> *(Luxemburg 1905, 3)*

Luxemburg held that revolutionary parties should not seek to lead the masses in the manner of a schoolmaster but instead stimulate their intellectual *enlightenment*. Shortly before, in 1904, she took issue with Lenin on the grounds that his organizational concepts are "imbued, not with a positive creative spirit, but with the sterile spirit of the night-watchman state" (Luxemburg 2004c, 256), which reduces the rank-and-file to docile, unthinking recipients of commands from above. And in 1905, in response to the split within the Russian Social Democratic Labor Party (RSDLP), she took sharp issue with the Bolsheviks for their sectarianism, referring to "the so-called Lenin faction's . . . somewhat 'Cossack' way of resolving a party dispute" (Luxemburg 2000c, 593).

However, such disputes on organizational questions did not define her attitude to Lenin or the Bolsheviks. More significant than the *form* of organization or the conflicts between respective groupings was the attitude toward the social forces in the actual revolution. And when it came to that she was much closer to the Bolsheviks than the Mensheviks. The latter mechanistically treated 1905 as a replay of what happened during the 1848 Revolutions, when the relatively weak and politically inexperienced working class was compelled to serve as a left-wing pressure group on the liberals. Luxemburg sharply opposed this, arguing that a new situation had arisen in Russia in which the *form* of the revolution is bourgeois-democratic while the *content* is proletarian. This was the same position promoted at the time by Lenin.

In February 1905 she wrote that "the true task of Social Democracy is *beginning*: to keep the revolutionary situation going *in permanence*" (Luxemburg: 2000d, 489) – one of the first references to "permanent revolution" among commentators on 1905. Yet she held "at the present moment the people are not in a position to take political power and carry out a socialist transformation" (Luxemburg 2000e, 531). Given her proximity to the Bolsheviks on this question, it is no accident that she became so close to Lenin as to spend several weeks with him in Finland in 1906, where she composed *The Mass Strike, the Political Party, and the Trade Unions*. This suggests that "[t]owering above all her criticism [of Lenin], as well as her approval, was not the question of organization but the concept of revolution . . . the organizational question took a subordinate place throughout the next decade" (Dunayevskaya 1981, 58).

Such commonality of views was not to last. By 1908 she grew increasingly critical of the Bolsheviks over what she viewed as their overemphasis on armed insurrection that bypasses mass deliberation. She wrote in a remarkable essay of 1908 entitled "Lessons of the Three Dumas,"[6]

> The leadership of the Russian and Polish proletariat goes into battle having no illusions that it can gain power through Jacobin methods, let alone be capable of immediately introducing social equality. . . . But the absence of illusions strengthens rather than weakens the revolutionary proletarian. The Russian proletariat does not expect any final redemption from the creation of a [democratic] Republic; instead, it views it as an indispensable instrument and the pathway to its salvation. In addition, today's working class will not be deceived that it can in any way bring down absolutism by establishing a dictatorship on its behalf, that is, a socialist system. A socialist revolution can only be the result of an international revolution, and the results that the Russian proletariat can reach in the present revolution depends on the degree of social development of Russia itself.
>
> *(Luxemburg 2015c, 263)*

Luxemburg is here discussing revolution not simply in terms of spontaneity or the relation between spontaneity and organization, *but in relation to the content of a new society*. Such a society cannot, she insists, be forced into existence through "dictatorial" measures that vitiate the need for the fullest and freest democratic expression. A democratic republic is needed, in her view, to prepare the masses for the fullest expression of democracy that will be needed to make socialism a reality. Here we encounter one of the distinctive marks of her concept of revolution, which will later be forcefully projected in her critique of the Bolsheviks in her 1918 *The Russian Revolution*.

Class Consciousness and Organization

Luxemburg repeatedly emphasizes revolutionary consciousness as an engine of revolution – revolutionary *class*-consciousness. The same cannot be said of national consciousness. Rejection of calls for national self-determination defined her politics from beginning to end. This did not stop her from being a foremost opponent of imperialism (her magnum opus, *The Accumulation of Capital*, traces out the integrality of imperialism and the logic of capital).[7] Nor did it stop her from fervently opposing the dehumanization of indigenous peoples and other victims of imperialism and speaking passionately in their defense – a rarity among even her most revolutionary associates.[8] There was no Eurocentrism on Luxemburg's part when it came to viewing the impact of colonialism on the non-Western world.[9] Nevertheless, she rejected the claim that opposition to imperialism by colonized peoples generates progressive nationalist demands that could bring them alongside the proletariat as builders of a new society. For her, they were victims of imperialism, not active subjects who could uproot it. That task, she insisted, was reserved for a proletariat free of national sentiments.

The reasons for this stubborn rejection of national self-determination cannot detain us here.[10] But Lenin was on to something when he said her position indicates that she "applies Marxian dialectics only halfway" (*LCW* 22: 316). Her failure to identify the dialectical negation residing *within* the phenomenon of imperialism may reflect an overall tone-deafness to philosophical matters (she never engaged in a direct study of Hegelian thought, despite her many evocations of "the dialectic").

It may seem that Luxemburg's reduction of revolutionary consciousness to class-consciousness extends to a lack of interest in feminism. But such is not the case. It is true that she eschewed suggestions to focus on "the Woman Question." But that was not because of lack of interest in the issue but rather a refusal to allow the male leaders of the party to sideline her from engaging in the broader theoretical and political issues that they considered their turf. Her writings on women are more extensive than often acknowledged, ranging from articles on women's struggles[11] to essays raising broader theoretical issues, such as the relation between productive and unproductive labor. She wrote,

> [In capitalism] only that work is productive which produces surplus value . . . while all the toil of the women and mothers of the proletariat within the four walls of the home is considered unproductive work. This sounds crude and crazy, but it is an accurate expression of the crudeness and craziness of today's capitalist economic order.
>
> *(Luxemburg 2004d, 241)*

And following the German Revolution of 1918, in preparing to launch a new Communist Party of Germany, she wrote to Clara Zetkin,

> Now about the agitation on women's issues! Its importance and urgency is as clear to us exactly as it is to you. Actually, at the first meeting of our top leadership we decided, at my suggestion, to put out a women's paper as well . . . it is such an urgent matter! Every day lost is a sin.
>
> *(Luxemburg 2011b, 481)*

To be sure, Luxemburg did not explore many issues that later became of central concern to second wave feminism, and she refrained from affirming women's struggles as having a validity independent of the class struggle. But she was far more open and flexible on this issue than on the national question – which is one reason an increasing number of contemporary feminist thinkers have called attention to her insights in this area.[12]

In any case, in 1910 Luxemburg's position on an assortment of issues led her to break from Karl Kautsky, whom she accused of soft-peddling opposition to imperialism and compromising revolutionary principles for parliamentary advantage. Unlike her polemic with Bernstein in 1898–99, this time she stood virtually alone; even Lenin and Trotsky opposed her break from Kautsky. This raises some important issues regarding organization. Many have argued that Luxemburg was hamstrung by not paying sufficient attention to organization – especially as compared with Lenin. However, Lenin's attentiveness to organization did not prevent him from failing to catch Kautsky's opportunism in 1910 (which he was later to regret). Moreover, it is hard to argue that Luxemburg paid little attention to organization, given her intensive work in the Polish movement with the SDKPiL (not to mention her work in the SPD).[13] Luxemburg was no stranger to the unheralded grind of party building. If anything, the opposite was the case – she very nearly fetishized the role of a single, *unified* party.[14] As she stated in a letter to Roland-Holst, a leftist who broke from the Dutch Social Democratic Party in 1909,

> A splintering of Marxists (not to be confused with differences of opinion) is fatal. Now that you want to leave the party, I want to hinder you from this with all my might. . . . We cannot stand outside the organization, outside contact with the masses. The worst working-class party is better than none.
>
> *(Luxemburg 1999, 307–8)*

Why this insistence on holding to the unity of a party that she already knew was headed in the wrong direction? The answer lies in what was always foremost to her concept of revolution – namely, that socialism could only be created through the conscious support of the *majority* of the working class. And since most workers remained in the SPD, that is where left-revolutionaries needed to be. In other words, she simply could not abide by the idea of a minority taking power *on behalf* of the workers.

Luxemburg never deviated from her insistence on securing majority working class support as the fundamental prerequisite for a successful seizure of power. She wrote in December 1918, just weeks before her death:

> The Spartacus League is not a party that wants to come to power over the mass of workers or through them . . . [it] will never take over governmental power except in response to the clear, unambiguous will of the great majority of the proletarian mass of all of Germany, never except by the proletariat's conscious affirmation of the views, aims, and methods of struggle of the Spartacus League.
>
> *(Luxemburg 2004h, 356–57)*

Toward the New Society

Luxemburg's tendency to fetishize a united party proved to be highly problematic – especially in light of the great betrayal of 1914 and her initial reluctance to break from the SPD in the years that followed. But what largely motivated her – insistence on majority working class support for socialist revolution – retains its relevance, especially given what happened after the Bolshevik seizure of power in 1917. She supported the October Revolution, even though knew it did not have majority support, because the situation facing the Bolsheviks offered them no other choice. However, in 1918 she sharply critiqued them for making a virtue out of necessity by proceeding as if democratic governance by the working class was completely dispensable. In *The Russian Revolution* she famously castigates Lenin and Trotsky for shutting down freedom of expression, establishing the Cheka and moving toward a single party state. "The basic error of the Lenin-Trotsky theory," she held,

> is that they too, just like Kautsky, oppose dictatorship to democracy . . . [we need to] exercise a dictatorship of the *class*, not of a party or of a clique – dictatorship of the class, that means in the broadest public forum on the basis of the most active, unlimited participation of the mass of the people, of unlimited democracy.
>
> *(Luxemburg 2004e, 308)*

And this is because "socialism will not and cannot be created by any government, however socialistic. Socialism must be created by the masses, by every proletarian. Only that is socialism, and only thus can socialism be created" (Luxemburg 2004g, 368).

Here we confront the core of Luxemburg's concept of revolution – the notion that the form of revolutionary transformation must correspond to the content of the socialist society it aims to establish. This is a hard standard to live up to, as Luxemburg discovered early in 1919, when she supported the Spartacus League's abortive uprising even though she knew it did not have majority working class support. However, the difficulty in concretizing the principle does not make the principle any less compelling.

Luxemburg's refusal to compromise on the need to keep the principle firmly in view – even when dealing with a revolution surrounded by internal and external enemies and invaded by over a dozen imperialist powers – is precisely what makes her, for all her faults, such a beacon for our time. What we need today is her independent spirit that lets nothing get in the way of affirming our humanist values, our aspirations for democratic governance and our quest for new human relations. These are not mere idealist paraphernalia that be dispensed with once the ripe fruit of political power is dangling before us. They must be held onto and advanced at all costs . . . because when we fail to do so, the grandest of dreams can turn into the most horrific of nightmares.

Notes

1. See Luxemburg (2013), which includes the first full English translation of *Introduction to Political Economy* and her lectures on economics from the German Social Democratic Party's (SPD) school from 1907 to 1914. See also Luxemburg (2015a, 2015b), new translations of *The Accumulation of Capital* and the *Anti-Critique*.
2. For a recent expression of this, see Holloway (2015, 8): "To relegate the emancipated wealth of which Marx speaks in the *Grundrisse* to a post-capitalist future is to locate communism in an after-the-revolution future, rather than understanding it as the current raging struggle of communizing."
3. See Hudis (2012, 2013) for a critical analysis of Luxemburg's limitations on this issue.
4. Many of her articles and essays from 1905 and 1906 have only recently been identified and published in German (see Luxemburg 2014, 2017). Many more in Polish have yet to be published at all. Volumes 4, 5 and 6 of the English-language *Complete Works of Rosa Luxemburg*, published by Verso Books, will contain all of these writings on revolution. All quotations from her writings of 1905 to 1908 below will appear in these volumes.
5. See her letter to Jogiches of 1 November 1905: "You see, since yesterday I've been involved with *Vorwärts* on a daily basis, having to start from 4 in the afternoon" (Luxemburg 1999, 228).
6. This twenty-three-page essay was originally published anonymously in a Polish periodical and has only recently been identified and published (in German translation) – Luxemburg (2015c). It will appear in English translation in the forthcoming Vol. 5 of the *Complete Works*.
7. For an analysis of this, see Hudis (2014).
8. Compare, for instance, Lenin's marginal comment in his copy of Luxemburg's *Accumulation of Capital*: "The description of the torture of Negroes in South Africa is noisy, colorful, and meaningless. Above all, it is anti-Marxist" (quoted in Nettl 1966, II, 533).
9. For a fuller substantiation of this, see Hudis (2010).
10. For one of many efforts to come to grips with this issue, see Lichtheim (1966, 57–58): "It was the one issue on which she stood ready to break with her closest associates and to fly in the face of every authority, including that of Marx. . . . On this point, and on this point alone, she was intractable. . . . One of the strangest aberrations ever to possess a major political intellect." See also Dunayevskaya (1981, 51–65).
11. See Luxemburg (1902): "Whoever needs convincing that women are just as capable as men of experiencing both citizenship in its highest sense and the noblest of civic virtues would do well to study the history of the liberation struggles that have shaken Russia since the abolition of serfdom."
12. See especially Rose (2015), and the essays by Holmstrom and Alvarado-Díaz in Ehmsen and Scharenberg (2017).

13. The secondary literature on Luxemburg suffers from lack of attentiveness to her activity within the Polish movement. Her writings from the Polish revolutionary press total 3,000 pages – very little of which has been available in either German or English (the bulk of it has not even been reproduced in Polish). Her work in the Polish movement shows, I would argue, that far from being uninterested or evasive on matters of organization, Luxemburg often handled relations in the SDKPiL with as firm a centralist hand as Lenin used in the RSDLP. For a detailed discussion of this, see Hudis (2018).
14. The one exception was Luxemburg's insistence on maintaining her own *Polish* party, despite numerous pleas (including from some of her closest colleagues) to unite with the Polish Socialist Party, or at least the PPS-Left. But that was because those organizations, in her view, suffered from the disease of nationalism – the consideration that, in her mind, always overrode all other ones.

Bibliography

Adler, Georg, Peter Hudis, and Annelies Laschitza, eds. 2011. *The Letters of Rosa Luxemburg*. London and New York: Verso Books.

Alvarado-Díaz, Alhelí de María. 2017. "Heroine of the Revolution." In Ehmsen and Scharenerg 2017, 43–50.

Bernstein, Eduard. 1993 (1899). *The Preconditions of Socialism*. Cambridge: Cambridge University Press.

Datta Gupta, Sobhanlal. 2015. *The Socialist Vision and the Silenced Voices of Democracy: New Perspective, Part I: Rosa Luxemburg*. Kolkata: Seribaan.

Dunayevskaya, Raya. 1981. *Rosa Luxemburg, Women's Liberation, and Marx's Philosophy of Revolution*. Champaign-Urbana: University of Illinois Press.

Ehmsen, Stefanie, and Albert Scharenberg, eds. 2017. *Rosa Remix*. New York: Rosa Luxemburg Stiftung.

Holloway, John. 2015. "Read Capital: The First Sentence, or, *Capital* Starts with Wealth, Not with the Commodity." *Historical Materialism* 23(3): 3–26.

Holmstrom, Nancy. 2017. "Rosa Luxemburg: A Legacy for Feminists?" In Ehmsen and Scharenerg 2017, 32–36.

Hudis, Peter. 2010. "Accumulation, Imperialism, and Pre-Capitalist Economic Formations: Luxemburg and Marx on the Non-Western World." *Socialist Studies/Études Socialistes* 6(2): 75–91.

Hudis, Peter. 2012. "Rosa Luxemburg's Concept of a Post-Capitalist Society." *Critique: Journal of Socialist Theory* 40(3): 323–35.

Hudis, Peter. 2013. *Marx's Concept of the Alternative to Capitalism*. Chicago: Haymarket.

Hudis, Peter. 2014. "The Dialectic of the Spatial Determination of Capital: Rosa Luxemburg's *Accumulation of Capital* Reconsidered." *International Critical Thought* 4(4): 474–90.

Hudis, Peter. 2018. "Luxemburg and Lenin." In *Handbook of Leninist Political Philosophy*, edited by Tom Rockmore and Norman Levine, 201–29. Basingstoke: Palgrave Macmillan.

Hudis, Peter, and Kevin B. Anderson, eds. 2004. *The Rosa Luxemburg Reader*. New York: Monthly Review Books.

Lenin, V.I. 1964. "On the Junius Pamphlet." In *LCW* 22: 305–19.

Lichtheim, George. 1966. "Rosa Luxemburg." *Encounter* (June): 55–49.

Luxemburg, Rosa. 1902. "Russische Arbeiterinnen im Kampf." *Die Gleichheit: Zeitschrift für die Interessen der Arbeiterinnen* 12(9 and 23).

Luxemburg, Rosa. 1905. "Pod znakiem Socjaldemocracji." *Czerwony Sztandar* (24 March).

Luxemburg, Rosa. 1999. *Gesammelte Briefe*. Edited by Annelies Laschitza. Band 2. Berlin: Dietz Verlag.

Luxemburg, Rosa. 2000a. *Gesammelte Werke*. Edited by Annelies Laschitza, et al. Band 1.2. Berlin: Dietz Verlag.

Luxemburg, Rosa. 2000b. "Aus dem literarischen Nachlass von Karl Marx." *Gesammelte Werke* 1(2): 462–76.

Luxemburg, Rosa. 2000c. "Russische Parteistreitigkeiten" (June 23, 1905). *Gesammelte Werke* 1(2): 592–94.

Luxemburg, Rosa. 2000d. "Nach dem ersten Akt" (February 4, 1905). *Gesammelte Werke* 1(2): 485–90.

Luxemburg, Rosa. 2000e. "Eine Probe aufs Exempel" (March 1905). *Gesammelte Werke* 1(2): 528–32.

Luxemburg, Rosa. 2004a. "Social Reform or Revolution." In Hudis and Anderson 2004, 128–67.

Luxemburg, Rosa. 2004b. "The Mass Strike, the Political Party, and the Trade Unions." In Hudis and Anderson 2004, 168–99.

Luxemburg, Rosa. 2004c. "Organizational Principles of Russian Social-Democracy." In Hudis and Anderson 2004, 248–65.

Luxemburg, Rosa. 2004d. "Women's Suffrage and Class Struggle." In Hudis and Anderson 2004, 237–42.

Luxemburg, Rosa. 2004e. "The Russian Revolution [1918]." In Hudis and Anderson 2004, 281–311.

Luxemburg, Rosa. 2004f. "The Junius Pamphlet: The Crisis in German Social Democracy." In Hudis and Anderson 2004, 313–41.
Luxemburg, Rosa. 2004g. "Our Program and the Political Situation." In Hudis and Anderson 2004, 357–72.
Luxemburg, Rosa. 2004h. "What Does the Spartacus League Want?" In Hudis and Anderson 2004, 349–57.
Luxemburg, Rosa. 2011a. "To Leo Jogiches" (18 December 1899). In Adler, Hudis, and Laschitza, eds. 2011, 119–21.
Luxemburg, Rosa. 2011b. "To Clara Zetkin" (24 November 1918). In Adler, Hudis, and Laschitza, eds. 2011, 480–82.
Luxemburg, Rosa. 2011c (1911). "Peace Utopias." In Day and Gaido 2011, 441–58.
Luxemburg, Rosa. 2013. *The Complete Works of Rosa Luxemburg, Vol. I: Economic Writings 1*. Edited by Peter Hudis. London and New York: Verso.
Luxemburg, Rosa. 2014. *Gesammelte Werke*. Edited by Annelies Laschitza and Eckhard Müller. Band 6. Berlin: Dietz Verlag.
Luxemburg, Rosa. 2015a (1913). "The Accumulation of Capital: A Contribution to the Economic Theory of Imperialism." In *The Complete Writings of Rosa Luxemburg, Volume II, Economic Writings 2*, edited by Peter Hudis and Paul Le Blanc. London: Verso.
Luxemburg, Rosa. 2015b (1921). "The Accumulation of Capital, or, What the Epigones* Have Made Out of Marx's Theory: An Anti-Critique." In *The Complete Writings of Rosa Luxemburg, Volume II, Economic Writings 2*, edited by Peter Hudis and Paul Le Blanc. London: Verso.
Luxemburg, Rosa. 2015c. "Lehren aus den drei Dumas" (May 1908). In *Arbeiterrevolution 1905/06: Polnische Texte*, edited by Holger Politt. Berlin: Dietz Verlag, 245–67.
Luxemburg, Rosa. 2017. *Gesammelte Werke*. Edited by Annelies Laschitza and Eckhard Müller. Band 7. Berlin: Dietz Verlag.
Nettl, J.P. 1966. *Rosa Luxemburg*. 2 vols. Oxford: Oxford University Press.
Rose, Jacqueline. 2015. *Women in Dark Times: From Rosa Luxemburg to Marilyn Monroe*. London: Bloomsbury.

PART III

Second Foundation

6

SECOND FOUNDATION: MARXISM IN THE ERA OF THE RUSSIAN REVOLUTION

Alex Callinicos

Marxism at War

The outbreak of the First World War in early August 1914 led to a drastic and divisive effort to redefine the nature of Marxism. This was true at the political level. First, the shock of most of the main parties of the Second International supporting their governments' participation in the war and then of the Russian Revolution of October 1917 split the global socialist movement into rival revolutionary and reformist wings, a fracture consolidated by the proclamation of the Communist International in 1919. But this political polarization was accompanied by efforts to re-conceptualize Marxism itself in an effort to trace theoretically the origins of what the revolutionaries regarded as the betrayal of August 1914 and also to isolate what was intellectually distinctive about the Bolsheviks' political project. Two of the efforts to re-found Marxism in this way – György Lukács's *History and Class Consciousness* (1923) and Antonio Gramsci's effort to present Marxism as a "philosophy of praxis," culminating in his *Prison Notebooks* (1929–35) – were so powerful and original that their influence has outlasted the dramatic and violent context of revolution and counter-revolution in which they were written.

Historians always argue about how profound a break with the past apparent discontinuities actually represent. The same doubt certainly applies to the Marxism of the Third International, if one understands by this not merely these self-consciously innovative works but also the more "orthodox" writings of central figures in the Bolshevik Party such as Lenin, Trotsky and Bukharin. To characterize this process as "re-*foundation*" implies that it involved returning to a project that had been previously founded. But the fact it required "*re*-foundation" implies some creative effort both to render visible what was essential to that project and to re-inject new life to it. Of course, identifying what is essential in fact involves selection and therefore controversy. We can see this at work in *The State and Revolution* the most celebrated text of Lenin, whose thought scholars such as Lars T. Lih argue is a direct continuation of the "orthodoxy" developed by Kautsky and German Social Democracy. Lenin's starting point by contrast is the systematic distortion of Marx's and Engels's writing on the state in the era of the Second International (1889–1914):

> During the lifetime of great revolutionaries, the oppressing classes constantly hounded them, received their theories with the most savage malice, the most furious hatred and the most unscrupulous campaigns of lies and slander. After their death, attempts are

> made to convert them into harmless icons, to canonize them, so to say, and to hallow their *names* to a certain extent for the "consolation" of the oppressed classes and with the object of duping the latter, while at the same time robbing the revolutionary theory of its *substance*, blunting its revolutionary edge and vulgarizing it. Today, the bourgeoisie and the opportunists within the labor movement concur in this doctoring of Marxism.
>
> (LCW *25: 390)*

Therefore the text is devoted to a systematic presentation of Marx's and Engels's writings on the state and to demonstrate how key elements – the necessity to "smash" the capitalist state apparatus, the withering away of the state in the transition to communism and the significance of the Paris Commune of 1871 as inaugurating a radically democratic form of state that could provide the political framework for this transition – were indeed "omitted, obscured or distorted" by the likes of Bernstein and Kautsky. But this work of recovery is intended also to extend and update the Marxist theory of the state in the light of Russian revolutionary experience. *The State and Revolution* is unfinished (in a famous postscript Lenin explains that he was interrupted by the October Revolution: "It is more pleasant and useful to go through the 'experience of revolution' than to write about it", *LCW* 25: 497). But it is clear that he intended to conclude the text by demonstrating that, as he had already argued in April 1917,

> a state of the Paris Commune type, one in which a standing army and police divorced from the people are *replaced* by the direct arming of the people themselves . . . is the type of state which the Russian revolution *began* to create in 1905 and in 1917. A Republic of Soviets of Workers', Soldiers', Peasants', and other Deputies, united in an All-Russia Constituent Assembly of people's representatives or in a Council of Soviets, etc., is what is *already being realized in* our country now.
>
> (LCW *24: 68)*

Recovery and innovation are thus closely connected. We see the same process at work in Lenin's *Philosophical Notebooks*, based primarily on his reading of Hegel's *Science of Logic* in the summer and early autumn of 1914, the very moment when the Great War broke out and the Second International imploded.[1] It is here that he writes: "*Aphorism:* It is impossible completely to understand Marx's *Capital*, and especially its first chapter, without having thoroughly studied and understood the *whole* of Hegel's *Logic*. Consequently, half a century later none of the Marxists understood Marx!!" (*LCW* 38: 180). Given the centrality of the critique of political economy to Marx's project, and the importance of Lenin's reading of *Capital* to his own writings on the agrarian question in Russia, this is no mere philological observation: Lenin is firing a critical arrow at Marxism as it had hitherto been practiced. Another aphorism develops the point: "Marxists criticized (at the beginning of the twentieth century) the Kantians and Humists more in the manner of Feuerbach (and Büchner) than of Hegel" (*LCW* 38: 179). The only example Lenin cites is that of Georgi Plekhanov, founder of Russian Marxism but by then a bitter opponent of the Bolsheviks, but it is clear the point is a more general one: the dominant stance of the Marxism of the Second International was that of the naturalistic materialism that was a powerful force in 19th-century, Western intellectual culture (Ludwig Büchner was a leading German exponent). Compared to the subjective idealism of Hume and Kant, Hegel's absolute idealism offers a superior insight into the role of human practice in connecting thought and the world. So Lenin comments:

> Remarkable: Hegel comes to the "Idea" as the coincidence of the Notion and the object, as *truth, through* the practical, purposive activity of man. A very close approach

> to the view that man by his *practice* proves the objective correctness of his ideas, concepts, knowledge, science.
>
> (LCW *38: 191)*

It matters less whether Lenin is correctly interpreting Hegel here than that he is echoing here Marx himself in the first "Thesis on Feuerbach":

> The chief defect of all previous materialism (that of Feuerbach included) is that things, reality, sensuousness are conceived only in the form of the *object, or of contemplation*, but not as *sensuous human activity, practice*, not subjectively. Hence, in contradistinction to materialism, the *active* side was set forth abstractly by idealism – which, of course, does not know real, sensuous activity as such.
>
> (MECW *5: 24)*

Lenin in the *Philosophical Notebooks* thus draws close to two of the main distinguishing features of the "Marxism of subjectivity" that emerges after the Russian Revolution – a positive appreciation of Hegel and the priority accorded to practice (which was reflected, for example, in Gramsci's retranslation of the "Theses on Feuerbach" into Italian). There were anticipations before 1914, most notably perhaps in the writings of the Italian philosopher Antonio Labriola, who declared that

> the *philosophy of practice* . . . is the pith of historical materialism. It is the immanent philosophy of things about which people philosophize. The realistic process leads from life to thought, not from though to life. It leads from work, from the labor of cognition, to understanding as an abstract theory, not from theory to cognition.

Labriola also strikes a Gramscian note when he says that, in conceiving "man as a social and historical being," historical materialism "marks also the end of naturalistic materialism" (Labriola 1912, 60).

Despite his influence on Gramsci, and on others who took the revolutionary side in the great socialist schism after August 1914, Labriola was an academic who never joined the Italian Socialist Party and who was ambivalent about the polemic provoked by Bernstein's revisionism and sympathetic to Italian colonialism.[2] What turned comparatively muted notes in pre-1914 Marxism into the powerful current of revolutionary Hegelianism was the polarization engendered by the First World War and its aftermath, in which the divisions within the socialist movement became entangled in the violent antagonism between revolutionary left and counter-revolutionary right that killed Rosa Luxemburg, sent Lukács into exile and condemned Gramsci to a fascist prison – before stoking the fires of another, even more destructive, general war.[3]

The resulting reconfiguration of Marxism involved substantive changes. Probably the most important was the theory of imperialism, incubated in the years before 1914 by thinkers as diverse as the left-Liberal J.A. Hobson, the Austro-Marxist Rudolf Hilferding and the champion of the German revolutionary left Rosa Luxemburg (see chapter 3). Lenin's pamphlet *Imperialism, the Highest Stage of Capitalism* offered a synthesis, drawing especially on Hobson and Hilferding, as well as on a mass of empirical material. The geopolitical rivalries that led to the First World War, Lenin argues, are a consequence of structural changes in capitalism arising from the growing concentration and centralization of capital: "In its economic essence imperialism is monopoly capitalism" (*LCW* 22: 298). His most original contribution is the idea of uneven development, which Lenin describes as "an absolute law of capitalism" (*LCW* 21: 342). The thought is not simply that different states and regions develop at different tempos but that the tempos change, destabilizing the existing distribution of economic and military power and therefore rendering impossible the kind of peaceful capitalist division of the world that Kautsky envisages in his theory of ultra-imperialism. This analysis – developed in a more theoretically systematized form by Nikolai Bukharin in *Imperialism and World Economy* (1917) – points toward the political conclusion that justified the October Revolution and the formation of the Third International: capitalism in its imperialist phase is inescapably driven to hugely destructive conflicts such as the Great War, which are symptoms of its inability further to develop the productive forces. Socialist revolution has therefore become a historical necessity.[4]

Reconceiving Historical Necessity

But the reconfiguration of Marxism involved, among other things, an interrogation of the meaning of "historical necessity," which Kautsky had understood as the "natural necessity" on whose behalf the class struggle acted as the agent of the inevitable downfall of capitalism and triumph of socialism. It is surely significant that both Lukács and Gramsci selected for specific criticism Bukharin's *Historical Materialism* (1921), which they took to be symptomatic of the naturalistic materialism dominant in the Second International (and re-emerging the Third) with which they thought it essential to break. A critique of historical inevitability is then the first of three themes – the other two are hegemony and ideology/reification – through which we will explore the distinctive kind of Marxism that emerged in the era of the Russian Revolution. Even the revolutionary leaders most formed within the intellectual culture of the Second International inflected the notion of historical necessity by admitting – indeed stressing – the possibility of alternatives. The most famous example is offered by Rosa Luxemburg in her *Junius Pamphlet* (1916) against the First World War:

> We stand today, as Friedrich Engels prophesied more than a generation ago, before the awful proposition: either the triumph of imperialism and the destruction of all culture, and, as in ancient Rome, depopulation, desolation, degeneration, a vast cemetery; or, the victory of socialism, that is, the conscious struggle of the international proletariat against imperialism, against its methods, against war.
>
> *(Luxemburg 2004, 321)*

Louis Althusser comments that this kind of formulation implies that

> history doesn't tend – "naturally" – and solely towards socialism, for history doesn't seek the realization of a goal. . . . Yes, our "civilization" can die on the spot, not only without moving to a higher "stage," nor regressing to a lower stage, but in piling on all the suffering of a delivery that never ends, and of an abortion that is not a deliverance.
>
> *(Althusser 2018, Kindle locs. 1012, 1021)*

In his writings in 1917 Lenin presents the same dilemma in a sharper and more immediate form. From example, in *The Impending Catastrophe and How to Combat It*, drafted in the early autumn of that year, Lenin writes:

> The war has created such an immense crisis, has so strained the material and moral forces of the people, has dealt such blows at the entire modern social organization that humanity must now choose between perishing or entrusting its fate to the most revolutionary class for the swiftest and most radical transition to a superior mode of

production. . . . The war is inexorable; it puts the alternative with ruthless severity: either perish or overtake and outstrip the advanced countries *economically as well*. . . . Perish or forge full steam ahead. That is the alternative put by history.

(LCW *25: 367–68)*

Presenting alternatives can function as a call to action. Luxemburg appeals for "the conscious struggle of the international proletariat." Lenin in autumn 1917 had a more immediate audience in mind, the leadership of the Bolshevik Party, whom he was trying to convince to organize an insurrection. On 6 November, the day before the seizure of power, he warns the Bolshevik Central Committee: "History will not forgive revolutionaries for procrastinating when they could be victorious today (and they certainly will be victorious today), while they risk losing much tomorrow, in fact, they risk losing everything" (*LCW* 26: 235). There is no assurance of inevitable victory here. Already in his response to the Russian Revolution of February 1917 Lenin had written:

There are no miracles in nature or history, but every abrupt turn in history, and this applies to every revolution, presents such a wealth of content, unfolds such unexpected and specific combinations of forms of struggle and alignment of forces of the contestants, that to the lay mind there is much that must appear miraculous.

(LCW *23: 297)*

By the autumn of the same year he was arguing that such "abrupt turns" could offer the prospect of decisive advance – the achievement of soviet power – or equally decisive defeat – not merely economic collapse but successful counter-revolution. Rather than swim with the tide, as Kautsky had suggested, revolutionary socialists must know how to recognize and seize the moment when it comes. This requires a party that monitors the situation closely, ready to respond quickly to "abrupt turns in history," and to spring into action. This is a conception of history that invites an activist understanding of Marxism.

The revolutionary dramas with which Luxemburg and Lenin had to grapple didn't afford them the luxury of reflecting extensively on the implications of this kind of posing of alternatives for the broader understanding of Marxism. Others did, most notably Gramsci, albeit in a context of defeat. Famously his immediate reaction to the October Revolution was to call it "the revolution against Marx's *Capital*" demonstrating that history did not have to "follow a predetermined course" in which bourgeois revolution and the development of capitalism must necessarily precede socialist revolution: "The Bolsheviks reject Karl Marx, and their explicit actions and conquests bear witness that the canons of historical materialism are not so rigid as might even have been and has been thought" (Gramsci 1977, 34).

There is an air of somewhat forced paradox about this celebrated article. The mature Gramsci shows himself in his *Prison Notebooks* to be a very careful reader of *Capital*, with a sophisticated understanding of Marx's tendential law of the rate of profit to fall as involving an interplay of tendencies and counter-tendencies (most notably the struggle by capitalists to increase relative surplus-value through productivity-increasing innovations). This interpretation, developed in his critique of the liberal Hegelian philosopher Benedetto Croce in Notebook 10, informs one of the most important notes of all, "Analysis of Situations. Relations of Forces" in Notebook 13, where he decisively breaks with any suggestion that the triumph of socialism is inevitable. It is here that that Gramsci puts forward his conception of organic crisis:

A crisis occurs, sometimes lasting for decades. This exceptional duration means that incurable structural contradictions have revealed themselves (reached maturity), and

> that, despite this, the political forces which are struggling to conserve and defend the existing structure itself are making every effort to cure them, within certain limits, and to overcome them. These incessant and persistent efforts (since no social formation will ever admit that it has been superseded) form the terrain of the "conjunctural" [*occasionale*], and it is upon this terrain that the forces of opposition organize.
>
> *(Gramsci 1971, 178; Gramsci 1975, III, 1579–80; Q13 §17)*

Organic crises arise from "incurable structural contradictions" defined by the struggle between the tendency of the rate of profit to fall and its counter-tendencies. Gramsci had already dismissed Croce's claim that

> if the law regarding the fall in the rate of profit were established exactly, as its author believed, it "would mean neither more nor less than the automatic and imminent end of capitalist society." There is nothing automatic and even less imminent about it.
>
> *(Gramsci 1995, 432; Gramsci 1975, II, 1283; Q10 II §36)*

Now he hammers home the point:

> It may be ruled out that immediate economic crises of themselves produce fundamental historical events; they can simply create a terrain more favorable to the dissemination of certain modes of thought, and certain ways of posing and resolving questions concerning the entire subsequent development of national life.
>
> *(Gramsci 1971, 184; Gramsci 1975, III, 1587; Q13 §17)*

The detonation of economic contradictions thus creates the context in which rival political formations based on antagonistic class forces contend, each seeking to impose their own resolution of the crisis, with no implication that the victory of any one of these collective actors is predetermined.

The Conflict of Hegemonies

One effect of this rethinking of Marxism is to make politics a creative process, since it is here (and more broadly in the superstructure generally) that, as Marx put it in a passage that Gramsci frequently quoted, "human beings become conscious of this conflict [i.e., in the economic base] and fight it out" (*MECW* 29: 263; translation modified). This brings us to the second of our three themes, hegemony, which is central to Gramsci's mature thinking in prison. In a pathbreaking (though controversial) essay Perry Anderson shows that the concept entered the international socialist movement through debates among Russian Marxists before 1917, where it served to refer to the relationship of political leadership that the working class would exercise over the peasantry in what Lenin and the Bolsheviks still understood as a bourgeois-democratic revolution against the Tsarist autocracy (Anderson 2017a; see also Anderson 2017b). Indeed, in his entry on Lenin, Lars T. Lih argues that the concept of hegemony can be seen as the unifying theme of his thought.

Gramsci takes over this Bolshevik understanding of hegemony: it informs, for example, the argument in his final major pre-prison texts, the Theses of the Lyons Congress of the Communist Party of Italy (PCdI) in January 1926 and "Some Aspects of the Southern Question." In the latter text, defending the approach he taken with his comrades in the *Ordine Nuovo* group in Turin in 1919–20, he writes:

> The Turin comrades posed concretely the question of the "hegemony of the proletariat": ie of the social base of the proletarian dictatorship and of the workers' state. The proletariat can become the leading (*dirigente*) and the dominant class to the extent that it succeeds in creating a system of class alliances which allows it to mobilize the majority of the working population against capitalism and the bourgeois state. In Italy, in the real class relations which exist there, this means the extent to which it succeeds in gaining the consent of the broad peasant masses.
>
> *(Gramsci 1978, 443)*

But already in this text Gramsci is already introducing new content to the concept of hegemony, which no longer refers simply to the kind of alignment of forces the Bolsheviks achieved in October 1917, when they were able, as Lenin put it, to "neutralize the peasantry" by adopting the program of the Social Revolutionary Party and encouraging them to seize the land of the nobility and gentry (*LCW* 30: 263). Gramsci draws on Croce to rethink hegemony as "ethico-political": it marks the threshold a class crosses when it ceases to function merely at the "economic-corporate" level of defending its particular material interests within a pre-given social structure and asserts its claim to lead society not merely by exercising coercive power (what Gramsci calls "domination") but by persuading other subaltern classes that it represents the universal interest. Hegemony thus encompasses moral and intellectual leadership as well as domination; correlatively, the concept of the state is expanded to incorporate civil society. As André Tosel puts it, civil society

> is a mediating social formation but "private" in point of law. It organizes itself by means of apparatuses of hegemony that assure the decisive social functions, such as education, social security, the media, associative life, religions, the systems of parties and of unions, conceptions of the world. These functions are articulated on the state but rest on the production of consensus. They are – extraordinary formula – "the 'private' drama of the state" [*trama "privato" dello Stato*] and it is they that assure the becoming-state of a fundamental class. Hence the famous and sibylline equations: "State = civil society + political society, in other words hegemony protected by the armor of coercion."
>
> *(Tosel 2016, 159–60, quoting Gramsci 1971, 263, 1975, II, 764; Q6 (VIII) §88)*[5]

Socialist revolution is therefore neither the product of ineluctable economic forces nor a moment of insurrectionary fervor. It requires an immense creative effort to formulate a conception of the world that can articulate and legitimize the working class's aspiration to hegemony and to construct institutions that can inculcate this conception among workers, thereby forging a "collective will," and win to their side other oppressed and exploited classes, in part by incorporating elements of the latter's conceptions of the world, in part through concessions to their material interests. Central to this undertaking is the revolutionary party – the "Modern Prince," as Gramsci calls it in tribute to Machiavelli, which recruits, trains and organizes the "organic intellectuals" of the proletariat, and through them seeks to increase the weight in workers' consciousness of the communist conception of the world implicit in their collective labor in production and weaken the influence of the bourgeois and even more ancient conceptions of the world.

But this effort – which Gramsci could only project from prison – would have to confront "the political forces which are struggling to conserve and defend the existing structure itself are making every effort to cure them, within certain limits, and to overcome them." These would be making their own efforts to reconstruct bourgeois hegemony. Gramsci seeks to capture these efforts through the concept of passive revolution, which he initially took up to characterize the Risorgimento, the protracted process of interstate wars, diplomatic maneuvers and revolutionary initiatives that unified Italy in the mid-19th century on the basis of a series of compromises between the Northern industrial bourgeoisie and the Southern landed aristocracy. His distinctive analysis of the intellectuals as the social category whose role is to articulate and organize hegemony originated in part in Gramsci's appreciation of Italy's incomplete bourgeois revolution, in which the subordination of the Southern peasantry depended on the role of "traditional intellectuals" inherited from the old regime, above all the Catholic clergy.

But Gramsci comes to spread the concept of passive revolution onto a far larger canvass, understanding it as "molecular changes which in fact progressively modify the pre-existing composition of forces, and hence become the matrix of new changes" (Gramsci 1971, 109; Gramsci 1975, III, 1767; Q15 (II) §6). Applied to Gramsci's own situation, where the revolutionary wave whose highpoint came in October 1917 had been defeated, passive revolution refers to attempts to defend the existing capitalist mode of production and avert its overthrow by incorporating some of the pressures to socialize the productive forces. This reflects

> the necessity for the "thesis" [capitalism] to achieve its full development, up to the point where it would even succeed in incorporating part of the antithesis itself [socialist revolution] – in order, that is, not allow itself to be "transcended" in the dialectical opposition.
>
> *(Gramsci 1971, 110; Gramsci 1975, III, 1768: Q15 (II) §6)*

In the era of counter-revolution and global depression that defined the years between the world wars, passive revolution took two main forms, fascism, which combined elements of economic planning with the systematic repression of the workers' movement, and what Gramsci called "Americanism and Fordism," but which reached its climax with Franklin Roosevelt's New Deal, the reorganization of the liberal capitalism that had failed in Europe on the basis of mass production and the transformation of proletarian subjectivity to accommodate its rhythms (see especially Tosel 2016, 121–39).

Ideology, Reification and Totality

Gramsci's reflections on passive revolution are the most powerful and concrete demonstration that there is nothing automatic about the ascent of the workers' movement to revolutionary consciousness. In the absence of a revolutionary party that works intensively to construct a "historical bloc" articulating base and superstructures together on the basis of proletarian hegemony, the consciousness of members of the subaltern classes is likely to be so internally contradictory as to induce paralysis rather than praxis:

> When one's conception of the world is not critical and coherent but disjointed and episodic, one belongs simultaneously to a multiplicity of mass human groups. The personality is strangely composite: it contains Stone Age elements and principles of a more advanced science, prejudices from all past phases of history at the local level and intuitions of a future philosophy which will be that of a human race united the whole world over.
>
> *(Gramsci 1971, 324; Gramsci 1975, II, 1376; Q 11 (XVIII) §12)*

Acknowledging that the formation of revolutionary consciousness is problematic takes us to the third theme, ideology, the domain of the superstructure where "human beings become conscious of this conflict and fight it out." For Gramsci, ideologies (his usage is not consistent) are popularizations of class-specific conceptions of the world whose propagation via the activities of parties and intellectuals helps to transform the class in question into a collective subject aspiring to hegemony. The formation of class consciousness for Gramsci is thus an intentional and conflictual process, a struggle between rival conceptions of the world corresponding to competing hegemonic projects.

Class consciousness is also central to the work of Lukács, as is indicated by the title of his most famous work. But, whereas Gramsci focuses on deepening the problematic of hegemony he inherited from Lenin and the Bolsheviks, Lukács starts in the central essay of *History and Class Consciousness*, "Reification and the Consciousness of the Proletariat," from a close reading of Marx's *Capital* and in particular the theory of fetishism. This isn't what Althusser would later call an "innocent" reading free of theoretical and philosophical presuppositions. *History and Class Consciousness* is informed by Lukács's political experience as a leading figure in the abortive Hungarian Revolution of 1919 and (till the late 1920s) in the Hungarian Communist Party. Also, just as Gramsci articulated his version of Marxism in dialogue with Croce and other Italian Hegelian philosophers, Lukács engages with some of the classics of German sociology such as Max Weber's *Economy and Society* and Georg Simmel's *The Philosophy of Money*. This engagement predates his embrace of Marxism in 1918 but continues to inform *History and Class Consciousness*.

Both Weber and Simmel offered highly sophisticated diagnoses of modernity (see Callinicos 2007, chs. 7 and 8). For Weber the course of European history is dominated by a process of rationalization in which different aspects of social life are increasingly organized on the basis of instrumental rationality – in other words, the use of scientific knowledge to select the most efficient means for achieving a given end. The most important instances of this process are the rise of modern capitalism, and the bureaucratization of both public and private life. Weber understands capitalism in terms not dissimilar to Marx's as "the rational capitalistic organization of (formally) free labor" (Weber 1992, xxxiv), where "[s]trict capital accounting is further associated with social phenomena of 'shop discipline' and the appropriation of the means of production, and that means: with the existence of a 'system of domination'" (Weber 1978, I, 108). But he believes socialist revolution would simply swallow up the whole of society in a single bureaucratic organization; there is no escape from the "iron cage" of rationalized modernity (Weber 1992, 123).

Simmel's focus is apparently narrower, but his conclusions are similar. This is because he sees money as the quintessence of the relativity that, according to him, is constitutive of reality itself. Adopting a subjective theory of value, he argues that exchange is "the economic-historical realization of the relativity of things" (Simmel 2011, 107). Accordingly, "if the economic value of objects is constituted by their mutual relationship of exchangeability, then money is the autonomous expression of this relationship" (Simmel 2011, 127). Therefore,

> [t]he more the life of society becomes dominated by monetary relationships, the more the relativistic character of existence finds its expression in conscious life, since money is nothing other than a special form of the embodied relativity of economic goods that signifies their value.
>
> *(Simmel 2011, 556)*

Simmel detects a similar process of rationalization at work in modern life to that analyzed by Weber, but sees it as driven by the increasing dominance of money as an end in itself (here he draws close to Marx) and leading to the triumph of objectivity over subjectivity:

> money is everywhere conceived as purpose, and countless things that are really ends in themselves are thereby degraded to mere means. But since money itself is an omnipresent

> means, the various elements of our existence are thus placed in all-embracing teleological nexus in which no element is either first or last. Furthermore, since money measures all objects with merciless objectivity, and since its standard of value so measured determines their relationship, a web of objective and personal aspects of life emerges which is similar to the cosmos with its continuous cohesion and strict causality . . . since the whole structure of means is one of a causal connection viewed from the front, the practical world too is increasingly becomes a problem for the intelligence. To put it more precisely, the conceivable elements of action become objectively and subjectively calculable rational relationships and is so doing progressively eliminate the emotional reactions and decisions which only attach themselves to the turning points of life.
>
> *(Simmel 2011, 467–68)*

One can see a direct parallelism between this last passage and what Marx writes in *Capital* about

> that inversion [*Verkehrung*] of subject and object which already occurs in the course of the production process itself. We saw in that case how all the subjective productive forces of labor present themselves as productive forces of capital. On the one hand, value, ie the past labor that dominates living labor, is personified into the capitalist; on the other hand, the worker conversely appears as mere objectified labor power, as a commodity. This inverted relationship necessarily gives rise, even in the simple relation of production itself, to a correspondingly inverted conception of the situation, a transposed consciousness, which is further developed by the transformations and modifications of the circulation process proper.
>
> *(CIII: 136)*

But here the inversion of subject and object starts in production, with the appropriation of the worker's labor by the capitalist, and is one aspect of commodity fetishism, where "the relationships between the producers, within which the social characteristics of their labors, take on the form of a social relation between the products of labor" (*C*I: 164). For Marx this transposition is a consequence of the fact that in capitalism the products of labor take the form of commodities made to be sold. The economic relationships among autonomous but interdependent commodity producers are necessarily mediated by the exchange of their products on the market.

> To the producers, therefore, the social relations between their private labors appear as what they are, ie they do not appear as direct social relations between persons in their work, but rather as material [*dinglich*] relations between persons and social relations between things.
>
> *(CI: 165–66)*

Fetishism thus involves both social reality and its representation: the result is both the naturalization of social relationships and their being experienced as fragmented, as "the threads of the inner connection get more and more lost, the relations of production becoming independent of one another and the components of value ossifying into independent forms" (CIII: 967).

Lukács's brilliance consists in taking over much of the content of Weber's and Simmel's diagnoses but setting them in the context of Marx's critique of capitalism and more particularly the theory of commodity fetishism. The unifying theme is that of reification (*Verdinglichung*, *Versachlichung*), the transformation of social relations into things, or, more precisely, into unrelated fragments that are understood in a partial and naturalistic way. What is thereby denied to the agents of capitalist society is any understanding of this society as a whole:

> It is evident that the whole structure of capitalist production rests on the interaction between a necessity subject to strict laws in all isolated phenomena and the relative irrationality of the total process. . . . The capitalist process of rationalization based on private economic calculation requires that every manifestation of life shall exhibit this very interaction between details which are subject to laws and a totality ruled by chance.
>
> *(Lukács 1971a, 102)*

This antinomy between fragmentation and totality is crucial for Lukács. Trapped in reification, individuals experience society as a medley of disconnected parts. Bourgeois thought, from the empirical social sciences to the most advanced philosophy, merely reproduces the tension between knowable parts and unknowable whole. Marxism, however, allows a rational insight into the structure of the whole: "In the teeth of all these isolated and isolating facts and partial systems, dialectics insists on the concrete unity of the whole" (Lukács 1971a, 6). But this ability to grasp capitalism as a totality is not a mere voluntarist affirmation of faith – it stems from the structure of capitalist society. Lukács develops what I have elsewhere called a "perspectival conception of ideology" (Callinicos 2007, 206–9). In other words, individuals' beliefs about society are shaped less by some active process of intervention, say by Gramsci's institutions of civil society, and more by their specific position in a social structure constituted by class antagonism. The bourgeoisie and its intellectual representatives are unable to understand the nature of capitalist society because they view this society from the standpoint of the exploiters – for whom it is crucial that this exploitation is concealed.

But the worker's perspective on capitalism is different. Lukács drew here on two potentially independent thoughts. The first is, as Martin Jay points out, the 18th-century Neapolitan philosopher "Giambattista Vico's celebrated 'verum-factum' principle, which stated that knowledge of the true was itself dependent on the making of the objects of that knowledge" (Jay 2012, 5). This is what Lukács himself calls "the grandiose conception that thought can only grasp what it has itself created" (Lukács 1971a, 39). Capital and the surplus-value that feed it are created by the workers' labor, and there they alone can understand the nature of the social totality that they have made. The second thought arises from the nature of capitalism as a system of generalized commodity production dependent on the transformation of labor power into a commodity that creates the working class in the first place:

> The worker can only become conscious of his existence in society when he becomes aware of himself as a commodity . . . his immediate existence integrates him as a pure naked object into the production process. Once this immediacy turns out to be the consequence of a multiplicity of mediations, once it becomes evident how much it presupposes, then the fetishistic forms of the commodity system begin to dissolve: in the commodity the worker recognizes himself and his own relations with capital. Inasmuch as he is incapable of raising himself above the role of object his consciousness is the *self-consciousness of the commodity*; or in other words it is the self-knowledge, the self-revelation of the capitalist society founded upon the production and exchange of commodities.
>
> *(Lukács 1971a, 168)*

It is thus the very abjection of the worker, her reduction to the status of "absolute commodity," that makes it possible for her class to understand and overthrow capitalism:

> The purely abstract negativity in the life of the worker is objectively the most typical manifestation of reification, it is the constitutive type of capitalist socialization. But for this very reason it is also *subjectively* the point at which this structure is raised to consciousness and where it can be breached in practice.
>
> *(Lukács 1971a, 172)*

The working class is indeed the "identical subject-object of the social and historical processes of evolution" (Lukács 1971a, 149). From being completely objectified within production, workers can, through their practice of class struggle that disrupts the structure of reification, become increasingly conscious of their role as at once creators and gravediggers of capitalism.

The status of Marxism thus becomes not so much the "scientific socialism" of the Second International but the conscious and systematic articulation of the workers' self-consciousness and therefore of the self-consciousness of capitalist society. But Lukács also transformed the concept of orthodoxy – a highly contested concept both between the Second and Third Internationals and within the revolutionary camp itself. He contemptuously spurned the old argument between Kautsky and Bernstein over whether or not Marx's predictions about the evolution of capitalism had been empirically corroborated or refuted:

> Let us assume for the sake of argument that recent research had "disproved" once and for all every one of Marx's individual theses. Even if this were to be proved, every serious "orthodox" Marxist would still be able to accept all such modern findings without reservation and hence dismiss all of Marx's theses in toto – without having to renounce his orthodoxy for a single moment. Orthodox Marxism, therefore, does not imply the uncritical acceptance of the results of Marx's investigations. It is not the "belief" in this or that thesis, nor the exegesis of a "sacred" book. On the contrary, orthodoxy refers exclusively to *method*.
>
> *(Lukács 1971a, 1)*

And central to method is what Sartre would call totalization: "*The primacy of the category of totality is the bearer of the principle of revolution in science*" (Lukács 1971a, 27, emphasis in original). So whereas Gramsci took over Marx's distinction between base and superstructure but sought to reconceptualize it by conceiving the (pluralized) superstructures as the various institutions of civil and political society, Lukács displaced the distinction altogether, at least in his most abstract reflections. Marx's anchoring of the social totality in production, conceived as the unity of the interaction of humans and nature via the labor process and of the social relations of production, still present in Gramsci, plays little role in *History and Class Consciousness*. Lukács's rediscovery of the labor-nature metabolism when he read Marx's *Economic and Philosophic Manuscripts of 1844* helped to prompt the intellectual shift that informed his later writings, which form the subject of Bianca Imbiriba Bonente's and Joao Leonardo Medeiros's entry.

Critique in the Absence of the Proletariat

But the central problem with *History and Class Consciousness* lies elsewhere, in the Messianic role it assigns the proletariat as the "identical subject-object" of history, an empirically existing social class effectively substituting for Hegel's Absolute Spirit. Lukács was of course aware that the actual working class lacked the required self-consciousness. He distinguished between "actual" and "imputed" class consciousness:

> Class consciousness consists in fact of the appropriate and rational reactions "imputed" to a particular typical position in the process of production. This consciousness is, therefore, neither the sum nor the average of what is thought or felt by the single individuals who make up the class.
>
> *(Lukács 1971a, 51)*

How then to get from one to the other? *History and Class Consciousness* offers only the most condensed and abstract answers to this question. And the years between the two world wars unfolded, the plausibility of its conception of the proletariat diminished. On the one hand, after a temporary stabilization during the 1920s, capitalism descended into its greatest economic crisis, which resulted, not in the renewed revolutionary wave predicted by the Comintern, now firmly subordinated to Moscow, but the victory of reaction in its most extreme forms: to fascism already installed in Italy were added National Socialism in Germany and, at the end of the 1930s, the Franco dictatorship in Spain. On the other hand, the consolidation of the Stalin regime in the USSR, culminating in the atrocious years between 1927 and 1938 when agriculture was forcibly collectivized, heavy industry vastly expanded on the backs of an atomized working class, and the Communist Party itself decimated during the Great Terror, represented a very different outcome from that expected amidst the great revolutionary hopes at the end of the First World War. Trotsky, exiled from the USSR and eventually murdered by a Stalinist agent, became the great, though isolated champion of the revolutionary tradition that seemed to have triumphed in 1917.

Gramsci's reflections on passive revolution must be seen as a response to this conjuncture, and they seem to encompass the possibility of a socialist version, in which a planned economy is constructed, but under siege and tightly controlled from above:

> So an unprecedented concentration of hegemony is necessary, and hence a more "interventionist" government, which will take to the offensive more openly against the oppositionists and organize permanently the "impossibility" of internal disintegration – with controls of every kind, political, administrative etc., reinforcement of the hegemonic positions of the dominant group, etc.
>
> *(Gramsci 1971, 239; Gramsci 1975, II, 802; Q6 (VIII) §138)*

But Gramsci's map of passive revolution remains within the framework of what Lukács argued was the unifying premise of Lenin's thought: the actuality of the revolution (Lukács 1970). This comes out clearly in this magnificent passage:

> The philosophy of praxis . . . does not aim at the peaceful resolution of existing contradictions in history and society but is the very theory of these contradictions. It is not the instrument of government of the dominant groups in order to gain the consent and exercise hegemony over the subaltern classes; it is the expression of these subaltern classes who want to educate themselves in the art of government and who have an interest in knowing all truths, even the unpleasant ones, and in avoiding the (impossible) deceptions of the upper class and – even more – their own.
>
> *(Gramsci 1995, 395–96; Gramsci 1975, II, 1319–20; Q10II §41 XII)*

Philosophically Lukács and Gramsci grappled with the horns of the same dilemma, well stated by Andrew Feenberg, who argues that the philosophy of praxis affirms that "the social subject must take over all the same powers that individual subjects enjoyed in the old philosophy. Somehow reality is to be understood in an essential relation to a subject situated within it and dependent on it" (Feenberg 2014, Kindle loc. 196). Maintaining Marxism's status as a critique of political economy requires that there is a gap between this collective revolutionary subject and the empirical reality of capitalist society. But in Lukács's case the gap is so great as to be unsustainable. Gramsci offered instead an "absolute historicism" that refused to accord to concepts such as truth an epistemological status stronger than that of intersubjective agreement, without explaining how he could then avoid a collapse into sociological relativism.

The *Prison Notebooks* were only published after the Second World War. *History and Class Consciousness*, by contrast, had an immediate impact after its publication in 1923. It has even been suggested that Martin Heidegger's *Being and Time* was written partly in response to Lukács's book (Arato and Breines 1979, 203–4). But, in part because of the political conditions outlined earlier, in part because of the philosophical difficulties that led Lukács himself to renounce what he later called his "attempt to out-Hegel Hegel" (Lukács 1971b, xxiii), it was his diagnosis of reification that carried conviction rather than the affirmation of the actuality of revolution. This is evident most notably in the work of the Frankfurt School, which developed around the Institute for Social Research at Frankfurt University during the 1920s. Under the directorship of Max Horkheimer, the Institute concentrated on studying the workings of the superstructure, and especially on what Horkheimer and his chief collaborator Theodor Wiesengrund Adorno would call, in their most famous work, *Dialectic of Enlightenment* (1944/1947), the culture industry. The Frankfurt School were heavily indebted to Lukács for his critique of reification and commodity fetishism, but were increasingly skeptical of the working class's potential as a revolutionary subject. Even before the National Socialist seizure of power that drove them into exile, Horkheimer anatomized what he called "The Impotence of the German Working Class" in the face of the Great Depression, which divided those workers still in jobs and reluctant to risk them, who tended to support the Social Democrats, from the deeply alienated unemployed, apparently permanently excluded from production, and open to the appeals of both the Communists and the Nazis: "The capitalist process of production has thus driven a wedge between the interest in socialism and the human qualities necessary to its implementation" (Horkheimer 1978, 61–65, 62).

In his celebrated essay "Traditional and Critical Theory" (1937), Horkheimer contrasts the Marxist method to "traditional theory," which reflects the intellectual fragmentation caused by the division of labor. Yet he denies that the working class has any privileged epistemological access to the totality:

> Even the situation of the proletariat is, in this society, no guarantee of correct knowledge. The proletariat may indeed have experience of meaninglessness in the form of continuing and increasing wretchedness and injustice in its own life. Yet this awareness is prevented from becoming a social force by the differentiation of the social structure which is still imposed on the proletariat from above and by the opposition between personal [and] class interests which is transcended only at very special moments. Even to the proletariat the world superficially seems quite different than it really is.
>
> *(Horkheimer 1972, 213–14)*

The thinkers associated with the Frankfurt School deepened the interrogation of historical necessity that was one of the characteristics of the revolutionary Hegelianism of the 1910s and 1920s. The key text here is Walter Benjamin's "On the Concept of History," written in 1939–40, at the darkest moment of the 20th century, when it seemed that the future belonged to Hitler and Stalin. For Benjamin, the course of history is a cumulative catastrophe, progress the myth that corrupted Social Democracy, revolution a Messianic irruption into the linear time of bourgeois normality that seeks to avenge past suffering, not realize a radiant future. Yet there remains in Benjamin an affirmation, however despairing, of the actuality of the revolution. For Adorno and Horkheimer in *Dialectic of Enlightenment* the process of reification is projected backwards far into the past, while its power in the present renders collective resistance null. In *Negative Dialectics* (1966) Adorno condemns the method of totalization that Lukács made definitive of Marxism as the expression of an idealist rage against nature's resistance to human domination. As Henry Pickford shows later, Marx's critique of political economy nevertheless continued to be a fundamental reference point for Adorno, who was an important influence on the *neue Marx Lektüre* that developed in west Germany in the 1960s and 1970s as part of the emergence of a new revolutionary left.

All the same, the Frankfurt School pioneered a version of Marxism located no longer in the workers' movement but in the academy. Indeed, their relative indifference to class analysis meant they had little concrete to say about the National Socialism that had driven them into exile: Trotsky's much more directly political writings on Hitler's rise remain the classic Marxist engagement with fascism (Trotsky 1971). The expression "Critical Theory" – originally intended at least in part as a euphemism for Marxism that could act as protective cover in times of persecution – becomes, particularly in the hands of Jürgen Habermas, who established himself as the dominant figure in the "second generation" in postwar West Germany – the name of an alternative approach. This process of distanciation from substantive Marxist theory has continued into the present, with Axel Honneth, leading figure in the so-called third generation, seeking to detach the problematic of reification from the Hegelian Marxist framework in which Lukács formulated it (Honneth 2012).[6]

More broadly, the period between the wars saw the definitive pluralization of Marxism: now counterposed were not only the versions associated with Social Democracy and the new orthodoxy installed in the Communist parties with the institutionalization of "Marxism-Leninism," but the dissident Marxisms that contested them both, associated with such names as Trotsky and Bordiga, and the more academic discourses pioneered by the Frankfurt School. Orthodox Communism remained overwhelmingly dominant in terms of social power and mass influence, but, as the 1960s would show, the future of Marxism did not lie with it.

Notes

1. See, on Lenin's reading of Hegel, Althusser (1971), Löwy (1993) and Kouvelakis (2007).
2. My understanding of Labriola's significance for Gramsci is heavily dependent on Bernstein (2015, ch 1) and Tosel (2016, ch III). Feenberg (2014) addresses the whole tradition of the "philosophy of praxis" from the perspective mainly of the young Marx and Lukács.
3. The German left Communist Karl Korsch was another important contributor to the reconfiguration of Marxism after the First World War: see Korsch (1970, 2016).
4. See Callinicos (2018).
5. The attribution to Gramsci of an "expanded" or "integral" conception of the state incorporating civil society is controversial: compare Anderson (2017a), Buci-Glucksmann (1980) and Thomas (2009).
6. Kouvelakis (2019) emphasizes the break between the project of Critical Theory as originally developed by Horkheimer in the 1930s and its subsequent evolution, especially in the hands of Habermas and Honneth, who eradicated the despairing anti-capitalism in which Horkheimer and Adorno persisted after 1945.

Bibliography

Adorno, Theodor W. 1973 (1966). *Negative Dialectics*. London and New York: Routledge.
Althusser, Louis. 1971. "Lenin before Hegel." In *Lenin and Philosophy and Other Essays*, 103–20. London: NLB.

Althusser, Louis. 2018. "Livre sur l'imperialisme (extraits)." In *Écrits sur l'histoire*, edited by G.M. Goshgarian. Paris: Presses universitaires de France.
Anderson, Perry. 2017a (1977). *The Antinomies of Antonio Gramsci*. London: Verso.
Anderson, Perry. 2017b. *The H-Word: The Peripeteia of Hegemony*. London: Verso.
Arato, Andrew, and Paul Breines. 1979. *The Young Lukács and the Origins of Western Marxism*. London: Pluto.
Benjamin, Walter. 2003. "On the Concept of History." In *Selected Writings*, edited by Michael W. Jennings. Vol. 4, 389–400. Cambridge, MA: Harvard University Press.
Bernstein, Aaron. 2015. "From the Theses on Feuerbach to the Philosophy of Praxis: Marx, Gramsci, Philosophy, Politics." PhD Thesis, King's College London.
Buci-Glucksmann, Christine. 1980. *Gramsci and the State*. London: Lawrence and Wishart.
Bukharin, N.I. 1969 (1921). *Historical Materialism: A System of Sociology*. Ann Arbor: University of Michigan Press.
Bukharin, N.I. 1972 (1917). *Imperialism and World Economy*. London: Merlin.
Callinicos, Alex. 2007. *Social Theory: A Historical Introduction*. 2nd edn. Cambridge: Polity.
Callinicos, Alex. 2018. "Lenin and Imperialism." In *The Palgrave Handbook of Leninist Political Philosophy*, edited by Tom Rockmore and Norman Levine, 457–82. London: Palgrave Macmillan.
Feenberg, Andrew. 2014. *The Philosophy of Praxis: Marx, Lukács and the Frankfurt School*. London: Verso.
Gramsci, Antonio. 1971. *Selections from the Prison Notebooks*. London: Lawrence and Wishart.
Gramsci, Antonio. 1975. *Quaderni del carcere*. Edited by Valentino Gerratana. 4 vols. Turin: Einaudi.
Gramsci, Antonio. 1977. *Selections from the Political Writings 1910–1920*. London: Lawrence and Wishart.
Gramsci, Antonio. 1978. *Selections from the Political Writings 1921–1926*. London: Lawrence and Wishart.
Gramsci, Antonio. 1995. *Further Selections from the Prison Notebooks*. London: Lawrence and Wishart.
Honneth, Axel. 2012. *Reification: A New Look at an Old Idea*. Oxford: Oxford University Press.
Horkheimer. Max. 1972. *Critical Theory: Selected Essays*. New York: Continuum.
Horkheimer, Max. 1978. *Dawn & Decline: Notes 1926–1931 and 1950–1969*. New York: The Seabury Press.
Horkheimer, Max, and Theodor W. Adorno. 2002. *Dialectic of Enlightenment*. Stanford: Stanford University Press.
Jay, Martin. 2012. "Introduction to Axel Honneth." In *Reification: A New Look at an Old Idea*. Oxford: Oxford University Press.
Korsch, Karl. 1970 (1923). *Marxism and Philosophy*. London: NLB.
Korsch, Karl. 2016 (1938). *Karl Marx*. Leiden: Brill.
Kouvelakis, Stathis. 2007. "Lenin as a Reader of Hegel." In *Lenin Reloaded: Toward a Politics of Truth*, edited by Sebastian Budgen, Stathis Kouvelakis, and Slavoj Žižek, 164–204. Durham, NC: Duke University Press.
Kouvelakis, Stathis. 2019. *La critique défaite: Emergence et domestication de la Théorie critique*. Paris: Éditions Amsterdam.
Labriola, Antonio. 1912 (1898). *Socialism and Philosophy*. Chicago: Charles H. Kerr.
Lenin, V.I. 1964a (1917). "Imperialism, the Highest Stage of Capitalism." *LCW* 22: 185–304.
Lenin, V.I. 1964b (1918). "The State and Revolution: The Marxist Theory of the State and the Tasks of the Proletariat in the Revolution." *LCW* 25: 385–497.
Löwy, Michael. 1993 (1976). "From the 'Logic' of Hegel to the Finland Station." In *Changing the World: Essays in Political Philosophy from Karl Marx to Walter Benjamin*, 77–90. Atlantic Highlands, NJ: Humanities Press.
Lukács, György. 1970 (1924). *Lenin: A Study on the Unity of His Thought*. London: NLB.
Lukács, György. 1971a (1923). *History and Class Consciousness: Studies in Marxist Dialectics*. London: Merlin.
Lukács, György. 1971b. "Preface to the New Edition (1967)." In Lukács 1971b, ix–xxxix.
Luxemburg, Rosa. 2004. "The Junius Pamphlet: The Crisis in German Social Democracy." In *The Rosa Luxemburg Reader*, edited by Peter Hudis and Kevin B. Anderson, 313–41. New York: Monthly Review Books.
Simmel, Georg. 2011 (1900). *The Philosophy of Money*. London: Routledge.
Thomas, Peter. 2009. *The Gramscian Moment: Philosophy, Hegemony, and Marxism*. Leiden: Brill.
Tosel, André. 2016. *Étudier Gramsci: Pour un Critique Continue de la Révolution Passive*. Paris: Éditions Kimé.
Trotsky, Leon. 1971. *The Struggle against Fascism in Germany*. New York: Pathfinder Press.
Weber, Max. 1978 (1922). *Economy and Society*. 2 vols. Berkeley: University of California Press.
Weber, Max. 1992 (1904–5). *The Protestant Ethic and the Spirit of Capitalism*. London: Routledge.

7
GYÖRGY LUKÁCS (1885–1971)

Bianca Imbiriba Bonente and João Leonardo Medeiros

The description of György Lukács's arrest by Russian troops in 1956 is a well-known episode of the life of the Hungarian Marxist philosopher. Having been asked by the KGB officer if he was carrying a weapon, Lukács answered "yes" and presented a pen (Kadarkay 1991, 434). This is undoubtedly a good story, but it contains a basic fault: it is simply not true.[1] Nevertheless, the tale is a good insight into Lukács's biography – filled with important events, but controversial to the point of admitting diverging reconstitutions.

Lukács is often accused of collaborating with Stalinism, of sectarianism, of aesthetical conservatism, and many efforts have been made to show that these accusations are far from fair (see Tertulian 1993). One thing is certain: his life is too long, intense and controversial to be summarized in a few words. Even Lukács's most famous biography is not able to record the dimension of his life's trajectory. For instance, it only mentions incidentally the book to which Lukács dedicated the last twenty-five years of his life (Kadarkay 1991, 464–65).

What must not be forgotten is that throughout Lukács's life his intellectual activity was expressed not only through texts, but also through more than fifty years of militant praxis. Born the son of a rich banker, Lukács became an internationally recognized Communist leader. Depending on the period of his life, he could be described as minister, exile, sentenced to death, philosopher, professor or activist of the Hungarian Communist Party. What unifies his kaleidoscopic life is his aversion to capitalist society and, after 1917, his faith in the communist revolution.

Regarding his intellectual activity, there is a discussion on the number of turning points during his sixty-five years of almost uninterrupted production. There are indisputably two breaks. The first one happens after the Russian Revolution, when Lukács becomes a Marxist.[2] Lukács himself identifies a second break in the early 1930s, when his philosophical attitude radically changes. The turning point in his intellectual trajectory was his contact with Marx's *Economic and Philosophic Manuscripts*, in 1930. He was a visiting scholar at the Marx-Engels Institute in Moscow when the *Manuscripts* were being prepared for publication. This means that he was one of their first interpreters (Lukács 1971c, xxxvi–xxxvii). Many analysts have understood this shift as an *ontological* turn: an explicit search for the objective foundations of social existence that would make it possible to grasp its defining procedural determinations (tendencies) and to distinguish them from historical contingency.[3]

Yet, there is a discussion on the continuity of his thought and work from this second rupture up to his death in 1971. Some renowned interpreters convincingly refer to an interlude between approximately 1931 and 1961.[4] According to them, in the huge Marxist production of this period, the ontological orientation is present but still latent.[5] After 1961, the ontological issues clearly take on a central and explicit position in the thought of Lukács, and this serves as inspiration for a ruthless criticism of his early work, including *History and Class Consciousness* (*HCC*) and *The Theory of the Novel*.[6] This was certainly a response to the crisis of Marxism and the socialist project, and probably also influenced by Lukács's reading of Ernst Bloch's (1961) and Nicolas Hartmann's (1949) books. Considering the existence of a rupture in Lukács's intellectual development, the question is: which phase should be prioritized in a posthumous reassessment? Taking into account the influence of Lukács on Marxism and on social thought in general, the answer is his early production – particularly *HCC*. However, if the idea is to represent the entirety of his oeuvre, indisputably the massive production that Lukács himself conceived as his contribution to Marxism should receive more space and attention. Whether judged in terms of theoretical consistency or simply by the number of pages or years dedicated to it, Lukács's mature ontological work is the best representation of his thought.

History and Class Consciousness

It would be a mistake, however, to undermine the historical and theoretical importance of Lukács's early production. In the history of Marxism, Lukács's contribution during the first period is a turning point in the Marxist analyses of subjectivity, as it is expressed within the domains of ideology or in the arts and culture. In spite of its own internal contradictions, *HCC* successfully escapes from opposing poles of revisionism and economic determinism, dominant in the period of the Second International. The book contains at least four very important theoretical developments.

First, Lukács emphasizes the category of totality. This is a radical attack on economic determinism, since the center of the analysis (that is, of the object reflected in it) lies in the historical web of social relations and not on a single domain, no matter how important it may be (Lukács 1971c, xx).

Second, Lukács's conception of method as the defining principle of the Marxist "orthodoxy" is a radical attack on revisionism as first developed by Eduard Bernstein. Of course, the method is always thought by Lukács as an expression of the object's immanent structure and dynamics. It is possible, hence, immediately to answer the kind of criticism that claims the historical contingency of Marxism: there are no sacred theoretical principles, except those implied by the object reflected in the theory. On the other hand, resorting to method – dialectics – opens the door to welcome Hegel. As is widely known, *HCC* is one of the first contributions in the Marxist tradition that recognizes Hegel as an inevitable source for understanding Marx (Lukács 1971b, 27).

Third, there is in *HCC* an ontological orientation, especially in Lukács's way of dealing with false forms of consciousness (for example, Lukács 1971b, 49–50, 104, 112, 127–28). His understanding of ideology in terms of "false consciousness" is quite naive when compared to that found in the complex theory of subjectivity advanced in his mature work. It is, nevertheless, able to explain that the "false consciousness" always plays a role in social reproduction, at least if it is really socially rooted. In *HCC*, Lukács associates the ideological forms of consciousness of the capitalist society to the phenomena of reification and commodity fetishism, and to the particular reaction of each class to them (Lukács 1971b: 213, n32). The critical explanation of the social objectivity of consciousness is the main principle of the kind of criticism that he describes as ontological critique in his later production.

Finally, *HCC* is one of the first readings of volume I of *Capital* in which the theory of value is immediately connected to the theory of estrangement (*Entfremdung*). Upon reviewing Marx's analysis of commodities, Lukács's emphasis lies on commodity fetishism, differently from most readings of the time. Before the publication of the *Grundrisse* in 1939–41, and even after that, Marx's theory of estrangement was held as a philosophical digression of the young Hegelian philosopher who suddenly appears in the end of chapter 1 of Capital, I. *HCC*, the work of Isaak Rubin (1972) and of Karl Korsch (1970) – all of them published in 1923 – are the first influential readings that diverge from this dominant interpretation.

There are, however, good reasons to accept Lukács's sharp self-criticism on the *HCC*. Several problems can be easily mentioned: the misconception of nature and natural sciences; the reference to the indefensible notion of identical subject-object;[7] the influence of voluntarist-idealist elements in the conception of ethics; connected to the latter, a messianic conception of the revolutionary role of the proletariat. In his posthumous book, the *Ontology of Social Being*, these and other serious faults of his early production undergo to a new treatment.

Lukács's Mature Ontology

Broadly speaking, the development of Lukács's Marxism from the 1930s onwards is related to the conditions of political praxis, which aroused in him a feeling of refounding Marxism. This took the form of a project: building a Marxist *Ethics*, based on the *Ontology*. It is a matter for a biographical discussion whether Lukács kept the project of the *Ethics* based on a materialist ontology intact or if he anticipated various developments of this project in the *Ontology* (see Lukács 1983, 135).

Lukács's *Ästhetik* (1963) is a first systematic attempt to connect an ontological conception of society to a materialist conception of values – in this case, aesthetic values.[8] This means that Lukács not only uses his specialized knowledge as a literary critic and theorist, but also that he takes a step forward to a new perspective. This book includes many important theoretical insights. For instance, the analysis of the Hegelian/Marxian categories of universal, particular and singular is still an unavoidable reference (Lukács 1966).

Another prominent trace in Lukács's *Ästhetik* is the role played by everyday thought and praxis in his understanding of aesthetic phenomena. The emergence and historical relevance of every single aesthetic process or object is always thought of in relation to the determinations of daily life. One should also recall Lukács's conception of the category of mimesis and the interesting parallel between the anthropomorphizing form of the artistic representation (mimesis) and the disanthropomorphizing form of scientific theories, which is useful to explain both art and science (Lukács 1966). Finally, the concrete analyses comparing the relationship between social reproduction to the possible development of the various forms of arts are also worth mentioning (Lukács 1966).

The *Ontology of Social Being* is "simply" an attempt to disclose those objects, structures and processes that can be properly recognized as defining society as a form of existence. Of course, these general determinations of society have to be expressed in the different particular historical social formations, though not necessarily in the same way (due precisely to the particular determinations that influence the phenomenal expression of those universal features).

In order to identify the general determinations of society, Lukács compares the mode of reproduction of this particular form of being – social being – to those of previously existing forms of being – organic and inorganic being – from which society emerges. Lukács makes it clear that this implies a notion of development as a process of emergence of determinations proper to the form of being in question.[9] To offer a synthetic image of the development of society, Lukács adopts Marx's expression "retreat of the natural boundary," that is, the emergence of increasingly "pure" objects, structures and processes and the development of the existing social objects toward an increased sociability.[10]

It is precisely this comparison between the mode of reproduction of society and the sphere of life that paves the way for recognizing labor as the central category of social existence and, thus, as the center in the ontology of social being. The recognition of the centrality of labor, as Lukács tirelessly repeats, is not a matter of value judgment, but the result of an analysis that opposes the particular form of material reproduction of human beings to that found in nature (Lukács 1980b, Section 2). It is important to mention that the centrality of labor in the ontology of social being is not identical to the prominent role it plays in capitalist society. This dominating role of labor is, as Marx demonstrated, an exclusive determination of this social formation.

Lukács's rare attempts to introduce the massive argument of his ontology in a brief presentation have always placed particular emphasis on the analysis of labor. This analysis has, at least, two great virtues. First, it is based on broadly known arguments of Marx in which he identifies the general determinations of labor when compared to analogous forms of biological reproduction (*CI*: ch. 7; *MECW* 28: 17–36). This contrast sheds light on the teleological character of labor, which responds to the active form of human reproduction as compared to the passive (instinctive) reproduction of other forms of life, including higher animals (Lukács 1980b, Section 1).

In *Capital*, after stressing the teleological nature of labor, Marx identifies and deals with its material presuppositions (*CI*: 283–91). Lukács's argument takes advantage of this development, but explores the dimension of subjectivity. Briefly speaking, Lukács demonstrates that both knowledge and value judgments are not just objectively founded but also intimately related to the social form of material reproduction. In other words, he shows that even those most primitive forms of labor have knowledge and value judgments as presuppositions, precisely due to their teleological character (Lukács 1980b, 26–33).

If teleology means "positing an end" (using the categories proposed by Lukács himself), previously and ideally defined in a world of causal determinations that would not produce the end by themselves, then it implies a "spiritual apprehension" of these determinations.[11] To connect means to ends, it is necessary that the subject of labor, for instance, recognizes that some stones are suitable to be converted into an axe and others are not, and that she or he registers somehow this recognition in the reflected "world" of consciousness. On the other hand, it is necessary that the subject of labor chooses among the existing objective alternatives, and this obviously demands a value judgment (some stones are useful/useless, good/bad etc.). This judgment comprises not only material causes of labor but also its subjective presuppositions (the conception of stones is efficient/inefficient, false/true etc.) and the activity in itself (it is efficient/inefficient, right/wrong etc.). This means that human reproduction does have values and judgments of behavior as inner moments (Lukács 1978b, 1980b, 26–33).

It is hard to minimize the importance of this particular moment in Lukács's social ontology. In a single movement, the author offers a way out of various false antinomies in the development of philosophy and social theory. First, he refuses the antinomy between empiricist (Humean, Benthamite etc.) and idealist (Kantian, Nietzschian etc.) ethics and demonstrates that the "ought," values and value judgments are objectively based. That is to say, the materialist ethics proposed by Lukács is underpinned by the ontology of social being. Second, the same argument serves as the raw material for a materialist analysis of the emergence and development of the various forms of knowledge, a process culminating in the emergence of science. In doing so, the relationship between science, praxis and the reproduction of society is immediately established in a very sophisticated way. Finally, Lukács unfolds his analysis of consciousness into a theory of ideology.

Ideology, Estrangement and Ethics

The last half of the monumental second volume of the *Ontology* is entirely dedicated to this theory of ideology and its implication to a theory of estrangement. Hence, Lukács returns to themes that are directly associated with his earlier thought: forms of consciousness that can be considered ideological (not only everyday conceptions but also scientific, philosophical, religious and artistic forms of consciousness) and estrangement as a distinguishing feature of capitalist sociability. However, his theories of ideology and of estrangement are no longer based on an *implicit* ontological conception of society, of values, of humanity etc., a conception with idealist traits. They are based on the Marxist ontology developed in the previous chapters of the book.

Both theories are very innovative, but still recognizably Marxist and, if it is possible to say, Lukácsian. In the case of ideology, the great novelty is the immediate association with the analysis of human praxis, particularly of everyday praxis, explained in the book. In the theory of ideology presented in the *Ontology*, Lukács's conception refers to the various forms of consciousness that allow individuals to move themselves among social contradictions[12] (Lukács 1986, 657).

The social foundation of these forms of consciousness is, to a certain extent, independent of their truth-content. As is clear not only in artistic praxis but also in religion and politics, many times truth or falsehood is not the defining moment of the ideological character.[13] It is also not the subversive or conservative nature of the message. What is really decisive is the capacity of the form of consciousness in question to act as a mobilizing factor of *social* activity, thus transcending the simple sphere of individuality.[14]

This conception of ideology is the cornerstone of Lukács's theory of estrangement, the theory that connects the abstract philosophy advanced in the book to its explicit political (revolutionary) implications. The author associates the phenomenon of estrangement with the material reproduction of society *and* with the "ideological complex." As Lukács puts it, "without the mediation of ideological forms, estrangement, no matter how massive the economic determination of its existence is, will never develop itself adequately and, for this reason, cannot be overcome in a theoretically correct and practically effective way" (Lukács 1986, 656).

The criterion to distinguish estranged forms of existence (and of consciousness) is, once again, social praxis. The analysis of labor shows that this exemplary form of practice involves not only ideas or real choices among real alternatives, but always *objectification*: literally, conversion of ideas into real (material or immaterial) objects. The decisive moment of this analysis, in terms of its importance for the theories of ideology and estrangement is that when Lukács associates objectification (*Objektivation/ Vergegenständlichung*) with alienation (*Entäußerung*). In his use of the latter, alienation is not a synonym of estrangement (*Entfremdung*), as is presumably the case in Marx (Vedda and Infranca 2012). In this regard, Lukács does not return to Hegel or even to his own early analysis (*HCC*, in particular); both analyses fail to distinguish, on the one hand, the categories of objectification and alienation, and, on the other, alienation and estrangement.[15] Lukács now conceives alienation as the counterpart of objectification and, as such, as an ontological determination of human praxis (Lukács 1986, 354).

What is at stake, thus, is to establish the difference between these two aspects of human praxis. As Lukács puts it,

> in objectification, man produces something practical, even if it is just the expression of his feelings by means of language . . ., while the aspect of alienation in the same [objectifying] act indicates that it was set in motion by a single man and that it expresses and influences his individual development.
>
> *(Lukács 1986, 464)*

Therefore, the term precisely refers to the externalization of aspects in the personality of the subject of praxis, an externalization that ultimately responds to the humanization of the objects and processes that constitute the world. When some human project is objectified, not only does something new emerge into reality, but it also emerges into reality as an objectified form of an aspect of the positing subject's personality. This is the case, to offer a simple example, of an instrument of production specially adorned in an artistic way.

Even if inextricably connected to the praxis of single individuals, the humanization of the world necessarily reacts back on the individuals themselves as a determination of social praxis. The development of human praxis means increasing its social content. This involves the process through which every single act depends on social objects, structures etc. and the process of diversification of the sphere of praxis. The development of praxis, hence, necessarily expresses itself as a development of the objectifications in the same sense: more various and socially complex objectifications take place. If alienation is the counterpart of objectification, this means that alienation tends to increase with social development, allowing a more open, diversified and complex expression of the aspects of the personality of human beings.

Finally to reach the phenomenon of estrangement, one needs only to recognize that the development of society in general, and of praxis in particular, is intrinsically marked by contradictions (Lukács 1986, 669). Directly following Marx, Lukács argues that the economic development of social existence involves at the same time a tendency to increase productivity, and therefore human capacities, and a tendency to develop human personality. The problem is that these two tendencies are frequently opposed. As it obviously happens in slavery *and in capitalism*, the development of capacities can assume not exactly the development of personality in (the majority of) individuals, but conversely its brutal repression. Estrangement, in Lukács's usage, is the word that captures precisely the "dialectical contradiction between the development of capacities and the development of personality" (Lukács 1986, 510).

If alienation is an ontological determination of praxis, estrangement is entirely historical. There is, in fact, no inner relation between the development of capacities and the repression of personality, no matter how often this has happened in history. This means at least three things. First, it means that there are various historical forms of estrangement. In each historical period, some forms prevail. Second, because it results from a social contradiction, estrangement always resolves itself into ideological forms. The historical character of estrangement expresses itself subjectively in the particular forms of ideology that allow individuals to deal with it in their daily practices. This is clearly the case of commodity fetishism.

Third, if estrangement is historical, then it is possible to think of a kind of society in which the contradiction between human capacities and personality is overcome.[16] Now, if the development of humanity needs to be understood as the development of the human species – as the development of human capacities *and* as the open expression of human personality in generic terms, then overcoming estrangement can be held to be an ethical project for humanity. There is no coincidence in the fact that Marx conceived communism, from the 1840s to his death, as a state of society in which "the free development of each is the condition for the free development of all" (*MECW* 5: 506).

Lukács's ethical project can be, thus, summarized in the following manner. It consists in a renewal of Marxism in a way that it can once again function as ideology. More precisely, the idea is to remove any trace of decadent (Stalinist/positivist and/or idealist) Marxism to turn it into a mobilizing factor for human praxis toward overcoming current forms of estrangement – those brought forth by capitalism. At a first glance, there is no difference between this formulation and that of HCC. This is a deceptive impression, however. Lukács's text is consciously historical. It is a reflection on socialism and Marxism written *after* the Stalinist period, in a time of crisis of Marxism and of disillusionment with socialism. The self-critical nature of Lukács's later production reflects the author's belief in the need for a deep critical reassessment of Marxism and of the communist project.

Notes

1. It is Lukács (1983, 132) himself that declares it to be false: "This is a legend," he says.
2. Before the Marxist turn, Lukács had already written several influential books: for instance, Lukács (2010, 1971a). The first Marxist texts are collected in the famous Lukács (2014, 1971b).
3. On the ontological turn, see: Oldrini (2002), Netto (2002), Lukács (1971c, 45–8), Tertulian (1971, 1988, 2002), and Mészáros (1995).
4. See Oldrini (2002), Vaisman (2007), Tertulian (1993, 1971).
5. The development of Lukács's ideas appear in the various topics he dealt with in the period, as recorded in the many important books published from 1931 to 1961: for instance, Lukács (1975, 1980a, 1962, 1963).
6. See Lukács (1986, 151, n. 8, 1971c). It is worth mentioning that, in the 1920s, Lukács wrote a defense of *HCC*, never published. See Lukács (2000) and Löwy (2011).
7. In HCC, Lukács takes the proletariat as "the identical subject-object of the historical process, i.e. the first subject in history that is (objectively) capable of an adequate social consciousness" (Lukács 1971b, 199). In his *Ontology*, on the contrary, Lukács rejects the identical subject-object as a "philosophical myth," arguing that it fuses two dimensions of the world that are separate in reality: the subjects of the reflecting consciousness and the objects reflected in it (Lukács 1978a, 28).
8. On Lukács's *Aesthetic*, see Vedda (2006) and Duayer (2008); and various chapters of Vedda and Infranca (2007).
9. It should be also clear that this notion of development does not describe a linear process, but the phenomenon of "uneven development" (Lukács 1978b, 129).
10. In the English translations of *Capital*, the same expression appears as "the receding of natural limits" (*CI*: 650).
11. Lukács rejects the absolute opposition between teleology and causality. As he demonstrates, in the labor process, both causality and teleology are present as presuppositions: see Duayer and Medeiros (2006). See also Infranca (2005).
12. Lukács also recognizes what he calls "high (or pure) forms of ideology," which are not necessarily related to contradictions of everyday life but to the development of the human species in itself. This is the case of philosophy, science and the arts (Lukács 1986, 411, 619).
13. Even in science (and philosophy), a form of praxis in which truth is the defining value, practical utility many times appears as a guiding value for theoretical development and as an epistemologically decisive criterion. Lukács's critique of neo-positivism (logical positivism) demonstrates precisely the social genesis and foundation of this instrumental justification of science, making sense of the ontological negation it necessarily implies. Crudely, a science with no principles or commitments is an ideological expression of the volatile and contradictory character of capitalist reproduction. (Lukács 1984, 343–70).
14. One of Lukács's best examples deals with the capacity of poetic creation to perform this mobilizing function. (Lukács 1986, 714).
15. See Lukács (1986, 501, 1971c, xii–xiii). Marx recognized these two aspects of human praxis, but never fixed them into separate categories of alienation and objectification: Lukács (1986, 505).
16. Overcoming means dialectical sublation (*Aufhebung*). There is no previous guarantee that the elimination of prevailing forms of estrangement does not lead to the emergence of more complex and sophisticated forms, even in socialism.

Bibliography

Bewes, Timothy, and Timothy Hall, eds. 2011. *Georg Lukács: The Fundamental Dissonance of Existence: Aesthetics, Politics, Literature*. London; New York: Continuum.

Bloch, Ernst. 1961. *Philosophische Grundfragen I. Zur Ontologie des Noch-Nicht-Seins*. Frankfurt: Suhrkamp.

Duayer, Juarez. 2008. *Lukács e a Arquitetura*. Niterói: Eduff.

Duayer, Mario, and João Leonardo Medeiros. 2006. "'Underlabouring' for Ethics: Lukács' Critical Ontology." In *Contributions to Social Ontology*, edited by Clive Lawson, John Latsis, and Nuno Martins, 148–72. London: Routledge.

Hartmann, Nicolai. 1949. *Neue Wege der Ontologie*. Stuttgart: W. Kohlhammer.

Infranca, Antonino. 2005. *Trabajo, Individuo, Historia. El Concepto de Trabajo en Lukács*. Buenos Aires: Herramienta.

Kadarkay, Arpad. 1991. *Georg Lukács*. Oxford: Blackwell.

Korsch, Karl. 1970. *Marxism and Philosophy*. London: NLB.

Löwy, Michael. 2011. "Revolutionary Dialectics against 'Tailism': Lukács' Answer to the Criticisms of History and Class Consciousness." In *Georg Lukács Reconsidered: Critical Essays in Politics, Philosophy and Aesthetics*, edited by Michael J. Thompson, 65–72. London and New York: Continuum.
Lukács, György. 1962 (1955). *The Historical Novel*. London: Merlin Press.
Lukács, György. 1963. *Die Eigenart des Ästhetischen*. Werke Band 11, 12. Neuwied: Luchterhand.
Lukács, György. 1966. *Estetica. I. La peculiaridad de lo Estetico*. Tomos 1 a 4. Barcelona and México, DF: Ediciones Grijalbo.
Lukács, György. 1971a (1916). *The Theory of the Novel*. London: Merlin Press.
Lukács, György. 1971b (1923). *History and Class Consciousness: Studies in Marxist Dialectics*. Cambridge, MA: The MIT Press.
Lukács, György. 1971c. "Preface to the New Edition (1967)." In Lukács 1971b, ix–xxxix.
Lukács, György. 1975 (1948). *The Young Hegel*. London: Merlin Press.
Lukács, György 1978a (1972). *Ontology of Social Being, Vol. 1: Hegel's False and His Genuine Ontology*. London: Merlin Press.
Lukács, György. 1978b (1972). *Ontology of Social Being, Vol. 2: Marx's Basic Ontological Principles*. London: Merlin Press.
Lukács, György. 1980a (1954). *The Destruction of Reason*. London: Merlin Press.
Lukács, György. 1980b (1973). *Ontology of Social Being, Vol. 3: Labour*. London: Merlin Press.
Lukács, György. 1983. *Record of a Life: An Autobiographical Sketch*. Edited by István Eörsi. London: Verso.
Lukács, György. 1984. *Zur Ontologie des gesellschaftlichen Seins*. Erster Band, Werke Band 13. Darmstadt: Luchterhand.
Lukács, György. 1986. *Zur Ontologie des gesellschaftlichen Seins*. Zweiter Band, Werke Band 14. Darmstadt: Luchterhand.
Lukács, György. 1995 (1968). "Die ontologischen Grundlagen des Menschlichen Denkens und Handelns." In *Objektive Möglichkeit. Beiträge zu Georg Lukacs' "Zur Ontologie des gesellschaftlichen Seins,"* edited by Rüdiger Dannemann and Werner Jung, 31–47. Opladen: Westdeutscher Verlag.
Lukács, György. 2000 (1996). *A Defence of History and Class Consciousness: Tailism and the Dialectic*. New York: Verso.
Lukács, György. 2010 (1910). *Soul and Form*. New York: Columbia University Press.
Lukács, György. 2014 (1919). *Tactics and Ethics (1919–1929)*. London and New York: Verso.
Mészáros, István. 1995. *Beyond Capital: Towards a Theory of Transition*. London: Merlinn.
Netto, José Paulo. 2002. "Georg Lukács: Um Exílio na Pós-Modernidade." In *Lukács e a Atualidade do Marxismo*, edited by Maria Orlanda Pinnassi and Sergio Lessa, 77–101. São Paulo: Boitempo.
Oldrini, Guido. 2002. "Em Busca das Raízes da Ontologia (Marxista) de Lukács." In *Lukács e a Atualidade do Marxismo*, edited by Maria Orlanda Pinnassi and Sergio Lessa, 49–76. São Paulo: Boitempo.
Rubin, Isaak Ilich. 1972 (1928). *Essays on Marx's Theory of Value*. Detroit: Black & Red.
Tertulian, Nicolas. 1971. "L'évolution de la Pensée de Georg Lukács." In *L'homme et la Societé*. Vol. 20, 13–36. Paris: Editions Anthropos.
Tertulian, Nicolas. 1988. "Lukács' Ontology." In *Lukács Today: Essays in Marxist Philosophy*, edited by Tom Rockmore, 243–73. Dordrecht: Reidel.
Tertulian, Nicolas. 1991. "Le Grand Projet de l'Éthique." *Marx Actuel* 10: 81–96.
Tertulian, Nicolas. 1993. "Lukács et le Stalinisme." *Les Temps modernes* (juin): 1–45.
Tertulian, Nicolas. 2002. "Lukács Hoje." In *Lukács e a Atualidade do Marxismo*, edited by Maria Orlanda Pinnassi and Sergio Lessa, 27–48. São Paulo: Boitempo.
Vaisman, Ester. 2007. "A Obra Tardia de Lukács e os Revezes de seu Itinerário Intelectual." *Revista Trans/Form/Ação – Revista de Filosofia* 30(2): 247–59.
Vedda, Miguel. 2006. *La Sugestión de lo Concreto: Estudios sobre Teoría Literaria Marxista*. Buenos Aires: Gorla.
Vedda, Miguel, and Antonino Infranca, eds. 2007. *György Lukács. Ética, Estética y Ontología*. Buenos Aires: Colihue.
Vedda, Miguel, and Antonino Infranca. 2012. "Introducción: Sobre la Génesis de la Categoría de Alienación." In *La Alienación: Historia y Actualidad*, edited by Miguel Vedda and Antonino Infranca, 9–30. Buenos Aires: Herramienta.

8

ANTONIO GRAMSCI (1891–1937)

André Tosel[1]

Antonio Gramsci was above all a revolutionary theorist. He projected the categories of Marxian "science" within the perspective of an action-science that recovered the question of the formation of a national-popular political will. Gramsci retrieved this theme in opposition to any deterministic interpretation of the critique of political economy, and indeed in opposition to any temptation to derive political and cultural superstructures from the economic base. He did so amidst a period of fire and blood in which the hope born of the October Revolution and the Leninist breakthrough deteriorated and ebbed away, caught as this hope was in the double vice of fascist dictatorship and the social-liberal takeover. "Statolatry" in the East threatened the expansive capacity of the Soviet experience, while amidst the organic crisis of the old liberal state fascist dictatorship imposed a violent form of restoration. In the West, this restoration tended to take the consensual form of a passive revolution. Here, a new state founded on the rationalization of the production process, as well as the formalization of the masses' dynamism by way of more democratic structures, succeeded both in imposing its own state practices and in reproducing the hegemony of the dominant classes. The problem of the state, and of the balance between the moments of force and consent was, indeed, a central one. This moreover raised questions as to the relevance of the Marxian and Marxist way of theorizing the relations between economics and politics. This provided the theoretical-strategic context in which Gramsci elaborated his original conception of the historical bloc and the producers' capacities to achieve hegemony.

The Primacy of Politics and the Split Within the Superstructure

Gramsci began by rejecting the economism of the Second International, as well as its reappearances in the Comintern after Lenin's death. The state is not simply an instrument of coercion in the hands of a class subject, as if the state somehow stood outside the capitalist relations of production that it serves to guarantee. Rather, it has a constitutive function in the formation of these classes and their development within the fundamental economic activities. "The historical unity of the ruling classes is realized in the state, and their history is essentially the history of states and groups of states" (Gramsci 1975, III, 2287–88; Q 25 (XXIII) §5).

The economic base does not represent a pre-formed entity bearing the outlines of the demands and political possibilities that might be derived from it through deduction, as if forming a "second world" lower in value and consistency. Rather, this base should be understood as a field of objective necessity, that is, of the external or externalized forces that crush and limit human initiative and "human freedom." The economic base is not a foundation that can be defined as *other*, as if it determined humans' activity without itself being defined by this activity. It is the whole set of conditions with which humans' will is confronted, as they either find material to work with therein, or encounter a resistance that they have to displace. It is grasped from the inside, through the action of opposed political wills that seek to fashion its structure in order to transform its characteristic circumstantial necessity into freedom. The relationship between necessity and freedom, or between economics and politics, takes precedence over its terms, which are never separate. Within this relationship, freedom – defined as the initiative of the will – is the term able to encompass the others. It is the will that has always already acted; and the experience of economic necessity reveals itself to the will, or freedom, in a relationship that constitutes the will itself.

The economic base does not exist alone and separate; rather, it dialectically reveals itself at the moment when there is a historic will to initiative. It thus reveals itself as already posited within the movement that elaborates the political superstructure. It is a foundation, but through and for this will. That is how we should understand what Gramsci calls the first, economic moment of the relationship of forces – for we should be led astray by the quasi-objectivist style of his formulations. For Gramsci,

> A relation of social forces which is closely linked to the structure, objective, independent of human will, and which can be measured with the systems of the exact or physical sciences. . . . This relation is what it is, a refractory reality.
> *(Gramsci 1971, 180–1; Gramsci 1975, III, 1583; Q 13, §17)*

We should understand that this objectivity belongs to an irreducibly practical dimension: it is the product of a prior moment of praxis, and it outlines the contradictory conditions for another, subjective moment of praxis, that is, that which brings social transformation. It is the object of a subject, the matter of its real action.

This objectivity of economic necessity (an objectivity that has to be transformed) delimits the sphere of what is objectively realizable through and for this determinate freedom – that is, the freedom proper to the associated wills that find in this objectivity the foundation of their own function within the relations of production. But the realization of the economic moment always proceeds by way of the properly political moment, which includes but also exceeds the state moment. This is the site of "an evaluation of the degree of homogeneity, self-awareness, and organization attained by the various social classes" (Gramsci 1971, 181; Gramsci 1975, III, 1583; Q 13, §17). It is also in this moment that freedom constitutes itself completely, through its effort to become a collective freedom. It does this when it takes on the determinate form of a social group capable of creating an expansive conformism, and of modeling this latter around asserted ends and practices, with an inflexible intransigence that is also prepared to make the necessary compromises. This freedom is realized in organization, that is, in the coordination of plural wills and of their institutionalization processes (class, party, nations, states). The "general productive laboring" activity that constitutes the heart of the economy proceeds by way of ethical-political action. It takes this route via ethical-political action in order to find its own unity therein, and it appears as the result of an activity that is conscious of its political ends. Production, in its historical form, interprets this activity through and in political action. Praxis is the passage from the economic to the political, the incessant transformation of a determinate necessity into a determinate freedom, the creation of forms of life. The historical bloc is a specific form of the unity of a permanent passage between the economic and political, which can never be presented as an inverse derivation of the economic starting out from politics. Rather, it is the relatively stable and yet transformable result of the very act of constituting the bloc.

Gramsci uses the category *catharsis*, an Aristotelian term that is also proposed by Benedetto Croce in the sense of the purification of the impulsiveness of life through the form of expression. Gramsci uses this category in order to think through this infinite passage from base to superstructure,

> the passage from the purely economic (or egoistic-passional) to the ethico-political moment, that is the superior elaboration of the structure into superstructure in the minds of men. . . . Structure ceases to be an external force which crushes man, assimilates him to itself and makes him passive; and is transformed into a means of freedom, an instrument to create a new ethico-political form and a source of new initiatives.
>
> *(Gramsci 1971, 366–67; Gramsci 1975, II, 1244; Q 10 II §6i)*

We should not be misled by the speculative allure of this theory, which appears as the philosophical support for the "science of politics" and of the state. The economic-political division can only be understood from the perspective of the distinction internal to the superstructure that determines this distinction and makes it operative. According to Gramsci's theory of the extended state, this superstructure should be broken down into civil society and political society. We can only understand the state's function in unifying the ruling classes if we break the political superstructure down into two, distinguishing the state in the narrow sense, or political society (PS), from the extended state, or civil society (CS). Does this mean that Gramsci was purely and simply returning to a Hegelian conception, later adopted by the young Marx and indeed maintained throughout his career in parallel with the base-superstructure pairing? At first glance this seems not to be the case: for CS surely refers not to the economic base, but to a superstructural sphere. And most importantly, in occupying this sphere it concentrates the properly ethical-political functions of freedom, of will, of spontaneous consent. Conversely, PS, or the state as an apparatus of constraint, configures the pole of imposed necessity.

This split reproduces the economic/political division, by pulling down the fully developed – but not narrowly state – moment of the political side, and making the state moment coincide with politics as coercion, which is not fully political. In a letter to his sister in law Tatania Schucht, Gramsci explained how a study that had initially concerned the question of the intellectuals had become a theory of the historic bloc, of catharsis, and of the breaking down of superstructures into CS and PS:

> my study also leads to certain definitions of the concept of the State that is usually understood as a political Society (or dictatorship, or coercive apparatus, meant to mold the popular mass in accordance with the type of production and economy at a given moment) and not as a balance between the political Society and the civil Society (or the hegemony of a social group over the entire national society, exercised through the so-called private organizations such as the Church, the unions, the schools, etc.); it is within the civil society that the intellectuals operate.
>
> *(Gramsci 1994, II, 67)*

It was Gramsci's reflection on the triumph of fascism and the halt imposed on the revolutionary process in the West that demanded this division between two types of superstructures. This reflection moreover allowed a comparative analysis of revolution as war of movement and as war as position, in turn leading to the well-known theme of hegemony. For Gramsci, the subaltern classes are confronted with a historic task in some senses homologous to that which was accomplished by the capitalist ruling classes. Like them, they must both dominate the antagonistic classes and lead the allied classes, by realizing the possibilities linked to their place within production. If a social group is to be able fully to exercise its domination, inscribed within the socio-economic production relations, it must most certainly occupy and transform the state, political society (PS), thus obtaining the means of "liquidating" the antagonistic groups or forcing them to submit. But this domination can only be realized if it is prepared before the seizure of power, through the formation of a capacity to lead the allied groups on all the terrains of civic, social and cultural life. Even once power is taken, it is only exercised if the dominant group continues to "lead" the allied groups (see Gramsci 1971, 57–58, 1975, III, 2010–11; Q 19 §24).

But what, precisely, does "lead" mean? It means organizing the whole set of "private" activities of what should be termed civil society, and being able to take the initiative in the ideal-ideological elaborations and practices engaged by the "hegemonic apparatuses." The state extends as a "hegemony armored with coercion"; it cannot live by force alone. It has to work through persuasion, through conviction, by securing consent over the forms, the modes, the content and the common sense of the fundamental "non-political" activities (experienced within the hegemonic apparatuses). So in the West the revolutionary wave crashed up against civil society (CS)'s system of fortresses, for this site of hegemony could serve as a rear base for reconquering the elements of the state that had fallen or been threatened over the course of the insurrections. And that was the reason why the seizure of state power in the East (Russia) was so much easier, precisely because there the state was everything and CS was embryonic. But it was only momentarily easy, for the task now posed was precisely to create these elements of CS, to use the state-dictatorship to build this hegemony without collapsing into a cult of the state.

For the modern masses, hegemony and the construction of the new historical bloc materialize in specific conditions. Even when we assume the general rule of the combination of force with consent, this pairing must also be grasped in terms of its asymmetry. If the new fundamental class becomes enormously more able to assimilate allied groups to itself, on account of its concentration and its place in economic relations, conversely it finds itself in a situation of objective inferiority relative to the modern ruling classes. These latter still dominate the economic mechanism, which is based on the private appropriation of the means of production and on the management of the profits of accumulation. They are moreover able to use the extended state (CS+ PS) to form and reproduce their own unity, according to the required balances. They produce elements that dominate common sense, useful instances of knowledge, and they can cement ideas and authorized practices in a commonly accepted conception of the world. That is how they simultaneously produce both politics and philosophy. For their part, the subaltern classes start off disaggregated on the political and ethical, intellectual and cultural terrain, at the same time as they are economically dominated as a dependent salariat of wage workers. They have no philosophical, ethical and political autonomy, and they have great difficulty in going beyond the economic-corporative level of historical activity:

> The subaltern classes, by definition, are not unified and cannot unite until they are able to become a "State:" their history, therefore, is intertwined with that of civil society, and thereby with the history of States and groups of States.
>
> *(Gramsci 1971, 52; Gramsci 1975, III, 2288; Q 25 §5)*

The Complexity of the Distinction Between State and Civil Society

It is this asymmetry that raises difficulties, and that explains the complexities of the CS/PS distinction. If CS is indeed the site of hegemony, it cannot constitute itself as a demiurgic will. If it extends the state into the private web of its apparatuses, it must also adapt to the economic possibilities in order to be able to realize them; a task that demands recourse to the state-dictatorship as an instrument. For it is the state that compels the incompletely hegemonic CS to adapt. The state apparatus, its army, its courts and its police, provides operational might to certain social forces, which direct this apparatus in order to transform CS, that is, so that it will realize these transformations in the economic sphere. This means that the CS/PS distinction can, indeed, be understood as an opposition, if the state compels this adaptation. This disqualifies any social-democratic interpretation of hegemony in terms of securing some minimum consensus through the normal use of democratic procedures alone.

Indeed, directing the hegemonic apparatuses is not solely enough to dominate, that is, to form a mode of production that liberates the collective labor power. If indeed state violence must be reduced to the minimum necessary level, it is impossible to fix this minimum *a priori*. Hegemony in CS is often partial. This demands a higher, instrumental use of the state in order to bring the elements of a new structure to bear, imposing them on rebellious elements of CS. The hegemonic process develops in two directions that are concretely in tension: one that goes in the direction political economy → CS → PS, and the other that goes in the direction PS → economy → CS. PS offers a superior and necessary technique. The distinction between CS and PS is not only, as Gramsci tells us, a "methodological" one; for it can also take the form of a real opposition. Proof of this is the example of the state introducing elements of planning into the economy, and the opposition that comes from certain elements from within CS. In this case it is CS that becomes the outpost, with PS functioning as its fragile rearguard.

In other words, CS and PS can swap their respective functions as earthworks or fortresses and front lines. If a dominant class can reorganize itself on the basis of the hegemonic apparatuses, in order then to reconquer the state apparatus, a class with a fragile but already real hegemony can also "use" the heights of the state apparatus to intervene in the economy and conquer further hegemony within CS. The state has a plastic character that demands not only that we break it down into CS and PS, but also that we alternately accord primacy to first one, then the other of these two terms. However, the real opposition cannot last. It signifies a crisis of hegemony that can be resolved only through a restored balance between the two terms, oriented toward their identification.

If we are properly to understand this tendency toward identification, we clearly have to expand our definition of CS and give it a greater degree of nuance. Far from reducing CS to the hegemonic apparatuses alone, that is, as the mediation between economics and politics, we have to understand it in terms of its link to the economy. And here we confront the fact that civil society is defined by the activity of socially determinate individuals who can identify with the state's goals precisely on the basis of this organic activity that is already assured within the economic structure. Civil society here partly regains the same sense it had in Hegel or in Marx, as an economic dimension that is both included in its extended-state function, and internally affected by the ethical-political moment. It is this web of determinations that makes for Gramsci's real and indeed complex originality. From this perspective, economic apparatuses like trade unions or institutions coordinating economic life as the "determinate market" also belong to CS.

The subaltern classes, which are disaggregated and at first excluded from the state, can thus only organize on the terrain of civil society, understood as economic activity and as a system of private activities where consent is produced. For example, the trade unions are both hegemonic apparatuses and economic agents. They pursue their activity at both the economic-corporate level and at the level of political relations, where they are confronted with state action. They are thus dominated on the determinate market and organized and ruled by the coercion-state. An "economic-corporate" unification is partial, limited as it is to demands for redistribution and rights to participation. The passage to the ethical-political moment is decisive: this is the moment of becoming-the-state, which proceeds by investing the hegemonic apparatuses, constituting a new common sense, producing a new (practice of) philosophy, and taking state power and exercising it. This is the moment when the intransigence manifested in the "spirit of separation" takes form from below, and organizes a new social conformity that is better able to assimilate.

The party form thus appears as the specific ethical-political instance of organization. Becoming-the-state appears as a political imperative, which is to be achieved through organization. The party is a school in which we acquire an ethical-political sense of the state. For the classes that are subaltern in CS, this is the first possible way of being a state. Organization is not a simple institutional process, but an act through which individual wills that are already linked at the level of economic relations, albeit a discontinuous and heteronomous way, become coordinated. This freedom, providing itself with discipline and organization, is not limited to the party alone. For it also has to be the state, that is, convince a plurality of other allied wills that are themselves more or less organized. If organization succeeds in making necessity into freedom, and if organization is a compulsory passage, it also entails risks of bureaucratization that can only be corrected through the continual development of this same freedom.

For a modern class that is subaltern but also a contender for hegemony, the only way forward is to answer the dilemma between the reproduction of disaggregation and the extended and universalized pursuit of the process of the state's ethical becoming. What allows the seizing of the extended state is the perspective, peculiar to the modern subaltern class alone, of a hegemony that is completely expansive in intensity. Sticking to the hegemonic form that has been developed by the current ruling class does not allow this. Yet this critical-practical perspective also relies on an analysis of the conjuncture and on the art of the possible. There is nothing to guarantee it. In the East nothing guaranteed that the new state would succeed in making the right compromises, especially given that it found itself in the unprecedented situation of representing classes poorer than the former dominant classes, with which it had to make compromises. And in the West nothing guaranteed against the capitalist ruling classes using the advantage constituted by their wealth and their mastery of economic life to reduce compromises to the minimum and allow a vast field of action for their own economic-corporate interest, at the risk of prompting the de-assimilation of the increasingly disaggregated masses. In so doing – coming into contact with the requirements of this new CS – PS itself transforms by reducing the necessary constraint to the minimum that is possible in the given historical situation. It tends to combine with CS, or even be absorbed into it, now that CS has become tendentially homogenous with the hegemonic class.

The "Integral State" as "Ethical State"

In the perspective of the new fundamental class's hegemony, and of the construction of its own historical bloc, the relations between CS and PS are no longer a matter of opposition, distinction and identification. Rather, they are ultimately to be understood as relations through which PS is absorbed into CS. Contrary to what Marx thought, and together with him the Marxist tradition of the Second International (Kautskyan orthodoxy) and the Third International (the Lenin of *The State and Revolution*), the state cannot disappear entirely. Rather, it is confronted with the indefinite task of becoming an ethical or educator state,

In reality, one must conceive of the state as "educator" insofar as it aims to create a new type or level of civilization. How does this come about? Despite the fact that the state essentially operates on economic forces, reorganizes and develops the apparatus of economic production, and innovates the structure, it does not follow that the elements of the superstructure are left alone to develop spontaneously through some kind of aleatory and spontaneous germination. In this field, too, the state is a "rationalization," an instrument of acceleration and Taylorization; it operates according to a plan, pushing, encouraging, stimulating etc. (Gramsci 1975, II, 978; Gramsci 1995, 273; Gramsci, 2011, III, 272; Q8 §62).

Extended into CS and indeed as CS, PS becomes the "integral state" that bases itself on CS in order to adjust it to the possibilities liberated by the economic structure and to bring about the coincidence between CS and the economic structure itself.

What now follows is the overcoming of the organic separation between the economic and the political, proper to capitalist modernity. A modernity, this, which reproduces the real subsumption of labor and its duplication in a state-representative democracy. The overcoming of this separation appears in outline even within capitalist modernity, because economic institutions are always political, and vice versa. Overcoming this consists of lifting the limits that modern society imposes on its own development, both by giving free rein to its own economic-corporate interests – to the point of de-assimilating wider layers of society – and because of its contradictory identification of its own ethical-political practices with the management of this de-assimilation. The bourgeois class crashes up against the internal limits of this unprecedented process, which it alone has been able to produce historically. The modern assimilation process comes under threat, and even risks grinding to a halt, on account of the "saturation" of a bourgeois class that has become incapable of assimilating new elements, or rather can only "assimilate" them on the model of exclusion and marginalization. The new class's horizon corresponds to the fact that it can

> posi[t] itself as apt to assimilate the whole of society – at, at the same time, is truly capable of embodying this process – . . . tak[ing] this notion of the state and the law to such a level of perfection as to conceive of the end of the state and the law, for the state and the law would serve no purpose once they had accomplished their task and been absorbed by civil society.
>
> *(Gramsci 1975, II, 937; Gramsci 2011, III, 234; Q 8 §2)*

Here we note that the end of the state means its absorption into civil society, which for its part is named the ethical state. This "correction" of Marx is a very substantial one.

Gramsci's reflection on the state, inseparable from his militant praxis, proceeds along a non-linear path from the opposition of PS and CS to their identification, and from the identification of the two to the absorption of PS by CS. The coming of a period of organic freedom cannot be reduced to the advent of a state that embodies a pure consensus. The educator-state imparts a consensus that is based on the spirit of separation, rooted in a fundamental class's position within production. The content of this consent is economic-political, and it develops through the permanent remolding of the unstable balance that links it to force. If democracy intervenes as a constitutive process, it cannot stabilize itself *a priori* in representative democratic politics alone. So here there is no idealism about democracy, as if it could be identified with a determinate system of rules that are fixed for all eternity.

Hence Gramsci did not theorize a separate state sphere. Rather, he theorized a state that ceaselessly re-composes itself as political society plus civil society. CS is first of all the site of the anticipation of the possibility of a regulated society, a transubstantiation of CS in a society where the modern prince of free initiative extends both qualitatively and qualitatively, and is institutionalized in a new determinate market characterized by elements of planning and the political regulation of production. The ethical state is that state that uses PS – open to the organized pressure from the advancing subaltern classes – as a higher technique for permitting CS, already undergoing hegemonic transformations, to pursue its activity by becoming an internalization of the economic base (assimilator-class) and making this an inherent condition of political will.

Gramsci does not provide any philosophy of history with a guaranteed happy ending. Instead, he proposes a dramatic theory of modernity's historic present. Seen through the dynamic relation between civil and political society, this present sees both a democratization of the moment of force and a continuing constraint exercised over the activities that belong to a wide span of civil society. The hegemony that has now been achieved does not unite society to the point that force disappears from the terrain of political will. So long as the state's existence remains necessary, there will still be an outer limit of the hegemonic construct. That is why civil society, grasped in its particular contradictions, retains an unconditional value, whereas the state has only a conditional value even if it appears as the ultimate moment of the realization of hegemony within civil society. Gramsci's specific concept of politics should therefore be understood as the infinite effort to reduce the margins of civil society which resist their assimilation by civil society itself and eliminate their coercive assimilation by political society.

Translated by David Broder

Note

1. *Editorial note*: We were delighted when André Tosel, the author of extremely important studies of Gramsci, agreed to write the entry for this handbook on Gramsci. Alas, he died suddenly in April 2017, before he had written the entry. In tribute we are publishing this text, which originally appeared as "Quelques distinctions gramsciennes: économie et politique, société et état." *La Pensée*, 301 (1995).

Bibliography

Gramsci, Antonio. 1971. *Selections from the Prison Notebooks*. London: Lawrence and Wishart.

Gramsci, Antonio. 1975. *Quaderni del carcere*. Edited by Valentino Gerratana. 4 vols. Turin: Einaudi.

Gramsci, Antonio. 1994. *Letters from Prison*. 2 vols. New York: Columbia University Press.

Gramsci, Antonio. 1995. *Further Selections from the Prison Notebooks*. London: Lawrence and Wishart.

Gramsci, Antonio. 2011. *Prison Notebooks*. Edited by Joseph A. Buttigieg. 3 vols. New York: Columbia University Press.

9
LEON TROTSKY (1879–1940)

Paul Le Blanc

Leon Trotsky was a central leader of the 1917 Russian Revolution, one of the founders of modern Communism and the Soviet state, as well as the central organizer and leader of the victorious Red Army during the Russian civil war (1918–22). He was also among those who fought against the degeneration of that revolution and movement brought on by the bureaucratic dictatorship led by Joseph Stalin. Trotsky himself – amid the difficult civil war years – had been in the forefront of advancing authoritarian policies that he and other revolutionaries had defended as necessary emergency measures to protect the early Soviet Republic. But by 1924 he was in the forefront of the struggle against the authoritarianism that was overwhelming the revolution's original goals.

While judged very severely by many who disagreed with him, his example and ideas have profoundly influenced successive generations of labor and socialist activists – but also scholars engaging with issues with which Trotsky dealt: dynamics of global history and world politics; the evolution of the USSR; the nature of bureaucracy; strategy and tactics of the labor movement; military theory and practicalities; questions of art, literature and philosophy; and more. His most influential works include *The History of the Russian Revolution*, offering a panoramic and detailed account of the overthrow of Russia's oppressive old order through the democratic and working-class insurgencies of 1917, and *The Revolution Betrayed*, an analysis of how the promising revolution was overcome through the crystallization of the Stalin regime.[1]

Biography

Lev Davidovich Bronstein was born in the Ukraine, then part of the Russian Empire, and in revolutionary movement adopted the underground name "Trotsky." He became known for his eloquence as a writer, but also as an orator – qualities inseparable from his role as a political activist. The scope of his thought and activism became quintessentially global.[2]

At the age of eighteen Trotsky first become active in the revolutionary socialist movement in the Russian Empire, and he was soon drawn to the revolutionary Marxist current around the newspaper *Iskra*, initiated by Vladimir Ilyich Lenin, George Plekhanov and Julius Martov. Initially close to Lenin, he broke with him when the newly reformed Russian Social Democratic Labor Party (RSDLP) split into Bolshevik and Menshevik factions in 1903, lining up with the anti-Leninist Mensheviks.

In the course of the revolutionary upsurge of 1905, in which he played a central role, Trotsky developed the theory of permanent revolution, which caused him to become independent of the Mensheviks in the complex factional line-up in the RSDLP. Although in some ways drawing closer to Lenin's Bolsheviks, he was a firm partisan of RSDLP unity and sharply opposed the creation of a separate Bolshevik party in 1912. With the outbreak of the First World War, he played a major role in organizing an international anti-war opposition made up of a diverse grouping of socialists from various countries gathered at a conference in Zimmerwald, Switzerland.

When the Russian Tsar was overthrown in February/March 1917 by a semi-spontaneous workers' uprising, Trotsky was living in exile in the United States. Hurrying back to Russia, he found that his thinking converged with that of Lenin: both favored a second revolution of workers and peasants to replace the coalition of pro-capitalist liberals and moderate socialists with a revolutionary socialist regime based on democratic councils (soviets). He joined Lenin's party, quickly becoming a central figure. With Lenin, he was a central leader of the October/November 1917 revolution, the organizer and leader of the Red Army that defended the early Soviet Republic in the face of civil war and foreign invasions, and a founder and leader of the Communist International.

In the 1920s, after Lenin's death (1924), Trotsky became one of the foremost defenders of the original ideas and ideals of the 1917 Revolution and of the early Communist movement against the bureaucratic regime that increasingly overwhelmed them. The left opposition that Trotsky helped lead was decisively defeated in 1927, and Trotsky found himself again in exile – first in Turkey, then Norway and France, and finally Mexico.

From exile, Trotsky labored to explain the meaning of the Russian Revolution and its bureaucratic degeneration. Warning against the failure of Communists and Socialists to form a united front against the rise of Hitler in Germany, he also distinguished himself, from 1936 onward, in exposing the crescendo of political repression, and the public "purge trials" of leading Communists orchestrated by the Stalin regime, following the 1935 assassination of Leningrad Communist leader Sergei Kirov. In 1938, he helped organize the Fourth International, made up of small revolutionary groups in various countries. He was assassinated by an agent of the Stalin regime two years later.

Trotsky's Marxism

In addition to an intensive study of Marx and Engels, Trotsky was influenced – as were all Russian Marxists – by George Plekhanov, Pavel Axelrod and Karl Kautsky, but also by the Hegelian-Marxist philosopher Antonio Labriola. He worked closely in the early 1900s with Alexander Helphand (Parvus), and was also influenced by the views of Rosa Luxemburg, among others, yet for the final two decades of his life he was especially influenced by Marxist perspectives associated with Lenin.

Defining features of Trotsky's thought included his development of the theory of uneven and combined development and the related theory of permanent revolution. These provided a distinctive orientation for socialist revolution in what would later be termed "under-developed countries" but ultimately in countries throughout the world. Central to this orientation was an understanding of revolutionary internationalism – seeing the global political economy, and consequently the fates and struggles of all working classes and oppressed peoples, as indissolubly interlinked.

These perspectives guided Trotsky and others in the making of the October Revolution of 1917. They were also evident in the founding and development of the Communist International (Third International) in 1919–22, within which (along with Lenin and others) Trotsky blended the struggle for reforms and the struggle for revolution through application of the united front tactic. Such perspectives were central to Trotsky's increasingly profound critique, from 1923 onward, of the bureaucratic degeneration within the Soviet Republic. This was also inseparable from Trotsky's exposure of and opposition to what he saw as the poisonous and murderous characteristics of Stalinism as reflected in the Moscow trials and massive repression in the Soviet Union in the late 1930s.

Beginning in the 1920s Trotsky also contributed to the development of a Marxist analysis of fascism – particularly the version that arose in Germany represented by Adolf Hitler's Nazi movement, which came to power in 1933. His views on how best to prevent or defeat the victory of fascism, were related to the united front perspectives that he, Lenin, and others had advanced in the early years of the Communist International. He opposed this to what he perceived as the sectarian refusal in 1930–34 by affiliates of the Communist International to build working-class united fronts to resist the rise of Hitler; he later sharply criticized what he viewed as the Communist International's class-collaborationist "People's Front" policy of 1935–39. Each of these very different orientations, advanced one after the other under Stalin's leadership, contained built-in dynamics of defeat, Trotsky insisted.

Trotsky, resistant to the conversion of his ideas into a dogmatic "orthodoxy," insisted that political perspectives must be based on "facts throwing light on the real situation and not of general formulas that might be applied equally well to Paris or Honolulu" (Trotsky 1974, 58). At the same time, his analyses of 20th-century developments, and his strategic and tactical orientation, would prove to be powerfully influential on multiple continents.

Uneven and Combined Development and Permanent Revolution

According to Trotsky, there is an obvious and simple law of history that has profoundly important consequences. This is the law of uneven development: different areas and different countries are just that – different. While all of Europe had been dominated by some variety of feudalism, and while all of Europe was affected by the development of the capitalist market, the different regions had their own particular characteristics. For various reasons, technological and cultural and ideological innovations arose first in one area and then had an impact on other areas at different times – leading to uneven development in the history of Europe as a whole. Trotsky argued that this "general law" of *unevenness* in the historical process led to another "general law" – *combined development*, a drawing together of different historical stages, "an amalgam of archaic with more contemporary forms" (Trotsky 2017, 5).

Uneven and combined development guaranteed that the dynamics of the bourgeois-democratic revolution, and the transition to a capitalist social order, would be quite different in other parts of Europe and the world than had been the case in France at the end of the 18th century. This framed the conceptualization of the theory of permanent revolution, which Trotsky first articulated as an approach for the peculiarities of Russia, but which he later concluded had relevance for the rest of the world.

The rise and industrial development of capitalism has done three things – according to both Marx and Trotsky. First, there was a process sometimes known as "primitive accumulation," which involved a horrific and murderous displacement and oppression and brutal exploitation of masses of peasants and indigenous peoples on a global scale. Second, there has been a massive process of proletarianization – making a majority of the labor force and population into a modern working class (those whose livelihood is dependent on selling their ability to work, their labor-power, for wages). This working-class majority is the force that has the potential power, and the objective self-interest, to replace the economic dictatorship of capitalism with the economic democracy of socialism – and the awareness of all this is what Marxists mean when they speak of workers' *class-consciousness*. Third, the spectacular technological development generated by capitalism – the ever self-renewing Industrial Revolution – creates the material basis for a new socialist society.

> As Marx put it in 1845, the creation of this high level of productivity and wealth "is an absolutely necessary practical premise [for communism] because without it want is generalized, and with want the struggle for necessities begins again," generating a competition for who gets what, and then "all the old crap" starts all over again.
>
> *(Trotsky 1937, 56; see* MECW *5: 49)*

Drawing from Marx, Trotsky and a growing number of his Russian comrades came to see the coming revolution in backward Russia in this way. The democratic struggle against the semi-feudal Tsarist autocracy would only be led consistently and through to the end by the small but growing Russian working class in alliance with the peasant majority – and the success of such a revolution would place the organizations of the working class into political power. There would be a natural push to keep moving in a socialist direction (with expanding social improvements for the masses of people) – although the socialism that Marx had outlined and that the Russian workers were fighting for could not be created in a single backward country.[3]

But a successful Russian revolution would help push forward revolutionary struggles in other countries, and as these revolutions were successful – especially in industrially more advanced countries such as Germany, France, Italy and Britain – the Russian workers and peasants could join with comrades in a growing number of countries to development of a global socialist economy that would replace capitalism and create a better life and better future for the world's laboring majority. This is why Lenin, Trotsky and their comrades labored to draw revolutionaries and insurgent workers from all around the world into the Communist International, to help advance this necessary world revolutionary process for international socialism: because socialism cannot triumph if it is not global.

Analysis of Stalinism

Trotsky's analysis clearly emerges from the fundamental analysis of Karl Marx eighty years earlier. It is also inseparable from the basics of his own theory of permanent revolution.

But the anticipated revolutions in other countries were not successful, and seven years of relative isolation – with military invasions, foreign trade boycotts, civil war and economic collapse, and other hardships – had three results. First, the projected government by democratic councils (soviets) of workers and peasants was delayed as the overwhelming social-political-economic emergency brought about what was originally seen as a temporary dictatorship by the Communist Party. Second, a massive bureaucratic apparatus crystallized in order to run the country and administer the economy. As Trotsky would later explain in *The Revolution Betrayed*, when there aren't enough necessities to go around, there is rationing and people

> are compelled to stand in line. When the lines are very long, it is necessary to appoint a policeman to keep order. Such is the starting point of the power of the Soviet bureaucracy. It "knows" who is to get something and who has to wait.
>
> *(Trotsky 1937, 112)*

While some of the Communists remained absolutely dedicated to the original ideals and perspectives that had been the basis for the 1917 revolution, there were many who became corrupted or compromised or disoriented. Stalin was a central figure in the increasingly authoritarian bureaucratic apparatus, and along with the brilliant but disoriented Nikolai Bukharin, he dis-attached the idea of socialism not only from democracy, but also from the revolutionary internationalism that is at the heart of Marxism, advancing the notion of building socialism in a single country – the Soviet Union. Trotsky and his co-thinkers denounced this notion as "a skinflint reactionary utopia of self-sufficient socialism, built on a low technology," incapable of bringing about genuine socialism (Trotsky 1970b, 45–46). Instead, "all the old crap" would start all over again.

But it was Stalin who won this battle, fiercely repressing Trotsky and the left opposition. Unlike an eventual majority of Oppositionists who renounced their beliefs in a vain hope of remaining relevant to future developments and possible struggles in the Communist Party and the USSR, Trotsky and a hardcore of co-thinkers refused to capitulate to Stalin. Trotsky himself was expelled from the Soviet Union in 1929, and most of the hardcore were sent to forced labor camps and eventually executed in the late 1930s.

Bukharin and others had envisioned building their "socialism in one country" slowly and more or less humanely, but they were outmaneuvered and smashed politically by Stalin and those around him who decided to initiate a so-called revolution from above – a forced collectivization of the land and rapid, authoritarian industrialization process (all at the expense of the peasant and worker majority) to modernize Russia in the name of "socialism in one country." Peasant resistance was dealt with brutally, and famine resulted. Worker resistance was also savagely repressed. All critical discussion in the Communist Party was banned. All independent and creative thought and expression – in education, art, literature, culture – throughout the country gave way to authoritarian norms that celebrated the policies and personality of Stalin.

Although claiming that the modernization policies they oversaw added up to socialism, and that they were the loyal and rightful heirs of Lenin and the 1917 revolution, Stalin and his functionaries in the increasingly massive bureaucratic apparatus enjoyed an accumulation of material privileges, with authority and a lifestyle that placed them far above the majority of the people. As Trotsky put it,

> it is useless to boast and ornament reality. Limousines for the "activists" [that is, the bureaucrats], fine perfumes for "our women" [that is, wives of the bureaucrats], margarine for the workers, stores "de luxe" for the gentry, a look at delicacies through the store windows for the plebs – such socialism cannot but seem to the masses a new re-facing of capitalism, and they are not far wrong. On a basis of "generalized want," the struggle for the means of subsistence threatens to resurrect "all the old crap," and is partially resurrecting it at every step.
>
> *(Trotsky 1937, 120)*

Despite the unending pseudo-revolutionary propaganda, and positive improvements in economic and social opportunities for some workers, there was widespread suffering and dissatisfaction within the population. Many in the USSR remembered the democratic and egalitarian ideals of the revolutionary cause and some remained committed to these. Dissident Communists who had capitulated to Stalin, and even some who had supported him, were deemed untrustworthy by the regime. Such dynamics finally exploded in the late 1930s – with many of Lenin's old comrades accused of treason, forced to confess in public show trials, and executed. Hundreds of thousands more veteran Communists were denounced, arrested, and either shot or sent to forced labor camps, where many died under horrific conditions.

Some of Trotsky's followers in various countries broke with him over the best way to analyze such developments. Some claimed that Stalin's USSR simply represented a form of capitalism (*state capitalism*), while others insisted that it was a new form of class society (*bureaucratic collectivism*). Trotsky insisted, however, that it was a *degenerated workers' state*. By this he meant that it still retained some positive features: a nationalized, planned economy, with certain social gains still worth defending. He added, however, that such things could only be defended if the working class carried out a political revolution.[4]

"It is not a question of substituting one ruling clique for another, but of changing the very methods of administering the economy and guiding the culture of the country," Trotsky explained. "Bureaucratic autocracy must give place to Soviet democracy." This must involve freedom of expression, multiple parties, free elections and genuine democracy in the workplaces and in the soviets (Trotsky 1937, 289).

A failure to rescue revolutionary Russia through working-class democratization and the spread of socialist revolution to other countries, he predicted, would eventually ensure the collapse of the Soviet Union and the re-establishment of capitalism, to the detriment of a majority of the people there.

Fascism and the Triumph of Hitler

For Trotsky, the global economic devastation of the Great Depression set the stage for the playing out of what Rosa Luxemburg had predicted amid the First World War – either workers' revolutions in various countries bringing humanity forward to a socialist future, or a downward slide into barbarism, represented by extreme authoritarianism and the murderous destruction of a Second World War. Fascism represented such extreme authoritarianism, the rise of its most virulent form, Nazism in Germany, which Trotsky explained by tracing several convergent developments.

Nazism's growing mass base came largely from what Trotsky viewed as "petty bourgeois" layers: farmers, shopkeepers, civil servants, white-collar employees who did not want to be "proletarianized" and were becoming increasingly desperate for an alternative to the grim status quo and the deepening economic crisis. They, and some "backward" layers of the working class, were for various reasons alienated from the "Marxism" associated with both the massive German Communist Party and the even more massive Social-Democratic Party rooted in majority sectors of the country's working class. Elements from these alienated social sectors were drawn to a plebeian movement steeped in the ideological witch's brew of super-patriotic nationalism and racism prevalent in much of late 19th-century and early 20th-century Germany, blended with vague anti-capitalist rhetoric and fierce anti-Semitism.

The Nazis drew considerable material support from substantial elements within the upper classes (aristocrats, financiers, industrialists) who detested Social Democrats and trade unions and who genuinely feared the possibility, particularly with the devastating economic downturn, of the sort of Communist revolution that had triumphed in Russia a dozen years before. The mass political movement the Nazis were building provided a counter-weight and ultimately a battering ram to smash the Marxist threat.

An essential ingredient in the growth of Nazi mass appeal was the failure of the major parties of the working-class left to provide a revolutionary solution to the problems afflicting society – the Social-Democrats thanks to the reformist and opportunistic moderation of their own bureaucratic leaders, the Communists thanks initially to their woeful inexperience, later compounded by the sectarian blunders of early 1930s Stalinism, which denounced all left-wing forces not in the Communist International as "social-fascists" who were more dangerous than Hitler.

To the extent that left-wing organizations and parties proved ineffective and impotent, Trotsky argued, petty bourgeois layers will be vulnerable to fascist appeals, drawing the more conservative layers of the working class along with them – which is exactly what was happening in regard to the Nazi movement, as masses of Germans were attracted by Hitler's sweeping authoritarian certainties. According to Trotsky, history had shown (for example, in 1917) the extent to which revolutionary vanguard layers of the working class were able to mobilize the working class as a whole into effective struggles going in a socialist direction, growing elements of the petty bourgeoisie would be drawn leftward.

Revolutionary Strategy and Tactics

Trotsky's call in the early 1930s for a *united front* of Social-Democrats and Communists (as well as the dissident fractions of each) in Germany drew on a conceptualization to which the Communist International of the early 1920s had been won by Lenin, Trotsky himself and others – a tactical approach that was integrally connected to a revolutionary strategy. This notion was based in an understanding that the organized working class, although divided between reformists and revolutionaries, could defend and advance its interests through a fighting unity, the united front. Within this context the revolutionaries, as the most effective fighters, could ultimately win the adherence of a working-class majority.

This dynamic had played out in Russia in 1917, when a coup attempt by the reactionary General Kornilov in August was defeated by united working-class action, in the course of which the effective and militant Bolsheviks won predominant influence within the working class. That, in turn, had set the stage for the socialist revolution of October 1917. "Should the Communist Party be compelled to apply the policy of the united front, this will almost certainly make it possible to beat off the fascist attack," Trotsky argued. "In its own turn, a serious victory over fascism will clear the road for the dictatorship of the proletariat" – that is, for the working class to take political power and initiate a transition to socialism (Trotsky 1971, 97–98, 254).

In addition to breaking the Nazi threat and bringing a revolutionary transition in Germany, such a revolutionary development would likely generate similar revolutionary upsurges and transitions elsewhere, and by ending the USSR's isolation, thereby also helping to overcome the influence of Stalinism there and in the world Communist movement. In addition to pushing aside the twin tyrannies of Hitlerism and Stalinism, the question is naturally raised whether such developments might have prevented the Second World War.

Beginning in 1935, the world Communist movement under Stalin announced that the primary task was to push back fascism and prevent a new world war by forming far-reaching alliances (including coalition governments) between Socialists and Communists and pro-capitalist liberals – under the banner of "the People's Front." Trotsky argued this made incoherent any pretense at Marxist analysis, insisting that it could not realize its own stated goals of stopping fascism and war. In France and Spain, such governments were established. The problem with this, according to Trotsky, was that fascism arose out of the crises of capitalism, just as imperialism and war arise out of the natural dynamics of capitalism. To preserve the unity of the People's Front, it was necessary to repress the uncompromising militancy of the working-class struggles – but this was the force needed to end both capitalism and the threat of fascism.

In seeking to develop what he termed a *transitional program* that could guide revolutionaries as the 1930s gave way to the 1940s, Trotsky outlined three sectors of world revolution – the advanced capitalist countries, the degenerated workers' state, and the less developed countries exploited and oppressed by imperialism (Trotsky 1977). In each he sought to identify immediate, practical economic struggles and democratic struggles in which masses of laboring and oppressed peoples could struggle uncompromisingly for their interests around demands with revolutionary implications, forming a transition from an oppressive status quo to a liberating socialist future.

Trotsky has become a particularly important figure in the Marxist pantheon. This is in part because he represents a heroic vision thanks to his role in leading the Russian Revolution and his lonely struggle against its degeneration. But his theoretical contributions were also very significant. Trotsky's perspectives are inseparable from those of Marx and Engels, Luxemburg, Lenin and others. Yet within the evolving Marxist tradition, different revolutionaries came to certain insights and clarifications before others. Various theorists also gave a distinctive articulation to certain ideas: Gramsci's discussion of "hegemony" and Luxemburg's description of the "mass strike," as well as Lenin's insights on the "revolutionary party" and on the "worker-peasant alliance," are a few of the examples that come to mind. Trotsky's "permanent revolution" perspective certainly belongs in this category. Also, unlike the others mentioned, Trotsky lived as late as 1940, which enabled him to make certain contributions not allowed to them. What sociologist C. Wright Mills once said of Marx's ideas also seems relevant to those of Trotsky: "To study his work today and then come back to our own concerns is to increase our chances of confronting them with useful ideas and solutions" (Mills 1962, 35).

Notes

1. Chattopadhyay (2006), Hallas (2003) and Knei-Paz (1980).
2. Trotsky (1970a), Deutscher (2015) and Le Blanc (2015).
3. Trotsky (1969), Löwy (1981) and Dunn and Radice (2006).
4. Twiss (2015) and Van der Linden (2009).

Bibliography

Chattopadhyay, Kunal. 2006. *The Marxism of Leon Trotsky*. Kolkata: Progress.
Deutscher, Isaac. 2015. *The Prophet: The Life of Leon Trotsky*. London: Verso.
Dunn, Bill, and Hugo Radice, eds. 2006. *100 Years of Permanent Revolution: Results and Prospects*. London: Pluto Press.
Hallas, Duncan. 2003. *Trotsky's Marxism and Other Essays*. Chicago: Haymarket.
Knei-Paz, Baruch. 1980. *The Social and Political Thought of Leon Trotsky*. Oxford: Oxford University Press.
Le Blanc, Paul. 2015. *Leon Trotsky*. London: Reaktion Books.
Löwy, Michael. 1981. *The Politics of Combined and Uneven Development: Trotsky's Theory of Permanent Revolution*. London: Verso.
Mills, C. Wright. 1962. *The Marxists*. New York: Dell.
Trotsky, Leon. 1937. *The Revolution Betrayed*. Garden City, NY: Doubleday, Doran and Co.
Trotsky, Leon. 1969. *Permanent Revolution, and Results and Prospects*. New York: Merit Publishers.
Trotsky, Leon. 1970a. *My Life, an Attempt at an Autobiography*. New York: Pathfinder Press.
Trotsky, Leon. 1970b. *The Third International After Lenin*. New York: Pathfinder Press.
Trotsky, Leon. 1971. *The Struggle against Fascism in Germany*. New York: Pathfinder Press.
Trotsky, Leon. 1974. "Summary of the Discussion." In *Writings of Leon Trotsky, 1934–35*, edited by George Breitman and Bev Scott, 58–64. New York: Pathfinder Press.
Trotsky, Leon. 1977. *The Transitional Program for Socialist Revolution*. New York: Pathfinder Press.
Trotsky, Leon. 2017 (1930). *The History of the Russian Revolution*. London: Penguin.
Twiss, Thomas M. 2015. *Trotsky and the Problem of Soviet Bureaucracy*. Chicago: Haymarket.
Van der Linden, Marcel. 2009. *Western Marxism and the Soviet Union*. Chicago: Haymarket.

10
AMADEO BORDIGA (1889–1970)[1]

Pietro Basso

The imposing figure of Amadeo Bordiga passes through two completely different periods of both 20th-century and communist movement history. The leader of the Communist Party of Italy (*Partito Comunista d'Italia*, PCd'I) and an influential member of the Third International, Bordiga was center stage in the period starting with the great carnage of World War I and culminating in the revolutionary cycle triggered by the October Revolution. An even more devastating world war inaugurated the second period of Bordiga's activity – a time characterized by a strong and sustained capitalist development. Bordiga had a marginal political role then, but he carried out a deep and original reconstruction of Marxist revolutionary thought. Albeit still little known, or very much misinterpreted by bitterly hostile Stalinists, Bordiga's work made its mark on 20th-century and communist movement history.

The Fight Against Reformism (1911–20)

Bordiga was born on 13 June 1889 in Resina, near Naples, from a half-aristocratic and half-bourgeois family. He was only a twenty-one-year-old engineering student when he joined the Italian Socialist Party (*Partito Socialista Italiano*, PSI), founded in 1892. The context of his early political education was marked by a fundamental contradiction. Naples, just like the rest of Italy, was experiencing a state-supported swift industrialization leading to the growth of a politically involved new proletariat. But a sub-reformist leadership was affecting Neapolitan socialism – an extreme version of a national phenomenon. The local leadership dedicated themselves to electoral plotting with anti-socialist forces, and their freemason partners supported imperialist militarism.

Because of this contradiction, Bordiga and a few other comrades quit the local PSI Federation and found the Carlo Marx Revolutionary Socialist Circle on 2 April 1912. They studied Marx's thought while campaigning among industrial workers. They also took part in elections putting forward militant candidates who were devoted to the socialist cause and rejected any compromise with bourgeois parties. The Carlo Marx Circle dissolved only two years later – but not before obtaining the dissolution of the Naples Federation from the 1914 PSI Congress in Ancona as well as a declaration of incompatibility between socialism and freemasonry. The circle of Naples Marxists led by Bordiga got thus to be acknowledged across the country for both its theoretical force and political intransigence, and became a model to the Youth Socialist Federation.

Bordiga's relationship with the PSI at the national level was equally complicated. The beginning of the 20th century saw some influential figures like Turati, Treves, Kuliscioff and Bissolati shape a clear *reformist* agenda. Despite essentially sharing Bernstein's views, the PSI's reformists kept referring to socialism as the goal, however remote, of their actions. But what they actually meant by socialism was the *widening of democracy* within the limits of existing institutions. The class struggle was regarded as a *law-abiding peaceful* way of boosting this evolutionary process, with elections being the key events.

The young Bordiga rejected this view, but he remained for a decade in the PSI, as its rank and file included the most militant factory and farm workers. Following the 1911 Italo-Turkish war over Libya, an *intransigent tendency* appeared within the PSI, with Bordiga playing an active role in it. His tireless contribution proved crucial, eventually leading, some years later, to the programmatic and political foundation of the PSI Communist Abstentionist Fraction. Their targets were both reformism and the maximalist tendency led by Giacinto Menotti Serrati, which was critical of reformism and yet unable to separate from it. During this fight, Bordiga anchored his approach in the principles of Marxist communism. His internationalist conception of the class struggle was based on a constant monitoring of the international labor movement. In response to the collapse of the Second International at the outbreak of the First World War, Bordiga was to be among the first to call for a completely new international organization (Bordiga 1998, 257).

The political struggle that forged an Italian communist left fed itself off both the proletarian opposition to Italy joining World War I, the "Red Week" of June 1914, and the *biennio rosso* of 1919–20 – the widespread working class unrest at the end of the First World War that made Italian society teeter on the brink of insurrection. During those years, Bordiga and his comrades faced the sudden about-turn of the *Avanti!* chief-editor Benito Mussolini, who shifted his support from neutralism to interventionism in October 1914. They stuck resolutely to revolutionary defeatism even in the harsh atmosphere when Italy seemed to face military defeat in autumn 1917. They then opposed the law-abiding, conciliatory and corporatist agenda set out by union leaders and PSI MPs. The party – they claimed – came before unionism or parliamentary groups; and it had to foster social conflict with a view to preparing a socialist revolution, which alone can free the proletariat from class oppression.

Bordiga's group therefore welcomed the Russian revolution and spread its message. According to Bordiga, "the revolution has dealt a mighty blow to the *nationalist* conception of the war" because by crushing their own militarism the Russian proletarians have set an example and encouraged German proletarians to follow in their steps. Moreover, "while everybody was leaving it for dead," socialism had proved to be very much alive. On 28 February 1918, Bordiga wrote that from "free Russia," where a double revolution had occurred, socialism was delivering an international message that concerns the capitalist order at world level: "The International Social Revolution is on the agenda of History" (Bordiga 1998, 411–25).

The struggle against reformism came to a climax that shook up the PSI. Reflecting the popularity of soviet power among the working classes, the party chose to join the Third International in 1919. The communist fraction and Bordiga wrongly believed they could get the PSI maximalist majority to cut the umbilical cord with the reformists. In Bordiga's view, the Bolsheviks had won thanks to their intransigence toward both bourgeois parties and "socialist fractions," and that was a model to follow. But the majority of the PSI were reluctant to burn their bridges with reformists; they were stuck with uncertainty in the face of that historical turning point.

There is some evidence contradicting the common belief that Bordiga was doctrinaire, sectarian and distant from workers' feelings. First, he knew that his group was bound to split from the PSI, and yet spared no effort to make Serrati's maximalists come over to his side, while actively tightening links with militant proletarians, including rural workers. Second, Bordiga was convinced that taking part in elections collided with preparing a revolution, and yet he accepted the Third International's policy of rejecting abstentionism. Third, Bordiga believed that the Turin group *Ordine Nuovo* led by Antonio Gramsci was workerist and idealist in nature, and yet worked to have them participate in the foundation of the new Communist Party (PCd'I).

Bordiga, the PCd'I and the Third International (1921–26)

The new party was eventually born in Livorno in January 1921. As Bordiga pointed out, *it was born late*, that is to say, after the revolutionary process reached its peak in Russia and Europe. As for Italy, by the time the PCd'I saw the light of day, class struggle was falling away while the fascist movement was growing stronger and stronger, and was about to crush the newborn Party. However, the PCd'I was not insignificant at all as a political force. It boasted over 42,000 members in 1921, most of whom were maximalist left-wing proletarians who had streamed into the PSI during the 1919–20 period. During the succeeding years of gathering reaction (1921–23), Bordiga's energetic leadership worked to turn this party's rank-and-file into a cohesive and centralized organization that rejected all personal scheming and groupism, and proved able to defend itself physically from fascism's assaults.

Another remarkable feature of the Bordiga-led PCd'I was its active and critical participation in the Third International (which Lenin personally encouraged: Pannunzio 1921, 13–14). No other West European Communist party asked so resolutely that the International actually led the revolutionary struggle of the working class across all countries. However, it was in this troubled relationship with the Third International leadership that the young Italian left showed its weaknesses. Its approach was firmly anchored in Marxist principles, and yet failed properly to inspire the *actual* political action of the party. The Italian left Communists did not have an in-depth understanding of how workers' struggles were developing, which translated into a somewhat crude use of tactics. The same applies to their theoretical and practical approach to the question of the Comintern tactic of the "united front" with the social democratic parties, which they interpreted only as "unity in the trade unions" without any "political united front." This "rigid" approach, however, stemmed from the vital need of the newborn Communist Party to disentangle itself from a maximalist mishmash systematically watering down revolutionary principles and practice. The PCd'I leaders had rapidly to provide political training to young militants who had just turned to the communist perspective. Similarly, they displayed a "rigid" attitude toward international politics, fearing that Moscow's excessive tactical flexibility would harm the Third International's strategy and basic principles, as eventually happened.

1923 was Bordiga's and his comrades' *annus terribilis*. The fascist "witch-hunt" of Communists started, and Bordiga spent most of the year in prison. This is also when the International dissolved the PCd'I's Executive Committee in a *coup de force*, accusing it of fatally hindering fusion with the PSI. While the Mussolini regime was suppressing the party's press, state repression, political firings, rocketing unemployment and fascist aggressions were wiping out PCd'I's proletarian ranks. In this context, a three-year tense confrontation began between Bordiga and both Moscow and the new Gramsci-led PCd'I leadership. The latter eventually prevailed and marginalized Bordiga. The Lyon Congress of January 1926 brought about an almost complete re-foundation of the PCd'I. At the following Enlarged Plenum of the Comintern's Executive Committee (ECCI), February 1926, Bordiga *alone* stood up to the overall Comintern policy, driven by the principle of "socialism in one country."

At the time of the Lyon Congress the working-class movement and the left wing of the International were losing ground dramatically. The whole European proletariat had already been defeated despite its valiant efforts in Hungary, Germany, Italy and Bulgaria. In Moscow, Stalin and Bukharin had already prevailed over the "United Opposition" of Zinoviev, Kamenev and Trotsky. In Lyon, the new centrist PCd'I majority made some heavy accusations against Bordiga's leadership, which, they argued, failed to prevent the victory of fascism because of their sectarian view and the refusal of the "united front." Bordiga's leadership was then blamed for being unable to analyze real social facts and power relations between classes. Allegedly, it could not tell a reactionary situation from a democratic one, and took a pedagogical and propagandistic approach to political action. Bordiga's seven-hour speech in reply was equally robust. The new leadership's "opportunist" course, he argued, was "poisoning" the party, paving the way to its "disintegration and degeneration"; the leadership refused to realize that the democratic bourgeoisie helped bring fascism into power; they shirked the leadership responsibility of the party by following proletarians' temporarily low mood; they addressed all rural producers indiscriminately instead of talking to farm laborers first; they subjected the minority to a humiliating discipline (Peregalli and Saggioro 1998, 83 ff.).

At the Sixth Enlarged Plenum of the ECCI in Moscow, Bordiga was even more marginalized, and once again responded with what E.H. Carr called a "powerful, though solitary, assault" (Carr 1964, 502) on the triumphant Stalinist leadership of the Russian party and the Third International. Bordiga addressed them with a fundamental question of principle, with crucial practical consequences: who is entitled to talk and make decisions about the perspectives of socialism in Russia – the Russian party alone, or the whole International? Only a few days before the Bolshevik leadership had requested that other delegates should not raise the "Russian question." Bordiga had a memorable verbal crossfire with Stalin during the meeting with the Italian delegates, and gave an equally memorable speech at the ECCI's Plenum. He asked Stalin some awkward questions about the workers' opposition in Leningrad, the concessions to middle peasants, the campaign against Trotsky, and Stalin's disagreement with Lenin over crucial issues. To top it off, Bordiga asked the Russian leader what would happen in Russia if no revolution broke out in Europe for some time. To Bordiga, Russian issues were not "inherently Russian"; they were the business of the international Communist movement instead. Consequently, the International as a whole should have made decisions about these issues.

Bordiga's 23 February speech at the ECCI's Plenum expanded on this point, as he now criticized the entire International's politics as well as its role in the Russian party. He argued "The great experience of the Russian party is invaluable indeed, and yet we need *something more besides*"; that is, the knowledge of the conditions for "demolishing the capitalist, liberal and parliamentary state" in the advanced countries, since the modern democratic state can defend itself better than the authoritarian ones, and it is *far more effective* in making proletarians turn to opportunism. Defeating such a strong, experienced enemy as the European democratic bourgeoisies requires *more than the mere* existence of Communist parties, which – Bordiga argued – had then to "rally huge masses around them." In sum, while agreeing on the theses of the Third Comintern Congress in 1921 that had mapped out a strategy based on using the united front tactic, he rejected their tactical applications because they harmed the "specific nature" of Communist parties thereby weakening their capacity of conquering the masses. Bordiga also criticized the influence affecting decision-making in Russia of middle peasants and *nepmen* exploiting the new market mechanisms introduced in 1921, and claimed that all Comintern sections should take part in the debate over the future of the Russian revolution, also on account of the growing pressure of world capitalism against it. Bordiga therefore condemned the "bolshevization" of the Communist parties as a pretentious attempt to replant the "Russian model" everywhere. He also criticized the underlying idea that there was such a thing as an organizational formula for "solving the problem of revolution." Finally, in Bordiga's opinion both the appearance of factions within the Comintern and the mounting insubordination against it were not the cause but rather the symptom of a severe crisis, and the Comintern's resorting to humiliation and violence – a true and not in the least revolutionary "reign of terror" – would only make things worse (Peregalli and Saggioro 1998, 119).

After 1945: Against Both "State Marxism" and Financial-Thermonuclear Imperialism

On 20 November 1926 Bordiga was arrested and placed in confinement in Ustica with dozens of other PCd'I members, including Gramsci. He was then transferred for some months to Palermo prison to be eventually put back in confinement in Ponza until 1929. In March 1930, he was expelled from the party for "factionalism" and for "supporting, defending and embracing the Trotskyist opposition." In 1937, the Communist leader Palmiro Togliatti wrote, in unforgettable prose, that "Bordiga is now living in Italy as a Trotskyist skunk protected by the police and by fascists, and hated by workers in the way that a traitor has to be hated" (Togliatti 1972b, 29, 36). Actually, Bordiga was expelled from the professional register of engineers by the fascists and could therefore not run his own firm. From 1929 to the end of the 1960s, he lived modestly, practicing his profession "with great civil courage and technical competence," exposing "the disastrous Neapolitan urbanistic policy" (Gerosa 2006, 9). Bordiga had already quit political activity by the time of his expulsion from the PCd'I. He would live in voluntary seclusion until the end of 1944, turning down Karl Korsch's invitation to coordinate with other left-wing communists across Europe as well as all invitations to leave Italy. Nor would he remotely join in the political work of his comrades from the left, who had fled in exile to France and Belgium, and had founded the group called the Fraction and the journals *Prometeo* and *Bilan*. At first Bordiga believed there was a chance to get the International back on track, which meant waiting, but then he persuaded himself that a *historic* defeat had occurred, which required much meditation.

This was not without consequences. Bordiga's separation from both the proletarian movement and the sparse groups challenging Stalinist and social-democratic hegemony seriously affected the political organizational work he eventually resumed in the second postwar period. Compared with the years 1911–26, a much wider gap appeared between theory and organizational work as well as between program and political intervention. The weakness of the theoretical work Bordiga did in the postwar period lies in the very conception of the class-party relationship: the party acquired such a dominant and equally abstract role, in fact, that the reality of class just disappeared. According to Bordiga, for instance, "the party is the only remaining actual organ that defines the class, fights for the class, will rule for the sake of the class in due course and sets up the end of all governments and classes" (Bordiga 1953a, *passim*),[2] as though the party was a demiurge that molds the class and the revolutionary process.

However, the forced isolation from industrial proletarians the Italian communist left had to suffer after World War II may well account for Bordiga's views on the party. Meanwhile, the Communist Party (now the *Partito Comunista Italiano*, PCI) was becoming the mass party of the Italian working class. But, as Togliatti put it in 1944, the "new party" was now conceived as a "*national* Italian party" that had to deal with the "problem of the emancipation of labor within the frame of our national freedom and life," in order to make the "the salvation, the resurrection of Italy" come true (Togliatti 1972a, 69–70). This reformist and socio-nationalist party scrupulously thwarted all attempts to spread revolutionary Marxism among the workers' movement. The PCI succeeded in that endeavor quite easily because of the general improvement in workers' living conditions and the extension of democratic rights, which, however, was also achieved thanks to workers' fights. Albeit partially and temporarily, there actually was an "integration" of the working masses within the democratic institutions.

Bordiga's theoretical and political weaknesses does not detract from the value of the theoretical work he carried out throughout the second postwar period with the help of a few Italian and French comrades (Bruno Maffi, Giuliano Bianchini, Ottorino Perrone, Susanne Voute as well as Jacques Camatte and Roger Dangeville during Bordiga's last years). The essence of Bordiga's work in this period lies in a *fresh return to the critique of political economy*, that is, a Marxist-based analysis of the evolution of contemporary capitalism, which addresses, more particularly, the "socialist" USSR and US super-capitalism – the two cornerstones of the new world order. Moreover, and at the same time, Bordiga's analysis brings into focus the distinctive traits of socialism and communism – both disfigured by the triumphant march of anti-Marxist "state Marxism."

Bordiga wrote about the USSR on several occasions, animated as he was by the conviction that "Marxism is the theory of the counter-revolution." In other terms, Marxism is able to unravel the mystery of a revolution that got "crumpled" up, and eventually "vanished." Bordiga's research went beyond individual actors, specific Russian laws and institutions, and the ideological expressions of the counter-revolution. In his view, a "double-revolution" occurred in 1917 Russia; the nature of its state-capitalism is essentially capitalist, not socialist; the socio-economic structure of Stalin's Russia is that of "state capitalism mixed with private enterprise, whereas the latter develops by lessening the former"; the complex kolkhoz system prevailing in the countryside ultimately is a "sub-bourgeois formula," as production units are still "welded" to the institution of the family; rather than actually planning things, "Soviet-type economic planning" just records what has already happened, and it has nothing to do with socialism, because it relies on capitalist criteria like wages and profits, money and monetary accounting.

Bordiga's conclusion clearly echoes Marx's line of reasoning: one should not confuse capitalism with private property in the means of production. There may not be private property, or just a little of it. However, we do not get anywhere near to socialism when the production of goods and the reproduction of society embody the logic of the market, the wage relation and corporation: "the beast is the enterprise, and not the fact that someone owns it" – this is Bordiga's razor-sharp metaphor. Nor is socialism anywhere to be seen when dead labor dominates living labor, with a network of capitalist interests and groups operating within the country and tightening links with global market powers. All this has nothing to do with "popular socialism." This is about developing capitalism in Russia instead, and tackling its trend toward stagnation. Sooner or later, the protagonists would confess all (Bordiga 1976, 1990).

As for the US "world superpower," Bordiga carried out a well-documented and caustic analysis of that "plutocratic monster that keeps under its classic iron heel our proletarian comrades." Bordiga destroyed the image popular after 1945 of the US as the "hope for humanity" and the land of "people's capitalism." He anticipated where capitalism was actually going. The more capitalism becomes parasitic – he points out, the faster it "shifts from productive techniques to speculative maneuvers." The US is the emblem of this process. Armed with its massive money supply, the super-dollar and the monopoly of capital, it conquers the world, including Europe. Roughly hidden beneath a *façade* of "democratic issues," pacifism and calls for freedom, are the "imperial programs" of the most devastating militarism ever, a true monster-state.

This is what Bordiga calls the new "*financial-thermonuclear imperialism*." The new imperialism, he argued, will not necessarily affect mass consumption, but will fail to narrow "the income inequality gap . . . between metropolises and colonial and vassal states, as well as between advanced industrial areas and backward agrarian areas, or those of primordial agriculture." Furthermore, *and* "*above all*," it will not be able to tackle the inequality gap "between social classes of the same country, including the one where the prince of imperial capitalism raises its slave-dealing banner." In other words, the US will not be able to eradicate any of their own historical scourges, starting with the condition of African Americans (Bordiga 1950).

Looking Forward

Bordiga thus gave a sharp portrait of the two universal models of capitalism peacefully competing with each other on the world stage while fruitlessly struggling with their insoluble internal antagonisms. In the postwar period, he also turned to the awakening of the peoples of the Global South. He had overlooked it in the 1920s, but in the early 1960s he wrote: "Perhaps the whirlwind march of our yellow and black brothers, which keeps increasing in pace and intensity, will make up for the half century we have lost" (Bordiga 1973, 53). This theoretical and historical research pursued tirelessly by Bordiga led him to envisage that a revolutionary scenario would unfold as early as the mid-1970s (Bordiga 1953b, 28–30).

He accordingly laid out a topical set of immediate revolutionary measures to be imposed in Western countries, involving reducing the share taken by investment goods in the total product and cutting overall production, "raising the costs of production" in order to pay higher wages for less labor-time, cutting the working day by at least half in order to absorb unemployment and antisocial activities, "authoritarian control of consumption" to combat advertising and consumerism, replacing commodified social security with support for non-workers, shifting construction in order to spread homes and workplaces more evenly across the countryside, attacking professional specialization, and subordinating education and the media to the communist state. Happily contrasting with his own self-portrait as a mere imitator of Marx fighting all innovators, Bordiga sketched out an *up-to-date* revolutionary program. This is a program for our times, unless "the common ruin of the contending classes" occurs. . . .

Notwithstanding his theoretical and political weaknesses, Amadeo Bordiga will be center stage in a still-to-come genuine history of the communist movement. Few Marxists have understood so deeply the international nature of both the proletarian revolution and the way to socialism. Even fewer realized so soon that Stalinism was leading to a complete distortion of the strategy and the program of the International. Almost no one has probably been able to depict so vividly the distinctive characteristics of the socialist and communist society. In addition, at a time when the "US model" was at its peak Bordiga unveiled the horrid traits of the new imperialism and the inherent link between democracy and militarism. Meanwhile, opposing "socialist" productivism he showed as early as the 1950s that Marx's and Marxist *critique* of political economy is from the outset an *ecological critique* of capitalism, as it brings into question nature's and the species' relation to capital, and not just the capital/wage labor relation.

Some historians have argued that Bordiga saw better far than near. If this is the case, then we should regard him as a revolutionary explorer of the 21st century.

Notes

1. Dedicated to the memory of Silvio Serino, who first introduced me to the figure of Amadeo Bordiga long ago. I would like to thank Roberto Taddeo for reviewing the first draft and his constructive criticism.
2. The idea of the "one-class, one-party revolution" is perplexing, as it assumes a "pure" revolutionary scenario in which proletarians fight alone against all non-proletarian classes.

Bibliography

Arfé, Gaetano. 1977. *Storia del socialismo italiano*. Milano: Mondadori.

Basso, Pietro, ed. 2020. *The Science and the Passion of Communism: Selected Writings of Amadeo Bordiga 1912–1965*. Leiden: Brill.

Bordiga. Amadeo. 1950. "Imperialismo 'vecchio' e 'nuovo.'" *Battaglia comunista* 3.

Bordiga. Amadeo. 1953a. "L'invarianza storica del marxismo, falsa risorsa dell'attivismo." *Sul filo del tempo* (May).

Bordiga, Amadeo. 1953b. "Il programma rivoluzionario immediato nell'Occidente capitalista." *Sul filo del tempo* (May).
Bordiga, Amadeo. 1970. *In difesa della continuità del programma comunista*. Milano: Edizioni il programma comunista.
Bordiga, Amadeo. 1973. *"L'estremismo malattia infantile del comunismo," condanna dei futuri rinnegati*. Milano: Edizioni il programma comunista.
Bordiga, Amadeo. 1976. *Struttura economica e sociale della Russia d'oggi*. Milano: Edizioni il programma comunista.
Bordiga, Amadeo. 1990. *Russia e rivoluzione nella teoria marxista*. Milano: Edizioni il programma comunista.
Bordiga, Amadeo. 1992. *America*. Torino: Editing.
Bordiga. Amadeo. 1998. *Scritti 1911–1926. La guerra, la rivoluzione russa e la nuova Internazionale 1914–1918*. Genova: Graphos.
Carr, Eduard H. 1964. *A History of Soviet Russia: Socialism in One Country 1924–1926*. London: MacMillan and Co.
Gerosa, Luigi. 2006. *L'ingegnere "fuori uso." Vent'anni di battaglie urbanistiche di Amadeo Bordiga. Napoli 1946–1966*. Presentazione di M. Fatica. Formia: Fondazione A. Bordiga.
Gramsci, Antonio. 1967. *Scritti politici*. Roma: Editori Riuniti.
Gramsci, Antonio. 1971. *La costruzione del partito comunista*. Torino: Einaudi.
Martinelli, Renzo. 1977. *Il Partito comunista d'Italia 1921–1926*. Roma: Editori Riuniti.
Pannunzio, Giovanni. 1921. *Ciò che ho visto nella Russia bolscevica (giugno-settembre 1920)*. Torino: Libreria editrice dell'Alleanza Cooperativa Torinese.
Peregalli, Arturo, and Sandro Saggioro. 1998. *Amadeo Bordiga. La sconfitta e gli anni oscuri (1926–1945)*, Milano: Colibrì.
Storia della sinistra comunista. Dal II al III Congresso dell'Internazionale Comunista: settembre 1920 – giugno 1921. 1986. Vol. 3. Milano: Edizioni il programma comunista.
Togliatti, Palmiro. 1972a. *Il partito*. Roma: Editori Riuniti.
Togliatti, Palmiro. 1972b. *Antonio Gramsci*. Roma: Editori Riuniti.

11
WALTER BENJAMIN (1892–1940)

Enzo Traverso

Walter Benjamin is generally associated with the tradition of Western Marxism, whose main features Perry Anderson depicted forty years ago in a famous essay: a privileged focus on philosophy and aesthetics rather than on economy, history and politics, as well as a "retreat" into a theoretical realm without any organic link with the workers' movement and the organized political left (Anderson 1976). Within the Frankfurt School in exile, to which Benjamin belonged as a marginal member, his position was certainly the most radical. Like Herbert Marcuse, he did not share the political resignation of the leading members of the Institute – Max Horkheimer and Theodor W. Adorno – who considered as ineluctable both universal reification and the advent of a totalitarian, "administered society." Instead of nourishing a pervasive skepticism toward class struggle, his criticism of instrumental reason carried palingenetic and revolutionary expectations whose primary source lay in messianic Judaism. Benjamin certainly was not the only Marxist thinker to emphasize the revolutionary potentialities of religion, but – thus prefiguring in some respects the Latin American Liberation Theology – he elaborated a kind of political theology grounded on a complete symbiosis between Marxism and messianic Judaism.

A Synthesis of Revolutionary Marxism and Jewish Messianism

If Benjamin's embrace of Marxism was not exceptional at all in inter-war Germany, especially for "pariah" Jewish intellectuals excluded from the Weimar academy, his trajectory was quite unique. During the First World War, he broke with the nationalism of most youth movement associations – he fled to Switzerland in order to avoid his conscription – but in 1918–19 he remained indifferent to the German and Hungarian revolutions, which he depicted as "childish aberrations." He came across Marxism only in 1924 thanks to Asja Lacis, a Latvian Communist he met in Capri, who introduced him to Bertolt Brecht and communist theory. More than Marx's writings, which he assimilated partially and superficially, the works that proved the most influential in shaping his reception of Marxism were probably György Lukács's *History and Class Consciousness* (1923), Karl Korsch's *Marxism and Philosophy* (1923) and Leon Trotsky's *History of Russian Revolution* (1930–32).

It is worth mentioning that Benjamin's discovery of Marxism did not produce any significant break in his intellectual itinerary. He integrated it into his own thought as a kind of theoretical and political layer that harmoniously joined two others already solidly rooted: romantic anti-capitalism and messianic Judaism. Shared by many German intellectuals of his generation, romantic anti-capitalism expressed a rejection of modernity as a mechanical civilization based on purely quantitative values, built on instrumental rationality, the enemy of any spirituality and finally imprisoning human life within a hostile world (a diagnostic summarized by the Weberian famous image of the "iron cage"). However, differently from the most widespread versions of *Kulturkritik* generally oriented toward "cultural pessimism," nationalism and political conservatism from Oswald Spengler to the Conservative Revolution, Benjamin's romantic anti-capitalism merged with messianic Judaism, focusing on the idea of community and leaning to redemptive hopes. Deeply influenced by the works of his friend Gershom Scholem, a historian of Kabbala who moved to Palestine in the mid-1920s, this religious current took an anarchist flavor and prepared Benjamin to embrace a Marxist form of political radicalism that, preserving its religious roots, distinguished him from the dominant trends of both Judaism (assimilated and politically conformist) and Marxism (rigorously atheistic). In 1929, he mentioned Franz Rosenzweig's *The Star of Redemption* (1921) and Lukács's *History and Class Consciousness* as two complementary books that "remained living," the second offering "the most organic and the most complete work of Marxist theory." In other words, Benjamin was at first indifferent and later increasingly opposed to any conception of Marxism as a "scientific" theory of economy, history and society. In his eyes, it was rather the accomplishment of a liberation's hope whose goals were essentially ethical and spiritual – an ideal of justice, community and fraternity – and transcended purely economic worries: socialism was not an economic necessity but answered an ancestral search of equality. What he found in Marxism was at the same time a "political practice" and "a binding attitude" (Benjamin 1994, 248).

As several critics emphasize, communism did not replace romantic and messianic anarchism in Benjamin's thought; they rather merged together, engendering a new and original configuration in which Jewish theology and secular Marxism coexisted, dialectically intermingled. In a letter to Scholem of 1926, he claimed this highly heterodox syncretism explaining that, in his view, "radical politics" (communism) finally worked "on behalf of Jewry" (Benjamin 1994, 301). Scholem defined this "dual identity" as Benjamin's "Janus face" (Scholem 1981, 209). In summarizing their conversation on the relationship between Marxism and Judaism, he synthesized the position of his friend in this way:

> He said that his Marxism still was not dogmatic but heuristic and experimental in nature, and that his transposition into Marxist perspectives of the metaphysical and even theological ideas he had developed in the [previous] years . . . was meritorious, because in that sphere they could become more active.
>
> *(Scholem 1981, 261)*

The final and most effective link between the two parts of his thought, Benjamin concluded, would have been supplied by the revolution itself.

Messianic Judaism conferred to this interpretation of Marxism an apocalyptic and eschatological dimension: social and political liberation through class struggle and socialist revolution posited by classical Marxism coincided with messianic redemption. Instead of completing a historical process – the run of civilization from the Stone Age to a liberated and affluent society – socialism meant the cataclysmic advent of a post-historic age, of a new messianic time that radically broke with previous history and civilization. In 1921, probably influenced by the writings of Rosenzweig and Sorel, Benjamin wrote an enigmatic text on violence clearly oriented toward nihilistic anarchism. Depicting history as a continuous display of oppressive violence, he imagined the irruption in the realm of history of a "divine violence" that destroyed any political order based on law and created its own legitimacy (Benjamin 1996–2003, 1, 234–52). A few years later, this vision – as radical as abstract, not to say metaphysical – of redemptive violence, took a new formulation through the language of Marxism. "Divine violence" became the proletarian revolution, rooted in a social and historical subject. In 1929, Benjamin defended Marxist communism that furnished the aesthetic and spiritual revolt of Surrealism with a "methodical and disciplinary preparation for revolution." Communism was a form of "organized pessimism," that is, a complete rejection of the capitalist order, which offered a political outcome to "the radical conception of freedom" first elaborated by Bakunin and then rediscovered by surrealism in the 20th century (Benjamin 1996–2003, 2/1, 216). Revolution answered spiritual aspirations but its accomplishment had nothing metaphysical; it was a social and political process embodied by real human beings. One of Benjamin's most Marxist texts, his address at the Paris Institute for the Study of Fascism (1934), analyzed the role of the intellectuals and artists in the class struggle emphasized that they should not clarify their attitude *to* the conditions of production of a given society, but rather their position *in* them. Instead of expressing their solidarity with the proletariat, they should commit themselves to the conflicts of their time as *producers*, becoming part of the class struggle. Any remotely contemplative attitude like that of the writers of the New Objectivity under the Weimar Republic did not overcome a bourgeois horizon and perpetuated a "counterrevolutionary function." His conclusion sounded like a slogan: "revolutionary struggle is not between capitalism and spirit; it is between capitalism and the proletariat" (Benjamin 1996–2003, 2/2, 770, 772, 780).

Of course, this symbiosis of messianic Judaism and secular Marxism created tensions and a permanent movement from one to the other styles of thought. In spite of his romanticism, Benjamin was neither indifferent nor hostile to modern technology. In one of his most famous essays, "The Work of Art in the Age of Mechanical Reproduction" (1936), he pointed out the emancipatory potentialities of industrial production. On the one hand, the aesthetic creations of mass society (notably photography and cinema) had irreversibly lost the "aura" of classical art, which was irreducibly singular and not susceptible to any serialization; on the other hand, however, they possessed an intrinsically "democratic" character and contained the premises of an emancipated art, no longer reserved to the ruling classes or a privileged elite (Benjamin 1996–2003, 3, 101–33). Differently from the illusions of all apologists of Progress, for Benjamin technology did not warrant a radiant future and could even, according to the logic of instrumental reason, become a tool of human and social regression. But this did not justify its obscurantist rejection: against fascism, which transformed technology into a "fetish of doom," socialism must use scientific knowledge as a "key of happiness" (Benjamin 1996–2003, 2/1, 321). This obviously meant building harmonious relationships between technology and nature, which he called a "generous mother" quoting Johann Jakob Bachofen. In a fragment of *One-Way Street* (1928), he wrote that modernity had broken the "cosmic experience" of humankind, separating it from nature by technical means. Capitalism had destroyed their originally harmonious relationship and "turned the bridal bed into a bloodbath" (Benjamin 1979, 59). The Great War had clearly proved that science and technology had become means of destruction and this diagnostic led to a political conclusion:

> If the abolition of the bourgeoisie is not completed in an almost calculable moment in economic and technical development (a moment signaled by inflation and chemical warfare), all is lost. Before the spark reaches the dynamite, the lighted fuse must be cut.
>
> *(Benjamin 1979, 80)*

Twelve years later, in his "Theses on the Concept of History" (1940), he depicted "progress" by the famous allegorical image of the "Angel of History" who, irresistibly pushed by a storm toward the sky, observed frightened and impotent a landscape of ruins growing up continuously under his eyes. Progress was a catastrophe celebrated by the continuous cortège of the victors (Benjamin 1996–2003, 4, 392).

The Critique of Historicism and Social Democracy

It is precisely in his "Theses," a highly cryptic text, that Benjamin's attempt to find a synthesis between messianic Judaism and secular Marxism reached its most accomplished form. Using two allegorical figures of romantic literature, an "automaton" disguised as a Turkish puppet and a hidden "hunchback dwarf," he argued that socialism could prevail only if historical materialism (the automaton) was able to revitalize itself with the spiritual resources of theology (the dwarf). Alone, both of them were sterile, as either an empty mechanism or an illusory, mystical escapism from the profane world. In his prolegomena to this text, he pointed out that Marx had "secularized the idea of messianic time (*messianische Zeit*)" in his vision of the "classless society" (Benjamin 1996–2003, 4, 401).

Differently from more widespread forms of romantic nationalism or religious conservatism, whose nostalgia longed for supposedly organic social hierarchies and authoritarian political institutions, Benjamin's critique of modernity did not aim at restoring the past. His wistfulness for the bygone times was rather a detour through the past looking for the future. Far from rehabilitating absolutism or feudalism, his romantic anti-capitalism was utopian, directed to overcome the bourgeois order toward socialism. In his essay "Paris, Capital of the Nineteenth Century" (1935), he described a dialectical tension between the image of the classless community of a forgotten past and the future of an emancipated society. The most ancient age survived in the "dream images" (*Wunschbilder*) of human beings, where they joined utopian expectations:

> Corresponding to the form of the new means of production, which in the beginning is still ruled by the form of the old (Marx), are images in the collective consciousness in which the new is permeated with the old. These images are wish images. . . . In the dream in which each epoch entertains images of its successor, the latter appears wedded to elements of primal history [*Urgeschichte*] – that is, to elements of a classless society. And the experiences of such a society – as stored in the unconscious of the collective – engender, through interpenetration with what is new, the utopia that has left its trace in a thousand configurations of life, from enduring edifices to passing fashions.
>
> *(Benjamin 1996–2003, 3, 33–34)*

Benjamin's conception of history was radically opposed to *historicism* (that is, in his lexicon, a form of positivism he identified with scholars like Leopold Ranke and Numa Denis Fustel de Coulanges). For historicism, the past was a closed continent and a definitely completed process; it simply meant the accumulation of dead stuff ready to be ordered chronologically, archived and put into a museum. To this conception he opposed a different vision of history as an open temporality. According to Benjamin, the past is at the same time permanently threatened and never definitively lost; it haunts the present and can be reactivated.

Historicism was a form of "empathy with the victors" based on the "indolence of the heart" (Benjamin 1996–2003, 4, 391). Against this approach that accepted as ineluctable the victory of the rulers, he defended a dialectical and redemptive relationship with the past, which could be brought back by working through the contradictions of the present. Benjamin called "recollection" or "remembrance" (*Eingedenken*) this process of reactivation of an unfinished past. Of course, rescuing history did not mean coming back and remaking it; it meant rather changing the present. In other words, to salvage the past, human beings had to renew and realize the hopes of the vanquished, to give a new life to their wishes and expectations. Whereas historicism defended a purely linear and chronological vision of history as *khronos*, a "homogeneous and empty time," historical materialism advocated a dialectical conception of history as *kairos*, that is an open, restless and changing temporality.

Benjamin depicted social democracy as the political equivalent of historicism. Its ineffectiveness was rooted in a vision of history as a quantitative accumulation of productive forces according to which economic growth meant social progress and the advent of socialism appeared as an ineluctable outcome of civilization. In the culture and practice of social democracy, progress was not a potentiality of science and technology, it was actually an ineluctable and irreversible result, "something that automatically pursued a straight or spiral course." Nothing, he observed, had "corrupted the German working class so much as the notion that it was moving with the current" (Benjamin 1996–2003, 4, 393). This conception was antipodal to Marx's theory, Benjamin explained, which did not view the "oppressed class" as the harbinger of material progress but rather as "the avenger that completes the task of liberation in the name of generations of the downtrodden" (Benjamin 1996–2003, 4, 394). In 1937, he devoted a long essay to Eduard Fuchs, a leftist collector and art historian, which actually was a radical critique of the Marxism of the Second International. Since the end of the 19th century, German social democracy had reinterpreted Marxism in the light of social-Darwinism and evolutionism, drawing the conclusion that both its principles and even its tactics corresponded to "natural laws." "History assumed deterministic traits: the victory of the party was 'inevitable'" and therefore the party itself became more and more reasonable, moderate, polite, incapable of taking any risk: it was paralyzed by its own "stalwart optimism." Against the soporific effects of these principles and practices, Benjamin pointed out the virtues of the 19th-century French revolutionary tradition:

> France as the ground of three great revolutions, as the home of exiles, as the source of utopian socialism, as the fatherland of haters of tyranny such as Michelet and Quinet, and finally the soil in which the Communards are buried.
>
> *(Benjamin 1996–2003, 3, 273–74)*

Rescuing the past meant seizing its emergence in what Benjamin called "now-time" or "actualization" (*Jetzt-Zeit*), the dialectic link between the bygone time and the utopian future: "what has been (*Gewesene*) comes together in a flash with the now (*Jetzt*) to form a constellation" (Benjamin 2002, 462). This meeting between past and present condensed itself into ephemeral but intense images. Thus, the concept of "now-time" designated the disruptive moment in which the continuum of chronological time broke up and the past suddenly emerged in the present. In his manuscript of the *Arcades Project*, he compared this clash to "the process of splitting the atom" in order to "liberate the enormous energies of history that are bound up in the 'once upon a time'" (Benjamin 2002, 463). The concepts of "now-time" and "recollection" suggest a symbiotic relationship between history and memory. In this sense, according to Benjamin, history was not only a "science" but also, and perhaps above all, "a form of recollection (*Eingedenken*)." Conceived in this way, it resulted in a montage of "dialectic images" (*Denkbilder*) rather than in a linear narrative (typical of historicism).

In the fourteenth thesis of 1940, Benjamin defined revolution as "a tiger's leap into the past" that took place in the realm of history, that is, in a given society with its antagonistic class relations and political conflicts: "The same leap in the open air of history is the dialectical one, which is how Marx understood the revolution" (Benjamin 1996–2003, 4, 395). And revolution was a potentiality, not the automatic result of historical development. The alternative was fascism, which threatened both the present and the past, the living human beings and their ancestors. In a passage that implicitly evoked Rosa Luxemburg's warning "socialism or barbarism," he pointed out that, far from being condemned by a supposed historical law, fascism "had not ceased to be victorious" (Benjamin 1996–2003, 4, 391).

In *The Class Struggles in France* (1850), Marx defined revolutions as the "locomotives of history" (*MECW* 10: 122). This metaphor suggested a teleological vision of history as a linear acceleration, as a movement going ahead on established rails, which Karl Kautsky codified at the end of the 19th century by interpreting Marxism as a doctrine of social progress. History moved onward through a conflict between productive forces and property relations, a contradiction that revolutions sublated dialectically by establishing a superior stage, in a lineal sequence that culminated in socialism. In the prolegomena to his "Theses," Benjamin suggested a completely different idea of revolution: "Marx says that revolutions are the locomotives of history. But perhaps it is quite otherwise. Perhaps revolutions are an attempt by the passengers on this train – namely, the human race – to activate the emergency brake" (Benjamin 1979, 80). Instead of pushing history toward "progress," they stopped its movement, by breaking its chain of violence. In one of his fragments on Baudelaire (*Zentralpark*), he wrote that revolutionary action, like that carried out by Blanqui in the 19th century, did not "presuppose any belief in progress" but rather the "determination to do away with present injustice" (Benjamin 1996–2003, 4, 188). In *The Arcades Project*, he announced a radically anti-positivistic historical materialism that would have "annihilated in itself the idea of progress": its "founding concept was not progress but actualization (*Jetzt-Zeit*)" (Benjamin 1996–2003, 4, 402). Revolution was a jump into the future by salvaging the past. Instead of accelerating history on its present course, it was a change of civilization, as the passage from a historical to a messianic temporality. In terms of political theology, one could define it as messianic redemption: the passage from the *civitas terrena* to the *civitas dei*.

Revolution as Redemption

These views put Benjamin in a very peculiar position in both Marxist and Jewish traditions. On the one hand, he simultaneously rejected the teleological interpretations of historical materialism and reformulated Marx's idea of communism as the end of prehistory and the beginning of true history (*Geschichte*), which implied a self-emancipated society of free and equal human beings (Hering 1983, 166). On the other hand, Benjamin clearly departed from all inherited forms of messianic theology, which posited redemption as God's irruption in history that human beings should wait, not provoke or induce. For Benjamin, on the contrary, the messianic interruption of the linear course of history was the result of revolutionary action. As Herbert Marcuse pertinently observed, this vision tried to overcome dialectically the traditional conflict between religious chiliasm and atheistic socialism in a synthesis in which "redemption became a materialist political concept: the concept of revolution" (Marcuse 1975, 24). In short, revolution was the core of a reinterpretation of Marxism built around three interconnected themes: a critique of *historicism* (linear temporality), a critique of *deterministic causality* (automatic social change) and a critique of the *ideology of Progress* (both a teleological philosophy and a politics of impotence). In short, Benjamin's Marxism was a theory of historical discontinuity and messianic breaks.

There is no doubt that the radicalism of this philosophical and political statement was rooted in a tragic historical context. Benjamin wrote his "Theses" between the end of 1939 and the beginning of 1940, just after being liberated from a French internment camp for "enemy aliens" and a few months before the French defeat, his flight from Paris and his suicide in Portbou at the Spanish border. In that historical conjuncture, after the defeat of the Spanish Republic, the Soviet-German pact and the outbreak of the Second World War, when the victory of fascism seemed almost ineluctable, a revolutionary option appeared as an act of faith. Messianic hopes fulfilled the vacuum left by the failure of antifascism. In other words, this synthesis between Marxism and messianic Judaism was an alternative to both social democracy and Stalinism, the hegemonic forces of the left that had proved unable to stop the rise of fascism. This critique of the dominant currents of the left was probably one of the sources of his intellectual attraction to both radical conservatism and heretic communism. His intransigent rejection of any form of right-wing politics did not impede him from reading passionately the works of radical right-wing legal and political theorist Carl Schmitt, with whom he tried to establish a dialogue during the Weimar Republic (Heil 1996; Agamben, 2005, 52–64). To a large extent, his political posture reversed Schmitt's political theology, insofar as, mirroring each other, both of them focused on the historical confrontation between revolution and counterrevolution. In his "Theses," Benjamin explicitly claimed a "state of exception" (*Ausnahmezustand*) as the necessary condition for preparing the struggle against fascism, which he allegorically named the "Antichrist," a figure of Christian theology that in Schmitt's lexicon meant Bolshevism (Benjamin 1996–2003, 4, 391, 392).

In the Marxist field, his sympathies went to Trotsky. Many of his friends pointed out his admiration for the author of *History of the Russian Revolution*, a book he read voraciously, "with a breathless excitement" (Benjamin 1994, 393). His conversations with Bertolt Brecht in Denmark show that, whereas the dramatist expressed his skepticism with respect to Stalin and the Moscow trials, Benjamin defended Trotsky (Benjamin 2003, 117–18; Wizisla 2009, 28–29; Kraft 1972, 69). Shifting from testimonies to the more recent scholarship, it is worth mentioning Terry Eagleton, for whom Trotsky's politics completed Benjamin's philosophy: "What remains an image in Benjamin becomes a political strategy with Trotsky" (Eagleton 1981, 178). Revolutionary Marxism itself, one should observe, discovered Benjamin much later (see Eagleton 1981; Callinicos 2004; Bensaïd 1990; Leslie 2000; Löwy 2005), but significantly contributed to emphasizing the political dimension of a thinker whose reception had focused almost exclusively on the fields of aesthetics and literary criticism.

Swinging between Marxism and messianic Judaism, between Moscow and Jerusalem, or even, to mention his own friends, between Brecht and Scholem, but simultaneously rejecting both Stalinism and Zionism, Benjamin remained an outsider. In 1926, his trip to Moscow resulted in a deep disappointment – he met Asja Lacis in a hospital and discovered a country completely oriented toward modernization (Benjamin 1986) – and he never seriously planned on joining Scholem in Jerusalem. Neither Brecht nor Scholem understood his "Theses on the Concept of History," which seemed to them either a Marxist document enveloped by a hermetic and useless theological language (full of "metaphors and Judaisms" Brecht 1993, 159) or a superb messianic text corrupted by Marxist references to the class struggle. For the second generation of critical theory (Habermas), this attempt to fuse political radicalism and religion was dangerous and ineluctably condemned to failure. But perhaps these approaches are quite sterile: Benjamin's restless thought did not wish to build a doctrine. Its openness to different forms of subversion and rebellion, from anarchism to surrealism, from messianic theologies to heretical communism, was a singular, personal path. Finally, it has become a fruitful premise for a critical renewal of Marxism since the end of the 1970s, when Benjamin's legacy crossed the borders of aesthetic and literary criticism and entered the "canon" of Western Marxism.

Bibliography

Agamben, Giorgio. 2005. *State of Exception*. Chicago: University of Chicago Press.
Anderson, Perry. 1976. *Considerations on Western Marxism*. London: New Left Books.
Benjamin, Walter. 1979. *One-Way Street and Other Writings*. London: New Left Books.

Benjamin, Walter. 1986. *Moscow Diary*. New York: Harvard University Press.
Benjamin, Walter. 1994. *The Correspondence of Walter Benjamin 1910–1940*. Edited by Gershom Scholem and Theodor W. Adorno. Chicago: The University of Chicago Press.
Benjamin, Walter. 1996–2003. *Selected Writings*. Edited by Michael W. Jennings. 4 vols. Cambridge, MA: Harvard University Press.
Benjamin, Walter. 2002. *The Arcades Project*. Cambridge, MA: Harvard University Press.
Benjamin, Walter. 2003. *Understanding Brecht*. London: Verso.
Bensaïd, Daniel. 1990. *Walter Benjamin: Sentinelle messianique*. Paris: Plon.
Brecht, Bertolt. 1993. *Journals 1934–1955*. London: Methuen.
Callinicos, Alex. 2004 (1987). *Making History: Agency, Structure, and Change in Social Theory*. 2nd edn. Leiden: Brill.
Eagleton, Terry. 1981. *Walter Benjamin: Or Towards a Revolutionary Criticism*. London: New Left Books.
Heil, Susanne. 1996. *Gefährliche Beziehungen: Walter Benjamin und Carl Schmitt*. Stuttgart: Metzler Verlag.
Hering, Christopher. 1983. *Die Rekonstruktion der Revolution: Walter Benjamins messianischer Materialismus in der Thesen "Über den Begriff der Geschichte."* Frankfurt/Main: Peter Lang.
Kraft, Werner. 1972. "Über Benjamin." In *Zur Aktualität Walter Benjamins*, edited by Siegfried Unseld, 59–69. Frankfurt: Suhrkamp.
Leslie, Esther. 2000. *Walter Benjamin: Overpowering Conformism*. London: Pluto Press.
Löwy, Michael. 2005. *Fire Alarm: Reading Walter Benjamin's "On the Concept of History."* London: Verso.
Marcuse, Herbert. 1975. "Revolution und Kritik der Gewalt. Zur Geschichtsphilosophie Walter Benjamins." In *Materialen zu Benjamin Thesen "Über den Begriff der Geschichte,"* edited by Petr Bulthaup, 23–27. Frankfurt: Suhrkamp.
Scholem, Gershom. 1981. *Walter Benjamin: The Story of a Friendship*. New York: Schocken Books.
Wizisla, Erdmut. 2009. *Walter Benjamin and Bertolt Brecht: The Story of a Friendship*. New Haven: Yale University Press.

12
THEODOR W. ADORNO (1903–69)

Henry W. Pickford

In memory of Jonathan Hess

Continuing the Critique of Political Economy

The relationship between Marx and Theodor W. Adorno, and more generally Frankfurt School Critical Theory centered around the Institute for Social Research under the direction of Max Horkheimer, warrants reappraisal. This is so not least because more primary materials (Adorno's university lecture courses, seminar protocols by students etc.) and interpretive studies have become available, including work by the "*neue Marx-Lektüre*" circle.[1] Moreover, scholars are revising the story of the Frankfurt School to include students of Adorno – such as Alfred Schmidt, Hans-Georg Backhaus and Helmut Reichelt – who developed the sometimes muted but recognizably Marxian presence within Adorno's writing and teaching. The issue is further complicated by the historical development of Marxism itself, as instanced by Engels's anecdote that, as French so-called Marxists emerged in the late 1870s, Marx reportedly asserted: "Ce qu'il y a de certain c'est que moi, je ne suis pas Marxiste" (*MECW* 46: 353).

Earlier scholarship concluded that Adorno had left Marx and Marxism by the late 1930s. Martin Jay holds that "Horkheimer and Adorno, however broad the scope of their interests and knowledge, were never really serious students of economics, Marxist or otherwise" and "although Horkheimer and Adorno still used language reminiscent of Marxism . . . they no longer sought answers to cultural questions in the material substructure of society" (Jay 1973, 152, 258–59). For Perry Anderson Adorno's "Western Marxism" is characterized by its abandonment of political practice and turn to philosophical questions of epistemology and aesthetics, resulting in "method as impotence, art as consolation, pessimism as quiescence" (Anderson 1976, 93). And Jürgen Habermas flatly states "Adorno did not engage with political economy" (Habermas 1983, 109, translation modified).[2]

Yet Adorno and other members of the Frankfurt School took themselves to belong to the Marxist tradition.[3] Adorno drew the contrast between on the one hand a scientistic and positivistic Marxism that conceived of societal laws mechanistically, the *Diamat* (dialectical materialism) against which he persistently inveighed, and on the other hand Critical Theory that did not abandon Marxism but rather adhered to Marx's original project: a critique of political economy, a capacious field of inquiry that along with "the economic" included what would become political science, sociology and social psychology. Adorno identified Marx's "political economy" as the missing dialectical "point of indifference" between the seemingly autonomous contemporary disciplines of economics and sociology: that "the economic relationships between people, though ostensibly of a purely economic, calculable nature, are in reality nothing but congealed interpersonal relationships" based on exchange for "the real self-preservation of human society"; and that "the tendency of capital, the concentration of capital . . . determines the structure of our society down to the level . . . of the most delicate subjective behavior" (Adorno 2000a, 141–43).[4]

As early as 1925 Adorno gravitated to Marxism,[5] and after he formally joined the Institute for Social Research in 1937, protocols of discussions between Adorno and Horkheimer from the 1940s, 1950s and 1960s attest to their ongoing concern to specify their evolving relationship to Marx and the critique of political economy. For instance, in the 1956 conversations Adorno acknowledges "I have always wanted to . . . develop a theory that remains faithful to Marx, Engels and Lenin, while keeping up with culture at its most advanced" (Adorno and Horkheimer 2011, 103). And shortly before his death in 1969, he and Horkheimer were again summarizing the ways in which Critical Theory remains Marxist (see appendix). A careful examination of Adorno's works shows the presence of Marx throughout his writings and university courses, from his 1931 inaugural lecture "On the Actuality of Philosophy," in which the critique of commodity fetishism illustrates Adorno's program of philosophical interpretation, to his 1968 text "Late Capitalism or Industrial Society," in which he argues that Western society is increasingly industrialized with respect to forces of production but remains immured within capitalist relations of production; sprinkled throughout Adorno's writings are statements like "a critical theory of society [is] represented prototypically by that of Marx" (Adorno 2000a, 145).

For this brief chapter, we may discern two ways in which to understand Adorno's Marxian relationship to political economy, which are dialectically related: each informs and corrects the other. In his 1962 seminar "Marx and the Basic Concepts of Sociological Theory" Adorno delineates two ways to understand the critique of political economy:

> What does critique of political economy mean in Marx? (1.) Critique of the classical theory of liberalism. (2) Critique of the economy itself. That is, critique of the self-understanding of liberalism . . . as well as a [critique] of liberalism itself. Marx is concerned with an immanent critique of liberalism . . . Liberal theory is confronted with its own claim with regard to the act of exchange. "You say that equivalents are exchanged, that there is a free and just exchange, I take your word, now we shall see how this turns out!" This is immanent critique.
>
> *(Adorno 2018, 5; cf. Backhaus 2000)*

The first kind of critique of political economy criticizes classical political economy *as* theory, as society's conceptual self-understanding that is revealed to be self-contradictory immanently, that is, in terms of its own concepts and normative standards, whereas the second kind of critique criticizes the object itself: socio-economic reality as it is described by the science of political economy.[6] This double-character of critique of political economy proves a helpful heuristic for understanding Adorno's relationship to Marxism.

From Liberal to Monopoly Capitalism

For Adorno and other Institute members, critique of political economy in the sense of the economy itself meant recognizing contemporary structural changes in socio-economic reality that represented the transition of "high," "liberal" or "free market" capitalism of the 19th century into phenomena variously theorized as "late," "monopoly," "administered" or "state" capitalism. Beginning with the global crisis of 1873, industries such as railroads and power utilities consolidated into trusts and monopolies that coordinated more closely with the state. One of the Institute's economists, Friedrich Pollock, observed that during the inter-war years in Soviet Russia, fascist Germany and New Deal United States state planning and regulation sought in differing ways and degrees to administer production, circulation and consumption, resulting in greater bureaucratization and unification of political, social and economic life-contexts, and the emergence of the new social category of "the masses."[7] Whereas during the liberal phase of capitalism the proletariat was "half outside" society, now society was becoming entirely "integrated" or – as Weber pointedly formulated it – "societized" (*vergesellschaftet*) in either a totalitarian or democratic form (Adorno 1989). An essential agent of this societalization is the "culture industry," which replaces the social-critical role of autonomous art in the 19th century and instead "intentionally integrates its consumers from above" (Adorno 1991b, 85) through standardization of content and rationalization of distribution, resulting in the passive consumption of ideological products that reinforce conformist attitudes and effacing the "cultural lag" Marx posited between cultural superstructure and economic base.[8] As a result of these structural changes under late capitalism, no external standpoint exists from which criticism could be leveled, a position that Adorno maintained throughout his intellectual life:

> Material production, distribution, consumption are administered jointly. . . . Everything is now one. The totality of the processes of mediation, which amounts in reality to the principle of exchange, has produced a second, deceptive immediacy. This enables people to ignore the evidence of their own eyes and forget difference and conflict or repress it from consciousness. . . . No overall social subject exists . . . all social phenomena today are so completely mediated that even the element of mediation is distorted by its totalizing nature. It is no longer possible to adopt a vantage point outside the mechanism that would enable us to give the horror a name; one can tackle it only where it is inconsistent with itself.
>
> *(Adorno 2003b, 124, translation modified)*

Whereas Pollock argued that administered capitalism in effect neutralized economic crises including class conflicts, Adorno faulted him for "the undialectical assumption that a non-antagonistic economy is possible in an antagonistic society" (Adorno and Horkheimer 2004, 139).[9] Relying on classical Marxian theory, he held that class was defined strictly by the objective "position of people in the production process" (that is, its relationship to means of production),[10] a division that had sharpened under late capitalism, although accompanied by more potent means of ideological veiling and an intensified asymmetry in societal power that rendered the emergence and likely efficacy of a proletarian class consciousness nearly impossible, *pace* Lukács's (1971) theory:

> The latest phase of class society is dominated by monopolies; it tends toward fascism, the form of political organization worthy of it. While it vindicates the doctrine of class struggle with its concentration and centralization, extreme power and extreme impotence directly confronting one another in total contradiction, it makes people forget the actual existence of hostile classes. . . . The total organization of society by big business and its ubiquitous technology has taken such utter possession of the world and the imagination that even to conceive of the idea that things might be otherwise calls for an almost hopeless effort.
>
> *(Adorno 2003a, 96)*

Furthermore, no appeal to basic human needs can be made because needs are thoroughly societally mediated: nature and history are inextricably intertwined (Adorno 2006b, 2017).[11] For these reasons the concept of class requires dialectical differentiation, because "its basis, the division of society into exploiters and exploited, not only continues unabated but is increasing in coercion and solidity" while "the oppressed who today, as predicted by the [Marxian] theory, constitute the overwhelming majority of mankind are unable to experience themselves as a class" (Adorno 2003a, 97).[12] Similarly, non-economic political domination is revealed in the increasing division between corporate monopolies and other "exploiters" that sunders class unity among the bourgeoisie: "the ruling class disappears behind the concentration of capital" (Adorno 2003a, 99). The development of class consciousness as the prerequisite for social transformation is hindered by material ameliorations from the welfare state, governmental regulation, mass entertainment etc., that is, by non-economic factors that materially and ideologically mask the persistence of structural class antagonism or reinforce its ineluctability as "second nature" through the implicit threat of sheer power. For Adorno this indicates the larger context of self-preservation and domination within which the narrowly conceived sphere of "the economic" under liberalism once functioned and which has now been usurped by administered society itself:

> Even political economy, the conception of which [Marxian] theory grimly gave to liberalism, is proving to be ephemeral. Economics is a special case of economizing, lack prepared for domination. The laws of exchange have not led to a form of rule that can be regarded as historically adequate for the reproduction of society as a whole at its present stage. Instead, it was the old form of rule that had joined the economic apparatus so that, once in possession, it might smash it and thus make its own life easier. By abolishing the classes in this way, class rule comes into its own. In the image of the latest economic phase, history is the history of monopolies. In the image of the manifest act of usurpation that is practiced nowadays by the leaders of capital and labor acting in consort, it is the history of gang wars and rackets. . . .
>
> But the ruling class is not just governed by the system; it rules through the system and ultimately dominates it. The further modifying factors lie outside the system of political economy but are central to the history of domination. In the process of liquidating the economy, they are not modifying factors but the essence.
>
> *(Adorno 2003a, 100, 104)*

This diagnosis motivates Adorno's and Horkheimer's early masterwork, *Dialectic of Enlightenment*, which is often read as a speculative work of anthropology and philosophy of history in its genealogical account of the emergence and ascendency of instrumental (Max Weber's "purposive") rationality in the West. While the second edition removed the more explicit Marxian terminology exhibited in the original work,[13] one can still read it as a proto-history of bourgeois subjectivity and rationality that constitute unthematized presuppositions of classical political economic theory such as the instinct for self-preservation, means-ends reasoning and labor as the subjugation of nature. Those who claim the Frankfurt School abandoned Marxism often identify *Dialectic of Enlightenment* as marking that departure, but in a posthumously published 1969 sketch for a new foreword to the book Adorno accounts for the shift in focus with Marxian historical-materialist analysis:

> While the book does not conceal its descent from materialist dialectics, it had already dissociated itself from the latter's orthodoxy. With the avoidance of executed economic

> analyses, which would be required in many cases, the concept of domination was used, heretically against the polemic in *Anti-Dühring* by Engels. The deviation from purely economical thinking nevertheless has its economic ground. The object of Marxian political economy was liberalism as reality and ideology. With its advancement to an economy that indeed leaves intact the pseudo-market but otherwise depends on the powers that control production, which also determine circulation and distribution, the liberal laws of the market lose their significance; as a result so too did the economic concept of the economy. Domination has always existed in political economy. The sale of the commodity labor-power, from which Marx deduced the class relationship, in truth presupposes it as the coercion to sell one's labor-power. Therefore domination no longer is of no explanatory use because of its abstractness; rather it is the form [*Gestalt*] into which economical reason has descended, long corroded by irrationality.
>
> *(Adorno 2003c, 7–8)*

Adorno follows Marx in *Capital* (CI: 270–80) in identifying the reciprocal determination between domination and "the economic" narrowly construed. Moreover, that relationship is subject to historical-materialist change, just as the Institute analyzed the transformation in capitalism from its high liberal to its late, administered phase.

An Immanent Critique of Conceptual Fetishism

The second and more pervasive way in which Marx informs Adorno's writings is as a dialectical critique of classical political economy *as* theory. Adorno emphasizes that Marx's *Capital* serves as a critique of the concepts and theories of classical political economy that sought to justify capitalism: "the laws of movement of society, that are positively applied in Hegel or Smith or Ricardo, are then criticized by Marx, and as a consequence the categories to which he brings society are critical categories" (Adorno 2008, 79). In this sense *Capital* undertakes ideology critique of the discourse of political economy by criticizing immanently its central categories such as commodity, value, money and capital, by which society understands itself falsely. Adorno's (1966) magnum opus *Negative Dialectics* can be read in part as a critique of political economy in this Marxian tradition, as an immanent critique of the epistemological categories at work in capitalism.

Society for Adorno is constituted by the relationship of exchange, which presupposes the category of abstract equivalence. In *Capital* Marx shows that the commodity and the labor represented in the commodity each have a "double-character" that is "crucial to an understanding of political economy" (CI: 132): the use-values and qualitative properties of commodities are disregarded in that their value is expressed as abstractly equivalent exchange-values; and similarly the differences in the concrete labors that produce commodities are abstracted into units of average socially necessary labor time that, as the value of the commodities, render them exchangeable. Adorno, following the work of his friend Sohn-Rethel[14] emphasizes that this process of "real abstraction" is presupposed in practical acts of exchange: "One cannot arrive at relationships of exchange without a moment of conceptuality. . . . The conceptuality in the relationship of exchange is itself a kind of facticity," or second nature (Adorno 2018, 3–4, cf. 2000a, 32) as "the law of value that comes into force without men being conscious of it" (Adorno 1973, 300; cf. 316). In real abstraction what appears identical in the form of abstract equivalence is "non-identity under the aspect of identity," his definition of "contradiction" (Adorno 1973, 5). Categories such as the principle of exchange, abstract equivalence and identity-thinking unfold the immanent historically specific contradiction, the "social a priori" (Adorno 1973, 190) underlying bourgeois political economy. Marx's analysis uncovers non-identity within central concepts of political economy. With regard to the bourgeois concept of freedom, workers are free to sell their labor-power yet, dispossessed of the means to live and the means of production, they have no choice but to sell themselves: the exchange of labor-power for a wage is both free and unfree. So too the value of the purchased commodity labor-power is both the value of its reproduction as it is consumed and the surplus value produced from its consumption: the exchange of labor-power for a wage is both just and unjust.

The general mystification of central concepts of political economy that masks such non-identity Adorno calls "conceptual fetishism" in identity-thinking, for which he offers a historical-materialist account:

> The exchange principle, the reduction of human labor to its abstract universal concept of average labor time, has the same origin as the principles of identification. It has its social model in exchange and exchange would be nothing without identification. . . . The spread of the principle imposes on the whole world an obligation to become identical, to become total.
>
> *(Adorno 1973, 146)*

That is, identity-thinking in epistemology merges with the exchange-principle in economic praxis through the cognitive judging of abstract equivalents. In the context of Kantian epistemology, according to which objectively valid knowledge claims rely on the subsumption of intuitions under concepts and categories of judgment, we can discern in fact two different criticisms at work here in Adorno. First, a predicative judgment of perception amounts to the conceptual prescinding from the qualitatively particular, sensuous intuition, and can be considered a form of cognitive domination. But second, once such a cognitive act of the understanding has been executed, the resulting judgment is available for use in syllogistic reasoning, and it is this operation that amounts to an abstract equivalence between the non-equivalent referents of those perceptual predications: the sensuous particulars or their intuitions.

Just as exchange-value, the abstraction of labor time exerted in producing a commodity, is not an inherent property of the thing but rather the socially necessary form in which objects appear under capitalism, so too identity-thinking imputes the abstract identity between non-identical particulars via the universal – the concept – under which they are subsumed. And just as according to Marx a commodity has a use-value, its inherent properties that potentially satisfy human needs, so too a concept has its intrinsic or "emphatic idea": the set of properties, the situations, the objects that ideally would fulfill the concept in what Adorno calls "rational identity." Just as Marx does not abstractly negate the concepts of political economy but rather immanently criticizes them to drive them beyond their present contradiction (e.g., that exchange of labor-power is both just and unjust, both free and unfree), so too Adorno argues that

> if comparability as a category of measure were simply annulled, the rationality that is inherent in the exchange principle – as ideology of course, but also as a promise – would give way to direct appropriation, to force, and nowadays to naked privilege of monopolies and cliques. When we criticize the exchange principle as the identifying principle of thought, we want to realize the ideal of free and just exchange. To date, this idea is only a pretense. Its realization alone would transcend exchange. If critical theory has unmasked it for what it is – an exchange of things that are equal and yet unequal – then the critique of the inequality within equality aims also at equality . . . if

> no person were denied a part of his living labor anymore, then rational identity would be achieved, and society would have transcended identity-thinking.
>
> *(Adorno 1973, 146–47, translation modified; cf. Adorno 2011, 221–22)*

By taking the emphatic idea of a concept not only as ideology but also as an indeterminate promise, Marx and Adorno perform a twofold immanent critique in which present conditions are shown to contradict the reigning ideology and – rather than being abstractly negated for failing to represent reality – the ideology is taken "at its word," as an indeterminate promise of its realization.[15] Such a transcendence of abstract exchange and identity-thinking might be glossed by Marx's underdetermined but equally proleptic and particularist ideal espoused in his 1875 critique of the Gotha Program: "from each according to his ability to each according to his needs" (*MECW* 24: 116).[16] Similarly, transcending identity thinking would aim for "unreduced experience" via epistemic acts that non-coercively modulate between particular and universal, intuition and concept: "Utopia would be above identity and above contradiction; it would be a togetherness in diversity" (Adorno 1973, 154). To this would correspond the fulfilled promise implicit in the idea of a "just exchange" of labor-power: "To go beyond the principle of exchange means at the same time to *fulfill* it: no one should receive less than the equivalent of the average societal labor" (see Appendix).

So Adorno's turn to epistemology and sociology is not a departure from Marx, but rather a deepening of Marx's critique of political economy, now directed at the contradictions and domination within the objective and subjective conditions that underlie abstract equivalence and commodity exchange. By situating these concepts in their specific historical and social context, as Marx did with value, labor and property, Adorno's analysis is recognizably materialist. As he wrote to Thomas Mann:

> Basically the task is not to confront philosophy with dialectical materialism in an external and dogmatic fashion, but rather to grasp this materialism as the very truth of philosophy in its objectivity. That this has never properly been done before, I am convinced, is in large part responsible for what has become of Marxism.
>
> *(Adorno and Mann 2006, 62)*

Adorno's project to grasp the materialism within philosophy also aligns him with the two most influential Marxist writers directly preceding him, who in 1923 investigated the role of Hegelian philosophy in Marx's thought: György Lukács's *History and Class Consciousness*, and Karl Korsch's *Marxism and Philosophy*, whose epigraph quotes Lenin: "We must organize a systematic study of the Hegelian dialectic from a materialist standpoint" (Korsch 1970, 29). Adorno too saw this project as developing Marx's critique of political economy by criticizing its philosophical categories. As he said at the conclusion of his seminar on Marx and sociology: "The genius of Marx consisted precisely in the fact that, filled with disgust he tackled exactly that which he found disgusting: the economy" (Adorno 2018, 11).[17]

Notes

1. Interpretive studies include Johannes (1995), Demirović (1999), Negt (2000) and most importantly Braunstein (2011). On the *neue Marx Lektüre* see: www.radicalphilosophy.com/article/the-neue-marx-lekture.
2. For similar judgments see Dubiel (1985, 105) and Kolakowski (2005, 1091, 1103).
3. On the early Frankfurt School's relation to Marxism, see Kautzer (2017).

4. Cf. Horkheimer's judgment that "Economism, to which Critical Theory is often reduced, does not consist in giving too much importance to economy, but in giving it too narrow a scope" (Horkheimer 1972, 249).
5. Of conversations with Walter Benjamin about Marx Adorno wrote to Alban Berg: "To tell you that politically it has brought me decisively closer to communism perhaps offers a drastic clarification of the development" (Adorno and Berg 2005, 50).
6. Marx directed his critique of political economy "at the substance" of society, that is, the "social production and reproduction of the life of society as a whole" (Adorno 2000a, 84, 141; cf. also Adorno 2016, 618, and Jarvis 2004).
7. The central texts by Pollock in this regard are 1932, 1941a and 1941b; cf. also Horkheimer (1978). In theorizing the transition from liberal to monopoly capitalism Pollock drew on the important work of Hilferding (1981).
8. See Horkheimer and Adorno (2002, 94–136) and Adorno (1991a, 53–113). But cf. Adorno (2008, 108–13) for a dialectical theory of integration (social conformism) and disintegration (antagonism reduced to conflicts between powerful cliques).
9. Cf. Wiggershaus (1998, 280–91) and Hammer (2006, 54–65), and Neumann's reservations regarding Pollock's economic analysis: Neumann (1944).
10. Adorno (2008, 196–200, 2000b, 189).
11. Hence Adorno speaks of "dialectical anthropology"; cf. https://virtualcritique.wordpress.com/2017/08/15/henry-pickford-on-fabian-freyenhagens-adornos-practical-philosophy/
12. For related thoughts regarding the evanescence of class-consciousness see Adorno (1970–86, 8, 187, 1984, 113–115, 193–4, 1989, 272–4, 1993, 13–14, 2000a, 22–5, 2008, 52–66, 2011, 164).
13. See Horkheimer (1985, volume 5, 13–290) and the annotations, the editor's afterword and the essay by Willem van Reijen and Jan Bransen in Horkheimer and Adorno (2002). Institute members in American exile exercised caution in expressing their Marxist views, just as they did in pre-war Germany: cf. Kracauer's advice to Adorno in 1931 that "more than every other theory Marxism demands tactical cunning" (Adorno and Kracauer 2008, 282).
14. Sohn-Rethel (1978) argued in historical materialist fashion that "real abstraction" in exchange constituted "social synthesis" as well as the cognitive synthesis of scientific rationality that should be developed in socialist society, contrary to Adorno's suspicions of such rationality. Cf. Engster and Schlaudt (2018).
15. Indeterminate because the concept's fulfillment will vary with historical-material conditions; cf. Pickford (2002, 2018). An example from the positivism dispute: "The concept of society, which is specifically bourgeois and anti-feudal, implies the notion of an association of free and independent human subjects for the sake of the possibility of a better life and, consequently, the critique of natural societal relations. The hardening of bourgeois society into something impenetrably and inevitably natural is its immanent regression" (Adorno 1976, 25). For a similar interpretation of Marx's critique of the categories of political economy see Horkheimer (1985, vol. 12, 438), discussed in Jarvis (1998, 48–52).
16. Adorno also identifies certain virtues, including generosity, pity and gratitude, "in which one gives more than one receives," contrary to the rational principle of exchange (Adorno 2016, 575–76) and anticipating an abundance of goods to be achieved by the forces of production. On the other hand Adorno criticizes Marx's account of the emancipatory role of technology: "The unleashing of the forces of production, a feat of spirit mastering nature, has an affinity to the violent domination of nature" (Adorno 1973, 306, translation modified) examined in *Dialectic of Enlightenment*.
17. For helpful comments on a previous draft, my thanks to Alex Callinicos and Iain Macdonald.

Bibliography

Adorno, Theodor W. 1969 (2003). "Zur Spezifikation der kritischen Theorie." In *Adorno. Eine Bildmonographie*, edited by Theodor W. Adorno Archiv, 290–92. Frankfurt am Main: Suhrkamp.
Adorno, Theodor W. 1970–86. *Gesammelte Schriften*. Edited by Rolf Tiedemann. 20 vols. Frankfurt: Suhrkamp.
Adorno, Theodor W. 1973 (1966). *Negative Dialectics*. London and New York: Routledge.
Adorno, Theodor W. 1976. "Introduction." In *The Positivist Dispute in German Sociology*, edited by Theodor W. Adorno et al., 1–67. New York: Harper.
Adorno, Theodor W. 1984. *Minima Moralia*. London: Verso.

Adorno, Theodor W. 1989. "Society." In *Critical Theory and Society: A Reader*, edited by Stephen Eric Bronner and Douglas MacKay Kellner, 267–75. New York: Routledge.

Adorno, Theodor W. 1991a. *The Culture Industry: Selected Essays on Mass Culture*. New York: Routledge.

Adorno, Theodor W. 1991b. "Culture Industry Reconsidered." In *The Culture Industry: Selected Essays on Mass Culture*, 85–92. New York: Routledge.

Adorno, Theodor W. 1993. "Messages in a Bottle." *New Left Review* 1(200): 5–14.

Adorno, Theodor W. 2000a. *Introduction to Sociology*. Stanford: Stanford University Press.

Adorno, Theodor W. 2000b. "Sociology and Empirical Research." In *The Adorno Reader*, edited by Brian O'Connor, 174–91. Oxford: Blackwell.

Adorno, Theodor W. 2003a. "Reflections on Class Theory." In *Can One Live after Auschwitz?*, edited by Rolf Tiedemann, 93–110. Stanford: Stanford University Press.

Adorno, Theodor W. 2003b. "Late Capitalism or Industrial Society?" In *Can One Live after Auschwitz?*, edited by Rolf Tiedemann, 111–25. Stanford: Stanford University Press.

Adorno, Theodor W. 2003c. "Aus einem Entwurf 'Zur Neuausgabe' der *Dialektik der Aufklärung*, Frankfurt a.M, Februar, 1969." In *Frankfurter Adorno Blätter VIII*, edited by Rolf Tiedemann, 7–8. Munich: edition text + kritik.

Adorno, Theodor W. 2006a. *History and Freedom*. Cambridge: Polity.

Adorno, Theodor W. 2006b. "The Idea of Natural History." In *Things Beyond Resemblance: Collected Essays on Theodor W. Adorno*, edited by Robert Hullot-Kentor, 252–69. New York: Columbia University Press.

Adorno, Theodor W. 2008. *Philosophische Elemente einer Theorie der Gesellschaft*. Edited by Tobias ten Brink and Marc Phillip Nogueira. Frankfurt: Suhrkamp.

Adorno, Theodor W. 2011. *Philosophie und Soziologie*. Edited by Dirk Braunstein. Frankfurt: Suhrkamp.

Adorno, Theodor W. 2016. *Philosophische Terminologie*. Edited by Henri Lonitz. Franfurt: Suhrkamp.

Adorno, Theodor W. 2017. "Theses on Need." *Adorno Studies* 1(1): 103–4.

Adorno, Theodor W. 2018 (1997). "Marx and the Basic Concepts of Sociological Theory: From a Seminar Transcript in the Summer Semester of 1962." *Historical Materialism* 26(1): 1–11.

Adorno, Theodor W., and Alban Berg. 2005. *Correspondence 1925–1935*. Edited by Henri Lonitz. Cambridge: Polity.

Adorno, Theodor W., and Max Horkheimer. 2004. *Briefwechsel*. Vol. 2. Edited by Christoph Gödde and Henri Lonitz. Frankfurt: Suhrkamp.

Adorno, Theodor W., and Max Horkheimer. 2011. *Towards a New Manifesto*. London: Verso.

Adorno, Theodor W., and Siegfried Kracauer. 2008. *Briefwechsel*. Edited by Wolfgang Schopf. Frankfurt: Suhrkamp.

Adorno, Theodor W., and Thomas Mann. 2006. *Correspondence 1943–1955*. Edited by Christoph Gödde and Thomas Sprecher. Cambridge: Polity.

Anderson, Perry. 1976. *Considerations of Western Marxism*. London: NLB.

Backhaus, Hans-Georg. 2000. "Über den Doppelsinn der Begriffe 'politische Ökonomie' und 'Kritik' bei Marx und in der Frankfurter Schule." In *Wolfgang Harich zum Gedächtnis*, edited by Stefan Dornuf and Reinhard Pitsch. Vol. 2, 10–213. Munich: Müller und Nerding.

Braunstein, Dirk. 2011. *Adornos Kritik der politischen Ökonomie*. Bielefeld: Transcript.

Demirović, Alex. 1999. *Der nonkomformistische Intellektuelle. Die Entwicklung der Kritischen Theorie zur Frankfurter Schule*. Frankfurt: Suhrkamp.

Dubiel, Helmut. 1985. *Theory and Politics: Studies in the Development of Critical Theory*. Cambridge, MA: MIT Press.

Engster, Frank, and Oliver Schlaudt. 2018. "Alfred Sohn-Rethel: Real Abstraction and the Unity of Commodity-Form and Thought Form." In *The Sage Handbook of Frankfurt School Critical Theory*, edited by Beverley Best, Werner Bonefeld, and Chris O'Kane, Vol. 1, 284–301. London: Sage.

Habermas, Jürgen. 1983. *Philosophical-Political Profiles*. Cambridge, MA: MIT Press.

Hammer, Espen. 2006. *Adorno and the Political*. London: Routledge.

Hilferding, Rudolf. 1981 (1910). *Finance Capital: A Study of the Latest Phase of Capitalist Development*. London: Routledge.

Horkheimer, Max. 1972. *Critical Theory: Selected Essays*. New York: Seabury Press.

Horkheimer, Max. 1978. "The Authoritarian State." In *The Essential Frankfurt School Reader*, edited by Andrew Arato and Eike Gebhardt, 95–117. Oxford: Blackwell.

Horkheimer, Max. 1985. *Gesammelte Schriften*. Edited by Alfred Schmidt and Gunzelin Schmid Noerr. 18 vols. Frankfurt: Fischer.

Horkheimer, Max, and Theodor W. Adorno. 2002. *Dialectic of Enlightenment*. Stanford: Stanford University Press.
Jarvis, Simon. 1998. *Adorno: A Critical Introduction*. New York: Routledge.
Jarvis, Simon. 2004. "Adorno, Marx, Materialism." In *The Cambridge Companion to Adorno*, edited by Tom Huhn, 79–100. Cambridge: Cambridge University Press.
Jay, Martin. 1973. *The Dialectical Imagination: A History of the Frankfurt School and the Institute of Social Research, 1923–1950*. Berkeley: University of California Press.
Johannes, Rolf. 1995. "Das ausgesparte Zentrum. Adornos Verhältnis zur Ökonomie." In *Soziologie im Spätkapitalismus. Zur Gesellschaftstheorie Theodor W. Adornos*, 41–67. Darmstadt: Wissenschaftliche Buchgesellschaft.
Kautzer, Chad. 2017. "Marx's Influence on the Early Frankfurt School." In *The Palgrave Handbook of Critical Theory*, edited by M.J. Thompson, 43–64. New York: Palgrave Macmillan.
Kolakowski, Leszek. 2005 (1978). *Main Currents of Marxism*. New York: W. W. Norton.
Korsch, Karl. 1970 (1923). *Marxism and Philosophy*. London: NLB.
Lukács, Gyorgy. 1971. *History and Class Consciousness*. London: Merlin.
Negt, Oskar. 2000. "Adorno als Marxist." In *Leiden beredt werden lassen. Beiträge über das Denken Theodor W. Adornos*, edited by Joachim Perels, 9–26. Hannover: Offizin.
Neumann, Franz. 1944. *Behemoth: The Structure and Practice of National Socialism, 1933–1944*. Revised edn. New York: Octagon.
Pickford, Henry. 2002. "The Dialectic of Theory and Praxis: Late Adorno." In *Adorno: A Critical Reader*, edited by A. Rubin and N. Gibson, 312–41. Oxford: Blackwell.
Pickford, Henry. 2018. "Riddlework (I): Adorno's Model of Critique." In *Der aufrechte Gang im windschiefen Kapitalismus: Kritikmodelle im Gegenwartskapitalismus*, edited by Rüdiger Dannemann, Henry Pickford, and Hans-Ernst Schiller, 67–92. Wiesbaden: Springer.
Pollock, Friedrich. 1932. "Die gegenwärtige Lage des Kapitalismus und die Aussichten einer planwirtschaftlichen Neuordnung." *Zeitschrift für Sozialforschung* I(1): 8–27.
Pollock, Friedrich. 1941a. "State Capitalism: Its Possibilities and Limitations." *Studies in Philosophy and Social Science* IX(2): 200–25.
Pollock, Friedrich. 1941b. "Is National Socialism a New Order?" *Studies in Philosophy and Social Science* IX(3): 440–55.
Sohn-Rethel, Alfred. 1978. *Intellectual and Manual Labour. A Critique of Espistemology*. Atlantic Highlands: Humanities Press.
Wiggershaus, Rolf. 1998. *The Frankfurt School. Its History, Theories and Political Significance*. Cambridge, MA: MIT Press.

APPENDIX

Theodor W Adorno and Max Horkheimer, "On the Specification of Critical Theory" (31 March 1969)

1. Integration of the subjective factor. "The cement." Necessity of a psychological surplus beyond the objective economy, in order to hold society together.
2. Marxism as Critical Theory means, that it [Marxism] cannot become hypostatized, not simply philosophy. The philosophical questions are *open*, not predetermined by ideological worldview [*Weltanschauung*].
3. Critical Theory does not refer to totality but *criticizes* it. But that also means that it [Critical Theory] according to its contents is anti-totalitarian, with all political consistency.
4. Critical Theory is no ontology, no positive materialism. Within its concept is that the satisfaction of material needs is a necessary but not the sufficient condition of an emancipated society. The realized materialism is at once also the abolition of materialism as the dependence on blind material interests.

   To go beyond the principle of exchange means at the same time to *fulfill* it: no one should receive less than the equivalent of the average societal labor.
5. For Critical Theory science [*Wissenschaft*] is one among other societal forces of production and interwoven with the conditions of production. It itself is subject to that reification against which Critical Theory is arrayed. It [*Wissenschaft*] cannot be the measure [*Maß*] of Critical Theory, and Critical Theory cannot be science as Marx and Engels postulated it.
6. This means as much as that in Critical Theory Marxism must critically reflect on itself, without it being weakened. It is irreconcilable with positivism. Positivism is a restricted form [*Gestalt*] of reason. Its unreason is immanently ascertainable. Critical Theory is motivated by an altered concept of reason.
7. Against Marxism as metaphysics Critical Theory takes dialectic incomparably more *seriously* than established Marxism. This is valid above all for ideology. Critical Theory cannot deal with [*abfertigen*] the superstructure from above. The concept of ideology, as that of societally necessary illusion, contains within itself the concept of a correct consciousness. Not all mind [*Geist*] is ideology. Critical Theory means immanent critique also of mind.

8. Critical Theory is motivated by the interest in a society worthy of human beings, in this respect practical. But Critical Theory must not be measured according to praxis as a *thema probandum*; objectivity of truth, reason are authoritative to it. Critical Theory does not hypostatize a unity of theory and praxis, which under the present society is not at all possible. Between theory and praxis there is no continuum.

(Theodor W. Adorno Archive 2003, 292; my translation)

13
HERBERT MARCUSE (1898–1979)

Arnold L. Farr

Revolutionary Theory in Non-Revolutionary Times

In 1906 Benedetto Croce published his book *What is Living and What is Dead of the Philosophy of Hegel*. We may ask this same question today regarding Marx and Marxism. Karl Marx has had an even greater and more universal impact than Hegel and he also considered his philosophy historical. However, at first glance it seems that history has been friend and foe to Marx. Marx's apparent prediction of the collapse of capitalism whether as a result of the proletarian revolution of by capitalism's own contradictions have not been borne out by history. The revolutions that did occur either failed to destroy capitalism or they gave birth to new forms of totalitarianism and oppression. Further, it seems like the working class has passively accepted their subaltern position in the capitalist system.

On the other hand, while there has been no successful global revolution against capitalism, there continue to be sporadic revolts such as the Occupy movement that indicate a degree of social unrest. Further, due to its contradictions, capitalism tends toward crisis from time to time, thereby causing more instability. However, these crises are often resolved by the intervention of political power, thereby vindicating Marx's critique.

Given the failure of many of Marx's predictions, the rise of Stalinism, the crisis of Marxism itself, many have asked what is living and what is dead in Marx? Answering such a question requires a profound knowledge of Marxian theory. I don't believe that the question can be answered by composing a list of ideas or propositions from Marx's work that one finds living or dead. What is living in Marx does not allow such an approach. In this chapter I simply want to lay out the approach to Marxism and Marxian theory developed by Herbert Marcuse. Marcuse's form of critical theory saves Marxism and Marxian theory and shows that it is still the correct theory of capitalism while at the same time subjecting Marxism and Marxian theory to a transformative critique.

Herbert Marcuse began writing during a period of history that had witnessed several failed attempts at revolution, the rise of totalitarianism in the name of Marxism, the rise of fascism and the development of passivity in the working class. To read Marx at that time was to read a revolutionary theory in a non-revolutionary time. Of what value could such a theory be? Marcuse believed that Marxian theory was still valuable and contained the most adequate critique of capitalism. While he was quite aware of some problems in Marx's theory, these problems could be corrected within the framework of the theory itself. As a historical theory, Marxism would always have to adjust itself to the historical moment. By always adjusting his views as history demanded Marcuse believed that he was still carrying out the critical project initiated by Marx.

The Three Cs of Critical Theory

Marcuse quite often referred to Marx's philosophy as Critical Theory, thereby identifying it with his own project. Marcuse's interpretation of the function of critical theory is what allowed him to correct and save Marxian theory within the framework of that theory. Douglas Kellner has provided us with a very helpful tool for understanding and evaluating the task of critical theory. He follows Marcuse's own vision of Critical Theory and develops what he calls the three Cs of critical theory.

> The ultimate goal and fundamental interest of critical theory is a free and happy humanity in a rational society. What is at stake is the liberation of human beings and the development of their potentialities (N [Marcuse 1968], 145f). This project requires radical social change; consequently all of critical theory's concepts are geared towards social practice. From a methodological point of view, critical theory is at once to *comprehend* the given society, *criticize* its contradictions and failures, and to *construct* alternatives.
>
> *(Kellner 1984, 122–23)*

Where Marx and Marcuse converge and differ is indicated in the function of the three Cs of critical theory in their works. There are four issues to which I will apply the three Cs from the perspective of Marx and Marcuse. They are revolutionary consciousness, the working class or proletariat, subjectivity and revolution.

Marcuse's Freudian Revision of Marxian Theory

With any theory, we ought to inquire about the goal of the theory and whether the theory itself contains all of the necessary tools to fulfill its own mission. If the goal of Marxian theory is the liberation of the working class from the chains of capitalist alienation, then the theory must explain and remedy the historical resistance by the working class to the revolutionary action that would free them. At the level of comprehension Marx knew that as the capitalist controlled the means of production she also controlled the means of intellectual production. He writes:

> The ideas of the ruling class are in every epoch the ruling ides, i.e. the class which is the ruling material force of society is at the same time its ruling intellectual force. The class which has the means of material production at its disposal has control at the same time over the means of mental production, so that thereby, generally speaking, the ideas of those who lack the means of mental production are subject to it.
>
> *(*MECW *5: 59)*

The preceding passage entails the theory of ideology or false consciousness that is so important to many Marxists. The very idea that the ruling class can control ideas or intellectual production suggests that they have a way of shaping the consciousness or mental development of the working class. However, Marx did not pursue this line of inquiry. Instead, he provided us with a theory of revolution based on the collapse of capitalism due to its own contradictions. In this context we get a very detailed critique of political economy. Second, Marx seemed to assume that the proletariat would soon find their exploitation and alienation intolerable and would then rise up and overthrow capitalism.

It is this latter assumption that led Marcuse to attempt a Freudian revision of Marxian theory. Somehow, the working class had not only internalized the values of the ruling class, they began to identify with them. Marcuse used psychoanalysis at two distinct levels. At one level he used it to understand and critique the social, political, emotional and psychological mechanisms by which people are repressed and led to identify with their oppressors. At another level Marcuse searches for a biological or instinctual basis for resistance and liberation. This second level will be addressed in the next section of this chapter. For now I want to examine the identification of the worker with the ruling class.

Marcuse's *One-Dimensional Man* can be read as a form of ideology critique. It attempts to answer the question of why the working class has not developed class consciousness or revolutionary consciousness as Marx and many Marxists had hoped. The first sentence of the first chapter is very striking. It reads: "A comfortable, smooth, reasonable, democratic unfreedom prevails in advanced industrial civilization, a token of technical progress" (Marcuse 1964, 1).

In a 1978 interview with Bryan Magee Marcuse expressed his disagreement with Marx's belief that the proletariat would rise up and throw off their chains by saying that "we know today that it is not the case that the proletariat have nothing to lose but their chains, they have considerably more to lose" (Magee 1977). Here's Marcuse comprehension of capitalist society differs from Marx's. Hence, historical circumstances demand a revision of Marxian theory. *One-Dimensional Man* is an inquiry into the social, political and psychological mechanisms that dupes the working class into passively accepting its alienated and exploited status. According to Marcuse, the system gives the worker just enough to keep him satisfied. Life tends toward the trivial under the façade of freedom and unity. While the worker is not free, the abundance of goods and trivial recreation when he is not working creates the illusion of freedom and equality.

> The people enter this stage as preconditioned receptacles of long standing; the decisive difference is in the flattening out of the contrast (or conflict) between the given and the possible, between the satisfied and the unsatisfied needs. Here, the so-called equalization of class distinctions reveals its ideological function. If the worker and his boss enjoy the same television program and visit the same resort places, if the typist is as attractively made up as the daughter of her employer, if the Negro owns a Cadillac, if they all read the same newspaper, then this assimilation indicates not the disappearance of classes, but the extent to which the needs and satisfactions that serve the preservation of the Establishment are shared by the underlying population.
>
> *(Marcuse 1964, 8)*

In this passage we see the problem of identification at work. The sharing or common interests in goods and forms of entertainment creates a false sense of unity and equality. The 2016 presidential election in the US provides an example of this as many poor white working class people identified with and voted for a billionaire candidate whom they interpreted as being down to earth like them. The need by members of the working class to identify with the rich and powerful results in an erasure of the space for critical consciousness.

Today this private space has been invaded and whittled down by technological reality. Mass production and mass distribution claim the *entire* individual, and industrial psychology has long since ceased to be confined to the factory. The manifold processes of introjection seem to be ossified in almost mechanical reactions. The result is, not adjustment but *mimesis*: an immediate identification of the individual with *his* society and, through it, with the society as a whole (Marcuse 1964, 10).

Although Marx was right in claiming the in every era the ideas of the ruling class are the ruling ideas, it seems that Marx was not aware of how deeply these ideas would enter into the psyche of the working class. He was not aware of the degree to which the potential for the development of critical/revolutionary thought could be put under erasure. Further, Marcuse points out the way in which capitalist society can produce then meet false needs. Capitalist society is organized in such a way that the working class receives a certain degree of satisfaction.

Revolutionary Subjectivity in Non-Revolutionary Times

In some ways it seems like Marcuse and the Frankfurt School turned away from Marx. This may be true regarding some members of the Frankfurt School but it is not true for Marcuse. It is the case that unlike Marx, Marcuse did not develop a critique of political economy. He did not have to. For Marcuse, the critique of political economy provided by Marx was basically correct with the exception of a few problems. What was most in need of revision in Marx was his theory of revolution. I will say more about that in the next couple of sections. What was needed when Marcuse was writing was not another critique of political economy but rather a critique of culture, political organization, the new social mechanisms of repression etc. This is why Marcuse and others turned to Freud. It seemed that capitalist society had developed in such a way that the Marxian/Marxist theory of revolution and of the rising class consciousness of the working class were false. Marcuse and the Frankfurt School have often been accused of abandoning the working class and the vision of a proletarian revolution. This may be true for some members but not for Marcuse. However, the theory of revolution as well as the notion of the working class would be revised by Marcuse.

The revolution that Marx and Marxists anticipated required the development of class consciousness or revolutionary subjectivity. The failure of such to develop among the working class as defined by Marx suggests that the time was not revolutionary. However, Marcuse never gave up on the possibility of the development of revolutionary subjectivity (Farr 2009, 15–36). This brings us to the second use of Freud in Marcuse's work. Freudian psychoanalysis not only helped disclose the mechanisms of repression that put under erasure the development of revolutionary subjectivity. It also provided Marcuse with insight into the potential development of radical or revolutionary subjectivity in non-revolutionary times. Marcuse simply extends Freud's drive theory beyond Freud's own use of it. However, this extension is made possible by Freud himself. Freud acknowledges that the work of repression is never complete. Repression requires repetition. This means then, that the repressed drive is always there trying to assert itself (Freud 1949, 84–97).

For Marcuse this means that there is always a space for resistance. In *Eros and Civilization* and several other places Marcuse will use Freud to develop an emancipatory theory of phantasy and imagination as sources of resistance. With the help of Freud and the many social and political revolts taking place all over the world Marcuse was able to repackage the Marxian theory of revolution. The student protests of the 1960s, the civil rights movement, the women's rights movement, the environmentalist movement, the hippies etc. were all examples of a revolt against repression, war, waste and oppression. These protests were proof that even in a repressive society and in a non-revolutionary time the instinctual structure of many human individuals cried out against this repression. People could still imagine a qualitatively better society. Hence, the development of revolutionary consciousness was still possible. With the critical contribution of psychoanalysis to Marcuse's theory and the influence of contemporary struggles for freedom and a better society Marcuse was forced to rethink the nature of the working class. The Marxian and Marxist notion of the proletariat was no longer applicable.

Beyond the Proletariat

Rather than give up on the working class as the potential revolutionary force in capitalist society, a new understanding of the working class in its more recent form must replace the Marxian/Marxist concept of the proletariat. Marcuse advanced beyond the Marxian/Marxist concept of the proletariat in two ways. First, Marcuse argued for an expanded concept of the working class. Second, he saw revolutionary consciousness develop in what he called catalyst groups. These were groups fighting against forms of oppression that were not merely economic. Regarding the expanded working class. Marcuse argued: "The working class is still the 'ontological' antagonist of capital, and the potentially revolutionary Subject: but it is a vastly expanded working class, which no longer corresponds directly to the Marxian proletariat" (Marcuse 2014, 392). Developments in late capitalism have altered the nature of the working class. Here again is where proper comprehension of society leads to a new form of critique as well as the construction of a solution that differs from that of Marx and the Marxists. In late capitalism industrial laborers no longer make up the majority of the working class. Workers in late capitalism expect and receive a slightly higher standard of living than the typical industrial laborer. They also require more education. With developments in late capitalism comes the formation of a new group of workers whom we know as white collar workers.

Marcuse writes:

> White collar employees, technicians, engineers, and the steadily growing private and public bureaucracy which assures the creation as well as realization of surplus value. All these have to sell their labor power and are separated from the control of the means of production. In this greatly enlarged working class, the gap between intellectual and material labor is being reduced, knowledge and education are generalized; however, these achievements are invalidated to the degree to which the system reproduces itself through the productivity of *unproductive* labor, which does not increase the social wealth, but rather destroys and abuses it through the production of waste, planned obsolescence, a self-propelling armament industry, management of consciousness and subconsciousness, etc.
>
> *(Marcuse 2014, 392)*

With late capitalism the labor force is constituted less by the industrial laborer or the proletariat and more by a new professional class to whom the Marxian concepts of alienation and exploitation still apply because they do not control the means of production. They also work for a wage that they do not have the power to determine. However, even this new development in capitalism does not lead to a rejection of the idea of revolution. In fact, Marcuse finds new hope for the development of revolutionary consciousness in the white collar worker. The level of education required for some white collar workers as well as the amount of intellectual work that they must engage in makes possible what Marcuse following Rudolf Bahro calls "surplus consciousness" (see Bahro 1978). Surplus consciousness is a form of consciousness that goes beyond the form of consciousness required for mere material production. As such, it is capable of entertaining thoughts that cannot be completely contained by the capitalist attempt to whittled down human consciousness to that form of consciousness needed for mere material production. Hence, surplus consciousness has the potential to develop into revolutionary consciousness as the white collar worker has greater potential to imagine a qualitatively better society (Marcuse 2014, 397).

While there are still several factors in capitalist society that work to prohibit progressive social change there is one in particular that Marcuse draws attention to that must be discussed in the context of revising the Marxian/Marxist notion of the working class. Marcuse was aware of the role that racism played in controlling the working class. In his *Paris Lectures* Marcuse claims that: "In the United States there has always been, to put it mildly, a competition and an antagonism between white labor and Black labor. This is still skillfully exploited, sometimes even in the unions themselves" (Marcuse 2015, 67). Marcuse never develops this preceding idea in any detail and this is not the place to do it here. Suffice it to say that one of the main strategies by capitalists has been to divide and conquer the working class. The purpose of such a strategy is to hinder the development of revolutionary consciousness in the working class by putting them at war against each other.

There is one more area where Marcuse looks for revolutionary subjectivity beyond the proletariat. Being consistent with the historical nature of Marxian theory, Marcuse paid attention to the many struggles for social transformation that very developing around the world. For example; the Black struggle for freedom, the struggle for women's rights, environmentalism etc. The various groups engaged in these struggles were called "catalyst groups" by Marcuse (Marcuse 1969, 51).

Revolution or Reform?

Marcuse believed that Marx's theory was a theory of revolution. Critical Theory, if it is to remain within the Marxian framework must also be revolutionary. However, the theory of revolution must be modified in light of historical developments. Marcuse never completely gave up on the working class as potential revolutionary class. Having been accused of abandoning the working class, he writes:

> I never said that the working class can be replaced by any other class in the transition from capitalism to socialism. I have never said that, for example, these students could be such a replacement. What I did say is that under the pressure of integration and in the place of a still not actually revolutionary working class, the preparatory educational political work of such groups as these students assumes all-important significance.
>
> *(Marcuse 2015, 8)*

Marcuse's use of the term "integration" refers to conformity to the nation's present culture not racial integration. This was the main theme of *One-Dimensional Man*, as I discussed earlier. Since the general population had internalized the values of the dominate group Marcuse looked for the potential development of revolutionary consciousness wherever he could find it. Although today and even in Marcuse's day academic institutions tend to conform to the nation's present culture, Marcuse believed that these institutions were perhaps the last hope for the development of revolutionary consciousness. He also called for new forms of education and establishing new institutions. He writes:

> What is at stake in the process of establishing these institutions, in the process of working out the new social relationships, what is at stake is a radical transformation of all basic values of Western civilization. A radical transformation of all basic values of Western civilization, which, as you know, was and still is a patriarchal civilization. This is only

to indicate the place which the discussion of the women's movement will have in the context of what to submit to you.

(Marcuse 2015, 9–10)

In some ways, Marcuse's theory of revolution is even more radical than that of Marx.

In the preceding passage he calls a radical transformation of all basic values of Western civilization. In Marcuse's view the revolution must go well beyond an economic revolution. It demands a lot more than the working class gaining control of the means of production. Capitalism has been able to prohibit the Marxian/Marxist revolution because of its ability to shape culture, values, the psyche of the worker or the very consciousness of the individual. Therefore, we must transcend the values imparted by capitalism to our society. A qualitatively new and better society demands a new type of human being. In a lecture entitled "Marxism and the New Humanity: An Unfinished Revolution" Marcuse argues that the transition from capitalism to socialism requires "a new type of man, with new needs, [and] the capability of finding a qualitatively different way of life" (Marcuse 2014, 343).

In *An Essay of Liberation* Marcuse frames this requirement for a new human being in terms of human beings developing a new sensibility. Again, Marcuse's point is that capitalism goes beyond being merely an economic system. It is an economic system wherein those who own and control the means of production benefit from the total control of every aspect of the life of the individual. Hence, the ideas of the ruling class work to produce forms of subjectivity that can be manipulated and controlled. This form of subjectivity must be dismantled and reconstructed for emancipatory purposes. The human individual under socialism cannot be the same as the human individual under capitalism. It is the form of *Praxis* or the struggle against violence, waste, exploitation etc., that the new sensibility develops as the negation of the entire Establishment (Marcuse 1969, 25). Invoking Freud's theory of the drives here, repressed drives are never completely subdued by the process of repression, they continue to assert themselves often via the imagination. The imagination is always capable of presenting us with the image of a liberated society and a better way of life. Such an image presents a challenge to the present order of things and provides the basis for the development of revolutionary subjectivity. As we have seen, this urge to revolt occurs among many different groups who are dealing with various form of oppression. The end of *An Essay on Liberation* calls for the development of solidarity among all of the catalyst groups, who all belong to the expanded working class.

Marcuse's notion of the expanded working class, the concept of catalyst groups, as well as his call for solidarity between all oppressed groups all represent an attempt to construct an alternative for our society that is based on his historically informed comprehension and critique. As capitalism expands it alters the nature of labor and other social forces. Marxian theory, as a historical theory, must be modified to remain relevant as capitalism is modified. Marcuse maintained revolutionary hope by always looking for new possibilities for revolution that were capable of responding to new developments in capitalism and capitalist society in general.

Bibliography

Bahro, Rudolf. 1978. *The Alternative in Eastern Europe*. London: Verso.

Farr, Arnold L. 2009. *Critical Theory and Democratic Vision: Herbert Marcuse and Recent Liberation Philosophies*. Lanham, MB: Lexington Books.

Freud, Sigmund. 1949. "Repression." In *Collected Papers*, edited by Ernest Jones. Vol. 1, 84–97. London: The Hogarth Press.

Kellner, Douglas. 1984. *Herbert Marcuse and the Crisis of Marxism*. London: Macmillan and Co.

Magee, Bryan. 1977. "Herbert Marcuse and the Frankfurt School." www.youtube.com/watch?v=vm3eu ZS5nLo. Print version in *Men of Ideas: Some Creators of Contemporary Philosophy*. London: BBC Books.
Marcuse, Herbert. 1964. *One-Dimensional Man: A Study of Advanced Industrial Society*. Boston: Beacon Press.
Marcuse, Herbert. 1966. *Eros and Civilization*. Boston: Beacon Press.
Marcuse, Herbert. 1968. *Negations: Essays in Critical Theory*. Boston: Beacon Press.
Marcuse, Herbert. 1969. *An Essay on Liberation*. Boston: Beacon Press.
Marcuse, Herbert. 2014. *Marxism, Revolution, and Utopia*. London and New York: Routledge.
Marcuse, Herbert. 2015, *Herbert Marcuse's 1974 Paris Lectures at Vincennes University*, edited by Peter-Erwin Jansen and Charles Reitz. Frankfurt and Kansas City, MO: CreateSpace.

PART IV

Tricontinental

14
TRICONTINENTAL: MARXISM OUTSIDE EUROPE

Vijay Prashad

Only at the end of his life did Karl Marx leave the shores of Europe and travel to a country under colonial dominion. This was when he went to Algeria in 1882. "For Musalmans, there is no such thing as subordination," Marx wrote to his daughter Laura Lafargue. Inequality is an abomination to "a true Musalman," but these sentiments, Marx felt, "will go to rack and ruin without a revolutionary movement" (*MECW* 46: 242). A movement of revolutionary understanding would easily be able to grow where there was this cultural feeling against inequality. Marx did not write more about Algeria or about Islam. These were observations made by a father to his daughter. But they do tell us a great deal about Marx's sensibility.

There was no room in Marxism for the idea that certain people needed to be ruled because they were racial or social inferiors. In fact, Marxism – from Marx's early writings onward – always understood human freedom as a universal objective. Human slavery and the degradation of human beings into wage slavery awoke in Marx his prophetic indignation. One of Marx's most famous passages in *Capital* (1867) pointed out that the "rosy dawn of the era of capitalist production" should not be found in the antiseptic bank or factory. The origin of capitalism had to be found – among other processes – in "the extirpation, enslavement and entombment in mines of the aboriginal population, the beginning of the conquest and looting of the East Indies, the turning of Africa into a warren for the commercial hunting of Black skins" (*CI*: 915). Capitalism grew and was sustained by the degradation of humanity. No wonder, then, that anti-colonialism would play such an important role in the Marxist movement.

Once you drift outside the boundaries of the North Atlantic region – from Europe to the United States of America – the categories of Marxism had to be stretched and the narrative of historical materialism had to be enhanced. Otherwise, people would be adopting categories that – surely – had universal application but were not applied in the same way everywhere. Few Marxists adopted the continents of dialectical and historical materialism without translation into their own contexts and into their own dilemmas. That has been one of the richest elements of the Marxist tradition, and one that is very rarely considered.

Lenin

When Marxism traveled outside the domain where Marx first developed the theory, it had to engage with what Lenin called in 1920 "the very gist, the living soul, of Marxism – a concrete analysis of concrete conditions" (*LCW* 31: 166). In fact, Lenin's contribution opened the door for the assessment of Marxism outside Europe. Lenin was not alone in this understanding of the need for a "concrete analysis of concrete conditions," for a creative interpretation of Marxism for different social contexts. A decade after Lenin, the Cuban intellectual and revolutionary Julio Antonio Mella understood that the mood of the time was for socialism – "The cause for socialism in general is the cause of the moment: in Cuba, in Russia, in India, in the United States and in China – everywhere." But the "only obstacle" for socialism was "in knowing to adapt it to the reality of different environments." Marxists must not, Mella wrote, "make 'servile copies of revolutions made by other people in other climates'" (Mella 1975, 87–88). That would be wooden and impossible.

The Italian Marxist Antonio Gramsci wrote wryly that the revolution in Russia was a "revolution against *Capital*," meaning a revolution against the premonitions in Marx's mature work (Gramsci 1977, 34). But this was not entirely the case. Revolutions in the advanced capitalist states did not occur for a variety of reasons, and the main successful revolutions came in peasant societies – what Lenin called the "weakest link" in the capitalist order. This was itself an elaboration of Marx's full theory, of the considerations of ideology as much as of structure. It was the "labor aristocracy" in the advanced states that hindered the subjective side of the ledger, even as objectively these states bore the conditions for revolution. That subjective side – the agitation in the masses, the existence of a party, the development of a creative Marxism – came about for a host of reasons in the weakest links, from Russia in 1917 to Cuba in 1959.

The revolutionary, Mella wrote, need not repeat Lenin; the revolutionary must follow Lenin's advice, to be creative with Marxism. The revolutionary should not treat Marxism as a theology – to follow it to the letter – nor should the revolutionary treat every individual case as exceptional. The point was to understand the nature of capitalist universality alongside the rich history of each country, to develop a dialectical understanding of the universal and the particular, of capitalist social relations alongside how these emerged in each location. That is what Lenin had done, which contributed to the unfolding of the revolution in Russia.

Peasant societies such as Mexico and India, China and southern Africa grasped Lenin's translation of Marxism from the context of the factory into the fields. Lenin worked out the contradictions of capitalism in Russia (*The Development of Capitalism in Russia*, 1899), which allowed him to understand how the peasantry in the sprawling Tsarist Empire had a proletarian character. It was based on this that Lenin argued for the worker-peasant alliance against Tsarism and the capitalists. Lenin understood from his engagement with mass struggle and with his theoretical reading that the social democrats – as the most liberal section of the bourgeoisie and the aristocrats – were not capable of driving a bourgeois revolution let alone the movement that would lead to the emancipation of the peasantry and the workers. This work was done in *Two Tactics of Social Democracy in the Democratic Revolution* (1905). *Two Tactics* is perhaps the first major Marxist treatise that demonstrates the necessity for a socialist revolution, even in a "backward" country, where the workers and the peasants would need to ally to break the institutions of bondage. These two texts show Lenin avoiding the view that the Russian Revolution could leapfrog capitalist development (as the populists – *narodniki* – suggested) or that it had to go through capitalism (as the liberal democrats argued). Neither path was possible nor necessary. Capitalism had already entered Russia – a fact that the populists did not acknowledge – and it could be overcome by a worker and peasant revolution – a fact that the liberal democrats disputed. The 1917 Revolution and the Soviet experiment proved Lenin's point.

Having established that the liberal elites would not be able to lead a worker and peasant revolution, or even a bourgeois revolution, Lenin turned his attention to the international situation. Sitting in exile in Switzerland, Lenin watched as the social democrats capitulated to the war-mongering in 1914 and delivered the working-class to the world war. Frustrated by the betrayal of the social democrats, Lenin wrote an important text – *Imperialism* – which developed a clear-headed understanding of the growth of finance capital and monopoly firms as well as inter-capitalist and inter-imperialist conflict. It was in this text that Lenin explored the limitations of the socialist movements in the West – with the labor aristocracy providing a barrier to socialist militancy – and the potential for revolution in the East – where the "weakest link" in the imperialist chain might be found. Lenin's notebooks show that he read 148 books and 213 articles in English, French, German and Russian to clarify his thinking on contemporary imperialism. Clear-headed assessment of imperialism of this type ensured that Lenin developed a strong position on the rights of nations to self-determination, whether these nations were within the Tsarist Empire or indeed any other European empire. The kernel of the anti-colonialism of the USSR – developed in the Communist International (Comintern) – is found here. It is what drew in anti-colonial militants from the Dutch East Indies to the Andes.

A Heroic Creation

In the Andes (in South America), Jose Carlos Mariategui (1894–1930) wrote in 1928: "We do not wish that Socialism in America be a tracing and a copy. It must be a heroic creation. We must, with our own reality, in our own language, bring Indo-American socialism to life" (Vanden and Becker 2011, 129). What did Mariategui do? He read his Marx and his Lenin – and he studied deeply in the social reality of the Andes. Lenin's theory of the worker-peasant alliance provided a fundamental addition to his Marxism. "The socialist revolution in a mainly agrarian country like Peru in the 1920s," he wrote, "was simply inconceivable without taking into consideration the insurgent mobilization of indigenous rural communities that were challenging the power of large land-owners (*latifundistas*) who were responsible for keeping alive old forms of economic exploitation." The agent of change in Peru among the producing classes had to include the indigenous rural communities whose population was mainly Amerindian. To seek the insurgents among the minuscule industrial sector of Lima alone would be to go into battle with capital with one hand tied behind the back. This is an echo of Lenin's call for worker and peasant unity, but with the indigenous communities now in the framework.

Were the indigenous rural communities capable of a socialist movement? In the 1920s, when Mariategui was writing, the prevailing intellectual fashion with regard to the rural communities was *indigenismo*, or Indianness – meaning a cultural movement that revived and celebrated Amerindian cultural forms but did not seek to explore their transformative potential. *Indigenismo* defanged the Amerindians and romantically saw them as culture producers but not history producers. Mariategui reinterpreted their history in a more vibrant way – looking backward at Inca primitive socialism and current struggles against the *latifundistas* as resources for social transformation. "The thesis of a communist Inca tradition is," he wrote, "the defense of a historical continuity between the ancient Inca communal way of life and the Peruvian communist society of the future." Mariategui's Andean socialism was never a restoration of the past, of a primitive communism of an ancient Inca world. "It is clear that we are concerned less with what is dead than with has survived of the Inca civilization," he wrote in 1928. "Peru's past interests us to the extent it can explain Peru's present. Constructive generations think of the past as an origin, never as a program." In other words, the past is a resource not a destination – it reminds us of what is possible, and its traces show us that elements of that old communitarianism can be harnessed in the fight against colonial private property relations in the present. When Marxism came to the Third World, it had to be supple and precise – learn from its context, understand the way capitalism morphs in new venues and explore the ways for social transformation to drive history.

Marxism would have died an early death in places like the Andes if it did not take seriously the concrete conditions of the workers as well as the social aspirations of national self-determination. The tentacles of imperialism gathered firmly around the sovereignty of countries like Peru, suffocating them with credit and warships, forcing the people into lives of great indignity. To improve the conditions of work and life as well as to capture the necessity of anti-colonial nationalism meant that Marxist-inspired movements had to merge the struggle of nationalism to that of socialism. It had to urge on the movements that remained within the horizon of capitalism – those that sought to improve the conditions of life – and to urge on the movements for more representation in government – those that sought to enter systems that remained under imperial control. It was these emancipatory demands – drawing on old messianic ideas and anarchism as well as Marxism – that would bring together the currents of anti-colonial nationalism and socialism in the colonies and semi-colonies into what we are calling Third World Marxism.

It is important to pause here and digest a fact that is often not considered when one is looking at the world of Marxism. Many of those who became Marxists in the colonial world had never read Marx. They had read in various cheap pamphlets about Marx and had confronted Lenin as well in this form. These were workers such as the Cuban worker Carlos Baliño (1848–1926), who introduced his fellow Cubans to Marx. Books were too expensive, and they were often difficult to get (the role of the censor needs to be central to this story). People like Baliño, China's Li Dazhao (1888–1927), India's Muzaffar Ahmed (1889–1973) and Iraq's Yusuf Salman Yusuf, or Fahd (1901–49) came from humble backgrounds with little access to the kind of European education needed to grasp Marx's work. But they knew its essence. They learned it in bits and pieces, often from agents of the Communist International (Fahd derived his Marxist education from the Comintern's Piotr Vasili) or from sojourns at the University of the Toilers of the East in the USSR. They did not come from bourgeois families, did not earn stipends from their parents nor did they get the opportunity to study the width of Marxism and find their way through scholarship. They came to Marxism from the factory floor and the agriculturalist's field, from the prisons of the colonial rulers and the nationalist cells to which they flocked. They drew from what they learned and developed their theories about both imperialism and capitalism from that reading and from their experience.

These were men and women who came to radicalism through their affection for the people, understanding that anti-colonialism had to be part of their framework but so too did the social revolution. It would not be enough to eject the colonizer and elect the bourgeoisie to take the colonizer's place. Both had to go. It is why many of these radicals formed parties to the left of the bourgeois nationalists but not so far to their left that they did not participate together in anti-colonial actions. Baliño, for instance, played a key role alongside Julio Antonio Mella (1903–29) to form the Communist Party of Cuba in 1925. Drawing from the work of José Marti (1853–95), Baliño and Mella fused anti-colonialism nationalism with their own understanding of and aspiration for socialism. As Isabel Monal – editor of *Marx Ahora* – put it, Baliño and Mella brought together national liberation and socialism into a dialectical unity since "none believed in the illusion of the supposed progressive role of a washed-up bourgeoisie" (Monal 2004/5, 21). This was a view shared across the colonized world. Most Marxist movements in the colonized world struggled with the question of the native bourgeoisie – whether to see it as even partially progressive or to see it as inherently reactionary once in power. Parties split on these lines, the Comintern argued till dawn along them.

The Comintern tried to be supple, but its limited knowledge of the world meant it ended up being far too dogmatic to be always useful. By the late 1920s, the Comintern suggested the creation of a Black Belt in the southern region of the United States, Native Republics in South Africa and an Indian Republic along the Andean region of South America. From Moscow, it appeared as if the nationalities theory could be easily transported to these distant lands. For South America, the theory was debated at the First Latin American Communist Conference held in Buenos Aires in June 1929. Fierce debate broke out here, with the Comintern's preferred position being opposed by Mariategui's associates. "The construction of an autonomous state from the Indian race," Mariategui wrote, "would not lead to the dictatorship of the Indian proletariat, nor much less the formation of an Indian State without classes." What would be created is an "Indian bourgeois State with all of the internal and external contradictions of other bourgeois states." The preferred option would be for the "revolutionary class movement of the exploited indigenous masses," which was the only way for them to "open a path to the true liberation of their race." The debate on goals and strategy became so fierce that this was the only Latin American Communist Conference to be held. "The indigenous proletariat await their Lenin," Mariategui wrote. He meant not a Lenin as such, but a theory that could emerge from the movements to lead them against the rigid structures of the past and present.

This was not always the lesson that was learned. But it is our lesson now.

Against Our Backwardness

Revolutionaries in the colonies and the semi-colonies had to confront the problem of backwardness. Few saw the intervention of the colonial powers as progressive, since these European colonial powers typically collaborated with the worst elements in colonial societies to maintain power – the landlords, the clergy and the traditional intellectuals. Colonial social policy frequently lay a heavy hand on social development, freezing old forms of hierarchy and creating new ones in the name of tradition. Simultaneously, colonial policy impoverished society, plundering social wealth toward the North Atlantic states and creating social deserts in areas that once had rich cultural dynamics. What was left was backwardness – an impoverishment of belly and spirit.

Bourgeois nationalists confronted this backwardness by denying it, by glorifying ancient traditions mainly. This kind of revivalism only deepened the backwardness, stifling the development of the colonized economy and its society. Revolts of the peasants and the workers pushed the bourgeois nationalists to understand that the task of political independence had to be seen as central, but it should not be isolated from the social revolution, the revolution against the economic and cultural conditions of backwardness put in place by the colonial powers and by the landed aristocracy and landed bourgeoisie.

The Egyptian socialist – Salama Musa (1887–1958) – is emblematic of an early revolutionary consciousness in the colonies. Musa was struck by the hierarchies of his society and of the apparent futility of his times. There were two obstacles to progress – the colonial powers (mainly Britain) and traditionalism. Both prevented Egyptian society from developing out of its impasse, with education systems atrophied, with hunger general and with religious thought pushed as the authentic Egyptian ideology. Musa was not convinced that the *Nahda*, the enlightenment of the Arabs, would be sufficient since it did not seem to be able to break away from traditionalism and the heavy weight of colonialism. What did Musa mean when he wrote, "Although the sun rises in the East, the light, however, comes from the West"? (Ibrahim 1979, 348). Did he mean that the West was the font of reason? Actually, his thought process was far more sophisticated, having journeyed in his youth through Nietzsche and the idea of the superman. It was not that reason came from the West, but that the West – with its theft of resources and its ability therefore to develop socially – had produced developments in thought (Marxism, Fabian Socialism) that should be engaged with in places such as Egypt. It was necessary not to dig oneself into a hole of nativism nor to adopt the ideology of the colonial masters. The point was to find frameworks and concepts from the best of reason to develop a critique of one's society. This was what Musa attempted in his *Our Duties and the Tasks of Foreign Countries* (1930) as well as in his *Gandhi and the Indian Revolution* (1934) and *Egypt: the place where civilization began* (1935).

The idea of "backwardness" (*takhalluf*) is not easily dismissed. To critique Western thought for its disdain for the colonies was insufficient for revolutionaries, since their task was to develop a theory and a praxis for how to exit from the hard reality of backwardness. Hassan Hamdan (1936–87), known as Mahdi Amel, directly tackled this problem. In one his early essays – "Colonialism and Backwardness" (*al-Tariq*, 1968) – Mahdi Amel wrote:

> If you really want our own true Marxist thought to see the light, and to be capable to see reality from a scientific perspective, we should not start with Marxist thought itself and apply it to our own reality, but rather start from our reality as a foundational movement.

If one starts one's analysis with the historical development of society and its own cultural resources "only then can our thought truly become Marxist." The reality of colonial backwardness had to be explored and Marxism had to be elaborated to take that backwardness into account.

Arabs bore the stigma of being "backward," Mahdi Amel wrote. It was as if they were not capable of anything but failure. But the ruin of Arabs was not because of any essential aspect of their culture but because of what had befallen them. Colonial rule for a hundred years would alter the structure of politics and economics as well as society. Old Arab notables would be side-lined or absorbed into a new world where they were merely the representatives of forces that lived elsewhere. The new elites that emerged represented external forces, not their own populations. When Paris sneezed, they caught a cold. The United States' ambassador became more important than elected officials. (An old joke that used to do the rounds: "Why is there no revolution in the United States? Because there is no US embassy there.") The experience of backwardness was not the fault of Arabs, Mahdi Amel suggested, but it was the way in which their lives had been structured. Marxism had to take this idea seriously, he argued.

At this time the Pakistani scholar Hamza Alavi had offered his theory of the colonial mode of production; in India there was a debate over the modes of production; and the Egyptian Marxist Samir Amin had produced work on tributary mode of production. Like them, Mahdi Amel saw backwardness not in cultural terms, but in terms of the way the global order had been structured – with the South to provide raw materials and markets, while the North would produce the finished goods and earn the bulk of the social wealth. The feeling of backwardness reflected this order. The political mess in the South was also related to this economic subordination. All these thinkers – with greater or lesser success – tried to provide a theory of how this is so.

Tricontinental Marxism

In 1948, the UN founded a special agency for Latin America – Economic Commission for Latin America (CEPAL) – whose work over the course of the next two decades inaugurated the "dependency school" of unequal development. The *cepalismo* – or the approach of CEPAL – pointed toward the structural obstacles for the development of Latin America. Indeed, wrote its most prolific director – Raúl Prebisch – the countries of Latin America were trapped in a cycle of dependency to the old colonial powers. Producers of primary goods and borrowers of capital, Latin American states were caught in a subordinate position. The terms of trade between the Latin American states and the old colonial powers advantaged the latter, since prices of primary goods – such as barely processed food – peaked faster than prices of manufactured goods (and services). Neither Prebisch nor most of his team were Marxist, but there was no question that the dependency tradition influenced a generation of Marxists and left nationalists across Latin America. Two decades after Prebisch's important 1948 CEPAL manifesto, a younger generation of Marxists (Ruy Mauro Marini, Theotonio dos Santos and Andre Gunder Frank) developed dependency theory – a key arena for the growth of Third World Marxism.

These theorists argued against the older position that Latin America wallowed in feudalism or semi-feudalism – and so that Latin America needed a capitalist jolt to move toward modernity. The *dependencia* school, drawing from *cepalismo*, was of the view that the world capitalist system had absorbed Latin America into its orbit in a subordinate position not in the 20th century, but from the start of the period of colonization. Alongside the *dependencia* school was the work of people such as Samir Amin, who argued that capitalism created a polarity in the world between the old colonial centers and the old colonized periphery. Amin argued – in 1956 – that the process of accumulation of capital on a world scale had shaped the agenda of the periphery, had forced the peripheral countries to adapt to the needs and interests of the center. This is what Amin called "unilateral adjustment." It meant that the policy framework for the newly independent states had already been constrained into dependency to capitalist globalization. The possibility of an exit from capitalist globalization and from the illusion of development seemed remote without a full break from the tentacles of unilateral adjustment, a break that Amin called "delinking."

It was this trend – from *cepalismo* to Samir Amin's theory of delinking – that provided the theory for the national liberation struggles from Cuba outwards. In 1966, the Cuban government hosted a range of revolutionary states and national liberation movements for the Tricontinental Conference. Conversations at the conference remained mainly at the political level – with the speeches defending the armed conflicts of the national liberation forces from Vietnam to Guinea Bissau and with speeches against the reproduction of poverty by US-led imperialism. But there was little discussion of Marxist theory or of the world economic order. That was taken for granted. It was clear to the national liberation forces that Marxism was their touchstone and that variants of dependency theory were their shared framework. Fidel Castro's speeches of the 1960s reveal his reliance upon the range of thought from *cepalismo* to delinking, from dependency theory to breaking unilateral adjustment. It was this broad understanding of the development of underdevelopment that drew an alliance between non-aligned states with different class alignments to the New International Economic Order, the UN General Assembly Resolution of 1973 that pledged to reshape world relations outside unequal exchange not only in trade but also in finance.

To break the imperialism of finance – the ugliness of debt, the crisis that would break out in 1983 – was central to this Marxist vision of the world. Castro would often say – as he did in 1985 when he inaugurated a world movement against global debt – that a "new international economic order" must be founded to "eliminate the unequal relations between rich and poor countries" to "ensure the Third World its inalienable right to choose its destiny, free of imperialist intervention and of exploitative measures in international trade" (Castro Ruiz 2016). Castro, like the other Tricontinental Marxists, had no illusions about the bourgeoisie and oligarchy in the South – people who had a class alignment with imperialism rather than against it. Theirs was not a national liberation that would hand over power to the bourgeoisie and oligarchy, but one that would accelerate revolutionary forces beyond the bourgeois state. Given that the most revolutionary classes in the periphery were often the most excluded, it would be a betrayal of history to send them back to the fields and factories after they had provided the political basis for a reconstruction of social relations.

Against the Past, Toward the Future

Debates around dependency theory and unequal exchange went from Santiago (Chile) to New Delhi (India). It was important for Marxists in this part of the world – the periphery according to the geography of dependency theory – to study closely the process of accumulation on a world scale (as Amin's book title put it), but also the class relations inside their countries that refracted international power relations. Creative Marxism was the need of the hour, but so too was suspicion of the national bourgeoisie that would often use its peripheral status to exploit its own workers against the metropolitan bourgeoisie. Disagreements in international Communism that broke out between the USSR and the People's Republic of China as well as the Socialist Federal Republic of Yugoslavia took place with these issues on the table, and they had an impact on left movements across the South. In India, for instance, the debate within the Communist movement that ran from 1951 to 1964 was sharp and learned. One section – the minority – argued that the Indian bourgeoisie could be an ally at time of the Indian working-class and peasantry because of its peripheral status, and that the USSR was the center of the world revolution. Another section – the majority of the movement – was of the view that the Indian bourgeoisie was unreliable as an ally to the workers and peasants and that the USSR was a fraternal country but not the font of revolutionary theory and praxis. This debate led to a split in the Indian communist movement in 1964, with produced the Communist Party of India (CPI) – the minority – and the Communist Party of India (Marxist) or CPIM – the majority.

Inside the CPIM, one of the main theoreticians was EMS Namboodiripad (1909–98). EMS, as he was known, was a radical in the Indian freedom struggle and one of the very youthful leaders of the Congress Socialist Party – a socialist component of the anti-colonial freedom platform, the Congress Party. Born in what would become Kerala, EMS and the other members of the Congress Socialist Party in his state joined the Communist Party of India. In 1957, EMS led the Communist Party of India to victory in the state elections in Kerala. Deep structural changes were put in place in Kerala, which earned the ire of the bourgeoisie, which – in collusion with the CIA – overthrew the EMS ministry in 1959. Meanwhile, EMS continued to study and write original work on Indian history and politics. He would make the argument that it was necessary to engage India's theoretical traditions and its history from a Marxist perspective to draw out concepts and dynamics essential to the Indian revolution. In other words, both historical materialism and dialectical materialism should not be adopted from the European tradition without serious reconstruction.

From his 1939 report to the Malabar Tenancy Enquiry Committee to his 1970s essays on caste and class, EMS explored the Marxist method to interpret the history and society of India. For historical materialism – the historical narrative laid out by Marx – society moved through two stages, from slavery to feudalism, and then from feudalism to capitalism, in anticipation of a future stage, from capitalism to socialism. Nothing like this happened in India. "India remained tied to the same old order," EMS wrote,

> under which the overwhelming majority of the people belonged to the oppressed and backward castes. This is the essence of what Marx called India's *unchanging* society where the village was not touched by the wars and upheavals at the higher levels.
>
> *(Namboodiripad 2010, 74)*

Caste society and the hegemony of Brahmanism had a most pernicious impact on Indian society. The caste system not only kept the oppressed masses in thrall, the ideological hegemony of Brahmanism resulted in a sustained stagnation of science and technology, and therefore, ultimately, of the productive forces as well. This process weakened India, leaving the door wide open for European colonialism. As EMS put it, "the defeat of the oppressed castes at the hands of the Brahmanic overlordship, of materialism by idealism, constituted the beginning of the fall of India's civilization and culture which in the end led to the loss of national independence."

The stagnation of Indian history from the time of Adi Shankara in the 8th century was encapsulated in the caste-based feudal society. This caste order with its religious justifications was able to contain its contradictions. This meant that while challenges to the caste order by rebellion did occur across Indian history, none of these rebellions were able to frontally assault caste and break caste hierarchy in any substantive way. Neither British colonialism nor the Indian bourgeoisie in the postcolonial state had any real appetite to smash caste. The conversion of feudal landlords into capitalist landlords and the conversion of tenant serfs into the agrarian proletariat did not break the back of feudalism. The transformations merely superimposed capitalist social relations upon the caste-based feudal order. "In India," EMS wrote, "many of the forms of exploitation of the pre-capitalist system are continuing, some in the original and some in changed forms. There exists along with these a new system of exploitation as a result of capitalist development." The agrarian proletariat, because of the old feudal relations, experienced harsh pauperization – the poor in the fields getting poorer as old feudal customs allowed landlords to transfer all the burdens of agriculture on their workers, while reaping all the profits – little of it re-invested to modernize agriculture in any way.

Pre-capitalist social formations cultivated by colonialism and by the national bourgeoisie had to be systematically undermined by the people's movements of independent India. EMS traced the potentialities within Indian society, finding opportunities for social progress and brakes against it. Cognizant of the special oppression of caste and of religious majoritarianism in Indian society, EMS fought against the organizing of people based on these very lines; one cannot fight caste oppression on caste lines. Instead, caste oppression had to be fought by organizing people into unified class organizations that understood and emphasized the special role of caste in Indian society. As he put it in his essay on caste and class,

> We had then and still have to fight a two-front battle. Ranged against us on the one hand are those who denounce us for our alleged "departure from the principles of nationalism and socialism," since we are championing "sectarian" causes like those of the oppressed castes and religious minorities. On the other hand, are those who, in the name of defending the oppressed caste masses, in fact, isolate them from the mainstream of the united struggle of the working people irrespective of caste, communities and so on.
>
> *(Namboodiripad 2010, 107)*

But the tonic of unity was not meant to dissolve questions of social indignity experienced by oppressed castes, by women, by *adivasis*, by those who experienced the violence of class hierarchy alongside the violence of other hierarchies. These questions had to be at the table. It took the Communist movement in India many decades to wrestle with the precise balance between the need for unity of all exploited people and for special emphasis on certain kinds of oppressions along lines of social division. The initial organizational route proposed by Indian Communism was to use the platform of class organizations openly to attack caste oppression, religious majoritarianism and feudal male chauvinism. But soon it became clear that this was insufficient.

The working class is not made up of unmarked bodies of workers. It is made up of people with experiences of social hierarchies and indignity who require particular emphasis to fight those hierarchies. This is why Indian Communism would eventually develop organizational platforms – such as the All-India Women's Democratic Association (AIDWA) and the Tamil Nadu Untouchability Eradication Front – that would concentrate attention on the specific hierarchies that needed to be combatted alongside the class demands of the left. The point is made clearly by Brinda Karat, a leader of the CPIM and a former president of AIDWA,

> A mechanical understanding of class is often problematic. When Marx said, workers of the world unite he was not speaking of male workers. We are unable to integrate the multiple forms of the double burden that working women face as an integral part of our struggle. All successful revolutions have shown the critical role of working women in the revolution. We know the February revolution in Russia was started by the huge street demonstrations of women workers. Apart from gender, in our experience in India, within the working classes, there are sections which face added oppression and discrimination on the basis of caste, with a large section of the so-called untouchables, the Dalits, relegated to the lowest rungs of the social ladder. Caste acts as an instrument for the intensification of the extraction of surplus value of the Dalits. Somewhat similar is the assault on the rights of *Adivasi* communities (tribal communities) with the corporate grab of land, forests, destruction of histories, cultures, languages, and ways of life. No class struggle in India can succeed without at the same time challenging the birth based hierarchical caste system against Dalits or the specific issues that *Adivasi* workers face. I think this would be equally relevant on the question of race, religious-based discrimination or even against immigrants in other countries. These aspects have grown in the last century and working-class struggles which ignore these aspects damage and weaken themselves laying themselves open to legitimate charges of being racist or casteist. Thus, class-consciousness must necessarily include the consciousness of the specific exploitation that workers may face because of their caste or racial origins or because of their gender.
>
> (*Karat 2017*)

Reading the South

One of the limitations of our understanding of Marxism is the assumption that "theory" is produced in Europe and in North America, while "practice" takes place in the Global South. Revolutionaries in the South are assumed to write tracts and manuals, fleeting notes on their movements, but not to contribute to Marxism in a substantial way. One is often told, what did Mao, Ho Chi Minh and Che Guevara write of real importance? Manuals of revolutionary wars are useful, but they are not decisive toward an understanding of the mutations of capitalism and imperialism. Part of this is arrogance. The other part is a lack of understanding of the tempo of work demanded by our movements of our intellectuals and leaders. Perry Anderson wrote decades ago that "[t]he hidden hallmark of Western Marxism as a whole is . . . that it is a product of *defeat*" (Anderson 1976, 42). Marxism in the South was not so categorically defeated as a political movement. It continues to struggle forward, its leadership rooted in these struggles, not yet banished from the frontlines into professorships. Their texts are not always elaborated in a high theoretical manner, written as they are by candlelight as the sound of protest cascades around them. The work has to be taken seriously and studied for its form and its content, for the innovations imbedded in these texts that carry forward revolutionary thought in a creative manner.

Note

This chapter draws from a chapter in **Red Star Over the Third World** (*LeftWord Books, 2017 and Pluto Press, 2018*).

Bibliography

Anderson, Perry. 1976. *Considerations on Western Marxism*. London: NLB.

Castro Ruiz, Fidel. 2016 (1985). "The Debt Is Unpayable." www.cadtm.org/Fidel-Castro-The-debt-is-unpayable

Gramsci, Antonio. 1977. *Selections from the Political Writings 1910–1920*. London: Lawrence and Wishart.

Ibrahim, Ibrahim A. 1979. "Salama Musa: An Essay on Cultural Alienation." *Middle Eastern Studies* 15(3): 346–57.

Karat, Brinda. 2017. "The Russian Revolution is still Relevant Today." *Indo-Brit* (8 November). http://indobrit.org/the-russian-revolution-is-still-relevant-today-brinda-karat/

Mella, Julio Antonio. 1975. *Documentos y articulos*. La Habana: Instituto Cubano del Movimiento Comunista y la Revolución de Cuba. Instituto Cubano del Libro.

Monal, Isabel. 2004/5. "Cuban Foundational Marxist Thought." *International Journal of Political Economy* 34(4): 11–23.

Namboodiripad, E.M.S. 2010. *History, Society and Land Relations: Selected Essays*. New Delhi: LeftWord Books.

Vanden, Harry E., and Marc Becker, eds. 2011. *José Carlos Mariátegui: An Anthology*. New York: Monthly Review Press.

15

VLADIMIR ILICH LENIN (1870–1924)

Lars T. Lih

In her eulogy to Lenin after his death in 1924, his widow Nadezhda Krupskaya remarked on his lifelong commitment to

> the grand idea of Marx: the idea that the working class is the advanced detachment of all the laborers and that all the laboring masses, all the oppressed will follow it. . . . Only as *vozhd* [leader] of all the laborers will the working class achieve victory.
>
> (*Lih 2011, 14*)

Krupskaya's words well express both the strategic and the emotional heart of *hegemony*, the term used by Bolsheviks to describe the core of their outlook.[1] Lenin's commitment to the hegemony strategy was strongly intertwined with his empirical reading of class forces in Russia at a particular time and place, and he never elaborated it in the books most familiar to foreign readers such as *Imperialism* or *State and Revolution*. Nevertheless, Bolshevism and its impact on world history cannot be understood without grasping the evolution of the hegemony strategy, starting with its origins in classical Marxism and ending with Lenin's final articles in 1923.

Marxist Origins of the Hegemony Strategy

In the *Communist Manifesto*, Marx repeatedly stressed the vital importance of combining partial goals with final goals:

> The Communists fight for the attainment of the immediate aims, for the enforcement of the momentary interests of the working class; but in the movement of the present, the Communists also represent and take care of the future of that movement.
>
> (MECW *6: 518*)

This outlook gave rise to a double tactical imperative: fight alongside partial allies for partial goals, but at the same time do not confuse these partial goals with the permanent aims of the worker revolution.

Behind this abstract formulation lay a deep concern with one essential partial goal: conquering political freedom by overthrowing repressive absolutist regimes (the democratic or "bourgeois" revolution). Political freedom was needed to prepare the proletariat for its historical mission of taking state power and introducing socialism. Enlightenment and organization: these concepts form the leitmotif of Marx and Engels from the 1840s to the end of their lives, whatever the exact words (Marx in 1864: "united by combination and led by knowledge"; Engels in 1890: "united action and discussion"). This commitment to enlightenment and organization of an entire class on a national scale a large and growing section of the socialist movement had a vital interest in political freedom (free press, right of assembly etc.) and therefore in the anti-absolutist revolutions needed to acquire them.

Political freedom was only a means to the final goal of socialism – but an absolutely essential means. According to Marx, the proletariat and those who believe in its mission must strive to install and expand political freedom by means of temporary alliances with whatever class forces are empirically available to accomplish this task. Over the course of the second half of the 19th century, the same tactical imperative gave rise to different empirical answers. In 1848, Marx and Engels thought the bourgeoisie *had* to carry out the democratic revolution: "Let them know in advance that they are only working in our interest. They still cannot for that reason give up their fight against the absolute monarchy, the nobility and the clergy. They must conquer – or already go under" (*MECW* 6: 528). In contrast, an immature worker movement was relegated to the role of junior partner.

As the century progressed, the two men observed the decline of the revolutionary fervor of the bourgeoisie and the rise of a strong and class-conscious proletariat. These two developments were deeply intertwined, since the bourgeoisie's failure of nerve was diagnosed as a fear of a strong and independent proletariat. The logic of this evolution in class relations was aptly summed up by Karl Kautsky: In Russia,

> the proletariat is no longer an appendage and tool of the bourgeoisie, as it was in bourgeois revolutions, but an independent class with independent revolutionary aims. But wherever the proletariat comes forth in this way, the bourgeoisie ceases to be a revolutionary class.
>
> *(cited in Lih 2017a)*

Thus by the end of the 19th century, the key elements of the hegemony strategy were in place. Already in his book-length commentary on the 1892 Erfurt Program of the German Social Democratic Party (SPD) – a book that was fundamental for Russian Social Democracy, including Bolshevism – Kautsky had set forth the basic propositions underlying the hegemony strategy (for citations and discussion, see Lih 2006, 96–101). First, political freedom as a crucial although partial goal:

> These freedoms [freedom of association, of assembly, of the press] are light and air for the proletariat; he who lets them wither or withholds them – he who keeps the proletariat from the struggle to win these freedoms and to extend them – that person is one of the proletariat's worst enemies.
>
> *(Kautsky 1965, 219)*

Furthermore, Social Democracy becomes "the representative not only of the industrial wage-laborers but of all the laboring and exploited strata – and therefore the great majority of the population, what is commonly known as 'the *Volk*'" (*Volk* is equivalent to *narod* in Russian, the common people).

The hegemony outlook was central to Marx-inspired Russian Social Democracy from the very beginning. Georgii Plekhanov's shift from populism to Marx was directly inspired by the

Manifesto's critique of apolitical "True Socialism" and particularly the sentence from the *Manifesto* quoted earlier, which proclaimed that "in the movement of the present, the Communists also represent and take care of the future of that movement." The *Manifesto* helped Plekhanov realize that he could fight for an anti-tsarist but non-socialist revolution without abandoning socialism as his central goal – in fact, he fought for political freedom *because* socialism was his central goal (Baron 1963, 67–77).

In 1889, in an address presented to the International Socialist Congress in Paris, Plekhanov pronounced what was later regarded as the foundational formulation of the hegemony strategy: "The revolutionary movement in Russia can triumph only as the revolutionary movement of the workers. There is not and cannot be any other way out for us." In this formulation, "the Russian revolution" refers to the democratic revolution aimed at bringing down the tsar and instituting political freedom. Plekhanov's prophecy was not idle talk: there is a direct line from the tactical principles of the *Communist Manifesto* to the political agitation of Russian Social Democracy and from thence to the Manifesto of October 1905 that granted some measure of political freedom to Russia.

From 1900 to 1904, the *Iskra* group within Russian Social Democracy took up the banner of the hegemony strategy. The core of this group was the editorial board of the underground Social Democratic newspaper *Iskra* (The Spark) that included Plekhanov from the older generation as well as younger underground activists such as Lenin and Julius Martov. The *Iskra* group set itself the task of creating a national party structure that despite its underground status would enable the proletariat to be a leader in the rapidly advancing day of reckoning with the tsar. The Russian Social Democrats were inspired by a very concrete political model: the German Social Democratic party (SPD) and its impressive and innovative use of the opportunities opened up by Germany's relative political freedom: an extensive press, rallies and demonstrations, electoral campaigns, worker societies of all kinds.

The new type of underground built up by the local Social Democratic activists and idealized by Lenin in *What Is To be Done?* (1902) was aimed at applying these techniques to the extent possible in absolutist Russia. The old type of underground had tried to wall itself off from society so that it could carry out assassination plots and the like. The aim of the new type was to connect to the workers by as many threads as possible while still preserving protection from police harassment. But the ultimate aim of this underground was to make itself unnecessary by overthrowing the tsar. The political motto of Lenin's *Iskra* group (and later Bolshevism) can be paraphrased as follows: Let us build a party as much like the German SPD as possible under repressive conditions so that we can overthrow the tsar and become even more like the SPD.

Lenin's commitment to the full hegemony strategy during the *Iskra* period is best manifested by his 1903 pamphlet *To the Rural Poor* (*LCW* 6: 361–432). Lenin's motivation for writing the pamphlet was to fulfil the task of proletarian leadership of the *narod*. Although he explains to the peasant the *final* goal of socialism, he lays greater emphasis on the *partial* goals that are in the direct interest of the *narod* as a whole. Lenin asserts that the socialist proletariat and only the socialist proletariat can lead the *narod* to accomplish these partial goals. In a key assertion, he asked the rhetorical question "What do the Social Democrats want?" and answered: "First and foremost, the Social Democrats want political freedom."

The Hegemony Scenario

According to Lenin, the hegemony scenario was not some sort of Bolshevik peculiarity, but rather the straightforward application of the principles of "revolutionary Social Democracy" to the special case of Russia. He therefore was tremendously enthusiastic when an article by Karl

Kautsky – the "*vozhd* [leader] of the German revolutionary Social Democrats" (*LCW* 11: 365–75) – appeared in late 1906 entitled "Driving Forces and Prospects of the Russian Revolution." Lenin acclaimed this article as "a brilliant vindication of the *fundamental principles* of Bolshevik tactics" and promptly arranged for a Russian translation accompanied by his own commentaries. His endorsement allows us, indeed compels us, to see Kautsky's article as a canonical statement of the hegemony scenario.[2]

The hegemony scenario was first and foremost an empirical analysis of Russian society Kautsky stated the essential empirical hypothesis underlying the scenario as follows:

> The revolutionary strength of Russian Social Democracy and the possibility of its victory rests on this community of interests [*Interessengemeinschaft*] between the industrial proletariat and the peasantry – but this same factor establishes the limits to the possible utilization of this victory.
>
> *(Lih 2017a)*

In his commentary, Lenin quotes these words and adds

> this means, not the socialist dictatorship of the proletariat, but the democratic dictatorship of the proletariat and peasantry . . . what is important here, of course, is not this or that formula used the Bolsheviks to describe their tactic, but the essence of this tactic, totally affirmed by Kautsky.
>
> *(*LCW *11: 365–75)*

Lenin's particular formulation arose out of polemics in spring 1905 and found expression in his pamphlet *Two Tactics in Russian Social Democracy in the Democratic Revolution* (*LCW* 9: 15–115). It can be unpacked as follows: We Bolsheviks believe that only a "worker-peasant dictatorship" – that is, a revolutionary government or *vlast* based on the popular classes – can carry the revolution "to the end," that is, achieve the full measure of the vast democratic transformation of Russia now achievable. Therefore, if the opportunity arises, the Social Democrats should certainly participate in such a government. Our Social Democratic critics remind us that the proletariat can rule alone only when socialism is possible. Of course! We are talking about the *democratic revolution* that will install the political freedom vitally necessary for the struggle for socialist revolution. Thus the class dictatorship we advocate is a *democratic dictatorship*: one based on "the democracy" (the popular classes) and limited to the partial but still hugely ambitious goal of thorough democratic transformation. By its very nature, a worker-peasant class alliance cannot move directly to socialism. (Lenin's insistence on this point was partially aimed at the non-Marxist Party of Socialist Revolutionaries).

Thus the community of interests between worker and peasant set certain limits to what could be accomplished while preserving the alliance. These limits, however, were *empirical* and as such *open-ended*. The open-ended nature of the worker-peasant alliance is crucial for later developments.

But the heart of the hegemony scenario was never the *limits* imposed by the alliance but its vision of *class leadership*. As Kautsky emphasized,

> The age of *bourgeois* revolutions, that is, of revolutions in which the bourgeoisie was the driving force, is over – in Russia too. . . . The bourgeoisie does not belong to the driving forces of the present revolutionary movement in Russia and to this extent we cannot call it a bourgeois one.

As Lenin summed up: "the fundamental principle of Bolshevik tactics" was "a bourgeois revolution, brought about by the proletariat and the peasantry despite the instability of the bourgeoisie" (*LCW* 11: 365–75).

Hegemony was the fundamental issue that separated Bolshevik and Menshevik wings of Russian Social Democracy. One Menshevik activist (Alexander Martynov) asserted that "the hegemony of the proletariat is a harmful utopia"; a Bolshevik activist (Iosif Stalin) responded that "the hegemony of the proletariat is not a utopia, it is a living fact, the proletariat is actually uniting the discontented elements around itself" (Stalin 1946–1953, 2: 1–13). The Menshevik rejection of the hegemony scenario was not primarily due to a blind commitment to abstract doctrine but rather to their own reading of class forces in Russia, which led them to stress the unreliability of the peasant as an ally and the dangers of isolation from other anti-tsarist forces.

The hegemony scenario as outlined by Kautsky, Lenin and Trotsky in 1906 also had international implications. The more complete the victory of the Russian anti-tsarist revolution, the more powerful would be the reverberations in Western Europe. Since Western Europe, unlike Russia, was on the eve of a truly socialist revolution, a successful worker revolution there would tremendously accelerate Russia's advance toward socialism – such was the hope.

Wager on Hegemony

Any great political undertaking can be viewed as a wager that a particular reading of social forces is correct. In 1917 and the years following, the Bolsheviks staked their political survival on the hegemony scenario and its central prediction: the socialist proletariat could successfully defend the revolution by providing leadership to the peasants on the basis of a profound community of interests. The Bolsheviks had to face bitter disillusionment in many ways during those years, but the underlying wager on hegemony paid off.

The slogan of 1917 – All Power to the Soviets! or *Vsya vlast sovetam!* – was a translation of the hegemony scenario into the concrete circumstances of 1917. The system of soviets that sprang up during and after the February revolution was the only possible institutional form of the worker/peasant *vlast* envisioned by the hegemony scenario. The imperialist war – the central issue in Russian politics in 1917 – was not addressed in the canonical formulations of 1906, but the war only strengthened the logic behind the scenario by making liberal leadership all the more unviable. In his argument in favor of an immediate assumption of full power, Lenin pointed to a wave of peasant revolts in late summer and early autumn as a de facto rejection of socialist "agreementism" [*soglashatelstvo*], that is, allowing the liberal elite reformers to retain control of the revolution. Thus the assumption of full power by the soviets in October 1917 was made possible by a workable version of proletarian leadership of the peasant majority.

The basic thrust of Lenin's April Theses – replacement of the "bourgeois" Provisional Government by a worker-peasant state authority based on the soviets – was not controversial among Bolsheviks (for an analysis of Bolshevik discussion of the April Theses, see Lih 2017b). The relation between Lenin's own ideas about "steps toward socialism" and the hegemony scenario is set forth in a crucial article from late April 1917, "A Basic Question" (for text and commentary, see Lih 2017c). Lenin's aim was to show that his Theses did not have the dire implications alleged by critics such as Plekhanov. He strongly reaffirmed a central proposition of the earlier hegemony scenario: Russia's peasant majority made the introduction of socialism impossible for the nonce. This fact, however, did not detract from the necessity and urgency of full soviet power, since a *vlast* based on the overwhelming majority of the country was an imperative of any genuine democracy.

Lenin went on to argue that Russia's peasant majority need not imply that "steps toward socialism" could not be taken here and now. By "steps toward socialism," Lenin primarily meant policies of state economic regulation that everyone agreed were needed to combat the war-induced economic crisis. Despite their claims to the contrary, the liberal-dominated Provisional Government would never truly implement such policies, precisely because they prepared the ground for real socialism.

A close look at these arguments shows that Lenin's seeming innovation followed closely the logic of hegemony: the socialist proletariat, and only the socialist proletariat, is able to accomplish crucial partial goals in the name of ultimate goals. The liberals in 1917 were incapable of any truly effective response to the crises of 1917, just as earlier they had been incapable of solving Russia's agrarian question or of attaining full-throated political freedom. In contrast, the socialist proletariat would not be inhibited from implementing needed policies energetically and ruthlessly. Furthermore, the new government could ensure that the peasants gave their support on the basis of genuine understanding and assent.

In the civil war that followed the October revolution, the hegemony scenario faced its most severe test. Although Menshevik leader Fedor Dan remained hostile to Bolshevism, his direct observations in 1920 confirmed the ultimate success of the wager on hegemony: "To defend the land he has seized against the possible return of the landlord, the peasant Red Army man will fight within the greatest heroism and the greatest enthusiasm" (Dan 2016, 82). But the peasants could hardly have constituted an effective fighting force unless they had been given political leadership by a political party based on the urban branch of the *narod* – a party that was able to use the essential elite skills of the officers even while ensuring that the officers had no political influence, especially on the central question of peasant land. The Red Army was Bolshevik hegemony in action.

Indeed, the core insight of the hegemony scenario proved more robust than even its proponents imagined. As pointed out in the title of an article published in *Pravda* on 7 November 1920 by Evgenii Preobrazhensky for the third anniversary of the October revolution, the "middle peasant" turned out to be the "Social Base of the October Revolution":

> Over the whole course of the civil war, the middle peasantry did not go along with the proletariat with a firm tread. It wavered more than once, especially when faced with new conditions and new burdens; more than once it moved in the direction of its class enemies. [But] the worker-peasant state, built on the foundation of an alliance of the proletariat with 80% of the peasantry, already cannot have any competitors for the *vlast* inside the boundaries of Russia.

Hegemony and Socialism

The hegemony scenario in its original form had envisioned only one way of moving past the obstacle to socialist transformation seemingly created by Russia's peasant majority: a socialist revolution in Europe that would enable radical solutions to Russia's agrarian problems. By the middle of 1919, Bolshevik leaders faced the unpleasant realization that they could not count on revolution in other European countries in the near future. Given the logic to the hegemony scenario, the Bolsheviks had to choose among the following alternatives:

- give up on the socialist project and define the regime as purely democratic
- continue to stake everything on international revolution
- go forward with the socialist project against the opposition of the peasant majority
- defer any project of socialist transformation that alienated the peasantry
- devise "steps toward socialism" that could carry the peasants all the way to socialism.

We must restrict ourselves at present to a necessarily simplified overview of the evolution of Lenin's own views. Of course, Lenin did not abandon the socialist project, but he did explicitly affirm that the democratic achievements of the revolution were more impressive than genuinely socialist change. This realization, a commonplace among Bolshevik leaders generally, should *not* be tied to the introduction of the New Economic Policy (NEP) in spring 1921. Even during the height of so-called war communism in 1919–20, the Bolsheviks did not hide the fact that very few steps had been taken on the long path to socialism.

Starting in mid-1919, the actual foreign policy of Soviet Russia turned more and more decisively away from any short- or middle-term hopes for European revolution. Nevertheless, the inevitability of global revolution remained an important source of confidence in the ultimate victory of socialism. The hegemony scenario itself was deemed to have international significance on two levels. On the global level, Soviet Russia saw itself as the natural political leader of the primarily peasant countries of "the East." On a national level, the hegemony scenario was applied to those countries thought to be undergoing a democratic revolution.

Of course, the Bolsheviks had no desire to clash with the peasantry over socialist transformation. At the height of the civil war in 1919, Lenin went out of his way to condemn in the strongest terms possible any possible use of coercion for the purpose of furthering socialist transformation in the countryside: "There is nothing more stupid than the very idea of violence in the area of property relations of the middle peasantry" (*LCW* 29: 210–11). Thus at the heart of the evolution of the hegemony scenario after 1917 were the last two alternatives listed earlier: defer any project of socialist transformation that alienated the peasantry and devise "steps toward socialism" that could carry the peasants all the way to socialism.

Whenever forced to choose between socialist ideals and peasant support, the Bolsheviks chose peasant support. Immediately after the October revolution, they gained peasant support by letting the peasants break up large estates (much to the scorn of Western socialists, who saw the breakup of large production units as economic regression). In 1919, they moved away from "class war in the villages" to an accommodation with "middle peasants." In 1920, they based long-term agricultural policy on small-scale peasant agriculture rather than socialist experiments. In 1921, they retreated further by allowing free trade in grain. This New Economic Policy must therefore be seen as the natural continuation of essential Bolshevik policy, and *not* as a sudden realization that peasant interests had to be taken into account (as it is often portrayed in the scholarly literature).

Lenin also drastically revised his map of "steps toward socialism" in the countryside. His original hopes had been for rapid progress toward collective production from *within* the village: the poorer peasantry would pool together their land to form communes (*kommuny*) or take over landowner estates and run them as "state farms" (*sovkhozy*) and thus reveal the advantages of socialism to the rest of the peasantry. The only problem was – as Lenin realized with growing dismay – the actual communes and state farms were *negative* examples that pushed the peasantry *away* from socialism. In January 1920, at the height of his disillusionment with *sovkhozy* and *kommuny*, Lenin read an article by the Bolshevik engineer Gleb Krzhizhanovsky on the vast potential of Russia's electrification. This new strategy for leading the peasantry down the path to socialism is the inner meaning of Lenin's famous slogan from late 1920: "Communism is soviet power plus electrification of the whole country."

In his final articles from early 1923, Lenin openly asserted that the Russian *narod* (people, primarily peasantry) could be led all the way to socialism:

> Strictly speaking, there is "*only*" one thing we have left to do and that is to make the population so "enlightened" that they understand all the advantages of everybody

participating in the work of the cooperatives and that they organize this participation. "*Only*" that. . . . But to achieve this "only," there must be a veritable transformation [*perevorot*]: a whole period of cultural development for the entire mass of the *narod* [*narodnaia massa*].

(LCW *33: 467–75)*

Conclusion

The hegemony strategy was the heart of Bolshevism. On one level, this strategy arose out of an empirical application of basic tactical principles that go back to the *Communist Manifesto*. On another level, the strategy resonated with the vision of a vast popular revolution in which one section of the Russian *narod* provided political leadership to another section. Both levels find expression in Krupskaya's words: "the grand idea of Marx: the idea that the working class is the advanced detachment of all the laborers and that all the laboring masses, all the oppressed will follow it."

Notes

1. For a survey of all the various other meanings of "hegemony," see Anderson (2017). In his lifetime Lenin called himself by his birthname, Vladimir Ilich Ulyanov, or "N. Lenin"; only posthumously were the two names fused: see the opening pages of Lih (2011).
2. For the text of Kautsky's article and commentaries by Trotsky and Lenin, see Day and Gaido (2009). For further analysis, see Lih (2017a).

Bibliography

Anderson, Perry. 2017. *The H-Word: The Peripeteia of Hegemony*. London: Verso.

Baron, Samuel. 1963. *Plekhanov, the Father of Russian Marxism*. Stanford, CA: Stanford University Press.

Dan, Fedor. 2016. *Two Years of Wandering: A Menshevik Leader in Lenin's Russia*. Edited by Francis King. London: Lawrence and Wishart.

Day, Richard, and Daniel Gaido, eds. 2009. *Witnesses to Permanent Revolution: The Documentary Record*. Leiden: Brill.

Kautsky, Karl. 1965 (1892). *Das Erfurter Programm*. Berlin: Dietz Verlag.

Lih, Lars T. 2006. *Lenin Rediscovered*: *What Is To be Done? In Context*. Leiden: Brill.

Lih, Lars T. 2011. *Lenin*. London: Reaktion Books.

Lih, Lars T. 2017a. "The Proletariat and its Ally: The Logic of Bolshevik 'Hegemony.'" https://johnriddell.wordpress.com/2017/04/26/the-proletariat-and-its-ally-the-logic-of-bolshevik-hegemony/

Lih, Lars T. 2017b. "Thirteen to Two: Petrograd Bolsheviks Debate the April Theses." https://johnriddell.wordpress.com/2017/07/20/thirteen-to-two-petrograd-bolsheviks-debate-the-april-theses/

Lih, Lars T. 2017c. "A Basic Question: Lenin Glosses the April Theses," https://johnriddell.wordpress.com/2017/08/15/a-basic-question-lenin-glosses-the-april-theses/

Stalin, J.V. 1946–1954. *Works*. Moscow: Foreign Languages Publishing House.

16
JAMES CONNOLLY (1868–1916)

Kieran Allen

James Connolly is an iconic figure in Irish society. He is celebrated in song and has a train station, a hospital and schools named after him. He was one of the key leaders of the Easter 1916 rebellion that began the overthrow of British imperialism. After its suppression, a wounded James Connolly was strapped to a chair and executed by a British firing squad. That alone guaranteed him a place in the pantheon of Irish heroes. Yet the fact that one of the main instigators of the 1916 Irish rising was a Marxist was largely hidden from the population. Official nationalist Ireland went to great lengths to ignore this inconvenient fact. As late as1968, for example, a prominent Irish historian, Owen Dudley Edwards, made the astounding claim that Connolly was "one of the best and most enlightened apologists the Catholic Church has since the industrial revolution" (Edwards 1971, 29).

Connolly's own followers did not help. The Irish Transport and General Workers Union, which he led, suppressed some of his writings, including those celebrating British working class solidarity with Irish workers. After Irish independence, they formed an alliance with the Catholic bishops in an anti-communist crusade that targeted any genuine left-wing sentiment. The mere mention of Connolly's Marxism was an anathema. However even his Communist Party biographer, Desmond Greaves, found difficulties in Connolly and criticized him for tending "to deny any progressive significance to the capitalist class" (Greaves 1976, 242). Greaves was a supporter of the "stages theory," which suggested that workers should first unite with the progressive national bourgeoisie to fight for national liberation. Connolly, unfortunately, did not subscribe to this dogmatic schema.

James Connolly was born into a working-class family and grew up in an Irish slum in Cowgate, Edinburgh. Poverty drove him into the British army at the age of fourteen and he was sent to serve in Ireland. When he heard that his regiment was being transferred to India, he deserted and returned to Scotland. There he became active in the socialist movement and gravitated to its most revolutionary wing.

In 1896, he responded to an advertisement seeking a socialist organizer in Dublin and took up the position. He then set about forming the Irish Socialist Republican Party but when this collapsed in 1903, he emigrated to the US. There his revolutionary views led him to a sectarian organization, Daniel De Leon's Socialist Labour Party, which formally appeared to share his outlook. However, he soon broke with this insular organization and became an organizer with the Industrial Workers of the World. This was inspired by syndicalist ideas that had developed in a number of countries in the aftermath of the first Russian Revolution of 1905.

Connolly returned to Ireland and became a union organizer with the newly formed Irish Transport and General Workers Union where he played a major role during the great lock-out of 1913. When Home Rule for Ireland appeared to be in sight, he proposed the formation of a Labour Party – but he died before this project came to full fruition. Nevertheless he joined the "broader left" Independent Labour Party (I) but some of the difficulties that accompany such formations emerged in 1914. It refused to oppose the war and some of its prominent members supported the Allied cause. Connolly was among a tiny handful of socialists who believed that the war was produced by a barbaric system that had to be overthrown by revolution. His internationalism was elementary. He wrote: "To me the socialist of another country is a fellow patriot as the capitalist of my own is a natural enemy" (Connolly 1914c).

That desire for revolution led him to align with the most intransigent elements within Irish republicanism that followed the dictum that "England's difficulty was Ireland's opportunity" and were preparing for armed rebellion. Subsequently, Connolly faced many criticisms from the British left for participating in the 1916 rebellion. Lenin, however, defended the rising, noting that even if it was led by the "petty bourgeoisie with all its prejudices" (Riddell 1984, 377), it was a legitimate revolt against imperialism. He did not, however, discuss Connolly's specific role within it. Connolly's subsequent execution was actively encouraged by his enemies within the Irish employer class (Mitchell and O'Snodaigh 1985, 26).

Connolly and Second International Marxism

James Connolly's politics were shaped by the Marxism of the Second International. This was often characterized by an economic determinism and a belief in the inevitability of socialism. Connolly explicitly defended "the doctrine of economic determinism" in polemics with a Catholic priest (Connolly 1973, 75). However, Connolly was a rebel within this tradition in important and productive ways.

For one thing, he stood decisively on its left wing. He was an ardent advocate of revolution, even when others were moving to a notion of gradual reform. When the miners' leader, Keir Hardie, was forming the British Labour Party, Connolly argued that:

> It's not a Labour Party the workers need. It's a revolutionary party pledged to overthrow the capitalist class in the only way it can be done by putting up barricades and taking over factories by force. There is no other way.
>
> *(Nevin 2005, 24)*

He despised the gradualism of the Fabians denouncing their attempt to "emasculate the working class movement . . . by substituting the principle of municipal socialism and bureaucratic State control for the principle of revolutionary reconstruction" (Howell 1986, 43).

Neither Hardie nor the Fabians were Marxists but some within the Second International who were also taking the first tentative steps to managing capitalism. Connolly belonged to the "clear cuts" within the socialist movement who opposed any dilution of revolutionary principles. He opposed the participation of the French socialist Millerand in a government of "republican defense" on 1899. His vision of socialism was sharpened by a profound understanding that it had to arise from the self-activity of the working class. He rejected all attempts to equate socialism with mere state ownership. He wrote:

> Socialism properly implies above all things the co-operative control by the workers of the machinery of production; without this co-operative control the public ownership by the State is not Socialism – it is only state capitalism.

> To the cry of the middle-class reformers, "make this or that the property of the government" we reply "Yes, in proportion as the workers are ready to make the government their property."
>
> *(Connolly 1972, 27–28)*

The Turn to Syndicalism

This equation of socialism with the self-activity of workers led Connolly to embrace a militant syndicalism. This involved both a leftward break with the dominant tradition of the Second International – and a regression in terms of ideological struggle. The economic determinism of the Second International led to passivity in its political practice. Its principal methodology became the dissemination of propaganda in order to solidify the electoral base of socialist parties. Working class struggle took second place to the building of a political machine that could take power via the parliament. In practice this approach led to a separation of politics from economic struggles, which mirrored the dichotomy within bourgeois society itself. Politics was to consist of voting while the capitalists kept hold of economic power. Economic activity by workers was hemmed into the confines of "industrial relations" pursued by increasingly moderate and bureaucratic unions. At its Stuttgart Congress in 1907 the Second International formally recognized this fundamental separation stating that "it falls to [the parties] of Social Democracy to organize and lead proletarian political struggle. It is the task of union organization to coordinate and lead working class economic struggles" (Gluckstein 1983, 25).

Connolly's own instincts was to challenge the growing passivity of the Second International and his embrace of syndicalism was his way of putting working class self-activity at the center of a strategy for change. His experience of the Industrial Workers of the World convinced him of the merits of revolutionary unionism and he transferred this experience to Ireland when he became an organizer with the Irish Transport and General Workers Union. Connolly summed up its strategy as follows:

> No consideration of a contract with a section of the capitalist class absolved any section of us from taking instant action to protect other sections when said sections were in danger from the capitalist enemy.
>
> Our attitude always was that in the swiftness and unexpectedness of our action lay the chief hopes of temporary victory, and since permanent peace was an illusionary hope until permanent victory was secured, temporary victories were all that need concern us.
>
> *(Connolly 1914a)*

This type of class struggle trade unionism was crucial to organizing vast numbers of casual and the precarious workers. Conventional trade unionism that played by the rules of "industrial relations" stood little chance of success. However, there were also weaknesses in the strategy. The syndicalist approach was modeled on how the bourgeoisie developed its economic power within the structures of a feudal society. Connolly thought that the industrial power of workers could develop in a similar way. Militant trade unionism would lead to workers' control so that every factory would eventually become a "fort wrenched from control of the capitalist class and manned with soldiers of the Revolution" (Connolly 1971, 40). The transition to a socialist society would occur by taking stock of the number of factories that workers controlled and proclaiming a lock-out of the capitalist class.

Unfortunately workers cannot accumulate economic power in the same way that the bourgeoisie did under feudalism. Theirs is based on capital and money – workers' power is based on solidarity, confidence and political clarity. Connolly had also grossly underestimated the role of the state in propping up capitalist rule. This became apparent in 1913 when the full force of the state machine was deployed to break up the growing strength of the ITGWU during a massive employer lock-out.

Connolly's turn to syndicalism led him to play down the ideological struggle among workers. He thought that "industrial unity" among workers was the key to political unity and the elimination of "political scabbery" (Connolly 1971, 41). However, reformist ideas did not simply parallel the contours of craft unionism. Reformist ideas arise organically within capitalist society from the lack of confidence and fatalism among workers and the control that the rich exercise overt the means of mental production. They were not confined to either a "labor aristocracy" as Lenin suggested or craft unionism as Connolly argued. However, despite Lenin's faulty theory of reformism he still embarked on building a revolutionary party that developed a cadre capable of challenging bourgeois ideas.

Connolly's syndicalism, however, led in the opposite direction. Political organization became a mere propaganda supplement to revolutionary trade unionism and was neglected. After the defeat of the workers during the 1913 lock-out and the subsequent rise of war fever in 1914 among a section of Dublin workers, Connolly focused on the Irish Citizens Army – a workers' militia formed as a defense unit against police violence during the lockout- as his principal vehicle. This was a key factor in his decision to participate in the 1916 rising in the particular manner in which he did. His involvement ensured that socialist ideas entered the republican psyche of Irish society in the longer term. But the absence of a Marxist party formed around Connolly's politics also ensured that the red flag was often submerged beneath the green.

Socialism and the Struggle for Irish Freedom

Despite this, Connolly's major contribution to Marxism was the manner in which he opposed imperialism and the consequent divisions it created among workers. Connolly was one of the few members of the Second International who lived in a colony. The dominant grouping within it suggested that as the working-class movement in the colonies was weak – mainly due to the lack of industrial development – they would have wait until the socialist movement in the metropolitan countries would bring change. In practice, this also meant that socialists within the colonies should abstain from any involvement in struggles for national freedom. These, it was implied, were nationalist diversions that could only be removed after the metropolitan countries brought economic development and subsequently granted independence. Only after this long process had been completed could the struggle for socialism begin in earnest.

Connolly disputed this and boldly proclaimed that Irish freedom and socialism were interlinked. He insisted that socialists, no matter what their background, should support the independence and freedom of Ireland. Previously, there had been a "gas and water" grouping around the Belfast labor leader, William Walker. This tended to take an abstentionist position on Irish freedom, with Protestants tending to favor unity within the empire and Catholics tending more toward Home Rule for Ireland. By contrast, the program of the ISRP asserted that "[t]he subjection of one nation to another as of Ireland to the authority of the British crown is a barrier to the free political development of the subjected nation and can only serve the exploiting classes of both nations" (Ryan 1948, 186).

However, Connolly went further and broke decisively with the mechanical model of how countries were to progress. In his view, there were not a set of stages whereby there, first, had to be a period of industrial development spearheaded by a nationalist bourgeoisie before a struggle for socialism could commence. Quite the opposite. The myriad problems that imperialism brought on a country like Ireland – not least sectarian divisions within the workers' movements that divided Protestant and Catholic – could only be overcome in the course of a struggle for socialism. The ISRP program therefore went on to state that "the national and economic freedom of the Irish people must be sought in the same direction, viz, the establishment of an Irish socialist republic" (Ryan 1948, 186).

One reason was that the putative agent for leading a struggle for national freedom, the local bourgeoisie, has none of the revolutionary instincts that their forefathers had during the French Revolution of 1789. They had become tied into imperial power structures and feared their "own" poorer masses more than they resented the inferiority heaped on them by their imperial masters. Connolly wrote his classic book, *Labour in Irish History* (1910), to illustrate this principle by showing how the wealthy Irish "were tied by a thousand economic strings in the shape of investments binding them to English capitalism as against every sentimental attachment drawing them towards Irish patriotism." The working class, he concluded, were the "incorruptible inheritors of the fight for Irish freedom" (Connolly 1987, 24).

This challenge to both British imperialism and the Irish rich brought him into conflict with the leaders of Irish nationalism. These attempted to promote the broadest unity of the Irish nation in order to win Home Rule or autonomy within the empire. Connolly, however, favored full independence but opposed the idea of a "union of classes" that would unite rich and poor in a fight for Irish independence. Criticizing the call for nationalist unity vigorously, he wrote:

> The cry for a "union of classes" is in reality an insidious move on the part of our Irish master class to have the powers of government transferred from the hands of the English capitalist government into the hands of an Irish capitalist class and to pave the way for this change by inducing the Irish worker to abandon all hopes of bettering his own position.
>
> *(Connolly 1898)*

Instead, he argued that the struggle for Irish freedom needed to be led by workers and culminate in a "workers' republic." He advanced two further reasons why this was necessary. If the working class were to really mobilize for Irish independence, Connolly suggested, that they would not stop, having achieved a capitalist republic. They would go further and fight for social as well as national freedom. To the objection that a fight for a socialist republic would frighten off potential allies, he made the following reply:

> It may be pleaded that the ideal of a Socialist Republic, implying, as it does, a complete political and economic revolution would be sure to alienate all our middle-class and aristocratic supporters, who would dread the loss of their property and privileges. What does this objection mean? That we must conciliate the privileged classes in Ireland! But you can only disarm their hostility by assuring them that in a free Ireland their privileges will not be interfered with. That is to say, you must guarantee that when Ireland is free of foreign domination, the green-coated Irish soldiers will guard the fraudulent gains of capitalist and landlord from "the thin hands of the poor" just as remorselessly and just as effectually as the scarlet-coated emissaries of England do today.
>
> On no other basis will the classes unite with you. Do you expect the masses to fight for this Ideal?
>
> *(Ryan 1948, 34)*

The other reason Connolly advocated a socialist solution to Ireland's national question was because of the sectarian divisions inside the working class itself. Connolly witnessed these divisions at first hand in July 1912, when Edward Carson's violent opposition to Home Rule led to pogroms in Belfast. Three thousand workers were expelled from their jobs, a fifth of them dubbed "rotten Prods" because of their socialist or Liberal sympathies. Connolly vigorously opposed Orange supremacism and was adamant in defending the right of Ireland to Home Rule, even if he thought this did not go far enough in the direction of independence.

As the Home Rule movement grew in influence due to its alliance with the Liberal Party in Britain, the partition of Ireland was increasingly suggested as the "compromise" to deal with the sectarian divisions. Connolly, however, warned against partition arguing that it would produce "a carnival of reaction" that would help "the Home Rule and Orange capitalists and clerics to keep their rallying cries before the public as the political watch cries of the day" (Connolly 1914a, 1914b).

But while opposing loyalism and the partition of Ireland, Connolly wanted openly to appeal to Protestant workers. The way to do this, he thought, was not to placate the reactionary sentiments of the Orange Order but to show how its sectarianism divided workers. He thought that only the prospect of a socialist Ireland could hold any appeal to Protestant workers. There was, quite simply, no future for Protestant workers in a capitalist Ireland under the green flag. He wrote

> When the Sinn Feiner speaks to men who are fighting against low wages and tells them that the Sinn Féin body has promised lots of Irish labor at low wages to any foreign capitalist who wished to establish in Ireland, what wonder if they come to believe that a change from Toryism to Sinn Feinism would simply be a change from the devil they do know to the devil they do not.
>
> *(Connolly 1909)*

These were highly sophisticated and advanced position but there was a blind spot in Connolly's analysis. In his historical writings, Connolly suggested that a form of primitive communism existed in Ireland before the conquest by Britain. Private ownership and capitalism were, therefore, colonial imports and undoing the conquest required a return to common ownership. This romanticization of Ireland's past was combined with a mistaken prediction about how the overproduction of goods on the world market had "rendered impossible the rise of another industrial nation in Europe" (Connolly 1972, 13). As a consequence of this analysis, Connolly came to believe that earnest republicans had to move in the direction of socialism. Living before the ascent of national liberation movements to state power, Connolly had believed that the republican tradition could be won over to the left. History was to prove him wrong on this point. National liberation movements might subsequently adopt the language of socialism but their agenda was about capital accumulation rather the working class emancipation.

Connolly's life is often summed up by the manner of his leaving it. His involvement in the 1916 rising has been various described as an abandonment of socialism (Morgan 1988) or a final, belated recognition of the wisdom of a stages approach to national liberation (Greaves 1976). It was neither. The manner in which he was involved in the rising was rather the crystallization of all of Connolly's revolutionary instincts with some of his theoretical weaknesses.

In August 1914, the First World War broke out and Connolly immediately saw it as a product of an imperialist order that had grown out of a profit-driven system. He was appalled at the way the leaders of the Second International had succumbed to chauvinism and supported their own respective country's war efforts. He summed up his own attitude by stating that "the signal of war ought to have been the signal of rebellion . . . when the bugle sounded the first note for actual war, their notes should have been taken as the tocsin for social revolution" (Connolly 1915).

He was determined to act, to foment an insurrection. He wanted to strike a blow both for Irish freedom and to undermine the imperialist world order. He thought that a revolt in Ireland against the British Empire would have a ripple effect around the world. Connolly's problem was that the labor movement had been crushed in the 1913 Lockout and had neither the political or organizational coherence to embrace his vision. His syndicalist perspectives had been disoriented. He had no coherent revolutionary organization around him. His impatience led him to the Irish Republican Brotherhood and he became one of main instigators of an uprising. He cajoled, mocked and urged the IRB to take on the road of insurrection. Eventually, after an apparent "kidnapping," he reached agreement with its leaders on practical plans. However, the price was that he entered the rising on republican terms. There was no call for working class mobilization or independent socialist propaganda.

In Connolly's mind, there was not the slightest intention of taking part in a "blood sacrifice" and regarded all such talk as that of a "blithering idiot" (Reeve and Reeve 1978, 274). Even while joining with his IRB allies, Connolly urged his supporters to "hold on to their guns as those with whom we are fighting may stop before our goal is reached. We are for economic as well as political liberty" (Greaves 1976, 403).

His tragedy was that his vision largely died with him, and the newly independent Ireland was shaped more by the ideas of Arthur Griffith, a right-wing ideologue of Sinn Féin whose main ambition was to create a Gaelic Manchester. Griffith had opposed the rising, but his concept of a free-market society that showed little concern for trade union rights won out after the counter-revolution of 1922 that coincided with the formation of the Irish Free State and a bloody civil war.

James Connolly was a wonderful propagandist but not always a consistent theoretician. His Marxism showed certain limitations particularly when it came to an analysis of religion or family structures under capitalism. But when it came to courage, he was second to none. And nowhere was this more in evidence than in his firm belief that socialists in the "backward" colonies were not condemned to await pre-set patterns of History. They could fight openly for working class self-emancipation and bring about national liberation from imperialism.

That vision is still relevant today when it comes to a strategy for dealing with sectarianism – itself a bitter fruit of imperialist intervention. Rather than waiting for moderate leaders to promote understanding of an Orange and Green tradition, socialists oppose the institutionalization of communal politics. They challenge all forms of supremacist ideologies within the working class – but do so from a perspective of class interests rather than nationalism. That outlook owes much to the original vision of James Connolly.

Bibliography

Connolly, James. 1898. "The Re-Conquest of Ireland." *Workers Republic* (2 September).

Connolly, James. 1909. "Sinn Fein, Socialism and the Nation." *Irish Nation* (23 January).

Connolly, James. 1914a. "Labour and the Proposed Partition of Ireland." *Irish Worker* (14 March). https://www.marxists.org/archive/connolly/1914/03/laborpar.htm

Connolly, James. 1914b. "Industrial Unity and Political Division in Ireland." *Forward* (21 March). https://www.marxists.org/archive/connolly/1914/03/iupoldiv.htm

Connolly, James. 1914c. "Continental Revolution." *Forward* (15 August). www.marxists.org/archive/connolly/1914/08/contrev.htm

Connolly, James. 1915. "Revolutionary Unionism and War." *International Socialist Review* (March). www.marxists.org/archive/connolly/1915/03/revunion.htm

Connolly, James. 1971. *Socialism Made Easy*. Dublin: Plough Books.

Connolly, James. 1972. *Erin's Hope and the New Evangel*. Dublin: New Books.
Connolly, James. 1973. "Labour, Nationality and Religion." In *James Connolly: Selected Political Writings*, edited by Owen Dudley Edwards and Bernard Ransom, 59–126. London: Jonathan Cape.
Connolly, James. 1987. *Labour in Irish History*. London: Bookmarks.
Edwards, Owen. 1971. *James Connolly: The Mind of an Activist*. Dublin: Gill and Macmillan.
Gluckstein, Donny. 1983. "The Workers' Council Movement in Western Europe." *International Socialism* 2(18): 3–29.
Greaves, C. Desmond. 1976. *The Life and Times of James Connolly*. London: Lawrence and Wishart.
Howell, David. 1986. *A Lost Left: Three Studies in Socialism and Nationalism*. Manchester: Manchester University Press.
Mitchell, Arthur, and Padraig O'Snodaigh. 1985. *Irish Political Documents 1916–1919*. Dublin: Irish Academy Press.
Morgan, Austin. 1988. *James Connolly: A Political Biography*. Manchester: Manchester University Press.
Nevin, Donal. 2005. *James Connolly*. Dublin: Gill and MacMillan.
Reeve, Carl, and Ann Barton Reeve. 1978. *James Connolly in the United States*. Atlantic Highlands, NJ: Humanities Press.
Riddell, John. 1984. *Lenin's Struggle for a Revolutionary International*. New York: Monad.
Ryan, Desmond. 1948. *Socialism and Nationalism*. Dublin: Three Candles.

17
JOSÉ CARLOS MARIÁTEGUI (1894–1930)

Mike Gonzalez

José Carlos Mariátegui was not well served by those who claimed his legacy after his early death. Three generations later, his Marxism has proved stronger than its distortions.

A radical in his early teens, a declared socialist in his early twenties, he returned from a three year journey through Europe early in 1923, "a convinced and committed Marxist." He had just over eight years of life left – which makes his contribution as a thinker and an organizer all the more extraordinary. He shaped the early working class movement in Peru, reinterpreted Marxism for the reality of Latin America and challenged both reformism and the sectarianism of the Comintern.

> In the struggle between two systems, between two ideas, we don't see ourselves as spectators, nor are we seeking a third way. . . . Although socialism was born in Europe, it is a world movement from which no country that moves within the orbit of civilization can stand aside.[1]

"My Stone Age"

José Carlos was born in Moquegua, the son of an indigenous seamstress and an aristocratic father who abandoned his mother, leaving her to care for José Carlos and his two siblings. In 1902 (he was eight) the boy suffered an injury to his leg that required an operation, and that would prove a lifelong torment. The family moved to Lima to be near the French hospital where he spent four months in treatment, remaining more or less housebound for the next four years. But he turned that to advantage, reading voraciously in both Spanish and French.

At fifteen, he found work as a printer's apprentice on the newspaper *La Prensa*. Within a year, using the name Juan Croniqueur, he was writing both parliamentary reports and "*crónicas*," a form that combined social commentary and cultural observation. He was drawn by the avant-garde artistic circles of Lima and briefly shared their characteristic fin-de-siecle *ennui*. He was critical of a middle class he found self-indulgent and shallow, but expressed admiration for the decadent poet Abraham Valdelomar and his *Colónida* group. This was Mariátegui's "stone age."

The 19th century booms in guano and nitrate had briefly fueled economic growth in Peru, but it was stopped in its tracks by the Pacific War with Chile in 1879–83 and the loss of the port of Tacna. Foreign capital financed the phase of recovery and by the beginning of the 20th century had appropriated Peru's mines, coastal export agriculture and oil. The ruling elite, acting through the Civilista Party, was content to benefit from external finance, though a radical wing under Augusto Leguía argued for national economic development. The First World War raised demand for Peru's exports, but dramatically increased the cost of living for the working class. The early trade unions, led by anarchists, grew in response and the Rumi Maqui rising in 1916 marked the beginning of new communal resistance in the Andes. With the end of the war, and the consequent decrease in production, working class resistance intensified.

In 1918–19 Mariátegui published two short-lived papers, *Nuestra Epoca* and *La Razón*, which actively supported the general strike in May. When Leguía became president two months later and conceded some key workers' demands Mariátegui was carried through the streets by workers. Yet within weeks Leguía turned to repression, and in October sent José Carlos on an extended "information-gathering" trip to Europe. It was a punishment, but a double-edged one.

Art and culture remained central to his thinking, and he regarded the best of the avant garde as rebels against the fallacies of bourgeois reason. But Juan Croniqueur had given way to José Carlos Mariátegui, the socialist.

Europe

He arrived early in 1920 in a Europe still responding to the promise of the Bolshevik revolution. In Italy, a new order was emerging in the form of the workers councils in the occupied factories; the sheer excitement of it emerges his *Letters from Italy* (Mariátegui 1969). He was present at the conference of the Italian Socialist Party (PSI) at Livorno in 1921, where the Communist Party was formed after a split. Gramsci was marginalized in the debates at Livorno, though he went with the new party. While in Italy Mariátegui read *L'Ordine nuovo*, the journal edited by Gramsci and his Turin comrades. Mariátegui's biographer, Guillermo Rouillon, asserts that José Carlos, Falcón and two others "went to see Gramsci seeking his political advice during their stay in Rome" (Rouillon 1963, 91). The four later formed the first Peruvian communist group, though it was mainly symbolic. He visited Berlin and Vienna and Paris before his return, meeting and interviewing intellectuals, artists and political leaders, including Hilferding and Gorki, as well as furiously reading Marx, Weber and Nietzsche (Mariátegui 1970).

On his return early in 1923, Mariátegui was invited to give a series of lectures on his European experience at the Universidad Popular, set up by the student movement mainly as a center for working class education. His classes offered a Marxist interpretation of the revolutionary moment in Europe and, for the first time, of the history of Latin America and its reality. There was no socialist tradition in Peru, so his was a creative and original project.

His lectures, published as *History of the World Crisis* are a fine example of popular education and an admirable synthesis of European history over the previous twenty years (Mariátegui 1959). Two strands emerge in the lectures and the articles collected in *The Contemporary Scene* (Mariátegui 1925). The first is his observation of a bourgeois order in a decline and decadence that also embraced the mechanical Marxism of the Second International. Socialism, he writes, "has become bourgeois." Even the institutions of the worker's movement had absorbed bourgeois ideology and its perception of politics as negotiation and consensus. In the aftermath of the Great War, this clash between capitals, he argued, "workers should ask themselves whether they want to rebuild capitalism and bourgeois society, so that in forty or fifty years time, or perhaps less, a new conflagration will produce more carnage" (Mariátegui 1959, 16). The comment was characteristically prescient.

Peru in early 1923 was a society in crisis. The promised modernization of the economy had occurred only in the sense that foreign capital dominated the key enclaves of the economy. The working class, which included the factory and service workers of Lima-Callao, the miners in the Central Valley and the textile workers of the southern city of Cuzco, probably numbered around forty thousand to fifty thousand of whom some 5 percent were unionized. In the export agriculture sector, where the Gildemeister and Larco estates were among the largest estates, workers, largely from the highland areas, were essentially kidnapped by contractors and held captive by a debt peonage system. Forty percent of the population was indigenous, living in the Andean regions where they worked as virtually enslaved labor for the regional landowners, the *gamonales*. As Mariátegui analyzed it in his *Seven Essays*, the Peruvian economy combined a modern sector directly linked to the external market, with an economy he described as "semi-feudal," in which relations of servitude prevailed.

The anarchist-dominated Universidades Populares were not the easiest terrain for Mariátegui to begin forging the instruments, organizational and theoretical, that would produce the social revolution in Peru. Nonetheless, José Carlos's project was the development of a Marxist *politics*, a strategy for building a revolutionary movement. His writing and his activism were all dedicated to this end. While the Latin American revolution could not be a "copy or imitation" of the Western experience, neither could it grow in isolation from the working class movements elsewhere in the world:

> Internationalism exists as an ideal because it is the new, emerging reality. . . . A capricious, impossible utopia, however beautiful, never moves masses. The masses are moved and inspired by that theory which offers an imminent objective, a credible end, . . . a new reality in process of becoming.
>
> (*Mariátegui 1959, 156*)

Mariátegui already refers here to an ideal, a theory – terms that anticipate a central, and controversial, concept in his work – the *myth*. In his 1925 essay "Man and Myth," written while recovering from the amputation of his right leg, he develops this idea. His Marxism was a philosophy of praxis. The direct link to Gramsci has been made by many commentators, and is fundamental, but Mariátegui will have taken the concept from Labriola via his reading of Sorel. Though he met and was impressed by Gramsci during his time in Italy, Gramsci's major theoretical elaborations on the theme came later – and Mariátegui did not live to read them. The connection, then, is in a shared understanding of Marxism, and a coincidence of concerns, though Gramsci's use of the concept comes only in his *Prison Notebooks*.

> Marxism as a "philosophy of praxis" is necessarily concerned with the critical exploration of the forms of activity, organization and ideas that emerge and are contested within the politics of everyday life. As such it is inherently involved with the evaluation of the strategies and tactics of movements and parties.[2]

That evaluation drew important conclusions from the Italian experience; Mariátegui felt that the left had underestimated fascism. It was, as he put it in his "Biography of Fascism" (Mariátegui 1964), a counter-revolutionary practice that offered a reactionary utopia in a time of crisis embodied. The failure of the bourgeois leadership of the European trade unions disarmed the working class at this critical moment. But most fundamentally, the split within the Socialist Party had isolated the Marxists, the revolutionaries, from a significant section of the class. Thus there was a limited challenge to a bourgeois hegemony that embraced both the bourgeoisie itself and a significant layer of the workers movement. The alternative future that the actions of the most advanced sectors of the Italian working class had placed on the table of history during the factory occupations, was confused and lost.

Mariátegui's response took the form of a manifesto "May Day and the United Front" (1924). Reiterating that "we are still too few to divide ourselves" he argued passionately that

> [t]he united front does not annul the personality, does not annul any of those who make it up. . . . Everyone should work for his own credo. But all should feel united by class solidarity, bound together by the struggle against the common adversary, tied by the same revolutionary will.
>
> *(Vanden and Becker 2011, 342–43)*

Myth

The concept of "the revolutionary will" points to another constant in Mariátegui's developing Marxism: "Man, as philosophy defines him, is a metaphysical animal. He does not live productively without a metaphysical conception of life. Myth moves man in history" (Mariátegui 1964, 19). In another essay, "Materialist Idealism," his analysis of the proliferation of quasi-mystical doctrines adopted by the bourgeoisie in the aftermath of war is withering; "the best sign of the health and power of socialism as the source of a new civilization is . . . its resistance to all these spiritualist ecstasies" (Mariátegui 1967, 102). His concept of myth, in contrast, derived from the writings of Georges Sorel, whom he admired throughout his life, as did Gramsci. For Robert Paris, a pioneering Mariátegui scholar, the Peruvian was "an ambiguous Sorelian." Mariátegui found in Sorel's writing a critical account of bourgeois rationalism, an anti-reformist skepticism about the state and an emphasis on the significance of workers' self-activity. But he did not accept Sorel's worldview entirely; indeed he clashed with the anarchist supporters of Sorel at the Universidad Popular and afterwards.

What Mariátegui took from Sorel was a concept that allowed him to address the significance of ideas and cultural and historical memory in shaping the consciousness of "the multitude," the protagonist of the social revolution.[3] He meant something far broader than theory, or faith – elsewhere he calls it a passion – forged in struggle but directed at a future society. For the proletariat, socialist revolution is the myth. For beyond the struggle to improve the material conditions of life is what Oshiro Higa, in his extraordinary study (Oshiro Higa 2013, 108), describes as "anticipatory consciousness," a category sometime interchangeable with "imagination." Despite his earlier formulation, this is not actually metaphysical or religious, for "it has moved from heaven to earth." The difference between the idealists he had earlier criticized and the idealism of the present is that "Idealism can only prosper when a social class becomes the instrument of its realization" (Mariátegui 1964, 46).

This was not an abstraction. The Latin American reality, and the Peruvian in particular, demanded a Marxism able to respond to very different externalities from Europe. Mariátegui did not propose a different revolutionary subject, but rather a broader perception of that subject in which other social layers and classes could identify with and participate in the social revolution impelled by the laboring classes, the proletariat. The bourgeoisie had abandoned its own myth – of progress in theory and in practice. The First World War had left it in ruins, and the confusion and decadence of the ruling class in both Europe and Latin America made a mockery of all bourgeois utopians. To the extent that they existed, they were rebels against bourgeois optimism itself – the surrealists, the Bohemians like Chaplin, the poets and especially the great César Vallejo, for whom God was an old man throwing dice and the future an unanswered question.

Against this Mariátegui set a Marxist politics of working class organization, of unity of all those exploited and oppressed by capitalism where the proletariat remained a tiny minority of the class. Forty percent of Peru's people were indigenous; no social revolution was conceivable without them. They were not, as they had been seen historically by Europe and were still regarded by many on the left, external to the global capitalist order. His *Seven Essays* (1928) are dedicated to a careful materialist proof of their economic inclusion and their corresponding ideological marginality.

Seven Essays

The Conquest of the Americas was not a heroic enterprise. But, with rare exceptions, the collapse of the Aztec and Inca imperial theocratic orders produced little in the way of sustained resistance. After Bartolomé de Las Casas's 16th-century defense of the Indian, the indigenous communities effectively disappeared from the European view until the late 19th century and the emergence of the movement called "indigenismo." Why it arose when it did, to criticize the mistreatment of indigenous peoples, is a complex issue, but it was in essence a moral critique aimed at the landowning classes. Mariátegui recognizes the humanism of the indigenista intellectuals, like Clorinda Matto de Turner. The poet Manuel González Prada (1844–1918), an anarchist influential at the turn of the century, exposed the ill-treatment of the Indians, yet shared the view of their passivity and lack of consciousness, arguing that independence had simply continued the colonial system that had corrupted both the dominant and the dominated classes. He could not, as Mariátegui did, conceive of the indigenous communities as active builders of an alternative future.

Mariátegui located them firmly within the global Peruvian society rather than as more or less exotic outsiders; their exploitation was integral to the economy and the prevailing relations of production. The education that the earlier generation of indigenistas had recommended for them did not touch the central cause of their alienation – the appropriation of the land by the *gamonales*, the rapacious rural landowners to whom they were subject. Their freedom was not a matter of consciousness alone, but of transforming an economic system that rested on their labor and denied them land.

There could be no social revolution without them, because their absence would signal that socialism did not mean the transformation of the whole of society for the benefit of its majorities. But they could not be won to the revolution by an offer of absorption into a Western colonial system into which they had already been assimilated as slave labor. Thus the ideology of revolution must in its turn embrace a lived experience beyond its original material basis in the west. Marxism, as Mariátegui endlessly insisted, was a philosophy of revolutionary praxis that could take root in different soils. The liberation of the indigenous peoples

> is the task of socialism. Only socialist doctrine gives a modern and constructive sense to the socialist cause which, located in its real social and economic terrain and raised to the level of a creative and realistic politics can count for its fulfillment on the will and discipline of the class that today is appearing in our historical process – the proletariat.
> *(Mariátegui 1928, 188)*

Peru was especially suited to this new enterprise because bourgeois individualism has no resonance among the indigenous people. The Peruvian bourgeoisie was weak, indolent and submissive to Western capitalism; it had not been capable of developing a hegemonic project that might win sections of the working class. Beyond that, and critically, Mariátegui argued, indigenous traditions are by their nature collective. In the essay "The Problem of the Indian" he develops what others would later describe, not always helpfully, as "Inca socialism." There were those among his contemporaries, most notably Luis Valcárcel, who did advocate the recreation of the

Inca world in confrontation with a wider society, racially defined. Earlier Indian risings, notably the Tupac Amaru rebellion of the late 18th century, were led by descendants of the Inca aristocracy, and were restorationist.

What would draw the history of indigenous resistance and a revolutionary socialist project together were two things; the specific struggle against capitalist relations of production in regard to land, and the pre-Hispanic traditions of community and collective labor and cooperation that the ancient system of land ownership, the *ayllu*, had rested on and that had survived the collapse of Inca autocracy within popular culture. The *ayllu* was a social formation that embraced every generation and every sector of the population (including the sick and the aged) in a single unit whose resources and products were equally shared. It also included a kind of tithe to the Inca aristocracy and the empire – so it coexisted historically with an autocratic system and was subordinated to it. Conquest, however, destroyed the old Inca hierarchy but left the communities still organized around these traditions. These shared values, furthermore, did not derive from any metaphysical precepts, and certainly not from the deification of the emperor. These shared ideals, this *myth*, as Mariátegui described it, offered a tangible and anticipatory vision of a socialist society.

He emphasizes that history cannot be unlived, nor the past regained. But the future can and will be built out of the experiences of resistance, rebellion and collective hope merged into a revolutionary project. He adds,

> There are those shallow theorists whose only opposition to socialism is that capitalism hasn't completed its mission in Peru. How surprised they must be when they realize that the function of socialist government of the nation . . . will be largely to carry through capitalism, or at least those historically necessary possibilities still to be realized, as they are required by social progress.

The scientific and technical advances achieved under capitalism will be taken and used for different purposes. They are after all a legacy of all humankind. But they will cease to be instruments of exploitation. In Latin America, he argued, the tasks that had fallen to the bourgeoisie in Europe would now be realized by a socialist revolution. This sounds very like Trotsky's theory of permanent revolution. Mariátegui expressed admiration for both Lenin and Trotsky on many occasions, though he continued to repeat the Comintern's line on Trotsky until very late in his life – when he began to make contact with the French Trotskyists around Pierre Naville. But despite his formal position it may well be that the coincidence of ideas fueled the Comintern's suspicion of him.

Seven Essays was in every sense a practical analysis, against a background of growing working class organization – the second Congreso Obrero, or Workers' Congress, convened in 1926. In that same year Mariátegui founded the extraordinary journal *Amauta* (the name given to wise men in Inca society), as an open platform for debate on the left, a vehicle for the dissemination of the ideas of the new indigenism, as well as a new platform for the discussion about art and politics taking place across the movement worldwide. It was extremely influential; its sales of 4000 an issue probably represented many more readers among workers and intellectuals. In Peruvian terms it was a meeting point between the socialists who met every weekday evening at Mariátegui's home in Washington Izquierda Street and the circles around Haya de la Torre and his Apra organization.

José Carlos had worked with Apra through most of the twenties, but increasingly distrusted Haya's version of Marxism and his personal ambition. When in 1928 Haya formed the PNP, an electoralist front with elements of the bourgeoisie and imperialism, it precipitated an important clarification of Mariátegui's position. The second series of *Amauta*, which began after Mariátegui's arrest and detention by Leguía for his role in a supposed Communist plot, opened with an editorial, "An Anniversary and a Balance Sheet," that declared:

> The Latin American Revolution will be nothing more and nothing less than . . . a phase of the world revolution. . . . We certainly do not want socialism in Latin America to be a copy or imitation. It should be a heroic creation.
>
> *(Vanden and Becker 2011, 128, 130)*

The last phrase is probably the most-quoted part of his writings. It points again to the idea that revolution is driven by a struggle over material conditions and the distribution of resources, but also by an ideal, a vision of the future, a myth.

Mariátegui founded his Peruvian Socialist Party in 1928, in reaction to Haya's attempted appropriation of that political space. He continued to resist the growing pressure from the Comintern for the creation of a Communist party; instead he argued for a Communist cell active within the PSP. There is considerable debate about why Mariátegui responded in this way. The least convincing is that he was afraid of repression; this was a man whose energy and commitment to the socialist cause never abated despite the pain he was constantly suffering. The more plausible explanation is that he was concerned that a still small left within a small working class, where other currents (like Apra and anarchism) were still influential, could be all too easily isolated *politically*, especially from the indigenous resistance whose role in the social revolution he regarded as pivotal.

Mariátegui's last work was his *Defense of Marxism*, written against *Beyond Marxism* (1927) by the Belgian social democrat (and later Nazi collaborator) Henri de Man. De Man was, as Mariátegui described him, a disenchanted reformist who discussed Marx while ignoring the October revolution. His book, while widely read at its moment was essentially a return to the mechanical Marxism of Bernstein. His Marx is a determinist and little more than a historian of a capitalism that has now moved on from his original characterization. For Mariátegui, by contrast, Marxism was both theory and practice, both material and ideal, in combining a rigorous and continuing analysis of the material reality and an understanding of the creative possibilities of a new world.

In his final months an ailing Mariátegui sent three papers to the Latin American Communist Conference held in Buenos Aires in 1929, including "On Anti-Imperialism," an attack on Haya and his "Peruvian Version of the Kuomintang" and "On the Question of Race," an elaboration of his thinking on the indigenous question. His representatives, Julio Portocarrero and Hugo Pesce, were coldly received. The conference was dominated by Codovilla, leader of the Argentine Communist Party, in the spirit of Third Period Stalinism. Mariátegui's conception of the "united front" could have little in common with the sectarian thesis of "class against class"; his discussion of Indian America had little resonance with a conference bent on applying a European model, and a Stalinist one at that, that was indifferent to the Andean nations. There was no "Peruvian reality" in their view, only the semi-colonial world. When Mariátegui refused to accept the twenty-one conditions required for affiliation to the Communist International, he was attacked and marginalized. The Comintern's insistence on arguing for separate indigenous republics made mock of Mariátegui's strategy and isolated the left from the indigenous struggle for more than a generation. As he complained to Samuel Glusberg, "they are trying to create a vacuum around me, scaring off anyone who comes near me."[4]

Mariátegui died in Lima in April 1930. Shortly after his massive funeral took over the city, the Communist Party was formed under the leadership of the sinister Eudocio Ravines and

Amauta became a mouthpiece for a virulent anti-Trotskyism. Yet two generations later, the collapse of Stalinism and the rise of indigenous resistance movements of unprecedented strength brought Mariátegui's ideas, and his practice, back from the wilderness. The socialism of the 21st century advocated by Hugo Chávez in Venezuela explicitly referenced his notion of a participatory socialism and his creative and expansive Marxism. It was once again becoming clear that the Latin American revolutions, each specific in their emergence and their histories, could not be anything but aspects of a world revolution in which the "actuality of revolution" would once again demonstrate its diversity and its compelling necessity.

Notes

1. Mariátegui (2012b, 533).
2. Personal communication from Colin Barker.
3. He was using the term in the sense that Marx and Engels spoke of "the masses." Its use here is not be confused with the way the term is used by Hardt and Negri.
4. Letter of 21 November 1929 in Mariátegui (1964, 673).

Bibliography

Flores, Galindo A. 1992. *La agonía de Mariátegui*. Lima: Ed Revolución.
Flores, Galindo A. 2010. *In Search of an Inca: Identity and Utopia in the Andes*. Cambridge: Cambridge University Press.
Gonzalez, Mike. 2018. *In the Red Corner: The Marxism of Jose Carlos Mariátegui*. Chicago: Haymarket.
Mariátegui, José Carlos. 1925. *La escena contemporánea*. Lima: Amauta.
Mariátegui, José Carlos. 1928. *Siete Ensayos de interpretación de la realidad peruana*. Lima: Amauta.
Mariátegui, José Carlos. 1959. *Historia de la Crisis Mundial*. Lima: Amauta.
Mariátegui, José Carlos. 1964. *El alma matinal*. Lima: Amauta.
Mariátegui, José Carlos. 1967. *Defensa del marxismo*. Lima: Amauta.
Mariátegui, José Carlos. 1969. *Cartas de Italia*. Lima: Amauta.
Mariátegui, José Carlos. 1970. *Figuras y aspectos de la vida mundial*. Lima: Amauta.
Mariátegui, José Carlos. 1984. *Correspondencia*. Lima: Amauta.
Mariátegui, José Carlos. 2012a. *Complete Works/Obras Completas*. www.marxists.org
Mariátegui, José Carlos. 2012b. *Mariátegui Total*. Vol. 1. Lima: Amauta.
Melis, Antonio. 1999. *Leyendo a Mariátegui*. Lima: Amauta.
Oshiro Higa, J. 2013. *Razón y mito en Mariátegui*. Lima: Congreso del Peru.
Rouillon, Guillermo. 1963. *Bio-bibliografía de José Carlos Mariátegui*. Lima: UNMSM.
Sulmont, Denis. 1977. *Historia del movimiento obrero en el Peru 1890–1977*. Lima: Tarea.
Vanden, Harry E., and Marc Becker, eds. 2011. *Jose Carlos Mariátegui: An Anthology*. New York: Monthly Review Press.

18
MAO ZEDONG (1893–1976)

Dhruv Jain

Mao Zedong was born in a village in Hunan Province, south-central China. Despite being the son of a relatively wealthy farmer, Mao became involved in anti-Qing dynasty politics as a liberal republican. He later became a Communist and the Chairman of the Central Committee of the Communist Party of China (CPC). He is regarded to be the founding father of the People's Republic of China. He is also one of the most controversial figures of the 20th century due to his promulgation of policies like the Great Leap Forward campaign (1958–62) and the Great Proletarian Cultural Revolution (1966–76), which unintentionally contributed to the deaths of millions of people. These policies were animated by a series of theoretical innovations collectively referred to as "Mao Zedong Thought." The significance of these theoretical developments are contested with some accusing Mao Zedong Thought of being a variant of Stalinism, while others differentiate between the two. Furthermore, there is a consensus that Mao's thought is a combination of Chinese and Marxist traditions, although there is no agreement to the extent and contours. Here Mao and his political thought are examined with respect to Marxism, especially in relation to Soviet Marxism. While explaining Mao's theoretical innovations and differentiating between him and Stalin on several key questions, there also is an acknowledgment that significant similarities exist, including the development of a cult of personality, and the limitations on democracy and political freedom.

The Road to Damascus (1912–27)

Mao briefly joined the 1911 October revolution that overthrew the Qing dynasty.

> Not yet exposed to Marxism, Mao became an idealist liberal, convinced that if individuals cultivated themselves, an unjustly and imperfectly governed world could be transformed into an ideal political community presided over by intelligent and upright leaders.
>
> *(Karl 2010, 10)*

Only in 1918, while working in Beijing University as a library clerical worker, was he introduced to Marxism (Karl 2010: 14). By mid-1920, he had organized a Communist group in Hunan, which helped constitute the CPC in 1921 (Karl 2010, 18).

In 1923 Mao successfully organized tin and coal miners in Anyuan and Hankou Canton Railway workers, leading to his promotion to the Central Committee in Shanghai (Karl 2010, 23). Before departing however, warlords destroyed the movement (Karl 2010, 23). In Shanghai, Mao worked under the auspices of the Comintern's United Front strategy. The Comintern advocated that the CPC function as a "bloc within" with the nationalist Kuomintang party, that is, they "would retain a subordinated organizational identity, but no independent overarching structure" (Karl 2010, 24). In 1925 Mao went to Shaosan, effectively withdrawing from politics (Karl 2010, 27–28). Fortuitously, peasant unions spontaneously formed and, by the summer of 1925, he was working in the peasant movement, although violent repression caused him to flee to Canton (Karl 2010, 29).

Mao restarted his Communist activities in Canton. Because of his pro-peasant perspectives, he was assigned to study peasant movements and he returned to Hunan in early 1927 to study the movement there. In two essays, "Analysis of the Classes in Chinese Society" and "Report on an Investigation of the Peasant Movement in Hunan," Mao renovated classical Marxist interpretations of the peasantry's role (Meisner 1997, 189). He was convinced that the peasantry could play a central role in China's revolution.

In April 1927, the Kuomintang leader Chiang Kai-Shek ordered the massacre of his former Communist allies and their sympathizers. Over one million were killed (Karl 2010, 33).

Preliminary Experiments (1927–35)

Following the 1927 massacre, Mao and the Red Army established a revolutionary base area in the Jinggangshan Mountains in northwestern Jiangxi province. Mao and Zhu De – in-charge of Red Army daily operations – experimented with the practices and policies that would characterize Mao Zedong Thought, including innovating a strategy that emphasized organizing the peasantry and surrounding the cities, rather than relying on urban-based movements (Karl 2010, 36).

However, his ideas remained a minority position within the CPC and he was instructed by the Central Committee, led by the Moscow-educated Li Lisan, to adopt a military strategy that advocated dispersing the Red Army into small bands (Karl 2010, 39). Mao rejected these orders and pursued his own strategy of luring the enemy deep into guerrilla zones where the Red Army enjoyed the advantage because the enemy was forced to disperse, thus making them easier to attack despite asymmetric numbers and military technologies (Karl 2010, 40). These became central features of his strategy of protracted war. Irrespective of the success that this strategy enjoyed, Mao and Zhu were forced to abandon Jinggangshan and re-establish themselves in early 1930 in Ruijin city, southern Jianxi province.

Li ordered Mao and Zhu to attack Changsa, the capital of Hunan province. "This order derived from Li's belief that the Red Army's only utility was to launch assaults on cities, rather than to build a revolutionary movement slowly in rural base areas" (Karl 2010, 40). The attack was a disaster and the Red Army was destroyed. The defeat exacerbated tensions on the Central Committee, resulting in Mao and his compatriots, over time, rejecting the "Li Lisan Line." In 1931 Mao declared the formation of the Jiangxi Soviet. Simultaneously Mao's preferred military tactics defeated four Nationalist extermination campaigns and he implemented his land reform and social policies, including literacy programs, marriage and divorce reforms, and public hygiene campaigns (Karl 2010, 45).

In October 1933, Chiang Kai-Shek finally encircled the Jiangxi Soviet. The Comintern agent, Otto Braun, and Zhou Enlai decided to abandon it in the summer of 1934 (Karl 2010, 46). In July, the Red Army broke through the Nationalist encirclement and escaped (Karl 2010, 47). The

Long March had begun. The Red army was consistently attacked in the following months, resulting in half of the columns being defeated (Karl 2010, 47). Reaching Zunyi city in Guizhou province, the army held a conference, which saw Mao's rise to prominence and the removal of most of the Moscow-led party leadership (Karl 2010, 47). He also decided that they would seek refuge in their most remote base area, Yan'an in Shaanxi Province. They only arrived in October 1935.

Yan'an, the Civil War and Mao Zedong Thought (1935–49)

In Yan'an Mao would again implement many social and land reform policies, such as cooperative production. Furthermore, along with Chen Boda, his Soviet-trained philosopher secretary, he systematically studied Marx and Soviet economic and philosophical texts. Thus, Mao developed a political ideology, which in the Party Reform campaign waged in 1942–43, was called "Mao Zedong Thought."

Two essays written in these years, "On Practice" and "On Contradiction," are central to Mao's political thought. Both essays were intended to defeat "dogmatists" within the party, whom Mao identifies as the CPC leadership between 1931 and 1934. Mao explains his inductive method in "On Practice" when he writes:

> Discover the truth through practice, and again through practice verify and develop the truth. Start from perceptual knowledge and actively develop it into rational knowledge; then start from rational knowledge and actively guide revolutionary practice to change both the subjective and the objective world.
>
> *(Mao 1965a, 308)*

In effect, there is a constant dialectic between practice and the development of Truth, which then can only be verified as Truth through further practice.

In "On Contradiction," Mao explains that, in contradistinction to the Deborin school of Soviet philosophy, contradictions pervade everything. Thus, he insists that contradictions are internal to every object and subjective thought. Contradictions are universal. Thus, despite invoking Stalin positively, Mao effectively rebukes him, as he argues that there remain contradictions between classes in the USSR. This insight undergirds Mao's later theory of permanent revolution. However, every contradiction and its aspects is also particular and its attributes are relative to this particularity. Under given conditions, several different aspects co-exist within a given object and are in contradiction to one another, which results in one aspect transforming into another, thus causing change. Complex phenomena, like Chinese society, are riven with numerous contradictions, however, one contradiction is "primary." Mao writes, "one of them is necessarily the principal contradiction whose existence and development determine or influence the existence and development of the other contradictions" (Mao 1965a, 331). This principal contradiction, at a given time, "plays the leading role," however, the principal contradiction can always change depending on which of the different aspects within the contradiction transforms. Mao here introduces the idea of "uneven development." Aspects within a contradiction can develop unevenly from one another, which will then affect which aspect supersedes the other (Mao 1965a, 333). Finally, Mao introduces the idea of antagonistic and non-antagonistic contradictions. Mao argues that antagonism is but one form of the "struggle of opposites" that characterizes contradictions (Mao 1965a, 345). The struggle between the bourgeoisie and the working classes can become an antagonistic contradiction if the class struggle develops, whereas there can contradictions among the people that are non-antagonistic (Mao 1965a, 344). Antagonistic contradictions can become non-antagonistic, and vice versa.

Mao developed these themes in a 1938 report entitled, "On the New Stage," which warned party members about dogmatism and emphasized the need to study and learn how to apply a "Marxism that has taken on a national form," which in the Chinese context constitutes a "sinification of Marxism" (Mao 2004, 539). The sinification of Marxism has two components: the critical reception of classical Marxism and the process of understanding and reflecting on China's history and present. Mao argues that "the theories of Marx, Engels, Lenin, and Stalin are universally applicable," but simultaneously cautions his audience that "[we] should not regard their theories as dogma but as a guide to action" (Mao 2004, 537). By a "guide to action," he means that Chinese Communists should study "the standpoints and methods by which Marx and Lenin observed and resolved problems" (Mao 2004, 538). Mao effectively wants fellow Communists to adopt the Marxist method without necessarily adopting the conclusions that the classical Marxists may have arrived at. However, the study of the classical Marxist corpus, Mao suggests, should be accompanied with the study and critical summation of the history of China (Mao 2004, 538). Returning to the idea that contradiction has a particularity ascribed to it, and the idea of uneven development, he posits that, "*It* [China] *has its own laws of development*, its own *national characteristics*, and many precious treasures" (Mao 2004, 538). The critical evaluation of China's history epistemologically requires the recognition that conventional Marxist categories themselves need to be adapted to fully capture its laws of development and national characteristics, otherwise Marxist theory will have become a dogma.

This adaptation of Marxist categories and Marxism, Mao notes, means that "we must constitute ourselves the heirs to this precious legacy" (Mao 2004, 538). For Mao, this process is vital for honing one's capacity to effectively and creatively apply Marx's and Lenin's "the standpoints and methods" to understand Chinese history, and arrive at solutions to present political problems. He points out, "*Conversely, the assimilation of this legacy becomes a method that* aids considerably in guiding the present great movement" (Mao 2004, 538). Reconfiguring Marxism in this way is vital for the efficacy and success of practice. This Mao explains is a "concrete Marxism" in opposition to an "abstract Marxism" or a "foreign formalism" as it is a "Marxism that has taken on a national form, that is, Marxism applied to the concrete struggle in the concrete conditions prevailing in China" (Mao 2004, 539). This concrete Marxism in the Chinese context was referred to as Mao Zedong Thought.

This concrete Marxism, as exemplified in Mao's (1965c) essay, "New Democracy,"

> referred to an economic and political formation . . . suitable to China's needs; but more significantly it also represented the insertion of a new stage in historical progress appropriate to all societies placed similarly to China in the world.
>
> *(Dirlik 1997, 73; see Mao 1965c)*

While the Chinese revolution was part of the global revolution, the peculiarities of the "semi-feudal semi-colonial" conditions that China experienced meant that national liberation was a principal task. Also, it introduced a new stage in the immediate post-revolutionary society that was not socialism, but a new state system, a new economy and new national culture led and developed by the CPC. Furthermore, as he outlines in a 1938 speech, "On Protracted War," these conditions mean that the road to victory was through the military strategies that he and Zhu had been developing in the year prior.

Mao in 1937 entered into a second United Front with Chiang and the Nationalist party, but this time as a distinct entity. The United Front would break down in 1941. By 1945 Mao and the People's Liberation Army had driven the Japanese out of China and by 1949 had defeated Chiang and the Nationalist party. The People's Republic of China was born.

Problems in Socialist Construction, De-Stalinization and the Great Leap Forward (1949–62)

During the 1950s, Mao increasingly focused on the problem of socialist construction, especially finding alternatives to Stalinist economic, political and ideological orthodoxies (Meisner 1997, 191). This need was compounded by Nikita Khrushchev's "Secret Speech," which began the process of formal de-Stalinization in the USSR. The debate about Stalin in international polemics from 1956 until 1962 between the Chinese and the Soviets revealed deep tensions about how to de-Stalinize from the left, rather than the right, as evidenced in the debate about the Soviet theory of "peaceful coexistence" with the West, which culminated in the Sino-Soviet split. Simultaneously, Mao introduced his own theory of permanent revolution that sought to address problems of socialist construction, while emphasizing an alternative economic policy that focused on revolutionizing the relations of production and superstructure of the masses. Mao put this theory into practice in January 1958 when he announced the Great Leap Forward campaign, which sought, through the mobilization and politicization of the mases, to improve general well-being and social wealth by increasing agricultural outputs and industrialization. Despite the failures of the Great Leap Forward, the first decade of post-liberation China saw significant improvements. The 1950–52 land reforms provided a solid foundation for a decade of industrial growth, population expansion, subsidized housing, universal medical care, improved educational opportunities and so on (Karl 2010, 85).

Following Khrushchev's "Secret Speech," Mao insisted that the criticism of Stalin ought to be done in such a manner that reflected both his positive and negative contributions. Mao was unwilling to state that the Stalin period was without any positive achievements, as he feared that too sharp a criticism would be detrimental to the Chinese's government's stability. Simultaneously Mao significantly differed with Stalin. Mao, focusing on the cult of personality and the centralization of power, criticized Stalin for broadening of repression of dissidents, inadequate preparation for the war against fascism, his attitude toward the peasantry and giving incorrect advice to other Communist parties in the international Communist movement. However, Mao and his compatriots became increasingly bellicose in their exchanges with the Soviet Union in 1960–62 over foreign policy, especially given Soviet advocacy for peaceful coexistence between communist and capitalist blocs, and the peaceful transition to socialism in capitalist countries. Mao and his compatriots thus argued that the critique on Stalin was intended to introduce a reformist politics, and, in effect, was a de-Stalinization from the right, not the left.

Returning to the question of dealing with dissidents and peasants, Mao in his 1957 speech, "On the Correct Handling of Contradictions Among the People," emphasized the importance of recognizing antagonistic and non-antagonistic contradictions among the people, which differed from Stalin who regarded all contradictions to be antagonistic. He also called for a "people's movement to critique the Party and Party methods" (Karl 2010, 95). This movement took the form of the 100 Flowers campaign. "Newspapers published at first tentative and then increasingly vituperative criticisms of unjust Party methods, incredible inefficiency, poor planning, inadequate attention to everyday life and people's needs, and so on" (Karl 2010, 96). Intellectuals soon joined the movement as well. However, the movement was withdrawn a few weeks after being launched because "some critics went beyond the boundary of political discussions and demanded more than the party (and Mao) was willing to tolerate" (Wu 2014, 32). Party leaders alarmed by the extent of dissatisfaction being expressed pressurized Mao to disown the campaign, and was accompanied by house arrests, purges and social exclusion of so-called rightist elements (Wu 2014, 32–33). It did not however, result in the same widespread violent repression as Stalin's purges.

Given Mao's conviction in the universality of contradictions, even within socialist societies, he argued for a theory of permanent revolution. Mao believed that given the persistence of these contradictions it would always be necessary to engage in revolutionary struggles. Mao however, was quick to distance his own concept of permanent revolution from Leon Trotsky's. Mao said,

> I stand for the theory of permanent revolution. Do not mistake this for Trotsky's theory of permanent revolution. In making revolution one must strike while the iron is hot – one revolution must follow another. . . . Trotsky believed that the socialist revolution should be launched before the democratic revolution is complete.
>
> *(Mao 1974, 94)*

Upon one revolution being completed, Mao believed it was essential that another revolutionary cycle begin.

Mao put into practice his theory of permanent revolution, using an alternative economic program, in the Great Leap Forward campaign. Mao explained in 1958 that the initial phase of Chinese economic development had uncritically copied from the USSR because of dogmatism and inexperience, in most affairs except for agrarian collectivization, light industrial production and commerce (Mao 1974, 98). The CPC had not implemented any of the policies they had pursued in Yan'an, especially decentralized production. He was encouraged however by the success of the voluntary agricultural collectivization campaign (Knight 2007, 220). Thus, while Mao thought that the development of the productive forces was essential, he argued contra Stalin that it was not the technical level that mattered, but the relations of production and ideology in practice.

> The success of the Great Leap Forward was therefore predicated on Mao's theoretical belief that changes in the relations of production and superstructure, combined with an alternative strategy for economic development, would bring about a rapid advance of the Chinese economy.
>
> *(Knight 2007, 230)*

The Great Leap Forward was a failure. The steel produced in the decentralized agrarian backyard furnaces was useless, and crops were not harvested due to the diversion of attention from agrarian production to light industrial production. This was aggravated by two years of national calamities (Meisner 1999, 237). "The combination of enthusiasms and irrational initiatives, along with Mao's increasing dismissal of criticism of himself, his policies, and theories produced a tragic situation in 1959" (Karl 2010, 106). Between 1959 and 1961 there were between fifteen to twenty million deaths due to starvation (Karl 2010, 107). The immediate effect of this was that Mao's economic innovations were reversed, the People's Communes scaled back and Mao's power was greatly diminished in the early 1960s.

The New Bourgeoisie and Great Proletarian Cultural Revolution (1966–76)

By mid-1966, Mao had become increasingly dissatisfied with the direction of the Chinese transition to socialism. He believed that the polices adopted in the aftermath of the Great Leap were fostering the development of a new bourgeoisie. Mao's proposed theory of a "new bourgeoisie" however was incoherent and "in fact contained several interconnected but markedly different interpretations" (Wu 2014, 36). Furthermore, Mao's theory focused primarily on the distribution and manifestations of power, especially bureaucratic privileges, rather than the political structures that gave rise to such power distributions (Wu 2014, 36). This meant that Mao's theory of "new bourgeois elements" focused on "ideologically deviant individuals or factions" and other politically suspicious elements, like speculators or academics (Wu 2014, 37).

> Last, although Mao often warned that cadres might become a new privileged stratum, he in fact never portrayed this group as an emerging ruling class. Mao was careful to define the targets of the Cultural Revolution as elements in the party that had taken the capitalist road.
>
> *(Wu 2014, 38)*

Able to muster only limited support for his views in the Party and state apparatuses, Mao "launched a ferocious attack on many of his comrades and the party organizations allegedly under their control by appealing directly to the masses and calling for rebellion" (Wu 2014, 19). He called on students in particular to "bombard the headquarters," that is, attack Mao's opponents in their positions of authority. The Great Proletarian Cultural Revolution (GPCR) was launched. The resulting Red Guard movement mobilized large numbers of youth to challenge all those who opposed them. The Red Guards were a unique form of political organization inasmuch as they were supposed to be permanent extra-party formations (Group in Charge of the Great Proletarian Cultural Revolution 1970, 146). However, "the absence of clearly defined objectives and targets resulted in the degeneration of the movement into pervasive factional conflicts" (Wu 2014, 50).

Furthermore, many of the class contradictions and resultant grievances that existed came to the fore and the mass movements quickly took on a life of their own outside of Mao's control. Indeed, workers articulated economic grievances that included complaints about: depressed wages and poor working conditions, especially increased labor regimentation and forced overtime; the rustication policy that resulted in 200,000 youth being sent to the countryside in 1957–66 to maintain population control; and the "strategy of national economic accumulation" that relied on disciplined temporary workers who often were women (Wu 2014, 99–105). However, when groups of rebel workers captured state power in Shanghai in 1967, Mao, despite welcoming the seizures, was adamant that they should only control political affairs, and that economic and administrative affairs ought to be managed by the disposed staff (Wu 2014, 121).

Recognizing the extent of the disorder, by 1968–69 Mao sought to stabilize the situation. The army, the only institution relatively unscathed by GPCR infighting, was sent into the schools and factories. The mass movements were demobilized on Mao's orders, and a series of purge campaigns that only concluded in 1972 were carried out that resulted in the arrest of hundreds of thousands (Wu 2014, 200–201). The excesses of the GPCR did much to discredit the movement. At the 1969 9th party Congress, Lin Biao, a PLA commander and key advocate for the cult of personality around Mao, was designated successor. However, by 1970, Mao became concerned about the increased role of the military in civilian life, especially "as it as it had stepped into the vacuum created by the gutting of the Party," and verbally attacked Lin Biao (Karl 2010, 145). In 1971, under mysterious circumstances, Lin Biao, his wife, and son boarded a jet to abscond to the Soviet Union. The jet crashed and everyone on board was killed. The Lin Biao incident further depoliticized the population and cast doubt on the entire GPCR (Wu 2014, 203–5). Mao's death in 1976 and the subsequent arrest of his closest collaborators, the so-called Gang of Four, officially brought the Cultural Revolution to a close. The successor regime under Deng Xiaoping abandoned Mao's policies, and implemented a modernization plan that liberalized the economy *and* loosened state control, effectively incorporating longstanding grievances, and thereby ensuring continued CPC rule (Wu 2014, 219–20).

Conclusion

Mao's political thought, or Mao Zedong Thought, was a consistently evolving body of work that attempted to resolve both problems that emerged in China's attempts to make a revolution in a society and context radically different than the European one in which Marxism had been founded. Furthermore, Mao sought to manage the transition to socialism in overwhelming peasant societies in the developing world without making the mistakes that characterized the Soviet experience. Mao's mistakes have done much to discredit him and his thought, however, it would be wrong to overlook his theoretical contributions and enduring legacy. He successfully developed a military strategy and political thought that was able to liberate China from Japanese imperialism and the Kuomintang. Furthermore, Mao made important steps in identifying central errors in the Soviet transition to socialism. Whereas, Stalin and the Soviet tradition viewed the Communist Party and socialist state as the guarantors of the revolutionary process, Mao argued that if guided by an erroneous line they could be a chief source of capitalist restoration. While the Soviet tradition abhorred disorder and mass movements were deemed acceptable only to the extent they were sponsored and directed by the Party-state, Mao emphasized the need for continuing revolutionary upsurges and campaigns under socialism and welcomed the independent, spontaneous activity of the popular masses as essential to the success of these efforts. However, Mao and his political thought remained incapable of providing a sufficient analysis of the contradictions and class differentiations in post-revolutionary societies, which meant that it was unable to safeguard the socialist transition in China. It is this contradictory legacy that makes Mao and his thought vital to study.

Bibliography

Dirlik, Arif. 1997. "Modernism and Antimodernism in Mao Zedong's Marxism." In *Critical Perspectives on Mao Zedong's Thought*, edited by Arif Dirlik, Paul Healy, and Nick Knight, 59–83. Atlantic Highlands: Humanities Press.

Group in Charge of the Great Proletarian Cultural Revolution. 1970 (1966). "Decision of the Central Committee of the Chinese Communist Party Concerning the Great Proletarian Cultural Revolution." In *Important Documents of the Great Proletarian Cultural Revolution in China*. Peking: Foreign Languages Press.

Karl, Rebecca. 2010. *Mao Zedong and China in the Twentieth-Century World*. Durham: Duke University Press.

Knight, Nick. 2007. *Rethinking Mao: Explorations in Mao Zedong's Thought*. Lanham, MD: Lexington Books.

Mao, Zedong. 1965a. *Selected Works of Mao Tse-Tung*. Vol. 1. Beijing: Foreign Language Press.

Mao, Zedong. 1965b (1927). "Report of an Investigation of the Peasant Movement in Hunan." In *Selected Works of Mao Tse-Tung*. Vol. 1, 23–59. Beijing: Foreign Language Press.

Mao, Zedong. 1965c (1940). "On New Democracy." In *Selected Works of Mao Tse-Tung*. Vol. 2, 339–84. Beijing: Foreign Language Press.

Mao, Zedong. 1974. *Mao Tse-Tung Unrehearsed: Talks and Letters, 1956–1971*, edited by Stuart Schram. Harmondsworth: Penguin.

Mao, Zedong. 2004. "On the New Stage." In *Mao's Road to Power: Revolutionary Writings 1912–1949 Vol. 6: The New Stage August 1937–1938*, edited by Stuart R. Schram and Nancy J. Hodes, 458–541. Armonk, NY: M.E. Sharpe.

Meisner, Maurice. 1997. "Stalinism in the History of the CCP." In *Critical Perspectives on Mao Zedong's Thought*, edited by Arif Dirlik, Paul Healy, and Nick Knight, 184–206. Atlantic Highlands, NJ: Humanities Press.

Meisner, Maurice. 1999. *Mao's China and after: A History of the People's Republic*. 3rd edn. New York: The Free Press.

Wu, Yiching. 2014. *The Cultural Revolution at the Margins: Chinese Socialism in Crisis*. Cambridge: Harvard University Press.

19

C.L.R. JAMES (1901–89)

Christian Høgsbjerg

The Black Trinidadian historian and writer Cyril Lionel Robert James (1901–89) was one of the 20th century's most remarkable Caribbean thinkers. He is perhaps best remembered as the author of the classic history of the Haitian Revolution, *The Black Jacobins* (1938), which analyzed the only successful mass slave revolt in human history, the transformation of the colonized slave society of Saint-Domingue into the world's first independent Black republic outside Africa from 1791 to 1804. In his native Trinidad, James also analyzed calypso and Carnival, helped pioneer the West Indian novel with *Minty Alley* (1936), campaigned for "West Indian self-government," wrote the first and still only biography of the pioneering leader of the Trinidad Workingmen's Association, *The Life of Captain Cipriani* (1932). In Britain, James perhaps most notably became a professional sports writer, reporting for what is now the *Guardian*, and wrote the classic social history of West Indian cricket, *Beyond a Boundary* (1963). Yet James's life and work ranged far beyond the boundaries of the Caribbean, and indeed he spent most of his life outside the Caribbean itself, with long notable sojourns in first Britain in 1932–38 and then the United States in 1938–53, and spent the last decade of his life in the 1980s in Brixton in London, in a flat above the offices of the *Race Today* Collective.[1]

Critically, James was also one of the 20th century's most cultured anti-Stalinist revolutionary Marxist theorists.[2] As David Widgery once memorably put it, James combined

> the historical eloquence of E.P. Thompson, the cricketing connoisseurship of John Arlott, the revolutionary ardor of Tony Cliff and the preciousness of John Berger, all mixed up with a wit and a way with paradox which is entirely West Indian.
>
> *(Widgery 1989, 122)*

During the Great Depression of the early 1930s – the greatest crisis of capitalism in its history – James, politically radicalizing as a young writer amidst mass unemployment and the rise of fascism, like many young literary intellectuals of his generation would move from liberal humanism to revolutionary socialism. Unlike many Marxists of his generation however, James did not join the international Communist movement but instead the tiny international Trotskyist movement. Soon after first joining up with organized Trotskyists in Britain in 1934, James wrote the pioneering study *World Revolution, 1917–1936: The Rise and Fall of the Communist International* (1937), was elected onto the International Executive Committee of the Fourth International at its founding conference in 1938 and met Leon Trotsky himself in Coyoacán, Mexico, in 1939 to discuss the strategy and tactics of Black liberation. At first in and then emerging out of the official Trotskyist movement while in the United States, as his authorized biographer Paul Buhle once put it, James developed into "one of the few truly creative Marxists from the 1930s to the 1950s, perhaps alone in his masterful synthesis of world history, philosophy, government, mass life and popular culture" (Buhle 1986, 81).

James remained a lifelong Marxist and humanist, and in interviews toward the end of his life would assert that his "greatest contributions" had been "to clarify and extend the heritage of Marx and Lenin" and "to explain and expand the idea of what constitutes the new society" (James 1986, 164). When asked "what would you most like to be remembered for" in an interview in 1980, James himself was quite explicit and unequivocal.

> The contributions I have made to the Marxist movement are the things that matter most to me. And those contributions have been political, in various ways; they have been literary: the book [on] *Moby Dick* [*Mariners, Renegades and Castaways* (1953)] is a study of the Marxist approach to literature. All of my studies on the Black question are [Marxist] in reality . . . on the whole, I like to think of myself as a Marxist who has made serious contributions to Marxism in various fields. I want to be considered one of the important Marxists.
>
> *(Dance 1992, 119)*

Theorizing Colonial Liberation

Born a Black colonial subject in the West Indies, James would not only witness the decline and fall of the British Empire over the course of his long life, but as a leading anti-colonialist activist would make a critical contribution to the process. In Britain during the 1930s he would evolve into a militant Pan-Africanist, working alongside figures like George Padmore, his boyhood friend from Trinidad and a former leading organizer in the Communist International, the Jamaican Amy Ashwood Garvey, first wife of Marcus Garvey, and the Kenyan nationalist Jomo Kenyatta in helping form and lead new organizations like the International African Friends of Ethiopia and the International African Service Bureau. James edited publications like *Africa and the World* and *International African Opinion* and wrote the pathbreaking *A History of Negro Revolt* (1938). Alongside his political campaigning, since arriving in Britain, James had also made time to research the Haitian Revolution – regularly visiting archives in Paris – and in 1934 he had turned his research into a remarkable anti-imperialist play focusing on Haiti's revolutionary leader, *Toussaint Louverture: The story of the only successful slave revolt in history*. This was staged at London's Westminster Theatre in 1936, with Paul Robeson starring in the title role. From James's discussions as a socialist activist with working-class audiences, he quickly learned that, as he put it in early 1936, "British Imperialism does not govern only the colonies in its own interests . . . it governs the British people in its own interests also" (James 1992, 66). As a Marxist in the Pan-Africanist movement, James worked to try to bring the growing resistance against British colonial rule across the Africa and the Caribbean together with the power of the industrial working class in the imperial metropolis of Britain.

In his masterful history of the Haitian Revolution, *The Black Jacobins*, James revolutionized understanding of not only Atlantic slavery and abolition but also race and empire more generally.[3] James stressed for the first time how race and class were intrinsically intertwined in colonial Saint-Domingue, and so class struggle was central to the tumultuous upheaval that was to be so critical to the abolition of the entire Atlantic slave trade.

> The race question is subsidiary to the class question in politics, and to think of imperialism in terms of race is disastrous. But to neglect the racial factor as merely incidental is an error only less grave than to make it fundamental.
>
> *(James 2001, 230)*

Indeed,

> had the monarchists been white, the bourgeoisie brown, and the masses of France black, the French Revolution would have gone down in history as a race war. But although they were all white in France they fought just the same.
>
> *(James 2001, 104)*

In a more sophisticated analysis of the relationship between capitalist accumulation and the barbarism of colonial slavery than what was soon to be advanced by his one-time student in Trinidad, Eric Williams, in *Capitalism and Slavery* (1944), James noted that the plantations and the slave ships were fundamentally modern capitalist institutions in themselves, things that did not just enrich but had been themselves formed by "the French bourgeoisie" and "the British bourgeoisie." He described the plantations as "huge sugar-factories" and the slaves as a proto-proletariat, indeed, "closer to a modern proletariat than any group of workers in existence at the time," and when they rose as "revolutionary laborers" and set fire to the plantations, he compared them to "the Luddite wreckers" (James 2001, 69, 71, 73).

Yet James's critical stress on Black agency – making the central plot of his "grand narrative" the dramatic transformation in consciousness and confidence of the Haitian masses – was combined with a masterful grasp of the totality of social relations in which they acted. His reading of the Marxist classics, above all Trotsky's *History of the Russian Revolution* (1930), saw James make a pioneering and outstanding application to the colonial Caribbean of the historical law of uneven but combined development of capitalism and the corresponding theory of permanent revolution. As Trotsky had noted in his *History*, the peculiarities resulting from the "backwardness" of Russian historical development had explained the "enigma" that "a backward country was the *first* to place the proletariat in power":

> Moreover, in Russia the proletariat did not arise gradually through the ages, carrying with itself the burden of the past as in England, but in leaps involving sharp changes of environment, ties, relations, and a sharp break with the past. It is just this fact – combined with the concentrated oppressions of czarism – that made the Russian workers hospitable to the boldest conclusions of revolutionary thought – just as the backward industries were hospitable to the last word in capitalist organization.
>
> *(Trotsky 2017, xvii, 9)*

Trotsky would always stress that "what characterizes Bolshevism on the national question is that in its attitude towards oppressed nations, even the most backward, it considers them not only the object but also the subject of politics" (Trotsky 1975, 180), and Trotsky had subjected the Chinese Revolution of 1925–27 to detailed analysis. Yet during the 1930s, as Michael Löwy has noted, the absence of "further major upheavals on an equivalent scale in the colonial world during Trotsky's lifetime" probably explains why Trotsky himself "never felt the political exigency to produce a further theorization of permanent revolution in the colonial theatre" (Löwy 1981, 86). James's greatest achievement in *The Black Jacobins* was to make just such a further theorization, demonstrating that just as "the law of uneven but combined development" meant the enslaved laborers of Saint-Domingue, suffering under the "concentrated oppressions" of slavery, were soon to be "hospitable to the boldest conclusions of revolutionary thought" radiating from the Jacobins in revolutionary Paris, so the Marxist theory of permanent revolution illuminated not just anticolonial struggles in the age of socialist revolution but also the antislavery liberation struggle in the age of "bourgeois-democratic" revolution. The bold Haitian rebels were, James insisted, "revolutionaries through and through . . . own brothers of the Cordeliers in Paris and the Vyborg workers in Petrograd" (James 2001, 224).

Throughout his study of the Haitian Revolution, James ably demonstrated that it was not simply an inspiring struggle on a tiny island on the periphery of the world system, but was inextricably intertwined with the great French Revolution throughout, pushing the revolutionary process forward in the metropole and investing notions of human rights with new meanings and universal significance. In writing about the Haitian Revolution, he rewrote the history of the French Revolution as well, challenging much conventional thinking outside of the Caribbean – including within the classical Marxist tradition up to that point. In *The Black Jacobins*, James fused classical and Marxist scholarship to resurrect a vivid panorama of the Haitian Revolution, stressing that it was not simply the greatest event in the history of the West Indies but took its place alongside the English Civil War, the American War of Independence and the French Revolution as one of the great world-historical revolutions in its own right, a revolution that had forever transformed the world and laid the foundation for the continuing struggle for universal human rights.

The Black Jacobins established James as one of the most eloquent and critical anti-imperialist figures of the 20th century. It is easier, James noted at one point in the book, "to find decency, gratitude, justice, and humanity in a cage of starving tigers than in the councils of imperialism" (James 2001, 229). James's thrilling and dramatic demonstration of how "the transformation of slaves, trembling in hundreds before a single white man, into a people able to organize themselves and defeat the most powerful European nations of their day" represented "one of the great epics of revolutionary struggle and achievement," was written ideologically to arm colonial liberation struggles (James 2001, xviii). At the close, James noted

> imperialism vaunts its exploitation of the wealth of Africa for the benefit of civilization. In reality, from the very nature of its system of production for profit it strangles the real wealth of the continent – the creative capacity of the African people.

Yet "the blacks of Africa are more advanced, nearer ready than were the slaves of San Domingo . . . the imperialists envisage an eternity of African exploitation: the African is backward, ignorant . . . they dream dreams" (James 2001, 303–4).

James's own lifelong anti-colonialism was also to be vindicated with the victories of national independence movements across Africa and the Caribbean after the Second World War, not least in Ghana under the leadership of Padmore's protégé Kwame Nkrumah and in Trinidad itself, with the rise to power of the People's National Movement (PNM) led by Eric Williams. Yet, James now seemed to shift away from classical Leninist anti-imperialist strategy and tactics to accommodate to the new situation of decolonization – decolonization without socialist revolution admittedly being something Lenin had not foreseen as a possibility in his study *Imperialism*. In *World Revolution*, James had approvingly quoted Lenin when he "called for 'determined war' against the attempt of all those quasi-Communist revolutionists to cloak the liberation movement in the backward countries with a Communist garb" (James 1937, 234). Yet now amidst decolonization, James refused to wage any such "determined war" and indeed showed a disastrous misjudgment of many autocratic leaders of "Pan-African Socialism," cloaking the likes of

Kwame Nkrumah in a communist garb, only then to have bitterly to break from those he had previously declared anti-capitalist revolutionaries on a par with Lenin.

Aside from playing a leading role in achieving a significant symbolic victory in the appointment of Frank Worrell as the first Black captain of the West Indian cricket team, James's return to Trinidad in 1958 to play his part in the movement toward independence was not a political success for him personally. As a supporter of Eric Williams, James became secretary of the Federal Labour Party, the governing party of the embryonic West Indies Federation, and took on editing the P.N.M. weekly paper *The Nation*. By 1960 however, as James detailed in his book *Party Politics in the West Indies* (1962) he had been forced to break with Williams as a result of the collapse of the West Indies Federation, and the latter's agreement to the retention of a US naval base at Chaguaramas and more general abandonment of non-alignment in favor of support for America in the context of the Cold War. In 1960, James gave a lecture series in Trinidad, published under the title *Modern Politics* (1960), which seem to reveal a return to a more classical Marxist understanding of imperialism as a system after the dashing of his high hopes in Third World nationalist movements.

> The passing of colonialism . . . is a sign of the weakness of the capitalist bourgeois state . . . nevertheless there is no question about it: the basic opposition to imperialism must come from the proletariat of the advanced countries.
>
> *(James 1973, 90)*

Theorizing Black Liberation

In 1938, James left Britain to go on a speaking tour for the American Trotskyist movement, and ended up staying in America for the next fifteen years. In 1939, James spent a week with Leon Trotsky himself in Coyoacán, Mexico City, in order to discuss how Marxists might convincingly answer "the Negro question," the question posed by the massive systematic racism suffered by Black people in America. Some of the specific campaigning ideas suggested at this meeting were indeed to be taken up in the civil rights movement of the 1950s. James for example suggested that racial

> discrimination in restaurants should be fought by a campaign. A number of Negroes in any area go into a restaurant all together, ordering for instance some coffee, and refuse to come out until they are served. It would be possible to sit there for a whole day in a very orderly manner and throw upon the police the necessity of removing these Negroes.

Trotsky agreed, adding that "Yes, and give it an even more militant character. There could be a picket line outside to attract attention and explain something of what is going on" (Breitman 1980, 40, 46). In 1948, James summarized his position, which built on Lenin's writings on national and colonial liberation, in "The Revolutionary Answer to the Negro Problem in the United States," a speech given at that years' convention of the American Socialist Workers' Party in support of the resolution "Negro liberation through revolutionary socialism" (of which James himself had been a central author):

> We say, number one, that the Negro struggle, the independent Negro struggle, has a vitality and a validity of its own; that it has deep historic roots in the past of America and in present struggles; it has an organic political perspective, along which it is

traveling, to one degree or another, and everything shows that at the present time it is traveling with great speed and vigor.

We say, number two, that this independent Negro movement is able to intervene with terrific force upon the general social and political life of the nation, despite the fact that it is waged under the banner of democratic rights, and is not led necessarily either by the organized labor movement or the Marxist party.

We say, number three, and this is the most important, that it is able to exercise a powerful influence upon the revolutionary proletariat, that it has got a great contribution to make to the development of the proletariat in the United States, and that it is in itself a constituent part of the struggle for socialism.

(*James 1996, 139*)

James's writings on Black liberation in the United States would later influence important groups such as the League of Revolutionary Black Workers in Detroit in the late 1960s. Though stressing Black self-organization, James never abandoned fighting for multi-racial working class unity, championing international socialism and workers' power as the key to universal emancipation. In his "Eightieth Birthday Lectures," organized by the Race Today Collective in 1981, James was challenged by a Black nationalist for having "a blind spot about the racism of the white working class" in British society. James responded,

it would be very strange if there wasn't some racism in the white working class because in any society the ideas that are dominant in the ruling class will find a reflection in the elements of those who work. But while you can accuse me of having a blind spot in regard to the racism of the white working class, I would say you have a much blinder spot in regard to the progressive, revolutionary element of the British working class . . . that is a much more powerful element.

(*Busby and Howe eds. 1984, 61*)

Theorizing State Capitalism and World Revolution

After Trotsky's murder in 1940, James under the pseudonym "J.R. Johnson" alongside Raya Dunayevskaya ("Freddie Forest") and Grace Lee Boggs, formed the "Johnson-Forest Tendency" within American Trotskyism in order to attempt to deal with the profound crisis the movement was now thrown into. The tendency made a highly original attempt to, as James wrote in *Notes on Dialectics* (1948) make a "leap from the heights of Leninism" (James 1980, 150) through breaking with orthodox Trotskyism and returning to the writings of Hegel, Marx and Lenin in order to face up to the new realities after the Second World War world. James's refusal to treat Trotsky's writings of the late 1930s as sacrosanct but instead attempt theoretically to develop Marxist theory so it could make sense of new realities has been concisely, critically analyzed elsewhere.[4] The Johnson-Forest Tendency were among the very first Marxists to incorporate the humanism of Marx's 1844 *Economic and Philosophic Manuscripts* into their Marxism, publishing the first English translations from them in 1947. They also aimed to "Americanize" Marxism and Bolshevism, and James's wide-ranging writings on culture and society in this vein included *American Civilization* (1949–50) and *Mariners, Renegades and Castaways* (1953) – a fascinating study of Herman Melville's *Moby Dick*.

It should be registered briefly however that their development of the theory of state capitalism – outlined in works like *State Capitalism and World Revolution* (1950) – to understand the Stalinist regimes enabled the Johnson-Forest Tendency, like the French group "Socialisme

Ou Barbarie" around Cornelius Castoriadis and the Socialist Review Group around Tony Cliff in Britain to preserve an orientation around Marx's central theoretical insight that the emancipation of the working class would be the conquest of the working class itself. As James and his co-thinkers put it in 1950, Stalinist Russia represented a "desperate attempt under the guise of 'socialism' and 'planned economy' to reorganise the means of production without releasing the proletariat from wage slavery" (James et al. 1986, 7).[5] While both Stalinists and orthodox Trotskyists held on to the notion that state ownership of the means of production meant the Stalinist regimes were "socialist," those Marxists like James who held to a theory of state capitalism were free to champion the struggles of workers under Stalinist tyranny fighting back against "their" states. The "Johnson-Forest Tendency" analyzed more global and systematic tendencies toward "state capitalism" and bureaucracy in the West as well during the mid-20th century in works like *The American Worker* (1947) and *The Invading Socialist Society* (1947), and so helped to restore to Marxism the importance of viewing society "from below," from the standpoint of the working class at the point of production.

The Johnson Forest Tendency (again like the Socialist Review Group and Socialisme ou Barbarie) also made a theoretical break from the ultimately elitist Stalinist and orthodox Trotskyist theory of the revolutionary party. This tended to arrogantly declare itself the solution to the "crisis of revolutionary leadership" and then dismiss as "backward" the vast majority of the working class for not suddenly rallying to its banner. Yet, unlike Cliff's Socialist Review Group, the Johnson-Forest Tendency (and for that matter Socialisme ou Barbarie) also steadily abandoned the rich Leninist and Bolshevik legacy of ideas on revolutionary organization. Though maintaining the need for some sort of revolutionary organization, the group now celebrated what James called "free creative activity" and "disciplined spontaneity" (James 1980, 118), the self-activity of the working class itself, autonomous of official political parties and trade union bureaucracies, as if these struggles in themselves could overcome what the leaders of the Johnson-Forest Tendency called the "crisis of the self-mobilization of the proletariat" (James et al. 1986, 58–59).[6]

In 1937, James had pointed out that "the pathetic faith the average worker has in the leaders of the organizations he has created is one of the chief supports of the capitalist system" (James 1937, 171). Yet, despite the fact that the postwar economic boom meant the grip of reformism over the Western working class movement grew stronger than ever as the system was able to deliver meaningful "reforms," James – inspired by first the rise of the Congress of Industrial Organizations in America and the Shop Stewards Movement in England and then the rebirth of Workers' Councils in the Hungarian Revolution of 1956 – now wrote instead as if reformist ideas and organizations were dead or dying. James nonetheless lived to see the eruption of Solidarity in Poland in 1980–81 and, just before his passing, the opening scenes of the 1989 revolutions in Eastern Europe. Such upheavals for James served not only as a vindication of his revolutionary democratic perspective of "socialism from below," but also a reminder of an elementary, essential truth – one James did so much to powerfully elucidate in all his work – that liberation from oppression and exploitation can only come from below, from the mass movements and class struggles of the oppressed and exploited themselves.

Notes

1. *Race Today* was edited by James's great-nephew Darcus Howe.
2. For more on James's life and work, see for example Bogues (1997), Buhle (1993), Høgsbjerg (2014), Rosengarten (2008), Smith (2010) and Worcester (1996).
3. For more on *The Black Jacobins*, see Forsdick and Høgsbjerg (2017).
4. For more discussions of James's mature Marxism, see for example Callinicos (1990), Le Blanc (2000) and Høgsbjerg (2006).

5. For more on James's theory of state capitalism, see Phelps (2006).
6. For more discussion of this, and a spirited defence of James's theory of the party, see Glaberman (1999).

Bibliography

Bogues, Anthony. 1997. *Caliban's Freedom: The Early Political Thought of C.L.R. James*. London: Pluto.
Breitman, George. ed. 1980. *Leon Trotsky on Black Nationalism and Self-Determination*. New York: Pathfinder.
Buhle, Paul. 1986. "Marxism in the USA." In *CLR James: His Life and Work*, edited by Paul Buhle, 81–104. London: Allison and Busby.
Buhle, Paul. 1993. *C.L.R. James: The Artist as Revolutionary*. London: Verso.
Busby, Margaret, and Darcus Howe, eds. 1984. *C.L.R. James's 80th Birthday Lectures*. London: RT Publications.
Callinicos, Alex. 1990. *Trotskyism*. Minneapolis: University of Minnesota Press.
Dance, Daryl Cumber. 1992. "Conversation with C.L.R. James [1980]." In *New World Adams: Conversations with Contemporary West Indian Writers*, edited by Daryl Cumber Dance, 109–19. Leeds: Peepal Tree.
Forsdick, Charles, and Christian Høgsbjerg, eds. 2017. *The Black Jacobins Reader*. Durham, NC: Duke University Press.
Glaberman, Martin, ed. 1999. *Marxism for Our Times: C.L.R. James on Revolutionary Organization*. Jackson: University Press of Mississippi.
Høgsbjerg, Christian. 2006. "Beyond the Boundary of Leninism? C.L.R. James and 1956." *Revolutionary History* 9(3): 144–59.
Høgsbjerg, Christian. 2014. *C.L.R. James in Imperial Britain*. Durham, NC: Duke University Press.
James, C.L.R. 1937. *World Revolution, 1917–1936: The Rise and Fall of the Communist International*. London: Secker and Warburg.
James, C.L.R. 1973. *Modern Politics*. Detroit: Bewick.
James, C.L.R. 1980. *Notes on Dialectics: Hegel, Marx, Lenin*. London: Allison and Busby.
James, C.L.R. 1986. "Interview." In *CLR James: His Life and Work*, edited by Paul Buhle, 164–67. London: Allison and Busby.
James, C.L.R. 1992. "Abyssinia and the Imperialists [1936]." In *The C.L.R. James Reader*, edited by Anna Grimshaw, 63–66. Oxford: Blackwell.
James, C.L.R. 1996. "The Revolutionary Answer to the Negro Problem in the United States [1948]." In *C.L.R. James on the "Negro Question,"* edited by Scott McLemee, 138–47. Jackson: University Press of Mississippi.
James, C.L.R. 2001. *The Black Jacobins: Toussaint L'Ouverture and the San Domingo Revolution*. London: Penguin.
James, C.L.R., Raya Dunayevskaya, and Grace Lee [Boggs]. 1986. *State Capitalism and World Revolution*. Chicago: Charles H. Kerr Publishing Company.
Le Blanc, Paul. 2000. "Introduction." In *C.L.R. James and Revolutionary Marxism*, edited by Paul Le Blanc and Scott McLemee, 1–37. New York: Humanity Books.
Löwy, Michael. 1981. *The Politics of Combined and Uneven Development: The Theory of Permanent Revolution*. London: New Left Books.
Phelps, Christopher. 2006. "C.L.R. James and the Theory of State Capitalism." In *American Capitalism: Social Thought and Political Economy in the Twentieth Century*, edited by Nelson Lichtenstein, 157–74. Philadelphia: University of Pennsylvania Press.
Rosengarten, Frank. 2008. *Urbane Revolutionary: C.L.R. James and the Struggle for a New Society*. Jackson: University Press of Mississippi.
Smith, Andrew. 2010. *C.L.R. James and the Study of Culture*. Basingstoke: Palgrave Macmillan.
Trotsky, Leon. 1975. *The Struggle against Fascism in Germany*. Harmondsworth: Penguin.
Trotsky, Leon. 2017 (1930). *The History of the Russian Revolution*. London: Penguin.
Widgery, David. 1989. *Preserving Disorder: Selected Essays, 1968–88*. London: Pluto.
Worcester, Kent. 1996. *C.L.R. James: A Political Biography*. New York: State University of New York Press.

20
MARXIST THEORY IN AFRICAN SETTLER SOCIETIES

Allison Drew

Claims about Marxism's weakness on the national question notwithstanding (Davis 1976, 10), African Marxists offered creative analyses of the national and closely linked land questions – contributions that have been largely neglected. Marxist influence in colonial Africa was diffused from coastal areas via ports and cities and along rail lines, which allowed the distribution of political propaganda. Its impact as a theory and a 20th century political movement was felt primarily in settler societies with urban proletariats, particularly South Africa and Algeria, colonized respectively by the British and French imperial states.

These countries showed profound similarities but also crucial differences that provided the parameters in which Marxist analyses took shape. Both experienced ruthless military conquest, the massive land expropriation of the indigenous people and the imposition of rigid sectional divisions. But Algeria's geographical proximity to Europe pulled it far more closely into European crises than South Africa. Moreover, Algeria had an indigenous Muslim landed elite that supported French colonization, and a significant section of its labor force migrated to France, becoming a displaced proletariat. South Africa, by contrast, lacked an indigenous black landed elite, racist laws stymied the development of a prosperous black peasantry and its labor migrated internally, within the country. Finally, Algeria was pulled between two aspirant global religions, Islam and Christianity, which reinforced the social and political divisions between the settler and indigenous populations. In South Africa, Christianity subsumed the localized indigenous religious beliefs, and social cleavages were cross-cutting, as blacks and whites often shared common religious values despite the pernicious racial inequalities.

This entry examines Marxist thinking in these countries during the 1950s, a decade of increasing anti-communist repression.[1] In South Africa the 1948 National Party electoral victory on an apartheid program accelerated racial polarization. The Cold War offered a convenient rationalization for repression; the 1950 Suppression of Communism Act squeezed the space available for public political discussions and protests. In Algeria, the outbreak of armed struggle in 1954 made open debate and public protests untenable. Due to the Cold War and the desire to placate the United States, the French state hunted Algerian Communists with disproportionate fervor. Despite these repressive conditions, Marxists nevertheless theorized the national and land questions, issues that were central to their national liberation struggles.

In both countries Marxist theory was introduced by socialist organizations, which in turn were influenced by their relationships with their imperial metropoles. The Communist Party of South Africa (CPSA) was founded as a national section of the Comintern in 1921. Although technically under the authority of the Comintern's Anglo-American Colonial Group, the CPSA operated as an autonomous party; its geographic distance protected it from undue British Communist interference. South African socialism crystallized into Communist and Trotskyist tendencies, and the organizational pluralism facilitated intellectual debate. By contrast, the *Parti communiste français* (PCF), launched in 1920, included three Algerian federations; only in 1936 was an autonomous *Parti communiste algérien* (PCA) formed. The PCF and later the PCA occupied all the political space on the anti-colonial left, the Socialist Party retaining its colonial heritage. Thus, the crucial discussions about the national and land questions were between the PCA and the PCF and the PCA and Algerian nationalists. Although Algerian Communists' dependency on their French counterparts initially hindered their theoretical development, the PCA's changing membership and the pressure of the war of independence led to important Algerian Marxist contributions.

Marxists in colonized societies invariably endorsed Lenin's view that the right to national self-determination was fundamental for democracy and working-class internationalism, typically interpreting national self-determination as independent statehood (Löwy 1976, 96). The French state claimed Algeria as part of France, but the Muslim majority lived as a conquered and oppressed people. Early 20th-century Algerian nationalists argued for equal rights within the French state, but by the Second World War they were demanding independence, while Algerian Communists oscillated between equality and independence. By contrast, despite South Africa's colonial origins, in 1910 it became a self-governing dominion of the British Empire. Marxist debates oscillated between those who saw the oppressed black majority as a colony needing self-determination and those who believed that national oppression could be resolved through full democratic rights for all.

South African and Algerian Marxists were influenced by the differing timing, interpretation and application of Comintern policies. In the 1920s, as the prospects of revolution in Europe waned, the Comintern gave more attention to anti-colonial and national liberation struggles, which were seen as means to undermine imperialism. The Comintern's 1928 Sixth Congress argued that peasant struggles could destabilize imperialism until capitalism's contradictions led to its collapse. For the Comintern, the national and land questions in colonized societies overlapped. Indeed, the two questions were inextricably linked: not only did the colonizers oppress the conquered nations, they often seized the land of the colonized and, as Frantz Fanon (1967, 34; translation modified) aptly noted, "the land . . . is the source of bread and, above all, dignity."

Marxism in South Africa

In South Africa, the Native Republic thesis introduced by the Comintern in 1927–28 lay the foundations for subsequent debates on the national and land questions. The thesis called for "an independent Native Republic, as a stage towards a workers' and peasants' government," positing a peasant-based rather than a proletarian struggle (Drew 2000, 96). Given Marxism's historic concern with the urban working class, the thesis caused great acrimony within the CPSA, catalyzing waves of expulsions and the development of a Trotskyist movement.

With the adoption of the urban-oriented People's Front and the outbreak of the Second World War, the CPSA put the Native Republic thesis aside and concentrated pragmatically on trade union and electoral activities. Consequently, despite their tiny numbers, Trotskyists played a disproportionate role in theorizing the national and land questions, arguing that the struggle to achieve democratic rights – whether franchise or land rights – would push the black majority towards a permanent revolution. They began with the problem of how to link urban and rural struggles – a challenge given the country's vast size and poor infrastructure. The organized urban proletariat – overwhelmingly white, racist and protectionist – could not be a working-class vanguard. Thus, Trotskyists stressed the significance of migrant labor to link urban and rural movements. For them, migrant labor's exposure to urban ideas made it a vanguard able to transmit political ideas from town to countryside.

But the two main Trotskyist groups, the Fourth International Organisation of South Africa (FIOSA) and the Workers Party of South Africa (WPSA) disagreed about whether to organize on the basis of objective class position or consciousness as reflected in beliefs and aspirations. The FIOSA's Moshe Noah Averbach (Mon 1997) argued that aside from minute numbers of farmers scattered about the cramped reserves – territory to which Africans were relegated – rural Africans had little or no land and were aspirant peasants only, while those on white farms were agricultural proletarians. This "tribal proletariat" – proletarian in outlook, peasant in aspiration – was the potential vanguard of an alliance of urban and rural workers jointly oppressed by their lack of democratic rights and united in their struggle against the color bar. By contrast, the WPSA saw the land question as the alpha and omega of the South African revolution. Arguing that the African majority's national aspirations flowed from land hunger, it proposed the slogan "Land and Liberty" – the demand of an 1870s Russian underground group. WPSA activists organized Africans in reserves on the basis of their land hunger, hoping to prevent capitalists from using migrant workers as strike-breakers.

Trotskyism's practical impact came from members of the Non-European Unity Movement (NEUM), notably the WPSA's Isaac Bangani Tabata, who campaigned for the All African Convention (AAC), a NEUM affiliate with a rural Eastern Cape constituency, and the FIOSA's Hosea Jaffe, a leading figure in the NEUM's predominantly Western Cape Anti-Coloured Affairs Department (CAD) movement. The NEUM was founded in 1943 on the basis of a Ten Point Programme of minimum democratic demands to be achieved on the basis of non-collaboration with the racial system. Point 7 called for "Revision of the land question," explaining that

> the relations of serfdom at present existing on the land must go, together with the *Land Acts*, together with the restrictions upon acquiring land. A new division of the land in conformity with the existing rural population, living on the land and working the land, is the first task of a democratic State and Parliament.

The 1950s was a decade of virtually continuous rural upheaval as Africans protested government intervention in the reserves. The AAC campaigned against the 1945 Rehabilitation Scheme, which entailed culling cattle and resettling people into reserve-based villages. Anti-Rehabilitation protests intertwined with struggles against the Tribal Authorities who collaborated with apartheid and accumulated wealth by so doing (Tabata 1997; Mbeki 1964, 34, 40–42).

AAC activists saw rural Africans as peasants or aspirant peasants, interpreting the abolition of restrictions on acquiring land as the right to buy and sell land. Tabata argued that rural Africans could not be mobilized on a slogan of nationalization as from their perspective the state's trusteeship of reserve land was tantamount to nationalization. Since the legal right to buy land without the means to do so could never satisfy land hunger, he maintained, rural Africans would eventually reject capitalism. Thus, the legal right to buy and sell land would become a pivot of a permanent revolution.

Tabata's stance was criticized by Jaffe and his Anti-CAD followers and by Trotskyists of Cape Town's Forum Club. Jaffe argued that Point 7 implied first, a democratic redivision of the land rather than socialist collectivization; secondly, legal equality on the land; and lastly, the right to buy and sell land. Redivision entailed the expropriation of large landowners, the abolition of white control of land and the allotment of land to smallholders on an equal household basis. Jaffe believed that migrant workers or "peasant-workers" would apply the technical and cooperative practices learned in their urban worksites to agricultural production, preferring individual titles to non-marketable land. The dispute became so heated that the NEUM split in December 1958.

The Forum Club's Kenneth Jordaan (1997a) maintained rural Africans were a proletarianized reserve labor force who no longer looked to land for subsistence. Unlike the bourgeoisies of classical democratic revolutions, he argued, South Africa's white bourgeoisie could never satisfy black democratic demands. The country's democratic struggle was "being waged without the bourgeoisie and against the bourgeoisie" (1959, 333). Precisely because South African capitalism was premised on the lack of democratic rights, democracy would undermine it.

Despite the AAC's hopes, Jordaan continued, industrial South Africa lacked the large peasantry upon which to develop a black farming class. Its bourgeoisie relied on the super-exploitation of proletarianized reserve-dwellers and would never allow them to withdraw from the labor market to develop as independent farmers. Thus, the AAC's position was not progressive from a working-class perspective, while the Anti-CAD's call to break up and redistribute large, productive capitalist landholdings was economically unviable, and its assumption that Africans had a prior land claim and would abandon industry to farm, utopian. In contrast to Tabata, Jordaan proposed nationalization to allow the continuation of large, mechanized farms, enabling a gradual transition to collectivization.

The CPSA had disbanded shortly before the Suppression of Communism Act. Seeking a space for debate, Communists and sympathizers formed the Johannesburg Discussion Club, whose proceedings published only one paper on the land question (Sanders 1997). In 1953 some former CPSA members regrouped as the underground South African Communist Party (SACP), which stressed the national over the class struggle and sought a close relationship with the African National Congress (ANC). In the mid-1950s Communists helped draw up the Freedom Charter, a democratic program similar to the Ten Point Programme, but with more social democratic content and without the stress on non-collaboration. Adopted by the Congress of the People in June 1955 and the ANC in 1956, its land clause stated: "The Land Shall Be Shared Among Those Who Work It!"

In March 1960 the outbreak of the Eastern Cape Phondoland uprising and the police massacre of unarmed Pan Africanist Congress (PAC) demonstrators at Sharpeville and Langa transformed the political terrain. A State of Emergency was declared on 30 March, and the ANC and PAC banned on 8 April. The SACP's Govan Mbeki was writing a book about Transkei politics, focusing on the evolving political consciousness manifested during the Phondoland uprising. Like Tabata, Mbeki recognized migrant labor's importance: The 1952 ANC-led Defiance Campaign had been successful in Port Elizabeth and East London, where migrant workers maintained close links with rural kin. Class differentiation in the reserves was growing slowly, but still limited, and both Tabata and Mbeki stressed the reserve population's political solidarity, rather than the impact of rural class differentiation on consciousness. They both saw the relationship of urban and rural protests as one of intense, short-lived urban protests periodically intersecting with slower, longer-lived rural protests.

In 1961 several South African groups launched sabotage attacks. But sabotage only intensified the state's crackdown. Influenced by the Phondoland uprising, Mbeki (1964, 130–31) proposed guerrilla struggle. He and his comrade Joe Slovo drafted a discussion document on the armed struggle. While Mbeki stressed the rural population's peasant aspirations, Slovo – like Jaffe – saw reserve dwellers as peasant-workers. Impressed by the Chinese revolution, Slovo felt it necessary to appeal to them on the basis of land hunger (Sanders 1997). This discussion, like that of the Trotskyists, was cut off by the arrest and imprisonment of the left-wing groups strategizing about armed struggle.

If the land question was crucial for South Africa's liberation struggle, so was the question of who constituted the South African nation. South Africa's distinctive feature was the legal codification of white supremacy, which divided the population into separate sectional groups – generally called national or racial groups. A key Marxist debate concerned whether to accept these groups as the starting point for political organizing or try to transcend them from the outset. Communists retained the Comintern's colonial conception. While aspiring to a non-racial society, they nonetheless operated within a multi-racial and multinational paradigm, exemplified by the ANC-led Congress Alliance. Yet differences emerged within the SACP. Influenced by Soviet thinking about the progressive role of national democratic movements in the Third World, Michael Harmel (1997) argued that South Africa was characterized by white monopoly capitalism with colonial conditions for the black majority – two nations in the same state. Lionel Forman (1992a), by contrast, argued that South Africa comprised nations and aspirant nations, and that working class policy must guarantee their right to territorial and administrative autonomy, along with individual freedom of movement. Forman distinguished between bourgeois nationalism and people's nationalism, suggesting that the black proletariat's rapid growth raised the possibility of a Chinese-type "people's movement."

Trotskyists recognized that racial divisions were internalized in popular consciousness, and this was reflected in the NEUM's federal structure, but they nonetheless maintained that there was one South African nation. Rejecting the colonial analogy, they argued that British imperialism had refashioned pre-capitalist remnants to produce a political dualism – democracy for whites and a slave colony for blacks. "The color bar is the iron hoop which binds together the whole structure of imperialist-capitalism," argued Averbach (Mon 1997, 326). Breaking the color bar would undermine this structure and lead to its collapse.

Communists used Stalin's (2012, chapter 1) empirical definition of nationhood: "a historically constituted, stable community of people, formed on the basis of a common language, territory, economic life, and psychological make-up manifested in a common culture" – despite the definition's obvious lack of fit with multilingual Africa and its variance with Lenin's distinction between oppressor and oppressed nations (Löwy 1976, 94–98). The NEUM (1951) staunchly rejected Stalin's definition, insisting: "All that is required for a people to be a nation is community of interests, love of their country, pride in being citizens of their country" (Karis and Carter 1977, 495). Nation-building must begin with principled rather than ad hoc unity against the *herrenvolk* (master race), insisted the NEUM. This required repudiating those who collaborated with the state's divide and rule policies.

Jordaan (1997a) countered that the basis for Non-European unity was the common lack of democratic rights – not color. The NEUM's emphasis on a *herrenvolk* master race obscured class divisions and implied that blacks and whites constituted two inherently antagonistic blocs. The modern racial system was the result of rapid imperialist intervention in a white settler society. The liberation movement's political demands must coincide with the economic tendency towards increasing black proletarianization, Jordaan insisted.

In an unusual exchange between Communists and Trotskyists at a 1954 Forum Club symposium, the SACP's Jack Simons (1992) argued, in contrast to Harmel (1997) and Forman (1992b), that South Africa's national question could not be solved by the traditional demands of oppressed nations for autonomy, self-determination or secession, but rather by legal and social equality. The color bar stifled the development of a black bourgeoisie and prevented any significant class differentiation amongst the oppressed, Simons noted. The working class would play the dominant political role within the liberation movement, which would, accordingly, reflect the common interests of all workers rather than specific group interests. This would reinforce South Africa's tendency to develop into one nation rather than a multinational society, he concluded.

Jordaan (1997b) similarly argued that South Africa was characterized not by conflicting nations, but by a dominant group oppressing other people of the same nation. Hence, the national question could not be solved through formal independence but through democracy; in this respect, the national and democratic struggles converged. South Africa's white bourgeoisie would not lead this democratic struggle, and unlike China, India and Indonesia, South Africa had no significant black bourgeoisie. Black South Africans were overwhelmingly workers or impoverished rural cultivators. The black proletariat, whose aspirations would inevitably conflict with capitalism, must lead the democratic struggle, resulting ultimately in a permanent revolution.

The SACP shelved discussion of the national question once it accepted the Freedom Charter, whose national clause proclaimed: "All National Groups Shall Have Equal Rights!" Despite its assumption of group rights, the Freedom Charter was open-ended enough to lend itself to a variety of interpretations. Nonetheless, it sparked a dispute within the ANC. The Natal ANC argued that the national clause emphasized racial divisions over nation-building. Similarly, Africanist Robert Sobukwe argued that multiracialism negated democracy by promoting group rather than individual rights, giving disproportionate representation to whites while denying the indigenous majority their rightful possession of the land (Karis and Carter 1977, 65–66, 317–20). Ultimately, just as the NEUM had fractured over the land question, the ANC fractured over the national question, as Africanists split off in 1959 to form the PAC, claiming undue white Communist influence.

SACP and ANC activists formed the armed struggle group *Umkhonto we Sizwe* (Spear of the Nation) on a non-racial basis, suggesting that Communists found multi-racialism increasingly impractical. The SACP's thinking, nevertheless, still reflected the Native Republic thesis. Its 1962 program maintained that South Africa was characterized by "colonialism of a special type," that national democracy was a precondition for socialism and that it should continue its alliance with the ANC. Like the Native Republic thesis, colonialism of a special type assumed a two-stage process based on a multi-class, multi-racial alliance for national liberation as a stage towards socialism.

Marxism in Algeria

If the Native Republic thesis provided the foundation for South African Marxist debates, in Algeria the demand for independence had an analogous impact. The political environment was extremely inhospitable to communism. The *côde de l'indigénat* (native code) compelled Muslim Algerians to strict obedience to the colonial regime, imposing harsh punishments for infractions that were not illegal in France but were unlawful in Algeria when committed by Muslims and making it illegal for them to join political parties. This made recruitment of indigenous Algerians exceptionally difficult. Repression made left-wing activism extremely risky. The Communist Party was banned twice during the colonial era and once again, following independence.

In May 1922 the Comintern published its *Appel de l'Internationale communiste pour la libération de l'Algérie et de la Tunisie* – a call for the liberation of Algeria and Tunisia. Noting the hazards posed by repression, the Comintern urged French workers to support the struggle of North African workers and French soldiers and sailors not to shoot them. In that way the French working class could assist the national revolution while attacking French imperialism.

But the call for independence led to increased repression by the French state and to a spate of resignations and expulsions from the PCF's Algerian region. Dissenting voices argued that a socialist revolution in France was a precondition for socialism in Algeria – especially given the backwardness of the Muslim landed elite. Nonetheless, by the decade's end, their numbers depleted, Communists in Algeria had accepted independence as policy.

However, the matter was re-opened in the late 1930s. With the PCF arguing that anti-fascist struggle necessitated a strong united France, independence was sidelined. In February 1939, as war clouds loomed over Europe, the PCF general secretary Maurice Thorez provided the rationale for Franco-Algerian unity, namely that Algeria was a "nation in formation" needing French guidance. While the PCF supported the right to self-determination, this right did not mandate separation. The PCA was the Algerian organization best-suited to lead this nation in formation because it was open to all, irrespective of religion, race, ethnicity or gender.

Most Algerian nationalists scornfully rejected the proposition that Algeria was not yet a fully formed nation. The PCA was divided over the thesis. However, with its advocates contending that at least Thorez spoke of an Algerian nation, albeit one in the process of development, in March 1939 the majority accepted it. Once the Second World War erupted, the union of France and Algeria was seen as even more necessary. Anti-fascism was counterpoised to anti-colonialism, which was constructed as divisive. Despite heated debates, the PCA ultimately followed the PCF. This position exacerbated tensions with the Algerian nationalist movement, which developed rapidly during the war, particularly after the November 1942 Anglo-American landing.

While the PCF emerged from the world war strengthened and, for many, heroic, this was not so for the PCA. Tensions between nationalists and Communists peaked following the May 1945 massacre of Algerians around Sétif and Guelma. The PCA initially claimed that the massacre had been precipitated by fascist provocateurs. But the massacre's scale – probably tens of thousands – compelled a rethink. From 1946 on the PCA gave greater attention to the national question – despite loyally maintaining the nation in formation thesis – and attracted young Algerians concerned that the nationalist parties were not addressing social justice issues. As increasing numbers of Algerians joined the PCA, they pushed the issue of national oppression.

Yet the postwar French state resisted any real reforms, and the *Front de libération nationale* (FLN) announced itself on 1 November 1954 with coordinated sabotage attacks across the country. Within months sabotage became a guerrilla war led by the FLN's *Armée de libération nationale* (ALN). When the FLN launched armed struggle from the rural, mountainous regions most urban Communists, having prioritized urban workers, were caught off guard. However, the PCA quickly provided clandestine support to the FLN, hoping to continue open political and trade union work for as long as possible. But it was under tremendous pressure from both inside and outside its ranks to join the armed struggle or risk increasing marginalization. In June 1955 it launched its own armed units, the *Combattants de la libération* (Liberation Soldiers), which later merged into the ALN. As the war ground on, open political discussion became impossible. When the government dissolved the PCA on 12 September 1955, Communists went underground or overseas. The mass arrests of August 1957 left Bachir Hadj Ali and Sadek Hadjères as the two remaining PCA political bureau members inside Algeria.

French troops used torture routinely, and while in prison the Marxist journalist and PCA member Henri Alleg wrote *La Question* (1958), the powerful account of his own torture that sparked an outcry in France and was read by South African Marxists such as Neville Alexander. The war's escalating intensity and the pressure from Algerian Communists compelled the PCA to develop its own distinctive position vis-à-vis French Communists, not least concerning the national question. Indeed, on 16 January 1956, with the war in full swing, the PCF's Léon Feix had finally admitted that Algeria's nation in formation was a nation in fact (Sivan 1976, 243–58).

In January 1957 the PCA launched *Réalités algériennes et Marxisme*, a theoretical journal whose name reflected the concern to apply Marxism to Algeria's specificities. The first issue was produced in Algeria, but underground publishing was too difficult, so the PCA's external wing in Prague took it over. Its second issue in 1958 included a substantial article by an anonymous contributor that showed the evolution of thinking on the national question compared to Thorez's nation in formation thesis. Algerian nationalism was rooted in love of land and liberty, values dating back to the Berbers, the author began. The Arabs had introduced Islam but allowed the Berbers to retain their customs and social organization, laying the basis for a multicultural Algerian nation. Capitalism had facilitated the territory's economic unification. But colonialism – by closing mosques and independent schools, imposing the French language and decreeing Arabic as foreign – had hindered the development of Algerian nationalism. Nonetheless, nationalism had leapt forward during the Second World War and been further fueled by the Sétif massacre (Anonymous 1958, 4, 9; Sivan 1976: 250–53).

The author implicitly recognized the limitations of Stalin's empirical definition of nationhood for transforming Algeria, modifying it to include subjectivity. Independent Algeria would include not only the Arabo-Berber people – who fit Stalin's criteria – but Jews and Europeans. Jews had lived in North Africa for centuries, and although the 1870 Crémieux Decree had split them off from Muslims, by identifying as Algerian they could become part of the Algerian nation and state. Similarly, Europeans would not be at home in France, but they could be integrated into the Algerian state as citizens and workers, and progressive Europeans, as part of the Algerian nation (Anonymous 1958, 17, 21).

The article contended that Communists had overestimated European workers' anti-colonialism, while underestimating the impact of their superior conditions vis-a-vis Algerian workers on their political consciousness. But Algeria was incontestably Arab, and this cultural imprint would inevitably increase after independence. Algerians would never accept incoming president Charles de Gaulle's approach to integration, and any positive relationship between France and Algeria necessitated that France recognize the Algerian nation. The equality of Algerians and Europeans was impossible under the colonial economic framework, which Algerians must break, concluded the author (Anonymous 1958, 23–29).

Just as the unrelenting war compelled Algerian Marxists to rethink the national question, so it pushed them to analyze the land question. Communists had been organizing peasants and agricultural workers for decades; November 1951 saw the first Algerian conference of agricultural workers, which adopted a charter of rights for land workers. Living underground during the war, Hadj Ali published an analysis of the land question that he presumably discussed clandestinely with his Communist wife Lucie Larribère and his comrade Hadjères, also in hiding. He began with the brutal French conquest and expropriation, followed by the concentration of land, the devastation of forestland and increased desertification. Alongside European landowners, indigenous feudal-like landowners continued their traditional exploitation while introducing capitalist methods. All this led to a major decline in peasant living standards, a fall in the number of sharecroppers and a sharp increase in agricultural workers. This resulted in widespread hunger, with peasants seeking work in Algerian and French cities (Hadj Ali 1961, 16–21).

Like their South African counterparts, Algerian peasants demanded "Land and Liberty," their support for the slogan indicating that Algeria's democratic struggle was at its base a peasant revolution. Like Mbeki, Hadj Ali stressed the rapidly developing political consciousness of rural people. Participation in the struggle helped the rural poor to throw off their inferiority complex vis-à-vis both the colonizers and the feudal elite. Thus, revolutionary organization developed very rapidly into a guerrilla struggle based on mutual reciprocity between the ALN and the rural poor. On the one side, peasants supplied food to the ALN, while agricultural workers contributed to the struggle at night after work. On the other, the ALN seized land abandoned by Europeans fleeing the war-torn countryside and redistributed it to peasants (Guerroudj 2013, 1, 13; Hadj Ali 1961, 11).

In contrast to Tabata and Mbeki's emphasis on rural solidarity, however, Hadj Ali stressed the political impact of rural class differentiation. The PCA and the working class needed the support of poor peasants, sharecroppers and agricultural workers, he began. It was also important to unite with middle peasants who had not betrayed the national liberation struggle, to win over small European cultivators, to neutralize medium-sized European farmers and isolate the large-scale European and Muslim landowners. Once the war was over, it was crucial to satisfy the aspirations of poor peasants and rural workers through the return of their stolen land and to give land to those who would work it. This accorded both with the national interest, he maintained, and with popular understanding of the Koran (Hadj Ali 1961, 12–13, 23–24, 28–29).

While the PCA believed that the war of independence was a peasant war for land, it nonetheless stressed proletarian leadership. Peasants were prone to "an ideology that expresses itself occasionally in acts of a distorted character, to the discredit of the just character of the national struggle . . . creating the impression of a chauvinist, racist, fanatical struggle." Proletarian leadership was required to control spontaneous violence (Hadj Ali 1969, 252–53; Taleb Bendiab 2015, 314–15). The difference with Fanon could not have been starker: "The starving peasant . . . is the first among the exploited to discover that only violence pays," claimed Fanon. Yet nationalist parties neglected peasants, who "alone are revolutionary, for they have nothing to lose and everything to gain" (Fanon 1967, 47).

The PCA's April 1962 independence program reflected the articles on the national and land questions. It stressed that the future Algeria would belong to all Algerians working together in a vibrant civil society for the national good. Algeria would be an independent sovereign democratic republic with a formal constitution enshrining human rights, the neutrality and noninterference of the state in religion, the mutual respect and tolerance of religious beliefs, the prohibition of racial discrimination and the full equality of women. It also advocated the expropriation of large land holdings without compensation. While nationalization and socialization of the principal means of production and collectivization of agriculture were not sufficient conditions for socialism, it maintained, they would provide its basis (PCA 1962, 16–17, 19).

In turn, the PCA program undoubtedly influenced the FLN's independence program, adopted at Tripoli in May-June 1962. The FLN program advocated a popular democratic revolution based on the leadership of the rural masses supported by the urban poor and middle class and reflecting socialist and collectivist values. The FLN's organ *El Moudjahid* (1961, 1962) had published extracts from Fanon's *Damnés de la terre* (*Wretched of the Earth*, Fanon 1967). Like Fanon, the Tripoli program's authors saw the peasantry as the leading force of what was first and foremost an agrarian revolution with three principal tasks: agrarian reform, agricultural modernization, and the restoration and conservation of natural resources (FLN 1962, 81–82, 112–13). The PCA and the FLN put forward very different notions of postwar Algeria, the former's reflecting political pluralism, and the latter's a one-party state. In November 1962, soon after independence, the FLN banned the PCA.

Conclusion

South African and Algerian Marxists responded creatively to the increasing repression of the 1950s. The spiraling repression compelled them to analyze their existing social conditions as a step towards envisioning their future societies. In both cases Marxists stressed the need for multicultural nations. However, their analyses of the national and land questions reflected their distinctive national conditions. Thus, in the absence of a significant African peasantry, South

African Marxists stressed the importance of migrant labor and rural solidarity, while their Algerian counterparts emphasized rural class divisions.

Their analyses were also affected by their geopolitical positions. South Africa's distance from Britain allowed the South African left to develop with relative autonomy, while the left's organizational pluralism stimulated Marxist thinking, although sectarian rivalries limited the impact of their theoretical contributions. By contrast, Algeria's geographic proximity to France allowed the PCF to maintain intellectual dominance for several decades. While the PCA's initial dependence on the PCF hindered its theoretical development, the influx of Algerian members and the rapidly evolving conditions during the war of independence compelled Algerian Marxists to develop their own distinctive positions.

Repression both stimulated and impeded theoretical work. On the one hand, repression intensified the need for theoretical analysis; on the other, faced with sweeping arrests and exile, continuing this work inside the two countries became increasingly risky. Whatever the weakness of European Marxism in addressing the theory of nationalism, colonialism – especially settler colonialism, with its national oppression and land expropriation – posed the national and land questions acutely. African Marxists took up the challenge.

Note

1. This discussion draws on Drew (1996, 2000, 2012, 2014, 2017).

Bibliography

Alleg, Henri. 1958. *La Question*. Paris: Minuit.

Anonymous. 1958. "Essai sur la nation algérienne." *Réalités Algériennes et Marxisme* 2 (July): 3–35.

Davis, Horace B., ed. 1976. *The National Question: Selected Writings of Rosa Luxemburg*. New York: Monthly Review.

Drew, Allison. 1996. "The Theory and Practice of the Agrarian Question in South African Socialism, 1928–60." *Journal of Peasant Studies* 23(2/3): 53–92.

Drew, Allison, ed. 1997. *South Africa's Radical Tradition: A Documentary History*. Vol. 2. Cape Town: Buchu, Mayibuye and University of Cape Town Press.

Drew, Allison. 2000. *Discordant Comrades: Identities and Loyalties on the South African Left*. Aldershot: Ashgate.

Drew, Allison. 2012. "Govan Mbeki's The Peasants' Revolt: A Critical Examination." In *Rural Resistance in South Africa: The Mpondo Revolts After 50 Years*, edited by Thembela Kepe and Lungisile Ntsebeza, 67–89. Leiden: Brill.

Drew, Allison. 2014. *We Are No Longer in France: Communists in Colonial Algeria*. Manchester: Manchester University Press.

Drew, Allison. 2017. "Comparing African Experiences of Communism." In *Cambridge History of Communism*, edited by Noman Naimark, Silvio Pons, and Sophie Quinn-Judge. Vol. 2, 491–517. Cambridge: Cambridge University Press.

Fanon, Frantz. 1967 (1961). *The Wretched of the Earth*. London: Penguin.

FLN. 1962. "Projet de programme pour la réalisation de la révolution démocratique populaire (adopté à l'unanimité par le CNRA à Tripoli en juin 1962." In *Les Textes fondamentaux de la révolution*. Algiers: Editions ANEP.

Forman, Lionel. 1992a (1954). "Discussion on South Africa's National Question." In *A Trumpet from the Housetops: The Selected Writings of Lionel Forman*, edited by Sadie Forman and André Odendaal, 176–79. London: Zed.

Forman, Lionel. 1992b (1954). "Nationalisms in South Africa." In *A Trumpet from the Housetops: The Selected Writings of Lionel Forman*, edited by Sadie Forman and André Odendaal, 180–84. London: Zed.

Guerroudj, Jacqueline. 2013. "Les Luttes Paysannes dans la Région de Tlemcen." *Socialgerie*.
http://www.socialgerie.net/spip.php?article1215

Hadj Ali, Bachir. 1961. "Le parti communiste algérien et le problème de la terre." *Réalités Algériennes et Marxisme* 6 (March): 11–29.

Hadj Ali, Bashir [sic]. 1969. "Algeria: Features of the Armed Struggle." In *Guerrilla Warfare and Marxism*, edited by William J. Pomeroy, 249–54. London: Lawrence and Wishart.

Harmel, Michael. 1997 (1954). "Observations on Certain Aspects of Imperialism in South Africa." *Viewpoints and Perspectives* 1(3). In Drew ed. 1997, 262–69.

Jordaan, K.A. 1997a (1951). "A Critique of Mr. W. P. van Schoor's 'The Origin and Development of Segregation in South Africa.'" *Discussion* 1(3). In Drew ed. 1997, 249–62.

Jordaan, K.A. 1997b (1954). "What Are the National Groups in South Africa? A Contribution to the Symposium." *Forum Club, Cape Town*. In Drew ed. 1997, 270–74.

Jordaan, K.A. 1997c (1959). "The Land Question in South Africa." *Points of View* 1: 1. In Drew ed. 1997, 325–39.

Karis, Thomas, and Gwendolen M. Carter. 1977. *From Protest to Challenge: A Documentary History of African Politics in South Africa, 1882–1964*. Vol. 3. Stanford: Hoover Institution.

Löwy, Michael. 1976. "Marxists and the National Question." *New Left Review* 1(96): 81–100.

Mbeki, Govan. 1964. *South Africa: The Peasants' Revolt*. Harmondsworth: Penguin.

Mon, A. [M.N. Averbach]. 1997 (1945). "A Comment on Trotsky's Letter to S.A." *Workers' Voice* 1(3). In Drew ed. 1997, 297–304.

NEUM. 1973 (1951). "A Declaration to the People of South Africa from the Non-European Unity Movement." In *From Protest to Challenge: A Documentary History of African Politics in South Africa, 1882–1964*, edited by Thomas Karis, 494–506, Vol. 2. Stanford: Hoover Institution.

PCA. 1962. *Programme du parti communiste algérien pour l'indépendance totale: La terre et le pain, le travail et l'instruction, la paix et la démocratie réelle, pour ouvrir la voie au socialisme*. Algiers: Edition "el houriyya."

Sanders, Z. [Zena Susser]. 1997 (1953). "Aspects of the Rural Problem in South Africa, Lecture Delivered to the Johannesburg Discussion Club on 1 December 1952." *Viewpoints and Perspectives* 1(1). In Drew ed. 1997, 316–21.

Simons, H.J. 1954 (1992). "Nationalisms in South Africa." In *A Trumpet from the Housetops: The Selected Writings of Lionel Forman*, edited by Sadie Forman and André Odendaal, 184–89. London: Zed.

Sivan, Emmanuel. 1976. *Communisme et nationalisme en Algérie, 1920–1962*. Paris: Fondation Nationale des Sciences Politiques.

Stalin, J.V. 2012 (1913). *Marxism and the National Question*. London: CPGB-ML. www.cpgb-ml.org/download/publications/stalin_marxism_and_national_question.pdf

Tabata, I.B. 1997 (1945). "The Rehabilitation Scheme: A New Fraud." In Drew ed. 1997, 304–14.

Taleb Bendiab, Abderrahim. 2015. *Écrire L'Histoire: Contribution à une Nouvelle Méthodologie de la Recherche Historique*. Algiers: Apic Éditions.

21
FRANTZ FANON (1925–61)

Leo Zeilig

Dying of leukemia in October 1961 in Washington, Frantz Fanon wrote letters to his close friends and family. To his friend Roger Taïeb, he wrote:

> We are nothing on earth if we are not first of all slaves to a cause, the cause of the people, the cause of justice and freedom. I want you to know that even at the moment when the doctors had despaired I thought again . . . of the Algerian people, of the people of the Third World, and if I held on, it is because of them.
>
> *(Cherki 2006, 237)*

Since his death Fanon has been appropriated for almost every cause. Five years after his death he emerged as the preferred theorist of the developing Black Power movement in the United States, influencing Bobby Seale and Huey P. Newton in the Black Panther Party. In the 1960s and 1970s Fanon was the quintessential third worldist. He was taken up by movements that looked to guerrilla struggle in the countryside and in the newly independent third world.

Most of Fanon's activism and writing was dedicated to revolutionary change. Soon after he moved to Algeria in 1953 he devoted himself the Front de libération nationale (FLN). He wrote about the ensuing revolutionary struggle in Algeria and how people were transformed by their involvement in the struggle for liberation. Relationships between men and women, families and their children, that had seemed frozen into the fabric of society and traditions, came apart in a process that Fanon described as "radical mutation" as the battle against the French rippled across Algerian society. Later Fanon saw how national liberation could become a curse, unless it was extended beyond the immediate goal of independence from former colonial powers and linked to regional and international processes of popular transformation.

Inside Martinique: Racism, War and France

Fanon was born in 1925 to a middle-class family in Martinique. His childhood was comfortable and relatively unremarkable. But life in Martinque permanently marked his identity. The island "department" of the French state was a place of excoriating racism. Its communities were, in Fanon's youth, divided into a small class of white planters and businessmen, the békés, mulatto and Black. On the island pigmentation and specifically the whiteness of the skin, to a large extent determined your trajectory in life, and your own sense of self-worth.

In 1944 Fanon fled Martinique to join the Free French. He served in Morocco, Algeria and finally in France. He had been taught to believe that he was French and schooled in the French Revolution and the Enlightenment, and the values of fraternity and equality. His experience of the war bought these illusions crashing down. After being demobilized, Fanon graduated quickly from his Fort-de-France Lycée and moved to Paris and eventually to Lyon where he studied medicine. In the city he attended the guest lectures of the philosopher Maurice Merleau-Ponty and was attracted by Merleau-Ponty's emphasis on lived-experience and how it could be used to explain the nature of the Black experience in France. He also read the philosopher Jean-Paul Sartre with fascination and critical passion – an engagement with Sartre that he maintained for the rest of his life.

Black Skin, White Masks

Fanon was no stranger to French racism. He started to write his first book, still a student of medicine, *Peau Noire, Masques Blancs* (Black Skin, White Masks). The book is an attempt to describe the "lived experience of a black person." It was published in 1952. Employing Sartre's work on antisemitism Fanon explains that being Black is made in confrontation with others. Race and racism, Fanon argues in the book, is a relationship of intersubjectivity that orbits around a superiority and inferiority complex, with whiteness at the center of a supposed superiority (Macey 2011, 41).

Fanon argues that he is cast into his blackness by racism, and becomes the categories, the insults and stereotypes of the racist:

> I was responsible for my body, responsible for my race, responsible for my ancestors. . . . He is all the clichés of anti-black racism: "the negro is stupid, the negro is bad, the negro is wicked, the negro is ugly."
>
> *(Fanon 1952, 116, 117)*

But as the Black person is also confined to his blackness by the racist gaze and insult, so the racist is trapped by his whiteness.

Using Hegel, Fanon appeals for a humanism that continues throughout his work, one that can only be acquired through recognition by others – the acknowledgment of the humanity of Black (and colonized) peoples in Europe, not bestowed as a benevolent gesture but seized and reached for in struggle and collective action. Recognition and humanity cannot be granted.

The colonial situation and "modern" racism involve a systematic denial of the humanity of the Black/"colonized" person. Humanity, for Black and white alike, can only be reached through a relationship that depends on recognition: "It is on that other being, on recognition by that other being, that his own human worth and reality depends" (Fanon 1986, 217). If the personhood of only the white person is acknowledged, then the Black person does not exist, is not present.

For Fanon, literally to be seen it is necessary to grasp and seize recognition: "this human reality in-itself-for-itself can be achieved only through conflict and through the risk that conflict implies" (Fanon 1986, 218). Only through such "conflict" can the non-person (the slave, the Black person confronting racism, the colonized) be realized.

For Hegel this risk was essential: "The individual, who has not staked his life, may, no doubt, be recognized as a person, but he has not attained the truth of this recognition as an independent self-consciousness" (Fanon 1986, 219). Fanon turns "risking life" into the necessity for conflict and struggle, some sort of as-yet-unclear collective action. In a sense this process involves doing battle for a human world; to create something other than "bare existence" requires a world of mutual recognition.

Slavery might be over, Fanon argues, but all that has happened is that the Black person "has been allowed to assume the attitude of a master," literally to eat at the master's table. *Liberation without a life-and-death struggle is no liberation at all.* Fanon is seeking something (uncertain as he still is in *Black Skin, White Masks*) much more fundamental, a world where there are no longer "slaves" or masters – a future of shared humanity, Black and white hand in hand. The former slave who can find in his memory no trace of the struggle "for liberty or of that anguish of liberty of which Kierkegaard speaks, sits unmoved before the tightrope of existence" (Fanon 1986, 221). It is necessary therefore for such a person to "forever absorb himself in uncovering resistance, opposition, challenge" (Fanon 1986, 222).

Here Fanon's analysis assumes a further depth. If the Black person – in such racist circumstances – is denied his humanity and depersonalized, then so is the white person. As the Fanon scholar Lewis Gordon has written, the white man is "anti-man" and needs also to discover humanity, "to emerge out of the ashes of the fact of his desiccation" (Gordon 1995, 12).

Fanon writes powerfully in his article on the "North African Syndrome" from the same period of "this man whom you thingify by calling him systematically Mohammed, whom you reconstruct, or rather whom you dissolve, on the basis of an idea." But such a process of "thingifying" also degrades and dehumanizes the racist, the master, the white man (his own humanity cannot not be fully realized and recognized). As Fanon concludes:

> If YOU do not demand the man, if YOU do not sacrifice the man that is in you so that the man who is on this earth shall be more than a body, more than a Mohammed, by what conjurer's trick will I have to acquire the certainty that you, too, are worthy of my love?
>
> *(Fanon 1970, 26)*

Simply put, if we do not recognize the humanity in the person who is before us, how can we can reclaim the humanity that is in us?

Fanon was still not clear on what this "struggle" would entail or how practically to seek recognition. The question of agency looms large; who will seize recognition and assert their humanity? The people of Algeria would help to actualize Fanon's philosophy. These fundamental ideas would emerge in other forms in all of Fanon's later work.

Algeria: Resistance and Repression

At the end of 1953 Fanon was employed as a psychiatrist in Blida-Joinville, a town a short distance from Algiers. Algeria was then a territory of metropolitan France firmly under the heel of French authority. Algeria had been, since 1848, French territory. Invaded by France in 1830, but not fully integrated for another eighteen years, as the French struggled to pacify "native" resistance. When "integration" finally took place the Arab-Berber (or *indigènes*) were not accorded French citizenship and remained subjects with few rights.

Fanon, writing to his brother, explained: "I'm going to Algeria. You understand: the French have enough psychiatrists to take care of their madmen. I'd rather go to a country where they need me" (Macey 2000, 203).

Through the Second World War there was a wave of working-class militancy in Algeria escalating until 1945. In many ways these strikes and demonstration infused with nationalist ideas and bread and butter demands were the first phase of a regional explosion of labor activism. In May 1945 Algeria was shaken by an uprising whose dimensions and violence were unparalleled. There were massive trade-union demos in Oran, Algiers and other cities. Across Algeria for two days after armistice celebrations "the whole area was out of military and administrative control" (Murray and Wengraf 1963, 53–4). The French were determined to gain the upper hand. On 8 May 1945 – as Europe was celebrating victory against the Nazis – in the town of Sétif, 250 km from the capital Algiers, there was a crackdown. After a series of pro-independence demonstrations between 20,000 and 30,000 Algerians were massacred by the French authorities in the surrounding areas in the east of the country (Planche 2006).

The FLN and Psychiatry

On 1 November 1954 a new group of radical nationalists, who became the Front de libération national (National Liberation Front), launched an "insurrection." The FLN was initially a small minority of Algerian nationalists committed to violent and armed confrontation with France. From early in its life, the FLN was a fairly ruthless organization. The FLN sought to maintain hegemony over its own forces and pacify potential competitors (Harbi and Stora 2004).

Fanon threw himself into the frenzy. If he had arrived a radical with vague notions of political action, he left Algeria three years later a revolutionary determined to dedicate his life to the Algerian cause. Soon after 1954 Fanon helped, with colleagues, to turn Blida-Joinville's fortress-like hospital into a place where wounded FLN fighters could be healed of the traumas of war and have their bodies stitched back together. Fanon ended up treating *both* war damaged French policemen – who wanted to see "nerve" specialists, so they could continue to torture "terrorist" suspects, as well as Algerian fighters. For a man widely and inaccurately regarded as the apostle of violence, he treated both with equal concern and in most cases kept their identities and confidences secret.

Conditions eventually became impossible at the hospital as the war and Fanon's involvement in it escalated. Toward the end of 1956 Fanon's cover was blown. He left for Tunisia; his wife, Josie, and young son following shortly afterwards. Days after the family left a bomb exploded outside their house in Blida.

Exile in Tunisia

Tunisia had become independent the previous year and quickly became the principal base for the FLN's exiled leadership. Fanon lived off and on in Tunis for the rest of his life. Together with other exiles he helped produce the organization's newspaper *El Moudjahid*. Pierre and Claudine Chaulet, who were close friends and fellow-militants of the FLN in Algeria, had also moved to Tunis. They vividly describe Fanon during his years in Tunis,

> Brilliant talker, charmer, adored using words from the medical and psychiatric lexicon to express the core meaning, seemed to have read everything, sometimes in a spin of words, taking lyrical flight, attentive to the reactions of his listeners, pushing sometimes reason to the point of paradox to provoke discussion and at the same time a disciplined militant, modest and accepting criticism of certain improper expressions or exaggerations.
>
> *(Interview 15 December, 2010)*

Fanon continued to work as a psychiatrist, publishing papers on his experiments, and attempting to reform the hospital regime in the two psychiatric units where he worked.

Year Five of the Algerian Revolution

Fanon wrote *L'An V de la Revolution Algerienne* (*Year Five of the Algerian Revolution*, published in English with the title *Studies in a Dying Colonialism*) in 1959. The book was an attempt to garner support for the FLN and engage with the French left. It was a publication of pro-Algerian and FLN propaganda, that celebrated the popular involvement in the war of liberation. The French left had equivocated and failed to support the FLN and the war. The French Communist Party was the largest force on the left and though the Algerian Communist Party actively supported the war against the French, the French party's pronouncements were scandalous. They argued that the revolution would take place, not in Algeria, but in France and Algerian nationalists must follow the political lead of the French proletariat. Algeria was not ready for independence.

Fanon's argument in the book was that the revolution had seen the extraordinary flowering of human capacity that overturned old attitudes, habits and the deeply embedded sense of colonial and racial inferiority.

Struggle – the *real struggle* – was the key for Fanon. This involved the popular participation of ordinary Algerians in the revolution. The book is part declaration of this popular ownership of revolutionary struggle, and the liberating wind sweeping through Algerian society. It is also, in part, a lyrical and poetic celebration of how people are, using Fanon's medical lexicon, "re-cerebralized" by revolution. For example, describing the transformation taking place between men and women, Fanon writes:

> The couple is no longer shut in upon itself. It no longer finds its end in itself. It is no longer the result of the natural instinct of perpetuation of the species, nor the institutionalized means of satisfying one's sexuality. . . . The Algerian couple, in becoming a link in the revolutionary organization, is transformed into a unit of existence.
>
> *(Fanon 1989, 114)*

Fanon argued that the strength of the Algerian revolution is not the number of patriots under arms rather it is the "hundreds of thousands of . . . Algerian men and women" who make up the revolt (Fanon 1989, 29) who have turned the future of the Algerian nation into a reality. "There is a new kind of Algerian man, a new dimension to his existence" (Fanon 1989, 30). The book tells a story of the transformation of human potential during revolutionary turmoil. Undiscovered capacities develop; cowed and humiliated people stand up against oppression; old customs of servility fall away. The "remodeling" of Algerians under the dynamics of the revolution transforms "the consciousness that man has of himself" (Fanon 1989, 30). Both oppressed and oppressor are fundamentally altered. The colonizers are dislodged from their perch of invulnerability, their convoys stoned, their forces attacked. Out-gunned by the French army, the revolution has one formidable force: the "radical mutation that the Algerian has undergone" (Fanon 1989, 32).

The case studies in the book that detail this "mutation" look to popular mobilizations: the role of the veil traditionally worn by women, the use of the radio, the Algerian family and medicine. In *Black Skin, White Masks*, seven years earlier, Fanon had written that the recognition of the Black person's humanity by the white racist world could only be achieved through collective effort and struggle. The exact nature of this "struggle" was ill defined, however. The young Fanon was caught between an individual assertion of his own value and an acknowledgment that mutual recognition and a new humanism would require collective struggle. *Studies in a Dying Colonialism* represents, in part, the resolution of these questions. The racism and inferiority of colonialism were undermined by collective engagement in the revolution, out of which a new Algeria, a new humanism and "recognition" of colonial subjects as agents in their own lives were beginning to emerge.

The Wretched of the Earth

Fanon was diagnosed with leukemia at the end of 1960 and knew immediately that he was dying. He pushed himself to almost inhuman lengths to write and influence a movement in which that he has begun to have serious misgivings and fears. *The Wretched of the Earth*, which he wrote in the last months of his life, shows Fanon as a revolutionary thinker in continual development. The book is extremely rich and complex.

The "Profiteering Caste"

Even though Fanon was intimately involved in the FLN, he drew critical lessons about the limitations of national freedom and independence. The book can be read as warning to Algeria – and the rest of the decolonized/ing world – about how the national bourgeoisie decay into

> a sort of little greedy caste, avid and voracious, with the mind of a huckster, only too glad to accept the dividends that the former colonial power hands out to it. This get-rich-quick middle class shows itself incapable of great ideas or of inventiveness. It remembers what it has read in European textbooks and imperceptibly it becomes not even the replica of Europe, but its caricature.
>
> (Fanon 1967, 141)

The Wretched of the Earth grasped the predicament that independence presented to the movements and leadership of national liberation. Postcolonial power was caught between an enfeebled national bourgeoisie – "caste of profiteers," was Fanon's preferred terms – and the limitations imposed on any newly developing nation in the modern world. In this context, he argued that it was inevitable that the new national bourgeoisies would act to suppress those in their own people whose demands could not be met within the existing economic and political system. The pseudo-bourgeoisie is not a real bourgeoisie. They own nothing Fanon tells us, and they will bring nothing. They have no national program of development, seeking simply to become the favored middlemen for metropolitan capital.

Fanon described how national freedom often became its opposite, the "curse of independence." There was one crucial event that drew back the curtains on independence. Fanon saw the Congo crisis unfold before him. A nationalist party was elected to power in 1960 in democratic elections promising real independence. But days after the official ceremony of independence the country ruptured. Two mineral rich provinces broke away, Katanga and Kasai, backed and armed by Belgium, the former colonial power. In January 1961, Patrice Lumumba, the leader of the nationalist Mouvement national congolais and the elected Prime Minister – whom Fanon had met at pan-Africanist conferences in Ghana and the Congo – was murdered by the Belgians and their Congolese "puppets" in Katanga. Real economic and political independence would not be countenanced by the parting colonial powers. The conclusion that Fanon drew was that Africa must craft its own tools and wage a relentless battle against imperial invasion *and* the "caste of profiteers" who usurp the powerful forces of national liberation.

Fanon also learned from Latin America, which had experienced independence generations before Africa's. Independence, he noted, had been keenly fought for, but hopelessly compromised. Fanon writes despairing in *The Wretched of the Earth*, "[t]he African bourgeoisie of certain underdeveloped countries have learnt nothing from books. If they had looked closer at the Latin American countries they doubtless would have recognised the dangers which threatened them" (Fanon 1967, 140). Fanon was a figure of the Black Atlantic, his life, experiences and thinking crisscrossed the Atlantic, picking up and developing insights from the Caribbean and the Americas, which then enriched and expanded his analysis of the struggles being fought in Africa.

The Peasantry or Workers?

Like many thinkers of his time, Fanon was influenced by Maoist interpretations of socialism, which emphasized the central role of the peasantry in revolutionary struggle while holding a deep suspicion toward the proletariat, which he believed had been effectively "bought off" with the profits of imperialist exploitation. Fanon wrote:

> the proletariat is the nucleus of the colonized population which has been most pampered by the colonial regime. The embryonic proletariat of the towns is in a comparatively privileged position. . . . In the colonial countries the working class has everything to lose; in reality it represents that fraction of the colonized nation which is necessary and irreplaceable if the colonial machine is to run smoothly.
>
> *(Fanon 1967, 86)*

It was to the peasantry that Fanon turned for his revolutionary agents:

> it is clear that in the colonial countries the peasants alone are revolutionary, for they have nothing to lose and everything to gain. The starving peasant, outside the class system is the first among the exploited to discover that only violence pays. For him there is no compromise, no possible coming to terms; colonization and decolonization a simply a question of relative strength.
>
> *(Fanon 1967, 47)*

There is a real sense in the book that the role Marx gave to the working class could be taken by the peasantry. This displays a failure to understand what Marx meant by the pivotal role of the working class and its relationship to the oppressed *and* capitalist production.

Though the idea of combining national democratic and social transformation into a permanent regional and global revolution was lost with the degeneration of the Russian revolution after 1917, Fanon's tantalizes us with insights into the role of the national bourgeoisie in a colonized and developing world setting. He also recognized the need in his last book to "enrich" the revolution with social transformation and that his project for a "new humanism" could only be achieved on a global scale – once the European proletariat stopped playing its game of "sleeping beauty."

iii) On Violence

It is on the chapter dedicated to violence in *The Wretched of the Earth* that Fanon has received his greatest misreading and denunciations. Fanon writes clearly that "at the level of individuals, violence is a cleansing force. It frees the native from his inferiority complex and from his despair and inaction; it makes him fearless and restores his self-respect" (Fanon 1967, 74). Shorn of its context these statements seem to extol violence, but this was not Fanon's intention. Fanon was writing about the necessity of resistance, which will involve violence, against overwhelming and violent odds. The experience of colonialism, Fanon explains, has been of unremitting violence, its overthrow will require force. Liberation without it is impossible – a cruel dream shimmering beautifully in the distance, always out of reach.

Violence used by the oppressed also has the therapeutic effect of ridding the colonialized of their deeply held feelings of inferiority. The colonizer can be hurt, their violence countered and broken. The result will be, as it is with all popular upheavals, a sense of strength and pride in their own value and self-worth – a collective struggle, involving violence but also an inherently personal transformation from inferiority to self-assertion and recognition. Therefore, any real struggle of the oppressed will require counter-violence. Non-violence Fanon writes is an invention of the colonial intelligentsia:

> Violence alone, violence committed by the people, violence organised and educated by its leaders, makes it possible for the masses to understand social truths and gives the key to them. Without that struggle, without that knowledge of the practice of action, there's nothing but a fancy-dress parade and the blare of trumpets. There's nothing save a minimum of re-adaptation, a few reforms at the top, a flag waving: and down there at the bottom an undivided mass, still living in the Middle Ages, endlessly marking time.
> *(Fanon 1967, 118)*

Fanon was thus not the apostle of violence, but its subtle and pragmatic analyst.

Endgame

After a momentary respite in the sickness, knowing that he had an incredibly short time to live, Fanon insisted on lecturing ALN troops in Ghaudimaou on the Tunisian/Algerian border. He used draft versions of the famous chapter in his last book "Pitfalls of National Consciousness." As important as their cause was, he argued, it had to be extended and deepened into the social and economic life of the new nation. Independence was no panacea and unless the transformation that these ALN troops were committed to was enriched and spread regionally and globally then national liberation would become a "curse" or a prison that would solve few of the problems that Algerian's had given their lives for.

Fanon's orientation to the countryside and the lumpen proletariat won him many supporters in the 1960s and 1970s but helped to limit his own alternatives. The real history of working-class action in the developing world has often been concealed. Fanon's role in helping to conceal this reality makes his legacy decidedly ambiguous.

Fanon belongs to the radical tradition of decolonization. Modestly he helped to promote and influence the FLN, but *Studies in a Dying Colonialism* and especially *The Wretched of the Earth* he had major impact on national liberation movements across the continent and the world. He was arguably the most important figure in the ideological struggle against colonialism in the 20th century.

Fanon unique from his contemporaries examined the dangers of postcolonial power. So, he wrote how after independence the aspirations of real independence are jettisoned. For much of Africa the seemingly radical structures of the nationalist revolution hardened into the Stalinist mold of the one-party state (Molyneux 1985). Fanon's contribution was posing questions and explaining the "curse" that national liberation would become for the new decolonized nations.

Bibliography

Cherki, Alice. 2006. *Frantz Fanon: A Portrait.* New York: Cornell University Press.
Fanon, Frantz. 1952. *Peau Noire, Masques Blancs.* Paris: Éditions du Seuil.
Fanon, Frantz. 1967. *The Wretched of the Earth.* London: Penguin.

Fanon, Frantz. 1970. *Towards the African Revolution*. London: Pelican.
Fanon, Frantz. 1986. *Black Skin, White Masks*. London: Pluto Press.
Fanon, Frantz. 1989. *Studies in a Dying Colonialism*. London: Earthscan.
Gordon, Lewis. 1995. *Fanon and the Crisis of European Man*. Abingdon: Routledge.
Harbi, Mohamed, and Benjamin Stora. 2004. *La guerre d'Algérie*. Paris: Robert Laffont.
Macey, David. 2000. *Frantz Fanon: A Biography*. London: Verso.
Macey, David. 2011. "I Am My Own Foundation: Frantz Fanon as a Source of Continued Political Embarrassment." *Theory, Culture and Society* 27(7–8): 33–51.
Molyneux, John. 1985. *What Is the Real Marxist Tradition?* London: Bookmarks.
Murray, Roger, and Tom Wengraf. 1963. "The Algerian Revolution (Part I)." *New Left Review* 1(22): 14–65.
Planche, Jean-Louis. 2006. *Sétif 1945: Histoire d'un massacre annoncé*. Paris: Perrin.

PART V

Renewal and Dispersal

22
READING *CAPITAL* IN 1968

Frédéric Monferrand

When Structures Descended Into the Streets

One of the distinctive features of the Marxist debates of the 1960 and 1970s is that they were conducted under the patronage of the mature Marx of *Capital* rather than of the young Marx of the *1844 Manuscripts* who had been so important for the previous generation. These decades indeed saw the publication or translation of hitherto unavailable drafts, manuscripts and chapters of the "critique of the political economy" such as the *Grundrisse* or the *Results of the Immediate Process of Production* that shed a new light on the genesis and structure of Marx's theory of the capitalist mode of production.[1] Yet, these materials would probably have come to naught if their publication did not intervene in a conjuncture that called for a profound renewal of Marxist theory and practice.

Two dates arguably mark the political beginnings of the 1960s: 1956, with the Soviet repression of the Hungarian uprising, which occasioned a deep crisis of the Communist movement and 1959, with the independence of Ghana, which launched a worldwide process of decolonization. The Hungarian events not only discredited the Soviet regime in the eyes of numerous Communist activists and fellow travelers. It also interrupted the "dogmatic slumber" of a new generation of militant intellectuals who, discontent with both the trivialities of an all-encompassing "dialectical materialism" and with its "humanist" ethical supplement, turned to *Capital* in order to ground emancipatory politics on a renewed theoretical basis. The decolonization process, on the other hand, raised the question as to whether Marx's critique of political economy still holds when the Western working class is not the sole revolutionary subject in sight. Forcing their way back into anti-capitalist theory and politics, from which they had been excluded by orthodox Marxism's Eurocentric and teleological conception of history, dispossessed peasants and oppressed peoples, colonized and racialized subjects imposed a new perspective on the capitalist mode of production. Consequently, the latter was to be depicted in Samir Amin's works on imperialism (Amin 1974), in Ruy Mauro Marini's theory of dependency (Marini 1969) or in Immanuel Wallerstein's world-system theory (Wallerstein 1979) as an always already global economy, structurally resting on the articulation of unequal forms of labor exploitation and political domination.

Now, as emphasized by Fredric Jameson, the anti-colonial and anti-imperialist struggles that were waged on the margins of the world system soon reflected back into its European and North

American centers, where they caused the emergence of new political imaginaries and antagonistic identities. The 1960s and 1970s can indeed be framed as a period when women, students, "marginals" and racial or sexual minorities all came to think of themselves as "inner colonized of the First World," thus entering a conflictual social fabric no longer solely dominated by the institutions of the labor movement (Jameson 2008, 485–87). It is this multiplicity of antagonistic subjectivities that would come to the fore of the political stage in 1968. Hence, while in the early 1960s capitalist societies could still appear to be locked down in the "iron cage" of mass consumption, political integration and technological rationalization, by the beginning of the 1970s they seemed to have cracked up under the joint pressure of anti-colonial struggles, working-class antagonism, student agitation and feminist activism. It is this dialectic of objective constraints and subjective liberation, of structural domination and practical experiment, – in short, of social transformation – that Jacques Lacan aptly, though ironically, captured when, reversing a famous slogan of the time, he stated that in '68, "structures did descend into the street."[2] In what follows, I would therefore like to use the issue of social transformation as the guiding thread of a schematic, indeed partial, examination of the some of the returns to Marx's *Capital* that emerged in the 1960 and 1970s.

Three Returns to Marx

Among these returns, three kinds of readings particularly stand out, if only by the importance they still have in the contemporary discussion of capitalism and its critique:[3] the Critical Theory-oriented reading developed by some of Theodor Adorno's students such as Hans-Georg Backhaus and Helmut Reichelt, which was later to be known as the *neue Marx Lektüre* ("New Marx reading," henceforth NML), the political reading promoted by Mario Tronti in *Operai e capitale* (*Workers and Capital*), and the epistemological reading elaborated by Louis Althusser and his students in *Reading Capital*. These readings share at least one important feature that distinguishes them from so-called traditional Marxism and justify their comparison: all three take the concept of "critique" in the subtitle of *Capital* – "Critique of Political Economy" – to imply a break with, rather than a continuation of classical political economy, so that they all consider that *Capital* should not be read as a political economy treatise but as a theory of capitalist social formations. It is on this common background that we can understand the differences between the NML, Tronti and Althusser. These differences concern, on the one hand, the actual kind of break with political economy that Marx is supposed to have accomplished and, on the other hand, the conception of capitalism this break implies. Let us briefly examine these differences, for they determine the way Backhaus, Reichelt, Tronti and Althusser address the issue of social transformation.

For the NML, Marx's break with political economy is fundamentally *ontological*. Where classical political economy merely aims at measuring quantitative proportions between labor, money and value, the critique of political economy aims at exposing the very constitution of these categories conceived of as abstract forms of socialization (Backhaus 1997, 41; Elbe 2006, 69). In this perspective, capitalism appears to be a system of autotomized social relations imposing themselves "behind the back" of those who reproduce them. For Tronti instead, Marx's break with political economy is *political*: it mainly consists in interpreting economic categories as categories of the class struggle, so that capitalism appears in *Workers and Capital* as a conflict-driven process of exploitation and of refusal of exploitation (Tronti 2006, 210–20). Finally, according to Althusser, the break with classical political economy accomplished in *Capital* is essentially *epistemological*. Rejecting any anthropological grounding of economic categories, Marx would inaugurate a new science of history in light of which capitalism appears as a historically specific set of social structures (economic, political and ideological) allotting places and functions to both subjects and objects (Althusser 1996, 396, 2015, 337; Balibar 1974, 109).

Now, as profound as they are, these differences can all be interpreted as various theoretical ways of addressing the practical issue of social transformation. In the following pages, I will first argue that the NML's emphasis on the autonomization of social relations is to be understood as a critical reflection on the objective conditions of (im)possibility of the radical transformation of society, that is, as a negative theory of revolution. Turning to Tronti's political reading of Marx, I will then argue that this negative theory of revolution ought to be complemented by a positive inquiry into the subjective conditions of social transformation. Finally, I will try to reconstruct Althusser's intervention as a structural theory of revolutionary conjunctures. With this, I aim neither at "synthesizing" these heterogeneous readings of Marx's *Capital*, nor at giving a comprehensive account of their respective contribution to Marxism. I merely hope to contribute to the contemporary "Post-Marxist" reappropriation of a particularly vivid period of political and theoretical elaborations and debates.

The *Neue Marx Lektüre*: A Negative Theory of Revolution

The claim that the NML has anything interesting to say about social transformation might sound counterintuitive for both formal and substantial reasons. On a formal level, Backhaus's *Dialektik der Wertform* and Reichelt's *Zur logischen Struktur des Kapitalbegriffs bei Karl Marx*, to cite but two of the seminal works of this tradition, present themselves as mere philological investigations into what Marx's critique of political economy "really is about" or rather, into how *Capital* volume I should be understood when it is compared to both its drafts (mainly the *Grundrisse* and the "*Urtext*" of *A Contribution to the Critique of Political Economy*) and to its first edition of 1867.[4] On a more substantial level, Reichelt's, but also Alfred Schmidt's readings of *Capital*, to mention another important participant in the debate, rest upon quite a sharp distinction between history and logic that seems to suit neither an account of capitalism's inner transformations nor an anticipation of its supersession into a different kind of society. Drawing upon Marx's claim to "present only the inner organization of the capitalist mode of production, in *its ideal average*, as it were" (CIII: 970), Reichelt and Schmidt indeed argue that the critique of political economy does not deal with the historical constitution of capitalism but with its constituted structures, that is to say: with the logical relations labor, value and surplus value maintain within a fully developed capitalist mode of production (Reichelt 1970, 126–36; Schmidt 1981, 33).

The relation of the NML to the issue of social transformation, however, does appear when Backhaus's and Reichelt's endeavor is referred to its political background. This endeavor stems from the inner debates of the West German student movements of the 1960–70s (*Endnotes* 2010). Mainly organized within the *Sozialistischer Deutscher Studentenbund* (SDS), the German New Left was roughly divided between two tendencies: an anti-authoritarian one, which mostly drew its inspiration from the Critical Theory of Adorno, Horkheimer and Marcuse, and a more traditional one, committed to the labor movement and anti-imperialist struggles, which relied on a more "orthodox" body of thought, including Marx's *Capital*. In this perspective, the NML can be described as an attempt to provide the "anti-authoritarian" tendency with an alternative reading of the critique of political economy developed within the framework of Critical Theory. In Horkheimer's seminal essay, "Traditional and Critical Theory" written for the seventieth anniversary of the first publication of *Capital*, this framework is clearly set out in Marxist terms. Critical Theory, Horkheimer explains, seeks the unity of theory and practice through the self-reflection of the ends and motives of proletarian struggles, so that the concept of critique is to be understood "in the sense it has in the dialectical critique of political economy" and Critical

Theory ought to be defined as "the intellectual side of the historical process of proletarian emancipation" (Horkheimer 1972, 206, 215). Even when, by the end of the 1940s, Adorno and Horkheimer irrevocably abandoned any trust in the revolutionary potential of working-class struggles, they still conceived of Critical Theory as an attempt to dissolve, through theoretical means, the structural factors that foster or impede the practical transformation of society.[5] It is therefore not surprising that the NML should place Marx's discussion of commodity fetishism at the core of its investigations.

The purpose of this discussion precisely is indeed to explain why commodity exchange and production appear as a necessary and self-evident way of satisfying social needs rather than as a historically specific and therefore transformable mode of production (CI: 164). In a Marxist perspective, this issue can be intuitively tackled in two different ways: (1) through a critique of the socially necessary illusions attached to the very practice of exchange, that is on the ground of a theory of ideology. (2) Through a critique of the lack of control people actually have on the social life process, that is on the ground of a theory of alienation. But, as Adorno points out in his 1962 seminar on Marx, which was decisive for the development of the NML, the originality of the critique of fetishism is precisely to combine these two kinds of explanation:

> On the one hand, commodity fetishism is an illusion; on the other, it is utmost/ultimate reality – and the superiority of the reified commodity [*der verdinglichten Ware*] over humanity stands as testament to this. That the categories of illusion are in truth also categories of reality, this is dialectic.
>
> *(Adorno 2018, 160)*

Backhaus was to take this reference to the dialectical character of the critique of commodity fetishism seriously. It is only when one interprets fetishism in light of the dialectic of the value-form, he argues, that one can properly grasp the central function this concept occupies in the mode of presentation (*Darstellungsweise*) of the categories of the critique of political economy (Backhaus 1997, 45). In the dense and often rewritten passages of *Capital* volume I devoted to this dialectic, Marx indeed traces the illusion that makes value appear as a "natural" property of things back to the very form of appearance (*Erscheinungsform*) of the exchange process. Already in a simple act of exchange, a given commodity expresses its abstract property of holding value in the material body of the use-value of another commodity. For this act of exchange to be repeatable at the level of society, there needs to be a commodity whose sole use-value is to allow for the generalized circulation of commodities and this commodity is money. This dialectical presentation of money shows that Marx's analysis in the beginning of *Capital* volume I presupposes the entirety of capitalist social relations, so that the "labor theory of value" does not deal with some pre-capitalist simple-commodity mode of production, as Engels would have it (CIII: 1028–45), but with "the most abstract, but also the most universal form of the bourgeois mode of production" (CI: 174). This means that "value" is not to be conceived of as a substance inherent in commodity units, but as a relation between products of labor that can only express themselves in a social form materialized as money (Heinrich 2004, 63–64). With money, the value-abstraction thus turns into what Alfred Sohn-Rethel calls a "real abstraction" (Sohn-Rethel 1978, 17–19). It acquires a thing-like materiality that definitively "conceals the social character of private labor and the social relations between the individual workers, making those relations appear as relations between material objects instead of revealing them plainly" (CI: 168–69).

The "social character of private labor" Marx is referring to is abstract labor, whose objectification in the exchange process constitutes the substance of value. At the beginning of *Capital*, value producing labor is deemed to be "abstract" because it is the result of a process of abstraction. It is what remains when one reduces qualitatively different use-value producing concrete labors to what they have in common: the fact of being mere expenditures of human labor-power (*CI*: 131–37). But then again, this abstraction is not an ideal, intellectual one, but a real, practical one, daily accomplished through the exchange process: "by equating their different products to each other in exchange as values, men [sic!] equate their different kinds of labor as human labor. They do this without being aware of it" (*CI*: 166–67). In this perspective, commodity-exchange is not only the form of appearance of capitalist social relations of production, whose historically specific character it conceals and therefore naturalizes (fetishism as ideology). It also accomplishes the "social synthesis," to use another Sohn-Rethelian phrase (Sohn-Rethel 1978, 35), between heterogeneous human activities that are thereby "form-determined" as value-producing activities, or abstract labor (fetishism as alienation). To put it briefly: the exchange relation is an autotomized form of socialization that both dispossesses individuals of any mastery on the social life process and generates illusions that ensures its own automatic reproduction. It is therefore not surprising that in *Capital* Marx should compare value to a "substance" which is also the "automatic subject" of its valorization (*CI*: 254–55). Commenting on the Hegelian overtones of this comparison, Reichelt writes:

> There is a structural identity between the Marxian notion of Capital and the Hegelian notion of Spirit. . . . In Marx's thought the expansion of the concept into the absolute is the adequate expression of a reality where this event is happening in an analogous manner. . . . Hegelian idealism, for which human beings obey a despotic notion, is indeed more adequate to this inverted world than any nominalistic theory wishing to accept the universal as something subjectively conceptual. It is bourgeois society as ontology.
>
> *(Reichelt 1970, 76–77, 80; see also Bellofiore and Riva 2015)*

According to Reichelt, Marx's uses of Hegelian figures of thought throughout the various drafts of the critique of political economy first meets methodological requirements. The dialectical mode of presentation of the categories of the critique of political economy – from the commodity to the double character of the labor contained within it, and from money to capital – finds in Hegel's *Logic* a model of logical coherence and systematicity. But, as the passage just cited makes clear, these methodological requirements are themselves pledged on socio-ontological ones:[6] the systematicity of *Capital* expresses the systematicity of Capital as a form of society. Hence, just as in Hegel's *Logic* the dialectical unfolding of concepts expresses the self-movement of the Idea, the mode of presentation of the categories in Marx's *Capital* expresses the self-movement of Capital itself, for which commodities, including human labor-power, are but mere forms of the valorization of value. In this perspective, one could argue that even the most technical pages dedicated by Backhaus or Reichelt to Marx's method are to be read as attempts to ground Adorno's "ontology of the wrong state of things" (Adorno 1973, 11) on the critique of political economy. In its turn, this negative ontology can be interpreted as a critical theory of the "objective-subjective constitution of social reality" under capitalism (Backhaus 1992, 57; Reichelt 2005, 39–58; Bonefeld 2014, 21–70). At the end of the day, what the NML demonstrates is indeed that capital is a socio-historical totality that preforms both the objects and the subjects of a damaged experience, where the former only appear as things to be produced and exchanged for money, while the latter only think and act as producers, exchangers or consumers.

Whether acknowledged or not, and despite its high level of abstraction, this negative ontology of capitalism is not without political, or rather anti-political, implications (*Endnotes* 2010). It envelops a negative idea of revolution, that is, an idea of what a revolution ought not to be if it is to be a truly radical transformation of society. In the NML's perspective, the supersession of the topsy turvy world of capital cannot be conceived of as the emancipation of, but rather as an emancipation from labor defined as the peculiar form that human activity takes once it is inscribed within the value-form.[7] Consequently, the revolution cannot be reduced to a mere transfer of property from the hands of the capitalists to the workers or their self-proclaimed representatives. Rather, it inseparably implies the abolition of autotomized forms of socialization such as value or money and a profound transformation of the way we relate to ourselves, to the world and to each other. But how, then, can individuals who are totally subjected to the value-form turn themselves into antagonistic subjects? Such is the question that the NML's ultimately raises but does not answer. Such is, in contrast, the issue Mario Tronti placed at the core of his reading of *Capital*.

Tronti's Workerism: A Phenomenology of Revolutionary Subjectivity

Published in 1966, *Workers and Capital* is unquestionably the main theoretical product of the Italian "red sequence." In it, Tronti lays the foundation for the workerist interpretation of the new cycle of struggles opened up by the massive influx of Southern unskilled workers in the big factories of Northern Italy then in full Fordist restructuring. At such a level of capitalist development, Tronti explains:

> the social relation is transformed into a moment of the relation of production, the whole of society is turned into an articulation of production, that is, the whole of society lives as a function of the factory and the factory extends its exclusive domination to the whole of society.
>
> *(Tronti 2006, 48)*

Adorno and his students would probably not have denied such a gloomy description of late capitalism (Chanson and Monferrand 2018). For Tronti, the process of subsumption of society under the logic of capitalist accumulation indeed produces a profound reorganization of every social spheres and practices. To take but a few examples that were all to be developed within the "autonomist" tradition of the 1970s, particularly by its feminist currents (Federici 2012): schools train labor-power to be exploited in the factory, the factory gives rise to the development of urban infrastructures, including means of communication and circulation as well as housing projects, and in these projects women's reproductive labor ensures the continuous availability of an exploitable labor-power. Yet, Tronti argues in a Lukácian way (Lukács 1971; Cavazzini 2013), this capitalist totalization of society is a contradictory process. On the one hand, it causes the historically specific character of capitalist social relations to appear as generic social ones, thus accomplishing the fetishization of capitalist society as a self-evident state of things. On the other hand, however, it is precisely when it has absorbed all social mediations that capital turns out to be exposed the most to proletarian insubordination. To say that "the factory extends its exclusive domination to the whole of society" is indeed to say that working class struggles at the point of production now have the power to disrupt the capitalist articulation of the social whole. Hence, where the capitalist objectification of social reality is considered by the NML to be the last word of the critique of political economy, it is only for Tronti half of the story *Capital* tells.

Reflecting upon the equivocity of Marx's concept of *Erscheinung*, which both means "appearance" and "semblance," Tronti argues that it is only from the bourgeois standpoint of the circulation of value that capital seems to have liquidated any possible opposition to its self-expanding process of valorization. Seen from the working class's standpoint of the production of value, however, the capitalist restructuring of social relations appears as what it is: a strategic moment in the class struggle that sees those who seek to reduce human activity to labor and those who refuse such a reduction on opposite fronts (Tronti 2006, 185). In this perspective, the *Doppelcharakter* of the categories of the critique of political economy – use value/exchange value, concrete labor/abstract labor, labor power/living labor, labor process/valorization process, constant capital/variable capital – ought to be referred to the class opposition these categories both reveal and conceal (Cleaver 1979, 51–66). Projecting the real dichotomy inscribed in the social space by the workers into the textual space of Marx's *Capital*, Tronti aims at uncovering the various mediations through which the commodity labor-power turns itself into an antagonistic working class.[8] He first does this on a historical level:

> We too have worked with a concept that puts capitalist development first, and workers second. This is a mistake. And now we have to turn the problem on its head, reverse the polarity, and start again from the beginning: and the beginning is the class struggle of the working class.
>
> *(Tronti 2006, 87)*

The claim that "the beginning is the class struggle of the working class" is here to be taken literally. For Tronti, the historical formation of the working class indeed precedes that of the capitalist class. The working class first appears on the historical stage as a mass of proletarians condemned by their "liberation" from both feudal ties and the means of production to sell their labor-power to individual capitalists. As soon as it is thrown into the production process, however, this mass of labor-power sellers starts to organize itself as a class of producers, thus forcing their employers to constitute themselves as a class unified by the need to control those it exploits. In a Trontian perspective, therefore, the capitalist class can be deemed to be "reactionary" in the rigorous sense that its very existence is but a mere reaction to the political formation of the working class. But this should not be taken to mean that the capitalist class is historically passive, quite the contrary. For as soon as they have made themselves into a class, the capitalists start using working-class antagonism as the driving force of capitalist development.[9]

According to Tronti, the best example of such a strategic use of antagonism is to be found in the first volume of *Capital*, parts 3 and 4. There, Marx shows how the workers' struggle for a "normal" working day introduces a qualitative leap in the conflictual relations between classes. On the one hand, this struggle accelerates the process of integration between State and Capital, and thus, the unification of the dominant class as a ruling class through the passing of "factory laws" that regulate working time. On the other hand, this struggle causes the transition from absolute surplus value extraction, based on the lengthening of the working day, to relative surplus value extraction, based on the machinery-induced increase in labor productivity, thus accelerating the concentration process of the working class (*C*I: 411–16, 643–44). At stake in Marx's analyses of the struggle for a "normal" working day, Tronti concludes, is therefore a "Copernican revolution": working class struggles should not be conceived of as functional moments of the economic development of capital. Rather, "the capitalist economic system" should be seen "as a moment of the political development of the working class" (Tronti 2006, 222).

This "Copernican revolution" leads Tronti to write the history of the "political development" in question as a *Bildungsprozess* through which the workers progressively build the power to interrupt the linear logic of capitalist development. It is therefore not surprising that the third part of *Workers and Capital*, the real center of the book, should contain a discussion of Hegel's *Phenomenology of Spirit* (Tronti 2006, 131–42). Just as in Hegel the individual consciousness' learning process goes through the same steps as that of Spirit, in Tronti the revolutionary becoming of the individual proletarian goes through the same steps as that of the class: from labor-power to productive labor and to working class.[10] If this is so, it is because at its highest level of development social capital reabsorbs its genesis within its structures, thereby transforming each and every social sphere into a site of struggle and of antagonistic subjectivation (Tronti 2006: 203). At stake in the Trontian "Copernican revolution" is therefore not only the history of the class struggle during the constitution of capitalism, but also the phenomenology of the various figures under which it is waged within a constituted capitalist society.

In the sphere of circulation, before entering the sphere of production, the worker faces the capitalist as a commodity seller who exchanges labor-power for money. In the sphere of distribution, after she got out of the sphere of production, she faces the state as a citizen receiving revenues. In both cases, the relation of the worker to her "other" (the capitalist, the state) presupposes the entirety of the capitalist social relations of production. Indeed, the money/labor-power exchange would not happen if the capitalist had not monopolized the social conditions of production and if the worker was not thereby condemned to sell the only commodity she owns to survive. And the state-regulated distribution of revenues is nothing but the political form of the class domination capital exercises over the whole of society. As a result, the spheres of circulation and distribution are the sites of struggle where the workers are the weakest. In these spheres, the class struggle cannot but take individualized and reformist forms, for the only demands an individual labor-power seller and wage-earner citizen can raise concern better employment conditions or a fairer distribution of the wealth of society among its members.

In the sphere of production, however, the worker is not exploited as an individual, but as an interchangeable member of an abstract "collective worker" (CI: 544–52). According to Tronti, the concrete labor of the individual is not made "abstract" by exchange. Or if it is, it is only as a presupposition of the real abstraction process it goes under as soon as it is incorporated into capital's machinery. As a result, Marx's claim that in capitalist society, "the general human character of labor forms its specific social character" (CI: 160) is to be interpreted as a political one: generalizing exploitation, capital socializes abstract labor as working class. Massifying production, it gives rise to what Sergio Bologna (1972) called the "mass worker." Dispossessed and unskilled, alien to workers' traditions and identities, hostile to traditional forms of political organization, this mass worker finds in the factory the site of struggle where it becomes possible to refuse her capitalist-imposed identity of labor-power seller and productive worker.

Just as the NML, therefore, Tronti insists that the revolutionary transformation of society does not require the emancipation of labor, but from labor. Contrary to the NML, however, he makes it clear that only those upon whom work is imposed can strategically refuse work where it is most necessary: at the point of production. There, the working class is the strongest, for the whole cycle of capital accumulation depends on its participation. There, the working class has no other demands to make but the revolutionary demand for power and the end of exploitation. Hence the workerist slogan: "the party in the factory" (Tronti 2006, 133).

As should be clear by now, "the factory" in Tronti does not only denote the center of the social totality, around which capital reorganizes each and every social spheres and practices. It also circumscribes the political scene where all social conflicts are totalized and simplified into an epochal antagonism opposing Workers and Capital (Balibar 2016). Now, it is precisely this idea – namely that the social whole and the political struggles that strive to dismember it are structured around a given "center" – that Althusser questioned in *For Marx* as well as in *Reading Capital.*

Althusser: A Structural Theory of Revolutionary Conjunctures

One could sum up the previous reflections as follows: where the NML focuses on capital's objective tendency to reproduce its domination over society, Tronti points to the working class's subjective counter-tendency to disrupt and transform the forms of this domination. The issue that still needs to be addressed is therefore that of the explosive encounter between these contradictory tendencies, that is, the issue of *revolutionary conjunctures*. In the Marxist tradition, this issue has been addressed in two ways: from the standpoint of a theory of the *event* and from the standpoint of a theory of *transition*. Despite the different political accentuations they imply – accentuation of the "communist" destruction of existing social relation on the one hand, accentuation of the "socialist" construction of new social relations on the other – these two perspectives both involve a determinate conception of the social structures that are to be dismembered by the revolution and of the inscription of this revolution within the historical continuity it is supposed to break with. This is why Althusser placed the problem of the articulation between history and structure at the core of his reading of *Capital*.

In "The Object of *Capital*," this problem is dealt with through the detour of a discussion of Marx's rupture with political economy. Where Smith or Ricardo took "the economy" to be a transhistorical sphere of human life grounded on human beings' needs and propensity to barter, Althusser explains, Marx understood it as a regional structure located within a larger, historically specific, global social structure (Althusser 1996, 363–71, 2015, 310–17). It can thus well be said that Marx "historicized" political economy. But this "historicizing" does not merely consists in situating the capitalist mode of production somewhere between feudalism and communism on a chronological timeline, according to the historicist prejudice of "the homogeneous continuity of time." Nor does it consist in taking capitalist society as a coherent whole whose parts (the economy, politics, aesthetics etc.) all belong to the same "epoch," according to the equally historicist prejudice of "the contemporaneity of time" (Althusser 1996, 276, 2015, 240–41). Indeed, Althusser argues, both these prejudices rest upon an "expressive" conception of totality, in light of which each social sphere and practice appears as the phenomenon of some essential principle, be it the Hegelian "Idea" or the Marxist "Labor/Capital" relation (Althusser 1996, 280–1, 2015, 244). Arguably, both the NML's and Tronti's depiction of the capitalist social totality can be taken as sophisticated examples of this "expressivist" model: the former, because it poses exchange relations as the form of manifestation of abstract labor, the latter because it places the factory at the center of "social capital." According to Althusser, the problem with this historicist-expressivist doublet is that it is *a-strategic*: picturing history as the maturation process of the contradiction between productive forces and relations of production would be bound to reduce real revolutionary experiments (the Paris Commune, the Bolshevik Revolution, the Cultural Revolution) to mere historical exceptions. Conceiving of social totality as the form of manifestation of a simple essence would make it impossible to *locate* the critical nodes where one can act on social contradictions and *anticipate* their becoming (Althusser 1969, 204). Regarding Tronti's thoroughly political reading of *Capital*, these criticisms might appear rather ill-placed. Yet, the fact remains that it is mostly for political reasons that Althusser insists that the object of *Capital* is not the temporal unfolding of a simple totality, but the specific historicity of a complex whole.

What characterizes this historicity is first and foremost its heterogeneity and non-synchronicity. Not only philosophy and science, literature and politics, all have their own particular history, but the economic "base" of society is itself temporally differentiated between the rhythm of development of the productive forces and the reproductive cadence of the relations of production (Althusser 1996, 283–85, 2015, 246–47). In this perspective, the growth of the productive forces can by itself provoke the implosion of the relations of production no more than a change in the economic base of society can mechanically produce a transformation of its superstructures, for none of these mutations coexists within a given simple historical time of reference. Now, according to Althusser, this temporal heterogeneity is the *index* of the complexity of the social whole, conceived of as a "structure articulated in dominance" (Althusser 1969, 202). To say that the social whole is a complex structure is to emphasize the real differences between the various instances (economic, political, ideological) it articulates. And to say that this complex structure is "articulated in dominance" is to highlight the unequal determination that each of these instances exercises upon the other, the elements they combine and the dynamic of the whole. Hence, the non-synchronicity of historical times is to be taken not only as the index but also as the *effect* of the causal relation existing between the various elements of the economic structure, and between this structure and the superstructure. Commenting on Marx's 1857 Introduction,[11] Althusser argues that this causality is neither transitive nor expressive, but "structural" or "metonymic" (Althusser 1996, 402–5, 2015, 342–44). This means that "the economy" does not act from the outside on ideological battles or political institutions, and the latter are no mere forms of manifestation of the former: the economic structure of society itself is affected by its own effects on superstructural instances. Going back to the example mentioned earlier, one can notice that in Marx's analysis of the struggle for the "normal" working day the state is forced by the class struggle at the point of production to act as a determining factor in the restructuring of the mode of production. At work "in the practical state" in this analysis is therefore the thesis of the "structural causality" of the global structure of society on its regional economic structure. A thesis that Balibar spells out as follows: "*the economy is determinant in that it determines which of the instances of the social structure occupies the determinant place*" (Balibar 1996, 452, 2015, 385, emphasis in original) Balibar's specific contribution to *Reading Capital* is precisely to have drawn the conclusions of this thesis regarding the problem of transition.

In "On the Basic Concepts of Historical Materialism," he insists that Althusser's insights into the non-contemporaneity of historical times forbid any evolutionist conception of revolutionary transitions as actualizations of capitalism's inner tendencies. Whether they concern the concentration process of capital or the socialization of the working-class, the production of an "industrial reserve army" or the tendency of the rate of profit to fall, Balibar argues, these tendencies do not push toward the "supersession" of the capitalist mode of production, but toward its reproduction (Balibar 1996, 555, 2015, 470). It may well be the case that this reproduction produces real changes in the elements that the mode of production combines, but it does not radically alter this combination. For example, the passage from manufacture to large-scale industry does imply a change in the productive forces, that is, in the relation of the worker to the means of production, but it involves no real change in capitalism's constitutive structure, which still opposes those who own the means of production and those who own nothing but their labor-power. It can therefore be argued that, making the "whole mode of production move with an immobile movement" (Balibar 1996, 544, 2015, 461), the reproduction process of capital is an ever-going process of *synchronization* of the various instances that compose the social whole, whereas the socialist transition is the process of their *de-synchronization*. But inasmuch as this desynchronizing process cannot be produced by the existing tendencies of the capitalist mode of production, it itself has to be rooted in a transitional mode of production. This transitional mode of production is then both characterized by the non-correspondence of the economic base and the political and ideological superstructure, and by the dominance of the latter over the former. In the last instance, making the revolution consists in transforming the economy in such a way that political and ideological struggles "occupy the determinant place" (Balibar 1996, 566–67, 2015, 478–79).

Maoist in spirit, this conclusion was to put Balibar in a difficult position. As he was later to explain, his discussion of transition is based on a generalization of the Althusserian notion of a "displacement" of social contradictions and conflicts (Balibar 1974, 228). Whereas in Althusser this notion is circumscribed to the sole "real historical present: the present of the *conjuncture*" (Althusser 1996, 293, 2015, 254), in Balibar it is used as a means of comparison between successive modes of production. Hence the claim that the dominant place occupied by the economy in capitalism is displaced to politics in the transitional mode of production. As a result, Balibar was led to reintroduce surreptitiously the "ideological" problematic of "periodization" in his sophisticated discussion of the problem of transition. Measuring social transformation up against the "immobile movement" of the reproduction of social relations, he ended up juxtaposing discrete modes of production on a chronological timeline. Denying any real historicity to capitalism, he eventually proved unable to account for the actual passage from one mode of production to the other (Elliott 2006, 148–50). With this "self-criticism," Balibar sends us back from transition to event, or, to put it in Althusserian terms, from "structural causality" to "overdetermination."

Elaborated in *For Marx*, the concept of "overdetermination" is meant to account for the conditions of possibility of revolutionary events. Althusser reflected upon the circumstances that made the Bolshevik Revolution possible: the contradictory position of Russia, both an imperialist and semi-colonial country, on the world market, the coexistence of an "advanced" capitalist mode of production in the cities and of a "backward" feudal mode of production in the countryside. In his view, these circumstances cannot be disregarded as mere contingent obstacles to the necessary unfolding of the Labor/Capital contradiction. Making up the material texture of history, these circumstances are rather proof that the "principal contradiction" never exists nor appears as such on the historical stage. For the Labor/Capital contradiction is always "overdetermined," both determining and determined by the international situation it is part of, the political institutions within which it develops, and the ideological representations under which it is lived and dealt with. This means that the class struggle neither exists *behind* nor *alongside* other types of struggles, say, to stick to the 1917 example, anti-war or democratic movements, but always *under* these political forms, which give it in return its historical effectivity. What makes social movements antagonistic or non-antagonistic, functional or disruptive, is therefore not their "purely" economic character but, on the contrary, their ability to make a strategic use of their very "impurity," that is, of their overdetermined character. In this perspective, a conjuncture is "revolutionary" when social contradictions are not merely "displaced" from one instance to the next, but are made to "condense" and "fuse" into a "ruptural unity" (Althusser 1969, 99, 211).

However, this "ruptural unity" ought not be conceived of as the simple and sudden outer manifestation of the complex and latent inner articulation of the social whole, for this whole is never actually unified except for when it is dismembered by the revolutionary event. In other words, it is only from the standpoint of past or anticipated insurrections – from the standpoint of the memory or hope of a radical transformation of society as a whole – that social relations can be endowed with the unity of a totality. On the one hand, social structures thus exist nowhere but through the conjunctures in which they are reinforced or disturbed. On the other hand, these conjunctures are themselves structured by the changes of power relation between forces that occupy various social places and belong to heterogeneous historical times (Montag 2013, 93). This means that structures have always already descended into the street, where the materiality of historical becoming is uncovered as necessarily contingent. How, then, does one practically impose another direction to this becoming? Such is the question that was on the horizon of the three readings of *Capital* I roughly examined in this chapter. That the same question should be raised more than fifty years after these readings were elaborated surely is testimony to the non-contemporaneity of historical time.

In Lieu of a Conclusion: Fifty Years Later

I have tried to show in this chapter that the issue of social transformation can be used as a heuristic way to lay out and compare the readings of *Capital* developed at the same time by the neue Marx-Lectüre, Tronti and Althusser. If one were to evaluate these readings, one would therefore have to examine their ability to account for their social context of elaboration as well as to participate, through theoretical means, to its practical transformation. Now, what is striking in this regard is that while "1968" symbolizes a time when a multiplicity of antagonistic subjectivities asserted themselves, the working class seems to be the sole political figure acknowledged by the readings of *Capital* I have surveyed. It would be wrong, however, to conclude from this that these readings are simply outdated. For they all provide useful tools for dealing with what is probably the main issue contemporary emancipatory politics inherited from the 1960–1970s: the issue of the combination of a diversity of experiences of struggle, determined by heterogeneous factors and aiming at specific objectives. Hence, the NML reminds us that this diversity of particular struggles is the other side of the now hardly deniable universality of the value-form, so that anti-capitalism might appear as what gives "in the last instance" a minimal coherence to the various attempts at changing the world that we know of today. In Tronti, on the other hand, one finds a political method for interpreting the transformations of capitalism from the standpoint of those who are striving to flee from its domination. A method according to which the issue of the encounter between different locus of struggles is to be dealt with at the level of the communicability of antagonistic practices rather than on the level of ideological unity. But it is perhaps Althusser's theory of the "overdetermined" character of each and every social conflict that deserves the most to be actualized today. This theory indeed suggests that the anti-capitalist struggle is not an already constituted type of struggle, existing alongside other types of struggles such as anti-racist or anti-sexist ones, to which it should then be articulated. Rather, anti-capitalism is transversal to all social conflicts, overdetermined by them and polarizing them in return, so that the politically relevant question is not "what kind of struggle should be given priority to?" but "how to promote an anti-capitalist standpoint in each and every social conflict?"

Notes

1. The *Grundrisse* was published in German in 1939, but were mostly discussed after the 1968 publication of Rosdolsky's classic study, *The Making of Marx's "Capital"* (Rosdolsky 1977). In Italy, the *Grundrisse* was published in 1970, but important parts of the translation, especially the so-called Fragment on Machines, were already published in 1964 in the workerist journals *Quaderni Rossi* and *classe operaia*. In France, the *Grundrisse* was translated in 1967–68 by the Bordigist Roger Dangeville, while Jacques Camatte, another Bordigist, wrote the first commentary in French of the *Results of the Immediate Process of production* (Camatte 1976). However, one fragment of the *Grundrisse*, "Forms which precede the capitalist mode of production," had already been translated by Yves Duroux and Jean-Claude Milner for Althusser's 1964–65 seminar on *Capital*, which was to be published under the title *Reading Capital*.
2. The phrase was pronounced during the discussion that followed the lecture Michel Foucault gave in 1969 at the Société Française de Philosophie: "Qu'est-ce qu'un auteur?" (Foucault 1983).
3. For various recent comparative studies of these *Capital* readings, see Carlino and Cavazzini (2014), Sotiris (2015), Baronian (2017) and Pitts (2018).
4. As both Backhaus and Reichelt recall, it is their discovery, in 1963, of a rare copy of the 1867 edition of *Capital* volume I in the library of a student accommodation in Frankfurt that launched the program of the *NML* (Backhaus 1997, 29; Reichelt 2008, 11).
5. Hans-Jürgen Krahl's description of Critical Theory testifies to the way the radical students of the Frankfurt School received it. Critical Theory, he writes, is "a doctrine, whose statements construe society from the standpoint of its transformability" (Krahl 2008, 228).
6. To put it in Chris Arthur's words: "the *logical* framework has *ontological* import" (Arthur 2004, 9).
7. One of the virtues of Moishe Postone's *Time, Labor and Social Domination* precisely is to make the critique of labor that is more or less implicit in the NML "canonical" texts explicit (Postone 1993).
8. Antonio Negri will apply the same political method of reading to Marx's *Grundrisse* (Negri 1991). Already in *Workers and Capital*, Tronti claims that "it is in the *Grundrisse* that Marx shows the best understanding of [the] problem" of the political passage from labor-power to working class (Tronti 2006, 211).

9. The historical initiative Tronti attributes to the capitalist class as a political subject is particularly clear in the analyses devoted to the New Deal in the "post-scriptum of problems" he added to the 1970 edition of *Workers and Capital*, which announces his turn from the autonomy of the working class to the "autonomy of the political." On this, see Davide Gallo Lassere's entry in this volume.
10. Hence the writing, by Nanni Balestrini, of a workerist *Bildungsroman*: *We Want Everything!* in which one follows the journey of a young proletarian from misery to revolutionary politics (Balestrini 2016). The Hegelian presuppositions of Tronti's conceptual and political construction were criticized by Raniero Panzieri, a founding member of the first workerist journal *Quaderni rossi*, whose split gave rise to the foundation of *classe operaia* where some of the essays that compose *Workers and Capital* were first published (Panzieri 1973, 302).
11. "In all forms of society there is one specific kind of production which predominates over the rest, whose relations thus assign rank and influence to the others. It is a general illumination which bathes all the other colours and modifies their particularity. It is a particular ether which determines the specific gravity of every being which has materialized within it" (G: 106–7).

Bibliography

Adorno, Theodor W. 1973 (1966). *Negative Dialectics*. London and New York: Routledge.

Adorno, Theodor W. 2018 (1997). "Marx and the Basic Concepts of Sociological Theory: From a Seminar Transcript in the Summer Semester of 1962." *Historical Materialism* 26(1): 1–11.

Althusser, Louis. 1969 (1965). *For Marx*. London: Allen Lane.

Althusser, Louis. 1996 (1965). "L'objet du *Capital*." In Louis Althusser, Étienne Balibar, Roger Establet, Pierre Macherey, and Jacques Rancière. *Lire "Le Capital,"* 245–418. Paris: Presses Universitaires de France.

Althusser, Louis. 2015 (1965). "The Object of *Capital*." In Louis Althusser, Étienne Balibar, Roger Establet, Pierre Macherey, and Jacques Rancière. *Reading Capital: The Complete Edition*, 215–356. London: Verso.

Amin, Samir. 1974. *Accumulation on a World Scale: A Critique of the Theory of Underdevelopment*. New York: Monthly Review Press.

Arthur, Christopher J. 2004. *The New Dialectic and Marx's "Capital."* Leiden: Brill.

Backhaus, Hans-Georg. 1992. "Marxian Social Economy as Critical Theory." In *Open Marxism*, edited by Werner Bonefeld, Richard Gunn, and Kosmas Psychopedis. Vol. 1, 54–92. London: Pluto.

Backhaus, Hans-Georg. 1997. *Dialektik der Wertform. Untersuchungen zur Marxschen Ökonomiekritik*. Freiburg: Ça ira Verlag.

Balestrini, Nanni. 2016. *We Want Everything*. London and New York: Verso.

Balibar, Étienne. 1974. *Cinq études du matérialisme historique*. Paris: Maspero.

Balibar, Étienne. 1996 (1965). "Sur les concepts fondamentaux du matérialisme historique." In *Lire "Le Capital*", edited by Louis Althusser, Étienne Balibar, Roger Establet, Pierre Macherey, and Jacques Rancière, 419–568. Paris: Presses Universitaires de France.

Balibar, Étienne. 2015 (1965)."On the Basic Concepts of Historical Materialism." In *Reading Capital: The Complete Edition*, edited by Louis Althusser, Étienne Balibar, Roger Establet, Pierre Macherey, and Jacques Rancière, 357–480. London: Verso.

Balibar, Étienne. 2016. "Un point d'hérésie du marxisme occidental. Althusser et Tronti, lecteurs du *Capital*." *Période*. http://revueperiode.net/un-point-dheresie-du-marxisme-occidental-althusser-et-tronti-lecteurs-du-capital/

Baronian, Laurent. 2017. "Sous les pavés, *Le Capital*. Le problème du travail dans l'opéraïsme et la *Neue Marx-Lektüre*." *Période*. http://revueperiode.net/sous-les-paves-le-capital-le-probleme-du-travail-dans-loperaisme-et-la-neue-marx-lekture/

Bellofiore, Riccardo, and Tommaso Redolfi Riva. 2015. "The *Neue Marx-Lektüre*: Putting the Critique of Political Economy Back into the Critique of Society." *Radical Philosophy* 189: 24–36.

Bologna, Sergio. 1972. "Class Composition and the Theory of the Party at the Origins of the Workers' Council Movement." *Telos* 13: 4–27.

Bonefeld, Werner. 2014. *Critical Theory and the Critique of Political Economy*. London: Bloomsbury.

Camatte, Jacques. 1976. *Capital et Gemeinwesen. Le 6° chapitre inédit du "Capital" et l'œuvre économique de Marx*. Paris: Spartacus.

Carlino, Fabrizio, and Andrea Cavazzini. 2014. "Althusser et l'opéraïsme. Notes pour l'étude d'une 'rencontre manqué.'" *Période*. http://revueperiode.net/althusser-et-loperaisme-notes-pour-letude-dune-rencontre-manquee/

Cavazzini, Andrea. 2013. *Enquête ouvrière et théorie critique. Enjeux et figures de la centralité ouvrière dans l'Italie des années 1960*. Liège: Presses Universitaires de Liège.

Chanson, Vincent, and Frédéric Monferrand. 2018. "Workerism and Critical Theory." In *The Sage Handbook of Frankfurt School Critical Theory*, edited by Beverley Best, Werner Bonefeld, and Chris O'Kane, Vol. 3, 1302–13. London: Sage.
Cleaver, Harry. 1979. *Reading "Capital" Politically*. Brighton: Harvester.
Elbe, Ingo. 2006. "Zwischen Marx, Marxismus und Marxismen: Lesarten der Marxschen Theorie." In *"Das Kapital" neu lesen. Beiträge zur radikalen Philosophie*, edited by Jan Hoff, Alexis Petrioli, Ingo Stützle, and Frieder Otti Wolf, Frieder, 52–71. Münster: Westfälisches Dampfboot.
Elliott, Gregory. 2006. *Althusser: The Detour of Theory*. Chicago: Haymarket.
Endnotes. 2010. "Communization and Value-Form Theory." *Endnotes* 2. https://endnotes.org.uk/issues/2/en/endnotes-communisation-and-value-form-theory
Engels, Frederick. 1981. "Supplement and Addendum to Volume 3 of *Capital*." In *CIII*, 1028–47.
Federici, Silvia. 2012. *Revolution at Point Zero. Housework, Reproduction and Feminist Struggle*. Oakland: PM Press.
Foucault, Michel. 1983. "Qu'est-ce qu'un auteur?" *Littoral* 9: 3–32.
Heinrich, Michael. 2004. *An Introduction to the Three Volumes of Karl Marx's Capital*. New York: Monthly Review Press.
Horkheimer. Max. 1972. *Critical Theory: Selected Essays*. New York: Continuum.
Jameson, Fredric. 2008 (1984). "Periodizing the 60s." In Fredric Jameson. *The Ideologies of Theory*, 483–515. London: Verso.
Krahl, Hans-Jürgen. 2008. *Konstitution und Klassenkampf. Zur historischen Dialektik von bürgerlichen Emanzipation und proletarischer Revolution. Schriften, Reden und Entwürfe aus den Jahren 1966–1970*. Frankfurt: Verlag Neue Kritik.
Lukács, Georg. 1971. *History and Class Consciousness: Studies in Marxist Dialectics*. London: Merlin.
Marini, Ruy Mauro. 1969. *Subdesarrollo y revolución*. Mexico: Siglo XXI Editores.
Montag, Warren. 2013. *Althusser and His Contemporaries: Philosophy's Perpetual War*. Durham, NC: Duke University Press.
Negri, Antonio. 1991. *Marx Beyond Marx: Lessons on the "Grundrisse."* Brooklyn: Autonomedia.
Panzieri, Raniero. 1973. *La ripressa del marxismo-leninismo in Italia*. Milan: Nuova edizioni operaie.
Pitts, Frederick Harry. 2018. *Critiquing Capitalism Today: New Ways to Read Marx*. London: Palgrave Macmillan.
Postone, Moishe. 1993. *Time, Labor and Social Domination: A Reinterpretation of Marx's Critical Theory*. Cambridge: Cambridge University Press.
Reichelt, Helmut. 1970. *Zur logischen Struktur des Kapitalbegriffs bei Karl Marx*. Frankfurt: Europäische Verlangsanstalt.
Reichelt, Helmut. 2005. "Social Reality as Appearance: Some Notes on Marx's Conception of Reality." In *Human Dignity: Social Autonomy and the Critique of Capital*, edited by Werner Bonefeld and Kosmas Psychopedis, 31–68. Farnham: Ashgate.
Reichelt, Helmut. 2008. *Neue Marx-Lektüre: Zur Kritik sozialwissenschaftlicher Logik*. Hamburg: VSA-Verlag.
Rosdolsky, Roman. 1977. *The Making of Marx's "Capital."* London: Pluto.
Schmidt, Alfred. 1981. *History and Structure: An Essay on Hegelian-Marxist and Structuralist Theories of History*. Cambridge, MA: The MIT Press.
Sohn-Rethel, Alfred. 1978. *Intellectual and Manual Labor: A Critique of Epistemology*. Atlantic Highlands, NJ: Humanities Press.
Sotiris, Panagiotis. 2015. "Althusserianism and Value-Form Theory: Rancière, Althusser and the Question of Fetishism." *Crisis and Critique* 2(2): 166–94.
Tronti, Mario. 2006. *Operai e capitale*. Rome: Derive Approdi.
Wallerstein, Immanuel. 1979. *The Capitalist World-Economy*. Cambridge: Cambridge University Press.

23
JEAN-PAUL SARTRE (1905–80)

Sam Coombes

The general overall trajectory of Sartre's career is well known, as is the fact that by no means all of it sits easily or unquestionably in the "Marxist" category, at least not in any classic sense of that term: from the libertarian semi-anarchist phenomenologist positions of the 1930s to Sartre's awakening to the importance of history at the start of World War II; to existentialist humanism tending increasingly toward Marxism in the postwar years, and polemical debates with the French Communist Party; to the Communist fellow-traveling years (1952–56); to the work that came to be seen as epitomizing "Sartre's Marxism," the first volume of the *Critique of Dialectical Reason* (1960); to ultimately a rather dichotomous positioning on Sartre's part that on the one hand saw him produce the gargantuanly erudite *Family Idiot* and on the other involve himself in militant Maoist-tending political activism.

The *Critique* remains Sartre's most sustained engagement with Marxist philosophy and, in the absence for many years (in fact until the early 1980s) of works such as *The War Diaries* (1983 [1939–40]) and *Notebooks for an Ethics* (1983 [1947–48]), was understandably taken by many commentators to signal a marked rupture with Sartre's earlier and especially pre-war works. One central reason for this reading was the assumption that *Being and Nothingness* (1943), Sartre's most sizeable theoretical work of the 1940s, was very largely expressive and representative of all the key tenets of his thought in the "early" period. But for all that Sartre was voluble and loquacious, he was often also tantalizingly elliptical. One only has to consider the number of unfinished and unpublished manuscripts throughout his career, and those instances in which what would appear to be a topic of absolutely central importance to a given theoretical discussion is sidelined in a few short sentences, to take cognizance of the fact that Sartre's expositions of his ideas are often far from complete.

Being and Nothingness, Sartre's magnum opus of the early period of his career, is presented as a work of "phenomenological-ontology," an attempt to describe the ontological freedom and situatedness of the individual subject principally in his or her surrounding local context. Despite its focus on ontology, or questions relating to being, *Being and Nothingness* does in fact contain claims that are highly suggestive for ethics, the reader being only briefly informed that the implications of Sartre's ontological claims for ethical conduct will have to await a subsequent work. This work, published posthumously as *Notebooks for an Ethics*, never saw light of day in the period and hence successive generations of Sartre commentators associated Sartrean ethics with the overarchingly inauthentic outlook and exclusively negative view of interpersonal relations expressed in *Being and Nothingness*, in ignorance of the positive ethics of generosity and reciprocity that he had formulated in the interim period. Quite how Sartre became the passionate advocate of socialism that he did in *What Is Literature?* (1948) while being assumed to continue believing that "hell is other people" (*No Exit* [1945]) would only become fully apparent after his death.

There has long been debate about the way in which the early humanist Marx relates to the later economics-focused Marx of *Capital*. The prevalence of later Engelsian-derived dialectical materialism, or Diamat, in the Stalinist era gave rise to the commonly held view in both Communist and liberal circles that Marxian theory, supposed to enjoy the status of scientific truth, did not contain ethical and moral presuppositions. There is a noticeable lack of discussion of these fields in Marx's writings, Marx, as Yvon Quiniou reminds us, stressing the primacy of politics in relation to morality, often presented as of a piece with bourgeois ideology.[1] Quiniou argues that an "ethical normativity" can nevertheless be clearly detected in Marx's thought, problematic though it in some ways is: "Its presence is evident: Marx explicitly acknowledged its pivotal role in the shaping of his theoretico-practical itinerary" (Quiniou 2002, 65). R.G. Peffer confirms this reading, referring to reconstructing Marx's "implicit moral theory" despite the difficulty posed by the "submerged character" of Marx's moral views (Peffer 1990, 4).

Taking this idea of continuity in Marxian thought as a basis, there are good reasons for viewing the early Sartrean conception of the subject as in important respects reminiscent of that of the early Marx of the *Economic and Philosophic Manuscripts of 1844*, which had become available in France in 1937–38. Marx had stressed the centrality of creative labor to the human condition opposing creative labor to alienation. As Sartre was to do later, the early Marx highlighted the importance of subjective agency and self-realization. This ethical humanist Marxist view of the subject accords well with the Sartrean insistence, stretching from Sartre's earliest theoretical writings of the 1930s through to the *Critique* and beyond, on the fundamental inalienability of the freedom of the individual. Even in the *Critique* Sartre was to reject notions of absolute historical determination or of any sort of collective consciousness (Flynn 1984, 110), despite for many years by this stage having accepted the idea that individuals were fully conditioned by their circumstances. If the Marxist Sartre of the *Critique* accepts entirely Marx's dictum that "[m]en make their own history, but . . . they do not make it under circumstances chosen by themselves" (*MECW* 11: 103), this is a view that can be traced back in his writings until at least 1945 and arguably even the *War Diaries* (1939–40).

In what follows, it is hence the continuity in Sartre's thinking rather than rupture that will be the guiding thread. The *Critique of Dialectical Reason*, as well as being a major stand-alone contribution to Marxist theory, will be presented as to some extent the logical outcome and culmination point of many years of development in Sartre's intellectual itinerary. It is worth noting in this regard that even as late as an interview of 1975 Sartre declared an abiding fidelity to the conception of the translucidity of consciousness that he had set out more than thirty years previously in *Being and Nothingness*, and generally showed himself not to be in disagreement with many of his fundamental earlier claims (Schlipp 1981, 23). Critical studies appraising the extent to which the claims of the *Critique* conform to classic Marxist categories are numerous (Desan 1965; Flynn 1984). I will address some of these issues but as a logical extension of a broader discussion of Sartre's development toward Marxism in the post–World War II period.

Sartre's Turn Toward Marxism

The first explicit references to concepts that can be clearly associated with Marxist thinking are to be found in Sartre's *War Diaries*. In one passage of scathing self-criticism Sartre comments that "I am undoubtedly a monstrous product of capitalism, parliamentarism, centralization and the civil service" (Sartre 1984, 292). As Sartre's self-analysis in the diaries develops there is more broadly a perceptible shift in the direction of the sort of opposition between the abstract and the concrete of material conditions that is commonly to be found in classical Marxism. Sartre wonders how he had been able during the 1930s to turn a blind eye to the influence that objective circumstances could exert over his freedom: "this way of mine of taking refuge at the top of the tower, when it is being attacked from below, and of looking down without so much as blinking" (Sartre 1984, 473).

Sartre's rejection of his pre-war bourgeois self in the name of a newfound acknowledgment of material and social conditions of possibility was to take a more explicitly theoretical formulation in his postwar writings, and indeed a formulation that was soon to start anticipating the schemas of the *Critique of Dialectical Reason* in key ways. "For fifteen years now," Sartre later remarked in an interview of 1960, "I have been looking for something: it is a matter . . . of giving a political foundation to anthropology" (Sartre 1971, 9) and it is in the founding text to the *Temps Modernes* journal that he both rejects the 19th-century liberal conception of rights as inadequate and explains that man is best understood as a synthetic whole, that is as a totality (Sartre 1948, 23), which involves acknowledging not only that he is necessarily in situation but also that he is conditioned by his economic circumstances and by his social class. Such situational constraints encroach much more significantly on subjective freedom than those discussed in *Being and Nothingness*.

Sartre calls for a synthetic anthropology, indicating that ontological freedom, though not reducible to or determined by situation, nevertheless cannot simply transcend the conditioning it produces. The synthetic conception of reality is opposed to "analytical" thought, these contrasting categories corresponding to proto-Marxist thought on the one hand and bourgeois and liberal thought on the one hand on the other. Man understood as a synthetic whole is a totality, but Sartre goes on to formulate for the first time a position that would remain central to his existential Marxism until the *Critique* and beyond: Sartre argues that the capacity for subjective self-determination must nevertheless be safeguarded: "I can accept without difficulty that a man, even though his situation conditions him completely, can be a locus of irreducible indeterminacy." In the *Critique*, Sartre describes his method as "regressive-progressive and analytico-synthetic" (Sartre 1982, 88). Although the regressive-progressive method would accord a more central place to the dialectical interaction between the free subject and his socio-historical situation than the position Sartre advances in the founding text to *Les Temps Modernes* does, the basic idea of the subject who is conditioned by history and yet free to act upon and change her circumstances remains the same.

In 1946, Sartre produced a text entirely devoted to questions of Marxist philosophy and political practice, entitled "Matérialisme et révolution," which has tended not to receive the full attention it merits in the critical literature. In this text, and notably in a revised version of 1949 in which a number of footnotes concerning Marx were added, Sartre effectively recuperates the thought of Marx, saving it from the clutches of mechanistic Stalinist doctrine. Stalinist Marxism, in its insistence on a rigidly deterministic conception of historical change, effectively writes the free subject out of history, thereby rendering the revolutionary project at the heart of Marx's thought impossible, Sartre observes. Stalinist Diamat, he concludes, is a debased and crude version of the theory contained in Engels's *Anti-Dühring* (1878) in its attempt to ally a flat assertion of material reality to the dialectical schema contained in Hegel's *Logic*: historical change becomes a function of a dialectics of nature, whereas in the later Marx the dialectic had been interpreted much more loosely. The revolutionary, Sartre ripostes, must be ontologically free if he is to have any chance of emancipating himself from his constraining socio-economic situation; however socio-economically unfree the worker might be, he remains free to make choices such as whether or not to revolt. The distinction that Sartre maintains here and throughout this text between the subjective and the political types of freedom is the direct descendant of that established between freedom in situation and ontological freedom in *Being and Nothingness*.

The influence of Maurice Merleau-Ponty on Sartre's thinking during the postwar years was pivotal in the development of his political thought, even if their itineraries were ultimately to lead them in contrasting directions, Merleau-Ponty away from explicit support for Marxism while Sartre toward a number of years of fellow-traveling with the Communist Party (1952–56 notably). Sartre was later to acknowledge openly his indebtedness to his erstwhile political editor at the *Temps Modernes* in his obituary for Merleau-Ponty (1961). Moreover, in the mid 1940s when Sartre and the French Communist left were caught in a deadlock of mutual misunderstanding and misrepresentation, Merleau-Ponty played the role of intermediary in debate, his position being close enough to both to illuminate the inadequacies of each side. He stood almost entirely alone[2] in his insistence on the compatibility of existentialism and Marxism and was the only thinker in the immediate postwar years who argued forcefully for their reconciliation.

The Cold War, Marxist Aesthetics and Socialist Ethics

If the fellow-traveling years (1952–56) are largely put to one side as essentially an error of judgment on Sartre's part (as they are commonly recognized to be), Sartre's most significant Marxist writings prior to the *Critique* are constituted by a cluster of texts written in the late 1940s. The themes central to *What Is Literature?* (1950 [1948]), the posthumously published *Notebooks for an Ethics* (1983) and *Dirty Hands* (1948) link up in manifold ways and indicate an evolution in Sartre's political thought that involves developing perspectives on both aesthetics and ethics. Also of note in this period is Sartre's attempt to form a political group, the "Rassemblement Démocratique et Révolutionnaire" (R.D.R.) in 1948 whose objective was to create a cross-party association unifying leftists seeking to escape the growing East-West Cold War polarity and envisage an independent role for Europe. The R.D.R. proved short-lived, partly because of the intense fire it immediately came under from the P.C.F., but it offers evidence of Sartre's willingness to implicate himself in active politics. It also puts his fellow-traveling period of the 1950s into a fresh perspective clearly suggesting as it does that if Sartre was ultimately to side whole-heartedly with Soviet-led Communism during the Cold War years, accepting such a polarity was not his preferred choice.

Notebooks for an Ethics essentially comprise two principal thematic focuses, on the one hand a dialectics of history that in fact builds on earlier tentative reflections on the topic in the *War Diaries* and anticipates that of the *Critique*, and on the other a socialist ethics that reverses the negative ethics of *Being and Nothingness* and, in its instantiation in *Dirty Hands*, is reminiscent of the Marxist ethics set out by Trotsky in *Their Morals and Ours* (1938), which Sartre had learned of when reading the writings of Merleau-Ponty. As regards historiography, however, whereas Merleau-Ponty's inquiries into the "sens" (i.e., meaning or direction) of history in *Sense and Non-Sense* (1948) were ultimately limited to explaining the ambiguity and unpredictability of the existential present, from *Notebooks* through to the *Critique* Sartre endeavors to elaborate an existentialist version of the Hegelian dialectic so as to propose a new global account of history's forward movement. In *Notebooks*, moreover, it is not only history that is understood as having a fundamentally political dimension. Certain key questions of ethics are similarly presented as intertwined with matters of political theory and practice: "Morality today *must* be revolutionary socialist" (Sartre 1992, 18), claims Sartre in the first notebook of the series. Moreover, in many places in *Notebooks*, Sartre presents questions of history and of ethics as interconnecting:

"Morality must be historical" (Sartre 1992, 12); "The end of History will be the advent of Morality" (Sartre 1992, 91). Sartre hereby intertwines historiography, ethics and politics, as the latter two categories are conceived of as being thoroughly imbricated in the historical dialectic, which is already understood as a dialectic of individual subject and history as it will subsequently be in the *Critique*.

The "Morality" Sartre refers to is by definition a socialist morality of solidarity and reciprocity. This historicized, politicized morality is in *Notebooks* also a positive conception of intersubjective ethics that overturns the exclusively negative morality of *Being and Nothingness*. Sartre had argued that our habitual state is an inauthentic one in which we seek omnipotence in the form of psychological ascendancy over others; in other words, Sartre had concluded, we seek to be like God. Once the project to be like God, following the ethical conversion Sartre had referred to in *Being and Nothingness*, is cast aside, relations characterized by generosity, gift-giving and even love become possible. The individual subject no longer needs to seek to ground herself in the world in the manner of the "spirit of seriousness" and need no longer concoct narratives for himself in order to conceal from himself uncomfortable truths (*mauvaise foi*). In a state of "pure" rather than "impure reflection," it becomes possible for the subject to commit him or herself fully not just ontologically (which as Sartre had explained in *Existentialism is a Humanism* was always inevitable) but also ethically and politically. In its political dimension, commitment for Sartre now means active engagement in the direction of attempting to ensure that socialism becomes a political reality.

What Is Literature? is known for being the archetypal Sartrean assertion of the need for commitment in writing. Flaubert and Goncourt had been charged as responsible for the repression that followed the Paris Commune in the founding text of the *Temps Modernes* (1946) because they had not written a word against it, and *What Is Literature?* confirms a tendency in Sartre's thinking in this period toward a certain functionalist reductionism with respect to prose writing. However, in marked contrast with the criterion of "ideological correctness" imposed in the USSR by Andrei Zhdanov, which dictated that artistic production should be ideologically aligned with Communist ideology, Sartre's politicization of prose is founded on the idea of the total responsibility of the prose writer. In *Existentialism Is a Humanism* Sartre had adhered explicitly to the Kantian universalist notion that one could not want freedom for oneself without seeking to ensure it for others at the same time; one could only enjoy genuine freedom if others also were free. And as Sartre equates the political ideal of socialism with greater emancipation for all, then it follows that on his view the prose writer, whose use of prose as opposed to poetry commits him inevitably one way or the other in any case, must actively strive to encourage his readers to militate in favor of socialism.

These conceptions of ethics, politics, responsibility and commitment come together in the debates that lie at the heart of *Dirty Hands* (1948). Although described by Sartre as nonpartisan (Howells 1988, 90), that is as about politics rather than politically committed, the centerpiece of the work is Sartre's examination of questions of principles versus pragmatism, and ends versus means, which lie at the heart of classic Marxist political philosophy and had been articulated with particular clarity by Trotsky in *Their Morals and Ours*. Trotsky was perhaps the most notable advocate of the idea that the Marxist worldview was not an amoralism, as scientistic Marxists and Marxism's liberal critics would have it, but rather was founded on an alternative conception of morality. Sartre's *Notebooks* contain a nine-page discussion of the work, but its influence on his thinking can be perceived much more broadly in the blend of historiography, ethics and politics that characterizes his reflections throughout. Its influence is also vital to *Dirty Hands* (1948) whose central action, the assassination of a revolutionary political leader named Hoederer, had in any case been inspired by the murder of Trotsky in 1940 (De Beauvoir 2001, 209–10).[3]

The accusation of "amoralism" levelled at Marxism and Bolshevism by liberal democrats, Trotsky argued, was founded on a limited and historically naive conception of morality. Marxism's liberal critics failed to see that sets of moral values were relative to their historical context and to the stage the class struggle had reached. The bourgeois democratic conception of morality was that which corresponded to the era of progressive capitalism. As this era came under threat from the rise of the working class, however, a new type of morality came into focus, which Trotsky termed "the morality of proletarian revolution" (Trotsky et al. 1973, 23). This conception, founded on the class struggle, the dialectical materialist view of history and the goal of a future socialist revolution, was mistakenly charged with being an amoralism because it did not acknowledge the principles of bourgeois morality. In *Dirty Hands* Hoederer, whose outlook Sartre commented was the only one that seemed to him to be a laudable one, demonstrates to the young bourgeois idealist Hugo that his moral purism and insistence on principles has nothing to do with the type of politicized ethics that he and his comrades defend.

The Crystallizing of a Dialectics of Subject and History

Sartre's dialectic is founded on the idea of an interactive relationship between the individual subject and his or her historical context. In later interviews Sartre was to date his interest in dialectics to the immediate postwar years (Schlipp 1981, 18) and it is well known that his first serious contact with the work of Hegel was stimulated by the research of Alexandre Kojève on the German philosopher during these years. In the *Critique*, the Sartrean version of the dialectic is given expression notably through the "progressive-regressive" method. Sartre sets dialectical reason against analytical reason, the former being a more detailed and sophisticated version of the synthetic conception of man that he had argued for in the founding text of the *Temps modernes*. In the *Critique* the focus is more squarely on the "regressive" moment, the aim of which being to work one's way back to the component parts of a given entity under scrutiny. Via this "regressive" movement back to all the components and conditioning of a social, historical and economic nature that lead to that entity having become what it now is, that is, a synthetic totality, we can gain a better understanding of its actions and possibilities in the present. Conditioning, however all encompassing, is never synonymous for Sartre with rigid social determinism though as is demonstrated by the example he gives of French writer Paul Valéry: "Valéry is a petit bourgeois intellectual, no doubt about it. But not every petit bourgeois intellectual is Valéry" (Sartre 1968, 56). Any given individual has the capacity through his or her actions to move beyond the possibilities apparently allowed by his or her socio-historical conditioning.

Sartre's dialectic is clearly of a very different variety from the more abstractly Hegelian version integral to Stalinist Diamat, which involved a philosophically unconvincing marriage of Hegelian dialectics as articulated in the *Logic* with a flat assertion of materialism. But it also contrasts with that of the mature Marx, despite the allegiance that Sartre declares to Marxian thought near the start of *Search for a Method* (1957), the immediate theoretical predecessor to the *Critique* and reaffirmed at the start of the same volume (Sartre 1982, 822). Whereas Marx, as Henri Lefebvre pointed out, reintroduced a version of the dialectic to explain the relationships between economic categories in the process of generating capital (Lefebvre 2012), Sartre's focus is the dialectical working of human praxis in a milieu of scarcity. Praxis begins to assume the alienated characteristics of scarcity itself in the "practico-inert" field (a concept that in the later Sartre's work substitutes by and large for the material and human collectivities that assume the passive character of "seriality"). However, seriality is countered by the positive praxis by which what Sartre terms the "group in fusion" comes into being. Whereas the concept of the "series" expresses intersubjective alienation as in the well-known example Sartre gives of individuals constituting only obstacles to each other in a bus queue rather than engaging in relations of solidarity, the "group in fusion" spontaneously comes together with a common purpose as in the case of what took place in the Quartier Saint Antoine shortly before the storming of the Bastille. In such moments the shackles of social alienation are cast off and individuals work together in a spirit of solidarity. However, groups themselves are subject to the alienating power of the practico-inert. In order to achieve consistency and greater efficacity, over time they become organizations. Some of the spontaneity of the original group formation is lost but in the interests of effectively promoting more clearly defined goals. Via this process, though, the group ultimately becomes an institution and hence exhibits the reified and alienating qualities of the practico-inert and of seriality from which it first emanated. Sartre hereby highlights the constant risk of the encroachment of reification and alienation in the very processes working toward revolutionary change themselves; indeed, his Marxist existentialism was to remain more intrinsically revolutionary in character than the Marxism of established leftist political formations of the day, the French Communist Party in particular.

The Family Idiot (1970) was to focus more on the "progressive" moment in the dialectic than the *Critique*, seeking to account for Flaubert as an emanation from his historical context as well as in constant dialectical interaction with it. By this time, Sartre's existentialist humanist Marxism had come under heavy fire from the structuralists and notably the structuralist Marxists inspired in particular by the work of Althusser. Much of his Marxist writing was produced moreover when his leading contemporary Merleau-Ponty had abandoned the idea of lending active support to Marxism; Merleau-Ponty proceeded to deliver a scathing attack on Sartre's position in *The Adventures of the Dialectic* (1974 [1955]). Whatever the merits of these critiques, and of the subsequent decentering of the subject by thinkers who came in one way or another to be associated with poststructuralism (Derrida, and later Badiou for example), Sartre's ethical humanist outlook and particular subject-historical formulation of the dialectic from 1945 onward continues to occupy a central place in mid-20th-century attempts to revamp, reformulate and add to the conceptual apparatus of classical Marxism.

Notes

1. This point was defended by Quiniou in "La Morale de Marx," a paper given at Université Paris VIII (25 January 2001).
2. Michael Kelly (1999, 5–6) suggests that Lefebvre's overt hostility to Sartre's thought in his full-length study *L'Existentialisme* masked important areas of common ground shared by the two thinkers.
3. Ian Birchall (2004, 85–6) provides a detailed and convincing examination of the evidence substantiating the link with the assassination of Trotsky.

Bibliography

Birchall, Ian. 2004. *Sartre against Stalinism*. Oxford: Berghahn.
De Beauvoir, Simone. 2001. *The Prime of Life*. London: Penguin.
Desan, Wilfred. 1965. *The Marxism of Jean-Paul Sartre*. New York: Doubleday.
Flynn, Thomas. 1984. *Sartre and Marxist Existentialism*. Chicago: Chicago University Press.
Howells, Christina. 1988. *Sartre: The Necessity of Freedom*. Cambridge: Cambridge University Press.
Kelly, Michael. 1999. "Towards a Heuristic Method: Sartre and Lefebvre." *Sartre Studies International* 5(1): 1–15.
Lefebvre, Henri. 2012 (1948). *Le Marxisme*. Paris: Presses Universitaires de France.
Merleau-Ponty, Maurice. 1961. *Sense and Non-Sense*. Evanston, IL: Northwestern University Press.
Merleau-Ponty, Maurice. 1974. *The Adventures of the Dialectic*. London: Heinemann Educational.
Peffer, R.G. 1990. *Marxism, Morality and Social Justice*. Princeton, NJ: Princeton University Press.
Quiniou, Yvon. 2002. *Etudes matérialistes sur la morale*. Paris: Editions Kimé.
Sartre, Jean-Paul. 1948. "Présentation des *Temps Modernes*." In *Situations II*, 7–30. Paris: Gallimard.

Sartre, Jean-Paul. 1968 (1957). *Search for a Method*. New York: Vintage.
Sartre, Jean-Paul. 1971. *Situations IX*. Paris: Gallimard.
Sartre, Jean-Paul. 1981–93. *The Family Idiot*. Chicago: University of Chicago Press.
Sartre, Jean-Paul. 1982 (1960). *Critique of Dialectical Reason*. Vol. 1. London: Verso.
Sartre, Jean-Paul. 1984. *War Diaries: Notebooks from a Phoney War, November 1939–March 1940*. London: Verso.
Sartre, Jean-Paul. 1989a. "Dirty Hands." In *No Exit and Three Other Plays*. London: Vintage Books.
Sartre, Jean-Paul. 1989b. "No Exit." In *No Exit and Three Other Plays*. London: Vintage Books.
Sartre, Jean-Paul. 1992. *Notebooks for an Ethics*. Chicago: University of Chicago Press.
Sartre, Jean-Paul. 2003 (1943). *Being and Nothingness*. London: Routledge.
Sartre, Jean-Paul. 2007. *Existentialism Is a Humanism*. Paris: Broché.
Schlipp, Paul Arthur, ed. 1981. *The Philosophy of Jean-Paul Sartre*. LaSalle, IL: Open Court.
Trotsky, Leon, John Dewey, and George Novack. 1973. *Their Morals and Ours: Marxist vs. Liberal Views on Morality*. New York: Pathfinder Press.

24
LOUIS ALTHUSSER (1918–90)

Maria Turchetto

Louis Althusser, after his schooling in Algiers and Marseilles, entered the École Normale Supérieure (ENS) as a student in 1939. Enlisted and taken prisoner in 1940, he spent the war in captivity. In 1945 he resumed his studies at the ENS, in the Faculty of Philosophy, and in 1948 he became a maître assistant; he would remain a philosophy teacher there until 1980. 1948 is also the year he joined the French Communist Party (PCF). His communist militancy is important to understand his theoretical commitment, never divorced from the political one. As he says in one of his conversations with Fernanda Navarro:

> I wanted to intervene in France in the French Communist Party, which I joined in 1948, in order to struggle against triumphant Stalinism and its disastrous effects on my Party's politics. At the time, I had no choice: if I had intervened publicly in the *politics* of the Party, which refused to publish even my philosophical writings (on Marx), deemed heretical and dangerous, I would have been, at least until 1970, immediately expelled, marginalized and left powerless to influence the Party at all. So there remained only one way for me to intervene politically in the Party: by way of *pure theory* – that is, *philosophy*.
>
> *(Althusser 1994a, 30, 2006, 253)*

And later on:

> the Party could not expel me anymore, because my directly political interventions were grounded in Marx, whom I interpreted in "critical and revolutionary" fashion. Marx protected me even in the Party, thanks to his status as the "sacrosanct father" of our thought.
>
> *(Althusser 1994a, 34, 2006, 256: translation modified)*

The interpretation of the "philosophy of Marx" proposed by Althusser was truly "critical and revolutionary": a true theoretical revolution with respect to the Marxism of the time. Another great figure of French culture, Michel Foucault, has taught us to be wary of the "cultural unities" given by common sense or tradition and invited us to look for discontinuities within them, break them up and use the fragments to build new unities and new orders. Even the "author" represents a merely empirical cultural unity, which a theoretical point of view – and not simply a biographical one – can legitimately break up. Althusser conducts this operation on Marx, separating a "mature Marx" from a Marx still strongly conditioned by Hegelianism.[1] It was a heretical operation, certainly swimming against the stream during the years in which it was conducted – when the "young Marx" was in vogue in philosophical studies – but which would prove to be of great rigor, even at the philological level. The operation brings to the fore *Capital* volume I, the "work on which Marx has to be *judged*" (Althusser 1971, 71), rather than texts such as the *Economic and Philosophic Manuscripts of 1844*, whose nature as notes rather than real elaborations was later highlighted; rather than occasional writings or "fragments" that were made to weigh more than the whole of *Capital* (such as the letter to Kugelmann or the "Fragment on Machines" in the *Grundrisse*, on which entire theoretical edifices were erected); but also rather than *Capital* volumes II and II, which we know today were extensively interpolated by Engels.

Fully to understand the "revolutionary" scope of the interpretation of Marx proposed by Althusser, it is indeed important to place it in the framework of Marxism after the Second World War:[2] a strongly *dualistic* framework. On the one hand, "orthodox" Marxism dominated; this is the version that enjoyed the imprimatur of Moscow and that I will call – using an Althusserian term – *economistic* Marxism. On the other hand, "heterodoxy" was represented by a Marxism that I will call *philosophical*, a term that seeks to hold together the two faces of this Marxism identified by Althusser, namely humanism and historicism. Althusser produces a critique that affects both fronts.

Better to identify the two Marxisms that "fill the world" after World War II, against which Althusser carves out a different position, we can refer to an Italian author, Claudio Napoleoni, who in the same years spoke of "two Marxes," "Marx the scientist" and "Marx the philosopher," identifying the first with an economist of the classical school (a continuer of Smith and Ricardo) dominated by the procedures of science, the second with a theorist of "alienation," in a sense very close to that of the Frankfurt School (Napoleoni 1985). With this distinction Napoleoni captured, in my opinion, not so much the two souls of Marx as the two souls of 20th-century Marxism: the economistic one, which can be traced back to Kautsky (or even Engels), and the philosophical one, whose main matrix resides firmly in the Frankfurt School.

The Critique of Economistic Marxism

Let's consider, very briefly, the characteristics of economistic Marxism, which I would define, as a first approximation, to counterpose it to the Marxian program of the "critique of political economy," *a political economy without critique*. The two cornerstones of this conception are: the reductive interpretation of the Marxian notion of *production relations* and the role of motor of history attributed to the *productive forces*.

The relations of production are understood by orthodox Marxism exclusively as relations of *property* and *exchange*: in other words, as relations of distribution and circulation. So capitalism is given by the binomial private property/market (a binomial in which the first term is "unjust" and the second "irrational") and socialism by the antithetical couple public property/planning. Now Marx had accused the classical economists of having concentrated their analysis on distribution and circulation relations, ignoring production: ignoring its *social* character, reducing it to a mere technical fact. Orthodox Marxism restores this "blindness" to production, in spite of the Marxian critique. In this the orthodox Marxists – and not Marx – continue the classical economists, and are almost exclusively readers of *Capital* volumes II and III (dedicated to circulation and distribution), while they ignore in fact volume I (dedicated to the "immediate process of production," that is to say considered in abstraction from the mediating movements of circulation and distribution).[3] For Orthodox Marxism, how wealth is produced becomes once again inessential: what matters, from the social point of view, is how it circulates and is distributed. Production returns to being a merely technical, socially inert and neutral background; on the contrary, something intrinsically "useful," whatever the form of society within which it takes place.

Grafted on here is the idea of the productive forces of universal history, a true secular religion, a legend or "grand narrative" about the destiny of man established by orthodox Marxism.[4] According to this legend, the history of humanity is the history of the continuous and progressive development of the productive forces. The various forms of society promote or hinder this development, which however is destined to prevail: the social relations that block it will be overwhelmed and overcome. According to orthodox Marxism, capitalist relations (i.e., private property and the market) initially had a propulsive role, but then they ended up turning into fetters on the development of the productive forces: for this reason, capitalism is destined to fall. For this reason, the goodness and the superiority of socialism are measured by the *productivity* of this system: the noble race with the West is thus unleashed over who will make more wheat, weapons and sputniks. . . .

The Althusserian critique is based on the revival of the Marxian concept of *production relations*: much of *Reading Capital* is dedicated to redefining this concept. According to Althusser, with the concepts of "mode of production" and "production relations" Marx effected a break with the classical school in economics, placing himself on a new terrain in epistemology (producing a new conception of how the knowledge of society and of history develops, very distant from the 19th-century conception) and in science (investigating a new object, production itself, seen in its historical specificity).

The production relations are defined by Althusser *functionally*, that is, with reference to the functional roles that are created in production:

> the structure of the relations of production determines the places and functions occupied and adopted by the agents of production, who are never anything more than the occupants of these places, in so far as they are the "bearers" (*Träger*) of these functions. The true "subjects" (in the sense of constitutive subjects of the process) are therefore not these occupants or functionaries, are not, despite all appearances, the "obviousnesses" of the "given" of naïve anthropology, "concrete individuals," "real men" – but *the definition and distribution of these places and functions. The true "subjects" are these definers and distributors: the relations of production*. . . . But since these are "relations," they cannot be thought within the category subject. And if by chance anyone proposes to reduce these relations of production to relations between men, i.e., "human relations," he is violating Marx's thought, for so long as we apply a truly critical reading to some of his rare ambiguous formulations, Marx shows in the greatest depth that the relations of production . . . are irreducible to any anthropological inter-subjectivity – since they only combine agents and objects in a specific structure of the distribution of relations, places and functions, occupied and "supported" by objects and agents of production.
> *(Althusser 1996c, 393, 2015, 334–35)*

From this step we begin to understand that what it means to say that production is "a process without subject," an Althusserian phrase as famous as it is little understood. And we come to know that the relations of production are not merely intersubjective relationships: they are functions that shape the *subjects* (determining their role, their place in society – in a dominant or subordinate position, to begin with) as much as objects, the "things":

> These relations of production determine the connections between the different groups of agents of production and the objects and instruments of production, and thereby

> they simultaneously divide the agents of production into functional groups, each occupying a definite place in the production process. The relations between the agents of production are then the result of the typical relations they maintain with the means of production (object, instruments).
>
> *(Althusser 1996c, 388, 2015, 331)*

This means, among other things, that *the relations of production shape the productive forces* – the instruments, the technique, the science itself, which therefore cannot be thought of as separate and neutral.

This is the true heart of the Althusserian critique of economistic Marxism. It would be worthwhile to dwell at length on this point, but I will limit myself here to underlining the theoretical and political importance of this critique, highlighting two consequences. The first is the unprecedented possibility of *critique of "real socialism"* that derives from this approach. At a time when the anti-Communists spoke of totalitarianism and lack of freedom, attributing these aspects to the very nature of "socialism," while the Communists spoke at most of "degeneration" of socialism due to the "cult of personality," Althusser's analysis involves a judgment that sounds even paradoxical to the common sense of the time: the society of so-called real socialism is in fact *capitalist*, since nothing has changed in it at the level of the mode of production – literally, of *how* production is organized – and of the *relations of production*, that is, of the functional relationships involved in production. It would be above all Charles Bettelheim who would develop this consequence of the Althusserian critique, in works such as *Class Struggles in the USSR*, in my opinion still unsurpassed (Bettelheim 1974).

The second consequence is an unprecedented possibility of *critique of science* "from within." Productive force par excellence – therefore "neutral" and even "progressive" par excellence, at most twisted "from the outside" to the goals of capitalist profit making – science (and above all the *Big Science*, that linked to space and nuclear research) had become something untouchable for Marxism: for orthodox Marxism, engaged in the emulation of Western technical-scientific achievements; but also for heterodox "philosophical" Marxism, which limited itself to juxtaposing a pallid "humanism," incapable of criticizing disquieting "scientism" on its own terms. But I will dwell on these limits of philosophical Marxism in the next section. Here I am especially interested in pointing out this enormous potential of the Althusserian critique, which makes it possible to link the form of scientific discourse to the structure of production relations, and which provides the rationale, among other things, for works such as *Philosophy and the Spontaneous Philosophy of the Scientists* (Althusser 1974).

The Critique of Philosophical Marxism

And now we come to philosophical Marxism: to the Frankfurt School, first of all, which in my opinion represents its high point. The products of this school (Habermas and the followers of hermeneutics) remained far below the original Frankfurt program. In fact, if orthodox Marxism presents itself, as to its theoretical coordinates, as an eminently 19th-century form of thought (a mixture of classical economics and philosophy of history), the Frankfurt School definitely belongs to 20th-century thinking. A problematic above all links it to the latter: one that, to use an expression of Max Weber's, I will define as the question of the "sciences in an era of specialization." The sciences are many and specialized, and there is no "philosophy" capable of summarizing them, of presenting their overall design. Faced with this problem, the Frankfurt School offers an original solution: the "Critical Theory" that the scholars belonging to the *Institut für Sozialforschung* propose does not in fact have to do with philosophy understood in the traditional sense. What they seek to bring forward is, in fact, a project of *social research* oriented toward "current society as a whole"; but since "society as a whole" cannot be assumed as an immediate object of research, because of the growth of social mediations that characterizes the contemporary era, this cognitive task can only be addressed from a plurality of disciplinary points of view: economics, psychoanalysis, anthropology, sociology etc. "Critical Theory" is what unifies the different approaches in three dimensions: a methodological reflection ("critical" means, in this context, the capacity for internal self-reflection on its own foundations, the explication of its conceptual and practical assumptions, caution toward pre-established methodologies); the assumption of a *point of view* that orients knowledge ("critical" means here to embrace the idea of an emancipated society as a point of reference); the identification of a kind of *privileged object* of analysis, represented by the "alienated" social relationships that characterize contemporary society ("Critical Theory" tends to become in this sense a "theory of alienation" that traces the latter not only on the level of economic relations, but also on those of politics, culture, everyday life, the very instinctual structure in the individual subject).

This third dimension represents in my opinion the weak point of the Frankfurt School: the idea of "alienation" that pervades social relations at all levels and in all areas (and pervades them *more and more*) in fact ends up making "society as a whole" an "expressive totality" – to use the terminology adopted by Althusser in *Reading Capital* (Althusser 1996c, 402–3, 2015, 342). The limitation that derives from this is that society thus conceived, if it is not susceptible to economistic "reductions," is not even "structurable."

The Frankfurtian approach thus falls under two targets of the Althusserian critique. First, the critique of historicism, to the extent that the expressive contemporaneity introduced by the extended concept of "alienation" (a concept that brings everything back to a single "inner essence" of which the elements of the whole are "phenomenal forms of expression") leads to a cumulative continuity of historical time (Althusser 1996c, 402, 2015, 342): society becomes more and more alienated, therefore less and less decipherable as the alienation spreads to new areas.[5] Second, the critique of humanism, to the extent that the subject of "alienation" is no longer a *class*, but *man*.

For Althusser

> In 1845, Marx broke radically with every theory that based history and politics on an essence of man. This unique rupture contained three indissociable elements.
>
> (1) The formation of a theory of history and politics based on radically new concepts: the concepts of social formation, productive forces, relations of production, superstructure, ideologies, determination in the last instance by the economy, specific determination of the other levels, etc.
> (2) A radical critique of the *theoretical* pretensions of every philosophical humanism.
> (3) The definition of humanism as an *ideology*.
>
> *(Althusser, 1996a, 233, 1969, 227)*

Aleatory Materialism

The last period of Althusserian reflection, following the tragedy of 1980,[6] sees a radicalization above all of the critique of historicism. In the decade between 1980 and his death in October 1990, the French philosopher no longer dared to speak. The texts relating to "aleatory materialism" will be published only posthumously.

The radicalization concerns, on the one hand, the now explicit rupture with respect to orthodox Marxism that enjoys the imprimatur of Moscow: no longer constrained by his membership of the PCF, Althusser openly disavowed "dialectical materialism," understood as a form of encyclopedic knowledge built in the Soviet academies:

> the immense, ridiculous and stillborn work of the Benedictines of historical materialism and dialectical materialism, all official Soviet philosophy and that of its emulators in the countries of real socialism and of many ordinary party philosophers of Marxist theory in Western countries.
>
> *(Althusser 2000, 49)*

On the other side, Althusser makes explicit the operation of breaking the cultural unity represented by the author that we mentioned at the beginning, playing not only Marx against the Marxist tradition, but also Marx against Marx himself, arguing that

> In fact, we find two absolutely unrelated conceptions of the mode of production in Marx.
>
> The first . . . recurs in the famous chapter on primitive accumulation, the working day, and so on, and in a host of minor allusions, to which I shall return, if possible. It may also be found in the theory of the Asiatic mode of production. The second is found in the great passages of *Capital* on the essence of capitalism, as well as the essence of the feudal and socialist modes of production . . .; and, more generally, in the "theory" of the transition, or form of passage, from one mode of production to another.
>
> *(Althusser 2000, 105–6, 1994b, 570, 2006, 197)*

The Althusserian rereading of *Capital* volume I, part 8, on primitive or original accumulation emphasizes the nature of the historical reconstruction that is undermined by every "philosophy of history," understood as a necessary path of humanity in progress. In fact, the conditions of the genesis of capitalism – that is, the existence of a class of "free" workers, that is, free from feudal relations and without means of production, and the existence of a class of capital-owners – are not presented by Marx as the result of a single historical process: there is not a "law of history" that transforms feudalism into capitalism according to a unique logic and direction, but there are many differentiated historical paths, out of step in time, which progress and sometimes regress in different times, ways and places, proceeding for a long time without meeting significantly and without showing any necessitating logic.

One path is the history of the *genesis of the proletariat*: fundamentally, it is the story of the "expropriation of the rural population and their expulsion from the land," which includes different processes in different countries and at different periods. For England alone Marx identifies at least three significant stages susceptible to various causal interpretations: the dissolution of feudal remnants between the 15th and 16th centuries, part of a larger process of strengthening the monarchy; the massive transformation of cultivated lands in pasture around the end of the 15th century, following the development of the wool trade; subsequently an important stage is represented by the expropriation of church property following the Reformation; finally, starting from the 18th century, an important role is played by the legislative activity of the State in dismantling the residual publicly owned and communal properties (through the enclosures, laws fencing off common lands) and in the control of the expropriated rural population (laws against vagabondage and forcing the landless to work). The history of the *genesis of capital* is yet another path: the extremely varied and complex history of the formation of large masses of wealth in the form of money. Marx reconstructs in particular the history of usurer's capital and that of merchant capital, the latter mainly linked to the exploitation of conquered territories and colonies, and therefore to an essentially *unequal* exchange.

Capitalism is therefore not a necessary step the march of humanity in progress, but – to use the terminology coined by Althusser in these texts – the result of the contingent and "aleatory" "encounter" of different processes, of "elements that are independent of each other, each resulting from its own specific history, in the absence of any organic, teleological relation between these diverse histories" (Althusser 2000, 109, 1994b, 572, 2006, 199), an encounter that nevertheless "takes hold," giving rise to a system capable of reproduction.

The Influence of the Althusserian Interpretation

The influence of the original interpretation of Marx that Althusser proposed is very important and far from exhausted in its effects.

Recall, in the first place, the radical criticism of "real socialism," which, as I pointed out, derives from the revival of the Marxian notion of production relations. The question of the "nature" of the so-called socialist countries, debated especially in the 80s of the last century, after the fall of the Berlin Wall became and remained almost a dead letter: a sort of great removal for the entire left at international level, with the only relevant exception, already mentioned, of the works of Charles Bettelheim in France and of his pupil Gianfranco La Grassa in Italy. A return to the problem cannot be separated from the Althusserian elaboration.

Second, the centrality attributed by Althusser to the notion of production relations at the time resonated with at least two important strands of critical thought: the critical analysis of the organization of work and technique, both in the 1970s (with Braverman (1974) but also with the early work of Raniero Panzieri[7] and *Quaderni Rossi*) and in subsequent years, addressing in this case the phenomena of Toyotism and technology based on IT and electronics (for example with the works of Benjamin Coriat in France [Coriat 1979, 1991] and of Paola Manacorda in Italy [Manacorda 1984]); and an original approach to the questions of science and technology starting from some innovative works by Italian scientists, among whom I acknowledge first of all Marcello Cini.

Today Althusser's influence, far from being exhausted, also invests other sectors, also thanks to the conspicuous revival of publications and translations of Althusserian texts that have remained unpublished until now. In addition to the field of psychoanalysis (to the well-known "Freud et Lacan" other texts have been added on the subject (Althusser 1964, 1996b) in recent years, it is important to resume the political reflection of an Althusser who, starting from the middle of the 1970s, was the careful and lucid witness of a profound transformation that radically changed the "party form" (Althusser 2016).

Translated by Alex Callinicos

Notes

1. Starting with the texts brought together in *For Marx* in 1965 (Althusser 1996a, 1969), in particular "On the Young Marx" and "The '1844 Manuscripts' of Karl Marx."
2. Let us follow, in this regard, Althusser's guidance: every philosophical position, to have significant effects, must be placed in the context of different and conflictual positions: "[a philosophy] exists only insofar as it occupies a position it occupies, and it only occupies this positions insofar as it has conquered it in the thick of an already occupied world. It therefore insofar as this conflict has made it something distinct [*différence conflictuelle*]" (Althusser 1998, 68, 1976, 165–66).
3. Harry Braverman also laments the absence in the Marxist tradition of a reflection on *Capital* volume I (Braverman 1974, 9).
4. Starting with Friedrich Engels: significant, in this sense, is the "Supplement and Addendum," written on the occasion of the first publication of *Capital* volume III, in which Engels revives – and unfortunately proposes as an "authentic interpretation" of the Marxian text – a history of humanity. It is marked precisely by the development of the productive forces and the expansion of exchange: a path from

"savagery" to "civilization" (to resume the terminology derived from Lewis Morgan and employed by Engels himself in *The Origin of The Family, Private Property and the State*) or from a hypothetical "primitive communism" to developed communism, culmination and "end" of history.

5. It is not by chance that the logical conclusion drawn by the Frankfurt School is pessimistic: late capitalism destroys the "classical subject" that could have undertaken the historical task of emancipation.
6. On 16 November 1980, Althusser killed his wife Hélène Rytmann, strangling her. He was declared mentally ill at the time of his actions and admitted to a psychiatric clinic. Beginning in July 1982, at the Soisy-sur-Seine clinic and then in his Parisian apartment, he resumed writing. In a few weeks, he wrote a dozen texts that deal partly with the political conjuncture, partly on what he himself called "aleatory materialism" or "materialism of the encounter." The texts – which Althusser intended to collect in a book – have been published in several languages including the Italian edition edited by Vittorio Morfino and Luca Pinzolo (Althusser 2000).
7. On the continuity between Panzieri's and Althusser's readings of the notion of production relations, see Turchetto (1995).

Bibliography

Althusser, Louis. 1964. *Freud et Lacan*. Paris: Edition Gallimard.

Althusser, Louis. 1969 (1965). *For Marx*. London: Allen Lane.

Althusser, Louis. 1971. "Preface to *Capital* Volume I." In *Lenin and Philosophy and Other Essays*, 69–102. London: NLB.

Althusser, Louis. 1974. *Philosophie et philosophie spontanée des savants*. Paris: Maspero.

Althusser, Louis. 1976. *Essays in Self-Criticism*. London: NLB.

Althusser, Louis. 1994a. *Sur la philosophie*. Paris: Edition Gallimard.

Althusser, Louis. 1994b. "Le courant souterrain du materialism de la recontre." In Louis Althusser. *Écrits philosophiques et politiques*, edited by François Matheron. Tome 1, 539–80. Paris: Stock/IMEC.

Althusser, Louis. 1996a (1965). *Pour Marx*. Paris: Edition La Découverte.

Althusser, Louis. 1996b. *Psychanalyse et sciences humaines*. Paris: Libraire Générale Française/IMEC.

Althusser, Louis. 1996c (1965). "L'objet du *Capital*." In Althusser Louis, Étienne Balibar, Roger Establet, Pierre Macherey, and Jacques. *Lire "Le Capital,"* 245–418. Paris: Presses Universitaires de France.

Althusser, Louis. 1998. *Solitude de Machiavel*. Paris: Presses Universitaires de France.

Althusser, Louis. 1999. *Machiavelli and Us*. London: Verso.

Althusser, Louis. 2000. *Sul materialismo aleatorio*. Milano: Unicopli.

Althusser, Louis. 2006. *Philosophy of the Encounter: Later Writings, 1978–87*. London: Verso.

Althusser, Louis. 2015 (1965). "The Object of *Capital*." In *Reading Capital: The Complete Edition*, edited by Althusser, Louis, Étienne Balibar, Roger Establet, Pierre Macherey, and Jacques Rancière, 215–356. London: Verso.

Althusser, Louis. 2016. *Les vaches noires. Interview imaginaire*. Paris: PUF.

Althusser, Louis, Étienne Balibar, Roger Establet, Pierre Macherey, and Jacques Rancière. 1996 (1965). *Lire le Capital*. Paris: Presses Universitaires de France.

Althusser, Louis, Étienne Balibar, Roger Establet, Pierre Macherey, and Jacques Rancière. 2015 (1965). *Reading Capital: The Complete Edition*. London: Verso.

Bettelheim, Charles. 1974. *Les luttes de classes en URSS. De 1917 à 1923*. Paris: Maspero.

Braverman, Harry. 1974. *Labor and Monopoly Capital: The Degradation of Work in the Twentieth Century*. New York: Monthly Review Press.

Coriat, Benjamin. 1979. *L'atelier et le chronomètre. Essai sur le taylorisme, le fordisme et la production de masse*. Paris: Christian Bourgois.

Coriat, Benjamin. 1991. *Penser à l'envers*. Paris: Christian Bourgois.

Manacorda, Paola Maria. 1984. *Lavoro e intelligenza nell'età microelettronica*. Milano: Feltrinelli.

Napoleoni, Claudio. 1985. *Discorso sull'economia politica*. Torino: Boringhieri.

Turchetto, Maria. 1995. "Ripensiamento della nozione 'Rapporti de produzione' in Panzier." In *Ripensando Panzieri trent'anni dopo. Atti del convegno Pisa 28/29 gennaio 1994*, edited by Salvatore D'Albergo, 19–26. Pisa: BFS.

25

MARIO TRONTI (1931–)

Davide Gallo Lassere

Scrutinizing the world through political eyes; confronting history first, and only then engaging with theory; seeking not so much immersion in a tradition of thought but the tools with which to organize struggle. This, broadly speaking, is the approach developed by Mario Tronti throughout his life. A thinking political actor rather than a political thinker, the author of the founding text of workerism systematically works to implode the separation between theory and practice. According to Tronti, theory is always political, and politics is always theoretical; it is on the basis of practices that theory is produced and theory can and must express political productivity. As he stated in an early article,

> if *Capital* is simultaneously a scientific work and a moment of political action which shifts the objective reality of things, we may argue that even the October Revolution or the Paris Commune are both also simultaneously great movements of practice and powerful theoretical discoveries.
>
> *(Tronti 1959, 12–13)*

In spite of the significant turning points encountered over time, from conflict rooted in the materiality of class to a metaphysical vision of conflictuality, this style of militancy, which fuses theoretical research and political action, has come to be recognized as one of the defining characteristics of Tronti: from his debut in the Ostia branch of the Italian Communist Party (PCI) when he critiqued the long-standing Communist leader Togliatti's interpretation of Gramsci, to his latest essay *Dello spirito libero* and his taking up the post of Senator of the Italian Republic on the benches of the Democratic Party. A feeling of fateful belonging to a part of the social world that – once defeated by the forces of history – is marked by tragic traits. If, effectively, the last century witnessed the full swing of the titanic confrontation that took place on a global scale between workers and capital, the anthropological catastrophe that followed the defeat of Communism demands a radical reconstruction of thought and action. It is the sequence of these historic events that fueled Tronti's work: from 1960s workerism to confrontation with theological tradition; via the discovery of the autonomy of the political; a reading of the classics of history of thought; a study of bourgeois, worker and conservative revolutions; reflections on the Great and the Minor Twentieth Centuries; critique of actually existing political democracy and the search for an antagonistic realism.[1]

Within and Against

Operai e capitale (Workers and Capital) is the cornerstone of autonomist Marxism. Written in an assertive and paratactic style, lacking both subordinate clauses and concessive conjunctions, the categorial force of this coming-of-age book gives rise to a practical method of thinking so rigorous and devoted to the real that it provided an invaluable ethical and political lesson to the militant-intellectuals of the workerists. Proceeding via thesis, affirming by avoiding demonstration, expressing the density of social and political relations in an incisive and trenchant language: this is how Tronti draws – in a Brechtian manner – the "line of conduct" against the "plan of capital" at the moment when the factory has invaded the whole of society.[2]

In order to gain an overall understanding of the plurality of the contents of this complex work, which has played a major theoretical and political role in Italy and beyond, it is therefore necessary to read the succession of different chapters through which the volume is articulated in parallel with the evolution of the social and political situation of the country, and of the divisions which marked the operaist group. Far from being a homogeneous work, *Operai e Capitale* is in fact composed of

1. an introduction from the end of 1966, when the *classe operaia* experiment was already coming to an end;
2. three analytical chapters, the "first hypotheses," which appeared in the reviews *Il mondo nuovo* and *Quaderni rossi*, in 1962–63;
3. four political chapters, "a new type of political experiment," the editorials of the journal *classe operaia*, all from 1964;
4. the "first theses" of 1965;
5. the postscript of the second edition, from 1970, which announced the entry onto the battlefield of the autonomy of the political.

Once the diagnosis of neocapitalism has been developed in the opening chapters – particularly in the chapters "The Factory and Society" and "Social Capital" – Tronti threads the whole of the work with theoretical and political shifts that are in direct contact with the dynamic of social struggles in Italy. These shifts allow us to decipher, simultaneously, Tronti's double movement from and toward the Italian Communist Party and his breaking with his fellow workerists, first, Raniero Panzieri (his departure from the *Quaderni rossi*), and then Romano Alquati, Sergio Bologna and Toni Negri (the end of *classe operaia*).

This work of his youth concentrates previous studies on Gramsci and the logic of capital from which the primacy of the subject over the object[3] is already visible, and proposes a reading of "Marx Yesterday and Today." As previously stated, for Tronti "the first hand-to-hand combat of theory is not with another theory, but with history" (Tronti 2008c, 9). It's the urgent need to transform the world that necessitates the stress-testing of the concept. The "Marxian purification of Marxism" to which the workerists aspired therefore entails a confrontation not between Marx and other thinkers or between Marx and his epoch, but between Marx and Fordist, Keynesian, and Taylorist capitalism: "it is necessary to judge *Capital* by *contemporary capitalism*" (Tronti 2006a, 32, 27). The "Initial Hypotheses" of this daring use of Marx beyond Marx, as it will come to be described, therefore set about to dissect the context of the early 1960s. Granted new impetus by a renaissance of workers' struggles – particularly the strikes and blockades for the 1962 collective renegotiation of contracts at the Fiat plant in Turin, which immediately overflowed into the riots of the Piazza Statuto[4] – these analytical hypotheses cast a critical eye over the political-industrial landscape of the time by insisting on the struggle-development-crisis triptych.

According to the writings of Tronti that were published in the *Quaderni rossi*, it's the power of wage struggles that pushes capital to innovate organizationally and technologically and to socialize the productive forces and in so doing, capital actually promotes the most favorable conditions for it to come under fire. Indeed, the more capital valorizes itself, the more it finds itself forced to incorporate the working class into the process of accumulation, thereby structuring it as a potential force of opposition: "*within* society and at the same time *against* it . . . which is precisely the condition of workers as a class in the face of capital as a social relation" (Tronti 2006a, 11). The struggles for pay raises and improved working conditions – just like the struggles for the working day described by Marx in chapter 10 of *Capital* – define a substantial modification of the composition of capital and incur an extension and intensification of the processes of subsumption of society and of its valorization in capitalist terms, making the workers coordinated in the factories the true keystone of the system.

> At the highest level of capitalist development the social relation becomes a *moment* of the relation of production, and the whole of society becomes an *articulation* of production; in other words, the whole of society exists as a function of the factory and the factory extends its exclusive domination over the whole of society.
>
> *(Tronti 2006a, 48)*

From an analytical point of view, we must consider (1) the growing integration, implemented by state and capitalist agents, of the production-distribution-exchange-consumption cycle; (2) the progressive subordination of "all political relations to social relations, all social relations to relations of production and all relations of production to factory relations" (Tronti 2006a, 48, 51). Whereas, from a political perspective, we should reverse the approach and consider "the State from the perspective of society, society from the perspective of the factory and finally the factory from the point of view of the worker" (Tronti 2001, 51). The famous "Copernican revolution" of workerism, which consists in examining social struggles as the motor of capitalist development, making the latter a variable dependent on the former,[5] led the militant-intellectuals of the group to reformulate the relation between "class and party." "A New Style of Political Experiment," condensed into the watchword "Lenin in England" aimed precisely to again place "the party in the factory" (Tronti 2008a) – the beating heart of the societies of the time – and, from this nerve center of neocapitalist command, to attack and seize the state apparatus by breaking down the dichotomy between economic struggles and political struggles. Since the traditional workers' movement was subordinated to capitalist planning – with the union functioning as a channel of communication between workers and bosses, and the party providing external support to government rule – the workerists who were grouped around Tronti aimed for *the autonomous organization of struggles within the factory*, and it was this aim that determined the departure of Tronti and others from the editorial board of the *Quaderni rossi*.

In order to obstruct reformist maneuvers, Tronti and those comrades of his who gathered in *classe operaia* sought to deploy "an old tactic in the service of a new strategy." The increasingly combative nature of worker contestation – "1905 in Italy" – inspired the group to take a distance from the institutions of the traditional workers' movement. The slogan "Lenin in England" in fact represents "the search for a new practice for a workers' party: . . . the organization of the working class at its highest level of political development" (Tronti 2006a, 93). This original line of action necessitated an unprecedented form of organization, capable of strengthening and radicalizing, intensifying and accelerating workers' practices of contestation. In order to hamper stability and provoke a genuine political crisis – a crisis of power and not a simple crisis of government – "it is necessary to exacerbate the wage dynamic," "affect the productivity of work," "bring together the most urgent moment of workers' struggles and the most critical point of a situation's evolution" (Tronti 2006a, 99–100). It is only through applying pressure at "the highest levels of struggle" that it is possible to achieve victory, because "the link which will break will not be the one where capital is weakest but where the working class is strongest" (Tronti 2006a, 118). Spontaneous behaviors of insubordination by workers thus constitute the strategy, while the revolutionary party must reconquer the tactical moment, which means collecting, communicating and organizing the diffuse refusals of work until they establish a genuine crisis of the state machine. The bet of the workerists was that the specific situation of the Italian laboratory – "where we find ourselves simultaneously in the presence of both a sufficiently advanced capitalist economic development and a very high political development of the working class" (Tronti 2006a, 159) – would configure itself as the epicenter of revolution in the West, since economic struggles, through their application of pressure on the distribution of surplus value, impact directly on political stability: they acquired an authentically subversive dimension and became politically unsustainable.

The central chapters of *Operai e capitale*, written in 1964 (at the same time as the death of Togliatti, the internal restructuring of the PCI and a number of powerful workers' struggles), mark the move from a consideration that revolves around the link between factory/society to a reflection that focuses on the factory/politics network, meaning: the transition from the analysis of capitalism to the theory of revolution. The "Initial Theses" of 1965 (notably the opening essay "Marx, Labor Power, Working Class"), the true heart of the volume, consolidate this perspective from a historical-philosophical point of view. They examine retrospectively the elements heretofore articulated in order to push them further by discussing them more effectively. It is in this way that (1) the return to origins and to Marxian texts is rendered more consistent; (2) their importance for an understanding of the present roots itself in an archeology of the struggles of the 19th century; (3) an opening onto a new political phase becomes clearly visible, in the foreground of which we can observe the confrontation between, on the one hand, the "strategy of refusal," which involves the self-negation of workers as workers, and, on the other, "the two reformisms, of capital and of the workers' movement" (Tronti 2006a, 90).[6]

From Heresy to Prophecy

The *political reading* of the labor theory of value articulated in *Operai e capital* (Tronti 2006a, particularly 220–28 and 262–65), which identifies the working class as the vital, and therefore potentially deadly, element for capital, is supported by the "Hot Autumn" of 1969. However, the outcome of this impressive experience – which saw wage rises combined with strikes, blockades and sabotage bring Italian society to the edge of a crisis of the system – confirmed the idea that pushed Tronti to decree the end of the experiment of *classe operaia*. According to Tronti and the workerist group who rejoined the PCI, the savage antagonism of a refusal to work was not enough; what was also necessary was the proposal of an organized political force capable of rising to the highest spheres of the state, in order to occupy the institutions, take power and govern society, through the positive affirmation of its own perspective and own needs (Tronti 1977a). *Verfassung* rather than *Konstitution*; State-form and not simple constitutional charter. The "Postscript of Problems" to the second edition of *Operai e capitale*, guided by an analysis of English neoclassical economics, of the historical role of German social democracy and of the reforms of the US New Deal, broadens the spectrum of the themes dealt with by laying the ground for the autonomy of the political, which captured Tronti's attention for a whole decade. The constellation of historical-theoretical motives that informed this problem is concentrated on the moments of crisis and transition in which economic dynamics are subjected to the hold of the political. The early 1970s capitalist response to social struggles, the authoritarian response (Italy, Germany) or the reformist response (USA, UK) of the 1920s and 30s to the worker and soviet threats, the brilliant tactical coup of Lenin in taking the Winter Palace and the New Economic Policy that followed, but also the processes of primitive accumulation and the modern bourgeois revolutions: are all examples of the political mastery of economic laws that must be carefully examined in order to sharpen the weapons of critique and the critique of the weapons.

Whether as a lever of stabilization, as during the long peace of a hundred years of the 19th century (Tronti 1975), or as a catalyst for social mutations,[7] as in the aforementioned experiences, the political – which interlaces the upper strata of the ruling classes, parties, culture, people – insists on the contradictions that are at work in a given social formation in order to provide them with a partial solution. Machiavelli, Hobbes, Hegel and Schmitt; Weber, Lenin and Keynes; the Great War, 1917, and the Great Depression, thus become the test benches on which the validity of this thesis is tried. If the working class wants to beat capital, it has to commit itself to the heart of a double arena, the factory *and* the state: workers against capital, on the one hand, organized workers' movement against the ruling bourgeois classes, on the other. In effect, the intelligence of capital is not only visible in the field of technological and organizational innovation, but also at the institutional level; it does not restrict itself to regulating and planning accumulation, but it also possesses a character that is eminently tactical and strategic. In moments of crisis, the initiative of capital is in fact susceptible of operating an "advancement of the political terrain in relation to society" (Tronti 1977a, 60). According to Tronti, in order to make concrete a radicalization of the revolutionary perspective, it is therefore necessary to envisage the implementation of a workers' use of the state machinery. From this perspective, the refrain "from wage, to party, to government" does not outline – at least from the perspective of Tronti's intentions – the form of a mediating withdrawal under the aegis of capital, but points directly to the overturning of the dominant foundations and social relations; he aims to revive political action at the height of socio-economic confrontation in order to avoid the capitalist metabolization of workers' demands, or any kind of heterogeneity of aims.[8] According to Tronti, only *the force that directs politically the processes of social transformation* can be the victor. Whereas any abandonment of the political (institutions, government, state) to the hands of the adversary condemns the workers' movement to restrict itself to sectoral changes, which are always susceptible to being recovered and assimilated by capital as it regains its dynamic.

It is in this way that the relative failure of the social struggles of the 1960s-70s, caused by their inability to lead the assault at the heart of power, ratifies the twilight of politics; it concludes the definitive movement away from the Great toward the Minor Twentieth Century:

> from workers' struggles to the movements of contestation, like a red curtain falling and closing the theatre of an era. For us, and for many others, it seemed on the other hand that an era was just beginning. Delightful illusion. . . . The red on the horizon was really there: except that it was not the red of breaking dawn, but the dimming light of a setting sun.
>
> *(Tronti 1998, 23)*

According to Tronti, what failed the "students and workers united in struggle" was a political realism that was fit for the challenges posed by the state and by capital. This lack of practical and theoretical experience on the part of the revolutionary movement and on the part of Marxism could and should have been compensated by the study of the conservative tradition and of reactionary thinkers. In order to complement the "Marxist monotheism" (Tronti 1977b, 20, 54–55) of the critique of political economy, Tronti embarked on a lengthy undertaking to translate the Marxist categories and vocabulary to the level of the political: political cycle, primitive accumulation of the political, theory of political collapse, *homo democraticus*, critique of political democracy etc.

This conceptual tradition, whose spiritual fathers are Karl Marx and Carl Schmitt,[9] results in a reconfiguration of the reform/revolution dialectic. Beyond a revisiting of the heroic history of the workers' movement – the true depositary of revolutionary memory from which the younger generations could draw – and beyond the confrontation between religious and theological thought, the Marxian *zur kritik* of Marxism articulated by the elder Tronti returns to a phrase already present in *Operai e capitale*: "on the bending road of practice, you must slow down; on the straight line of theory, accelerate" (Tronti 2015b, 6). No revolutionary thought and practice that aim to be resolutely realist can afford to avoid or ignore the mutations of the situation – social, economic, political, cultural and anthropological – and of the radically unfavorable relation of forces to the demands for liberation. From this framework, politics that aims to obstruct the course of history, rather than accelerate it, must restrain their demons, slow their rhythm, reconstitute the forces of opposition and organize them with a view to a long transition. As the penultimate of the "Theses on Benjamin" emphasizes: "I see more *katechon* than *eschaton* in the '*what is to be done?*' which follows the end of modern politics" (Tronti 1998, 209).[10] If, in spite of all that was negative in the practical attempts of the Great Twentieth Century, "we cannot go backwards in relation to the 11th thesis on Feuerbach" (Tronti 1992, x), the revolution, rather than being the act by which we take power, adopts henceforth the traits of the process by which we manage power: "we must be reformists first, and only after, revolutionaries." This is the theoretical and political legacy of the career of Mario Tronti, that "lightning bolt without thunder!" (Tronti 2016).

Final Considerations

Taking as his point of departure the double overturning that assigns the working class (instead of capital and the party) with both the role of driving force in historical development and the function of strategist in political struggle, Tronti ends up with positions that can leave us perplexed. If the idea of an industrial subsumption of the social implies the fact that factory struggles are revolutionary because they call the whole of society into question, after the turn to the autonomy of the political, this same idea determines the necessity of a transition to the institutional level in order to counter the capacity of capital to "recover" or "integrate" struggles. Over the course of Tronti's journey the diagnosis shared by 1960s Marxism of capitalism as a logic that has swallowed all social spheres, leads therefore to distinct political conclusions, as though Tronti might have explored all the possible political articulations of the thesis of the becoming-social of the factory. Beyond the dubious replies Tronti provides, we can nonetheless ask whether the questions he poses are the right ones: is there really any justification for such a separation between the social and the political? Is the search for a central subjectivity always unavoidable? Must we continue to think and to act on the basis of binary distinctions, as with those that imply the friend/enemy opposition (workers and capital, or, on another level, women and men, white and non-white people etc.)? We could, in effect, argue that the challenges of the present confront us with the need of struggles to re-articulate the horizontality of movements with the verticality of forms of autonomous organization in order to bring together a plurality of subjectivities that have specific needs and experiences. This being said, it nevertheless remains true that many of the problems tackled by Tronti retain their urgency and relevance. Among others: the unity of theory and practice in the form of the politicization of all questions of an intellectual nature; the taking up of a partial and partisan point of view that is the only one up to the task of accessing an understanding the totality of capitalist social relations and transforming them radically; the critique of all progressive visions of history; or, also, the elaboration of an approach that is resolutely anti-economistic and anti-sociological.

Notes

1. Cf. the monograph published on Tronti's work written in 2014 by Franco Milanesi, *Nel Novecento*. Cf. Also, the anthology edited in 2018 by Matteo Cavalleri, Michele Filippini and Jamila Mascat, especially their long introduction, pp. 11–65.
2. *Operai e capitale* has now been published in English: Tronti (2019). On the decisive influence of this work for young workerists, cf. the interviews in *Gli operaisti* edited by Guido Borio, Francesca Pozzi and Gigi Roggero in 2005 and *L'operaismo degli anni Sessanta*, edited by Giuseppe Trotta and Fabio Milana. These two volumes are excellent introductions to workerism. For an exhaustive introduction in English, see Wright (2017).
3. Cf. Tronti (1958, 1961, 1976).
4. An excellent book on the Italian "red sequence" was published by Nanni Balestrini and Primo Moroni in 1987.
5. "We too have worked with a concept that puts capitalist development first, and workers second. This is a mistake. And now we have to turn the problem on its head, reverse the polarity, and start again from the beginning: and the beginning is the class struggle of the working class. At the level of socially developed capital, capitalist development becomes subordinated to working class struggles; it follows behind them, and they set the pace to which the political mechanisms of capital's own reproduction must be tuned" (Tronti 2006a, 87).
6. Cf. also, Tronti (2008b).
7. Cf. the study of Hobbes, Cromwell and the historical genesis of capitalism in Tronti (1977b).
8. The most interesting considerations can be found in "Sul '68, tutto è stato detto," in Tronti (2001, 81–100).
9. Cf. *"Karl und Carl"*, in Tronti (1998, 151–64).
10. For Tronti, the politics of *eschaton* correspond to the traditional Marxist-Hegelian view of historical struggle: the acceleration of historical tendencies internal to capitalist society will bring about communist society as the "end of history." To counter this, he opposes a politics of the *katechon*, which corresponds to a slowing down of the historical tendencies of capitalism in order to defer their disastrous consequences.

Bibliography

Balestrini, Nanni, and Primo Moroni. 1987. *La orda d'oro*. Milan: Feltrinelli.
Borio, Guido, Francesca Pozzi, and Gigi Roggero, eds. 2005. *Gli operaisti*. Rome: DeriveApprodi.
Cavalleri, Michele, Michele Filippini, and Jamila Mascat, eds. 2018. *Il demone della politica*. Bologna: Il Mulino.
Milanesi, Franco. 2014. *Nel Novecento*. Turin: Mimesis.
Tronti, Mario. 1958. "Alcune questioni attorno al marxismo di Gramsci." In *Studi gramsciani*, edited by Istituto Antonio Gramsci, 305–21. Rome: Editori Riuniti.
Tronti, Mario. 1959. *Marxismo e sociologia*. Rome: Istituto Gramsci. Now in Tronti, Mario. 1961. "Studi recenti sulla logica del *Capitale*." *Società* 6: 881–903.
Tronti, Mario. 1975. *Hegel politico*. Rome: Istituto della Enciclopedia italiana.
Tronti, Mario. 1976. "Tra materialismo dialettico e filosofia della prassi." In *La città futura*, edited by Alberto Caracciolo and Giovanni Scalia, 139–86. Milan: Feltrinelli.
Tronti, Mario. 1977a. *L'autonomia del politico*. Milan: Feltrinelli.
Tronti, Mario, ed. 1977b. *Stato e rivoluzione in Inghilterra*. Milan: Saggiatore.
Tronti, Mario. 1978. "Quattro inediti di Mario Tronti." *Metropolis*. 2 (June): 77–9.
Tronti, Mario. 1992. *Con le spalle al futuro*. Rome: Editori Riuniti.
Tronti, Mario. 1998. *Il tramonto della politica*. Turin: Einaudi.
Tronti, Mario. 2001. *Cenni di Castella*. Florence: Cadmo.
Tronti, Mario. 2006a (1966). *Operai e capitale*. Roma: Derive Approdi.
Tronti, Mario. 2006b. *Politica e destino*. Rome: Sossella editore.
Tronti, Mario. 2008a (1965). "Il partito in fabbrica." In Trotta and Milana, eds. 2008, 461–76.
Tronti, Mario. 2008b (1963). "I due riformismi." In Trotta and Milana, eds. 2008, 306–9.

Tronti, Mario. 2008c. "Noi operaisti." In *L'Operaismo degli anni Sessanta*. Edited by Trotta, Giuseppe, and Fabio Milana, 5–60. Rome: DeriveApprodi.
Tronti, Mario. 2015a. *Dello spirito libero*. Rome: Il Saggiatore.
Tronti, Mario. 2015b. *In nuove terre per antiche strade*. www.centroriformastato.it/wp-content/uploads/tronti_nuove_terre.pdf
Tronti, Mario. 2016. *Cari compagni*. www.euronomade.info/?p=7366
Tronti, Mario. 2019 (1966). *Workers and Capital*. London: Verso.
Trotta, Giuseppe, and Fabio Milana, eds. 2008. *L'Operaismo degli anni Sessanta*. Rome: DeriveApprodi.
Wright, Steve. 2017. *Storming Heaven: Class Composition and Struggle in Italian Autonomist Marxism*. London: Pluto.

26

ERIC HOBSBAWM (1917–2012)

George Souvlis

Eric Hobsbawm is possibly the only historian who has been equally praised for his work and criticized for the politics he endorsed throughout his life. Even today, most accounts display a polemical zeal against his political stance that even ardent Cold Warriors would have been hesitant using in the public debates of the time. This chapter is an attempt to offer a temperate though critical understanding of the relationship between Hobsbawm's politics and his work as a historian. If we are to grasp this complicated relationship effectively, we need to distinguish between the Marxist methodology that he used as his main, not though exclusive, analytical framework, and his popular-frontist understanding of politics as well as his support for the USSR in the postwar era. The former was not reducible to the latter, or vice versa. The Marxist analytical tools were chosen according to the demands of the research he was undertaking; Hobsbawm's politics was an outcome of his politicization during the 1920s and 1930s in the ranks of the Communist International. Although both aspects were indeed, in some senses, inextricably linked, they also displayed a relative autonomy.

Hobsbawm's work can thus be divided into four analytically distinct historical phases, which will be discussed in what follows. The first section covers the years of Hobsbawm's formation, the inter-war period and World War II. The following section examines his intellectual production during the 1960s, a decade in which he wrote some of his most influential studies, building on the interests of the British Marxist tradition that has been named "history from below." The third section reconstructs his tetralogy on the formation of the modern world. The final section is devoted to the political debates in which he was involved from the 1980s onwards, a period during which Eric Hobsbawm acquired the status of a public intellectual.

Hobsbawm's Formative Years

Eric Hobsbawm was born in Alexandria on 9 June 1917, a few months before the October Revolution and one and a half years before the conclusion of World War I, a moment that signaled the end of empires and the formation of modern nation-states. Both parents – an Austrian mother and a British father – were Jewish. The first twenty years of his life can be described as the outcome of these two wider historical processes. Hobsbawm became a Communist as he grew up in a Europe polarized between communism and the far right. In mid-1931 – a few months before official unemployment figures in Germany reached the historical peak of six million – the orphaned Eric and his sister moved to Berlin in order to live with their aunt and uncle (Hobsbawm 2002, 43; Wilde 2013). In autumn 1932 he joined a Communist secondary-school students' organization, the *Sozialistischer Schulerbund* (Hobsbawm 2002, 63). This political engagement in the Communist cause would last until the end of his life, even if in changing forms. In 1933 Eric and his sister moved to London (Hobsbawm 2002, 76). After finishing school, he started his undergraduate degree at King's College, Cambridge, where he studied history. Here he encountered Marxist historical analysis and joined the student branch of the Communist Party of Great Britain (Hobsbawm 2002, 100). The most crucial political experience for Hobsbawm and many of his peers happened between 1934 and 1939, in the years of the Popular Front, when the Communists sought to build an anti-fascist alliance with social-democratic and liberal bourgeois parties. As he acknowledged in his autobiography, this had a lasting influence on him throughout his life: "Popular Front politics continues to determine my strategic thinking in politics to this day" (Hobsbawm 2002, 218). However, the Popular Front did not influence only the way in which he perceived politics, but also, to a certain degree, the type of historiography that he practiced. The Comintern's ideological policy was based on analyses that linked the conjunctural political assessments of that time with struggles and figures from the past.

The echoes of this approach were illustrated by the efforts of the Communist Party Historians' Group, of which Hobsbawm was a prominent member. The Group sought to unearth the past traditions, experiences and struggles of the British people in order to create a political lineage that could inform the politics of its own time. In other words, this group made a conscious effort to produce an invented counter-hegemonic approach to the history of the British nation, which could challenge the dominant narrative and become politically inspirational. The Group also engaged into structural interpretations of social change, most importantly the famous debate on the transition from feudalism to capitalism that took place in the 1940s and 1950s (Hilton 1976). Hobsbawm contributed to this discussion with his seminal articles on the crisis of the 17th century. These pieces offered an interpretation of the delayed capitalist transition in Britain that took into account that the English Revolution took place almost two centuries before the Industrial Revolution. Drawing on the debates within the Historians Group, and more precisely on Maurice Dobb's studies, he argued that the general feudal crisis of the 17th century created the conditions for the emergence of a series of rebellious actions the most successful of which led to the overthrow of the English monarchy and the establishment of the first successful bourgeois revolution (Hobsbawm 1954a, 1954b).

Writing People's History

Hobsbawm's first monograph was *Primitive Rebels: Studies in Archaic Forms of Social Movement in the 19th and 20th Centuries* (Hobsbawm 1971). This groundbreaking study focuses on the different ways in which traditional societies – and more precisely, specific groups of people with know-how in weaponry – react to market integration. The time span that the study covers is the last thirty years of the long 19th century. During this period, the logic of the market was economically embedded throughout the world via imperialist forms of domination. Politically, a series of nation-states began to emerge in Europe, a process that was completed with the end of World War I and the two revolutions of 1917. However, these processes did not unfold without resistance from below, from people who experienced the dissolution of their societies as markets became entrenched. These traditional forms of rebellion corresponded to the historical context in which they emerged. Hobsbawm examines thus the predecessors of the modern revolutionaries. The main concept on which the study builds is the "social bandit," referring to those

> peasant outlaws whom the lord and state regard as criminals, but who are considered by their people as heroes, as champions, avengers, fighters for just, perhaps even leaders of liberation, and in any case men to be admired, helped and supported.
>
> *(Hobsbawm 1971, 13)*

The "social" dimension of banditry points then to the explicit class connotations of Hobsbawm's argumentation.

These bandits are indeed structurally bound to the peasantry; they are its defenders, to the extent that the rule of law has not yet been universalized, leaving several social layers exposed to the contradictions that emerged in the transitory phases of state building. The political outlook of the bandits was a "primitive" one, corresponding to the class they represented. Their repertoire of action, informed by traditional values, attempted to bring back the previous order of things and not to build a new one. These features make them different from the modern labor movement, which is organized as a class for itself, with a specific ideology (socialism) and with the aim of transforming the existing order of things into a new one that will qualitatively differ from its predecessor.

Published a decade later, *Bandits* (1969) built upon themes and issues raised in *Primitive Rebels*. The topic of social protest is also central to *Captain Swing*, co-written with George Rudé, which reconstructs, as the title suggests, the history of the English agricultural wage laborers' uprisings of the 1830s (Hobsbawm and Rudé 1975). The laborers, like the social bandits, did not aim at revolution but at the restoration of the previous order of things (Hobsbawm and Rudé 1975, 65). This, among other factors, led to the defeat of the movement, though the struggle did not go to waste (Hobsbawm and Rudé 1975, 281, 282).

Hobsbawm's next book, *Labouring Men* (1964), was a collection of essays focused on collective action, but this time of a modern type. Three main themes are examined in this study: the transformation of traditional political action into modern forms of organization; the role of religion in 19th-century British society and more precisely among the working classes; and the impact – or, more accurately, the non-impact – of Marx's theories on the making of the Labour Party. Hobsbawm's most significant contribution in this volume is his refinement of the concept of the "labor aristocracy." This refers to an upper and privileged stratum of the manual working class, which for many Marxist scholars is also a basis for explaining working-class activity in Victorian and Edwardian Britain and beyond. According to Hobsbawm, the labor aristocracy as a historical phenomenon emerges

> when the economic circumstances of capitalism make it possible to grant significant concessions to its proletariat, within which certain strata of workers manage by means of their special scarcity, skill, strategic position, organizational strength, etc., to establish notably better conditions for themselves than the rest.
>
> *(Hobsbawm 2012)*

Between 1840 and 1890, in Britain, a new layer of skilled workers emerged in industrial sectors such as cotton-textiles and metal-working "where machinery was imperfect and depended on some significant manual skill" (Hobsbawm 1964, 282–83). This specialized category of workers were the most effective in establishing unions that used their training "to make their labor artificially scarce, by restricting entry to their profession" (Hobsbawm 1964, 290–91).

Hobsbawm's later collection, *Worlds of Labour* (1984b), develops similar themes and topics to *Labouring Men*, though by then labor history had become established as discrete field of research. However, Hobsbawm's studies on labor history were not informed by the normative ideal of value-free research that had long reigned among historians and that dominated the field of social sciences in the postwar era, but by an explicit political commitment. Researching and writing for the labor movement, for Hobsbawm, should rather be combined with sound scholarship: the task of academic historians should be "to consolidate the new territories won by the committed" (Hobsbawm 1959, 72).

The Tetralogy of the Modern World

While Hobsbawm's studies on banditry and the British labor movement established him as an authoritative historian within Marxist circles and the academic world, his tetralogy on the making of the modern world – especially its last volume, *Age of Extremes* – was responsible for his work's journey from the academic world to the public sphere. This made him, all around the world, one of the most noted and widely read historians of the last three decades. It was written over a time span of more than thirty years (*The Age of Revolution* was published in 1962 and *Age of Extremes* thirty-two years later in 1994). This time distance between the writing of the four volumes had an impact on the narration, the epistemology and the politics underpinning the project.

The first and second volumes are each structured in two major sections on "developments" and "results." There is an implicit "materialist," if not Marxist, message in the architecture of these volumes. The developments are economic, then political and military, while the results are expressed in social structures, then political ideologies and finally in the cultural level, science, religion and arts (Elliott 2010). The first volume of the tetralogy focuses on the "dual" revolution that largely shaped the modern world as we know it now: the Industrial and French revolutions (Hobsbawm 1996, ix). The former was responsible for the establishment of economic liberalism, the latter for its political form: the modern institutions through which the popular will was expressed, with parliament being the most prominent (Hobsbawm 1996, 2–3). In Hobsbawm's "long 19th century," the bourgeoisie was the class that best expressed these values and realities. It was the central political actor that consciously asserted its domination throughout this century by establishing an efficient legal-political system of property relations, as it slowly but steadily sidelined the *ancien régime*.

The second volume, *The Age of Capital*, focuses, as its title indicates, on the ascendancy of global capital between 1848 and 1875. In this period, the European bourgeoisie lost its progressive political role as it compromised with the conservative-aristocratic status quo put under threat by the working classes. Indeed, by that time, these latter achieved a far more effective level of organization than the one they had at the beginning of the century, when the Industrial Revolution had not yet spread throughout the continent (Elliott 2010, 93). According to Hobsbawm's apt description of this shift, "The British (industrial) revolution had swallowed the French (political) revolution" (Hobsbawm 1995, 15). The political promises of 1789 were forestalled and the aims of the 1848 revolutions, far from being fulfilled, remained an open chapter for the next generations of revolutionaries. These defeats explain the capitalist advance that took place in the following decades. The technological innovations that accompanied this new cycle of capitalist accumulation allowed a new expansive phase in new lands outside the European continent. By the end of this period, the capitalist integration of the globe was almost complete.

The *Age of Empire* (1987) is the last of Hobsbawm's three volumes on the long 19th century. It studies how the century of the triumph of capitalism ended with the cataclysm of the Great War. The imperial expansion that took place over the last quarter of the 19th century was the capitalist solution to the crisis of profitability of 1873 to 1896. It gave shape to a world governed by a combined and uneven development between dominant and dominated states, a geopolitical equilibrium that changed substantially only with the liberation movements that emerged during the postwar period. In this period, European governments started one after the other to give up *laissez-faire* policies and adopt protectionist tariffs. In Hobsbawm's narrative of imperialist development, capitalism takes a specific shape as an outcome of internal contradictions. The subaltern classes' response to the storm of the crisis was to organize in trade unions, (working-class) parties and peasant cooperatives (for the agrarian population) or to emigrate to the New World. This was a potentially explosive situation for liberal elites, forcing them to include the new working class parties in the national parliaments. These parties constituted the chief parliamentary opposition in most European countries during this period.

The culmination of Hobsbawm's synthesis of the making of the modern world is *Age of Extremes: The Short Twentieth Century (1914–1991)*. In this study there is an explicit and structuring chronological periodization in three dialectically interlinked phases. The first, "The Age of Catastrophe," extends from the First to the Second World War. The second, "The Golden Age," covers the first quarter of the postwar period up till the oil crisis of 1973, the affluent period of the Western capitalist world with the emblematic welfare state, a product of Keynesian regulation. The third phase, "Landslide," is the era of neoliberal order where the global economy became dominated by international banks and multinational corporations outside the control of nation-states.

"The Age of Catastrophe," for Hobsbawm, was dominated by the two world wars and the two main social movements that challenged the established liberal order – Fascism and Communism. While the First World War started as an inter-imperialist conflict for global hegemony between the dominant powers of the period, it unintentionally gave rise to its potential political gravediggers – the Bolsheviks, and the nationalists who soon transformed into fascists – who assumed political leadership in several states and within two decades abolished liberalism, both economically (through protectionist policies) and politically (through proletarian and authoritarian dictatorships). This process was accelerated by the financial crisis of 1929. In a liberal world that was collapsing without any adequate systemic response to its crisis, the Soviet Union was the only real alternative to fascism.

The dominant feature of the "Golden Age" that followed the "Age of Catastrophe" was the systemic antagonism between the US and USSR, the so-called Cold War (Hobsbawm 1994, 226). This worked as an ideal arena for an expansive capitalist accumulation, in turn accounting for the long economic boom. An integral aspect of the stability of the new geopolitical order was the decolonization process that took place after 1945. Both superpowers were opposed to the old type-colonialism and attempted to integrate the countries of Africa and the other continents into their own spheres of influence.

Two global shifts, one economic and one political, put an end to this phase, inaugurating the "Landslide" between 1973 and 1991. The first is the paradigm shift from an organized to an unorganized form of capitalism – in other words, the arrival of the neoliberal order – and the second is the collapse of the USSR. The image of the new world order that Hobsbawm provides is rather bleak. The economic stability of the previous decades was replaced by recurrent periodic crises that put in doubt all the certainties (employment, social security, pensions etc.) of the postwar Western world. The role of states in this new conjuncture was reduced significantly, with their fate now dictated by international financial capital and its needs. The planned economies of the Third World experienced equal if not bigger difficulties. In many cases, these economies could not sustain themselves, so they resorted to IMF financing that "adjusted" them to the new global order. The collapse of the socialist world – both the Russian and the Yugoslav versions – can also be explained with reference to this shift. But the sea-change of the 1970s that swept across the world is not interpreted with tools deriving from historical-materialist analysis. Absent, then, are both types of causal explanation used within a Marxist framework – the horizontal structure of antagonism between capitals, and the vertical conflict between labor and capital.

From Just a Marxist to a Public Intellectual?

The third phase of Hobsbawm's career encompasses the period between his retirement from Birkbeck in 1982 to the end of his life in 2012. In the context of the Thatcherite attack on the working class in Britain, a shift took place from Hobsbawm's role as an intellectual that acted within the circles of the British left to that of a public intellectual at a larger stage. Despite being a member of another party, Hobsbawm played a key role within the debate on the future of the Labour Party and its strategy in the 1980s, with his numerous articles for *Marxism Today*, the theoretical journal of the CPGB. The Party had lost by that time its specific identity and seemed to function more like a think-tank attempting to influence Labour. Hobsbawm's lack of belief in class politics and his rise as an intellectual figure enjoying a large audience were significant in this regard. In his view, one of the reasons for Labor's failure was its left's insistent focus on a classical class-based analysis. The appropriate political response in the new conjuncture should rather consist in the formation of an anti-Thatcherite front including the right-wing split from Labour – the SDP – and their Liberal allies, also conceived as "anti-Thatcher forces" (Hobsbawm 1984a, 10).

Almost two decades later Hobsbawm came back re-discussing some aspects of the issues he touched in the 1980s with his collection *How to Change the World: Tales of Marx and Marxism* (2011). It was his last book published while he was still alive. In contrast to what the title suggests, this was not a manual for global proletarian revolution but a collection of his own texts on the intellectual history of Marx (part 1) and Marxism (part 2). The second part devoted particular attention to Gramsci: after Marx, the Marxist figure who most influenced the British historian.

Hobsbawm suggests that Marx's work should be approached both as an engagement with the conjuncture and as an attempt to connect theory and praxis in a constructive way (Hobsbawm 2011, 11). Given the differences between Marx's and the present times, for Hobsbawm, the classical writings' strategic instructions have a limited value for current struggles: he considers them

> dangerous even to use . . . as a set of precedents. . . . What could be learned from Marx was his method of facing the tasks of analysis and action rather than ready-made lessons to be derived from classic texts.
>
> *(Hobsbawm 2011, 89)*

The British historian did not have however the same hesitations over Gramsci, who, he believed, could still inform socialist strategic perspectives. The Sardinian Communist, in his view, was the "most original thinker produced in the West since 1917" (Hobsbawm 2011, 316). Hobsbawm attempted to offer an open-ended take of his work:

> He is a Marxist, and indeed a Leninist, and I don't propose to waste any time by defending him against the accusations of various sectarians who claim to know exactly what is and what is not Marxist and to have a copyright in their own version of Marxism.
>
> *(Hobsbawm 2011, 316)*

A careful reading of Hobsbawm's account shows that he was close to the version of Gramscianism that developed within and around the CPGB, where "Gramsci is squarely a post-Leninist, a theorist of broad alliances which are negotiated rather than pre-given, popular-democratic and not just class alliances. He is the theorist of war of position rather than frontal assault on the state" (Forgacs 1989, 83).

Adopting this line of reasoning Hobsbawm argues that

> naturally the winning of hegemony, so far as possible, before the transfer of power is particularly important in countries where the core of ruling-class power lies in the subalternity of the masses rather than in coercion. This is the case in most "Western" countries, whatever the ultra-left says, and however unquestioned the fact that in the last analysis, coercion is there to be used. As we may see in, say, Chile and Uruguay, beyond a certain point the use of coercion to maintain rule becomes frankly incompatible with the use of apparent or real consent, and the rulers have to choose between the alternatives of hegemony and force, the velvet glove and the iron fist.
>
> *(Hobsbawm 2011, 327–28)*

From this quote it appears that, rather than offering an open-ended reading of Gramscian Marxism, Hobsbawm launches a polemic against an understanding of the transition to socialism that promotes coercion as an equally necessary aspect as consent. Equally problematic seems to be his conception of hegemony. Rather than the affirmation of the worldview and capacity to lead of the working class at the core of a new historical bloc, hegemony is limited to the constitution of broad popular coalitions.

Conclusion

Hobsbawm was an erudite historian, whose work was mainly, though not exclusively, informed by the Marxist tradition. Concepts from other historiographical traditions were also integrated in his approach of historical research, if not always consciously. The Marxism he used as a historian did not follow closed nomothetic theoretical schemas but open-ended concepts and flexible mediations. The main criterion for the selection of these concepts was the object itself, how it could be used more effectively to grasp the historical phenomena that he sought to understand. The politics with which he was affiliated was derived from the CPGB and more precisely its Popular-Frontist strategy, which he endorsed throughout his life across the different historical conjunctures. Hence, critics like Michael Burleigh, arguing that Hobsbawm's historical work has to be rejected because of his support for the USSR and other Stalinist states, should not be taken seriously since they do not take into account the difference between these two levels (Burleigh 2012). The reason why most of his critics took this kind of view was not because he endorsed the USSR, but because of his non-acceptance of neoliberalism and his refusal to reject Marxism as a valid analytical repertoire, especially after the collapse of the Soviet world. Until the end of his life, Hobsbawm searched for answers to the very complex problems confronting humanity as a result of its capitalist conditions, even when the political alternatives he was familiar with had disappeared. He thus subscribed to Marx's call for "ruthless criticism of all that exists." His answers were not always persuasive, but this did not prevent him asking these questions in difficult times. He thus realized Edward Said's definition of the intellectual as

> someone whose place is publicly to raise embarrassing questions, to confront orthodoxy and dogma (rather than to produce them), to be someone who cannot easily be co-opted by governments or corporations, and whose raison d'être is to represent all those people and issues that are routinely forgotten or swept under the rug.
>
> *(Said 1996, 11)*

Bibliography

Burleigh, Michael. 2012. "Eric Hobsbawm: A Believer in the Red Utopia to the Very End." *Telegraph* (1 October). www.telegraph.co.uk/news/politics/9579092/Eric-Hobsbawm-A-believer-in-the-Red-utopia-to-the-very-end.html
Elliott, Gregory. 2010. *Hobsbawm: History and Politics*. London: Pluto.
Forgacs, David. 1989. "Gramsci and Marxism in Britain." *New Left Review* 1(196): 70–88.
Hilton, Rodney, ed. 1976. *The Transition from Feudalism to Capitalism*. London: NLB.
Hobsbawm, Eric. 1954a. "The General Crisis of the European Economy in the 17th Century." *Past & Present* 5(1): 33–53.
Hobsbawm, Eric. 1954b. "The Crisis of the 17th Century – II." *Past & Present* 6(1): 44–65.
Hobsbawm, Eric. 1959. "Commitment and Working Class History." *Universities & Left Review* 6: 71–72.
Hobsbawm, Eric. 1964. *Labouring Men: Studies in the History of Labor*. London: Weidenfeld & Nicolson.
Hobsbawm, Eric. 1971. *Primitive Rebels: Studies in Archaic Forms of Social Movement in the 19th and 20th Centuries*. Manchester: Manchester University Press.
Hobsbawm, Eric. 1984a. "Labour: Rump or Rebirth?" *Marxism Today* (March): 8–12.
Hobsbawm, Eric. 1984b. *Worlds of Labour: Further Studies in the History of Labour*. London: Weidenfeld & Nicolson.
Hobsbawm, Eric. 1987. *The Age of Empire, 1875–1914*. London: Weidenfeld & Nicolson.
Hobsbawm, Eric. 1994. *Age of Extremes: The Short Twentieth Century 1914–1991*. London: Abacus.
Hobsbawm, Eric. 1995 (1975). *The Age of Capital, 1848–1875*. London: Weidenfeld & Nicolson.
Hobsbawm, Eric. 1996 (1962). *The Age of Revolution, 1789–1848*. New York: Vintage Books.
Hobsbawm, Eric. 2002. *Interesting Times: A Twentieth-Century Life*. New York: Pantheon Books.
Hobsbawm, Eric. 2011. *How to Change the World: Tales of Marx and Marxism*. London: Little Brown.
Hobsbawm, Eric. 2012. "Lenin and the 'Aristocracy of the Labor.'" *Monthly Review* 64(7). https://monthlyreview.org/2012/12/01/lenin-and-the-aristocracy-of-labor/
Hobsbawm, Eric, and George Rudé. 1975. *Captain Swing*. New York: W. W. Norton & Company.
Said, Edward. 1996. *Representations of the Intellectual: The 1993 Reith Lectures*. New York: Vintage Books.
Wilde, Florian. 2013. "Divided They Fell: The German Left and the Rise of Hitler." *International Socialism* 2(137). http://isj.org.uk/divided-they-fell-the-german-left-and-the-rise-of-hitler/

27

NICOS POULANTZAS (1936–79)

Bob Jessop

Nicos Aristides Poulantzas was a Greek Marxist whose widely influential intellectual and political career was spent in Paris. He taught sociology at the University of Paris VIII (Vincennes) from 1968 until his tragic suicide in 1979. He was also a member of the Greek Communist Party of the Interior, a reformist party aligned with Eurocommunism (see Poulantzas 1979a). Among many contributions to Marxist theory and strategy, he is best known for his work on state power. Although this reputation is largely due to a much-cited but misleading epistemological debate[1] with Ralph Miliband, another Marxist political theorist, his key substantive contributions as a state theorist stem from his relational account of state power. Another controversy in which he was involved concerned the implications of changes in postwar capitalism for classes and class struggle.[2] Unfortunately, a focus on these disputes in state and class theory has hindered a fuller, more nuanced appreciation of Poulantzas's overall contribution to Marxist theory and practice and the significant shifts in his position of diverse issues.

Intellectual Career

After completing a law degree at Panteion University of Social and Political Sciences in Athens, Poulantzas studied law successively in Munich, Heidelberg and Paris, where he settled. There he wrote a Sartre-inspired PhD on the unity of fact and value in Marxist legal philosophy and legal theory (Poulantzas 1965). He then began to develop a view of the capitalist type of state and political struggle that owed much to the postwar discussion of Gramsci's prison notebooks, notably their insights into hegemony, and to postwar Italian Marxist thought more generally. He soon integrated these topics into an account of the relative autonomy of the capitalist state that was influenced by Althusser's structural Marxism (Poulantzas 1973; for background, see Althusser 1969; Althusser and Balibar 1970). Inspired by political events such as the Greek coup d'état in 1967 and May 1968 in France, he turned to strategically relevant topics such as fascism and military dictatorships, the changing contours of imperialism and social class relations, and the role of parties and social movements in modern capitalism (1974a, 1975, 1976a, 1978b, 1979b). His final studies addressed problems posed by the latest crises in Marxist theory and practice, the challenges of Foucault's analyses of power and resistance, and the collapse of state socialism.

Poulantzas was highly attuned to changing conjunctures and this is reflected in some remarkable shifts in his philosophical position, theoretical focus and strategic concerns. Like Marx, his intellectual trajectory moved from legal philosophy to the state and then to political economy. His studies of constitutional and administrative law had a lasting influence on his analysis of the institutional matrix of the state. In contrast to Marx, however, who built on the legacies of German philosophy, Poulantzas was inspired by trends in contemporary French philosophy: first, Sartre and existentialism, then Althusser and structuralism, and, finally, Foucault and the micro-physics of power. Politically he was initially attracted to existential Marxism, then to a Gramscian inflection of Marxism-Leninism, prompting calls for working-class hegemony led by a vanguard party, and, finally, to a left Eurocommunist position that was committed to party and class alliances at the base as well as to a close articulation of direct and representative democracy. These shifts were related to philosophical fashion but they were primarily driven by his attempts to interpret and explain the significance of political trends and shocks in France, Greece and elsewhere (Jessop 1985).

On the State and State Power

Ignoring his PhD thesis, which Poulantzas seems to have consigned to the "gnawing criticism of the mice" in that he stated, when his fame grew, that it would not be republished (1978b, 86n), Poulantzas's first monograph was *Political Power and Social Classes* (1973, hereafter *PPSC*) This sought to provide the theoretical framework for answering the question initially posed by the Bolshevik legal theorist Evgeny Pashukanis: why, in the capitalist state, "political domination is constantly absent from its institutions." In other words, why it "presents itself as a popular-class-state [with its legitimacy based on] the ensemble of formally free and equal individuals-citizens and on the popular sovereignty and secular responsibility of the state towards the people" (1973, 123; cf. 1978b, 49; compare Pashukanis 1978, 139). He argued that the separation between the economic and political regions in the capitalist mode of production – the basis on their respective relative autonomies – and the exclusion of extra-economic coercion from the labor market and labor process enabled an end to direct class rule. This created the conditions for struggles to establish the "normal" form of the capitalist state, that is, one that is *formally adequate* to capitalist political domination, even if it is not statistically normal. This is the modern representative state, which offers a flexible framework to unify the long-term political interests of an otherwise fissiparous power bloc, disorganize the subaltern classes, and secure popular consent based on plausible claims to represent the national-popular interest and deliver economic concessions. In *PPSC*, this analysis was developed in three steps: first, Althusser's structural Marxism provided the theoretical rationale for the relative autonomy of the political region in capitalist social formations; second, legal theory provided the concepts to describe the state's formal institutional architecture as the instantiation of the political region and the terrain of political class struggle; and, third, a close reading of classic texts by Marx, Engels, Lenin and, above all, Gramsci provided the concepts for the analysis of the struggle for hegemony within the power bloc and/or over the people.

Curiously, the Poulantzas-Miliband debate turned on epistemological issues. An Althusserian critique of Miliband's attempted empirical proof of the class nature of state personnel and policies in *The State in Capitalist Society* (1969) was countered by a critique of Poulantzas's theoreticism and (hyper-)structuralism that took for granted what had to be proved. The protagonists missed the juridico-political and Gramscian aspects of Poulantzas's analysis and how Miliband's book moved from provocative empirical evidence to an increasingly sophisticated theoretical analysis of the state in capitalist society (see Jessop 2007). This flawed debate set back state theory for many years because it diverted attention from the enduring aspects of Poulantzas's work and the shared interest of both theorists in Gramsci's analysis of hegemony and ideological apparatuses.

PPSC offered a general theoretical analysis focused on the *normal* form of the capitalist state, namely, the bourgeois democratic republic. It included brief case studies of alternative paths toward this state form and an outline periodization that noted a shift from a transitional absolutist state suited to mercantilism via a liberal state adequate to competitive capitalism to an interventionist state appropriate to monopoly and state monopoly capitalism. Assuming in this text – an assumption later abandoned – that the economic region of a capitalist social formation followed its own logic, Poulantzas focused on the state's crucial general political function. This was to organize and consolidate the hegemony of one fraction of capital within the power bloc and to facilitate the organization of hegemony over the popular masses.

Poulantzas's next monograph studied fascism and dictatorship (1974a). Prompted by debates on whether the Greek military dictatorship was fascist and how to resist it, Poulantzas explored the nature of exceptional regimes (i.e., regimes that suspended democratic rule, whether fascist, military or Bonapartist) and the strategic errors committed by the Comintern in assessing fascism. He based his theoretical and strategic analysis on a detailed account of successive phases of fascism as a social movement and political regime and how these corresponded to offensive and defensive steps in the class struggle. He also emphasized the historical specificity of fascist regimes as responses in weak links in the imperialist chain during the transition to the dominance of monopoly capitalism and its associated interventionist state. Germany and Italy were latecomers to capitalism and their outward expansion depended on developing the strength to repartition a world already divided among other metropoles (Lenin 1964). Fascism emerged because normal (democratic) means for the circulation of hegemony were blocked by complex political and ideological crises and the prevailing balance of forces excluded resort to a military dictatorship or a Bonapartist bureaucratic despotism. German and Italian fascist regimes not only aimed to shift the domestic balance of forces in favor of monopoly capital but also to advance its interests in the inter-imperialist struggle for domination. The analysis developed a sophisticated account of the interaction between changes in the imperialist chain and factors internal to each society. It also highlighted the complexity of the multiple crises that affected these weak links and their (in)ability to resolve these crises through the normal play of class forces in democratic regimes.

The collapse of the dictatorships in Greece, Portugal and Spain prompted Poulantzas to write *Crisis of the Dictatorships* (1976a) to develop his theoretical analysis of the imperialist chain, rivalries between the US and European Economic Community for economic and political influence in Southern Europe, and the class contradictions at the heart of the state. It also drew appropriate lessons from the nature of their collapse and the left's strategic failures to exploit this conjuncture to consolidate a left-leaning democratic transition and prepare the ground for later struggles for democratic socialism. His analyses had some influence in the Iberian Peninsula as Portugal and Spain experienced political renewal and generated more general interest in his work in Latin America.

The second and third steps in Poulantzas's analysis in *PPSC*, that is, its reliance on juridico-political categories to describe the specificity of the capitalist type of state and on classic Marxist concepts, especially from Gramsci, for its class analysis, were retained in his last monograph, *State, Power, Socialism* (1978b, hereafter *SPS*). But Althusser was displaced by a return to Marx's revolutionary materialism. Two features were crucial here. One is the correlation between the form of appropriation of surplus labor and the form of sovereignty and dependence (CIII: 927); and the other is the insistence that "capital is not a thing, but a social relation between persons which is mediated through things" (CI: 932). Thus, Poulantzas explored the formal adequacy of the modern state in maintaining economic exploitation and political domination and, in this context, defined the state, too, as a social relation. He rejected the view that the state is an entity – whether a docile instrument or rational subject. For, "like 'capital', *it is rather a relationship of forces, or more precisely the material condensation of such a relationship among classes and class fractions, such as this is expressed within the State in a necessarily specific form*" (1978b, 128–29, italics in original). He suggests that *state power* (not the state apparatus) is a *form-determined* condensation of the changing balance of forces in political and politically relevant struggle. This underpinned his claim to have finally completed Marx's theory of the state, the absence of which is almost a commonplace in discussion of Marx's legacy (Poulantzas 1978a).

A further influence in *SPS* was Foucault's work on power as a social relation, the dialectic of power-resistance and the coupling of power/knowledge. Poulantzas acknowledged the inspiration of his language and ideas but stressed this came from Foucault as an analyst of power – not as an epistemologist or methodologist. Foucault's analyses reinforced the Greek's developing insights that the state's structural powers or capacities cannot be understood by focusing on the state alone – even assuming one could precisely define its institutional boundaries. For, considered as an institutional matrix rather than as a real (or fictive) subject, the state comprises an ensemble of centers, branches and apparatuses that offer unequal chances to different forces within and outside the state to act for different political purposes. Moreover, although this ensemble has distinctive resources and powers, it also has distinctive vulnerabilities and depends on resources produced beyond its boundaries. This means that the powers of the state are always conditional and relational.

SPS also built on Poulantzas's analyses of fascism and military dictatorships and other work to argue that a new normal type of capitalist state was emerging to replace the interventionist state. This was authoritarian statism. This is now "*permanently and structurally characterized by a peculiar sharpening of the generic elements of political crisis and state crisis*" rather than showing intermittent signs of short-term, conjunctural crisis. In brief, authoritarian statism involves "intensified state control over every sphere of socio-economic life combined with radical decline of the institutions of political democracy and with draconian and multiform curtailment of so-called 'formal' liberties" (1978b, 203–4). More specifically, Poulantzas argued that the principal elements of authoritarian statism and its implications for representative democracy comprise: first, a transfer of power from the legislature to the executive and the concentration of power within the latter; second, an accelerated fusion between the three branches of the state – legislature, executive and judiciary – accompanied by a decline in the rule of law; third, the functional decline of political parties as the main channel for political dialogue with the administration and as the major forces in organizing hegemony; and finally, the growth of parallel power networks cross-cutting the formal organization of the state and holding a decisive share in its various activities and linking the state to capitalist interests (1975, 55–7, 1978b, 217–31). This new form of state existed in metropolitan and dependent capitalist states alike but could take different forms: more neo-liberal in France, for example, more authoritarian in Germany (cf. Poulantzas 1979a, 199). Thus, while highlighting these general tendencies, Poulantzas added that they varied in intensity, were not inevitable and could be resisted and reversed.

The basis of this claim was elaborated in an essay on "The Crisis of the State" (1976b). Distilling the lessons from his studies of exceptional regimes as well as the state in contemporary metropolitan formations, Poulantzas argued that, while the generic elements of crisis are constantly reproduced in capitalist societies, crises only emerge when these elements condense into a distinct conjuncture and develop according to specific rhythms (1976b, 21–22, 28). He analyzed economic crises, political crises and organic crises and their conjunctural specificities. And he concluded that political crises were primarily rooted in the field of political class relations and only secondarily in the defects of specific political institutions (1976b, 23, 28).

Critique of Political Economy and Class Analysis

As he developed a more comprehensive, relational analysis of the state and state power, Poulantzas became more interested in traditional Marxist economic themes. He made important contributions to debates on changes in the contemporary phase of imperialism, the changing forms of internationalization and fractionation of capital, the nature of productive and unproductive labor, the composition of the proletariat, the rise of the new petty bourgeoisie, the changing forms of the manual-mental division of labor, the internationalization of the state and new forms of state intervention, especially regarding economic crisis-management and political and ideological crises, and much else besides. These themes were prominent in his work on *Classes in Contemporary Capitalism* (1975), which developed new concepts for analyzing contemporary capitalism and, on this basis, proposed changes in democratic socialist strategy. These reflections were further elaborated in *SPS*, which combined classical Marxist political economy and his insights into contemporary imperialism.

Building on his interpretation of fascism, Poulantzas intensified his analysis of the development of imperialism. Whereas the export of capital is more important in imperialism than trade in commodities, its current phase marked a shift from (1) capital export *to colonies* to exploit *raw materials* or *develop new export markets* to (2) capital export within the *metropolitan zone* in the form of *direct investment* to seize every opportunity to *directly exploit labor* in the dominant regions to counter the global tendency of the rate of profit to fall (1975, 1976a, 10–12). This shift began in the immediate postwar period and was consolidated in the 1960s (1976a, 12). It altered the traditional division between "town-industry-metropoles" and "countryside-agriculture dominated formations." It created a spatial division of labor *within* productive capital itself, increases the importance of manufactured goods in foreign trade, and promotes a worldwide industrialization of agriculture. Nonetheless these developments do not suspend capital's crisis-tendencies. On the contrary, based on developments in the 1960s and early 1970s, Poulantzas identified a crisis of imperialism that affected the whole imperialist chain and not just, as widely believed at the time, a crisis of US hegemony in Europe (1975, 87, 1974b, 1975, 1976a, 1978).

His main argument was that the general crisis of imperialism leads to internal divisions and strategic differences on how best to reorganize the balance of power among different metropoles under US hegemony. This was reflected in inter-imperialist contradictions inside each metropolitan center and, indeed, the fractions of capital most integrated into the circuits of contemporary imperialism – which he described as the interior bourgeoisie to distinguish them from the national bourgeoisie and comprador capital (1975, 28–29). However, for Poulantzas, in Europe and elsewhere, the principal contradiction in imperialism was the antagonism between the popular masses and their respective bourgeoisies and states (1975, 86–88, 155). This was evident in the emphasis in all metropoles on "international competitiveness" and, in this context (or on this pretext), on a politics of austerity to roll back past economic and social concessions to dominated classes. It follows that inter-imperialist contradictions were secondary and should not be allowed to divide subordinate classes on national lines – especially as they were reproduced inside each national formation because of the differential ties of the interior bourgeoisie to fractions of capital in other economic spaces. This required, he concluded, a new kind of united and popular front against imperialism *tout court*. Poulantzas hoped his analysis would shift the terms of left-wing debate within the European Economic Community, especially France, and reorient political strategies to promote democratic socialism. As we have seen, this analysis was extended to dependent or peripheral Fordism in his work on southern Europe (1976a, 9–10, 41). And, in a posthumously published essay, he reflected on dominated or dependent capitalist formations elsewhere in the imperialist chain (1980).

More generally, as Poulantzas returned to key themes in the critique of political economy, he analyzed the labor process in terms of a complex economic, political and intellectual division of labor and examined social classes from the viewpoint of their *extended* reproduction in different sites of struggle and over time rather than focusing exclusively on class relations in production. Yet, even as he sought to expand the field of class analysis and class struggle and to maintain the primacy of the latter in social transformation, he remained trapped within classical Marxist political economy with its commitment to economic determination in the last instance and the primacy of the working class as a revolutionary subject. In a period of the "crisis of Marxism" and in response to his changing approach to the state, he eventually began to question these fundamental tenets of Marxism and try to move beyond them (see Poulantzas 1979a).

The Motor-Force of Political Involvements

The key to explaining these theoretical shifts and their strategic implications is Poulantzas's attempts to understand and influence left-wing strategy in Greece and France. Two key turning points in his native Greece were the military coup in April 1967 and its eventual collapse in July 1974 under the weight of its own internal contradictions rather than through direct mass struggles. The coup posed the crucial difference between democracy and dictatorship and led to a more active political role. Its collapse confirmed Poulantzas's growing suspicion that the state was far from monolithic and that class struggle penetrated deep into its core. Thus his principal concerns regarding Greece were to understand its military dictatorship, the conditions leading to its overthrow, the absence of working class hegemony in the democratization process, and the scope for moving from an anti-dictatorial alliance to an anti-imperialist, anti-monopoly alliance. More generally, he came to advocate a left Eurocommunist strategy to intensify the contradictions internal to the state as well as mobilize the popular masses outside the state to prepare for the eventual democratic transformation of the entire state system. For France, May 1968 was a crucial moment and led Poulantzas to reject a structuralist approach that left little scope for social agency. He was especially concerned in the 1970s with how to win left unity around an anti-monopoly, democratic socialist program. Much of his work therefore involved developing theoretical and political justifications, initially, for class alliances (especially between proletariat and new petty bourgeoisie rather than between worker and peasant); and, later, for forging links between traditional class struggles and the radical demands and resistance of new social movements. The collapse of the Union de la Gauche between the Socialist and Communist parties in France in 1977 was the final straw that led Poulantzas to turn away from a simple faith in proletarian struggles and the leading role of the vanguard communist party. He now advocated a more complex and challenging alliance strategy that was not only *pluriclassiste* but also *pluripartiste*. This did not privilege the working class or communist party and highlighted the autonomous role of non-class forces and social movements in the struggle for democratic socialism (1978b, 1979a, 1979b).

In this way Poulantzas arrived at his final political position. He called for a combination of struggles within the state as well as at a distance from the state to modify the balance of forces as well as struggles to transform the state; and he advocated a combination of representative and direct democracy as the best means to avoid the statist degeneration of socialism that had occurred in the Soviet bloc.

The Significance of Poulantzas for Marxism

These conclusions point to Poulantzas's significance in the Marxist tradition. For he was almost alone among postwar Marxists to address the unanswered questions in Western Marxism as identified by Perry Anderson:

> What is the real nature and structure of *bourgeois democracy* as a type of State system, that has become the normal mode of capitalist power in the advanced countries? What type of *revolutionary strategy* is capable of overthrowing this historical form of State – so distinct from that of Tsarist Russia? What would be the institutional forms of *socialist democracy* in the West, beyond it? Marxist theory has scarcely touched these three subjects in their interconnection
>
> *(Anderson 1976, 103).*

These topics preoccupied Poulantzas from 1964 until his death in 1979. *Political Power and Social Classes* addressed the real nature and structure of bourgeois democracy. *Fascism and Dictatorship* dealt with fascist regimes and organized labor's failure to check their rise or overthrow them. It also contrasted the "normal" mode of capitalist power in advanced capitalist formations and various "exceptional" modes of bourgeois political domination. His third and fourth books, *Classes in Contemporary Capitalism* and *Crisis of the Dictatorships*, related problems of revolutionary strategy to democratic and exceptional regimes in both advanced and dependent capitalist countries. And *State, Power, Socialism* reviewed the current threats to bourgeois democracy and the institutional forms that socialist democracy might assume in the West. Poulantzas also tackled these subjects "in their interconnection." He also addressed four other key issues mentioned by Anderson: the meaning and position of the nation as a social unit and its relationship to nationalism; the laws of motion of capitalism as a mode of production and the forms of crisis specific to these laws; the true configuration of imperialism as an international system of economic and political domination; and state socialism. In short, he was an unusual Western Marxist and, while the answers he implicitly provided to Anderson's questions may need revision in the light of 40 years of further theoretical work and further changes in contemporary capitalism, his key conceptual and strategic innovations remain valuable and deserve the renewed critical appreciation that they have attracted in recent years and, of course, as Poulantzas would have wanted, critical elaboration.

Notes

1. See especially (Poulantzas 1969, 1976c; Miliband 1970, 1973; for commentaries, see Aronowitz and Bratsis 2002; Jessop 2007; and Gallas et al. 2011).
2. This held especially for the exact boundaries, size and continuing primacy of the working class as well as the nature and political significance of the new middle classes.

Bibliography

Althusser, Louis. 1969 (1965). *For Marx*. London: Allen Lane.
Althusser, Louis, and Étienne Balibar. 1970 (1968). *Reading Capital*. 2nd edn. London: NLB.
Anderson, Perry. 1976. *Considerations on Western Marxism*. London: NLB.
Aronowitz, Stanley, and Peter Bratsis, eds. 2002. *Paradigm Lost: State Theory Reconsidered*. Minneapolis: University of Minnesota Press.
Gallas, Alexander, Lars Bretthauer, John Kannankulam, and Ingo Stützle, eds. 2011. *Reading Poulantzas*. London: Merlin.
Jessop, Bob. 1985. *Nicos Poulantzas: Marxist Theory and Political Strategy*. Basingstoke: Macmillan.
Jessop, Bob. 2007. "Dialogue of the Deaf: Reflections on the Poulantzas-Miliband Debate." In *Class, Power and the State in Capitalist Society: Essays on Ralph Miliband*, edited by Paul Wetherly, Clyde W. Barrow, and Peter Burnham, 132–57. Basingstoke: Palgrave.
Lenin, V.I. 1964 (1917). "Imperialism, the Highest Stage of Capitalism." *LCW* 22: 185–304.
Miliband, Ralph. 1969. *The State in Capitalist Society*. London: Weidenfeld & Nicolson.
Miliband, Ralph. 1970. "The Capitalist State: Reply to Poulantzas." *New Left Review* 1(59): 53–60.
Miliband, Ralph. 1973. "Poulantzas and the Capitalist State." *New Left Review* 1(82): 83–92.

Pashukanis, E.B. 1978. *Law and Marxism: A General Theory*. London: Ink Links.
Poulantzas, Nicos. 1965. *Nature des choses et droit: Essai sur la dialectique du fait et de la valeur*. Paris: R. Pichon et R. Durand-Avzias.
Poulantzas, Nicos. 1969. "The Problem of the Capitalist State." *New Left Review* 1(58): 67–78.
Poulantzas, Nicos. 1973 (1968). *Political Power and Social Classes*. London: NLB.
Poulantzas, Nicos. 1974a (1970). *Fascism and Dictatorship: The Third International and the Problem of Fascism*. London: NLB.
Poulantzas, Nicos. 1974b. "Internationalization of Capitalist Relations and the Nation-State." *Economy & Society* 3(2): 145–79.
Poulantzas, Nicos. 1975. *Classes in Contemporary Capitalism*. London: NLB.
Poulantzas, Nicos. 1976a (1974). *Crisis of the Dictatorships*. 2nd edn. London: NLB.
Poulantzas, Nicos. 1976b. "Les transformations actuelles de l'État, la crise politique et la crise de l'État." In *La Crise de l'État*, edited by Nicos Poulantzas, 19–58. Paris: Presses Universitaires de France.
Poulantzas, Nicos. 1976c. "The Capitalist State." *New Left Review* 1(95): 63–83.
Poulantzas, Nicos. 1978a. "Les théoriciens doivent retourner sur terre." *Les nouvelles litteraires* (26 June).
Poulantzas, Nicos. 1978b. *State, Power, Socialism*. London: Verso.
Poulantzas, Nicos. 1979a. "Interview with Nicos Poulantzas." *Marxism Today* (July): 194–201.
Poulantzas, Nicos. 1979b. "L'état, les mouvements sociaux, le parti." *Dialectiques* 28: 7–16.
Poulantzas, Nicos. 1980. "Research Note on the State and Society." *International Social Science Journal* 32(4): 600–608.

28
SAMIR AMIN (1931–2018)

Yousuf Al-Bulushi

Globalizing Marxism, Delinking From Eurocentrism

Samir Amin, who died in August 2018, was a Marxist political economist and public intellectual with a global knowledge of the history of capitalism. Amin, of Egyptian and French origin, was a leading figure in dependency theory and world-systems analysis. His main strength lay in his ability to extend the Marxist framework in order to understand global capitalism from the specific vantage point of formerly colonized countries in Africa, Asia and Latin America.

Amin began his activism as a Communist in Paris while a student at Sciences Po. He then returned to Nasser's Egypt, continuing to work with the Communist Party and developing lasting ties with the Bandung movement, whose members were heavily socialist. His ideas first gained currency in this conjuncture, at the height of the national liberation movements in the Global South and a time when the end of colonial rule defined Africa as a region. In 1973, he helped establish the Council for the Development of Social Research in Africa (CODESRIA) and became its first director. In later years he would become involved with the World Social Forum. Amin continued to engage in a variety of anti-capitalist projects throughout the Global South until the end of his life, including an attempted revival of the non-aligned movement. In Senegal, where he spent much of his time, he headed the Africa Bureau for the Third World Forum.

In this entry, I outline Amin's major contribution of a Marxist theory from the Global South. I focus on the following concepts: dependency, the uneven geography of the world system, Eurocentrism, globalized value, imperialism and delinking. In elaborating the trajectory of his thought, I introduce the increased attention in his writing over time to the prospect of multipolarity. The chapter closes with a discussion of the need to expand upon his proposal for geopolitical delinking with a more profound epistemic delinking and a further diversification and globalization of Marxist theory.

Dependency Theory and the Uneven Geography of the World System

Amin is best known as a world-systems theorist through his work on dependency. This was the subject of his 1958 PhD dissertation and his two most influential books: *Accumulation on a World Scale* (1974a), a critique of conventional development economics, and *Unequal Development*

(1976), a study of the social formations of peripheral capitalism. Both books played an important part in the neo-Marxist interventions in development studies in the 1970s.

Amin criticized the liberal field of development studies because of its assumption that national economies take precedence over the world economy. But he also argued that a neo-Marxist analysis of development necessarily differed from Marx's own theory, which needed to be historicized as primarily an analysis of the world's core countries. The task of neo-Marxists, stressed Amin, was to understand the capitalist system as a historically evolving world economy and to grasp how it constrains development in the periphery. Together with Giovanni Arrighi, Walter Rodney, Harold Wolpe and others, he participated in the debates about the transition to capitalism among Marxists and the race-class debates that raged throughout Southern Africa during the 1970s and 1980s (Hart 2007; Amin 1974b, 1985). In a move that paralleled later Marxists like Moishe Postone (1993), he claimed that Marx's writings on non-Western societies should be historicized and understood as products of his delimited 19th-century European context, rather than simply applied word-for-word directly in the present. The combined influence of debates around the recently published *Grundrisse* (1973), pre-capitalist formations and Althusser's notion of articulation came together to open new conceptual ground for understanding the articulation between different modes of production in peripheral capitalism (Amin 1985; Sayre 2008). Distinguishing between abstract, synchronic modes of production and concrete, historical social formations, Amin extended Marx's key concepts with the benefit of a much more expansive body of knowledge about Africa, Asia and Latin America than Marx had at his disposal in the 19th century. Amin argued that the various modes of production overlapped and existed synchronously, rather than evolving in a historical/teleological sequence. A social formation, on the other hand, constituted a concrete "complex involving several modes of production" (1974b, 68).

As capitalism globalized, it nonetheless did so according to an uneven development whereby the core social formations relied upon imperialist power to engage in hyper-exploitation over peripheral social formations. This explained the lack of economic dynamism in peripheral countries and their structural ties to core processes of accumulation and wealth generation. Peripheral social formations were characterized by (1) the dominance of agrarian capital, (2) a local bourgeoisie comprised primarily of merchants, (3) high levels of inequality and (4) partial proletarianization accompanied by high levels of unemployment and underemployment. The latter are due to the separation of the producers from the means of production in the absence of a national bourgeoisie capable of leading an internally oriented process of accumulation. Peripheral growth based on this model will inevitably stagnate due to its reliance on a volatile primary sector geared toward export, and a limited domestic market of luxury consumption. In sum, although dependency can take different forms, it is fundamentally an insurmountable condition for the vast majority of countries with peripheral social formations.

While in the colonial period exploitation occurred primarily through the extraction of raw materials and the mobilization of cheap supplies of labor, in the contemporary era exploitation is also facilitated by the core's five crucial monopolies over technology, finance, natural resources, media and communications, and weapons of mass destruction (Amin 1997). Monopolistic control over these strategic sectors, resources and institutions "annuls the impact of industrialization in the peripheries" (Amin 1997, 5).

Against Eurocentrism, for a "Modernity Critical of Modernity"

Amin developed a pioneering analysis of Eurocentrism in his eponymous 1989 text. He uncovered an internal critique of modernity's Eurocentrism in the 19th century writings of Marx.

> The distinctive feature of Eurocentrism is either to view the particular European way of articulating nation, state, and classes as a model that reveals the specificity of the European spirit (and, therefore, a model for others to follow, if they can) or the expression of a general law that will be inevitably reproduced elsewhere, even if delayed.
> *(Amin 2009a, 256)*

Modernity had hitherto been understood as constituting the triplet of liberty, equality and property, a fundamentally bourgeois ideology that equated the market with democracy. The right-wing libertarian strain of modernity – developed by 19th-century liberal Claude Frédéric Bastiat and later elaborated by Friedrich von Hayek in the 20th century – would even go so far as to abandon the ethical imperative of equality all together. In a direct attack on such formulations, Marx had established an alternative tradition of modernity that Amin terms "modernity critical of modernity."

This critical approach challenged hegemonic narratives that can only claim ancient Greece and Rome as part of "Europe" after severing their obvious ties to and embeddedness in Southwest Asia and North Africa. Amin was here engaged in a debate with Eurocentric Marxists whose teleological analysis of a progressive sequence of modes of production – Greco-Roman slavery, European feudalism, Western capitalism – reproduces the Hegelian idea that capitalism could only have emerged within the European world (Moghadam 1989). This Eurocentric framing, according to Amin, ironically overlaps with Third World cultural nationalists who reject Marxism as inapplicable to their societies because it is supposedly only applicable to Europe. As such, Amin's critique of Eurocentrism differs from many others because he is searching for a more properly global account of modernity that will allow Marxist theory to apply universally.

Modes of Production, Capitalism/Imperialism and Globalized Value

Amin's unique approach informs his intervention in the 1970s in the Marxist debates over the transition between different historical modes of production. These debates occurred while the decolonization movements challenged the idea of a single, Eurocentric path from capitalism to socialism. Amin's intervention took the form of updating what he saw as Marx's inadequate theorization of the feudal and Asiatic modes of production. In his view, using the concept of feudalism to describe various pre-capitalist modes of production risked Eurocentrism because that concept was designed for Europe and not the non-European world. Similarly, the concept of the Asiatic mode of production could imply an ahistorical Orientalist understanding of the world empires as the natural sites of stagnant despotism. In their place, Amin proposed the concept of a "tributary mode of production" to capture the variety of forms of elite struggle for power through the non-economic extraction of surplus from the peasantry (Amin 2009a, ch. 4, 1976).

In the periphery, capitalism only partially displaces the tributary mode of production and is instead articulated with it in many cases. As capitalism develops, the law of value polarizes the world into a center and a periphery. Imperialism should therefore be understood as a permanent feature of capitalism from its inception to the present day, rather than as a mere phase in its development (2006, 3). However, Amin argues that capitalism/imperialism takes different forms depending on the relation between center and periphery. He explains this mutation of capitalism/imperialism through the law of value, which itself mutated from its simplest form (the production of expensive outputs at the center with low cost inputs at the periphery) to its advanced form, which, in the post-1975 era of generalized monopoly capitalism, he calls "globalized value." Amin's law of globalized value – according to which Northern capital is able to appropriate "imperialist rent" thanks to the differences in real wages between center and periphery – represents an attempt to finish Marx's planned fifth and sixth volumes of *Capital* on international trade and the world market (2013b). It is an appropriate response to the "de-localization" strategy capital began to deploy in the 1970s through the neoliberal outsourcing of production to a value chain scattered across both poor and rich countries. Amin's theory of globalized value also intervenes in current debates regarding the return of extractivism throughout Africa and Latin America in particular, and it adds to the calls for a re-theorization of the role of rent in contemporary capitalism.

Crisis, Multipolar Delinking and the Limits of Culturalism

Amin adheres to the world-systems school's thesis that capitalism entered a terminal crisis starting in the 1970s. Contemporary processes of globalization have their origin in this period of crisis and have continued to seek temporary spatial fixes to the periodic internal crises of capitalist growth. The most recent crisis, which began in the housing sector of the United States in 2007 and proceeded to spread throughout the broader global economy, is merely the latest phase in this long-term decline of the world system.

Relatively high rates of growth in China, India and Brazil cannot compensate in aggregate for the slow rates of growth in the historically dominant triad of the US, Europe and Japan. Monopoly capital has entered a generalized phase in which its power is expressed in totalizing fashion. This monopoly is held over the five previously discussed institutions of control, technology, finance, natural resources, media and communications, and weapons of mass destruction, rather than simply over economic property, and Amin cites Jonathan Nitzan's and Shimshon Bichler's *Capital as Power* (2009) positively in this regard. Under the waning leadership of the US military, the collective imperialism of the triad is now forced to recognize that it cannot manage global capitalism through increasing reliance upon direct force. For Amin and his fellow world-systems thinkers, the increasingly violent military campaigns of the United States and its allies merely highlight their inability to manage a system in decline.

Indeed, the 2007–8 economic crisis gave way to a long series of rebellions and revolts starting in 2011. Amin's own work adds a lot to our understanding of these anti-systemic movements. The global character of capitalism, in his view, has transformed the class struggle into a global struggle that demands a corresponding project of "delinking." Delinking, for Amin, requires the formation of South-South alliances. To delink, countries of the Global South should give priority to their domestic needs rather than to those of international capital. It is only when the peripheral countries are able to neutralize the effects of external economic interaction that development strategies can succeed. Amin believes in the strong role of states in the delinking process. But a tension emerges here in his analysis as he oscillates between state-based programs of delinking and national popular delinking movements among the people (2006, 106–107).

While delinking appears to parallel the politics of the Bandung and Tricontinental era, Amin believes such a repetition of the past is no longer possible, given the concentration of control achieved by the imperialist triad. On the other hand, he believes the efforts of national popular movements from below will also run aground without the buffer of a regional bloc at the level of the inter-state system capable of shielding such movements from the imperialist interventions and disruptions of the US and its allies. The recent slow demise of the Latin American pink tide and the Bolivarian Alliance for the Peoples of Our America (ALBA) is a good example of the structural bind that Amin's project of delinking found itself in. It also provides evidence that his oscillation between popular delinking and state delinking was likely a product of the structural impediments to change in the world system, rather than any inadequacy in his own analysis. As he put it: "The challenges to the construction of a genuinely multipolar world are more serious than many 'alter-globalization' movements imagine" (2006, 146).

He nonetheless persisted in his proposal for the construction of a counter-hegemonic geopolitical bloc to challenge the dominance of the triad. Since the US and Western Europe have been the principal proponents of the idea that "there is no alternative" to neoliberalism (TINA), Amin remained hopeful that China or Russia would break from these Atlantic powers. While the events of recent years have only added credence to this possibility, Amin also acknowledged that with respect to economic policy, Russia remains firmly tied to a neoliberal alliance in its role as a primary commodity exporter to Europe, having failed to revive its struggling industrial base. Despite this, he believed that progress at the national and global scales could only occur once the rule of oligarchies based in the rich world – dependent upon the five monopolies mentioned previously – was overturned.

Amin understood the Islamist movements of the past few decades as compatible with capitalism rather than as constituting a genuinely anti-imperialist challenge, something that is periodically argued on both the right and the left. He was careful to challenge the racist Western assumption that political Islam represents "an inevitable result of the irruption of culturally and political backward peoples on to the [political] arena" (2003c, 166). But he did believe that political Islam provided a form of cultural identity that replaced a more useful class identity. "By encouraging culturalist responses," Amin argued, "globalization strategies make as much use as they can of diversity inherited from the past" (2003c, 166). Nonetheless, it remains unclear whether Amin believed religious ideas – in this case Islam – could play *any* role in shifting the geography of reason away from Europe. It is fair to say that Amin did not believe any of the *existing* forms of political Islam posed a serious alternative. However, at times he referred to the possibility of a convergence between radical political movements and theologies of liberation (Amin 2009a, 22).

Marxist Revolutions and the Long Transition to Socialism

Throughout his life, Amin remained an unapologetic proponent of state socialism as a liberatory project. Like all post–Cold War socialisms, his vision of socialism had to engage critically with the actually existing socialisms of the 20th century. Amin was more sympathetic than most other Marxist theorists toward the 20th-century revolutions in Russia and China. He believed the Soviet experiment ultimately collapsed in the face of overwhelming sabotage from imperialist countries and because of the paradoxical success of its authoritarian industrialization and militarization programs. Nonetheless, in his view the Leninist theory of the weakest link was vindicated by the fact that the Russian and Chinese revolutions occurred not in Europe but in relatively peripheral countries that were characterized by agrarian rather than industrial economies. This fact necessitated sustained attention to the prospect of worker-peasant alliances.

Amin tended not to place much credence in the idea that other leaders besides Stalin might have guided the USSR along a more liberatory path, as the problems that led Stalin down the road of authoritarian collectivization were largely structural. These structural challenges continue to confront all anti-systemic movements today and take the form of balancing the imperative of modernization with social needs. Amin proclaimed that only "academic Marxists," far removed from the difficult practical choices faced by those who actually take state power, can easily dismiss the Soviet state under Stalin (2016, 78). The extreme forms of violence carried out by the Soviet state were, in his view, no worse than the parallel forms of primitive accumulation embarked upon by the capitalist powers. He also argued that workers in the USSR benefitted much more than their Western counterparts from the social mobility and wealth socialization that the Soviet phase of primitive accumulation accomplished.

Despite this defense of the Soviet project, and true to his Third Worldist loyalties, Amin believed that Mao's vision was ultimately superior to that of the Russian revolutionaries. Mao's superiority was evidenced by his maintenance of the worker-peasant alliance and his insistence upon a popular democratic rather than a national bourgeois road to development. Challenging the fashionable and growing attention paid to the urban question at the turn of the 21st century, Amin built on this Maoist platform by repeatedly emphasizing the ongoing importance of the agrarian question and the necessity of food sovereignty, arguing that they belonged at the forefront of any revolutionary strategy for peripheral countries. And in looking back on the successes and ultimate failures of 20th century actually existing socialisms, he took a longer-term view in arguing that the path toward socialism would entail a "long transition." In short, unlike his three counterparts in the world-systems gang of four – Immanuel Wallerstein, Andre Gunder Frank and Giovanni Arrighi – Amin was generally positive about the coming to state power of the socialist movement in the 20th century. Despite acknowledging the abuses of power, the lack of democracy and the dogmatisms produced by state socialism, he still believed that "the USSR and China did delink" for a time period, and that they benefitted tremendously from this delinking (Amin et al. 2006, 183).

Thinking With and Beyond Samir Amin's Global Marxism: Epistemic Delinking and the Local-Global Continuum

Amin's elaboration of the concepts of center and periphery emphasizes exploitation in the international arena rather than at the point of production. This focus has led to two subsequent problems in his theory. First, it dictated his obsessive focus on imperialism. Giovanni Arrighi, David Harvey and others who take production as the starting point of analysis criticize the old conceptualization of imperialism whereby production is concentrated within a particular state or empire. Indeed, Amin's overemphasis on the center exploiting the periphery neglects the fact that the production process now also happens at a global scale, in the fragmented parts of global value chains (Cowen 2014). Responding to such criticisms, Amin redeployed the concept of monopoly capitalism, and argued that the precise place of production is not as important as the fact that there remains a geographical core/center in the world system that still dominates through monopolies (Amin 2013a, 15–42).

This incessant focus on a center exploiting its periphery is nonetheless one of the potential pitfalls of the delinking project. Amin's alter-globalist solution takes recourse to a South-South alliance aiming to delink from the center. But this overemphasis on a single center – what he called the triad of the United States, Europe and Japan – downplays the negative impact of centers in the South itself that exploit other countries in the South. In other words, Amin's work underemphasizes regional centers of exploitation – what Wallerstein calls semi-peripheries – such as the Gulf states in the Middle East, South Africa in Southern Africa, Brazil in South America and China throughout the world. The focus on globally polarized centers and peripheries, moreover, can lead to a similar neglect of exploitation *within* Third World nation-states. Despite his criticism of the bourgeoisie for exploiting nationalism to cover for class struggle, Amin failed to dwell extensively on how elites within each state use their power to exploit other classes and to accumulate in close collaboration with the center. While his concept of re-compradorization opens the door to such a discussion, it remains tied to the broader global center-periphery relation, rather than to equally important contradictions *internal* to a given society. And although Amin was quite right to situate the class struggle within the international arena, internal contradictions in peripheral formations also play a major role in making these countries dependent, blocking the path to socialism. Amin's theory therefore did not delve deeply enough into how the dialectic between internal and systemic contradictions determines both the path of these countries and that of capitalism at a global scale (Surin 2001, 2009). In other words, it continued to emphasize an abstract global scale rather than the entirety of the local-global continuum (Darian-Smith and McCarty 2017).

This leads us to the second main shortcoming of Amin's theory, namely his attachment to and ongoing support for modernity, universalism and its stages of development. Amin's approach to the study of the world system and his adherence to many of the central principles of modernity are closely interrelated. In this respect, at least, he remained a somewhat orthodox Marxist who believed that the development of capitalism would eventually lead to a final stage of communism. In other words, one might argue that Amin *has not gone far enough* with delinking (Robinson 2011). A more radical project might entail a complete epistemic delinking, something Sylvia Wynter (2003), Walter Mignolo (2007), Ramón Grosfoguel (2007) and others in the decolonial school have proposed. But this epistemic delinking would need to be explored within, alongside, and at times beyond the Marxist project. It would imply a heretical line of thought that currents such as the Black radical tradition (Robinson 1983; Wynter 2003) exemplify best. An anti-capitalist delinking might also require forms of "dispersed power" (Zibechi 2010) that challenge the univocity of power emanating from states by emphasizing a plurality of counter-powers operating at scales both below and above the nation-state. At his weakest, Amin's recourse to a strong state and a secular modernity drove him to tacitly endorse the 2013 coup against the Muslim Brotherhood led by the authoritarian General Abdel Fattah el-Sisi in Egypt and to support the 2013 French invasion of Mali. Amin was certainly right to point out the elitist nature of Islamist movements like the Brotherhood. But perhaps – as Amin himself hinted at in his study of Eurocentrism – this position too quickly forecloses a politics that is critical of capitalist Islamic movements while at the same time open to the possibility of a decolonial convergence between politics and radical spirituality.

If we take Amin's work holistically, however, his study of Eurocentrism attacks Western universalism as imperialist, and instead argues that the world is divided into overlapping social formations comprised of agglomerations of communal, tributary and capitalist modes of production. One can argue that there is a tension between his rejection of the developmentalist narrative and his infatuation with modernity and a seemingly inevitable socialist revolution. In this regard, his vision of socialism was based on a relatively traditional model of economic development where the fruits of growth would be redistributed to working people rather than concentrated in the hands of a few. While he was aware of the ecological problem posed by capitalism (Amin 2009b) he largely left this issue to other thinkers within the Marxist and world-systems traditions to elaborate (Belamy Foster 2000; Moore 2015). Another often-cited challenge to Amin's formulation of center and periphery concerns the rise of China. In this regard, however, the ideas of his fellow travelers in world-systems analysis – such as Giovanni Arrighi – help demonstrate that China's rapid rise need not be viewed as a contradiction of the central tenets of world-systems analysis (2007).

Amin's work remains an inspiration to theorists seeking to globalize Marxism. His writings challenge Eurocentric Marxism while offering a rigorous account of the structural uneven development underpinning the world-system. Amin's contributions go beyond political economy to the study of culture, history and the epistemology of Eurocentrism, while offering us some of the constitutive elements of an alternative, more properly universal, paradigm for liberatory politics.

Bibliography

Amin, Samir. 1974a. *Accumulation on a World Scale: A Critique of the Theory of Underdevelopment*. 2 vols. New York: Monthly Review Press.

Amin, Samir. 1974b. "Modes of Production and Social Formations." *Ufahamu: A Journal of African Studies* 4(3): 57–85.

Amin, Samir. 1976. *Unequal Development: An Essay on the Social Formations of Peripheral Capitalism*. New York: Monthly Review Press.
Amin, Samir. 1982. "Class and Nation: Historically and in the Present Crisis." *Science and Society* 46(1): 91–93.
Amin, Samir. 1983. "Expansion or Crisis of Capitalism?" *Third World Quarterly* 5(2): 361–85.
Amin, Samir. 1985. "Modes of Production, History and Unequal Development." *Science and Society* 49(2): 194–207.
Amin, Samir. 1990. *Delinking: Towards a Polycentric World*. London: Zed Books.
Amin, Samir. 1991. "The Ancient World-Systems versus the Modern Capitalist World-System." *Review* 14(3): 349–85.
Amin, Samir. 1996. "The Challenge of Globalization." *Review of International Political Economy* 3(2): 216–59.
Amin, Samir. 1997. *Capitalism in the Age of Globalization*. London: Zed Press.
Amin, Samir. 1998. *Specters of Capitalism: A Critique of Current Intellectual Fashions*. New York: Monthly Review Press.
Amin, Samir. 1999a. "Capitalism, Imperialism, Globalization." In *The Political Economy of Imperialism*, edited by Ronald M. Chilcote, 157–68. New York: Springer.
Amin, Samir. 1999b. "For a Progressive and Democratic New World Order." In *Globalization and the Dilemmas of the State in the South*, edited by Francis Adams, Satya Dev Gupta, and Kidane Mengisteab, 17–32. Basingstoke: Palgrave Macmillan.
Amin, Samir. 2000. "The Political Economy of the Twentieth Century." *Monthly Review* 52(2): 1–17.
Amin, Samir. 2001a. "US Hegemony and the Response to Terror." *Monthly Review* 53(6): 20–22.
Amin, Samir. 2001b. "Imperialism and Globalization." *Monthly Review* 53(2): 6–15.
Amin, Samir. 2003a. "World Poverty, Pauperization, and Capital Accumulation." *Monthly Review* 55(5): 1–10.
Amin, Samir. 2003b. "Confronting the Empire." *Monthly Review* 55(3): 15–23.
Amin, Samir. 2003c. *Obsolescent Capitalism: Contemporary Politics and Global Disorder*. London: Zed Books.
Amin, Samir. 2004a. "Globalism or Apartheid on a Global Scale?" In *The Modern World-System in the Longue Durée*, edited by Immanuel Wallerstein, 5–30. Boulder, CO: Paradigm Publishers.
Amin, Samir. 2004b. *The Liberal Virus: Permanent War and the Americanization of the World*. London: Pluto.
Amin, Samir. 2006. *Beyond US Hegemony: Assessing the Prospects for a Multipolar World*. London: Zed Press.
Amin, Samir. 2007. "Political Islam in the Service of Imperialism." *Monthly Review* 59(7): 1.
Amin, Samir. 2008. *The World We Wish to See: Revolutionary Objectives in the Twenty-First Century*. New York: Monthly Review Press.
Amin, Samir. 2009a (1989). *Eurocentrism: Modernity, Religion and Democracy: A Critique of Eurocentrism and Culturalism*. New York: Monthly Review Press.
Amin, Samir. 2009b. "Capitalism and the Ecological Footprint." *Monthly Review* 61(6): 2–4.
Amin, Samir. 2010a. *The Law of Worldwide Value*. New York: Monthly Review Press.
Amin, Samir. 2010b. *Ending the Crisis of Capitalism or Ending Capitalism?* Oxford: Fahamu/Pambazuka.
Amin, Samir. 2010c. *Global History: A View from the South*. Oxford: Fahamu/Pambazuka.
Amin, Samir. 2010d. "Exiting the Crisis of Capitalism or Capitalism in Crisis?" *Globalizations* 7(1–2): 261–73.
Amin, Samir. 2013a. *The Implosion of Contemporary Capitalism*. New York: Monthly Review Press.
Amin, Samir. 2013b. *Three Essays on Marx's Value Theory*. New York: Monthly Review Press.
Amin, Samir. 2016. *Russia and the Long Transition from Capitalism to Socialism*. New York: Monthly Review Press.
Amin, Samir. 2017. *October 1917 Revolution: A Century Later*. Milton Keynes: Daraja Press.
Amin, Samir, Giovanni Arrighi, Andre Gunder Frank, and Immanuel Wallerstein. 1982. *Dynamics of Global Crisis*. New York: Monthly Review Press.
Amin, Samir, Giovanni Arrighi, Andre Gunder Frank, and Immanuel Wallerstein. 2006. *Transforming the Revolution: Social Movements and the World-System*. New Delhi: Aakar Books.
Arrighi, Giovanni. 2007. *Adam Smith in Beijing: Lineages of the 21st Century*. London: Verso.
Cowen, Deborah. 2014. *The Deadly Life of Logistics: Mapping Violence in Global Trade*. Minneapolis: University of Minnesota Press.
Darian-Smith, Eve, and Philip McCarty. 2017. *The Global Turn: Theories, Research Designs, and Methods for Global Studies*. Oakland: University of California Press.
Foster, John Bellamy. 2000. *Marx's Ecology: Materialism and Nature*. New York: Monthly Review Press.
Grosfoguel, Ramón. 2007. "The Epistemic Decolonial Turn: Beyond Political Economy Paradigms." *Cultural Studies* 21(2–3): 211–33.
Hart, Gillian. 2007. "Changing Concepts of Articulation." *Review of African Political Economy* 34(111): 85–101.
Mignolo, Walter. 2007. "Delinking: The Rhetoric of Modernity, the Logic of Coloniality, and the Grammar of De-Coloniality." *Cultural Studies* 21(2–3): 449–514.

Moghadam, Val. 1989. "Against Eurocentrism and Nativism." *Social and Democracy* 5(2): 81–104.
Moore, Jason. 2015. *Capitalism in the Web of Life*. London: Verso.
Nitzan, Jonathan, and Shimshon Bichler. 2009. *Capital as Power*. New York: Routledge.
Postone, Moishe. 1993. *Time, Labor, and Social Domination: A Reinterpretation of Marx's Critical Theory*. Cambridge: Cambridge University Press.
Robinson, Andrew. 2011. "An A–Z oftheory: Samir Amin," Ceasefire Magazine. https://ceasefiremagazine.co.uk/in-theory-amin-2/
Robinson, Cedric. 1983. *Black Marxism: The Making of the Black Radical Tradition*. Chapel Hill: The University of North Carolina Press.
Sayre, Nathan. 2008. "Assessing the Effects of the *Grundrisse* in Anglophone Geography and Anthropology." *Antipode* 40(5): 899–920.
Surin, Kenneth. 2001. "Dossier on *Empire*." *Rethinking Marxism* 13(3–4): 89–94.
Surin, Kenneth. 2009. *Freedom Not Yet: Liberation and the Next World Order*. Durham: Duke University Press.
Wynter, Sylvia. 2003. "Unsettling the Coloniality of Being/Power/Truth/Freedom." *CR: The New Centennial Review* 3(3): 257–337.
Zibechi, Raul. 2010. *Dispersing Power: Social Movements as Anti-State Forces*. Oakland: AK Press.

29
IMMANUEL WALLERSTEIN (1930–2019)

Marcel van der Linden

Immanuel Wallerstein grew up in a relatively privileged and politically conscious New York family. Already at a young age he became active in the liberal American Veterans Committee and the United World Federalists, but he kept aloof from left-wing politics. In an autobiographical note he explained:

> The Social-Democrats convinced me that almost everything they said about the Communists was correct – the evils of Stalinism and terror, the unprincipled swervings of the world party line, the langue de bois. But at the same time the Communists convinced me that almost everything they said about the Social-Democrats was correct – the chronic cave-ins to Western nationalisms, the incredible weakness of their opposition to capitalist polarization, the lack of serious militancy concerning racial injustice. Politically, this created many dilemmas for me, with which I have had to wrestle ever since.
>
> *(http://iwallerstein.com/intellectual-itinerary/)*

Though very interested in the anti-colonial movement in India at the time, Wallerstein decided to become an Africanist after having attended in 1951 an international youth congress in which several African delegates participated. Wallerstein's first monographs reflect this interest: *Africa, The Politics of Independence* (1961), *The Road to Independence: Ghana and the Ivory Coast* (1964) and *Africa: The Politics of Unity* (1967). While doing his research he spent time in Paris. In the French capital he became acquainted with political radicals from the Global South and with historians around the innovative journal *Annales* (Brick 2015). His African studies made him understand the important world-political issues better. Afterwards Wallerstein wrote that

> In general, in a deep conflict, the eyes of the downtrodden are more acute about the reality of the present. For it is in their interest to perceive correctly in order to expose the hypocrisies of the rulers. They have less interest in ideological deflection.
>
> *(Wallerstein 1974b, 4)*

Gradually Wallerstein's views evolved, until by the 1970s he arrived at a global historical-sociological approach. The first major result of this development was *The Modern World-System, I: Capitalist Agriculture and the Origins of the European World-Economy in the Sixteenth Century*

(1974). This magnum opus, which was reprinted many times, and appeared in fourteen languages, laid the foundations for Wallerstein's so-called world-systems analysis – combining four influences in particular: the historiography of the *Annales* school (above all Fernand Braudel); sociological thinking about systems presupposing the coherence and functionality of all their elements; long wave theory in economics; and dependency theory, which postulates relations of structural dependency between the capitalist "core" and "periphery."

The essence of Wallerstein's world-systems approach has been described many times, and by now has become part of textbook knowledge:

- Since the 16th century the European (capitalist) world system has extended to the whole world.
- It is characterized by *one* international division of labor and *multiple* political units (states).
- The system is an interdependent whole consisting of a core, a periphery that is exploited by the core through unequal exchange, and a semi-periphery that is economically located halfway between the core and periphery.
- The system is dynamic; there is upward mobility through which a peripheral region can over time become a semi-peripheral or core region, and there is also downward mobility.
- Inside the core, there is fierce competition among states striving for global hegemony. There have been three occasions when a core state succeeded in becoming hegemonic in world commerce for a short period of time: the Dutch Republic in the 17th century, Britain in the 19th century and the United States after 1945.
- The system develops in long cycles of rise and fall.
- It is capitalist; that is, the economy is based on market production for profit.
- Since the 19th century, virtually every corner of the world has been integrated into the system, even including apparently feudal or "socialist" regions.

Shortly after *The Modern World-System, I* had appeared, in September 1976, the Fernand Braudel Center for the Study of Economies, Historical Systems, and Civilizations opened its doors at the State University of New York – Binghamton under Wallerstein's directorship. The new institution had a flying start; after only three months, it presented its "Proposed Research Programs" in a substantial booklet. In the summer of 1977, the first issue of its journal *Review* was published. That same year, a section on the "Political Economy of World-Systems" (PEWS) inspired by the Braudel Center was established within the American Sociological Association. The PEWS section has held annual conferences and published their proceedings ever since. Since 1979, the Center has sponsored a book series called "Studies in Modern Capitalism" together with the Maison des sciences de l'homme of Paris, published by Cambridge University Press. The "message" of Wallerstein's new approach was effectively spread this way, not only by the master himself, but also by many co-thinkers and students, including Giovanni Arrighi, Terence K. Hopkins, Beverly Silver, Joan Smith, Dale Tomich and many others.

In later years Wallerstein elaborated his approach much further. He published three more volumes of *The Modern World System* (in 1980, 1989, 2011), plus a stream of articles and other books on related topics. His theory has become one of the most discussed contributions to the social sciences of the past century. Its influence has been strongest among sociologists and political scientists – though that influence appears to be declining now and is "overtaken by new realities and more fashionable theoretical paradigms" (El-Ojeili 2014, 2) – but historians only rarely feel drawn to it. Robert DuPlessis's (1978, 12–13) observation is still valid:

> unlike, say, E.P. Thompson's *The Making of the English Working Class*, whose publication marked a fundamental rupture in labor history and indeed in social history as a whole,

forcing reconceptualizations among all who followed, irrespective of ideological or scholarly allegiance, the continuing discussion of Wallerstein's work is not indicative of its significant assimilation either by Marxists or by other historians.

Marx and Marxisms

Wallerstein was a co-founder and till his death a member of the Marxist Sociology section of the American Sociological Association. Although Marx was always a major inspiration for him, he kept a critical distance from Marx, whom he considered as

> the most interesting thinker of the 19th century by far, but one insufficiently delinked from classical economics. In any case, we are in the 21st century and must make use of him while moving beyond him on questions he didn't face.
>
> *(Wallerstein, personal communication, 13 April 2017)*

Wallerstein distinguishes three Marxian eras. First, the era of Marx himself, until his death in 1883. Second, the era of the so-called orthodox Marxism from the 1880s to the 1950s (Kautsky, Lenin, Stalin), when Marxism became "a relatively codified set of ideas, which in its worst moments was reduced to a catechism." And third, since the 1950s,

> the era of a thousand Marxisms, the era of Marxism "exploded." In this era not only is there no orthodoxy but it is also hard to say that any version is even dominant. Marxism is being used to paper over so many different worldviews that its content seems very diluted indeed.
>
> *(Wallerstein 1986, 1301–2)*

During the third era,

> we cannot rely on the acquired wisdom of the second era. No doubt there is wisdom there, but we have to tear it into very small bits in order to reassemble it in forms that are usable. Not to do so is simply to fall further into the monumental culs-de sac in which, as of the 1960s, both orthodox Marxism and scientific social science found themselves.
>
> *(Wallerstein 1986, 1307)*

While during the second era intellectuals were supposed to guide the rebellious forces, during our third, contemporary, era

> The task before us is precisely to place the activities of the intelligentsia (i.e., social science) and the activities of political organizations in a framework in which, in tension and tandem with each other, they illuminate the historical choices rather than presume to make them.
>
> *(Wallerstein 1986, 1307–8)*

The third era enables us to approach Marx critically, while simultaneously respecting his anti-capitalist drive. Implicitly, Wallerstein's works are an attempt to develop such a critical perspective.

Wallerstein's Marxism is an idiosyncratic Marxism, in which the volumes of *Capital* play an insignificant role. His approach is "a major modification of the traditional Marxist approach, rather than a simple application of accepted Marxist principles" (Shannon 1989, 11). The theory of value, with its many aspects and implications, is only indirectly present, in the notion of "unequal exchange," which is never explained.[1] I will discuss briefly a few core elements of Wallerstein's approach, and their relationship with more traditional Marxist interpretations.

Capitalism

Wallerstein defines capitalism loosely as "a system of production for sale in a market for profit and appropriation of this profit on the basis of individual or collective ownership" (Wallerstein 1974a, 66). According to this approach it does not matter what the social relations *within* the production system look like (whether there is, for example, serfdom or wage labor); what matters is only a type of economic behavior that is oriented toward sales of commodities and profit making. This interpretation goes back to Adam Smith, and is the reason why some critics call it "Neo-Smithian Marxism" (Brenner 1977). The more orthodox approach defines capitalism (or the capitalist mode of production) as generalized commodity production. This interpretation means that capitalism exists, when not just goods and services *created* by the production system take the form of commodities, but also that the *inputs* of that system – including labor power, raw materials and means of production – are purchased as commodities. In this view capitalism is the progressing circulation of commodity production and distribution, such that not just products of labor, but also means of production and labor-power itself acquire the status of commodities.

Against his classical Marxist critics Wallerstein argued that the narrow definition is an expression of methodological nationalism, because it emphasizes developments *within* separate states, while capitalism is a *global* phenomenon:

> For the orthodox Marxists, . . . [the] "economy" was a national construct. Classes were national. It was countries that could be labeled either capitalist or not. This debate was fundamental. . . . In my view, capitalism was the characteristic of a world-system, of the specific variety I called a "world-economy." Classes were classes of this world-system. State structures existed within this world-system.
>
> *(Wallerstein 2011, xx)*

Wallerstein's broad definition allows him to see the beginnings of the capitalist "modern world-system" in the 16th century, while classical Marxists date these beginnings two centuries later.[2]

Bourgeoisie

Marxists distinguish several types of capitalists: merchants, industrial entrepreneurs, rentiers and more. Wallerstein argues that this is a mistake.

> Just like workers who live in households which merge revenue from multiple sources (only one being wages), the capitalists (especially big ones) live in enterprises which in reality merge revenues from many sources of investment – rents, speculation, trading profits, 'normal' production profits, financial manipulation.
>
> *(Wallerstein 1979, 131)*

Since all these different revenues come in money form, their origin does not matter to capitalists.

In many ways capitalists no not behave as schematic Marxists believe. Capitalists are ultimately not interested in competition, but in monopolies: obtaining important profits is easiest if there is only one seller.

> Any time the world-economy is expanding significantly, one will find there are some 'leading' products that are relatively monopolized. . . . It is from these relatively monopolized products that great profits are made and large amounts of capital can be accumulated.
>
> *(Wallerstein 2016, 192)*

Capitalists are also not interested in the free flow of the factors of production (commodities, labor, capital), but want some of these flows to be restricted. Capitalists do not abhor state intervention, but "have always and consistently sought to utilize the state machineries and welcomed the concept of political primacy" (Wallerstein 1991b, 145). And successful capitalists don't want to remain capitalists: "the primary objective of every 'bourgeois' is to become an 'aristocrat,'" and to transform profit into rent (Wallerstein 1991b, 146).

Proletariat

Wallerstein has an equally catholic approach when it comes to the working class. He insists on a wide range of modes of labor control within capitalism, which are characteristic of different locations within the global division of labor. With characteristic boldness, he advanced a new definition of the proletariat. In his eyes proletarians are all "those who yield part of the value they have created to others" and "In this sense there exists [sic] in the capitalist mode of production only bourgeois and proletarians. The polarity is structural" (Wallerstein 1979, 289). This approach "eliminates as a *defining* characteristic of the proletarian the payment of *wages* to the producer" (Wallerstein 1979, 289). The key point is that products of labor are *commodified*, and that this commodification can occur in many different ways. A diversity of "modes of labor control" therefore exists within the modern world system. Wallerstein distinguishes several such modes, including slavery (a "kind of indefinitely lasting work obligation of one person to another from which the worker may not unilaterally withdraw"); "coerced cash-crop labor" (i.e., "a system of agricultural labor control wherein the peasants are required by some legal process enforced by the state to labor at least part of the time on a large domain producing some product for sale on the world market"), self-employment and share-cropping (Wallerstein 1974b, 91, 1989, 164).

Because economic relations vary between the core, the periphery and the semi-periphery, the combinations of modes of labor control that prevail in each of these spheres also vary. The core areas have integrated economies with relatively capital-intensive production and high levels of productivity, in which wage labor and medium-sized yeomen predominate (Wallerstein 1979, 38). The periphery features export-driven commerce with relatively weakly developed domestic markets and highly labor-intensive production, in which slavery and coerced cash-cropping labor predominate. The semi-periphery trades with both core areas and the periphery, and has on average moderately capital-intensive and moderately labor-intensive production; share-cropping among other forms plays a major role. Variations in the predominant modes of labor control are thus an essential feature of the capitalist world system:

> Free labor is indeed a defining feature of capitalism, but not free labor throughout the productive enterprises. Free labor is the form of labor control used for skilled work in core countries whereas coerced labor is used for less skilled work in peripheral areas.

> The combination thereof is the essence of capitalism. When labor is everywhere free, we shall have socialism.
>
> *(Wallerstein 1974b, 127)*

It is above all the market mechanism of supply and demand that determines the specific mix of modes of labor control in a given region. "It is always a choice [for the employer] about the optimal combination of machinery (dead labor) and living labor" (Wallerstein 1980, 174). The employer considers which alternative is "optimal and politically possible *in the short run*": (1) wage labor, (2) coerced cash-crop labor, (3) slavery, (4) share-cropping, (5) tenancy or (6) additional machinery (Wallerstein 1974b, 127).

Class Struggle

Strategies of resistance and survival of subaltern groups or classes have never occupied a central place in Wallerstein's world-system approach. There is little analysis to be found in his work about, for example, the interaction between slave rebellions and modes of slave exploitation. His neglect of social protest is sometimes even compounded by negative evaluations of it. This is particularly true of workers' movements. Already early on Wallerstein was an admirer of Frantz Fanon, a theorist well known for his lack of appreciation for the rising workers' movements in colonial countries (Wallerstein 1968, 1979, 250–68). Generalizing Fanon's perspective, Wallerstein says:

> Has it not been true . . . of the majority of workers' movements that their strength and their cadres have been drawn from a segment of the working population which was somewhat "better off," whether this segment were technically independent artisans or more highly paid skilled (and/or craft) wage workers? The search for those who truly had nothing to lose but their chains . . . leads us today to what is variously called the subproletariat, the lumpenproletariat, the unskilled (often immigrant) workers, the marginal, the chronically unemployed.
>
> *(Wallerstein 1989, 108)*

Alongside this argument based on social stratification, Wallerstein has a second reason for his low opinion of labor movements. Thanks to their form of organization, he maintains, they are powerless in face of the world system. The capitalist economy is a world economy, and the working class *an sich* (in itself) is therefore by definition a world class. On the other hand, "classes *für sich* [for themselves] organize themselves (or perhaps one should say disorganize themselves) at the level of the territorial states" (Wallerstein 1977, 105), because political power is organized in the capitalist world system through states. The world working class is thus the victim of a fundamental, insoluble dilemma, which makes it impossible for its "movements" to operate effectively on a global scale.

Immizeration

Marx observed not only class *struggle*, but also class *polarization*, accompanied by progressing immizeration of the proletariat. Class polarization is for Wallerstein an empirical fact. If one focuses exclusively on the *current* revenues of bourgeois and proletarians, that is without income from inherited sources (capital, property, privileges etc.), then

> the distinction being one between those (the bourgeois) who live off the surplus-value which the others (the proletarians) create [. . .], then one can argue indeed that over

> the centuries more and more persons have come to be located unambiguously in one or the other category and that this is the consequence of a structural process which is far from completed.
>
> *(Wallerstein 1991a, 129)*

Immizeration was Marx's "most radical and most daring hypothesis, and thereupon the hypothesis that has been the most vigorously denounced" (Wallerstein 1984, 94). Especially after 1945 many anti-Marxist intellectuals showed that Marx's hypothesis was wrong, and that the living standard of industrial workers in Western countries has improved significantly over the years. This criticism was correct, and Marxists largely stopped defending Marx in this respect. The immizeration hypothesis seemed to be refuted by history itself. But:

> Marx was far more astute about the *longue durée* than we often give him credit for being. The fact is that polarization is a historically correct hypothesis, not a false one, and one can demonstrate this empirically, provided we use as the unit of calculation the only entity which really matters for capitalism, the capitalist world-economy. Within this entity there has been over four centuries not merely a relative but even an absolute polarization of classes.
>
> *(Wallerstein 1991a, 127–28)*

Conclusion

Wallerstein's world-systems approach stimulated many responses. Some fundamental objections to it have been put forward by critics over the years. Perhaps the most important one is that it is anachronistic: it projects characteristics of 19th and 20th century world capitalism back on the three preceding centuries. International trade with colonies was indeed one of the foundations of economic growth in Western Europe, but only from the late 18th century on. "Between 1450 and 1750, historians now generally agree, core-periphery trade was neither extensive nor unusually profitable, and as few industries relied upon imported raw materials, foreign trade exerted little pressure toward specialization in the domestic economies" (DuPlessis 1978, 20). Partly for this reason, Wallerstein's concept of "unequal exchange" is polyvalent. On top of that, the whole construction is structuralist and functionalist in character.

- First, the world-system approach exhibits a strong tendency toward determinism, in the sense of a vision of history in which the existing division of labor completely determines other developments. Some of Wallerstein's own collaborators have advanced similar criticisms. Giovanni Arrighi argued that world-system analysts cannot claim anymore that class relations and class conflicts are reducible to core-periphery relations.

  > The sooner world-systemists stop seeking an explanation for almost everything in core-periphery relations and their temporal equivalent – A-B phases of Kondratieffs and suchlike cycles – the better for the credibility of their analyses to anybody who is not already a true believer.
  >
  > *(Arrighi 1998, 121)*

- Second, the theory´s determinism remains implicitly Eurocentric: it suggests that the requirements of the core capitalist region entirely *determine* what happens in the periphery. Clearly these two weaknesses are linked to each other. Many authors have pointed out that reality is in truth much more complicated. In his study of early modern viniculture,

Tim Unwin (1993, 262) stresses the need "to incorporate social, political and ideological factors alongside economic ones in any explanation of the emergence of a modern world-system." Many other authors have put forward similar arguments (e.g., Stern 1988; Washbrook 1990). This criticism has been also adopted to some extent in recent years by collaborators of the Braudel Center itself. William Martin, one of Wallerstein's prominent second-generation collaborators, wrote: "What we have not achieved, I think we must frankly admit, is a conceptual rendering of this world-wide, historical process of class formation – we remain still prisoners of an outward movement from Europe and the United States" (Martin 2000, 244).

- Third, the loose definition of capitalism used by Wallerstein, on the basis of sale for profit and appropriation of profit obscures the fact that capitalism is based on *competition* among commodity owners. Competition is, in Marx's words, "the basic law" of capitalism that "governs the general rate of profit" (CIII: 127–28).[3] These qualifications make clear not only that Wallerstein often takes an extremely sweeping (and therefore vague) view of the meaning of capitalism and its operational logics, implausibly including even the former Soviet Union as "capitalist." It is also that a fundamental aspect of the dynamics of capitalism (the quest to maintain and increase profits forced on capital by constant competition) disappears from view.

Despite these failings the world-systems approach can be an important source of inspiration. Its special value is that it persistently tries to make connections visible among developments in different locations in the world, transcending parochial outlooks. The approach could, however, be made much more persuasive if it considered history as a relatively open-ended process, in which social formations are shaped by global *and* local forces, and it treated capitalism less as a closed system, and more as a dynamic, contradictory process.

As Steve Stern rightly comments: "Wallerstein's work raises provocative and weighty issues and contributes specific historical and theoretical insights whose value should not be overlooked even if one concludes that the general paradigm is fundamentally flawed" (Stern 1988, 889). In this sense, Wallerstein has had an exceptionally stimulating impact on numerous fields of study across more than four decades.

Notes

1. Apparently Wallerstein was inspired by Emmanuel (1972). But the extensive debates about this approach (see for example Mandel 1975; Raffer 1987) find no echo in his writings.
2. Marx, however, called the Dutch Republic "the model capitalist country of the seventeenth century" (*CI*: 916).
3. See also Marx (*G*: 650): "*Free competition* is the relation of capital to itself as another capital, i.e. the real conduct as capital."

Bibliography

Arrighi, Giovanni. 1998. "Capitalism and the Modern World-System: Rethinking the Nondebates of the 1970s." *Review* 21: 113–29.

Brenner, Robert. 1977. "The Origins of Capitalist Development: A Critique of Neo-Smithian Marxism." *New Left Review* 1(104): 25–92.

Brick, Howard. 2015. "Peasant Studies Meets the World System: Eric Wolf, Immanuel Wallerstein, and Visions of Global Capitalism." In *Lineages of the Literary Left: Essays in Honor of Alan M. Wald*, edited by Howard Brick, Robbie Lieberman, and Paula Rabinowitz, 291–329. Ann Arbor MI: University of Michigan Library.

DuPlessis, Robert S. 1978. "The Partial Transition to World-Systems Analysis in Early Modern European History." *Radical History Review* 39: 11–27.
El-Ojeili, Chamsy. 2014. "Reflections on Wallerstein: The Modern World-System, Four Decades on." *Critical Sociology*: 1–22.
Emmanuel, Arghiri. 1972. *Unequal Exchange: A Study of the Imperialism of Trade*. London: NLB.
Mandel, Ernest. 1975. *Late Capitalism*. London: New Left Books.
Martin, William G. 2000. "Still Partners and Still Dissident after All These Years? Wallerstein, World Revolutions and the World-Systems Perspective." *Journal of World-Systems Research* 6(2): 234–63.
Raffer, Kunibert. 1987. *Unequal Exchange and the Evolution of the World System: Reconsidering the Impact of Trade on North-South Relations*. New York: Palgrave Macmillan.
Shannon, Thomas Richard. 1989. *An Introduction to the World-System Perspective*. Boulder, CO: Westview Press.
Stern, Steve. 1988. "Feudalism, Capitalism, and the World System in the Perspective of Latin America and the Caribbean." *American Historical Review* 93: 829–72.
Unwin, Tim. 1993. "Wine in the Early Modern World System: Profit, Production and Exchange." In *The Early-Modern World System in Geographical Perspective*, edited by Hans-Jürgen Nitz, 248–64. Stuttgart: Steiner.
Wallerstein, Immanuel. 1968. "Fanon, Frantz." In *International Encyclopedia of the Social Sciences*. Vol. 5, 326–7. New York: Macmillan & Free Press.
Wallerstein, Immanuel. 1974a. "Dependence in an Interdependent World: The Limited Possibilities of Transformation Within the Capitalist World Economy." *African Studies Review* 17: 1–27.
Wallerstein, Immanuel. 1974b. *The Modern World-System, I: Capitalist Agriculture and the Origins of the European World-Economy in the Sixteenth Century*. New York: Academic Press.
Wallerstein, Immanuel. 1977. "How Do We Know Class Struggle When We See It? Reply to Ira Gerstein." *The Insurgent Sociologist* 7(2): 104–6.
Wallerstein, Immanuel. 1979. *The Capitalist World Economy*. Cambridge: Cambridge University Press, and Paris: Editions de la Maison des Sciences de l'Homme.
Wallerstein, Immanuel. 1980. *The Modern World-System II: Mercantilism and the Consolidation of the European World-Economy, 1600–1750*. New York: Academic Press.
Wallerstein, Immanuel. 1984. "Marx and History: Fruitful and Unfruitful Emphases." *Thesis Eleven* 8: 92–101.
Wallerstein, Immanuel. 1986. "Marxisms as Utopias: Evolving Ideologies." *American Journal of Sociology* 91(6): 1295–308.
Wallerstein, Immanuel. 1989. *The Modern World-System III: The Second Era of Great Expansion of the Capitalist World-Economy, 1730–1840s*. San Dieg, CA: Academic Press.
Wallerstein, Immanuel. 1991a. "Marx and History: Fruitful and Unfruitful Emphases." In Étienne Balibar and Immanuel Wallerstein. *Race, Nation, Class: Ambiguous Identities*, 125–34. London and New York: Verso. (Originally in *Thesis Eleven* 8: 92–101.)
Wallerstein, Immanuel. 1991b. "The Bourgeois(ie) as Concept and Reality." In *Race, Nation, Class: Ambiguous Identities*, edited by Étienne Balibar and Immanuel Wallerstein, 135–52. London: Verso.
Wallerstein, Immanuel. 2011. "Prologue to the 2011 Edition." In Immanuel Wallerstein. *The Modern World-System, I: Capitalist Agriculture and the Origins of the European World-Economy in the Sixteenth Century*. With a New Prologue, xvii–xxx. Berkeley and Los Angeles: University of California Press.
Wallerstein, Immanuel. 2016. "Capitalism as an Essential Concept to Understand Modernity." In *Capitalism: The Reemergence of a Historical Concept*, edited by Jürgen Kocka and Marcel van der Linden, 187–204. London: Bloomsbury Academic.
Washbrook, David. 1990. "South Asia, the World System and World Capitalism." *Journal of Asian Studies* 49: 479–508.

30

G.A. COHEN (1941–2009)

James Furner

G.A. Cohen was a philosopher who developed both a distinctive Marxist theory of history, and a distinctive ethics. Within Marxist circles, he is most renowned for the conception of history eloquently propounded in his first book, *Karl Marx's Theory of History: A Defence* (*KMTH*) (1978). For others, Cohen's later, ethical writings are the central focus, in particular the essays posthumously collected in *On the Currency of Egalitarian Justice* (2011), which defend a "luck egalitarian" approach to distributive justice; and a sustained critique of John Rawls's theory of justice, entitled *Rescuing Justice and Equality* (2008). As the latter, too, opens by claiming Marx's socialist conviction as a guiding inspiration (Cohen 2008, 1), any summary of Cohen's thought must address the relation between his early theory of history, and his later ethics. For Cohen, Marxism is a theory of history concerned with empirical fact. "Scientific socialism offers no ideals or values to the proletariat" (Cohen 2001, 64). In his own judgment, then, Cohen's intellectual trajectory is that of an "ex-Marxist" (2001, 105).

The Theory of History

KMTH focuses on the relationship between material productive power, and the social relations of production that constitute an economic structure. Adopting Marx's 1859 Preface to *A Contribution to a Critique of Political Economy* (*MECW* 29: 261–65) as its guide, *KMTH* defends a technological version of historical materialism founded on two theses: the development thesis and the primacy thesis (Cohen 1978, 134). The development thesis says that productive power tends to develop throughout history. The primacy thesis says that the nature of a society's relations of production is explained by the level of development of its productive power. Together, the theses entail that existing productive power develops, and that relations of production will persist only so long as they continue to promote its development. Should the existing relations of production come to fetter the development of productive power (*MECW* 29: 263), the theses entail that they will be replaced by relations that promote it.

The development thesis asserts a general tendency in conditions of scarcity; it is "of the nature of the forces to develop" (Cohen 1978, 134). Any defense of the development thesis must therefore appeal to something with a suitably general presence. *KMTH*'s defense rests on asocial premises about human nature, and an appeal to the historical record. Human beings, *KMTH* says, are "somewhat rational," that is, somewhat disposed to use their know-how to employ the means of satisfying "compelling wants they have" (Cohen 1978, 152). Further, their intelligence enables them to modify nature, to make their wants easier or less costly to satisfy. As human beings' situation has been one of scarcity, that is, the objects of their wants have required undesirable labor to produce, their reason has led them to acquire knowledge, and to use it to improve their situation, "for not to do so would be irrational" (Cohen 1978, 153). To counter the objections that mitigating scarcity might not be the rational thing to do all things considered, or that society may not do what is rational, *KMTH* appeals to the historical record: regression in the level of productive power has been rare, while growth has been frequent. *KMTH* claims that, if this record is "better explained" by the rationality of mitigating scarcity having considerable weight than by "inertia . . . alone" (and inertia cannot explain growth), we may infer that the rationality of mitigating scarcity has sufficient weight to make the development thesis plausible (Cohen 1978, 155).

The significance of *KMTH*'s defense of the development thesis is that it entails a refinement of its primacy thesis, which is itself a particular version of the idea that productive power explains relations of production. If the development thesis is true, but, as on the *KMTH* defense, facts about the effect of relations of production on agents' desire to mitigate scarcity, and thereby on productive power, do not belong to that defense, these facts must still be consistent with it. They are consistent with it only if the effect of relations of production is to promote the development of productive power. As *KMTH* offers a relation-independent defense of the development thesis, the only way for it to respect such facts *and* to uphold the asymmetry between powers and relations asserted by its primacy thesis is to incorporate the function of relations of production for the development of existing productive power into its primacy thesis. So refined, *KMTH*'s primacy thesis says: a society's relations of production are as they are because, being so, they serve to develop its productive power (Cohen 1978, 160).

KMTH's version of the 1859 Preface's claim that the economic structure explains a legal and political superstructure (*MECW* 29: 263) incorporates a parallel refinement. If, as *KMTH*'s primacy thesis says, the explanation of relations of production is superstructure-independent, then, as legal and political phenomena nonetheless affect these relations, this effect must be consistent with *KMTH*'s primacy thesis. It is consistent with *KMTH*'s primacy thesis only if legal and political phenomena serve to secure relations of production that promote the development of productive power. Accordingly, *KMTH*'s version of the doctrine of basis and superstructure says: a society's legal and political systems are as they are because, being so, they serve to secure relations of production that develop its productive power (Cohen 1978, 231–32).

KMTH defends its primacy thesis and doctrine of basis and superstructure using a form of explanation called functional explanation. In a functional explanation, what is taken to be explanatory is a dispositional fact, that is, a fact of hypothetical conditional form "if *e*, then *f*." Cohen's preferred term for functional explanation is thus "*explanation by disposition*" (1986, 225). An adherent of functional explanation, or explanation by disposition, is someone who holds that it is justified to believe that a dispositional fact is explanatory provided enough instances confirm the statement of a law incorporating it, even "in the absence of a theory as to *how*" (Cohen 1978, 266) the dispositional fact is supposed to contribute to the explanation. Suppose it is claimed, for example, that capitalist relations of production functionally explain the rule of law state. The relevant law to be confirmed (amending Cohen 1978, 260) is then:

> IF it is the case that if a rule of law state were to exist at t_1,
> then it would help secure capitalist relations of production at t_2 that promote the development of productive power,
> THEN a rule of law state exists at t_3

An adherent of functional explanation holds that confirmation of this law justifies a belief that the existence of a rule of law state is explained by this dispositional fact (that, were a rule of law state to exist, it would help secure capitalist relations of production that promote the development of productive power), even without a theory of how it is supposed to contribute to the explanation.[1]

The Contradiction of Advanced Capitalism

According to *KMTH*'s theory of history, if capitalism is to perish, that can only be because its economic structure comes to fetter the development of productive power. But *KMTH*'s theory of history is plausible only if the rationality of mitigating scarcity is weighty. Its weight would have to be doubted if there were cause to expect a transition away from capitalism in which it did not supply actors' preponderant motivation. So, insofar as *KMTH* is to give us reason to believe that capitalism will be replaced by socialism, it must argue that fettering occasions a transition to socialism motivated by the rationality of mitigating scarcity. This argument must also uphold *KMTH*'s judgment that the "unbroken development" of productive power is one of capitalism's specific characteristics (Cohen 1978, 155). The argument takes the form of an analysis of a "distinctive contradiction of advanced capitalism" (Cohen 1978, 297–325).

KMTH measures the level of productive power by the workable time (in principle more extensive than the time actually worked) that would remain "after the laboring time required to maintain the producers has been subtracted" and if existing productive power was put to "optimal use" (Cohen 1978, 61, 56). Time freed up by the development of productive power need not be devoted to *undesirable labor*, however, and that is the key to the contradiction of advanced capitalism. Although the development of productive power need not be reflected in expanding output, capitalism's competitive dynamic will never allow the development of productive power to be channeled to reduce toil (Cohen 1978, 306). At some stage, then, capitalism's inherent bias for output expansion over toil reduction will generate a "welfare"-based reason to choose a socialist economic structure (Cohen 1978, 310). Not to choose it would be to fail to identify the means of one's "satisfaction" (Cohen 1978, 319). One problem with this argument, however, is that *KMTH* says people exhibit the rationality of mitigating scarcity by employing the means of satisfying the wants they have, not by pursuing the options that would bring them satisfaction (compare Cohen 1978, 152, 319).

KMTH's normative justification of socialism is, relatedly, that a socialist economic structure is necessary for freedom, understood as the active cultivation of one's talents. The mass of humankind have remained "unfree" under all previous social forms, because starved of the "opportunity to cultivate their talents" (Cohen 1978, 204). By channeling productivity gains to reduce toil, a socialist economic structure redirects the development of productive power in accordance with a "theory and practice of leisure" (Cohen 1978, 320). Socialism thereby ends capitalism's "spiritual alienation" (Cohen 1988, 119).

Revisions to the Theory of History

Cohen's subsequent writings offer both clarifications and revisions of *KMTH*'s arguments, as well as criticisms of historical materialism. The clarifications and revisions appear in essays from the 1980s collected in Cohen's second book, *History, Labour and Freedom* (*HLF*) (1988). Later works, such as *If You're An Egalitarian, How Come You're So Rich?* (2001), adopt a more critical posture.

One clarification concerns the development thesis. *KMTH*'s claim that, if the rationality of mitigating scarcity helps explain the historical record better than inertia alone, then it has sufficient weight to support the development thesis, is unconvincing. The weight of a type of rationality is only confirmed by the historical record if it explains the latter *satisfactorily*. *HLF* implicitly concedes this, just by seeking to clarify how the historical record exhibits this rationality. The rationality of mitigating scarcity may be exhibited by an act that replaces an inferior productive power with a superior one. But it may also be exhibited, *HLF* says, by an act that retains a relation of production because it is productivity-enhancing, or that replaces it in order to use a superior productive power whose use it prevented (Cohen 1988, 24, 91). Second, *HLF* distinguishes the "reason operative in the mind of the person(s) who caused better forces to be adopted" from the "underlying reason for productive progress" (Cohen 1988, 22). Even if, for example, in capitalism, capitalists adopt superior productive power to make profits, others may exhibit the rationality of mitigating scarcity by choosing to retain a productivity-enhancing capitalist economic structure in order to mitigate scarcity. In reply to Andrew Levine's and Erik Olin Wright's (1980) critique of *KMTH*, Cohen complains that his argument for the development thesis is misinterpreted if it is taken to imply *either* that the direct object of an act that exhibits the rationality of mitigating scarcity need be a productive power, *or* that those who introduce superior productive power need be motivated by it (1988, 23–25).

KMTH's defense of the development thesis faces another problem, however. The historical record cannot confirm that the rationality of mitigating scarcity is relation-independent if it confirms that class position (or social factors explained by class position) explains actors' attempts to mitigate scarcity by adopting (relations that permit) superior productive powers. Yet this is what it must confirm, given that it is logically possible for there to be a type of society in which members acting on a desire to mitigate their condition of scarcity would retain a type of economic structure that had ceased to develop productive power, due, for example, to coordination problems frustrating collective agency, or to the risk that repression of attempts to institute new relations would destroy productive power. It is inadequate to reply that, "for material reasons," such logically possible societies are "contingently unlikely" (Cohen 1988, 101; cf. Cohen 1982, 253–73). The historical record does not cease to confirm that social factors have a role in explaining the weight of the rationality of mitigating scarcity if they are themselves materially explained. Rather, their material explanation and role only allows the historical record to confirm the weight of an argument for the development thesis that includes a social premise. Any such argument undermines *KMTH*'s version of historical materialism, however. If the case for the development thesis is relation-dependent, then the development thesis cannot be used, as in *KMTH* (Cohen 1978, 158–59), to ground *KMTH*'s primacy thesis.

Second, *HLF* distinguishes "restricted" and "inclusive" variants of the technological version of historical materialism that *KMTH* defends, and affirms the former. The restricted variant holds that history is, *among other things*, a process marked by *KMTH*'s development thesis and primacy thesis (Cohen 1988, 158). It refrains from claiming that these theses are central to history, in the sense of explaining major developments in non-economic spheres. It holds, more modestly, that the theses explain enough about these spheres to forestall the objection that the historical record disconfirms *KMTH*'s theses. *HLF* recommends the restricted variant on two grounds: it is easier to defend *KMTH*'s version of historical materialism from the charge that it neglects phenomena that (1) reflect "the need for self identification,"[2] or (2) express the creative side of human nature, if its explanatory ambition is restricted (Cohen 1988, 169–71).

Third, *HLF* implies that socialism can be judged superior to capitalism even if the transition to socialism *disconfirms* *KMTH*'s primacy thesis. Whether fettering is the hindrance of the development or the use of productive power, or, as Cohen now says, "*used* productive power . . . in the future" (1988, 117), an adequate fettering claim compares an existing structure unfavorably to a feasible alternative (1988, 111–17). Yet, *KMTH*'s account of the transition to socialism says that people will choose socialism to impart a more satisfying *direction* on the use and development of productive power, rather than to increase its rate of development, or use it more efficiently. If that is true, a transition to socialism will *not* confirm *KMTH*'s primacy thesis, *unless* (following *HLF*'s conception of fettering) people choose socialism to reduce toil at a point where socialism's expected use of the productive power it would develop by some future date would free up more surplus workable time than would capitalism's expected use of the productive power capitalism would develop by that date. Accordingly, it is *possible* "to concede that capitalism develops the productive forces more quickly" than socialism would, and so to drop any claim of fettering against capitalism, "while insisting that socialism . . . offers a better way of life" (Cohen 1988, 120–21), and arises for *that* reason.

In *HLF*, Cohen reports that its reservations about *KMTH*'s version of historical materialism do not weaken his belief that socialism is "both desirable and possible" (1988, 132). Cohen notes that this belief does not depend on "theses about the whole of human history" (1988, 132). The preceding summary suggests something stronger: *KMTH*'s arguments for its historical theses could be rejected *as they apply to the transition from capitalism to socialism* without weakening any belief one might have that *KMTH*'s contradiction of advanced capitalism explains or justifies a transition to socialism.

Cohen's later, critical posture toward historical materialism laments its "*obstetric* conception of political practice" (2001, 43). If x is a desirable future state of affairs, then an obstetric_1 conception of political practice is one that assumes both that x will occur without a positive contribution from agency A, and that it is rational for A to help bring x about (just as it is rational for a midwife to help an "expectant mother" give birth) (Cohen 2001, 43). Second, an obstetric_2 conception of political practice assumes that, on the occasion of dysfunctionality in a social form, the latter will have itself developed the means for its replacement (just as midwives "deliver the form that develops *within* reality") (Cohen 2001, 50).

Marxists adopt an obstetric_1 conception of political practice if they regard socialism as being bound to occur even without the agency of those who have good reason to help bring it about. Yet *even those* who believe socialism is *inevitable* need not adopt an obstetric_1 conception of political practice, if they believe in its inevitability because eventually there are bound to be enough people with good reason to bring it about who will act rationally (cf. Cohen 1988, 55–56). Cohen says Marxists adopt an obstetric_2 conception of political practice by assuming that a "single set of people," possessing all the characteristics required for people to have both the capacity and interest to overthrow capitalism, are bound to become a majority as capitalism advances (2001, 72, 107–8). But this is merely *one* absurd (because alliance-eschewing) logically possible form an obstetric_2 socialist practice *could* take. Cohen contrasts obstetric_2 socialist practice with "utopian desig[n]," that is, with writing "recipes" of "*what* one is trying to achieve" (2001, 77). This, too, is confused. If a social form develops the means for its replacement, organizational principles exhibited in struggles prompted by its dysfunctionality may belong to the means it supplies.

Equality and Community

Equality barely features in *KMTH*, as either a desideratum of a good society or a motivation for revolution. *KMTH*'s "indictment" of advanced capitalism is "based on considerations wholly independent of its severe domestic inequality" (Cohen 1978, 297). To anticipate: *KMTH* would indict advanced capitalism even if its distribution of goods and labor burden, correcting for unchosen disadvantage, were equal. Several factors lie behind Cohen's later interest in equality.

First, an interest in equality arises indirectly from *KMTH*'s version of historical materialism. The latter predicts a transition to socialism, and requires that it be rational. But how can it be rational for an actor to participate in a socialist revolution if they believe that socialism is inevitable? Cohen's answer is to "*reduce the burden on other revolutionaries in the task of achieving what they all seek*" (1988, 63). An ethos of equality in the struggle for socialism is sustained by the identity socialists assume when they join the revolutionary movement.

Second, as Cohen came to distance himself from his version of Marxism, he could take an interest in issues that that Marxism neglected. "Marxism," *HLF* says, sees history as a process of liberation from scarcity and "oppression" (Cohen 1988, vii), class oppression in particular (Cohen 1978, 214; 1988, 140). Yet a concern with equality is broader than an opposition to oppression, of whatever kind. Not every kind of inequality is *imposed* by an advantaged group on a disadvantaged group. Distancing himself from his Marxism, Cohen could take an interest in equality as such.

A third impulse, characterized by Cohen as "the central normative problem that Marxists did not have to face in the past" (2001, 108), is the need to offer a coherent condemnation of both exploitation *and* poverty. If there is less overlap of the exploited and the needy than there once was (Cohen 1995, 155), it is now an urgent practical problem to reconcile the justification of relief from poverty (for producers and non-producers alike) that underpins the welfare state, with condemnation of exploitation, which, Cohen believes, Marxism has based on a producer's claim to the product they create (2001, 106, 1988, 226–29).[3]

Finally, *KMTH*'s discussion of communism reports Marx's and Engels's condemnation, in *The German Ideology* (*MECW* 5: 79), of the fact that for proletarians, "the condition of their existence, labor, and with it all the conditions of existence governing modern society, have become something accidental" (Cohen 1978, 131). To offer a luck egalitarian approach to distributive justice as a contribution to a socialist ethics (Cohen 2009, 17; 2011, 102) is in keeping with one reading of this condemnation.

Luck egalitarianism is the doctrine that says that distributive justice consists in equalizing access to advantage. It seeks "to correct for *all* unchosen disadvantages" (Cohen 2009, 17–18). "Unchosen" disadvantage is "disadvantage for which the sufferer cannot be held responsible, since it does not appropriately reflect choices that he has made or is making or would make" (Cohen 2011, 13). Two disadvantages in particular call for remedy: "exploitation and brute luck" (Cohen 2011, 5). Exploitation is an unreciprocated transfer that inherits its injustice from an ownership structure that is unjust because its inequality is unchosen, for example, because people are born into it (Cohen 2011, 120). Bad brute luck consists in unchosen shortfalls, liabilities or expensive tastes (Cohen 2011, 30), relative to the social average. Some people are more fortunately endowed than others, in terms of external assets and/or natural talent; and some have "*expensive tastes*: they need unusually large doses of resources to achieve an ordinary level of welfare" (Cohen 2011, 17). Uniting the luck egalitarian attitude to both wrongs is a desire to equalize the conditions in which agents are to exercise "responsibility" (Cohen 2011, 19). Luck egalitarianism thereby seeks to incorporate "the most powerful idea . . . of the antiegalitarian Right" (Cohen 2011, 32).

Cohen recommends socialism as a mode of organization that combines the luck egalitarian approach to distributive justice with "a principle of community" (2009, 12).[4] The latter requires that "people care about, and, where necessary and possible, care for, one another" (Cohen 2009, 34–35). Two points are stressed. First, community involves "a communal form of reciprocity," where "I serve you . . . because you need or want my service, and you, for the same reason, serve me" (Cohen 2009, 38).[5] Second, the principle of community condemns a state of affairs in which agents are disposed to withhold vastly superior resources from those whose lack of access leads them to suffer. The principle of community tempers responsibility with a communal spirit while "forbidding certain inequalities that the egalitarian principle permits" (Cohen 2009, 12).

One concern a Marxist may have about Cohen's luck egalitarian approach to justice, even if it is so tempered, is that it condemns capitalist behavior only indirectly, by condemning the unequal distribution that is its present condition. It cannot condemn all logically possible capitalisms, for example, "cleanly generated" (Cohen 1995, 161) capitalisms arising from initial egalitarian distributions of external resources and natural talent (Furner 2015, 27–29).[6] While Cohen's luck egalitarianism may justify compensation for "those who hate work" (2009, 21), it is consistent with a dynamic of capital accumulation. One thing uniting Cohen's theory of history and his later ethics, therefore, is their respective failure to explain or indict *KMTH*'s contradiction of advanced capitalism.

Cohen and Analytical Marxism

Finally, a note on Analytical Marxism, the project in whose name Cohen came to offer his work (2000, xvii–xxviii; cf. 1988, xii). Cohen defines Analytical Marxism by two views: (1) there is no specifically dialectical mode of reasoning; (2) all social explanations are to appeal to entities whose constituents are individual behaviors (2000, xxiii). Cohen's work does not always observe (2). One example must suffice: the concept of "*collective* unfreedom" (Cohen 1988, 269).[7] Cohen says the proletariat is forced to sell its labor power, and hence is collectively unfree, because each of its members is free to escape his or her class position "*only on condition that the others do not exercise their similarly conditional freedom*" (1988, 263, 2011, 161). Through the phrase "*similarly conditional*," collective unfreedom is defined by constituent *relations*. Critics of Analytical Marxism may mine Cohen's works for arguments against it.

Notes

1. For a persuasive critique of functional explanation, see Sayer (1987, ch. 5).
2. For a rebuttal of Cohen's parallel charge against Marx (1988, 137–44), see Furner (2011, 200–8).
3. For criticism of that belief, see Furner (2018, chs 1 and 8).
4. A further, undeveloped aspect of Cohen's ethics is a small-c conservative attitude to value (2013, 143–74).
5. For a critique of this notion, see Furner (2018, ch. 7).
6. On Cohen's own reservations (2011, 142–3), see Vrousalis (2015, 96–8).
7. For more examples, see Furner (2018, ch. 2).

Bibliography

Cohen, G.A. 1978. *Karl Marx's Theory of History: A Defence*. Oxford: Clarendon Press.
Cohen, G.A. 1986. "Walt on Historical Materialism and Functional Explanation." *Ethics* 97(1): 219–32.
Cohen, G.A. 1988. *History, Labour, Freedom*. Oxford: Clarendon Press.
Cohen, G.A. 1995. *Self-Ownership, Freedom and Equality*. Cambridge: Cambridge University Press.
Cohen, G.A. 2000. *Karl Marx's Theory of History: 2000 Edition*. Oxford: Oxford University Press.
Cohen, G.A. 2001. *If You're an Egalitarian, How Come You're So Rich?* Cambridge, MA: Harvard University Press.
Cohen, G.A. 2008. *Rescuing Justice and Equality*. Cambridge, MA: Harvard University Press.
Cohen, G.A. 2009. *Why Not Socialism?* Princeton: Princeton University Press.
Cohen, G.A. 2011. *On the Currency of Egalitarian Justice*. Princeton: Princeton University Press.
Cohen, G.A. 2013. *Finding Oneself in the Other*. Princeton: Princeton University Press.
Cohen, Joshua. 1982. "Review of Karl Marx's Theory of History." *Journal of Philosophy* 79(5): 253–73.
Furner, James. 2011. "Marx's Sketch of Communist Society in *The German Ideology* and the Problems of Occupational Confinement and Occupational Identity." *Philosophy and Social Criticism* 37(2): 189–215.
Furner, James. 2015. "Marx with Kant on Exploitation." *Contemporary Political Theory* 14(1): 23–44.
Furner, James. 2018. *Marx on Capitalism: The Interaction-Recognition-Antinomy Thesis*. Leiden: Brill.
Levine, Andrew, and Erik Olin Wright. 1980. "Rationality and Class Struggle." *New Left Review* 1(123): 47–68.
Sayer, Derek. 1987. *The Violence of Abstraction: The Analytical Foundations of Historical Materialism*. Oxford: Basil Blackwell.
Vrousalis, Nicholas. 2015. *The Political Philosophy of G. A. Cohen: Back to Socialist Basics*. London: Bloomsbury.

31
FREDRIC JAMESON (1934–)

Robert T. Tally Jr.

Fredric Jameson is the leading Marxist literary and cultural critic in the United States and, arguably, in the English-speaking world in the late 20th and early 21st centuries. In a career that spans more than sixty years, Jameson has produced some twenty-five books and well over a hundred essays in which he has demonstrated the versatility and power of Marxist criticism in analyzing and evaluating an enormous range of cultural phenomena, from literary texts to architecture, art history, cinema, economic formations, psychology, social theory, urban studies and utopianism, to mention but a few. As Colin MacCabe has observed, "nothing cultural is alien to him" (1992, ix).

Jameson's complete oeuvre might be summed up as "a continuous and lifelong meditation on narrative, on its basic structures, its relationship to the reality it expresses, and its epistemological value when compared with other, more abstract and philosophical modes of understanding" (Jameson 1971, 173), the very words Jameson himself used to describe György Lukács's career. But Jameson is not merely an American Lukács, even if he shares with this predecessor a commitment to formal enquiry bolstered by a powerfully Hegelian historical dialectic. Jameson's vast range of interest and prodigious learning has enabled him to authoritatively weigh in on an extraordinary number of topics and debates, such that it seems that Jameson's criticism has remained at the cutting edge of every literary and cultural movement to appear in the late 20th century. In many respects, however, Jameson's work has remained remarkably consistent even as he ventured into always novel areas of cultural theory and practice over more than six decades. With each new cultural or theoretical phenomenon encountered – existentialism, structuralism, semiotics, poststructuralist theory, deconstruction, third cinema, postmodern architecture, postcolonialism, globalization and so on – Jameson has advanced and built upon his ecumenically Marxist theory. In his own version of the Hegelian *Aufhebung*, Jameson's writings simultaneously cancel, preserve and elevate the objects of cultural criticism.

Jameson is at once undoubtedly *avant-garde* and seemingly old-fashioned. His project analyzes and evaluates the cultural landscape with an almost up-to-the-minute calibration, while always situating these interventions in a consistent yet flexible and complex system through which may be glimpsed that totality that ultimately gives meaning to each discrete element within it. Yet Jameson has insisted upon the value of formal analysis, paying particular attention to matter of style (even descending to the level of individual sentences), a practice that might have appeared to be retrograde in the face of the fashionable theories, new historicisms and cultural studies of the day. In this way, Jameson seems to be a hip, ultra-contemporary postmodern theorist and a traditional, almost 19th-century thinker, all at the same time. Among the wide variety of concepts and practices for which Jameson is best known, his commitment to a properly Marxist cultural criticism, his conception of the political unconscious in literature, his extraordinarily influential theories of postmodernism, and his concept of cognitive mapping stand out prominently.

Marxism as the Untranscendable Horizon of Contemporary Thinking

A number of important 20th-century, European Marxist theorists were first introduced to American audiences through Jameson's work. Jameson's earliest writings on Sartre in the 1950s critically assessed France's leading intellectual at the very moment when Sartrean existentialism would become an influential presence in American literature and philosophy. During the 1960s, and culminating in his monumental 1971 opus, *Marxism and Form*, Jameson was among the first in the United States to write about such thinkers as Adorno, Benjamin, Bloch and Lukács, often before their works had been translated into English. Then, as a scholar of French and German culture so attuned to 20th-century European thought, Jameson was ideally positioned to recognize and respond to the explosion of theory in the 1970s. In *The Prison-House of Language* (1972), *Fables of Aggression* (1979) and *The Political Unconscious* (1981), he deftly articulated such topics as the linguistic turn in literature and philosophy, the concepts of desire and national allegory, and the problems of interpretation and transcoding in a decade when continental theory was beginning to transform literary studies in the English-speaking world. Jameson's essays of the 1970s and early 1980s gave insight into the ostensibly strange, new ideas associated with structuralism, poststructuralism, psychoanalysis, semiotics and critical theory.

Jameson's early works were self-conscious attempts to bring various traditions of what would become known as Western Marxism into the critical discussions taking place in the United States and elsewhere. Beginning with his first book, a seemingly apolitical investigation of Sartre's style, Jameson explored a Marxist tradition of cultural criticism largely unknown to American readers. In his second and third books, Jameson explicitly attempted to introduce German and French critical theory to an audience that not only had little to no native, operable, Marxian intellectual culture, but whose popular view of Marxism was at best simplistic and at worst a grotesque misrepresentation.

> The whole ambition of *Marxism and Form* [was] to make available in English some of those traditions, and to make it more difficult for people to entertain these clichés and caricatural ideas of what Marxism was on the cultural level.
>
> *(in Jameson 2007b, 154)*

Marxism and Form included lengthy chapters on Adorno, Lukács and Sartre's *Critique of Dialectical Reason*, with slightly briefer discussions of Benjamin, Marcuse and Bloch, and concluded with a long, programmatic essay on the prospects and character of a truly dialectical criticism. In *The Prison-House of Language*, published one year later and originally conceived as part of the overall project of *Marxism and Form*, Jameson addresses Russian formalism and French structuralism, examining from a Marxist perspective the "linguistic turn" in critical theory made possible by Ferdinand de Saussure's influential *Course in General Linguistics*. In the three early books, then, Jameson established himself as one of the leading critics of continental criticism and theory, largely through his engagement with other writers. Although he was not literally translating works from French or German into English, Jameson here fulfilled the task of the translator by bringing these foreign ideas across the linguistic, philosophical and historical divide and making them available for use on new shores.

Marxism and Form, along with *The Prison-House of Language*, established Jameson as both a leading Marxist intellectual and one of the most prominent literary critics in the United States. At a moment when "theory" was beginning to infiltrate major academic literary journals and university curricula, Jameson's critical interventions were both timely and transformational. In his writings, Jameson coolly assessed the shifting territories and terminologies associated with continental theory, as well as its influence on more traditional forms of literary criticism, while he energetically lobbied for the priority of a Marxist approach. In a seminal 1971 essay, "Metacommentary," Jameson attempted to outflank in advance many of the emerging methodologies by observing that the literary text, by virtue of its inherently social production and existence in language, comes to us as an always and already interpreted thing. As such, any particular interpretative method – New Critical, psychoanalytic, semiotic, deconstructive etc. – limits itself to a particular kind of hermeneutic model that cannot but ignore a more basic question of why we need to interpret in the first place (see 2008, 7). Any commentary upon a given literary text must involve metacommentary, which for Jameson stands as another code word for the project of dialectical criticism itself. Ian Buchanan has suggested that metacommentary is a cornerstone of the entire Jamesonian enterprise (Buchanan 2006, 12–16), and, although Jameson refrains from emphasizing the specifically Marxian content of his argument there, in this early and quite public intervention Jameson serves notice that the only theoretical practice capable of making sense of literature, which itself represents various attempts to make sense of one's experience in an unrepresentable social totality, is Marxism.

Borrowing a well-known expression from Sartre, Jameson names Marxism as the "untranscendable horizon" of critical thinking in the contemporary world.[1] Elsewhere, he also asserts that history itself is this "untranscendable horizon"; but it amounts to the same thing, as Marxism is the preeminent discourse by which History with a capital "H" might be disclosed. In his 1979 essay "Marxism and Historicism," Jameson invokes this conception as the basis for his eclectic or holistic embrace of other literary theories and methods within his own Marxist framework. Noting that various schools of interpretation focus upon certain themes – for example, language or communication for structuralism, desire for Freudianism, temporality for phenomenological approaches, archetypes for myth criticism and so on – Jameson explains that no intelligent contemporary Marxism will wish to exclude or repudiate any of the themes just listed, which all in their various ways designate objective zones in the fragmentation of contemporary life. Marxism's "transcendence" of these other methods therefore does not spell the abolition or dissolution of their privileged objects of study, but rather the demystification of the various frameworks or strategies of containment by means of which each could lay claim to being a total and self-sufficient interpretive system. To affirm the priority of Marxist analysis as that of some ultimate and untranscendable semantic horizon – namely the horizon of the *social* – thus implies that all other interpretive systems conceal a *seam* that strategically seals them off from the social totality of which they are a part and constitutes their object of study as an apparently closed phenomenon (2008, 452).

Whereas linguistic, psychological, ethical, or political methodologies and theories are still valuable inasmuch as they provide a handle by which to grasp these extremely important elements of social experience, only Marxism, properly understood, aims at apprehending the social totality that both conditions individual experience and evades individual perception.

The Political Unconscious

A similar theory is outlined in the opening pages of *The Political Unconscious: Narrative as a Socially Symbolic Act*, in which Jameson conceives of Marxism as

> that "untranscendable horizon" that subsumes such apparently antagonistic or incommensurable critical operations, assigning them an undoubted sectoral validity with itself, and thus at once canceling and preserving them.
>
> *(1981, 10)*

The aim is ultimately to disclose the unseen or repressed historical dimension of both lived experience and the representations of reality in literary and cultural texts. But, as Jameson makes clear, history cannot be experienced and understood in itself, as a thing or even as a story, but may only be uncovered through the processes of narrative, which, famously, Jameson takes to be "the central function or *instance* of the human mind" (1981, 13). Drawing upon Althusser's conception, itself derived from Spinoza, of the "absent cause," Jameson proposes that

> history is *not* a text, not a narrative, master or otherwise, but that, as an absent cause, it is inaccessible to us except in textual form, and that our approach to it and to the Real itself necessarily passes through its prior textualization, its narrativization in the political unconscious.
>
> *(1981, 35)*

Working through the phases or horizons of textual interpretation, from the timely symbolic act to broader social system and on to the vast spatiotemporal territory of human history, the hermeneutic process of *The Political Unconscious* arrives at "a space in which History itself becomes the ultimate ground as well as the untranscendable limit of our understanding in general and our textual interpretations in particular" (1981, 100). But for Marxists history must be understood as "the experience of Necessity," no longer in terms of its content (as in an older discourse of "needs," such as food and shelter) but as

> the inexorable *form* of events. . . . History is what hurts, it is what refuses desire and sets inexorable limits to individual as well as collective praxis, which its 'ruses' turn into grisly and ironic reversals of their overt intentions.
>
> *(1981, 102)*

Understood in this way, the methodological and hermeneutic program of *The Political Unconscious* to uncover the historical dimension that had been obscured or repressed in cultural texts themselves, as in other interpretive practices, may be seen as a critique of ideology or false consciousness, however much Jameson, perhaps rightly, wishes to avoid the implications of these older slogans in other respects. In disclosing the narrative of history, the critic may also orient his or her vision toward a utopian alternative.

In the conclusion, revealingly titled "The Dialectic of Utopia and Ideology," Jameson discusses how his innovative conception of a political unconscious is also very much a part of the "classical" Marxian ideology-critique and points toward a comprehensive sense of class consciousness. But Jameson's position expands and refines this project, proposing that "*all* class consciousness," including that of the ruling class, is fundamentally utopian, insofar as it expresses "the unity of a collectivity" in an allegorical or figurative manner (1981, 289–91). It becomes clear that even the reactionary or conservative political positions of a class (and, of course, of the narratives produced by members of that class) maintain a utopian kernel that cannot be ignored by a properly dialectical criticism. Criticizing the moralism that he finds objectionable in many radical philosophies and methods, Jameson avers that "any Marxist analysis of culture . . . can no longer be content with its demystifying vocation to unmask and to demonstrate the ways in which a cultural artifact fulfills a specific ideological mission," but must seek "to project" a cultural object's "simultaneously Utopian power" (1981, 291). Hence, he identifies "bad faith" on the part of Marxists or other critics who neglect that ultimate lesson of the dialectic, that is, the dialectical reversal, in which the negative and the positive may be combined in the unity of opposites. In apprehending the coexistence of both positive and negative, utopian and ideological, one also concedes that the work, as well as the interpreter, is situated within the nightmare of history. Jameson's political unconscious may be seen as another means by which we orient ourselves within and attempt to map the social totality.

Postmodernism

Fearlessly and unexpectedly wading into the troubled waters of the postmodernism debates in the early to mid-1980s, Jameson immediately became the central theorist of this famously decentered cultural phenomenon, and his books and essays of this era addressed the postmodern in art, architecture, cinema, literature, philosophy, politics, social theory and urban studies, to name just a few of the areas. His *Postmodernism, or, the Cultural Logic of Late Capitalism* (1991), which incorporated his famous 1984 essay of that name as its first chapter, helped to reorient the postmodernism debates; moreover, Jameson demonstrated the power of Marxist theoretical practice to make sense of the system underlying the discrete and seemingly unrelated phenomena. By the early 1990s, Jameson had become an unavoidable theorist and critic for anyone engaged in contemporary literary and cultural studies, broadly conceived. Grounding the seemingly groundless postmodernism in the material condition of a postcolonial epoch of globalization, as well as in the economics of postindustrial capital and financialization, Jameson's work helped to redefine the millennial moment, the ramped-up war on terror and the pervasive uncertainty attendant to the present historical conjuncture.

During this time, Jameson not only offered a nuanced and rather generous reading of postmodernism, which in contrast to Habermas's intervention did not ultimately reject the *nouveau* theory in favor of a retrofitted Enlightenment sensibility, but which, in Jameson's words, attempted to "outflank" it, to force postmodernism to come to terms with its historical situation and, thus, to incorporate it into a properly Marxist, dialectical system of thought. Unlike some of postmodernism's critics on the left, such as Terry Eagleton or Alex Callinicos (to name two of the best), Jameson did not reject postmodernism or the claims of postmodernity; on the contrary, at times he might have been justly accused of celebrating postmodernism. With respect to postmodernism, Jameson is less interested in whether postmodern art or theory is a positive or negative development and more interested in what it represents to our ongoing investigations of the social totality or world system. Postmodernism also clearly indicates something historical, and for Jameson the concept has value as a way of periodizing our present situation, of making it available to us as a meaningful conception of our own place in a broader history, which is one of the crucial ideas he had suggested in his essay "Periodizing the 60s" (Jameson 2008, 512–13). In the evocative title to what is probably his most famous essay (and later book-title), Jameson supplies his answer: postmodernism is the cultural logic of late capitalism.

Possibly the most striking aspect of Jameson's approach to postmodernism is his insistence that it be imagined as a system at all. For both enthusiasts and detractors of postmodern art, architecture, literature and theory, postmodernism was understood as unsystematic and, moreover, as anti-systematic, as in Jean-François Lyotard's argument that postmodern thought eschews those grand narratives of modernity, which are themselves then conceptualized as systems (Lyotard 1984). Further, by connecting the apparently disparate phenomena to a global economic system, late or multinational capitalism, Jameson grounds the concept in what the older Marxist tradition understood as the economic base. Once postmodernism is envisioned as "the cultural logic of late capitalism," Jameson's dialectical critique of this or that postmodern characteristic or text takes on greater historical significance, for the seemingly local or isolated occurrence can be situated in a vaster structure or narrative. By periodizing the postmodern, assessing it as a cultural dominant and identifying many of its key features (e.g., the waning of affect, a nostalgia for the present etc.), Jameson was able to "outflank" the previous theories of the postmodern and to *capture* postmodernism for Marxism, as Perry Anderson has put it (1998, 54).

Cognitive Mapping

At the conclusion of his influential essay on postmodernism, Jameson famously calls for a project of cognitive mapping on a global scale (see 1991, 54), and the notion of cognitive mapping has become one of Jameson's most celebrated concepts. Although situated in the context of a "new spatiality implicit in the postmodern" (1991, 418), the idea had been with Jameson a long time. For example, Jameson had used the figure of the map, more or less metaphorically connected to narrative itself, as a means of projecting a totality as early as the 1960s and 1970s. And although he refrained from using the term as much in his post-2000 writings, the idea of cognitive mapping can be gleaned in such later works as *Valences of the Dialectic* (2010), *Antinomies of Realism* (2013) and *Raymond Chandler: Detections of Totality* (2016b). Arguably, in fact, Jameson's entire critical endeavor could be connected to the project of cognitive mapping (see Tally 2014).

Jameson's famous illustration of the postmodern transmogrification of social space is found in his analysis of the Westin Bonaventure hotel in Los Angeles, a postmodern edifice in which the traditional markers of entrances or exits, indeed of inside or outside, are bewilderingly obscured. After discussing the floor plan, elevators, lobby and other quotidian elements of the place, Jameson concludes that "this latest mutation in space – postmodern hyperspace – has finally succeeded in transcending the capacities of the individual human body to locate itself, to organize its immediate surroundings perceptually, and cognitively to map its position in a mappable external world" (1991, 44). Jameson quickly shifts from the perceptual confusion of an individual in a scarcely legible lived space, which after all is a fairly common though no less angst-ridden experience known as "being lost," to the far vaster, abstract space of a global system, which is nevertheless the absent cause or conditioning horizon of this discrete building in Los Angeles in which the individual subject feels "out of place." A sort of existentialist crisis of representation, this cartographic anxiety requires the coordination of one's individual perspective with some sense of the larger social totality.

Jameson's proposed solution, an aesthetic of cognitive mapping, famously combines the concepts of "wayfinding" and "imageability" in the urban planner Kevin Lynch's *The Image of the City* with Althusser's theory of ideology as "the representation of the subject's *Imaginary* relationship to his or her *Real* conditions of existence." In Lynch's analysis, the anxiety an individual experiences in not being able to navigate the urban environment is heightened by the lack of clear landmarks or paths, so the pedestrian seeks to form a mental image of the city for use in moving about its spaces. But moving beyond the simpler navigation of a building's or a city's spaces, Jameson connects this cognitive mapping with Althusser's theory of ideology, in which one may form a "situational representation" of the individual subject in relation to "that vaster and properly unrepresentable totality which is the ensemble of society's structures as a whole" (1991, 51). Cognitive mapping, while still grounded in the material and spatial relations of postmodern lived experience, is thus another attempt to represent that vast, social totality. In this sense, Jameson has conceded that *cognitive mapping* "was in reality nothing but a code word for 'class consciousness' . . . of a new and hitherto undreamed of kind" (1991, 418), one suited to the vicissitudes of worldwide proletarianization in the epoch of globalization.

The 21st century has called for new ways of imagining both the past and the future, as Jameson nicely indicates in the title of his extended analysis of the utopian impulse, *Archaeologies of the Future* (2005), while it has also opened up a space for renewed attention to such putatively superannuated subjects as modernism, the dialectic itself, Hegel and Marx, and perhaps realism, allegory and myth, to follow the chronologically complicated trajectory of Jameson's recent and forthcoming books, including what remains to be published in Jameson's not yet complete project, titled *The Poetics of Social Forms* (see Cevasco 2012, 89). Throughout all of this, Jameson's mapping project has emphasized the need for a sense of totality, which in turn has made possible new ways of understanding and engaging with the world system in the era of late capitalism. From that point, the dimly descried or implicit alternatives to "what is" are not only imaginable in some sense, but are made to appear almost inevitable, even if we cannot quite delineate the contours of this utopian vision.

Conclusion

As this condensed *précis* demonstrates, Jameson has consistently found himself near the center of the most current cultural and critical controversies of the day, moving with remarkable agility through the theoretical thickets of existentialism, structuralism, poststructuralism, postmodernism and globalization. Yet, throughout all of these interventions, Jameson has been among the more resolutely traditional Marxist theorists and critics. For instance, when faced with a rising tide of virulent anti-Hegelianism from both the left and the right, Jameson has embraced both Hegel and the dialectic, going so far as to reinterpret contemporary theories and critical practices as merely so many instances of the dialectical unity of opposites, thereby absorbing any errant positions in his overall system. Moreover, to speak more generally, Jameson's commitment to a properly literary critical project, even when he ventures into other disciplinary fields, might also be deemed old fashioned. In a somewhat post-literary age, with media theory and cultural studies usurping the roles previously played by literary criticism and literary history, Jameson's criticism and theory, especially in its attention to narrative, form, genre and tropes, appear to represent an almost perversely Luddite perspective. Even when he has ventured into architecture, film, visual arts, or media criticism, Jameson has always done so as a literary critic, paying closest attention to the forms and functions normally associated with narrative fiction. Despite his remarkable breadth of cultural inquiry, Jameson in some respects remains the student of Erich Auerbach, his teacher in graduate school at Yale University in the 1950s, and of the great philological tradition of the early 20th century. From his earliest writings to his most recent, Jameson has been concerned above all with the ways in which individual expressions relate to forms, which in turn derive their force and significance from the totality of social, political and economic relations at work in a given mode of production. For Jameson, the critical perspective peculiar to literary criticism enables a properly Marxist critique of the world system.

Note

1. "I regard Marxism the untranscendable philosophy for our time" (Sartre 1982, 822).

Bibliography

Anderson, Perry. 1998. *The Origins of Postmodernity*. London: Verso.

Buchanan, Ian. 2006. *Fredric Jameson: Live Theory*. London: Continuum.

Callinicos, Alex. 1989. *Against Postmodernism: A Marxist Critique*. Cambridge: Polity Press.

Cevasco, Maria Elisa. 2012. "Imagining a Space That Is Outside: An Interview with Fredric Jameson." *The Minnesota Review* 78: 83–94.

Eagleton, Terry. 1996. *The Illusions of Postmodernism*. London: Verso.
Habermas, Jürgen. 1987. *The Philosophical Discourse of Modernity: Twelve Lectures*. Cambridge, MA: MIT Press.
Jameson, Fredric. 1961. *Sartre: The Origins of a Style*. New Haven: Yale University Press.
Jameson, Fredric. 1968. "On Politics and Literature." *Salmagundi* 2(3): 17–26.
Jameson, Fredric. 1971. *Marxism and Form: Twentieth-Century Dialectical Theories of Literature*. Princeton: Princeton University Press.
Jameson, Fredric. 1972. *The Prison-House of Language: A Critical Account of Structuralism and Russian Formalism*. Princeton: Princeton University Press.
Jameson, Fredric. 1979. *Fables of Aggression: Wyndham Lewis, the Modernist as Fascist*. Berkeley: University of California Press.
Jameson, Fredric. 1981. *The Political Unconscious: Narrative as a Socially Symbolic Act*. Ithaca: Cornell University Press.
Jameson, Fredric. 1990a. *Late Marxism: Adorno, or, the Persistence of the Dialectic*. London: Verso.
Jameson, Fredric. 1990b. *Signatures of the Visible*. London and New York: Routledge.
Jameson, Fredric. 1991. *Postmodernism, or, the Cultural Logic of Late Capitalism*. London: Verso.
Jameson, Fredric. 1998a. *The Cultural Turn: Selected Writings on the Postmodern, 1983–1998*. London: Verso.
Jameson, Fredric. 1998b. *Brecht and Method*. London: Verso.
Jameson, Fredric. 2001. *A Singular Modernity: Essay on the Ontology of the Present*. London: Verso.
Jameson, Fredric. 2005. *Archaeologies of the Future: The Desire Called Utopia and Other Science Fictions*. London: Verso.
Jameson, Fredric. 2007a. *The Modernist Papers*. London: Verso.
Jameson, Fredric. 2007b. *Jameson on Jameson: Conversations on Cultural Marxism*. Edited by Ian Buchanan. Durham, NC: Duke University Press.
Jameson, Fredric. 2008 (1988). *The Ideologies of Theory*. London: Verso.
Jameson, Fredric. 2009. *Valences of the Dialectic*. London: Verso.
Jameson, Fredric. 2010. *The Hegel Variations: On the Phenomenology of Spirit*. London: Verso.
Jameson, Fredric. 2011. *Representing Capital: A Reading of Volume One*. London: Verso.
Jameson, Fredric. 2013. *The Antinomies of Realism*. London: Verso.
Jameson, Fredric. 2015. *The Ancients and the Postmoderns: On the Historicity of Forms*. London: Verso.
Jameson, Fredric. 2016a. *An American Utopia: Dual Power and the Universal Army*. Edited by Slavoj Žižek. London: Verso.
Jameson, Fredric. 2016b. *Raymond Chandler: The Detections of Totality*. London: Verso.
Lyotard, Jean-François. 1984 (1979). *The Postmodern Condition: A Report on Knowledge*. Minneapolis: University of Minnesota Press.
MacCabe, Colin. 1992. "Preface." In Jameson. *The Geopolitical Aesthetic: Cinema and Space in the World System*, ix–xvi. Bloomington and London: Indiana University Press and the British Film Institute.
Sartre, Jean-Paul. 1982 (1960). *Critique of Dialectical Reason*. Vol. 1. London: Verso.
Tally, Robert T., Jr. 2014. *Fredric Jameson: The Project of Dialectical Criticism*. London: Pluto.
Wegner, Phillip E. 2014. *Periodizing Jameson: Dialectics, the University, and the Desire for Narrative*. Evanston: Northwestern University Press.

32
DANIEL BENSAÏD (1946–2010)

Darren Roso

Born in Toulouse to a Franco-Algerian Jewish family in 1946, Bensaïd had his formative political experience amid a battle within the French Communist Party. This ended in his expulsion in 1965, and his participation in the upheavals of May 1968. He was a founding member of the Jeunesse Communiste Révolutionnaire and the Ligue Communiste Révolutionnaire – of which he became a leading theoretician. Integral to the official Communist thinking of Bensaïd's time was the notion that history is pushed forward solely by the mechanics of capitalist development: an unbending line from the French Revolution to the Russian, and a communism beyond capitalism. Orthodox Trotskyism also had weaknesses: a philosophical vocabulary that extolled the virtues of time. Bensaïd carried out an immanent critique of this optimism and its central assumptions of a simple time-lag between the "subjective factor" in history and the latter's overripe objective conditions and of the long-term tendency for the working class to become homogenous and conscious as a result of industrial development.

There was a qualitative breakthrough in his theoretical work at the end of the 1980s, when he aligned interventionist politics with the notion of discordant temporalities. During his tenure at the philosophy department of the University of Paris-8, he lectured on Marx's *Capital, Grundrisse* and *Theories of Surplus-Value*, accumulating the material for his masterworks *Marx l'intempestif* (Bensaïd 2002) and *La Discordance des Temps* (1995). He became one of the most creative Marxists in France, developing a framework in which three interlocking themes were fundamental: messianic reason, Marx's discordant times and politics as a strategic art.

Messianic Reason

Bensaïd was perhaps drawn to Jewish messianic thought by Fritz Mauthner's *Critique du langage* (Bensaïd 2013, 285). Bensaïd's first printed mention of Walter Benjamin appears to be in *Stratégie et partie* (1986), but his engagement with Benjamin bore fruit only with the collapse of Stalinism in the Eastern bloc. His book *Walter Benjamin, sentinelle messianique* (1990) grappled with a specific problem: if history marches forward, why are there periods of obvious retreat? This was a major reason why Benjamin's "On the Concept of History" had attracted the attention of a number of intellectuals in the Fourth International. Michael Löwy, for example, hailed the work as the greatest breakthrough since Marx's "Theses on Feuerbach" (Löwy 1985, 59). Bensaïd drew on Benjamin to represent history as a terrain of uncertainty and bifurcation. Benjamin's critique of the "homogenous and empty time" of historical progress made way for a messianic vision in which history, according to Bensaïd, was transformed "from a time of necessity to a time of possibilities" (Bensaïd 2002, 88). "Messianic time" is a notion that admits the possibility of absolute ruptures in history, a notion that Bensaïd tied to his concern with a more classical Marxist vision of political struggle.

Benjamin's temporal categories are structured around the present, within which the past and the future are embedded and the immediately possible is contested. "In the constellation of eras and events," Bensaïd wrote, "the present indefinitely appeals to another present, in a discontinuous interplay of echoes and resonances" (Bensaïd 2002, 86). This triply organized present scans "the field of what is potential from the vantage point of its 'maybes,' and invents new opportunities" (Bensaïd 2002, 55). Bensaïd contrasted Benjamin's Messiah with Ernst Bloch's Utopia. For the latter, history was like an unsinkable ship in a tempest – a vessel rising and falling on the waves, but always reaching its pre-determined destination. In Utopia, the future, the approaching port, is the dominant category. For Benjamin, the constant navigation – the present – is key. Bloch's position downplays political strategy; Benjamin's messianism contains an interventionist strategic predisposition: politics attains primacy over history.

The maritime metaphor begins to break down when we think about history. A ship's navigator can find their fixed position, their "present," through aggregating "circles of position" through observing celestial bodies in all directions. But with historical memory, the present constantly redefines and rearranges past bodies because all historical writing is partisan. History can be written from the vantage point of the victors or the vanquished, for example. More than that, objects of memory are not fixed like the stars, but in need of rearrangement: as we confront new situations, old reference points often need to shift if we are to make (correct) sense of the present. And exactly which reference points are relevant is always contested. As Benjamin argued, this means "appropriating a memory as it flashes up in a moment of danger," sparking the flames of hope in the past in order to wrestle the stock of tradition away from those that threaten it (Benjamin 2003, 391).

From Benjamin, Bensaïd was led to Péguy, Proust, Blanqui, Kafka and the Surrealists. He fashioned a new representation of history that is an infernal repetition of catastrophe, unless subjected to messianic interruption. Central to messianic reason are concepts that express "the tension and anxiety of what is merely possible" (Bensaïd 2002, 88). In this representation of history, optimism and pessimism, the possible and the actual, are locked in a tense dialectical embrace. For Bensaïd, strategic thought aspires to resolve the contradiction, neither succumbing to a sense of historical inevitability nor becoming lost in some voluntarist notion of a will to power that could overcome the limitations of the real world.

Bensaïd was responding to a century marked more by trauma than triumph. With the defeats of the workers' movement and increasing neoliberal atomization, class memory had suffered as a result of the slow political, social and cultural breakup of its bearers, becoming Marrano-like (Spanish Jews forced to convert to Catholicism, but who continued to practice their Judaic faith in secret). Small, heretical revolutionary traditions certainly contained memories worth defending. But they had to be brought to bear on new developments, Bensaïd believed, because historical memory doesn't rejuvenate spontaneously just because the time is ripe. This was the Péguyist dimension of Bensaïd's thought: commodified modernity is an anti-memory that leaves tradition to the ruins of history.

The "obscure disaster" (the collapse of the Eastern Bloc) reversed the situation classical Marxists had faced at the turn of the 20th century, when "optimism had only been possible in the camp of the rising working class and its theorists" and when the destructive tendencies of capitalism were balanced by the elation of the struggle – the "the auspicious and victorious rise of the working class in its trade union and political action," as Luxemburg wrote (Badiou 2013; Luxemburg 2015, Kindle loc. 5065). By contrast, the end of the 20th century brought melancholy rather than jubilation.

Bensaïd wanted to safeguard "socialism from below" from the ruins of Stalinism (Draper 1966). He went a step beyond Fourth International leader Ernest Mandel, who, "[g]lued to his principle of hope, his mythology, refusing to bury the world of yesterday and reconsider the commitment of a lifetime," thought that the fall of the Berlin Wall marked the end of a dark historical interlude and that "the revolution was starting up again at the point where it had halted with the murder of Rosa Luxemburg" (Bensaïd 2013, 285, 264). In contrast to this optimism, Bensaïd wrote, in a 1991 LCR manifesto, that history "does not know parentheses" (Ligue Communiste Révolutionnaire 1991, 30). The cycle opened by the Russian Revolution was over; no new popular revolution in the East could be expected to reconnect to October.

Marx's Discordant Times

Bensaïd's reading of Marx in the late 1980s and early 1990s was an attempt "to rediscover the categories that would make it possible to face a major crisis of historical time" (Bensaïd 2013, 287). His philosophical vocabulary expanded to include notions such as "*bifurcation*," "*contretemps*" (for our purposes, this can be translated as "discordance of times"), "*the untimely*," "*the melancholic wager*," "*slow impatience*" and "*broken time*," which theoretically align history to strategy and rid it of determinist residues. The deployment of this philosophical vocabulary was bound up with real world political problems.

Bensaïd recognized that the defeats inflicted on the workers' movement weren't momentary setbacks, but of a prolonged nature. His concern with discordant times was twofold. First, he rejected deterministic readings of class struggle (the idea that workers will inevitably enter into struggle and become politically conscious of their historic tasks). In reality, exploitation brings uneven development: sections of the working class enter the struggle at different moments and with varying intensities, retreat into passivity, don't enter the struggle at key moments, or even end up supporting counter-revolutionary movements. Second, he argued that Marx's *Capital* theoretically represented a "contradictory conceptual organization of social time," which deconstructed a transcendental view of time and consolidated a "representation of a rigorously immanent history" (Bensaïd 2002, 74). Marx's conceptualization of capital's temporalities made historical development intelligible as a field in which strategic intervention can take place. The theoretical assault on sociological determinism and on faith in the organic development of class consciousness opened a new window into Marx's writing of history, which was a theoretical revolution introducing *contretemps* and *non-contemporaneity*. Insisting on the discordance of temporalities – that is, that no concrete social formation is reducible to the homogeneity of its dominant production relation and that the unification of the subalterns into a historic bloc is a political fact to fight for, not a preordained eventuality, Bensaïd's interpretation of Marx placed politics at the point where discordant times intersect, aligning politics to *contretemps*.

The central claim of this interpretation is that Marx rejected a fetishized (religious) representation of history. Marx's criticism of the speculative philosophy of history – his polemics against the young Hegelians in *The Holy Family* and *The German Ideology* and his demolition of Proudhon's ideological representation of history in *The Poverty of Philosophy* (1847) – was pioneering in this regard. Bensaïd's interpretation owed much to Benjamin: history and time do nothing. Politics has primacy over, yet is immanent in, a history shorn of its religious representation.

Bensaïd was aware that Marx left only a few comments about his method. Where he did leave notes, as in the introduction to the *Grundrisse*, they were undeveloped. Notes six and seven were most striking from Bensaïd's point of view, and complemented Trotsky's notion of uneven and combined development (Bensaïd 2007). Note six spoke of "*the uneven development of material production relative to e.g. artistic development*. In general, the concept of progress [is] not to be conceived in the usual abstractness" (*G*: 109). Note seven put necessity into a dialectical relation with contingency, without which there could be neither history nor events.

Marx's critique of historical reason went hand in hand with the critique of political economy. From the *1844 Manuscripts* to *Capital*, his research project had deciphered the rhythms immanent to the logic of capital. He forged a new representation of time as a social relation. *Capital* unpacks the multiplicity of temporalities within the capitalist mode of production. The first volume presents time in terms of capitalist production: "[The] disciplinary methods reveal a linear time . . . an 'evolutive' time [that correlated to] a new way of administering time and making it useful, by segmentation, seriation, synthesis and totalisation" (Foucault 1976, 160). The second volume presents the cyclical time of circulation. And the last volume presents the organic time of capital, the unity of the time of production and circulation. With respect to cycles, turnovers and crises, Bensaïd made use of Henryk Grossman's insight: "First of all, [Marx] had to fashion all the conceptual categories relative to the time factor: cycle, turnover, turnover time, turnover cycle. He criticized classical theory for having neglected the time factor" (Bensaïd 2002, 74).

Bensaïd developed his ideas about crisis in *The Time of Crises (and Cherries)* (1995) and his long preface to *Les Crises du capitalisme* (2009). One of the major questions posed by the return of serious economic crises in the 1970s regarded the conditions under which another boom could take place. Bensaïd argued that it is no use prophesying about the system's "final crisis"; Marx demonstrated that capitalist production butts against its own immanent barriers and that crises are inevitable – not that they cannot be overcome. Bensaïd underlined how Marx moved from one determinate abstraction to another, *Capital* moved from a very abstract account of the core features of capitalism toward its concrete appearance by progressively lifting simplifying assumptions and approximating real historical crises: "While a good number of readers believe they have found a complete theory of crises in Volume I or II, Marx never interrupts the dialectic of abstract and concrete, of possibility and actuality, of structure and history" (Bensaïd 2016, 15). Economic crisis is tied to production, circulation and the reproduction of the system and its specific temporalities. But the resolution of a crisis is only partially an economic matter. The material effects of crisis and the discordance of temporalities create the space in which contingent political events in a sense "interrupt" history. Here, class struggle is fundamental: it determines the shape and the outcome of crises. Economic logics determine the "enigmatic patterns of historical time, which is the time of politics" (Bensaïd 2002, 77).

Bensaïd's critique contains two related fronts: opposition to an optimistic sociological determinism and opposition to the philosophical representation of the working class characteristic of Marx's early works. The first rested on a "sociological wager," which speculated that the growth and concentration of industry would result in a corresponding growth in combativity and consciousness of the class. Bensaïd did not agree with this line of argument because it lacked the moment of interventionist political practice. The second, the perilous dialectic of object and subject, of in-itself and for-itself, has philosophical implications. It belongs "to the philosophical representation of the working class characteristic of the early works" (Bensaïd 2002, 115), present in the famous letter to Arnold Ruge of September 1843, in which Marx evokes the "consciousness" that the world – Marx hadn't yet named the working class – "*has to* acquire, even if it does not want to" (*MECW* 3: 144). In the *Introduction to a Contribution to the Critique of Hegel's Philosophy of Right*, the working class was named the emissary of this speculative mission. Bensaïd, however, rejected the idea that the working class is "compelled as proletariat to abolish itself" because its "fate is in some sense determined by its being":

> the *Grundrisse* and *Capital* present themselves as a labor of mourning for ontology, a radical deontologization, after which no space remains for any "world beyond" [*arrière-monde*] whatsoever, any dual content, any dualism of the authentic and the inauthentic, science and ontology. There is no longer any founding contrast between Being and existence, nothing behind which there lies concealed some other thing that does not come to light. The appearance of the commodity, of social labor-time, of classes, is inextricably the appearance and the travesty of their being: Being is resolved into existence, class essence into class relations. Reduced to a pathetic philosophical incantation, the obscure disclosure of the in-itself in the for-itself evaporates in its own conceptual impotence.
>
> *(Bensaïd 2002, 116)*

Again, Bensaïd's theoretical arguments were responses to the downturn of the 1980s and the collapse of the Berlin Wall. These events exposed a problem for the Marxist left. The standard economic optimism (combining determinist evaluations of rising working-class consciousness with catastrophist notions of economic crisis) and the more immediate expectations of the political period from 1968 – that the limitations of left-reformism would be exposed, leading workers en masse to revolutionary conclusions – were shown to be misplaced.

Politics as a Strategic Art

Postwar orthodox Trotskyism had made a fetish of Trotsky's *Transitional Program*. But not only is there an absence in history of absolute compulsion, there is also no programmatic bridge that can serve as a substitute in bringing the working class to political consciousness. Though the *Transitional Program* recognizes that political intervention and ideological battles are necessary, it still contains a certain determinism – if only there is the right leadership, then workers, through the course of left reformism exposing itself, will be won to the revolution. Through excessive use, postwar orthodox Trotskyism turned this into a dogma and fell into political idealism. Trotsky's document was mired in a determinist faith:

> [The] laws of history are stronger than the bureaucratic apparatus. . . . As time goes on, their desperate efforts to hold back the wheel of history will demonstrate more clearly to the masses that the crisis of the proletarian leadership . . . can be resolved only by the Fourth International.
>
> *(Trotsky 1974, 74)*

Bensaïd's "strategic art of politics" was an alternative to the uses and abuses of the *Transitional Program*. Mandel, for instance, ended up with the kind of faith in time that Bensaïd rejected. Fetishizing the document meant oscillating between a subjectivist voluntarism and an objectivistic determinism, as Bensaïd explained in *Marx l'intempestif* and in his "Critical Introduction to the Marxism of Ernest Mandel" (2007). The fetish was connected to a vision of history in which the struggles of the working class inevitably led to experiences that would only confirm the correctness of the ideas of orthodox Trotskyism. Bensaïd was critical of this vision, writing:

> Certainly, the owl of Minerva is said to only take flight at dusk, but the difficulties of class consciousness stem much more from the effects of the alienation of labor and commodity fetishism than to a reassuring time lag, suggesting that consciousness will come late, but will necessarily come.
>
> *(Bensaïd 2010, 163)*

In Bensaïd, the discordance of temporalities becomes the key to "strategic reason" – an art of the present and conceptualization of struggle irreducible to sectarianism or opportunism. In the face of each concrete situation, strategic reason chooses between many possibilities. But only through calculated political intervention can the possible emerge from the actual.

Bensaïd broke with the familiar language of positivist Marxism and reaffirmed a vision of politics as an art of the possible. He had a singular political vision compared with contemporaries such as Rancière, Badiou, Laclau and Mouffe, Holloway and Negri. He did not ontologize the emancipatory subject or retreat from politics to ontology (or aesthetics), and he criticized anti-political illusions. He did not think politics was circumscribed to rare events. He did not uncritically praise social movements. He did not dissolve the moment of politics into an amorphous mass of identities. He did not degrade the moment of revolutionary rupture by engaging in vague talk about hegemonic processes. He thought of politics as a strategic art, an organizer of emancipatory horizons that proposed concrete arguments about how to win.

Integral to Bensaïd's Marxism was his concern with "the broken time of politics and strategy" (Bensaïd 2002, 23). In the thick of the mêlée of "time stretched and torn apart; concentrated, staccato, broken" was the strategic operator – a political form that could organize retreats and advances, take the initiative and mediate discordant times – with a thorough implantation in the working class. Political forms are historically specific, whether propaganda organizations, leagues or mass parties, but each in their own way form part of a conceptual network structuring the political field, which includes class consciousness, the relations of class forces, alliances and the revolutionary crisis.

Lenin and the Bolsheviks showed that political power can be seized by the working class, that strategic orientation is possible, that an unfavorable balance of forces can be upset and that the illusory march of time can be broken. The political field is not a linear continuation of social life or a simple reflection of the economic struggle. It condenses and displaces social antagonisms to a higher level because, ultimately, state power has to be confronted if human emancipation is to be realized. Bensaïd's personal notes in *Le spectacle, stade ultime du fétichisme de la marchandise* give a clear picture of his political vision:

> The problem of politics, conceived strategically and not in a bureaucratic way, consists in grasping the junctures of crisis and favourable moments to overturn this asymmetry [between rulers and ruled]. In order to do that, we must accept working in the contradictions and real relations of force, rather than believe, illusorily, to deny them or subtract ourselves from them. Because the subalterns (or the dominated) are not outside of the political domain of struggle and domination is never full and absolute. The outside is always inside. Freedom pierces the very heart of the arrangements of power. Practice brings experience and specific knowledge, capable of providing the arms of an alternative hegemony. And the norms of domination can be broken by an event that results neither from the necessity of the social order, nor from the action of a subject historically predestined, nor from a theological miracle, but from ordering practical political battles, engaging the clutch of the movement that tends to abolish the present state of things.
>
> *(Bensaïd 2011, 40)*

This vision is bound to an appreciation of Lenin's grasp of political representation, mediation and strategic intervention. The emphasis placed upon broken time is very important. The strategic art of politics necessitates a party that can play the role of a "strategic operator" that adjusts to changing situations – putting forward initiatives that rise to the occasion.

This is a positive argument for a politics of the oppressed, explored in depth in *Le pari mélancolique* (1997) and *Éloge de la politique profane* (2008). Generalized commodity fetishism and exploitation turn oppressed producers into physically and intellectually stunted beings. In the "ordinary run of things" submission begets submission. But if the unfolding of time heals no wounds, how can a class subjected to drudgery and alienation emancipate itself? "The answer" – which is common property of the classical Marxist tradition – "is found in political confrontation and class struggle: only struggle can break this vicious circle" (Bensaïd 2002, 105). Political confrontation is a necessary part of the answer to the crisis of historical time because it forges new knowledge and rearranges the historical/memorial landscape as it rallies resistance into a working class aspiration for total control over the world it creates.

The politics of the oppressed must cautiously keep a distance from the state, while not being absolutely outside of it. In his long introduction to *Inventer l'inconnu* (2008) Bensaïd showed how Marx's critique of modernity introduced new conceptions of politics, representation, the state and democracy. But the problems of the relationship between the wage relation, legal form, political representation and bureaucracy have been objects of debate throughout the conflicting histories of Marxism. For Bensaïd, *Democracy Against the State* (the title of Miguel Abensour's book) had to include the strategic moment of struggles for emancipation, which could move beyond the bureaucratic representative state and invent another idea of citizenship and democracy. Socialism strives toward the "withering away" of the state and its replacement by a socialized political power of the producers and oppressed, as a step toward the realization of freedom.

Fins et Suites

Bensaïd's Marxism tied politics to a set of specific theoretical conditions – Benjamin's critique of historical progress and the discordance of times in Marx's research project – in order to refound an anti-deterministic politics, always with an aim to overthrowing the capitalist order. His interventionist political vision is defined by risk; it takes the form of a melancholic wager (an insight he drew from Lucien Goldmann's *The Hidden God*). The wager has a long and subterranean history. Those who recognized the tragic nature of the quest for human liberation often repressed the insight as a sign of weakness; for official Stalinism, tragedy was treason "calculated to subvert the morale of the front lines" (Steiner 1996, 343–44). The melancholic side of the wager is Bensaïd's innovation – it is coupled with the break from optimistic, teleological narratives of Marxism. Left-wing melancholia, a theme now further developed in Enzo Traverso's beautiful book by the same name, is the mark of a generation of revolutionary intellectuals who thought they had the ready-made scientific keys to unlocking the enigmas of emancipation, but who suffered political defeat. The outcome of their experience was a healthy and lucid dose of doubt that did not allow the tragedy inherent in political action to collapse into a distant and conservative melancholy. Bensaïd tells us that time is not on our side, while asking us not to shy away from the calculated political risks required to change the world.

Bibliography

Badiou, Alain. 2013 (1998). *D'un désastre obscur – Droit, Etat, Politique*. La Tour-d'Aigues: l'Aube.
Benjamin, Walter. 2003. "On the Concept of History." In *Selected Writings*, edited by Michael W. Jennings. Vol. 4, 389–400. Cambridge, MA: Harvard University Press.
Bensaïd, Daniel. 1990. *Walter Benjamin: Sentinelle Messianique*. Paris: Plon.
Bensaïd, Daniel. 1995. *La Discordance des temps: Essais sur les crises, les classes, l'histoire*. Paris: Éditions de la passion.
Bensaïd, Daniel. 2002 (1995). *Marx for Our Times*. London: Verso.
Bensaïd, Daniel. 2007. *Eloge de la politique profane*. Paris: Albin Michel.

Bensaïd, Daniel. 2010. "Thirty Years after: A Critical Introduction to the Marxism of Ernest Mandel." In *Strategies of Resistance*, edited by International Institute for Research and Education, 156–67. London: Resistance Books.
Bensaïd, Daniel. 2011. *Le spectacle, stade ultime du fétichisme de la marchandise*. Paris: Éditions Lignes.
Bensaïd, Daniel. 2013. *An Impatient Life*. London: Verso.
Bensaïd, Daniel. 2016. "The Time of Crises (and Cherries)." *Historical Materialism* 24(4): 9–35.
Bensaïd, Daniel, Ugo Palheta, and Julien Salingue. 2016 (1986). *Stratégie et parti*. Paris: Les Prairies ordinaires.
Draper, Hal. 1966. "The Two Souls of Socialism." *New Politics* 5(1): 57–84.
Foucault, Michel. 1976. *Discipline and Punish: The Birth of the Prison*. London: Penguin.
Ligue Communiste Révolutionnaire. 1991. *A la gauche du possible*. Paris: La Breche 1991.
Löwy, Michael. 1985. "Revolution against 'Progress': Walter Benjamin's Romantic Anarchism." *New Left Review* 1(151): 42–59.
Luxemburg, Rosa. 2015a (1913). "The Accumulation of Capital: A Contribution to the Economic Theory of Imperialism." In *The Complete Writings of Rosa Luxemburg*. Volume II: *Economic Writings 2*, edited by Peter Hudis and Paul Le Blanc. London: Verso.
Steiner, George. 1996. *The Death of Tragedy*. New Haven: Yale University Press.
Trotsky, Leon. 1974. *The Transitional Program for Socialist Revolution*. New York: Pathfinder Press.

PART VI

Beyond Marxism?

33

BEYOND MARXISM? THE "CRISIS OF MARXISM" AND THE POST-MARXIST MOMENT

Stathis Kouvelakis

Two centuries after his birth, Marx's image in the mainstream media and academic circles can be summed up by the motto "Marx is alive but Marxism is dead." The Marx who is still alive is usually presented as an "economist" who provided a lucid view of capitalism and of its internal contradictions. This view has periodically re-emerged in the decades that followed the collapse of the Soviet bloc: each time a crisis breaks out, representatives of the mainstream confess that somehow "Marx was right," or, at least, more lucid than those economists who, once more, have proved unable to foresee the coming crisis and its long-term effects in contemporary societies. Thus, shortly after the start of the 2008 recession, Nouriel Roubini, a senior economist for the Clinton administration, the IMF and the World Bank, declared to the *Wall Street Journal*: "Karl Marx had it right. At some point, capitalism can destroy itself" (Roubini 2011). More recently, commenting on the impact of new digital technologies, the Bank of England governor Mark Carney said that "we have exactly the same dynamics as existed 150 years ago – when Karl Marx was scribbling the *Communist Manifesto*" (Drury 2018). Debatable as they might be in terms of their analytical value, such statements reveal however that the idea of a structural contradiction within capitalism still seems inseparable from the name of the author of *Capital*.

The unexpected international success of the French economist Thomas Piketty's book *Capital in the Twenty-first Century* (Piketty 2014) is a deeper symptom of the impact of the Great Recession on mainstream public opinion. Piketty, a self-avowedly non-Marxist supporter of social-democracy, demonstrates with a wealth of empirical data a tendency to the concentration of wealth that is inherent to the "normal" functioning of capitalism. The tendential divergence between the rate of return to capital and the rate of growth leads to social polarization if the state doesn't intervene, via taxation, to attenuate the effects of the accumulation of assets at the top of the social ladder. By contesting the belief in the progressive character of this system, a cornerstone of bourgeois common sense since Bernard Mandeville and Adam Smith, this approach raises an even more serious challenge to the legitimacy of the system than the simple recognition of the inevitability of crises.

Piketty's conclusion is that taxing wealth is necessary to avoid the economic and social instability fueled by the polarization within advanced Western societies between a tiny minority of asset-owners and the working majority. What in previous circumstances would look like a moderate social-democratic redistributionist proposal, and indeed considered as such by Piketty's critics from the left (Duménil and Lévy 2014, 2015; Lordon 2015), proved nevertheless sufficient for the defenders of neoliberal orthodoxy to make its author appear as a "modern Marx" (*The Economist* 2014). It is true that, despite Piketty's firm denial of any Marxian or Marxist influence (Chotiner 2014), the title of the book, as well as its length and long-term historical perspective, indicates at least an implicit ambition to compete with the 19th-century German thinker. Its success – nearly three million copies sold worldwide – resonated strongly with the anti-inequality agenda put forward by the Occupy movement. It confirmed the loss of legitimacy of neoliberalism in the very area in which it has most successfully captured the public mind in its heyday.

The paradox of this renewed acceptance of Marx's vision of capitalism is that it goes together with an almost consensual rejection of any version of the political project defended by its author. The reasons are all too obvious: the collapse of the regimes that claimed his legacy combined with the turn toward a national but nevertheless ruthless form of capitalism where parties claiming to be "communist" are still in power – with Cuba standing (temporarily?) as a solitary exception. The weekly *Die Zeit*, Germany's most serious outlet of the liberal left, summed up this common sense of the time in its dossier published under the characteristic title "Hatte Marx doch recht?" (Was Marx right?) The guiding line was that despite all "the new enthusiasm for Marx, history teaches that his dream of the overthrow of circumstances in reality ended catastrophically" (Nienhaus 2017). Still, according to the same publicist, Marx might prove useful even at a political level by providing capitalism with a brake on its own self-destructive tendency, which the rising forces of right-wing "populism" can only reinforce: "The world should still make an effort to continue to discredit Marx, the revolutionary predictor. To do that, one should necessarily read Marx, the analyst, and Marx, the world economist" (Nienhaus 2017).

The reference to Marx in the current mainstream discourse thus testifies its own internal contradiction: the perception of capitalism's structural deficiencies, the loss of legitimacy of the policies implemented since the Reagan-Thatcher era – even in the eyes of some fractions of the elite – only strengthen the belief in the insuperable character of the system. The ultimate proof lies in the fact that the only conceivable usefulness of the most radical critique ever launched against this system is to prevent its "self-destruction," that is, to serve its perpetuation. Even left social scientists such as Wolfgang Streeck, a sociologist of Weberian inspiration, cannot see any alternative to the current state of crisis. His notion of an "end of capitalism" points exactly to this situation: an endless *Götterdämmerung* of capitalism during which it goes down a path of continuous decay with no solution in sight (Streeck 2016, 57–58). This situation, according to Streeck, derives from a structural factor, that is, the capacity of a globalized and finance-dominated capitalism to prevent the emergence of forces able to challenge the system as such. His conclusion takes the form of an aporia: although the question of an alternative to capitalism, and not simply of a better "variety" of it, should be left open, there seems to be no effective agency capable of taking on such an endeavor (Streeck 2016, 235).

The "Crisis of Marxism"

This pervasive pessimism could be interpreted as a consequence of the collapse of Soviet communism, a dark variant of the (in)famous "End of History" thesis formulated by Francis Fukuyama in the immediate aftermath of the event. A longer-term historical perspective shows however that the aporia of the "desirable yet impossible alternative" significantly predates the demise of "really existing socialism." Even more interestingly, it came from within Marxism and was formulated by some of the main protagonists of the theoretical debates of the 1960s and 1970. In November 1977, at a conference organized by the Italian dissident communist daily *Il manifesto*, its director Rossana Rossanda, declared in her opening statement that "the very idea of socialism, not as a generic aspiration but as a theory of society, a different mode of organization of human existence, is fading from view" (Rossanda 1977). According to Rossanda, this crisis of the perspectives of the labor movement

> goes beyond the purely political domain and invests the realm of theory itself. It is a crisis of Marxism, of which the *nouveaux philosophes* are the caricature, but which is experienced by immense masses as an unacknowledged reality. Marxism – not as a body of theoretical or philosophical thought, but as the great idealistic force that was changing the world – is now groaning under the weight of this this history.

However, for her, "whatever the nature of the post-revolutionary societies [of 'really existing socialism'], they can and must be interpreted and that Marxism offers a reliable instrument for doing this." To be up to this task, Marxism needs to understand that "the Gulag is the product neither of a philosophy nor of a pure idea of power and politics." Hence the necessity to analyze the economic and social processes that unfolded in the years following the October revolution, instead of recycling the abstract debates on the Leninist party and on "relation between the vanguard and the masses."

In his own intervention, which became the most famous of this conference, Louis Althusser confirmed Rossanda's diagnosis of the conjuncture while offering a much darker view of the capacity of Marxism to overcome its crisis. For him, "something has 'snapped' in the history of the labor movement between its past and present, something which makes its future unsure" (Althusser 1977). This rupture is referred to the fact that "there no longer exists in the minds of the masses any 'achieved ideal,' any really living reference for socialism." The "crisis of Marxism" originates in the Stalinist era, during which Marxism was entrenched into a series of ossified formulae, but Stalinism also blocked it insofar as it seemed able to provide practical solutions and build "socialism in one country," eventually extending it to an entire geopolitical bloc.

However, unlike Rossanda, the French philosopher seems more than doubtful about the capacity of Marxism to "provid[e] a really satisfactory . . . explanation of a history which was, after all, made in [its] name" – "almost an impossibility" as he states it. The reason for that lies ultimately *within* Marxism and cannot, as suggested by Rossanda, be resolved by the study of historical conjunctures in the light of Marxist categories. In 1973, in his first – and very belated – attempt to provide an explanation for this phenomenon, Althusser had characterized Stalinism as an essentially *theoretical* "deviation" that should be analyzed as the "posthumous revenge of the Second International, as a revival of its main tendency," that is, as a "special form" of "economism" (Althusser 1976, 89). Four years later, the roots of the problem are located in the writings of Marx, Lenin and Gramsci. The previous self-confident affirmations on Marxism as the "new science of the continent History" (Althusser 1971, 15) gives way to the enumeration of a seemingly endless series of "gaps" and "enigmas." The theoretical unity of *Capital* is seen as "largely fictitious" and its theory of exploitation suspected of carrying a "restrictive conception . . . hindering the broadening of the forms of the whole working class and people's struggle" (Althusser 1977). The status of philosophy and of dialectics in Marx is an "enigma," as is his relation to Hegel. No theory of the state, nor of the workers organizations is to be found in Marx, Lenin or in the entire "Marxist heritage." Gramsci's attempt to fill those gaps with the "little equations" of the *Prison Notebooks* on hegemony (as a combination of force and consent) just sound "pathetic."

This systematic demolition makes the statements on the "crisis of Marxism" as a moment of "possible liberation and renewal" appear as purely rhetorical. In a private letter sent a few months later to his friend Merab Mamardachvili, Althusser refers to his intervention at the Venice conference as a "masked talk," a desperate attempt to "dyke up the waters somewhat"

(Althusser 2006, 3). He discounts even his own work as nothing more than "a little, typically French justification, in a neat little rationalism bolstered with a few references (Cavaillès, Bachelard, Canguilhem and, behind them, a bit of the Spinoza-Hegel tradition), for Marxism's (historical materialism's) pretension to being a science" (Althusser 2006, 3). He also confesses that he's tempted by a definitive retreat to silence, since what he could work on is

> nothing of importance in a time when one must be armed with enough concrete knowledge in order to be able to speak of things like the state, the economic crisis, organizations, the "socialist" countries, etc. I don't have this knowledge and I have to, like Marx in 1852, "begin again at the beginning," but it's late for this, given my age, fatigue, lassitude, and also solitude.
>
> *(Althusser 2006, 5)*

This "radical loss of morale," to quote Perry Anderson's words (Anderson 1983, 29), should not be seen as an individual case – despite the highly tragic dimension of Althusser's destiny – but rather as a symptom of an epochal turn in the conjuncture. The course of events showed that Althusser and those who spoke of the "general crisis of Marxism" (Haider and King 2017) had foreseen the downturn of the revolutionary energies more clearly than those who, like Anderson, saw it as a phenomenon "confined to Latin Europe," essentially caused by the defeat of the Eurocommunist strategy pursued by the local Communist parties and supported by most of the Marxist intelligentsia of those countries (Anderson 1983, 76–77). The inglorious collapse of the Eastern European "really existing socialism," followed by the meltdown of the Western Communist parties, the turn to capitalism of the Third World "socialist" or "non-aligned" regimes and the accelerated integration of social-democracy in the neoliberal order, signaled the end of the historical cycle initiated by the October revolution. The idea of Marxism as a reflective form of unity of revolutionary theory and praxis, and of communism as the "*real* movement that abolishes the present state of things" as Marx and Engels famously put it in the *German Ideology* (*MECW* 5: 49), became more problematic than ever before. The "crisis of Marxism" was over, leaving the future perspective of Marxism in a state of radical uncertainty.

The "Post-Marxist" Moment

In a way, Anderson's judgment castigating "the veritable *débandade* of so many leading French thinkers of the Left since 1976" (Anderson 1983, 32) has been vindicated. Indeed, unlike its predecessor of the late 19th/early 20th century, sparked by the controversy around Eduard Bernstein's "revisionism," the late 20th-century "crisis of Marxism" produced little of significance compared to the controversies that made Marxism a living tradition throughout its history (Kouvelakis 2005a). In his 1983 essay, Anderson had already pointed out that what Marxism in crisis shared with its predecessor ("Western Marxism" in the Andersonian terminology) was the "poverty of strategy" (Anderson 1983, 28). More recently, Daniel Bensaïd elaborated on the "eclipse of strategic reason" as the central dimension of Marxism's retreat from the 1980s onwards (Bensaïd 2007). What now appears clear is that the definitive collapse of Marxist "orthodoxy" – which only survives as a farcical pastiche in the institutes of the Chinese CP – also led to the dislocation of the various forms of "heterodoxy," if not as purely intellectual arguments at least as forces capable of intervening in the course of events.

Let's pursue the comparison between the two "fin-de-siècle" crises of Marxism a bit further. The late 19th century "revisionist" attack on the official doctrine of German Social Democracy – the model party of the entire international socialist movement – triggered a high-profile debate on the nature of the transformations of contemporary capitalism, the validity of the *Zusammenbruchstheorie* ("breakdown theory") as the cornerstone of the "orthodox" strategy, the evolution of class structure in Western societies, the role of mass action, cooperatives, reforms and elections. These were the issues on which Bernstein, Hilferding, Kautsky, Labriola, Luxemburg, Sorel and many others (including major non-Marxist intellectuals such as Benedetto Croce and Werner Sombart) argued, drawing antagonistic approaches with long-lasting consequences within Marxism and the workers' movement.

Nothing of that sort came out of the "crisis of Marxism" of the late 1970s and early 1980s. As can be seen from the interventions of Rossanda and Althusser that set the terms of the debate, at no moment was the shared diagnosis of the strategic impasse in the West and the failure of Stalinism and its avatars in the East situated within the wider perspective of the ongoing transformation of capitalism on a world scale. The term "capitalism" is indeed remarkably absent from those exchanges, anticipating its eclipse from academic and public debate in the period that followed. Indeed, what came quickly to prevail, at least in Latin Europe and in the areas where Marxism was the most influential in the previous period, is Althusser's theoreticist approach, which located the reasons of the crisis in the "gaps" and "enigmas" of the Marxian and Marxist canon. Despite the body of work produced by left historians of the Soviet Union such as Moshe Lewin, Rossanda's call for a historical-materialist analysis of the conjunctures that led to the emergence of Stalinism and the defeat of socialist revolution in the West remained unanswered at a properly theoretical level. Rather than the promised reflective and self-critical renewal, the introverted character of the debate launched by the "crisis of Marxism" internalized and amplified the historical defeat of which it was both an anticipatory sign and a symptom.

It then comes as no surprise that the "new revisionism" that emerged from that crisis, under the label of "Post-Marxism," amounted to a form of disintegration from within of the dominant Western Marxist paradigm of the previous period, that is, Althusserianism. In the radically transformed "postmodern" atmosphere of the 1980s and after, the search for the ultimate unity of a "structured totality" came to be seen as at best irrelevant, and most commonly as an expression of a desire for "closure" that can only pave the way to "totalitarianism." The "overdetermination" of conjunctures becomes pure "contingency," the "materiality of ideology" is turned into a discourse-based ontology of the "social" guaranteeing its radical "indeterminacy." As Fredric Jameson underlined, this move should itself be seen as part of the broader shift from what is called "structuralism" to "poststructuralism," a shift that marks the passage to a new period at the political, the cultural and the economic levels. The central notions of the 1960s theoretical revolution, from semiotics and structural anthropology to anti-humanist Marxism,

> fall-back into a now absolutely fragmented and anarchic social reality . . ., as so many more pieces of material junk among all the other rusting and superannuated apparatuses and buildings that litter the commodity landscape and that strew the "collage city," the "delirious New York" of a postmodernist late capitalism in full crisis.
>
> *(Jameson 2008, 506)*

Let us examine more closely how these themes have played out in what should undoubtedly be considered as the manifesto of this 1980s "Post-Marxism," Ernesto Laclau and Chantal Mouffe's *Hegemony and Socialist Strategy* (Laclau and Mouffe 1985).[1]

Their starting point is quite similar to Bernstein's "revisionism": the question of "revolutionary agency," with its "historical-sociological" and political-strategic implications. Marxism's unsurmountable flaw, according to Laclau and Mouffe, is to consider as a given the existence of a unified social subject, the working class, in charge of a historical mission, the revolutionary overthrow of capitalism. This vision is grounded in a deterministic vision of social relations, which sees the centrality of class struggle (and the corresponding form of consciousness) as guaranteed by the "determination in the last resort by the economy." In a word, Marxism is guilty of "essentialism" and, as a consequence, increasingly unable to grasp the forms of subjectivation that prevail in contemporary conjunctures. "Essentialism" is actually nothing more than an attempt, as illusory on the analytical plane as it is vain at a practical level, to fill the constitutive indeterminacy of the social and the ensuing decentered character of the forms of subjectivation. No wonder then that the working class never fulfilled its alleged historical mission. Marxism is thus left in disarray when confronted with the fragmented and open configuration of the "new social movements" (such as feminism, ecology, sexual and ethnic minorities), irreducible to any class essentialism.

Even worse, Marxism should also be held responsible both for the authoritarianism inherent in the Leninist type of organization and for the totalitarian regimes that claimed its legacy. A number of features, all seen as intrinsic to Marxian and Marxist theory, has inevitably led to this historical disaster. At first, class essentialism cannot be dissociated from a purely instrumental conception of democracy and of civil liberties. Marxists are expected to fight for them as long as they are useful for them seizing power, but, as such, their class nature is seen as irretrievably "bourgeois." Therefore, once in power, the proletariat "would be the first to abolish them once the 'bourgeois-democratic' stage [of the revolution] was completed" (Laclau and Mouffe 1985, 55). Second, Marxism extends the "ontological primacy granted to the working class" from the social to the political level. The Leninist party and, eventually, the state dominated by that party act as the sole legitimate leadership of the broader masses regrouped under the hegemony of the revolutionary class. Hence a "predominantly external and manipulative character" of the leadership, displaying "an increasingly authoritarian practice of politics" (Laclau and Mouffe 1985, 56). But this ontological primacy of class was also extended to an epistemological privilege. The party becomes the depository not only of political correctness but also of science. Once Marxists are in power, their vision led directly to totalitarianism, defined as the forced unification of law, power and knowledge under the auspices of a "unitary people" (Laclau and Mouffe 1985, 187). Laclau and Mouffe emphasize that the

> possibility of the authoritarian turn was, in some way, present from the beginning of the Marxist orthodoxy; that is to say, from the moment, in which a limited actor – the working class – was raised to the status of a "universal class."
>
> *(Laclau and Mouffe 1985, 57)*

Marxism is doomed to disaster by its desire to "suture" the social, that is, to reduce – if necessary through violence – its constitutive openness under a single, unitary, meaning, provided by the alleged truth of revolutionary class consciousness.

As opposed to Marxism, Post-Marxism as defined by Laclau and Mouffe categorically rejects class determinism to emphasize the constitutive role of discursive articulations and the indeterminacy of the social. Discourse holds a sort of ontological primacy since "our analysis rejects the distinction between discursive and non-discursive practices" (Laclau and Mouffe 1985, 107) insofar as nothing can be considered as external to discourse and/or irreducible to discursive articulations – including the economy (Laclau and Mouffe 1985, 76–77). As a notion, "discourse" is thus equivalent to the Heideggerian "Being" (filtered by Derrida's "deconstruction"), whose meaning remains always hidden and therefore adequate to the "impossibility of the real" (Laclau and Mouffe 1985, 129), the impossibility of achieving the fullness of a "presence," of a fixed essence that would amount to its closure. It is only through the practice of discursive articulation that the openness of the social can give rise to forms of political subjectivation, but always and solely in a contingent, partial and temporary mode. "Hegemony" is the proper name of this practice: it consists in establishing chains of equivalence between the heterogeneous demands emerging from the social and transforms the very identity of the terms that come under this articulatory relation. This approach, obviously at odds with anything Gramsci ever thought under the same term, thus makes intelligible the irreducible plurality of political subjects that succeed the defunct centrality of workers while contributing positively to their emergence.

Liberal Democracy as the Ultimate Horizon

Laclau's and Mouffe's theoretical ambition goes however further than an epistemological claim. The task they attribute to Post-Marxism is to turn the theory and practice of hegemony decisively in the direction of democracy. The relation between the two terms appears indeed as an ambivalent one, subjected to a tension between a "democratic and an authoritarian practice of hegemony" (Laclau and Mouffe 1985, 57). From the outset the political space of modernity appears as divided between these two modes of subjectivity. The modern political actor corresponds to a "popular subject position," constituted by the chain of equivalence defining an "us" as opposed to "them." Its logic is the two of an antagonism. But antagonism is irreducibly plural, it cannot be subsumed under any single, allegedly "objective," contradiction. The "democratic subject position" recognizes this impossibility and opens up a common space, in which these antagonisms can only coalesce in a partial and contingent way through their articulation with other elements. Ecological, feminist, national or workers' movements can therefore take many, sometimes diverging, forms depending on the way they are discursively articulated. The logic of the "democratic subject position" isn't the two but the many, the radical pluralism of identities: "pluralism is radical only to the extent that each term of this plurality of identities finds within itself the principle of its own validity" (Laclau and Mouffe 1985, 167). We are here in the field of the multiplicity of Wittgensteinian "language games" (Laclau and Mouffe 1985, 179) understood as a proliferation of discursive operations across an increasingly complex social terrain made of fragmented and autonomous spheres. This multiplicity should be preserved at all costs since its negation would amount to that "suture of the social," which is the original sin of Marxism but, also, as we shall now see, of right-wing authoritarianism.

This dual character of the political space leads therefore to a fundamental consequence: the relation between the two modes of political subjectivity is of complementarity but also of tension. The creative character of politics requires the deployment of the logic of equivalence. But the antagonism carried by that logic can potentially constitute a threat to pluralism, and, as a consequence to democracy as the common ground which allows the differentiation (of "separation of spaces") that is required by the construction of equivalences to operate. Equivalence and plurality need therefore to limit each other, and, most significantly, the first should never pretend, or be allowed, to absorb the second. This imperative can also be formulated as the necessity to "balance" equivalence by autonomy, or "equality" by "liberty." It doesn't take much effort to recognize here the terms in which liberalism has always framed the question of democracy: the threat of an egalitarian democracy that would undermine the "separation of spaces" – in Marxist terms the (relative) separation of the political and the economic as the distinctive dimension of capitalism[2] – should be removed, or at least contained, in order to preserve the space of liberty. As stated by Laclau and Mouffe,

> the demand for *equality* is not sufficient, but needs to be balanced by the demand for *liberty*, which leads up to speak of a radical and *plural* democracy. A radical and

> non-plural democracy would be one which constituted *one* single space of equality on the basis of the unlimited operation of the logic of equivalence and did not recognize the irreducible moment of plurality of spaces. This principle of the separation of spaces us the basis of the demand of liberty. It is within it that the principle of pluralism resides and that the project for a plural democracy can link up with the logic of liberalism
>
> *(Laclau and Mouffe 1985, 184).*

The specter looming behind this threat is nothing else than revolution, not only socialist revolutions but also the French Revolution – at least in its Jacobin moment[3] – held as equally responsible for the totalitarian path eventually pursued by Stalinism. It is essential to understand, according to the authors of *Hegemony and Socialist Strategy*, that the "logic of totalitarianism" is a "new possibility which arises in the very terrain of democracy" (Laclau and Mouffe 1985, 186). Its impulse comes from the tendency of the logic of equivalence to expand, and this happens when "it ceases to be considered as one political space among others and comes to be seen as the centre, which organizes and subordinates all other spaces" (Laclau and Mouffe 1985, 186). As history has shown, "every attempt to establish a definitive suture and to deny the radically open character of the social which the logic of democracy institutes leads to what [Claude] Lefort designates as 'totalitarianism'" (Laclau and Mouffe 1985, 187). This is why every temptation to seek "a nodal point around which the social fabric can be reconstituted" should be categorically rejected (Laclau and Mouffe 1985, 188). But this is precisely what the "classic concept of revolution, cast in the Jacobin mold" is about, since

> it implied the foundational character of the revolutionary act, the institution of a point of concentration of power from which society could be "rationally" reorganized. This is the perspective which is incompatible with the plurality and the opening which a radical democracy requires.
>
> *(177–78)*

Such a perspective is equally shared by Marxism and Jacobinism:

> this change introduced by Marxism [class] into the principle of social division maintains unaltered an essential component of the Jacobin imaginary: the postulation of one foundational moment of rupture, and of a unique space in which the political is constituted.
>
> *(Laclau and Mouffe 1985, 152)*

"Totalitarianism" exists however also in a symmetrical right-wing version, that of fascism's "authoritarian fixing of the social order" (Laclau and Mouffe 1985, 188). Totalitarianism as such is therefore "a *political logic* and not a type of social organization" and this is "proved by the fact that it cannot be ascribed to a particular political orientation" (Laclau and Mouffe 1985, 187). This position is the logical consequence of the radical decoupling of the political from any socio-economic determination and its reduction to a discursive construction. Fascism and communism differ to the extent that they represent different "particular political orientations," corresponding to different "types of social organization," however this opposition is of secondary importance (hence the use of the term "particular" to refer to their respective "political orientations") compared to what both share: a common desire "to establish a definitive suture and to deny the open character of the social which the logic of democracy institutes" (Laclau and Mouffe 1985, 187). It is not difficult to trace in this "anti-totalitarianism" a variant of the

Cold War discourse that became dominant during the Thatcher-Reagan era. Far from being a new (or even a 20th-century) construction this anti-totalitarianism is the heir a liberal tradition descending in a straight line from Burke's and Tocqueville's view of the French Revolution as a catastrophe resulting from a desire to rebuild society from scratch, that is, according to "abstractions" and "preconceived systems" (Losurdo 2015).

The "radicality" of "radical democracy," as Laclau and Mouffe name their project, should therefore not be confused with any notion of "revolution." They make it clear that by the term "radical alternative" they are

> evidently not referring to a "revolutionary alternative," involving the violent overthrow of the existing state, but to a deepening and articulation of a variety of antagonisms, within both the State and civil society, which allows a "war of position" against the dominant hegemonic forms.
>
> *(Laclau and Mouffe 1985, 75)*

Rather than Gramsci, the literal but actually superficial reference, the model for this "war of position" is provided by Alexis de Tocqueville's notion of "democratic revolution" as a movement of expansion of rights into new spheres within the limits imposed by the respect of "pluralism" and of the "separation of spheres" (Laclau and Mouffe 1985, 160–63). This "revolution" was conceived by the French liberal thinker as the movement of a gradual but continuous erosion of traditional hierarchies, as a movement of permanent mobility and circulation of individuals and wealth across the social ladder. Likewise, for the theorists of Post-Marxism, it allows the questioning of "relations of subordination" both by "old" and "new" social movements and the extension of "rights" to new fields. The "new social movements" (ecology, feminism, minorities) appear however as the most appropriate vehicles for such a strategy, since they are explicitly based on non-class principles and flexible modes of identity and alliance formation. They appear therefore as the driving social force within societies characterized by an increasing autonomization of social activities. However, really existing workers' struggles (as opposed to the illusory messianic vision of the proletariat) can and should also be understood in that way. These struggles, dismissed as "reformist" by Marxists, "correspond more in reality to the mode adopted by the mobilizations of the industrial proletariat than do the more radical earlier struggles" (Laclau and Mouffe 1985, 157). Their modernity lies in the fact that, contrary to the radically hostile to capitalism visions of the semi-artisans still caught in the preindustrial imaginary depicted by E. P. Thompson in *The Making of the English Working Class*, "the relations of subordination between workers and capitalists are thus to a certain extent absorbed as legitimate differential positions in a unified discursive space" (Laclau and Mouffe 1985, 157).

This last formulation is particularly revealing of the way "radical democracy" is ultimately understood as a struggle between "logics" contesting existing forms of inequality and subordination but always within an unchanged overall framework. This unnamed totality turns out being nothing else than capitalism, the system in which the "legitimate differential positions" of workers and capitalist can as it were persist in their being. Indeed, only capitalism allows the "openness of the social" based on the separation of spheres which constitutes the indispensable condition for "political pluralism", or, in other terms, for the "institutional diversity and complexity which characterizes a democratic society" (Laclau and Mouffe 1985, 190–91). It is therefore perfectly consistent with their line of thought to define "the task of the Left" as a move "to deepen and expand [liberal-democratic ideology] in the direction of a radical and plural democracy" (Laclau and Mouffe 1985, 176). The claim made twice, and almost in passing, about the necessity to "put an end to the capitalist relations of production," as "*one* of the components of a project for radical democracy" (Laclau and Mouffe 1985, 178; italics added) and without this entailing the "elimination of other inequalities" as its consequence (192), appears thus as little more than a rhetorical gesture aimed at giving a residual left-wing flavor to an enterprise of systematic demolition of the very idea of anti-capitalism as the basis for any consistent emancipatory project.

The Revenge of Totalization

Laclau's and Mouffe's 1985 book and the work that followed on "agonism" and "populist reason" had a long-lasting impact not only in the intellectual debate but also in the new political sequence opened-up by the 2008 crisis, as testified by the rise of "left-populist" movements in Europe such as Podemos and France Insoumise. Many of its themes are shared other theorists who, notwithstanding divergent theoretical frameworks and political conclusions, found themselves in agreement with what it breaks from – class politics, the critique of political economy – as well as with some of the positive elements that take center stage: a version of the "linguistic turn" and the rehabilitation of the categories of political liberalism. Habermas's theory of "communicative action," Honneth's "politics of recognition," Foucault's notions of "power" and "discursive formations" (but also his late fascination with ordoliberalism) are obvious cases of such an evolution. In their work from the 1980s onwards, even figures who kept closer ties with Marxism and anti-capitalism such as Toni Negri followed a partly convergent trajectory, elaborating on themes such as "immaterial labor," the "multitude" as the new subject of politics and the expansion at the world-scale of the US constitution as the horizon of social movements in the new reality of an allegedly post-imperialist and post-national "Empire." "Post-Marxism" became thus the name of a broader constellation that expressed a substantial part of the "objective Spirit," to quote Hegel's term, of the historical moment marked by the defeat of the revolutions of the 20th century.

Not that everyone agreed with this turn of events. The Post-Marxism advocated by Laclau and Mouffe was, as could be expected, met by strong rebuttals coming from Marxist theorists, with Ellen Meiksins Wood and Norman Geras making the most significant contributions (Wood 1986; Geras 1990). What came essentially under criticism was their distorted understanding of Marxist concepts and their thinly disguised belief in the virtues of liberal democracy. The paradox here is that, despite the intensity of the polemics, Marxists and Post-Marxists shared the same terrain, that of a conceptual discussion moving in the terrain of intellectual history and Marxist theory, with some sparse references to the political conjuncture of the moment in order to denounce the toothless politics attributed to Post-Marxists. Thus, although most of the Marxist reaction to Post-Marxism was driven by a strong rejection of Althusser,[4] it adopted de facto the "theoreticist" approach of the "crisis of Marxism" expressed by the French philosopher. These polemics have little, if anything, to offer concerning the transformations that capitalism, the state and the social structure were undergoing in the 1980s. At a moment of deep retreat of the left and of social movements, critical thinking and emancipatory politics came out even weaker from the late 20th century "crisis of Marxism."

A new picture only started emerging when the contradiction created by the fall of "really existing socialism" and the now unchallenged domination of neoliberal capitalism at a global scale began to unfold. Various trends, each with a distinctive temporality, converged, shifting gradually the terms of the debate.

The first of these is the dissent that developed from within the Post-Marxist constellation. Its most significant expression was Slavoj Žižek's turn toward a critique of the theoretical matrix from which his previous work had developed (Žižek 1999; Butler et al. 2000). Although Žižek's entire trajectory is grounded on the writings of Althusser and Lacan, his fondness for Hegel and for dialectical thinking always made him always appear as a highly atypical poststructuralist. From the late 1990s onwards, he moved to an internal but systematic contestation of the positions of Laclau and Mouffe, enlarged to those of other figures such as Judith Butler or Jacques Rancière. Starting from a notion assimilating subjectivity to the Hegelian labor of negativity, Žižek now affirms the necessity of a global alternative to capitalism. He thus rejects the compulsive Post-Marxist insistence on the radical "openness" and "indeterminacy" of the social, emphasizing that capitalism acts as the force closing violently the possibilities of the Real by imposing the centrality of class antagonism. He thus comes to share Fredric Jameson's long-standing view that totalization isn't a matter of choice but something imposed by the existing, albeit unrepresentable, totality that is capitalism.

The closure inherent in the prevailing social order can only be broken by the foundational act of a revolutionary subject, who bets on the constitutive void of a given situation, a vision reminding us of Sartre's notion of freedom as an act bringing nothingness to the world, mediated by Alain Badiou's theory of the Event. Leninist politics is thus rehabilitated, much to the chagrin of Laclau, not as offering the right theory of the party but as the model of an act of radical rupture opening up the possibility of a new order, of which the moment of the October revolution still provides the standards (Žižek 2004). Notwithstanding significant problems of internal consistency (see Callinicos 2001), and a persistent lack of strategic thinking – in line with the "poverty of strategy" of Western Marxist thought – Žižek's evolution can be seen as an attempt to articulate decisionism to the reinstatement of the dialectical categories of necessity and contingency (the Hegelian movement of the concept posing its own presuppositions), as a necessary tool for the understanding of historical processes – another strong rebuttal of the Post-Marxist/postmodern cult of "contingency."

This break from within Post-Marxism reveals the internal instability of this constellation, deriving from the reactive character inscribed in its very name. The ambition to supersede Marxism while inheriting its ambition of a theory linked to a form of emancipatory project – even if the totalizing dimension and the notion of "emancipation" itself came under heavy criticism – proved more fragile than what was widely accepted in the first decades that followed the end of the "short 20th century." However, this crack wouldn't have sufficed to change the terms of the debate had Marxist theory not proved remarkably resilient throughout the period when (nearly) all sides proclaimed its death had arrived. A number of thinkers of the generation of the 1960s and the 1970s, mostly based in the world of Anglophone academia, persisted in providing ambitious totalizing analyses of the fundamental aspects of the transformations of the existing mode of production.

To name just a few, let's start with Fredric Jameson and his notion of "postmodernism" as the "cultural logic of late capitalism." Faithful to the categorical imperative of Marxism "Always historicize!" (Jameson 1981, 9), intensified by an "unslaked thirst for totalization" (Kouvelakis 2005b), Jameson offered a vast typology of this pervasive restructuring of social experience characterized by a dehistoricized and dislocated (or "depthless") sense of space and time. As an immanent expression of a distinctive stage of capitalism, the all-pervasive postmodern *logic* – rather than specific currents or artistic styles identifiable as "postmodernist" – acts as a powerful counterweight to the emergence of class consciousness (or "cognitive mapping" in Jameson's terms).

Inspired by the work of Henri Lefebvre and other thinkers of the historical-materialist tradition (such as Engels and Rosa Luxemburg), David Harvey has developed the (so far) most systematic Marxist theory of space as the terrain in which the mode of production displaces and temporarily resolves its own structural contradictions – through a process of constant production of "spatio-temporal fixes." Harvey extended his theory to a periodization of capitalism, exploring the specificities of the current moment in his analysis of neoliberalism and the "new imperialism." At a more empirical level, Mike Davis provided extraordinary vivid accounts of the formation of these new forms of high-capitalist hyper-spaces, from California's dystopic "city of quartz" and the urban artefacts of Dubai to the "gated communities" booming around the globe or sprawling of slums in the cities of the Global South. Davis's preoccupations resonate with a rising body of work from theorists such as Paul Burkett, John Bellamy Foster, Michael Löwy and Andreas Malm on capitalism's role in the ongoing environmental catastrophe, the ecological dimension of Marxian thought and the eco-socialist alternative.

This strongly "spatial" Marxism explains the strong presence of a critically oriented research in most university departments of geography and urban studies and acts as an inspiration for activists involved in innumerable struggles contesting capital's spatial order. It is supplemented by the renewal of Marxist political economy retraced by Alex Callinicos in "Hidden Abode: The Marxist Critique of Political Economy," in this volume. The realities of financialized capitalism were the object of systematic scrutiny by economists such as François Chesnais, Gérard Duménil, Cédric Durand, Costas Lapavitsas and Anwar Shaikh even before the 2008 Great Recession, which, as noted previously, triggered a broader attention to the Marxist understanding of contemporary capitalism and its crises. A widely similar picture emerges from the fields of international relations, labor studies and of the theory of the neoliberal state and the world legal order. Even if a strong philosophical current continued to produce an important and innovative body of work (mostly in Italy and France, around figures such as Domenico Losurdo, André Tosel and Daniel Bensaïd), it cannot be said anymore that the type of Marxist theorizing that flourishes in the Western world shares the essential characteristics once attributed by Anderson to "Western Marxism" (Anderson 1976). Although clearly an heir of the 20th-century heterodoxies associated with that tradition, it has decisively stopped concentrating on its essentially aesthetical and speculative themes to pick up the thread of research on political economy and social and political theory.

This renewal of Marxism signals a new intellectual conjuncture and testifies to its capacity to withstand the challenges posed by its protean Other, capitalism, and by the failures of the experiments conducted in its name. It comes however at a cost, that of retreating into an essentially academic sphere, accentuating the problematic relation to political practice that characterized the previous configuration. In that sense, the "crisis of Marxism," as a diagnosis on the crisis of the perspectives of the socialist and communist project, is still with us and will remain as long as a new victorious experience of emancipatory struggle hasn't come into being. But one should also keep in mind that what initially appears as a purely intellectual phenomenon often turns out to be the anticipatory sign of a deeper historical trend. The future of Marxism as an active force aiming at changing the world could thus still surprise.

Notes

1. Although attributed to a large number of thinkers – the Wikipedia article on the notion lists no fewer than thirty-five names, even very unlikely ones (Abdullah Öcalan, Pierre Bourdieu or Paulo Freire) – most of those who claimed the label of "Post-Marxism" came from the Althusserian tradition: Étienne Balibar, Barry Hindess, Paul Hirst, Gareth Stedman-Jones to name a few. Most of the themes of Post-Marxism and of the broader "poststructuralist" constellation can be identified in currents coming from other Marxist backgrounds, the such as Italian post-operaismo, Indian Subaltern Studies, versions of postcolonialism etc. The shared prefix "post" is an infallible sign of their common belonging to the constellation of "poststructuralism" or, better even, of the "postmodern condition," to quote Jean-François Lyotard's original formulation (Lyotard 1984).
2. See Wood (1981).

3. Laclau and Mouffe only praise the French Revolution, following Hannah Arendt, François Furet and Claude Lefort to whom they refer themselves, for its "1789 moment," that is for inaugurating a "new mode of institution of the social," symbolized by the Declaration of the Rights of Man seen as providing the discursive basis for the "struggles for political liberty" (Laclau and Mouffe 1985, 155). This is typically the traditional liberal view of the Revolution, always carefully separating the "good" 1789 moment from the "bad" 1793 one, the former representing the conquest of liberty and the latter standing for the drift toward "tyranny" and "totalitarianism."
4. For a different perspective see, however, Elliott (1986).

Bibliography

Althusser, Louis. 1971. "Philosophy as a Revolutionary Weapon." In Louis Althusser. *Lenin and Philosophy and Other Essays*, 13–26. London: New Left Books.

Althusser, Louis. 1976. "Reply to John Lewis." In *Essays in Self-Criticism*, 33–99. London: NLB.

Althusser, Louis. 1977. "The Crisis of Marxism." viewpointmag.com/2017/12/15/crisis-marxism-1977/

Althusser, Louis. 2006 (1978). "Letter to Merab Mamardachvili." In Louis Althusser. *Philosophy of the Encounter: Later Writings 1978–1987*, edited by François Matheron and Olivier Corbet, 1–6. London and New York: Verso.

Anderson, Perry. 1976. *Consideration on Western Marxism*. London: NLB.

Anderson, Perry. 1983. *In the Tracks of Historical Materialism*. London: Verso.

Artus, Patrick. 2018. "La dynamique du capitalisme est aujourd'hui bien celle qu'avait prévue Karl Marx." *Natixis Flash Economie* (2 February). research.natixis.com

Bensaïd, Daniel. 2007. *Eloge de la politique profane*. Paris: Albin Michel.

Bidet, Jacques, and Stathis Kouvelakis, eds. 2008. *Critical Companion to Contemporary Marxism*. Chicago: Haymarket.

Butler, Judith, Ernesto Laclau, and Slavoj Žižek. 2000. *Contingency, Hegemony, Universality: Contemporary Dialogues on the Left*. London: Verso.

Callinicos, Alex. 2001. "Review of Slavoj Žižek, *The Ticklish Subject*, and Judith Butler, Ernesto Laclau and Slavoj Žižek, *Contingency, Hegemony, Universality*." *Historical Materialism* 8: 373–403.

Chotiner, Isaac. 2014. "Thomas Piketty: I Don't Care for Marx." *The New Republic* (6 May).

Drury, Colin. 2018. "Mark Carney Warns Robots Taking Jobs Could Lead to Rise of Marxism." *Independent* (14 April). independent.co.uk/news/uk/home-news/mark-carney-marxism-automation-bank-of-england-governor-job-losses-capitalism-a8304706.html

Duménil, Gérard, and Dominique Lévy. 2014. "Économie et politique des thèses de Thomas Piketty. I. Analyse critique." *Actuel Marx* 56: 164–79.

Duménil, Gérard, and Dominique Lévy. 2015. "Économie et politique des thèses de Thomas Piketty: II. Une lecture alternative de l'histoire du capitalisme." *Actuel Marx* 57: 186–204.

The Economist. 2014. "A Modern Marx: Capitalism and Its Critics." economist.com/news/leaders/21601512-thomas-pikettys-blockbuster-book-great-piece-scholarship-poor-guide-policy

Elliott, Gregory. 1986. "The Odyssey of Paul Hirst." *New Left Review* 1(159): 81–105.

Geras, Norman. 1990. *Discourses of Extremity: Radical Ethics and Post-Marxist Extravagances*. London: Verso.

Haider, Asad, and Patrick King, eds. 2017. "The Crisis of Marxism" [Texts by Louis Althusser, Etienne Balibar, Christine Buci-Glucksmann, Nicos Poulantzas, Rossana Rossanda]. viewpointmag.com/2017/12/18/the-crisis-of-marxism

Jameson, Fredric. 1981. *The Political Unconscious: Narrative as Socially Symbolic Act*. London: Methuen.

Jameson, Frederic. 2008 (1984). "Periodizing the 60s." In Fredric Jameson. *The Ideologies of Theory*, 483–515. London and New York: Verso.

Kouvelakis, Stathis. 2005a. "The Crisis of Marxism and the Transformation of Capitalism." In Bidet and Kouvelakis 2008, 23–38.

Kouvelakis, Stathis. 2005b. "Fredric Jameson: An Unslaked Thirst for Totalization." In Bidet and Kouvelakis 2008, 697–710.

Laclau, Ernesto, and Chantal Mouffe. 1985. *Hegemony and Socialist Strategy*. London: Verso.

Lordon, Frédéric. 2015. "Why Piketty Isn't Marx." *Le Monde diplomatique* (May).

Losurdo, Domenico. 2015. *War and Revolution: Rethinking the 20th Century*. London: Verso.

Lyotard, Jean-François. 1984 (1979). *The Postmodern Condition: A Report on Knowledge*. Minneapolis: University of Minnesota Press.

Nienhaus, Lise. 2017. "Karl Marx: Er ist wieder da." *Die Zeit* (May). zeit.de/2017/05/karl-marx-kapitalismus-probleme-rechtspopulismus-ungleichheit last accessed April 4 2018.

Piketty, Thomas. 2014. *Capital in the Twenty-First Century*. Cambridge, MA: Harvard University Press.
Rossanda, Rossana. 1977. "Power and Opposition in Post-Revolutionary Societies." viewpointmag.com/2017/12/15/power-opposition-post-revolutionary-societies-1977/
Roubini, Nouriel. 2011. "Roubini Warns of Global Recession Risk." *Wall Street Journal* (11 August). wsj.com/video/roubini-warns-of-global-recession-risk/C036B113-6D5F-4524-A5AF-DF2F3E2F8735.html last accessed April 4 2018.
Streeck, Wolfgang. 2016. *How Will Capitalism End? Essays on a Failing System*. London: Verso.
Wood, Ellen Meiksins. 1981. "The Separation of the Economic and the Political in Capitalism." *New Left Review* 1(127): 66–95.
Wood, Ellen Meiksins. 1986. *The Retreat from Class: A New "True" Socialism*. London: Verso.
Žižek, Slavoj. 1999. *The Ticklish Subject: The Absent Centre of Political Ontology*. London: Verso.
Žižek, Slavoj. 2004. *Revolution at the Gates: Zizek on Lenin: The 1917 Writings*. London and New York: Verso.

34
RANAJIT GUHA (1923–)

Alf Gunvald Nilsen

A pioneer of critical postcolonial historiography, Ranajit Guha was born in 1923 into a landed family in what is now Bangladesh.[1] Due to his father's legal practice in Calcutta, his family was protected from the impact of the general decline of landlordism in the Bengal countryside, which intensified greatly in the late colonial era (see Chatterjee 1984; Bose 1986). In the mid-1930s, he was sent to Calcutta for his secondary education, and later on began his university studies at the revered Presidency College. In a context characterized by the Second World War, a devastating famine, and communal violence, Guha was exposed to the political currents of the times – most significantly, perhaps, a nascent Communist movement whose ranks he would soon join (see Bhattacharya 2014; Mukherjee 2015). At Presidency College, he also developed an interest in the historical origins of the Permanent Settlement Act – that is, the colonial legal regime that established a specific form of landlordism in Bengal in the 1790s – which would result, much later, in his first book, published in 1963, *A Rule of Property for Bengal* (Guha 1996). He also came under the influence of the historian Susobhan Sarkar, who was a member of the Communist Party of India and one of the first scholars to introduce the work of Antonio Gramsci to an Indian audience.

After completing his Master's degree in history from the University of Calcutta in 1946, he became a full-time member of the Communist Party of India (CPI) and relocated to Paris, where he spent six years working as an organizer at the secretariat of the World Federation of Democratic Youth. He returned to India in the early 1950s to take up a series of teaching jobs, before relocating to Britain in 1959, working first at the University of Manchester and later at the University of Sussex. It was in Brighton that the nucleus of what has become known as the Subaltern Studies project began to crystallize, as Guha brought together a younger generation of historians for regular discussions about South Asian historiography. Spurred in part by Guha's encounter with Maoist activists in the early 1970s as well as his observations of the crisis of the Indian polity that was brought on by Indira Gandhi's imposition of Emergency rule from 1975 to 1977, this project was as much a critique of the foundations of the postcolonial republic as it was a pathbreaking intervention in the scholarly craft of history-writing (see Nilsen 2017a, ch. 1). Guha edited the *Subaltern Studies* series from 1982 to 1989 – a period during which he was based at the Australian National University in Canberra. In later years, his attention turned to phenomenological questions in historiography – asking, in essence, what it might entail to recover a past appropriated by colonialism.

The Politics of Critique

In order to truly understand the full significance of the Subaltern Studies project that Guha spearheaded and forged the template for, it is necessary to appreciate the politics of the historiographical critique that he and his co-travelers developed in their writing about popular struggles in colonial India. The best starting point for doing so is arguably Guha's own political writings – many of which appeared in the magazine *Frontier* in the 1970s (see Guha 2009).

In these writings, Guha, of course, was intervening in an explosive conjuncture in India's postcolonial history. India was deeply embedded in the global revolt of 1968, which in the postcolonial states of the South found its expression in new social movements that took aim at the institutionalized elite politics practiced in these states (Watts 2001, 172). In India, this was expressed in the Naxalite movement's guerrilla war against the Indian state from 1967 until the early 1970s and in the growth of a series of militant movements and protest waves in the 1970s (Banerjee 1984; Ray 2012; Omvedt 1993). This in turn was closely tied to the collapse of the nation-building model developed under independent India's first prime minister, Jawaharlal Nehru, in the shape of economic stagnation and the breakdown of the Congress Party's political legitimacy and consensus formation mechanisms (Frankel 2005).

In this context, Indian authorities resorted to coercion and authoritarianism in order to prevent the eruption of a revolutionary situation. In Guha's home state of West Bengal, where the Naxalite revolt had begun in 1967, this was manifest in a profoundly violent crackdown on Maoist activists and insurgents. This crackdown, in which custodial torture played a central role, became the target of sharp criticism in an article that Guha penned for *Frontier* in 1971: "For all who care," he wrote angrily, "it is time to wake up to the fact that, so far as political torture is concerned, we already have a bit of Algeria in West Bengal" (Guha 2009, 565). The resort to torture and coercion, as well as the acquiescence of the liberal Bengali bourgeoisie, Guha argued, were symptomatic of the colonial origins of Indian liberalism:

> our liberalism since its very inception in the early nineteenth century grew up with distinctly collaborationist traits expressed, above all, in a servile reliance on and unswerving faith in *Law and Order – the most formal expression of the culture of the ruling class.*
>
> *(Guha 2009, 574)*

Five years later, in an article published in *Journal of Contemporary Asia*, Guha developed a critique of the Emergency that took aim at what he perceived to be the liberal self-deception contained in the argument that the sudden authoritarian turn in the Indian polity had to be understood in terms of Indira Gandhi's personal and psychological idiosyncrasies:

> The truth is that nothing has been well with Indian democracy ever since its inception and that the present Emergency is merely a climactic act in a process going back to the very circumstances of the birth of the Indian republic.
>
> *(Guha 2009, 579)*

The Indian republic, he went on to argue, was established as "a decolonized but undemocratic state" and state violence was foundational to its emergence – most clearly evident in the mobilization of military force against the Communist-led peasant insurrection in Telangana (see Roosa 2001). And since its inception, despite the liberal tenor of Nehru's political credo, the Indian state had relied on coercion in many forms in order to ensure the reproduction of elite rule – for example, through the use of pre-emptive detention, the steady expansion of the police apparatus, suppression of democratic expressions of popular discontent, and the torture of political prisoners by the police. "Thus it will be fair to conclude," Guha (2009, 597) claimed, "that democracy in India has long been dead if it was ever alive at all."

The Subaltern Studies Project

"The historiography of Indian nationalism has for a long time been dominated by elitism – colonialist elitism and bourgeois-nationalist elitism." This is how Guha (1982, 1) announced the arrival of the Subaltern Studies project on the academic stage. Both colonial and nationalist historiographies, he argued, shared the assumption that "the making of the Indian nation and the development of the consciousness – nationalism – which informed this process, were exclusively or predominantly elite achievements." In opposition to this elitism, Guha (1982, 4) asserted the existence of a "politics of the people" that constituted an "autonomous domain," parallel to and isolated from the elites' mental world and sphere of influence:

> For parallel to the domain of elite politics there existed throughout the colonial period another domain of Indian politics in which the principal actors were not the dominant groups of the indigenous society or the colonial authorities but the subaltern classes and groups constituting the mass of the laboring population and the intermediate strata in town and country – that is, the people.
>
> *(Guha 1982, 4)*

This politics found expression in the countless uprisings and protest movements that developed among the small peasants and indigenous populations of the Indian village and among India's dawning urban proletariat in the course of the nineteenth and the first half of the twentieth century.

A new historiographical approach, Guha argued, was needed in order to establish and understand the nature and dynamics of the domain of subaltern politics – and this was not just an intellectual imperative.[2] For, as Guha (1982, 6) saw it, the struggles of India's subaltern groups were not capable of propelling "the nationalist movement into a full-fledged struggle for national liberation." This in turn meant that independence arrived in the form of a "*historic failure of the nation to come to its own*" (Guha 1982, 7) – a historic failure that was write large in the lapses and limits of bourgeois democracy that had been the target of critique in Guha's political writings, as discussed previously.[3] Ultimately, then, the Subaltern Studies project was not just a quest to restore popular agency as an autonomous force in India's struggle for independence, but also a research program that intended to shed light on the historical origins and political economy of India's postcolonial state.

In intellectual terms, the Subaltern Studies project was nourished by the intersection between British Marxist historiography and Antonio Gramsci's perspectives on hegemony and popular resistance (see Ludden 2002b; Chaturvedi 2000b). The goal of writing "history from below" was drawn from the British Marxist historians' analysis of the bourgeois revolution in England and the transition to industrial capitalism (see Hill 1975; Thompson 1966). The assumption that subaltern political consciousness and repertoires of action constituted an autonomous domain was taken from Gramsci's program (1971, 52) for the study of what he called "subaltern classes" (see Green 2011). However, Guha – who left the CPI in 1956, in protest against the Soviet invasion of Hungary – did not conceive of the project as a straightforward exercise in Marxist historiography. In his seminal essay "The Prose of Counter-Insurgency," which was published in the second volume of *Subaltern Studies*, Guha (1983a) argued that the presentation of peasant revolts in dominant Indian historiography as spontaneous events erases insurgent forms of consciousness and experience, and thus also the meanings that the insurgents ascribed to their own actions. This, he argued, was also the case with the orthodox Marxist understanding of the history of the independence struggle, since it replaces the actual subaltern insurgent with an abstraction frequently entitled "Worker-and-Peasant" (Guha 1983a, 33).

Guha's quest to uncover the subjective experience and consciousness of peasant rebels under the Raj yielded the highly influential study *Elementary Aspects of Peasant Insurgency in Colonial India* (Guha 1983b). Colonial rule, Guha argued, subjected the Indian peasantry to the domination of the state, the landlord and the moneylender, and the overthrow of this triumvirate in turn became the main objective of peasant insurgency – and it was a deeply conscious objective:

> The peasant obviously knew what he was doing when he rose in revolt. . . . By trying to force a mutual substitution of the dominant and the dominated in the power structure it left nothing to doubt about its own identity as a project of power.
>
> *(Guha 1983b, 9)*

Underpinning and animating these revolts was a general form of insurgent consciousness, which Guha deciphered and conceptualized in terms of six elementary aspects: negation, that is, the rejection of the inferiority and stigma attributed to subaltern groups by dominant groups; ambiguity, that is, engaging in acts that dominant groups label criminal in order to upend established symbolic hierarchies; modality, that is, the ways in which peasant revolts is enacted through practices that are public, collective, destructive and total; solidarity, that is, the coming together of insurgent groups on the basis of class, caste, regional and ethnic affinities; transmission, that is the ways in which peasant revolts would spread through the use of signs and symbols; and territoriality, that is, the manner in which a sense of belonging to a lineage and habitat pitted insurgent peasants against alien enemies. These, he argued, were the constitutive elements of "a consciousness which informed some historic actions aimed at turning the rural world upside down" (Guha 1983b, 337).

Dominance Without Hegemony and Beyond

Elementary Aspects quite possibly embodies the ambition of the template that Guha laid out in his introduction to the first volume of *Subaltern Studies* in its fullest form – namely, to define "a subaltern consciousness separate from hegemonic cultural forms, and rooted in myth, religion, and magical belief, that was realised in the practice of rural resistance" (Sivaramakrishnan 2002, 217). In the way that it accomplishes this task, the book also testifies to the profoundly binary structure of Guha's thought, which is evident, as K. Sivaramakrishnan has put it, in the tendency to decipher social phenomena in terms of "structured oppositions" (Sivaramakrishnan 2002, 217; see also O'Hanlon 2002).

This tendency was also strongly evident in Guha's further development of his critique of elitist historiography – most importantly in his long and important essay "Dominance Without Hegemony and Its Historiography," which appeared in the sixth volume of *Subaltern Studies* (Guha 1989).[4] In this essay, Guha effectively formulated a thoroughgoing critique of the emergence and trajectory political modernity in India. Hegemony, for Guha, was the hallmark of the political in Western capitalist democracies. In this context, he argued, the bourgeoisie had gained the consent of subaltern groups as it emerged at the helm of the struggle against feudalism. Following the paradigmatic bourgeois revolutions in England and France, a hegemonic liberal political culture was crafted that incorporated subaltern groups within the ambit of democratic nation-states. In contrast, the colonial state established by the British in India rested fundamentally on coercion: "As an absolute externality, the colonial state was structured like a despotism, with no mediating depths, no space provided for transactions between the will of the rulers and that of the ruled" (ibid., 274). Furthermore, the political culture that emerged under the Raj was one in which its key idioms of rule were mediated through precolonial political traditions. As a consequence, Guha argued, colonial rule failed to generate a hegemonic political culture: "For, under conditions of dominance without hegemony, the life of civil society can never be fully absorbed into the activity of the state" (Guha 1989, 72).

This analysis, of course, connects with and elaborates Guha's claims about the historic failure of the Indian nation to truly come into its own in the wake of the freedom struggle. The Indian bourgeoisie, he argued, was unwilling and unable to dislodge semi-feudal structures of power and willingly struck compromises with their British overlords:

> The destruction of the colonial state was never a part of their project. They abjured and indeed opposed all forms of armed struggle against the raj and settled for pressure politics as their main tactical means in bargaining for power.
>
> *(Guha 1989, 213–14)*

As he put it in a subsequent essay, the willingness to compromise and accommodate with landlordism and the colonial state also meant that the nationalist movement also failed "to assimilate the class interests of peasants and workers effectively into a bourgeois hegemony" (Guha 1992, 102). This, of course, went a long way toward explaining the deficiencies that Guha identified in his political writings on the postcolonial Indian state – and he believed dominance without hegemony was intrinsic to this form of state as well (Guha 1989, 307).

Reflecting, arguably, a more general turn in the Subaltern Studies project, Guha's later work came to focus on meta-questions pertaining to postcolonial historiography.[5] In a particularly poignant essay entitled "The Small Voice of History," he singles out for critique the manner in which the ideology of the state – or what he calls statism – has come to "determine the criteria of the historic" (Guha 1996, 1). In Indian historiography, he argues, statism was bequeathed to the educated elite through colonialism, but, precisely because colonial rule never gained hegemonic status, the history of India's civil society "would always exceed that of the Raj, and consequently an Indian historiography of India would have little use for statism" (Guha 1996, 3). In its place, Guha argued that it was necessary to listen to "the small voices which are drowned in the noise of statist commands" (Guha 1996, 3). These voices, he argued, were unlikely to fit those historiographical designs – be they colonial, bourgeois or Marxist[6] – that privilege one specific societal contradiction over all others. In making this argument, Guha was in fact returning to a concern that he had grappled with already in the mid-1980s, in the essay "Chandra's Death," in which he asked what it might mean for historiography that was attentive toward "the small drama and fine detail of social existence, especially at its lower depths" (Guha 1987, 138).[7] Ultimately, such a historiography was necessary in order for "the colonized to recover their past appropriated by conquest and colonization" (Guha 2002, 2).

A Critical Assessment

Any critical assessment of Guha's work – as well as the wider Subaltern Studies project – needs to take its point in a foundational acknowledgment of it pivotal and pathbreaking nature. Besides the signal achievement of directing critical scholarly attention toward the significance of popular politics and mobilization from below in the history of modern India, Guha and the Subaltern

Studies project have also debates and dialogues that have been of singular importance in terms of pushing the conceptual boundaries of the study of subalternity, subaltern politics and hegemony – not just in India but in the Global South more generally (see Nilsen and Roy 2015). Many of these advances have occurred, I would argue, despite the best efforts of Marxist academics, who too often have been preoccupied with denouncing Guha and his fellow-travelers for their departures from Marxian orthodoxy (see, for example, Alam 2002; Singh et al. 2002).

This, of course, does not absolve Guha from criticism from a Marxist point of view. As I have pointed out elsewhere, there is, despite the invocations of Gramsci in the opening essay in the first volume of *Subaltern Studies* and in *Elementary Aspects of Peasant Insurgency in Colonial India*, very little that is actually Gramscian about Guha's understanding of subalternity and hegemony (see Nilsen 2017a, ch. 1). First of all, Gramsci did not conceive of subalternity and the political agency of subaltern groups as constituting an autonomous domain. On the contrary, subalternity is a form of adverse incorporation in hegemonic formations, and the collective action of subaltern groups gravitates around engaging institutional ensembles, framing claims through discourses, and mobilizing through political forms that are commensurable with the reproduction of unequal structures of power: "Subaltern groups are always subject to the activity of ruling groups, even when they rebel and rise up: only 'permanent' victory breaks their subordination, and that not immediately" (Gramsci 1971, 55; Gramsci 1975, I, 299–300; Q3 (XX) §14; see also Nilsen and Roy 2015; Green 2002; Roseberry 1994). This also means that the binary that Guha proposes between state ideologies and subaltern forms of consciousness is false. Subaltern groups, as Adam Morton (2007, 62) puts it, are fundamentally "intertwined with processes of state formation" and, consequently, state ideologies become "sites of protracted struggle as to what they mean and for whom" when subaltern groups mobilize to contest their adverse incorporation in a hegemonic formation (Corrigan and Sayer 1985, 6; see also Nilsen 2015; Mallon 1995).

Second, Gramsci's acute understanding of the negotiated character of hegemony – that is, the insight that hegemonic processes advanced through the construction of "unstable equilibria" of compromise between dominant and subaltern groups (Gramsci 1971, 182; Gramsci 1975, III, 1584; Q13 (XXX) §17) – is entirely absent in Guha's work. This is most evident in his theorization of India's colonial political modernity as a case of dominance without hegemony. As Vivek Chibber (2013) has pointed out, Guha's contrast between the development of political modernity in the West and in colonial India is deeply problematic.[8] In terms of Western political modernity, the link between bourgeois revolutions and political liberalism is very tenuous. The bourgeois revolutions in France and England, Chibber argues, created "an oligarchic state with an expanded scope for political participation – but only for members of the ruling order that had hitherto been excluded" (2013, 77). Ultimately, the inclusion of subaltern groups in these new political orders was an achievement of mobilization from below, rather than an intrinsic feature of bourgeois hegemony: "For more than a century after the new states were installed, laboring classes had to wage unceasing struggle to gain any substantial political rights – the very rights that Guha seems to associate with a hegemonic order" (Chibber 2013, 87). Subalterns, in other words, are not passive in their adherence to the hegemony of dominant groups, and hegemony must therefore be understood as an incomplete process that must be constantly be "renewed, recreated, defended, and modified" (Williams 1977, 112).

Ultimately, what is missing in Guha's work, and in the Subaltern Studies project more generally, is a dialectical conception of the internal relationships between dominant and subaltern groups and the practices through which they seek to exercise and legitimate power and resistance within a historically defined set of social relationships. This, I hasten to add, is not merely a scholastic criticism. On the contrary, it is a criticism that is moored in ambitions that are very similar to those that led Guha to his intellectual program for a subaltern historiography in the first place – namely to produce knowledge that is relevant to the imperative of bringing about progressive social change. This ambition will be better served by a perspective that sees power and resistance as relational practices, and which understands subaltern politics as a process that arises and develops through the appropriation and reinterpretation of dominant ideologies and active use of existing political institutions and practices. Through such a perspective, in my view, we can come closer to the actual terrain that subaltern groups move on as they develop their oppositional projects. And by doing this, we can initiate a debate on the possible limitations of such political practices – a discussion that in turn can play a role in the further development of oppositional practices capable of breaking with institutionalized power relations and their ideological legitimation.

Notes

1. This biographical introduction is based on Chatterjee (2009) and Amin and Bhadra (1994).
2. As Partha Chatterjee (2009, 13) notes, the initial statement of this intellectual program was made in Guha's critical analysis of the Bengali play *Neel Darpan*, which was published in the *Journal of Peasant Studies* in 1974. Challenging its status in the Indian nationalist imagination, Guha (2009, 180) argued that the play merely "shows where the liberal stands at the time of a peasant revolt: he stands close to the power of the state seeking cover behind the law and the bureaucracy."
3. What Guha is alluding to here is the idea that India's struggle for independence is best understood in Gramscian terms as a passive revolution – that is, as a molecular transformation toward capitalist modernity, which reproduces the economic and political position of precapitalist ruling classes. This idea was more fully articulated at a later stage in the work of Partha Chatterjee (1986, 1993) and Sudipta Kaviraj (1997).
4. This was the last volume in the series that was edited by Ranajit Guha.
5. Toward the late 1980s, publications in the series became ever more strongly marked by theoretical debates about historiography in postcolonial contexts and analyses of discursive power in colonial situations. This turn was signaled by Gayatri Chakravorty Spivak's interventions in the collective's work, as well as by Edward Said's foreword to the *Selected Subaltern Studies* edited collection, which introduced an American audience to the series in 1988. See Sarkar (1997), Chapter 3 for an insider's critique of this turn in the project.
6. Interestingly, a key butt of Guha's critique in this essay is P. Sundarayya's standard history of the Telangana movement, a text that he cited approvingly in his 1976 article on the flawed nature of Indian democracy.
7. It is significant of course, that both in "Chandra's Death" and "The Small Voice of History," it is precisely the dynamics of gender relations in subaltern communities and subaltern movements that enable Guha to tease out these small dramas and fine details.
8. This does not, of course, entail that Chibber's critique and the Marxist approach that he proposes are unproblematic. As I have argued elsewhere, his perspective is deeply marred by an entrenched Eurocentrism that does little to help us build the many passages that should run between Marxism and postcolonialism: Nilsen (2017b); see also Lazarus (2016) and Hitchcock (2015).

Bibliography

Alam, Javed. 2002. "Peasants, Politics and Historiography: Critique of New Trend in Relation to Marxism." In Ludden, ed. 2002a, 43–57.

Amin, Shahid, and Gautam Bhadra. 1994. "Ranajit Guha: A Biographical Sketch." In *Subaltern Studies VIII: Writings on Indian History and Society*, edited by Shahid Amin, and Gautam Bhadra, 222–25. New Delhi: Oxford University Press.

Banerjee, Sumanta. 1984. *India's Simmering Revolution: The Naxalite Uprising*. London: Zed Books.

Bhattacharya, Sabyasachi. 2014. *The Defining Moments in Bengal, 1920–1947*. New Delhi: Oxford University Press.

Bose, Sumanta. 1986. *Agrarian Bengal: Economy, Social Structure and Politics, 1919–1947*. Cambridge: Cambridge University Press.

Chatterjee, Partha. 1984. *Bengal, 1920–1947: The Land Question*. Calcutta: K. P. Bagchi.

Chatterjee, Partha. 1986. *Nationalist Thought and the Colonial World: A Derivative Discourse*. New Delhi: Oxford University Press.

Chatterjee, Partha. 1993. *The Nation and its Fragments*. New Delhi: Oxford University Press.

Chatterjee, Partha. 2009. "Editor's Introduction." In Ranajit Guha. *The Small Voice of History: Collected Essays*, 1–18. Ranikhet: Permanent Black.

Chaturvedi, Vinayak, ed. 2000a. *Mapping Subaltern Studies and the Postcolonial*. London: Verso.

Chaturvedi, Vinayak. 2000b. "Introduction." In *Mapping Subaltern Studies and the Postcolonial*, edited by Vinayak Chaturvedi, vii–xix. London: Verso.

Chibber, Vivek. 2013. *Postcolonial Theory and the Specter of Capital*. London: Verso.

Corrigan, Paul, and Derek Sayer. 1985. *The Great Arch: English State Formation as Cultural Revolution*. Oxford: Basil Blackwell.

Frankel, Francine. 2005. *India's Political Economy, 1947–2004: The Gradual Revolution*. New Delhi: Oxford University Press.

Gramsci, Antonio. 1971. *Selections from the Prison Notebooks*. London: Lawrence and Wishart.

Gramsci, Antonio. 1975. *Quaderni del carcere*. Edited by Valentino Gerratana. 4 vols. Turin: Einaudi.

Green, Marcus. 2002. "Gramsci Cannot Speak: Presentations and Interpretations of Gramsci's Concept of the Subaltern." *Rethinking Marxism* 14(3): 1–24.

Green, Marcus. 2011. "Rethinking the Subaltern and the Question of Censorship in Gramsci's *Prison Notebooks*." *Postcolonial Studies* 14(4): 387–404.

Guha, Ranajit. 1982. "On Some Aspects of the Historiography of Colonial India." In *Subaltern Studies I: Writings on Indian History and Society*, edited by Ranajit Guha, 1–8. New Delhi: Oxford University Press.

Guha, Ranajit. 1983a. "The Prose of Counter-Insurgency." In *Subaltern Studies II: Writings on Indian History and Society*, edited by Ranajit Guha, 44–84. New Delhi: Oxford University Press.

Guha, Ranajit. 1983b. *Elementary Aspects of Peasant Insurgency in Colonial India*. New Delhi: Oxford University Press.

Guha, Ranajit. 1987. "Chandra's Death." In *Subaltern Studies V: Writings on Indian History and Society*, edited by Ranajit Guha, 135–65. New Delhi: Oxford University Press.

Guha, Ranajit. 1989. "Dominance without Hegemony and Its Historiography." In *Subaltern Studies VI: Writings on Indian History and Society*, edited by Ranajit Guha, 210–309. New Delhi: Oxford University Press.

Guha, Ranajit. 1992. "Discipline and Mobilize." In *Subaltern Studies VII: Writings on Indian History and Society*, edited by Partha Chatterjee and Gyanendra Pandey, 69–120. New Delhi: Oxford University Press.

Guha, Ranajit. 1996. "The Small Voice of History." In *Subaltern Studies IX: Writings on Indian History and Society*, edited by Shahid Amin and Dipesh Chakrabarty, 1–12. New Delhi: Oxford University Press.

Guha, Ranajit. 2002. *History at the Limit of World-History*. New York: Columbia University Press.

Guha, Ranajit. 2009. *The Small Voice of History: Collected Essays*. Ranikhet: Permanent Black.

Guha, Ranajit, and Gayatri Chakravorti Spivak, eds. 1988. *Selected Subaltern Studies*. New York: Oxford University Press.

Hill, Christopher. 1975. *The World Turned Upside Down: Radical Ideas During the English Revolution*. London: Penguin Books.

Hitchcock, Peter. 2015. "*Postcolonial Theory and the Specter of Capital* by Vivek Chibber (Review)." *The Comparatist* 39: 355–64.

Kaviraj, Sudipta. 1997. "A Critique of the Passive Revolution." In *State and Politics in India*, edited by Partha Chatterjee, 45–87. New Delhi: Oxford University Press.

Lazarus, Neil. 2016. "Vivek Chibber and the Spectre of Postcolonial Theory." *Race and Class* 57(3): 88–106.

Ludden, David, ed. 2002a. *Reading Subaltern Studies: Critical History, Contested Meaning and the Globalization of South Asia*. New Delhi: Permanent Black.

Ludden, David. 2002b. "Introduction: A Brief History of Subalternity." In Ludden, ed. 2002a, 1–42.

Mallon, Florencia. 1995. *Peasant and Nation: The Making of Postcolonial Mexico and Peru*. Berkeley: University of California Press.

Morton, Adam David. 2007. *Unravelling Gramsci: Hegemony and Passive Revolution in the Global Political Economy*. London: Pluto.

Mukherjee, Janam. 2015. *Hungry Bengal: War, Famine and the End of Empire*. New Delhi: C Hurst & Co.

Nilsen, Alf Gunvald. 2015. "For a Historical Sociology of State-Society Relations in the Study of Subaltern Politics." In *New Subaltern Politics: Reconceptualizing Hegemony and Resistance in Contemporary India*, edited by Alf Gunvald Nilsen and Srila Roy, 31–53. New Delhi: Oxford University Press.

Nilsen, Alf Gunvald. 2017a. *Politics from Below: Essays on Subalternity and Resistance in India*. New Delhi: Aakar Books.

Nilsen, Alf Gunvald. 2017b. "Passages from Marxism to Postcolonialism: A Comment on Vivek Chibber's *Postcolonial Theory and the Specter of Capital*." *Critical Sociology* 43(4–5): 559–71.

Nilsen, Alf Gunvald, and Srila Roy. 2015. "Reconceptualizing Subaltern Politics in Contemporary India." In *New Subaltern Politics: Reconceptualizing Hegemony and Resistance in Contemporary India*, edited by Alf Gunvald Nilsen and Srila Roy, 1–27. New Delhi: Oxford University Press.

O'Hanlon, Rosie. 2002. "Recovering the Subject: Subaltern Studies and Histories of Resistance in Colonial South Asia." In Ludden, ed. 2002a, 135–86.

Omvedt, Gail. 1993. *Reinventing Revolution: New Social Movements and the Socialist Tradition in India*. New York: East Gate.

Ray, Raka. 2012. *The Naxalites and Their Ideology*. New Delhi: Oxford University Press.

Roosa, John. 2001. "Passive Revolution meets Peasant Revolution: Indian Nationalism and the Telangana revolt." *Journal of Peasant Studies* 28(4): 57–94.

Roseberry, William. 1994. "Hegemony and the Languages of Contention." In *Everyday Forms of State Formation: Revolution and the Negotiation of Rule in Everyday Mexico*, edited by Gilbert M. Joseph and Daniel Nugent, 355–66. Durham, NC: Duke University Press.

Sarkar, Sumit. 1997. *Writing Social History*. New Delhi: Oxford University Press.

Singh, Sangeeta, Minakshi Menon, Pradeep Kumar Datta, Biswamoy Pati, Radhakantha Barik, Radhika Chopra, Partha Dutta, and Sanjay Prasad. 2002. "*Subaltern Studies II:* A Review Article." In Ludden, ed. 2002a, 58–107.

Sivaramakrishnan, Kalyanakrishnan. 2002. "Situating the Subaltern: History and Anthropology in the Subaltern Studies Project." In Ludden, ed. 2002a, 212–55.

Thompson, E.P. 1966. *The Making of the English Working Class*. New York: Vintage.

Watts, Michael. 2001. "1968 and All That . . ." *Progress in Human Geography* 25(2): 157–88.

Williams, Raymond. 1977. *Marxism and Literature*. Oxford: Oxford University Press.

35
JÜRGEN HABERMAS (1929–)

Alex Demirović

Since the 1960s, Habermas has been regarded as one of the more prominent representatives of Critical Theory and, in this respect, also as a Marxist, given that critical theory sits comfortably within the tradition of Western Marxism and the representatives of earlier Critical Theory regarded themselves as critical, non-dogmatic Marxists up to their later work (Anderson 1976). For Herbert Marcuse and Theodor W. Adorno, this is obvious. The latter explicitly emphasized the connection: "That is tantamount to saying that, if is not to be watered down, Marxism must critically reflect itself in Critical Theory" (Adorno 1969, 292). For Max Horkheimer, this continuity is masked by a multiplicity of critical commentaries on and disassociations from the New Left. Habermas, by contrast, has clearly distanced himself from earlier Critical Theory and from Marxism since the 1970s and spoken of a paradigm shift that he brought about by adapting critical social theory. In scientific-theoretical terms, there was thus a rupture between older Critical Theory and Marxism, on one hand, and his own theory, on the other.

According to his claim, Habermas aspired to guide Critical Theory from its status as a philosophy of history toward becoming a normal science. In his own perspective his theory no longer has any internal theoretical connection with earlier Critical Theory. In addressing the issue, Stefan Müller-Doohm (2014, 69) claims that Habermas is not developing Marxist theory or Critical Theory further in the way that Horkheimer and Adorno had intended: "Habermas is not passing on any theory but rather developing something entirely new, something completely different," which cannot be rooted in historical materialism.

Yet despite – or precisely because of – the paradigm shift he claims, Habermas's self-conception includes maintaining a connection to Marxism. He presents Lukács's *History and Class Consciousness* as the path to the young Marx – the Marx of the early economic-philosophical works and the *Grundrisse*, "Marx as theoretician of reification" (Habermas 1985, 167–68). That connection has also shaped his own theoretical program: as he emphasizes, Habermas is concerned with reformulating the reification theorem without getting into the aporias that he sees in Horkheimer and Adorno (Habermas 1984, 366). Marx's critique of political economy had little impact on Habermas's theory. He stressed that he referred to various parts of Marx's theory from the standpoint of his own systematic interests in various contexts and in light of various issues. He owes, as he says, that systematic interest to Western Marxism (see Habermas 1985, 216).

Marx is integrated into a philosophical history perspective; Habermas claims to understand Marx better than Marx understood himself and aims for a social theory at a higher level. That is not inherently wrong: the capitalist social formation has changed quite extensively since Marx's time and exegetic repetition of Marx's thought will not lead to a more precise understanding of its concrete conditions. But Habermas's reference indicates a disassociation or a break from Western Marxism and from Marx. If he praises Marx for being a classic (like Adam Smith or Hegel) because there is still *something* to be learned from him "despite the passing of time and the different historical circumstances," that praise is poisoned by his historicization of Marx's theory (Habermas 2014, 151). He considers Marx's scientific revolution (and value theory in particular) to be unreasonable and his theory to be empirically suspect.

These reflections offer clues as to what might be understood as Habermas's specific Post-Marxism (Demirović 2011). He does not denounce Marx's theory as the ideology of a political tendency but rather understands it as a significant contribution to modern social scientific discussion and a moment of universalism. The insights and claims he articulates need to be updated to a new historical level of social development. This will happen by critically examining and revising Marx's concepts and empirical analyses and placing them in a new theoretical context. The concept of critique loses its meaning as critique of capitalist society for the purpose of overcoming it.

Communicative Reason

What was the perspective from which Habermas received Marx? What is his specific and new theoretical project? It is a project of practical philosophy – a theory of communicative action. That theory does not seek to object to the moral norms of reality but rather to comprehend them as moments of societal reproduction and an evolutionary learning process; practical considerations of interests, needs and values should be internally linked with reason and therefore with a validity claim that has explanatory potential. It is an argument elaborated against earlier Critical Theory. According to Horkheimer, reason should evolve from labor. Habermas understands this as meaning that the process of appropriating nature leads to an objectifying stance and a kind of insight and rationality that permit a technical utilization of nature. Correspondingly, a multitude of social processes are reorganized around these technical processes. If the lifeworld is "rationalized" in accordance with this instrumental rationality, it is coterminous with the "institutionalization of a sovereignty that becomes politically unrecognizable: the technical rationality of a social system of purposive-rational action does not reveal its political content" (Habermas 1968, 49, 1987a, 187).

Habermas agrees with Marcuse's notion that the relations between productive forces and the relations of production have historically changed due to the development of productive forces and that therefore a science-based rationality can no longer be used to gauge a critique. Nonetheless, he rejects Marcuse's critique of the domination of technology, which extends Marx's argument that the development of machines under the conditions of capitalist accumulation is a weapon against workers. Due to his critique of Max Weber's theory of rationality, Habermas does not agree with a domination-critical interpretation such as this. If Marcuse is correct, then there must be alternative paths to technical development. Habermas contests this with arguments that he adopts from Arnold Gehlen, according to which people have the elements of purposive-rational action embodied in their hands and feet, eyes, ears and brains. Technical artefacts are just an extension of these organs. Therefore, technology is "our technology" without alternative (Habermas 1968, 55–57). In Habermas's view, Marcuse makes a categorical error in that he understands nature as a counterpart to a fraternal, symbolically mediated communication. Both technically supported, purposive-rational action as well as inter-subjective communication have a universalistic character and are "projects of the human species as a whole" (Habermas 1968, 57).

Habermas translates Marcuse's critique back into the culture-critical thought he had addressed in *Theory and Practice*, namely that purposive-rationally oriented systems are a problem if they encroach on society and spread to the totality of the way of life. Habermas thus gives precedence to cultural meaning, cultural interpretations and communicative relations of understanding, and socially integrative processes of meaningful action over systemically integrated ramifications of action, such as labor, exchange or administration. He conceives the functional subsystems of economy and politics as modern differentiations derived from everyday communications in the lifeworld. Labor is understood as a success-oriented, purposive-rational, and instrumental activity and not a cooperative practice in which individuals work together, are consciously coordinating and planning their activity, and have a common culture of collaboration. For Habermas labor therefore contrasts with communicative action. He implausibly tailors certain concepts to stipulate in advance that the appropriation of nature through labor cannot be democratically organized. Habermas thereby develops an almost Polanyian problematic: the establishment of a borderless, liberated technical rationality that is successful in principle must be countered with a more comprehensive rationality that has the power to push back and re-confine any society-threatening, success-oriented, functionalist and bisected rationality. Only reason can stand up to reason. The remedy for the pathologies of modernity is thus to be found in reason itself.

This thinking is contextualized by the fact that Habermas is defending the need to peel away from the production- and consciousness-philosophical paradigm of the Marxist tradition. According to his understanding, that paradigm necessarily leads to fundamental doubts about modern rationalization processes and, ultimately, to pessimism. The reason is that this paradigm yields a cultural-critical diagnosis of the times according to which the economic system generated through ever greater scientific-technical resources becomes overwhelming and alienated from individuals such that it becomes increasingly difficult to conceive of correcting that development. But that perspective only accounts for half of modernity, disregarding processes of political and cultural rationalization as well as differentiation of subsystems and the intractable logic of their actions, which have led to democracy, autonomous art and a universalistic orientation for the actions of individuals. In opposition to those assumptions Habermas proposes a reformulation of the concept of reason, which he expects will make a comprehensive concept of modernity possible. Modernity is characterized by a worldview rationalization through decentering the relations to the world: the objective world that is the object of a success-oriented action, the inter-subjective world in which action is oriented to rapprochement, and finally the subjective world that is linked with an expressive-dramaturgical action. An action is rational if the validity claims raised in any dimension (i.e., the truth of statements about the objective world, the correctness of norms that are said to be inter-subjectively applicable, or the veracity of expressions of subjective experience) have a basis that can be communicatively contested through arguments.

Submission to a cognitive-instrumentally limited rationality must be avoided; Habermas argues for integration of this rationality and for equilibrium and successful interaction between these three ways of relating to the world and types of action (Habermas 1984, 73–74). The question he poses for himself is this: how can this form of instrumental rationality be reclaimed without simultaneously compromising the differentiation of systemic processes that characterizes modernity? According to Habermas, that would be the objective of Marxism, which ultimately seeks to annul the evolutionary progress of functional differentiation by once again burdening the economic and the political-administrative system with moral and political arguments, thereby disrupting success-oriented action. Habermas bases his fastidious conception of reason in language generally and speech acts specifically. Speech acts consist of three dimensions; instrumental rationality is only one of them. In their speech acts, participants in an interaction negotiate situational interpretations and come to a consensus that a sentence is true because it corresponds to an objectivity in a world outside and enables successful action.

Every speech act also includes a second dimension: that of the inter-subjective relations of the participants in the communication. The speech act presupposes that the individuals are equal participants in communication and, likewise, have a right to participate in a discussion with arguments and can question and challenge validity claims that have been raised. This is a matter of truth-analogous discussions about the correctness of the practical action of participants in communication. Also crucial in this case is the fact that moral correctness is not assessed according to substantive considerations but rather to considerations that evolve as consensus in communication practice. Ultimately, each speech act also makes a claim to expressive authenticity. This means that individuals speak with a posture of veracity and therefore take the sentences they utter seriously and commit themselves to their meaning.

In all three dimensions, compatible action is motivated by the fact that specific and contestable validity claims are made each time. It is therefore critical for a communicative action that the speakers in a speech action not only simultaneously adopt the three relations to the world but also that they do so in a reflexive sense because they relativize their utterances against the possibility that their validity might be contested. With their utterances, they thereby assume an interpretive framework in which they can and want to achieve understanding. Language becomes what it always already is: the medium of action coordination. In quite idealistic terms, speech in itself aims at understanding.

In all three dimensions, if consensus did not already implicitly exist, it is the outcome of a discussion that can be carried out quite contentiously. In that case, a negative opinion contests a validity claim and demands an explanation. This can ultimately cause the discursive process, the object of a discussion, or the participants themselves to become the object of deliberation.

In terms of rationality and action theory, it is important for Habermas that modernity can be denoted by a differentiation of three relations to the world, three types of action, and three forms of rationality. Validity claims arise in all three dimensions. The fact that the validity of each validity claim can be communicatively contested both motivates and coordinates action. I would therefore like to understand Habermas as a theorist in the social contract tradition. This is because each speech act produces inter-subjective conditions. They constitute contractual offers that speakers communicatively commit to honoring in the event of an objection to the validity claims raised in a given speech act. Speakers assume an obligation to reciprocity, given that their speech acts can motivate conversation partners to connecting actions only under the condition that they can expect a justification discourse about facts or norms. This interactive relationship constitutes a basic sociality and universality that lies deeper than the class divide and unequal distribution of goods; it forms a universalist criterion with which to evaluate every society. From this perspective, Marx's is a subordinate theory that is insufficiently complex from the outset, because, by focusing on labor, it only analyzes the instrumental dimension of modernity and neglects what is essential. According to Habermas, it therefore only continues the functionalist self-misunderstanding of modernity itself.

Habermas's relationship to the "linguistic turn" in philosophy and the speech act theory inaugurated by J. L. Austin creates problems for him that are similar to those found in Ernesto Laclau and Chantal Mouffe. The reference to language and a universal-pragmatic reconstruction of speech acts requires a speaker position beyond history; at this level of language, history does not occur and sociality becomes a logical construction. In principle, Habermas must accept that action is always coordinated through everyday communication in the lifeworld. Communicative socialization is built into the linguistic mechanism of the reproduction of the species (Habermas 1984, 397). In this sense, history fulfills its telos in reaching modernity and comes to its terms when the relations to the world and the rationalities that are always already contained within language are evolutionarily differentiated and balance each other. Incidentally, the uncanny and mutually misunderstood proximity of Habermas's approach, on one hand, and Laclau's and Mouffe's, on the other, is remarkable given that neither side recognizes the other's theories. Apart from the linguistic ahistoricity and the claim that they are each ultimately constructing theories of politics and democracy from the ruins of Marxism, this also affects their shared Post-Marxism and the crisis explanations with which they diagnose their era: bureaucratism and consumerism, ultimately even the significance of an ahistoric theory of conflict in both approaches, namely agonistics in Laclau and Mouffe and yes/no statements and public discussion in Habermas (see Demirović 2017).

Social Theory

In deference to the reification theorem, Habermas assumes that social power relations can only retain their objectivity as long as society does not discuss them in the public sphere. The pressure of reasonable arguments can disturb and alter reified conditions (Habermas 1972, 307). He reformulates this strategy of critique along the lines of communication and rationality theory because he regards the implication of the philosophy of consciousness to be incorrect – namely the implication that a critique can ultimately make an individual's conditions completely transparent to that individual. This would specifically mean that controversial validity claims and discursive negotiation of situational interpretations are no longer necessary. The modern differentiation of instrumental action would also be revoked. The idea of a normative critique of capitalist conditions based on communication theory is thus linked to a specific perception of society.

Habermas's theorizing, which is universally designed, historicizes Marx's partisan theory. The empirical developments of capitalist social formation and the theoretical discussions since Marx become criteria for assessing and reformulating Marx's theory. Habermas thereby takes up an external perspective, but one that is associated with a claim to execute Marx's program better than Marx himself and to reconstruct that program under new social conditions. He assumes that Marx's thinking is appropriate to liberal capitalism, but that the crisis processes in the dynamics of capitalist development themselves lead to a reorganization of society and demand (both with and against Marx) a new theory to fit the time. In Habermas a critical distinction between the liberal and organized stages of capitalism is necessary to explain the expansion of the circulation of societal reproduction, in which the state plays a new and significant role. Consequently, the understanding of crisis expands as well. For Habermas, "crisis" is not only an objective outcome, it must also be subjectively experienced. The relevant question for him is how the relationship of systemically integrated and socially integrated action is constituted.

There is a tension in class societies between the unequal distribution of socially generated wealth and the legitimacy of that inequality. Its legitimation is supported by norms and systems of justification (Habermas 1976, 20). Liberal capitalism has also to cope with this problem. It has been characterized by the differentiation of a self-regulating economic system from the political system. The apolitical sphere of capital's self-management is governed through money. The state takes on an array of functions intended to ensure the preconditions for the reproduction process. In the sphere of the market, a strategic-utilitarian morality and a technical-instrumental action orientation develop. Equivalency of exchange and the principles of fairness and performance become the fundamental ideology of bourgeois society. The conditions of production no longer require legitimation from above; the law of value exercises class domination anonymously and apolitically. This is how the systemic integration of the economic system and social integration – that is, the exercise of functions appropriate to systemic processes and action based on subjective consent – are carried out simultaneously (Habermas 1976, 51–52; Habermas 1987a, 335–36). This frees the political order from its obligations of legitimation. In this sphere, it is to some extent possible to develop universalist norms that not only appeal to generalizable interests but also imply that these norms should be the outcome of a discursively achieved consensus. The ruling class can no longer see itself as a ruling class. Society is directed toward scientific rationalization and in such a way that the universalist norms (i.e., freedom and equality) are realized. This makes it sensitive to the contradiction between norm and reality and creates pressure to continuously improve and approach universalism. At the same time, liberal capitalist society is prone to economic crises that present a direct threat to its identity and, because the norms of equality and freedom are not honored, lead directly to crises of social integration.

Late capitalism represents a reaction to the economic and social crises of liberal capitalism. The state can no longer be understood in terms of superstructure; it intervenes in economic circulation and thereby fundamentally changes systemic processes. According to Habermas, the law of value no longer applies because wages are negotiated politically. The working class is socially integrated through corporatist agreements and by means of mass democracy. The way of life based on political abstentionism, privatization and consumerism is the result of a relatively high standard of living. By intervening in the economy by means of money and law in order to smooth out (and even to prevent) crisis dynamics, the state moves those dynamics onto the terrain of the political administrative system, which finds then itself confronted with the problem of ungovernability. This includes not only management problems but also crises of legitimation, given that the democratic state is dependent upon mass loyalty, which it can no longer access through cultural tradition and must instead create anew in each public debate.

Conceptually, Habermas's analysis implies that the capitalist mode of production consists of economic relations alone. It is augmented by a second relationship: the political administrative system. Habermas does not understand the state as a capitalist state. Between these two subsystems, controlled by means of money and power respectively, and the institutionalized forms of the lifeworld there are the relations of exchange pertaining to the benefits of the economy (income, goods) and the state (organization, decision-making), versus labor and management or, above all, demands and loyalty. Public debate mediates individuals' interests, desires and interpretations of the lifeworld relative to the functional subsystems and ensures cohesion between systemic and social integration. In other words, thoroughly adversarial public debates ensure society's cohesion. Modern societies are characterized by the fact that the lifeworld asserts its primacy "in relation to the subsystems separated out of its institutional orders" (Habermas 1987a, 345). But this creates tensions that lead Habermas to reformulate the concept of reification. He criticizes Marx, on one hand, for failing to distinguish between systemic and social integration and thus for not developing a concept for the specific tensions at the boundaries of these fields. On the other hand, Marx is guilty for having seen reification only in its economic dimension and not also in its political dimension. Habermas does not want to understand reification (in the Lukáscian sense) as a product of social labor, as a "sensible-supersensible" (*sinnlich-übersinnlich*) thing endowed with its own independent existence. He differs from the Marxist tradition in that he does not criticize the separation of economy and politics that become autonomous subsystems; he considers this distinction to be a "higher and evolutionarily advantageous level of integration" (Habermas 1987a, 339).

Instead, he argues that the relation of "the objective, social, or subjective world" is unilaterally prejudiced through systemic processes (Habermas 1987a, 187). Accordingly, Habermas conceives of reification as the subsystems' encroachment on the vernacular coherencies of the lifeworld, which consequently disrupt cultural reproduction. This is because production of commodities as well as the state's performance in the form of money and law imply specific abstractions from individuals' concrete demands. While traditional sensuous resources are undermined by modern rationalization processes, everyday processes for understanding the lifeworld (in which meaning can be regenerated) are simultaneously colonized through bureaucratic and consumerist encroachments. Nonetheless, Habermas believes in the existence of a sphere of understanding-oriented action that has simultaneously developed through the differentiation of the formally organized domains of action of the economy and the state apparatus and that, within this sphere, cohesion is re-established at a higher level of differentiation between instrumental, moral and expressive moments (Habermas 1987a, 329, 339–40).

Habermas explicitly draws an anti-Marxian conclusion from these considerations. He rejects a program of a reappropriation of dead labor by living labor and the destruction of the media-steered subsystems of the economy and the state. His theory aims to argue critically against a functionalist rationality only insofar as the subsystems exceed the boundaries of the subsystems in such a way that it encroaches on the lifeworld and elicits social pathologies. Nevertheless, he does not plead for the dissolution of the systems into the lifeworld as a Marxist complex theoretical approach would do in favor of free and self-determined new forms of social organization and differentiation; rather Habermas argues only for a restoration of the primacy of the lifeworld over the subsystems. Social pathologies are seen now as a fundamentally unavoidable feature of modernity. However, systemic chains of action should not be abandoned but subjected to pressure through the resistance of the lifeworld and public debates that besiege the political system and can be reprogrammed, constrained, or corrected by means of moral and legal norms. The balance of systems and lifeworld has to be recovered to limit the destructive effects of systemic operations. Habermas's theory has not the aim to overcome social contradictions systematically produced by the capitalist mode of production but to restore always in vain an equilibrium that will always and ever again be disordered by the functionalist logic of the subsystems. Contemporaries should give up the premodern idea of a final exit from this fate and should modestly define the lifeworld and accept and enjoy the efficiency of the subsystems.

Habermas's theorizing invokes the long-term success of social democratic reformism since World War II. It was obviously formulated at a moment when the Keynesian welfare state had already fallen into crisis. He put his social theory forward during the twilight of Fordist capitalism. It became apparent in the early 1980s that the growing ecological crisis could no longer be regarded as foreign to the system. Confronted with ungovernability, the strengthening of the labor movement and the social movements of the 1970s, a neoliberal reaction emerged, leading to the termination of the class compromise by the bourgeoisie, the erosion of democratic institutions, the polarization between rich and poor, and a myriad of state encroachments on the individual's life-contexts. The law of value asserted itself with a vengeance, wage-labor expanded globally to an unprecedented extent, and the state proved to be the apparatus of bourgeois power in a significant way. If Habermas hoped that his theory, although outdated due to the development of capitalism into neoliberalism, would at least be able to slow the process, his aspirations have fallen short: it has neither been carried forward nor updated. Habermas's critique of Marx has ultimately contributed to the defeatism of reason when faced with the challenges of social theory.

Bibliography

Adorno, Theodor W. 2003 (1969). "Zur Spezifikation der kritischen Theorie." In *Adorno. Eine Bildmonographie*, edited by Theodor W. Adorno Archiv, 290–92. Frankfurt am Main: Suhrkamp.

Anderson, Perry. 1976. *Considerations on Western Marxism*. London: NLB.

Demirović, Alex. 2011. "Postmarxismus." In *Politische Theorie und Politische Philosophie. Ein Handbuch*, edited by Martin Hartmann and Claus Offe, 58–59. Munich: C.H. Beck.
Demirović, Alex. 2017. "Radical Democracy and Socialism." In *Rethinking Democracy: Socialist Register 2018*, edited by Leo Panitch and Greg Albo, 298–321. London: Merlin.
Habermas, Jürgen. 1968. *Technik und Wissenschaft als "Ideologie"*. Frankfurt am Main: Suhrkamp.
Habermas, Jürgen. 1972. *Theorie und Praxis*. Frankfurt am Main: Suhrkamp.
Habermas, Jürgen. 1976. *Legitimation Crisis*. London: Heinemann.
Habermas, Jürgen. 1983. *Philosophical-Political Profiles*. Cambridge, MA: MIT Press.
Habermas, Jürgen. 1984. *The Theory of Communicative Action, Vol. 1: Reason and the Rationalization of Society*. Boston: Beacon Press.
Habermas, Jürgen. 1985. *Die Neue Unübersichtlichkeit*. Frankfurt am Main: Suhrkamp.
Habermas, Jürgen. 1987a. *The Theory of Communicative Action, Vol. 2: Lifeworld and System: A Critique of Functionalist Reason*. Boston: Beacon Press.
Habermas, Jürgen. 1987b. *The Philosophical Discourse of Modernity: Twelve Lectures*. Cambridge: Polity Press.
Habermas, Jürgen. 2014. "Entgegnung [auf Ingo Elbe]." In *Habermas und der Historische Materialismus*, edited by Smail Rapic, 151–53. Freiburg im Breisgau: Alber.
Müller-Doohm, Stefan. 2014. "[Beitrag zur] Diskussion." In *Habermas und der Historische Materialismus*, edited by Smail Rapic, 203–16. Freiburg im Breisgau: Alber.

36

ERNESTO LACLAU (1935–2014) AND CHANTAL MOUFFE (1943–)

Geoff Boucher

The work of Ernesto Laclau and Chantal Mouffe is a strikingly innovative departure from Althusserian Marxism, one that is inspired by the Gramscian category of hegemony and influenced by the poststructuralist philosophies of Derrida, Foucault and Lacan. Laclau's and Mouffe's theory of discourse is intended as a replacement for both classical and Althusserian Marxism, where "discursive practice" takes the place of social practice and "social antagonism" substitutes for class contradictions. The aim of their Post-Marxist theory is to bring radical social theory and socialist strategy into a new epoch, one characterized by increasing social complexity (rather than the simplification of class contradictions) and proliferating political conflicts (rather than class polarization). It is also to renew the vision of the left after the failure of the proletarian dictatorships, by resigning from the communist ideal of post-political social harmony and accepting instead the permanence of the democratic contestation of social relations. Laclau's and Mouffe's theoretical contributions, both jointly and separately, have been provocative but controversial, exercising a significant influence on poststructuralist inspired social theory, but attracting polemical refutations from Marxist critics. The aim of the present chapter is to render Laclau's and Mouffe's theory intelligible for a materialist audience with a working knowledge of Marxism, and to outline some of the most important criticism.

Laclau and Mouffe aim to reimagine the project of the left by abandoning what they call the "Jacobin Imaginary" of Leninist politics, embracing instead a conception that is "radically libertarian and infinitely more politically ambitious than the classical left" (Laclau and Mouffe 1985, 152). They advocate the egalitarian linking-up of struggles against oppression, the preservation of pluralism within left-wing politics, and democratic citizenship as a progressive social cement. Describing radical-democratic politics in terms of an extension and deepening of the Democratic Revolution of Modernity, Laclau and Mouffe advocate equality, liberty and solidarity, in the context of a self-limiting revolution that would happen within democratic, rather than insurrectionary, frameworks. By contrast with classical socialism, they insist that complete equality and total liberty are the opposed poles of totalitarianism and atomization, so that democratic politics consists in a dynamic equilibrium between these poles. Despite the fact that their signature work had a controversial reception on the left, Laclau and Mouffe insisted that their Post-Marxism was not – as alleged (Geras 1990) – "an ex-Marxism without substance," but was at least as much Post-*Marxist* as *Post*-Marxist. Although their initial interventions were polemically aimed against the Leninist "Jacobin Imaginary," after the initially hostile response to radical-democratic politics on the left abated, Laclau and Mouffe switched to contesting the "neutralization of the political" in mainstream political philosophy. In sharp critiques of liberal conceptions of the social contract and deliberative democracy, of communitarian solidarity and theories of recognition, Mouffe in particular has insisted on an "agonistic" vision of politics as contestation rather than redistribution or reconciliation.

Perhaps the most strikingly innovative aspect of radical democratic politics is its solution to the problem of the addressee of critical theory, after the eclipse of the classical proletariat as historical subject. For Laclau and Mouffe, collective agents – that is, political subjects – are formed through discursive operations that, not surprisingly, strongly resemble the Gramscian category of hegemony. According to Gramsci, this happened through cementing social alliances by means of ideological representations and political compromises, in an exercise of "ethico-political leadership," which involved the identification of the national or popular interest with the generalized interests of the alliance partners. Collective agents become political subjects to the extent that they fuse sectoral interests into a generalized interest, creating corporate identities, and they become hegemonic to the degree that their control of the ideological and political landscape compels subaltern groups to formulate demands within the reigning social alliance's definition of the national-popular interest. What Laclau and Mouffe add to all of this is a description of the process in terms of a theory of discourse that breaks from the assumption of social groups as natural kinds with necessary forms of political representation. This allows for the possibility of arbitrary relations between political identities and social locations, in the context of multiple, overlapping and crisscrossing, hegemonic struggles, reflecting not only the emergence of the "new social movements," but also other novel mobilizations of the late 20th and early 21st centuries.

The Deconstruction of Marxism

Laclau's and Mouffe's key theoretical innovation is a poststructuralist reinvention of the concept of social practice as "discourse," something that allows them to theorize antagonism, hegemony, dislocation and exclusion in ways that go beyond Althusserian Marxism. They arrive at this through a critique of Marxism that is worth briefly looking at, not because its claims are exceptionally rigorous, but because this renders intelligible a set of contentions that are otherwise potentially confusing.

According to Laclau and Mouffe, classical Marxism was an "evolutionary paradigm," centered upon the concept of "historical necessity," unfolding through the "endogenous laws" operating in the "economic base" (Laclau and Mouffe 1985, 7–46). The result was an ascending sequence of economically determined historical stages, characterized by eventual economic stagnation and class polarization, culminating in the revolutionary transformation of society after the seizure of state power. The final stage of history ends with proletarian revolution, followed by post-capitalist societies. Now, the fundamental conviction of Laclau and Mouffe is that of the failure of this model, but their key evidence is not really the disintegration of "actually existing socialism" in the former USSR and Yugoslavia, or the authoritarianism of Chinese Communism. Instead, their target is the way that the economic reductionism and class essentialism of the model assigns to every social fraction and superstructural element – ideologies, parties, institutions – a single and clear class significance. They maintain that the model's failure is legible in the theoretical and practical efforts of 20th-century socialist movements to cope with the challenge of developments that indicate social complexity rather than a simplification of antagonisms. These include the ramification of social strata, the proliferation of "non-class antagonisms," new social movements and ambiguous ideological formations.

Laclau and Mouffe interpret Gramsci's concept of hegemony as a response to political fragmentation – itself the result of a proliferation of social forces and a multiplication of political agents that defied the classical model of class polarization – leading to a strategy involving the formation of social alliances (Laclau and Mouffe 1985, 65–71). In philosophical terms, they argue, this implied the supplementation of the economistic logic of historical necessity governing classical Marxism with a logic of political contingency. However, the effects of this supplement were limited when the need to constitute social alliances in order to form a historic bloc was recaptured within the class model, through the notion that only "fundamental classes" could provide political leadership (Laclau and Mouffe 1985, 69). At the same time, the category of hegemony implied a gradual acknowledgment that "class unity" is in fact the symbolic condensation of an ideological identity around a political symbol, one that is in principle arbitrary in relation to the social field. Laclau and Mouffe conclude that "intellectual and moral leadership constitutes, according to Gramsci, a higher synthesis, a collective will, which, through ideology, becomes the organic cement unifying a historical bloc" (Laclau and Mouffe 1985, 67). Political subjects are no longer classes but social alliances, which do not take power, but become the state by becoming hegemonic, that is, the historic bloc controls the normative and institutional framework of society by maintaining relations of consent and coercion throughout society (Laclau and Mouffe 1985, 67).

For Laclau and Mouffe, if Gramsci's concept of hegemony confronted the economic reductionism of classical Marxism, then Althusser's concept of overdetermination challenged its class essentialism. The Althusserian notion of the "relative autonomy" of the "structural instances" (economic, political, juridical, ideological) of the social formation conceptualizes social practices in each of these different levels of society as driven by regionally specific developmental dynamics. Accordingly, the significance of a political, juridical or ideological element – such as a party, law or myth – cannot be directly reduced to the class contradictions of the economic foundation and assigned a singular belonging (as, for instance, "bourgeois ideology"). Instead, political, juridical and ideological conflicts, arising through local contradictions, but influenced by the effects of the other instances, had to be related to the complex whole of the social formation through a concept of multiple causation that Althusser borrowed from Freud, namely, "overdetermination." For Althusser, overdetermination meant a *weighted* multiple causation, one that retained the principle of economic determination in the final instance in a complex way. Not surprisingly, Laclau and Mouffe reject the notion of economic determination as a residue of class essentialism, but they are not content to remain – as fellow ex-Althusserians, Barry Hindess and Paul Hirst, had done – with the notion of multiple causation operating between the *membra disjecta* of the Althusserian social formation (Hindess and Hirst 1977). Instead, following a complex deconstructive critique of the concept of structure and its economic taproot in Althusserian Marxism, Laclau and Mouffe propose to reconstruct left-wing critique through discourse theory. Rejecting any distinction between articulation of language and practice on materials, on the grounds that these are merely differentiations in the "social production of meaning" (Laclau and Mouffe 1985, 107), they set forth the category of discourse, which is supposed to supersede the Marxian paradigm of labor as the model of social practice.

Discursive Practice, Hegemonic Articulation and Social Antagonism

For Laclau and Mouffe, the field of institutionally constructed social practices is diacritically structured, "like a language," that is, it consists solely of differences between economic, political, juridical, ideological – and so forth – practices, "without positive terms" (Laclau and Mouffe 1985, 99). From this perspective, the meaning of a social practice is not constituted through its functional relation to nature and/or society, but, rather, is given solely by its relationship to the institutional network consisting of other practices. Further, the structural locations that determine the material interests of social agents are the same thing as the institutional practices that they perform, so that the identity of groups consists in the ensemble of economic, political, juridical, ideological – and so forth – practices that constitutes their subject-positions, or, social roles. As a consequence, every social agent has a particular identity that is, in the final analysis, differentially defined within the relational complex of the ensemble of social practices that makes up the relevant institutional apparatus. Because the field of social practices is differentially structured, Laclau and Mouffe describe this as "discourse" and propose that an "articulation" is "any practice establishing a relation among elements such that their identity is modified as a result of the articulatory practice" (Laclau and Mouffe 1985, 105). They insist that discursive articulation "must pierce the entire material density of the multifarious institutions" it operates on (Laclau and Mouffe 1985, 109), because "discourse is a real force which contributes to the moulding and constitution of social relations" (Laclau and Mouffe 1985, 110).

Laclau and Mouffe propose a distinction between "differential" articulations, which assign social identities to agents within a politically neutral field of differences, a "discursive totality," and "equivalential" articulations, which antagonistically render entire fields of agents equivalent to one another, in relation to a "constitutive outside." That is achieved by articulating all of the particular identities onto a political symbol, a "floating signifier," a signifier that acts to represent the discursive totality to itself and to its outside. They argue that the antagonistic articulation of a discursive totality in opposition to other discursive totalities is necessary and therefore inevitable, so that all social identities are incomplete, perforated by antagonism. Actually, that follows directly from the idea that the floating signifier that "represents" a discursive totality must be differentially defined in relation to another signifier, namely, the floating signifier of another discursive totality.

Describing the process whereby a discursive totality forms as "suture," Laclau and Mouffe conclude that "there is no social identity fully protected from a discursive exterior that deforms it and prevents it becoming fully sutured" (Laclau and Mouffe 1985, 105). Conversely, "this [discursive] exterior is constituted by other discourses," which constitute a "field of discursivity" surrounding every discursive totality, so that every discursive totality must have a "constitutive outside" (Laclau and Mouffe 1985, 146 n.20). Turning this around one more time, the formation of a discourse involves "cutting out" the "regularity in dispersion" of a differentially related ensemble of discursive practices, a partial totality, from the "field of discursivity" surrounding it, something that happens by articulating all of these practices to a floating signifier (Laclau and Mouffe 1985, 113). Examples of floating signifiers are things like "freedom," "communism," "democracy" and so forth, signifiers that "float" because the articulation of multiple subject-positions onto them empties them of content, transforms them into political blanks, or surfaces of inscription, whose content depends solely on the struggles that become connected with them.

Discursive totalities are best grasped as social alliances whose political identity is formed through antagonistic equivalence ("us" and "them"), which means that every identity is relationally determined, or rendered incomplete, by the necessary existence of an antagonistic identity against which it is defined. However, "every antagonism, left free to itself, is a floating signifier, a 'wild' antagonism which does not predetermine the form in which it can be articulated to other elements in a social formation" (Laclau and Mouffe 1985, 171). What this means can best be exhibited by discussing the way that Laclau and Mouffe underscore the novelty of their concept by pointing out the difference between social antagonism, structural "real opposition" and class contradiction. Where class contradictions are grasped through a dialectical logic governed by historical necessity, real oppositions imply a radically external observer capable of viewing society as a whole. By contrast, social antagonisms are regulated by a logic of political contingency that prevents the closure of the social, its existence as a complete totality, therefore ruling out both dialectical progression and neutral metalanguage (Laclau and Mouffe 1985, 125). Laclau and Mouffe propose that there are two main types of antagonism – popular antagonisms and democratic antagonisms. Popular antagonisms divide social space into two opposed camps, while democratic antagonisms make the world increasingly complex (Laclau and Mouffe 1985, 133).

Laclau and Mouffe theorize the operation of hegemonic articulation as involving the consolidation of a social alliance in the modern locus of political power, the "empty place" of popular sovereignty created by the democratic revolutions, which is not exactly the same as "taking state power" or "winning the elections" (Laclau and Mouffe 1985, 152–59). That is because, for Laclau and Mouffe, by creating equivalences between the demands of alliance partners, and simultaneously defining the alliance in opposition to some antagonist, hegemony involves the expansion of a discourse into a horizon of social meaning. Laclau focuses especially on the way that this involves the tendential "emptying out" of the particular identities of alliance partners, as their subject positions are articulated equivalentially onto floating signifiers whose generality increases as the alliance expands. But Laclau also insists that recognition of the constitutive nature of the gap between a particular project and the impossibility of fully incarnating the universal is the condition of possibility for democratic politics (Laclau 1995, 46). Indeed, the "Jacobin temptation" that constitutes totalitarian politics is the idea that the empty place of modern power can be permanently occupied by a social force that incarnates the universal directly, which is why Laclau and Mouffe connect classical Marxism with the "Jacobin Imaginary."

Strongly influenced by Claude Lefort's notion of the constitutive role of the political (rather than the economic) in the formation of societies, both Laclau and Mouffe draw upon his theory of the "empty place of power" in democratic modernity. For Lefort, the modern substitution of the sovereignty of the people for the sacred body of the premodern sovereign involves an evacuation of the locus of power, which reveals that the political is that symbolic place where society is cemented by creating a myth of unification around some universal value. It is political symbolism – the ability to signify in the name of the absent fullness of community – that is the "empty place of power," indicating that this is a dominant ideology, or "social imaginary," and not an institutional site (Laclau and Mouffe 1985, 155).

Laclau's and Mouffe's intervention met a controversial reception on the left, and Laclau's *New Reflections on the Revolution of Our Times* and Mouffe's *The Return of the Political* are mainly dedicated to the defense and elaboration of their initial perspective. The central charges levelled by Marxist critics were that Laclau's and Mouffe's theory of discourse, with its refusal of the practice/material distinction was idealist (Geras 1990, 61–126), inflated the category of ideology beyond plausible restrictions (Callinicos 1985; Palmer 1990; Wood and Foster 1997), and lapsed into moral relativism with anti-socialist political implications (Harris 1992, 1996; Wood 1998). In response, Laclau alleged that the Marxist criticism involves "an illegitimate detour through the referent" to arrive at a pre-discursive materiality, denounced the "rationalist dictatorship of the Enlightenment" and affirmed that truth is relative to a discourse and political decisions are situation specific (Laclau 1990, 4, 97–133).

The Challenges of Right-Wing Decisionism and Left-Wing Populism

Following the controversial reception of *Hegemony and Socialist Strategy*, Mouffe turned to interventions in mainstream political philosophy, centered on the validity of social mobilization and political contestation for a robust democracy. Laclau, meanwhile, addressed the contention of that work that, for radical democracy, "the fundamental concept is that of democratic struggle," whereas political populism is either derivative or authoritarian (Laclau and Mouffe 1985, 137). These interventions spanned conjunctures very different from those that prompted the emergence of Post-Marxism, and they placed in question some of Laclau's and Mouffe's fundamental assumptions.

In *The Return of the Political* (1992), Mouffe adopted the notion, first developed by pro-Nazi legal theorist Carl Schmitt, of a "neutralization of the political," to describe the "post-political," bipartisan consensus between conservatives and liberals (including New Labour) that emerged after the disintegration of "actually existing socialism." In subsequent essays on democratic citizenship as a form of social solidarity for democratic politics, and the necessity of pluralism for an agonic conception of political decision-making, Mouffe confronted the "challenge of Carl Schmitt" for radical democracy (Mouffe 1999). On the surface, the relation of the negation of identity that is set up by the connection between social antagonism and constitutive outside is strongly reminiscent of Schmitt's notion of politics in terms of the friend-enemy distinction. Although both Laclau and Mouffe insist that they are not "left Schmittians," Mouffe accepts that Schmitt's militarization of politics along existential lines has conceptual affinities to the Post-Marxist insistence on the permanence of politics (Mouffe 2009, 13–14). The fundamental question at stake here is not just about "decisionism," that is, the link between contingent articulations and a conception of the political as arbitrary – it also concerns the ethico-political disturbance that is a logical entailment of the Laclavo-Mouffian position, namely, that a politics of liberation must involve *exclusion*.

The difference, Mouffe maintains, between her and Schmitt, is pluralism. She accepts the idea of a tension between popular sovereignty and democratic contestation, but rejects the Schmittian idea that these could be reconciled in a politically homogeneous plebiscitary democracy that is reliant on the existential negation of some external enemy. Mouffe argues that the achievement of homogeneity would prevent the emergence of contestation and decision within the political community, so that pluralism is a crucial component of democratic politics, and she invokes the need for a civic culture that converts antagonists into adversaries rather than enemies (Mouffe 1999, 39–55). Instead of excluding political antagonisms as "irrational," radical democratic hegemony would entail the promotion of activist citizenship – a militant political subjectivity – that would support a radical democratic government through mass mobilizations within the framework of democratic contestation. For Mouffe, "within the constitutive ethico-political principles of modern democracy," antagonists are to be treated as democratic adversaries, whereas for Schmitt they are regarded as enemies of society (Mouffe 1992a, 30).

Yet against John Rawls's notion of a rational consensus, Mouffe argues that democratic institutions should allow political disagreements to take an adversarial form, acknowledging that these are generated within constitutive tensions between liberty and equality, democracy and sovereignty, rather than just a clash of ideas susceptible to rational adjudication. She insists that despite appearances, this is not a Rawlsian "overlapping consensus," but rather involves a political consensus on basic democratic values and procedures while allowing dissent over the interpretation of the precise meaning of these values and procedures (Mouffe 1992b, 3–4) (Mouffe 1996). For Mouffe, democratic citizenship is a social cement, involving political engagement, a pluralistic ethos and a culture of solidarity with strangers, which she advocates as the foundation for a new left-wing political imaginary (Mouffe 1992b, 3–4).

To theorize this strategy, Mouffe proposes a deconstructive synthesis "beyond liberalism and communitarianism" that might reconcile individual liberties with complex equality in a new form of political subjectivity. According to her, Rawls cannot tolerate real political dissent (Mouffe 1992b, 45–67), while Michael Walzer's concept of complex equality implies the elimination of social antagonism (Mouffe 1992b, 84–92). She rejects both the liberal theory of the state as a neutral instrument and the communitarian postulate of the primacy of a substantive community, and wants to combine the liberal notion of democratic citizenship with the communitarian concept of the partiality of the state ((Mouffe 1992a, 28–32). What she calls "agonistics" is a political art of judgment about how to participate in democratic contestation as a partisan without succumbing to the temptations of the neutralization or the militarization of the political (Mouffe 2013, 1–18).

Meanwhile, Laclau was confronting the implications of the claim that radical-democratic hegemonic strategy involves "the struggle for a maximum autonomization of spheres [of struggle] on the basis of the generalization of the equivalential-egalitarian logic" (Laclau and Mouffe 1985, 167). There is a coalition-building intention in that statement, alongside a difficult tension between difference and equivalence that is both logical and rhetorical. In *Contingency, Hegemony, Universality* (2000), Laclau sought to catalyze the formation of a "popular front" around post-structuralist influenced, left-wing theory, between himself, Judith Butler and Slavoj Žižek. Here, he reiterates that "there is no future for the left if it is unable to create an expansive universal discourse, constructed out of, not against, the proliferation of particularisms of the past few decades" (Butler et al. 2000, 306). Laclau's interventions involve a restatement of fundamental theses about hegemonic articulation and social antagonism, in the context of an elaboration of the way that the articulation of partial struggles to a floating signifier involves a tendential universalization, if not a categorical universalism (Butler et al. 2000, 82–86, 191). But in the end, the dialogue is upstaged by Žižek's intervention, who had already accused Laclau of "left Schmittianism" (Žižek 1999, 172, 174–82), and now raises a basic question: why is the *socialist* revolution prohibited, when the modern epoch arises from the democratic *revolution* (Butler et al. 2000, 93)? How is this not resignation to capitalism as the "only game in town" (Butler et al. 2000, 95)?

Laclau's work *On Populist Reason* (2005) might be seen as a spirited response to this sort of question, one that rejects class struggle for populist politics, and which embraces the formalist implications of the semiotic and rhetorical approach (Laclau 2005, 129–32, 153–54). Where Mouffe had defended the role of the new social movements, Laclau now defended left-wing populist movements and parties (such as Podemos in Spain and Syriza in Greece, though both emerged later than his book) as vital for democratic politics rather than a menace to it (Laclau 2014, 139–80). Intriguingly, in *The Rhetorical Foundations of Society*, Laclau follows up on the earlier remark that "the sociological equivalent of that to which rhetoric is opposed [i.e., logic] is a notion of social actors as constituted by well-defined interests and rationally negotiating with an external milieu" (Laclau 2005, 12). From the perspective of such social logics, populism symbolizes irrationality, whereas from a perspective according to which hegemonic articulations involve metaphors and metonymies, and the identity of agents is politically constituted, the construction of national-popular unity around ideological symbols is the elementary operation of social structuration (Laclau 2014, 139–40).

Bibliography

Butler, Judith, Ernesto Laclau, and Slavoj Žižek. 2000. *Contingency, Hegemony, Universality: Contemporary Dialogues on the Left*. London: Verso.

Callinicos, Alex. 1985. "Postmodernism, Post-Structuralism, Post-Marxism?" *Theory, Culture & Society* 2: 85–101.

Geras, Norman. 1990. *Discourses of Extremity: Radical Ethics and Post-Marxist Extravagances*. London: Verso.

Harris, David. 1992. *From Class Struggle to the Politics of Pleasure: The Effects of Gramscianism on Cultural Studies*. London: Routledge.

Harris, David. 1996. *A Society of Signs?* London: Routledge.
Hindess, Barry, and Paul Hirst. 1977. *Mode of Production and Social Formation: An Auto-Critique of Precapitalist Modes of Production*. London: Macmillan and Co.
Laclau, Ernesto. 1990. *New Reflections on the Revolution of Our Time*. Londo: Verso.
Laclau, Ernesto. 1995. *Emancipation(s)*. London: Verso.
Laclau, Ernesto. 2005. *On Populist Reason*. London: Verso.
Laclau, Ernesto. 2014. *The Rhetorical Foundations of Society*. London: Verso.
Laclau, Ernesto, and Chantal Mouffe. 1985. *Hegemony and Socialist Strategy: Toward a Radical Democratic Politics*. London: Verso.
Mouffe, Chantal. 1992a. "Citizenship and Political Identity." *October* 61: 28–32.
Mouffe, Chantal. 1992b. *The Return of the Political*. London: Verso.
Mouffe, Chantal. 1996. "Democracy, Power and the 'Political.'" In *Democracy and Difference*, edited by Seyla Benhabib, 245–56. Princeton: Princeton University Press.
Mouffe, Chantal. 1999. "Carl Schmitt and the Paradox of Liberal Democracy." In *The Challenge of Carl Schmitt*, edited by Chantal Mouffe, 39–55. London: Verso.
Mouffe, Chantal. 2009. *The Democratic Paradox*. London: Verso.
Mouffe, Chantal. 2013. *Agonistics: Thinking the World Politically*. London: Verso.
Palmer, Bryan. 1990. *Descent into Discourse: The Reification of Language and the Writing of Social History*. Philadelphia: Temple University Press.
Wood, Ellen M. 1998. *The Retreat from Class: A New "True" Socialism*. 2nd edn. London: Verso.
Wood, Ellen M., and John Bellamy Foster, eds. 1997. *In Defense of History: Marxism and the Postmodern Agenda*. New York: Monthly Review Press.
Žižek, Slavoj. 1999. *The Ticklish Subject: The Absent Centre of Political Ontology*. London: Verso.

37
ANTONIO NEGRI (1933–)

Timothy S. Murphy

Antonio Negri is a philosopher and militant who emerged from the innovative political and social movements that shook Italy – and Europe more generally – in the 1960s and 1970s to become the most influential Italian radical thinker since Antonio Gramsci. Born into a Communist family in Padua before World War II, he studied philosophy of law and constitutional law at the University of Padua and later at the universities of Oxford and Tübingen. From 1956 to 1979 he was professor of state doctrine at the University of Padua, and served as director of the university's Institute of Political Science from 1967 to 1973; he was also a research director at the National Research Center in Rome from 1969 to 1979. He was imprisoned from 1979 to 1983 and again from 1997 to 2003 on politically motivated charges of involvement with terrorism; he spent the interval between those prison terms in exile in France, where he taught at the University of Paris VIII and the Collège international de philosophie and did sociological research for the French government. Since his release in 2003 he has worked as an independent scholar based in Paris.

Constituent and Constituted Power

Negri's theoretical work is sometimes described as Marxist, in that he has continued to draw upon Marxian categories, concepts and methods throughout his career, and sometimes as Post-Marxist, in that he consistently articulates the need for both theorists and militants to go "beyond Marx" (as in the title of his 1979 book *Marx Beyond Marx*). The seeming paradox is resolved when we recognize that for Negri, the only way to go "beyond Marx" is to go through Marx, that is, to use Marxian analytical techniques in order to re-invent Marxian concepts – or even invent new concepts – for the recent stages in social history that Marx could not accurately foresee. In *Marx Beyond Marx*, which collects the lectures he gave at the École normale supérieure in Paris at the invitation of Louis Althusser, Negri interprets Marx's emphasis on antagonistic subjectivity in the *Grundrisse* as a fertile method for going beyond the rigid objectivism of *Capital* that had been extolled in different ways by Karl Kautsky and Althusser himself. In *Factory of Strategy* (1977), Negri extracts from Lenin's conception of the soviet a broader method for deriving concrete forms of political organization from the characteristics of the determinate social formation into which that organization aims to intervene, thus using Lenin himself to move beyond the vanguardism that has come to define conventional Leninism.

Although he has often been criticized for this practice of reading by more orthodox Marxists, deconstructive critics and historians of philosophy, Negri applies the same method of locating within a thinker's work the tools for going beyond his or her conclusions to Baruch Spinoza in *The Savage Anomaly* (1981) and *Subversive Spinoza* (1992), to poet-philosopher Giacomo Leopardi in *Flower of the Desert* (1987), and to the transatlantic revolutionary tradition (Machiavelli, Harrington, Jefferson and the Federalists, Rousseau and the French Revolutionaries) in *Insurgencies* (1992). It also plays an important role in his ongoing collaboration with Michael Hardt that has so far produced five major interventions into the debate over post-Fordism, neo-liberalism and globalization: *Empire* (2000), *Multitude* (2004), *Commonwealth* (2009), *Declaration* (2012) and *Assembly* (2017). This method, which he calls the "method of the tendency" in his political writings (see Negri 2005, 26–30) and the logic of "time to come" [*tempo avvenire*] in his metaphysical works (see Negri 2003, 161–65), finds its historical basis in his dualistic and antagonistic conception of modernity. Negri locates the theoretical advent of modernity in Machiavelli's distinction between *fortuna*, a conception of time as homogeneous, empty and repetitive (in Walter Benjamin's sense), which serves to measure the objective accumulation of knowledge, power and wealth acquired through class exploitation, and *virtù*, a conception of time as unpredictably disjointed by the eruption of subjective innovation in the form of art, science and political struggle (see Negri 2004, ch. 2). The former conception gives rise to the statist tradition of philosophical modernity (Descartes, Kant, Hegel and their followers), focused on the hierarchies of constituted power, while the latter gives rise to an asymmetrical, insurrectionary counter-tradition (Spinoza, Marx, Nietzsche, Foucault, Deleuze and Guattari) that focuses on the immanence of constituent power and refuses to be reduced to dialectical synthesis. Negri dedicated the earliest and most conventional stage of his academic career to analyzing the statist tradition (the only example of this stage available in English is *Political Descartes*, Negri 1970), and the past fifty years to excavating and realizing the possibilities of the counter-tradition.

From Militancy to Imprisonment

While still a student Negri became active in local Socialist politics in the Veneto, but the turning point of his career was his encounter with the dissident Socialist Raniero Panzieri, who convinced him to study Marx and later to join the editorial board of the journal *Quaderni rossi* (*Red Notebooks*). During the early 1960s Panzieri's circle sought to renew Italian working-class militancy following the disappointments of the immediate postwar years by studying the new conditions of labor in the Fordist factories that were fast becoming the dominant economic paradigm in formerly agricultural Italy. Militant sociologists such as Romano Alquati articulated the link between the new technical composition of the class – how it actually worked on the factory floor – and its political composition, that is, its organization as a political force outside the factory through its unions and parties. Such studies revealed to Panzieri and his younger colleagues Negri and Mario Tronti that a profound disagreement between workers and their party and union representatives was arising over whether to participate in conventional parliamentary politics and contract negotiations, and that new forms of political organization were needed to match the class's new subjective composition, particularly the unrestrainable militancy that manifested itself following the Piazza Statuto riots of 1962. From that point forward, Negri's primary focus as a theorist has been the analysis of new subjective forms among workers and the proposal of new structures for their effective political organization under the changing conditions of late capitalism.

As a young academic, Negri wrote scholarly studies of the statist ideology that Hegel, Kant and the historicists Wilhelm Dilthey and Friedrich Meinecke manifest at the same time that he was becoming involved with Socialist Party administration in Padua, but the two activities rarely intersected. Once he began to study Marx, at Panzieri's urging, the division between his professional and political activities began to break down: while he was leading discussion groups with factory workers at Porto Marghera, he was also writing essays analyzing the neutralization of labor within the Italian constitution of 1948 (see Hardt and Negri 1994, ch. 3). Over the course of the 1960s and 1970s he increasingly fused the roles of theorist and militant, to the point that each critical analysis was conceived and carried out collaboratively within the framework of the particular militant group and periodical with which he was associated at the moment of composition. At the same time, the Padua Institute of Political Science, which he directed, became a center for radical investigation, debate and planning, a counter-university within the university.

Disagreements with Panzieri over the direction of *Quaderni rossi* had led Negri and Tronti to resign from that journal in 1964 and found their own, *classe operaia* (Working Class), in which Tronti famously articulated the "workerist hypothesis" of working-class historical priority for the first time. That conception, which Negri more than anyone else has extended in new directions over the past five decades, forms the basis for the workerist Marxism (also known as autonomist Marxism) that spread across Western Europe – especially France and Germany – during the 1970s. Further splits in the Italian far left followed. While Negri was helping to found the non-union workers' group *Potere operaio* (Workers' Power) in 1969, Tronti decided to join the Italian Communist Party (PCI) in order to influence it from the inside (a strategy he shared with Massimo Cacciari and others, the failure of which became apparent over the course of the 1970s as the PCI became increasingly obsessed with policing its own left wing in order to join a governing coalition with the center-right Christian Democrats). The entry into Italian political debate of feminists, students, gay/lesbian activists and ecologists during the early 1970s precipitated a crisis in factory-centered Workers' Power, which disbanded in 1973 to make way for the broader "movement of movements" called *Autonomia* (*Autonomy*).

Negri initially affiliated himself with Autonomy's most hierarchical and conventionally Leninist wing and worked to construct a concept of the centralized workers' party adapted to the crisis of Fordism, but with the rise of "red terrorism" to match the long-standing "black terrorism" of Italian fascism, he realized that the emerging class composition of decentralized production and flexible work could not be constrained either within conventional Leninist categories or within Fordist relations of production. Whereas the professional worker of the original soviets embodied sophisticated skills necessary for production with simple machines and relied upon similarly skilled professional revolutionaries to organize their political struggle, and the deskilled Fordist mass worker of midcentury had formally delegated political activity to his/her party and union, the emerging socialized worker of post-Fordism refused to permit delegation or representation, either by capitalist management or by a centralized party (see Negri 2014, 2005). The emergence of the socialized worker, the direct conceptual precursor to the multitude of Negri's later collaborations with Hardt, corresponded to the shift from the formal subsumption of society by capital, in which older forms of production were allowed to persist under capitalist management, to its real subsumption, in which capitalist relations invaded and reshaped every aspect of production in all areas (see *CI*, 1019–38).

In another of the paradoxes that inflect his career, just as Negri was moving beyond conventional Leninism in both theory and practice, he was arrested on 7 April 1979 and accused of running a classically Leninist vanguard organization, the clandestine terrorist group Red Brigades; he was also accused of masterminding the kidnapping and assassination of former Italian prime minister Aldo Moro and of "armed insurrection against the powers of the state," as one warrant put it. Along with dozens of other high-profile militant intellectuals, he was incarcerated on the orders of a PCI-affiliated magistrate as part of that party's attempt to burnish its law-and-order credentials in anticipation of the "Historic Compromise" that would finally allow the PCI to join the governing coalition. Within a year thousands of other militants were arrested on similar charges and subjected to collective trials, resulting in the collapse of the Italian radical counterculture. Negri remained in prison for over four years awaiting trial, as the charges against him changed from month to month. Shortly after the start of his trial, in summer 1983, he was elected to parliament as a representative of the small, left-libertarian Radical Party; he was freed to take his seat, but when the legislature took up a bill to revoke his immunity, he fled to Paris, where he remained in exile for fourteen years. During that interval, he was found guilty in absentia at trial, but his original sentence of thirty years was reduced on appeal to thirteen years. In 1997 he voluntarily returned to Italy to serve his remaining sentence, and he was released on parole in 2003.

Multitude Against Empire

During his Parisian exile, Negri continued to theorize militant subjectivity and organization in books such as *Insurgencies*, although his uncertain status as a political refugee prevented him from participating in French political life. In 1984 Jacques Derrida and Jean-François Lyotard invited him to become a founding member of the Collège international de Philosophie, and in 1986 he met American Michael Hardt (b.1960) and began collaborating with him on the journal *Futur antérieur* and the book *Labor of Dionysus* (1994). However, their second book collaboration, *Empire* (2000), brought them a wider readership than any Negri had known in Italy. In that book Hardt and Negri propose two new concepts for grasping the historical transformation the global economy has undergone over the past fifty years: in place of the Leninist notion of imperialism functioning according to the direct nexus between metropolis and colony, they articulate the new logic of empire, which operates without direct colonial rule through global structures of capital flow, computerized commodity production and neoliberal doctrine, and in place of the industrial proletariat as the central subject of history to which all other subjective forms are subordinate, they nominate the multitude, a decentered and non-hierarchical collective subject defined not by its common essence or experiences but rather by the radical singularity of its constituents. In a restatement of Tronti's original workerist hypothesis, Hardt and Negri assert that the multitude, by means of its incorrigible insubordination, calls empire into being: since the nation-state, which emerged in its modern form as a function of classical imperialism, has proven itself during the postwar period to be incapable of guaranteeing smooth and predictable capitalist growth in the face of expanding worker demands, its formal sovereignty must be overdetermined and eroded by supranational institutions such as the World Bank, International Monetary Fund, transnational corporations and other globalizing structures. The result is a global system with no governing center, not even the US as "sole superpower" since it experiences capital flight, neoliberal restructuring and the erosion of sovereignty just as other nations do (see Hardt and Negri 2000, part 2).

Empire is not only a structure of governance but also a new mode of production that Hardt and Negri, adapting Foucault's late work, label "biopolitical production." This means that the cutting edge (though not necessarily the bulk) of capitalist production has shifted from material commodities to immaterial ones, including forms of intellectual property like software, data and digital media on the one hand and, on the other, social and/or affective forms of interpersonal care such as training, health maintenance, customer service and hospitality, as well as collaborative research and development. The logic and techniques of such recursive, information-driven social labor now permeate even the most material sectors of production such as agriculture, construction and industry. At the same time, the erosion of welfare-state programs and the privatization of public services compel individuals seeking work to become "entrepreneurs of themselves," in other words to view themselves as capitalist micro-firms who must constantly remodel themselves in order to compete on a labor market whose safety net is being withdrawn. This becoming-biopolitical of production, in which social life in the aggregate is both the subject and object of capitalist exploitation, has two opposed consequences: it results in the extension and intensification of exploitation as the division between labor time of production and leisure time of reproduction (as well as other traditional divisions) dissolves, but at the same time it relies upon the autonomous development and deployment of the intellectual, affective and social wealth of collaborating subjects. While the former produces new pathologies, the latter makes possible militant organizational initiatives independent of capital's command. Biopolitical production reveals the production of subjectivity and its suspension between the poles of exploitative subjection and autonomous subjectivation to be the basis for all other levels of production (see Hardt and Negri 2000, part 3).

The theory of empire was quickly taken up for debate and application within a wide range of left movements around the world, most notably the *Tute bianche* (White Overalls) in Italy, groups involved with the World Social Forums, and those protesting G7/G8 meetings; later, elements of it would also be adopted by groups within the Occupy movement. Praised by *Time* as a major innovation in social theory and denounced by the *Wall Street Journal* as evil, Hardt and Negri's work faced criticism from the left that generally took one of two forms. On the one hand, traditional Marxist critics such as Samir Amin, Atilio Boron and Ellen Meiksins Wood denied that the current global form of capitalism showed any meaningful divergences from classical imperialism, and hence they castigated the notion of empire either a mystification of superficial changes to imperialist logic or as a thinly veiled manifesto of capitalist triumphalism that the working class should reject. On the other hand, critics working in postcolonial theory, feminism and gender studies often accepted Hardt and Negri's claims regarding the decentering of sovereignty in empire but disputed the validity of their claims regarding the inclusiveness of the multitude, insisting instead on the continuing centrality of racial and gender hierarchies to the operations of multinational capital.

Other critics claimed that the US-organized wars in Afghanistan and Iraq inspired by the 9/11 events disproved Hardt and Negri's hypothesis of eroded national sovereignty, but the emergence of a resilient insurgency, the globalization of terror and the repeated systemic economic crises that followed revealed the impossibility of unilateral sovereign action on the part of the US. Recognition of this brought them additional readers attracted by their accounts of asymmetrical or "network" warfare under empire and of cosmopolitanism and fundamentalism as inversely parallel responses to globalization. While *Multitude* (2004) focused primarily on clarifying ambiguities in and responding to critics of the previous book, *Commonwealth* (2009) joined the revived debate over the common that sprang up following the dotcom and subprime crises. For Hardt and Negri, the common is betrayed and pillaged equally by socialist economies, which emphasize public or state ownership, and capitalist ones that fetishize private or individual ownership. The common as they conceive it appears in two forms: first, the environment and natural resources of the earth, which are governed by a logic of scarcity, and second, the collaborative social production of human subjects, governed by the logic of abundance, both of which are systematically objectified and expropriated by global capital. In their most recent collaboration, *Assembly* (2017), Hardt and Negri refine their model of empire by describing contemporary capitalism as an extractivism of the common, in that the growing self-organization and autonomy of productive subjects (what they now provocatively call the "entrepreneurship of the multitude") prevents capital from controlling them too closely if it wants to avoid restricting productivity, thus it must treat the results of biopolitical production as if they were natural resources to be directly appropriated. This is one reason why financial markets have come to dominate the processes of globalization, since they command all forms of production abstractly and at a distance from the internal articulations of production processes. A corollary of this extractivist model is the recognition that both primitive accumulation and formal subsumption, once thought to have been relegated largely to the past, remain crucial features of contemporary uneven development.

Hardt and Negri propose a number of strategies and tactics for the struggle against this new leviathan. *Empire* concludes somewhat mutedly by endorsing three universal rights that the multitude must claim: the right to global citizenship, the right to a guaranteed income, and the right to reappropriate the results of its own production. *Commonwealth* concludes by exhorting the multitude to replace the rigid, constituted institutions that according to Althusser and Foucault produce docile subjects with fluid, constituent institutions of singular subjectivation for the purposes of self-governance. *Assembly* repeats this exhortation and expands it into a demand for non-sovereign institutions of plural counter-power, which can only be constructed in the wake of destituent projects aimed at overturning the rule of finance capital. Hardt and Negri outline the possibility of a money of the common that would resist becoming capital and promote the foundation of social unions, essentially updates of the International Workers of the World, that could call broad-based social strikes as a means of registering the power of the multitude. Since *Assembly*'s primary aim is to draw organizational lessons from leaderless social movements like Occupy and Black Lives Matter, its central proposal is for movements of the multitude to invert the traditional relationship between strategy, which has conventionally been conceived as global and the province of hierarchical leaders, and tactics, which are normally considered local and intended to be carried out by the rank and file. Instead, Hardt and Negri suggest that strategic plans and decisions be reserved to the multitude as a whole, through structures of direct democracy, while tactics alone would be left to leaders to execute. This notion represents the coming to fruition of Negri's revisionary Leninism of the 1970s, when he proposed that the role of the party be reconceived as subordinate to the democratic management of needs within the working class as a whole.

In their 2019 essay "Empire, Twenty Years On," Hardt and Negri further extend and enrich their decentered model of global governance and contestation by drawing upon intersectional analysis – the practice, pioneered by Black feminism, of transposing the forms of resistance to regimes of exploitation previously considered external to one another (such as racism, sexism, heterosexism, class warfare, ecological conflict etc.) into a single apparatus of struggle composed of subjects who internalize all such forms without establishing a hierarchy among them – in order to find a means of turning the multitude into what they call "class prime," that is, neither the 19th- nor the 20th-century conception of the industrial working class, but class as a non-reductive potentiality of organization that has been diversified and multiplied by its members' passage through the multitude (Hardt and Negri 2019).

Global Struggle

Hardt and Negri's work continues to influence debates both within and outside the English-speaking world. Negri has been an advocate of European integration since his youth, though he has also criticized the European Union's structural complicity with empire (see Negri 2008a, part two). Both Hardt and Negri have long taken a keen interest in the rise of a regional bloc of left governments in Latin America; Hardt's earliest militant activities took place in that region, and in 2005 Negri and Giuseppe Cocco of the Federal University of Rio de Janeiro published an analysis, based in biopolitical theory, of the limitations of the underdevelopment and dependency theories that have dominated Latin American left politics throughout most of the 20th century (see Negri and Cocco 2005). Although Hardt and Negri are closest in terms of theory and practice to Luiz Inácio "Lula" Da Silva and the Brazilian Workers' Party (with which Félix Guattari was also affiliated in its early days) and they have taught regularly in that country and in Bolivia, they also visited Venezuela several times at the invitation of officials in the Hugo Chávez government, appearing in televised debates as well as at academic conferences on the politics of the multitude (see Negri 2008b, ch. 10). From Hardt's and Negri's viewpoint, the recent crises that have struck the Latin American bloc are the result of the incompleteness both of those governments' engagement with the social movements that originally brought them to power and of their efforts to restructure democratic institutions once in power.

Although Negri is now in his late eighties and is not permitted to visit the US as a consequence of his prison record, he continues to collaborate with radical thinkers and militants throughout the rest of the world in order to find points of alliance between their singular struggles and his own. In 2015 he published the first of three volumes of memoirs that describe those collaborations in detail (Negri 2015b). Even critics who strongly disagree with his theories acknowledge the indefatigability of his commitment to social transformation and respect his continual willingness to put himself at risk in order to pursue it.

Bibliography

Hardt, Michael, and Antonio Negri. 1994. *Labor of Dionysus: A Critique of the State-Form*. Minneapolis: University of Minnesota Press.

Hardt, Michael, and Antonio Negri. 2000. *Empire*. Cambridge: Harvard University Press.

Hardt, Michael, and Antonio Negri. 2004. *Multitude: War and Democracy in the Age of Empire*. New York: Penguin Press.

Hardt, Michael, and Antonio Negri. 2009. *Commonwealth*. Cambridge: Harvard University Press.

Hardt, Michael, and Antonio Negri. 2012. *Declaration*. New York: Argo Navis.

Hardt, Michael, and Antonio Negri. 2017. *Assembly*. Oxford: Oxford University Press.

Hardt, Michael, and Antonio Negri. 2019. "*Empire*, Twenty Years On." *New Left Review* 2(120): 67–92.

Negri, Antonio. 1991a (1979). *Marx Beyond Marx: Lessons on the Grundrisse*. Brooklyn: Autonomedia.

Negri, Antonio. 1991b (1981). *The Savage Anomaly: The Power of Spinoza's Metaphysics and Politics*. Minneapolis: University of Minnesota Press.

Negri, Antonio. 1999 (1992). *Insurgencies: Constituent Power and the Modern State*. Minneapolis: University of Minnesota Press.

Negri, Antonio. 2003. *Time for Revolution*. New York: Continuum.

Negri, Antonio. 2004 (1992). *Subversive Spinoza: (Un)Contemporary Variations*. Manchester: Manchester University Press.

Negri, Antonio. 2005 (1997). *Books for Burning: Between Civil War and Democracy in 1970s Italy*. New York: Verso.

Negri, Antonio. 2006 (1970). *Political Descartes: Reason, Ideology and the Bourgeois Project*. New York: Verso.

Negri, Antonio. 2008a. *Empire and Beyond*. Cambridge: Polity Press.

Negri, Antonio. 2008b. *Goodbye Mr. Socialism*. New York: Seven Stories.

Negri, Antonio. 2014 (1977). *Factory of Strategy: Thirty-Three Lessons on Lenin*. New York: Columbia University Press.

Negri, Antonio. 2015a (1987). *Flower of the Desert: Giacomo Leopardi's Poetic Ontology*. Albany: SUNY Press.

Negri, Antonio. 2015b. *Storia di un comunista*. Edited by Girolamo De Michele. Milan: Ponte alle Grazie.

Negri, Antonio, and Giuseppe Cocco. 2005. *Glob(AL): Biopoder e luta em uma América Latina globalizada*. Rio de Janeiro: Editora Record.

38

ALAIN BADIOU (1937–)

Jason Barker

Alain Badiou's relation to Marxism has been one of the defining characteristics of a philosophical career spanning some fifty years. There is little to be said of Badiou's political philosophy – or "metapolitics" – that doesn't bear on the theoretical reinvention of Marxism that began with Louis Althusser in the late 1950s, and that Badiou, as one of Althusser's students at the École normale supérieure (ENS) between 1955 and 1960, played an important hand in shaping.

On first impressions Badiou's political trajectory might be characterized as a "leftward march." Consider his setting up with Emmanuel Terray of a student section of the Socialist Party at the ENS; the split of the minority over its opposition to the Algerian war and his subsequent involvement in founding the Parti Socialiste Unifié (PSU) in 1958; his 1960s activism in the latter organization; his setting up of the (Maoist) Union des communistes de France marxiste-léniniste (UCFml) in 1970, followed by the Organisation Politique in 1985 and its "politics without party"; and, finally, his more recent preoccupation with the "idea of communism." However, in philosophical terms, throughout this entire period, Badiou's avowed Marxism has, broadly speaking, held firm to the same set of convictions.

First, there has been his principled opposition to the French Communist Party (PCF), which, unlike several of the Marxist philosophers of his generation, he opposed from the beginning of the Sino-Soviet split. Second, his fidelity to communism as an invariant form of political organization, whether it be transversal or contingent in relation to any presumed Marxist orthodoxy. Badiou might certainly be described as a "Post-Marxist" – and even "post-Maoist" (Bosteels 2005) – in adhering to a heterodox, crisis-ridden and "degenerate" Marxism that positively embraces its own antagonisms, contradictions and inconsistencies the better to adapt to the class struggle in novel and inventive ways (see Badiou 2009b, 1985). "I believe," as Badiou will declare in *Metapolitics*, "to put it quite bluntly, that Marxism doesn't exist." The "breaks" that define Marxism's discontinuous histories – since each one is "different in kind" – have the effect of rendering Marxism "the (void) name of an absolutely inconsistent set, once it is referred back, as it must be, to the history of political singularities" (Badiou 2005b, 58). Badiou sees no contradiction between this "inexistence" and "inconsistency" and the discursive capacity of Marxism to fashion and deploy revolutionary subjects in pursuit of emancipatory and egalitarian goals (as indeed it is the discursive capacity of psychoanalysis to fashion and deploy analysands in pursuit of existential goals).

There are at least three consecutive phases of Badiou's philosophy from which a particular Marxist problematic can be inferred in each case. In what follows I shall present an indicative summary.

Epistemological Phase

The first phase dates from Badiou's involvement in the Cercle d'Epistémologie and its accompanying journal the *Cahiers pour l'analyse* from 1967–69; and, more famously, his participation in Althusser's Philosophy Course for Scientists at the ENS, which lasted from November 1967 until 13 May 1968 when rapidly unfolding political events would prevent him from concluding his lecture, which was eventually published in 1969 as *The Concept of Model*.

Badiou's epistemological phase is Althusserian in its concern with establishing a theory of science as well as attending to the Althusserian (and Stalinist) distinction between historical materialism and dialectical materialism. Historical materialism, or the science of history, is, as Althusser will declare in 1969, a science of history as "a process without a subject" (Althusser 1972, 183). Badiou concurs that "there is no subject of science."

> Foreclosure, but of nothing, science may be called the psychosis of no subject, and hence of all: universal by right, shared delirium, one has only to maintain oneself within it in order to be no-one, anonymously dispersed in the hierarchy of orders. Science is the Outside without a blind-spot.
>
> (Badiou 2012a, 171–72)

Badiou's epistemology aims to establish a theoretical basis for the differentiation of science and ideology. In *The Concept of Model* Badiou, following the American philosopher W.V.O. Quine, contends that both formal and empirical scientific models are two varieties of the same idealist and positivist dogma regarding the distinction between material reality and its representation. Against the representative fallacy of science and its ideological outside, in other words, Badiou's materialist epistemology aims to establish the irreducible autonomy of singular sciences, their discontinuous historicities, against all adherence to the transcendent discipline of a "natural" philosophy. For Badiou, so-called dialectical materialism is not a master science. Instead, the dialectic is immanent to the real movement, so to speak, of demonstrations and proofs that characterize the productivity of scientific experimentation. Just as true science has no ideological outside, there is equally no philosophy for containing the subjectless historicity of singular science. As Badiou remarks, "Science is the veritable archi-theatre of writing: traces, erased traces, traces of traces; the movement where we never risk encountering this detestable figure of Man: the sign of nothing" (Badiou 1969, 174). Where science is concerned Man, no less than Marxism, is a void name.

Badiou's novel application of mathematics, which will resurface in his mature philosophy, is certainly not to be confused with any naïve attempt to deduce the fundamental "laws" of capital accumulation, economic cycles etc. from natural processes. It was precisely this "naïve" conviction that drove Marx to interrogate the contradictory formulas of differential calculus (Marx 1983). Moreover, where Engels was able to describe mathematics as an abstract science "concerned with creations of thought, even though they are reflections of reality" (*MECW* 25: 495), the epistemological reality Badiou wants to unleash "is of a piece with an effective scientific practice" (Badiou 2007, 22). For Badiou, given the "process without subject or goal," representation is anathema to science. The task therefore, in the context of an epistemological break, is to establish a consistent rule-governed axiomatic for the determinate manipulation of mathematical symbols, one that remains indifferent to all representational content; all "reflections of reality." Strict mathematical formalization, to the extent of subtracting logical manipulation from inference, and working toward complete internal demonstration of its systems, would equally serve as a model for "making history": singular histories unencumbered by grand narratives; or systems that operate, as Turing's imaginative interpretation of Hilbert's decision problem would have it, as computing machines capable of generating a yes or no response on arbitrary input. For Badiou mathematics is the most adapted of discourses to the singularity of scientific invention; an invention that Badiou identifies with the ideological (re)production of historical materialism. "No signifying order can envelop the strata of [science's] discourse" (Badiou 2012a, 173). In the immediate aftermath of May 68 this will prove to be a deeply unfashionable if not irrelevant conviction, not least for Badiou himself.

Maoist Phase

In the aftermath of May 1968 Badiou would set about rescinding his Althusserian credentials and assailing his former teacher's positions. The foreword to *The Concept of Model*, written in December 1968, sums up the new situation:

> Even today, the somewhat 'theoreticist' accents of this text hearken back to a bygone conjuncture. The struggle, even when it is ideological, demands an altogether different style of working and a combativeness both lucid and correct [juste]. It is no longer a question of taking aim at a target without striking it.
>
> *(Badiou 2007, 3)*

By mid-decade Badiou's "lucid and correct" line will surface in several essays sharply critical of Althusser and the PCF's seemingly implacable stranglehold over French Marxism and leftist politics. Four stand out. The first significant intervention is *Theory of Contradiction* (1975). No longer is it a question of conceptualizing the "class struggle in theory" through "internal systematic necessity" (Badiou 1975, 15). Instead, in this Maoist register, Badiou defers to the dynamic and dialectical transformation of theory in practice. The lucid and correct line, after all, requires "serving the people." Where previously the historical laboratory had been attuned to the Science of the "Outside without a blind-spot," now the historical laboratory answers to the exalted expansion of class struggle and its mass experiments. There can be no knowledge that is not grounded in the dialectical interplay between theory and practice, which Badiou qualifies as "reason in revolt" (Badiou 1975, 21–25).

The second essay, "Of Ideology" (1976), co-authored with Badiou's fellow UCFml militant Francois Balmès, addresses Althusser's botched self-criticism and his substantialist theory of ideology. Althusser's attempt to unite Marxism and psychoanalysis in accounting for "ideology in general" is a bourgeois obfuscation of the fact that ideology is divided by dominant and dominated class interests. "The dominant ideology, Marx says, is the reflection of the practices of class domination. It expresses the 'material relations,' it is not a specific function, operating in the element of the unconscious" (Badiou 1976, 19). There is bourgeois class domination only because it meets with proletarian resistance (46).

The third essay of his Maoist trilogy, "The Rational Kernel of the Hegelian Dialectic" (1978), written in collaboration with Joël Bellassen and Louis Mossot, is a translation and commentary on an extract from the Chinese philosopher Zhang Shiying's 1972 work *Hegel's Philosophy*. The presentation, which sets Badiou and his collaborators' annotations beneath Zhang's text, provides a running commentary on Zhang's work in defense of the strong Hegel, the materialist one of the *Logic*, against revisionist interpretations (Althusser's Hegel is once more the target here). But like Jacques Derrida's literary experiment *Glas* the text is also an exercise in dialectical spacing, a reading "between" Hegel in China and Hegel in France, and an implicit demonstration of the "one divides into two" maxim, of scission proliferating over synthesis. As intriguing as the text is on both sides of the divide, and for exhibiting Badiou's by now trademark juxtaposition of unlikely bedfellows – Mao and Lacan – it is difficult to imagine this work ever having risen out of obscurity had it not been for the seminar series that Badiou began to deliver at the University of Paris-VIII Vincennes in 1975, and whose proceedings would eventually be published in 1982 as *Theory of the Subject*.

Although well and truly a philosophical work inspired by Lacan's seminars, *Theory of the Subject* is heavily inscribed with its political conjuncture. Badiou's theory is one part combat against Althusser, Deleuze and the anti-Marxist New Philosophers, and one part rectification of their revisionist interpretations of dialectical materialist categories (identity and difference, affirmation and negation, antagonism and contradiction, unity and scission . . .). Its primary feature is the highly unusual and poetic nature of its author's demonstrations where, for instance, in Mallarmé's *Un coup de dés* one derives the "vanishing cause" of the structural dialectic; or where the *Oresteia* of Aeschylus provides the formula for the dialectics of destruction. As wildly esoteric and "metaphorical" as such associations might appear, Badiou's method aims to arrest the metaphors and metonyms of language and its errant significations and seize communist revolution in the precision of a mathematical formula. Badiou, as a mathematical philosopher, has always been inclined to take the "algebra of revolution" quite literally. To this end, through its formulation of the impossible surfaces of revolution, *Theory of the Subject* adapts and expands the topological (as opposed to algebraic) representations of the imaginary-symbolic-real triad familiar to readers of Lacan. As for the subject, Badiou identifies it with the Marxist party – taken in its "historical emergence" rather than in its ossified "democratic" incarnation (Badiou 2009b, 41) – under the aegis of the "minimal and purified political heterogeneity" (Badiou 2009b, 44) of the Maoist organizations that organically materialized in May 68. What remains of Marxism, in the strict dialectical terms of the text's conceptual vocabulary, is its degenerate nature, which is the inverse measure of its political transformation.

Philosophical (Meta-ontological) Phase

Being and Event (1988) marks a decisive departure from any explicitly Marxist problematic. As with *Theory of the Subject* the book's metaphysical content is minimally defined. Both books are works by an epistemological anti-realist less concerned with "objectivity" and "reality" than with the conceptual means of their subversion. If logic and mathematics are the means then this is due to the systematicity of Badiou's thinking. However, it's worth stressing that such systematicity is not remotely confined to the discourses of logic and mathematics. A great mathematical theorem such as Paul Cohen's independence proof of the Continuum Hypothesis contains

> a concentration of thought, an inventive beauty, a surprise of the concept, a risky rupture, in a nutshell, an intellectual aesthetic that we can, if we choose, compare to the greatest poems of our century, to the politico-military audacity of a revolutionary stratagem, or to the most intense emotions of an amorous encounter.
>
> *(Badiou 1999, 54)*

As for systematicity, if in our nihilist times "the 'systematic form' of philosophy is henceforth impossible" then one would do well to note that "[t]his anti-systematic axiom today is systematic" (65). However, in sharp contrast to *Theory of the Subject*, in *Being and Event* Badiou divorces such systematicity from Marxist topology and replaces it with what he terms an ontology of situations. Recall that in his epistemological phase Badiou endeavored to construct non-representational and non-ideological mathematical structures in aiming for complete internal consistency. However, this paradigm of scientificity remained tied to a historical materialist ideology of the production and reproduction of knowledges that by the time of *Theory of the Subject* was no longer amenable to a revolutionary theory of the subject: "Science of history? Marxism is the discourse with which the proletariat sustains itself as subject. We must never let go of this idea" (Badiou 2009b, 44).

Being and Event takes the purification and concentration of revolutionary practice one stage further by "desuturing" Marxism, whether in the guise of politics or science, from philosophy (Badiou 1999, 63). Although not remotely downplaying Marxism's real-subjective triumphs, Badiou will henceforth seek to preserve for philosophy an unbounded space of novelty and invention, of thinking in and for itself, where even the name "event" bespeaks the kind of philosophical egalitarianism that the Marxist signifier "revolution," weighed down by its historicist baggage, can no longer support. The event can be seized in four generic truth domains: art, science, politics, love. In *Being and Event* the domain Badiou is chiefly concerned with is ontology, the "science of being qua being." Commentaries and interpretations of the book and its conjuncture are now legion, but on the basis of what I have said so far the rather audacious thesis that lies at its heart is relatively straightforward to summarize. I will do so by mentioning first the thesis and then what I take to be its principal corollary.

1. Ontology = mathematics. This equation does not assert that being comprises a substantive "mathematical architecture," the ideal forms that Plato believed underlie observable reality (Badiou 2005a, 8). Badiou's interest in mathematics has always remained tied to the question of its discursive practice, of the purely logical procedures that facilitate thinking at its most highly impersonal and "abstract," rather than the technical application of mathematics to fields beyond itself, whether it be to other discourses or else some feature of objective reality or phenomenology. Since Heidegger the privileged site of access to being has been poetry. By contrast Badiou will argue that since the birth of philosophy in ancient Greece mathematics has been "legible even in Parmenides' poem in its usage of apagogic reasoning" (Badiou 2005a, 10). Ontology as mathematics strips being of its poetic aura, of its being-there (*Dasein*), to the point of its own deductive consistency. However, if such has always been the case then Badiou's philosophical (or meta-ontological) thesis that ontology = mathematics only receives its true force with the advent of Zermelo-Fraenkel set theory including the axiom of choice (ZFC), whose nine axioms "concentrate the greatest effort of thought ever accomplished to this day by humanity" (Badiou 2005a, 499). Set theory in its ZFC formalization is for Badiou the system most adapted to the thinking of infinite multiplicity which, as far as being qua being is concerned, is all there is to think.
2. Ontology is a situation. The bland simplicity of the proposition belies its profound complexity and the welter of obstacles that ZFC has had to overcome since its inception in the early part of the 20th century to attain the status of an axiomatic science (it hasn't overcome them all). The evental novelty that Badiou claims for his thesis ontology = mathematics hinges on the fact that "ontology can be solely the theory of inconsistent multiplicities as such" (Badiou 2005a, 28). The challenge in *Being and Event* is to describe any situation solely on the basis of the nine axioms of ZFC. The only "outside" to such an excoriating or "subtractive" conception of ontology and its ability to "count as one" any situation is quite literally "nothing." Here Badiou's philosophical reference point is Parmenides and the

> assertion that "if the one is not, nothing is" (Badiou 2005a, 31–37). The statement is not remotely nihilist. It is an axiom that attests to "the theory of inconsistent multiplicities as such" and to the fact that being can be described with complete indifference or absolutely no relation to "what" is being described (set theory proceeds from the difficult and counterintuitive idea that "set" can be conceived as any collection). But in order for his thesis ontology = mathematics = a (singular) situation to hold one must prove that the ZFC system is indeed consistent; in other words, that the system is a machine that can process every input, or articulate any collection as nothing other than multiples of multiples (Badiou 2005a, 29).

Now, it so happens that according to Gödel's First Incompleteness Theorem, ZFC cannot be both consistent and complete. "The coherency of ontology – the virtue of its deductive fidelity – is in excess of what can be demonstrated by ontology" (Badiou 2005a, 360). Nonetheless, and decisively, the fact that the consistency of ontology is undecidable will incline Badiou to decide in favor of its consistency at the expense of its completeness. Having reached the point where he can describe such "excess," or the inconsistency of ontology, as a "virtue," Badiou then pursues its "deductive fidelity" to his chosen model of ZFC philosophically, or in language and concepts adapted to exploring the evental novelty of situations that ordinarily comprise nothing but multiples of multiples. Aside from both its mathematical and conceptual meditations, *Being and Event* contains numerous "textual meditations" on eleven key thinkers from the history of philosophy: Plato, Aristotle, Spinoza, Hegel, Mallarmé, Pascal, Hölderlin, Leibniz, Rousseau, Descartes and Lacan). Intriguingly Marx doesn't figure among them. However, in one of the book's key "conceptual meditations" Badiou will introduce a typology of multiplicities in which "the State of the historico-social situation" is identified with "excrescence" ("the law that guarantees that there is Oneness" or "the guarantee that the one results in everything" (Badiou 2005a, 105–6); the bourgeoisie with "normality" ("presented economically and socially, and re-presented by the state" (109); and the proletariat with "singularity" (the presented multiple in a situation that remains unrepresented by the State).

Published in 2006 and as its title makes clear, *Logics of Worlds: Being and Event 2* is the sequel to its illustrious predecessor. Where the first instalment concentrates on the ontological/mathematical parameters of the formal axiomatic system, Badiou presents the second as the occasion for supplementing mathematico-ontological discourse with a "logic of appearing of truths." Where the first book sought to establish the structure or axiomatic of ontology and its consistency as a singular situation, the second seeks to furnish ontological structure with truths, to account for their appearance in "worlds" and the composition of their "atemporal meta-history" (Badiou 2009a, 9). With the re-adoption in *Logics of Worlds* of the dialectical materialism previously used in *Theory of the Subject*, and which Badiou contrasts with "democratic materialism" and "its denial of any hierarchy of ideas" (Badiou 2009a, 9), the author locates his system in a more explicitly political conjuncture; or, more accurately, in the divided conjuncture of universal politics and global culture. "Democratic materialism," as he proclaims disparagingly, "has a passion for history; it is truly the only authentic historical materialism" (Badiou 2009a, 509).

> Contrary to what transpires in the Stalinist version of Marxism – a version that Althusser inherited, though he disrupted it from within – it is crucial to disjoin the materialist dialectic, the philosophy of emancipation through truths, from historical materialism, the philosophy of alienation through language-bodies. To break with the cult of genealogies and narratives means restoring the past as the amplitude of the present. I already wrote it more than twenty years ago, in my *Theory of the Subject*: History

> does not exist. There are only disparate presents whose radiance is measured by their power to unfold a past worthy of them.
>
> *(Badiou 2009a, 509)*

The technical detail of Badiou's concentration of category theory and topoi in *Logics of Worlds* exhausts the power of abbreviation. None can be provided here. But the sequel or sequential nature of this monumental work does raise a significant methodological question regarding its supplementary nature that goes to the very heart of Badiou's greater speculative project. As Justin Clemens notes in his review of the work, "What does it mean to write a philosophical sequel?"

> If you add a proposed second volume, that hardly constitutes a sequel; a systematic work in no matter how many volumes is not a sequel. In philosophy, a sequel perhaps implies that the "original" was in some way a failure, somehow deficient, requiring supplementation or correction – and yet, somehow, the intervention you can't help but follow.
>
> *(Clemens 2006, n.p.)*

Although Marx's "project" was arguably neither systematic nor philosophical, the fact that Marx's lifelong endeavor to complete a critique of political economy never reached fruition – or never rose above the critique of bourgeois political economy – carries with it a certain irony, one reminiscent of the tragic (or perhaps epic) history that Marx himself satirized in the *18th Brumaire*. "As one knows," writes Badiou more recently, "Capital had to be pursued and undoubtedly achieved through an exhaustive consideration of what a social class, and finally the proletariat, is" (Badiou 2016, 45). As Clemens argues, it is no coincidence that the task of achieving perfect systematicity entails holding firm to the philosophical absolute. This absolute and Badiou's "didactics of eternal truths" herald a return, at least since the publication of *The Meaning of Sarkozy* in 2007, (see Badiou 2010, 2008) not to Marxist philosophy, but to the dialogue between Marxism and communism and the question of "communist invariants," that Badiou and Balmès introduced in *Of Ideology* (1976).

The communist invariants contain the subjective kernel of what Badiou identifies in more general terms as the idea of communism (see Badiou 2008). Arguing against Engels's famous account in *The Peasant War in Germany* of the historical precursors of working-class revolution in "advanced" industrial societies, Badiou puts forward an un-Marxist, anti-philosophical and utopian interpretation of revolt consistent with the disparate temporalities and transhistorical truths introduced in *Logics of Worlds*. "Popular revolts" in this conception amount to a traversal of the "disjoined worlds, incommensurable appearances, different logics" (Badiou 2009a, 21) of the "mass rebel (Spartacus, Müntzer or Túpac Amaru)" (27).

The extent to which communism can operate both under the aegis of such singularity and independently of Marxism was the subject of an intervention by Antonio Negri, delivered at the Idea of Communism conference in Berlin in 2010 and entitled "Is It Possible to Be Communist Without Marx?" (Negri 2011). Notwithstanding Badiou's lifelong admiration for the militant figure named Marx, today he is quite content to confirm that "in my classification of truths there is no place for something like Marxism" (Badiou 2016, 12).

Bibliography

Althusser, Louis. 1971. "Ideology and Ideological State Apparatuses: Notes towards an Investigation." In *Lenin and Philosophy and Other Essays*, 121–74. London: NLB.

Althusser, Louis. 1972. "Marx's Relation to Hegel." In *Politics and History: Montesquieu, Rousseau, Hegel and Marx*, 161–86. London: New Left Books.
Badiou, Alain. 1975. *Théorie de la contradiction*. Paris: Maspero.
Badiou, Alain. 1985. *Peut-on penser la politique?* Paris: Seuil.
Badiou, Alain. 1999 (1989). *Manifesto for Philosophy*. New York: SUNY.
Badiou, Alain. 2005a (1988). *Being and Event*. London: Continuum.
Badiou, Alain. 2005b. *Metapolitics*. London: Verso.
Badiou, Alain. 2007 (1969). *The Concept of Model: An Introduction to the Materialist Epistemology of Mathematics*. Melbourne: Re.press.
Badiou, Alain. 2008. "The Communist Hypothesis." *New Left Review* 2(49): 29–49.
Badiou, Alain. 2009a (2006). *Logics of Worlds*. London: Continuum.
Badiou, Alain. 2009b (1982). *Theory of the Subject*. London: Continuum.
Badiou, Alain. 2010 (2007). *The Meaning of Sarkozy*. London: Verso.
Badiou, Alain. 2012a (1969). "Mark and Lack: On Zero." In Hallward and Peden 2012, 159–86.
Badiou, Alain. 2012b (1968). "Infinitesimal Subversion." In Hallward and Peden 2012, 187–208.
Badiou, Alain. 2013 (1998). *D'un désastre obscur – Droit, Etat, Politique*. La Tour-d'Aigues: l'Aube.
Badiou, Alain. 2016. *Qu'est ce que j'entends par le marxisme?* Paris: Editions sociales.
Badiou, Alain, and François Balmès. 1976. *De l'idéologie*. Paris: Maspero.
Badiou, Alain, Joël Bellassen, and Louis Mossot. 1978. *Le noyau rationnel de la dialectique hégélienne*. Paris: Maspero.
Barker, Jason. 2002. *Alain Badiou: A Critical Introduction*. London: Pluto.
Bhattacharyya, Anindya. 2012. "Sets, Categories and Topoi: Approaches to Ontology in Badiou's Later Work." In *Badiou and Philosophy*, edited by Sean Bowden and Simon Duffy, 79–96. Edinburgh: Edinburgh University Press.
Bosteels, Bruno. 2005. "Post-Maoism: Badiou and Politics." *Positions: East Asia Culture Critique* 13(3): 576–634.
Clemens, Justin. 2006. "Had We But Worlds Enough, and Time, This Absolute, Philosopher . . ." *Cosmos and History: The Journal of Natural and Social Philosophy* 2(1–2). www.cosmosandhistory.org/index.php/journal/article/view/39/78
Engels, Frederick. 1987a (1850). "The Peasant War in Germany." *MECW* 10: 397–482.
Engels, Friedrich. 1987b (1877–8). "Anti-Dühring: Herr Eugen Dühring's Revolution in Science." *MECW* 25: 1–309.
Hallward, Peter. 2003. *Badiou: A Subject to Truth*. Minneapolis: University of Minnesota Press.
Marx, Karl. 1983 (1968). *Mathematical Manuscripts*. Edited by S.A. Yanovskaya. New York: New Park.
Negri, Antonio. 2011. "Is It Possible to Be Communist without Marx?" *Critical Horizons* 12(1): 5–14.

PART VII

Unexplored Territories

39
GLOBAL MARX?

Gayatri Chakravorty Spivak

Since 1978, my teaching of Marx, and my awareness that the text was written in German, was short on secondary scholarship but interactive, attempting to move with a diversified and changing world. Brilliant projects like David Harvey's (2016) distant learning summary of Marx's writing become complicit with the technological will to power through knowledge. What is it to "know" what Marx wrote? "Knowing" Marx's writings preserves the old conviction that the idea of knowledge is knowledge about knowledge, halting Thesis 11 before its end: the supplementary task is to try to change the world. "Knowing" work must be supplemented by the double-bind of one-on-one teaching possibly producing collectivities: Thesis 3 (*MECW* 5: 4). The supplement is dangerous, because it suggests that what is offered as a totality is incomplete and introduces the incalculable, since all must forever look beyond, to an undisclosable future of use – "poetry . . . from the future" (*MECW* 11: 106). My own work is so openly supplemental that I need fear no ancestor-worship. It is in that spirit that I have asked the question of global Marxism.

Attempting to move with a diverse and changing world and acknowledging Marx's own acknowledgment of the limit of his thinking in the differences among the many drafts for and the actual reply to Vera Zasulich in 1881, I attempt to situate Marx's urbanist teleology, as others have before me.[1]

My argument circles around Antonio Gramsci's well-known remark, in *Prison Notebook* number ten:

> The proposition contained in the Preface to *A Contribution to the Critique of Political Economy* to the effect that men [*sic*] acquire consciousness of structural conflicts on the level of ideologies should be considered as an affirmation of gnoseological [*gnoseologico*] and not simply psychological and moral value. From this, it follows that the theoretical-practical principle of hegemony has also gnoseological significance. . . . The realization of a hegemonic apparatus, in so far as it creates a new ideological terrain, determines a reform of consciousness and of methods of knowledge. . . . When one succeeds in introducing a new morality in conformity with a new conception of the world, one finishes by introducing the conception as well; in other words, one determines a reform of the whole of philosophy.
>
> *(*MECW *29: 61–65; Gramsci 1975, II, 1249–50; Q10 (XXIII) II §12; Gramsci 2000, 19)*

Our general idea about Marxism is usually a violent change in governance, dependent upon regime change, the will and wisdom of a leader, supported by a responsible government. What we have seen over the last hundred years is that the success of the system depends a great deal on the power of the people – either in education or resistance – in conjunction with the capacity of the head of state to protect his or her national economy over against the incursions of the global economy in the interest of redistribution.

This model could not be fully followed by the great revolutions of the 20th century because the diversified populations of the Russian empire and China, the two mammoths of Eurasia, were not equally resistant or educated, largely rural rather than urban, too dependent upon charismatic leaders, as were the Balkans, and their idea of gender empowerment was too mechanical.

Today, the charismatic leader supported or challenged by a resistant or motivated population model is threatened by the impersonal anti-humanist selective absolutism of global capitalism. The supposedly well-educated peoples of the European socialist or social-democratic sector are either remodeling the resources of the welfare state in reaction against what is elegantly called the "visible minorities," moving into those "developed" spaces by the vicious inequalities and violence/corruption attendant upon the abstract march of capital harnessed to unregulated greed, and/or against the miniature globality of the European "Union," a collection of debtor and creditor states. The postcolonial nations are neo-patrimonial, using the structures of democracy to preserve the status quo. Economic growth has no connection to social inclusion.

Marx knew the nature of capital, even if he did not know our worldly modernity. He said that capital, if it could, would want to move *mit Gedankenschnelle*, at the speed of thought (*G*: 548, 631). With the silicon chip, capital can move at an even greater speed. The neuro-ethicists can so far only describe how the brain behaves in the modes of right and wrong. They have not been able to upgrade the computer in the head, although silicon technologists affirm that the newest model robots can be programmed for empathy.

I attended many sessions at the May 2016 World Economic Forum on Africa in Kigali, Rwanda. "Africa's Fourth Industrial Revolution" was run in a brisk British way. Jon Ledgard, Director of "Afrotech and Future Africa" at the École Polytechnique Fédérale de Lausanne and founder of RedLine droneports and cargo drone network, spoke of the fact that roads and railways will not be constructed in Africa in the foreseeable future, and the skies were underused. (A previous session was devoted to liberalizing air travel.) Therefore, said Mr. Ledgard, transportation should take place via drone ports, which would house robots. Apparently one was already under contract for such a thing, or perhaps I misunderstood and it was already open, in Rwanda.

The entire discourse at the Forum reminds one of Marx's remark in "The Trinity Formula," that those who promote the unlimited social productivity of capital alone can fortunately forget the theft of "surplus value" (*CIII*: 953). Steve Resnick and Rick Wolff (1987) have taught us how to go back and back and back along the chain of these promises and once again arrive at the fact of the theft of surplus value that allows capitalism to flourish. This apart from the fact that today to take for granted that roads and railways were not to be built on the ground soon resembles somewhat the removal of possibility-thinking from rural Africa with the advent of oil.

"Who will build the drones?" Another participant, Neil Gershenfeld from MIT, answered "fab-labs": working the digital to assure that you can yourself build anything you want to, changing 2D to 3D. In answer to a question from a young African about joblessness in Africa today, he told us that we should change the idea of how to get things, that getting a job and making money in order to get things was not the only way. You could make what you wanted.

"Launching a new fab lab requires assembling enough of the hardware and software inventory to be able to share people and projects with other fab labs," says part of the online promo. Apply here Rick Wolff's lesson of working back to the theft of surplus value.

You will remember the astonishment of folks like James Steuart and Adam Smith at facing the sudden invention of a way of working that is not to make things for yourself or for a person who wanted you to make a thing for himself or herself but rather to make objects in great quantities for selling and making money, over and over again. James Steuart gave the name "industry" to this way of working, unlike anything known before. There are pages, particularly the first pages of the *Wealth of Nations*, full of exclamation points.[2] The great surprise, having to change the idea of making. Now here, within that last framework, is being offered, at the tip of technology, ways of going back to the other way, except through a denial that that historical framework was still at work and would displace itself with this new bit of digital idealism. There is no room for discussing this here, especially since I myself am unprepared to do so. But I place this here as an extreme form of the promise of globalization with which distance learning is complicit. Just change the idea of the interaction of learning – its transference – and you can know what Marx really thought, while you are in a position to make your computer in a fab lab.

What escapes the program (we have spoken of robots) is the contingent as such. The pursuit of the contingent is the edge of the technological will to power through knowledge. However, the power to be surprised by the contingent is now becoming less and less available because of the global disincentive for imaginative training. It is within this lack that I will locate the persistent necessity for something that can, somewhat unrecognizably, be called "global Marx." Is it the most accurate name for what I will describe? That question is contained in the question mark in my title: "Global Marx?"

Before I join the pursuit of the contingent, I want to go back to Antonio Gramsci's comment on the Preface to *A Contribution to the Critique of Political Economy*: "Marx's proposition . . . should be considered as an affirmation of gnoseological value."

"Gnoseological": in the logic of gnosis, knowing; a word-fragment that is still in colloquial English use: diagnosis, prognosis, words related to healing or the impossibility of healing – the double bind of healing.

Quintin Hoare and Geoffrey Nowell-Smith translate Gramsci's *gnoseologico* as "epistemological." "Actually between 'gnoseological' and 'epistemological' there is no difference," Italian political philosopher Michele Spanò writes.[3] Yet they are two different words. Therefore their so-called identity is a heterotautology. In this difference-as-identity of a smooth translation I will place the globalizability of Marx today.

"Gnoseological": learn to talk the talk well; "epistemological": learn to re-imagine myself as knower and the object of knowing as knowable in order to try to walk the walk.

I have said earlier that "gnoseological" in diagnosis and prognosis carries the double bind of healing as the impossibility of healing, not only in individual but also social "abnormalities." For those unfamiliar with "double bind," let us call it living within equally insistent contradictory instructions. Gramsci recognizes that Marx wishes to introduce the worker into the double bind of the contamination of manual labor by intellectual labor – not only the knowledge of the technology of capital, but its gnoseology – so that any worker could become a "dirigent." This is the task of the new intellectual in the party as well as civil society. Leadership training for all.

Marx's "Preface" was written in 1859. The body of the never completed continuation of *A Contribution* was written between 1861 and 1863. This was as much a preparation for *Capital* volume I as were the multilingual notebooks known as the *Grundrisse*, first published in 1939. As we know from Marx's letter to Engels of 1862, amidst all of this, he discovered the secret of surplus-value, which he describes in *Capital* I as the "*Sprengpunkt*" or "pivot of his critique," and everything changed (*CI*: 132; translation modified). He discovered the secret of reproductive heteronormativity, that every excess in the human and upper primate emerges out of the differences between needing and making. Marx described it in human terms: the worker advances the capitalist his labor and the capitalist repays less then he gets out of it since the worker needs less than s/he makes. He also describes it in rational terms: labor power is the only commodity which, when consumed, produces value.

The "Preface" to *A Contribution to the Critique of Political Economy* belongs to a period before Marx's preoccupation with the unique logic of surplus value. Here the emphasis is indeed on gnoseology, to *know* that ideology is a more conflictual text than the scientifically precise economic base and to tease out that relationship. However, this text already lays down the possibility of backtracking from gnoseology – knowing and laying down the right stuff, David Harvey – to epistemology – constructing civil society as the object of knowledge, because it does not preclude the inclusion of the writer's own ideological production and because it makes us move toward being folded together "within the framework of the old society," emphasizing the complicity with the prevailing relations of production (*MECW* 29: 263). For the "Preface" is nothing if not an account of epistemological performance: how a student of philosophy with a minor in jurisprudence puts himself to school to become the writer of the text it would introduce. Our last step as teachers and students of Marx is to open this apparently end-stopped narrative into the persistence of the run-on – a continuing commitment to the historic and generational.

Why, in a text about global Marxism, am I mentioning the World Economic Forum at all? It is to forge a practice that acknowledges complicity, not always with our consent, in every detail of the corporatist operation of the globe today. I cannot know what a cosmopolitical revolution would look like. But I do know that its principal agent can no longer be imagined as the internationally conscientized collective agent helping actively in a change in state-structure. In spite of Resnick's and Wolff's already-mentioned demonstration of the continuing importance of the theft of surplus-value upon which stands industrial capitalism; we have to admit that industrial capitalism is no longer produced by the definitive working class of the 19th and early 20th centuries. Facing global capitalism, the struggle for "another world" is staged in the discontinuous confrontation of the misnamed international civil society and the subalternized citizen, within which labor, with international solidarity undone by nationalism and the factory floor "pulverized" by electronic resources, has its own discontinuous place.[4] The WEF is also gnoseological, by way of the techniques of knowledge management. I want to conclude with the critique of knowledge management by way of opening Marx to globality, with a question mark. This is why I have here marked a complicity – a folded togetherness – of 19th-century confidence in scientific socialism and 21st-century confidence in the social productivity of globalized capital with the 20th-century disaster area of communo-capital complicity, as carefully studied in Resnick and Wolff's (2002) Marxist analysis of the former Soviet Union.

The World Economic Forum is basically engaged in "improving the state of the world" through Development, that is, insertion into the circuit of capital with no critical subject-formation (Spivak 2018). The goal is to enhance corporate social responsibility by folding it into the field of values such as "human dignity" and "common good." Assigning such values to one and all reflect the absolute failure of the epistemological effort toward grasping the heterogeneity of the developer and the developee – not to mention between the research methods of R&D on the one hand and, on the other, Policy. Any serious consideration of a just world has to consider the relationship between Policy and socialization, a very far epistemological cry from "the general will of the global." This where a global Marx must allow its tight focus upon the proletarian to waver into the classed, gendered, raced (non)citizen.

II

The first part, then, is about where we go, and how we intervene, in order to have the least little bit of impact in the global policy field: Research and Development, international civil society, World Economic Forum. What can become of Marx's vision in this sorry collection of underdevelopment-sustaining mechanisms supporting capitalist ambition and greed? The Trades Union Advisory Committee of the nation-state-oriented Organization for Economic Co-operation and Development (currently focused on industrial nation-states) – a haven upon that hapless terrain – must still talk about establishing friendly relations with business and collective bargaining, job security rather than revolution.

This second part, by contrast, is about an academic debate. This is one of two broad academic debates regarding Marx: a) Can Marx be followed today; and b) Should Marx be considered a humanist or materialist?

My position on Balibar's *Philosophy of Marx* (1993) is just a taste of the first debate.

Etienne Balibar is the felicitous heir of Marx within the Marxist tradition in its proper place of origin and development – a French philosopher deeply trained in German classical philosophy. I am fortunate enough to be able to call him my friend. At his suggestion, I have consulted his brilliant book, *The Philosophy of Marx*.

I write as a woman with no institutional training in philosophy, with thirty years of work in a backward district of West Bengal, where the general social oppression of the landless illiterate outcastes and aboriginals was certainly ameliorated by the Communist-Party-Marxist, the party in power that also engaged in goon politics in certain rural sectors and lost the elections after thirty-four years. My involvement with Western Marxism is through the soft margins of the US left, a rather different story. I owe a great deal to Resnick and Wolff for achieving that entry.[5] Before I put together my response to Balibar's challenge in his magisterial and wise slim book, I should perhaps put this section in contact with the previous one and repeat that my discussion of the Global Future Council on Ethics and Values at the World Economic Forum is an indication of the politically incorrect effort required to rectify (*pace* Balibar) persistently the digital idealism of Antonio Negri and Michael Hardt's massive volumes that posit a "multitude" automatically produced, advanced now into a consideration of social media as agent of change.[6] The World Economic Forum shares this view.

My ignorant alliance with my learned friend is by way of his conviction that one must "argue" with Marx. I also do agree with him that "Marxism is an improbable philosophy today" (Balibar 2014, 118), and so make peculiar contacts. Even if improbable, Marxism is not more impossible than anything else.

Rather than follow Marx to the letter, I harness my Marxist engagements to the tendency to go as far as possible:

> De Man goes on to say that the shift from history to reading typical of his generation "could, in principle, lead to a rhetoric of reading reaching beyond the canonical principles of literary history which still serve, in this book, as the starting point of their own displacement." "Reaching beyond" can mean displaced to another place. How far beyond? As far as I pull, in these times? Altogether elsewhere? At least into an understanding, as the best universities counsel students to cut their dissertations to market demands, that an aesthetic education inevitably has a meta-vocational function?
>
> *(Spivak 2012a, 34)*

Comparably, as our best philosophers call Marxism improbable, pull Marx into the global economy, the belly of the beast, to suggest that repeatedly rectified ingredients for a doctrine, recognized as such, may be what we need to make Marxism work in a globalized situation where the first wave of Marxist experiments are coming undone?

Like Balibar, I do not think Marx "postmodern." In the spirit of Thesis 3, I think changeful task is "persistent," adding to the thought of Marx, Gramsci, Balibar and all my brothers, the dimension of generational turnover, a gendered concern of a teacher of other people's children. Interpretation is originary, each a halfway house with the "walk the walk" – the point is to change the world – imperative included and leading beyond – the dangerous supplement.

Balibar perceives the ambiguities, contradictions and amphibologies in Marx. He makes the important suggestion that "no theorist, when he has effectively found something new, can *re-cast* his own thinking. . . . Others will do that" (2014, 112; other perceptions on 21, 27, 33, 92, 102 and *passim*). For me, this is the double binds that are the very defining character of life, action, thought – the condition of impossibility as the only available condition of possibility, a persistent rewriting of improbability.

Before I learned the lesson of the double bind in the late seventies, I taught and wrote in another way, what in Balibar becomes dismissive: "Revolution and science (revolution in science, science of revolution): . . . [this] alternative was never resolved by Marx. This also means that he never accepted sacrificing the one to the other, which is a mark of his intransigence" (Balibar 2014, 115). I taught it as "the heterogeneous dialectic of knowing and doing" (Spivak 1987, 50),[7] an asymmetry that opens to action.

Marx thought Hegel calculated everything for the mind. Therefore for the heterogeneous dialectic of knowing and doing, we go not to *The Science of Logic*, as Lenin had suggested, but to "The Beautiful Soul" in *The Phenomenology of the Spirit*, which Lacan describes as metonymic of psychoanalysis.[8]

Marx was haunted by Hegel; not a question of his being a Hegelian or not. Ever since finishing his doctorate, he was interested in finding out the economic reality of life under capitalism. Taken by the brilliance of Hegel's method, it was the phenomenology of capital that he attempted to work out. Phenomenology, not onto-phenomenology. The lesson we learn is that capitalism is for capital's sake and therefore unreal. Hence the socialist use of capital cannot be just for capital's sake alone.[9]

As soon as he understood that capitalism is based on the theft of surplus value, Marx also understood that the play of capital and labor was in terms of contentless value, and that the contents that appear along the line of play as moments of realization, were always traces or forms of appearance – *Erscheinungsformen*. There are some who think of land in this land-grabbing phenomenology of primitive accumulation as completely real. Marx quotes Ovid in heavy mockery: "and now in addition the ground, inorganic nature as such, *rudis indigestaque moles* 'a rough unordered mass' in its full sylvan primordiality. Value is labor. So surplus-value cannot be earth" (CIII: 954; translation modified).

Yet, in *The 18th Brumaire of Louis Bonaparte* Marx distinguishes the revolution of the 19th century as content rather than phrase: "Previously the phrase went beyond the content; [in the social revolution of the 19th century] the content goes beyond the phrase" (*MECW* 11: 106; translation modified). This is close to a passage in "Beautiful Soul," where Hegel is writing about "the moral intuition of the world [*Weltanschauung*]": "[T]he antinomy . . . that there is a moral consciousness, and that there is none, or that the validation of duty [for Marx socially just action] lies beyond consciousness, and conversely, takes place *in* it."

This was seen by Hegel to be "a contradiction . . . by content." And when this thinking

> in which the non-moral consciousness counts for moral, and its accidental knowing and willing is taken as fully potent, felicity granted to it by way of grace [perhaps a

reference to Kant's metaleptic invocation of "effect of grace" in the Appendix to the *Critique of Pure Reason*]

– it is seen as a contradiction "by form" (Hegel 1977, 383; translation modified).[10]

Marx, for whom phenomenological definition has become part of mental furniture, is here choosing the double bind of the antinomy of ideology: we can/we cannot – for the social revolution of the 19th century as "content" – over the "formal" reconciliation of the antinomy in the mere "phrase" of the revolutions of the past: we can do good. This is also an indication that socialism is not just the use of abstract average labor power to build a just society, for the abstract by definition has no content. There would be content in the 19th-century revolution – the poetry of the future – not just abstract planning, a point to which we return later.

Everybody knows that *Geist* is hard to translate. It is clear, however, that it is not consciousness – *das Bewusstsein* – and not reason – *die Vernunft*. Like capital, *Geist* by itself cannot "do." Hegel charts the course of its estrangements in Part C.BB of *Phenomenology*. However, when it is contaminated by *Gewissen* – psychologistically (and unfortunately) only translatable into English as "conscience" – it can only stage the "doing." Marx finds in this predicament of self-consciousness, instantiated in this constellation, the fact of human beings making their own history but not able to choose their roles. *Geist* shot through with *Gewissen* can hold *Wissen* and *Wollen* – knowing and willing – but not actually know and will. This counterintuitive way of a spatializing structure is hard for Marx's English translators to grasp. But let us continue: *Bewusstsein* or consciousness cannot really think good and bad, although programed to think it can and must. On the other hand, it must have the conviction, and it must talk about this conviction collectively, and thus it can bring about abstract collective consciousness. Of course Marx, not a Hegelian, did not act this out in such detail, but all the generalizing convictions – all the writing, the talks, the meetings – use this in action, even as they emphasize the separation of individual subjectivity – in the vanguard or the masses – from its ideological production. Since Marx is not obliged to show that he is a correct or incorrect Hegelian, this rough ironic parallel between *Gewissen* (conscience) and ideology cannot easily be discarded.

Hegel uses the words *Tat, Tätigkeit, Tun, handeln, Handlung,* – German words for doing or action – to show if duty was being done. Of course the word *Arbeit* or work/labor is never used. This is where Marx staged the phantasmagoria of the action of labor power, and in his work, unlike in Hegel, the dialectic becomes heterogeneous, in contrast to Hegel, for whom the separation between knowing and doing is kept brilliantly and counterintuitively intact.

From time to time Hegel warns that the staging of the phenomenology of *Geist* into human psychological types short-circuits the account of the march of philosophy. But the text often seems to ask for this transgression. Marx, as Fanon later more vividly, steps into this transgression and attempts to move the system away from "the mind alone."

Balibar charts Marx's lifetime move from an evolutionist history toward its undoing – by way of the experience and study of failed revolutions (1848, 1871), and the tendency of left movements to move away from Marx's methods, and, finally, the out-of-system (or anti-systemic) potentialities of the agricultural communes in Russia. The consequence of this chain of displacements is described this way by Balibar: "I am tempted, rather, to believe that Marx never, in fact, had the time to construct a doctrine because *the process of rectification went faster*" (Balibar 2014, 117). I see this as Marx's great gift, autodidact as he was, acquiring knowledge as new needs opened up, not only to be constrained to but creatively to be able to learn from his mistakes – again a chain into which we can, transindividually and responsibly, insert ourselves.[11] A persistent set of epistemological performative instructions kept overtaking the stern requirements of a gnoseology. Given the *Aufhebung* into globalization, this persistence is our difficult guide.

The thinking of globality requires thinking the contemporary. "In globalization every site is contemporary," I have written elsewhere, "and yet also unique. We therefore call it a double bind" (Spivak 2012a, 510). Balibar is able to grasp this intuition of globality in Marx: "communal form was '*contemporary*' (a term to which Marx insistently returned) with the most developed forms of capitalist production, the technique of which it would be able to borrow from the surrounding 'milieu'" (Balibar 2014, 108). Expanding our field of activity beyond the "pulverized" factory floor is part of such borrowing.

For Christine Buci-Glucksmann (1980, 348, 351), this particular thought of globality is still in the future. However, her reading of Gramsci reading Marx "beyond the letter" and her rendering of gnoseology as epistemology ("they are the same thing," says Michele Spanò) through Gramsci's idea of the "critico-practical act," are deeply resonant with my own.

In *The 18th Brumaire of Louis Bonaparte*, Marx suggests that the real long-term result of the French Revolution was, paradoxically, to strengthen the power of the executive. Some of us have felt the long-term result of the great revolution in China and Russia was to bring about a globalizable world. Following in the same great narrative mode, it can be said that, just as the Industrial Revolution made capitalist colonialism necessary, so does the technological revolution make global governance necessary. And just as monopoly capitalist colonialism did not exactly resemble mercantile capitalist colonialism – because of the difference, say, between British colonialism in Africa and India and Spanish colonialism in Latin America, so does this haphazard global governance not resemble a magnified world state, on the model of nation-state governance. The world's charter is written by finance capital. World trade is financialized. The Anthropocene flourishes through greed. Climate is changed drastically.[12] Victims of inequality suffer natural and social disasters more drastically than those not. Class apartheid in education produces rape-culture and bribe-culture above. Stoppage of imaginative training produces rape-culture and bribe-culture below. Democracy is exported on the spear-point of trade blackmail and war. In spite of the abstractions of finance, the bull market is driven by affect: investor confidence. And the subprime crisis is driven by family values.

Behavioral economics, attempting to thicken rational choice, is no match for this ethical catastrophe. If international socialism died of an ethics-shaped hole, global capitalism, although it is not as embarrassed to talk the ethical talk, will continue to live with the same terminal disease – an ethics-shaped hole.

Into this void steps the World Economic Forum, wanting to turn capitalism toward social justice with inadequate imaginative resources but an acknowledgment of complicity in the narrow sense ("we alone have done this"). Its strongest tradition of amelioration is sustainable underdevelopment, a phrase I have already used.

The World Economic Forum is a large, nonprofit, private sector organization, admonishing civil society; examining the decimation of the constitutional state; considering redress to corporate, military and extra-state violence, consequences of inequality and climate change, to name a few. It attempts to re-think technology by making it sit down with Amnesty International and Africa. It moves from local, national, to regional, perhaps to access the global. Access to global, in spite of digital idealists, is not a certainty here. It is not prepared to be taught what it cannot know – how not to control top-down.

The distance in kind between the top (WEF and Columbia University), the bottom (the largest sectors of the electorate – "citizens!" – in Africa and Asia) and the hapless middle (undocumented immigrants) makes the task of the teacher complex. The international civil society – confusing equality with sameness and thus denying history or teaching income-production and thus serving capital – is useless. Here one invokes the complicity – folded-togetherness – of fund-raising radicals and the corporate world. Of Research and Development I have written previously. It is upon this rough terrain that Gramsci's "new intellectual" must push the question mark in "global Marx?" into a possibility, supplement the question mark as copula – gnoseology into epistemology over and over again, working by the surreptitious light of the hidden declarative: "This is happening." (We remind ourselves that the supplement fills a need but also shows up the incompleteness of what it supplements. Here the intellectual's tendency is to remain, as a "beautiful soul," in the question mark forever.)

Before I had participated in Abu Dhabi, and in response to the Occupiers of Wall Street as well as W.E.B Du Bois, Gandhi and others on the General Strike, I wrote:

> Like Rosa Luxemburg, we can perhaps claim that the citizens' strike is no longer a step back toward the bourgeois revolution. Our example is not just Occupy Wall Street, a citizen's strike which started in 2007 as no more than a first move, but also the Eurozone and the "broad Left" in Greece, shoring up after financial disaster as a result of the capitalist policies of the creditor state/debtor state policies of the European Union. If, at the inauguration of the International Working Men's Association [at a meeting of trade unionists where Marx introduced the word International into the Workingmen's Association], Marx had felt that workers should keep abreast of international politics and diplomacy enough to intervene, then at this moment of capitalism's negation the citizen, the agent of the general strike redefined, must keep abreast of the laws regulating capital.
>
> *(Spivak 2014b, 12–13)*

Now, it is the citizen and the corporatist who acknowledge complicity in seemingly turning capital to social, the baseline of socialism. (Gender is still caught in family values – read sanctioned rape and reproduction – in most of the world. That is future work.)

Let us stop for a moment on the "seemingly," the semblance of an unmediated interest in social justice. As I have urged before, the corporatist actually works to preserve the interest of capital. The epistemological undertaking is therefore for the 99 percent, the citizens.

The 99 percent's rearrangeable desire, then, should be in the embrace of the teacher's agential slot for the electorate – often from within a liberation theology (more future work here to gender theology into the intuition of the transcendental, "belief" to imagination). There is a deep interest in inequality and the "slaves" involved in the commodities we enjoy, on all impressionistic sides, opening to Marx's insight of the fetish-character of the commodity, with a rough and ready idea of the social relations of production and no understanding of surplus-value.[13] However, the point now is to see the subaltern as subject ungeneralizable by the Forum, their numbers replenished as capital marches on, not just proletarian as universal subject.

As Marx had counseled a homeopathy of reification – appropriate the quantification of labor to turn capital into the service of the social – so does my wary move toward the nature of corporate benevolence acknowledge a homeopathy: the undoing of the distinction between public and private about which we at US universities worry endlessly. And, as Crystal Bartolovich comments:

> Subjected to tutelage of breakfast cereal and branded peer pressure throughout their lives, students are rarely going to be transformed into revolutionaries in fifteen weeks, no matter how "radical" their English or sociology professors may be [Bartolovich does not mention that their radicalism does not shun the complicity of corporate fundraising for project support]. Nevertheless, coming out of a generally conservative climate into the liberal university, bright students can develop their "critical-thinking" skills in

> ways useful to business and government so long as they don't think too critically for too long – something that corporate elites do not appear to be concerned will happen. They know their professors are small fish in a very big pond.
>
> (*Bartolovich 2013, 44*)

Ours is an invitation to get out of this acceptance of powerlessness as normal, to stop us-and-them-ing, to acknowledge complicity, and act the conjuncture.

III

In closing I will emphasize that the agent of production of the social today is the citizen rather than the wage-worker as such. The subaltern voter and the subalternized citizen need to be welcomed into the Marxist struggle of moving capital into the social incessantly. The fact that the subaltern can vote and be "developed" (not just robbed of indigenous knowledge and DNA) has made a huge conjunctural change that is usually ignored. The internationally divided, often adversely gendered, hopelessly exploited proletariat is of course also a member of this lowest stream of citizenship. To produce in this large, ungeneralizable global subaltern group a rearrangement of the petty bourgeois "mania to get rich" (*MECW* 3: 238) into a socialist desire to build a just world is the (im)possible task. "Socialism is about justice, not development," I can hear Teodor Shanin declaim.[14] In 1844, the Hegelian statement that conviction spoken and discussed (in *Sprache* and *Rede*) creates a general consciousness is noted as ignoring class divisions and conflicts by the young Marx. As Marx kept "rectifying," the result of this possible general consciousness is presumed to undo the proper names of modes of production. This intuition remains in the very late Marx: "If both wages and surplus-value are stripped of their specifically capitalist character – then nothing of them remains, but simply those foundations of the forms that are common to all social modes of production." We will come back to this passage.

The epistemological cut between the early humanist and the later materialist Marx (Althusser 1969) is too tight. The materialist Marx discovers the importance of the use of the abstract average as the "social" of socialism. The centrifugality or *Zwieschlächtigkeit* of the commodity, his own specific discovery, will allow the worker/citizen to restrain her/himself to contain the march of capital. But simply having the abstract tool (gnoseology) is not enough. While "normality" works by greed, or at least self-interest, even if enlightened, the socialized worker/citizen must want this self-restraint in the interest of social collectivity. Here Marx's unexamined humanism, sustained throughout the abstract materialist work (canny enough to know practically that the workers have petty bourgeois ideologies), sustains his conviction that this self-restraint will follow workers' ownership of "the means of production." It goes without saying that human rights intervention, although necessary in the short run, generally working toward restoration of often unknown rights by shaming states through public interest litigation, does not enter the epistemological task required by Marx's hope and plan, as Gramsci understood.

Let me add the aporia between liberty (autonomy, self-interest) and equality (alterity, unconditional hospitality), bringing forward some points I have made earlier. The democratic structure, body count, one equals one is arithmetical and impoverished. It does not produce a democratic society. The democratic structure presupposes a democratic society – a performative contradiction. This is why most postcolonial nations are neo-patrimonial: using the structures of democracy to preserve structures of patronage, bribe-culture, sustained by rape-culture; and preserving class-apartheid in education, so that votes as body count can be counted on indefinitely. This performative contradiction, therefore, invites us to make mind-sets change, an epistemological performance – a call to teachers.

We interrogate the absurdity of arithmetic equality, one person one vote, given the race-class-gendered unevenness of subject-production. Indeed, even if we achieved the impossibility of an absolutely egalitarian race-class-gender situation, 1=1 would remain an underived disability count of the "normal" human body, "able" always approximate and depreciating (like capital) within this inflexible arithmetic as the "majority" moves from birth to unevenly spaced death, other "majorities" shoving the sociograph at the same time. This does not disqualify democratic principles, but rather points at the difficulty of any claim to an affective collective solidarity in the name of political agency within the constraints of democratic principles. It is an insoluble problem. The solution is not to ignore it; however you want to understand the declarative. To remind the world of such inconveniences is the task of the humanities.

The irreducible conditionality of the human animal sits uneasily and irresolvably within the abstractions of democratic rationalist unconditionality. The two cross unevenly as life-expectancy is marked by class, gender and race. It certainly cannot be solved by informal markets or voting blocs. The preceding paragraphs suggest that the arithmetic structure of democracy requires for democratic functioning not only an informed electorate, but a basic imaginative flexibility, allowing for an epistemological performance where the least "disabled" subject knows that the world is not intended primarily for it, and that its way of knowing is contingent. The relationship between Marx*ism* as we know it and this post-anthropocentric epistemological perception – rather different from the easily declared post-humanism of the sustainable underdevelopers of environmentalism – is too massive to be launched here. I will content myself with another word on the formation of democratic judgment.

One-on-one and collective; a more careful alternative to consciousness-raising of various sorts: vanguardism to promote class-consciousness; organizing for collective bargaining and job security; legal awareness seminars; citizenship training; identitarian voting-bloc pre-party formation; gender-babble encompassing all. One-on-one pedagogy for collectivity, millennially tested within race-class-gender parameters, is the equivalent of what classroom teaching could be today: the careful work of learning and rearranging desires to contain the march of capitalism and to respect the rights of others who do not resemble me. Yet the politically correct formulas that circulate within our crowd are extended only to our self-consolidating other, not further. I give you an example from my limited but deep and intimate study: the six rural elementary schools that I have been teaching and training at for decades now.

The social groups there, including my teachers and co-workers, are fully aware of millennial caste-oppression, but know nothing about colonialism, which departed seventy years ago. They have never seen white people. The schoolbooks are not written for them, so the gender and multiculture (religion) banalities have to be taught straight. Gender and religious common ground must be dealt with outside of the classroom. And Europe cannot be ignored.

I try to make the groups friendly with the wretched map of the world on the back cover of the old geography book. No map of the world in the new government textbooks. I point at the northwestern corner of the huge Eurasian continent and tell them that that is Europe and that though so small, it won. I discuss with them how they won and even use such mid-Victorian examples as James Watt watching the lid dance on the pot of boiling water: the emergence of the rationality of capital – the beginning of industrial capitalism – accessible apparently to a high school student. I can then begin to introduce into the style of pedagogy the lesson of using capital for socialism. For, although until ten years ago the party in power was Communist-Party-Marxist, the secret of the theft of surplus-value was not taught in school or in the party office.[15] There is no factory floor. And yet they vote.

I remind myself not to be an "improver" (hard for a teacher) and discuss with my increasingly more aware co-workers (male and female teachers and supervisors) from these social groups the fact that I am not drawing profits from the work for and with them. Although they are not well acquainted with the world map and know nothing about colonialism, and have not seen any factories of any significant size, they do understand what profit or *munafa* is. They are subaltern, they have no special psychological essence, they are not "the East," or "the Non-West," or yet, awful phrase, "the Global South"; they are examples of a general argument that notices that they vote in a postcolonial nation that they do not know as such.

The argument from Eurocentrism now belongs to another class that must also deal with a limiting concept of "Europe" in global capitalism, that Europe is a part of a much larger world now. Europe's moment was historically important but not all-consumingly determining. Not everyone has to have a correct interpretation of the English and French revolutions. It is enough to think of the relationship between the Chartists and the Reform Bills, even Labour and New Labour; of the 18th Brumaire, even Aimé Césaire and Frantz Fanon versus Valéry Giscard d'Estaing. The sun rises at different times upon the globe today. When the stock exchange closes in London, it must wait for Tokyo and then Mumbai, and in-between opens the turbulent and unstable speculative "marriage of socialism and capitalism," where the "turnover rates are ten times higher," altogether different from the sober decision for a mixed economy taken in the New Economic Policy in 1921. The beginning of the end: without the epistemological support imagined by Du Bois, Gramsci, Fanon, this leads to a wild eruption of the uniformization/universalization of capital rearing to break through, like the steam in the steam-engines that we traveled by in my childhood and adolescence: Shanghai and Shenzen.[16]

These are examples where our politically correct formulas might not work. Yet even here, one can teach epistemological performance through a rearrangement of the desire for an impossible self-enrichment, which only gels into petty bourgeois ideology in the most cunning. Marx-via-Gramsci-limited by Zasulich must be extended here; and it must be remembered that the subaltern is by definition not generalizable. My example will not travel to details of socio-cultural life in other parts of India, as they will not to the large and diversified sectors of the subaltern in Africa, in Latin America. This is the one-on-one. The collectivity is the entry into citizenship, which will destroy subalternity. The citizen as such is generalizable, as is the proletarian as such. That is the displaced global Marx. For the diversified ungeneralizable unverifiable singular aesthetic, we do not look to Marx.

And yet.

Many committed readers of Marx feel that *Capital* volume III is both continuous with and transgressive from volumes I and II. One of the most famous "transgressive" passages is the invocation of "the realm of freedom." In closing, we will read it together to suggest that Marx's robust unexamined humanism, developed from the early task of correcting Hegel ("[t]he only labor which Hegel knows and recognizes is *abstract mental* [*geistige*] labor"; *MECW* 3: 333), so far felt as the *Zwieschlächtigkeit* or centrifugality in the word "social" – the abstract average and yet the place of human development – here gives us an empty space – "the realm of freedom" (*C*III: 958–59) – which we can occupy to introduce the incalculable, the supplement always considered dangerous by mechanical Marxists – imaginative training for the ungeneralizable singular aesthetic – persistent preparation for the ethical reflex – the absence of which in general education brought the first set of revolutions to heel.[17]

The passage invites careful reading.

In *Capital* I, Marx proposes counter intuitively that exchangeability is already present in nature ("[i]n considering the labor process, we began by treating it in the abstract, independently of its historical forms, as a process between man and nature"; *C*I: 643). This presupposition, never relinquished, supplies the basis for the broader proposition that labor is a human fact – the argument that can be broadened to the proposition that we can make more than we need in *every* act of life and thought. Marx, interested only in the economic sphere, compliments capital:

> It is one of the civilizing aspects of capital that it extorts this surplus labour in a manner and in conditions that are more advantageous to the development of labor powers, to social relations and to the creation of elements for a renewal on a higher plane than under the earlier forms of slavery, serfdom, etc.
>
> *(CIII: 958; translation modified)*

It is important that he is not speaking of capital*ism* here. In this passage Marx is looking forward to the socialist use of capital. I am thinking especially of phrases such as "*gesellschaftliche Verhältnisse*," where the adjective could almost be "socialist" and the noun is the more philosophical *Verhältniss* – suggesting a philosophically correct structural position rather than the more colloquial *Beziehung* (relationship); and of *höhere Neubildung*, which is almost *Aufhebung* or sublation. This is what capital does. And the problem, once again, is that the capital*ist* use simply "disappears." This is where our globally diversified effort can teach and practice Marxism by persistently *de*-humanizing greed as the *primum mobile* – the dangerous supplement, one-on-one yet collective.

In the next movement of this rich paragraph, Marx once again generalizes, bringing all modes of production together, bringing *Gemeinschaft* and *Gesellschaft* together. Here is the loss of the proper names of modes of production as a subjunctive goal, a blow to gnoseology. Marx brings up once again that exchangeability begins in nature. Before capital, nature ruled the human like a blind power. In socialized capital, "associated producers govern" this originary exchangeability, "human exchange of material [*Stoffwechsel*, usually "metabolism," translates literally into "exchange of material"] with nature in a rational way" (translation modified). And the entire world, all modes of production together, is the realm of necessity that supports human development for its own sake. This is the site of the epistemological struggle, where the question mark becomes the copula that opens the supplement that displaces itself, and continues questioning, again and again. And, if in the globalized practice of marxism (small m), the agent for turning capital to socialist uses must be the citizen, for Marx s/he remains the worker. Therefore, our passage ends with the effort to provide more time for the realm of freedom, which will no doubt be released if the realm of necessity is socialized.

No doubt. Marx's description of such a prepared realm of necessity is without reference to the epistemological – one-on-one yet collective – struggle required to produce a general will for social justice.

Here is the passage.

First Marx takes the small peasant (the least likely candidate) as proof of the illusion that capitalism is the norm. Then he shows us how easy it is to disprove this illusion by painting that effortless picture of a socialist state.

> Because a form of production that does not correspond to the capitalist mode of production [the self-employed small peasant] can be subsumed under its forms of revenue (and up to a certain point this is not incorrect), the illusion that capitalist [structural] relationships are the natural [structural] relationships of any mode of production is further reinforced. If however one reduces wages to their general basis, i.e. that portion of the product of his labor which goes into the worker's own individual consumption; if one frees this share from its capitalist limit and expands it to the scale of consumption that is allowed on the one hand by the existing social productivity (i.e. the social productive

> power of his own labor as effectively social) and on the other hand required for the full development of individuality; if one further reduces surplus labor and surplus product, to the degree needed under the given conditions of production, on the one hand to form an insurance and reserve fund, on the other hand for the constant expansion of reproduction in the degree determined by social need; if, finally, if one includes in both (1) the necessary labor and (2) the surplus labor . . . that those capable of work must always perform for those members of society not yet capable, or no longer capable of working – i.e. if one strips both wages and surplus-value of their specifically capitalist character – then nothing of these forms remains, but simply those foundations of the forms that are common [*gemeinschaftlich*] to all social [*gesellschaftlich*] modes of production.
>
> *(CIII: 1015–16)*

Today efforts at imagining social justice are seldom more than top-down efforts at preserving the movement of global capital: Development as "insertion into the circuit of capital without subject-formation." To imagine the Gramscian lesson in this globalized conjuncture, the "leftist" polarization of subject-formation and the collective abstraction of capital/social must be persistently undone by the new intellectual in a class-, gender- and race-sensitive way. The move to socialize capital cannot be assured by "a shorter working day." The forming of the subject for the ethical reflex, which is housed in the responsible outlines of a general will for socialization in the fullest sense, on the broad relief map of the globe, sometimes undone by centuries of extrinsic and intrinsic violence, inhabited by many first languages, is obliged to recognize, if necessary in the idiom of the subaltern, that, as I have insisted previously, the contingent, beyond programming, rises in the difference between need and capacity to make, and cannot be caught by knowledge management. Today's methodology of choice can be fearlessly confronted only if it becomes the deep background of a classroom teaching to rearrange desires, teaching also the risks of walking the walk that would then begin to be desired.

The invaluable work toward a will to justice is destroyed by a confidence in so-called toolkits and templates. The desire for such speedy solutions must be rearranged with the training of the imagination, to understand that to change gnoseology to epistemology today we must first understand that the toolkit closes off the contingent. If the toolkit is telling the top how to help the bottom, the bottom is thought as needing no more than material aid for income production and the reduction of poverty. Movements that are advertised as "from below" need to have their leadership/vanguard structure carefully read. This remote, infinitely complicated struggle cannot be assigned to knowledge management.

The new intellectual must teach how to make toolkits – even on the subaltern level – as halfway houses to be undone by the contingent rather than offer toolkits as a solution to the problem of action. Some of us have been criticizing the UN for example on the use of platforms of action to diffuse and manage violence against women. Some of us have been criticizing the mere statisticalization of such things as development and progress. All of this has to be integrated into a persistent critique of knowledge management so that meetings to achieve solutions do not work as if for children, with leaders who divide collectivities into groups, with instructions to produce lists of items that are collected as the groups are put back together. This is not the way that the imagination will be trained for epistemological performance so that unconditional ethics can be introduced to move capital into social justice. This is the work that we must continue to do persistently in order to make "Marxism" global.

I want to close with a word on gender. Within scientific socialism the empowerment of gender was stiffly rational. One can get proof of this in the writings of Alexandra Kollontai (1980) and latter day writers such as the Chinese feminist Dai Jinhua (2002).

Today gender empowerment through micro-credits and financial independence – taking employability as the bottom line of human dignity – follows the same sort of autonormative agenda. Here gendering as the type case of reproductivity must be acknowledged. Just as in the epistemological project of *Capital* I, the worker was invited to rethink himself epistemologically as agent of production rather than victim of capitalism, so also, and on a broader base, women must understand that men take more and give less and that women are not themselves the victims of phallocentrism but the agent of production. The need for legitimate passage of property must not be the excuse for keeping them in confinement. Integrating this to capitalism takes us from Engels through Thomas Piketty (2014) into listening to the gendered subaltern subject. If you think this is bio-politics, try to imagine more flexibly.

And a envoi: globality is my brief, and I have tried to attend to it, with a question marking the need for a persistent and effortful move from gnoseology to epistemology, from knowledge management to intellectual labor, from rational choice to imagination, moving poison to medicine, capital to social, rearranging desires as the generations pass. I have referred to a contemporary vanguard, the Global Futures Council of the World Economic Forum. The subtext: that work must be supplemented by the production of the subaltern intellectual: focused, local, intense work, attempting to produce in the largest sectors of the global electorate an understanding of the importance of the right to intellectual labor – a labor that is almost impossible to teach in the face of millennial cognitive damage, in the face of the imperative to obedience. At the World Economic Forum, Klaus Schwab, the Founder and Executive Chairman, spoke of moving from and between the local to the national into the regional, in preparation for the global. The subaltern are people who have not been welcomed into all the nationalisms of the previous centuries and yet also, in some sectors, have become multinational now as labor export, often undocumented. There one does not practice or teach leadership, but learns to follow how to teach. But that is another talk, another walk, another theater. I have given you a hint of it, speaking of my rural teaching.

For now, think that limit as center, not margin, as we part company.

Notes

1. *MECW* 24: 346–71; see also Baer (2006, Chapter 1) and Spivak (2012b), although this does not reference Zasulich.
2. Even a sober passage such as "Do we see every day . . . employment of their time and talents." throbs with this surprise (Steuart 1966, 468; see also Smith 1976).
3. Private correspondence with the Author.
4. Word used in unpublished conversation with the editor of *Asia Labor Monitor* in 2001.
5. They were the first and perhaps the only economists to see any value in my work, as reflected in my class-notes-based essay "Scattered Speculations on the Question of Value," first published in *Diacritics*, 1985.
6. Most expansively developed in Michael Hardt and Antonio Negri in *Multitude* (2004).
7. In a bolder formulation, Jean-Luc Nancy declares: "'To speak of freedom' is accordingly to suspend philosophy's work. And this is in fact the very possibility of a 'philosophizing'" Nancy (1994, 3).
8. Hegel, *The Science of Logic* (2010). "It is impossible completely to understand Marx's *Capital*, and especially its first chapter, without having thoroughly studied and understood the *whole* of Hegel's *Logic*. Consequently, half a century later none of the Marxists understood Marx!" (*LCW* 38: 180); Hegel (1977) and Lacan (2006, 242).
9. I cite here Amina Mohamed, currently running for the position of Chairperson of the African Union Commission and Alicia Bárcena, the Executive Secretary of the U.N.'s Economic Commission for Latin America and the Caribbean, neither noticeably Marxist, yet both pushing for sustainable development driving the market rather than vice versa, as is the case now.
10. The form-content move is a classic advancing manoeuver in the *Phenomenology*. See Hegel (1977, 399) and passim. Already in 1844, Marx roughly alludes to this section of the *Phenomenology*: "[t]he 'unhappy consciousness,' the 'honest consciousness,' the struggle of the 'noble and base consciousness,'

etc. etc., these separate sections contain . . . the *critical* elements" (*MECW* 3: 332). Our (Marx's) task is to supplement intellectual with manual labor.

11. For the transindividual, see Balibar (2014, 30).
12. Dipesh Chakrabarty's (2016) brilliant current work points the way to acknowledging the subject/agent bind into planetarity. However, given his theoretical base, he is obliged to ignore the challenges of the heterogeneity of knowing and doing.
13. A moving example of this interest is "Are My Hands Clean?" by Sweet Honey in the Rock (1988), https://www.youtube.com/watch?v=ev733n-5r4g.
14. Unpublished conversation with the author.
15. Theft of surplus value is not mentioned in Mao's groundbreaking essay on the peasant revolution in Hunan province (Mao 1965b). Early Bolsheviks often made the point that the Russian revolution was better than the German because it involved both workers and peasants. For Gramsci's "subalterns" – not to be confused with "proletariat" – too, there was no factory floor.
16. Spivak (2014a); description of Shanghai and Shenzen taken from Wong (2006).
17. Even here, Marx notices the usefulness of the method: "Hegel's standpoint is that of modern national economy [*modernen Nationalökonomen*]" (*MECW* 3: 333, translation modified). Marx himself proceeds from "national" to "political" economy in subsequent writings.

Bibliography

Althusser, Louis. 1969 (1965). *For Marx*. London: Penguin.

Balibar, Étienne. 2014 (1993). *The Philosophy of Marx*. London: Verso.

Bartolovich, Crystal. 2013. "Small Fish, Big Pond." *Academe* 99(6): 41–4.

Buci-Glucksmann, Christine. 1980. *Gramsci and the State*. London: Lawrence and Wishart.

Chakrabarty, Dipesh. 2016. "Humanities in the Anthropocene: The Crisis of an Enduring Kantian Fable." *New Literary History* 47: 83–98.

Conisbee Baer, Benjamin. 2006. "Ghost-Work: Figures of the Peasant and the Autochthon in Literature and Politics." Dissertation, Columbia University.

Dai, Jinhua. 2002. *Cinema and Desire: Feminist Politics and Cultural Politics in the Work of Dai Jinhua*. London: Verso.

Gramsci, Antonio. 1975. *Quaderni del carcere*. Edited by Valentino Gerratana. 4 vols. Turin: Einaudi.

Gramsci, Antonio. 2000. *The Gramsci Reader: Selected Writings*. Edited by David Forgacs. New York: New York University Press.

Hardt, Michael, and Antonio Negri. 2004. *Multitude: War and Democracy in the Age of Empire*. New York: Penguin Press.

Harvey, David. 2016. "Reading Marx's *Capital* with David Harvey." http://davidharvey.org/reading-capital/

Hegel, G.W.F. 1977. *Phenomenology of Spirit*. New York: Oxford University Press.

Hegel, G.W.F. 2010. *The Science of Logic*. Cambridge: Cambridge University Press.

Kollontai, Alexandra. 1980. *Selected Writings*. New York: Norton.

Lacan, Jacques. 2006. "The Function and Field of Speech and Language in Psychoanalysis." In *Écrits*, 197–268. New York: W. W. Norton.

Lederman, Rena. 2016. "Fieldwork Double-Bound in Human Research-Ethics Reviews: Disciplinary Competence: Or Regulatory Compliance and the Muting of Disciplinary Values." In *The Ethics Rupture: Exploring Alternatives to Formal Research-Ethics Review*. Edited by Will C. van den Hoonaard and Ann Hamilton, 43–72. Toronto: University of Toronto Press.

Mao, Zedong. 1965b (1927). "Report of an Investigation of the Peasant Movement in Hunan." In *Selected Works of Mao Tse-Tung*. Vol. 1, 23–59. Beijing: Foreign Language Press.

Nancy, Jean-Luc. 1994. *The Experience of Freedom*. Stanford: Stanford University Press.

Piketty, Thomas. 2014. *Capital in the Twenty-First Century*. Cambridge, MA: Harvard University Press.

Resnick, Stephen A., and Richard D. Wolff. 1987. *Knowledge and Class: A Marxian Critique of Political Economy*. Chicago: University of Chicago Press.

Resnick, Stephen A., and Richard D. Wolff. 2002. *Class Theory and History: Capitalism and Communism in the USSR*. New York: Routledge.

Smith, Adam. 1976 (1776). *An Inquiry into the Nature and Causes of the Wealth of Nations*. Oxford: Oxford University Press.

Spivak, Gayatri Chakravorty. 1985. "Scattered Speculations on the Question of Value." *Diacritics* 15(4): 73–93.

Spivak, Gayatri Chakravorty. 1987. "Speculations on Reading Marx: After Reading Derrida." In *Post-structuralism and the Question of History*, edited by Derek Attridge et al., 30–62. Cambridge: Cambridge University Press.
Spivak, Gayarti Chakravorty. 1988a. "Subaltern Studies: Deconstructing Historiography." In Guha and Spivak 1988, 3–32.
Spivak, Gayarti Chakravorty. 1988b. "Can the Subaltern Speak?" In *Marxism and the Interpretation of Culture*, edited by Cary Nelson and Lawrence Grossberg, 271–313. Basingstoke: Macmillan.
Spivak, Gayatri Chakravorty. 1999. *A Critique of Postcolonial Reason: Towards a History of the Vanishing Present*. Cambridge, MA: Harvard University Press.
Spivak, Gayatri Chakravorty. 2012a. *An Aesthetic Education in an Era of Globalization*. Cambridge: Harvard University Press.
Spivak, Gayatri Chakravorty. 2012b. "What's Left of Theory?" In *An Aesthetic Education in an Era of Globalization*, 191–217. Cambridge, MA: Harvard University Press.
Spivak, Gayatri Chakravorty. 2014a. "Penny for the Old Guy." *Cambridge Review of International Affairs* 27(1): 184–203.
Spivak, Gayatri Chakravorty. 2014b. "General Strike." *Rethinking Marxism* 26(1): 9–14.
Spivak, Gayatri Chakravorty. 2018. "Development." In *Political Concepts: A Critical Lexicon*, edited by J.M. Bernstein, Adi Ophir, and Ann Laura Stoler, 118–30. New York: Fordham University Press.
Steuart, James. 1966 (1767). *An Inquiry into the Principles of Political Economy*. London: Oliver and Boyd.
Wong, Susan M.L. 2006. "China's Stock Market: A Marriage of Capitalism and Socialism." *Cato Journal* 26(3): 389–424.

40
ANGELA DAVIS (1944–)

Andrew T. Lamas

Angela Davis became a global symbol of resistance in the early 1970s, at the height of the confrontation between the American state and the Black Power movement. A philosophy professor and Communist Party activist, she was forced into hiding, captured, jailed and falsely charged with capital offenses because of her association with George Jackson and other Black political prisoners at Soledad State Prison in northern California. After an international campaign, she was acquitted in June 1972. Davis has continued to support movements of resistance in the US and around the world, and she is particularly passionate about the Palestinian cause and prison abolition. Trained in various Marxist traditions, she activates the revolutionary, anti-reductionist elements of Marxism and the Black Radical Tradition by contributing to the development of a critical liberatory praxis – a Black Radical Feminism (or Abolition Feminism) that negates the erasure of difference and conceptualizes who matters in a way that points toward the creation of broad solidarities of resistance.

Beyond Economic Reductionism

Although there is a current of Marxist thought regarding racism, sexism and other forms of oppression that is vulnerable to the charge of economic reductionism, Davis's Marxism – which took shape in the last decades of the 20th century as Black Radical Feminism – is as textured, layered and complex as the experiences of those struggling to live in and change the world. In Karl Marx's thought, labor exploitation is intrinsic to capitalism. Analysis of multiple oppressions is often juxtaposed to exploitation theory. Davis demonstrates not only that it is possible but that it is necessary to consider the ways that multiple oppressions connect with processes of exploitation in the lived experience – historically and contemporaneously – of poor and working peoples around the world, whether the circumstances are those of slavery, wage labor, or other forms of the capital-labor relation and social reproduction. She maintains that these connections, if brought to the level of political consciousness, may provide foundation and motivation for collective resistance.

Against more dominant understandings (particularly in the United States) of intersectionality and multiple oppressions analysis, Davis maintains the necessary relation between the struggle for socialism and the struggle against exploitation and oppression. In this regard, her long-standing critiques of mainstream feminism – not only for its bourgeois racial and class biases but also its gender reductionism – parallel her similar critiques of other reductions, such as nationalisms – including Black cultural nationalism – but not when such are organized against heteropatriarchy, casteism, capitalism, colonialism and imperialism.

Davis's Black Radical Feminism may be understood as simultaneously an affirmation and extension of (1) an evolving, open Marxism – through a renovation of Marcusean Critical Theory (itself a radicalization of the Frankfurt School's Critical Theory) and (2) the Black Radical Tradition – in essence arguing that these traditions maintain their critical legitimacy and political potency to the extent that they embrace the analyses, insights and commitments of Black Radical Feminism. With reference to her mentor Herbert Marcuse's concept of the Great Refusal, Davis writes that "Marcuse must be acknowledged for reinterpreting Marxism in ways that embrace the liberation struggles of all those marginalized by oppression." She continues:

> What is clear to me is the deep connection between the Great Refusal and the abolitionist movements that have been and remain so important to freedom struggles in the Americas and elsewhere. We use the term *Black Radical Tradition* to associate the activist and scholarly work of the current moment with the anticapitalist analyses and radical demands of what progressive historians call the *Long Black Freedom Movement*. If the Great Refusal entails principled opposition to injustice and repression, then the Black Radical Tradition – a tradition that emanates from the theories and practices of Black liberation in the Americas – can certainly be described as a salient historical manifestation of the Great Refusal. This tradition has been embraced not only by people of African descent but also by those who eschew assimilation into oppressive structures and support the liberation of all people.
>
> *(Davis 2017, viii)*

For Davis, Black Radical Feminism's focus on multiple oppressions is in keeping with a non-reductive Marxist commitment to understand the totality in order to comprehend the parts. As György Lukács argues in 1921, "It is not the primacy of economic motives in historical explanation that constitutes the decisive difference between Marxism and bourgeois thought, but the point of view of totality" (Lukács 1971, 27). More concretely, Louise Thompson Patterson, a Black Communist, writing in the Communist Party-USA journal *Woman Today* in 1936, observes: "Over the whole land, Negro women meet this triple exploitation – as workers, as women, and as Negroes" (Patterson 1936, 30). Revolutionary subjectivity – the development of which is a central challenge for critical pedagogy – is most meaningfully developed when the parts are understood in their relation to the whole, both as connected in subjugation and potentially through solidarity to liberation. As Marcuse, the Marxist who perhaps most profoundly articulates the totalizing nature of capitalist modernity and its implications for resistance, famously says, "The Great Refusal takes a variety of forms" (Marcuse 1969, vii). In other words, the present situation necessitates the heterogeneity of political struggle.

Radical philosophy, for Davis, is about theorizing praxis. Her thought champions the political priority of building solidarities to engage collectively in confrontations with reaction in all of its manifestations – from heteropatriarchy and white supremacy to capital's class rule. This is why the Combahee River Collective, informed in part by Davis's earliest work, develops, in 1977, the concept of "identity politics" (Taylor 2017) – not as a joke or pejorative, but as a critical concept with explanatory power for understanding the actual, historical development of capitalism and the solidarities required for effective resistance.

The violence of heteropatriarchy, the ravages of class domination, and what W.E.B. Du Bois calls the "problem of the color-line" (Du Bois 1996, 15) are unique but not special – in that they are, in important ways, commonly destructive. If the terms of gender, sexuality, race and class are defined appropriately – that is, in accordance with the actual workings of systems and structures of power in the world and with the actual lived experiences of oppressed and exploited peoples – then, gender, sexuality, class and race are different ways of talking about many of the same things – the destruction of people and planet.

Solidarity Without Erasure

Solidarity without erasing difference is the keystone in Davis's philosophy of praxis. For her, capitalism simultaneously obscures, flattens and erases differences and also relies upon them for the creation of hierarchies that enable domination, dispossession and accumulation. The resistance to capitalism – the struggle for liberation, democracy and equality in its socialist form – necessitates the organization of powerful solidarities that at once enable the free expression of who we are in our commonalities *and* in our differences. For Davis, understanding the particular experiences of diverse peoples – Black women, indigenous women, Dalit women and other poor and working people – is important not only as a matter of respect but because doing so is necessary to get critical theory right and to forge the solidarities required for making progress toward a more liberatory existence. This entails, among other things, learning how people (despite and because of their differences) are negated (differently and similarly) by the interaction of exploitative and oppressive systems. The expression of who we *differently* are – when appropriately contextualized and organized – may enable a refusal of capitalism's one-dimensionalizing commodification of our distinctions. At the same time, however, concern with difference may be overemphasized to such a degree that commonalities of class, humanity and life are denied or obscured, thus negating possibilities for forming solidarities with sufficient power to challenge capitalism in its fullness and complexity.

Karl Marx, too, seeks to understand the actual, historical basis for capitalism, coming very close indeed to theorizing *racial* capitalism – a conceptualization that is today associated with Cedric Robinson, whose works, such as *Black Marxism: The Making of the Black Radical Tradition* (1983), directly influences Davis. Marx, in his late twenties, writes the following in *The Poverty of Philosophy* (1847):

> Direct slavery is just as much the pivot of bourgeois industry as machinery, credits, etc. Without slavery you have no cotton; without cotton you have no modern industry. It is slavery that gave the colonies their value; it is the colonies that created world trade, and it is world trade that is the precondition of large-scale industry. Thus slavery is an economic category of the greatest importance.
>
> (MECW *6: 167)*

Marx's thought probes not only the ways in which slavery shapes – and is shaped by – capitalist production but also the ways in which class, nationality and race are categories of significance not only for theoretical analysis but also political praxis. In a similar vein, for Davis, class reductionism, race reductionism, nationalist reductionism, gender reductionism etc. must be rejected – given the historical record and contemporary situation – both on grounds of critical reason and of political necessity.

Identity and Solidarity

For capitalism and its discontents, identity – as concept and political project – is fraught with complexities. A central thread, unmistakably woven throughout Davis's theoretical contributions and political interventions, is her critical reflection on identity's relation to the perpetual nightmare of capitalist accumulation, its multiple oppressions, and the unresolved legacies of slavery, such as the prison system and death penalty.

> Such structurally racist institutions visit their violence on all of the people within their clutches regardless of the individual's race or ethnicity. In other words, we have to conceptualize racism in a different way. While racism is about bodies, it is not only about bodies. It is also about structures. Institutions can be racist even as they act upon bodies that may not be racially marginalized.
>
> *(Davis 2013, 436)*

In Davis's work, this central thread also connects to the prospects of resistant, liberatory solidarities. She labors mightily to influence how identity is understood because, in her analysis, what is at stake is liberation. For her, identities are less about individuals as such and more about the systemically structured, interconnected, social relations through which life is experienced. Where difference is used as a basis for the construction of identity hierarchies, where human subjects are formed by, among other things, hegemonic power's imposition of identity-based stamps of superiority and subordination, humanity – both in what humans share in common and in genuine difference – is subject to erasure. Such socially constructed identities are less descriptive of individuals than revealing about historical and spatial, context-dependent, expressions of hierarchical relations, which, as regards class, race, gender, sexuality (and more) in the capitalist epoch, develop as interlocking, intersecting, simultaneous asymmetries of power.

> Fundamentally, the roots of homophobia are very much connected to the roots of racism, which are connected to the roots of sexism, and to the roots of economic exploitation. It is not coincidental that the same forces that will picket an abortion clinic or inflict violence on abortion providers are the same ones who have tried to prevent integrated schools. These ultra-right forces . . . are also the same forces responsible for violence against gays and lesbians, and for a fraudulent analysis holding homosexuals responsible for the so-called breakdown of the family. If one simply looks at the ties established among our enemies, there should be a greater awareness of the need to build a united movement. After all, we are challenging a common adversary.
>
> *(Davis 1989, 80)*

But, as regards the politics of struggle against this dehumanizing matrix, what matters more than *who you are* is *what you do*; or, put more pointedly, *what you do – and how and what you resist – is who you really are.*

This radical understanding has put Davis at odds with mainstream positions on identity. She argues that identity recognition can be detoured, for example, into the dead ends of mainstream feminism – what she has referred to as a "white, bourgeois feminism" – a (neo)liberal feminism that is not antiracist and not anti-capitalist, that does not comprehend the processes that generate the precarity and impoverishment of the vast majority of the world's people, and that is used to promote policies that actually widen inequalities, promote imperialist interventions and block the formation of solidarities to resist exploitation and oppression.

Critique of False Universals

On the occasion of the fortieth anniversary of a speech Marcuse gave at the University of Pennsylvania, and fortuitously also amidst the Occupy Wall Street (OWS) protests, Davis spoke in Philadelphia in 2011.

> That which clearly differentiates the Occupy movement from the movements of the 1960s, which created the terrain on which Herbert Marcuse theorized radical activism, is its explicit effort to be inclusive. Virtually everyone can identify with the 99%. ["We are the 99%" was a political slogan popularized during Occupy.] During the 1960s, movements tended to be specific. In the youth movement, for example, you were not supposed to trust anyone over thirty, except perhaps Herbert Marcuse [laughter], who was seventy at the time [laughter]. There was the Black movement, the women's movement, the Chicano movement. . . . One of the difficult challenges of the 1960s and the early 1970s was that of coalition building. The fact that relations among movements – the antiwar movement, the Black movement, the women's movement – were framed as coalitional was indicative of the inability to grasp the organic interrelationships of these issues. Today, many of us effortlessly speak about intersectionality, thanks primarily to the work of women of color feminism. We can conceptualize these issues not as discrete, disconnected issues whose relationship we have to mechanically orchestrate but, rather, as issues that are already crosshatched, overlaid, intersectional patterns. Class, race, gender, sexuality, ability, and other social relations are not simplistically separate. They can never remain uncontaminated by each other: so, when the OWS movement appeals to the 99%, which is constructed in relation to economic criteria, we ought to be already aware that the class hierarchies that produce this differentiation between the super rich and the rest of us are already shot through with gender and race and sexual hierarchies.
>
> There are those who say that the Occupy Wall Street movement has been so successful thus far because economics transcends race. Have you heard that? But economic relations do not transcend race. They are enabled by, and they reflect, racial hierarchies. . . . All of which is to say that the Occupy movement will have to be very careful about resisting the seductions of false universals.
>
> *(Davis 2013, 435–36)*

Davis's critique of false universals should not be interpreted as a critique of the long march toward a common humanity in a future, difference-respecting, ecosocialist commonwealth, but rather as a critical suspicion – given that, historically, universals are so typically proclaimed in bad faith, masking the perpetuation of unjust hierarchies. Marx, who first criticized Hegel's nomination of the Prussian civil service as the universal class representing the interests of all in the society, later adopted the notion of the *universal class* as a way of theorizing the significance of the proletariat's role in class struggle. Importantly, Davis criticizes the idea of the working class as the universal class *when* that class is not understood as constituted by the fullness of humanity's oppressed laboring producers and reproducers. Her critique operates against any such exclusions where, for instance, Black women and other women of color – their struggles, their labor, their critiques, their very humanity – are submerged and rendered invisible.

For Davis, ahistorical and aspatial abstractions – such as identitarian reductions – are cast aside, so that historical capitalism in its totalizing reality (as Marcuse theorized) can be seen for what it is – a classed, raced and gendered phenomenon that exploits identity, creates and exacerbates inequalities, sows division and destruction, while reaping power and profit. Though hegemonic, the system is rife with contradictions and cracks, thereby generating conditions (possibilities) for liberated consciousness, radical subjectivity and collective revolutionary agency, but also for virulent forms of reaction, from racism, misogyny and anti-immigrant scapegoating to other forms of State and State-sanctioned violence against radicals and "dangerous elements," and, ultimately, fascism.

Identity manipulation is a primary feature of capitalist ideology and capital accumulation. It operates dialectically – amidst hierarchies and through scapegoating mechanisms – as both *identity recognition* and *identity negation*, with each featuring an ideological cover for accumulation.

- Identity recognition is promoted in its multicultural form of equality (e.g., *All people – culturally different as they may be – are created equal.*) and in its post-Fordist form of consumer empowerment (e.g., *All people, as consumers, have abundant opportunities to express themselves – differently and uniquely – through their free, creative choices in the marketplace.*). The actual deployment of identity recognition for capital accumulation and the maintenance of class rule, however, is accomplished through the manipulation of difference (e.g., *White men of property up here. Laboring Black women down there.*). Marcuse conceptualizes such liberal inclusiveness as "repressive desublimation," a mode of appropriation that fetishizes and commodifies the many, different Others – flattening out the distinctions between "that which is" and "that which is not" and "extend[ing] liberty while intensifying domination" (Marcuse 1964, ch. 3).
- Identity negation, in its nationalist form of mystification (e.g., *We are all in this together*), is coupled with erasure and dispossession – regardless of identity and despite difference – through the process of commodification, which is the foundational mechanism for capital accumulation. What Marxists call commodification is what Martin Luther King Jr. calls "thingification" (King 1967, 131). In the end, no difference is respected: labor is dehumanized as commodity; animals are sliced and packaged as commodity; earth, too, is denaturalized as mere commodity.

Of course, ironically, capitalists understand all of this. It is in their operating manual. Simply put, the capitalist knows what the Marxist knows: identity is a social construct with a material force, masking underlying realities of major significance and value. While racism is directly linked to the economic process of capital accumulation and the reproduction of class divisions, it is also a political means by which capitalist elites organize hegemonic power in the society – by mobilizing whiteness across class lines. The capitalist unacquainted with Du Bois's classic work, *Black Reconstruction in America* (1935), would nonetheless recognize its conceptual scheme, very well understanding Du Bois's choice of forsaking a beginning chapter on "The Worker" (as in an opening move of intellectual abstraction by a class reductionist) and, instead, composing *two* initial chapters on labor – the first on "The Black Worker" and the second on "The White Worker." For "The Planter" (the title of chapter 3 – referencing white, slave-owning capital), the point is clear: by cultivating a shared *racial* relation with the White worker, the capitalist undertakes *class* exploitation of both White worker and Black worker, all the while disrupting the development of cross-race, class-based unity – the most significant threat to racial capitalism. In 1870, Marx makes the same point when explaining English capital's manipulation of English and Irish labor.

> This antagonism is artificially kept alive and intensified by the press, the pulpit, the comic papers, in short, by all the means at the disposal of the ruling classes. *This antagonism* is the *secret of the impotence of the English working class*, despite its organisation. It is the secret of the maintenance of power by the capitalist class. And the latter is fully aware of this.
>
> *(MECW 43: 475; emphasis in original)*

Genderlessness

Davis's critique rejects any suggestion that historical capitalism has a gender-blind and race-blind mode of operation. Perhaps nothing makes this point better than what is here called her concept of genderlessness.

This concept does not work like class reductionism to render gender, sexuality and other social formations invisible or ultimately irrelevant for understanding capitalist development and systems of domination. Quite the contrary. Genderlessness is a concept for understanding commodification as a process that is at once women-destroying and thing-creating, Black-destroying and thing-creating, humanity-destroying and thing-creating, species-destroying and thing-creating, nature-destroying and thing-creating.

Genderlessness is not typically associated with Davis's thought. The concept would appear antithetical to the Black Radical Feminism with which she is associated. If the feminist project is conceptualized as addressing the gendered experience of human existence, amidst the asymmetries of power in patriarchal, misogynist society, then all the more curious that the concept of genderlessness is evoked in her classic *Women, Race and Class*. In the chapter entitled "Standards for a New Womanhood," which, among other things, takes historians to task for failing in their studies of slavery in the United States to explore concretely "the multidimensional role of Black women within the family and within the slave community as a whole" (Davis 1981, 4), Davis – always critically contextualizing the present situation within its historical contexts of lived, material experience – writes:

> The enormous space that work occupies in Black women's lives today follows a pattern established during the very earliest days of slavery. As slaves, compulsory labor overshadowed every other aspect of women's existence. It would seem, therefore, that the starting point for any exploration of Black women's lives under slavery would be an appraisal of their role as workers.
>
> The slave system defined Black people as chattel. Since women, no less than men, were viewed as profitable labor-units, they might as well have been *genderless* as far as the slaveholders were concerned.
>
> *(Davis 1981, 5, emphasis added)*

In contrast to the unqualified assumption regarding the ubiquity of the gendered division of labor, Davis notes the historical data that in the middle of the 19th century, in the United States, "seven out of eight slaves, men and women alike, were field workers" (Davis 1981, 5). In reflecting further on 19th-century slavery in the most southern states – the Deep South – Davis concludes:

> For most girls and women, as for most boys and men, it was hard labor in the fields from sunup to sundown. Where work was concerned, strength and productivity under the threat of the whip outweighed considerations of sex. In this sense, the oppression of women was identical to the oppression of men.
>
> *(Davis 1981, 6)*

A distinguishing trait of Davis's critical scholarship is that actual, material, historical contradictions are reflected in her theoretical analysis, so she is able to articulate how what bell hooks calls the "white supremacist, capitalist, patriarchal class structure" (hooks 1984, 18) operates through processes that, at once – equally and differentially – subjugate. If one notes that Davis has observed the ways in which Blacks were and were not gendered, then the theoretical framework of her Black Radical Feminism is coming into view.

Objectification of a subject is a project of hollowing out, flattening, conforming, converting, consuming, erasing – a project of ruling and exploiting. That the subject is, for purposes of the process of objectification, diminished as a subject and even at times considered invisible, no longer existent or worthy of existence, or at least, not so as a subject but only in an owned and objectified form, in no way speaks to the necessary truth of the matter – as this is only one side of the equation. Oppression can generate, or be opposed by, resistance. What is diminished may – though reduced – exist nonetheless in a more concentrated and potent form and, through resistance, realize a powerful subjecthood – not only for oneself but for oneself as part of a community of others similarly situated – as dramatically conveyed by Frederick Douglass and Angela Davis in their respective autobiographies.

Women's oppression is such that the subject's gender is denied, rendering the person as a mere commodity and quantum of labor for production – that is, *genderless;* however, that genderlessness is very likely produced by putting gender and race – and more – to work in some way or other: "The license to rape emanated from and facilitated the ruthless economic domination that was the gruesome hallmark of slavery" (Davis 1981, 175). As per its conditions and requirements, the capitalist process of commodification acknowledges and uses – but also denies and negates – the subject's identities.

Each negation is unique, but, in the end – once quantified as a dehumanized, denatured unit of production, no one is special. In an important sense, then, we experience a common negation, though – most definitely – it is differentially applied and suffered; but, nonetheless, there is here a kind of equality in objectification, erasure and one-dimensionalization. The recognition of such – in our theory and practice – can be a powerful basis for building the solidarities on which our liberation depends.

In opposition to a crude Marxism, Davis would not agree with the following reductionist claim: *Once capitalism is overcome, racism and sexism would be eradicated*; however, she would agree with this assertion: *Overcoming capitalism is necessary for the eradication of racism and sexism*:

> I have never been one to assume that the advent of socialism by itself will emancipate women or automatically free Black people from the constraints of racism. But socialism does provide a much more effective basis on which to develop campaigns that can eventually wipe out both the institutional and the attitudinal expressions of sexism [and other oppressions].
>
> *(Davis 1989, 77)*

Bibliography

Davis, Angela Y. 1974. *An Autobiography*. New York: Random House.

Davis, Angela Y. 1981. *Women, Race & Class*. New York: Vintage Books.

Davis, Angela Y. 1989. "Complexity, Activism, Optimism: An Interview with Angela Y. Davis." *Feminist Review* 31: 66–81.

Davis, Angela Y. 2013. "Critical Refusals and Occupy." *Radical Philosophy Review* 16(2): 425–39.

Davis, Angela Y. 2017. "Abolition and Refusal." In *The Great Refusal: Herbert Marcuse and Contemporary Social Movements*, edited by Andrew T. Lamas, Todd Wolfson, and Peter Funke, vii–xi. Philadelphia: Temple University Press.

Du Bois, W.E.B. 1935. *Black Reconstruction in America: An Essay Toward a History of the Part Which Black Folk Played in the Attempt to Reconstruct Democracy in America, 1860–1880*. New York: Harcourt, Brace and Company.

Du Bois, W.E.B. 1996. *The Souls of Black Folk*. New York: Modern Library.

hooks, bell. 1984. *Feminist Theory: From Margin to Center.* Boston: South End Press.
King Jr., Martin Luther. 1967. *Where Do We Go from Here: Chaos or Community?* Boston: Beacon Press.
Lukács, György. 1971 (1923). *History and Class Consciousness: Studies in Marxist Dialectics.* London: Merlin.
Marcuse, Herbert. 1964. *One-Dimensional Man: A Study of Advanced Industrial Society.* Boston: Beacon Press.
Marcuse, Herbert. 1969. *An Essay on Liberation.* Boston: Beacon Press.
Patterson, Louise Thompson. 1936. "Toward a Brighter Dawn." *Woman Today* (Communist Party-USA).
Taylor, Keeanga-Yamahtta, ed. 2017. *How We Get Free: Black Feminism and the Combahee River Collective.* Chicago: Haymarket.

41

LISE VOGEL (1938–) AND SOCIAL REPRODUCTION THEORY

Tithi Bhattacharya

Lise Vogel's *Marxism and the Oppression of Women: Towards a Unitary Theory* was published in 1983, at a particularly inopportune moment for both Marxism and the question of women's oppression. In the U.K. a Conservative government, led by Margaret Thatcher, was re-elected by a landslide majority. A year later the pattern would be repeated in Vogel's own country, the United States, with a sweeping second victory for Ronald Reagan in 1984. While the now familiar social relations of neoliberalism were still in formation, the next few decades would offer great challenges for Marxists in general and Marxist feminists in particular.

Ironically, however, the early 1980s were not bad for a different version of feminism. Bourgeois feminism flourished and revivified a long dormant positive theoretical relationship between capitalism and women's empowerment. The way out of women's oppression, it was argued, was to compete and succeed *within* capitalism, as opposed to resisting or even questioning the system. Vogel's text offered some critical, even pioneering, answers to this very relationship between capitalism and women's oppression. The dominant conservative politics of the times and the rise of postmodernism within academic left circles however meant that her work and the theoretical innovations she proposed remained unexplored by most.

The republication of *Marxism and the Oppression of Women* (*MOW*) in 2013 reintroduced Vogel in an era of Marxist renewal but also situated her in a particular inflection of Marxist feminism, known popularly now as Social Reproduction Theory (SRT). For a new generation of feminists and gender activists in the Anglophone world, marked as they were by new social movements from Occupy to the Arab Spring, Social Reproduction feminism was a bridge into Marxism. MOW creatively illuminated for them the deeply gendered nature of capitalist social relations.

The Personal, the Political and the Theoretical

Born in 1938, Lise Vogel was a child of parents active on the US left in the 1930s and 1940s. Her own politics were nurtured and shaped in the fires of the civil rights movement of the 1960s. She started her undergraduate degree as a mathematics student at Harvard, but soon lost interest in the discipline, partly due to the culture of the all-male Mathematics Department. After spending some time in Paris, she decided to switch to art history. While studying in Boston she joined the Student Nonviolent Coordinating Committee (SNCC) and headed South as a volunteer to teach in the Freedom Schools and help with voter registration. Arrested more than once, for her role in voter registration and later in the anti-Vietnam War protests, when Lise Vogel finally came back to the North and joined academia, she had been permanently marked by her times. She recalled her time as a Junior Fellow at Dumbarton Oaks in Washington D.C.:

> Coming from Mississippi, I was struck not just by the hierarchies that permeated the workings of the institute but my colleague's virtually unquestioning acceptance of them. White administrative and clerical staff serviced the Fellows' every academic need . . . [a]nd Black women . . . took care of all domestic tasks. Well before the . . . appearance of the women's liberation movement, I . . . sensed the convergence of race, class and gender subordination . . . I particularly recall my horror . . . when the women, mothers all, appeared early Christmas morning to make us breakfast.
>
> *(Vogel 1995, 11)*

It is important to underscore both the antiracist roots of Vogel's radicalization as well as the concrete activism that she continued to participate in within the newly developing women's movement. A sense of the systemic totality of capitalism engendered for her generation a political conclusion that the fates of all were conjoined and hence solidarity with, not charity toward, the oppressed was the *sine qua non* of all struggle. "Thirty or forty years ago" Vogel writes "in contrast to today, it seemed agonizingly clear that the fates of all Americans were tied – that none could be free so long as some were bound" (Vogel 1995, 15).

If we read Vogel's mature work against the canvass of this personal history, the shades of her theoretical palette emerge with great clarity. First, as though a tribute to the work of Black women at her research institute, invisible labor and the invisible laborer is a central analytical concern for Vogel. In this, she follows in the footsteps of socialist feminists of a preceding generation who sought to establish the material roots of women's oppression under capitalism through what later became known as the domestic-labor debate.[1] But Vogel departs from this tradition in what could be considered her second major theoretical building block.

Second wave feminists such as Betty Friedan and Simon de Beauvoir, to paraphrase Marx, had only *described* the world. Undoubtedly it was a rich, complex and necessary description, allowing a generation of women to recognize and "name" their oppression. But this left finding an *explanation* for that oppression to the next generation of socialist feminists, which they found to be in domestic labor. Vogel was dissatisfied with this account for its explanatory power came from, what can be called, a division of labor analysis. To risk simplification, this tradition claimed that women were oppressed because of their marginalization from social production and the disproportionate burden of work they bore in the domestic sphere. This, to Vogel, appeared to be a surface level analysis – the effect of processes that had their cause somewhere else. From this criticism of earlier theory, Vogel developed what she called a "social reproduction perspective" (Vogel 1995, 85).

The fundamental insights of a social reproduction perspective, following Marx, are (a) that the labor expended for the production of commodities (at the point of production) and the labor expended for the "production" of people or workers who produce such commodities, are part of the same capitalist totality and intrinsically relational; and relatedly (b) that the working class family is the primary, but not the only, site for the reproduction of labor power or the reproduction of the working class as a whole. The domestic sphere thus cannot be seen simply as congeries of domestic labor or housework but "rather, [as] a particular set of activities involving the maintenance and replacement of the bearers of labor power and of the working class as a whole" (Vogel 1995, 86).

Third, and crucially, Vogel's activist past always reveals itself as the bedrock on which her theoretical scaffolding is built. The social reproduction perspective cannot be separated from strategic implications for anti-capitalist action. While social reproduction of labor power is essential to capitalist production, Vogel shows it to be also a major impediment to capitalism as it does not itself create surplus value and thereby directly fuel capitalist accumulation. Over the long term, struggle emerges between capital and labor with the former seeking to reproduce labor power at minimum cost and the latter fighting to win the best conditions for its own renewal. While production of value is woven into the fabric of capitalism, Vogel's analysis shows, so is class struggle.

Marxism and Social Reproduction Theory: An Integrated Relation

Social reproduction theory is a theoretical integration of gender into capitalist production relations. It is important to stress that SRT insists on theoretical integration as opposed to a simple combination, the former procedure suggesting an internal relation while the latter an external one.[2] Vogel chose a founding text of the historical materialist tradition, Engels's *The Origin of the Family Private Property and the State*, to show the externality of Engels's theorizing on gender and the need to provide a corrective. *Origin of the Family* was of course considered the authoritative text on women's oppression within Marxism. In an iconoclastically titled essay, "Engels: A Defective Formulation," Vogel argued that Engels's account of the relationship between social production and women's oppression was plagued by theoretical ambiguity and externality, hence open to serious misinterpretation.

The passage that Vogel took most exception to was one wherein Engels wrote of human life necessarily assuming a "twofold character: on the one hand, the production of the means of subsistence, of food, clothing and shelter and the implements required for this; on the other hand, the production of human beings themselves, the propagation of the species." Further on this dual process, Engels elaborated that the social organization of a particular era or stage of human history was "determined by both kinds of production: by the stage of development of labor, on the one hand, and of the family, on the other" (*MECW* 26: 131–32).

Since Marxists have criticized Vogel for being overtly dismissive of Engels in this essay (Ginsburgh 2014), it is important to pause and clarify what Vogel is objecting to in this formulation.

She is not disputing the twofold character of human life that Engels outlines in *Origin*, or Marx and Engels gestures toward in the *German Ideology* previously. What she is objecting to is that in *Origin* Engels fails to clarify the *relationship* between social production and "the production of human beings." In the absence of a discussion as to how the two processes relate, the relative weight of each, or the possibility of determining effects of one on the other, it appears as though, writes Vogel, "the production of human beings constitutes a process that has not only an autonomous character, but a *theoretical weight equal to that of the production of the means of existence*" [emphasis mine] (Vogel 2013, 33). If both processes are equally weighted, as a reading of Engels might suggest, this opens the door, Vogel correctly warns, to the "dual system" theories that have plagued the socialist feminist movement for decades.[3]

How Does SRT Rescue Historical Materialism From This Externality?

This is where Vogel's careful deployment of the term "unitary" in the very title of *MOW* assumes a certain centrality. She unites the effects of sexism with its cause and she does so in analytically unexpected ways.

It should be stated at the outset, that all of Vogel's theoretical work is acutely sensitive to the *experience* of sexism. Indeed, she credits the socialist feminist tradition, of which she is otherwise critical, of countering both (1) an idealist tendency, "which trivializes the issue of women's oppression as a mere . . . lack of rights and ideological chauvinism," and (2) a crude economistic model that similarly underplays "psychological and ideological issues, especially those arising within the family." In other words, in the context of the preceding discussion, she does not reject or underplay Engels's analytical emphasis on the significance of the family, or reproduction of human life within the site of the family in the understanding of women's oppression. What she establishes forcefully, that Engels in this particular text is silent on, is the *relationship* between the production of commodities and the reproduction of human life, or, as she puts it in *MOW* the "inseparability of the reproduction of individuals from overall social reproduction" of capital (Vogel 2013, 60).

In a startlingly original move, Vogel uses as her methodological model a text that had hitherto not been considered particularly illuminating about gender oppression – *Capital*. David McNally and Susan Ferguson, in their remarks on MOW, recognize the importance of this course of action. Any "serious Marxist account of women's oppression in capitalist society," they write, "is obliged to reckon with the central theoretical categories" that Marx offers in *Capital* (Vogel 2013, xviii).

The two questions that Vogel seeks to answer are whether gender-sex and class were "parallel issues" (Vogel 1995, 33), and what, if any, was the relationship between the two. *Capital* provided Vogel with the conceptual tools she needed to answer those questions. Again, McNally and Ferguson are useful here in showing the architecture of Vogel's methodology via *Capital*:

> Marx's critical procedure in *Capital* disclosed a series of interrelated concepts – the commodity, value, money, capital, labor-power, surplus-value, and so on – that were designed to illuminate the deep structural processes through which the capitalist mode of production reproduces itself. . . . By raising the problem of women's oppression within the categorical framework of *Capital*, and by doing so in more than an *ad hoc* fashion Vogel opened a new direction for socialist-feminist research.
>
> *(Vogel 2013, xviii)*

To go back to the questions; she answers them in three interrelated ways. First, following *Capital*, Vogel centralizes *the concept of labor power* in her analysis as the "unique commodity" whose status is both distinctive under capitalism and indispensable for an anti-capitalist practice. It is worth quoting her fully in her own words:

> In capitalist societies, labor power takes the form of a commodity and the reproduction of labor power has specific features, shaped in the workings of capitalist social reproduction. At its heart is working class women's historically evolved, disproportionate responsibility for domestic labor . . . Capitalism stamps this domestic labor with its own character: as in no other mode of production, maintenance and replacement [of labor power] tasks become spatially, temporally and institutionally isolated from the sphere of production, with serious consequences for relations between working class women and men and for the nature of women's oppression.
>
> *(Vogel 1995, 86)*

The argument about labor power as the analytical causeway between social production and social reproduction is deceptively simple. It exists in its broad outlines in *Capital*, albeit undeveloped by Marx himself. It unfolds in the following way.

> Labor power is the source of surplus value or profit under capitalism. But in order for labor power to exist and be constantly renewed such that it can be put to "work," it

> must be "reproduced." Reproduction of labor-power, while not a form of production itself, is "a condition of production, for it reposits or replaces the labor-power necessary for production."
>
> *(Vogel 2013, 144)*

There are, in the main, three ways in which such reproduction takes place: (1) through activities that regenerate the worker outside the production process, for example, food, sleep and other care work in the home, but also through other services such as education, health care or a public transport system than can and do contribute to the value of her labor power; (2) through generational replacement, that is, birth; (3) through activities that maintain and regenerate non-workers (within the working class), for example, children, and adults who are out of work for a multiple reasons ranging from old age, disability or unemployment.

While private households within the working class are the primary sites for the reproduction of labor power, such reproduction also takes place, Vogel insightfully comments, in "labor-camps, barracks, orphanages, hospitals, prisons, and other such institutions" (Vogel 2013, 159). Similarly, while birthing children may be the dominant form of renewing the workforce, Vogel also recognizes the role of immigration, slavery and other forms of forced labor in the social reproduction of the working class.

Having established the importance of labor power as a concept, Vogel then builds on it to delineate the second element of her argument, *the role of biological reproduction* and the family unit within capitalism. Women's ability to bear children (or put in SRT terms – their ability generationally to replace labor power) creates the conditions for their oppression under capitalism. Vogel, we must be clear, is not making a biologically determinist argument. Instead, she is pointing toward the *social organization* of biological capacity, which is both historical and specific to particular regions and communities. In reality, Vogel provides us with a vitally anti-essentialist, not to mention possibly trans-inclusive, argument about biological reproduction. She is drawing attention not to female biology but to capitalism's need for generational replacement of labor power. It is capital's dependence on specific bodily functions, such as child birth, lactation etc., that shapes privatized social reproduction and reinforces the enduring form of the male-dominated household under capitalism. The biological differences between a male and female body are only important here because of the ways in which such difference are articulated and organized by capital. Further, such an argument implies that it is ultimately irrelevant whether biological childbearing functions are carried out by cis or trans women, even if the latter phenomenon is never generalized within the social form.[4] As long as such functions are required and organized by capital, women's oppression, and by extension gender oppression and violence, will continue to exist.

The preceding two arguments, combined, clarify for us the conceptual category of division of labor, a source of confusion in the socialist feminist tradition. The dual system perspective takes "the . . . emphasis on the sex-division of labor and on the family as critically important phenomena which are not, however, firmly located with respect to overall social reproduction" (Vogel 2013, 136). SRT, on the other hand, hewing more closely to Marx's elaboration of the capitalist mode of production as a whole, integrates the historical organization of the division of labor within a generalized argument about the wage form. This integrative approach, as opposed to an additive one, has tremendous consequences for SRT and brings us to the final dimension of Vogel's argument, the *determinant effect of wage labor on the reproduction of labor power* within capitalist totality.

That the household, and domestic labor performed within it, played a significant role in capitalism was not in itself a novel argument that Vogel was making. Vogel's close attention to

Capital, however, allowed her to develop and correct two previous approaches to the question. The first, was the status accorded to domestic labor in the domestic labor debate that argued that domestic labor was value producing. The second, argued by socialist feminists, was that women's disproportionate share of domestic labor was the source of women's oppression. The first proposition had been conclusively refuted well before the publication of *MOW* (Smith 1978). But her rejection of domestic labor as value-producing, combined with the theoretical integration of the household within the structures of capitalist production, marked the singular innovation of Lise Vogel. This was significant for several reasons.

One, it put to rest all transhistorical arguments about men oppressing women for purely ideological reasons. Second, it did more than analyze the capitalist family, it situated the family form as a requirement for capitalist production thus explaining why the family, irrespective of the role of particularly sexed bodies within it, continued to produce female-subordinated gender norms. Capitalism, in its productive and juridical forms, needed the next generation of workers to be reproduced in the family and thus was compelled to regulate the biological capacity of women and female sexed bodies. As Vogel puts it, "it is the responsibility for the domestic labor necessary to capitalist social reproduction – and not the sex division of labor or the family *per se* – that materially underpins the perpetuation of women's oppression and inequality in capitalist society" (Vogel 2013, 177). Capitalism, far from being a gender-neutral system, was thus a highly gendered one.

Third, in revealing the relationship between the social relations of reproduction of labor power and the social relations of production of commodities, SRT was able to settle a crucial strategic question for anti-capitalist practice. Was it possible to achieve women's liberation under capitalism? To this Vogel responded with a decisive "no." Since women's oppression was located, not in the sphere of exchange, but in the "hidden abode" of production, it was capitalist production relations – the subordination of labor to capital, or the wage form – that needed to be abolished in order for women's oppression to cease.[5] In an argument closely following Lenin, Vogel, unpacked the contradictory nature of equality under capitalism. The fight for equality, say between women and men in the workplace, was never a "useless exercise in reformism." Instead, such battles had two dialectically opposite tendencies. On the one hand, they reduced differences between members of the working class thus creating the potential for a united struggle on the basis of solidarity. On the other hand, any robust struggle for reforms, inevitably revealed to those engaged in them, the horizons of what capitalism will allow within its existent relations: "for the further democratic rights are extended, the more capitalism's oppressive social and economic character stands revealed . . . then battle for equality [then] can point beyond capitalism" (Vogel 1995, 87).

It is perhaps in charting concrete political strategies for an anti-capitalist struggle, that Vogel's account was most criticized. When Vogel first presented her social reproduction perspective in a 1979 essay for the journal *Monthly Review*, two leading Marxist feminists, Johanna Brenner and Nancy Holmstrom, wrote a strong critical response. According to them, Vogel's perspective, with its emphasis on the social reproduction of capital having conditioning effects on the form of the household, in effect subordinated the role of the household and reproduced the "subordination of women's needs and interests to those of men." Brenner and Holmstrom claimed that Vogel took "class struggle, properly understood, to be central, which makes unity of the revolutionary forces the major task." In opposition to this view, they argued that women were "oppressed as women, not just as members of the working class" and "that women have interests that are not only different from those of men but also in conflict with them" (Brenner and Holmstrom 1983). Thus, they concluded, women's self-organization into women-only organizations, on a cross class basis, was not only important but necessary for a revolutionary socialist project.

Contemporary theorizing on what constitutes "class struggle" from a social reproduction perspective have refuted Brenner's and Holmstrom's claims on the issue and reinforced Vogel's theoretical procedure of establishing the centrality of class struggle.[6] Not only do Brenner and Holmstrom, by implication impute to class struggle a narrow, economistic view, they also draw unnecessary cleavages between workplace struggles (presumably "class struggle") and social struggles that arise outside of the point of production (such as anti-imperialist or feminist struggles).

Vogel, in her response, restated her position about the wage form having conditioning impulses on the form of the household and not the other way around. She also reminded her readers of her argument about capitalist equality, for it is through that aspect of the argument, she pointed out, that the question of cross class organizations could be resolved. While the lack of formal equality with men might draw bourgeois women in common struggle with working class women, Vogel pointed to the important fractures such a movement could generate internally for the bourgeois section was likely to regard "equality of women and men within capitalist society as a sufficient goal" (Vogel 1995, 87). Vogel in 1983 was prophetically anticipating Lean-In Feminism and its advocates! She was also not willing to be an analytical hostage to the question of a women's only organization. While she was not averse to such a form, she correctly saw this question as a "strategic orientation flowing from concrete analysis rather than an abstract principle of socialist organization" (Vogel 1995, 89).

Next Steps

It is not mere coincidence that Vogel's work was rediscovered in the era of neoliberalism and has attained immense popularity since. At a time when working class struggle at the point of production, and union density globally, are both at a historic low, SRT's emphasis on the imbricated relationship between production and reproduction has energized a new generation of scholars and activists. They have interpreted SRT's strategic lesson to be that social struggles about the lived conditions of the working class (such as water charges, housing or police brutality) need not remain politically cordoned off from workplace struggles and indeed can permeate or spark them. Both the French and the Russian revolutions started as bread riots led by women.

Similarly, the importance SRT accords to the totality of capitalist social relations make it possible to imagine new directions of research applying SRT to questions of race, immigration and sexuality that go beyond mere descriptions of these and other oppressions.

There was a certain untimeliness to Vogel's theoretical project when it first appeared in the inhospitable 1980s. But it is perhaps best to apply Giorgio Agamben's notion of contemporaneity to her work. Agamben argues that those who are truly contemporary, "who truly belong to their time," are those "who neither perfectly coincide with it nor adjust themselves to its demands." But precisely "through this disconnection and anachronism, they are more capable than others of perceiving and grasping their own time" (Agamben 2009, 40). Lise Vogel's contribution to Marxism resonates with this contemporaneity and relevance.

Notes

1. A section of feminists in the 1970s and 1980s argued that domestic labor produced value under capitalism and hence ought to be waged. The two major texts that elaborated this position were Dalla Costa (1973) and Fortunati and Spencer (1995). The best refutation of this argument, within the Marxist framework, is by Smith (1978).
2. See Ollman (1971) on internal relations in Marxism.
3. Dual systems theory was first advanced by Heidi Hartmann in 1979. Hartmann claimed that patriarchy and capitalism were two autonomous systems interacting with each other. This formulation was then

further developed into triple systems theory, for example by Sasha Roseneil (1994) and Sylvia Walby (1990), including racism as a third system.

4. Feminists such as Anne Fausto-Sterling have argued that this "two-sex model," that is, male and female only, is neither stable or universal (Fausto-Sterling 1993).
5. Marx uses the term "hidden abode" to describe the sphere of production that is not visible (CI: 279–80).
6. See Bhattacharya (2015).

Bibliography

Agamben, Giorgio. 2009. *"What Is an Apparatus?" and Other Essays*. Stanford: Stanford University Press.

Bhattacharya, Tithi. 2015. "How Not to Skip Class: Social Reproduction of Labor and the Global Working Class." *Viewpoint Magazine*. www.viewpointmag.com/2015/10/31/how-not-to-skip-class-social-reproduction-of-labor-and-the-global-working-class/

Bhattacharya, Tithi, ed. 2017. *Social Reproduction Theory: Remapping Class, Recentering Oppression*. London: Pluto.

Brenner, Johanna, and Nancy Holmstrom. 1983. "Women's Self-Organization: Theory and Strategy." *Monthly Review* 34: 34–46.

Dalla Costa, Mariarosa, and Selma James. 1973. *The Power of Women and the Subversion of the Community*. Bristol: Falling Wall Press.

Fausto-Sterling, Anne. 1993. "The Five Sexes: Why Male and Female Are Not Enough." *The Sciences* 33: 20–24.

Fortunati, Leopoldina, and Jim Fleming. 1995 (1981). *The Arcane of Reproduction: Housework, Prostitution, Labor and Capital*. Brooklyn: Autonomedia.

Ginsburgh, Nicola. 2014. "Lise Vogel and the Politics of Women's Liberation." *International Socialism* 2(144): 137–39.

Hartmann, Heidi. 1979. "The Unhappy Marriage of Marxism and Feminism: Towards a More Progressive Union." *Capital and Class* 8: 1–34.

Ollman, Bertell. 1971. *Alienation: Marx's Conception of Man in Capitalist Society*. Cambridge: Cambridge University Press.

Roseneil, Sasha. 1994. "Gender." In *Developments in Sociology*, edited by Michael Haralambos and Martin Holborn, 87–103. Ormskirk: Causeway Press.

Smith, Paul. 1978. "Domestic Labor and Marx's Theory of Value." In *Feminism and Materialism: Women and Modes of Production*, edited by Annette Kuhn and Annemarie Wolpe, 198–219. Boston: Routledge.

Vogel, Lise. 1995. *Woman Questions: Essays for a Materialist Feminism*. New York: Routledge.

Vogel, Lise. 2013 (1983). *Marxism and the Oppression of Women: Toward a Unitary Theory*. Chicago: Haymarket.

Walby, Sylvia. 1990. *Theorizing Patriarchy*. Oxford: Basil Blackwell.

42
STUART HALL (1932–2014)

Colin Sparks

Stuart Hall was a prominent left-wing public intellectual and the person most responsible for transforming a parochial British literary discourse into what is now known internationally as cultural studies. Hall has been the subject of many studies, and these tend to give contradictory accounts of his relationship to Marxism. Helen Davis, for example, emphasizes the influence of Marxism throughout his career (Davis 2004, 14). James Proctor, on the other hand, tends to marginalize the Marxist dimension and argues that Hall is best understood as someone whose positions were always shifting and "incomplete" and that his work is "full of contradictions, discrepancies and U-turns" (Proctor 2004, 8). These views are not necessarily incompatible: Hall did indeed have a serious engagement with Marxism and, perhaps, Post-Marxism, but he was an "unapologetic revisionist"' throughout his career (Davison et al. 2017, 5). The aim of this entry is to trace through Hall's own writings the main points of his contact with other explicitly Marxist theorists, the concepts he developed as a result of those contacts, and the uses to which he put them.

Hall came to the UK as a student in 1951 from his native Jamaica. According to his own accounts, although he was familiar with the work of Marx, a more important influence upon his political education was the Guild Socialism of G.D.H. Cole (Hall 2010, 79–80). Hall was active in the left-wing student milieu and a prominent member of a group of independent socialists who, in 1957, founded a journal, *Universities and Left Review* (ULR).

It was in *ULR* that Hall published his first substantial engagement with Marxism, in the 1958 essay "A Sense of Classlessness" (Hall 1958). Hall's argued that capitalist production was changing: while the old heavy industries remained important in terms of employment, new, more technologically oriented, industries reconstituted the working class, undermining the type of alienation produced by the older forms of manual labor analyzed by Marx in the *Economic and Philosophic Manuscripts*. The newer forms of labor involved greater individual expertise and greater personal investment in the productive process.

> In the circumstances of which Marx wrote, a brutalized working class within a severe work-discipline were unconscious of the nature of their alienation: today, alienation of labor has been built-in to the structure of the firm itself. "Joint consultation" and "personnel relations" is a form of false consciousness, part of the ideology of consumer capitalism, and the rhetoric of scientific management.
>
> *(Hall 1958, 28)*

The first effect of this change in the economic structure was that workers in these industries now possessed a "form of false consciousness" that led them to a much greater degree of investment in their labor and an identification with the organizations for which they worked.

The second effect was that capitalism after 1945 transformed the conditions of large sections of the working class. They increasingly lived in new houses, in new places and commanded greater disposable incomes. Increased purchasing power meant workers had become not only the producers of commodities but also their consumers. This new power to consume had "been so built in to capitalism that it has become the most significant relationship between the working class and the employing class" (Hall 1958, 28).

Hall followed Raymond Williams and Richard Hoggart in arguing that the traditional working class had created communities based on common experiences of deprivation and mutual solidarity. New opportunities for consumption brought not only physical objects but also their associated role as "insignias [sic] of class and status" (Hall 1958, 29). Hall argued that in place of the collective identities characteristic of the older working class communities, the new age brought a more differentiated "series of lifestyles" that allowed individuals and their families to signify their social status through their consumption choices. The "horizontal" patterns of mutual dependence and respect that Williams had argued in *Culture and Society* were the motivating forces of socialist organizations, were being replaced by a version of the middle-class "ladder" of individual advancement in which "life is now a series of fragmented patterns of living for many working-class people" (Williams 1961; Hall 1958, 31). The old motors of class-consciousness, if not the realities of class exploitation, had been defused by affluence: "where the subjective factors determining 'class consciousness' alter radically, a working class can develop a false sense of 'classlessness.'" As a consequence, citing Hoggart's dense account of life in a classic manual working class community, Hall argued that "socialism cannot develop as a set of ideas or as a program without a matrix of values, a set of assumptions, a base in experience, which gives them validity" (Hoggart, 1957; Hall 1958, 32).

On its publication, Hall's self-described "rather over-dramatized and badly written piece" provoked critical responses of varying degrees of orthodoxy and hostility, from, among others, E.P. Thompson, Ralph Samuel and, in the pages of *Labour Review*, Cliff Slaughter (Hall 1959, 50; Thompson 1959; Samuel 1959; Slaughter 1959). Hall accepted some of the criticism, but remained adamant as to the importance of his argument that,

> in a period when the majority of the working force has ceased to be "production workers" in the old sense, we need a different or modified set of criteria for explaining (to others and ourselves) what "exploitation" means – and therefore some rather new concepts to apply to the term "class struggle."
>
> *(Hall 1959, 51)*

The essay, however, remains a valuable starting point for understanding Hall's subsequent relationship to Marxism, as well as the character that he imparted to cultural studies. Very often the formulations that Hall was later to give to these issues was different from, and sometimes the reverse of, the ways in which he discussed them in this early essay, but the underlying issues remain more or less the same.

The most obvious prefigurative indicator is the insistence on the increasingly fragmented character of the working class. In its first iteration, "difference" is due to choices made in consumption, but it anticipates later formulations that were central to Hall's mature work. The second indicator is his attention to the ways in which people conceive of the world, here described in terms of "false consciousness." In later formulations, this was a concept he rejected in favor of a theory of ideology, but the concern remains. The third indicator is his self-proclaimed "revisionism" with regard to the relationship between "base and superstructure" (Hall 1958, 32). Hall here cited the *Economic and Philosophic Manuscripts* since "at least in the earlier writings on 'alienation' we need to give a different weight or emphasis to 'superstructure' than we would imagine simply from a study of *Capital*" (Hall 1958, 32). This is an evaluation of Marx he would later reverse, but the concern with the problematic relationship between material production and cultural phenomena would become central to Hall's theoretical positions.

At the end of 1959 *ULR* merged with *The New Reasoner* to form *New Left Review*, with Hall as the first editor. The journal's approach might best be summarized as a socialist humanism with a strong emphasis on analyzing "the superstructure." Hall wrote in the introductory editorial: "The humanist strengths of socialism – which are the foundations for a genuinely popular socialist movement – must be developed in cultural and social terms, as well as in economic and political" (Hall 1960a, 1).

After his departure from the editorship of *New Left Review* at the end of 1962, the emphasis in Hall's work shifted toward the development of the "cultural and social terms" that he identified as central to the socialist project. The work Hall produced during this period, particularly after he joined the Centre for Contemporary Cultural Studies (CCCS) at the University of Birmingham in 1964, demonstrates relatively little direct engagement with Marxism. When Marxism did reappear in Hall's writing, in the aftermath of 1968, it was at first largely in passing. Hall's introduction to first issue of the CCCS's journal *Working Papers in Cultural Studies* (WPCS) mentions Edward Thompson (alongside Hoggart and Williams), Adorno and Marx as the key influences on the work of CCCS, while his substantive article, a critical response to the Weberian account of cultural studies developed by Alan Shuttleworth, cites Sartre and the *Economic and Philosophic Manuscripts*, but none are treated systematically (Hall 1971a, 1971b, 102) The brilliant essay "The Social Eye of the *Picture Post*" in the second issue of *Working Papers in Cultural Studies*, is indebted to Roland Barthes but contains no evidence of an engagement with Marx (Hall 1972). His famous "break into complex Marxism" was, however, undoubtedly under way by this time, facilitated by an engagement with structuralism, and in particular with Claude Lévi-Strauss (Hall 1980a, 25, 2016, 54–73).[1]

The development of Hall's thought during this period is most fully articulated in the famous book *Policing the Crisis* that he and four of his students published in 1978. It is a collective work, and while Hall was clearly the guiding intelligence, it equally clearly bears the traces of different authors, so it must be read with caution if we are seeking evidence of Hall's own developing theoretical position. Alongside a close engagement with a number of Marxist themes, there are many of the issues that were central to the work of CCCS in the early 1970s, for example the idea of the "moral panic" borrowed from critical criminology (Cohen 2011).

The book, the authors state, is "about mugging . . . our aim has been to examine 'mugging' from the perspective of the society in which it occurs" and the analysis therefore involved an extremely wide range of questions, from Marx's ideas about productive and unproductive labor through to the analysis of television news (Hall et al. 1978, 328). "Mugging" was a term for street crime, often involving violence, which was imported from the US in the early 1970s and used to describe a supposed epidemic of young Black men robbing white people. The central argument of the book was that the social and economic settlement established by the 1945 Labour government had been eroded in the course of the 1960s. It was no longer an appropriate way for the ruling class to exercise its control of society socially, culturally or economically (Hall et al. 1978, 252). In its place was emerging an authoritarian framework aimed at subordinating the whole society ruthlessly to the rule of capital (Hall et al. 1978, 315).

The importance of "mugging" was that it mobilized themes that permitted a section of the ruling class to re-establish their moral and intellectual leadership of society in a new way. It focused a wide range of "social, moral and ideological dissent" through a lens of racism that, then as now, commands widespread popular support (Hall et al. 1978, 320). The emergence of Margaret Thatcher in 1975 as the leader of the Conservative Party meant "that those half-formed specters which once hovered on the edge of British politics proper have now been fully politicized and installed in the vanguard, as a viable basis for hegemony" (Hall et al. 1978, 316). This identification of Thatcher as the standard bearer of new form of hegemony resting upon popular authoritarianism and steadily evolving into what it today known as neoliberalism forms one of the major themes of Hall's engagement of Marxism up until his death

Hall's theoretical relationship with Marxism in this period is most clearly expressed in a series of lectures he delivered at the University of Illinois in 1983, and it is from that work that most of this discussion is drawn. Some of the other texts from around that time display a different emphasis, but they share the same underlying conception of Marxism.

Hall's first debt in reworking Marxism was to Louis Althusser. Hall claimed that his work represented "an immense theoretical revolution" (Hall 2016, 126) and that "it is impossible to think about culture or the debates in cultural theory outside the continuing effect of the Althusserian intervention" (Hall 2016, 114). He did not, however, "become an Althusserian" but instead took a number of key elements that he worked into his own distinctive position.

The appropriation of Althusser involved a reversal of positions that Hall had previously held and that he recognized had been fundamental to the New Left and cultural studies. Both the commitment to socialist humanism and the stress upon Marx's youthful writings were explicitly rejected by Althusser and Hall. Althusser, following structuralist principles, had theorized the "decentering of the subject" (Hall 2016, 100–101). This implied a sharp break from both the humanistic Marxism of New Left writers like Thompson and the more diffuse humanism Hall identified as common to the version of cultural studies advanced by Hoggart and Williams (Hall 1980b, 64).

The second borrowing was Hall's rethinking of the relationship between base and superstructure. Althusser, famously, bracketed out the issue of determination until the "lonely hour of the last instance." In place of analyzing the ways in which the economy determined the shape and content of other elements in society, Hall took from Althusser the concepts of the specificity of different levels of the social formation, overdetermination and relative autonomy (Hall 2016, 104–10). Hall used these together with the concept of articulation developed by Ernesto Laclau, to argue that "individual ideological elements have no necessary 'class-belongingness,'" and that there is "no necessary correspondence" between different levels of the social formation, for instance between the economic and the cultural (Hall 1980c, 174). These elements could, however, under some circumstances, be articulated with social positions (Hall 2016, 123). The consequences of these borrowings are that

> the model is much more indeterminate, open-ended, and contingent than the classical position. It suggests you cannot "read off" the ideology of a class, or even sectors of a class, from its original position in the structure of socioeconomic relations. But it refuses to say that it is impossible to bring classes or fractions of classes, or indeed other kinds of social movements, through a developing practice of struggle, into articulations with those forms of politics and ideology which allow them to become historically effective as collective social agents.
>
> *(Hall 2016, 124)*

The consequence of this re-theorization of the relationship between ideology and social class as the contingent result of social struggle is that Marxism, against what Hall defined as the teleological bent of its orthodox versions, can only be thought of as being "without guarantees" (Hall 1983).

Hall also adopted Althusser's rejection of ideology as "false consciousness," which stood in direct contrast to the views earlier advanced by Hall himself. His appropriation was, again, not uncritical: he rejected, for instance, Althusser's subsumption of civil society under the state in the concept of "ideological apparatuses" (Hall 2016, 132–34). The element that he found most valuable was the notion that ideologies are "systems of representations materialized in practices" working through "hailing" the individual as a subject (Hall 2016, 39–40). The implication is that the adoption of an ideology by any social grouping can only be effective if

> it is the articulation, the non-necessary link, between a social force which is making itself and the ideology or conceptions of the world which makes intelligible the process they are going through, which bring onto the historical stage a new social position and political position, a new set of social and political subjects.
>
> *(Hall 2016, 146)*

The final major borrowing was from Antonio Gramsci, specifically from the *Prison Notebooks*. As pre-figured in *Policing the Crisis*, Hall took from Gramsci the theory that in the advanced capitalist countries of the West the central mechanisms through which the ruling class ensured its continued control over society were ideology and culture. Through successfully presenting their ideology and culture as the natural way of thinking and behaving, as common sense, the dominant class presented itself as the rightful leader of society. To the extent that they managed to obtain the consent of at least a part of the dominated classes to their continued rule, the dominant classes exercised hegemony over society:

> hegemony refers to the ways in which those elements that rule politically and dominate ideologically . . . do so by having the capacity to mobilize popular forces in support. . . . Hegemony entails the formation of a bloc, not the appearance of a class. It is precisely the establishment of the ascendancy of a particular historic bloc or the formation over the society as a whole that constitutes hegemony, and this can only be accomplished if that bloc is able to generalize the interests and the goals of a particular group so that they come to command something like popular recognition and consent.
>
> *(Hall 2016, 170)*

The achievement of hegemony was always unstable and subject to contestation from other social groups. The classical Marxist stress upon working class activity was no longer the fulcrum of this contestation since the historical evidence was that "non-problematic forms of the class struggle and class belongingness have simply refused to appear" (Hall 2016, 186). In place of class struggle, one central locus for contesting capitalist hegemony was cultural life: "there can be no sustained establishment of counter-hegemonies without their articulations in culture and ideology. Cultural politics and ideological struggle are the necessary conditions for forms of social and political struggle" (Hall 2016, 189–90). In order to conduct such cultural interventions, it was necessary to abandon the orientation upon social class and to oppose the "power bloc" with a much broader conception of "the people": "the people versus the power bloc: this, rather than 'class-against-class,' is the central line of contradiction around which the terrain of culture is polarized" (Hall 1981, 238).

The theoretical framework sketched here is one that underlay, with different inflections, all of the work that Hall undertook from the mid-1970s to his death in 2014. The extent to which he retained parts of it, particularly those derived from Gramsci, is attested in an interview he gave near the end of his life, in which he states "'Gramscian' is about the only title I own" (Hay 2013, 16).

There was, after the 1980s, a bifurcation in Hall's analytic work. He was best known for his role as one of the leading writers for the British Communist Party's theoretical journal, *Marxism Today*, whose editor, Martin Jacques, claimed was "easily the most influential political magazine in Britain between 1978 and 1991" (Jacques n.d.).[2] Hall developed the ideas outlined in *Policing the Crisis* into a comprehensive analysis of British politics. He extended the scope to the broader notion of the "neoliberal revolution," which encompassed not merely Thatcher and Reagan but Blair and Cameron (Hall 2011). Alongside famous articles like "The Great Moving Right Show" and "The State: Socialism's Old Caretaker"[3] there were a stream of less-remembered interventions. For example, in December 1985, the article "Re-alignment – For What?" rehearses his objections to the "hard left" in terms that distil his overall position:

> [Their] model has committed us over the years to an analysis which no longer has at its center an accurate description of contemporary social, economic or cultural realities. Second, it has attached us to a definition and a model of how change occurs in society which in no way adequately reflects the actual social composition of the class forces and social movements necessary to produce it or democratic realities of our society. Third, it is no longer able to politicize and develop the majority experiences and dispositions of the popular forces which the Left must enlist. Fourth, it is wedded to an automatic conception of class, whereby the economic conditions can be transposed directly on to the political and ideological stage.
>
> *(Hall 1985, 14)*

Even in the last articles published in his lifetime, in the magazine *Soundings*, Hall retained his emphasis upon the primacy of cultural struggles and the "battle of ideas" in order "to shift the direction of popular thinking" (Hall and O'Shea 2013, 23).

The other major strand of Hall's work was the development of cultural studies. The famous works on the encoding/decoding model of news had, in its own development, mirrored his 1970s development from Barthesian structuralism to Gramscian Marxism but in later works he laid increasing emphasis upon identity:

> Increasingly, the political landscapes of the modern world are fractured in this way by competing and dislocating identifications – arising, especially, from the erosion of the "master identity" of class and the emerging identities belonging to the new political ground defined by the new social movements: feminism, black struggles, national liberation, anti-nuclear and ecological movements.
>
> *(Hall 1992, 280)*

Through the concept of identity, Hall went on to develop a body of work on Black culture, and particularly Black visual culture (Hall and Gilroy 2007). Hall had, for obvious reasons, always been aware of the issues of difference, notably racism, in British culture: the first issue of *NLR* had carried Hall's article on the role of the *ULR* Club in helping defend the West Indian community in Notting Hill from attacks by racist and fascist elements (Hall 1960b). Beyond personal experience, however, this concern was motivated by the legacy of Althusser who had enabled

Hall to "live in and with 'difference'" (Hall 2016, 119). The racism of modern societies, he argued, was founded precisely upon this "fear . . . of living with difference" (Hall 1992, 17). The stress upon analyzing difference allowed Hall to give much greater attention to the construction of identities that underlie perceptions of difference and provide a key to "how are people from different cultures . . . to make some sort of common life together . . .?" (Hall 2007, 150–51).

To return to the point where this entry began, it is correct *both* to say that Hall was seriously engaged with Marxism and that in important respects he shifted his position on major theoretical issues during the course of his career. There is, however, a deeper question of how far Hall's different interpretations of Marxism were in fact addressed to an underlying and pre-existing set of concerns. Despite Hall's explicit refusal to follow the insights of writers like Foucault and Derrida to their conclusions, there is a sense that the radical and very consistent displacement of the classic definition of class as defined by relationship to the means of production, combined with his sense of the multiplicity of social positions available in contemporary society, meant that Hall could be considered as a pioneer of Post-Marxism long before the term itself was ever coined.

Notes

1. So far as I can tell, the first mention of Althusser in Hall's published work is in his essay "The Determination of News Photographs" in *Working Papers in Cultural Studies 2* (Hall 1972).
2. Davis quotes Hall stating in a private communication that "One of the conditions of Hall joining the editorial board was that neither he nor his colleague [the playwright] David Edgar should be required to join the Communist Party" (Davis 2004, 133).
3. These articles, alongside other well-known pieces, are usefully collected in *Stuart Hall: Selected Political Writings* (Davison et al. 2017).

Bibliography

Cohen, Stanley. 2011. *Folk Devils and Moral Panics: The Creation of the Mods and Rockers*. Abingdon: Routledge.

Davis, Helen. 2004. *Understanding Stuart Hall*. London: Sage.

Davison, Sally, David Featherstone, and Bill Schwarz. 2017. "Introduction: Redefining the Political." In *Stuart Hall: Selected Political Writings: The Great Moving Right Show and Other Essays*, edited by Sally Davison, David Featherstone, Michael Rustin, and Bill Schwarz, 1–15. Durham, NC: Duke University Press.

Hall, Stuart. 1958. "A Sense of Classlessness." *Universities and Left Review* 1(5): 26–32.

Hall, Stuart. 1959. "The Big Swipe." *Universities and Left Review* 1(7): 50–52.

Hall, Stuart. 1960a. "Introducting NLR." *New Left Review* 1(1)(January–February): 1.

Hall, Stuart. 1960b. "ULR Club at Notting Hill." *New Left Review* 1(11)(January–February): 71–72.

Hall, Stuart. 1971a. "Introduction." *Working Papers in Cultural Studies* (1): 1–2.

Hall, Stuart. 1971b. "A Response to 'People and Culture.'" *Working Papers in Cultural Studies* (2): 97–102.

Hall, Stuart. 1972. "The Social Eye of the 'Picture Post.'" *Working Papers in Cultural Studies* (2): 71–120.

Hall, Stuart. 1980a. "Cultural Studies: Two Paradigms." *Media, Culture and Society* 2(1): 57–72.

Hall, Stuart. 1980b. "Cultural Studies and the Centre: Some Problematics and Problems." In *Culture, Media, Language: Working Papers in Cultural Studies*, edited by Stuart Hall, Dorothy Hobson, Andrew Lowe, and Paul Willis, 15–47. London: Hutchinson.

Hall, Stuart. 1980c. "Popular-Democratic versus Authoritarian Populism: Two Ways of Taking Democracy Seriously." In *Marxism and Democracy*, edited by Alan Hunt, 157–85. London: Lawrence Wishart.

Hall, Stuart. 1981. "Notes on Deconstructing 'the Popular.'" In *People's History and Socialist Theory*, edited by Raphael Samuel, 227–40. London: Routledge.

Hall, Stuart. 1983. "The Problem of Ideology: Marxism without Guarantees." In *Marx: A Hundred Years On*, edited by Betty Matthews, 57–86. London: Lawrence and Wishart.

Hall, Stuart. 1985. "Realignment: For What?" *Marxism Today* (December): 12–17.

Hall, Stuart. 1992. "Race, Culture and Communications: Looking Backward and Forward at Cutlural Studies." *Rethinking Marxism* 5: 10–18.

Hall, Stuart. 2007. "Living with Difference: Stuart Hall in Conversation with Bill Schwarz." *Soundings* 37: 148–58.
Hall, Stuart. 2010. "Life and Times of the First New Left." *New Left Review* 2(61): 177–96.
Hall, Stuart. 2011. "The Neoliberal Revolution." *Soundings* 48: 9–27.
Hall, Stuart. 2016. *Cultural Studies 1983: A Theoretical History*. Durham, NC: Duke University Press.
Hall, Stuart, and Alan O'Shea. 2013. "Common-Sense Neoliberalism." *Soundings* 55: 8–23.
Hall, Stuart, Chas Critcher, Tony Jefferson, John Clarke, and Brian Roberts. 1978. *Policing the Crisis: Mugging, the State and Law and Order.* Basingstoke: Macmillan.
Hall, Stuart, and Paul Gilroy. 2007. "Preface." In *Black Britain: A Photographic History*. London, edited by Stuart Hall and Paul Gilroy, 5–10. London: Saqi Books.
Hay, James. 2013. "Interview with Stuart Hall." *Communication and Critical/Cultural Studies* 10(1): 10–33.
Hoggart, Richard. 1957. *The Uses of Literacy*. London: Charro & Windus.
Jacques, Martin. n.d. "*Marxism Today* Introduction." http://banmarchive.org.uk/collections/mt/index_frame.htm
Proctor, James. 2004. *Stuart Hall*. London: Routledge.
Samuel, Ralph. 1959. "Class and Classlesness." *Universities and Left Review* 1(6): 44–50.
Slaughter, Cliff. 1959. "The 'New Left' and the Working Class." *Labour Review* 4(2): 49–54.
Thompson, E.P. 1959. "Commitment in Politics." *Universities and Left Review* 1(6): 50–55.
Williams, Raymond. 1961. *Culture and Society 1780–1950*. Harmondsworth: Penguin.

43
JUDITH BUTLER (1956–)

Terrell Carver

Judith Butler is a widely read philosopher and prominent public intellectual. Her academic work has been influential in relation to gender studies, most notably in a reversal of the sex-gender relationship as previously understood. Also considered a founder of queer theory, she undertook a thorough conceptualization of heteronormativity as a pervasive power-structure in society (Chambers and Carver 2008). Her political activities since the terrorist acts of 11 September 2001 in the US, and her interventions as a Jew in the politics of Israel-Palestine, have attracted global attention. In her thoughtful and provocative journalism, and public speaking and media appearances, she presents herself as a philosophically informed, left-leaning advocate for democracy, human rights and the rule of law (Schippers 2014, 53–57, 131–36).

Butler does not identify as a Marxist or Post-Marxist. Nonetheless in the philosophical works she cites, and methodologically in her engagements, there are substantial commonalities. The intellectual heritage in German idealism on which Butler draws is itself common to Marx's own intellectual development, and indeed this mode of philosophizing also figures in the reception of his work. Idealism also permeates the philosophers through which Butler commonly develops her views, given that they, like Marx, are also critical of it in various ways (Schippers 2014, 5–12). There is thus no great difficulty finding Marx's presence in Butler's work, even if by unacknowledged analogy. Conversely, reading Butler into Marx might appear anachronistic, and there is certainly no suggestion here that for Butler such a rereading of Marx would be of much interest. Butlerian readings of Marx, however, have a place in the reception of her work, and he emerges refreshed from this exercise (Carver 1998, 24–42).

Marx was also a political activist and public intellectual, though the alignment of Butler with Marx in those respects provides more contrast than congruence. Marx threw his life into communist/socialist politics, which was contextualized for him in the German states where he grew to maturity. After his post-revolutionary removal to London in 1849, his activism was still largely focused in that direction. While highly influential in committees and organizations that drew socialist movements together across national boundaries, he operated with his closest associates in a German-French network. As an émigré in Britain he had few native associates and only tenuous connections with local politics. Within those contexts he promoted internationalism and the formation of a global movement of workers, and it is in that way that his activism has been posthumously and eponymously appreciated (Claeys 2018).

Other than as a radical journalist and newspaper editor in the Rhineland, and in a burst of activity in the revolutionary years 1848–49, Marx had little role as a public intellectual. He had isolated moments of notoriety in connection with the post-revolutionary communist trials in Cologne, and very occasional and very brief notices in the Anglo-American press. During his lifetime a handful of political works in German and French were circulated in limited print-runs for a small, mainly German-speaking readership. He also wrote as a foreign correspondent for left-leaning papers from New York to Vienna. But as a socialist activist he reached many more readers with the documents authored in the 1860s and early 1870s for the International Working Men's Association (Musto 2014, 1–68).

Butler's career as a political activist and public intellectual, unlike Marx's, has developed almost entirely within the framework of her philosophical interests, and generally within an academic career. In that role public engagement and political protest are largely distinct from partisan electioneering and office-holding service. However, Butler has pushed against conventional limits within those terms. She has provocatively confronted individuals and groups with her views in highly politicized circumstances, exposing herself to threats and occasional physical abuse, together with concomitant risks and anxieties. Her speeches, interviews and publications have been highly critical of the US-led Global War on Terror and subsequent military interventions in Iraq and Afghanistan (Butler 2009). She has decisively supported the pro-Palestinian, anti-Zionist Boycott/Divest/Sanctions movement that aims to end Israeli occupation and settlement policies, protesting that they conflict with international law and violate human rights (Butler 2004a, 2013, 2014, 2017).

Like Marx's political pamphlets and activist journalism, Butler's work is profoundly critical and philosophically sophisticated. Unlike Marx, who was an outspoken communist/socialist and atheist, Butler has not operated within such a clearly defined political program and closely defined network. And again, unlike Marx, she has had much greater exposure to the global public as an intellectual, commanding respect in much wider circles and in much more varied contexts. Since the early 1990s she has capitalized on her intellectual achievements in gender studies and queer theory, deploying her authority as a philosopher and so counteracting what might otherwise be mere notoriety (Butler 1997a, 2000, 2004b).

Key to Butler's rise as a public intellectual was her initial engagement with feminism, itself a global political movement, broad based, involving millions of women, and not many men, in highly varied struggles. In her 1990 debut book in this field, Butler turned major intellectual resources loose on what were then politicized debating points, but more in activist circles than in academia. Her ideas are still not well understood within feminist and queer movements, let alone accepted there, even though her name is widely recognized. In academia those who do or would understand her writings were often little-inclined to read female authors, and even less inclined to read debates within feminist circles. In academic feminism, however her works are now canonical, and in that frame she generates considerable media interest.

It was Butler's critical engagement with feminism that drew her into a widely circulated controversy. These exchanges arose within the Marxist/Post-Marxist debates and struggles that set a unifying socialist politics of class struggle against the centrifugal forces of identity politics. New social movements, organizing on the basis of nationality, ethnicity/race, gender and sexuality, posed the political and theoretical challenges through which Post-Marxism arose, pithily formulated and defended in Laclau and Mouffe (1985). Nancy Fraser (1995, 1998) framed this confrontation theoretically in relation to the concept of justice, arguing that redistribution – with obvious links to Marxist class analysis via a transformative social democratic politics – was necessarily fundamental to other concerns, such as an identity politics of cultural recognition on liberal inclusionary terms (Schippers 2014, 26–27). Butler's counterblast was determinedly political to the present, rather than reverential to a tradition, arguing that any unity within "the Left" had to be forged through practices of contestation rather than declared by fiat and exclusion. Philosophically her riposte was also characteristic: identities are not constituted out of apparent differences to be taken for granted, but rather apparent differences are the condition of possibility for – in a nod to Laclau and Mouffe – unifying and productive articulations (Butler 1998, 36–37).

Butler's reputation as a formidable and challenging intellect, and her determination to be a provocative public intellectual, have combined to give her a global political presence that Marx might possibly have envied. Marxism, as an inspiration to international communist movements and national liberation struggles, created global recognition for Marx, albeit posthumously, when his thought and image were manipulated in sometimes shocking ways. Since then, his name commands both demonization and reverence. Butler does not occupy this position in her own life and probably will not be constructed that way *post mortem*. Nonetheless as public intellectuals and political activists there is a traceable overlap between the two.

Idealist Philosophers and the "Linguistic Turn"

Since the 1870s and 1880s Marx has been presented, initially by his friend and sometime co-author Friedrich Engels, as a philosopher of nature, history and thought, and a materialist in some dialectical sense. In Engels's exposition Marx's materialism departed in a quasi-Hegelian way from conventional empiricisms, but was ontologically similar to them in presuming that all existence was necessarily material, even consciousness. By the turn of the 20th century dissenting voices, even within Marxist movements, were finding this philosophical system less than fully defensible in itself, and not fully consistent with Marx's own writings. More seriously, dialectical or even historical materialism might be inconsistent with whatever theory and method was thought to be intrinsic to his intellectual and political project.

Among other considerations such skepticisms highlighted the claimed elision in Marxism between a foundational materialism and an economic determinism. Determinism was said to be foundational to a scientific materialism of matter-in-motion, whereas the exposition of the materialist interpretation of history – which was Engels's coinage in a book review of 1859 – relied on socio-historical activities of production, consumption, distribution and exchange (*MECW* 16: 465–77). Assertions of the necessary congruence of a materialism of material things in a physical sense, but also of economic activities involving human agents with material resources, were plausible to some but unconvincing to others, and have therefore been debated ever since (White 1996).

Engels published Marx's manuscript "Theses on Feuerbach," after the author's death, as evidence for the materialism that he assigned to Marx. Marx's uniquely important breakthrough of 1845 followed on – so Engels averred forty years later – from Feuerbach's influential, self-styled materialist inversion of Hegel's thorough-going philosophical idealism (*MECW* 26: 353–98). Marx's "Theses" dismiss conventional materialisms outright as merely "contemplative," and he mounts an effective critique of Feuerbach's outlook as in that way insufficiently social and historical. Marx's own "new [materialism]," as he says in his "Theses," would be otherwise. In that regard he praises contemporary idealism for developing the "*active* side" (*MECW* 5: 35; emphasis in original). This was a point taken by Engels but transmuted into claims that matter – and indeed everything that exists – is intrinsically in contradictory and transformative motions. In Engels's view, law-like regularities can be inferred, and in principle predicted, from this quasi-Hegelian ontology of material motion. However, alternative versions of Hegelianism, discovered within or projected into Marx's writings, found other ways to incorporate the "active side," praised by Marx in his "Theses," into a way of reading most or all of his work (Jay 2016).

Butler's philosophical education was rooted in early study of idealist philosophies, notably Hegel, his French reception in works by Alexandre Kojève and Jean Hyppolite, and the German phenomenologists, notably Martin Heidegger and Edmund Husserl. Her interest in the philosophy of subjectivity was worked out in a close reading of Hegel's *Phenomenology of Spirit* (or *Mind*), and extended to an engagement with psychoanalysis, notably through the works of Sigmund Freud and Jacques Lacan (Butler 1997b, 2012 [1999], 2015; Lloyd 2007, 13–22). This is seemingly distant from Marx's intellectual engagement with political economy, though not so alien from his appreciation of the "active side" in philosophical idealism. His early critical discussion of Hegel's *Phenomenology* itself makes this connection (*MECW* 3: 326–46). These editorial extracts from Marx's rough notebooks were posthumously published only in 1932 and were part of the Hegelian reception of Marx in France and Germany. Marx's early manuscripts, though, were highly marginal and indeed anathema to the established Marxisms of the time. Rather similarly Foucault's archaeological structuralism, and later historicizing genealogical studies, bear some analogical relationship to Marx's critical concerns with power, institutions and oppression. Foucault's thinking also bears a direct if decidedly unorthodox relationship to Marx's thorough historicizing of politics, law, morality, religion and social consciousness generally. Butler's debts to, and critiques of, Foucault are very well attested (Lloyd 2007).

Eschewing a lengthier engagement with Marx, Butler put her alignment with extreme brevity: "the critical point of departure is the historical present, as Marx put it" – though Butler does not say where (1999, 8). The short and selective account of Continental Marx-reception in the 1930s through the 1970s, recounted earlier, sets the scene for Butler's apparent non-engagement with Marx, and indeed – despite her specific intellectual interests – it offers a way of rereading Marx in a Butlerian manner.

Performativity/Citationality/Repetition

Butler's interest in subjectivity was clearly a personal one in which she reveled in the substantive uncertainties exposed in phenomenological examinations of consciousness. She was also fully on board with the stylistic forms through which language was stretched and remolded to express such anxieties. Philosophical accounts of the desiring subject were thus arising for her within the conceptually limber and innovatory protean approach to language that Hegel had originated. Butler could have had a career as a psychoanalytically informed phenomenologist, had she pursued this interest in the conventional manner of (apparently) de-gendered philosophizing. However, through her feminism she was forewarned and anxious, and moreover self-confessedly angry and rebellious, over the putatively heterosexual identity and reproductive destiny ascribed to her as a woman (Butler 1999, vii–xxvi).

Butler's exact route to the performatively titled *Gender Trouble* (1990) has been recounted by herself in terms of selected personal experiences. Something like the intellectual genealogy constructed earlier was also certainly part of it. Her intellectual and personal engagement with feminism was not an obvious route for her, particularly given her evident interest in philosophy, or more generally academia, as a career. The title of the book alludes to John Waters's notoriously vulgar film *Female Trouble* (1974), and it hints at the nature of Butler's engagement with feminist politics of the 1980s. She was determinedly critical, rather than determined to be on-side, other than in her own way. As her reception developed in the 1990s, this stance of hers was returned in a blaze of notoriety.

Working from philosophical premises quite alien to most in the feminist movement, even in academia, Butler attacked what had been an ark of the covenant in social science, at least since the 1950s, and well attested by social science, psychology, psychoanalysis and medical science

(Repo 2016). This commonplace, considered by many to be foundational to modern feminism, was the sex-gender distinction: bodily sex is biologically given, whereas social behavior – derived from it and thus corresponding to it – was malleable. Thus, some ways of being a woman could be quite different from those currently established by social institutions, conventions, norms and etiquettes.

In an argument of stunning originality and deeply felt transgression, Butler simply reversed these presumptions and relocated the critical potential for feminism over and beyond gender. In doing so she turned the familiar materialist certainty of the sexed body into a phenomenological effect of the rather less certain workings of the "active side," as Marx might have put it. This "active side" resides in human minds, as consciousness, language and social activities intertwine. It constitutes the meaning-making that constructs the world we – as desiring subjectivities – struggle to know. Rather surprisingly, especially to Butler herself, this largely unfamiliar and wholly counterintuitive view – that gendered thinking tells us what sex is, and not the reverse – took off. The initial reception was generally hostile, on both intellectual and political grounds. But with repetition in succeeding works, and with considerable personal commitment, this performative approach to gender has a distinct place in feminism and feminist theory. And it is approvingly cited as a founding moment in queer theory as well (Giffney and O'Rourke 2016 [2009]). Butler, of course, resists such pigeon-holing categorizations but has political views and projects aligning with both interests, as well as others focused on a variety of issues and campaigns.

Performativity was the concept through which Butler explained this new, reversed view of the sex-gender relationship. Rather like Marx's dismissal of conventional materialisms, it disposes entirely of any "contemplative" referential correspondence of concept to object: "A performative is that discursive practice that enacts or produces that which it names" (Butler 1993, 13). Or specifically in relation to gender: "There is no gender identity behind the expressions of gender; that identity is performatively constituted by the very 'expressions' that are said to be its results" (Butler 1999, 33). Indeed, buried in lengthy and erudite footnotes, Butler rereads Marx's "Theses on Feuerbach" into her core understanding of performativity, saying that he "calls for a materialism which can affirm the practical activity that structures and inheres in the object as part of that object's objectivity and materiality." She then interprets the "Theses" indirectly: "*If* materialism were to take account of praxis as that which constitutes the very matter of objects, and praxis is understood as socially transformative activity, then such activity is understood as constitutive of materiality itself" (Butler 1993, 250 n5; my emphasis).

Butler's note provides a somewhat nervous explication of an equivocal claim in her text: for Marx, she writes, "'matter' is understood as a principle of *transformation*, presuming and inducing a future" (Butler 1993, 31; emphasis in original). However, she prefaces this proposition with the qualifier "when." This "when" suggests that possibly elsewhere in his works Marx had other ideas about matter and materiality. This is most probably Butler's nod to the controversies sketched earlier concerning the conventional materialism that Engels and others had ascribed to Marx in order to make his writings congruent with their conceptions of scientificity. And, as mentioned previously, a focus on "the material" was taken to underscore the Marxist understanding of his preoccupation with economic activities. However, it was not part of Butler's various intellectual projects and prioritized political concerns to defy Marxists with a reinterpretation of Marx.

Performativity for Butler operates as a repetition, and indeed she denies that one-off performances are actually possible. This repetitive practice of citation is crucial to Butler's original anxieties concerning subjectivity, namely the way that subjectivity is somewhat stabilized through naturalization. She refers here to the way that identity-forming practices, such as gender, are psychologically internalized as oneself and thus sedimented in consciousness. Thus gender as a performative marks an understanding that citational practices materialize a binary distinction that defines a difference termed male and female. This constitutive understanding is projected into bodies that must therefore conform to a life-defining division, and so a reproductive duality is then inscripted into biological sciences. Butler puts this very powerfully and with a political sting:

> The process of that sedimentation or what we might call materialization will be a kind of citationality, the acquisition of being through the citing of power, a citing that establishes an originary complicity with power in the formation of the "I."
>
> *(Butler 1993, 15, 2005)*

The more usual route to explaining Butler's concept of performativity, such that her reversal of the sex-gender relationship becomes plausible, is through J.L. Austin's philosophy of the speech-act and the "linguistic turn" predicated in various ways on the philosophies of Jacques Derrida and the later work of Ludwig Wittgenstein. These are sources – among a plethora of others – that Butler acknowledges herself (Butler 1993, 246 n9). The relationship between those philosophers and any overt engagement with Marx is even more tenuous, though doubtless not absent, given the ubiquity of some version of Marx and/or Marxism in 20th-century intellectual life (Kitching and Pleasants 2002). The route taken here through Hegelian idealism, via Marx himself in the "Theses on Feuerbach," and within the subsequent phenomenological tradition, is somewhat less obvious or intelligible to Anglophone readers. Yet the overlaps between these idealisms backs up the "linguistic turn" route to Butler's concept. Moreover, this demonstrable commonality between Butler and Marx, rather than presumed difference, is the hermeneutic key here. And on the basis of that commonality, it is possible to construct a Butlerian reading of Marx.

Class/Commodity/Money

A Butlerian reading of Marx, however, will not – as constructed here – have any specific connection with sex, gender, feminism, heteronormativity or the politics of marginalized queers. Marx doesn't specifically prefigure the political debates through which these conceptualizations have become salient. And his engagements with the feminisms of his time were subjected to a communist class critique by himself and by most of his associates. His comments on the situation of women are pungently political but expressed rather in passing. His speculative interest in a new relationship between the sexes was occasionally stated, but never followed up in any detail (Carver 2004, 205–26). Engels's efforts in this direction largely postdated Marx's death. A Butlerian reading of Marx will therefore not arise in an obvious way.

Performativity as a philosophical explication of the way that language, consciousness, social activity, power and disciplinary normativities arise, however, is transferrable. Taking this approach to Marx's work resolves any number of puzzles: the problem of political agency as merely subjective, in relation to class position as evidently objective; the supposed conflict between a voluntarist rhetoric of action and a presumption of economic determinism; the apparent psychologism of commodity fetishism as opposed to the foundational positivism of value-theory; the mysterious silence about communism or even socialism as an ultimate goal versus the fervently detailed denunciations of working-class exploitation under capitalism. A performative perspective on these referential terms – class, commodity, capital – tells us that they have no reality beyond the repetitive citational social practices through which they are made to make sense and through which meaningful social activities arise. And indeed in that way they become naturalized as commonsensical. The same rereading can be applied to the other concepts that Marx used, as listed in part previously.

On this reading of Marx, his reconceptualization of human history as self-transformative does not so much echo Hegelian idealism, which he denigrated as mystified and mystifying, as prefigure or indeed instantiate Butler's performativity. Thus humans have variously constructed practices that materialize and successively transform life-sustaining and culturally enhancing needs in a self-reflexive way. Moreover in his *Economic and Philosophic Manuscripts of 1844* Marx commented on the historical transformation of the human senses and physical morphology through repetitive, materializing practices (*MECW* 3: 298–306). These supposed certainties become contingent on human agency and less than fully predictable, even within constraints, as he said in 1852 in a notable political intervention, *The Eighteenth Brumaire of Louis Bonaparte*: "Men make their own history, but they do not make it just as they please" (*MECW* 11: 103). Marx's rhetoric, even when parodic and satirical, is intended to promote action so that human agents will performatively effect a communist transformation in social relations and individual subjectivities.

It is language through which social activities, particularly those of everyday production and consumption, constitute experiential realities that materialize meanings in the world. As distinctions are repetitively naturalized, they become commonsensical, even identity-forming. On this view Marx's class binaries – or variations on these – align with Butler's conception of gender binaries – or variations on these. Or in other words the human body as sexed is no more an unchangeable material reality than is the valorized object as commodity. As Marx put it succinctly: "The mysterious character of the commodity-form consists therefore simply in the fact that the commodity reflects the social characteristics of men's own labour as objective characteristics of the products of labour themselves, as the socio-natural properties of these things" (*CI*: 164–65).

Marx's reversal of naturalized common sense was not that of sex-gender but of market forces in relation to human agents. He argued that through a communist transformation of socio-productive activities humans will come to control their own creations. That transformation would put an end to the pseudo-social relations of domination that these material/immaterial objects have come to exercise over human lives. This takes place through the production of commodities for the market, the accumulation of monetary capital, and the financial speculations that transcend state boundaries.

Recounted in a recent commentary on Marx, the following passage could just as well be about the gender hierarchy naturalized in the sexed body:

> Of course, as Marx says, "a single individual can, by chance cope . . . with" these "thingly relations of dependence"; however, "the mass of those dominated by them cannot, since their very existence expresses the subordination, and the necessary subordination, of the individual to them."
>
> *(Roberts 2017, 101)*

As with Butler the repetitive citation of relations of dependence naturalizes subjectivities that – in relation to a transformative politics – are hard to shift collectively. Nonetheless through an on-going politics that is necessarily performative, social institutions and individual subjectivities have changed and are changing. And as both thinkers were aware – at least on this reading of Marx – nothing guarantees that power-shifts land in exactly the right place.

Bibliography

Benhabib, Seyla, Judith Butler, Drucilla Cornell, and Nancy Fraser. 1995. *Feminist Contentions: A Philosophical Exchange*. New York: Routledge.

Butler, Judith. 1993. *Bodies That Matter: On the Discursive Limits of "Sex."* Milton Park: Routledge.

Butler, Judith. 1997a. *Excitable Speech: A Politics of the Performative*. New York: Routledge.

Butler, Judith. 1997b. *The Psychic Life of Power: Theories in Subjection*. Stanford: Stanford University Press.

Butler, Judith. 1998. "Merely Cultural." *New Left Review* 1(227): 33–44.

Butler, Judith. 1999 (1990). *Gender Trouble: Feminism and the Subversion of Identity*. Milton Park: Routledge.

Butler, Judith. 2000. *Antigone's Claim: Kinship between Life and Death*. New York: Columbia University Press.

Butler, Judith. 2004a. *Precarious Life: The Powers of Mourning and Violence*. London: Verso.

Butler, Judith. 2004b. *Undoing Gender*. Milton Park: Routledge.

Butler, Judith. 2005. *Giving an Account of Oneself*. New York: Fordham University Press.

Butler, Judith. 2009. *Frames of War: When Is Life Grievable?* London: Verso.

Butler, Judith. 2012 (1999). *Subjects of Desire: Hegelian Reflections in Twentieth-Century France*. New York: Columbia University Press.

Butler, Judith. 2013. *Parting Ways: Jewishness and the Critique of Zionism*. New York: Columbia University Press.

Butler, Judith. 2014. "On Israel, Palestine and Unacceptable Dimensions of the Status Quo: Interview with Dan Falcone for *Truth Out*." www.truth-out.org/news/item/26946-judith-butler-on-israel-palestine-and-unacceptable-dimensions-of-the-status-quo

Butler, Judith. 2015. *Senses of the Subject*. New York: Fordham University Press.

Butler, Judith. 2017. "Preface to Jewish Voice for Peace." In *On Anti-Semitism: Solidarity and the Struggle for Justice*. Chicago: Haymarket.

Carver, Terrell. 1998. *The Postmodern Marx*. Manchester: Manchester University Press.

Carver, Terrell. 2004. *Men in Political Theory*. Manchester: Manchester University Press.

Chambers, Samuel A., and Terrell Carver. 2008. *Judith Butler and Political Theory: Troubling Politics*. Milton Park: Routledge.

Claeys, Gregory. 2018. *Marx and Marxism*. London: Pelican.

Fraser, Nancy. 1995. "From Redistribution to Recognition? Dilemmas of Justice in a 'Post-Socialist' Age." *New Left Review* 1(212): 68–93.

Fraser, Nancy. 1998. "Heterosexism, Misrecognition and Capitalism: A Response to Judith Butler." *New Left Review* 1(228): 140–49.

Giffney, Noreen, and Michael O'Rourke, eds. 2016. *The Ashgate Research Companion to Queer Theory*. Milton Park: Routledge.

Jay, Martin. 2016. *Reason after Its Eclipse: On Late Critical Theory*. Madison: University of Wisconsin Press.

Kitching, Gavin, and Nigel Pleasants. 2002. *Marx and Wittgenstein: Knowledge, Morality and Politics*. Milton Park: Routledge.

Laclau, Ernesto, and Chantal Mouffe. 1985. *Hegemony and Socialist Strategy: Towards a Radical Democratic Politics*. London: Verso.

Lloyd, Moya. 2007. *Judith Butler: From Norms to Politics*. Cambridge: Polity Press.

Musto, Marcello, ed. 2014. *Workers Unite! The International 150 Years Later*. London: Bloomsbury.

Repo, Jemima. 2016. *The Biopolitics of Gender*. Oxford: Oxford University Press.

Roberts, William Clare. 2017. *Marx's Inferno: The Political Theory of Capital*. Princeton: Princeton University Press.

Schippers, Birgit. 2014. *The Political Philosophy of Judith Butler*. Milton Park: Routledge.

White, James D. 1996. *Karl Marx and the Intellectual Origins of Dialectical Materialism*. Basingstoke: Macmillan.

44
ECOLOGICAL MARXISM

Camilla Royle

The state of the biosphere is undoubtedly one of the most pressing concerns of the 21st century. But, while there have been numerous high-profile UN conferences in order to address climate change, very little has been done given the scale of the problem. Global leaders seem determined to continue to expand aviation, subsidize the fossil fuel industry and utilize more extreme forms of fuel, be it oil from Canadian tar sands or shale gas extracted by fracking in the U.K. Furthermore, climate change denial is undergoing something of a revival, represented most strikingly by Donald Trump's presidency. Climate change is not the only pressing environmental issue. Animal and plant species are being lost at an unprecedented rate (see Dawson 2016); air pollution remains a global health risk; and zoonotic diseases, plastic in the oceans and toxic contamination of crop plants have been identified as emerging issues of concern (UNEP 2016).

Marxists from a range of disciplinary backgrounds including philosophy, economics, history, anthropology, geography and the natural sciences have engaged with questions of nature and the environment. Many of them have found the basis for a sophisticated analysis in the dialectical and historical materialist method of Marx and Engels themselves (Holleman 2015). But Marx's substantive contributions, especially in *Capital*, have also been built on and developed. This chapter will highlight some of the approaches to ecological Marxism developed over the last fifty years. It will address three broad themes: the early attempts by James O'Connor and Ted Benton to reconcile Marxist ideas with those of the environmental movement; the "second-stage eco-socialism" that developed in response to this first stage and the production of nature approach, before going on to note some recent areas of controversy.[1]

What Is Ecological Marxism?

But, before dealing with the controversies, it is worth restating some points of agreement. Marx and Engels were clear in seeing humans as part of nature. Furthermore, their worldview was predicated on understanding relationships between real human beings living in different types of societies: "The first premise of all human history is, of course, the existence of living human individuals. Thus the first fact to be established is the physical organization of these individuals and their consequent relation to the rest of nature" (*MECW* 5: 31). This suggests that for Marx and Engels the issue of the natural environment is a starting point for analysis, not something added on as an afterthought. But at the same time as being *of* nature, Marx also refers to humans as acting "upon external nature," consciously manipulating the natural world and in the process changing themselves. Humans "oppose" themselves to nature, so nature can be thought of here as a *differentiated* unity (*CI*: 283–84, see also the discussion in Henderson 2009, 266–70).

Beyond making generalizations about the labor process, Marx is of course also concerned with understanding and critically analyzing capitalism, a dynamic system driven by accumulation for accumulation's sake and characterized by competition between capitals. Many of the ecological Marxists surveyed here have asked why capitalism specifically is so ecologically destructive; many have concluded that mere tinkering will not be enough to address systemic environmental problems. Marxists share an interest in how human societies have changed throughout history, how a future society might operate differently and how to bring about such a change. As opposed to liberal approaches that emphasize individual actions and consumption patterns, ecological Marxists are more concerned with society as a whole. Therefore, ecological Marxism is, arguably, defined by an appreciation of how differing relationships *between* humans necessitate different ways of relating to the rest of the living and non-living world.

In this spirit, Marxist environmental historians have thrown light on changing human-environment relations. For example, Martin Empson (2014) uses several historical examples to demonstrate the lasting effects past humans have had on the landscape and how, for example, the shift from feudal to capitalist production relations in Europe had a profound effect on the organization of agriculture. In a similar vein, *Fossil Capital* by Andreas Malm deals more specifically with the introduction of steam engines in Britain in the 19th century. Malm's central argument is that steam power replaced water power not because steam was a superior technology but because it allowed capitalists to establish an urban workforce and utilize a predictable energy supply. This suited capitalist interests at the time and was resisted by workers. For Malm, the type of energy a society uses was, and continues to be, a site of class struggle (Malm 2016).

As well as historical materialism, dialectics has been thought of as a guiding theme for ecological Marxists. There is much debate about the role of dialectics in Marxism and particularly whether there are dialectical processes in nature. Here suffice it to say that dialectics is a way of thinking about the world that emphasizes dynamism and contradiction and considers the world as a totality (see Harvey 1996, ch. 2). Marx's own conception of the human relationship with nature as an evolving and differentiated unity can be thought of as an example of such a dialectical worldview at work.

However, despite their many points of agreement, ecological Marxists have often differed on quite fundamental issues. Noel Castree points out that Marxian theories of nature have "see-sawed between naturalistic and social constructionist positions" (Castree 2000, 5). At one extreme of a continuum it is possible to emphasize social relations to such an extent that "nature" is viewed as having no external existence outside of human society. At the other extreme are positions that try to bring nature back in, reasserting the materiality of the non-human world, but that can fall prey to a form of environmental determinism whereby human societies are viewed as being simply molded by the natural environment. The human-centric position has sometimes been conflated with philosophical idealism, and more naturalistic approaches with materialist philosophies. For Castree, both approaches are dualist, in other words they assume that nature and society are two distinct realms. They may differ in whether nature or society is seen as the explanatory pole but neither escapes this fundamental limitation to our capacity to understand environmental questions.

An Unexplored Territory?

Ecological Marxists have developed their approach in relation to and in response to the growth of environmentalism as a social movement. This is often associated with several events of the

1960s, including the release of Rachel Carson's 1962 book *Silent Spring*, which exposed the effects of pesticides, and Roger Payne's haunting recordings of whale song, which inspired the Greenpeace "Save the Whales" campaign. However, there was and continues to be, some debate as to the extent to which Marxism can contribute to discussions of the biosphere (Harribey 2005), especially as in the late 20th century the Soviet Union was claiming to espouse Marxist principles while being responsible for disasters such as the draining of the North Aral Sea. Likewise, environmentalism has sometimes seemed to be a middle class concern especially as the environmentalisms of the 1960s and 1970s often adopted notions of "limits" to economic growth, which seemed at odds with working class demands for better living conditions.

Writing in 1981, Ted Benton referred to deep-rooted "tensions and oppositions" that had led to the socialist left taking an ambiguous or even hostile stance toward the environmental movement. Some viewed this as a problem with Marx himself. He was seen as a Promethean thinker, concerned with increasing material production in order to satisfy human needs with little regard for the environmental consequences (see Burkett 2014, 147). Marx saw value as deriving from labor power. Therefore, some have been skeptical that a Marxist framework can account for a situation of scarcity of natural resources that are not valued. As we shall see, the value issue continues to be debated today.

Benton (1981) argued that Marxism is hindered by several key limitations that left it inadequate to engage fully with the findings of environmental thinkers. For example, in Marx's discussions of the labor process he emphasizes processes whereby humans consciously manipulate raw materials in order to produce new items, for example making a table from wood. But, Benton contends, not all labor processes are like this. Much of agriculture involves humans playing an eco-regulatory role, in other words applying labor in order to optimize the conditions for a transformation to take place – for plants to grow perhaps. Furthermore, there are variations in the extent to which raw materials *can* be freely and intentionally manipulated – thus the amount of heat we receive from the sun is absolutely non-manipulable. And of course all raw materials ultimately depend on appropriation from nature and will run out if they are not replenished. Benton argues that these omissions in the Marxist approach limit its ability to recognize external limits to the development of human societies.

James O'Connor, founder of the journal *Capitalism, Nature, Socialism*, proposed that capitalism is characterized by two contradictions (O'Connor 1988). The first, between the forces and relations of production, is internal to capitalism. The second contradiction occurs when capitalism undermines its own conditions of existence by damaging the natural environment, which is considered external to capital. This ultimately results in greater costs for capital (adapting to drought by installing artificial irrigation might represent such a cost); this impairs its profitability and results in a tendency toward crisis (1988, 13). In O'Connor's terms, the second crisis is one of underproduction in the sense that capitalism undervalues the conditions of production, treating them as if they are freely available. For O'Connor, conditions of production are treated as commodities but are not themselves "produced" capitalistically (Harribey 2008, 192). O'Connor, like Benton, explicitly counterposes his ecological Marxism to what he refers to as traditional Marxism. However, second-stage ecosocialists have questioned such distinctions.

"Second-Stage Ecosocialism"

At the end of the 20th century, two major contributions to ecological Marxism were published: *Marx's Ecology* by John Bellamy Foster (2000) and Paul Burkett's *Marx and Nature: A Red and Green Perspective* (2014 [1999]). Foster and Burkett have referred to themselves as part of a second stage of ecosocialist thought, classifying many of their predecessors as the first stage. Second-stage ecosocialism is, they argue, characterized by a shift from trying to reconcile divergent red and green strands of thought toward reaffirming Marx's own ecological worldview. Foster's choice of title is telling: *Marx's Ecology*, not Marxism *and* ecology.

Foster traces the materialist influences on Marx's philosophy, including the Greek philosophers Democritus and Epicurus (the subject of Marx's doctoral dissertation) and the soil science of Justus von Liebig. According to Foster, the concept of "metabolism" is central to Marx's understanding of the labor process (Foster 2000, 157). The labor process is "first of all, a process between man and nature, a process by which man, through his own actions, mediates, regulates and controls the metabolism between himself and nature" (*CI*: 283). Humans satisfy their needs by appropriating from nature and must maintain a constant relationship with the natural world in order to survive, at the very least humans need to exchange material and energy with their external environments. However, when humans are alienated from their own ability to labor, as occurs in capitalism, this leaves them no longer able to regulate their relationship with nature, therefore creating a rift in the metabolic process.

Like Foster, Burkett bases his analysis on a close reading of Marx's own texts. He argues that, far from advocating a Promethean domination of nature, Marx was fully aware of the role of natural processes in contributing toward wealth or use value, and viewed human labor power itself as a natural as well as a social force (Burkett 2014). Responding to Benton's comments about eco-regulatory processes, Burkett contends that Marx *does*, in fact, distinguish between eco-regulatory and other forms of production at various points in his writings. The reason he does not begin his discussion in *Capital* with this form of labor is because his analysis starts with a trans-historical concept of human labor, whereas eco-regulation is specific to agricultural societies (Burkett 2014, 42–45).

Perhaps more fundamentally, Burkett has placed value theory at the center of an ecological Marxism. According to Marx, there are three forms of value: use value, exchange value and a third known simply as value. Use value can be thought of as a "social combination of labor and nature to satisfy human needs" (Burkett 2014, 79–80). But, in order to understand how capitalism works, Marx introduced the concept of value as the abstract labor time embodied in commodities. For workers, the value of their labor power is separate from (and lower than) the value of the goods or services they produce, allowing the capitalist to take the difference as surplus value and make a profit. Without this exploitation of labor, capitalism cannot exist. Bees produce a use value when they make honey that humans consume but do not produce value (see Kallis and Swyngedouw 2017, for a further discussion).

Burkett points out that it is capitalism, therefore, that treats nature as a free gift without value. This is not a normative statement on the part of Marx. For Burkett, critics who say that Marx devalues nature are in danger of missing the ecological core of his worldview. The increasing subordination of use value in favor of value within capitalism as it drives to increase profits is enabled by the exploitation of workers' labor power but use value remains a "necessary moment of value production" (Burkett 2014, 83). In short, capitalism relies on nature but is structurally unable to value it. This is a source of contradiction or tension that helps explain why the system is so ecologically destructive.

More recently, Huber has used Marx's value theory to criticize projects aimed at allocating monetary value to "ecosystem services," for example where firms buy up plots of forest and market them as a profitable investment opportunity. These valuation schemes seem destined for failure when it comes to solving our environmental problems as capitalism is ill-equipped to value services such as the carbon sequestration performed by a forest. It has no way of valuing processes outside of labor and production (Huber 2017).

Urban Political Ecology and the Production of Nature

At the same time as thinkers have debated Marx's theory of value, another group of scholars have developed their own somewhat distinctive approach. Geographer David Harvey famously stated that "there is nothing unnatural about New York City" (Harvey 1996, 186), a claim that challenges the common sense association of nature with rural or wilderness areas. For thinkers like Harvey much more attention should be paid to ecosystems constructed by humans: who is constructing them, toward what purpose and in whose interests? As Marx and Engels imply, there is little, if any, untouched nature out there in any case: "the nature that preceded human history . . . is nature which today no longer exists anywhere" (*MECW* 5: 40). Harvey draws attention to the active role humans play in constructing our own environments; for Henderson (2009, 269), this is in line with Marx's own view. Recall that for Marx human labor necessarily transforms the natural world. As this must include the labor that occurs in cities, people in urban areas are relating to nature when they live their everyday lives. Nature isn't just something encountered on a visit to the countryside.

Neil Smith makes the point even more forcefully when he says that humans "produce" nature (Smith 1984). As he readily admits, this very idea seems to go against all our assumptions, nature is "the epitome of that which neither is nor can be socially produced" (Smith 2007, 22). However, Smith's point is not that humans literally "produce" mountains but that nature cannot be understood as external to capitalist production: if aspects of nature are not already circulating as commodities, they have the potential to be commodified and are therefore subjected to capitalist logics. In this process, produced nature assumes some of the characteristics of capital itself. What is more, humans are constantly producing new entities – from acidified oceans to genetically modified organisms; it is not possible to prise apart what is "natural" and what is artificial about these "socio-natural" admixtures. Smith's view is clearly distinct from O'Connor's position that the conditions for capitalist production are not "produced."

For Smith, capital's production of nature has intensified dramatically in the last few decades as a new range of ecological commodities has been developed. For example, legislation in the US means that people are compensated for preserving wetland habitats and there is now a market in "wetland credits." This is a shift from the way nature had previously been commodified, for example when wood is removed from a forest to be made into a table, to one where a wetland is commodified precisely because it remains embedded in its (socially produced) natural environment (Smith 2007). Marx distinguished between the formal and real subsumption of labor. In the former, workers enter into a relationship with capital but retain some autonomy over the labor process; with the latter, there is a more intensive relationship whereby the ways in which workers perform their work are themselves transformed (CI: 429–32). For Smith, the distinction between formal and real subsumption can also be applied to nature in order to make sense of a situation where nature itself is now being transformed to make it more productive.

The thinkers discussed in this section tend to reject the notion that the conditions of production are external to capitalism or that human society encounters natural limits (Castree 2000). As Smith sees it, the very idea that nature is external to society is an ideological notion that has arisen with modern capitalism (Smith 1984).

Debating World Ecology

Continuing this sharp opposition to dualism, Jason W. Moore has made an ambitious attempt to rethink ecological Marxism and develop what he refers to as world-ecology (Moore 2015). First, Moore proposes that ecological Marxism will be ineffectual if it rests on a dualism. Instead capitalism ought to be seen as developing *through* nature in a continual process whereby humans and environments are constantly making each other. Dualism can only further capitalist aims for it is the ideology of a separate non-human world that helps enable that world to be quantified and rationalized and therefore subjected to appropriation by capital (Moore 2015, 2). For Moore, even sophisticated Marxist interpretations such as the metabolic rift theory adopt a "soft dualism" when they invoke a relationship *between* humanity and nature and talk of a rift or break in this relationship.

Second, Moore hopes to combine a version of Marxist value theory with a global environmental history. While maintaining that it is the labor power of exploited workers that produces surplus value in capitalism, Moore adds that unpaid work, including the "work" provided by non-human natures, is "appropriated" by capitalism, a process that contributes to the formation of capitalist value as it makes labor power cheaper. For example, it becomes cheaper to employ workers if they are able to harvest firewood for fuel at no cost. In this Moore owes some of his ideas to the social reproduction theories developed by Marxist feminists who drew attention to the role of unpaid human labor (for example by women in the home) in reducing costs for capitalists.

For Moore, capitalism has, over centuries, reconfigured non-human nature, a process that does not produce value in itself but produces the relations that make the production of value possible. Moore suggests that 20th-century capitalism has relied on a strategy of creating cheap inputs, but these "cheaps" are now getting more expensive. Therefore capitalism will therefore imminently reach a crisis, perhaps even a terminal crisis.

Andreas Malm has sharply criticized Moore, arguing that it is necessary to distinguish between the social and the natural in order to locate the social sources of environmental problems. He also takes issue with Moore's hopeful assessment that capitalism will soon grind to a halt as its own contradictions become unmanageable, pointing out that capitalism tends to offload its problems onto the working class rather than dissolving itself when it encounters a crisis (Malm 2019). John Bellamy Foster and his colleagues have also criticized Moore's thinking. Foster argues that Moore's ideas are dangerous in that they downplay any analysis of the ways in which human societies emit waste products into their external environments (including the greenhouse gases that cause climate change). Therefore, while Foster accepts that socio-natural relations are in some sense internal, he says that a dialectical approach also needs a conception of the external relationship *between* society and nature to enable us to recognize the appearance of rifts in the metabolic process arising with capitalism (Foster 2016, see also Holleman 2015; Foster and Burkett 2018). For second stage ecosocialists such as Foster, Holleman and Burkett, it is crucial to understand society and nature as existing in a relationship mediated by human labor. Foster also says that the production of nature thesis is social constructionist and that it denies "any meaningful, materialist conception of nature" (Foster 2016, 399). For Foster this approach "subsumes" nature into society. And its adherents are too quick to dismiss any discussion of the properties of the biosphere outside of human influence as dualism.

Castree would surely disagree with Foster's assessment that the production of nature approach is social constructionist. He has argued, on the contrary, that it "circumvents the absolutisms of either natural limits conservatism or social constructionist utopianism" (Castree 2000, 28). For Castree, one advantage of the production of nature framework is that it allows for an understanding of the ways in which different environments are capitalized in historically and geographically specific ways. Harvey has also raised objections to Foster's approach, accusing him of dealing in "apocalyptic proclamations" and "doomsday scenarios" (1996, 195). For Harvey, Foster emphasizes environmental destruction to the point where it seems that environmental problems are insurmountable, leading to pessimism and inertia among activists.

A Future for Ecological Marxism

In conclusion, ecology and the environment continue to be areas of lively debate for Marxists. Partly this reflects the fact that the environmental social movements or the issues they deal with have not gone away. Hundreds of thousands of people have taken part in protests on environmental issues including worldwide marches against Trump's climate policies in spring 2017. As Naomi Klein (2014) reports, movements taking direct action to oppose environmental destruction have sprung up around the world, from the oil fields of the Niger Delta to Standing Rock in the US (Klein 2014, 293–336). These protests were surpassed in 2019 by the wave of international school strikes inspired by Greta Thunberg and gaining increasing trade-union support and the mass direct action organized by Extinction Rebellion. This new wave of environmentalism is noteworthy for its emphasis on social justice. Some have also specifically blamed capitalism for the world's environmental problems with Klein's own book subtitled *Capitalism vs the Climate* becoming an international bestseller.

In 2016 geologists proposed to rename the current geological epoch the "Anthropocene," to reflect the extent and intensity of the effects of human activity on Earth system processes. This finding might seem to confirm Marx's assertion that there is little untouched "nature" in existence. On the other hand, the term Anthropocene has been critiqued from the left as an abstraction that treats all humans as equally implicated in environmental destruction. The Anthropocene is just one area of fruitful inquiry for ecological Marxists. Other areas for future research might include applying Marxist work on racism and colonialism to understand the unevenly distributed consequences of environmental problems, researching workers' movements around environmental demands, developing a Marxist approach to animals/animal welfare and studying proposed technological solutions to climate change. Over the last 50 years ecological Marxists have addressed issues that Marx and Engels would never have come across in their own lifetimes. For some this means that Marxism must travel beyond its original preoccupations. However, for others, the outlines of an ecological approach can already be discerned in Marx and Engels's own writings.

Note

1. It is only possible to offer a brief outline, which will of course contain many omissions, notably this chapter focuses on the work of North American and European writers with which I am most familiar. It has also been necessary to attempt to try to divide up ecological Marxists into different schools of thought, which unavoidably simplifies issues greatly.

Bibliography

Benton, Ted. 1981. "Marxism and Natural Limits: An Ecological Critique and Reconstruction." *New Left Review* 1(178): 51–86.

Burkett, Paul. 2014 (1999). *Marx and Nature: A Red and Green Perspective*. Chicago: Haymarket.

Castree, Noel. 2000. "Marxism and the Production of Nature." *Capital & Class* 24(3): 5–36.

Dawson, Ashley. 2016. *Extinction: A Radical History*. New York: OR Books.

Empson, Martin. 2014. *Land and Labour: Marxism, Ecology and Human History*. London: Bookmarks.

Foster, John Bellamy. 2000. *Marx's Ecology: Materialism and Nature*. New York: Monthly Review Press.

Foster, John Bellamy. 2016. "Marxism in the Anthropocene, Dialectical Rifts on the Left." *International Critical Thought* 6(3): 393–421.

Foster, John Bellamy, and Paul Burkett. 2018. "Value Isn't Everything." *International Socialism* 2(160): 39–76.

Harribey, Jean-Marie. 2005. "Ecological Marxism or Marxian Political Ecology?" In *Critical Companion to Contemporary Marxism*, edited by Jacques Bidet and Stathis Kouvelakis, 189–208. Leiden: Brill.

Harvey, David. 1996. *Justice, Nature and the Geography of Difference*. Oxford: Blackwell.

Henderson, George. 2009. "Marxist Political Economy and the Environment." In *A Companion to Environmental Geography*, edited by Noel Castree, David Demeritt, Diana Liverman, and Bruce Rhoads, 266–93. Oxford: Wiley-Blackwell.
Holleman, Hannah. 2015. "Method in Ecological Marxism." *Monthly Review* 67(5): 1–10.
Huber, Matt. 2017. "Value, Nature, and Labor: A Defense of Marx." *Capitalism, Nature, Socialism* 28(1): 39–52.
Kallis, Giorgos, and Erik Swyngedouw. 2017. "Do Bees Produce Value? A Conversation between an Ecological Economist and a Marxist Geographer." *Capitalism, Nature, Socialism* 29(3): 1–15.
Klein, Naomi. 2014. *This Changes Everything: Capitalism vs the Climate*. London: Allen Lane.
Malm, Andreas. 2016. *Fossil Capital: The Rise of Steam Power and the Roots of Global Warming*. London: Verso.
Malm, Andreas. 2019. "Against Hybridism: Why We Need to Distinguish between Nature and Society, Now More Than Ever." *Historical Materialism* 27(2): 156–87.
Moore, Jason W. 2015. *Capitalism in the Web of Life: Ecology and the Accumulation of Capital*. London: Verso.
O'Connor, James. 1988. "Capitalism, Nature, Socialism: A Theoretical Introduction." *Capitalism, Nature, Socialism* 1(1): 11–38.
Smith, Neil. 1984. *Uneven Development: Nature, Capital, and the Production of Space*. Oxford: Blackwell.
Smith, Neil. 2007. "Nature as Accumulation Strategy." *Socialist Register 2007: Coming to Terms with Nature*: 16–36.
UNEP. 2016. *UNEP Frontiers 2016 Report: Emerging Issues of Environmental Concern*. Nairobi: United Nations Environment Programme.

45
HUEY P. NEWTON (1942–89)

John Narayan

Introduction: The Black Panther Party Is a Marxist-Leninist Party!

In November 1970, Black Panther Party (BPP) leader Huey P. Newton gave a lecture at Boston College where he introduced his theory of intercommunalism. Founded in Oakland, California in 1966 the BPP had gained a loyal local following with its resistance to racist police brutality and its idea of "policing the police." The Party was thrust into the national spotlight when Newton was convicted and imprisoned in 1968 for the voluntary manslaughter of an Oakland policeman.[1] The onset of the "Free Huey Campaign" and the assassination of Martin Luther King in 1968 in turn rendered the BPP the public face of US Black Power. Between 1968 and 1970 the Party ballooned to more than forty chapters across a vast sway of US cities. This saw the BPP forge strong national and international support through a politics of revolutionary armed self-defense against the US state and a commitment to anti-imperialism (Bloom and Joshua 2013; Spencer 2016). Having been significantly weakened by the violent effects of the FBI's Counter Intelligence Program (COINTELPRO) against Black radicalism, Newton used the 1970 lecture as an opportunity publicly to shift the BPP's ideology away from a perception of armed struggle against the US state and toward the idea of a wider project of creating anti-racist and anti-imperialist solidarity (Brown 1992; Hilliard 1993). Articulated in the midst of revolutionary struggle at home in the US, and beyond in the Third World, intercommunalism saw Newton narrate the Black liberation struggle through the Marxist theory of imperialism.

This should have been no surprise. The BPP had been inflected with Marxist thought since its inception in October 1966. Continuing the tradition of Black anti-imperialism, the BPP had always connected the struggle of the Black community with a wider struggle of other oppressed communities within the US and around the globe (Bloom and Joshua 2013: 311–12; Singh 2004).[2] The Party's use of Marxism, however, was open ended and evolved in response to geo-political and geo-economic changes throughout the late 1960s and early 1970s. As Newton punchily put it:

> Some people think they are Marxist-Leninists but they refuse to be creative, and are, therefore, tied to the past. They are tied to a rhetoric that does not apply to the present set of conditions. They are tied to a set of thoughts that approaches dogma – what we call flunkyism.
>
> *(Newton 2002, 165)*

Newton's theory of intercommunalism can be seen as the apex of the Party's contribution to Marxist theory through its rearticulating of Marxist theories of imperialism through the Black liberation struggle.[3] Moreover, Newton's theory of intercommunalism provides a proto-theorization of neoliberal globalization. Although Newton did not predict the entirety of the neoliberal social order, his theory provides one of the first accounts of the reconfiguration of the colonial/imperial relationships between the center and periphery of the global economy, the global spread of multinational corporations and capitalist social relations, the end of state socialism, and the attack on welfare capitalism across advanced economies. Newton saw these processes as taking shape in his immediate context, but it was his belief that the effects of these processes would increase in vivacity as reactionary intercommunalism brought the world into ever-closer capitalist interconnection and interdependence. Unfortunately, posterity has been unkind to Newton's thought, which has largely been ignored for the last forty years. Even with the recent historical reappraisal of the Black Power movement, and specifically the BPPs political legacy, Newton remains one of the most neglected neo-Marxists of the 20th century.

This entry seeks to retrieve Newton's neo-Marxist theory of intercommunalism and its narration of the emergence of a truly global form of capitalism. The first section narrates the disarticulated form of global capitalism Newton saw emerging in the mid-20th century and the effects he envisioned for communities across the world. The second section focuses on what Newton saw as the political implications of reactionary intercommunalism for radical politics both within the US and the Third World. The conclusion reflects on the legacy of Newton's Marxism and how Newton's vision can help to illuminate both the past and future of global capitalism.

Reactionary Intercommunalism: Empire's Disarticulated Capitalism

Huey P. Newton's formulation of what he called reactionary intercommunalism is essentially a reflection on the reality of postwar US hegemony and its relationship to imperialism. As Newton outlined, the geo-political ramifications of World War II had seen the US penetrate the former holdings of European imperial empires and reshape the global economy in its own interests. The postwar concentration of global production capabilities and raw materials in the hands of its economically powerful and increasingly multinational corporations, combined with the technological superiority of its military and the dominance of its emergent mass media, meant that the US now resembled an imperial "empire" rather than a nation-state (Newton 2002: 151–53). However, Newton put forward that US empire differed from the "primitive empire" of the Romans, or even modern European imperial empires, because of its unrivalled global reach:

> the evidence shows very clearly that the United States is not a nation, for its power transcends geographical boundaries and extends into every territory of the world. Through modern technology the United States can control the institutions of other countries. Hence, so long as it can control the political forces, the cultural institutions, the economy, the resources and military of other countries at will and for the narrow interests of a small clique then we cannot say that America is a nation any longer – it is an Empire.
>
> *(Newton 1972a, 7)*

The "ruling circle," which Newton located in the nexus between corporate and government power, now held unprecedented direct or indirect power over every nation on earth. This, in turn, saw the US economy become a base for an 'international bourgeoisie' and international corporate power (Newton 2009, 200). As a result, the characteristics of nationhood, such as "economic independence, cultural determination, control of the political institutions, territorial integrity, and safety," no longer existed for both the US state or those beyond the US state. The interconnection of the world with the interests of the US empire and its international bourgeoisie meant that Third World nations, and even former European imperial powers, now bent to the "weight" of its interests, "yielding theoretical national sovereignty" (Newton 2002, 170).

Newton's narration of the end of modern sovereignty could be taken as short hand for similar neo-Marxist critiques of postwar US geo-political hegemony and neo-imperialism in the now much feted era of "embedded liberalism." In particular, one could see Newton's work within the lineage of Mandel's (1975) *Late Capitalism* and its idea of "super-imperialism," and Baran and Sweezy's *Monopoly Capital* (1966). However, Newton's idea of reactionary intercommunalism seems to go beyond the idea of American Empire contained within these works.[4] Newton labelled the US Empire "reactionary intercommunalism" because he foresaw the interconnection of the entirety of the world's communities under a truly global form of capitalism (Newton 2002, 187). Moreover, reactionary intercommunalism marked a fundamental change in the nature of imperialism. Such a regime did not seek simply to replicate Europe's imperial exploitation of resources in the non-white nations of the Third World, but also mitigate the problems of capitalist under-consumption and overproduction by developing a world market and global base of labor and consumption. The imperial innovation of the reactionary intercommunalism thus centered on its ruling circle's realization that "they cannot send U.S. troops everywhere" and that "peaceful co-option" was the best way to preserve the capitalist system (Newton 2002, 256–58, 300).[5]

This, in turn, shifted the practice of imperial rule from the occupation of land and native populations to the spread of technology, markets and potential consumers. The proof of this rearticulation of imperial rule was to be found in fundamental changes to the global economy and the geography of industrial production. Newton argued that Western multinational corporations had begun transplanting advanced industrial technologies from the First World to the Third World to help create a global commodity and consumption chain. This disarticulated Fordism now meant that multinational corporations did not care whether nations claimed to be communist, or indeed anything else, as long as "Ford can build its motor company in their territory" (Newton 2002, 261). Along with this shift in the geography of production, the spreading ideology of capitalist social relations in the non-capitalist world fostered ever-greater pools of potential labor and consumers.

Newton believed that the effects of reactionary of intercommunalism would be disastrous for both the First and Third World populations. In the First World Newton foresaw that the nature of welfare capitalism would be disrupted due to the effects of reactionary intercommunalism's disarticulated Fordism and technological advancement. Newton argued that technological innovation (automation, robotics, cybernetics), even more than global labor arbitrage, would eradicate the need for expensive wageworkers in the First World. The technological automation and the spatial reconfiguration of industrial production of reactionary intercommunalism would see the "increase of the lumpen-proletariat and the decrease of the proletariat" in the West and the likely dismantling of the welfare state as ruling circle sought to maximize profits and share of income (Newton 2002, 193). Reactionary of intercommunalism would essentially end the Western postwar era settlement between labor and capital.

In the Third World Newton predicted not only the spread of capitalist production, technology and forms of consumption but also an increased rate of super-exploitation. This centered on Western-based multinational corporations transplanting but "still controlling" the new geography of production and exploiting new found pools of labor in the Third World. This process would see "growth without development" with increased capital flows from the Third World back into the First World. A regime supported by self-enriching "comprador agents" in Third World nation-states across Africa, Asia and Latin America (Newton 2002, 253). Newton argued that non-white elites now bowed to the power and ideology of empire and would readily oppress and exploit their own people in order to secure their own position and wealth (Newton 2002, 302).

Newton concluded that reactionary of intercommunalism meant that all nation-states and their populations had now become a "collection of communities," with no "superstructure of their own" other than global capitalism. Although these collections of communities suffered different material realties, reactionary intercommunalism now saw people of all cultures "under siege by the same forces" of empire. Newton took reactionary intercommunalism to mean that there was now only "differences in degree" between the material realties of Black Americans and other exploited communities across the world (Newton 2002, 170–72).

Revolutionary Intercommunalism: Survival Pending Revolution

Newton, believed that global revolution, what he called "revolutionary intercommunalism," was possible due to the very ontology of reactionary intercommunalism. Revolutionary intercommunalism was founded on the belief that attempts to fight reactionary intercommunalism through forms of nationalism or even internationalism were pointless. Newton asserted that the economic, technological and political reality of reactionary intercommunalism meant that nations could not reassert their former forms of sovereignty in order to practice nationalism or internationalism (Newton 2002, 187).

The only solution to a situation to such a "distorted form of collectively," Newton contended, where the "superstructure of Wall Street" appropriated the wealth that all global communities of "labor" produced, was to liberate all of the communities of the world. Revolutionary intercommunalism was therefore the socialist process of redistributing economic and political power to all communities in order to disperse such economic and political power to benefit all the earth's people (not peoples). In this future scenario, humanity would become "one community and then transform the world into a place where people will be happy, wars will end, the state itself will no longer exist." This process of revolutionary intercommunalism, Newton believed, could be discerned in the emergence of Third World liberation movements and radical social movements in the First World in the late 1960s and 1970s (Prashad 2008).

Yet, if Newton espoused the potential emergence of a revolutionary intercommunalism among all those communities exploited by reactionary intercommunalism, he also saw that the socio-economic conditions generated by the latter did not necessarily lead toward this outcome. Newton abandoned the idea of violent armed revolution because he believed that the effects of reactionary intercommunalism were creating ideological disunity both within, and beyond, the US. On one hand Newton feared that capitalist social relations would be taken as the only cure for capitalist inequality. This would see capitalist social relations presented as the only alternative to the material poverty of the Third World:

> The difference, however, is everybody in America has a television, a car, and a relatively decent place to live. Even the lowest of the low do not live anywhere near the level of the poor of the world. . . . Those who support the so-called socialist states will begin to be swayed by the introduction of U.S. consumer market into their socialist countries.
>
> *(Newton 2002, 264)*

This highlighted how reactionary intercommunalism marked the move from the struggle over imperial control of land and territory to a struggle to "accommodate the needs and desires of people with concessions to U.S. technology, its might and the infiltration, thereby, of imperialist ideology." The power of reactionary intercommunalism to grant proletarianization among the dispossessed was accompanied by the power to encourage possible revolutionary subjects to dream "of mink coats and two-car garages" (Newton 2002, 265).

As noted earlier, Newton also believed that the expansion of proletarianization in the Third World and the technological fix of capitalism would disrupt the Fordist compact between labor and capital in the First World. Moreover, Newton suggested that reactionary intercommunalism would disrupt the racial settlement of US welfare capitalism (Newton 2002, 193). Reactionary intercommunalism would see the real "integration" of "black unemployables," who through racist discrimination were purposefully cut out of the economy, and "the white racist hard hat" who could not now be "regularly employed" due to the changes to technological base and geographic spread of global capitalism (2002, 193). This was not the end of racial capitalism, both within and beyond the US, but rather the boomeranging of conditions found in the Third World and the US ghettos, such as state retrenchment, precarious employment and extreme poverty, back into the general white population of the US and rest of the First World:

> Reactionary intercommunalism perceiving the interrelationship of all natural phenomena, including all human beings, seizes upon the phenomena in an attempt to distort the balance in its favor. This exploitation has led to enormous profits and power in the short run. But in a split second, historically, the super industrial engines of the imperialist, reactionary intercommunalists have come to grief, and even the populations of the Anglo-American Empire itself are in the process of being "nativized" and pauperized.
>
> *(Newton 2002, 317)*

Although Newton recognized this process as disrupting the racial foundations of US welfare state capitalism, he also saw its likely effects as the perpetuation of nationalism, xenophobia and racism among and between the US populace. For example, Newton "hoped" that the white majority would "join forces" with minority populations who had already been deemed "unemployable." But Newton's (2002, 193) assertion that white Americans continued to see Black Americans as a "threat," despite the change in their "objective" economic circumstances, disclosed the prevalent anti-revolutionary and regressive effects of reactionary intercommunalism. The processes linked to reactionary intercommunalism thus served to perpetuate forms racial disunity between the US populace and foreclosed the emergence of a revolutionary subject.

The negative reaction of oppressed people to the plight of other oppressed people brought home for Newton how the reactionary intercommunalism hollowed out the means and resources of communities to grasp the global contours of their oppression and common humanity. This transpired not only because the key sites for hegemonic battle within civil society often systemically discriminated against or denied access to oppressed groups. But also because the very processes of reactionary intercommunalism, such as the dismantling of welfare capitalism and lumpenproletarianization in the First World and spreading of capitalist production and proletariatinzation in the Third World, now led to the co-opting or destruction of the very socio-economic, cultural and political institutions that could facilitate revolutionary intercommunal subjectivity among the people (e.g., unions, socialist nation-states).

Newton's perception of the divisive effects of reactionary intercommunalism saw him pivot the activities of Panthers away from armed confrontation with the US state and toward what he called "survival programs." These programs, which included initiatives such as free breakfasts for school children, employment centers, health clinics and the Black Panther newspaper, were designed to address the basic needs of a Black community that had been racially excluded from the spaces and spoils of US welfare capitalism and which had been further marginalized by economic and political changes associated with reactionary intercommunalism. However, Newton also believed that the survival programs could help facilitate the Black community's consciousness and understanding of reactionary intercommunalism and engender revolutionary intercommunalism:

> All these programs satisfy the deep needs of the community but they are not solutions to our problems. That is why we call them survival programs, meaning survival pending revolution. We say that the survival program of the Black Panther Party is like the survival kit of a sailor stranded on a raft. It helps him to sustain himself until he can get completely out of that situation. So the survival programs are not answers or solutions, but they will help us to organize the community around a true analysis and understanding of their situation. When consciousness and understanding is raised to a high level then the community will seize the time and deliver themselves from the boot of their oppressor.
> *(Newton 2002, 339)*

The Panthers' programs served to raise consciousness and understanding through practice as well as ideology. Survival programs not only usurped the effects of reactionary intercommunalism but also created new and novel institutional forms of intercommunal co-operation and collaboration that provided democratic empowerment for subjugated communities.[6] While the Party, through its various chapters across the US, often initiated programs, the day-to-day running of them often involved the wider community, local businesses and professionals such as doctors and nurses. The Panthers' survival programs therefore sought to "raise consciousness in the form of the people participating in a program they had put together themselves to serve themselves" (Hilliard 2008, 34). Newton's orientating of the Panthers toward survival programs is best seen as an attempt to secure the material and ideological survival of the very communities that could achieve revolutionary intercommunalism in the face of processes that he believed would materially and ideologically eviscerate such revolutionary potential. Newton thus presents a re-theorization of the Gramscian concept of the war of position in the context of global capitalist empire, which insists that if revolution is to ever become a reality such a strategy must focus on "survival pending revolution" (Narayan 2017b).

Conclusion: The Legacy of Huey P. Newton's Marxism

Historians of the BPP have often downplayed the significance of Newton's theory of intercommunalism on BPP praxis (see Spencer 2016; Bloom and Joshua 2013). But Newton's reconceptualization of imperialism as reactionary intercommunalism and the need to adapt a strategy of survival pending revolution seem to prove otherwise. BPP community programs became the lynchpin of the Party from 1971 onwards and became the most visible aspects of the Party's Black Panther Newspaper. Indeed, Newton's idea of revolutionary intercommunalism and its questioning of whether nationalism, whether white or non-white, was a solution to contradictions of global capitalism also filtered into the Party's most hallowed document: the Ten Point Program. These would see the reconceptualization of some of the Black Nationalist overtones of some of the twenty points that made up the Program's evocations of "What We Want" and "What We Believe In" toward a vision of the Party that was based around revolutionary intercommunalism. The ultimate sign of this being the Party's dropping of a reference to a UN plebiscite on the future of Black self-determination in the US and the adding of the call for the "community control of modern technology" (Spencer 2016, 139–42). Newton's theory of intercommunalism thus cemented and clarified the BPP's Marxist inflected anti-imperialism and its vision for a future beyond capitalism and racism.

Yet, the impact of Newton's Marxism stretches beyond the 1970s and into our own present. Newton's theorization of reactionary intercommunalism is best read as a proto-theorization of what we have come to call neoliberal globalization (Narayan 2017a, 2017b). Newton's narration of how the interests of corporate capital, technological advancement and a new geography of industrial production would lead to deindustrialization, precarious employment, welfare state retrenchment and an orgy of profit in the First World has essentially come to pass (see Harvey 2005). Although Newton's narrative of how Third Worldism would be defeated through Western neo-imperialism, elite enrichment and the expansion of capitalist forms of production, consumption and exploitation in the Third World is also eerily prescient (see Prashad 2013; Smith 2016).

If we accept the premise that Newton offers a proto-theorization of neoliberal globalization, then it becomes clear that the mainstream narrative about the rise of neoliberalism also needs rewriting. The common narration of neoliberalism places the start of the discourse at the Mont Pelerin Society in the mid-20th century and the operationalization of such discourse in sites such as Chile (1973), New York (1975), UK (1979), US (1976/1980); and then via the IMF the exporting such a doctrine across the planet (see Harvey 2005; Klein 2007; Jones 2012). Whereas these popular narratives of neoliberal globalization focus on the interlinked processes of the dismantling of welfare capitalism and lumpenproletarianization in the First World and spreading of capitalist production and proletarianization in the Third World, the effects on the racialized effects of neoliberal globalization are usually an afterthought.

Newton's neo-Marxist theorization of reactionary intercommunalism forces us to reconsider both the time-line of these events and the centrality of race in the unfolding of neo-liberalism in the US and beyond. Newton's theorization radically differs from the usual narrative, arguing that the processes of neoliberal globalization would shatter the racialized settlement of Fordism in the US and wider Western world. This reflects Newton's view that reactionary intercommunalism, or what we call neo-liberalism, is as much a racial moment as an economic moment. Indeed, in the midst resurgent racist and xenophobic authoritarian populism across the Global North in response to the effects of neoliberal globalization, Newton's Marxism appears as prescient as ever (Narayan 2017a).

What Newton's Marxism and its theorization of neoliberal globalization bring to light is that there can be no simple return to supposed benign forms of welfare capitalism or state power. These prior forms of capitalism not only have their own crimes of domination (racism, imperialism, patriarchy) that must be transcended rather than repeated. The current order, as Newton understood 40 years ago, requires new alternative revolutionary intercommunal institutions and forms of life that could achieve liberation for all. But this can only happen through reimagined and reorganized institutions (welfare, employment, economy) that are grounded in revolutionary intercommunal values. As our neoliberal present increasingly fractures communities across the globe into antagonistic relationships, and further co-opts or destroys their communal institutions of resistance, it may be high time to return to the history of the BPP and Newton's Marxism for our own form of survival pending revolution.

Notes

1. As a result of public pressure through the "Free Huey" campaign's questioning of the state's evidence, and two subsequent re-trials with hung juries, Newton was released in August 1970: Portions of this entry first appeared in Narayan 2017b; thanks to Sage Publications for permission to include them here.

2. The Panthers created alliances with a plethora of US social movements such as the student led anti-Vietnam War and Peace movements, Latino groups like the Young Lords Organisation and poor white American groups like the Young Patriots Organisation. On the global front the purpose with the "peoples of world" pursuing nationhood, such the National Liberation Front in South Vietnam (NLF), the Mozambique Liberation Front (FRELIMO) and Palestinian Liberation Organisation (PLO).
3. Not all of Newton's audience that day, and in the months that followed, were enamoured with a theory that cast Black liberation within Marxist terminology. See Heynen (2009) for how intercommunalism was itself challenged within the Black Panther Party.
4. Baran and Sweezy, for example, only list one European country (Greece) and do not include Japan within conceptions of American Empire. One could also find links between Newton and Panitch's and Gindin's (2013) contemporary work on US empire. These parallels were also made during Newton's lifetime. In Box 47, Folder 9 of the Dr. Huey P. Newton, Dept. of Special Collections, Stanford University, one can find a transcript of Immanuel Wallerstein's presentation at an annual meeting of the ASA in 1972 of his now famous paper "The Rise and Future Demise of the World Capitalist System: Concepts for Comparative Analysis" (Wallerstein 1974). Scribbled on the front of it is a note to Huey from a "David" that reads "Dear Huey, the framework of this analysis is very close to yours – I thought you might find it interesting."
5. Reactionary intercommunalism does not preclude the use of militarism to achieve such co-option. Moreover, Newton saw US military power as a form of "policing" that held similarities with policing of Black communities to uphold capitalist exploitation.
6. A common misconception about the Panthers' community programs is that they were solely for the Black community and not truly intercommunal. Although the Panthers embedded these programs in communities of Black people, they often offered their services to the whole of society. This often saw other communities of color and poor white communities access Panther programs such as the free medical centers.

Bibliography

Baran, Paul, and Paul Sweezy. 1966. *Monopoly Capital*. New York: Monthly Review Press.

Bloom, Joshua, and Waldo E. Martin. 2013. *Black against Empire: The History and Politics of the Black Panther Party*. Berkeley: University of California Press.

Brown, Elaine. 1992. *A Taste of Power: A Black Woman's Story*. New York: Pantheon Books.

Harvey David. 2005. *A Short History of Neo-Liberalism*. Oxford: Oxford University Press.

Heynen, Nik. 2009. "Bending the Bars of Empire from Every Ghetto for Survival: The Black Panther Party's Radical Anti-Hunger Politics of Social Reproduction and Scale." *Annals of the Association of American Geographers* 99(2): 406–22.

Hilliard, David. 1993. *This Side of Glory: The Autobiography of David Hilliard and the Story of the Black Panther Party*. Boston: Little Brown.

Hilliard, David, ed. 2008. T*he Black Panther Party: Service to the People Programs*. Albuquerque, NM: University of New Mexico Press.

Jones, D.S. 2012. *Masters of the Universe: Hayek, Friedman, and the Birth of Neo-Liberal Politics*. Princeton: Princeton University Press.

Klein, Naomi. 2007. *The Shock Doctrine: The Rise of Disaster Capitalism*. London: Penguin.

Mandel, Ernest. 1975. *Late Capitalism*. London: Verso.

Narayan, John. 2017a. "The Wages of Whiteness in the Absence of Wages: Racial Capitalism, Reactionary Intercommunalism and Rise of Trumpism." *Third World Quarterly* 38(11): 2482–500.

Narayan, John. 2017b. "Huey P. Newton's Intercommunalism: An Unacknowledged Theory of Empire." *Theory, Culture and Society* 36(3): 57–85.

Newton, Huey. P. 1972a. "Intercommunalism: A Higher Level of Consciousness." Unpublished manuscript. Dr. Huey P. Newton Foundation Inc. collection, M0864. Dept. of Special Collections, Stanford University Libraries, Stanford, California.

Newton, Huey P. 1972b. "Merrit College Lecture Series 1 and 2." Unpublished Manuscript. Dr. Huey P. Newton Foundation Inc. collection, M0864. Dept. of Special Collections, Stanford University Libraries, Stanford, California.

Newton, Huey P. 2002. *The Huey P. Newton Reader*. New York: Seven Stories Press.

Newton, Huey P. 2009 (1972). *To Die for the People*. San Francisco: City Light Books.

Panitch, Leo, and Sam Gindin. 2013. *The Making of Global Capitalism: The Political Economy of Global Empire*. London: Verso.
Prashad, Vijay. 2008. *The Darker Nations: A People's History of the Third World*. New York: The New Press.
Prashad, Vijay. 2013. *The Poorer Nations: A Possible History of the Global South*. London: Verso.
Singh, Nikhil Pal. 2004. *Black Is a Country: Race and the Unfinished Struggle for Democracy*. Cambridge: Harvard University Press.
Smith, John. 2016. *Imperialism in the Twenty-First Century: Globalization, Super-Exploitation and Capitalism's Final Crisis*. New York: Monthly Review Press.
Spencer, Robyn C. 2016. *The Revolution Has Come: Black Power, Gender and the Black Panther Party in Oakland*. Durham, MV: Duke University Press.
Streeck, Wolfgang. 2014. *Buying Time: The Delayed Crisis of Democratic Capitalism*. London: Verso.
Wallerstein, Immanuel. 1974. "The Rise and Future Demise of the World Capitalist System: Concepts for Comparative Analysis." *Comparative Studies in Society and History* 16: 387–415.

46

CHANDRA TALPADE MOHANTY (1955–) AND THIRD WORLD FEMINISM

Feyzi Ismail

Third World feminism developed partly in response to the second-wave feminist movements of the 1960s that emerged mainly in the West, and which tended to portray the experience of white, Western, middle and upper-class women as the predominant experience of all women. Third World feminism advanced a critique of such a "global sisterhood" (Morgan 1984; Mohanty 1984), which is based on the idea of a common oppression and victimhood (hooks 1986) and therefore shared values and aspirations, but which underestimates class interests, racial oppression, imperialism and the colonial experience. More than academic critique, however, it was real tensions within the feminist movements that forced a reckoning with questions of class, race and imperialism. While some women's liberation activists in the West during this period drew inspiration from the powerful national liberation movements taking place in the colonies (Aguilar 2015), Third World feminists such as Audre Lorde, bell hooks, Patricia Hill Collins, Hazel Carby, Chandra Mohanty and others, challenged the sexism of Black male patriarchs and the racism of mainstream feminism. They looked to the civil rights movement and to the history of Black women's contributions to feminist thought and organizing. In doing so, they also developed intellectual roots independent of second-wave feminism. Third World feminism aimed both to appreciate difference, and to forge commonalities across borders in the fight against oppression.

Third World feminism later influenced the development of postcolonial feminism, which emerged in the 1980s with the postmodern turn. Postcolonial feminism critiqued Western feminism by emphasizing the complexity and diversity of women's oppression and by deconstructing representations of women in nationalist discourses as symbols of traditional, ostensibly pristine, pre-colonial times. It sought to call attention to women's struggles against patriarchal colonial legacies. The anti-imperialist and anti-racist campaigns of mass resistance against the postcolonial state have been central to both Third World feminism and postcolonial feminism. Third World feminists also claimed that the simultaneous oppression of sexism, racism and capitalism resulted in a "triple jeopardy" (Aguilar 2015) for Third World women. The preoccupation of these feminisms, including transnational feminism – which also rejects the "global sisterhood" paradigm – has been how to build solidarity across borders. Transnational feminism draws on postcolonial feminism, using "the politics of location" (Rich 1984; Grewal and Kaplan 1994; Alexander and Mohanty 1997) as a method with the potential both to deconstruct dominant hierarchies of identity, power and privilege, and to construct solidarity between women in different geographical contexts. The term "transnational" was intended as an alternative to "global" and "international" (Swarr and Nagar 2010, 4), and although it is not always "a radical category or one that speaks to a transformative or liberatory praxis" (Alexander and Mohanty 2010, 43), transnational feminism is also used to describe the activism associated with the theory.

The neglect of the experience of women in the Global South by Western feminism was captured most strikingly in the seminal essay by Chandra Talpade Mohanty, "Under Western Eyes: Feminist Scholarship and Colonial Discourses," written in 1984 and updated in 1991. In it, Mohanty interrogates the construction of "Third World" women by feminists in privileged positions of global knowledge production in Western universities, who were inclined to universalize female experience, idealize Western women's own freedoms relative to non-Western women, and essentialize women of color as passive victims, effectively silencing historical and contemporary feminist struggles taking place in the Global South. Mohanty insisted on using the term "Third World" as it retains a connection to colonialism and contemporary forms of economic and geopolitical domination, and yet "is meant to suggest a continuous questioning of the designation" (Mohanty 1984, 354). The original connotations of the Third World as a project were, of course, redemptive and even revolutionary (Prashad 2007), connected as they were to political movements prior to and following decolonization.

The aim of the essay was not limited to making a culturalist argument about ethnocentrism (Mohanty 1984, 336) but criticized the class position of certain Western feminists and the separatist strategies of a certain strand of feminism: "It was intended both as a critique of the universalizing and colonizing tendencies of feminist theorizing and as a methodological intervention arguing for historicizing and contextualizing feminist scholarship. 'Under Western Eyes' had a clear political purpose" (Mohanty 2013, 975–76). Although based in Western academia herself, Mohanty argues that feminist scholarship must be linked to political practice, and much of her work has focused on building dissent within the neoliberal academy and on organizing in the struggles around racism, war, immigrants and refugees, incarceration and civil rights in the US and beyond.

In contrast, mainstream feminism – or "free-market feminism" according to Alexander and Mohanty (1997, xv) – has served to reinforce racism and marginalize the concerns of working-class women by focusing on the backwardness of culture, tradition and religion as ostensibly holding back women in the Global South. A failure to develop an analysis of the state and to recognize the role of Western states in capitalist expansion and imperialist aggression has meant that elite, Western feminists have often been at the forefront of promoting military intervention, for example, by advocating for the liberation of women through the War on Terror following 9/11 (Eisenstein 2009, 174; Riley et al. 2008, 11). The legacy of Third World feminism has been both the denunciation of imperialism, in particular of the Western interventions in Afghanistan and Iraq, and the misogynistic practices upheld by those who dismiss feminism as a Western ideology.

Situating Mohanty's work and Third World feminism in an analysis of class, race and imperialism, and of working-class organization, this entry contributes to assessing the contributions of Third World feminism and what a Marxist perspective and the centrality of the capital-labor relation offers to anti-imperialist and anti-racist organizing across borders. The following sections elaborate on questions that women's movements throughout history have consistently grappled with: the need for recognizing difference but also building solidarities across difference, gendered struggles against the state and colonial rule, women's labor in the global economy and strategies for resistance.

Universalism and Difference

If Western feminism tended to universalize the conditions and experience of women, overlooking distinctions of race, nationality, class and other differences and their influence on women's rights, desires and capacity to organize, it followed that the solutions it proposed – such as equal pay, legal rights, abortion etc. – would be applicable to all women, without considering the diversity of historical contexts and backgrounds. Mohanty develops an important polemic against this position and against the notion of a universal patriarchy that views women as an undifferentiated group and in which all men oppress all women. The assumption that women are a homogenous category sharing the same oppression limits feminist scholarship into binary divisions between men who possess power and therefore dominate and women who lack power. If sexual difference is the central division in society then "the implication is that the accession to power of women as a group is sufficient to dismantle the existing organization of relations" (Mohanty 1984, 351). But women are not "essentially superior or infallible" (1984, 351) on the basis of their biology. Mohanty rejects a universal patriarchal framework as the central mode of exploitation because it suggests either "an international male conspiracy or a monolithic, ahistorical power hierarchy" (1984, 335). Rather what is needed, in her view, is an analysis of the exploitation of Third World women workers by multinational capital (Mohanty et al. 1991, 30), in terms that reveal the sexualization and racialization of the work that women do. This would both challenge the ideological construction of "women's work" as a naturalized category and press toward realizing the potential for women workers to exercise their agency.

Third World feminist scholarship more broadly has sought to address the relationship between the cultural and ideological construction of what it means to be a woman and the real experiences of women – living, material subjects with distinct collective histories. For much of mainstream Western feminist scholarship, conversely, this relationship is constructed on the basis of assumptions about the Third World – a geography bound by monolithic and static notions of patriarchy, culture and history – and Third World women. This ultimately homogenizes the complexity and conflict in women's lives and ignores the power that is exercised by Western feminism itself. In what Mohanty describes as "the colonialist move" (Mohanty 1984, 349), Western feminists become the true subjects of history, while non-Western women remain at the level of study, objects lacking history, political agency and subjectivity. Western women are then defined as the arbiters, those who judge other women according to Western standards. Ultimately, Mohanty argues, without the construction of the "Third World woman" as traditional, domestic, veiled, family oriented etc., the self-representation of Western women as liberated cannot be sustained.

The corollary of mainstream feminist analysis is that it limits an understanding through which to develop the practical possibilities of women and men fighting together against a system that shapes the social relations that produce women's oppression. Prioritizing gender over race, nationality and class, for example, would discount the potential of Black women organizing with Black men against racial oppression, or women and men organizing within national liberation movements against colonialism. For Third World women and Black women, the experience of sexism was profoundly racialized, and race was as critical a question as gender. In the US, for example, the idea that women's liberation could not be separated from Black liberation was recognized as early as the 1830s: women were being brought into the factory system and began to make connections between the erosion of their role as producers in the home together with the rising ideology of womanhood – in which being a wife and mother were ideals (Davis 1983, 32) – and the slave system. Both served the interests of capital accumulation. More recently, Black feminist organizations such as the Combahee River Collective, formed in 1974 and steeped in a context of economic and social crisis, introduced the term "identity politics" in a landmark statement issued in 1977 to describe the interlocking oppressions that Black women face (Taylor 2017), such that gender oppression cannot be the sole basis on which the movement is built. The task – which was unresolved by the collective – was how to work across difference and on what basis.

The critique of an abstract feminist universalism aimed to subvert the historical connection between colonialism and patriarchy, emphasizing context, particularities of experience and history, and local politics. Only once these factors were identified and revealed could solutions to division be found. In analyzing these contradictions in mainstream feminist theory, Mohanty not only contributed to opening the space for historical analysis but pointed to the need for collective struggle and solidarity across difference, one that is both anti-capitalist and anti-imperialist (Mohanty 2003b). But Mohanty also develops a critique of the local and emphasizes aspects of the universal that remain necessary. She calls for a systemic critique of the neoliberal, postmodernist assumption that grand narratives are reductionist and neglectful of difference. For Mohanty, the need for theory in analyzing the universal is crucial in order "to address fundamental questions of systemic power and inequalities and to develop feminist, antiracist analyses of neoliberalism, militarism, and heterosexism as nation-state-building projects" (Mohanty 2013, 968). Mohanty argues for an explanatory account of the systemic nature of power, but it is her engagement with women's concrete struggles that grounds this theory in the workings of power and material reality (Mohanty 2003b). In noting that the Israeli state's occupation of Palestine is supported by US economic and military aid, for example, and that Israel has now become the largest arms supplier to India, Mohanty denounces the political uses of Islamophobia in countries like the US, Israel and India and the entanglement between humanitarianism, NGOs and militarism (Mohanty 2011). Her work on Palestine is instructive of how attention to local struggles contributes to a universal understanding of the workings of the capitalist system. Feminist scholarship, according to Mohanty, must focus on making the connections between capitalist exploitation, militarization and "the gendered violence of securitized states" (2011, 77), while highlighting spaces for resistance and organizing, particularly by women as they sustain daily life under punishing conditions.

Colonialism, Nationalism and Women's Oppression

Taking place alongside feminist struggles in the West, the struggle for women's emancipation in the colonies was bound up in the struggle for national liberation and formed an essential part of the struggle for democracy. Women in the Third World were making connections between women's liberation and national liberation: they resented their roles as cultural symbols of the nation, often promoted by male nationalist reformers, but also rejected colonialist modernity, which aimed to liberate women from traditional and oppressive social practices for the purposes of developing them as cheap sources of labor (Jayawardena 2016, 8). From the 1980s, a growing body of scholarship emerged in relation to the history of organizing for women's liberation in the colonies (Jayawardena 2016), and to the feminist consciousness that had developed in response to colonialism and imperialism. Colonial rule attempted to naturalize the idea of the white, masculine figure embodying the power of the empire, sanctioned by a system of laws and practices and imputed with superiority and moral significance: the "authority, discipline . . . and self-sacrifice" (Mohanty et al. 1991, 17) of white men rendered colonized people incapable of self-government. Mohanty argues that as colonial rule was fundamentally about economic surplus extraction from the colonies, the colonial state needed sexualized, racialized and violent institutions and ideologies to legitimate practices of ruling.

Not only did racism and the erasure of the history of the colonies serve to legitimize colonialism, aggravating existing inequalities and creating new ones, but the economic interests of both the colonial powers and local elites could be served through patriarchal practices regulating the sexuality of women and their entry into the labor force and politics (1991, 19–20). The enduring tensions between the interests of middle and upper-class women and working-class women in the colonies were visible from the outset: the construction of middle-class womanhood – and the limited social reforms accompanying it, such as literacy and education, property rights and the ending of polygamy – was often tied to a bourgeoisie that wanted to "promote stable family life as a cornerstone of capitalist development" (Jayawardena 2016, 256). As capitalist expansion and the forcible opening up of markets reinforced class divisions and deepened capitalist social relations of production and reproduction, the emerging national bourgeoisies responded either by organizing to expel the colonial powers through nationalist movements involving the working classes, or by negotiating with the colonial powers to secure more profitable positions for themselves.

While some women accepted traditional roles in the postcolonial era, many working-class women recognized the potential for revolutionary movements – including in Algeria, Cuba, Egypt, India, Vietnam and elsewhere (Prashad 2007, 57) – to bring about the end of all oppression (Jayawardena 2016). In most cases, however, women revolutionaries were unable to use the national liberation movements to press for a wider revolutionary consciousness, and gains such as women's suffrage were achieved within the parameters set mainly by male nationalist reformers. After independence, it was often these national bourgeoisies who would take over as rulers in order to consolidate a labor supply for capital accumulation, but which also needed women to perform the domestic labor that would ensure the reproduction of labor power within the household.

The need for women's labor produced contradictory dynamics. On the one side, allowing women's entry into the workforces of modernizing nations meant that traditional practices restricting mobility and enforcing seclusion had to be moderated (Jayawardena 2016). On the other side, once postcolonial reforms worked to stabilize the capital-labor relation in the productive sphere, they reinforced women's roles in the domestic sphere. For both foreign and national capitalists, women – and in particular women of color in the Global South – continue to be the cheapest sources of labor, whether for agriculture or industry. Here lies the contemporary universal experience of working-class women: as modernization and capitalist development needs women workers to fill the ranks of the reserve army of labor, the exploitation and oppression of women serves to push wages down. Gender and racial discrimination deepen exploitation and oppression both in the Global North and South, but the experience of labor, across borders, is interconnected.

Women's Labor Under Capitalism

The exploitation of Third World women and the power of their agency have been significant themes of analysis for Mohanty. Drawing on the work of Mies (1982) and her study of lace makers in Narsapur, India, Mohanty reiterates Mies's argument that defining women as housewives in relation to men and categorizing women's work in the household as "leisure" facilitated the accumulation of capital (Mohanty 2003a, 149). Mies (1982) argues that the feminization of production – defined as growing numbers of women entering the global labor force as employment conditions for both women and men have become increasingly casualized, flexible and poorly paid – meant that women were producing for the world market and became a lucrative source of profit for local businessmen. From this observation, however, Mies argues that production relations are built on relations of reproduction, and that because women subsidize the wages of their husbands, the primary source of exploitation is men: "it is precisely this unequal and exploitative relationship between men and women which enables the total system to perpetuate itself" (Mies 1982, 109). But as Gilliam (1991, 229) argues, the "issue was not about men's oppression of women, but about the impact of unequal and international labor structures on family relations." Ideological processes at work in contemporary production serve to reinforce "normative understandings of femininity, womanhood, and sexual identity" (Mohanty 2003a, 152), particularly in global value chains that seek immigrant women as sources of cheap labor-power, who are purported to be unskilled and disciplined, and able to tolerate repetitive, tedious work.

In both the Global North and South, it is women's labor, productive and reproductive, that is increasingly relied on as jobs are cut, wages decline and government budgets for welfare are slashed (Eisenstein 2009, 15). Capitalist relations of production structure relations of reproduction and the sexual division of labor on a global scale, ensuring that the subordinate position of women – both as low-paid workers in the sphere of production and unpaid for their reproductive work – is profitable for the system. As the reproduction of labor power is essential for the reproduction of capitalism, the oppression of women – including racism other manifestations of oppression – is located in the needs of capital. The class location of women, including class differentiation between women, is crucial to define (German 2018), particularly as women in the Global South form the bulk of the world's working class, whether or not they are temporarily outside paid work.

While acknowledging the objective interests of Third World women based on their social location and experience as workers, Mohanty argues against what she claims is a narrow definition of class struggle – that between capital and labor – and against trade union methods based primarily on "the class interests of the male worker" (Mohanty 2003a, 143). Yet by rejecting definitions of capital and labor as "no longer totally accurate or viable" (2003a, 161), Mohanty foregrounds the challenge of articulating common interests at the level of subjective needs and desires, which she argues have a transformative dimension, while underplaying the objective interests of women workers in the capitalist system. Grounding the identity of women workers in histories of race, gender and caste (2003a, 167) is essential, but in organizing women workers across borders or within them, the objective category of class must be central to the "revolutionary basis for struggles against capitalist recolonization" (2003a, 168) that Mohanty calls for. Mohanty's call will only have real purchase if a class perspective is used, which avoids reifying gender to the point where men are seen as the source of the exploitation of women, as two distinct classes (Gilliam 1991, 216). Ultimately, political unity and resistance must be combined with concrete strategies based on objective, material conditions, and an analysis of the workings of capitalism, to which capital and labor are central. A critique that is not only about equal access within the system but also transformation of the system must start from an analysis of the global economy built on the paid and unpaid labor of women, particularly women of color in the Global South.

Strategies for Resisting the Capitalist State

In presenting the complexities of the experience of women under capitalism, the theoretical contributions of Mohanty and Third World feminist scholarship in general have been significant. The challenge for feminism is how to build a genuinely transnational movement that respects difference, universalizes on the basis of working-class solidarity and is oriented toward transforming capitalist social relations in their totality. One of Mohanty's preoccupations has been the need for decolonizing knowledge production in the neoliberal academy (Mohanty 2013, 975). This has involved an analysis of both the general and the specific: the transnational reach of neoliberal academic culture but also a concrete and place-based narrative that includes organizing against it. The extent to which Mohanty's work has influenced an understanding of feminism that is based on "solidarity and resistance to empire and global capital" (Mohanty 2013, 984), depends on the development of a coherent strategy, both at the level of the nation-state (Herr 2014) and beyond. Needless to say, the academy cannot be the only or even the main space of struggle. Not only does Mohanty place a great deal of emphasis on organizing, she argues against academic feminism "whereby the boundaries of the academy stand in for the entire world and feminism becomes a way to advance academic careers rather than a call for fundamental and collective social and economic transformation" (Mohanty 2003a, 6). It is this political approach, insisting on concrete and collective struggle rather than an overemphasis on subjective experience, that can offer a basis for emancipation.

In the early 1990s, Mohanty argued that "the nation-state is no longer an appropriate socio-economic unit for analysis" (Mohanty et al. 1991, 2) because of the dominance of transnational corporations and because factories were migrating in search of cheap labor. This was not a rejection of the role of the state as such, as Mohanty noted that working-class women and women of color have often been subjected to intervention by the state in their personal lives through, for example, sterilization programs, and must deal with the fact that a disproportionate number of Black men are drafted into the army and incarcerated (1991, 9). States are militarized and own the means of organized violence, and as such can reinforce racism and sexism as they discipline populations in the mediation of capital accumulation (Alexander and Mohanty 1997, xxiii–xxiv). Since women's movements have always been part of and develop in relation to the wider social movements of society at a particular time (Jayawardena 2016, 10), constructing alliances across borders and within borders – across race, culture, identity and sexuality – and on the basis of class solidarities against the nation-state, are vital.

Following the launch of the War on Terror, Mohanty and others (Riley et al. 2008) have drawn attention to how women and women's groups have been central to organizing against imperialist wars, interrogating the use of feminism to justify war and highlighting the connections within contemporary imperialism between foreign policy objectives and domestic racism, increased surveillance and austerity. Women have been at the forefront of Black Lives Matter, Standing Rock, the International Women's Strike following the election of Trump and the climate justice movement, among countless other movements. The strength of Mohanty's work is that it has been interventionist: to develop "a feminist anticapitalist critique that constitutes a radical intervention in a neoliberal academic culture and corporate academy" (Mohanty 2013, 977) but, crucially, one that is advanced in conjunction with the movements against capitalism. It is the latter – and how the work and legacy of Third World feminism has been taken up in the movements and by activists, rather than in academic establishments – that has contributed to developing strategies that have the potential to confront the core of capitalist production and build national and international solidarity along class lines, within which gender and racial equality are central.

Bibliography

Aguilar, Delia D. 2015. "Intersectionality." In *Marxism and Feminism*, edited by Shahrzad Mojab, 203–20. London: Zed.

Alexander, M. Jacqui, and Chandra Talpade Mohanty. 1997. *Feminist Genealogies, Colonial Legacies, Democratic Futures*. New York: Routledge.

Alexander, M. Jacqui, and Chandra Talpade Mohanty. 2010. "Cartographies of Knowledge and Power: Transnational Feminism as Radical Praxis." In *Critical Transnational Feminist Praxis*, edited by Amanda Lock Swarr and Richa Nagar, 23–45. Albany: SUNY Press.

Chew, Huibin Amelia. 2008. "What's Left? After 'Imperial Feminist' Hijackings." In *Feminism and War: Confronting US Imperialism*, edited by Robin L Riley, Chandra Talpade Mohanty, and Minnie Bruce Pratt, 75–90. London: Zed.

Davis, Angela Yvonne. 1983. *Women, Race and Class*. New York: Random House.

Eisenstein, Hester. 2009. *Feminism Seduced: How Global Elites Use Women's Labor and Ideas to Exploit the World*. Boulder: Paradigm Publishers.

German, Lindsey. 2018. "Marxism, Class and Women's Oppression." *Critical and Radical Social Work* 6(2): 141–57.

Gilliam, Angela. 1991. "Women's Equality and National Liberation." In *Third World Women and the Politics of Feminism*, edited by Chandra Talpade Mohanty, Ann Russo, and Lourdes Torres, 215–36. Bloomington: Indiana University Press.

Grewal, Inderpal, and Caren Kaplan, eds. 1994. *Scattered Hegemonies: Postmodernity and Transnational Feminist Practices*. Minneapolis: University of Minnesota Press.

Herr, Ranjoo Seodu. 2014. "Reclaiming Third World Feminism: Or Why Transnational Feminism Needs Third World Feminism." *Meridians: Feminism, Race, Transnationalism* 12(1): 1–30.

hooks, bell. 1986. "Sisterhood: Political Solidarity between Women." *Feminist Review* 23: 125–38.

Jayawardena, Kumari. 2016 (1986). *Feminism and Nationalism in the Third World*. London: Verso.

Mies, Maria. 1982. *The Lace Makers of Narsapur: Indian Housewives Produce for the World Market*. London: Zed.

Mohanty, Chandra Talpade. 1984. "Under Western Eyes: Feminist Scholarship and Colonial Discourses." *Boundary* 2: 333–58.

Mohanty, Chandra Talpade. 2003a. *Feminism without Borders: Decolonizing Theory, Practicing Solidarity*. Durham: Duke University Press.

Mohanty, Chandra Talpade. 2003b. "'Under Western Eyes' Revisited: Feminist Solidarity through Anticapitalist Struggles." *Signs: Journal of Women in Culture and Society* 28(2): 499–535.

Mohanty, Chandra Talpade. 2011. "Imperial Democracies, Militarised Zones and Feminist Engagements." *Economic and Political Weekly* 46(13): 76–84.

Mohanty, Chandra Talpade. 2013. "Transnational Feminist Crossings: On Neoliberalism and Radical Critique." *Signs: Journal of Women in Culture and Society* 38(4): 967–91.

Mohanty, Chandra Talpade, Ann Russo, and Lourdes Torres, eds. 1991. *Third World Women and the Politics of Feminism*. Bloomington: Indiana University Press.

Morgan, Robin, ed. 1984. *Sisterhood Is Global: The International Women's Movement Anthology*. New York: The Feminist Press.

Prashad, Vijay. 2007. *The Darker Nations: A People's History of the Third World*. New York: The New Press.

Rich, Adrienne. 2003 (1984). "Notes Toward a Politics of Location." In *Feminist Postcolonial Theory: A Reader*, edited by Reina Lewis and Sara Mills, 29–42. New York: Routledge.

Riley, Robin L., Chandra Talpade Mohanty, and Minnie Bruce Pratt, eds. 2008. *Feminism and War: Confronting US Imperialism*. London: Zed.

Swarr, Amanda Lock, and Richa Nagar, eds. 2010. *Critical Transnational Feminist Praxis*. Albany: SUNY Press.

Taylor, Keeanga-Yamahtta, ed. 2017. *How We Get Free: Black Feminism and the Combahee River Collective*. Chicago: Haymarket.

PART VIII

Hidden Abode

47

HIDDEN ABODE: THE MARXIST CRITIQUE OF POLITICAL ECONOMY

Alex Callinicos

> The process of the consumption of labor-power is at the same time the production process of commodities and of surplus-value. The consumption of labor-power is completed, as in the case of every other commodity, outside the market or the sphere of circulation. Let us therefore, in company with the possessors of money and of labor-power, leave this noisy sphere, where everything takes place on the surface and in full view of everyone, and follow them into the hidden abode of production, on whose threshold there hangs the notice "No admittance except on business." Here we shall see, not only how capital produces, but how capital is produced. The secret of profit-making must at last be laid bare.
>
> The sphere of circulation or commodity exchange, within whose boundaries the sale and purchase of labor-power goes on, is in fact a very Eden of the innate rights of man. It is the realm of Bentham, Freedom, Equality and Property . . .
>
> As we leave this sphere of simple circulation or the exchange of commodities, . . . a certain change takes place, so it appears, in the physiognomy of our *dramatis personae*. Who was previously the possessor of money now strides out in front as a capitalist; the possessor of labor-power now follows as his worker. The one smirks self-importantly and is intent on business; the other is timid and holds back, like someone who has brought his hide to market and now has nothing else to expect but – a hiding.
>
> (CI: 279–80; translation modified following Furner 2018, 172–73)

This famous passage from *Capital* Volume I stands at the hinge of the book, at the end of the first two parts, where Marx sets out his theory of value and surplus value, and thus before his detailed demonstration in the rest of the book that the capitalist process of production is one of relentless exploitation and accumulation, driving bourgeois society toward economic crisis, social polarization and revolution. It offers an epitome of Marx's overall argument across the three volumes of *Capital.*[1] Particularly in volume I, part 1, "Commodities and Money," Marx is concerned particularly with the sphere of circulation, where commodities are bought and sold on the market. Here "everything takes place on the surface and in full view of everyone." Circulation is, in other words, the realm of appearances. The opening sentence of the book declares: "The wealth of societies in which the capitalist mode of production prevails *appears* as an 'immense collection of commodities;' the individual commodity *appears* as its elementary form" (CI: 125; emphasis added). These appearances are systematized and given pseudo-scientific form in what Marx calls "vulgar economy," the precursor to modern neoclassical economics, which portrays economic actors as rational consumers each seeking maximally to realize their preferences.

In volume I, chapter 1, "The Commodity," Marx sets out an alternative theoretical perspective, based on the labor theory of value. He affirms, in other words, that commodities exchange according to the socially necessary labor-time required to produce them, and shows how money emerges spontaneously in the process of commodity exchange as one commodity assumes the specialized role of universal equivalent, in which the values of all the commodities are expressed. Finally, in section 4 of this chapter, "The Fetishism of the Commodity," Marx argues that the appearances of capitalism as a system of generalized commodity production are systematically distorted, with the social relations among commodity producers represented as the relationship between the products of their labor as they are exchanged on the market. But this powerful reconceptualization of the circulation process leaves a major puzzle, which Marx addresses in part 2, "The Transformation of Money into Capital." Capital is self-expanding value, a quantity of money that, at the end of the investment cycle (if all goes well), increases: in the general formula of capital, M – C – M'. But where does this extra money, the capitalist's profit, come from? The circulation process can't provide the answer, Marx argues. The exchange between capitalist and worker on the labor market appears to be a transaction between free and equal commodity owners. But underlying this "Eden of the innate rights of man" is the real inequality between the capitalist "possessor of money" and the worker, whose only productive resource is his or her labor-power. To uncover the "secret of profit making" we must explore therefore the process of production. For the labor-power the worker sells to the capitalist is the commodity that when used to produce other commodities through the worker's labor creates new value. So long as the worker, when employed by the capitalist to produce commodities, creates more value than is represented by his or her labor-power – surplus-value, in other words – the capitalist makes a profit. This profit, then, derives from the exploitation of wage-labor.

The antagonism in the immediate process of production between capital and wage-labor – in other words, not just individual capitalist and worker, but two classes defined by their opposed positions in the relations of exploitation – constitutes the core of the capitalist mode of production. It gives the lie to the self-presentation of bourgeois society, promoted by how things appear in the circulation process, as one realizing the ideals of freedom and equality (see *G*: 163–65). We can see here why Marx understands his analysis of the capitalist mode of production as a *critique* of political economy as a form of bourgeois ideology. But this doesn't mean Marx has finished with circulation. In part 7 of *Capital*, volume I, he addresses the accumulation of capital: the competitive pressure the "many capitals" into which the capitalist class is divided subject each other compels each to reinvest much of the surplus-value in improved and expanded methods of production. Competitive accumulation imparts capitalism with the revolutionary dynamic that Marx and Engels praise in the *Communist Manifesto*, driving the development of the productive forces – and also the recurring crises with which this intertwined. But accumulation also embroils capital in circulation, to hire the workers and purchase the equipment and raw materials required to reproduce the system. Hence volume II is devoted to the circulation process of capital – both the individual circuits that the different kinds of capital, productive, commodity (retailing) and money (finance), all must undergo, and the proportions that must hold between the sectors producing means of production and those producing means of consumption if reproduction is to take place.

The object of volume III is the unity of the production and circulation processes. It is at this level that it is possible to understand the trajectory of capitalism as a totality – notably in part 3, which is devoted to the law of the tendential fall in the rate of profit regulating the cycle of boom and slump. But at the same time, because economic actors are implicated in circulation, where all that counts is turning a profit, the fetishistic representation of capitalism reaches its apogee in what Marx calls (in the original subtitle he gave the volume) the "figures [*Gestalten*] of the total process" (Marx 1992). The source of profits in the exploitation of labor in production is obscured as the different forms of non-productive capital, as well as the owners of real estate and other property titles are able to appropriate a share in the surplus value extracted by the productive capitalists. Toward the end of *Capital*, III, Marx discusses what he calls the trinity formula, an ancestor of the neoclassical production function that originates in Adam Smith's concept of natural price as the price where capital, land and labor are compensated at their "natural" rates. But this idea, which assigns revenue to what we would now call the factors of production on the basis of their supposed contribution to the production of output rests on a category mistake that confuses technology and social relations: "the ostensible sources of the wealth annually available belong to completely disparate spheres and have not the slightest analogy with one another. Their mutual relationship is like that of lawyer's fees, beetroot and music" (*C*III: 953). The actual source of profit in in the appropriation of surplus labor in production is systematically obscured as surplus value is fragmented into the more superficial configurations of interest, net profit and rent.

Here again we see how critique of ideology and of political economy go together in Marx. Circulation is at once an indispensable dimension of the capitalist economic system and the necessary source of imaginary representations of that system. Both its specific properties and its distorting effects must be included in a proper analysis. Something parallel, and also related, is to be found in Marx's theory of money in *Capital* I, which involves much more than the conception of money as a commodity (in his day, usually gold), embracing in particular a detailed account of the different functions of money that culminates in an account of credit and world money. The importance that Marx attributes to this is underlined by his criticism of classical political economists such as Adam Smith and David Ricardo for ignoring "the form of value, which in fact turns value into exchange value," and focusing exclusively on "the analysis of the magnitude of value" (*C*I: 174 n34). By the form of value Marx means particularly the effects of capitalism's nature as a system of generalized commodity production where the products of labor circulate as commodities bought and sold on the market, particularly the necessity of money.

This leads to the phenomenon of fetishism since the relations between the different units of production are mediated by the circulation of their products of the market and the fluctuations of these products' prices on the market. Circulation may be the realm of semblance, but the representations it generates – the "configurations" of profit, interest, rent and the like – are necessary semblances that allow economic actors to orient themselves and calculate in everyday market transactions. As Adorno puts it, "on the one hand, commodity fetishism is an illusion, on the other, it is utmost/ultimate reality" (Adorno 2018, 160).[2] Failure to grasp the significance of the form of value leads according to Marx to "economists who are entirely agreed that labor time is the measure of the magnitude of value, hav[ing] . . . the strangest and most contradictory ideas about money, that is, about the universal equivalent in its finished form" (*C*I: 174 n34). For Marx, by contrast, money and credit play a critical role in his theory of crises, though this is only developed in an incomplete and disorganized form in *Capital*, III, Part 5.

So Marx develops an account of the capitalist mode of production that simultaneously gives primacy to production but analyzes it as necessarily articulated with circulation (Fine and Harris 1979). The complexity of his argument gives rise to a tension that we can see acted out in the subsequent history of Marxist political economy. Failure to keep the different elements of the argument in balance can lead to in the direction of what I have called substantialism and etherealism (Callinicos 2014, 16–17). Substantialism follows in the path of Marx's great predecessors, above all Ricardo. In other words, for them the labor theory of value (hereinafter LTV) is simply an empirical quantitative theory of the behavior of prices, profits, wages and other magnitudes in a capitalist economy. One consequence is often the neglect of or confusion about money with which Marx taxed the classical political economists. This is very much the dominant tendency in Marxist political economy, though the very use of the expression "Marxist political economy," as opposed to Marx's own description of his project as the critique of political economy, is a sign of the extent to which substantialism has prevailed in practice (see the excellent history in Howard and King 1989, 1992). Alternatively, and to an important degree in reaction, theorists have thematized the problem of the form of value, but often to the extent of offering merely a meta-commentary on *Capital* that provides little or nothing in the way of analysis of capitalist development. What follows is necessarily a highly selective account of how this has played out in the history of Marxist political economy.

Pioneers – Hilferding, Rubin, Luxemburg and Grossman

The publication of Engels's edition of *Capital*, III, in 1894 proved to be a turning point, provoking criticism from the mainstream orthodoxy of what was in the process of becoming neoclassical economics, but also inspiring a series of works that sought to build on Marx's achievement. Of these the most important in terms of both its intellectual quality and its influence is undoubtedly Rudolf Hilferding's *Finance Capital*, which his fellow Austrian Marxist Otto Bauer greeted on its publication in 1910 as that of "almost an additional volume of *Capital*" (Bauer 2011a, 416). Gramsci later complained that pre-1914 Marxism polarized between "[t]he so-called orthodox tendency, represented by Plekhanov, . . . who . . . relapses into vulgar materialism," and "its opposite: the tendency to connect the philosophy of praxis to Kantianism and to other non-positivist and non-materialist philosophical tendencies" (Gramsci 1971, 387; Gramsci 1975, II, 1508; Q11 (VIII) §70). He has in mind here in particular Austro-Marxism, the current of Marxist thought that flourished around the Austrian Social Democratic Party in the late 19th and early 20th centuries. While in many ways in both theoretical substance and political practice close to Kautsky and the SPD, they sought to give Marxism a more sophisticated philosophical grounding by drawing on the neo-Kantian philosophy widely prevalent at the time.

Austro-Marxism thus bears some analogies to the revolutionary Hegelianism of Lukács and Gramsci after the First World War. But in reality the Austro-Marxists remained philosophically close to the prevailing positivism of the day. We can see this, for example, in the sophisticated and perceptive review Hilferding wrote of Marx's *Theories of Surplus Value*, edited by Kautsky from the *Economic Manuscript of 1861–63*. He is quick to spot Hegel's influence: "If we now examine the presentation of all three volumes in terms of their method, to start with we get a big surprise: this is Hegel! What Marx brings to the presentation is the self-development of economic science" (Hilferding 2018a, 279). But he then seeks to reinterpret Hegel using the philosophy of science developed by the great Austrian physicist Ernst Mach, who sought in *The Science of Mechanics* to explain the conceptual development of the sciences through the idea of the "economy of thought" – in other words, the function of theory is to summarize as efficiently as possible the empirical data provided by observation. (By contrast, one of the main aims of Lenin's *Materialism and Empirio-Criticism* was to combat Mach's influence on Russian Marxists: Lecourt 1973). So Hilferding writes: "What in Hegel is the self-development of the Idea, appears here [in Marx] as a biological-natural property of thought that constitutes a condition for scientific progress" (Hilferding 2018a, 289). The influence of positivism on Hilferding can also be seen in the famous passage in the preface to *Finance Capital* where he affirms the autonomy of Marxist science from socialist values:

> In logical terms Marxism, considered only as a scientific system, and disregarding its historical effects, is only a theory of the laws of motion of society. . . . The socialist

> outcome is a result of tendencies which operate in the commodity-producing society. But acceptance of the validity of Marxism, including recognition of the necessity of socialism is no more a matter of value judgment than it is a guide to practical action. For it is one thing to acknowledge a necessity, and quite another thing to work for that necessity.
>
> *(Hilferding 1981, 23)*

The contrast is stark here with Marx's conception of the critique of political economy, where the interrogation of bourgeois ideology is inseparable from the analysis of capitalist production relations. This doesn't prevent from Hilferding having a sophisticated understanding of *Capital*. Thus he shares with Isaak Rubin a recognition of the importance of Marx's concept of form-determination (*Formbestimmtheit*) that is normally missing in substantialist versions of Marxist political economy:

> the product, in its social-formal determination [*gesellschaftlichen Formbestimmtheit*], is no longer a product of the production process that simply owes its natural properties to the changes made to it for the purpose of its intended use; instead, it is a product of the production *relations* in which its producers stand.
>
> *(Hilferding 2018b, 368; compare Rubin 1972, 37)*

As Riccardo Bellofiore shows later, Rubin systematically thematizes the problem of form, thus establishing a strong claim to be the founder of what has recently come to be known as value-form theory: "the basic notions or categories of political economy express the basic *social-economic forms* which characterize various types of production relations among people and which are held together by the things through which these relations among people are established" (Rubin 1972: 31).

Ruben's brilliance is confirmed by the recent publication in English of hitherto unpublished or untranslated texts (see Day and Gaido 2018). But – whether because of his own intellectual preferences or because his precarious position as a Menshevik in Bolshevik Russia – he remained the author of the first great commentary on *Capital*, *Essays on Marx's Theory of Value*, rather than seek to apply or develop Marx's categories by studying capitalism. By contrast, Hilferding's grasp of the issue of form in *Capital* is present in his own masterwork, *Finance Capital*. This has three main features: (1) a sophisticated and detailed restatement and development of Marx's own theory of money and credit; (2) an extension of Marxist value theory to analyze the workings of the stock market, notable for its introduction of the category of promoter's profit, which refers to the share of surplus-value that the organizers' of initial public offerings can appropriate (Hilferding 1981, 107–16); and (3) a systematic account of the transformations undergone by capitalism thanks to the growing concentration and centralization of capital, expressed in the emergence of cartels and monopolies and in the development of finance capital itself,

> [t]he dependence of industry on the banks. . . . An ever-increasing part of the capital of industry does not belong to the industrialists who use it. They are able to dispose of capital only through the banks, which represent the owners. On the other side, the banks have to invest an ever-increasing part of their capital in industry, and in this way they become to a greater and greater extent industrial capital. I call bank capital, that is, capital in money form which is actually transformed in this way into industrial capital, finance capital.
>
> *(Hilferding 1981, 225)*[3]

It is in (2), the most innovative part of *Finance Capital*, that Hilferding pays the most attention to differences in form, for example, between money capital that is loaned to productive capitalists in exchange for interest, and fictitious capital such as shares, whose price is the capitalized dividend, which in turn is a claim on the surplus value created by labor in production. Marx's "figures of the total process" thus assume a new and even more oblique shape. But it is (3), the account of finance capital that had the real impact. Hilferding subtitled his book *A Study of the Latest Phase of Capitalist Development*, and it was as an account of what he would later call "organized capitalism" that it had enormous influence. Opinions differed over where the greater organization of capitalism would lead. Kautsky drew on Hilferding in developing his theory of ultra-imperialism, according to which capitalists would increasingly cooperate economically across state borders, therefore removing the necessity for geopolitical competition among them. Bukharin by contrast argued that the process of organization would culminate in the fusion of finance capital and nation-state, leading to an intensification of interstate rivalries and more inter-imperialist wars such as that between 1914 and 1918. Hilferding himself was more cautious pointing to both how the emergence of finance capital and associated developments such as the growth of overseas investment and the increasing links between the bourgeoisie and the state fed Great Power rivalries and the restraining effects of the international cooperation among capitalists and the advances made by the socialist movement. Lenin was less influenced by Hilferding than by the left-liberal J.A. Hobson, but drew on *Finance Capital* when developing his own account of the "latest phase" in *Imperialism, the Highest Stage of Capitalism.*

Rosa Luxemburg offered a radically different analytical framework for theorizing capitalist imperialism in *The Accumulation of Capital* (1913). She develops a critique of Marx's reproduction schemes in *Capital* II, which offer no explanation, she claims, of where in a purely capitalist economy the effective demand to realize the surplus value that is invested, in conditions of accumulation (or, as Marx calls it, expanded reproduction), to purchase additional means of production and employ additional workers comes from. She concludes that this flaw is not merely a theoretical anomaly but reflects the fact that "the accumulation of capital as a historical process, in all its relations, is contingent on noncapitalist social strata and forms" (Luxemburg 2015a, Kindle loc. 6710). This has two crucial implications – first,

> the dialectical contradiction that the movement of capital accumulation requires an environment of noncapitalist social formations, that it is in a constant process of metabolism with the latter as it proceeds, and that it can only exist as long as it finds itself in this milieu.
> *(Luxemburg 2015a, Kindle loc. 6715)*

Second, imperialism, "the expansion of capital from the old capitalist countries into new regions and the competitive economic and political struggle among those for these new areas," represents a drive forcibly to incorporate "noncapitalist social strata and forms" in search of markets (Luxemburg 2015b, Kindle loc. 9002). Hence the subtitle of Luxemburg's book – "*A Contribution to the Economic Theory of Imperialism*":

> But the more capitalist countries there are that take part in this chase after other regions as sources of accumulation, the fewer remaining noncapitalist regions there are, the fewer areas still open to the worldwide expansion of capital, and thus the more embittered becomes the competitive battle between different groups of capital for these regions as sources of accumulation, and thus the battle campaigns or other expeditions on the world arena become more and more transformed into a chain of economic and political catastrophes: worldwide economic crises, wars, and revolutions.
> *(Luxemburg 2015b, Kindle loc. 8964)*

Thus, like Lenin, but on a completely different theoretical basis, Luxemburg sought to demonstrate that imperialism was not, as Kautsky and Hilferding suggested, an optional "policy" for capital, but a necessary consequence of the course of capitalist development. In explaining capitalist development as dependent on an external noncapitalist "third party," she makes explicit an assumption common to other Marxist theorists of imperialism, Hilferding and Lenin as well, that *Capital* analyzes a national economy, ignoring both the evidence to the contrary in Marx's text and his extensive writings on colonialism, which he treats as immanent in the process of capital accumulation (Pradella 2013). But, then and now, very few Marxists have accepted Luxemburg's critique of Marx's reproduction schemes. Roman Rosdolsky, though sympathetic to Luxemburg's and Grossman's theories of breakdown, points to her failure to understand that Marx is concerned to establish the possibility of extended reproduction under highly restrictive conditions explored at a high level of abstraction. She rightly pointed out that "Marx's schemes of extended reproduction disregard all those changes in the mode of production which are caused by technical progress," but

> it cannot be concluded from this "failure" of the schemes of reproduction (as she supposed), that accumulation is completely "impossible," but simply that any revolution in the productive forces which takes place on a social scale must bring the given state of equilibrium of the branches of production to an end and lead, via all kinds of crises and disturbances, to a new temporary equilibrium.
>
> *(Rosdolsky 1977, 495, 496)*

Or, as Marx himself puts it, the

> conditions for the normal course of reproduction, whether simple or on an expanded scale, . . . turn into an equal number of conditions for an abnormal course, possibilities of crisis, since, on the basis of the spontaneous pattern of this production, this balance is itself an accident.
>
> *(CII: 571)*

Defining the conditions of equilibrium is a means to identifying the circumstances of its breakdown. But Luxemburg's misunderstanding was a fertile one. We can see this in three respects. First, in *The Accumulation of Capital* she offers a powerful historical account of the conquest and transformation of precapitalist societies by European capitalism in the last decades of the 19th century. In somewhat the same spirit (though on a different theoretical basis), Utsa and Prabhat Patnaik have recently developed a theory of imperialism as the subordination and exploitation, first through colonialism, now via neoliberalism, of the petty producers of the tropical South by the advanced capitalist economies of the temperate North (Patnaik and Patnaik 2016). Second, Henryk Grossman took Bauer's attempt to demonstrate, against Luxemburg, that Marx's scheme of extended reproduction was coherent, and sought to show that successive rounds of accumulation on Bauer's assumptions would lead eventually to the economic breakdown of capitalism (Bauer 2011b, Grossman 1992). Unlike Luxemburg, Grossman relies on Marx's argument in *Capital*, III, that the rising organic composition of capital – in other words, the ratio between constant capital invested in means of production and variable capital used to employ wage-laborers – would lead to a fall in the average rate of profit, but his thesis is broadly congenial to her in its hostility to what Rosdolsky calls "the neo-harmonist interpretation of Marx's theory" (Rosdolsky 1977, 491). Neither Grossman nor Luxemburg imagined that capitalism would automatically collapse by virtue of the internal economic barrier that they believed they had discovered. Both expected what Luxemburg called the "chain of economic and political catastrophes" that the approach to this barrier provoked would bring about the overthrow of capitalism long before it was reached. Third, Luxemburg pioneered within the Marxist tradition an exploration of the problems capitalism might face in generating sufficient effective demand to purchase all the commodities produced – what is sometimes called underconsumptionism. This was of course within mainstream economics the great theme of Maynard Keynes's *General Theory of Employment Interest and Money* (1936), but his arguments were anticipated in the early 1930s by Luxemburg's fellow Pole and Marxist Michal Kalecki (Kalecki 1967; Kowalik 2014). Paul Sweezy in his hugely influential *A Theory of Capitalist Development* also argues that "what Marx at one place calls 'the fundamental contradiction' of capitalism" lies in the fact that it "attempts to expand production without any reference to the consumption that can alone give it meaning" (Sweezy 1942, 174–75).

Neither Luxemburg nor Grossman was offering a theory of the business cycle, that is, of capitalism's regular movement between boom and slump, which Marx was among the first to discover (though Grossman argues that this cycle is generated by the counter-tendencies to economic breakdown). Here again Hilferding was highly influential in stressing the role played by "disproportional relations [that] arise in the course of the business cycle arising from disturbances in the price structure" (Hilferding 1981, 266). These disproportionalities occur between different sectors of the economy, and in particular what Marx called Departments I (means of production) and II (means of consumption). Although Hilferding mentions Marx's law of tendential fall in the general rate of profit, so hotly discussed by more recent Marxist political economists, he doesn't foreground it. Among the Marxists of the Second and Third Internationals, only Grossman and Gramsci seem to have taken this law seriously. Explaining crises by disproportionalities forced the rest to confront the implications of the increasing "organization" of capitalism that Hilferding had made a leading theme of *Finance Capital*. Both he and Bukharin drew the conclusion that the economic and political dominance of monopolies and cartels and their integration with the state allowed capital to regulate and limit the disproportions in the economy and their disruptive effects – although Bukharin insisted that the political contradictions between rival "state capitalist trusts" continued and indeed grew more intense. Their faith in the possibility of what Hilferding called a "general cartel" regulating disproportions left both unable to explain the Great Depression of 1929–39, still the greatest systemic crisis in the history of capitalism. Bukharin's fellow Bolshevik, Evgeny Preobrazhensky did offer an explanation, by arguing that the growth of monopoly capitalism made it increasingly difficult to dispose of obsolete fixed capital therefore making crises more serious and harder to overcome (Preobrazhensky 1985). But this represented a final flash of creativity before the long night of Stalinism descended, during which both Bukharin and Preobrazhensky were murdered. Their deaths were matched further westwards by Luxemburg's assassination by a proto-Nazi militia after the German Revolution of November 1918 and Hilferding's murder by the Gestapo in Paris following the fall of France.

Contemporary Debates: Crises, Profitability, and Financialization

Stalinism and fascism by no means introduced a complete caesura in the history of Marxist political economy. In the United States, the *Monthly Review* journal edited by Sweezy provided a framework in which serious intellectual work continued. As *Monopoly Capital*, the title of Sweezy's best-known work (co-written with Paul Baran), illustrates, they continued the exploration of the changes wrought in capitalism by the concentration of economic power that Hilferding had inaugurated.[4] But Baran's own work focused on one of the main preoccupations of postwar economics, the problem of development – or rather of the relative *lack* of development and continued economic dependence of the new sovereign states emerging from the ruins of the European colonial empires in Africa and Asia, which he diagnosed as a product of the continuance of imperialist domination of the South (Baran 1973). This allowed the *Monthly Review* team both to identify with Third World revolutionary movements and to engage in fruitful dialogue with (and often publish) the work of Marxist economists in the South – for example, Samir Amin and Ruy Mauro Marini, who, as their entries in this Handbook show, sought systematically interrogate the economic mechanisms that trapped both recent ex-colonies and Latin America (most of which had become nominally independent in the early 19th century) in continuing dependence and poverty. Such approaches represented a radicalization of the "structuralist" critique of North-South economic relations already developed by Latin American developmental economists in the 1950s. Against the background of decolonization and Third World liberation struggles Marxist political economy experienced an internationalization that was reflected in the impact of works like *How Europe Underdeveloped Africa*, by Walter Rodney, the Guyanese intellectual and activist assassinated in 1980 (Rodney 1972). This body of work provoked a number of theoretical debates – for example, over the argument developed by Arghiri Emmanuel and (in a more nuanced way) by Amin than the persisting dependence of the South was a consequence of a global process of unequal exchange that systematically transferred value to the advanced capitalist economies (Emmanuel 1972; Amin 1973, 1974).

These and related debates contributed to a broader revival of Marxist political economy in the 1960s and 1970s. This has to be seen against the background of, as Frédéric Monferrand argues elsewhere in this Handbook, a widespread "return to Marx" that involved alternative readings of *Capital*. One of these, the German *neue Marx Lektüre*, involved a return to the problem of the value-form that had been explored by Hilferding and (much more intensively) by Rubin at the beginning of the 20th century. The bulk of Marxist political economy hitherto had been overwhelmingly focused on theorizing and empirically documenting the actual trends in capitalist development. The *neue Marx Lektüre*, drawing on the Frankfurt School critique of capitalism, was reinforced by the publication of an English translation of Rubin's *Essays in Marx's Theory of Value*, and by the gradual appearance of Marx's unpublished economic manuscripts, starting with the *Grundrisse*. It encouraged a focus on commodity fetishism, which in the work of, for example, John Holloway, became the key to the entire Marxist critique of capitalism as a process of fragmentation and alienation (Holloway 2002). But, as we shall see, the problem of value-form has been much less cordoned off from Marxist political economy in recent decades than it was at the beginning of the 20th century.

For most Marxist economists in the North the more immediate issue in the 1970s was to explain the symptoms of economic crisis that Western capitalism was showing – and which contributed to the wave of political radicalization that had created the context for the revival of Marxism in the first place. There was widespread agreement that the major Western economies – above all the US – were facing a crisis of profitability. But views differed on what this entailed. Some theorists relied on Marx's argument in *Capital* III, that the rising organic composition of capital would cause a fall in the rate of profit (for example, Mandel 1975). But they had to explain why this was happening then and why capitalism had experienced the longest and strongest boom in its history between 1948 and 1973. One answer was provided by the theory of the permanent arms economy, according to which the very high levels of peacetime arms expenditure at the height of the Cold War in the 1950s and 1960s had slowed down the rise of the organic composition of capital; since arms are neither means of production nor means of consumption their production need not increase the average organic composition. The decline in arms spending as the Cold War cooled in the course of the 1960s on this account explained the return of crises. The most sophisticated version of the theory of the permanent arms economy, by Michael Kidron and Chris Harman, presupposed Tony Cliff's interpretation of Stalinism as bureaucratic state capitalism, which implied that the Cold War was an inter-imperialist struggle like the two world wars (Kidron 1970; Harman 2009; Cliff 2003; Kuper 2018; Callinicos 2020). Like Hilferding, Lenin, Bukharin and Preobrazhensky before them, these theorists highlighted the structural changes undergone by 20th-century capitalism, what Kidron and Harman called the "ageing of the system," as the units of capital grow larger and more interwoven with the state.

Other Marxists preferred to offer what Robert Brenner calls "supply-side" explanations of the economic crises of the 1970s and 1980s (Brenner 1998). Most straightforwardly this rested on the claim that workers, well-organized and confident thanks to the full employment achieved in the advanced economies during the long boom of the 1950s and 1960s, were able to push up their wages, thereby causing a fall in the rate of profit (for an early statement of the argument, see Glyn and Sutcliffe 1972). This idea of a "profit squeeze" admitted of different interpretations. It dovetailed in with the basic thesis of the workerism pioneered by Mario Tronti, on the basis of a powerfully argued interpretation of *Capital*, that "the workers' struggle has always functioned as a dynamic moment of capitalist development" (Tronti 2006, 69). Or, as Harry Cleaver puts it,

> the working class is not a passive, reactive victim, which defends its interest against capitalist onslaught, and . . . its ultimate power to overthrow capital is grounded in its existing power to initiate struggle and to force capital to reorganize and develop itself.
> *(Cleaver 1979, 52)*

On this view, the profit squeeze was simply one aspect of a multi-dimensional "refusal of work" that was spreading beyond the factories to the whole of society. Antonio Negri explicitly reinterpreted Marx's law in these terms: "The law of the tendency to decline represents . . . one of the most lucid Marxist intuitions of the intensification *of the class struggle* in the course of capitalist development" (Negri 1991, 101).[5]

This posed the question of how this understanding of the profitability crisis related to Marx's account in *Capital*, III. Negri dismissed this as "economistic" and inferior to the earlier version of the theory of the falling rate of profit he claimed to find in the *Grundrisse*. For some Marxist economists, however, acceptance of a supply-side explanation of the crisis became part of a broader critique of Marx's value theory. An increasingly intense debate developed primarily (though not exclusively) in the English-speaking world about the "transformation problem," a matter of controversy since the original publication of *Capital* volume III in 1894 (for a comprehensive survey see Moseley 2016). When analyzing the capitalist process of production in volume I, Marx assumes that commodities exchange according to their values, that is, the socially necessary labor time required to produce them. But he drops this assumption when he comes to study the capitalist economy as a unity of production and circulation in volume III. The movement of capital between different sectors leads to the formation of an average rate of profit that represents a redistribution of surplus value from capitals with low organic compositions to those with high compositions. As a result, commodities exchange at their prices of production, that is, their values modified by this redistribution. For Marx the transformation is an example of his method of "rising from the abstract to the concrete" outlined in the 1857 Introduction to the *Grundrisse* (G: 101). It allows him to focus on the exploitation of labor and creation of surplus-value in the process of production abstracting from the complications of circulation, but then to introduce these when considering the differentiation of capital into competing "many capitals" and the distribution of surplus value among them and between different fractions of capital (Callinicos 2014, chs 2 and 3; Moseley 2016).

The debate centered on the criticism that Marx's transformation of values into prices of production was internally inconsistent because, while transforming the values of the output of a given cycle of production into prices of production, he left the value of the inputs, and more especially of the means of production, unmodified. This first objection surfaced in the early 20th century (Bortkiewicz 1949). But in the 1970s it became bound up with the reception of what was taken to be Piero Sraffa's alternative value theory, which generates a set of relative prices based on the real wage and physical coefficients of production (Sraffa 1960). Sraffa, it was contended, had made Marx's labor theory of value redundant, thereby offering a way out of the alleged inconsistency of the transformation (Steedman 1977).[6] This Sraffian or neo-Ricardian version of Marxist political economy had the effect of reinstating Ricardo's theory of profits, which treats wages and profits as inversely related, whereas Marx's more complex theory makes the rate of profit dependent on both the rate of surplus value and the organic composition of capital. From the Sraffian perspective, profit squeeze was the only possible explanation of crisis.

The controversy over Marx's value theory drove some Marxist economists beyond neo-Ricardianism toward more conventional post-Keynesian critiques of neoclassical orthodoxy that build on the work of Kalecki and Hyman Minsky among others (e.g., Minsky 2008). For others, however, the debate, often conducted in the language of algebra, encouraged the rejection of the substantialist reduction of Marx's value theory to its quantitative dimensions. For some this involved a close reading of *Capital* to demonstrate there was no "transformation problem" (for example, Kliman 2007; Moseley 2016). Others were attracted to some version of value-form theory. The greater availability of Marx's economic manuscripts stimulated often highly erudite and critical studies of his discourse. For Michael Heinrich, for example, *Capital* is less a quantitative empirical theory than "a critique of bourgeois social relations" but an incomplete one suffering from serious indeterminacies (Heinrich 2012, 35; see also Heinrich 1999). For others, attending to the form of value involved, as it had in Marx originally, addressing the role played by money and finance in contemporary capitalism, and therefore involved a continuation of, rather than the rejection of empirical research (for an early example, see Lipietz 1985). The increasing role that currency fluctuations, international capital movements and debt have been playing in the global economy in recent decades in any case encouraged this kind of focus on money and finance.

This shift was closely related to assessments of the new neoliberal version of capitalism as it became entrenched during the 1980s. How did it contribute to overcoming the crisis of profitability? Both neo-Ricardians and more orthodox Marxists could agree that this would require forcing up the rate of surplus value – increasing profits by exploiting workers more. But Marx himself stresses the importance of the destruction of capital, which has the dual effect of removing inefficient firms and reducing the organic composition of capital. Hence crises are functional to capitalism as "momentary, violent solutions for the existing contradictions, violent eruptions that re-establish the disturbed balance for the time being" (CIII: 357) and thus allow the process of capital accumulation to continue until the next turn in the "vicious circle" of boom and slump (Marx 2016, 364). These different theoretical perspectives inform Marxist appreciations of neoliberalism. David Harvey famously argues that "the evidence strongly suggests that the neoliberal turn is in some way and to some degree associated with the restoration or reconstruction of the power of economic elites" (Harvey 2005, 15). This most directly involved an offensive against organized labor in the advanced economies symbolized by Margaret Thatcher's defeat of the British coal miners' strike of 1984–85 and leading in the US, according to Brenner, to "a repression of wages without precedent during the last century, and perhaps since the Civil War" (Brenner 1998, 3). But the expansion of industrial production in the Global South, where workers would usually be paid much lower wages than their northern counterparts can be seen as part of the same process of raising the rate of exploitation (Smith 2015).

For supporters of the profit squeeze theory this increase in the rate of surplus-value was sufficient to constitute the resolution of the crises of the 1970s and 1980s (for example, Panitch and Gindin 2012). Other Marxist economists more sympathetic to Marx's own approach nevertheless agreed that capitalism had overcome its problems of profitability. They believed, however, that capitalism continued to suffer from major economic contradictions, but argued that these had shifted from production to finance (for example, Duménil and Lévy 2004, 2011; Lapavitsas 2013). Marxists in this way became contributors to a broader discussion of financialization – that is, the greater economic weight that finance has generally been accepted as having in the neoliberal era. There are different ways of understanding financialization (among the best discussions are Lapavitsas 2013; Fine 2014; Chesnais 2016; Durand 2017). For some (for example, Chesnais) it is a version of Hilferding's original finance capital, in which the banks and related institutions (the shadow banking sector of hedge funds and other kinds of investment fund) dominate the rest of the economy; for others (notably Lapavitsas) it is more a matter of finance gaining greater autonomy by emancipating itself from its traditional role of organizing loans for industrial and commercial firms. Another widely recognized aspect of the phenomenon is the penetration of finance into the rest of the economy – as industrial corporations become major financial actors in their own right – and into everyday life through housing and student loans and consumer credit (all of which can then be bundled together into securities and bought and sold on financial markets). Particularly in the wake of the 2007–8 financial crash and its aftermath, it is tempting to interpret the dysfunctions of financialization – particularly evident in the credit-driven housing bubble that preceded the crash – as the main source of capitalist economic instability today. Giovanni Arrighi proposed a particularly interesting version of this view. He combined a sophisticated version of supply-side theory, in which "an eminently systemic but political variable, . . . the power struggle in which the US government sought to contain, through the use of force, the joint challenge of nationalism and communism in the Third World," symbolized by the Vietnam War, "contributed to the profit squeeze," with the thesis that financialization was a symptom of the decline of American hegemony (Arrighi 2007, 134).

An alternative interpretation is offered by Marxists who argue that neoliberalism never fully overcame the crisis of profitability of the 1960s and 1970s. This was powerfully argued by Brenner a decade before the crash (Brenner 1998). He documented the relatively low rates of growth experienced by the advanced capitalist economies in the neoliberal era – a serious anomaly for the supply-side explanation given the compression of wages. Brenner argued that the "long downturn" reflected the fact that Western capitalism in the 1980s and 1990s had only experienced a partial recovery from the earlier crisis of profitability. Although sympathetic to the neo-Ricardian critique of Marx, he offered his own unorthodox theory of the falling rate of profit, which relied on the ability of established but relatively inefficient capitals to stay in business while accepting a low rate of profit, thereby depressing the aggregate rate of profit. But others defended Marx's own theory, arguing that neoliberalism failed to destroy capital on a sufficiently large scale fully and stably to offset the decline in the rate of profit in the 1960s and 1970s (Harman 2009; Carchedi 2011; Kliman 2011; Roberts 2016; Carchedi and Roberts 2018). The financial bubbles that developed between the late 1980s and the mid-2000s were ways of postponing the resulting economic collapse, but the reckoning finally came in 2007–8.

One can see this debate as a version of the tension between production and circulation that informs the passage from *Capital* I with which this chapter started. Marx himself sought to articulate both together in a complex totality. Harvey offers one way to do this in recent work that offers a multi-causal theory of crises. Drawing on Marx's analysis of the different circuits of productive, commodity and money capital in *Capital* II, he argues that these circuits offer different possibilities of crisis: "Blockage at any of these points will disrupt the continuity of capital flow and, if prolonged eventually produce a crisis of devaluation" (Harvey 2010, 47) – for example as a result of a wage squeeze, rising raw material prices, a lack of consumer demand, or the bursting of a financial bubble; the crash of 2007–8 represented the realization of the latter two possibilities. Supporters of the falling rate of profit theory rejected the underconsumptionism implicit in Harvey's analysis (e.g., Harvey 2017, 33), but they were able to find a place for finance in their own arguments. Brenner was criticized for neglecting finance in his initial account of the "long downturn" (Fine et al. 1999). But he later developed an innovative analysis of the Wall Street bubble at the end of the 1990s. This was a case of "stock-market Keynesianism": the inflated prices of securities increased the wealth of better-off households, thereby allowing them to achieve higher levels of borrowing and spending that could keep effective demand high and the economy growing despite the underlying problems of profitability; this was an argument that could be extended to the housing bubble in the US in the mid-2000s, as Brenner did (Brenner 2002, 2004). Despite Brenner's criticisms of Marx's value theory, his analysis has an affinity here to the way in which Marx in *Capital*, III, seeks to integrate the tendency of the rate of profit to fall with the fluctuations of financial markets, where bubbles allow the accumulation process to continue despite falling profitability, and crashes effect the destruction of capital necessary to allow accumulation to resume (Callinicos 2014, ch. 6). Harvey's earlier theory of crisis in *The Limits to Capital* somewhat analogously posits a process of displacement of the contradictions of the accumulation of productive capital first via the "financial fix" – the expansion of credit – and then through the "spatial fix" – the geographical restructuring of capitalism that is inseparable from the geopolitical rivalries driving imperialism (Harvey 1982, 2003).

Harvey's *The New Imperialism* was simply the most prominent in a wave of re-examinations of the Marxist theory of imperialism. A major point of controversy concerned whether inter-imperialist rivalries persisted, albeit in new forms, as Harvey and I contend (Harvey 2003; Callinicos 2009), or have been rendered obsolete, as Negri famously argues, announcing with Michael Hardt the emergence of a new transnational Empire (Hardt and Negri 2000); from a different theoretical perspective, Leo Panitch and Sam Gindin also contended that geopolitical conflicts among the advanced capitalist states had been transcended, thanks to their incorporation in the US "informal empire" (Panitch and Gindin 2012). The underlying pattern of controversy recalled the arguments between Lenin and Kautsky during the First World War. But undoubtedly the broader economic context has changed, thanks to the dramatic growth of industrial production in East and South Asia. Not only did this play its part of the development of geopolitical tensions, with China emerging as the most serious challenger to US hegemony yet seen, but the outsourcing of production by transnational corporations to take advantage of wage differentials between North and South has drawn renewed attention to the concept of super-exploitation so important to Marini's work (Smith 2015; Carcanholo 2017). Such discussions are hard to separate from the further development of the Marxist theory of international trade: accounts of unequal exchange between North and South require some account of the value transfers from "periphery" to "center" (for an important discussion see Carchedi 1991, chs. 6–8). The future of the Marxist critique of political economy is likely to depend on how successfully it captures not just the macro-patterns of crisis but also the complex transformations in production and trade that contemporary capitalism is currently undergoing. The search to elaborate, and deepen Marx's extraordinary synthesis continues.

Notes

1. For good introductions to Capital, see Choonara (2017), Fine and Saad-Filho (2010), and Foley (1986).
2. A similar appreciation of the importance of the theory of fetishism can be found in the early Lukács and also in the writings of Lucio Colletti: Colletti (1972, 1973, 1975).
3. For a recent assessment of *Finance Capital* see Lapavitsas (2013, ch. 4).

4. Also in the US, the exiled German left Communist Paul Mattick continued the approach pioneered by Grossman: see especially Mattick (1971).
5. Harder to classify was the "Regulation School," which emerged in France during the 1970s with a brilliant study of American capitalism by Michel Aglietta (1979). The basic thesis that the history of capitalism has involved different institutionally constituted "regimes of accumulation" was very influential, but the underlying theory of crisis, a revival of the old theme of disproportionalities between branches of production, was weak, and over time Regulation theory became little different from more mainstream ideas about "varieties of capitalism." For an important critique see Brenner and Glick (1991).
6. It's not clear that this interpretation accorded with Sraffa's own intentions, but for a powerful Marxist critique of his theory, see Salama (1975).

Bibliography

Adorno, Theodor W. 2018 (1997). "Marx and the Basic Concepts of Sociological Theory: From a Seminar Transcript in the Summer Semester of 1962." *Historical Materialism* 26(1): 1–11.

Aglietta, Michel. 1979. *A Theory of Capitalist Regulation: The US Experience*. London: NLB.

Amin, Samir. 1973. *L'échange inégal et la loi de la valeur: la fin d'un débat*. Paris: Éditions Anthropos-IDEP.

Amin, Samir. 1974. *Accumulation on a World Scale: A Critique of the Theory of Underdevelopment*. 2 vols. New York: Monthly Review Press.

Arrighi, Giovanni. 2007. *Adam Smith in Beijing: Lineages of the Twenty-First Century*. London: Verso.

Baran, Paul. 1973 (1957). *The Political Economy of Growth*. Harmondsworth: Penguin.

Bauer, Otto. 2011a. "Finance Capital." In Day and Gaido 2011, 413–39.

Bauer, Otto. 2011b. "The Accumulation of Capital." In Day and Gaido 2011, 713–43.

Bortkiewicz, Ladislaus von. 1949. "On the Construction of Marx's Fundamental Theoretical Construction in the Third Volume of Capital." In Eugen von Böhm-Bawerk, *Karl Marx and the Close of His System and Rudolf Hilferding, Böhm-Bawerk's Criticisms of Marx*, edited by Paul M. Sweezy, 199–221. New York: Augustus M. Kelley.

Brenner, Robert. 1998. "Uneven Development and the Long Downturn." *New Left Review* 1(229): 1–265.

Brenner, Robert. 2002. *The Boom and the Bubble: The US in the World Economy*. London: Verso.

Brenner, Robert. 2004. "New Boom, New Bubble." *New Left Review* 2(25): 57–100.

Brenner, Robert, and Mark Glick. 1991. "The Regulation Approach: Theory and History." *New Left Review* 1(188): 45–119.

Bukharin, N.I. 1972 (1917). *Imperialism and World Economy*. London: Merlin.

Callinicos, Alex. 2009. *Imperialism and Global Political Economy*. Cambridge: Polity.

Callinicos, Alex. 2014. *Deciphering Capital: Marx's Capital and Its Destiny*. London: Bookmarks.

Callinicos, Alex. 2020. "Chris Harman and the Critique of Political Economy." *International Socialism* 2(165): 37–55.

Carcanholo, Marcelo D. 2017. *Dependencia, superexplotación del trabajo y crisis: una interpretación desde Marx*. Madrid: Maia Ediciones.

Carchedi, Guglielmo. 1991. *Frontiers of Political Economy*. London: Verso.

Carchedi, Guglielmo. 2011. "Behind and Beyond the Crisis." *International Socialism* 2(132): 121–55.

Carchedi, Gugliemo, and Michael Roberts, eds. 2018. *World in Crisis: A Global Analysis of Marx's Law of Profitability*. Chicago: Haymarket.

Chesnais, François. 2016. *Finance Capital Today: Corporations and Banks in the Lasting Global Slump*. Leiden: Brill.

Choonara, Joseph. 2017. *A Reader's Guide to Marx's Capital*. London: Bookmarks.

Cleaver, Harry. 1979. *Reading Capital Politically*. Brighton: Harvester.

Cliff, Tony. 2003 (1948). "The Nature of Stalinist Russia." In *Selected Writings*. Vol. 3, 1–138. London: Bookmarks.

Colletti, Lucio. 1972. *From Rousseau to Lenin: Studies in Ideology and Society*. London: NLB.

Colletti, Lucio. 1973. *Marxism and Hegel*. London: NLB.

Colletti, Lucio. 1975. "Marxist and the Dialectic." *New Left Review* 1(93): 3–29.

Day, Richard B., and Daniel F. Gaido, eds. 2011. *Discovering Imperialism: Social Democracy to World War I*. Leiden: Brill.

Day, Richard B., and Daniel F. Gaido, eds. 2018. *Responses to Marx's Capital: From Rudolf Hilferding to Isaak Ilich Rubin*. Leiden: Brill.

Duménil, Gérard, and Dominique Lévy. 2004. *Capitalism Resurgent*. Cambridge, MA: Harvard University Press.

Duménil, Gérard, and Dominique Lévy. 2011. *The Crisis of Neoliberalism*. Cambridge, MA: Harvard University Press.
Durand, Cédric. 2017. *Fictitious Capital: How Finance Is Appropriating Our Future*. London: Verso.
Emmanuel, Arghiri. 1972. *Unequal Exchange: A Study of the Imperialism of Trade*. With Additional Comments by Charles Bettelheim. London: NLB.
Fine, Ben. 2014. "Financialization from a Marxist Perspective." *International Journal of Political Economy* 42(4): 47–66.
Fine, Ben, and Lawrence Harris. 1979. *Rereading Capital*. London: Routledge.
Fine, Ben, Costas Lapavitsas, and Dimitris Milonakis. 1999. "Addressing the World Economy: Two Steps Back." *Capital & Class* 23(1): 47–90.
Fine, Ben, and Alfredo Saad-Filho. 2010. *Marx's Capital*. London: Pluto.
Foley, Duncan K. 1986. *Understanding Capital: Marx's Economic Theory*. Cambridge, MA: Harvard University Press.
Furner, James. 2018. *Marx on Capitalism: The Interaction-Recognition-Antinomy Thesis*. Leiden: Brill.
Glyn, Andrew, and Bob Sutcliffe. 1972. *British Capitalism, Workers and the Profit Squeeze*. Harmondsworth: Penguin.
Gramsci, Antonio. 1971. *Selections from the Prison Notebooks*. London: Lawrence and Wishart.
Gramsci, Antonio. 1975. *Quaderni del carcere*. Edited by Valentino Gerratana. 4 vols. Turin: Einaudi.
Gramsci, Antonio. 1995. *Further Selections from the Prison Notebooks*. London: Lawrence and Wishart.
Grossman, Henryk. 1992 (1929). *The Law of Accumulation and Breakdown of the Capitalist System: Being also a Theory of Crises* (abridged). London: Pluto Press.
Hardt, Michael, and Antonio Negri. 2000. *Empire*. Cambridge, MA: Harvard University Press.
Harman, Chris. 2009. *Zombie Capitalism: Global Crisis and the Relevance of Marx*. London: Bookmarks.
Harvey, David. 1982. *The Limits to Capital*. Oxford: Martin Robertson.
Harvey, David. 2003. *The New Imperialism*. Oxford: Oxford University Press.
Harvey, David. 2005. *A Short History of Neoliberalism*. Oxford: Oxford University Press.
Harvey, David. 2010. *The Enigma of Capital and the Crises of Capitalism*. London: Profile Books.
Harvey, David. 2017. *Marx, Capital and the Madness of Economic Reason*. London: Profile Books.
Heinrich, Michael. 1999. *Die Wissenschaft vom Wert*. Münster: Westfälisches Dampfboot.
Heinrich, Michael. 2012. *An Introduction to the Three Volumes of Karl Marx's Capital*. New York: Monthly Review.
Hilferding, Rudolf. 1981 (1910). *Finance Capital: A Study of the Latest Phase of Capitalist Development*. London: Routledge.
Hilferding, Rudolf. 2018a (1911–12). "The Prehistory of Marxian Economics." In Day and Gaido, eds. 2018, 273–327.
Hilferding, Rudolf. 2018b (1905). "Karl Marx's Formulation of the Problem of Theoretical Economics." In Day and Gaido, eds. 2018, 262–77.
Holloway, John. 2002. *Change the World without Taking Power: The Meaning of Revolution Today*. London: Pluto.
Howard, M.C., and J.E. King. 1989 (1992). *A History of Marxian Economics*. 2 vols. London: Macmillan and Co.
Kalecki, Michał. 1967. *Selected Essays on the Dynamics of the Capitalist Economy*. Cambridge: Cambridge University Press.
Kidron, Michael. 1970. *Western Capitalism Since the War*. Harmondsworth: Penguin.
Kliman, Andrew. 2007. *Reclaiming Marx's "Capital": A Refutation of the Myth of Inconsistency*. Lanham, MD: Lexington Books.
Kliman, Andrew. 2011. *The Failure of Capitalist Production*. London: Pluto.
Kowalik, Tadeusz. 2014. *Rosa Luxemburg: Theory of Accumulation and Imperialism*. Basingstoke: Palgrave Macmillan.
Kuper, Richard. 2018. *Capitalism and Theory: Selected Works of Michael Kidron*. Chicago: Haymarket.
Lapavitsas, Costas. 2013. *Profiting Without Producing: How Finance Exploits Us All*. London: Verso.
Lecourt, Dominique. 1973. *Une crise et son enjeu: Essai sur la position de Lénine en philosophie*. Paris: Maspero.
Lenin, V.I. 1964 (1917). "Imperialism, the Highest Stage of Capitalism." In *LCW* 22: 185–304.
Lipietz, Alain. 1985. *The Enchanted World: Inflation, Credit and the World Crisis*. London: Verso.
Luxemburg, Rosa. 2015a (1913). "The Accumulation of Capital: A Contribution to the Economic Theory of Imperialism." In *The Complete Writings of Rosa Luxemburg, Volume II, Economic Writings 2*, edited by Peter Hudis and Paul Le Blanc. London: Verso.
Luxemburg, Rosa. 2015b (1921). "The Accumulation of Capital, or, What the Epigones* Have Made Out of Marx's Theory: An Anti-Critique." In *The Complete Writings of Rosa Luxemburg, Volume II, Economic Writings 2*, edited by Peter Hudis and Paul Le Blanc. London: Verso.
Mandel, Ernest. 1975. *Late Capitalism*. London: New Left Books.

Marx, Karl. 1992. "Das Kapital (Ökonomische Manuskript 1863–1865) Drittes Buch." In Karl Marx and Friedrich Engels, *Gesamtausgabe, Second Section*, Vol. 4, Part 2. Berlin: Dietz [*MEGA2* II/4.2].
Marx, Karl. 2016. *Economic Manuscript of 1864–1865*. Leiden: Brill.
Mattick, Paul. 1971. *Marx and Keynes: The Limits of the Mixed Economy*. London: Merlin.
Minsky, Hyman P. 2008 (1975). *John Maynard Keynes*. New York: McGraw-Hill.
Moseley, Fred. 2016. *Money and Totality: A Macro-Monetary Interpretation of Marx's Logic in Capital and the End of the "Transformation Problem."* Leiden: Brill.
Negri, Antonio. 1991 (1979). *Marx Beyond Marx: Lessons on the Grundrisse*. Brooklyn: Autonomedia.
Panitch, Leo, and Sam Gindin. 2012. *The Making of Global Capitalism: The Political Economy of American Empire*. London: Verso.
Patnaik, Utsa, and Prabhat Patnaik. 2016. *A Theory of Imperialism*. New York: Columbia University Press.
Pradella, Lucia. 2013. "Imperialism and Capitalist Development in Marx's *Capital*." *Historical Materialism* 21(2): 117–47.
Preobrazhensky, Evgeny A. 1985 (1931). *The Decline of Capitalism*. Armonk: M.E. Sharpe.
Roberts, Michael. 2016. *The Long Depression*. Chicago: Haymarket.
Rodney, Walter. 1972. *How Europe Underdeveloped Africa*. London: Bogle-L'Ouverture Publications.
Rosdolsky, Roman. 1977. *The Making of Marx's Capital*. London: Pluto.
Rubin, Isaak Ilich. 1972 (1928). *Essays on Marx's Theory of Value*. Detroit: Black & Red.
Salama, Pierre. 1975. *Sur la valeur*. Paris: Maspero.
Smith, John. 2015. *Imperialism in the 21st Century*. New York: Monthly Review.
Sraffa, Piero. 1960. *The Production of Commodities by Means of Commodities: Prelude to a Critique of Economic Theory*. Cambridge: Cambridge University Press.
Steedman, Ian. 1977. *Marx after Sraffa*. London: NLB.
Sweezy, Paul M. 1942. *The Theory of Capitalist Development*. Oxford: Oxford University Press.
Tronti, Mario. 2006 (1966). *Operai e capitale*. Roma: DeriveApprodi.

48
HENRYK GROSSMAN (1881–1950)

Rick Kuhn

Grossman's work developed interlocking Marxist approaches to scientific method; the contradiction between the use value and value aspects of capitalist production; economic crisis; and capitalism's breakdown tendency. His recovery and extension of Marx's analyses in these areas paralleled and were influenced by György Lukács's contributions to philosophy and Lenin's to political theory and practice.

Born in Kraków to a bourgeois Jewish family in 1881, Grossman became active in the Polish Social Democratic Party of Galicia (the large province of the Austro-Hungarian empire whose population was mainly Polish and Ukrainian) while at school. At university, he was a revolutionary Marxist and leader of students critical of the PPSD's nationalism and was involved in organizing Jewish workers, whom the party neglected. The Jewish Social Democratic Party of Galicia, of which he was the founding secretary and main theoretician, broke from the PPSD on May Day 1905. Its initial membership of around 2,000 expanded during the heightened working class struggles across the empire over economic and political demands, especially for universal suffrage, between 1905 and 1907.[1]

During the following period of subdued class struggles, having finish his first degree and moved to Vienna, Grossman was not involved in the increasingly reformist Social Democratic Workers Party of Austria, which had capitulated to the nationalism of the empire's dominant nations and was hostile to the JSDP. His higher degree and subsequent research, before and during World War I dealt with 18th-century economic policies and ideas, and the history of official social statistics in the Habsburg Empire. The principal product of these investigations, clearly while not explicitly Marxist in approach, was a detailed study of the empire's early trade policy for Galicia (Grossman 1914).

Grossman supported the Bolshevik revolution in Russia. A Leninist politics of working-class self-emancipation shaped the framework within which he formulated all his subsequent contributions to economic theory (Grossman 2018).[2] He moved to Warsaw in 1919. That year or earlier, he began to work on the Marxist theory of economic crises. He joined the Communist Workers Party of Poland in 1920.

For more than two years Grossman worked at the Polish Central Statistical Office, where he was in charge of the design of the first population census of the new republic and published several articles related to his work, before being appointed to a full professorship in economic policy at the Free University of Poland. His publications while there included a monograph on Simonde de Sismondi as a predecessor of Marx. Because of his political activity, particularly in the illegal Communist Party's front organizations, Grossman was arrested five times and did prison stretches of up to eight months.

Political repression pushed Grossman into leaving Poland for a well-paid post at the Institute for Social Research, associated with the University of Frankfurt at which he also taught. His period in Frankfurt, between 1925 and 1933, was Grossman's most productive. A series of essays and *The Law of Accumulation and Breakdown of the Capitalist System, Being Also a Theory of Crisis*, his best known work, dealt with Marxist economic theory (Grossman 2018, 1992).

Grossman stuck to the framework of his work in Warsaw and Frankfurt, developed before the terminal Stalinization of the international Communist movement, in his subsequent studies. That remained the case even when he identified with the Stalinist Soviet Union, from the end of the 1920s until the early 1930s and again from around 1936. His economic analyses were anathematized by in the international Communist movement.

In Parisian exile from 1933 until 1936, Grossman associated with dissident German Communist leaders of the Socialist Workers' Party of Germany and wrote a study of the emergence of the modern scientific worldview, which prompted his later and long unpublished monograph on René Descartes (both in Freudenthal and McLaughlin 2009). From Paris he moved to London and then, in 1937, to New York. In exile, Grossman also wrote further studies of French and English antecedents that highlighted distinctive and important aspects of Marx's economic theories, and offered a critique of bourgeois economics' shared fundamental assumptions, from Adam Smith to the still dominant neoclassical school (Grossman 2017c, 2017d, 2017e).

There was a break between Grossman and Max Horkheimer, the director of the Institute for Social Research and its US incarnation, in the early 1940s. Horkheimer's abandonment of historical materialism and not simply pessimistic but increasingly conservative outlook as well as Grossman's apologetic attitude to the Soviet Union, personal frictions and pay cuts were factors. In early 1949, Grossman took up a professorial chair at the University of Leipzig, the oldest in the Soviet Occupation Zone of Germany. He died the following year. Despite his efforts, none of his works was ever republished in east Germany, because they contradicted the Stalinist orthodoxy in economics.

The following sections examine some of Grossman's most important contributions to Marxism.

Method

The sorting of the myriad aspects of the reality that impinge on us according to their importance in influencing other aspects is intrinsic to scientific research, indeed to any intentional human activity. To understand falling bodies and develop the theory of gravity, for example, physicists "exclude the accidental and external influences of air" as a first step in their explanations. Such thought experiments, that is, initial abstraction away from less significant factors, are also a feature of economics as a science. But not all abstractions are accurate. Although Sismondi sometimes engaged in an anti-theoretical, empiricist rhetoric, Grossman pointed out that one of his most important criticisms of the classical political economy of Smith and Ricardo was that they abstracted from "*the essential elements* which characterize capitalist society." Contrary to the prevalent and superficial readings of his work, the Swiss economist's practice was far from empiricist. He developed François Quesnay's abstract model of reproduction, excluded survivals of previous modes of production, and concentrated on crucial relations that the mainstream economists did not include, particularly the nature of the capital–wage labor relationship (Grossman 2017b, 40, 42–43).

Grossman was the first to systematically explain the logical structure of Marx's *Capital*. The three volumes are governed by the "procedure of successive approximation" (*Annäherungsverfahren*). Marx strips away all the less important and relevant features that clutter our perception of capitalism, by making simplifying assumptions, in order to identify fundamental relations. Those assumptions are then successively lifted, so that the abstract insights are embedded in accounts closer to concrete reality. The model in the first volume abstracted, for example, from differences among the turnover times in the production of various commodities; competition among capitals; changes in the values of commodities; credit; changes in the value of money; systematic deviation of prices from values; differences in the organic compositions of capital among industries; and the concrete forms – industrial profit, commercial profit, interest, ground rent – taken by surplus value. In the course of the discussions in the second and third volumes, these and other aspects of empirical capitalism are introduced progressively to generate more complicated models, incrementally closer to the reality we perceive (Grossman 2013, 1992, 30–13). A failure to grasp Marx's method invalidated attempts to use his reproduction schemas in the second volume of *Capital* to explain economic crises both in terms of value disproportions alone and underconsumption.

In his studies of the origins of the scientific worldview and Descartes, Grossman also provided systematic evidence of the relationship between the development of machinery, stimulated by early capitalism, and modern science, physics in particular. Further, he demonstrated that Descartes's principal contribution to mathematics was designed to make it possible for a wider layer of people to make calculations that had previously been possible only for a small elite, just as machines had allowed less skilled workers to undertake tasks that previously only highly skilled artisans could complete (Grossman's essays in Freudenthal and McLaughlin 2009).

Use Value and Value

Ricardo and, before him, Smith mentioned use value only to go on to ignore it and construct theories of abstract exchange value. This abstraction had infamous consequences. In mainstream economics, the neglect of use value became even more pronounced in response to the left Ricardians' employment of classical theory to justify socialist conclusions.

Marx's transformation of Ricardo's economic categories was like his transformation of Hegel's dialectic. An important feature this reconfiguration was the systematic exploration, drawing on Sismondi, of the dual character of economic processes, including their material aspects, as opposed to Ricardo's one-sided concentration on them as abstract, value processes. This provided a means of grasping both the real relations behind the veil of appearances and the reasons for these misleading appearances.

A fundamental aspect of Marx's innovative analysis was the identification of human labor under capitalism as at once concrete labor, which creates the use values of specific commodities, and abstract labor, which generates commodities' value. Human labor is the use value of the commodity labor power, while labor power's value is the amount of abstract labor required to produce it. Capitalist processes of production are at once labor processes, through which specific kinds of concrete labor are applied, and value-creating (valorization) processes, in which quantities of socially necessary abstract labor are embodied into commodities.

But the use value and value aspects of capitalist relations were not simply discussed early in the first volume of *Capital* and then set aside, as many Marxist economists have assumed. Marx's method of successive approximation meant that, in *Capital*, the distinction between use value and value, gained at the most abstract level of analysis, permeates its increasingly concrete investigations, which progressively approach the complex real world (Grossman 2013, 1992,

147). Capital and the organic composition of capital, for example, also have dual characters. The organic composition of capital is the ratio between the value of human labor power and other inputs into production processes "in so far as it is determined by" "the relation between the mass of the means of production employed on the one hand, and the mass of labour necessary for their employment on the other" (the relation between the means of production as use values and living labor) "and mirrors the changes in the latter" (*CIII*: 762). The contradiction between the unlimited productive potential of the development of productive forces and the constraints on output imposed by capitalist relations of production also expresses that between the use value and value aspects of economic processes under capitalism (Grossman 1992, 123).

The neglect of use value or its confusion with exchange value has remained a feature of mainstream economics. Much of Marx's critique of vulgar economics, Grossman demonstrated, therefore also applies to its current, sophisticated and sophistical third, marginalist phase, preoccupied with psychology (the subjective theory of value) and mathematical technique, and popularly known as "economics."

There has been a long-running controversy over Marx's explanation of the way in which the values of commodities are transformed into "prices of production" as rates of profit equalize across industries with different organic compositions of capital. The neo-Ricardian Ladislaus von Bortkiewicz (1949) identified a "problem" in Marx's failure to assume that economic processes occur simultaneously, as in equilibrium models, and "solved" it by means of systems of equations based on precisely this assumption. Paul Sweezy's very influential *The Theory of Capitalist Development* popularized this "solution" among English-reading Marxists (Sweezy 1942, 109–28). The acceptance of Bortkiewicz's solution to the "transformation problem" embedded the fundamentally static, equilibrium approach of mainstream bourgeois economics in many Marxist economists' thinking. Subsequently, on the basis of this instantaneous, equilibrium methodology, not only non-Marxist economists but many Marxists also concluded that Marx's law of the tendency for the rate of profit to fall, the crux of his account of economic crises, was false. This refutation only holds if Marx's own "temporalist" approach, which eschews the implausible marginalist assumption of the simultaneous determination of the prices of inputs and outputs, is disregarded.

In contrast with the static framework of both classical political economy and its vulgar descendants, both of which assume that capitalism has a tendency to equilibrium, the dual nature of commodities, especially as applied to the commodity labor power, allowed Marx to grasp capitalism as a dynamic system. Grossman's recovery of Marx's critique of the way classical political economists and their vulgar successors assumed "the simultaneous rhythm of all economic processes" exposed many previous (and subsequent) Marxists' capitulation to bourgeois economics. They neglected the use value, therefore the time aspect of economic relations and reverted to pre-Marxist equilibrium analysis. In the process of resolving the transformation problem, between the 1980s and 2010s, the temporal single system and closely related interpretations, recapitulated the account Grossman provided of Marx's approach to capturing the dynamics of capitalism and his objections to the static methodology of vulgar Marxists (Kliman 2007; Moseley 2016).

Crisis and Breakdown

Grossman subjected the crisis theories of mainstream economists and most of his Marxist predecessors to sustained criticism in the course of identifying two complementary theories of crisis in Marx's work. The first explained capitalism's dynamic instability. The second, based on Marx's law of the tendency for the rate of profit to fall, accounted for capitalism's breakdown logic. Both were grounded in the contradictions between the capitalist production process as a labor process, creating use values, and as a process generating new values, in the form of surplus value. They account for the cyclical nature of crises and are counterposed to earlier Marxists' treatments of crises and/or capitalism's tendency to break down in terms of underconsumption (such as Cunow 1898; Kautsky 1902; Luxemburg 2015) and value disproportion (e.g., Hilferding 1927; Bauer 2011) alone.

In contrast to neo-harmonist, value-fixated accounts of the proportions required for stable capitalist growth, Marx's inclusion of material technical/use value conditions resulted in a radical theory of disproportionality with much more stringent and, in the real world, implausible conditions for capitalist equilibrium. Grossman described his recovery of this account of crisis under simple reproduction as "my chief contribution to Marxist theory" (Grossman 1947). While nothing like a book manuscript has survived, his published works contain elements of the argument, which built on his earlier, more general recovery of Marx's theory of radical disproportionality.

In the second volume of *Capital*, Marx dropped the preliminary assumption of equal production times (the periods required for the production of commodities) of all capitals and also introduced the complication of circulation time (the period commodities spend in the sphere of circulation before they are sold). Together production and circulation time constitute turnover time. Differences in turnover time are conditioned by the technical (i.e., use value) characteristics of production processes and the commodities they create. Even in the model of simple reproduction (i.e., without growth) in the second volume of *Capital*, which abstracts from the credit system among other aspects of the real world, crises are inevitable because of the use value distinction between fixed capital (embodied in commodities, like machines, that function in multiple cycles of the labor process) and circulating capital (commodities, like raw materials or wage goods, that are used up in one cycle). In some years, more fixed capital will have to be replaced than in others. But the model assumes a consistent level of output each year. Unevenness in the accumulation of fixed capital will tend to become cyclical, clumped together during some periods, generating booms, and thinning out during others, resulting in slumps.

Extending Marx's and Grossman's analysis, consideration of different kinds of fixed capitals, as use values, with different average life spans, can account for cycles of different periodicities. Hence there are cycles of investment in normal productive fixed capital and longer cycles of investment in larger scale fixed capital, infrastructure and buildings (Roberts 2016, 219–21). The existence of credit in the real world can even out fixed capital investments in different industries and enterprises, geographically, at a given time. It does not even out and may intensify fluctuations in fixed capital investment over time.

Furthermore, simple reproduction in value terms is not necessarily simple reproduction in terms of use values. Changed weather conditions in agriculture and large losses in output, due to unforeseen circumstances, in any industry can lead to a decline in the number of commodities produced while the living labor and the value of the means of production used to produce them, therefore their total value, are unchanged. Such a development will disrupt simple reproduction in other industries to which it provides inputs.

When the scale of reproduction expands and there is technological change, Grossman argued, the situation becomes even more complicated. Even if new investment is proportional across sectors, in value terms, without technological change, the scope for the growth in the number of commodities produced by different sectors can vary according to the use value characteristics of their output. So, for example,

> No one who finds two tractors sufficient for the cultivation of their land will buy four simply because their price has fallen by half, as the demand for tractors – *ceteris paribus* – is

> not dependent on their price alone but is, rather, determined by the cultivated area, that is quantitatively (Grossman 2017c, 533).

If technological change occurs, problems of proportion will arise even when investment is not increased or increases in the same value proportions in different industries. Should technological progress leap ahead in the steel compared to the car industry the quantity of steel will rise more rapidly than the number of cars. So, even though the car industry may have the capacity, in *value* terms, to purchase the same proportion of the steel industry's output as previously, its *technical* requirements for steel will not have kept up with the expanded production of steel. The previous equilibrium, on the basis of the previous value proportionalities, will be disrupted.

The material characteristics of the technology used in production also mean that there is a minimum amount of accumulated value that has to be invested in specific sectors. This, too, is an obstacle to simultaneous proportional expansion of production. For example, surplus value accumulated over a very short period may be sufficient to expand a clothing factory by an additional number of cutting and sewing machines. But a steel mill may have to accumulate over several years before it can invest in a new furnace and related equipment.

The contradiction between use value and value also underpinned Marx's theory of capitalist breakdown, which was another aspect of his account of periodic crises. A tendency to breakdown was, according to Marx, inherent in the capitalist mode of *production* but this has been denied by many Marxist economists for generations (Grossman 1992, 41; Grossman 2017c, 180–91).

Two circumstances facilitated Grossman's "reconstruction of Marx's theory of crisis and breakdown": recovering Marx's method of abstraction and successive approximation that structured *Capital*; and the investigations associated with his theory of radical disproportionality. Extrapolating Otto Bauer's reproduction schema (Bauer 2011), designed to refute Luxemburg's defense of the idea that capitalism tended to break down, demonstrated the effects of the breakdown mechanism that Marx had identified but had subsequently been neglected. Bauer's model itself broke down in its thirty-fifth cycle because of this mechanism: the tendency for the rate of profit to fall (Grossman 1992, 67–77).

Capitalism spectacularly expands the number of use values produced while reducing the value of individual commodities, by channeling a progressively higher proportion of investment into new technologies embodied in constant capital, as opposed to the purchase of living labor power. The ratio between the cost of constant capital used and the wages bill increases. Driven by competition among capitalists, this rising organic composition of capital expresses the progressive nature of capitalism, which increases the productivity of labor because workers using more sophisticated equipment etc. produce more commodities in a given time. But it is only living labor that creates new, surplus value. The rate of profit, the ratio between the newly created value embodied in surplus value (profits) and capitalists' total outlays, falls. The requirements for the accumulation of constant capital encroach on the surplus value available for the consumption of capitalists and/or workers' wages. Eventually there is insufficient surplus value to maintain any given rate of accumulation: the model breaks down. The onset of the breakdown is accelerated as the absolute value of individual, new items of constant capital grows (Grossman 2017c, 190, 1992, 74–82).

This analysis captures a long term tendency of the capitalist system. To approach the real-world pattern of growth more closely, Marx continued his investigation by identifying countertendencies, also inherent in capitalism and shaped by the dual nature of capitalist production, that slow or temporarily reverse the tendency for the rate of profit to fall (*CIII*: 317–75). These included the cheapening of both means of production and the items workers consume, a consequence of the increased productivity of labor; reduced turnover time; increases in the variety of use values, including through foreign trade; the transfer of surplus value from less to more developed territories through unequal exchange and profits from capital exports; and economic crises themselves, which devalue means of production, sold off cheap or left idle by bankrupt businesses. Grossman deepened and extended Marx's analysis of these and other countertendencies, including their relationship with imperialism.

The effects of the countertendencies mean that capitalism's tendency to break down takes the form of recurrent economic crises. While exploitation, the rate of surplus value, rises, and (up to a point) the mass of surplus value does increase, neither this nor the other countertendencies is sufficient to fully offset the effect of the rising organic composition of capital on the rate of profit in the long term. Both capitalism's tendency to break down and inherent crises, grounded in the distinctively capitalist dual nature of the production process, are expressions of the contradiction between the forces and relations of production (Grossman 2017c, 157–160, 191, 1992, 83–85, 123, 130–200). While theoretical refutations of Marx's and Grossman's account of the tendency for the rate of profit to fall have relied on the static assumptions of bourgeois economic theory, there is ample empirical evidence for its operation over the long run (Kliman 2007, 113–38; Roberts 2016, 12–29).

A myth that Grossman had a mechanical theory of capitalism's collapse and the transition to socialism was fabricated by Stalinist and social democratic reviewers of his *Law of Accumulation*. It was often associated with the implied or explicit accusation that Grossman was a proponent of political passivity. The myth was imported into the Anglophone literature by Paul Sweezy (1942, 211, 214). His epigones have continued to peddle it. No act of esoteric divination was or is necessary to establish the nature of Grossman's commitment to political activity culminating in workers' revolution or that he did not mechanically apply his model of capital accumulation. His positions were apparent in his political affiliations, explicit endorsement of Lenin's approach to revolution, and clearly expressed, not only in recently published responses to critics but also in his readily accessible publications, notably *The Law of Accumulation* and his discussion of the development of Marxism in *the* standard German economic reference work, but also a study originally published in English:

> [N]o economic system, no matter how weakened collapses by itself in automatic fashion. It must be "overthrown." . . . "[H]istorical necessity" does not operate automatically but requires the active participation of the working class in the historical process. . . . The main result of Marx's doctrine is the clarification of the historical role of the proletariat as the carrier of the transformative principle and the creator of the socialist society. . . . In changing the historical *object*, the *subject* changes himself.
>
> *(Grossman 2017d, 227)*

The point of the theory of capitalist breakdown, Grossman argued, was that it helped identify economic circumstances in which the working class could achieve political power. Lenin, he pointed out, had laid out the political preconditions for successful revolutionary action.

Notes

1. Detailed information about Grossman's life, as well as the context, content and impact of his work can be found in Kuhn (2007).
2. Unless otherwise indicated, all subsequent references to Grossman's work are in Grossman (2018), which includes Grossman (2013), all his essays in Grossman (2017a) and many more of his writings.

Bibliography

Bauer, Otto. 2011. "The Accumulation of Capital." In *Discovering Imperialism: Social Democracy to World War I*, edited by Richard B. Day and Daniel F. Gaido, 713–43. Leiden: Brill.

Bortkiewicz, Ladislaus von. 1949 (1907). "On the Correction of Marx's Fundamental Theoretical Construction in the Third Volume of *Capital*." In Eugen von Böhm-Bawerk and Rudolf Hilferding, *Karl Marx and the Close of His System and Böhm-Bawerk's Criticism of Marx*, edited by Paul Sweezy, 199–221. New York: Kelley.

Cunow, Heinrich. 1898. "Zur Zusammenbruchstheorie." *Neue Zeit* 17, 1(12, 13, 14): 356–64, 396–403, 424–30.

Freudenthal, Gideon, and Peter McLaughlin, eds. 2009. *The Social and Economic Roots of the Scientific Revolution: Texts by Boris Hessen and Henryk Grossmann*. Dordrecht: Springer.

Grossman, Henryk. 1914. *Österreichs Handelspolitik mit Bezug auf Galizien in der Reformperiode 1772–1790*. Wien: Konegen.

Grossman, Henryk. 1947. Letter to Christina Stead and Bill Blake, 4 and 5 May, Box 17, Folder 125, Stead Collection, National Library of Australia, Canberra.

Grossman, Henryk. 1992 (1929). *The Law of Accumulation and Breakdown of the Capitalist System: Being also a Theory of Crises* (abridged). London: Pluto Press.

Grossman, Henryk. 2013 (1929). "The Change in the Original Plan for Marx's *Capital* and Its Causes." *Historical Materialism* 21(3): 138–64.

Grossman, Henryk. 2017a. *Capitalism's Contradictions*. Chicago: Haymarket.

Grossman, Henryk. 2017b (1924). "Simonde de Sismondi and His Economic Theories." In Grossman 2017a, 33–86.

Grossman, Henryk. 2017c (1941). "Marx, Classical Political Economy and the Problem of Dynamics." In Grossman 2017a, 137–91.

Grossman, Henryk. 2017d (1943). "The Evolutionist Revolt against Classical Economics." In Grossman 2017a, 193–229.

Grossman, Henryk. 2017e (1948). "W. Playfair, the Earliest Theorist of Capitalist Development." In Grossman 2017a, 231–51.

Grossman, Henryk. 2018. *Works, Volume 1: Essays and Letters on Economic Theory*, edited by Rick Kuhn. Leiden: Brill.

Hilferding, Rudolf. 1927. *Die Aufgaben der Sozialdemokratie in der Republik*. Berlin: Vorstand der Sozialdemokratischen Partei Deutschlands. http://library.fes.de/prodok/fa-59843.pdf

Kautsky, Karl. 1902. "Krisentheorien." *Neue Zeit* 20, 2(2, 3, 4, 5): 37–47, 76–81, 110–18, 133–43.

Kliman, Andrew. 2007. *Reclaiming Marx's "Capital": A Refutation of the Myth of Inconsistency*. Lanham, MD: Lexington Books.

Kuhn, Rick. 2007. *Henryk Grossman and the Recovery of Marxism*. Urbana and Chicago: University of Illinois Press.

Luxemburg, Rosa. 2015 (1913). "The Accumulation of Capital: A Contribution to the Economic Theory of Imperialism." In Rosa Luxemburg, *The Complete Works of Rosa Luxemburg: Volume II, Economic Writings 2*, edited by Peter Hudis and Paul Le Blanc, 3–342. London: Verso.

Moseley, Fred. 2016. *Money and Totality: A Macro-Monetary Interpretation of Marx's Logic in Capital and the End of the "Transformation Problem."* Leiden: Brill.

Roberts, Michael. 2016. *The Long Depression*. Chicago: Haymarket.

Sweezy, Paul. 1942. *The Theory of Capitalist Development*. Oxford: Oxford University Press.

49

ISAAK ILLICH RUBIN (1886–1937)

Riccardo Bellofiore

Isaak Illich Rubin's *Essays on Marx's Theory of Value* (Rubin 1972) were part of the discussions about abstract labor and value in the 1970s. Rubin's argument, however, was very much misinterpreted. Rubin detected the crucial links in Marx's dialectical deduction of value, money and capital, without completely resolving its difficulties.

Rubin was born in Daugavspils, Latvia, then part of the Russian Empire, on 12 June, 1886.[1] He studied economics at the Faculty of Law in Saint Petersburg. He was part of the Jewish Bund, and then of the Mensheviks until 1924. He was arrested twice in 1921, and again in 1923, because of these affiliations, and was sentenced to three years in a concentration camp (the last year was commuted from jail to exile in Crimea). In 1919 he began a collaboration with David Riazanov on the collected writings of Marx. *Essays on Marx's Theory of Value* was published in 1923, the second edition in 1924. Translations worldwide were from the 1972 US translation of the 1928 third edition. The US edition was partial, missing a short Preface, the Introduction, an appendix on "Marxian terminology" (labor and value, "crystallization," thing and social function) and the "Answer to the Critics" (Dashkovskii, Shabs, Kon). A 1929 fourth edition added some lines to the Preface, and a rejoinder to Bessonov.[2]

Some hints on Rubin's intellectual trajectory were known from "Abstract Labour and Value in Marx's System": a 1927 article translated into German, and then into English (Rubin 1978). It was part of the 1920s debate in *Pod znamenem marksizma* (*Under the Banner of Marxism*). An important book edited by Richard Day and Daniel Gaido has been just published (Day and Gaido 2018): it includes important new material, and hopefully redefines the discussion. Particularly important are an unfinished 1926–28 long manuscript, *Essays on Marx's Theory of Money*, and "The Dialectical Development of Categories in Marx's Economic System" (another article in *Under the Banner of Marxism* from 1929).[3] In the 1920s Rubin published other important books and essays. Among them, *Physiocracy* (1925), *The History of Economic Thought* (1926, second augmented edition 1928: Rubin 1979) and *Contemporary Economists in the West* (1927).

Arrested in 1930 for conspiracy in establishing a "Union Bureau of Mensheviks," in 1931 he was condemned to five years imprisonment, then released in 1934, and sent to Kazakhstan. In 1937, he was shot on charges of supporting a Trotskyist plot.

Rubin Versus the Critics

Rubin was critical of the reduction of abstract labor to the *physiological* expenditure of energy, and advanced a *sociological* reading of Marx's theory, where the theory of *fetishism* is an essential component of the theory of value, and abstract labor is interpreted as a *purely social* objectivity. Critics lamented that the *material* dimension of production was forgotten, in favor of a Neo-Kantian "idealist" position like Franz Petry's. Between the first and second edition of his *Essays* Rubin *extended* the argument: deepening the qualitative inquiry about abstract labor, exploring the quantitative dimension of socially necessary labor time, going into the consideration of qualified labor, prices of production, productive and unproductive labor. The second edition soon ignited virulent criticisms. Rubin replied in the third edition proposing *categorical innovations*. The substantial changes – in chapter 12 (content and form of value) and in chapter 14 (abstract labor) – followed the 1927 article. In chapter 3 he merged another (1924) article from *Under the Banner of Marxism*, "Production Relations and Material Categories," which was part of the debate on planning.

For Rubin, the logical structure of political economy as science exhibits the social structure of capitalism. It is the *social nature of material categories* that constitutes Marx's "inner connection." Classical political economy accepts without questioning the estranged form of economic relations, that is, the objectified, ready-made form of things. In fact, the reification of production relations means that "things," or better the social form of the products of labor, serve as bearers of a determinate kind of production relations.

A position like this was frontally opposed to the reduction of abstract labor to physiological labor, and of social relations to material relations. This was for example the position by A. Kon (*Lectures in Political Economy, First Part: Theory of Value, Theory of Money, Theory of Surplus Value*, 1928). The abstraction of labor is a *mental* generalization from concrete labors, an abstraction *in thought* leading to the determination of physiological labor as labor "in general." Abstract labor is a *logical* notion prolonged in a measure of the *physiological* effort, immediately defining *a quantitative measure of the magnitude of value*. Abstract labor has therefore no special relation with the "commodity form," and it is a quantitative concept only because its base is a physical amount of physiological energy. That social relations are liable only to a qualitative inquiry was argued also by A.A. Voznesenskii ("How to understand the notion of abstract labor" (*Under the Banner of Marxism*, December 1925). On the same journal a similar position was maintained by I. Dashkovskii in "Abstract labor and Economic Categories" (June 1926). The labor "creating" value must have a distinct characteristic of being *social* labor, christened as "economic" labor by S. Shabs in his 1929 book *Problems of Social Labor in the Economic System – a Critique of the Essays on Marx's Theory of Value by I.I. Rubin*. The criticism was that Rubin collapsed abstract labor and social labor into one and the same category. The critics deny that *both* abstract labor and the substance of value are historically connected to commodity exchange: labor is distinguished as *concrete, abstract* (i.e., *physiological*) and *social*.

In the second edition Rubin sharply rejected the view that reduced abstract labor to physiological labor. Contrasting the first chapter of *Capital* (where indeed a "reduction" to physiological labor was followed by the dialectical deduction of the form of value in the third section) with the *Contribution to the Critique of Political Economy* (where there is no "reduction" of exchange value to value and then labor), Rubin admitted that Marx originated the misunderstandings by not distinguishing the inquiry into the content of value from that into the form of value. On the one hand, "value in general" logically exists *as if* it could be anterior and independent from the "form of value." On the other hand, the "form of value" *is* the key concept to understand a universalized exchange economy. Without the "form of value," the critics' "logical" understanding would be right, and "value" reduces to simple expenditure of labor.

The Path Away From a View of Abstract Labor as "Isolated" in the Sphere of Exchange

The critics however convinced Rubin of the risk that in the second edition of his book the theory of the "form of value" was wrongly advocated *against* the social existence of the essential dimension of value before final exchange. Ironically, it is exactly this conclusion, more faithful to the Rubin of the second edition than to the Rubin of the third edition, which since the 1980s was maintained by what is mistakenly labeled the "Rubin school."[4] Rubin emancipated himself from this risk through a thorough study of the critique that Marx mounted against the proto-marginalist Samuel Bailey in *Theories of Surplus Value*. The critique of Bailey has a major weight in Rubin (1979) and in a 1929 study of Marx and Bailey for the bulletin of the Marx-Engels Institute.

Marx criticized Bailey's "nominalism," arguing that value is not identical with exchange value as it is given in any idiosyncratic act of exchange. However, he is also critical of Ricardo's "substantialism," according to which value is reduced to the content, or substance of labor, a position that is blind to the form of value and money. Political economy follows an *analytical* method, moving *from exchange value to value to labor*: this must be complemented, like in Marx, by a *synthetic* exposition, *from labor to value to form of value to exchange value*. Marx asks *why* labor must be exhibited in that form, and therefore *which* is the labor *expressed* in exchange value. Value-as-form, distinct from value-as-content, is an abstract property of the commodity that has *not yet* materialized in a determinate "objectivity": it has not yet taken a concrete form. This will happen in money as "exchange value," that is, in "value-as-form" externalized and made autonomous. This movement *from* the inner *to* the outer *within* the circularity of capital will be at the heart of the *Essays on Marx's Theory of Money*.

Chapter 14 of the second edition of Rubin's book was the most attacked. Abstract labor was defined as "private" labor turning into social labor in the *distinct phase* of commodity exchange, *after* production. Critics countered that in any social allocation of labor there is the need to reduce labor to a common standard, and labor is *immediately social* in production. In the Preface to the third edition Rubin declares that he cut away the passages that gave his critics arguments to attribute to him points of view that he did not agree with. Rubin conceded to the critics that in any economy where there is a "social division of labor" there is the need of a social *equalization* of labor, but this latter must not be confused with abstract labor, which is an *historically specific* form of equalization. In a *socialist community* the planning bureau has to equalize individual labors, but this equalization is *secondary* relative to the socialization and quantitative allocation of labor. *In a commodity economy* it is the other way round, labor is *not* immediately social, it has to *become* social through the *indirect* equalization of individual labors in commodity market exchange. In both cases there is the presupposition of a physiologically equal labor, but in the former labor is socially equalized in a *direct* fashion, in the latter *it becomes social as long as it is made equal through the abstraction of labor in the exchange of "things."*

Critics' complaints are justified relative to the second edition:

> until the producer is concerned with his particular *concrete* labor, this labor is a *private* labor. It becomes social *only* in the act of exchange on the market, that is through the equalization of very different kinds of products of labor, that is through the form of *abstract* labor . . . abstract labor emerges *only* in the real act of market exchange. . . . Abstract labor is produced *only* in exchange. . . . Abstract labor is *created* in exchange.[5]

Among the positions that in the Preface to the third edition Rubin declares that he does *not* share there are exactly the predominance of exchange over production and enclosing abstract labor in the phase of exchange – positions associated with contemporary value-form theory.

The Third Edition: Abstract Labor as "Latent" in Immediate Production

In 1927–28 Rubin *radically reformulates his conception of abstract labor. Exchange* is now a *dual* notion: (1) a *particular* phase of the capitalist economic circuit; (2) the *specific form of production in capitalism as characterized by an ex-post socialization (Vergesellschaftung) in universal commodity-exchange.* Thus it *encompasses within itself the totality of production and exchange as successive moments*, in an alternating pattern. In this second connotation exchange is *the social form of reproduction*. *Before* actual exchange as a distinct phase, "private" producers need to consider (in the sphere of "representation"), the compulsion coming from their competitors. Thus, *already* in the phase of immediate production, commodities are equated with money. It is an *anticipated equalization of concrete labors as abstract labor*.

In this new theoretical configuration, abstract labor is *latent* in immediate production. It is true that the metamorphosis of concrete labors to abstract labor so far is *preliminary* and *ideal*, and that latent abstract labor has *yet to become actual* on the final commodity market: however, *the rigid opposition of "private" production versus "social" final validation* – still present in the second edition, and resurfacing today in many value form approaches – *becomes meaningless*. Without exchange on the commodity market there would not be abstract labor, but abstract labor is present as *objective potency* in production.[6] The abstraction of labor is a *process*, and value "comes into being" in the *unity* of production and circulation.

A closer look at other Rubin's works between 1927 and 1929 is essential here. In "Abstract Labor and Value" (1927), Rubin writes that value-as-content (i.e., labor) and the social form of value are *both* included in the notion of value. The social form of the product must be divided into two parts, one that has *not yet* acquired a concrete manifestation and one that has *already* acquired an independent existence. The former is *value-as-form*, which is included in value itself, and the latter is *exchange value* properly speaking, which is its exteriorization and "incarnation." In commodity production the *socialization of dissociated labors* takes the specific form of abstract labor, which is the "content" of value, first "objectified" ideally in the "form" of value, then "embodied" materially in the universal equivalent, money. The concept of value is related *backwards* to the social relations of commodity producers through (abstract) labor (in becoming) as value-as-content, and is related *forward* to real money as exchange value through value-as-form as ideal money.

In *Essays on Marx's Theory of Money* (1926–28) this train of thought is detailed. When products of labor are produced for sale, and commodity exchange is universalized, price formation is continuous because of the continuity of the process of reproduction. With *money as the measure of value*, the preliminary mental anticipation of the normal prices of commodities is an expression of their values. This ideal evaluation changes qualitatively the social nature of *both* product and labor. Since money (gold) is a commodity produced by labor, price tags are a quantitative determination of the expected value-content *before* final exchange. As in his book, Rubin refers to an "equilibrium" side of value theory, according to which, in *normal* conditions, the *expected* price is dependent on the *objective* conditions of productive forces: "technical" socially necessary labor time. Demand seems to be the primary force in market exchange, but in fact depends from the volume and character of production.

Commodities enter the market with a *given* exchange value corresponding to its price, though these expectations may be disappointed. With *money as means of circulation*, a change of form is going on: the "soul" of the commodity turns into gold, while continuing *its own* movement; the exchange ratio between gold and commodities is fixed at the point of production, in the *direct barter* of gold as a commodity against all other commodities. Since a commodity is equated with all other commodities *in advance*, a *preliminary* evaluation in terms of gold is also going on *in production*. With *hoards and means of payment*, money from fluid crystallizes in a *fixed* thing (a "chrysalis").

In his 1929 report published in *Under the Banner of Marxism*, Rubin traced the dialectical development of categories, sketching the entire theoretical structure of *Capital* built from the contradiction hidden in the commodity between use value and value. Each commodity "reveals" value through the equalization with the other products. *Only* money *embodies* direct and universal exchangeability, but every commodity, without yet really being converted into money, still has the *potential* or "ideal form" of money. In *money as ideal money (value-as-form)*, which *inheres* in the commodity, we reach the money-*existence* of the commodity itself. This nebulous and chimerical form becomes externalized in fluid and firm forms. In *money as real money* (exchange value as the form of value) we reach a social form that is frozen, ossified, crystallized and has coalesced with a thing: the *absolute* existence of value. Rubin very well understands that this "reification" expresses the *fetish character* dominant in a monetary commodity capitalist economy, which generates *fetishism* as the naturalization of those specific (but *real*) social properties "things" possess in that social reality. With *money as capital* we see that the exchange of equivalents in commodity circulation is only a "seeming" exchange. When the *chrysalis* (money as money) has turned into a *butterfly* (money as capital), the *ghost* (value within a commodity) has turned into a *vampire*: capital is self-expanding value because it "sucks" living labor from the living bearers of labor power.

One Step Back to Rubin, and Two Steps Beyond?

Rubin has been either misinterpreted or underrated. His book was probably translated too late; surely, his contribution has been forgotten or sidestepped too soon. Lucio Colletti's interpretation between 1968 and 1975 shows amazing similarities with Rubin, but the latter's book wasn't yet translated (though anecdotal evidence insists that Colletti may have had knowledge of it through his first Russian wife, Irina). Hans-Georg Backhaus, one of the founders of the German value-form school, confessed to Emilio Agazzi he read only the initial chapters of Rubin 1972 (on fetishism) only after having published the first two parts of the "Materialen zur Rekonstruktion der Marxschen Werttheorie": after reading the other chapters (on the form of value) on Agazzi's suggestion, he declared this would have saved him a lot of work.[7] Étienne Balibar provides thorough and convergent considerations about fetishism in his *The Philosophy of Marx*, without ever referring to Rubin.

The point is that the processual perspective on the abstraction of labor presented by Rubin is a decisive step forward. It has to be complemented with Claudio Napoleoni's writings of the early 1970s. For Napoleoni, the deduction of abstract labor from (commodity and monetary) exchange, as we find in the first chapter of *Capital*, should be brought together with the deduction of abstract labor as the living labor of the wage-earners commanded by capital in the phase of production, as we find in the *Grundrisse* (Napoleoni 1975). Napoleoni clarifies that within the category of abstract labor, as long as it is understood as labor which is *immediately* private and only *mediately* social, capitalist competition within sectors is part of the "essence." The "immediately private labors" equalized in exchange are the collective labors commanded by capitalist firms: from here Marx can build his views on firms' struggle to get extra-surplus value, which anticipate Schumpeter.

These considerations help overcome some of the limits of Rubin, who gives too much weight to simple commodity production. Rubin also does not see that monetary validation of commodities – the *ex post socialization in circulation* – goes together with what Marx defines the *immediate socialization* of labor in production. As again Napoleoni argued, once we reach the stage of the real subsumption of labor under capital, labor does not only *count* as abstract in commodity circulation: it already *is* abstract in capitalist production. The abstraction of labor becomes *practically* true, and "form determination" extends to the expenditure of labor; the use value dimension is "mediated" by value. Abstract labor "in becoming" within the immediate process of production becomes the Subject (the "self-acting Fetish") that *from* production is actualized *within* circulation (Rubin 2018b, 805).

The difficulty is that Rubin's compact argument builds on Marx's view of money as a commodity (produced by labor). If this link is cut out, *a gap between two worlds opens up*, as Michael Heinrich shows:[8] on the one side, production, with incommensurable use values and concrete labor, and on the other circulation, where monetary socialization and commensurability emerges.[9] *This conclusion cannot be accepted*. We need to transform the monetary (labor) theory of value into a *macro-monetary theory of capitalist production*: a perspective that stresses the financing of production as the *monetary ante-validation* that opens the way to an *anticipated commensurability* of economic magnitudes within immediate production, in the expectation of the *final validation* on the commodity market.

This interpretation of the "cycle" of money capital can build on the contributions of Augusto Graziani (1997a, 1997b) .[10] This research project emerged in the 1970s for social and political reasons. The rediscovery of the "centrality" of labor and production as a contested terrain accompanied radical struggles within the capitalist labor process. These struggles highlighted how reductive had been the conceptualization of the relation between labor power and living labor inherited from the various Marxisms. The "constitution" of the reified capitalist reality had to be brought back to the conflictual, and potentially antagonistic, nature of class relations in the "hidden abode" of production.

The Soviet Background

Fully to grasp what was at stake in the polemic around Rubin two issues must be dealt with. The first issue is that the dispute had very much to do with the controversies about *planning*. The anti-Rubin position was that behind the theory of value lies a trans-historical content, grounded in physical techniques and materiality: what was later labeled the "Marxism of the productive forces." For Rubin functions and social forms cannot be *reduced* to material production and *grounded* on the latter: they do not belong to the thing in itself, considered from a material point of view, but to things as part of a given social context. The first approach confuses the *technical* and *social* functions of things. Rubin's alternative approach had an immediate consequence: Rubin saw planning as based on an organic and clear outline of society's fabric, allowing thoughtful choices about the goals and finalities of the development of productive forces, in accord with actual social needs.

In "The Dialectical Development of Categories in the Marxian Economic System" (1929) the point is laid bare with great perspicuity. A social form springs from a simpler one because of changes in the material productive forces. *But it does not emerge in a void or as a mere passive mirror of the given state reached by the productive forces, outside any link with social forms and production relations among human beings.* The specific nature of the capitalist commodity economy lie in the circumstance that the social relations among people are not established with *reference to* but *by means of* things themselves. It is this which gives to production relations among people a "materialized," "reified" form, and gives rise to commodity fetishism, the confusion between technical-material and socio-economical aspects of the productive process. *Marx's method*, Rubin insists, treats *the object of inquiry not as ossified things, isolated one from another, but as fluid and dynamic processes, linked with each other.*

The second issue has to do with Marx's connection to Hegel. The polemic around Rubin intersected the philosophical controversy between "mechanists" and "dialecticians" in the Soviet Union of the 1920s. The dialecticians argued against the "reductionist" position according to which more complex phenomena can be reduced to simpler phenomena, and sided with Rubin. The Russian economist had expressed his position with great clarity in the third edition:

> *on the question of the relation between content and form, Marx took the standpoint of Hegel*, and not of Kant. Kant treated form as something external in relation to the content, and as something which adheres to the content from the outside. From the standpoint of Hegel's philosophy, the content is not in itself something to which form adheres from the outside. Rather, through its development, *the content itself gives birth to the form which was already latent in the content. Form necessarily grows out of the content itself.* . . . From this point of view, *the form of value necessarily grows out of the substance of value.*
>
> *(Rubin 1972, 117, emphasis in original)*

The overlapping of the debates in the end proved fatal to most of the protagonists. In 1930 Bessonov and Kon edited a collection with the resounding title *Rubinism or Marxism?* That same year, B. Borilin and A. Leont'ev published *Against Mechanist Tendencies in Political Economy* in defense of Rubin, which was attacked in *Pravda* and provoked an answer from 10 young economists pro-Rubin ("Materials for a discussion on theoretical economics"). But on 10 October 1930 *Pravda*, vigorously attacked both mechanists and Rubinists. Two later *Pravda* articles sought to eradicate the *Rubin'scina*. Stalin's "struggle on two fronts" had brought down the curtain.

Notes

1. Cf. Jasny (1972), Medvevev (1972), and Boldyrev and Kragh (2012).
2. On the contextualization of Rubin (1972) I am very much indebted to Takenaga (2007), Tagliagambe (1978) and Nisticò (1987).
3. I am grateful to Richard Day and Daniel Gaido for allowing me to read some chapters in their book in advance.
4. Eldred et al. (1984) is a paradigmatic example.
5. Takenaga (2007, 14), my emphases.
6. The allusion is to Aristotle's meaning of potency or potentiality as 'real' possibility. Aristotle distinguished between, on the one hand, mere possibility, which is pure conceivability, what is merely thinkable or mere "capacity to be" (ένδέχεσθαι), and, on the other, potency (δύναμιζ)or potentiality as concrete possibility, or real possibility, which is taken to be a real being inasmuch as it is capable of "coming to be" – namely the unfolding of a form already implicit and thus arriving at a higher level of being (cf. Metaphysics, Θ, 3 and 6).
7. Cf. Agazzi "Introduzione" in Eldred et al. (1984, 10–11).
8. Cf. Heinrich (1999).
9. Cf. Backhaus and Reichelt (1995), who assess critically the first edition of Heinrich (1999).
10. Graziani (1997b) is marred by a serious error in translation. Graziani distinguishes "denaro" (Geld in Marx: money in English) from "moneta" (Münze in Marx). The translator, except in one instance, translated both as money.

Bibliography

Backhaus, Hans-Georg. 1978. "Materialien zur Rekonstruktion der Marxschen Werttheorie." *Gesellschaft. Beiträge zur Marxschen Theorie* 11: 16–177.

Backhaus, Hans-Georg, and Helmut Reichelt. 1995. "Wie ist der Wertbegriff in der Ökonomie zu konzipieren? Zu Michael Heinrich: *Die Wissenschaft vom Wert*." *Beiträge zur Marx-Engels-Forschung. Neue Folge*: 60–94.
Boldyrev, Ivan, and Martin Kragh. 2012. "Isaak Rubin: Historian of Economic Thought during the Stalinization of Social Sciences in Soviet Russia." *Journal of the History of Economic Thought* 37(3): 363–86.
Calogero, Guido. 1949. "Possibilità and 'Potenza.'" In *Enciclopedia Italiana*. Roma: Istituto dell'Enciclopedia Treccani.
Day, Richard B., and Daniel Gaido, eds. 2018. *Responses to Marx's Capital: From Rudolf Hilferding to Isaak Illich Rubin*. Leiden: Brill.
Eldred, Michael, Marnie Hanlon, Lucia Kleiber, and Vokberth M. Roth. 1984. *La forma-valore. Progetto di ricostruzione e completamento del frammento di sistema di Marx*. Edited and Introduced by Emilio Agazzi. Palermo: Lacaita.
Graziani, Augusto. 1997a. "Let's Rehabilitate the Theory of Value." *International Journal of Political Economy* 27(2): 21–25.
Graziani, Augusto. 1997b. "The Marxist Theory of Money." *International Journal of Political Economy* 27(2): 26–50.
Heinrich, Michael. 1999. *Die Wissenschaft vom Wert*. Münster: Westfälisches Dampfboot.
Jasny, Naum. 1972. *Soviet Economists of the Twenties: Names to Be Remembered*. Cambridge: Cambridge University Press.
Medvevev, Roy. 1972. *Let History Judge: The Origins and Consequences of Stalinism*. New York: Knopf.
Napoleoni, Claudio. 1975. *Smith, Ricardo, Marx*. Oxford: Blackwell.
Nisticò, Gabriella. 1987. *"Introduzione" to the Italian Translation of Jasny 1972, xi–xxxviii*. Rome: Istituto della Enciclopedia Italiana.
Rubin, Isaak Ilich. 1972 (1928). *Essays on Marx's Theory of Value*. Detroit: Black & Red.
Rubin, Isaak Ilich. 1978. "Abstract Labor and Value in Marx's System." *Capital & Class* 2(2): 107–39.
Rubin, Isaak Ilich. 1979. *A History of Economic Thought*. London: Ink Links.
Rubin, Isaak Ilich. 2018a. "Essays on Marx's Theory of Money." In Day and Gaido 2018, 619–727.
Rubin, Isaak Ilich. 2018b. "The Dialectical Development of the Categories in Marx's Economic System." In Day and Gaido 2018, 728–817.
Tagliagambe, Silvano. 1978. *Scienza filosofia politica in Unione Sovietica 1924–1939*. Milano: Feltrinelli.
Takenaga, Susumu. 2007. "Sur les révisions de la seconde à la troisième édition des *Essais sur la théorie de la valeur de Marx* par I. I. Roubine: une phase dans la polémique de la valeur dans l'ex-Union soviétique dans les années 1920." Congrès Marx International V – Section Etudes Marxistes – Paris-Sorbonne et Nanterre.

50
PAUL MARLOR SWEEZY (1910–2004)

John Bellamy Foster

Paul Marlor Sweezy, in the words of John Kenneth Galbraith (1987, 189), was "the most noted American Marxist scholar" of the second half of the 20th century. The *Wall Street Journal* (1972) referred to him as "the 'dean' of radical economists." Sweezy's intellectual influence, which was global in its reach, lay chiefly in two areas: as a leading Marxist economist and sociologist, and as the principal originator of a distinct North American brand of socialist thought in his role as cofounder and coeditor of *Monthly Review* magazine. Like Marx and Schumpeter, Sweezy provided a historical analysis and critique of capitalist economic development, encompassing a theory of the origins, development and eventual decline of the system.

From Harvard and the New Deal to *Monthly Review*

Sweezy was born 10 April 1910, in New York.[1] His father, Everett B. Sweezy, was vice president of the First National Bank of New York, then headed by George F. Baker, a close partner of J.P. Morgan and Company. His mother, Caroline (Wilson) Sweezy was in the first graduating class of Goucher College in Baltimore. He had two older brothers, Everett, born 1901, and Alan, born 1907. All three brothers went to Exeter and then to Harvard. In the early years, Paul followed in the footsteps of his brother Alan. Both Alan and Paul were editors of the *Exonian* and then later presidents of the *Harvard Crimson*. Both studied economics at the undergraduate and graduate levels at Harvard. Paul had all but completed his senior year at Harvard when his father died in 1931, interrupting his studies. Consequently, he did not graduate (magna cum laude) until the following year in 1932. In 1931–32, however, having already finished his undergraduate studies, he began graduate courses in economics at Harvard.

In fall 1932 Sweezy went to England for a year's study at the London School of Economics (LSE). During school breaks he also studied for several months in Vienna. These experiences changed his life and outlook considerably. Like many he had been shaken by the onset of the Great Depression. His father had lost the greater part of his fortune in the 1929 stock market crash, although enough remained to ensure a comfortable existence. In Britain, Sweezy was awakened by the intellectual and political ferment in response to the deepening depression and Hitler's rise to power in Germany. His initial intention in attending the LSE was to work with the conservative economist Friedrich Hayek. However, in the heated debates then taking place, particularly among younger scholars from around the world, Sweezy found himself increasingly attracted to Marxism. Lectures that he attended by Harold Laski at the LSE and his reading of Leon Trotsky's *History of the Russian Revolution*, which had just been translated into English, were key influences inducing Sweezy's radical change in perspective.

In fall 1933 Sweezy returned to the United States to continue his graduate studies in economics at Harvard where the intellectual climate had been dramatically transformed. Marxism, which in his earlier years at Harvard had played no part in his education, had by then become an important topic of discussion. One big change was the arrival at Harvard of Joseph Schumpeter, one of the foremost economists of the 20th century. A conservative economist, Schumpeter nonetheless had enormous respect for the economics of Karl Marx, even taking Marx as a kind of model for his own attempt to construct a theory of capitalist economic development consistent with neoclassical orthodoxy. Sweezy became Schumpeter's teaching assistant and younger colleague. They forged a close and lasting friendship, despite their opposing viewpoints.

During these years Sweezy cofounded the journal *Review of Economic Studies* and published a series of important economic essays on issues of imperfect competition, the role of expectations in economic decisions and economic stagnation. After Keynes's *General Theory of Employment Interest and Money* was published in 1936, Sweezy became a very active participant in the Harvard discussions surrounding the Keynesian revolution in economic theory. At the same time, he married a young economist, Maxine Yaple, who was to become best known for her work *The Structure of the Nazi Economy* (M.Y. Sweezy 1941).

Sweezy worked for various New Deal agencies during Roosevelt's Second New Deal in the late 1930s. In 1937, he carried out an important study of "Interest Groups in the American Economy" for the National Resources Committee (NRC), which was published in 1939 as an appendix to the NRC's well-known report, *The Structure of the American Economy* (Sweezy 1939a). In opposition to Adolf A. Berle and Gardiner Means's claim that a large number of US firms were management controlled, Sweezy argued that it was possible to discern eight leading "interest groups" consisting of industrial and financial alliances. In the first group, he listed the investment banking firm of J. P. Morgan and Co. and its alliance with the First National Bank, in which his father had worked. Sweezy also carried out research for the Security and Exchange Commission on their study of monopoly in 1939, and for the Temporary National Economic Committee, which was charged with analyzing issues of competition and monopoly in the US economy in 1940.

In 1938 Sweezy was appointed an instructor/professor in economics at Harvard. He and his brother Alan helped in the founding of the Harvard Teacher's Union, a branch of the American Federation of Teachers. The following year he published his classic article, "Demand Under Conditions of Oligopoly," in the *Journal of Political Economy* (Sweezy 1939b). Here, in what became one of the key texts in imperfect competition theory, he introduced the famous "kinked demand curve" theory of oligopolistic pricing, which explained why prices in oligopolistic markets tend to go only one way – up. The kinked demand curve hypothesis arose of out of Sweezy's 1937 dissertation *Monopoly and Competition in the English Coal Industry, 1550–1850* (Sweezy 1938), which won Harvard's prestigious David A. Wells prize.

In addition to teaching the principles of economics and a course on corporations, Sweezy took over a course on the economics of socialism formerly taught by Edward Mason. It was in the process of developing the lectures for this class that he wrote his seminal work *The Theory of Capitalist Development: Principles of Marxian Political Economy* (1942). This classic treatise is still used to teach Marxian analysis to students in economics. It made a large number of pioneering contributions, including: (1) its emphasis on the qualitative value problem (juxtaposed to the quantitative value problem) in Marx's treatment of the labor theory of value; (2) its elaboration of the Bortkiewicz solution to the transformation problem (which Sweezy later translated from German – see Bortkiewicz 1949); (3) its discussion of economic crisis theory (including what was then called "underconsumption" or realization crisis theory); and (4) its treatment of monopoly capitalism. In the short introduction to his book Sweezy provided what was to be an influential explanation of Marx's method of abstraction and successive approximations.

The most important conclusion of *The Theory of Capitalist Development* had to do with the long-run stagnation of investment under capitalism, arising from a built-in tendency in the system toward the overaccumulation of capital – ultimately rooted in the limited consumption of the masses. "Stagnation," Sweezy (1942, 217) wrote "is the norm towards which [mature] capitalist production is always heading." Once this was understood, Sweezy explained, the whole crisis problem appeared in a new light. Emphasis at that point shifted from the question of what caused a long downturn (or secular stagnation), to its opposite: the *specific historical forces* countering this tendency, allowing the capitalist economy to continue to grow.

The Theory of Capitalist Development appeared in the same year as Schumpeter's (1942) *Capitalism, Socialism and Democracy* and the two works can be seen as two sides of a complex debate on the future of capitalism and socialism, with Schumpeter opposing the theories of monopoly capitalism, secular stagnation and vanishing investment opportunities. In his posthumously published *History of Economic Analysis*, Schumpeter referred numerous times to Sweezy, and in particular to *The Theory of Capitalist Development*. Schumpeter (1954, 885) "strongly recommended" Sweezy's book, "as an admirable presentation of Marx's (and most of the neo-Marxists') economic thought."

In the 1930s Sweezy was a member of the League Against Fascism and War and joined various popular front organizations. With the United States entering the Second World War after the attack on Pearl Harbor, Sweezy was anxious to play an active role in the fight against fascism. In fall 1942 he left Harvard to enlist in the army as an officer candidate. He was assigned to the Office of Strategic Services (OSS) working with Harvard economist Edward Mason. In late fall 1943, he was sent to London to join the Research and Analysis program of the OSS there, where his immediate superior was another noted US economist, Chandler Morse. Sweezy's chief role was to keep an eye on British economic policy for the US government. He met frequently with economist James Meade, who was in the British economic warfare agency. It was clear that the war would result in a reorganization of world economic relations and that the United States was interested in coming out of the war as the top dog. At that time, Britain was still considered to be the number two economy and the whole question of what to do with the British Empire had not yet been decided. Sweezy was later to look back on many of his experiences in this respect as reflecting Washington's concerted attempt to subordinate its allies (including Britain) under new order of US hegemony, as described in Gabriel Kolko's *The Politics of War* (Magdoff and Sweezy 1981, 185–87).

The Research and Analysis section of the OSS produced reports and analyses of developments in particular countries that were distributed to several hundred military agencies and commands in the European theatre of operations. The London branch of the Research and Analysis section had been publishing for some time a newsletter that was a weekly summary of what was happening in the Axis countries, derived mostly from the German press, but also from other occupied areas. This information was collected in neutral Portugal and then channeled into London. Sweezy began working on the newsletter and turned it into a monthly magazine – called *The European Political Report* – that drew on an expanded range of sources. The newsletter took an explicitly New Deal-leftist, antifascist stance. Together with Franz Neumann, Sweezy wrote an important 1943 report of the OSS on the effects of "Speer's Appointment as Dictator of the German Economy" (Neumann and Sweezy 2013).

Sweezy reached the rank of second lieutenant and was awarded the Bronze Star Medal in 1946. The citation specified that the medal was for his role as editor of *The European Political*

Report. After the war, he received a Social Science Research Council Demobilization grant, which was designed to allow scholars who had been in the military to resume their research. He settled in Wilton, New Hampshire, and married Nancy Adams, his second wife, who he had met in London in 1944. They had three children: Samuel Everett (born 1946), Elizabeth (Lybess) MacDougall (born 1948) and Martha Adams (born 1951).

Despite more than two years left on his contract at Harvard, Sweezy decided to resign his position, recognizing that there was little chance in the rightward political climate of the time that he would receive tenure, notwithstanding Schumpeter's strong support. Instead, he devoted himself to independent research, churning out a wide array of publications, including his famous contribution to the debate on the transition from feudalism to capitalism, in which he questioned the argument offered in Maurice Dobb's *Studies in the Development of Capitalism* (Hilton 1976). Sweezy's position in this debate was widely recognized (see Hobsbawm 1964, 46) as adhering closely to Marx's original position but was nonetheless criticized by some orthodox Marxists as placing too much emphasis on the development of commercial capital. However, his most important and lasting influence on the general debate lay in his stress on the two phases of the dissolution of feudalism and of the formation of the system of capital accumulation – seen as representing two distinct problems for a general theory of transition (Wood 1999, 30–35).

On 27 March 1947, Sweezy (2011) engaged in the famous Sweezy-Schumpeter debate at Harvard "On the Laws of Capitalism" and economic stagnation. Recalling this debate, decades later Paul Samuelson (1972, 710), referred to Sweezy as a "young Galahad" opposed to Schumpeter's "the foxy Merlin." Sweezy, Samuelson wrote,

> was the best that Exeter and Harvard can produce . . . [and] had early established himself as among the most promising economists of his generation. . . . Unfairly, the gods had given Paul Sweezy, along with a brilliant mind, a beautiful face and wit. . . . If lightening had struck him that night people would truly have said that he had incurred the envy of the gods.

In 1948, Sweezy chaired the New Hampshire campaign of the Progressive Party, whose presidential candidate was former US vice president Henry A. Wallace.

Sweezy had long wanted to start a socialist political magazine. During the early post–Second World War years, he was in frequent contact with Leo Huberman, whom he had known since the 1930s. Huberman was an accomplished labor educator, journalist and writer of best-selling histories of economic development and labor struggles. The renowned Harvard professor of literature F.O. Matthiessen, who had recently inherited some money, offered Huberman and Sweezy $5,000 each year for three years in succession to start a magazine. The result was *Monthly Review: An Independent Socialist Magazine*, the first issue of which appeared in May 1949 with an article by Albert Einstein entitled "Why Socialism?" (Einstein 1949). Sweezy was to edit *Monthly Review*, one of the world's renowned socialist publications, until his death in 2004.

Sweezy's radical political and intellectual activities brought the full wrath of McCarthyism down on him. In January 1954, he was subpoenaed by New Hampshire Attorney General Louis C. Wyman, who was charged by the state legislature with investigating "subversive activities." Wyman focused on a lecture that Sweezy had delivered at the University of New Hampshire. He was called upon to answer questions on the content of his lecture, turn over his lecture notes, report on his political views and political activities, and name the names of others with whom he had been associated, including Communists, members of the Progressive Party and fellow travelers of Communism. Sweezy issued his own statement on freedom of speech that he read to the committee. Following the strategy proposed by Einstein of utilizing an aggressive First

Amendment defense (see Foster 2017, 23–24), Sweezy refused to turn over his lecture notes, to provide information on the contents of his teaching, or to name names. He also flatly refused comment on the views of others or to judge people on the basis of how they defended themselves. He insisted on the need and right of some individuals to utilize the protection against self-incrimination offered by the Fifth Amendment to the US Constitution, and supporting all of those who defended their civil liberties. He forcefully challenged the right of the inquisitors to persecute those simply pursuing their political freedoms. He was cited with contempt of court and consigned to county jail. His case was appealed and wound its way through the state and federal courts until *Sweezy vs. New Hampshire* was decided in favor of Sweezy by the US Supreme Court under Earl Warren, in June 1957, representing one of a number of key decisions that spelled the end of McCarthyism (U.S. Supreme Court 1957; Simon 2000).

Following the Cuban Revolution, Huberman and Sweezy traveled to Cuba and published *Cuba: Anatomy of a Revolution*, the first major work to explain the socialist nature of the Cuban Revolution (Huberman and Sweezy 1960). This helped shape *Monthly Review*'s major focus on supporting third world revolutions.

Monopoly Capital, Stagnation and Financialization

Throughout the 1950s and 1960s Sweezy worked very closely with Paul Baran, professor of economics at Stanford University, himself one of the leading Marxist economists in the post-1945 period. Baran and Sweezy's (1966) *Monopoly Capital: An Essay on the American Economic and Social Order* was published two years after Baran's death. *Monopoly Capital* was a synthesis and development of ideas contained in Sweezy's *Theory of Capitalist Development* and Paul Baran's no less influential work *The Political Economy of Growth* (1957). As Sweezy (1987) later put it,

> The central theme [of *Monopoly Capital*] is that in a mature capitalist economy dominated by a handful of giant corporations the potential for accumulation far exceeds the profitable investment opportunities provided by the normal *modus operandi* of the private enterprise system. This results in a deepening tendency to stagnation, which, if the system is to survive, must be continuously and increasingly counteracted by internal and external factors. . . . In the author's estimation – not always shared, or even understood by critics – the new and original contributions of *Monopoly Capital* had to do mainly with these counteracting factors and their far-reaching consequences for the history, politics and culture of American society during the period from roughly the 1890s to the 1950s when the book was written. They intended it, in other words, as much more than a work of economics in the usual meaning of the term.

The key analytical device that Baran and Sweezy brought to bear to address these countervailing factors was the examination of the generation and absorption of economic surplus – a concept modeled after Marx's surplus value and intended to complement it – but freed from the usual association of the latter exclusively with the notion of profits + rent + interest. The economic surplus concept, in its most developed definition, meant the difference between the income that could be generated with existing economic and technological means and the underlying costs of productive labor. This allowed Baran and Sweezy to "follow the money," that is, to ascertain the statistical traces of the surplus (and of value relations more generally) in the more convoluted economic formation of monopoly capital – as compared to its freely competitive predecessor. In a monopoly-capitalist society, prone to excess capacity and the stagnation of production and investment, and thus faced with a chronic problem of surplus capital absorption, various countervailing factors were necessary to prop up and perpetuate the system. It therefore became essential to explore the ways in which the sales effort, the state (including military spending), finance and other factors entered in to absorb the excess (non-investible) surplus, and the larger ramifications for a regime of capital that was increasingly irrational. Sweezy was later to carry this analysis forward in various ways, including exploring the relation of deepening stagnation to the process of maturity in capitalist economies (see Sweezy 1981a).

Monopoly Capital was enormously influential within radical political economy in the United States and globally in the 1960s and 1970s, giving rise to a whole new tradition of Marxian analysis, developing up the present day, focusing on the dialectical interconnections between the concentration and centralization of capital, monopolization, surplus capital absorption, economic stagnation tendencies, militarism and imperialism, and financialization. Baran and Sweezy's views represented the initial core of the political economy of the New Left in the United States with the rise of the Union for Radical Political Economics in 1968. With the return of economic crisis and stagnation in the 1970s, Sweezy and Harry Magdoff, who replaced Huberman as coeditor of *Monthly Review* in 1969, following the death of the latter, wrote a series of five books (Magdoff and Sweezy 1977, 1981, 1987, 1988; Sweezy and Magdoff 1972) addressing the problem of what they called "stagnation and the financial explosion," defining the accumulation process in advanced capitalism. It was out of this that most of the contemporary radical analysis of financialization arose. It was Sweezy (1997, 3) who first referred to "the financialization of the capital accumulation process," and to "the triumph of financial capital" (Sweezy 1994). As Costas Lapavitsas (2013, 15–16) has noted, "close association of financialization [theory] with Marxism goes back at least to the insights advanced by the current of *Monthly Review*."

The Great Financial Crisis of 2007–9 led to increased interest in *Monopoly Capital* and the critical tradition it had spawned. This was followed by the publication of the two missing chapters of *Monopoly Capital* – "Some Theoretical Implications" and "The Quality of Monopoly Capitalist Society: Culture and Communications" (Baran and Sweezy 2012, 2013) – both of which had been left out of the published book. Baran and Sweezy's correspondence while writing *Monopoly Capital* was published as *The Age of Monopoly Capital: Selected Correspondence of Paul Baran and Paul M. Sweezy, 1949–1964* (Baran and Sweezy 2017).

Sweezy's contributions to Marxian theory in the last quarter of the 20th century, beginning with the economic crisis of the early to mid-1970s, fanned out to take on an even wider set of issues, responding to what Eric Hobsbawm (1994, 401) called "The Landslide" that affected to varying degrees the economies on both sides of the Cold War divide. Sweezy engaged in debates with Charles Bettelheim and others *On the Transition from Capitalism to Socialism* (Sweezy and Bettelheim 1972) and *Post-Revolutionary Society* (Sweezy 1981b), eventually taking the position that Soviet-type societies had evolved into class societies of new, unstable type. Whether they would return to the socialist road or revert to the capitalist road was an open question, to be determined by the class struggle. Among his notable contributions in this period, Sweezy defended the labor theory of value in the face of neo-Ricardian economics (Sweezy 1984). He also wrote on "Capitalism and the Environment" (Sweezy 1989a). Much of his work, meanwhile, was directed to the exploring the theory of imperialism, in which he providing numerous pioneering contributions to the dependency, world system and the globalization debates (e.g., Sweezy 1989b).

In his *Four Lectures on Marxism* (1981a), Sweezy addressed such issues as Marxian dialectics, the historical contradictions of capital accumulation, the falling rate of profit theory, competition and monopoly, imperialism, and the crisis in Marxism. As he wrote in that work, he had at an early age

> acquired a mission in life, not all at once or self-consciously but gradually and through a practice that had a logic of its own. That mission was to do what I could to make Marxism an integral and respected part of the intellectual life of the country [in the United States], or, put in other terms, to take part in establishing a serious and authentic North American brand of Marxism.
>
> *(Sweezy 1981a, 13)*

There is no doubt that he succeeded in that endeavor. As Immanuel Wallerstein (2004, 126) wrote upon Sweezy's death,

> Through the whole second half of the twentieth century, Paul Sweezy has stood for one thing unflinchingly: a combination of sober, uncompromising analysis of the realities of the political economy of the world-system with a commitment to socialist transformation, without toeing anybody's party line. He showed that one could be on the left, and effectively, and still be consistently intellectually honest. It was a rare achievement that will continue to inspire us all.

Note

1. Much of the following discussion is adapted from two previous publications (Foster 2004, 2017a).

Bibliography

Baran, Paul A. 1973 (1957). *The Political Economy of Growth*. Harmondsworth: Penguin.

Baran, Paul A., and Paul M. Sweezy. 1966. *Monopoly Capital*. New York: Monthly Review Press.

Baran, Paul A., and Paul M. Sweezy. 2012. "Some Theoretical Implications." *Monthly Review* 64(3): 24–59.

Baran, Paul A., and Paul M. Sweezy. 2013. "The Quality of Monopoly Capitalist Society: Culture and Communications." *Monthly Review* 65(3): 43–64.

Baran, Paul A., and Paul M. Sweezy. 2017. *The Age of Monopoly Capital: Selected Correspondence, 1949–1964*, edited by Nicholas Baran and John Bellamy Foster. New York: Monthly Review Press.

Bortkiewicz, Ladislaus von. 1949. "On the Construction of Marx's Fundamental Theoretical Construction in the Third Volume of Capital." In Eugen von Böhm-Bawerk, *Karl Marx and the Close of His System and Rudolf Hilferding, Böhm-Bawerk's Criticisms of Marx*, edited by Paul M. Sweezy, 199–221. New York: Augustus M. Kelley.

Einstein, Albert. 1949. "Why Socialism?" *Monthly Review* 1(1): 9–15.

Foster, John Bellamy. 2004. "The Commitment of an Intellectual: Paul M. Sweezy (1910–2004)." *Monthly Review* 56(5): 5–39.

Foster, John Bellamy. 2017. "Introduction." In Paul A. Baran and Paul M. Sweezy, *The Age of Monopoly Capital: Selected Correspondence*, edited by Nicholas Baran and John Bellamy Foster, 13–48. New York: Monthly Review Press.

Hilton, Rodney, ed. 1976. *The Transition from Feudalism to Capitalism*. London: NLB.

Hobsbawm, E.J. 1964. "Introduction." In Karl Marx, *Pre-Capitalist Economic Formations*, edited by E.J. Hobsbawm, 9–65. New York: International Publishers.

Hobsbawm, Eric. 1994. *Age of Extremes, the Short Twentieth Century 1914–1991*. London: Abacus.

Huberman, Leo, and Paul M. Sweezy. 1960. *Cuba: Anatomy of a Revolution*. New York: Monthly Review Press.

Lapavitsas, Costas. 2013. *Profiting without Producing: How Finance Exploits Us All*. London: Verso.

Magdoff, Harry, and Paul M. Sweezy. 1977. *The End of Prosperity: The American Economy in the 1970s*. New York: Monthly Review Press.

Magdoff, Harry, and Paul M. Sweezy. 1981. *The Deepening Crisis of U.S. Capitalism*. New York: Monthly Review Press.

Magdoff, Harry, and Paul M. Sweezy. 1987. *Stagnation and the Financial Explosion*. New York: Monthly Review Press.

Magdoff, Harry, and Paul M. Sweezy. 1988. *The Irreversible Crisis*. New York: Monthly Review Press.
Neumann, Franz, and Paul M. Sweezy. 2013. "Speer's Appointment as Dictator of the German Economy." In Franz Neumann, Herbert Marcuse, and Otto Kirchheimer, *Secret Reports on Nazi Germany*, edited by Raffaele Laudani, 48–60. Princeton: Princeton University Press.
Samuelson, Paul A. 1972. *Collected Scientific Papers*. Vol. 3. Cambridge, MA: MIT Press.
Schumpeter, Joseph A. 1942. *Capitalism, Socialism, and Democracy*. New York: Harper and Row.
Schumpeter, Joseph A. 1954. *History of Economic Analysis*. Oxford: Oxford University Press.
Simon, John J. 2000. "Sweezy v. New Hampshire: The Radicalism of Principle." *Monthly Review* 51(11): 35–37.
Sweezy, Maxine Y. 1941. *The Structure of the Nazi Economy*. Harvard: Harvard University Press.
Sweezy, Paul M. 1938. *Monopoly and Competition in the English Coal Trade, 1550–1850*. Cambridge, MA: Harvard University Press.
Sweezy, Paul M. 1939a. "Interest Groups in the American Economy." In U.S. National Resources Committee, *The Structure of the American Economy*, Part I, 306–17. Washington, DC: U.S. Government Printing Office.
Sweezy, Paul M. 1939b. "Demand under Conditions of Oligopoly." *Journal of Political Economy* 47: 568–73.
Sweezy, Paul M. 1942. *The Theory of Capitalist Development*. Oxford: Oxford University Press.
Sweezy, Paul M. 1953. *The Present as History*. New York: Monthly Review Press.
Sweezy, Paul M. 1981a. *Four Lectures on Marxism*. New York: Monthly Review Press.
Sweezy, Paul M. 1981b. *Post-Revolutionary Society*. New York: Monthly Review Press.
Sweezy, Paul M. 1984. "Marxian Value Theory and Crisis." In *The Faltering Economy*, edited by John Bellamy Foster and Henryk Szlajfer, 236–50. New York: Monthly Review Press.
Sweezy, Paul M. 1987. "Paul A. Baran." In *New Palgrave Dictionary of Economics*, edited by John Eatwell, Murray Milgate, and Peter Newman. Vol. 1, 188–89. London: Macmillan and Co.
Sweezy, Paul M. 1989a. "Capitalism and the Environment." *Monthly Review* 41(2): 1–10.
Sweezy, Paul M. 1989b. "U.S. Imperialism in the 1990s." *Monthly Review* 41(5): 1–17.
Sweezy, Paul M. 1994. "The Triumph of Financial Capital." *Monthly Review* 46(2): 1–11.
Sweezy, Paul M. 1997. "More (or Less) on Globalization." *Monthly Review* 49(4): 1–4.
Sweezy, Paul M. 1998. "*The Communist Manifesto* Today." *Monthly Review* 50(1): 8–10.
Sweezy, Paul M. 2011. "The Laws of Capitalism." *Monthly Review* 63(1): 12–14.
Sweezy, Paul M., and Charles Bettelheim. 1972. *On the Transition to Socialism*. New York: Monthly Review Press.
Sweezy, Paul M., and Harry Magdoff. 1972. *The Dynamics of U.S. Capitalism*. New York: Monthly Review Press.
U.S. Supreme Court. 1957. *Sweezy v. New Hampshire*, October Term 1956, *U.S. Reports, 1957* (354 U.S. 234).
Wallerstein, Immanuel. 2004. "Memorial Statement on Paul Sweezy." *Monthly Review* 56(5): 126.
Wall Street Journal. 1972. "The Unorthodox Ideas of Radical Economists Win a Wider Hearing." (11 February).
Wood, Ellen Meiksins. 1999. *The Origin of Capitalism*. New York: Monthly Review Press.

51
KOZO UNO (1897–1977)

Ryuji Sasaki and Kohei Saito

Introduction

Japan is one of the few capitalist countries where Marxism became quite dominant in academia after World War II, and Kozo Uno is certainly the most famous Japanese Marxist.[1] His systematic (re)interpretation of Marx's *Capital* inspired younger generations and formed a big group, the so-called Uno School. The members of this School, such as Sigekatsu Yamaguchi and Makoto Itoh, held professorial positions in the department of economics at the University of Tokyo, developing Uno's economic system and reinforcing its influence in the Japanese academia of the 1970s and 1980s, and even overseas. In recent years, however, Uno's influence has been rapidly shrinking. In this chapter we examine the prosperity and decline of the Uno School against the backdrop of Uno's own economic system and methodology. We first sketch the formation of Uno's economic system with reference to particularities of pre-war Japanese Marxism to specify Uno's historical and intellectual background. Our focus is then Uno's famous "three-level theory" (*sandankairon*),[2] explaining the relationship between basic theory and stages theory as a radical attempt to reinterpret Marx's *Capital* and to provide an attractive alternative to the traditional Marxism. Finally, Uno's political economy will be critically examined to reveal its own internal inconsistencies as a cause of the recent decline of the Uno School.

The Emergence of Uno's Political Economy

The emergence of Uno's thought is closely connected to the problem of how to comprehend the specificity of Japanese capitalism as a late-developing capitalist nation in the imperialist era. After studying in Germany, Uno started teaching economic policy at University of Tohoku in 1924. He realized that there was an immense difficulty directly to apply Marx's *Capital* to reality, and even more to explain Japanese capitalism. At the time, the biggest debate in pre-war Japan, known as the "controversy over Japanese capitalism" (*Nihon Shihonshugi Ronso*), took place and split Marxists into two groups, *Kozaha* (Lectures Group) and *Ronoha* (Labour-Farmer Group). It was over the historical stage Japan was going through. Protected by the national isolation policy during the Edo period (1603–1868), Japan was swallowed up by the storm of capitalist globalization quite late. Once the modernization process started after the 1868 Meiji Restoration, however, capitalism rapidly developed and Japan became an imperialist nation with its own colonial policies. This unique mixture of late-development and imperialist policies brought about a great divergence between the pattern of Japanese modernization and the explanatory scheme of Marx's *Capital*.

In fact, pre-war Japan had a number of unique economic, political and social characteristics: the absolutist state system pivoted around the emperor, and the capitalist system was based on semi-feudal landed property, strong militarism, the persistence of feudal patriarchal households and the absence of democratic institutions. Japanese Marxists sought to analyze these characteristics in order to conceptualize the best socialist strategy. The *Kozaha* group mainly consisted of members of the Japanese Communist Party (JCP), who argued that the Meiji Restoration was not a bourgeois revolution because Japanese society still remained semi-feudal. This group regarded the characteristics mentioned earlier as proof that Japan was a "military semi-serfdom" type of capitalism. They concluded that a bourgeois democratic revolution was first necessary before a socialist revolution. The *Ronoha* group, consisted of socialists opposing the JCP such as Hitoshi Yamakawa and Itsuro Sakisaka. They believed that Japanese society was already capitalist, and that immediate socialist revolution was possible. The "residues" of feudalism would sooner or later be eradicated by the further development of capitalism.

However, even after the great defeat of Japanese imperialism in 1945 and the "democratization" under Allied occupation, the specificity of Japanese capitalism continued in the form of developmentalism (*Kaihatsushugi*), which prioritized state-led industrialization and economic growth over the realization of liberal-democratic ideals. This constrained the theory and practice of the left and reproduced earlier debates between JCP and anti-JCP socialists in postwar Japan.

The pre-war debates had been interrupted by state violence. Uno, though politically not active, was also arrested with members of *Ronoha* in 1938, as his commitment to *Ronoha* was suspected by the state authority, but he actually supported neither group. He was later acquitted. In his view, neither side questioned the *direct applicability* of Marx's analysis in *Capital* to Japanese society. They simply took for granted the unilinear development of modes of production, and ended up one-sidedly emphasizing either the feudal or the capitalist elements in Japanese society. Consequently, in Uno's view, the specificity of Japanese capitalism was neglected and buried under ideological claims. Uno believed it necessary to explain these ambivalences precisely as the specificity of Japanese capitalism. In his view, *Capital* alone was not enough as an explanatory tool because it only dealt with universal characteristics of the capitalist mode of production observed in Britain but late-developers such as the US, Germany and Japan did not follow the model of British capitalism. Since capitalism as a world system had then reached the imperialist stage, and Japanese capitalism did not exist independently of it, the binary opposition of capitalism and feudal residues around which the debate between *Kozaha* and *Ronoha* pivoted was false and infertile, and the conceptual mediation of the imperialist stage was, so Uno argued, indispensable for its adequate understanding.

Uno's Critique of Orthodox Marxism

In this context, what decisively distinguishes Uno from his later followers is his precise reading of *Capital*. It is not exaggerating to say that Uno was the only figure within the Uno School who actually struggled with *Capital* to understand Marx's *own* intentions. By doing so, Uno from the very beginning sought to liberate Marx's critique of political economy from any ideology and to (re-)establish it as the true theoretical foundation of "scientific socialism." His attempt caused a big "shock" among Marxists who treated *Capital* like a socialist bible because he was not hesitant to add "critiques" and "improvements" to Marx's theory. Uno was not intimidated by vehement critiques and aimed at scientific understanding of capitalism.

Until the 1960s, Marxist debates in Japan were heavily dependent on the political context and were gravely distorted by ideological factors that pivoted around the political strategy taken up by the Comintern and the JCP. In this context, Uno's determined attitude to separate "theory" and "practice," as well as "science" and "ideology," can be seen as an attempt to go beyond the ideological mindset of Japanese Marxism even by criticizing and radically reinterpreting Marx's *Capital*.

But why, despite his iconoclasm, did Uno's system of political economy become so influential? One of the reasons is that he offered an attractive alternative to Stalinism for the New Left. Indeed, Uno criticized Stalin in his article "Economic Laws and Socialism," which was published five years before Nikita Khrushchev's critique of Stalin in 1956. In the wake of the worldwide crisis of Marxism that followed, Uno's ideas increased their influence.

First of all, Uno argued that a theory of pure capitalism called "*genriron*" (basic theory) must be self-sufficient without any practical demands. But this claim is clearly incompatible with the "unity of theory and practice" characterizing orthodox Marxism (Lukács 1971, 3). Uno determinedly rejected this approach because, in his view, it was impossible mechanically to apply theory to reality. While natural sciences could be directly applied to reality, for Uno this was not possible in the case of political economy. This is not a minor point because Stalin (1972, 2), in contrast, argued that the laws of natural sciences and political economy are identical in nature. Uno contended that scientific investigations of political economy simply reveal the economic laws and movements of capitalism. This is certainly a presupposition for any practice because socialist movements first need to know what exactly needs to be overcome. However, the general character of basic theory does not tell what kind of concrete strategies and tactics are effective in changing situations. Furthermore, practice must not intervene in theory because of the risk that political ideologies and concrete strategies would be legitimized in the guise of "science," which was common in orthodox Marxism and ultimately led to the abuse of power by the CP under the terror of Stalinism.

Second, another dogma of orthodox Marxism was the correspondence of "history and logic," influenced by the dominant view of historical materialism propagated by Engels (1970, 225). Even Hilferding replied to anti-Marxist critics that the opening chapters of *Capital* volume 1 deal with pre-capitalist societies with simple commodity production where the law of value is valid, while the law of price and average profit in volume 3 applies in capitalist society. In this vein, Stalin (1972, 3, 5) maintained that the economic laws of commodity production, if properly recognized, can be consciously applied to realize human freedom, "whether in capitalism or in socialism." Uno (1958, 176), in contrast, insisted that the aim of recognizing the economic laws of capitalism through Marx's critique of political economy is to "get rid" of them and replace them with new laws. Here again, Uno distanced himself from Stalin's direct identification of the laws of natural sciences and social sciences. Restricting the task of basic theory to the analysis of pure capitalism, Uno intended to conduct a scientific investigation of the law of the capitalist economy free from Stalinist ideologies.

Finally, by distinguishing "science" and "ideology," Uno relativized the ideological understanding of capitalism developed under the political antagonism between the JCP and anti-JCP groups. In this vein, he strove to construct a neutral scientific system as a "pure" theory of capitalism by excluding "impure" historical factors that should be treated in stages theory. In this vein, Uno established a theoretical system that sought to explain the uniqueness of Japanese capitalism. Its key is his "three-level theory" (Uno 1980, xxii–xxiii), to which we now turn.

Uno's Three-Level Theory

The first stage of Uno's system is, as already pointed out, "basic theory," which deals with the essential and general characteristics of the capitalist mode of production. Marx wrote in the

Preface to the first edition of *Capital* volume I that he used the "power of abstraction" like the "physicist" who "makes experiments under conditions which ensure that the process will occur in its pure state" (*CI*: 90). This pure state of capitalism is not an arbitrary abstraction. Uno argued that capitalism possesses the historical tendency of real abstraction, actively subsuming and transforming its external environment according to the logic of pure capitalism.

Uno, however, lamented that Marx himself did not follow what he said in the Preface: Marx's *Capital* mixed up the general characteristics of capitalism and historical developments that are not essential to the capitalist mode of production as such. Uno thus proposed to refine Marx's *Capital* by excluding historical descriptions in order logically to deduce and order the essential categories and the general economic laws of pure capitalism. This reconstruction of *Capital* counts as *genriron*'s main task.

The history of capitalism, for Uno, is a real process in which this purifying tendency of capitalism imposes its economic laws on its environment. Yet, according to Uno, Marx believed too much in capitalism's power to transform the entire world into its pure state exemplified by 19th-century Britain. This helped explain why Marx was not able to predict the historical divergence of late-developing nations that did not follow the same path as British capitalism, forming a world system that cannot be explained by Marx's *Capital* alone.

Consequently, it is not possible directly to apply *genriron* to a concrete analysis of capitalism as world system. A mediating step is required, and this is the task of the second stage of Uno's three-level analysis, "stages theory" (*dankairon*): The historical stages of capitalism are divided by Uno into "mercantilism," "liberalism" and "imperialism," and the imperialist era diverges in several ways from Marx's assumptions about pure capitalism in *Capital*, which, according to Uno, only covers the period up to the liberal stage. Thus, before the concrete "empirical analysis" (*genjobunseki*), the third and last stage of Uno's theory, it is necessary to develop the particular historical characteristics of imperialist capitalism in addition to the mercantilist and liberal ones, distinguishing each historical stage carefully. In Uno's view, Marx was unable to develop a proper stages theory. This was inevitable because Marx could not witness the actual development of capitalism as a world system. As German and US capitalism clearly showed, however, the logic of pure capitalism does not fully penetrate into late-developing countries. According to Uno, Lenin's *Imperialism* and Hiferding's *Finance Capital* instead offered a theoretical foundation of his stages theory. Indeed, the reformism debate within the German Social Democratic Party initiated by Eduard Bernstein was due to the difficulty of explaining German capitalism and imperialism by mechanically applying Marx's theoretical scheme to reality.

Uno's Methodology in *Genriron*

It is now helpful to consider Uno's *genriron* in more detail. *Principles of Political Economy* consists of "doctrine of circulation," "doctrine of production" and "doctrine of distribution," reconstructing the three volumes of *Capital* as a whole. Uno's method (1980, xix) emphasizes the importance of "economic form-determinations" (*ökonomische Formbestimmungen*) such as "value," "commodity" and "money."[3] This emphasis is fully compatible with Marx's method, as the analysis of economic forms, in fact, represents a fundamental characteristic of Marx's critique of political economy.[4]

But the difference between Marx and Uno is also visible. One may be justified in wondering whether Marx's analysis of the "commodity" in the first chapter of *Capital* volume I could be reconstructed as "doctrine of *circulation*," when Marx apparently talked about "abstract labor" as the substance of value and "private labor" as the historical condition for the emergence of commodity production. Why did Uno omit Marx's theory of reification?

In his *Theory of Value*, Uno dealt with this problem of reification and actually showed a correct understanding of Marx's approach. That is, he treated value as the objectification of abstract human labor in a situation of commodity production where the social division of labor is based on the private labors of private individuals without any prior coordination (Uno 1965, 108). However, Uno intentionally excluded from his *genriron* Marx's explanation of "why" value and the value-form emerge together with private labor (*CI*: 168).

To understand why Uno omitted Marx's discussion of reification, we must turn to Uno's treatment of Marx's value-form theory. Marx's theory deals with the issue how commodities can express the pure social objectivity of value by relating themselves to another use-value and by bestowing on it an equivalent form. In the first chapter of *Capital* volume I, "The Commodity," Marx clearly assumed actual commodity exchanges, but left outside his observation the proprietors of commodities who carry out these exchanges. This is because Marx intended to reveal the structure of the "language of commodities" (i.e., the logic of the value form), which exists regardless of one's will and desire (*CI*: 143). In the first chapter Marx aimed at explaining respectively "why" and "how" this logic of value form comes to exist.[5] The task of chapter 2, "The Process of Exchange," is then to analyze how individuals with concrete desires and wills behave under these form-determinations. This is why Marx discussed the "commodity owners" in the second chapter for the first time (*CI*: 178), showing how their behaviors and wills are always already conditioned by the reified power of commodities and money. Joachim Hirsch (2005, 40) clearly emphasizes this point: "In acting under social relations, social forms determine a direction of the general and structural cognition and behavior that individuals follow."

Uno, however, intentionally blurred the unconscious dimension of reification and the dimension of human praxis involving will and desire. Consequently, Marx's reconstruction of the language of commodities disappears in Uno's value-form theory. Uno (1980, 6) instead argued that value-form theory is actually about how *humans* with desires, bestow the form determination of an "equivalent form" on the desired object based on their "subjective evaluation," an interpretation that dissolved the unconscious dimension of the value-form into the language of commodity owners. Uno believed that the dimension of human desire is indispensable for value-form theory because commodity exchange would not take place at all without it.

Such a reinterpretation of Marx's *Capital* caused heated debates, among which Kuruma Samezo's *Marx's Theory of the Genesis of Money* (2018), which defended Marx's original argument, is the most famous. In any case, if the value-form can be simply deduced from commodity exchange, it is not necessary to deal with the problem of "private labor" that produces the commodity form and with "abstract labor" as the substance of value. This is why part 1 of Uno's *genriron* omitted Marx's discussion of reification and of abstract labor, so that he could reinterpret part 1 of *Capital* volume I as the "doctrine of circulation," as if it had nothing to do with labor.

Accordingly, Uno displaced the demonstration of the labor theory of value to the "doctrine of production," part 2 of *genriron*, which starts with the category of capital. Since Uno excluded the substance of value in his analysis of the commodity, he discussed value determination in the production process as follows (1980, 25): Capitalist A produces commodities that are not means of subsistence, and Capitalist B produces means of subsistence. Capitalist A pays wages (i.e., the cost of reproduction of labor-power) to wage laborers who work under him. If they cannot attain what they need for living from Capitalist B with the wage that Capitalist A paid to them, the relationship of reproduction cannot be realized. Reproduction is possible only when the products of Capitalist A and Capitalist B are exchanged in proportion to the socially necessary labor time required to produce them, and thus value is regulated by socially necessary labor time.

Uno therefore assumed that the ratio of exchange is determined by the relationship of physical replacement, which results in the ratio of exchange based on labor time. This approach is similar to Piero Sraffa's deduction of prices from the physical conditions of production. While Sraffians even treat labor as a physical quantity in order to build a consistent system, Uno rather unconsciously brings in physical quantities despite his assumption of the labor theory of value. As long as Uno excluded Marx's theory of form-determination, in fact, he seemed obliged to make recourse to a Sraffian approach, which is incompatible with Marx's own method (Kliman 2007).

These theoretical divergences in Uno's *genriron* from Marx's *Capital*, in our view, do not simply arise from of his careless misunderstanding of *Capital*. They were rather a byproduct of his unique method of rigorously separating "basic theory" and "stages theory" and ascribing to the latter the role of comprehending the historical development of capitalism. Of course, any empirical analysis cannot be conducted on the basis of a mechanical application of the general theory of the capitalist mode of production as explicated in *Capital*; theoretical mediations are necessary. But the problem with Uno's three-level theory stems from his unique separation of "logic and history." As seen previously, Uno first excluded all historical factors from *Capital* and established a basic theory consisting of economic laws of capitalism with an appearance of eternity. He then proceeded to the stages theory referring to the basic theory as the "theoretical criterion" to judge what is pure and what is impure. Separated from the logical analysis of capitalism in *genriron*, stages theory becomes a "typological" treatment of historical specificities consisting of various combinations of impure factors in reality. As Uno (1959, 21) wrote:

> What stages theory reveals is a typological understanding in contrast to what basic theory reveals as laws. It does not consist in a logical development starting from the simplest category, but analyzes with the aid of basic theory the central capitalist nations and its international relations within the development of capitalism and reveals specificities that distinguish different stages of its historical development.

As Uno reduced the world of *Capital* into an eternal system governed by economic laws, he had strictly to separate basic theory from the theories investigating the specificities of a real world full of contradictions, treating them as analyses of impure factors independent of the "eternal" economic laws. *Genriron* almost disappears in stages theory.

In Uno's stages theory, for example, imperialist policy is not explained in terms of a policy response to the contradictions of capital accumulation, as in classics such as Hilferding's *Finance Capital*, but as statism resulting from an external relation between capitalism and some impure factors of pre-modern societies. In Uno's view, late developers such as Germany and the US could quickly introduce more advanced productive forces: finance capital liberated these nations to some extent from the burdens involved in large fixed capital-investments, so that they could maintain a relatively constant increase of productive forces. Consequently, so Uno argued, without thoroughly dissolving the old social relations in rural areas, these countries kept a large amount of relative surplus population, which became the condition for the accumulation of capital. The profitability of finance capital increased under the existence of a large surplus population and its power was transformed into political power, resulting in imperialist policies. Thus, Uno's stages theory does not explain imperialism from contradictions between the expansion of capitalist power, which was elucidated in *Capital*, and historical developments after Marx's death, but simply from "impure" factors such as the availability of developed productive forces, joint-stock companies and remnants of pre-capitalist social relations.

The fundamental problem of Uno's stages theory can be summarized as follows: what appear as "impure" historical factors in *Capital* are actually concrete examples of the entanglements of economic form-determinations and the material world, as well as their disruptions and contradictions. In Uno's basic theory, there are no wage-laborers who are exposed to extreme instability under the law of capitalist accumulation, or driven into small and dirty apartments. There is no disruption of the metabolism between humans and nature as a result of the increase in the productive forces, the degradation of living environment in the cities or soil exhaustion in the countryside. These factors are completely excluded from Uno's basic theory, which conceives economic laws of capitalism as eternal ones, as long as Uno set the task of *genriron* to grasp the laws of the "capitalist commodity-economy as if it were an eternal self-perpetuating entity" (Uno 1980, 125). Correspondingly, "persons" that appear in Uno's system are capitalist subjects who have internalized the market logic and rationality as the personified economic categories, namely, *homo economicus*. As a result, the world that Uno depicted turns out to be very similar to that of bourgeois economics.[6]

It is true that Uno did not completely neglect the contradiction between the commodity form and persons, and recognized the "impossibility" of the commodification of labor-power (Uno 1953, 82, 99). Differently from Lukács (1971, 166), however, Uno views the contradiction in the commodification of labor simply as meaning that labor-power is a unique commodity that cannot be reproduced through the production process of capital. This contradiction does not lead to any radical transformation of the capitalist mode of production, but can rather be always resolved through periodic economic crises. For Uno (1953, 77), moreover, such economic crises occurred thanks to wage-increases. In other words, in Uno's *genriron* crisis is a manifestation of the periodical self-regulating mechanism of the capitalist mode of production: it never points to the historical destiny of capitalism. The capitalist mode of production is instead an eternal system with periodical business cycles, so ultimately it is a world of general equilibrium.

Since *genriron* does not provide tools for analyzing the specificities of institutions and policies that mediate these disruptions and contradictions, stages theory falls into a typological theory, which explains capitalist historical development simply by juxtaposing various policies and institutions. In Uno's interpretation, therefore, Marx's theory becomes a form of institutionalism.

Conclusion

As seen previously, Uno's three-level theory was pathbreaking as a critique of traditional Marxism in the 1960s and 1970s, providing an explanation to the particularity of Japanese capitalism and an alternative version of Marxism to the Stalinist one. It encounters new problems today, however. Uno's three-level theory was based on his insight that capitalism's power of penetrating into the material world is limited. Since pure capitalism would not exist, stages theory was supposed to examine impure factors under the capitalist world system. Yet as the reified power of capital increases under neoliberal globalization, "pure" capitalism seems to dominate all over the world. Nevertheless, in contrast to Uno's "pure" capitalism without contradictions, we live in a world full of violent exploitation of human life-power and destruction of nature. It is no coincidence that Marx's *Capital* attracts younger generations, while Uno's influence is declining because people are looking for principles of political economy that can explain the contradictions and disruptions of reality. Neither the capitalist world without contradictions in basic theory nor the typological ordering of capitalist societies in stages theory functions as an effective tool to analyze them.

Notes

1. This work was supported by JSPS Kakenhi Grant Number JP18K12188.
2. For recent discussions in English, see The Uno Newsletters (http://unotheory.org/).

3. Thomas Sekine, the translator of Uno's book, avoided translating the term "Bestimmung," which inevitably obscures Uno's (and Marx's) intentions.
4. For the concept of "economic form determination," see Heinrich (2012, 40–41).
5. As Lange (2014) argues, Samezo Kuruma offered a comprehensive critique of Uno with this distinction of "how, why, and through what."
6. This tendency becomes more apparent in the "Uno-Sekine approach." John R. Bell (2009, 8) writes: "We first 'one-dimensionalize' human beings, reducing them to Homo economicus (or to the capitalist as the personification of capital)." He even claims: "The law of value, by far the most important component of the definition of capitalism by capital itself, cannot be adequately accounted for in the absence of a general equilibrium of the capitalist economy" (140).

Bibliography

Bell, John R. 2009. *Capitalism and the Dialectic: The Uno-Sekine Approach to Marxian Political Economy*. London: Pluto.

Engels, Friedrich. 1970 (1859). "Karl Marx: *A Contribution to the Critique of Political Economy*," appendix to Karl Marx, *A Contribution to the Critique of Political Economy*, 218–27. New York: International.

Heinrich, Michael. 2012. *An Introduction to the Three Volumes of Karl Marx's Capital*. New York: Monthly Review Press.

Hirsch, Joachim. 2005. *Materialistische Staatstheorie: Transformationsprozesse des kapitalistischen Staatensystems*. Hamburg: VSA Verlag.

Kliman, Andrew. 2007. *Reclaiming Marx's "Capital:" A Refutation of the Myth of Inconsistency*. Lanham, MD: Lexington Books.

Kuruma, Samezo. 2018. *Marx's Theory of the Genesis of Money*. Leiden: Brill.

Lange, Elena Luisa. 2014. "Failed Abstraction: The Problem of Uno Kozo's Reading of Marx's Theory of the Value Form." *Historical Materialism* 22(1): 3–33.

Lukács, Georg. 1971. *History and Class Consciousness: Studies in Marxist Dialectics*. Cambridge: The MIT Press.

Stalin, J.V. 1972. *Economic Problems of Socialism in the U.S.S.R.* Peking: Foreign Language Press.

Uno, Kozo. 1953. *Kyokoron* [Theory of Crisis]. Tokyo: Iwanami Shoten.

Uno, Kozo. 1958. *"Shihonron" to Syakaisyugi* [Capital and Socialism]. Tokyo. Iwanami Shoten.

Uno, Kozo. 1959. *Marx Keizaigaku Genriron no Kenkyu* [A Study on Marx's Principles of Political Economy]. Tokyo: Iwanami Shoten.

Uno, Kozo. 1965. *Kachiron* [Theory of Value]. Tokyo: Aoki Shoten.

Uno, Kozo. 1980. *Principles of Political Economy: Theory of a Purely Capitalist Society*. Sussex: Harvester.

52

HARRY BRAVERMAN (1920–76)

Brett Clark and Stefano B. Longo

Harry Braverman, who in his younger years worked as a coppersmith and then as a pipefitter, was a devoted socialist, political economist and writer. During the era of McCarthyism and the Red Scare, from the late 1940s through the 1950s, Braverman often wrote articles, under the pseudonym Harry Frankel, for socialist publications. In 1953, he helped found and edit *The American Socialist*, where he provided an insightful analysis of labor and class in relation to the capitalist mode of production. He insisted that Marxism is "a broad theory of social development," necessitating an open-ended analysis, enriched by "application and re-interpretation in every period" (Braverman 1956). He demonstrated as much with his pathbreaking book, *Labor and Monopoly Capital: The Degradation of Work in the Twentieth Century*, first published in 1974.

A central goal of Braverman's work was to analyze and explain the principal causes of the relentless transformation of the labor process prevailing in the modern era. Prior to *Labor and Monopoly Capital*, conventional and liberal scholarship on work and labor often proposed that industrialization, rather than capitalism, defined the historic period associated with the rise of wage-labor; that technological innovation was socially neutral in its deployment and consequences or that its development increased the overall skills of workers; that the increase in wealth had enhanced the well-being of the general public; and that power had become more dispersed throughout society (Blauner 1964; Kerr et al. 1969). Braverman systematically overturned these presumptions, offering a historically rich analysis of the labor process itself in relation to the development of the capital system. In doing this, he stripped away the veil shrouding the hidden abode of work, in order to examine the dynamic relations of production and the organization of work, struggles between capital and labor, control over the labor process, the cheapening of labor, the deepening polarization between classes and the continuing alienation that characterized capitalist social relations.

The Division of Labor and the Labor Process

In volume 1 of *Capital*, Marx explained that "labor . . . is a condition of human existence which is independent of all forms of society; it is an eternal natural necessity which mediates the metabolism between man and nature, and therefore human life itself" (CI: 133). Likewise, Braverman (1998, 316–17) pointed out that "humanity is a working species," which must interact with the larger biophysical environment in order to acquire and produce the goods necessary to reproduce itself. Work was also recognized as an activity that could enhance human development. But, following Marx, he also stressed that the specific character and organization of work, and its potential to enrich human lives, is determined by distinct historical modes of production. Thus, any analysis of work in modern society must consider how the prevailing system of production – the capital system – has transformed labor, the labor process and production. Braverman demonstrated that the social system primarily served the needs of capital, fostering the accumulation of capital, rather than enhancing the human condition. Thus, the potential for human development is conceded to the dictates and criteria of market processes.

As an astute student of human history, Braverman understood that unequal power relations and social stratification were not unprecedented social phenomena. Earlier human civilizations involved production, commodities, exchange and divisions of labor, often between men and women, which had unequal consequences across various social divisions. What distinguished capitalism, according to Braverman (1998, 35–36), was the specific form related to "the purchase and sale of labor power." In order for this condition to arise, workers were increasingly divorced from the means of production, which included the dismantling of legal constraints associated with serfdom, forcing them to sell their labor power, in order to earn wages to then purchase the means of subsistence. Additionally, the central goal under this system was "the expansion of a unit of capital belonging" to the capitalist. Thus, the labor process itself became "a process of accumulation of capital," associated with a distinct hierarchical division of labor.

As Marx (1977) presented in *Wage-Labor and Capital*, workers sell their capacity to labor for a specific amount of time. Braverman (1998, 6, 39–40) explained that in this arrangement, "*the labor process has become the responsibility of the capitalist*," resulting in an antagonistic relationship. Capitalists assumed responsibility to manage the labor process, trying to organize the conditions in a manner that allowed for the continual enlargement of surplus, which resulted in the "*progressive alienation of the process of production*" from workers. He stressed that Marx keenly recognized that the incessant drive to expand the accumulation of capital led to constant transformations in production processes.

In *Labor and Monopoly Capital*, Braverman provided an extensive analysis of the historical development of the labor process. Early capitalist production, such as "putting out" systems, lacked regulation, coordination and predictability. Gradually, capital centralized production, allowing greater control over the process, such as the hours worked. In large industrial operations, capital progressively engaged in an "*analysis of the labor process*," which involved examining each step in the production process (Braverman 1998, 49–55). While the division of labor is common in all societies, Braverman stressed, "the division of labor in the workshop is the special product of capitalist society." As the scale of production increased, capital subdivided the labor process, assigning specific tasks to different workers, with the intent to reduce the labor time – and the wages – associated with each step. These moves broke up the production process. Rather than having workers with specialized skills, who influenced the form and manner of production, capital exerted control over it, "destroying the craft." Workers were dismembered, rendered interchangeable, reduced to detailed assignments or tedious tasks.

In his book, *On the Economy of Machinery and Manufactures*, Charles Babbage (1835) explained that capital benefitted greatly by subdividing the labor process, as this cheapened the costs of each step. In other words, simplification lowered the costs of purchasing labor power. The consequence, Braverman (1998, 57–58) indicated, was that

> every step in the labor process is divorced, so far as possible, from special knowledge and training reduced to simple labor. Meanwhile, the relatively few persons for whom special knowledge and training are reserved are freed so far as possible from the

> obligations of simple labor. In this way, a structure is given to all labor processes that at its extreme polarizes those whose time is infinitely valuable and those whose time is worth almost nothing.

The next significant transformation of the labor process involved the application of scientific management under monopoly capitalism. Extending Paul Baran and Paul Sweezy's (1966) analysis of monopoly capital, Braverman explained that in the late 19th century, giant corporations became the dominant economic organizations, creating an opportunity for the generalization of systemic, large-scale management of the entire production process to maximize surplus potential. Braverman documented the central role that Frederick Winslow Taylor played in developing and applying scientific management as a means to coordinate and control the labor process, which contributed to a vast extension in the division of labor. At various plants, Taylor analyzed in detail every step in the labor process, with the intent to establish exact precision in how every action was performed. He desired to eliminate rest and ease – and unnecessary movements – on the part of workers, in order to increase overall productivity performance. He established three guiding principles. The first principle is the "*dissociation of the labor process from the skills of the workers*" (Braverman 1998, 77–78). Managers collected all information regarding knowledge, techniques and skills related to work, which workers had traditionally known and applied to their trades. Then the labor process was examined to determine shortcuts and efficient techniques used in production. The result was that the labor process was no longer reliant upon the knowledge of workers, but on the decisions of management. The second principle is "*the separation of conception from execution*" (Braverman 1998, 78–80). Taylor fully embraced the Babbage principle to subdivide the labor process into small, detailed operations. Management dictated what was produced, how it was produced, and how many were produced within a given time period. Taylor proposed that all "brain work" on the part of the workers should be eliminated, which Braverman contended resulted in the "dehumanization of the labor process." Under such conditions, the workers were easier to train and could produce more, decreasing overall labor costs and increasing surplus. These steps lead to the third principle, which is the "*use of this monopoly over knowledge to control each step of the labor process and its mode of execution*" (Braverman 1998, 82–3).

The consequences of the scientific management of the labor process were extensive. Capital gained greater control over working time and the labor process, enhancing profits. As the labor process was simplified, capital was more readily able to mechanize production, so long as management was able to maintain tight control over operations and increase overall productivity. In this, technological development was not neutral, as it always took place within a specific social-historical context, which shaped its deployment. Craftsmanship was increasingly displaced, undermining a broad range of skills and knowledge among laborers. As a result, workers were dislocated, lowering labor costs, and could be more easily treated as if they were simply machines. They became more alienated from the labor process, the decisions being made regarding production, and the science and technologies employed. Braverman highlighted how all of these historic changes in the labor process contributed to the degradation of work, as experienced by the working class.

Braverman (1998, 96) proposed that the general tendencies that he documented regarding the labor process under monopoly capital were "continually extended to new areas of work." He demonstrated as much in his detailed discussion of clerical work, and its historical shift from a predominately male profession to a female one, as scientific management was applied in order to break apart the specialized tasks, to establish control over the labor process and to cheapen labor (Braverman 1998, 205–11, 217–26, 231–35). Computing helped mechanize some areas of clerical work. As the labor process was simplified and the volume of work increased, more demands were placed on clerical workers to be efficient task masters. "Secretarial work," while vital to operations, was deemed "wasteful" by those who occupied the top positions in the hierarchy of labor.

Labor and Monopoly Capital renewed interest in studies of the labor process. It stimulated debates regarding work and its relationship to capital, technology, culture and ideological conditions. Braverman was criticized for proposing a unilinear trend toward deskilling – a term he did not actually employ (Aronowitz 1978). In the closing chapter, "A Final Note on Skill," Braverman explained that the average level of skill and knowledge in society had increased, but it was increasingly concentrated in the hands of fewer people and embedded in machines. For the majority of society, skills were declining, as most training took place on the job. Braverman (1998, 307) described that

> with the development of the capitalist mode of production, the very concept of skill becomes degraded along with the degradation of labor and the yardstick by which it is measured shrinks to such a point that today the worker is considered to possess a "skill" if his or her job requires a few days' or weeks' training, several months of training is regarded as unusually demanding, and the job that calls for a learning period of six months or a year – such as computer programming – inspires a paroxysm of awe.

This brief training stood in stark contrast to the years of teaching associated with craft apprenticeships. Braverman recognized that class struggle, innovations and contradictions influence the labor process and its reorganization. At the same time, he identified a specific tendency regarding the division of labor and the labor process given the logic capital, especially during the era of monopoly capital.

Monopoly Capital, Marketing and the Universal Market

Braverman made a significant contribution to the monopoly capital tradition, as a systematic assessment of the historical development of the modern labor process had not been done. Throughout much of the book, he considered how the period of monopoly capital influenced the general operations of the economy and society as a whole. The increasing scale of commodity production and the mechanization of the labor process amplified concerns regarding the realization of surplus value (Baran and Sweezy 1966). Modern corporations had developed sophisticated structures of management of the labor process, but they also took on tasks associated with marketing and social coordination. Braverman (1998, 184–86) explained that these steps were undertaken to try to reduce uncertainty. As a result, marketing became a central component of monopoly capital, trying to induce demand for commodities.

As Thorstein Veblen (1923, 305–6) described,

> the fabrication of customers can now be carried on as a routine operation, quite in the spirit of the mechanical industries and with much the same degree of assurance as regards the quality, rate and volume of output; the mechanical equipment as well as its complement of man-power employed in such production of customers being held to its work under the surveillance of technically trained persons who might fairly be called publicity engineers."

Veblen indicated that corporations preyed upon the emotions of the public to expand sales, as part of a "covert regime." Further, John Kenneth Galbraith (1958) determined that monopoly capital, through its control of production and sales effort, exercised "producer sovereignty," dominating both production and consumption.

Advancing this analysis, Braverman (1998, 185) noted how marketing considerations were being incorporated into production, as far as design and packaging. Furthermore, marketing played an essential role in managing the attitudes and actions of the public, especially in light of planned obsolescence, whereby products are designed with a limited life, in order to increase overall consumption of commodities. He stressed that marketing is a fundamental part of organizing the public to the needs of the capital, and thus labor and production systems. Building on Braverman's argument, Michael Dawson (2003), in *The Consumer Trap*, examined how the expansion of marketing operations, which followed on the heels of Taylor's scientific management, operated as a force of class coercion. Marketing was a systematic effort by monopoly capital to direct the larger population, when they had "free time" away from work – which had become increasingly alienating and therefore unfulfilling – back to the market to spend their wages, with proposed promises of gratification through the purchase of commodities. Within his discussion of marketing, Dawson highlighted how the production of high-quality, durable goods would increase production costs, decrease overall sales since items would last longer, and reduce profits. Thus, monopoly capital thrived off of the production of low-quality, disposable commodities, which the workers produced in increasingly controlled, mechanized and deskilled environments – only to then be encouraged to purchase these items with the wages they earned.

In his analysis of "The Universal Market," Braverman (1998, 188–96) powerfully presented the penetration and expansion of capital into everyday life, whereby "the capitalist mode of production [under monopoly capital] takes over the totality of individual, family, and social needs and, in subordinating them to the market, also reshapes them to serve the needs of capital." He insisted that in order to comprehend modern society, it was necessary to address "how capitalism transformed all of society into a gigantic marketplace." Throughout much of human history, families engaged in a broad array of self-provisioning or communal exchanges to sustain themselves. Braverman pointed out that even during the early periods of capitalism, families met many of their own productive needs. Nevertheless, the historical tendencies accompanying capitalist development progressively dismantled these conditions and operations. The privatization of land and increasing urbanization of the human population made it increasingly impossible to maintain self-provisioning. The industrialization of food production and other household commodities lowered prices, which led "to the dependence of all social life, and indeed of all interrelatedness of humankind, upon the marketplace." Braverman detailed how the commodity form expanded into new realms, including "recreation, amusement, security, for the care of the young, the old, the sick, the handicapped," substituting what was previous produced or provided by individuals, households and communities. He proposed that before long the capitalist market was going to offer a broad range of services, including those that addressed emotional needs, seemingly becoming indispensable as conditions of modern life. While the expansion of the capital system created a "total dependence on the market," Braverman importantly stressed that this also meant that "all work is carried on under the aegis of capital and is subject to its tribute of profit to expand capital still further." He emphasized that this resulted in a greater portion of the population experiencing dehumanizing and degrading forms of work.

Contemporary Integration of Braverman's Analysis

In the forty-plus years since the publication of Braverman's *Labor and Monopoly Capital*, there is much that needs to be accounted for as far as changes in the labor process, management practices, technological developments and the capital system itself. At the same time, many scholars continue to demonstrate the importance of Braverman's analysis. In recent times, it is important to continue the analysis of the dynamics that Braverman described, where the increasing immizeration of workers often occurs outside the view of those gaining the most benefits from the processes driving the universal market. For example, R. Jamil Jonna (2015) reveals how Braverman's discussion of the degradation of labor under monopoly capitalism serves as a foundation for understanding the precariousness of workers and the internationalization of production. While not explicitly referencing Braverman, John Smith (2016), in *Imperialism in the Twenty-First Century*, provides a powerful account of how the simplification and control of the labor process undergirds the global labor arbitrage – the system of differential rates of exploitation in the hierarchy of nations that leads to the massive transfer of surplus from the Global South to the North. His work clearly depicts the degradation of labor that is associated with producing commodities – such as clothing, phones and food – which are destined to be consumed in the North, but are linked directly to the super-exploitation of workers in the South.

Important work has extended Braverman's argument to show how it is useful for understanding the historical decomposition and recomposition of the working class, and how this relates to precariousness among workers (Jonna and Foster 2014). In regard to the global digital economy, Ursula Huws (2003, 2014), drawing upon Braverman, examines the ways that so-called high-tech jobs were eventually restructured and fragmented to impose greater control and exploitation of these workers. She also considers how capital has been able to extend the commodification process to new realms through mobile devices and social networking.

While Braverman has been acknowledged as making an important contribution to feminist analysis, his work could be further enriched through serious engagement with social reproduction theory (Baxandall et al. 1976). As Nancy Fraser (2016, 102) explains, "social reproduction is an indispensable background condition for the possibility of economic [commodity] production in a capitalist society," where social reproduction and economic production are constituted as separate spheres. Here the dialectical relationship between expropriation and exploitation could be addressed more broadly, recognizing how social reproductive work within the household has played an important role in decreasing the value of labor and promoting the realization of surplus value (Chattopadhyay 1999; Foster and Clark 2018; Fraser 2014, 2017).

Another promising direction, as far as extending Braverman's analysis is concerned, is in the realm of ecological Marxism. John Bellamy Foster (1994), in *The Vulnerable Planet*, proposed that the degradation of labor also involved a similar process in regard to nature, as capital imposed its management strategies on the world as a whole to facilitate the accumulation of capital. This notion has become increasingly important, when considering that Marx defined labor as a metabolic relationship between humans and nature. Recent scholarship, which has been inspired by Marx and Braverman, examines how the capital system, with its distinct organization of the labor process, is creating metabolic rifts in natural cycles and process, leading to the spoliation of the Earth system (Foster 2000; Foster et al. 2010; Longo et al. 2015).

Conclusion

Braverman's *Labor and Monopoly Capital* helped revolutionize Marxist scholarship of the labor process and it continues to serve as a rich foundation for contemporary scholarship. His dialectical, historical-materialist method revealed important tendencies related to the development of monopoly capital, such as the overall degradation of work for the vast majority of humanity, which has resulted in extreme polarization between the classes. He remained steadfast that it is the conditions imposed by the capitalist mode of production that are the central causes of these social developments. Similar to Marx, Braverman contends that work needs to be liberated from the constraints of capital, which will allow for it to be a process that can facilitate human development, meet human needs and employ technology in a way that expands the realm of freedom (see also Foster 2017; Lebowitz 2006; Magdoff 1982). In this, work becomes meaningful and rewarding.

Bibliography

Aronowitz, Stanley. 1978. "Marx, Braverman, and the Logic of Capital." *Insurgent Sociologist* 8(2–3): 126–46.

Babbage, Charles. 1835. *On the Economy of Machinery and Manufactures*. 4th edn. London: Charles Knight.

Baran, Paul A., and Paul M. Sweezy. 1966. *Monopoly Capital*. New York: Monthly Review Press.

Baxandall, Rosalyn, Elizabeth Ewen, and Linda Gordan. 1976. "The Working Class Has Two Sexes." *Monthly Review* 28(3): 1–9.

Blauner, Robert. 1964. *Alienation and Freedom*. Chicago: University of Chicago Press.

Braverman, Harry. 1956. "Which Way to a New American Radicalism?" *The American Socialist* (April).

Braverman, Harry. 1998 (1974). *Labor and Monopoly Capital: The Degradation of Work in the Twentieth Century*. New York: Monthly Review Press.

Chattopadhyay, Paresh. 1999. "Women's Labor Under Capitalism and Marx." *Bulletin of Concerned Asian Scholars* 31(4): 67–75.

Dawson, Michael. 2003. *The Consumer Trap: Big Business Marketing in American Life*. Urbana: University of Illinois Press.

Foster, John Bellamy. 1994. *The Vulnerable Planet*. New York: Monthly Review Press.

Foster, John Bellamy. 2000. *Marx's Ecology*. New York: Monthly Review Press.

Foster, John Bellamy. 2017. "The Meaning of Work in a Sustainable Society." *Monthly Review* 69(4): 1–14.

Foster, John Bellamy, and Brett Clark. 2018. "Women, Nature, and Capital in the Industrial Revolution." *Monthly Review* 69(8): 1–24.

Foster, John Bellamy, Brett Clark, and Richard York. 2010. *The Ecological Rift*. New York: Monthly Review Press.

Fraser, Nancy. 2014. "Behind Marx's Hidden Abode: For an Expanded Conception of Capitalism." *New Left Review* 86: 55–72.

Fraser, Nancy. 2016. "Contradictions of Capital and Care." *New Left Review* 100: 99–117.

Fraser, Nancy. 2017. "Crisis of Care? On the Social-Reproductive Contradictions of Contemporary Capitalism." In *Social Reproduction Theory*, edited by Tithi Bhattacharya, 21–36. London: Pluto.

Galbraith, John Kenneth. 1958. *The Affluent Society*. Boston: Houghton Mifflin.

Huws, Ursula. 2003. *The Making of a Cybertariat: Virtual Work in a Real World*. New York: Monthly Review Press.

Huws, Ursula. 2014. *Labor in the Global Digital Economy: The Cybertariat Comes of Age*. New York: Monthly Review Press.

Jonna, R. Jamil. 2015. "Monopoly Capital and Labor: The Work of Braverman, Baran, and Sweezy as a Dialectical Whole." *Labor Studies Journal* 40(3): 262–74.

Jonna, R. Jamil, and John Bellamy Foster. 2014. "Beyond the Degradation of Labor: Braverman and the Structure of the U.S. Working Class." *Monthly Review* 66(5): 1–23.

Kerr, Clark, John T. Dunlop, Frederick Harbison, and Charles A. Myers. 1969. *Industrialism and Industrial Man: The Problems of Labor and Management in Economic Growth*. Cambridge, MA: Harvard University Press.

Lebowitz, Michael A. 2006. *Build It Now: Socialism for the Twenty-First Century*. New York: Monthly Review Press.

Longo, Stefano B., Rebecca Clausen, and Brett Clark. 2015. *The Tragedy of the Commodity*. New Brunswick: Rutgers University Press.

Magdoff, Harry. 1982. "The Meaning of Work." *Monthly Review* 34(5): 1–15.

Marx, Karl. 1977 (1849). "Wage Labor and Capital." In *MECW* 9: 197–228.

Smith, John. 2016. *Imperialism in the Twenty-First Century*. New York: Monthly Review Press.

Veblen, Thorstein. 1923. *Absentee Ownership and Business Enterprise in Recent Times*. New York: B.W. Huebsch, Incorporated.

53
RUY MAURO MARINI (1932–97)

Marcelo Dias Carcanholo and Hugo F. Corrêa

Ruy Mauro Marini was a Brazilian Marxist intellectual, well known up to the present for the role he played in the conception and development of dependency theory. Marini was born in Barbacena (in the state of Minas Gerais, Brazil) in 1932 and died in 1997, in Rio de Janeiro. He was never exclusively an academic or an activist, in the strict sense of the term. Maybe this is the reason why it is impossible fully to understand his theoretical thinking without considering his life history, which perfectly illustrates the history of postwar Latin America: first, the hope founded initially on a belief in development (through industrialization policies) and subsequently on a belief in the growing political rise of the left (whose heyday was the Cuban Revolution); later with the disappointment originating from the reorganization and violent repression promoted by the local bourgeoisies, which often took the form of authoritarian governments and in every case was momentarily successful in stifling the struggles in favor of social change.

A Latin American Marxist in the Era of Military Juntas

Marini moved to Rio de Janeiro at the age of 18, in 1950. There he studied Law at the University of Brazil and subsequently joined the Brazilian School of Public Administration. It was there also that he met the development sociologist Guerreiro Ramos, whose support would be crucial for the completion of his studies in France (between 1958 and 1960), where he had, among others, Charles Bettelheim and Maurice Merleau-Ponty as professors. Marini's academic education would be substantially influenced by the major repercussion that the Cuban Revolution had in France (where he was living at the time), and by the movement of renewal of Marxist thinking, critical of Soviet Marxism.

Back in Brazil, Marini helped found the POLOP (Marxist Revolutionary Organization – Worker's Politics) and started a career as a journalist, which he pursued until in 1962 he moved to Brasilia to join the recently launched University of Brasilia (UnB). There he would resume his studies on his doctorate, would start his career as a university professor, side by side with prominent figures in what would become dependency theory (as is particularly the case with Theotônio dos Santos, Vânia Bambirra and Andre Gunder Frank) and would maintain his militant activities until the political changes in Brazil brought about by the military dictatorship that swept the country in 1964, made such a trajectory impossible. This is the point where Marini's political biography and the history of Latin America find an interesting convergence. Politically active and teaching in the federal capital in 1964, Marini – like many other former professors of UnB – was targeted by the military in one of their first acts. Two arrests and some months of clandestinity later, Marini would travel to Mexico, destination of his first exile.

Marini's first stay in Mexico would be shortened, however, due to the atmosphere that prevailed in the continent. During this first stay, Marini could, like many other political exiles, test an alternative interpretation to the current explanations of the military coup in Brazil, one that did not ignore the role played by the United States and its foreign policy in the Brazilian political situation but did not privilege the external intervention as a simple exercise of arbitrariness, alien to the national reality. It tried to integrate the different factors into a single argument, whose deep roots lay in the national socio-economic structure itself.[1] The article that resulted from this effort was published in the North American journal *Monthly Review* in 1965 under the title "Brazilian 'interdependence' and imperialist integration" and was of fundamental importance in emphasizing the process of formation of social classes in dependent countries and in pointing critically to the nature of the relations sustained by Brazil in the Latin American continent. Marini here discussed for the first time what he called Brazilian sub-imperialism, a reflection of the development of Brazilian capitalism, whose exact expression was in the developmentalist ideology sustained by the military regime.

In this period, Marini also wrote his first influential book, *Subdesarrollo y revolución*, published with great success in Mexico in 1969 and disseminated immediately in several European countries, but banned in Argentina and Brazil. However, a short journalistic article of much less repercussion would turn out to be decisive in Marini's personal trajectory. This article dealt with Brazilian student movements and was coincidentally published in a context of serious social unrest initiated by Mexican students. This conflict would have its climax in the Tlatelolco massacre (2 October 1968), in which it is estimated that hundreds of students and civilians were assassinated by official repression and thousands of arrests were made. The article ended up by shaping Marini's destiny, as he was forced to renounce his condition of political exile in Mexico and leave the country in 1969.

Marini would live through his second exile in Chile, together with many other political exiles. There he experienced a moment of great intellectual and political effervescence with the creation of the *Unidad Popular*, a leftist political front that would elect Salvador Allende president of Chile the following year. Between 1969 and 1973, the period of his Chilean exile, Marini devoted most of his time to his activities of research and teaching at CESO (Center for Economic-Social Studies of the University of Chile) and to his militant activities with the MIR (Movement of the Revolutionary Left). Although Marini himself considered that his written production had been seriously affected by the dedication he showed in that context to his activities as a militant and a professor, it was during this period that he wrote his best-known book, *Dialéctica de la dependencia*, which had its origin in a course on Marxist theory and Latin American reality taught at CESO. The final text had as its hallmark a theoretical synthesis of Marini's activism: an original theoretical rejection of developmentalism (which saw industrialization as the way out of underdevelopment) and of Soviet Marxism (that still supported a stages strategy and the thesis of the alliance of classes in favor of a bourgeois revolution). At the same time, Marini concludes the book with a revolutionary call, which was not to be taken as a defense of an armed struggle, according to a so-called Foco Theory.[2]

Although we will only be able to assess the content of this book in more detail later, it is necessary to stress its importance and its relation to the social context in which it was produced. The final years of the 1960s and the beginning of the 1970s was the period of the most intense controversy concerning the so-called dependency theory. At that moment when developmentalism was giving clear signs of fatigue, sociological critiques abounded, giving voice to both revisionist

Latin American structuralists[3] and to critics such as those who formulated dependency theory. But while part of those criticisms would emphasize internal (endogenous) aspects of the Latin American social processes and culminate in a solution familiar with the old developmentalism,[4] Marxist dependency theory – elaborated not only by Marini, but also by Theotônio dos Santos, Vânia Bambirra, Andre Gunder Frank, among others – deemed the processes of national development incapable of realization within the context of the capitalist world economy.

The military coup that installed General Augusto Pinochet's regime in Chile, in 1973, determined the beginning of Marini's third exile. Back in Mexico, in 1974, Marini resumed his journalistic activities, as well as his militancy and teaching at the Universidad Nacional Autónoma de México (UNAM), giving continuity to the activities of education and research, and deepening his vision of the Latin American reality from the perspective elaborated in *Dialéctica*. During this period, which would extend until 1984, there was a process of dissemination of Marini's works,[5] at a moment when Latin American thinking flourished at UNAM. With the amnesty granted to political exiles in 1979 and the beginning of the process of political opening and democratization, Marini returned to Brazil in 1985, putting an end to twenty years of exile.

However, it might still be possible to mention a fourth period of exile, in this case, a kind of "intellectual exile." Marini's political and academic standpoints turned his works into one of the favorite targets of his opponents, especially when, as from the mid 1970s, onwards the criticisms of dependency theory piled up. Among these criticisms, none is as emblematic as the one expressed by Cardoso and Serra (1978). The reason for this is that although some of Marini's texts reached some prominence, circulating in clandestinity among the left during the dictatorship, Marini came back to Brazil as a virtually unknown author. Worse than that, he had been slandered in a critique, without being given an opportunity to reply, published in Brazil by Cebrap, an institute that had Fernando Henrique Cardoso, former professor of the University of São Paulo, once influenced by Marxism, and future neoliberal president of Brazil, as a major figure. Marini's work only received a more public acknowledgment in Brazil after his death. The rescue of Marxist dependency theory in Latin America has had in Marini one of its most important references since the beginning of the 21st century.

The Dialectic of Dependency

We must now turn to some of the main theoretical points of Marini's work. Marxist dependency theory is the term used to name the vision that bases itself on Marx's theory of capitalism, on the classical theory of imperialism and on some pioneering studies about the relationship between the center and the periphery. It interprets the dependent condition of peripheral societies as a natural unfolding of the logic of the functioning of the capitalist world economy. From its formulation on, for various reasons, this theory was disputed, not only by the hegemonic social theory, but also by a significant part of the more critical tradition of social thinking.

Dialéctica de la Dependencia is the work in which the framework of the Marxist dependency theory has achieved its most complete expression. Its objective was to systematize the main categories of what the dependent condition comprises from a Marxist standpoint. First, this means considering the differentiated position of the various economies in the logic of world capital accumulation as a specific theme, which cannot be confused with Marx's level of abstraction in *Capital*. What Marx discovered about capitalism in general at a global level is the starting point to investigate the specificities of dependent capitalism.

For this reason, the first part of the book, which deals with methodological issues, is crucial, though its importance is seldom acknowledged. For Marini, social theory often suffered from two deviations in the analysis of Latin American reality when faced with the mismatch between the abstract concepts and concrete facts. On the one hand, it failed to consider the concrete specificity of the reality, fitting it without mediation in the pre-established conceptual framework. In the context of Marxism, it meant to treat *Capital* as a manual that could completely explain all the social shaping of capitalism regardless of place and historical moment. On the other hand, the specificity of the context was exaggerated to such an extent that the conclusion was that Marxist theory was inadequate to explain contemporaneity.

Marini's theoretical proposal was to use Marx as a starting point – at a higher level of abstraction, and based on the understanding of the dialectical laws of capitalist economy – to unveil the specificity of its concrete manifestations in the context of Latin American reality. From that standpoint, Marini understood dependency as a condition of those nations whose economy was shaped by the development and expansion of other (imperialist) nations. Therefore, it was not the case, as believed by developmentalists, that these economies were underdeveloped due to poor capitalist development. On the contrary, it was exactly because of the dialectical development of capitalism on an international scale that there are central imperialist economies and dependent economies. The political unfolding of this thesis is substantial, especially in the historical context of the 1960s and 1970s. The dependent condition is inherent to capitalism. Therefore, the revolutionary fight against the first presupposes opposition to the second as well.

However, what are the structural features that shape this situation of dependency? Part of the surplus produced in dependent economies does not become part of the process of internal accumulation of capital, but part of the accumulation of the central economies. This process of value transfer is known in that historical context as unequal exchange.[6]

When explaining unequal exchange, Marini refers to two mechanisms. First, given that distinct capitals can produce the same commodities with different productivities, the commodities produced by these capitals will have different individual values: the higher the productivity, the lower the value. As all the commodities are sold at their market value, according to the amount of labor time socially required, capitals whose productivity is above average will appropriate extra surplus-value generated by the capitals with productivity below average.

The second mechanism reveals itself when the competition between distinct production sectors are considered. Those with an above average organic composition of capital will sell their commodities for production prices superior to the values produced by themselves, appropriating a surplus-profit. Marini relates this mechanism to the role of monopoly in the production of commodities with a higher composition of capital. Nevertheless, the presence of monopoly would be more related to a third mechanism, that is, the tendency of monopoly capital to be able to maintain market prices above production prices for longer periods of time, increasing their capacity to appropriate value not produced by it.

As capitals in dependent economies, in average, tend to present productivities below average, considering both the competition between and within sectors, part of the surplus-value produced by them would be appropriated by capitals from abroad. This structural condition, expressed in the differentials of productivity, forces capitals in dependent economies to compensate for this transfer of value to maintain the dynamism of their accumulation. Marini identifies the super-exploitation of labor-power as this compensation. This category is central to Marini's theory and would be specific to the dependent condition. Therefore, it is not a question of merely raising the exploitation rate, the rate of surplus-value, as any capitalist economy would tend to do for the reasons already identified by Marx. Rather it is a question of compensating for the transfer of value to the central economies, increasing the production of surplus-value and ensuring the internal accumulation of capital.

In *Dialéctica de la Dependencia*, the author also lists the means available to dependent economies' capital to super-exploit labor-power: the intensification of labor without a proportional raise in salaries; the extension of the working-day, also without compensation in wages; the expropriation of part of the time required for the reproduction of labor-power, which defines the value of this commodity. In other parts of his work, the author adds a fourth form according to which an increase in the value of labor-power is not accompanied by a rise in wages in the same proportion.[7]

Thus, the central category of super-exploitation in Marini represents a mechanism for compensating for the transfer of value to the central economies, and, at the same time, a way of raising the rate of surplus-value. The author's imprecision when using the same term to refer to both the category and the ways in which it can be achieved can help us understand many of the imprecisions in the contemporary debate on super-exploitation.[8]

According to Marini, this leads to a divide between a high sphere of consumption, related to (fractions of) social classes that benefit from this type of accumulation, and a lower sphere that suffers the consequences of super-exploitation. This differentiation in circulation determines a split cycle of capital in dependent economies. The lower sphere, with limited capacity of consumption, turns itself to internal production. However, as dependent economies are oriented to the world market, capital does not depend on it to realize the value of its commodities.

On the other hand, the high sphere of consumption would be more associated with external demand, which implies more imports and structural deficits in the balance of payments. This is the classical dynamics of dependency: transfer of values compensated by super-exploitation, which divides consumption spheres, which in turn reproduce the transfer of values. This cycle of capital is typical of primary export economies, and the form of this dependent condition changes according to the particular historical period of the international division of labor.

For Marini, however, the process of industrialization of the Latin American economies, consolidated in postwar years, only changed the form of dependency. So-called import substitution, so often praised by developmentalists, would not create its own demand, but would only define the internalization of some industrial stages – as a result of external shocks – to respond to the pre-existing demand of the high sphere of consumption. The process of industrialization would still present the structural component of dependency, even more so if we consider that its financing counted on mass participation of foreign capital. With productivity below the international average, the transfer of values would continue to take place, now aggravated by technological dependency and by the service of external capital, in the form of remittance of profits, dividends and servicing the external debt. Super-exploitation would continue to be necessary and circulation would go on being divided between an internal market, which would fulfill the needs of the lower sphere and part of the less complex technological needs of the high sphere, and the external market, more necessary each day to boost exports, both of primary and semi-processed goods.

The historicity of dependency, from the mid-20th century, showed that technological and financial dependency refuted the thesis that capitalist industrialization would solve the problems of underdevelopment. The political unfolding of this process supported Marini's conclusion that dependency could only be countered by a socialist revolution. More than ever, the choice of *socialist revolution* or *dependency* questioned frontally the programmatic alliance between nationalist developmentalism and the mechanical thesis of the official Communist parties.[9]

Many of the theoretical conclusions of *Dialéctica de la Dependencia* were important for Marini's later work. The best example of this may be the role of the category sub-imperialism, already elaborated in *Subdesarrollo y Revolución* but further developed in the 1970s. The author interpreted the inflow of foreign productive capital into some dependent economies as a transfer to those countries of some lower stages of the production process, which resulted in a rise of the organic composition of capital. This led to the replication of value transfer mechanisms typical of the world market to regional market relations. The dependent character of the sub-imperialist economies was not annulled by that fact, nor did it mean that national capitals were necessarily able to appropriate a surplus-profit. After all, the dependent economies already suffered the process of trans-nationalization, in such a way that transnational capitals, inserted in these dependent economies, could replicate the unequal exchange and, later on transfer again those values to the countries from where these capitals originated.

Critique and Assessment

Marini was heavily criticized from various perspectives.[10] On the one hand, he was accused of being a circulationist for failing to consider the capitalist feature of the social relations of production, as if dependency was restricted to a problem of value realization. As seen previously, this argument cannot be sustained because of the centrality that super-exploitation of labor has in his thinking. Another usual criticism is that of stagnationism.[11] Briefly, according to stagnationism, the extreme economic inequality in Latin America constituted a restriction of demand that hindered economic growth. In directing this criticism to Marini, the suggestion was that income leakage toward other countries would define a structural restriction to the growth of dependent economies. As seen previously, the super-exploitation of labor, as a compensation for the transfer of value, would make the process of accumulation of dependent capital more dynamic and therefore would not represent an obstacle to economic growth.

Another criticism, within Marxism itself, asserted that, on the one hand, Latin American specificity did not justify the formulation of specific laws for dependent capitalism, and on the other hand, that Marini proposed an overdetermination of dependent economies by external forces, when in fact he should try to understand how the dependent insertion in the world economy is determined, in the last instance, by internal conditions. Cueva (1974) assumes that this is the case when arguing that dependency theory underrates the internal specificities of each social formation in Latin America, reducing them to a mere consequence of its subordinate insertions in the world economy.[12]

It does not seem to us that identifying the real and concrete specificity of capitalist development in Latin America leads necessarily to disregarding the fact that, in the imperialist stage of capitalism, certain economies inserted themselves in a subordinate manner in the international division of labor. The issue of the dialectical articulation between the internal conditionings of each social formation and their dependent insertion in the world economy was not, at any moment, disregarded by Marxist dependency theory. Very much the opposite: this was one of its great merits, especially in Marini's thinking.

Some of those criticisms probably had their origin in the undifferentiated treatment of what can be called "the Weberian strand" of dependency theory and its Marxist interpretation.[13] Some others had their origin in an attempt to purge from the debate about dependency its most radical pole, that is, Marxist dependency theory.

Several reasons explain why Marxist dependency theory has regained momentum at present.[14] Maybe the main one is the historical context. The rise of neoliberalism, especially in Latin America, in the late 20th century deepened the mechanisms of value transfer and, therefore, the structural components of dependency. This happened in a new historical phase of capitalism, which defines a new form of manifestation of dependency itself. One of the most interesting lines of research into Marxist dependency theory, at present, is the analysis of the determinants of the crisis of contemporary capitalism, the form in which imperialism manifests itself specifically at the moment and as a result, the specific historical character of dependency nowadays.

Notes

1. According to Theotônio dos Santos (2009, 22): Marini's "contribution became more original when, after the 1964 coup d'état, he defined the importance of the coup to the generation of finance capital and its imminent hegemony over the Brazilian economy. At that moment, he forged the concept of sub-imperialism. It served to demonstrate that the incipient Brazilian finance capital, originated in the context of a heavy dependence on foreign capital, would have to face the contradiction between its expansionist tendency – search of new markets for its investments and its products – and its subordinate condition and dependence on international capital."
2. In the 1970s, Latin-American left movements were highly influenced by Regis Debray's thesis on the possibility of small guerrilla groups making social revolution and creating class consciousness in the struggle itself – as he thought had happened in Cuba. But Marini, as well as Vânia Bambirra and others, were severe critics of these ideas. See Debray (1967), Bambirra (1968) and Marini (1973).
3. The term refers to the members of ECLAC (Economic Commission for Latin America and the Caribbean), the most influential institution to foster Latin American industrialization from the 1950s onwards.
4. See for example Cardoso and Faletto (1979). See Marini's criticisms in Marini (1978, 1993).
5. The site www.marini-escritos.unam.mx contains the most complete collection of Marini's works.
6. The debate on unequal exchange in the 1970s starts with Arghiri Emmanuel's doctoral thesis (1972) and includes authors such as Charles Bettelheim, Samir Amin (1973) and Ernest Mandel (1975) among others.
7. See for example Marini (1979).
8. See for example the debate in issue n° 25 of the journal Razón y Revolución (2013), available in http://revistaryr.org.ar/index.php/RyR/issue/view/8
9. This thesis saw capitalist development as a pre-condition to socialist revolution in dependent economies, and therefore ended up proposing a tactical alliance between Communist parties and bourgeois supporters of developmentalism.
10. Some of them can be found in the aforementioned article by Cardoso and Serra (1978). Marini's reply, not published originally in Brazil, can be found in Marini (1978).
11. Stagnationism is a theory advocated by some thinkers in the mid-1960s, such as Celso Furtado (1965).
12. Cueva (1988) reconsiders the content of his original criticism, which later allowed a certain rapprochement with Marxist dependency theory, in notes written by him. See for example Bambirra (1978) and Marini (2005).
13. By "Weberian strand" we refer to the works such as those of Cardoso and Faletto (1979), which are implicitly based on Weber's criticism of Marxism, according to which the latter would slide into economism and would disregard the importance of politics.
14. Some important references in this process of revival can be found in Osorio (2004), Valencia (2005), and Almeida Filho (2013), for example.

Bibliography

Almeida Filho, Niemeyer, ed. 2013. *Desenvolvimento e dependência: cátedra Ruy Mauro Marini*. Brasília: IPEA.

Amin, Samir. 1973. *L'échange inégal et la loi de la valeur: la fin d'un débat*. Paris: Éditions Anthropos-IDEP.

Bambirra, Vania. 1968. "Errors of the Foco Theory." *Monthly Review* 20(3): 28–35.

Bambirra, Vania. 1978. *Teoría de la dependencia: una anticrítica*. México: Ediciones Era.

Cardoso, Fernando H., and Enzo Faletto. 1979. *Dependency and Development in Latin America*. Berkeley and Los Angeles: University of California Press.

Cardoso, Fernando H., and José Serra. 1978. "Las desventuras de la dialéctica de la dependencia." *Revista Mexicana de Sociología* 40(special issue): 9–55. doi:10.2307/3539682

Cueva, Agustín. 1988. *Las democracias restringidas de América Latina: elementos para una reflexión crítica*. Quito: Planeta.

Cueva, Agustín. 2008 (1974). "Problemas y perspectivas de la teoría de la dependencia." In *Entre la ira y la esperanza y otros ensayos de crítica latinoamericana*. Buenos Aires and Bogotá: CLACSO. http://biblioteca virtual.clacso.org.ar/clacso/se/20100830114245/05problemas.pdf

Debray, Régis. 1967. *Revolution in the Revolution? Armed Struggle and Political Struggle in Latin America*. New York: Grove Press.

Dos Santos, Theotonio. 2009. "Ruy Mauro Marini: um pensador latino-americano." In *A América Latina e os desafios da globalização: Ensaios em homenagem a Ruy Mauro Marini*, edited by Carlos E. Martins and Adrían S. Valencia, 21–26. São Paulo: Boitempo.

Emmanuel, Arghiri. 1972. *Unequal Exchange: A Study of the Imperialism of Trade*. With Additional Comments by Charles Bettelheim. London: NLB.

Furtado, Celso. 1965. *Development and Stagnation in Latin America: A Structuralist Approach*. Washington: Washington University, Social Science Institute.

Mandel, Ernest. 1975. *Late Capitalism*. London: NLB.

Marini, Ruy M. 1969. *Subdesarrollo y revolución*. México: Siglo Veintiuno Editores.

Marini, Ruy M. 1973. "Prólogo." In *La Revolución Cubana, una reinterpretación*, edited by Vania Bambirra. Santiago de Chile: Editorial Nuestro Tiempo.

Marini, Ruy M. 1974. *Dialéctica de la dependência*. México DF: Ediciones Era.

Marini, Ruy M. 1978. "Las razones del neodesarrollismo (respuesta a F.H. Cardoso y J. Serra)." *Revista Mexicana de Sociología* 40: 57–106.

Marini, Ruy M. 1979. "Plusvalía extraordinaria y acumulación de capital." *Cuadernos Políticos* 20: 18–39. www.cuadernospoliticos.unam.mx/cuadernos/contenido/CP.20/CP20.4.RuyMauro.pdf

Marini, Ruy M. 1993. "La crisis teórica." In *América Latina: integración y democracia*, 55–86. Caracas: Editorial Nueva Sociedad.

Marini, Ruy M. 2005. "Memória." In *Ruy Mauro Marini: vida e obra*, edited by Roberta Traspadini and João Pedro Stédile, 57–134. São Paulo: Expressão Popular.

Osorio, Jaime. 2004. *Crítica de la Economía Vulgar: reproducción del capital y dependencia*. México: Universidad Autônoma de Zacatecas.

Valencia, Adrián S. 2005. *América Latina: de crisis y paradigmas. La teoría de la dependencia en el siglo XXI*. México: Plaza y Valdés.

54
DAVID HARVEY (1935–)

Noel Castree

David Harvey is perhaps the most famous Marxist alive today – if not globally then certainly in the Anglosphere. His name is synonymous with key concepts such as the "spatial fix," "time-space compression," "accumulation by dispossession" and "the right to the city." Now in his ninth decade, he remains a remarkably energetic advocate of Marxism, both as a means to understand the dynamics of capitalism and as a guide to political action. He cuts a distinctive figure in three arenas. First, in his home discipline (Geography) he almost single-handedly introduced Marxist political economy to his peers in the early 1970s, going on to reveal its immense explanatory power and political relevance. He is undoubtedly Geography's most influential thinker ever, not only inspiring more than one generation of geographers but also helping to significantly improve Geography's reputation in the wider academic sphere. Second, his highly original theorization of capitalism as constitutively geographical helped add a largely missing dimension to Marx's otherwise ground-breaking work – and thereby to Marxism across the social sciences and humanities through the 1970s, 1980s, 1990s and noughties. He is, in other words, a highly distinguished Marxist as much as a celebrated geographer. Finally, more than virtually any other university-based Marxist alive today, Harvey has worked hard to reach out beyond the academy. Over the last ten years especially, he has given numerous presentations around the world to activists and politically minded citizens; he has also written a number of accessible books designed to demonstrate the analytical acuity of Marxist political economy; and he has a substantial website where his introductory course on *Capital* volume I is freely available to thousands of people. In sum, Harvey is a Marxist geographer, a geographical Marxist and a public advocate for Marxism in equal measure.

In this chapter I want to explore Harvey's contributions in each of these arenas. As we will see, the common denominator is Harvey's particular "brand" of Marxism (for want of a better word). For over 40 years he's stayed true to the letter and spirit of Marx's original writings, especially the later ones (i.e., those written from the late 1850s onwards). As he once noted retrospectively, "What I realized after [my book] *Social Justice and the City* . . . was that I didn't understand Marx, and needed to straighten this out, which I tried to do without too much assistance from elsewhere" (Harvey 2000a, 85). In other words, rather than (1) interpret Marx through the lenses fashioned by various post-classical Marxists (e.g., Gramsci, Sartre or Althusser) or (2) add insights and concepts to Marxism from other critical theories (like feminism) in order to create some version of Post-Marxism, Harvey has focused single-mindedly on the three volumes of *Capital* and the *Grundrisse*.

Whereas some critics see this as a weakness, Harvey remains convinced that classical Marxism is, despite its 19th-century origins, deeply relevant today. The tenacity with which he has held this conviction is hugely impressive given that Marxism, as both a critical theory and a political ideology, fell seriously out of favor during the middle decades of his long career. Where a number of his contemporaries, like Ernesto Laclau, evolved their Marxism significantly over time, Harvey has remained steadfast in the face of both attacks on his own work and more general critiques of Marxist analysis and politics. Whether this indicates intellectual conservatism or mental toughness on his part is a matter of perspective.

Despite his prominence as a Marxist, few synoptic accounts of his *oeuvre* exist. Those that do are now rather dated (e.g., Castree 2007), including an otherwise illuminating autobiographical essay (Harvey 2002). This chapter, however inadequately, tries to survey the metaphorical landscape of Harvey's thought. It outlines some of the key characteristics of his writings and situates them in various salient intellectual and societal contexts, drawing on years of critical engagement with Harvey's work (Castree 1996, 1996, 2001, 2006a, 2006b, 2006c, 2009; Castree and Gregory 2006).

David Harvey, Marx and Anglo-European Marxism

Harvey has published over twenty books and more than two hundred articles and chapters since his life-changing discovery of Marx's writings in the early 1970s (captured in *Social Justice and the City* [1973]). Two intertwined red threads connect them: frequent direct references to Marx's publications, concepts and insights, and very limited use of the work of other Marxists. Indeed, since his magisterial work of theory *The Limits to Capital* (1982), one might say that Harvey has self-consciously attempted "to read . . . on Marx's own terms" (Harvey 2010b, 1), standing-in for him over a century after his passing in order to show why Marx's anatomization of capitalism is anything but dated. This embodiment of Marx has been most evident in Harvey's annual seminar on *Capital* volume 1, given in various places (Baltimore, Oxford and New York among them) and now available online (http://davidharvey.org/reading-capital/).

Of course, this is not to say that Harvey has interpreted Marx "correctly." He's well aware that his is a particular "reading." But it is to say that he believes his interpretation is faithful to the spirit and letter of the late Marx, and that he's eschewed the sort of far-reaching modifications and extensions of Marx characteristic of, say, the Frankfurt School of critical theory. Consider the following examples.

First, since *The Limits* Harvey has never wavered in his commitment to Marx's theory of living labor as the source of the distinctive form that value assumes in capitalist societies. This "value theory of labour," as Diane Elson (1979) memorably called it, comprises an ensemble of key concepts characteristic of virtually all "classical" readings of Marx past and present. They include use and exchange value, socially necessary labor time, and concrete and abstract labor, among many others. These concepts are virtually ever-present in Harvey's writings, and form a contradictory unity that is central to his (and Marx's) account of capitalism as a crisis-prone mode of production riven with irresolvable tensions.

Second, there's abundant evidence that Harvey holds fast to a philosophy of internal relations, a processual understanding of the world and a dialectical mode of reasoning that are all especially characteristic of Marx's later works. They are evident in *The Limits* and all Harvey's subsequent sole authored works, with him even spelling them out in a manifesto of sorts in his book *Justice, Nature and the Geography of Difference* (1996: ch. 8). In several publications, drawing in part on Bertell Ollman's superb works on dialectics (*Alienation* [1970: part 1) and *Dance of the Dialectic* [2003]), Harvey has noted the important Hegelian heritage in all this, albeit turned "right side up." Harvey presents himself, most obviously in *The Condition of Postmodernity* (1989), as a thoroughly holistic theorist alive to the totalizing and contradictory behaviors of capitalism. In his career, he has used Marx to discuss everything from architectural symbolism to urban class struggle in Paris to the overseas ventures of the United States. Of course, Marx himself was similarly promiscuous in his topical range.

Third, during Harvey's engagement with Marxism over nearly five decades. it's notable that his publications have largely ignored, or else fired critical broadsides against, most other substantial readings of Marx. For instance, he had no truck with the so-called analytical Marxism that was burgeoning in some Anglophone universities in the 1990s (see Harvey 1986). He was also critical of the critical realist Marxism that, in the Anglosphere, evolved out of Althusser and Balibar's (1970) revisionist reading of Marx (see Harvey 1987). Where he *has* engaged in some detail with Marxist or Marxisant works, he has typically *incorporated* their insights into his classical version of Marxism rather than substantially altering it – examples are his use of French regulation theory in *The Condition of Postmodernity*, of Giovanni Arrighi's historical research in *The New Imperialism* (Harvey 2003), and of Raymond Williams's notion of "militant particularism" in an edited book on a labor struggle in Oxford (Hayter and Harvey 1993). These appropriations have tended to embroider his theory of capital accumulation rather than reformulate it.

Is it a sign of stubbornness that Harvey has not engaged systematically with the work of leading Marxists past and present? Some might say so. However, less negatively, one reason is surely the sheer difficulty Harvey encountered mastering Marx's writings between the early 1970s and the publication of *The Limits to Capital* – a major work of synthesis and extension that both unified elements of Marx's later works and added-in geography with theoretical rigor. I say this because on many occasions Harvey has talked of the first encounter with Marx's corpus as a "struggle" for any reader, and has frequently cited Marx's famous claim that "there is no royal road to science" (CI: 102). A deeply attentive student of all Marx's many later publications, Harvey may not so much be stubborn as keenly protective of the huge analytical and normative power that comes with knowing Marx's works intimately.[1]

A Marxist Geographer

So much for the classical cast of Harvey's Marxism. How has it allowed him to make formative intellectual contributions to Geography, his disciplinary home for much of his career? There is far too much to say by way of a full answer. Therefore, I will highlight just some of many ways in which he pioneered new thinking. To understand them we need, briefly, to say something about geography, as both subject matter and the discipline of that name.

Geography, as an academic pursuit, had a strong idiographic focus until the late 1960s. Its practitioners examined the confluence of multiple events and phenomena at particular points on the Earth's surface – an approach codified as "areal differentiation" in the influential book *The Nature of Geography* (by American Richard Hartshorne 1939). The subject matter of Geography was thus space-time complexity: variation, difference and uniqueness were its hallmarks. In 1968, Harvey offered among the first heavyweight challenges to this view in a methodological work of science called *Explanation in Geography* (Harvey 1968). This book argued that geographical similarity and order existed within and between otherwise different locations, and that the use of general theory, models and hypothesis-testing using replicable methods held the key to its discovery. It showed that geography could, as a "spatial science," share the same "nomothetic" ambitions for theoretical and empirical generalization as the social and environmental sciences. Indeed, it could "spatialize" the processes and relations those sciences studied.

This commitment to discerning order among apparent space-time variation persisted after his conversion to Marxism, as recounted in the two main parts of *Social Justice* (where he moved from "liberal" to "socialist" formulations). Using Marx's general theory of capital accumulation, Harvey sought, through the 1970s and 1980s, to integrate geography into it as a central element. For instance, both *The Limits* and *The Urbanization of Capital* (1985a) show that the creative destruction of physical landscapes is part of the metaphorical DNA of capital. This is not only because accumulation cannot occur on the head of a pin, but also because capital's compulsion to grow requires new infrastructure in both older and new sites of commodity production. Harvey theorized the role of different capitalists in this process and the way geography features in specific circuits of capital (e.g., for rentiers as land and physical property), and the interaction between circuits.

Harvey thus demonstrated to his disciplinary peers how and why questions of geography – fixed capital, territorial divisions of production and consumption, urban agglomeration and so on – are *theoretical* questions, not simply the preserve of empirical gazetteers. This is the same as saying that geographical phenomena have a *constitutive* role to play in the fundamental processes that give rise to them in the first place. Here, then, there is no distinction between "process" (capital accumulation) and "outcome" (spatial form) because the latter makes the former flesh and, once it exists, may affect the subsequent operations of the process in question. The tangible character that processes assume, or are realized through materially, are thus for Harvey elements of a unified reality.

This was a truly profound insight for geographers because, as Harvey has repeatedly observed, "the insertion of concepts of space . . . place, locale, and milieu into any of the supposedly powerful but spaceless social . . . theoretic formulations [currently existing] has the awkward habit of paralyzing the theory's central propositions" (1985a, xi). As a Marxist, Harvey has shown how the paralysis can be avoided, in the process rescuing the discipline of Geography from the stereotype that it is about the empirical mapping of essentially aspatial economic, social or political processes. Other Marxist geographers like Neil Smith and Richard Walker (his former PhD students) accompanied Harvey in this rescue operation, and have helped significantly increase the academic status of Geography, especially in the wider social sciences. Needless to say, not all geographers concurred, with Andrew Sayer (1985) arguing that "space" may well be constitutive but only in a contingent way that eludes theoretical specification.

A Geographical Marxist

If, until David Harvey and a few other radical geographers, Marxism was missing from academic Geography, so geography as subject matter was largely missing from the works both of Marx and leading Marxists through much of the 20th century. The signal exception was Henri Lefebvre, author of *The Production of Space* (1991). Like Lefebvre before him, Harvey insisted that "Historical materialism has to be upgraded . . . to historical-geographical materialism," Harvey 1985a, xiv). He was among the first Anglophone Marxists to do so, but his call was not really heard until after *The Condition* (1989) was published. This book's trenchant critique of postmodernism and its cross-disciplinary flavor made it something of a publishing success, and helped draw wide attention among Marxists to Harvey's earlier works like *The Limits* and *Consciousness and the Urban Experience* (1985b).

Unlike *The Condition*, with its rather loose and evocative notion of "time-space compression," these showed with rigor why Marxists simply have to accord geography a key analytical and normative role in their research. As Harvey long ago observed, not only was time given priority in most Marxist analysis (including much of Marx's writing) but space, to the extent Marxists considered it at all, was typically misunderstood. Like Lefebvre, Harvey challenged the "common-sense" Newtonian view of space: it is not simply an *absolute* dimension, that is, an empty container within which political economic processes operate. Instead, space is materially produced by different societies in different ways: it is *relational*. Space comprises qualitatively different physical forms that are, variously, proximate to, and distant from, one another according to the geographical scale these forms are organized at or materially inter-connected (towns, cities, regions, nation-states etc.). These forms and these scales are both the outcome and shaper of political economic processes that are general in nature. "Geographical space," Harvey (1985b, 144) asserts, "is always the realm of the concrete and particular." The question then arises: "Is it possible to construct a theory of the concrete and particular in the context of the universal and abstract determinations of Marx's theory of capitalist accumulation?"

As I noted in the previous section, Harvey's answer has been a resounding "yes" for many years. His numerous writings, like Lefebvre's, show why "space relations and geographical phenomena are fundamental material attributes that have to be present at the very beginning of the analysis" (Harvey 1985a, 33). This focus on space places Harvey in a minority within the Marxist tradition. But Harvey neither *prioritizes* space over time nor theorizes space and time *separately* as if they are relatively autonomous dimensions of capital accumulation. As Harvey (2006, xix, emphasis added) once put it, "materialism of any sort demands that . . . space-time-process be considered as a *unity* at the ontological level." This quest for unity, it seems to me, is what we need to pay attention to as his key contribution to Marxist thought.

It is evident in *The Limits*, though "linear" readers of the text might mistake Harvey for treating time and space discretely in his three sequential "cuts" at a "crisis theory" of capitalism. As I have explained in detail elsewhere (Castree 2009), a dialectical reading of *The Limits* yields the following insights. First, time is a socially constructed dimension that is *both* abstract and historical in capitalism (on which see Moishe Postone's [1993] magisterial book). Clock time and the times of lived experience get fused via the laws of competition, economic growth and restructuring endemic to capitalism. Second, for capitalism to propel itself forward in time it requires specific locations and elaborate connections between them (communication and transportation systems). These nodes and networks are, in turn, modifiers of the "force" exerted by socially necessary labor time and (this is Harvey's term) the "socially necessary turnover time" of capital.

In short, for Harvey capitalist time makes capitalist space, and capitalist space makes capitalist time. They are the medium and outcome of one another, the cause and consequence. And they are together necessary elements of capitalism, not contingent or merely "empirical" features. If Harvey's account of capitalism is correct, then it's no longer possible for analysts to ignore, or give priority to only one half of, the time-space dimension. What Bob Dodgshon (2008) calls "geographies of the moment" continually give-way to future spatialities, incrementally and otherwise. So it is that synchrony and diachrony, the here and there, the now and not-yet, the local and the global, bleed into one another incessantly in our world of creative destruction. As a result, Harvey shows us why classical Marxists (indeed any and all Marxists) must be students of space-time as a complex and contradictory *unity*, not of either history or geography.[2]

An Academic Marxist Reaching Beyond the Academy

In his pithy history of Marxism, Perry Anderson (1976) contrasted the immediate decades after Marx's death – where Marxism existed mostly outside the academy, was preoccupied with political economy and revolutionary strategy, and was rooted in working-class organizations – with the increasingly university-based Marxism that has prevailed in the West since 1945. Since the collapse of actually existing communism in 1989, that Marxism has been on the defensive within the academy, even though the critique of capitalism is as relevant now as ever (the causes, and fall out, of the 2007–8 global financial crisis being a prime example of why). Outside the academy it has lost any mass base it ever had, with the erosion of trade union membership and worker power in pretty much every capitalist democracy. Meanwhile "developing" countries tend to lack strong institutions representing working people.

The university has been Harvey's home his entire career. The space and time to read, think and write afforded him by positions at Bristol, Johns Hopkins, Oxford and CUNY has been utterly essential to his professional success. It has also, in recent years, given him a secure base from which to reach out into the wider society. Starting with his 2003 book *The New Imperialism* – an analysis of America's geo-economic maneuvering on the world stage – Harvey has written several accessible (albeit still high-level) analyses of current affairs – all of which operationalize his classical interpretation of capitalism's enduring dynamics (Harvey 2005, 2010a, 2014). During the same period he has given numerous talks in venues outside academia, and his website contains videos of his seminar about *Capital* volume 1 (accompanied by a published companion: Harvey 2010b).

These books, and the other communicative media he has used, have allowed him to do three things. First, keep the flame of (classical) Marxist thought alive outside the university world; second, show the importance of geography to audiences beyond academia; and third, show how geography matters to political organizing and decision-making about the reform (or overthrow) of capitalism. Space prevents me saying more about this last point, an increasingly important dimension of all Harvey's writing since his 2000 book *Spaces of Hope* (which was partly written after the first wave of anti-capitalist demonstrations in the late 1990s). Suffice to say that, for Harvey, the geography of capital and the geography of opposition movements are equally important considerations when determining, politically, what is necessary, desirable and feasible. Sadly, the signal lack of effective organizations to mobilize workers globally means that a more just form of capitalism – never mind a revolution against it – are nowhere in sight.

It is virtually impossible to judge how effective Harvey's activities as a public intellectual have been this last fifteen years or so. We might simply note with approval that he has been willing to leave the relatively safe havens of the lecture theatre and seminar room. He has shown us that there is an appetite for Marxist thought in the wider world, despite the virtual death of socialist politics since 1989. By engaging Marx's theoretical ideas with the realities of our time, Harvey has ultimately demonstrated the public value of critical political economy in an era of neoliberal hegemony. However, this said, the absence of an organized mass constituency for Marxist thinking means that Harvey, despite his best efforts, cannot function as an *organic* intellectual. Even if such a constituency existed, it's an open question whether a professional academic Marxist like Harvey could fully connect with it, or any parties or organizations intended to represent it. Furthermore, if Daniel Drezner's (2017) analysis of the "ideas industry" is right, Harvey's public outreach is occurring in a highly polarized ideational context – certainly in the US, where he resides. This means he may be preaching to the converted at a time where mutual learning among political rivals is in very short supply but greatly needed.

Conclusion

In his first book as a Marxist, Harvey memorably insisted that "It's irrelevant to ask whether concepts [and] categories . . . are 'true' or 'false.' We have to ask, rather, what it is that produces them and what they serve to produce" (1973, 298). Since then he has been insistent that all forms of knowledge – especially those that are hegemonic – enter fully into the constitution of the world they describe, explain or evaluate. Indeed, if he believed otherwise he would hardly have spent the last forty-plus years consciously promulgating Marxism. Let me end by flagging some of the perceived problems with Harvey's classical Marxism. His critics have, as it were, asked what has produced Harvey's corpus and what, through its signature characteristics, it has served to produce.

First, despite his willingness to use dialectical reasoning to extend the analytical frontiers of Marxism, there are some notable gaps in his theory and empirical analysis of capital accumulation. The biggest one is the capitalist state, despite frequent mentions of state power and strategy in all his published writings. Harvey has developed none of the in-depth conceptual understanding provided by Nicos Poulantzas (1978) or the likes of Bob Jessop (2002). How can the spatio-temporal dynamics of capital be properly understood, so too the prospects for socialism, absent such an understanding? (Jessop 2004). Though it may seem a little mean-spirited to upbraid him for not doing even more than he already has in his remarkable career, there is a real sense in which Harvey has refused to fundamentally evolve his Marxism since *The Limits* was published in 1982. In part, as I indicated earlier, this is because he has ignored much of the lively debate within continental and Anglophone Marxism that occurred through the 1960s to the 1990s – and which still occurs in universities today. For all its explanatory power, can Harvey's classical Marxism really be said to offer an adequate account of a capitalism that, in its empirical form, is very different indeed from that prevailing in Marx's time?

Second, outside Marxism, Harvey's work has had a mixed reception among leftists for good reason. For instance, the feminist cultural critics Rosalyn Deutsche (1991) and Meaghan Morris (1992) have suggested that Harvey is guilty of a specifically masculine desire to offer the "total analysis" of any situation and a blindness to politically progressive forms of difference irreducible to class identities and politics. For both critics, Harvey's work replays the "meta-theoretical" sins that for too long had allowed Marxism to squeeze-out other forms of left-wing thought and politics in the Western academy. In an apologia published in the journal *Antipode*, Harvey (1992) addressed these criticisms to some extent, and did so more fully in *Justice, Nature and the Geography of Difference*. However, as Melissa Wright (2006) and Cindi Katz (2006) pointed out, Harvey's work is not terribly good at grasping "over-determination," except at the level of rhetoric. An index of this fact is that Harvey – unlike at least one of his students (Richard Walker) – has never had much time for the philosophy of critical realism in which complex causality, path-dependence and uncertainty loom large as problems of theory and method (cf. Brown et al. 2001).

Perhaps the key message is this: for all his radicalism as a thinker, a certain conservatism marks Harvey's Marxism. It serves as a double-edged blade. On the one hand, it explains his intellectual consistency over a long period of time, which has garnered him respect as he walks the line between dogmatic rigidity and the ability to make his Marxism speak to the specifics of a fast changing world. But it also explains his seeming unwillingness to reconstruct the house of concepts that Marx built, let alone add wings fashioned out of non-Marxist materials.

Notes

1. See Callinicos (2006), for another account of Harvey's relation to academic Marxism past and present.
2. See Jessop (2006) for a less generous reading than my own of Harvey's success in theorizing the process-time-space trinity.

Bibliography

Althusser, Louis, and Étienne Balibar. 1970. *Reading Capital*. 2nd edn. London: NLB.

Anderson, Perry. 1976. *Considerations on Western Marxism*. London: NLB.

Brown, Andrew, Steve Fleetwood, and John Michael Roberts, eds. 2001. *Marxism and Critical Realism*. London: Routledge.

Callinicos, Alex. 2006. "David Harvey and Marxism." In Castree and Gregory, eds. 2006, 49–54.

Castree, Noel. 1995. "Theory's Subject and Subject's Theory." *Environment and Planning A* 27 (2): 269–97.

Castree, Noel. 1996. "Birds, Mice and Geography: Marxisms and Dialectics." *Transactions of the Institute of British Geographers* 21(2): 13–26.

Castree, Noel. 2001. "From Spaces of Antagonism to Spaces of Engagement." In *Marxism and Critical Realism*, edited by Andrew Brown, Steve Fleetwood, and John Michael Roberts, 187–214. London: Routledge.
Castree, Noel. 2006a. "The Detour of Critical Theory." In Castree and Gregory, eds. 2006, 247–69.
Castree, Noel. 2006b. "David Harvey's Symptomatic Silence." *Historical Materialism* 14(4): 35–57.
Castree, Noel. 2006c. "Geography's New Public Intellectuals?" *Antipode* 38(2): 396–412.
Castree, Noel. 2007. "David Harvey: Marxism, Capitalism and the Geographical Imagination." *New Political Economy* 12(1): 97–115.
Castree, Noel. 2009. "The Time-Space of Capitalism." *Time and Society* 18(1): 26–61.
Castree, Noel, and Derek Gregory, eds. 2006. *David Harvey: A Critical Reader*. Oxford: Blackwell.
Deutsche, Rosalyn. 1991. "Boy's Town." *Society and Space* 9(1): 5–13.
Dodgshon, Robert. 2008. "In What Way Is the World Really Flat?" *Society and Space* 26(3): 300–14.
Drezner, David. 2017. *The Ideas Industry*. Oxford: Oxford University Press.
Elson, Diane, ed. 1979 *Value: The Representation of Labour in Capitalism*. London: CSE Books.
Hartshorne, Richard. 1939. *The Nature of Geography*. Washington, DC: Association of American Geographers.
Harvey, David. 1968. *Explanation in Geography*. London: Edward Arnold.
Harvey, David. 1973. *Social Justice and the City*. London: Edward Arnold.
Harvey, David. 1982. *The Limits to Capital*. Oxford: Martin Robertson.
Harvey, David. 1985a. *The Urbanization of Capital*. Oxford: Basil Blackwell.
Harvey, David. 1985b. *Consciousness and the Urban Experience*. Oxford: Basil Blackwell.
Harvey, David. 1986. "Review of *Making Sense of Marx*, by Jon Elster." *Political Theory* 14(4): 686–90.
Harvey, David. 1987. "Three Myths in Search of a Reality in Urban Studies." *Environment and Planning D: Society and Space* 5: 367–76.
Harvey, David. 1989. *The Condition of Postmodernity*. Oxford: Basil Blackwell.
Harvey, David. 1992. "Postmodern Morality Plays." *Antipode* 24(4): 300–26.
Harvey, David. 2000a. "Reinventing Geography." *New Left Review* 2(4): 75–97.
Harvey, David. 2000b. *Spaces of Hope*. Edinburgh: Edinburgh University Press.
Harvey, David. 2002. "Memories and Desires." In *Geographical Voices*, edited by Peter Gould and Forest Pitts, 149–88. Syracuse: Syracuse University Press.
Harvey, David. 2003. *The New Imperialism*. Oxford: Oxford University Press.
Harvey, David. 2005. *A Short History of Neoliberalism*. Oxford: Oxford University Press.
Harvey, David. 2006. "Introduction." In *The Limits to Capital*, 2nd edn, iv–xxviii. London: Verso.
Harvey, David. 2010a. *The Enigma of Capital and the Crises of Capitalism*. London: Profile Books.
Harvey, David. 2010b. *A Companion to Marx's Capital*. London: Verso.
Harvey, David. 2014. *Seventeen Contradictions and the End of Capitalism*. London: Profile Books.
Harvey, David. 2016. "Reading Marx's *Capital* with David Harvey." http://davidharvey.org/reading-capital/
Harvey, David. 2017. *Marx, Capital and the Madness of Economic Reason*. London: Profile Books.
Hayter, Teresa, and David Harvey, eds. 1993. *The Factory and the City*. London: Mansell.
Jessop, Bob. 2002. *The Future of the Capitalist State*. Cambridge: Polity.
Jessop, Bob. 2004. "On the Limits of *The Limits to Capital*." *Antipode* 36(3): 480–96.
Jessop, Bob. 2006. "Spatial Fixes, Temporal Fixes and Spatio-Temporal Fixes." In Castree and Gregory, eds. 2006, 142–66.
Katz, Cindi. 2006. "Messing with 'The Project.'" In Castree and Gregory, eds. 2006, 234–46.
Lefebvre, Henri. 1991 (1974). *The Production of Space*. Oxford: Basil Blackwell.
Morris, Meaghan. 1992. "The Man in the Mirror." *Theory, Culture & Society* 9(3): 253–79.
Ollman, Bertell. 1971. *Alienation*. Cambridge: Cambridge University Press.
Ollman, Bertell. 1993. *Dance of the Dialectic*. Chicago: University of Illinois Press.
Postone. Moishe. 1993. *Time, Labor and Social Domination*. Cambridge: Cambridge University Press.
Poulantzas, Nicos. 1978. *State, Power, Socialism*. London: Verso.
Sayer, Andrew. 1985. "The Difference That Space Makes." In *Social Relations and Spatial Structures*, edited bv Derek Gregory and John Urry, 49–66. London: Macmillan and Co.
Wright, Melissa. 2006. "Differences That Matter." In Castree and Gregory, eds. 2006, 80–101.

PART IX

Marxism in an Age of Catastrophe

55

COVID-19 AND CATASTROPHE CAPITALISM

Commodity Chains and Ecological-Epidemiological-Economic Crises

John Bellamy Foster and Intan Suwandi

COVID-19 has accentuated as never before the interlinked ecological, epidemiological and economic vulnerabilities imposed by capitalism. As the world enters the third decade of the 21st century, we are seeing the emergence of catastrophe capitalism as the structural crisis of the system takes on planetary dimensions.[1]

Since the late 20th century, capitalist globalization has increasingly adopted the form of interlinked commodity chains controlled by multinational corporations, connecting various production zones, primarily in the Global South, with the apex of world consumption, finance and accumulation primarily in the Global North. These commodity chains make up the main material circuits of capital globally that constitute the phenomenon of late imperialism identified with the rise of generalized monopoly-finance capital (Foster 2019; Amin 2018). In this system, exorbitant imperial rents from the control of global production are obtained not only from the *global labor arbitrage*, through which multinational corporations with their headquarters in the center of the system overexploit industrial labor in the periphery, but also increasingly through the *global land arbitrage*, in which agribusiness multinationals expropriate cheap land (and labor) in the Global South so as to produce export crops mainly for sale in the Global North.[2]

In addressing these complex circuits of capital in today's global economy, corporate managers refer both to supply chains and value chains, with supply chains representing the movement of the physical product, and value chains directed at the "value added" at each node of production, from raw materials to the final product (Tarver 2020). This dual emphasis on supply chains and value chains resembles in some ways the more dialectical approach developed in Karl Marx's analysis of the *commodity chains* in production and exchange, encompassing both use values and exchange values. In the first volume of *Capital*, Marx highlighted the dual reality of natural-material use values (the "natural form") and exchange values (the "value form") present in each link of "the general chain of metamorphoses taking place in the world of commodities" (Marx 1978; *MECW* 36: 63; CI: 156, 215; CII: 136–37). Marx's approach was carried forward by Rudolf Hilferding in his *Finance Capital*, where he wrote of the "links in the chain of commodity exchanges" (Hilferding 1981: 60).

In the 1980s, world-system theorists Terence Hopkins and Immanuel Wallerstein reintroduced the commodity-chain concept based on these roots within Marxian theory (Hopkins and

Wallerstein 1986). Nevertheless, what was generally lost in later Marxian (and world-system) analyses of commodity chains, which treated these as exclusive economic/value phenomena, was the material-ecological aspect of use values. Marx, who never lost sight of the natural-material limits in which the circuit of capital took place, had stressed "the negative, i.e. destructive side" of capitalist valorization with respect to the natural conditions of production and the metabolism of human beings and nature as a whole (*CI*: 638). He indicated that the "irreparable rift in the interdependent process of social metabolism" (the metabolic rift) that constituted capitalism's destructive relation to the earth, whereby it "exhausted the soil" and "forced the manuring of English fields with guano," was equally evident in "periodical epidemics," resulting from the same organic contradictions of the system (*CIII*: 949–50; *CI*: 348–49).

Such a theoretical framework, focusing on the dual, contradictory forms of commodity chains, which incorporate both use values and exchange values, provides the basis for understanding the combined ecological, epidemiological and economic crisis tendencies of late imperialism. It allows us to perceive how the circuit of capital under late imperialism is tied to the etiology of disease via agribusiness, and how this has generated the COVID-19 pandemic. This same perspective focusing on the commodity and commodity chains, moreover, allows us to understand how both the disruption of the flow of use values in the form of material goods and the resulting interruption of the flow of value have generated a severe and lasting economic crisis. The result is to push an already stagnant economy to the very edge, threatening the toppling of the financial superstructure of the system. Finally, beyond all of this lies the much greater planetary rift engendered by today's catastrophe capitalism, exhibited in climate change and the crossing of various planetary boundaries, of which the present epidemiological crisis is simply another dramatic manifestation.

Circuits of Capital and Ecological-Epidemiological Crises

Remarkably, during the last decade, a new more holistic One Health-One World approach to the etiology of disease arose, mainly in response to the appearance of recent zoonotic diseases (or zoonoses) such as SARS, MERS and H1N1 transmitted to humans from nonhuman animals, wild or domesticated. The One Health model integrates epidemiological analysis on an ecological basis, bringing together ecological scientists, physicians, veterinarians and public health analysts within an approach that has a global scope. However, the original ecological framework that motivated One Health, representing a new, more comprehensive approach to zoonotic disease, has recently been appropriated and partially negated by such dominant organizations as the World Bank, the World Health Organization and the Centers for Disease Control and Prevention in the United States. Hence, the multisector approach of One Health was rapidly converted into a mode of bringing such varied interests as public health, private medicine, animal health, agribusiness and big pharma together to strengthen the response to what were regarded as episodic epidemics, while signifying a broad corporatist strategy in which capital, specifically agribusiness, was the dominant element. The result is that the connections between epidemiological crises and the capitalist world economy are systematically downplayed in what purports to be a more holistic model (Wallace et al. 2015; Wallace 2012; Zinsstag 2012; Galaz et al. 2015).

There thus arose in response a new, revolutionary approach to the etiology of disease, known as Structural One Health, building critically on One Health, but rooted rather in the broad historical-materialist tradition. For proponents of Structural One Health the key is to ascertain how pandemics in the contemporary global economy are connected to the circuits of capital that are rapidly changing environmental conditions. A team of scientists, including Rodrick Wallace, Luis Fernando Chaves, Luke R. Bergmann, Constância Ayres, Lenny Hogerwerf, Richard Kock and Robert G. (Rob) Wallace, have together written a series of works such as *Clear-Cutting Disease Control: Capital-Led Deforestation, Public Health Austerity, and Vector-Borne Infection* and, more recently, "COVID-19 and Circuits of Capital" (in this case by Rob Wallace, Alex Liebman, Luis Fernando Chaves and Rodrick Wallace) in the May 2020 issue of *Monthly Review*. Structural One Health is defined as "a new field, [which] examines the impacts global circuits of capital and other fundamental contexts, including deep cultural histories, have upon regional agroeconomics and associated disease dynamics across species" (Wallace et al. 2018: 2).

The revolutionary historical-materialist approach represented by Structural One Health departs from the mainstream One Health approach in (1) focusing on commodity chains as drivers of pandemics; (2) discounting the usual "absolute geographies" approach that concentrates on certain locales in which novel viruses emerge while failing to perceive the global economic conduits of transmission; (3) seeing the pandemics not as an episodic problem, or a random "black swan" event, but reflecting a general structural crisis of capital, in the sense explicated by István Mészáros in his *Beyond Capital*; (4) adopting the approach of dialectical biology, associated with Harvard biologists Richard Levins and Richard Lewontin in *The Dialectical Biologist*; and (5) insisting on the radical reconstruction of society at large in ways that would promote a sustainable "planetary metabolism" (Wallace et al. 2015, 70–72, 2020, 12; Mészáros 1995; Levins and Lewontin 1985). In his *Big Farms Make Big Flu* and other writings, Rob Wallace draws on Marx's notions of commodity chains and metabolic rift, as well as the critique of austerity and privatization based in the notion of the Lauderdale Paradox, according to which private riches are enhanced by the destruction of public wealth. Thinkers in this critical tradition rely on a dialectical approach to ecological destruction and the etiology of disease. (Wallace 2016, 60–61, 118, 120–21, 217–19, 236, 332; Wallace 2020; on the Lauderdale Paradox, see Foster et al. 2010, 53–72).

Naturally, the new historical-materialist epidemiology did not appear out of thin air, but was built on a long tradition of socialist struggles and critical analyses of epidemics, including such historic contributions as: (1) Frederick Engels's *Condition of the Working Class in England*, which explored the class basis of infectious diseases; (2) Marx's own discussions of epidemics and general health conditions in *Capital*; (3) the treatment by the British zoologist E. Ray Lankester (Charles Darwin and Thomas Huxley's protégé and Marx's friend) of the anthropogenic sources of disease and their basis in capitalist agriculture, markets and finance in his *Kingdom of Man*; and (4) Levins's "Is Capitalism a Disease?" (Foster 2020, 61–64, 172–204; Engels 1975; Lankester 1911, 31–33, 159–91; Levins 2000; see also Waitzkin 1983).

Especially important in the new historical-materialist epidemiology associated with Structural One Health is the explicit recognition of the role of global agribusiness and integration of this with detailed research into every aspect of the etiology of disease, focusing on the new zoonoses. Such diseases, as Wallace stated in *Big Farms Make Big Flu*, were the "inadvertent biotic fallout of efforts aimed at steering animal ontogeny and ecology to multinational profitability," producing new deadly pathogens (Wallace 2016, 53). Offshore farming consisting of monocultures of genetically similar domestic animals (eliminating immune firebreaks), including massive hog feedlots and vast poultry farms coupled with rapid deforestation and the chaotic mixing of wild birds and other wildlife with industrial animal production – not excluding wet markets – have created the conditions for the spread of new deadly pathogens such as SARS, MERS, Ebola, H1N1, H5N1 and now SARS-CoV-2. Over half a million people globally died of H1N1 whereas the deaths from SARS-CoV-2 will likely far exceed that (Wallace 2016, 49).

"Agribusinesses," Wallace wrote, "are moving their companies into the Global South to take advantage of cheap labor and cheap land," and "spreading their entire production line across the world" (Wallace 2016, 33–34). Avians, hogs and humans all interact to produce new diseases. "Influenzas," Wallace tells us,

> now emerge by way of a globalized network of corporate feedlot production and trade, wherever specific strains first evolve. With flocks and herds whisked from region to region – transforming spatial distance into just-in-time expediency – multiple strains of influenza are continually introduced into localities filled with populations of susceptible animals.
>
> *(Wallace 2016, 81)*

Large-scale commercial poultry operations have been shown to have much higher odds of hosting these virulent zoonoses. Value-chain analysis has been used to trace the etiology of new influenzas such as H5N1 along the poultry production commodity chain (Paul et al. 2013). Influenza in southern China has been shown to emerge in the context of "a 'historical present' within which multiple virulent recombinants arise out of a mélange of agroecologies originating at different times by both path dependence and contingency: in this case, ancient (rice), early modern (semi-domesticated ducks), and present-day (poultry intensification)." This analysis has also been extended by radical geographers, such as Bergmann, working on "the convergence of biology and economy beyond a single commodity chain and up into the fabric of the global economy" (Wallace 2016, 306; Wallace et al. 2015, 69, 71, 73).

The interconnected global commodity chains of agribusiness, which provide the bases for the appearance of novel zoonoses, ensure that these pathogens move rapidly from one place to another, exploiting the chains of human connection and globalization, with the human hosts moving in days, even hours, from one part of the globe to the other. Wallace and his colleagues write in "COVID-19 and Circuits of Capital":

> Some pathogens emerge right out of centers of production. . . . But many like COVID-19 originate on the frontiers of capital production. Indeed, at least 60 percent of novel human pathogens emerge by spilling over from wild animals to local human communities (before the more successful ones spread to the rest of the world).

As they sum up the conditions of the transmission of these diseases,

> The underlying operative premise is that the cause of COVID-19 and other such pathogens is not found just in the object of any one infectious agent or its clinical course, but also in the field of ecosystemic relations that capital and other structural causes have pinned back to their own advantage. The wide variety of pathogens, representing different taxa, source hosts, modes of transmission, clinical courses, and epidemiological outcomes, have all the earmarks that send us running wild-eyed to our search engines upon each outbreak, and mark different parts and pathways along the same kinds of circuits of land use and value accumulation.
>
> *(Wallace et al. 2020, 11)*

The imperial restructuring of production in the late 20th and early 21st centuries – which we know as globalization – was the result primarily of the global labor arbitrage and the overexploitation (and super-exploitation) of workers in the Global South (including the purposeful contamination of the local environments) for the benefit primarily of the centers of world capital and finance. But it was also driven in part by a global land arbitrage that took place simultaneously through multinational agribusiness corporations. According to Eric Holt-Giménez in *A Foodie's Guide to Capitalism*, "the price of land" in much of the Global South

> is so low in relation to its land rent (what it is worth for what it can produce) that the capture of the difference (arbitrage) between low price and high land rent will provide investors with a handsome profit. Any benefits from actually growing crops are secondary to the deal. . . . Land arbitrage opportunities come about by bringing new land – with an attractive land rent – into the global land market where rents can actually be capitalized.
>
> *(Holt-Giménez 2017, 102–5)*

Much of this was fed by what is called the Livestock Revolution, which made livestock into a globalized commodity based on giant feedlots and genetic monocultures (McMichael 2007, 180).

These conditions have been promoted by the various development banks in the context of what is euphemistically known as "territorial restructuring," which involves removing subsistence farmers and small producers from the land at the behest of multinational corporations, primarily agribusinesses, as well as rapid deforestation and ecosystem destruction. These are also known as 21st-century land grabs, accelerated by high prices for basic foods in 2008 and again in 2011, as well as private wealth funds seeking tangible assets in the face of uncertainty after the Great Financial Crisis of 2007–9. The result is the greatest mass migration in human history, with people being thrown off of the land in a global process of depeasantization, altering the agroecology of whole regions, replacing traditional agriculture with monocultures and pushing populations into urban slums (Araghi 2000).

Rob Wallace and his colleagues observe that historian and critical-urban theorist Mike Davis and others

> have identified how these newly urbanizing landscapes act as both local markets and regional hubs for global agricultural commodities passing through. . . . As a result, forest disease dynamics, the pathogens' primeval sources, are no longer constrained to the hinterlands alone. Their associated epidemiologies have themselves turned relational, felt across time and space. A SARS can suddenly find itself spilling over into humans in the big city only a few days out of its bat cave.
>
> *(Wallace et al. 2020, 6; see Davis 2006; Kouddous 2020)*

Commodity Chain Disruption and the Global Bullwhip Effect

The new pathogens generated unintentionally by agribusiness are not themselves natural-material use values, but rather are toxic residues of the capitalist production system, traceable to agribusiness commodity chains as part of a globalized food regime (Wallace 2016, 61).[3] Yet, in a kind of metaphorical "revenge" of nature as first depicted by Engels and Lankester, the ripple effects of combined ecological and epidemiological disasters introduced by today's global commodity chains and the actions of agribusiness, giving rise to the COVID-19 pandemic, have disrupted the entire system of global production (*MECW* 25: 460–61; Lankester 1911, 159). The effect of lockdowns and social distancing, shutting down production in key sectors of the globe, has shaken supply/value chains internationally. This has generated a gigantic "bullwhip effect" rippling up from both the supply and demand ends of the global commodity chains (Leonard 2020). Moreover, the COVID-19 pandemic has occurred in the context of a global regime of neoliberal monopoly-finance capital that has imposed worldwide austerity, including on public health. The universal adoption of just-in-time production and time-based competition in the regulation of global commodity chains has left corporations and facilities such as hospitals with few inventories, a problem compounded by urgent stockpiling of some goods on the part of the population. The result is extraordinary dislocation of the entire global economy.

Today's global commodity chains – or what we call *labor-value chains* – are organized primarily in order to exploit lower unit labor costs (taking into account both wage costs and productivity) in the poorer countries of the Global South where world industrial production is now predominantly located. Unit labor costs in India in 2014 were 37 percent of the US level, while China's and Mexico's were 46 and 43 percent, respectively. Indonesia was higher with unit labor costs at 62 percent of the US level (Suwandi 2019, 59–61; Smith 2016). Much of this is due to the extremely low wages in countries in the South, which are only a small fraction of the wage levels of those in the North. Meanwhile, arm's length production carried out under multinational corporation specifications, along with advanced technology introduced into the new export platforms in the Global South, generates productivity on levels comparable in many areas to that of the Global North. The result is an integrated global system of exploitation in which the differences in wages between countries in Global North and Global South are greater than the difference in productivities, leading to very low unit labor costs in countries in the South and generating enormous gross profit margins (or economic surplus) on the export price of goods from the poorer countries.

The enormous economic surpluses generated in the Global South are logged in gross domestic product accounting as *value added* in the North. However, they are better understood as *value captured* from the South. This whole new system of international exploitation associated with the globalization of production constitutes the deep structure of late imperialism in the 21st century. It is a system of world exploitation/expropriation formed around the global labor arbitrage, resulting in a vast drain of value generated from the poor to capital based in the rich countries.

All of this was facilitated by revolutions in transportation and communication. Shipping costs dived as standardized shipping containers proliferated. Communication technologies such as fiber-optic cables, mobile phones, the Internet, broadband, cloud computing and video conferencing altered global connectivity. Air travel cheapened rapid travel, growing by an annual average of 6.5 percent between 2010 and 2019 (Bello 2020; Mazareanu 2020). Around a third of US exports are intermediate products for final goods produced elsewhere, such as cotton, steel, engines and semiconductors (O'Neil 2020). It is out of these rapidly changing conditions, generating an increasingly integrated, hierarchical international accumulation structure, that the present global commodity-chain structure arose. The result was the connecting of all parts of the globe within a world system of oppression, a connectivity that is now showing signs of destabilizing under the impacts of the US trade war against China and the global economic effects of the COVID-19 pandemic.

The COVID-19 pandemic, with its lockdowns and social distancing, is "the first global supply-chain crisis" (Feltri 2020). This has led to losses in economic value, vast unemployment and underemployment, corporate collapse, increased exploitation and widespread hunger and deprivation. Key to understanding both the complexity and chaos of the present crisis is the fact that no CEO of a multinational corporation anywhere has a complete map of the firm's commodity chain. Usually, the financial centers and procurement officers in corporations know their first-tier suppliers, but not their second tier (that is, the suppliers of their suppliers), much less the third- or even fourth-tier suppliers. As Elisabeth Braw writes in *Foreign Policy*,

> Michael Essig, a professor of supply management at the Bundeswehr University of Munich, calculated that a multinational company such as Volkswagen has 5,000

> suppliers (the so-called tier-one suppliers), each with an average of 250 tier-two suppliers. That means that the company actually has 1.25 million suppliers – the vast majority of whom it doesn't know.
>
> *(Braw 2020)*

Moreover, this leaves out the third-tier suppliers. When the novel coronavirus outbreak occurred in Wuhan in China, it was discovered that 51,000 companies globally had at least one direct supplier in Wuhan, while five million companies had at least one two-tier supplier there. On 27 February 2020, when the supply chain disruption was still largely centered on China, citing a report by Dun & Bradstreet, the World Economic Forum declared that more than 90 percent of the Fortune 1000 multinational corporations had a tier-one or tier-two supplier affected by the virus (Betti and Hong 2020).

The effects of SARS-CoV-2 have made it urgent for corporations to try to map their entire commodity chains. But this is enormously complex. When the Fukushima nuclear disaster occurred, it was discovered that the Fukushima area produced 60 percent of the world's critical auto parts, a large share of world lithium battery chemicals and 22 percent of the world's three-hundred-millimeter silicon wafers, all crucial to industrial production. Attempts were made at that time by some monopoly-finance corporations to map their supply chains. According to the *Harvard Business Review*,

> executives of a Japanese semiconductor manufacturer told us it took a team of a 100 people more than a year to map the company's supply networks deep into the sub-tiers following the earthquake and tsunami [and the Fukushima nuclear disaster] in 2011.
>
> *(Choi et al. 2020)*

Faced with commodity chains in which many of the links in the chain are invisible, and where the chains are breaking in numerous places, corporations are faced with interruptions and uncertainties in what Marx called the "chain of metamorphoses" in the production, distribution and consumption of material products, coupled with erratic changes in overall supply demand. The scale of the coronavirus pandemic and its consequences on world accumulation are unprecedented, with the global economic costs still increasing. At the end of March 2020, some three billion people on the planet were in lockdown or social-distancing mode. Most corporations have no emergency plan for dealing with the multiple breaks in their supply chains (O'Leary 2020). The scale of the problem manifested itself in the early months of 2020 in tens of thousands of force majeure declarations, beginning first in China and then spreading elsewhere, where various suppliers indicate they are unable to fulfill contracts due to extraordinary external events. This is accompanied by numerous "blank sailings" standing for scheduled voyages of cargo ships that are canceled with the goods being held up due either to failure of supply or demand. Airline passenger flights all over the world decreased by around 90 percent, leading the major US airlines to leverage "the bellies and passenger cabins of their aircraft [in order to redirect them] for cargo flights, often removing seats and using the empty tracks to secure cargo" (Cosgrove 2020).

The economic fallout from the COVID-19 pandemic was widely forecast to cause a collapse of world trade comparable to the Great Depression of the 1930s. The dire effects of the disruption of global supply chains during the pandemic have been particularly evident with respect to medical equipment, where the US and other advanced economies are heavily dependent on Chinese producers. Many other goods are also now in short supply, while in the general chaos warehouses are overflowing with goods, such as fashion clothing, for which demand has plummeted. In the world of just-in-time production and time-based competition, inventories are generally reduced to a minimum to decrease costs. With no slack, auto and many retail supply chains in the United States saw a chronic shortage in supplies. By mid-April 2020, 81 percent of global manufacturing firms were experiencing supply shortages, evident in a 44 percent increase in force majeure declarations by March 2020 from the beginning of the year, before the emergence of the novel coronavirus, and a 38 percent increase in production shutdowns. The result is not only material shortfalls but a crisis in cash flow and hence a huge "spike in financial risks" (De Martino 2020).

For today's multinational corporations, which care little about the use values they sell provided they generate exchange value, the real economic impact of the disruption of supply chains is their effect on value chains – that is, on exchange value flows. Although the full value effects of the global supply-side disruption will not be known for some time, an indication of crisis this generates for accumulation can be seen in the losses in value that corporations have experienced. Hundreds of companies, including firms such as Boeing, Nike, Hershey, Sun Microsystems and Cisco, have encountered critical commodity chain disruptions in the last couple of decades. Capital has every reason to fear the consequences for valorization and accumulation. Everywhere, production is dropping and unemployment/underemployment is soaring as firms shed workers who in the United States are left simply to fend for themselves. Corporations are now in a race to pull in their commodity chains and provide some semblance of stability in what seems to be an all-encompassing crisis. Moreover, the disruption of the whole chain of metamorphoses involved in the global labor arbitrage threatens to engender a financial meltdown in a world economy still characterized by stagnation, debt and financialization.

Not the least of the vulnerabilities exposed is what is known as *supply-chain finance*, which allows corporations to defer payments to suppliers, with the help of bank finance. According to the *Wall Street Journal*, some corporations have supply-chain financing obligations that dwarf their reported net debt. These debts owed to suppliers are sold by other financial interests in the form of short-term notes. Credit Suisse owns notes that are owed by large US corporations such as Kellogg and General Mills. With a general disruption of commodity chains, this intricate chain of finance, which is itself the object of speculation, is inherently placed in a crisis mode itself, creating additional vulnerabilities in an already fragile financial system (Eaglesham 2020).

Imperialism, Class and the Pandemic

As we have seen, SARS-CoV-2, like other dangerous pathogens that have emerged or re-emerged in recent years, is closely related to a complex set of factors. These include: the development of global agribusiness with its expanding genetic monocultures that increase susceptibility to the contraction of zoonotic diseases from wild to domestic animals to humans; the destruction of wild habitats and disruption of the activities of wild species; and human beings living in closer proximity. There is little doubt that global commodity chains and the kinds of connectivity that they have produced have become vectors for the rapid transmission of disease, throwing this whole globally exploitative pattern of development into question. As Stephen Roach of the Yale School of Management, formerly chief economist of Morgan Stanley and the principal originator of the global labor arbitrage concept, has written in the context of the coronavirus crisis, what the financial headquarters of corporations wanted was "low-cost goods irrespective of what those cost efficiencies entailed in terms of [the lack of] investing in public health, or I would also say [the lack of] investing in environmental protection and the quality of the climate." The result of such an unsustainable approach to "cost efficiencies" is the contemporary global ecological and epidemiological crises and their financial consequences, further destabilizing a system that was already exhibiting an "excessive surge" characteristic of financial bubbles (Roach 2020).

At the time of writing, rich countries are at the epicenter of the COVID-19 pandemic and financial fallout, but the overall crisis, incorporating its economic as well as epidemiological effects, will hit poor countries harder. How a planetary crisis of this kind is handled is ultimately filtered through the imperial-class system. In March 2020, the COVID-19 Response Team of the Imperial College in London issued a report indicating that in a global scenario in which SARS-CoV-2 was unmitigated, with no social distancing or lockdowns, forty million people in the world would die, with higher mortality rates in the rich countries than in poor countries because of the larger proportions of the population that were sixty-five or older, as compared with poor countries. This analysis ostensibly took into account the greater access to medical care in rich countries. But it left out factors like malnutrition, poverty and the greater susceptibility to infectious diseases in poor countries. Nevertheless, the Imperial College estimates, based on these assumptions, indicated that in an unmitigated scenario the number of deaths would be in the range of fifteen million in East Asia and the Pacific, 7.6 million people in South Asia, three million people in Latin America and the Caribbean, 2.5 million people in sub-Saharan Africa and 1.7 million in the Middle East and North Africa – as compared with 7.2 million in Europe and Central Asia and around three million in North America (Imperial College COVID-19 Response Team 2020, 3–4).

Basing their analysis on the Imperial College's approach, Ahmed Mushfiq Mobarak and Zachary Barnett-Howell at Yale University wrote an article for the establishment journal *Foreign Policy* entitled "Poor Countries Need to Think Twice About Social Distancing." In their article, Mobarak and Barnett-Howell were very explicit, arguing that

> epidemiological models make clear that the cost of not intervening in rich countries would be in the hundreds of thousands to millions dead, an outcome far worse than the deepest economic recession imaginable. In other words, social distancing interventions and aggressive suppression, even with their associated economic costs, are overwhelmingly justified in high-income societies

– to save lives (Mobarak and Barnett-Howell 2020).

However, the same is not true, they suggested, for poor countries, since they have relatively few elderly individuals in their populations as a whole, producing, according to the Imperial College estimates, only around half the mortality rate. This model, they admit, "does not account for the greater prevalence of chronic illnesses, respiratory conditions, pollution, and malnutrition in low-income countries, which could increase the fatality rates from coronavirus outbreaks." But largely ignoring this in their article (and in a related study conducted through the Yale economics department), these authors insist that it would be better, given the impoverishment and vast unemployment and under-employment in these countries, for the populations not to practice social distancing or aggressive testing and suppression, and to put their efforts into economic production, presumably keeping intact the global supply chains that primarily start upstream in low-wage countries (Barnett-Howell and Mobarak 2020).

As Mike Davis argues, 21st-century capitalism points to "a permanent triage of humanity . . . dooming part of the human race to eventual extinction." He asks:

> But what happens when COVID spreads through populations with minimal access to medicine and dramatically higher levels of poor nutrition, untended health problems and damaged immune systems? The age advantage will be worth far less to poor youth in African and South Asian slums.

> There's also some possibility that mass infection in slums and poor cities could flip the switch on coronavirus's mode of infection and reshape the nature of the disease. Before SARS emerged in 2003, highly pathogenic coronavirus epidemics were confined to domestic animals, above all pigs. Researchers soon recognized two different routes of infection: fecal-oral, which attacked the stomach and intestinal tissue, and respiratory, which attacked the lungs. In the first case, there was usually very high mortality, while the second generally resulted in milder cases. A small percentage of current positives, especially the cruise ship cases, report diarrhea and vomiting, and, to quote one report, "the possibility of SARS-CoV-2 transmission via sewage, waste, contaminated water, air conditioning systems and aerosols cannot be underestimated."
>
> The pandemic has now reached the slums of Africa and South Asia, where fecal contamination is everywhere: in the water, in the home-grown vegetables, and as windblown dust. (Yes, shit storms are real.) Will this favor the enteric route? Will, as in the case of animals, this lead to more lethal infections, possibly across all age groups?
>
> *(Kouddous 2020)*

Davis's argument makes plain the gross immorality of a position that says social distancing and aggressive suppression of the virus should take place in rich countries and not poor. Such imperialist epidemiological strategies are all the more vicious in that they take the poverty of the populations of the Global South, the product of imperialism, as the justification for a Malthusian or social Darwinist approach, in which millions would die in order to keep the global economy growing, primarily for the benefit of those at the apex of the system. Contrast this to the approach adopted in socialist-led Venezuela, the country in Latin America with the least number of deaths per capita from COVID-19, where collectively organized social distancing and social provisioning is combined with expanded personalized screening to determine who is most vulnerable, widespread testing, and expansion of hospitals and health care, developing on the Cuban and Chinese models (Serrano 2020; Fuentes 2020).

Economically, the Global South as a whole, quite apart from the direct effects of the pandemic, is destined to pay the highest cost. The breakdown of global supply chains due to canceled orders in the Global North (as well as social distancing and lockdowns around the globe) and the refashioning of commodity chains that will follow, will leave whole countries and regions devastated. Here, it is crucial to recognize as well that the COVID-19 pandemic has come in the middle of an economic war for global hegemony unleashed by the Donald Trump administration and directed at China, which has accounted for some 37 percent of all cumulative growth of the world economy since 2008 (Roach 2020). This is seen by the Trump administration as a war by other means. As a result of the tariff war, many US companies had already pulled their supply chains out from China. Levi's, for example has reduced its manufacturing in China from 16 percent in 2017 to 1–2 percent in 2019. In the face of the tariff war and the COVID-19 pandemic, two thirds of 160 executives surveyed across industries in the United States have recently indicated that they had already moved, were planning to move, or were considering moving their operations from China to Mexico, where unit labor costs are now comparable and where they would be closer to US markets (Kapadia 2020). Washington's economic war against China is currently so fierce that the Trump administration refused to drop the tariffs on personal protection equipment, essential to medical personnel, until late March 2020.

Trump meanwhile appointed Peter Navarro, the economist in charge of his economic war for hegemony with China, as head of the Defense Production Act to deal with the COVID-19 crisis. In his roles in directing the US trade war against China and as policy coordinator of the Defense Production Act, Navarro has accused China of introducing a "trade shock" that lost "over five million manufacturing jobs and 70,000 factories" and "killed tens of thousands of Americans" by destroying jobs, families and health. He is now declaring that this has been followed by a "China virus shock" (Rappeport 2020; Ruccio 2020). On this propagandist basis, Navarro proceeded to integrate US policy with respect to the pandemic around the need to fight the so-called China virus and pull US supply chains out of China. Yet, since about a third of all global intermediate manufacturing products are currently produced in China, most heavily in the high-tech sectors, and since this remains key to the global labor arbitrage, the attempt at such restructuring will be vastly disruptive, to the extent that it is possible at all (Huang 2020).

Some multinationals that had moved their production out of China learned the hard way later that the decision did not "free" them from their dependency on it. Samsung, for example, has started flying electronic components from China to its factories in Vietnam – a destination for companies that are eager to escape the trade-war tariffs. But Vietnam is also vulnerable, because they rely heavily on China for materials or intermediate parts (Reed and Song 2020; Bermingham 2020). Similar cases have happened in neighboring South-east Asian countries. Capitalists like Cao Dewang, the Chinese billionaire founder of Fuyao Glass Industry, predicts the weakening of China's role in the global supply chain after the pandemic but concludes that, at least in the short term, "it's hard to find an economy to replace China in the global industry chain" – citing many difficulties from "infrastructure shortcomings" in Southeast Asian countries, higher labor costs in the Global North, and the obstacles that "rich countries" have to face if they want to "rebuild manufacturing at home" (Tang 2020).

The COVID-19 crisis is not to be treated as the result of an external force or as an unpredictable "black swan" event, but rather belongs to a complex of crisis tendencies that are broadly predictable, though not in terms of actual timing. Today, the center of the capitalist system is confronted with secular stagnation in terms of production and investment, relying for its expansion and amassing of wealth at the top on historically low interest rates, high amounts of debt, the drain of capital from the rest of the world, and financial speculation. Income and wealth inequality are reaching levels for which there is no historical analogue. The rift in world ecology has attained planetary proportions and is creating a planetary environment that no longer constitutes a safe place for humanity. New pandemics are arising on the basis of a system of global monopoly-finance capital that has made itself the main vector of disease. The state systems everywhere are regressing toward higher levels of repression, whether under the mantle of neoliberalism or neofascism.

The extraordinarily exploitative and destructive nature of the system is evident in the fact that blue-collar workers everywhere have been declared essential critical infrastructure workers (a concept formalized in the United States by the Department of Homeland Security) and are expected to carry out production mostly without protective gear while the more privileged and dispensable classes socially distance themselves (Krebs 2020). A true lockdown would be much more extensive and would require state provisioning and planning, ensuring that the whole population was protected, rather than focusing on bailing out financial interests. It is precisely because of the class nature of social distancing, as well as access to income, housing, resources and medical care, that morbidity and mortality from COVID-19 in the United States is falling primarily on populations of color, where conditions of economic and environmental injustice are most severe (Chambers 2020).

Social Production and the Planetary Metabolism

Fundamental to Marx's materialist outlook was what he called "the hierarchy of . . . needs" (*MECW* 24: 543). This meant that human beings were material beings, part of the natural world, as well as creating their own social world within it. As material beings they had to satisfy their material needs first, eating and drinking, providing food, shelter, clothing, and the basic conditions of healthy existence, before they pursue their higher developmental needs, necessary for the full realization of human potential (*MECW* 24: 467). Yet, in class societies it was always the case that the vast majority, the real producers, were relegated to conditions in which they were caught in a constant struggle to meet their most basic needs. This has not fundamentally changed. Despite the enormous wealth created over centuries of growth, millions upon millions of people in even the wealthiest capitalist society remain in a precarious condition in relation to such basics as food security, housing, clean water, health care and transportation – under conditions in which three billionaires in the United States own as much wealth as the bottom half of the population.

Meanwhile, local and regional environments have been put in danger – as have all of the world ecosystems and the Earth System itself as a safe place for humanity. An emphasis on global "cost efficiencies" (a euphemism for cheap labor and cheap land) has led multinational capital to create a complex system of global commodity chains, designed at every point to maximize the over-/superexploitation of labor on a worldwide basis, while also turning the entire world into a real-estate market, much of it as a field for operation of agribusiness. The result has been a vast draining of surplus from the periphery of the global system and a plundering of the planetary commons. In the narrow system of value accounting employed by capital, most of material existence, including the entire Earth System and the social conditions of human beings, insofar as these do not enter the market, are considered externalities, to be robbed and despoiled in the interest of capital accumulation. What has mistakenly been characterized as "the tragedy of the commons" is better understood, as Guy Standing (2019, 49) has pointed out in *Plunder of the Commons*, as "the tragedy of privatizing." Today, the famous Lauderdale Paradox, introduced by the Earl of Lauderdale in the early 19th century, in which public wealth is destroyed for the enhancement of private riches, has the entire planet as its field of operation (Foster and Clark 2020, 167–72).

The circuits of capital of late imperialism have taken these tendencies to their fullest extent, generating a rapidly developing planetary ecological crisis that threatens to engulf human civilization as we know it; a perfect storm of catastrophe. This comes on top of a system of accumulation that is divorced from any rational ordering of needs for the population in- dependent of the cash nexus. Accumulation and the amassing of wealth in general is increasingly dependent on the proliferation of waste of all kinds. In the midst of this disaster, a New Cold War and a growing likelihood of thermonuclear destruction have emerged, with an increasingly unstable and aggressive United States at the forefront. This has led the *Bulletin of Atomic Scientists* to move its famous doomsday clock to 100 seconds to midnight, the closest to midnight since the clock started in 1947 (Spinazza 2020).

The COVID-19 pandemic and the threat of increasing and more deadly pandemics is a product of this same late-imperialist development. Chains of global exploitation and expropriation have destabilized not only ecologies but the relations between species, creating a toxic brew of pathogens. All of this can be seen as arising from the introduction of agribusiness with its genetic monocultures; massive ecosystem destruction involving the uncontrolled mixture of species; and a system of global valorization based on treating land, labor, species and ecosystems as so many "free gifts" to be expropriated, irrespective of natural and social limits.

Nor are new viruses the only emerging global health problem. The overuse of antibiotics within agribusiness as well as modern medicine has led to the dangerous growth of bacterial superbugs generating increasing numbers of deaths, which by midcentury could surpass annual cancer deaths, and inducing the World Health Organization to declare a "global health emergency" (Angus 2019). Since communicable diseases, due to the unequal conditions of capitalist class society, fall heaviest on the working class and the poor, and on populations in the periphery, the system that generates such diseases in the pursuit of quantitative wealth, can be charged, as Engels and the Chartists did in the 19th century, with social murder. As the revolutionary developments in epidemiology represented by One Health and Structural One Health have suggested, the etiology of the new pandemics can be traced to the overall problem of ecological destruction brought on by capitalism.

Here, the necessity of a "revolutionary reconstitution of society at large," rears its head once again, as it has so many times in the past (*MECW* 6: 482). The logic of contemporary historical development points to the need for a more communal-commons-based system of social metabolic reproduction, one in which the associated producers rationally regulate their social metabolism with nature, so as to promote free development of each as the basis of the free development of all, while conserving energy and the environment (CIII: 949). The future of humanity in the 21st century lies not in the direction of increased economic and ecological exploitation/expropriation, imperialism and war. Rather, what Marx called "freedom in general" and the preservation of a viable "planetary metabolism" are the most pressing necessities today in determining the human present and future, and even human survival (*MECW* 1: 173; Wallace et al. 2020).

Notes

1. This chapter also appears in *Monthly Review* 72 (2) (June 2020).
2. On the global labor arbitrage and commodity chains, see Suwandi (2019, 32–33, 53–54). Our statistical analysis of unit labor costs was done collaboratively with R. Jamil Jonna, also published as Suwandi et al. (2019). On the global land arbitrage, Holt-Giménez (2017, 102–4).
3. On the significance of the concepts of the residual and residues for dialectics, see Bernal (1934, 103–4) and Lefebvre (2016, 299–300).

Bibliography

Amin, Samir. 2018. *Modern Imperialism, Monopoly Finance Capital, and Marx's Law of Value*. New York: Monthly Review Press.

Angus, Ian. 2019. "Superbugs in the Anthropocene." *Monthly Review* 71(2) (June).

Araghi, Farshad. 2000. "The Great Global Enclosure of Our Times." In *Hungry for Profit*, edited by Fred Magdoff, John Bellamy Foster, and Fredrick H. Buttel, 145–60. New York: Monthly Review Press.

Barnett-Howell, Zachary, and Ahmed Mushfiq Mobarak. 2020. "The Benefits and Costs of Social Distancing in Rich and Poor Countries." *ArXiv* (10 April). https://arxiv.org/abs/2004.04867v1

Bello, Walden. 2020. "Coronavirus and the Death of 'Connectivity.'" *Foreign Policy in Focus* (22 March). https://fpif.org/coronavirus-and-the-death-of-connectivity/

Bermingham, Finbarr. 2020. "Vietnam Lured Factories during Trade War, But Now Faces Big Hit as Parts from China Stop Flowing." *South China Morning Post* (28 February).

Bernal, J.D. 1934. "Dialectical Materialism." In *Aspects of Dialectical Materialism*, edited by Hyman Levy et. al., 89–122. London: Watts and Co.

Betti, Francisco and Per Kristian Hong. 2020. "Coronavirus Is Disrupting Global Value Chains. Here's How Companies Can Respond." *World Economic Forum* (27 February). https://www.weforum.org/agenda/2020/02/how-coronavirus-disrupts-global-value-chains/

Chambers, Lauren. 2020. "Data Show That COVID-19 Is Hitting Essential Workers and People of Color Hardest." *Data for Justice Project, American Civil Liberties Union* (7 April). https://data.aclum.org/2020/04/07/covid-19-disproportionately-affects-vulnerable-populations-in-boston/

Choi, Thomas Y., Dale Rogers, and Bindiya Vakil. 2020. "Coronavirus Is a Wake-Up Call for Supply Chain Management." *Harvard Business Review* (27 March).

Cosgrove, Emma. 2020. "FAA Offers Safety Guidance for Passenger Planes Ferrying Cargo." *Supply Chain Dive* (17 April). www.supplychaindive.com/news/coronavirus-FAA-cargo-planes-air-freight/576270/

Davis, Mike. 2006. *Planet of Slums*. London: Verso.
De Martino, Bill. 2020. "COVID-19: Where Is Your Supply Chain Disruption?" *Future of Sourcing* (3 April). https://futureofsourcing.com/covid-19-where-is-your-supply-disruption
Eaglesham, Jean. 2020. "Supply-Chain Finance Is New Risk in Crisis." *Wall Street Journal* (4 April).
Engels, Friedrich. 1975 (1846). "The Condition of the Working Class in England: From Personal Observation and Authentic Sources." In *MECW* 4: 295–596.
Feltri, Stefano. 2020. "Why Coronavirus Triggered the First Global Supply Chain Crisis." *Pro-Market* (5 March). https://promarket.org/why-coronavirus-triggered-the-first-global-supply-chain-crisis/
Foster, John Bellamy. 2019. "Late Imperialism." *Monthly Review* 71(3) (July–August): 1–19.
Foster, John Bellamy. 2020. *The Return of Nature*. New York: Monthly Review Press.
Foster, John Bellamy, and Brett Clark. 2020. *The Robbery of Nature*. New York: Monthly Review Press.
Foster, John Bellamy, Brett Clark, and Richard York. 2010. *The Ecological Rift*. New York: Monthly Review Press.
Fuentes, Frederico. 2020."Venezuela: Community Organization Key to Fighting COVID-19." *Green Left* (9 April).
Galaz, Victor, Melissa Leach, Ian Scoones, and Christian Stein. 2015. *The Political Economy of One Health*. STEPS Centre, Political Economy of Knowledge and Policy Working Paper Series.
Hilferding, Rudolf. 1981. *Finance Capital*. London: Routledge.
Holt-Giménez, Eric. 2017. *A Foodie's Guide to Capitalism*. New York: Monthly Review Press.
Hopkins, Terence, and Immanuel Wallerstein. 1986. "Commodity Chains in the World Economy Prior to 1800." *Review* 10(1): 157–70.
Huang, Cary. 2020. "Is the Coronavirus Fatal for Economic Globalization?" *South China Morning Post* (15 March).
Imperial College COVID-19 Response Team. 2020. *Report 12: The Global Impact of COVID-19 and Strategies for Mitigation and Suppression* (26 March). www.imperial.ac.uk/media/imperial-college/medicine/mrc-gida/2020-03-26-COVID19-Report-12.pdf
Kapadia, Shefali. 2020. "From Section 301 to COVID-19: How a Volatile China Changed Supply Chains." *Supply Chain Dive* (31 March). www.supplychaindive.com/news/coronavirus-china-tariff-trade-supply-chains/574702/
Kouddous, Sharif Abdel. 2020. "Mike Davis on Pandemics, Super-Capitalism, and the Struggles of Tomorrow." *Mada Masr* (30 March). https://madamasr.com/en/2020/03/30/feature/politics/mike-davis-on-pandemics-super-capitalism-and-the-struggles-of-tomorrow/
Krebs, Christopher C. 2020. "Advisory Memorandum on Identification of Essential Critical Infrastructure Workers." *U.S. Department of Homeland Security* (28 March). www.federalreserve.gov/supervisionreg/srletters/SR2006a1.pdf
Lankester, E. Ray. 1911. *The Kingdom of Man*. New York: Henry Holt.
Lefebvre, Henri. 2016. *Metaphilosophy*. London: Verso.
Leonard, Matt. 2020. "What Procurement Managers Should Expect from a Bull-Whip on Crack." *Supply Chain Dive* (26 March). www.supplychaindive.com/news/coronavirus-supply-chain-bullwhip-demand-grocery-medical-covid/574784/
Levins, Richard. 2000. "Is Capitalism a Disease?" *Monthly Review* 52(4) (September): 8–33.
Levins, Richard, and Richard Lewontin. 1985. *The Dialectical Biologist*. Cambridge, MA: Harvard University Press.
Marx, Karl. 1978. "The Value Form." *Capital and Class* 4: 134–50.
Mazareanu, E. 2020. "Annual Growth in Global Air Traffic Passenger Demand from 2006 to 2020." *Statista* (10 March). www.statista.com/statistics/193533/growth-of-global-air-traffic-passenger-demand/
McMichael, Philip. 2007. "Feeding the World." In *Socialist Register 2007: Coming to Terms with Nature*, edited by Leo Panitch and Colin Leys, 170–94. New York: Monthly Review Press.
Mészáros, István. 1995. *Beyond Capital*. New York: Monthly Review Press.
Mobarak, Ahmed Mushfiq, and Zachary Barnett-Howell. 2020. "Poor Countries Need to Think Twice about Social Distancing." *Foreign Policy* (10 April).
O'Leary, Lizzie. 2020. "The Modern Supply Chain Is Snapping." *Atlantic* (19 March).
O'Neil, Shannon K. 2020. "How to Pandemic Proof Globalization." *Foreign Affairs* (1 April).
Paul, Mathilde, Virginie Baritaux, Sirichai Wongnarkpet, Chaitep Poolkhet, Weerapong Thanapongtharm, François Roger, Pascal Bonnet, and Christian Ducrot. 2013. "Practices Associated with Highly Pathogenic Avian Influenza Spread in Traditional Poultry Marketing Chains." *Acta Tropica* 126: 43–53.

Rappeport, Alan. 2020. "Navarro Calls Medical Experts 'Tone Deaf' over Coronavirus Shutdown." *New York Times* (13 April). www.nytimes.com/2020/04/13/us/politics/peter-navarro-coronavirus.html

Reed, John, and Song Jung-a. 2020. "Samsung Flies Phone Parts to Vietnam after Coronavirus Hits Supply Chains." *Financial Times* (16 February).

Roach, Stephen. 2020. "This Is Not the Usual Buy-on-Dips Market." *Economic Times* (18 March). https://economictimes.indiatimes.com/markets/expert-view/central-bank-role-is-secondary-in-this-crisis-stephen-roach/articleshow/74686137.cms?from=mdr

Ruccio, David 2020. "China Syndrome." *Occasional Links and Commentary* (14 April). https://mronline.org/2020/04/16/china-syndrome/

Serrano Mancilla, Alfredo. 2020. "President Maduro: Venezuela Faces the COVID-19 with Voluntary Quarantine without Curfew or State of Exception." *Orinoco Tribune* (18 April). https://orinocotribune.com/president-maduro-venezuela-faces-the-covid-19-with-voluntary-quarantine-without-curfew-or-state-of-exception-interviewed-by-alfredo-serrano/

Smith, John. 2016. *Imperialism in the Twenty-First Century*. New York: Monthly Review Press.

Spinazza, Gayle. 2020. "It's Now 100 Seconds to Midnight." *Bulletin of Atomic Scientists* (23 January). https://thebulletin.org/2020/01/press-release-it-is-now-100-seconds-to-midnight/

Standing, Guy. 2019. *Plunder of the Commons: A Manifesto for Sharing Public Health*. London: Pelican.

Suwandi, Intan. 2019. *Value Chains: The New Economic Imperialism*. New York: Monthly Review Press.

Suwandi, Intan, R. Jamil Jonna, and John Bellamy Foster. 2019. "Global Commodity Chains and the New Imperialism." *Monthly Review* 70(10) (March): 1–24.

Tang, Frank. 2020. "American Factory Boss Says Pandemic Will Change China's Role in Global Supply Chain." *South China Morning Post* (15 April).

Tarver, Evan. 2020. "Value Chain vs. Supply Chain." *Investopedia* (24 March).

Waitzkin, Howard. 1983. *The Second Sickness*. New York: Free Press.

Wallace, Rob. 2012. "We Need a Structural One Health." *Farming Pathogens* (3 August).

Wallace, Rob. 2016. *Big Farms Make Big Flu*. New York: Monthly Review Press.

Wallace, Rob. 2020. "Notes on a Novel Coronavirus." *MR Online* (29 January). https://mronline.org/2020/01/29/notes-on-a-novel-coronavirus/

Wallace, Rob, Luke Bergmann, Richard Kock, Marius Gilbert, Lenny Hogerwerf, Rodrick Wallace, and Mollie Holmberg. 2015. "The Dawn of Structural One Health: A New Science Tracking Disease Emergence Along Circuits of Capital." *Social Science and Medicine* 129: 68–77.

Wallace, Rob, Alex Liebman, Luis Fernando Chaves, and Rodrick Wallace. 2020. "COVID-19 and Circuits of Capital." *Monthly Review* 72(1) (May).

Wallace, Rodrick, Luis Fernando Chavez, Luke R. Bergmann, Constância Ayres, Lenny Hogerwerf, Richard Kock, and Robert G. Wallace. 2018. *Clear-Cutting Disease Control: Capital-Led Deforestation, Public Health Austerity, and Vector-Borne Infection*. Cham, Switzerland: Springer.

Zinsstag, J. 2012. "Convergence of Eco Health and One Health." *Ecohealth* 9(4): 371–73.

56
AFTERWORD

Alex Callinicos

Overturning the Fetishism of Reality

We trust that this Handbook has established the intellectual and political richness of the Marxist tradition and its Post-Marxist offshoots (despite the many omissions we have regrettably been forced to make). But surveying what has been contributed is necessarily retrospective. So what can be said about the future of this tradition? Answering this question is complicated, because it involves looking both backward, to the diverse thinkers covered in the Handbook, and forward, to the traumatic reality of the present and the perhaps foreshortened future. But there are some things that one can say.

First, and as we noted in the Introduction, the critique of political economy has a busy future ahead of it. Even before the collapse precipitated by the COVID-19 pandemic, the advanced capitalist economies seemed stuck since the Global Financial Crisis of 2007–9 in a syndrome of slow growth, trapping central banks in easy money policies that may have prevented a 1930s-like depression, but that did not stimulate a strong revival – except in the financial markets, where cheap credit boosted security prices. Rather than the "emerging market" economies coming to the rescue, they seemed increasingly to have been sucked in; even the Chinese giant was losing its bounce before COVID-19 appeared in Wuhan in late 2019. The pandemic sparked a crisis that was waiting to happen (Choonara 2020).

Understanding how capitalism has found itself in what even mainstream economists have been calling "secular stagnation" and tracking the options it faces are now major tasks facing those working in the Marxist critique of political economy. And it's clear that this involves confronting old and new realities. For example, we have included entries on older and more recent theories of empire, imperialism and dependency. But how, building on these works, to unravel the particular forms of economic integration and capitalist development dominant today – in an era of the uneven industrialization of the Global South, the development of global production networks, the continued financial and military hegemony of the United States, the prevalence of old and new forms of extractivism across the South, the increasing inroads made by climate change, and the migratory movements driven by poverty, war and the search for a better life? This is an urgent and challenging question.

Second, one reason why it is better to talk about the critique of political economy than about Marxist economics is that this critique is *political*: it seeks in other words to demystify capitalism and its ideological representations the better to overthrow it. Lucio Colletti expressed this very well in his revolutionary days:

> in *Capital* . . . Marx does not restrict himself to criticizing the "logical mysticism" of the economists, their "trinity formula": Land, Capital, Labor. Their "fetishism" is explained by the fetishism of reality itself, that is of the capitalist mode of production. . . . In fact, reality itself is upside down. It is therefore not just a question of criticizing the way in which economists and philosophers have depicted reality. It is necessary to overturn *reality* itself – to straighten it up and "put it back on its feet." "Until now the philosophers have only interpreted the world: the point however is to change it."
>
> (Colletti 1972, 233)[1]

Today, what Marx called "the bewitched, inverted, and topsy-turvy world" of contemporary capitalism (CIII: 969; translation modified) embraces not simply the economic antagonisms referred to earlier, but also an increasingly toxic politics in which a fast-rising far right has been exploiting the failure of neoliberalism and left reformism to grab for power. This right represents a literally reactionary response to attempts to alleviate the oppressions on which classical Marxism is widely accused of being silent – gender, race, LGBT+, ecology. Donald Trump's racism and sexism is the paradigm case, but think also of the French conservative right's mobilization against equal marriage legislation and Jair Bolsonaro's drive to open the Amazon to mining and agrarian corporations. The neoliberal center, which paid lip-service at least to a jargon of "equality and diversity," has had its legitimacy undercut by the Global Financial Crisis, and is being squeezed from the right. So far there is no comparable pressure from the left. But Trump's and Bolsonaro's underlying commitment to neoliberal priorities has been most fully exposed in their callous and negligent handling of the COVID-19 pandemic in the interests of a thoroughly fetishistic conception of "the economy" counterposed to life itself.

What can Marxism say to this world? Answering this question is inseparable from addressing the debate between Marxism and Post-Marxism. For the latter, in different idioms, reproaches classical Marxism for "economism," "classism," "productivism" that prevent it from finding a proper place for non-class forms of oppression. We hope that this Handbook has complicated the picture, as Gayatri Chakravorty Spivak seeks to do in her chapter. Two particular themes have emerged in the different entries. The first is that of imperialism. In other words, capitalism as a global economic system involves a hierarchy of power in which the most "advanced" capitalist states dominate the rest and compete with each other to gain hegemony over other states (Harvey 2003; Callinicos 2009). The long Marxist exploration of imperialism, from Marx himself, Hilferding, Luxemburg and Lenin to Giovanni Arrighi and David Harvey, is of direct relevance to the present: the COVID-19 pandemic has intensified the competition between the declining hegemon, the United States, and China, fast-expanding in economic and military capabilities and increasingly seeking to accumulate soft power internationally. But, second, several of the thinkers included in this Handbook – for example, Fanon, Davis and Newton – have highlighted the constitutive relationship between imperialism and racism. Indeed, as we saw in "Foundation," Marx already pointed to the racialized division within the working class in Britain and the US arising from centuries of colonial domination and slavery.

The COVID-19 pandemic, analyzed by John Bellamy Foster and Intan Suwandi in the preceding chapter and further discussed later, has brought into sharper focus the dependence of contemporary economies, for all the "weightlessness" celebrated by postmodern theorists and neoliberals, on labor. It also pushes us to think about the division between productive and reproductive labor on which capitalism is built. In her entry Tithi Bhattacharya presented Lisa Vogel's pioneering contribution to social reproduction theory and in particular the role of women's domestic labor in ensuring the reproduction of labor-power. The pandemic, in forcing huge numbers of employees to perform their waged work from home, has highlighted the centrality of domestic labor as households, especially women, struggle both to keep their employers happy and to care for children, cook and clean; the separation of workplace and household that for Max Weber was a hallmark of modernity has at least temporarily broken down, certainly for many more affluent households, increasing the double burden of domestic and wage-labor on women. Meanwhile, while health and care workers (themselves overwhelmingly women) have struggled directly with the pandemic, large numbers especially of manual workers have been forced to carry on working, often more intensively and on a larger scale, usually in conditions where it is impossible to practice social distancing – in farms and factories, supermarkets and pharmacies, warehouses, delivery vans and lorries, refuse trucks, buses and trains. Twenty-first-century capitalism continues to rest on labor – and, in the main, manual labor, not the "immaterial labor" that Toni Negri and Michael Hardt claim is a sign of the incipient collapse of capitalism.

Contrary to his portrayal as Eurocentric, Marx identified as the agent of social transformation an always-already internationalized working class, formed in the global context of capitalist imperialism and crisscrossed by the divisions arising from racism and the victimization of migrants. The working class today is vastly bigger and even more internationalized. And, more visibly than in Marx's own day, the issues created by oppression on the basis of gender, gender identity, sexual orientation, race, nationality and religion are internal to this class. For example, as Feyzi Ismail shows in her entry, Chandra Mohanty has pioneered a Third World feminism that centers on the agency of working women in the South, in whose struggles resistance to gender oppression, imperialist domination and capitalist exploitation are inextricably interwoven. Other contributors to this Handbook have also stressed that the chances of any genuine socialist project becoming an alternative pole of attraction to the neoliberal center and the far right will depend on the development of an anti-capitalist politics that recognizes and mobilizes around issues of oppression, understanding them as part and parcel of the struggle against exploitation, poverty and austerity.

Nature's Revenge

These conflicts unfold against a horizon dominated by the process of climate change, which is accelerating at a terrifying pace and threatens the collapse of large-scale human societies, perhaps in the course of a few decades. Meanwhile, the COVID-19 pandemic, which sparked the biggest recession since the 1930s, has provided further evidence of capitalism's destructive relationship with nature, as Foster and Suwandi show. Their analysis is an instance of the Ecological Marxism Camilla Royle discussed in her entry, the rediscovery of Marx's own preoccupation with the environmental destruction caused by the blind process of capital accumulation (particularly in agriculture), and attempts (inevitably, sometimes diverging) to build on his arguments. Indeed, one might say that one crucial trajectory of Marxism in the past couple of decades is a growing preoccupation with the immanent tendency of capitalism toward catastrophe. Apart from Foster and his co-workers, centered on the journal *Monthly Review*, there is the work of Mike Davis. In *Ecology of Fear*, for example, he writes about "the dialectic of ordinary disaster" – floods, earthquakes, fires – in contemporary Los Angeles (Davis 1999, ch. 1). In *Monster at the Door* he prophetically warned of the danger of pandemics involving avian flu viruses – what he now calls "the plagues of capitalism" (updated edition Davis 2020).

Common to both Davis and Foster and his collaborators is an understanding of humankind's place in nature. Foster especially takes inspiration from Marx's famous description of the labor process as "the appropriation of what exists in nature for the requirements of man. It is the universal condition for the metabolic interaction (*Stoffwechsel*) between man and nature, the everlasting nature-imposed condition of human existence" (CI: 290; see especially Foster 2000; Saito 2017). On this conception, which can be traced back to Marx's *Economic and Philosophic Manuscripts of 1844*, the relationship between humankind and the rest of nature is mediated by their labor. It is from this perspective that Marx diagnoses capitalism's destruction of nature, notably in this now famous passage:

> large landed property . . . produces conditions that provoke an irreparable rift in the interdependent process between social metabolism and natural metabolism prescribed by the natural laws of the soil [*die einen unheilbaren Riß hervorbringen in dem Zusammenhang des gesellschaftlichen und natürlichen, durch die Naturgesetze des Bodens, vorgeschriebnen Stoffwechsels*]. The result of this is a squandering of the vitality of the soil, and *trade carries this devastation far beyond the bounds of a single country* (Liebig).
>
> *(Marx 1992, 753; CIII: 949; Marx 2016, 798; translation modified)*[2]

This problematic of the metabolic rift, considerably developed by Foster and his collaborators, has been criticized as positing a dualism of society and nature (Moore 2015). But this is a misunderstanding. Marx consistently treats humans as natural beings, belonging to and participating the natural world as a whole (Timpanaro 1976; Burkett 2014; Foster 2020). Conceiving nature as a unity is perfectly consistent with recognizing the operation of different causal mechanisms within it: the concept of emergence allows us to distinguish between different levels of the natural world, each with their own distinctive properties and mechanisms but interdependent, so that the human supervenes on the biological, which in turn supervenes on the chemical and physical (Callinicos 2006, 161–73). Conceptualizing the specificity of the causal mechanisms that constitute human societies is essential to the critical dimension of Marx's thought, which, as we have already noted, involves contesting the naturalization of historically contingent and transitory social relationships that we see at work in fetishism and locating these relationships in the context of the capitalist mode of production (Foster and Burkett 2018; Malm 2019). Climate change is simultaneously a physical process in which growing CO_2 and methane emissions cause global temperatures to rise and a consequence of modern industrial capitalism's reliance on fossil fuels to drive the accumulation process – what Andreas Malm calls "fossil capital" (Malm 2016; see also Angus 2016). The actual effects of the interaction of these social and physical mechanisms may be intermingled and appear in experience indistinguishable, but, from the perspective of the critique of political economy, analytically isolating these different mechanisms is crucial. To borrow Gramsci's concepts of *distinzione metodica* and *distinzione organica*, the physical and the social may both participate in the organic unity of nature, but methodologically it is necessary to distinguish between them (Gramsci 1971, 160; Gramsci 1975, II, 1590; Q13 (XXX) §18).

This perspective is very much in the spirit of this famous passage in Engels's *Dialectics of Nature*:

> Let us not, however, flatter ourselves overmuch on account of our human victories over nature. For each such victory nature takes its revenge on us. Each victory, it is true, in the first place brings about the results we expected, but in the second and third places it has quite different, unforeseen effects which only too often cancel the first . . . at every step we are reminded that we by no means rule over nature like a conqueror

> over a foreign people, like someone standing outside nature – but that we, with flesh, blood and brain, belong to nature, and exist in its midst, and that all our mastery of it consists in the fact that we have the advantage over all other creatures of being able to learn its laws and apply them correctly.
>
> (MECW *25: 460–61)*

Davis if anything goes further in thematizing the specificity of physical processes, gently reproaching Marx and Engels for, while recognizing that "nature has teeth with which to bite back against human conquest," failing to consider

> the possibility that the natural conditions of production over the past two or three millennia might have been subject to directional evolution or epic fluctuation, or that climate therefore might have its own distinctive history, repeatedly intersecting and over-determining a succession of different social formations.
>
> *(Davis 2016, 29)*

In a series of works he has explored the interaction between the political economy of capitalism – understood as a contradictory and exploitive system of capital accumulation – and the behavior of complex physical systems characterized by non-linear processes of transformation in which small differences in initial conditions may produce constantly amplified changes (see the classic discussion in Prigogine and Stenghers 1984). In one remarkable essay, Davis argues that we must conceive the Earth itself as an open system interacting with Near-Earth objects whose collisions with it contribute to "[e]volution by catastrophe. . . . Catastrophe replaces the linear temporal creep of microevolution with non-linear bursts of macroevolution. Comet showers accelerate evolutionary change by injecting huge pulses of sudden energy into biogeochemical circuits" (Davis 1996, 75). Climate change is proving to be an example of "evolution by catastrophe." Non-linear processes are at work here, where rising temperatures and their consequences increasingly don't take the form of gradual increases, but can be self-reinforcing and therefore accelerating. The warming of the Arctic is an example. This is a consequence of rising temperatures but, by reducing the amount of ice sheet reflecting back the rays of the sun, it speeds up global warming, so leading to further reductions in the ice surface and increases in temperature – one of the positive feedbacks that threaten to unleash climate catastrophe.

Indeed, catastrophe is no longer a prospect foreshadowed in the writings of ecological critics. It is here, invading our everyday life – the East African floods of 2019, the wildfires in the Amazon, Australia and the US West Coast, and now a pandemic that besieges us in our own homes and has unleashed what Adam Tooze calls "the first economic crisis of the Anthropocene," the new geological epoch characterized by the effects humankind is having on nature in changing the climate and causing mass extinctions (Tooze 2020).[3] We are embroiled in a dialectic of extraordinary disaster. And we now see that what was already familiar in past catastrophes – for example, the great famines of the colonial era, for example, Ireland 1845–49 and Bengal 1943–44. One thing common to these appalling episodes is that suffering was overdetermined by class: the poor perished on an enormous scale, while for the rich – landowners, capitalists, colonial administrators and commanders – it was a matter of business as usual. Famines are, notoriously, not natural catastrophes, but a product of social relations, and in particular of the inability of the poor to gain access to resources they need in order to survive (Sen 1981, and, for more specific studies, Woodham-Smith 1991; Davis 2001; Mukerjee 2010). Catastrophe is not an equalizer. As Bertolt Brecht puts it in his great poem "Questions of a worker who reads,"

"Even in fabled Atlantis/That night when the ocean engulfed it, the drowning/Roared out for their slaves" (Brecht 2019, 675).

We see this at work in the COVID-19 pandemic, where the intersection of class and race has acted as a ferocious selector for both mortality and impoverishment. A *New York Times* columnist wrote in May 2020:

> In a country where race and ethnicity often intersect with wealth and class, there are a cascade of other impacts, particularly economic ones, to remain conscious of.
>
> In a Pew Research Center survey conducted last month, 52 percent of low-income workers said they or someone in their household had lost a job or taken a pay cut as a result of the pandemic. But . . . 61 percent of Hispanic people agree with the statement, compared to 44 percent of African-Americans and just 38 percent of white people. . . . A McKinsey and Company report last month found: "Thirty-nine percent of jobs held by black workers, seven million jobs in all, are vulnerable as a result of the Covid-19 crisis, compared with 34 percent for white workers."
>
> *(Blow 2020)*

Similarly, Richard Horton writes, "COVID-19 has revealed, exploited, and accentuated deep socioeconomic and racial disparities in the UK" (Horton 2020). The Office of National Statistics has found that "Black males are 4.2 times more likely to die from a COVID-19-related death and Black females are 4.3 times more likely than White ethnicity males and females" (ONS 2020b). It also estimates that "the age-standardized mortality rate of deaths involving COVID-19 in the most deprived areas of England was 55.1 deaths per 100,000 population compared with 25.3 deaths per 100,000 population in the least deprived areas" (ONS 2020a).

This suffering is dwarfed by the impact of the pandemic in the Global South – summed up by the lockdown imposed chaotically and cruelly on India on 25 March 2020 by the Hindu chauvinist government of Narendra Modi, in which 140 million lost their jobs, mainly the working poor of the casual laborers and small traders, many of them driven from the cities and threatened with starvation. Arundhati Roy writes:

> Stripped of dignity and hope, these once self-respecting people travel hundreds of miles on foot, on bicycles or crammed illegally into private trucks like so much cargo. They have carried the virus with them, spreading it like bushfire to the remotest parts of the countryside. Many have died of hunger and exhaustion or been killed in accidents on their desperate journeys.
>
> *(Roy 2020)*

The Modi government's insistence on preserving fiscal rectitude recalls the cheese-paring Malthusianism of the British Treasury under Sir Charles Trevelyan during the Great Irish Famine of the 1840s (Kazmin and Singh 2020).

So Marxism can encompass intellectually the multiple dimensions of crisis – biological, economic and political – in which the world is currently embroiled, and trace their sources to the class antagonism that Marx diagnosed and that continues to structure our societies. The problem remains how to cross the bridge separating theory from practice. This isn't an abstract intellectual imperative: it's about offering an internationalist political alternative to the populist nationalism and outright fascism of the far right. The most hopeful development is the emergence of mass movements that are starting to demand the kind of systemic transformation required to halt or alleviate climate change (Callinicos 2019; Empson 2019). In the South the impact of climate change is being felt more directly, often pushing divided societies deeper into crisis. A theme common across continents is "extractivism" – the transnational process of extracting natural resources (agricultural as well as mineral), often in highly exploitative and environmentally destructive conditions, but increasingly reliant on advanced technology and integrated into global financial circuits, which is evokes resistance from the laboring classes it simultaneously displaces and incorporates (for mining, see Arboleda 2020). For example, the Algerian researcher Hamza Hamouchene describes some recent struggles in Tunisia by local communities, peasants, fisherfolk, workers and the unemployed as "social mobilisations surrounding resource extraction, connected to [the] global environmental justice movement. . . . [They] represent the *environmentalism of the poor* . . . a quest for environmental and social justice and a fight against the social exclusion, the violence and authoritarianism of neoliberalism and its elites" (Hamouchene 2019, 16). In two other North African societies deeply shaped by extractivism, Sudan and Algeria, economic and political grievances have fused in uprisings that have reawakened the revolutionary spirit of 2011 (Alexander 2020; Del Panta 2020). But in the North as well, struggles around the environment, social reproduction, unemployment and working conditions are likely to become intermingled in what will probably be the long crisis precipitated by the pandemic.

The evident conflict between the logic of capital and the urgent necessity of reconstructing our economies to begin to heal the metabolic rift from which spring the catastrophes now cascading on us offers probably the most promising terrain on which Marxist ideas, in no doubt some unanticipated form, can become a material force once again.

Notes

1. This duality is discussed further in my essay at the beginning of Part VIII, "Hidden Abode."
2. I'm grateful to Kohei Saito for pointing out that, not simply did Engels simplify this passage when editing *Capital* volume III, but that this simplification is, inexplicably, maintained in the English translation of Marx's *Economic Manuscript of 1864–65*, the original draft of volume III (Saito 2019).
3. Some Marxists contest the concept of the Anthropocene, but see the sensible treatments in Angus (2016) and Royle (2016).

Bibliography

Alexander, Anne. 2020. "Class, Power, and Revolution in Sudan." *International Socialism* 2(166): 37–64.
Angus, Ian. 2016. *Facing the Anthropocene: Fossil Capitalism and the Crisis of the Earth System*. New York: Monthly Review Press.
Arboleda, Martín. 2020. *Planetary Mine: Territories of Extraction under Late Capitalism*. London: Verso.
Blow, Charles M. 2020. "COVID-19's Race and Class Warfare." *New York Times* (3 May).
Brecht, Bertolt. 2019. *Collected Poems*. Translated and Edited by Tom Kuhn, David Constantine, and Charlotte Ryland. New York: Liveright Publishing Corp.
Burkett, Paul. 2014 (1999). *Marx and Nature: A Red and Green Perspective*. Chicago: Haymarket.
Callinicos, Alex. 2006. *The Resources of Critique*. Cambridge: Polity.
Callinicos, Alex. 2009. *Imperialism and Global Political Economy*. Cambridge: Polity.
Callinicos, Alex. 2019. "Betting on Infinite Loss." *International Socialism* 2(163): 3–18.
Choonara, Joseph. 2020. "Socialism in a Time of Pandemics." *International Socialism* 2(166): 3–32.
Colletti, Lucio. 1972. *From Rousseau to Lenin: Studies in Ideology and Society*. London: NLB.
Davis, Mike. 1996. "Cosmic Dancers on Earth's Stage? Permanent Revolution in the Earth Sciences." *New Left Review* 1(217): 48–84.
Davis, Mike. 1999. *Ecology of Fear: Los Angeles and the Dialectic of Disaster*. New York: Metropolitan Books.
Davis, Mike. 2001. *Late Victorian Holocausts: El Niño Famines and the Making of the Third World*. London: Verso.
Davis, Mike. 2016. "The Coming Desert: Kropotkin, Mars, and the Pulse of Asia." *New Left Review* 2(97): 23–43.

Davis, Mike. 2020. *The Monster Enters: Covid-19, Avian Flu, and the Plagues of Capitalism*. New York: OR Books.
Del Panta, Gianni. 2020. "The Roots of Algeria's Crisis." *International Socialism* 2(166): 65–84.
Empson, Martin, ed. 2019. *System Change Not Climate Change: A Revolutionary Response to Climate Change*. London: Bookmarks.
Foster, John Bellamy. 2000. *Marx's Ecology: Materialism and Nature*. New York: Monthly Review Press.
Foster, John Bellamy. 2020. *The Return of Nature: Socialism and Ecology*. New York: Monthly Review Press.
Foster, John Bellamy, and Paul Burkett. 2018. "Value Isn't Everything." *International Socialism* 2(160): 39–76.
Gramsci, Antonio. 1971. *Selections from the Prison Notebooks*. London: Lawrence and Wishart.
Gramsci, Antonio. 1975. *Quaderni del carcere*. Edited by Valentino Gerratana. 4 vols. Turin: Einaudi.
Hamouchene, Hamza. 2019. *Extractivism and Resistance in North Africa*. Amsterdam: Transnational Institute. www.tni.org/files/publication-downloads/web_maghreb_en_21-11-19.pdf
Harvey, David. 2003. *The New Imperialism*. Oxford: Oxford University Press.
Horton, Richard. 2020. "Independent Science Advice for COVID-19: At Last." *The Lancet* (9 May). www.thelancet.com/journals/lancet/article/PIIS0140-6736(20)31098-9/
Kazmin, Amy, and Jyotsna Singh. 2020. "India: The Millions of Working Poor Exposed by Pandemic." *Financial Times* (30 April).
Malm, Andreas. 2016. *Fossil Capital: The Rise of Steam Power and the Roots of Global Warming*. London: Verso.
Malm, Andreas. 2019. "Against Hybridism: Why We Need to Distinguish between Nature and Society, Now More Than Ever." *Historical Materialism* 27(2): 156–87.
Marx, Karl. 1992. *Das Kapital (Ökonomische Manuskript 1863–1865) Drittes Buch*. In Marx, Karl, and Friedrich Engels, *Gesamtausgabe, Second Section*, Vol. 4, Part 2. Berlin: Dietz [*MEGA2* II/4.2].
Marx, Karl. 2016. *The Economic Manuscript of 1864–1865*. Leiden: Brill.
Moore, Jason W. 2015. *Capitalism in the Web of Life: Ecology and the Accumulation of Capital*. London: Verso.
Mukerjee, Madhusree. 2010. *Churchill's Secret War: The British Empire and the Ravaging of India during World War II*. New York: Basic Books.
ONS (Office of National Statistics). 2020a. "Deaths Involving COVID-19 by Local Area and Socio-economic Deprivation: Deaths Occurring between 1 March and 17 April 2020." (1 May). www.ons.gov.uk/peoplepopulationandcommunity/birthsdeathsandmarriages/deaths/bulletins/deathsinvolvingcovid19bylocalareasanddeprivation/latest
ONS (Office of National Statistics). 2020b. "Coronavirus (COVID-19) Related Deaths by Ethnic Group, England and Wales: 2 March 2020 to 10 April 2020." (7 May). www.ons.gov.uk/peoplepopulationandcommunity/birthsdeathsandmarriages/deaths/articles/coronavirusrelateddeathsbyethnicgroupenglandandwales/latest
Prigogine, Ilya, and Isabelle Stengers. 1984. *Order Out of Chaos: Man's New Dialogue with Nature*. London: Heinemann.
Roy, Arundhati. 2020. "After the Lockdown: We Need a Reckoning." *Financial Times* (23 May).
Royle, Camilla. 2016. "Marxism and the Anthropocene." *International Socialism* 2(151): 63–84.
Saito, Kohei. 2017. *Karl Marx's Ecosocialism: Capitalism, Nature, and the Unfinished Critique of Political Economy*. New York: Monthly Review Press.
Saito, Kohei. 2019. "Marx and Engels: The Intellectual Relationship Revisited from an Ecological Perspective." Paper given at the Seminar in Contemporary Marxist Theory, King's College London, 6 November.
Sen, Amartya. 1981. *Poverty and Famines: An Essay on Entitlement and Deprivation*. Oxford: Clarendon Press.
Timpanaro, Sebastiano. 1976. *On Materialism*. London: NLB.
Tooze, Adam. 2020. "'We Are Living through the First Economic Crisis of the Anthropocene.'" *Guardian* (7 May).
Wallace, Rob. 2016. *Big Farms Make Big Flu: Dispatches on Influenza, Agribusiness, and the Nature of Science*. New York: Monthly Review Press.
Woodham-Smith, Cecil. 1991 (1962). *The Great Hunger: Ireland 1845–1849*. London: Penguin.

INDEX

Printed in Great Britain
by Amazon

62630934R00335